Page break	brk	brkPage1
Rectangle (shape)	shp	shpNamePanel
Subform/report	sub	subContact
Text box	txt	txtLoginName
Toggle button	tgl	tglForm

Tags for Access Basic Variables

Variable Type	Tag	Example
Container	con	Dim conTables as Container
Control	ctl	Dim ctlVapor As Control
Currency	cur	Dim curSalary As Currency
Database	db	Dim dbCurrent As Database
Document	doc	Dim docRelationships as Document
Double	dbl	Dim dblPi As Double
Dynaset	dyn	Dim dynTransact As Dynaset
Field	fld	Dim fldLastName as Field
Flag (Y/N, T/F)	f	Dim fAbort As Integer
Form	frm	Dim frmGetUser As Form
Group	gru	Dim gruManagers as Group
Index	idx	Dim idxOrderId as Index
Integer	int	Dim intRetValue As Integer
Long	lng	Dim lngParam As Long
Object	obj	Dim objGraph As Object
Parameter	prm	Dim prmBeginDate as Parameter
Property	prp	Dim prpUserDefined as Property
QueryDef	qdf (alternate: qrd)	Dim qdfPrice As QueryDef
Recordset	rec (alternate: rst)	Dim recPeople as Recordset
Relation	rel	Dim relOrderItems as Relation
Report	rpt	Dim rptYTDSales As Report
Single	sng	Dim sngLoadFactor As Single
Snapshot	snp	Dim snpParts As Snapshot
String	str	Dim strUserName As String
Table	tbl	Dim tblVendor As Table
TableDef	tdf (alternate: tbd)	Dim tdfBooking as TableDef
Type (user-defined)	typ	Dim typPartRecord As mtPART_RECORD
User	usr	Dim usrJoe as User
Variant	var	Dim varInput As Variant
Workspace	wrk (alternate: wsp)	Dim wrkPrimary as Workspace
Yes/No	ysn	Dim ysnPaid As Integer

Access Basic Variable Prefixes for Scope

Scope	Tag	Example
Local	(none)	intCustomerId
Static	s	sintAccumulate
Module	m	mcurRunningSum
Global	g	glngGrandTotal
Passed parameter	p	pstrLastName

FOR EVERY COMPUTER QUESTION, THERE IS A SYBEX BOOK THAT HAS THE ANSWER

Each computer user learns in a different way. Some need thorough, methodical explanations, while others are too busy for details. At Sybex we bring nearly 20 years of experience to developing the book that's right for you. Whatever your needs, we can help you get the most from your software and hardware, at a pace that's comfortable for you.

We start beginners out right. You will learn by seeing and doing with our **Quick & Easy** series: friendly, colorful guidebooks with screen-by-screen illustrations. For hardware novices, the **Your First** series offers valuable purchasing advice and installation support.

Often recognized for excellence in national book reviews, our **Mastering** titles are designed for the intermediate to advanced user, without leaving the beginner behind. A **Mastering** book provides the most detailed reference available. Add our pocket-sized **Instant Reference** titles for a complete guidance system. Programmers will find that the new **Developer's Handbook** series provides a more advanced perspective on developing innovative and original code.

With the breathtaking advances common in computing today comes an ever increasing demand to remain technologically up-to-date. In many of our books, we provide the added value of software, on disks or CDs. Sybex remains your source for information on software development, operating systems, networking, and every kind of desktop application. We even have books for kids. Sybex can help smooth your travels on the **Internet** and provide **Strategies and Secrets** to your favorite computer games.

As you read this book, take note of its quality. Sybex publishes books written by experts—authors chosen for their extensive topical knowledge. In fact, many are professionals working in the computer software field. In addition, each manuscript is thoroughly reviewed by our technical, editorial, and production personnel for accuracy and ease-of-use before you ever see it—our guarantee that you'll buy a quality Sybex book every time.

To manage your hardware headaches and optimize your software potential, ask for a Sybex book.

FOR MORE INFORMATION, PLEASE CONTACT:

Sybex Inc.
2021 Challenger Drive
Alameda, CA 94501
Tel: (510) 523-8233 • (800) 227-2346
Fax: (510) 523-2373

Sybex is committed to using natural resources wisely to preserve and improve our environment. As a leader in the computer books publishing industry, we are aware that over 40% of America's solid waste is paper. This is why we have been printing our books on recycled paper since 1982.

This year our use of recycled paper will result in the saving of more than 153,000 trees. We will lower air pollution effluents by 54,000 pounds, save 6,300,000 gallons of water, and reduce landfill by 27,000 cubic yards.

In choosing a Sybex book you are not only making a choice for the best in skills and information, you are also choosing to enhance the quality of life for all of us.

Microsoft Access® 2
Developer's Handbook

Ken Getz
Paul Litwin
Greg Reddick

SYBEX®

San Francisco · Paris · Düsseldorf · Soest

Acquisitions Editor: Joanne Cuthbertson
Developmental Editor: David Peal
Editor: Dusty Bernard
Project Editor: Kristen Vanberg-Wolff
Technical Editor: Helen Feddema
Book Series Designer and Production Artist: Suzanne Albertson
Production Artist: Lucie Zivny
Graphics File Manager: Aldo X. Bermudez
Desktop Publishing Specialist: Deborah Maizels
Proofreader/Production Assistant: Emily Smith
Indexer: Ted Laux
Cover Designer: Design Site

Portions of this book are derived from three articles published in *Smart Access,* a monthly publication owned
and published by Pinnacle Publishing, Inc.:

"Jet 2.0 Query Optimization and Rushmore," Paul Litwin, July, 1994
"Handle Errors in Access," Greg Reddick, February, 1994
"When Are Dynasets Updatable?," Paul Litwin, December, 1993

These articles are copyrighted by Pinnacle Publishing and the derived material appears here with Pinnacle's
express consent. For information about *Smart Access,* a monthly newsletter for users of Microsoft Access,
please contact Pinnacle Publishing at 18000 72nd Ave., So., Suite 217, Kent, WA 98032, or via telephone at
800-788-1900 or 206-251-1900.

Appendix A copyright ©1993–1994 by Stan Leszynski and Gregory Reddick. All rights reserved. Used by
permission. Appendix A is based on the article "Naming Objects in Microsoft Access: Version 2 of a Proposed Standard," published in *Smart Access*, August, 1993.

The illustration on p.1050 adapted with permission of Shapeware Corporation, from *Programming Visio,*
copyright ©1994 Shapeware Corporation.

Library of Congress Card Number: 94-67532
ISBN: 0-7821-1327-3

Manufactured in the United States of America
10 9 8 7 6

Without the support and understanding of Peter Mason, Alicia and Geoffrey Litwin, and Geralyne Rudolph, this book wouldn't have been possible. They provided editorial, emotional, and intellectual support when we had little to offer in return. To them we dedicate this book.

ACKNOWLEDGMENTS

This book wouldn't have been possible without the concerted effort of many individuals in addition to the authors. First of all, we'd like to thank Mike Gunderloy, Scott Alexander, Brian Randell, and Dan Haught, who made it possible to produce this book by helping in the writing of several chapters.

Mike Gunderloy contributed significantly to Chapter 11, "Developing Multiuser Applications," Chapter 13, "Providing an Elegant Interface," and Chapter 15, "Debugging Applications" and provided technical editing support on several other chapters. Mike provides daily support to CompuServe MSACCESS forum users and was recognized in 1994 as a forum MVP by Microsoft. He's a principal at Brooklyn, New York–based Pyramid Computers and is a regular contributor to *Smart Access*.

Scott Alexander was responsible for Chapter 12, "Developing Client-Server Applications." Scott is a Sunol, California–based consultant specializing in the development of Windows-based client-server systems and providing performance management services for large networks. He was also recognized as an MSACCESS forum MVP by Microsoft in 1994 and has written for *Smart Access*.

Brian Randell contributed significantly to Chapter 20, "Creating Libraries, Wizards, Builders, and Menu Add-Ins." Brian is development manager at Interface Management Services, Inc., in Claremont, California. He develops custom Microsoft Office–based fund-raising and accounting systems. Brian is another regular fixture on CompuServe.

Dan Haught contributed significantly to Chapter 6, "Using Data Access Objects." Dan is the product manager for FMS Inc. in Vienna, Virginia. He's the developer behind Total Access Analyzer, a hugely successful Access documentation add-in for Access. Dan is also a contributing editor for *Smart Access*.

We'd also like to thank the following individuals who provided technical editing support for one or more chapters and thus improved the text considerably: Joe Celko, Desmond Chek, Michael Corning, Jim Ferguson, Pamela Hazelrigg, Michael Hernandez, Joe Morris, David Oxstein, John Viescas, and Thomas Wagner.

Thanks to all the current and former members of the Access and Jet teams at Microsoft. In particular, the following individuals gave us early access to information, answered lots of technical questions, or reviewed chapters: Kim Abercrombie, Steve Alboucq, Neil Black, Steve Brandli, Kevin Collins, Dennis Comfort, Scott Fallon, Don Funk, Jim Hance, Ross Hunter, Michael Mee, Mark Moeller, Tad Orman, David Risher, Joe Robison, Monte Slichter, and George Snelling.

We'd also like to thank Stan Leszynski, who coauthored the naming conventions found in Appendix A.

Special thanks to the folks at Shapeware, particularly Jill Carlsen, for providing software and answers to some thorny interaction problems. We'd also like to thank Pinnacle Publishing, particularly Dian Schauffhauser, for making it possible to reprint material from *Smart Access* and for being understanding when newsletter deadlines were sometimes missed because of book deadlines. And we'd like to thank Erik Ruthruff at Application Developers Training Company for also cutting us some slack on his expectations during the first half of 1994, allowing us to spend time writing rather than training.

Of course, without the hard work and support of the fine people at SYBEX, this book would be nothing more than a dream. Special thanks go to SYBEX editors David Peal, Dusty Bernard, and Kris Vanberg-Wolff and our technical editor, Helen Feddema.

Finally, we'd like to thank our friends, significant others, and other family members who put up with us during an especially long and trying year.

CONTENTS AT A GLANCE

TABLE OF CONTENTS

PART IV Multiuser Development 743

PART VI   Interoperability   977

17 ACCESSING DLLS AND THE WINDOWS API   979

FOREWORD

The shipment of Microsoft Access 2.0 marked a fundamental change in the desktop database scene. For the first time a product could be a true single solution for any given application within a corporation. Access 2.0 is remarkably easy for both entry-level end users with ad hoc querying and reporting needs and for "power users" who may be creating workgroup applications. But it doesn't stop there! For example, Access 2.0 is one of the premier client/server tools on the market today. And with a programming model similar to that of Microsoft Visual Basic, it offers serious developers almost unlimited power in creating everything from information systems on up to sophisticated transaction-processing applications running against SQL Server or Oracle databases.

There is a plethora of books on the market for Access 2.0, most focused at the lower- or mid-range user. What Paul Litwin, Ken Getz, and Greg Reddick have accomplished is significant, though—they've created a reference, in their *Microsoft Access Developer's Handbook,* that can take the professional developer from ground zero to the clouds. Here is a book that does more than just provide technical information; it helps you become a better developer. The authors discuss topics in depth that many other books merely skirt or ignore altogether.

They delve deeply into the most powerful tips and tricks for creating powerful forms and reports and offer in-depth discussions of critical issues surrounding client-server and multiuser application development. Their coverage of application optimization and customization (via OLE 2.0, add-ins, Wizards, and builders) is where the serious developer really takes off.

I've known Paul for years and worked closely with all three authors long before we shipped Access 2.0. They know their stuff. If there are three authors especially qualified to write a book the advanced Access developer can use, it is these three. All are well-known within the Access community for their creative solutions and depth of understanding of Access as a development platform. Their book makes a great stride forward in exposing professional developers to the application power of Access 2.0.

Scott Fallon, Microsoft Access Product Manager

About the Authors

Ken Getz   is a programmer, technical writer, and educator. Formerly a member of the Ashton-Tate Framework III and IV development teams, he currently develops custom applications and tools using Microsoft Access, Visual C/C++, and Visual Basic. He's a 1993 and 1994 Microsoft MVP award winner, spending all his spare time on CompuServe, learning while answering many of the questions posted there. He teaches Access developer training classes for the Application Developers Training Company, and is a frequent speaker at technical conferences, including Tech*Ed '94 and '95. He's also a Contributing Editor for *Smart Access*. When not programming or writing, he turns his chair around and tickles the other keyboard, the grand piano filling the other half of his office. You can reach Ken on CompuServe at 76137,3650 or on the Internet at 76137.3650@compuserve.com.

Paul Litwin   is the owner of Seattle-based Litwin Consulting, a Microsoft Solution Provider specializing in Windows database solutions using Microsoft Access, SQL/Server, and Microsoft Office applications. Paul is the editor of *Smart Access*, a widely acclaimed monthly newsletter from Pinnacle Publishing for Access developers. He has written many articles and reviews for numerous publications. In early 1994, Paul was commissioned by Microsoft to write the Jet Engine White Paper. He also trains developers for the Application Developers Training Company and is a regular speaker at conferences including Windows Solutions and Tech*Ed. In his spare moments, Paul enjoys spending time with his family, running, and coaching his son's grade school soccer team. You can reach Paul on CompuServe at 76447,417 or on the Internet at 76447.417@compuserve.com.

Greg Reddick   is the President of Gregory Reddick & Associates, a Redmond, WA based consulting firm specializing in developing Windows programs in Microsoft Access, Visual Basic, and C/C++. Greg has done database development for the last 12 years. He worked as a Software Design Engineer at Microsoft and spent four years on the development team for Microsoft Access 1.0. After leaving Microsoft, he wrote *Access to Word*, an add-on for Access that performs mail merges with Word for Windows. He writes for *Smart Access* and is the co-author of the industry standard naming conventions for Access (which appear in Appendix A). Greg also travels internationally to perform training. This is his second book on Access. You can reach Greg on CompuServe at 71501,2564 or on the Internet at 71501.2564@compuserve.com.

INTRODUCTION

When it was released in late 1992, Microsoft Access took the database world by storm because of its aggressive $99 price. But when the dust settled after the first million were sold, many users and developers were pleasantly surprised to find a *real database* hidden beneath that ridiculously cheap price tag. Access 1.0 and the soon-to-follow modest upgrade, version 1.1, were certainly far from perfect, but users found an instantly usable product that broke down the walls of database accessibility. At the same time, almost overnight, a large and healthy developer community (that included the authors of this book) was born and began to develop professional applications that ran businesses of all sizes throughout the world.

Since its introduction, however, Microsoft has been working on the next major release— version 2.0—which hit the streets in May of 1994. This major overhaul of Access fixed most of the limitations and annoyances of version 1.x and made numerous improvements in the areas of usability, programmability, and extendibility.

Access 2.0 is a wonderfully powerful development platform, but like any powerful product, it takes considerable time to master. Fortunately for you, the three of us (plus a few others) have spent many months and countless hours tearing apart Access 2.0, exposing its undocumented secrets, and making it do things that few have imagined were possible—all for your benefit.

About the Book

This book is not a substitute for the Microsoft documentation, nor is it meant as a comprehensive reference manual. Instead, we strove to address the major issues that we feel will face most developers. When we had to choose whether to cover a given topic or feature—one has to stop somewhere—we tended to favor the undocumented or poorly documented versus the well documented.

Among the many topics we cover in the 23 chapters that make up this book are database and user interface design, queries, form design, report design, Access SQL, Access Basic, Code-Behind-Forms, data access objects, the Windows API, OLE 2.0,

DDE, creating Wizards, error handling, debugging, multiuser programming, developing client-server front ends, security, help systems, and performance tuning.

In addition to the text, this book includes the usual assortment of figures, examples, and tables. We also include lots of notes, tips, and warnings throughout the book to call special attention to certain features or "gotchas."

Is This Book for You?

This book is for the Access developer or someone who would like to become one. It doesn't matter whether you develop Access applications full time, as only one component of your job, or in your spare time during the evenings and weekends. What matters is that you take the product seriously and want your applications to be the very best.

If you only care to get your toes wet with Access and are happy to throw together quick-and-dirty applications that are automated with nothing more than a few macros, you probably don't need this book. But if you're ready to dive into the thick of Access and get down to the business of developing industrial-strength applications that utilize Access to its fullest, you've picked the right book.

What You Need to Know

For you to benefit most from an advanced book such as this, we've had to dispense with the fundamentals and make several assumptions about you. We assume that you already have a basic level of familiarity with the product. At a minimum, you should already be comfortable creating tables and simple queries, forms, and reports and have at least a rudimentary understanding of macros and Access Basic. If you aren't up to speed, you may wish to put down this book for the moment and spend some time with Access and the manuals (including the *Building Applications* guide), the Help system, or an introductory text such as *Understanding Microsoft Access 2* by Alan Simpson (SYBEX, 1994).

Conventions Used in This Book

It goes without saying that the professional developer must consistently follow *some* standard. We followed several standard conventions in this book to make it easier for you to follow along.

We have used the Leszynski/Reddick (L/R) conventions for the naming of Access objects, which has become the de facto naming standard in the Access development community. (One of the authors of this book, Greg Reddick, codeveloped the standard, which in part bears his name.) Even if you don't subscribe to the L/R standard, however, you'll likely appreciate the fact that it has been used consistently throughout the book. These conventions, which were first published in *Smart Access,* are included in their entirety in Appendix A and excerpted in the inside front cover of this book.

In addition to following the L/R standard, we have prefaced all functions, subroutines, and user-defined types that you may wish to use from your own code with the "glr" prefix and aliased all Windows API declarations using a "glr_api" prefix. These conventions should avoid naming conflicts with any existing code in your applications. If, however, you import multiple modules from various chapters' sample databases into a single database, you may find naming conflicts as a result of our using consistent naming throughout the chapters. In that case you'll need to comment out any conflicting API declarations or user-defined types.

To meet the constraints of the page size of this book, we have used the symbol ➡ to indicate a line of program code that was too long to fit on a single printed line but that must appear as one line in your code. For example, the following two printed lines need to be entered on a single line in Access:

```
MsgBox "This line of code won't fit on a single printed page.",
➡ 0, "Line Break Note"
```

About the Disk

The disk that comes with this book (attached to the inside back cover) is a valuable companion to the book. It includes all the chapter databases discussed in the book, as well as several extra goodies that should make your Access development work more efficient.

Installing the Disk

The sample disk contains a text file (README.TXT) and a self-extracting compressed file (_GLRFILE.EXE). To use the disk, you'll need to follow these steps:

1. Copy README.TXT and _GLRFILE.EXE to a new subdirectory of your hard disk. (README.TXT contains additional installation information.)

2. Extract _GLRFILE.EXE by typing

   ```
   _GLRFILE
   ```

   at the DOS prompt (or by using File ➤ Run in the Windows Program Manager).

3. Run the set of self-extracting compressed files this process creates. One of these files, _CHAPTER.EXE, contains all the sample chapter databases. (We've used the convention of preceding all self-extracting files with an underscore. This makes it easy for you to distinguish a self-extracting file from a normal executable file.)

4. Read README.TXT for more installation details.

What's on the Disk?

Each chapter database includes numerous examples that demonstrate techniques discussed in the chapter, as well as generic, reusable code you can use in your own applications. A sampling of what you'll find in the chapter databases follows:

- A Soundex function for performing sound-alike searches (Chapter 3)
- A set of functions for reading and writing the ColumnHeadings property of crosstab queries (Chapter 4)

- A SQL scratch pad form (Chapter 5)
- Lots of data access objects examples, including a form that simulates the database container (Chapter 6)
- Useful composite controls, like multiple-select list boxes and spin buttons (Chapter 7)
- An incremental search control, using a text and list box linked together (Chapter 7)
- A generic query by form creator, which works with any data input form (Chapter 8)
- Screen-resolution–independent forms and automatic scaling on resize (Chapter 8)
- A set of functions for tracking Access events to help debug the order of events as they occur (Chapter 8)
- A set of functions for retrieving printer capabilities (Chapter 9)
- A set of functions for creating your own right mouse button menus (Chapter 10)
- Expanding forms—like the Print Setup dialog, forms that take two shapes (Chapter 13)
- A function that asserts the state of your code; used to track down logic errors (Chapter 14)
- A demonstration application for creating a project organization chart in Visio using OLE Automation (Chapter 19)
- Instructions on how to provide your own font-choosing form (Chapter 21)
- A set of functions for managing security through DAO, including one that prints out all user accounts with blank passwords and another you can use to prevent a user from creating new databases (Chapter 22)

In addition to the chapter databases, several other free- and shareware files and programs can be found on the disk, including

- **A Help file reference to all the reusable Access Basic procedures on the disk:** This standard Windows Help file is a useful reference to all the generic, reusable routines found on the disk.

- **The SuperSpy freeware program for spying window classes:** This freeware utility, from SoftBlox, Inc. (1201 West Peachtree St. N.W., Ste. 3220, Atlanta GA 30309; CompuServe 71623,2066), makes it possible for you to dig around inside Access and discover the class names for each of the window types. You can use this information to your advantage when you need to programmatically control the Access environment.

- **The Access 2.0 Security Wizard from Microsoft:** Using this Wizard, which is discussed in Chapter 22, is the only way to ensure that your databases are absolutely secure.

How to Use This Book

While you may find it easiest to read the chapters in the order in which they appear in the book, it's not essential. One goal we strove for as we wrote the book was to make it so that you could pick up and read any individual chapter without having to have read through several other chapters first. Thus, the book is *not* a linear progression that starts with Chapter 1 and ends with Chapter 23. Instead, we have logically grouped together similar chapters, but otherwise (with a few exceptions) the chapters do not particularly build upon each other.

To make it easier for you to be able to jump from one chapter to another, we have included cross-references throughout the book.

While we've done a lot of the work for you, you'll get the most benefit from this book by putting the material to real use. Take the examples and generic routines found in the book and expand on them. Add and subtract from them as you incorporate them into your applications. Experiment and enjoy!

PART I

Overview of Access

CHAPTER

ONE

Access and the Access Architecture

- Why Access is the desktop database platform of choice

- Components of the Access architecture

- What's new in version 2.0

Chances are, if you're reading this book, you've already decided that Microsoft Access 2.0 is a worthy platform for your development endeavors. Chances are, you're right. Microsoft has created a serious, full-featured, and powerful development environment for creating database applications on single-user or networked personal computers. Microsoft estimates that sales of Access in 1993 doubled the PC database sales over the previous year, and they are hoping for like improvement in 1994.

Where Access Fits in the Desktop Database Market

Certainly, Access is not without competition. There are several other Windows-based database development environments to choose from. Borland's Paradox for Windows and dBASE for Windows 1.0 (which will probably have been released by the time you read this), as well as Powersoft's PowerBuilder, are also capable desktop database development packages. There's even competition within the ranks at Microsoft: both FoxPro and Visual Basic are competing with Access. We feel quite strongly, however, that if you want to manage databases on Windows-based PCs, Access is far and away the best tool for the job, period. Here are just some of the reasons why we have come to this conclusion:

- Access has the strongest support for the relational model. Its support for the dynaset, integrated data dictionary, referential integrity (including support for cascading updates and deletes), and SQL all bear witness to this fact.

- Access is primarily a nonprocedural environment, although it contains a powerful procedural language—Access Basic with data access objects—when you need it.

- With the introduction of version 2.0, Access exposes a rich event model and supports the manipulation of almost every property at run time.

- Access supports OLE 2 and was the first product to support the new OLE 2 Custom Controls.

- Access supports multiuser database sharing both in file-server and client-server environments. This means you can scale your applications from single-user to client-server with the same front-end tool.

- The Jet engine, the database engine behind Access, is a mature, well-architected, relational database engine based on 1990s technology. This is in marked contrast to some of the 1970s and '80s-based database engines that other products use.

- With the introduction of version 2.0, the Jet engine now includes Rushmore optimization technology borrowed from FoxPro. This new technology means that many complex queries will execute much more quickly than before.

- Access has a companion run-time package, included in the Access Developer's Toolkit, that you can use to distribute Access applications without paying royalties.

- Microsoft sold over a million copies of Access in the first year of its existence. No other company has sold so many copies of a brand-new database product so quickly.

- Microsoft is a financially sound company with a focused vision for the future. This cannot be said for some of its competitors.

- Microsoft has the biggest usability lab in the world, meaning that they don't just say something is more usable—they can *prove* it.

- Microsoft listens to Access users and developers and incorporates their suggestions in new versions of the product. Microsoft is also acutely aware of its competition, but it isn't so market driven that it ends up always playing catch-up like some of its competitors. Instead, Microsoft leads the market.

Simply put, of all these products, Access has the best combination of power, ease of use, extendability, and long-term market viability.

Opportunity Knocks

Microsoft marketing tells us that the vast majority of Access sales went to end users (as opposed to developers) either in the stand-alone package or as part of Microsoft Office Professional. This might tempt you to say, "Well, then, it's an end-user package, so I'm going to use Paradox for Windows instead." But you'd be closing the door on opportunity. It's just this popularity among end users that makes Access a perfect development platform. Of course, power users might be able to get things set up just fine in Access, but once they get past a certain point (and that point has moved a little higher in Access 2.0), they're going to need some help. When they see what Access is capable of, they'll want more, and their wants will usually exceed their grasp. That's where you, the Access developer, fit in. Most users can't be bothered with reading manuals or figuring out the complexities of programming. You will, after going through the material in this book, be prepared to handle many of the situations that end users will confront you with.

There's another side to this issue, too: you can deliver solutions onto users' desktops that they can tweak and extend themselves. In other words, you're empowering your users. Can you do this with Paradox, FoxPro, dBASE, or PowerBuilder? Probably not. If you're an in-house developer in a large corporation or government agency, empowering your users can be a big advantage. Even independent developers will have the occasional client who wants to be able to "play with things." This means you don't have to spend all your time perfecting the formatting of that report. Let your sophisticated power users do it instead.

What's New in Access 2.0

Access 1.0 really opened the eyes of many database developers. It was one of the first relational database products available for the Windows 3.x platform, and it was certainly the first to fill the needs of many developers, both corporate and independent. Besides its ease of use in getting started, it was very easy to create simple applications. It had some limitations when developers got past a certain point in their applications, and it had a severe limitation in that databases couldn't be larger than 128 megabytes. Access 1.1 fixed that limitation, expanding the maximum database size to 2 gigabytes, and fixed some other limitations, as well. Still, there were many professional features lacking. Programmers used to Visual Basic's nearly complete flexibility were stymied by Access' inability to change control and form properties at run time, for example. On the other hand, there was no simpler way to get data in and out of forms than Access, so developers worked around Access 1.x's limitations.

Access 2.0 provides great gains for developers. Although there are numerous improvements for end users, the greatest leap from 1.1 comes in the improvements for the development community. For the professional programmer, Access 2.0 adds features in almost every area of the product. All these improvements are discussed throughout the book. The following sections list some of the more important changes for the developer, grouped by area of functionality.

Forms: What's New

Developers now have much finer control over how forms look and behave. The myriad of improvements to forms include the following:

- New form layout properties allow you more control over window characteristics of the form. This makes it possible for you to control more of the look of the form while calling the Windows API far less.

- New control builders help you in creating the more complex controls. In addition, Access has added a method that allows you to add your own builders, attached to any property of the property sheet. Chapter 20, which discusses Wizards and builders, demonstrates this new feature.

- You now have the ability (finally!) to change almost any form or control property *while the form or report is running.* You can change colors, sizes, captions, data sources, and more, just as you might expect.

- You can exercise greater control over data editing on forms. For example, you can control whether or not users can add new rows. In addition, counter values are now added when you first add a new row, not when that row gets committed.

- Forms and controls have many more event properties. With this greatly expanded event model, your applications can react to mouse and keyboard, timer, and form resizing events, among many others.

- Event procedures (also called Code-Behind-Forms, or CBF, by most developers) are now stored in modules attached to the specific form or report. These modules, in which every procedure is private, allow you to encapsulate code within the form it works with, and they make programming with Access far closer to the Visual Basic programming model.

Reports: What's New

Compared with the changes to forms, the improvements made to reports are less dramatic. Nonetheless, they are all useful and include the following:

- You can now attach *menus* to reports.

- A new event model has added OnActivate and OnDeactivate report events and OnRetreat section events. These events make it possible, for example, for you to have different toolbars visible when the user moves from one open report to another.

- You can now change properties of the report and its controls at *run time*. From the section events (OnFormat, OnPrint and OnRetreat), you can change almost any property of any control or section on the report.

Tables and Queries: What's New

Access queries and the Jet engine have been given a major overhaul. Table design and relationships have also undergone major improvements. These changes include the following:

- A graphical relationship builder has been added.

- Attached tables now support relationships.

- Access now supports cascading updates and deletes.

- Support for descending indexes and unique multicolumn indexes has been added.

- Field properties have been improved. You can now *require* a value for a field. You also have true input masks and support for zero-length strings.

- Engine-level table validation rules have been provided.

- Access now supports union queries, subqueries, and data definition queries. It also supports SQL pass-through queries, which improves client-server support.

- Access 2.0 provides an improved SQL view.

- You can now create Top "n" queries, which retrieve a fixed number or percent of rows.

- With an improved dynaset model, most columns of most queries are now updatable.

- Rushmore query optimization technology has been added to the Jet database engine, which means that Jet can use multiple indexes when executing a query. This can result in considerable performance increases for complex queries.

Access Basic: What's New

Access Basic has been improved considerably in version 2.0. The major changes include the following:

- With DAO (data access objects), a superset of Visual Basic 3.0's data-manipulation language, you can now modify almost any property of any object in Access from Access Basic. You can create, delete, and modify any data object that's part of the Jet engine. In addition, you can finally retrieve any piece of information you'll need for the data objects Access uses, including the elusive Description property for tables and queries.

- As part of DAO, you can modify and inquire about security settings directly from Access Basic. In Access 1.x, you had no means of handling security programmatically. Now it's all handled in a straightforward manner using DAO.

- You now have more generic syntax for referring to Recordset objects. In Access 1.x you found yourself dealing with tables, dynasets, and snapshots all as separate objects. In Access 2.0, these are all subtypes of the Recordset datatype, making it simpler to work with objects of each type with the same code.

Other Improvements

The preceding sections haven't covered all of the improvements. Many more changes were made to the product, including the following:

- Access 2.0 provides support for OLE 2. Access now supports in-place editing and OLE automation.

- Access also supports the exciting new OLE custom controls (OLE's replacement for Visual Basic's .VBX control). These add-ins, appearing from many vendors, make Access as extensible as Visual Basic ever was. OLE custom controls are portable, can work with either 16- or 32-bit applications, and are the future of component application tools, as far as Microsoft is concerned. Access' support for these (it's the first application to be able to use them) gives Access a strong lead in the database "wars."

- An improved security model gives you much finer control over object permissions.

- With the integrated database documentor, you can now print out your table definitions and form properties.

- The Menu Builder takes the work out of writing menu macros.

- You can *customize* Wizard styles and create and hook into your own Wizards and builders much more easily.

The Access Architecture

Gaining a full grasp of Access requires an understanding of how it was designed and programmed. Access has many distinct components that make up its whole. Figure 1.1 shows these layers.

FIGURE 1.1:

Access architecture

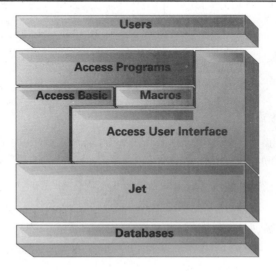

NOTE The block diagrams in this chapter are approximations; the relationships between components are certainly more complex than shown.

Users interface with Access using either the user interface tools or an Access program, which can be driven by macros, Access Basic, or a combination of the two. These components, in turn, make calls to the Microsoft Jet database engine to read or write rows of data.

Access consists of an executable file, MSACCESS.EXE, and a series of Dynamic Link Libraries (DLLs). The components fit together like a jigsaw puzzle to form Access. Access is designed this way for several reasons:

- If all of Access were in a single .EXE, all loaded at once, it would waste a considerable amount of RAM.

- This design allows Microsoft to independently test and ship each component.

- Code can be shared more easily with other Microsoft teams, such as the Visual Basic and Office teams.

- Packaged components (for example, the Jet engine, OLE, and Graph) can be shared with other programs.

The different components of Access are spread across numerous files on your disk. For example, the code for the Access User Interface and macros is in MSACCESS.EXE, Access Basic is in MSABC200.DLL, and Jet is in MSAJT200.DLL. There is a large number of supporting Dynamic Link Libraries and other files.

The Access User Interface

Access' user interface and appearance are layered on top of the low-level architecture, which is discussed in the section "The Access Internal Architecture" later in this chapter. The user interface (UI) presents the user with six kinds of objects in the familiar database container:

Tables

Queries

Forms

Reports

Macros

Modules

With the exception of attached tables, all data in a database is stored in one file, which, by default, uses the extension .MDB.

System Tables

Access stores all the interface objects, such as forms, as binary data. Rather than inventing a new scheme to store the binary data, Microsoft stores these objects in the database alongside the data. This *data dictionary* consists of a series of normally hidden tables called the *system tables*. The system tables include

MSysACEs

MSysColumns

MSysIMEXColumns

MSysIMEXSpecs

MSysIndexes

MSysMacros

MSysObjects

MSysQueries

MSysRelationships

Normally, Access hides these tables from the user. You can unhide them by setting the option Show System Objects in the Options dialog to Yes.

Almost the entire Access UI is devoted to manipulating these system tables. For example, in table design, creating a table creates a record in MSysObjects. Each new column created in the table adds a record to MSysColumns. Each new index adds a record to MSysIndexes.

In Version 1.x of Access, users could open the system tables and treat them like any other table, including writing to them. Version 2.0 prohibits users from writing directly to the system tables; reading from them is still allowed. This closed a gaping hole in the Access security scheme in which a knowledgeable user could reassign ownership of objects very easily.

The System Database

Each time Jet starts it looks to a particular database known as the System Database (or SystemDB file) for certain information. The SystemDB is, by default, called SYSTEM.MDA. This database contains information about the users in a workgroup. A *workgroup* is a group of users, with associated security information. (The Access UI also stores user preference information in the SystemDB.)

The fact that SystemDB is a separate file is important to remember because you must be careful to keep track of this database, as well as the databases that contain your data. The SystemDB file should be backed up at the same time that any other database is backed up. Losing a System Database can cause significant problems, especially if you've impemented security. You may be completely locked out of accessing your data if you cannot restore the SystemDB to its former state.

Chapter 22 describes Access security in depth, including how to manipulate security from Access Basic code using DAO.

Behind the Scenes: Other Objects

Access maintains several objects that are not among the six shown in the Database window. One of these objects is security information. Security information is stored in two places: the System Database and the MSysACEs system table. The System Database, as described in the preceding section, stores information about the users in a workgroup. The MSysACEs system table stores information about the particular objects for which a user has permissions.

Access also maintains the system relationships as another "hidden" object. These relationships are stored in the table MSysRelationships.

Access stores import and export specifications for the importing and exporting of ASCII text files in two additional system tables, MSysIMEXColumns and MSysIMEXSpecs. These tables are not created until you create the first import/export specification for a database. MSysIMEXSpecs contains one record for each import/export specification, storing general information regarding the specification. MSysIMEXColumns contains multiple records for each specification, with a record for each field to be imported or exported.

Access uses macros to design and store two other objects: menus and key assignments. In most ways these objects are treated as ordinary macros. They can even be run as macros. But if you specify a macro name in the MenuBar property of a form, Access creates the associated menu bar when you start the form. Similarly, specifying a keyboard macro in the options sets the keyboard assignments when Access is started.

The Access Internal Architecture

Beneath the user interface, Access consists of Access and Jet. Jet handles all the processing of rows of data; its architecture is discussed more fully in Chapter 16. Access handles everything else. The internal architecture of Access is depicted in Figure 1.2. These pieces include

MSACCESS.EXE

International DLL

OLE DLLs

MSINFO.EXE

Import Utility DLL

Utility Database

Other Libraries

Wizards

Cue Cards and Help

MSACCESS.EXE

MSACCESS.EXE, the central component of Access, drives each of the other pieces. It contains the code for most of the Access UI, including the windows you see.

Most chapters in this book relate to MSACCESS.EXE in one way or another, but Chapters 7 through 10 particularly concentrate on components related to MSACCESS.EXE.

International DLL

Microsoft made a considerable effort to isolate every item that needs to be translated in the Access UI. These items are stored in the International DLL. By replacing this single DLL, Microsoft can localize Access to another language. This ability drastically reduces the amount of time it takes to translate Access into another language since only this one DLL needs to be changed.

FIGURE 1.2:

A closer look at the Access internal architecture

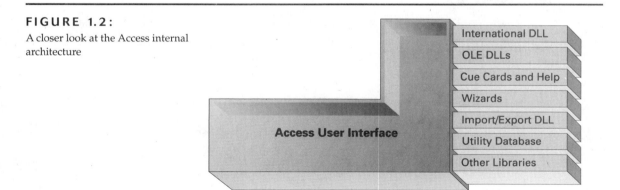

OLE DLLs and DDE

Object Linking and Embedding (OLE) is a standard model for creating and communicating between objects. It is the glue that binds together different applications. The OLE DLLs are really a part of the Windows operating system, but because they have been evolving so quickly, Microsoft ships the latest versions of these files with Access. Access ties into these libraries to perform tasks requiring OLE, including support for the new OLE custom controls.

One OLE application is installed with every copy of Access: MSGraph. Graph is an OLE server you can use to create data charts.

Chapter 19 looks at OLE in detail.

Although OLE is the interoperability method of the future, there is an older, less robust, and less full-featured method that has been around for several years called DDE (Dynamic Data Exchange). Many older applications still support only this interoperability standard, and many newer applications support both standards. Although it has its faults and can be frustrating at times to use, DDE has its place in the occasional Access application, certainly until OLE 2 becomes more pervasive and stable.

Using DDE with Access is the subject of Chapter 18.

MSINFO.EXE

When you select Help ➤ About Microsoft Access, Access 2.0 provides more information about the Windows environment than did earlier versions. It does this by activating a separate applet program, shared with other Microsoft Office applications, called MSINFO.EXE.

This application is essentially a Windows version of the DOS program, MSD. It can come in handy for debugging systems, but there are more complete third-party programs, such as TouchStone's CheckItPRO Analyst. Still, it is provided free, and since it's an .EXE file, you can invoke it yourself with a shell statement from Access Basic. For example:

```
intRet = Shell("c:\windows\msapps\msinfo\msinfo.exe")
```

Import/Export Utility DLL

Access can import tables from many kinds of data sources: FoxPro, dBASE, Paradox, Btrieve, and ODBC programs, such as SQL Server, using the Jet engine. But there are some kinds of data that Jet doesn't know how to process: ASCII, 1-2-3, and Excel, to name a few. Access is able to import tables from these data sources by using routines in MSAJU200.DLL.

Utility Database

The Utility database (UTILITY.MDA) is a special Access library database. Inside it are various utility forms and routines written in Access Basic. For example, the zoom box, import/export spec forms, and the Access Basic constants are stored here. For the most part, you can't tell whether the routines Access uses are part of the Access executable or are being interpreted by Access Basic. (There is one notable exception you might have run into: the zoom box won't work when you have an uncorrected Access Basic syntax error.)

Other Libraries

Access can install other libraries, including ones written by you or other developers; several libraries, for example, are discussed in Chapter 20 and are included on the disk that accompanies this book. These libraries allow you to extend the Access UI with your own code. Version 2.0 adds new features that make using libraries easier and more efficient (using Code-Behind-Forms, libraries now consume fewer resources), making libraries more practical than before. The version 2.0 Add-In Manager makes it much easier to load and unload custom libraries.

Chapter 20 describes how to create Access Basic libraries and other add-ins.

Wizards, Builders, and Menu Add-Ins

Wizards in Access are tools that help you (or more typically your users) perform tasks that are either complex or lend themselves easily to automation. An example of the first type of Wizard is one that creates combo and list boxes; an example of the second is one that creates a quick form.

Builders are tools that help construct a specific *property* (an attribute of an object) on an Access property sheet. You launch these tools by clicking a button that displays an ellipsis (...) after the property. For example, Access comes with a builder that helps you construct a menu bar, providing a means of automatically generating the needed macros that you would otherwise have to create yourself.

You can also create add-ins that are more general purpose than Wizards or builders. These tools are added to the File ➤ Add-Ins menu item and are always available from the File menu. In contrast, Wizards and builders are available only when the user is in a suitable context. For example, a property builder would be available only when the user is on that property. Wizards and builders provide some context information about the state of Access when they are invoked; menu add-ins do not receive any such information.

All of these tools are written in Access Basic and are described in detail in Chapter 20.

Cue Cards and Help

Access, of course, has an extensive Help file that runs using the standard Windows help engine (WINHELP.EXE). In addition, Access 1.0 introduced a new method for providing help, called *Cue Cards*. These extensions to the standard Windows Help system assist users in moving through the steps necessary to perform a design task.

You can create your own Help files that are called from your applications. Chapter 23 describes how to do this. Unfortunately, Microsoft has not yet introduced tools to help you create your own Cue Cards.

The Access Programming Model

The Access programming model uses an event-driven programming paradigm. *Event-driven programming* means that the programming language operates in response to actions that happen while a user is running a form or report. A relatively simple action by the user—moving the mouse over the form and clicking several controls, for example—will cause numerous events to fire. On any of these events, you can step in and perform some action. The code that is activated when an event occurs is called an *event handler*.

The more events Access generates when a user does something, the finer the control you have over Access since you can take control at any point where an event is generated. Access version 2.0 generates many more events than version 1.1.

The advantage of event-driven programming is that the user has more control over what occurs than under a traditional programming model. A user who wants to take look at a form that shows an interest calculation while the main loan form is up can do so. With some exceptions, Access applications don't determine the order of actions taken by the user. The Access event model is discussed in further detail in Chapter 8.

Access Basic

Access has two languages that can be used to drive it: Access Basic and macros. Macros are a simple script of actions for Access to perform. In contrast, Access Basic is a complete programming language based on the technology in Visual Basic. If you want to develop professional applications, you need to use Access Basic. You'll still need to learn all the macro actions since Access Basic doesn't provide replacement functions for some of them (for example, OpenForm and Hourglass), but these actions should be called from Access Basic procedures using the DoCmd statement. There are many reasons for using Access Basic: the availability of control structures, run-time error handling, and an extended command set, to name a few. In version 2.0 Access Basic now includes a rich data object hierarchy called data access objects, or DAO.

NOTE The vast majority of this book deals with Access Basic. You won't find much discussion regarding macros, except when you're required to use them: with menus, startup routines, and shortcut keys. These topics are covered in Chapter 10.

Calling the Windows API and Other DLLs

Every Windows program uses a set of functions provided by Windows called the Windows Application Programming Interface (API). These functions do everything from creating a window to reading an .INI file. These functions are reached through a number of DLLs that come with Windows. In Access Basic, most of these functions have been made a part of the programming language. For example, the Access Basic MsgBox() function calls the Windows MessageBox() function. However, not everything you can do with Windows can be done directly though standard features in Access Basic, so Access Basic provides a way to get at them directly.

In the same way that you can get to the Windows DLLs, you can get to any DLL. This ability allows you to extend Access Basic by writing procedures in other languages, such as C, that would normally be impossible in Access Basic alone.

The Windows API is used throughout the book, but Chapter 17 discusses it and other DLLs in particular detail.

A "Typical" Access Application

Applications developed in Access are made up of a number of components that are glued together with Access Basic. The typical (if such a thing exists) application might include these components:

Component	Description
Application database	Sits on the user's desktop. The application is started by an AutoExec macro that calls a startup Access Basic routine stored in a global module
Data tables	Stored in a data database that resides on the same machine or in a file-server or a client-server database
Main menu (or switchboard) form	Acts as the command center for the application and is opened by the startup routine. From here, various other forms, reports, and utility functions are called

Component	Description
Typical forms	Would contain code hooked into various form and control events that are stored in the form's Code-Behind-Forms module. Some of these procedures might call generic functions in global database modules or library modules. A macro-created custom menu bar would be attached to the MenuBar event of the form. Some forms might include embedded OLE objects—perhaps photos, sound, or AVI clips
Typical reports	Would be used to print columnar listings and summarization of data
Custom toolbars	Would change with the current context
Data source	For most bound forms and reports would be made up of queries
Custom, context-sensitive Help system	Would be hooked into forms, reports, and controls
Mail-merge routine that used DDE	Might be included to call Word for Windows or some other word processing program that in turn would use the calling database as its data source for the mail merge
Other utility functions	Would be written in Access Basic and called from the main menu form or other forms

Your own applications might include these features, and perhaps others. Each application would certainly have a different mix of features and might use other parts of Access, including its security model, DAO, OLE automation, OLE custom controls, and the Windows API. Much of this book focuses on helping you create each of these application components. You'll also find chapters to help you debug and optimize your applications.

Summary

Access is arguably the best desktop Windows database program on the market to-day. It has the right mix of features for both users and developers. It's easy to learn and use, but it's also built on a sound, modern relational database architecture and has the power and extendability to take you well into the 21st century.

This chapter has provided an overview of the Access architecture, showing how the pieces fit together to make the complete program. Understanding this architecture can help you to use Access to your advantage.

The components of the Access architecture include

- The Access user interface and each of its parts, including the database container objects, system tables, the System Database, and other hidden objects.

- The Access internal architecture, including each of the .EXE files and .DLL files that make up Access. These include MSACCESS.EXE, International DLL, OLE DLLs, MSINFO.EXE, Import Utility DLL, Utility Database, Wizards, builders, add-ins and other libraries, Cue Cards, and Help.

- The Access event-driven programming model, featuring Access Basic, data access objects, and the ability to call the Windows API and other DLLs.

Once you've grasped the Access architecture, you can proceed to understand how each component works and then move on to the job of putting together profes-sional-quality, bullet-proof applications. That is what the rest of this book is all about.

PART II

Manipulating Data

CHAPTER

TWO

Database Design

- Database design and normalization theory

- Designing your databases: a practical, 20-step approach

- Normalizing a poorly designed database

Database design theory is a topic that many people avoid learning; either they lack the time or they give up because of the dry, academic treatment the topic is usually given. If, however, creating database applications is part of your job, you're treading on thin ice if you don't have a solid understanding of relational database design theory.

This chapter begins with an introduction to relational database design theory, including a discussion of keys, relationships, integrity rules, and the often-dreaded normal forms. The chapter then presents a practical step-by-step approach to good database design and furnishes an example that demonstrates how to normalize an existing, poorly designed database.

The Relational Model

The relational database model was conceived in 1969 by E.F. Codd, then a researcher at IBM. The model is based on a branch of mathematics called set theory and logic. The basic idea behind the relational model is that a database consists of a series of unordered tables (or relations) that can be manipulated using nonprocedural operations that return tables. This model was in vast contrast to the more traditional database theories of the time, which were much more complicated and less flexible and were dependent on the physical storage methods of the data.

NOTE It is commonly thought that the word *relational* in the relational model comes from the fact that you *relate* tables to each other in a relational database. Although this is a convenient way to think of the term, it's not accurate. Instead, the word *relational* has its roots in the terminology that Codd used to define the relational model. The table in Codd's writings was actually referred to as a relation (a related set of information). In fact, Codd (and other relational database theorists) use the terms *relations, attributes,* and *tuples* where most of us use the more common terms *tables, columns,* and *rows,* respectively (or the more physically oriented—and thus less preferable for discussions of database design theory—*files, fields,* and *records*).

The relational model can be applied to both databases and database management programs themselves. The *relational fidelity* of database programs can be compared using Codd's 12 rules (since Codd's seminal paper on the relational model, the number of rules has been expanded to 300) for determining how DBMS products conform to the relational model. When compared with other database management programs, Access fares quite well in terms of relational fidelity. Still, it has a *long* way to go before it meets all 12 rules completely.

Fortunately, you don't have to wait until Access is fully relational before you can benefit from the relational model. The relational model can also be applied to the design of databases, which is the subject of the remainder of this chapter.

Relational Database Design

When designing a database, you have to make decisions regarding how best to take some system in the real world and model it in a database. This process consists of deciding which tables to create and what columns they will contain, as well as the relationships between the tables. While it would be nice if this process were totally intuitive and obvious, or even better automated, this is simply not the case. A well-designed database takes time and effort to conceive, refine, and build.

The benefits of a database that has been designed according to the relational model are numerous. Some of them are

- Data entry, updates, and deletions will be efficient.
- Data retrieval, summarization, and reporting will perform well.
- Since the database follows a well-formulated model, it behaves predictably.
- Since much of the information is stored in the database rather than in the application, the database is somewhat self documenting.
- Changes to the database schema are easy to make.

The goal of this chapter is to explain the basic principles behind relational database design and demonstrate how to apply these principles when designing a database using Access. This chapter is by no means comprehensive and certainly not definitive. Many books have been written on database design theory; in fact, many careers have been devoted to its study. Instead, this chapter is meant as an informal introduction to database design theory for the Access developer.

NOTE   For a more detailed discussion of database design, we suggest *An Introduction to Database Systems, Volume I,* by C.J. Date (Addison-Wesley); *SQL and Relational Basics* by Fabian Pascal (M&T Books); or *Database Processing: Fundamentals, Design, and Implementation* by David M. Kroenke (Macmillan).

Tables, Uniqueness, and Keys

Tables in the relational model are used to represent "things" in the real world. Each table should represent only one type of thing. These things (or *entities*) can be real-world objects or events. For example, a real-world object might be a customer, an inventory item, or an invoice. Examples of events include patient visits, orders, and telephone calls.

Tables are made up of rows and columns. The relational model dictates that each row in a table be unique. If you allow duplicate rows in a table, there's no way to uniquely address a given row programmatically. This creates all sorts of ambiguities and problems.

You guarantee uniqueness for a table by designating a *primary key*—a column that contains unique values for a table. Each table can have only one primary key, even though several columns or combinations of columns may contain unique values. All columns (or combinations of columns) in a table with unique values are referred to as *candidate keys,* from which the primary key must be drawn. All other candidate key columns are referred to as *alternate keys.* Keys can be simple or composite. A *simple key* is a key made up of one column, whereas a *composite key* is made up of two or more columns.

The decision as to which candidate key is the primary one rests in your hands; there's no absolute rule as to which candidate key is best. Fabian Pascal, in his book *SQL and Relational Basics,* notes that the decision should be based on the principles of minimality (choose the fewest columns necessary), stability (choose a key that seldom changes), and simplicity/familiarity (choose a key that is both simple and familiar to users). Let's illustrate with an example. Say that a company has a table of customers called tblCustomer that looks like the table shown in Figure 2.1.

FIGURE 2.1:

The best choice for primary key for tblCustomer would be CustomerId.

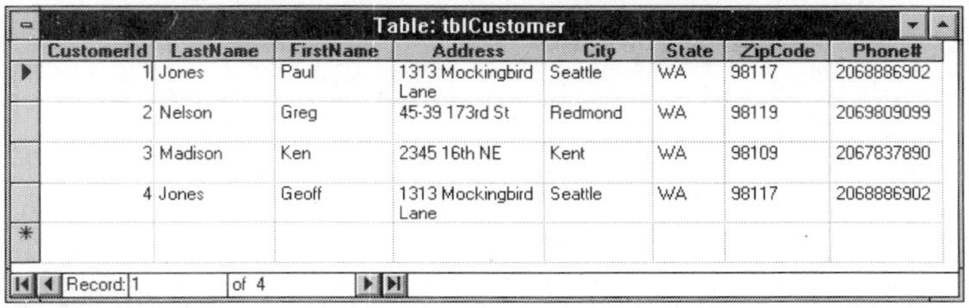

CustomerId	LastName	FirstName	Address	City	State	ZipCode	Phone#
1	Jones	Paul	1313 Mockingbird Lane	Seattle	WA	98117	2068886902
2	Nelson	Greg	45-39 173rd St	Redmond	WA	98119	2069809099
3	Madison	Ken	2345 16th NE	Kent	WA	98109	2067837890
4	Jones	Geoff	1313 Mockingbird Lane	Seattle	WA	98117	2068886902

Table: tblCustomer — Record: 1 of 4

Candidate keys for tblCustomer might include CustomerId, (LastName + FirstName), Phone#, (Address, City, State), and (Address + ZipCode). Following Pascal's guidelines, you would rule out the last three candidates because addresses and phone numbers can change fairly frequently. The choice between CustomerId and the name composite key is less obvious and would involve trade-offs. How likely would a customer's name change (for example, because of marriage)? Will misspelling of names be common? How likely is it that two customers will have the same first and last names? How familiar will CustomerId be to users? There's no right answer, but most developers favor numeric primary keys because names do sometimes change and because searches and sorts of numeric columns are more efficient than searches and sorts of text columns in Access (and most other databases).

Counter columns in Access make good primary keys, especially when you're having trouble coming up with good candidate keys and no existing arbitrary identification number is already in place. Don't use a counter column if you'll sometimes need to renumber the values (you won't be able to) or if you require an alphanumeric code (Access supports only Long Integer counter values). Also, counter columns make sense only for tables on the "one" side of a one-to-many relationship (see the section "Relationships" a little later in this chapter).

Foreign Keys and Domains

Although primary keys are a function of individual tables, if you created databases that consisted only of independent and unrelated tables, you'd have little need for them. Primary keys become essential, however, when you start to create relationships that join multiple tables in a database. A *foreign key* is a column in a table that references a primary key in another table.

Continuing the example presented earlier, let's say that you choose CustomerId as the primary key for tblCustomer. Now define a second table, tblOrder, that looks like the one shown in Figure 2.2.

CustomerId is considered a foreign key in tblOrder since you can use it to refer to a given customer (that is, a row in the tblCustomer table).

It is important that both foreign keys and the primary keys they reference share a common meaning and draw their values from the same domain. *Domains* are simply pools of values that columns are drawn from. For example, CustomerId is of the domain of valid customer ID numbers, which might in this case be long integers ranging between 1 and 50,000. Similarly, a column named Sex might be based on a one-letter domain equaling M or F. Domains can be thought of as user-defined column types whose definition implies certain rules that the columns must follow and certain operations that you can perform on those columns.

Access supports domains only partially. For example, Access will not let you create a relationship between two tables using columns that do not share the same datatype (for example, text, number, date/time, and so on). On the other hand, Access will not prevent you from joining the Integer column EmployeeAge from one table to the Integer column YearsWorked from a second table, even though these two columns are obviously from different domains.

Relationships

You define foreign keys in a database to model relationships in the real world. Relationships between real-world entities can be quite complex, involving numerous entities, all having multiple relationships with each other. For example, a family has multiple relationships among multiple people—all at the same time. In a relational database such as Access, however, you consider only relationships between pairs of tables. These tables can be related in one of three different ways: one-to-one, one-to-many, or many-to-many.

One-to-One Relationships

Two tables are related in a *one-to-one* (1→1) relationship if, for every row in the first table, there is at most one row in the second table. True one-to-one relationships seldom occur in the real world. This type of relationship is often created to get around some limitation of the database management software rather than to model a real-world situation.

In Access, 1→1 relationships may be necessary in a database when you have to split a table into two or more tables because of security or performance concerns or because of the limit of 255 columns per table. For example, you might keep most patient information in tblPatient but put especially sensitive information (for example, patient name, social security number, and address) in tblConfidential (see Figure 2.3). Access to the information in tblConfidential could be more restricted than for tblPatient. As a second example, perhaps you need to transfer only a portion of a large table to some other application on a regular basis. You can split the table into the transferred and the non-transferred pieces and join them in a 1→1 relationship. Tables in a 1→1 relationship should always have the same primary key, which will serve as the join column.

FIGURE 2.3:

The tables tblPatient and tblConfidential have a one-to-one relationship. The primary key of both tables is PatientId.

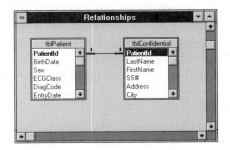

One-to-Many Relationships

Two tables are related in a *one-to-many* (1→M) relationship if, for every row in the first table, there can be zero, one, or many rows in the second table, but for every row in the second table, there is exactly one row in the first table. For example, each order for a pizza delivery business can have multiple items. Therefore, tblOrder is related to tblOrderDetails in a 1→M relationship (see Figure 2.4).

FIGURE 2.4:
There can be many detail lines for each order in the pizza delivery business, so tblOrder and tblOrderDetails are related in a one-to-many relationship.

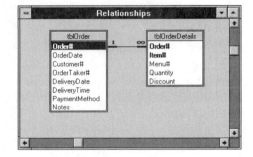

The 1→M relationship is also referred to as a *parent-child* relationship. 1→M relationships are the most commonly modeled relationship. They are also used to link base tables to information stored in *lookup tables*. For example, tblPatient has short one-letter DischargeDiagnosis codes that can be linked to a lookup table, tlkpDiagCode, to get more complete diagnosis descriptions (stored in DiagnosisName). In this case tlkpDiagCode is related to tblPatient in a 1→M relationship (that is, one row in the lookup table can be used in zero or more rows in the patient table).

Many-to-Many Relationships

Two tables have a *many-to-many* (M→M) relationship when, for every row in the first table, there can be many rows in the second table, *and* for every row in the second table, there can be many rows in the first table. M→M relationships can't be directly modeled in relational database programs, including Access. These types of relationships must be broken into multiple 1→M relationships. For example, a patient may be covered by multiple insurance plans, and a given insurance company covers multiple patients. Thus, the tblPatient table in a medical database would be related to the tblInsurer table using a M→M relationship. To model the relationship between these two tables, you would create a third table, a *linking table,* perhaps called tblPtInsurancePgm, that would contain a row for each insurance program under which a patient was covered (see Figure 2.5). Then, the M→M relationship between tblPatient and tblInsurer could be broken into two 1→M relationships. (tblPatient would be related to tblPtInsurancePgm, and tblInsurer would be related to tblPtInsurancePgm in 1→M relationships.)

FIGURE 2.5:
A linking table, tblPtInsurancePgm, is used to model the many-to-many relationship between tblPatient and tblInsurer.

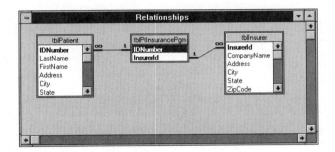

In Access, you specify relationships using the Edit ➤ Relationships command. In addition, you can create ad hoc relationships at any point, using queries.

Normalizing a Set of Tables

As mentioned at the beginning of this chapter, when designing databases you are faced with a series of choices. How many tables will there be and what will they represent? Which columns will go in which tables? What will the relationships between the tables be? The answer to each of these questions lies in something called *normalization,* the process of simplifying the design of a database so that it achieves the optimum structure.

Normalization theory gives us the concept of normal forms to assist in achieving the optimum structure. The *normal forms* are a linear progression of rules that you apply to your database, with each higher normal form achieving a better, more efficient design. The normal forms are

First Normal Form

Second Normal Form

Third Normal Form

Boyce Codd Normal Form

Fourth Normal Form

Fifth Normal Form

In this chapter we discuss normalization through Third Normal Form.

Before First Normal Form: Relations

The normal forms are based on *relations,* special types of tables that have the following attributes:

- They describe one entity.
- They have no duplicate rows; hence there is always a primary key.
- The columns are unordered.
- The rows are unordered.

Access doesn't require you to define a primary key for each and every table, but it strongly recommends that you do so. Needless to say, the relational model makes this an absolute requirement. In addition, tables in Access generally meet the third and fourth attributes listed above. That is, with a few exceptions, the manipulation of tables in Access doesn't depend on a specific ordering of columns or rows. (One notable exception is that encountered when you specify the data source for a combo or list box.)

NOTE For all practical purposes the terms *table* and *relation* are interchangeable, and we use the term *table* in the remainder of this chapter. However, we actually mean a table that also meets the definition of a relation.

First Normal Form

First Normal Form (1NF) says that all column values must be atomic. The word *atom* comes from the Latin *atomis,* meaning indivisible (or, literally, "not to cut"). 1NF dictates that for every row-by-column position, there exists only one value, not an array or list of values. The benefits from this rule should be fairly obvious. If lists of values are stored in a single column, there is no simple way to manipulate those values. Retrieval of data becomes much more laborious and less generalizable. For example, the table in Figure 2.6, tblOrder1, used to store order records for a hardware store, would violate 1NF.

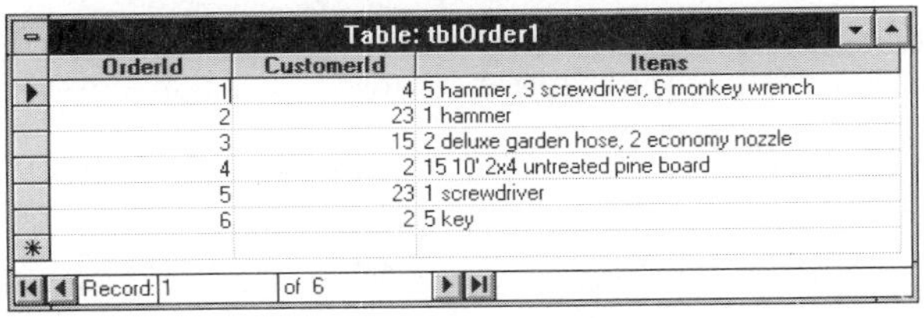

Table: tblOrder1

OrderId	CustomerId	Items
1	4	5 hammer, 3 screwdriver, 6 monkey wrench
2	23	1 hammer
3	15	2 deluxe garden hose, 2 economy nozzle
4	2	15 10' 2x4 untreated pine board
5	23	1 screwdriver
6	2	5 key

Record: 1 of 6

FIGURE 2.6: tblOrder1 violates First Normal Form because the data stored in the Items column is not atomic.

You'd have a difficult time retrieving information from this table because too much information is being stored in the Items field. Think how difficult it would be to create a report that summarized purchases by item.

1NF also prohibits the presence of *repeating groups,* even if they are stored in composite columns. For example, you might improve upon the same table by replacing the single Items column with six columns: Quant1, Item1, Quant2, Item2, Quant3, Item3 (see Figure 2.7).

FIGURE 2.7:

A better, but still flawed, version of the Orders table, tblOrder2. The repeating groups of information violate First Normal Form.

While this design has divided the information into multiple fields, it's still problematic. For example, how would you go about determining the quantity of hammers ordered by all customers during a particular month? Any query would have to search all three Item columns to determine whether a hammer was purchased and then sum over the three Quantity columns. Even worse, what if a customer ordered more than three items in a single order? You could always add more columns, but where would you stop—10 items, 20 items? Say that you decided that a customer would never order more than 25 items in any one order and designed the table accordingly. That means you would be using 50 columns to store the item and quantity information for each record, even for orders that involved only one or two items. Clearly, this is a waste of space. And someday, someone would want to order more than 25 items.

Tables in 1NF do not have the problems of tables containing repeating groups. The table in Figure 2.8, tblOrder3, is 1NF since each column contains one value and

FIGURE 2.8:

The tblOrder3 table is in First Normal Form.

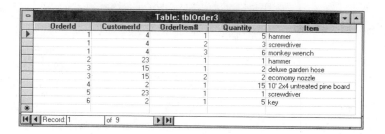

there are no repeating groups of columns. In order to attain 1NF, we have added a column, OrderItem#. The primary key of this table is a composite key made up of OrderId and OrderItem#.

You could now easily construct a query to calculate the number of hammers ordered. Figure 2.9 shows an example of such a query.

FIGURE 2.9:
Since tblOrder3 is in First Normal Form, you can easily construct a totals query to determine the total number of hammers ordered by customers.

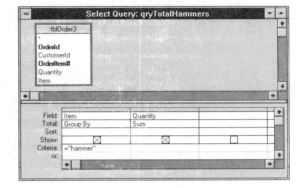

Second Normal Form

A table is said to be in Second Normal Form (2NF) if it is in 1NF and every non-key column is fully dependent on the (entire) primary key. Put another way, tables should store data relating to only one "thing" (or entity), and that entity should be described by its primary key.

The table shown in Figure 2.10, tblOrder4, is a slightly modified version of tblOrder3. Like tblOrder3, tblOrder4 is in First Normal Form. Each column is atomic, and there are no repeating groups.

To determine whether tblOrder4 meets 2NF, you must first note its primary key. The primary key is a composite of OrderId and OrderItem#. Thus, in order to be 2NF, each non-key column (that is, every column other than OrderId and OrderItem#) must be fully dependent on the primary key. In other words, does the value of OrderId and OrderItem# for a given record imply the value of every other column in the table? The answer is no. Given the OrderId, you know the customer

FIGURE 2.10:

The tblOrder4 table is in First Normal Form. Its primary key is a composite of OrderId and OrderItem#.

and date of the order, *without* having to know the OrderItem#. Thus, these two columns are not dependent on the *entire* primary key, which is composed of both OrderID and OrderItem#. For this reason tblOrder4 is not 2NF.

You can achieve Second Normal Form by breaking down tblOrder4 into two tables. The process of breaking a non-normalized table into its normalized parts is called *decomposition*. Since tblOrder4 has a composite primary key, decomposition is simple: put everything that applies to each order in one table and everything that applies to each order item in a second table. The two decomposed tables, tblOrder and tblOrderDetail, are shown in Figure 2.11.

Two points are worth noting here:

- When normalizing, you don't throw away information. In fact, this form of decomposition is termed non-loss decomposition because no information is sacrificed for the normalization process.

FIGURE 2.11:

The tblOrder and tblOrderDetail tables satisfy Second Normal Form. OrderId is a foreign key in tblOrderDetail that you can use to rejoin the tables.

- You decompose the tables in such a way as to allow them to be put back together using queries. Thus, it's important to make sure that tblOrderDetail contains a foreign key to tblOrder. The foreign key in this case is OrderId, which appears in both tables.

Third Normal Form

A table is said to be in Third Normal Form (3NF) if it is in 2NF and if all non-key columns are mutually independent. An obvious example of a dependency is a calculated column. For example, if a table contains the columns Quantity and PerItemCost, you could opt to calculate and store in that same table a TotalCost column (which would be equal to Quantity * PerItemCost), but this table wouldn't be 3NF. It's better to leave this column out of the table and make the calculation in a query or on a form or report instead. This saves room in the database and avoids your having to update TotalCost every time Quantity or PerItemCost changes.

Dependencies that aren't the result of calculations can also exist in a table. The tblOrderDetail table from Figure 2.11, for example, is in 2NF because all of its non-key columns (Quantity, ProductId, and ProductDescription) are fully dependent on the primary key. (That is, given an OrderID and an OrderItem#, you know the values of Quantity, ProductId, and ProductDescription.) Unfortunately, tblOrderDetail also contains a dependency between two of its non-key columns, ProductId and ProductDescription.

Dependencies cause problems when you add, update, or delete records. For example, say you needed to add 100 detail records, each of which involves the purchase of screwdrivers. This means you would have to input a ProductId code of 2 *and* a ProductDescription of "screwdriver" for each of these 100 records. Clearly, this is redundant. Similarly, if you decide to change the description of the item to "No. 2 Phillips-head screwdriver" at some later time, you will have to update all 100 records. As a further example, let's say you wish to delete all the 1994 screwdriver purchase records at the end of the year. Once all the records are deleted, you will no longer know what ProductId of 2 is since you've deleted from the database both the history of purchases and the fact that ProductId 2 means "No. 2 Phillips-head screwdriver." You can remedy each of these *anomalies*, however, by further normalizing the database to achieve Third Normal Form.

NOTE   An *anomaly* is simply an error or inconsistency in the database. A poorly designed database runs the risk of introducing numerous anomalies. There are three types of anomalies: insert, delete, and update. These anomalies occur during the insertion, deletion, and updating of rows, respectively. For example, an insert anomaly would occur if the insertion of a new row caused a calculated total field stored in another table to report the wrong total. If the deletion of a row in the database deleted more information than you wished to delete, this would be a delete anomaly. Finally, if updating a description column for a single part in an inventory database required you to make a change to thousands of rows, this would be classified as an update anomaly.

You can further decompose the tblOrderDetail table to achieve 3NF by breaking out the ProductId-ProductDescription dependency into a lookup table, as shown in Figure 2.12. This gives you a new order detail table, tblOrderDetail1, and a lookup table, tblProduct. When decomposing tblOrderDetail, take care to put a copy of the linking column, in this case ProductId, in both tables. ProductId becomes the primary key of the new table, tblProduct, and becomes a foreign key column in tblOrderDetail1. This allows you to join the two tables later using a query.

FIGURE 2.12:

The tbOrderDetail1 and tblProduct tables are in Third Normal Form. The ProductId column in tblOrderDetail1 is a foreign key referencing tblProduct.

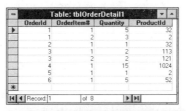

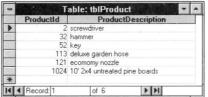

Higher Normal Forms

After Codd defined the original set of normal forms it was discovered that Third Normal Form, as originally defined, had certain inadequacies. This led to several higher normal forms, including the Boyce/Codd, Fourth, and Fifth Normal Forms. This book does not discuss these higher normal forms because the discussion would require the introduction of arcane terms and concepts and, more important, because all that extra effort gives you very little added value over 3NF. Instead we direct you to the books listed in the section "Relational Database Design" earlier in this chapter. Still, several points are worth noting here:

- Every higher normal form is a superset of all lower forms. Thus, if your design is in Third Normal Form, by definition it is also in 1NF and 2NF.

- If you've normalized your database to 3NF, you've likely also achieved Boyce/Codd Normal Form (and maybe even 4NF or 5NF).

- To quote C.J. Date, the principles of database design are "nothing more than *formalized common sense.*"

- Database design is more art than science.

This last item needs to be emphasized. While it's relatively easy to work through the examples in this chapter, the process gets more difficult when you are presented with a business problem (or another scenario) that needs to be computerized (or downsized). We outline an approach to take later in this chapter, but first we must discuss the subject of integrity rules.

Integrity Rules

The relational model defines several integrity rules that, while not part of the definition of the normal forms, are nonetheless a necessary part of any relational database. There are two types of integrity rules: general and database specific.

General Integrity Rules

The relational model specifies two general integrity rules: entity integrity and referential integrity. They are referred to as general rules because they apply to all databases.

The *entity integrity rule* is very simple. It says that primary keys cannot contain null (missing) data. The reason for this rule should be obvious. You can't uniquely identify or reference a row in a table if the primary key of that table can be null. It's important to note that this rule applies to both simple and composite keys. For composite keys, none of the individual columns can be null. Fortunately, Access automatically enforces the entity integrity rule for you; no component of a primary key in Access can be null.

The *referential integrity rule* says that the database must not contain any unmatched foreign key values. This implies that

- A row may not be added to a table with a foreign key unless the referenced value exists in the referenced table.
- If the value in a table that's referenced by a foreign key is changed (or the entire row is deleted), the rows in the table with the foreign key must not be "orphaned."

As defined by the relational model, three options are available when a referenced primary key value changes or a row is deleted:

- **Disallow:** The change is completely disallowed.
- **Cascade:** For updates, the change is cascaded to all dependent tables. For deletions, the rows in all dependent tables are deleted.
- **Nullify:** For deletions, the dependent foreign key values are set to null.

NOTE Access 2.0 lets you disallow or cascade updates or deletions of rows referenced by foreign keys. Prior versions of Access supported only the disallow option.

Access allows you to disallow or cascade referential integrity updates and deletions using the Edit ➤ Relationships command (see Figure 2.13). There is no Nullify option.

FIGURE 2.13:

Specifying a relationship with referential integrity between the tblCustomer and tblOrder tables using the Edit ➤ Relationships command. Updates of CustomerId in tblCustomer will be cascaded to tblOrder. Since the Cascade Delete check box hasn't been checked, deletions of rows in tblCustomer will be disallowed if rows in tblOrders would be orphaned.

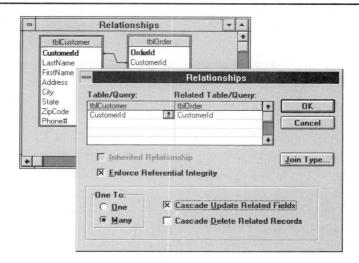

Database-Specific Integrity Rules

All integrity constraints that do not fall under entity integrity or referential integrity are termed *database-specific rules,* or *business rules.* These type of rules are specific to each database and come from the rules of the business being modeled by the database. Nonetheless, the enforcement of business rules is just as important as the enforcement of the general integrity rules discussed in the previous section.

NOTE Rules in Access 2.0 are now enforced at the engine level, which means that forms, action queries, and table imports can no longer ignore your rules. Because of this change, however, column rules can no longer reference other columns or use domain, aggregate, or user-defined functions. Access 2.0 supports the specification of a table rule you can use to check columns against each other.

Without the specification and enforcement of business rules, bad data will get into the database. The old adage, "garbage in, garbage out," applies aptly to the application (or lack of application) of business rules. For example, a pizza delivery business might have the following rules that would need to be modeled in the database:

- The order date must always be greater than the date the business started and less than the current date.

- The order time and delivery time can occur only during business hours.

- The delivery date and time must be greater than the order date and time.

- New orders cannot be created for discontinued menu items.

- Customer zip codes must be within a certain range (the delivery area).

- The quantity ordered can never be fewer than 1 or greater than 50.

- Non-null discounts can never be smaller than 1 percent or greater than 30 percent.

Access 2.0 supports the specification of validation rules for each column in a table. For example, the first business rule from the preceding list has been specified in Figure 2.14.

FIGURE 2.14:

A column validation rule has been created to limit all order dates to sometime between the first operating day of the business (5/3/93) and the current date.

Access 2.0 adds support for the specification of a global rule that applies to the entire table. This is useful for creating rules that cross-reference columns, as the example in Figure 2.15 demonstrates. Unfortunately, you're allowed to create only one global rule per table, which could make for some awful validation error messages (for example, "You have violated one of the following rules: 1. Delivery Date > Order Date. 2. Delivery Time > Order Time...").

FIGURE 2.15:

A table validation rule has been created to require that deliveries be made on or after the date the pizza was ordered.

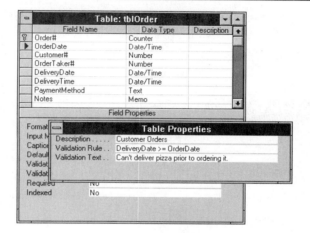

Although Access business rule support is better than most other desktop DBMS programs, it is still limited (especially in terms of the global-table rule), so you will typically build additional business rule logic into applications, usually in the data entry forms. This logic should be layered on top of any table-based rules and can be built into the application using combo boxes, list boxes, and option groups that limit available choices; form-level and field-level validation rules; and event procedures.

TIP
Use these application-based rules only when the table-based rules cannot do the job. The more you can build in business rules at the table level, the better, because these rules will always be enforced and will require less maintenance.

A Practical Approach to Database Design

As mentioned earlier in the chapter, database design is more art than science. While it's true that a properly designed database should follow the normal forms and the relational model, you still have to come up with a design that reflects the business you are trying to model. Relational database design theory can usually tell you what *not* to do, but it won't tell you where to start or how to manage your business. This is where it helps to understand the business (or other scenario) you are trying to model. A well-designed database requires business insight, time, and experience. Above all, it shouldn't be rushed.

> **NOTE**
>
> While designing your database in Access, you'll often need to print out table designs, relationships, integrity rules, and other elements of your design. Documenting your database in this way was very difficult using earlier versions of Access. Fortunately, version 2.0 introduces support for the printing of almost everything in the database schema. You can use the File ➤ Print Definition command from either Table Design view or the Edit ➤ Relationships dialog. You can also document your entire database, including forms, reports, queries, and other database objects, using the File ➤ Add-ins ➤ Database Documentor command.

To assist you in the creation of databases, we've outlined the following 20-step approach to sound database design:

1. Take some time to learn the business (or other system) you are trying to model. This usually means meeting with the people who will be using the system and asking them lots of questions.

2. On paper, write out a basic mission statement for the system. For example, you might write something like, "This system will be used to take orders from customers and track orders for accounting and inventory purposes." In addition, list the requirements of the system. These requirements will guide

you in creating the database schema (the definition of the tables) and business rules. Create a list that includes entries such as, "Must be able to track customer address for subsequent direct mail."

3. Start to rough out (on paper) the data entry forms. (If rules come to mind as you lay out the tables, add them to the list of requirements described in step 2.) The specific approach you take will be guided by the state of any existing system:

   - If this system was never before computerized, take the existing paper-based system and rough out the table design based on these forms. It's very likely that these forms will be non-normalized.

   - If the database will be converted from an existing computerized system, use its tables as a starting point. Remember, however, that the existing schema will probably be non-normalized. It's much easier to normalize the database *now* than later. Print out the existing schema, table by table, and the existing data entry forms to use in the design process.

   - If you are really starting from scratch (for example, for a brand-new business), rough out on paper the forms you envision filling out.

4. Based on the forms you created in step 3, rough out your tables on paper. If normalization doesn't come naturally (or from experience), you can start by creating one huge, non-normalized table per form that you will later normalize. If you're comfortable with normalization theory, try to keep it in mind as you create your tables, remembering that each table should describe a single entity.

5. Look at your existing paper or computerized reports. (If you're starting from scratch, rough out the types of reports you'd like to see on paper.) For existing systems that aren't currently meeting user needs, it's likely that key reports are missing. Create them now on paper.

6. Take the roughed-out reports from step 5 and make sure the tables from step 4 include this data. If information is not being collected, add it to the existing tables or create new ones.

7. On paper, add several rows to each roughed-out table. Use real data if at all possible.

8. Start the normalization process. First, identify candidate keys for every table and, using the candidates, choose the primary key. Remember to choose a primary key that is minimal, stable, simple, and familiar (see the section "Tables, Uniqueness, and Keys" earlier in this chapter). Every table must have a primary key! Make sure that the primary key will guard against all present and future duplicate entries.

9. Note foreign keys also, adding them if necessary to related tables. Draw relationships between the tables, noting whether they are 1→1 or 1→M. If they are M→M, create linking tables (see the section "Relationships" earlier in this chapter).

10. Determine whether the tables are in First Normal Form. Are all fields atomic? Are there any repeating groups? Decompose if necessary to meet 1NF.

11. Determine whether the tables are in Second Normal Form. Does each table describe a single entity? Are all non-key columns fully dependent on the primary key? Put another way, does the primary key imply all of the other columns in each table? Decompose to meet 2NF. If the table has a composite primary key, you should, in general, decompose the table by breaking apart the key and putting all columns pertaining to each component of the primary key in their own tables.

12. Determine whether the tables are in Third Normal Form. Are there any computed columns? Are there any mutually dependent non-key columns? Remove computed columns. Eliminate mutually dependent columns by breaking out lookup tables.

13. Using the normalized tables from step 12, refine the relationships between the tables.

14. Create the tables using Access. Create the relationships between the tables using the Edit ➤ Relationships command. Add sample data to the tables.

15. Create prototype queries, forms, and reports. While creating these objects, design deficiencies should become obvious. Refine the design as needed.

16. Bring the users back in. Have them evaluate your forms and reports. Are their needs met? If not, refine the design. Remember to renormalize if necessary (steps 8–12).

17. Go back to the Table Design screen and add business rules.

18. Create the final forms, reports, and queries. Develop the application. Refine the design as necessary.

19. Have the users test the system. Refine the design as needed.

20. Deliver the final system.

This list doesn't cover every facet of the design process, but it is useful as a framework for the process.

Normalizing a Database with Existing Data

From time to time you may be faced with having to normalize a poorly designed database. You can usually accomplish this without loss of data by using several action queries. For example, you could normalize the version of the orders table (tblOrder4) shown earlier in Figure 2.10, taking it from 1NF to 3NF, using the following steps:

1. Make a copy of your table and work on the copy. For example, we have made a copy of tblOrder4 and named it tblOrder5. At this time it's also a good idea to make a backup copy of the database. Store it safely in case you make a mistake.

2. Break out the item-related columns that are dependent on OrderItem# from tblOrder5 using a make-table query. This query, qmakOrderDetail5, will create tblOrderDetail5 and is shown in design mode in Figure 2.16. Don't delete any columns from tblOrder5 yet.

3. Move the product description information into a third table. Create this lookup table using a query based on tblOrderDetail5 with the Unique Values property set to Yes. You use this type of query because you want only one record created for each instance of the ProductId code. This query, qmakProduct5, is shown in design mode in Figure 2.17. It creates the tblProduct5 lookup table. Don't delete any columns from tblOrderDetail5 yet.

4. Open the three tables—tblOrder5, tblOrderDetail5, and tblProduct5—in Datasheet view and make certain they contain the required information. It's

FIGURE 2.16:

The qmakOrderDetail5 make-table query copies item-related data to a new table as part of the normalization process.

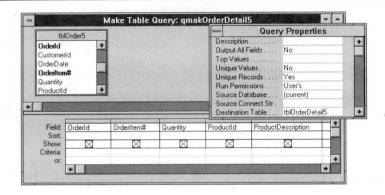

FIGURE 2.17:

The qmakProduct5 make-table query copies product-related data to a new lookup table as part of the normalization process.

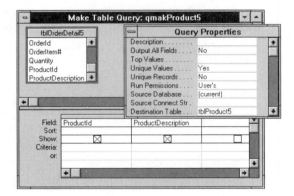

important that things look okay before you delete any columns from the tables. (You should still see duplicate rows in tblOrder5 and tblOrderDetail5, which you will fix later.) At this point you may find it helpful to create a select query that joins the three tables to help you make certain that all is well.

5. Create a third make-table query based on tblOrder5 to create the final order table, tblOrder5a. This query, qmakOrder5a, is shown in design mode in Figure 2.18. In this query include only columns that will be in the final orders table (OrderId, CustomerId, and OrderDate). Since tblOrder5 contains duplicate rows at this point, you must set the UniqueValues property to Yes.

FIGURE 2.18:

The qmakOrder5a make table query creates the normalized version of the orders table.

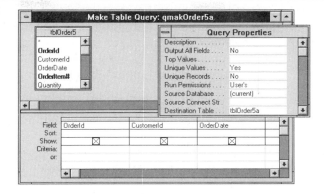

6. Create one more make-table query to create the final normalized version of the order details table, tblOrderDetail5a. This query, based on tblOrderDetail5, is shown in design mode in Figure 2.19. In this query include only columns that should remain in the final order details table (OrderId, OrderItem#, Quantity, and ProductId).

7. Open tblOrder5a, tblOrderDetail5, and tblProduct5, in turn, in Design view and define the primary key columns for each (OrderId, OrderId+OrderItem#, and ProductId, respectively).

FIGURE 2.19:

The qmakOrderDetail5a make-table query creates the normalized version of the order details table.

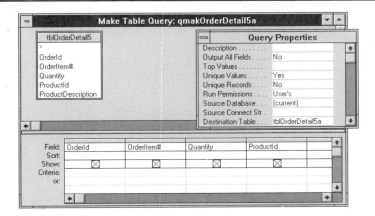

8. Create another select query that joins the three tables. If the result table looks okay, delete the original tables and rename the three new tables to their final names.

9. Create relationships between the tables using the Edit ➤ Relationships command. The screen in Figure 2.20 shows the relationships prior to renaming the tables.

FIGURE 2.20:

Relationships for the normalized tables, which are now in Third Normal Form

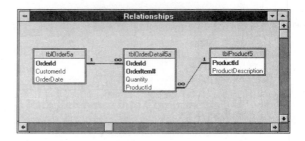

Breaking the Rules: When to Denormalize

Sometimes it's necessary to break the rules of normalization and create a database that is deliberately less normal than it otherwise could be. You'll usually do this for performance reasons or because the users of the database demand it. While this won't get you any points with database design purists, ultimately you have to deliver a solution that satisfies your users. If you do break the rules and decide to denormalize your database, it's important that you follow these guidelines:

- Break the rules deliberately; have a good reason for denormalizing.
- Be fully aware of the trade-offs this decision entails.
- Thoroughly document your decision.
- Create the necessary application adjustments to avoid anomalies.

When to Break the Rules

Here are several scenarios in which you might choose to break the rules of normalization:

You decide to store an indexed computed column, Soundex, in tblCustomer to improve query performance, in violation of 3NF (because Soundex is dependent on LastName). The Soundex column contains the sound-alike code for the LastName column. It's an indexed column (with duplicates allowed) and it's calculated using a user-defined function. If you wish to perform searches on Soundex code with any but the smallest tables, you'll find a significant performance advantage in storing the Soundex column in the table and indexing this computed column. You'd likely use an event procedure attached to a form to perform the Soundex calculation and store the result in the Soundex column. To avoid update anomalies, you'll want to ensure that this column cannot be updated by the user and that it is updated every time LastName changes.

To improve report performance, you decide to create a column named TotalOrderCost that contains a sum of the cost of each order item in tblOrder. This violates 2NF because TotalOrderCost is dependent on the primary key of tblOrderDetail, not on tblOrder's primary key. TotalOrderCost is calculated on a form by summing the column TotalCost for each item. Since you often create reports that need to include the total order cost but not the cost of individual items, you break 2NF to avoid having to join these two tables every time this report needs to be generated. As in the preceding example, you have to be careful to avoid update anomalies. Whenever a record in tblOrderDetail is inserted, updated, or deleted, you will need to update tblOrder, or the information stored there will be erroneous.

You decide to include a column, SalesPerson, in the tblInvoice table, even though SalesId is also included in tblInvoice. This violates 3NF because the two non-key columns are mutually dependent, but it significantly improves the performance of certain commonly run reports. Once again, you do this to avoid a join to the tblEmployee table, but it introduces redundancies and adds the risk of update anomalies.

This last point is worth elaborating on. In most cases when you denormalize, you will be required to create additional application code to avoid insert, update, and deletion anomalies that a more normalized design would avoid. For example, if you decide to store a calculation in a table, you'll need to create extra event procedure code and attach it to the appropriate event properties of forms that are used to update the data on which the calculation is based.

If you're considering denormalizing for performance reasons, don't always assume that the denormalized approach is the best. Instead, we suggest you first fully normalize the database (to Third Normal Form or higher) and then denormalize only if it becomes necessary for reasons of performance.

If you're considering denormalizing because your users think they need it, investigate the reason. Often they will be concerned about simplifying data entry, which you can usually accomplish by basing forms on queries while keeping your base tables fully normalized.

Summary

This chapter has covered the basics of database design in the context of Microsoft Access. Again, here are the main concepts:

- The relational database model, created by E.F. Codd in 1969, is founded on set theory and logic. A database designed according to the relational model will be efficient, predictable, self documenting, and easy to modify, and it will perform well.

- Every table must have a primary key that uniquely identifies rows in the table.

- Foreign keys are columns used to reference a primary key in another table.

- You can establish three kinds of relationships between tables in a relational database: one-to-one, one-to-many, or many-to-many. Many-to-many relationships require a linking table.

- Normalization is the process of simplifying the design of a database so that it achieves the optimum structure.

- A well-designed database follows the Normal Forms: First Normal Form requires all column values to be atomic; Second Normal Form requires every non-key column to be fully dependent on the table's primary key; Third Normal Form requires all non-key columns to be mutually independent.

- The entity integrity rule forbids nulls in primary key columns.

- The referential integrity rule says that the database must not contain any unmatched foreign key values.

- A well-designed database implements business rules and requires business insight, time, and experience.

- You can normalize a poorly designed database using a series of action queries.

- Occasionally, you may need to denormalize for performance.

CHAPTER

THREE

Select Queries and Dynasets

- How nulls affect query results

- Ins and outs of pattern-match searches

- Using joins, including inner, outer, and self joins

- Taking advantage of parameter queries

- Dynaset updatability

- Debugging your queries

In this chapter you'll learn about select queries and dynasets. The chapter covers details about fields and criteria, calculated fields, joins, query properties, and parameters. It also discusses the results of an Access select query—the dynaset—in detail, focusing on when it's updatable and when it isn't.

The Access Query: Beyond Read-Only Queries

In traditional DBMS programs, queries are usually thought of as an end-user concern, a way for the user to ask questions of the database, questions that the application programmer hasn't hard coded into the application. For example, in R:BASE, an application programmer might include the menu item query by example (QBE) to allow the user to perform ad hoc queries of the database. Beyond this, queries are not an integral part of R:BASE applications. Forms in R:BASE are almost always based on tables. Reports can be based on views (queries), but in R:BASE as well as practically every commercially available database program, views are read-only and cannot be used to edit data. Access is the first and, so far, only commercial database program to go beyond this read-only query paradigm. Access stores the results of most queries in *dynasets*—two-way updatable views of the underlying data. While this might not sound particularly astounding, the Access dynaset is truly a revolutionary programming achievement that you must understand in order to create applications that fully take advantage of the power of Access.

> **NOTE** For the newest version of R:BASE, R:BASE 4.5 Plus, which was released in the first quarter of 1994, Microrim added support for two-way updatable views similar to Access' dynaset. It's likely that other vendors will follow suit as they attempt to compete with Microsoft Access.

When working in Access, be aware that queries take a much more prominent role in application design than in many competing database programs. In most situations where a table is called for (for example, in a lookup table specification for a combo box control on a form, or for the source of a report), you can use a query instead.

Another exciting aspect of Access queries is that you can base queries on other queries, up to 50 levels deep. Thus, you can build upon the work you've already done and solve problems that cannot be addressed with a single query (without having to generate lots of temporary tables, as you must when using programs such as Paradox).

If you aren't used to working with queries, you need to rethink your application strategy. It is important to make queries an integral part of your applications. Simply put, any substantial application that fails to take advantage of the power of Access queries is not a very good one.

2.0 Query Enhancements

Access queries have been enhanced considerably in version 2.0. The modal SQL dialog box generated by the View ➤ SQL command has been replaced with the SQL view. Queries now have a much richer set of properties, including properties for each output field. Added support has been provided for union queries and subqueries (see Chapter 5). Dynaset updatability has been enhanced. New Query Wizards have been added. Data definition and SQL-specific queries have been added (see Chapter 5). Rushmore technology (borrowed from Microsoft FoxPro) speeds up many queries (see Chapter 16).

Select Queries:
The Bread and Butter
of Access Queries

The default query in Access is the *select query* since this is the most common type of query. You use select queries to ask questions of the database. You use *action queries*, on the other hand, to make batch changes to the database. *Totals queries* and *crosstab queries*, like select queries, are used to ask questions of the database, but the answers are placed in a static snapshot of the data rather than a dynamic table. Totals, crosstab, and action queries are covered in detail in Chapter 4. Two additional types of queries, SQL-specific queries and data definition queries, are discussed in Chapter 5.

NOTE In relational database terminology, a *view* refers to an abstract representation of one or more tables in a database. In standard SQL you create a view using the Create View command. In Access a *query* is equivalent to the relational view, but instead of the Create View command, Access uses a SQL Select statement for the query definition (or *querydef*). The term *dynaset* refers to the dynamic and updatable set of data (or view) returned by a query. The terms *view*, *query*, and *dynaset* are often used interchangeably. In this book we use the terms *query* and *querydef* to refer to the query's definition and *dynaset* and the more general *recordset* to refer to the results of a query.

Select queries are analogous to the SQL SELECT statement—they *select* data from one or more tables. Indeed, Access maps select queries directly to SQL SELECT statements.

The results of select queries in Access are displayed in *datasheets*. The set of data returned by a select query is referred to as a *dynaset*, which is short for *dynamic set*. Only select queries (in fact, only select queries *without* totals) return dynasets. The dynamic part of the Access dynaset comes from the fact that it is a two-way updatable view of the data that is stored in the base tables that make up the query. All other queries, including select queries with totals, create snapshots.

A Brief History of QBE

Access' Graphical Query By Example is a variant of the original query by example (QBE) that was first described by Moshe Zloof, working at IBM's Yorktown Heights Research Laboratory in the early 1970s. It wasn't until 1985, though, that QBE was popularized by Ansa with the introduction of Paradox. (Ansa and Paradox were purchased by Borland in 1987.) Since that time QBE has appeared in many database and related products, including dBASE, R:BASE, FoxPro, Superbase, and PageAhead's InfoPublisher, to name just a few. Although some of the products have strayed considerably from the standard (most notably, FoxPro), none, in our opinion, improved upon the standard—that is, until Access. Microsoft spent considerable time looking at the usability of QBE and took the standard to the next level of usability by moving the specification of join criteria off the QBE grid.

SQL View: Browsing and Changing SQL Commands

Access maps queries to structured query language (SQL) commands. At any point during the definition of a query, you can view the underlying SQL statements using the View ➤ SQL command (or by clicking the SQL toolbar button). When you choose this command, Access switches to SQL view. SQL view is not just for browsing the underlying SQL command, however. You can make changes to the SQL commands, and Access will change the query grid to correspond to the edited SQL statements.

If you make changes to the SQL statement that Access can't map to the query grid, query design mode is disabled. This doesn't necessarily mean that the query is syntactically incorrect. Union queries, subqueries, SQL pass-through, and data definition queries all have no counterpart in Access QBE.

If you prefer, you can ignore QBE entirely and directly enter SQL statements from scratch into an empty SQL view window. Developers well versed in SQL may prefer this method for creating queries. However, Access SQL is a unique dialect that differs substantially from the ANSI standard. So if you have previous experience with SQL, you may want to read Chapter 5 prior to this chapter for a discussion of the differences between Access and ANSI SQL.

If you are new to either SQL or QBE (or find Access' departures from the standards confusing), you'll likely find the SQL view invaluable. If, for example, you are comfortable with QBE but wish to learn more about SQL, just enter a query using QBE and then switch to SQL view to see how the SQL equivalent looks. On the other hand, if you have a long history of using SQL but you need to learn QBE, you can do just the opposite.

> **NOTE** This chapter presents many examples using both QBE and SQL. The complete explanation of the SQL syntax, however, is reserved for Chapter 5.

Fields and Criteria

Before getting into some of the more interesting aspects of queries, we will present a brief overview of the Query Design screen so we're all speaking the same language. Bear in mind, however, that this chapter is not a tutorial on queries; it assumes a basic familiarity with them.

> **NOTE** The examples in this chapter are taken from a database for a fictitious medical research study in the field of cardiology, CH3.MDB.

The screen in Figure 3.1 shows the qryFemalePts query in design mode. Let's examine the Query window for this query. The field list for the table tblPatient is located in the upper half of the screen. This half of the screen is known as the *table pane*. Several fields have been selected from the field list and dropped into the *query*

FIGURE 3.1:

The qryFemalePts query, a simple single-table query, in design mode. The field list for the tblPatient table is displayed in the upper half of the Query window. Four fields from tblPatient have been dropped onto the QBE grid, shown in the lower half of the window.

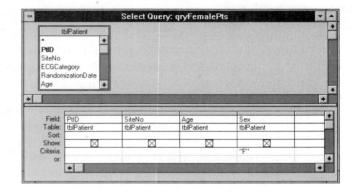

grid in the lower half of the query window. The string "F" has been entered onto the Criteria line under the field Sex. This single-table query returns all female patients. The screen in Figure 3.2 shows the resulting dynaset. The equivalent SQL SELECT statement is

```
SELECT  DISTINCTROW tblPatient.PtID, tblPatient.SiteNo,
tblPatient.Age, tblPatient.Sex
FROM tblPatient
WHERE ((tblPatient.Sex="F"));
```

FIGURE 3.2:

Datasheet returned by the qryFemalePts query. This query lists all female patients.

PtID	SiteNo	Age	Sex
14	4	67	F
9	4	67	F
97	5	82	F
6	5	34	F
76	5	49	F
214	3	73	F
217	4	67	F
218	4	68	F
15	4	62	F
56	2	43	F
88	8	58	F
94	2	78	F
145	2	66	F
34	2	63	F
18	1	49	F
219	1	69	F
220	5	66	F
226	1	59	F

Record: 1 of 18

> **TIP**
>
> To quickly place all of a table's fields in the query grid, drag the asterisk (*) at the top of a table's field list to the query grid. Alternately, you can double-click the title bar of a table's field list. This action causes the entire field list to be highlighted. Now you can move all the fields to the query grid by dragging any part of the highlighted list to the query grid.

Of course, you can create more complicated queries. The screen in Figure 3.3 shows the query specification for the qryFemaleSeniors&LongStay query, which selects records of female patients older than 65 or patients for whom the hospital stay (calculated as DischargeDate – RandomizationDate) is greater than six days. The equivalent SQL SELECT statement would be

```
SELECT  DISTINCTROW tblPatient.PtID, tblPatient.SiteNo,
tblPatient.Age, tblPatient.Sex,
tblPatient.RandomizationDate, tblPatient.DischargeDate,
[DischargeDate]-[RandomizationDate] AS HospitalStay
FROM tblPatient
WHERE ((tblPatient.Age>=65) AND (tblPatient.Sex="F")) OR
((([DischargeDate]-[RandomizationDate])>6));
```

FIGURE 3.3:

qryFemaleSeniors&LongStays query in design mode. This query returns all records for female patients of retirement age or those patients with hospital stays of a week or longer.

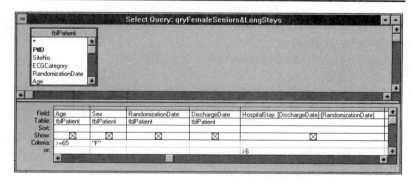

The screen in Figure 3.4 shows the dynaset resulting from this query. Note that criteria to be connected by the *And* operator (for example, tblPatient.Age>=65 AND tblPatient.Sex="F") are entered on a single line. Criteria to be connected by the *Or* operator are entered on separate lines. You can enter as many Or lines as needed.

FIGURE 3.4:

Datasheet returned by the qryFemaleSeniors&LongStays query

PtID	SiteNo	Age	Sex	RandomizationDate	DischargeDate	HospitalStay
93	4	72	M	4/1/93	4/8/93	7
14	4	67	F	4/19/93	4/23/93	4
9	4	67	F	6/11/93	6/16/93	5
97	5	82	F	4/27/93	5/3/93	6
214	3	73	F	11/15/93	11/23/93	8
216	3	35	M	11/30/93	12/27/93	27
217	4	67	F	1/4/94	1/8/94	4
218	4	68	F	1/18/94	1/25/94	7
15	4	62	F	12/18/93	12/25/93	7
56	2	43	F	7/19/93	8/19/93	31
86	8	56	M	4/5/93	5/5/93	30
94	2	78	F	2/2/94	2/5/94	3
145	2	66	F	6/22/93	6/28/93	6
219	1	69	F	2/4/94	2/11/94	7
220	5	66	F	3/2/94	3/6/94	4
223	2	71	M	3/1/94	3/8/94	7

Select Query: qryFemaleSeniors&LongStays

Record: 15 of 16

TIP

You can use fields in the specification of criteria but still hide them from the resulting dynaset by clearing the check box on the Show line. This can also be useful when you have dragged the asterisk field to the query grid and wish to specify criteria based on one of these fields. Simply drag another copy of the field to the grid and uncheck the Show check box for this second copy.

Table 3.1 shows examples of different types of criteria operators and expressions that you can use in queries.

TABLE 3.1: Examples of Query Operators and Expressions

Operator/ Expression	Example	Selects Records Where the Value
(none)	23.6	Equals 23.6 (No operator implies equality [=].)
=	= "Jones"	Equals "Jones". (The quotes are optional if there are no embedded spaces. If quotes are used, you can use either single quotes (') or double quotes ("). Text searches are case insensitive.)
<>	<> "Expired"	Is not equal to expired
>	> 23 November 1994	Is greater than 11/23/94 (You can enter date expressions in a variety of formats. Access encloses date expressions with the # symbol: #11/23/94#.)
<	< 45	Is less than 45
>=	>= 165	Is greater than or equal to 165
<=	<= 165	Is less than or equal to 165
Between	Between 1/1/50 and 12/31/59	Is a date that occurred during the 1950s
Like	Like "J*"	Begins with *J*. Thus, "Jones", "James", and "Joseph" would match (see Table 3.2)
Not	Not Like "J*"	Does not begin with *J*. The Not operator modifies other operators
Is Null	Is Null	Is null. Selects records in which this field is null (empty)
Is Not Null	Is Not Null	Is not null. Selects all records in which this field has some value

TABLE 3.1: Examples of Query Operators and Expressions (continued)

Operator/ Expression	Example	Selects Records Where the Value
And	Like "P*" and Not Like "*l"	Matches the pattern "P", but not where the value ends in "l". Thus, it would match the names "Peter" and "Pam" but not "Paul" or "Phil". Note that the And operator is rarely used within a single cell since a field cannot have more than one value at the same time. Exception: You can use And successfully with Like (as illustrated here) and with Between
Or	"Blue" or "Red" or "Green"	Is blue, red, or green. This expression using Or is equivalent to the next example, which uses the In operator
In	In("Blue", "Red", "Green")	Is blue, red, or green. This expression using In is equivalent to the preceding example, which uses Or
Date functions	Between Date() and Date()+30	Is a date between today (the system date) and 30 days from now
Other built-in functions	Right([LastName],4)="twin"	Equals "twin" for the four rightmost characters. Note that although this type of expression makes most sense when entered under the LastName column, you can enter it as criteria for any column (field)
User-defined functions	=Soundex([Litwin])	Is equal to the soundex Sound-alike code for the name "Litwin". (The CH3.MDB database includes the source code for this function in the module basSoundex.)

Specifying Pattern Match Criteria

Access' query syntax offers considerable flexibility in the specification of inexact patterns as criteria using the *Like* operator. You use the wildcard symbols to specify pattern matches. They are summarized in Table 3.2.

TABLE 3.2: Wildcard Characters and Examples of Their Use in Queries

Symbol	Matches	Example
?	Any single character	"b??r" matches "boar" and "bear" but not "bore", "bare", or "brier"
*	Zero or more characters	"b*r" matches "boar", "bear", and "brier" but still not "bore" or "bare"
#	Any single digit (0, 1, 2, 3, 4, 5, 6, 7, 8, or 9)	"## Elm St." matches "16 Elm St." and "34 Elm St." but not "9 Elm St." or "1A Elm St"
[characterlist]	Any single character in *characterlist.* If you use a hyphen in *characterlist,* you can specify a range of characters	"[m-p]ark" and "[mnop]ark" both match "mark", "nark", "oark", and "park" but not "bark"
[!characterlist]	Any single character not in *characterlist*	"[!gkz]ates" matches "lates" and "fates" but not "gates", "kates", or "zates"

> **NOTE**
> A *null* value in Access means that the field lacks a value. Unless a default value is defined for a field in a table, all fields in a new record start out as null. You can explicitly test for the presence of nulls using the *Is Null* operator or the *IsNull( )* function.

Here are some points to keep in mind when specifying pattern matches:

- You must include the Like operator when specifying pattern matches. If = (the equal sign) is used instead, the wildcard symbols are treated literally and the query returns records exactly matching the string instead. For example, if you specify ="Pa*rk", only records with values of "Pa*rk"—where the asterisk is included as a literal character, not a wildcard—are returned.

- The expression "Like '*'" returns all rows, *excluding* those with null values. (Prior to version 2.0, this criterion would include rows with null values.)

- For patterns of the form [*characterlist*], you may include within the brackets any ANSI character (including a space) except the [(right bracket) character.

- Ranges of characters must appear in ascending sort order. Thus, [9-0] will not match all digits. This needs to be rewritten as [0-9].

- Multiple ranges of characters in the form [*characterlist*] should not be delimited. For example, if you wish to match the digit 1, 2, 3, 7, 8, or 9, you would specify [1-37-9] as the pattern.

- For patterns of the form [!*characterlist*] (that is, match a character not in *characterlist*), the exclamation point must appear *inside* the brackets.

- If you wish to match the - (hyphen) character itself in a range of characters of the form [*characterlist*], place it as the first or last character in the *characterlist*. For example, to match any number or a minus sign, you could use [0-9-] or [-0-9].

- Unlike wildcard characters used at the DOS prompt, * works as expected anywhere in a string. (In DOS, asterisks really work as expected only if they are the last character of a string.) For example, in DOS, *a* matches *all* values; in Access, it matches any value that contains the letter *a* in any location within the string.

Criteria Placement and Evaluation

While optimizing a query, Access may reorder criteria. This may, in rare instances, affect the order of evaluation of complex expressions and thus may give you results that differ from what you expected. If you are unsure of how Access will process a query, use the SQL view to see how Access has interpreted your criteria.

Although it is natural to enter criteria within the criteria column to which an expression applies, you are not bound by this format. This flexibility is how Access is able to process functions in criteria specifications. For example, the "Other functions" example from Table 3.1:

```
Right([LastName],4)="twin"
```

might be entered in the LastName column, but it doesn't have to be entered there.

Access evaluates criteria expressions as follows:

- If an expression begins without an operator, the = operator is assumed.

- If an expression begins without a field name, the expression is assumed to apply to the current column.

- If an expression begins with a function name or a reference to another field, the current column is not assumed. Note, however, when using this syntax, that fields must be enclosed in square brackets to distinguish them from text strings.

For example, since qryFemalePts (see Figure 3.1) is selecting only females, there's no need to include Sex in the resulting dynaset. Thus, you could modify the query so that the Show check box was unchecked for the Sex field. The screen in Figure 3.5 shows this query in design mode.

FIGURE 3.5:

Design screen of the qryFemalePts1 query. This query returns all female patients.

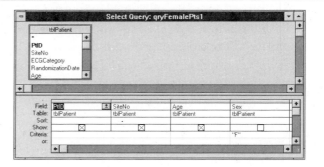

Alternately, you could choose not to include the Sex field (which is hidden in this example) at all in the query grid and instead enter this criterion under one of the other fields—for example, under Age. This version of the query, qryFemalePts2, is shown in Figure 3.6. Despite the different methods for defining the query, the dynasets and SQL statements of the two queries are identical. In fact, if you save qryFemalePts2, close it, and reopen it, you will find that Access has reformatted the query grid to look exactly like qryFemalePts1.

FIGURE 3.6:

Design screen of the qryFemalePts2 query. In this modified version of the qryFemalePts1 query (depicted in Figure 3.5), the criteria referencing Sex has been relocated under Age. The two queries, however, are equivalent.

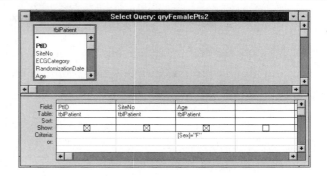

Calculations

Access does not directly support the creation of calculated fields in table definitions. In most situations where you would want to use a calculated field in a table, however, you can use a query instead. Access' queries support a variety of calculations (or expressions) using built-in functions, user-defined functions, and various text-manipulation operators. You can use expressions in the definition of fields or in the specification of selection criteria.

The format for a calculated query field is as follows:

CalculationName: Calculation

CalculationName is optional; if you do not include one, Access names the calculated field as Expr1, Expr2, and so on, but we recommend that you do not let Access name your fields. The name can include special characters and spaces but cannot include a : (colon) since this is the character that delimits a name from its calculation. When referring to calculated fields in forms, reports, or Access Basic, you use this name. This is why you won't want to use default names except for "quick and dirty" queries.

 Calculated fields can be used to rename a field. For example, to change the name of PtID to Patient ID#, add the calculated field Patient ID#: PtID to the query instead of the PtID field.

Some examples of query calculations are presented in Table 3.3.

TABLE 3.3: Examples of Expressions You Can Use As Calculated Fields in Queries

Expression	Returns
Expiration Date: Enrollment + 365	The date of enrollment plus 365 days
Expiration Date1: DateAdd("yyyy", 1, Enrollment)	The date of enrollment plus one year
Total Price: Price * 1.081	The price × 108.1% (or the price plus 8.1% tax)
LeastValue: IIf(([int1] < [int2], [int1], [int2])	int1 if int1 is less than int2; otherwise, this expression will equal int2
Full Name: [FirstName] & " " & [LastName]	The first and last names of a person separated by a space
Random Number1: Int((100 – 1 + 1) * Rnd + 1)	A random number between 1 and 100. Since the expression is interpreted by Access as a constant, however, Access computes it only once. Thus, all rows in the dynaset will contain the same random number
Random Number2: Int((100 – 1 + 1) * Rnd(Abs([PtId])) + 1)	A different random number between 1 and 100 for each row in the dynaset because by including a reference to a field, Access is forced to reevaluate the expression for each record
Soundex: Soundex([Last Name])	The Soundex sound-alike code for LastName, assuming this function was previously defined (see basSoundex in CH3.MDB)

Propagation of Nulls

In creating calculated fields based on fields that may contain null values, it is important to consider how nulls will affect the calculation. A null always evaluates as False in an expression, and Access propagates nulls unless the IsNull() function is used to explicitly handle nulls.

Consider the example of LeastValue from Table 3.3. Say that LeastValue will be used to create a calculated field based on the following five records:

int1	int2
9	1
7	93
Null	Null

int1	int2
Null	64
16	Null

LeastValue would then be equal to 1, 7, null, 64, and null, respectively. (In the preceding table, *Null* signifies a null value, not the string "Null".) Of course, the first three records make perfect sense. It is the last two records that return values that differ from what you would expect.

Let's examine how LeastValue is evaluated for the last two records:

IIf(Null<64, Null, 64) is evaluated as IIf(False, Null, 64), which becomes 64

IIf(16<Null, 16, Null) is evaluated as IIf(False, 16, Null), which becomes Null

Thus, it doesn't matter which field is the smaller of the two. Since a null is evaluated to False in any part of the IIf() condition, Access will always choose int2, no matter which field is null.

When dealing with nulls, you must ask yourself what you want to happen when nulls are present and then alter the expression using one or more IsNull() functions. In the preceding example, you would probably prefer one of the following two scenarios:

- A null value in one of the fields should always cause LeastValue to evaluate null. In this case, change the expression to

```
LeastValue1: IIf(IsNull([int1]+[int2]), Null,
➡ IIf([int1]<[int2], [int1],[int2]))
```

- A null value in one of the fields should always cause LeastValue to return the non-null field. In this case, change the expression to

```
LeastValue2: IIf(IsNull([int2]), [int1], IIf([int1]<[int2],
➡ [int1],
[int2]))
```

Nulls and Zero-Length Strings

In version 1 Access always converted fields containing only spaces to nulls. In version 2 spaces are handled differently, depending on the settings of the field's *Required* and *AllowZeroLength* properties. Version 2 also introduces the concept of a *zero-length string*, a string that is not null but has 0 length. Whether Access allows the entry of nulls or zero-length strings is dependent on the Required and AllowZeroLength properties. Table 3.4 details what happens when you enter a null (no entry), enter one or more spaces, enter any text and then backspace over the entire entry, or enter " " (two double quotes with no space between them) with each possible combination of these two properties.

TABLE 3.4: How Access Interprets Nulls, Spaces, and Other Entries for All Combinations of the Required and AllowZeroLength String Properties

Required Property Setting	AllowZero-Length-String Property Setting	Null Entry Becomes	One or More Spaces Becomes	Back Out of Entry Becomes	"" Becomes
No	No	Null	Null	Null	Disallowed
No	Yes	Null	Null	Null	ZLS
Yes	No	Disallowed	Disallowed	Disallowed	Disallowed
Yes	Yes	Disallowed	ZLS	ZLS	ZLS

Note: ZLS = ZeroLengthString

No matter what the settings of the Required and AllowZeroLength properties, Access always trims leading and trailing spaces from fields and never stores only spaces in a field. These spaces are always converted to either a null or a zero-length string. To search for a null in a query, use the Is Null operator. To search for a zero-length string, use " " (two double quotes with no space between them).

Sorting: Ordering the Dynaset

You specify sorting in queries by using the Sort row on the Access query grid. Sorting arranges the dynaset in an order that differs from the base tables. You can sort both indexed and nonindexed queries using table fields (although sorts of the former are usually faster). In addition, you sort the rows on calculated fields, although you will take a performance hit if you sort on calculated fields for large tables.

WARNING Access is inconsistent in the order in which it presents records when no sorting has been explicitly specified. For example, table datasheets always display the data in primary key order, but combo boxes display data in their natural order (that is, the order in which the records were entered). Queries without criteria follow the behavior of table datasheets, but the ordering Access chooses for queries with criteria or multitable queries (without explicit sorting) is hard to predict. To complicate the situation further, newer versions of Access may change the rules. Thus, it is important to *never* rely on the table's natural order for applications. If you need the data ordered in a certain way, sort it!

The specification of sorts is quite simple. Simply choose Ascending, Descending, or (not sorted) for a given field. If you choose (not sorted), the default, Access changes your choice to a blank entry when you tab out of the field.

For example, say you wished to change the qryFemalePts query (discussed earlier in this chapter and shown in Figures 3.1 and 3.2) so the dynaset was now sorted in ascending order by SiteNo and Age. Figure 3.7 shows such a query, qryFemalePtsSorted1. Its dynaset is displayed in Figure 3.8. The SQL is shown here. (Notice that sorting is translated into an ORDER BY clause for the SQL.)

```
SELECT  DISTINCTROW tblPatient.PtID, tblPatient.SiteNo,
tblPatient.Age, tblPatient.Sex
FROM tblPatient
WHERE ((tblPatient.Sex="F"))
ORDER BY tblPatient.SiteNo, tblPatient.Age;
```

FIGURE 3.7:

The query qryFemalePtsSorted1 demonstrates the use of sorting. In this query, dynaset records will be sorted in ascending order by SiteNo and then Age.

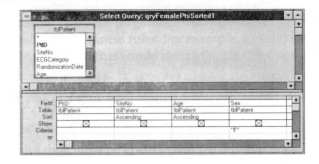

FIGURE 3.8:

Datasheet for the qryFemalePtsSorted1 query. Note that the records are sorted by SiteNo and then Age.

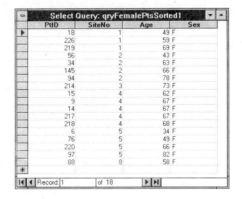

When you sort on multiple fields, Access orders the dynaset using the leftmost sorted field first and works its way from left to right with the remaining sorted fields. Thus, in the preceding query the records are ordered by SiteNo first and then Age. This means that sort order is tied to the order in which the fields are arranged in the query's dynaset. Fortunately, you can circumvent this limitation by dragging an extra copy of each field to be sorted to the query grid. Use one copy (with the Show check box cleared) for the specification of sorting and place it and all other sorted columns on the left-hand side of the query. Use the second copy (with the Show check box checked) for positioning the field in the dynaset.

Joins: Creating Multitable Queries

So far, we've limited the discussion to single-table queries. The real power of Access queries, however, is in multitable queries. The qryPtFollowup query, in design mode, is shown in Figure 3.9. This two-table query joins the tblPatient and tblFollowup tables on the field PtID in a one-to-many relationship. You might use this query to look at the status of patient follow-up visits for each site. The resulting dynaset is shown in Figure 3.10. If the relationship between these two tables had been previously defined using the Edit ➤ Relationships command, the join line would have been drawn automatically as soon as the tables were added to the query. For tables in which relationships have not been predefined, you will have to manually join the tables by dragging a line from one table to another.

FIGURE 3.9:

Two-table query, qryPtFollowup, shown here in design mode. The two tables, tblPatient and tblFollowup, are joined in a one-to-many relationship.

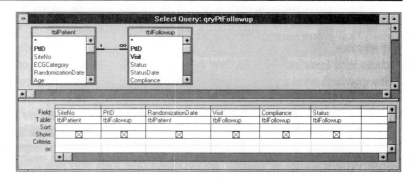

The SQL for qryPtFollowup is shown here. (Notice the JOIN clause, which is used in Access SQL to join two tables.)

```
SELECT  DISTINCTROW tblPatient.SiteNo, tblFollowup.PtID,
tblPatient.RandomizationDate, tblFollowup.Visit,
tblFollowup.Compliance, tblFollowup.Status
FROM tblPatient
INNER JOIN tblFollowup ON tblPatient.PtID = tblFollowup.PtID;
```

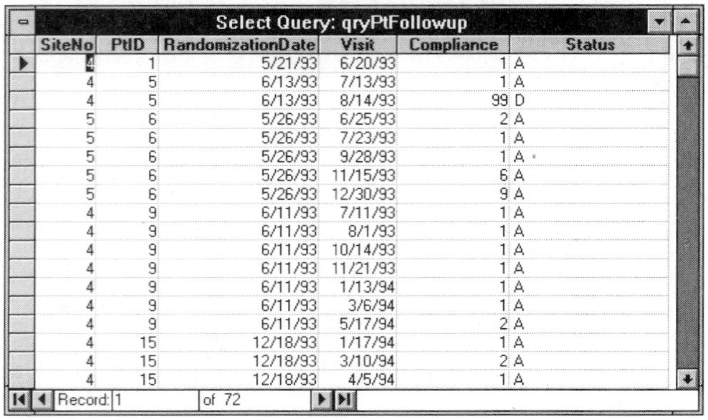

FIGURE 3.10:

qryPtFollowup datasheet with records formed by the join of the tblPatient and tblFollowup tables

SiteNo	PtID	RandomizationDate	Visit	Compliance	Status
4	1	5/21/93	6/20/93	1	A
4	5	6/13/93	7/13/93	1	A
4	5	6/13/93	8/14/93	99	D
5	6	5/26/93	6/25/93	2	A
5	6	5/26/93	7/23/93	1	A
5	6	5/26/93	9/28/93	1	A
5	6	5/26/93	11/15/93	6	A
5	6	5/26/93	12/30/93	9	A
4	9	6/11/93	7/11/93	1	A
4	9	6/11/93	8/1/93	1	A
4	9	6/11/93	10/14/93	1	A
4	9	6/11/93	11/21/93	1	A
4	9	6/11/93	1/13/94	1	A
4	9	6/11/93	3/6/94	1	A
4	9	6/11/93	5/17/94	2	A
4	15	12/18/93	1/17/94	1	A
4	15	12/18/93	3/10/94	2	A
4	15	12/18/93	4/5/94	1	A

Record: 1 of 72

NOTE

In version 1, Access did not support the definition of relationships for attached Access tables. In version 2 this limitation is no longer present. Thus, you can now define relationships between native and attached Access tables, and Access will draw the join lines for you in queries.

Joins will be easier to create if you follow these simple guidelines:

- Define primary keys for every table in the database.
- When creating foreign keys in related tables, use the same name you used for the primary key field it relates to.
- Define relationships for all one-to-many and one-to-one relationships in the database.

See Chapter 2 for a detailed discussion of relationships.

You don't have to stop with two tables. You can construct queries based on many tables. You might use more than two tables in a query in order to pull in descriptive labels from various lookup tables, to pull together data from multiple one-to-many relationships, or to join two tables in a many-to-many relationship.

You'll find that multitable queries become especially important if you've properly decomposed your database into fully normalized tables, as discussed in detail in Chapter 2. In fact, the whole process of normalization is dependent upon your ability to recompose (or denormalize) your tables through the use of queries.

For example, the tblPatient and tblMD tables in the CH3 database are related to each other in a many-to-many relationship. Doctors have multiple patients, and many patients have more than one doctor. If you needed to list each doctor and his or her patients, you would join these two "many" tables using a linking table, such as tblPtDoctors. The screen in Figure 3.11 shows a query, qryPtsByMD, that does just this. The first three tables in the table pane of the query represent this many-to-many relationship. The fourth table, tblPtConfidential, which is related to tblPatient in a one-to-one relationship, is also used in the query because the patient names are kept in this table. The resulting dynaset is shown in Figure 3.12.

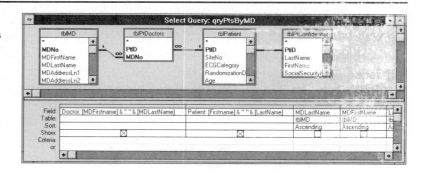

FIGURE 3.11:

The four-table qryPtsByMD query is used to list each doctor and his or her patients. tblMD and tblPatient have a many-to-many relationship. tblPatient and tblPtConfidential have a one-to-one relationship.

FIGURE 3.12:

qryPtsByMD datasheet. This query joins four tables to list each doctor and his or her patients.

The SQL statement for this four-table query with three joins is shown here:

```
SELECT  DISTINCTROW [MDFirstname] & " " &
[MDLastName] AS Doctor, [Firstname] & " " & [LastName] AS Patient
FROM (tblMD INNER JOIN (tblPatient INNER JOIN
tblPtDoctors ON tblPatient.PtID = tblPtDoctors.PtID)
ON tblMD.MDNo = tblPtDoctors.MDNo)
INNER JOIN tblPtConfidential ON tblPatient.PtID =
tblPtConfidential.PtID
ORDER BY tblMD.MDLastName,
tblMD.MDFirstName, tblPtConfidential.LastName,
tblPtConfidential.FirstName;
```

Inner and Outer Joins

By default, Access joins tables using an inner join. In an *inner join*, records are included in the dynaset only if a record in the first table matches a record in the second table. In addition to inner joins, Access supports two types of *outer joins*: left and right. In a *left outer join*, all records from the first (or left) table are included in the dynaset, even if some of the records from the first table do not match any records in the second table. As you might guess, the opposite is true for the right outer join. In a *right outer join*, all records from the second (or right) table are included in the dynaset, even if some of its records do not match any records in the first table. Another type of join, the *full outer join*, would include all matching records, plus all records that do not match from each of the two tables. This type of join is *not* supported by Access.

To create an outer join in Access, you double-click the join line connecting two tables. The Join Properties dialog box is displayed (see Figure 3.13) using a join between the tables tblPtSubset and tlkpECGCode. (The "tlkp" tag is used here to denote that this table is used only for the purposes of lookups. See the Introduction and Appendix A for more details on object-naming conventions.) In this dialog box, the options are as follows:

- The inner join (the default) is option 1. (Include only rows in which the joined fields from both tables are equal.)

- The left outer join option is option 2. (Include ALL records from tblPtSubset and only those records from tlkpECGCode in which the joined fields are equal.)

FIGURE 3.13:

The Join Properties dialog box for the join of tblPtSubset and tlkpECGCode is shown here for qryPtSubset_LJ_ECGCode. A left outer join has been selected for this query.

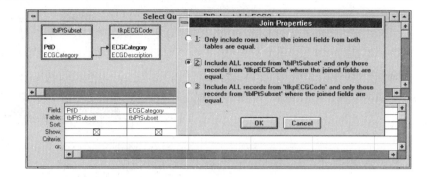

- The right outer join option is presented as option 3. (Include ALL records from tlkpECGCode and only those records from tblPtSubset in which the joined fields are equal.)

TIP

Which table is considered the "left" table for outer joins in the Join Properties dialog has nothing to do with the physical ordering of tables in the table pane of query design. For preexisting relationships, Access always designates the primary table (as defined using the Edit ➤ Relationships command) as the left table. For new joins, Access considers the table whose field you dragged the join line *from* to be the left table. For both types of joins, the actual physical order of the tables in the table pane is immaterial. For the sake of simplicity, however, it's a good practice to always put the primary table on the left side of any join lines. Following this scheme guarantees that option 2 of the Join Properties dialog is always the left outer join, no matter how you define *left*.

The three types of Access joins are best explained using an example. Say that we have two tables, tblPtSubset and tlkpECGCode. tblPtSubset consists of a subset of records from the tblPatient table, and tlkpECGCode is a lookup table that describes patient electrocardiogram (ECG) rhythm categories. For each record in tlkpECG-Code there can be zero, one, or many matching records in tblPtSubset. Thus, the two tables are related in a one-to-many relationship, with the lookup table being on the "one" side of the relationship. These two tables and their records are shown in Figure 3.14. The dynasets returned by an inner join of the two tables (qryPtSubset_IJ_ECGCode), a left outer join (qryPtSubset_LJ_ECGCode), and a right outer join (qryPtSubset_RJ_ECGCode) are shown in Figure 3.15.

FIGURE 3.14:

The records in tblPtSubset and tlkpECGCode

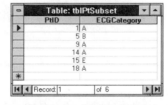

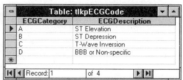

FIGURE 3.15:

A set of queries joining the tblPtSubset and tlkpECGCode tables. The inner, or natural, join, qryPtSubset_IJ_ECGCode, returns only matching records from both tables (shown at the top of the figure). In the middle of the figure is the left outer join query, qryPtSubset_LJ_ECGCode. The bottom is the right outer join, qryPtSubset_RJ_ECGCode.

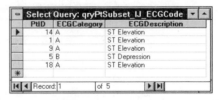

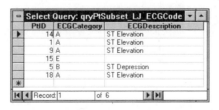

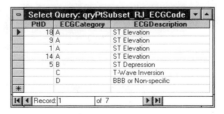

For the inner join query, qryPtSubset_IJ_ECGCode, only patients with matching records from both tables are included in the dynaset. You might use this query to create a list of all patients with a full text description of their ECG rhythms, but only if they had ECG rhythms as defined in tlkpECGCode.

The left outer join query, qryPtSubset_LJ_ECGCode, might be used to create a list of *all* patient records, even if a patient had an ECG rhythm that was not predefined in tlkpECGCode. Finally, the right outer join query, qryPtSubset_RJ_ECGCode, might be used to create a list of examples of every ECG rhythm category found in tlkpECGCode, plus those categories that didn't have any examples.

TIP   When an outer join has been selected, Access displays a line with an arrowhead at one end. For left outer joins, Access displays a right-pointing arrow at the right side of the join line (see Figure 3.13). Conversely, Access displays a left-pointing arrowhead at the left side of the join line for right outer joins. Confusing, isn't it? Not really, if you think of the arrow always pointing away from the table that includes all records and toward the table that includes only matching records.

Inner joins are, by far, the most common type of join. That's why they are also sometimes called natural joins.

Self Joins: Joining a Table to Itself

Sometimes it is necessary to join a table to itself in order to answer a question. Although *self joins* are not as common as intertable joins, they are nonetheless useful—for example, for answering certain types of queries where you have recursive relationships or where you wish to pull together and "flatten" multiple rows from a table. In a database in which you stored multiple addresses of a customer in separate rows of an address table, you could use a self join to pull together into a single record both home and work addresses. The trick to creating self joins in QBE is to alias the second copy of a table so that it is treated as if it were a separate table.

When you drop multiple copies of a table into a query, Access creates an alias so that each copy is uniquely named. For example, the second copy of tblMD would be named tblMD_1, the third copy would be named tblMD_2, and so on. You can change the alias of a table by altering the Alias property of the table's field list properties (see the next section).

For example, MDNo is the primary key for the table tblMD in CH3.MDB. This table also contains a column, DirectSuperior, that is used to note the MDNo of each doctor's supervisor. Thus, the table contains a recursive relationship between DirectSuperior and MDNo. (It's important that these two columns come from the same domain—that is, DirectSuperior must be based on the same domain as MDNo. See Chapter 2 for a discussion of domains.) Say you wished to view the names of all doctors and the names of their direct superiors, even if a doctor lacked a superior. This last requirement means that you need to use an outer self join to create the query. Self joins can use inner joins or left or right outer joins just like other (non–self-join) queries.

The Query Design view for such a query is shown in Figure 3.16. Its datasheet is shown in Figure 3.17, and its SQL is shown here:

```
SELECT DISTINCTROW tblMD.MDNo, tblMD.MDFirstName,
tblMD.MDLastName, Supervisors.MDNo AS SupervisorNo,
Supervisors.MDFirstName AS [Supervisor FirstName],
Supervisors.MDLastName AS [Supervisor LastName]
FROM tblMD LEFT JOIN tblMD AS Supervisors ON
tblMD.DirectSuperior = Supervisors.MDNo;
```

FIGURE 3.16:

The qryMDs&Supervisors query in design mode. This query joins tblMD to itself using a left outer join to produce a list of all doctors and their supervisors, even if they don't have a supervisor.

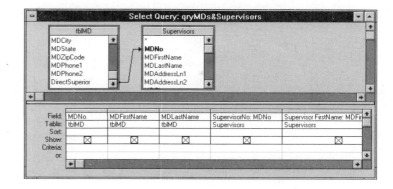

FIGURE 3.17:

The qryMDs&Supervisors datasheet displays all doctors and their supervisors.

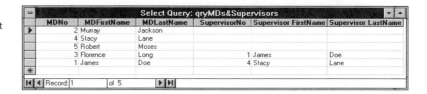

TIP You can define recursive relationships, like the one between DirectSupervisor and MDNo, using the Edit ➤ Relationships command. You can even have Access enforce referential integrity for recursive relationships so that, for example, users are prevented from entering a supervisor number for a supervisor that doesn't already exist.

Using Properties to Customize the Behavior of Your Queries

You can modify three sets of properties in queries: query, field list, and field properties. Each of the properties is summarized in Table 3.5 and discussed in the next sections.

TABLE 3.5: Properties Available for Select Queries

Property Set	Property	Description	SQL	Default Value
Query Properties	Description	Documents purpose of the query	*None*	*None*
	OutputAll-Fields	Places all fields from all tables/queries in the dynaset. Equivalent to using * for each table list. Use of this option may adversely affect the updatability of the dynaset	*	No
	TopValues	Returns only the top *n* or top *n* percent of rows. If *n* is entered as a percent value (for example, 75%), Access returns the top percentage. Otherwise, it returns the top number of rows	TOP *n* or TOP *n* PERCENT	Returns all rows per specified criteria
	Unique-Values	When set to Yes, Access returns only completely unique rows based on a comparison of all outputted fields. This option significantly slows down queries	DISTINCT	No
	Unique-Records	For certain types of queries, setting this property to Yes ensures that the dynaset is updatable (For most queries, however, this setting doesn't matter. See the section "The ALL, DISTINCTROW, and DISTINCT Predicates" in Chapter 5 for more details.)	DISTINCTROW	Yes

TABLE 3.5: Properties Available for Select Queries (continued)

Property Set	Property	Description	SQL	Default Value
	RunPermissions	Determines whether the query is run with the owner's (the person who created the query) set of permissions or the user's (the person running the query). Note that version 1.x defaulted to using the owner's permissions (See Chapter 22 for further details.)	WITH OWNERACCESS OPTION	User's
	SourceDatabase	You can use this property to specify that all of the query's base tables come from unattached tables in an external database. It's usually more efficient, however, to work with attached tables. Enter the subdirectory in which the database is located—for example, D:\DATA	FROM	(current)
	SourceConnectStr	Use this property with the Source Database property to specify the type of database to connect to (for example, dBASE IV, Paradox 3.5, and so on) for non-ODBC databases. For ODBC databases you must enter a product-specific connection string	FROM	*None*
	RecordLocks	Type of multiuser record locking to use for the dynaset (No Locks, All Records, or Edited Record) (See Chapter 11 for more details.)	*None*	No Locks

TABLE 3.5: Properties Available for Select Queries (continued)

Property Set	Property	Description	SQL	Default Value
	ODBC-Timeout	Time in seconds to cancel query if ODBC server doesn't respond. Not applicable for non-ODBC tables	*None*	60
Field List Properties	Alias	An alternate temporary name given to a table. You must use it when creating self joins	AS	*Table/query name*
	Source	Similar to the Source Database and Source Connect Str query properties. Use Source instead of the query properties if you will be using multiple unattached external tables from different sources. Enter in the format *database-path "database-type;"* for non-ODBC databases. For ODBC databases, you must enter a product-specific connection string	FROM	*None*
Field Properties	Description	Description of field for documentation purposes only	*None*	*None*
	Format	The display format for the field—for example, general, date, currency	*None*	For table fields, the field's Format property from the table. For calculated fields, *none*

TABLE 3.5: Properties Available for Select Queries (continued)

Property Set	Property	Description	SQL	Default Value
	Decimal-Places	For numeric fields, the number of decimal places to display	*None*	For table fields, the field's Decimal Places property from the table. For calculated fields, *none*
	InputMask	A template for masking user input—for example, 999-99-9999 for social security numbers	*None*	For table fields, the field's Input Mask property from the table. For calculated fields, *none*
	Caption	The caption or title for the field that will be displayed in the query's datasheet or the default label on a form	*None*	For table fields, the field's Caption from the table. For calculated fields, *none*

Query Properties

Query properties are the most general and apply to the entire query. You can use query properties, for example, to change settings for multiuser locking, to create "top n" queries, and to output unique records only.

Field List Properties

Field list properties apply to the source table's field lists. You would use these properties to create an alias for a table or to specify use of an external file as the source of a table.

(You can also use a related query property for this purpose—see the section "Using Properties to Indicate External Data Sources" a little later in this chapter.)

Field Properties

Field properties apply to individual output fields and affect the appearance of the fields. The field properties from a source table's table design properties (Format, DecimalPlaces, InputMask, and Caption) are normally inherited by the query. You may wish to adjust these properties or create properties for those fields that lack these properties. Once you modify a field's property in a query, the "inheritance link" is broken between the table and the query.

Normally, field list properties are inherited from the underlying field's property set. This inheritance link is a *hot* one-way link, so that if you later change a table's property, the query will reflect the change also—that is, unless you change the property on the *query*. Once you change a property—for example, changing the Format property for a General number to Currency—the link from the underlying table will be broken for that property (only).

Using Properties to Indicate External Data Sources

There is some overlap between Field List properties and Query properties regarding external data sources. Use the SourceDatabase and SourceConnectStr query properties when all the query's field lists (tables) are coming from a single source database (or subdirectory, in the case of non-ODBC sources). If the query is using data from multiple data sources, you would use the Source field list property instead (which combines SourceDatabase and SourceConnectStr into one string).

When using attached tables of any type, you *don't* use these properties. Instead, treat attached tables as if they were local Access tables. In fact, it is preferable and usually more efficient to use attached tables.

Using Top Value Queries

Top value queries are a feature introduced in version 2.0. You create top value queries by entering either a whole number (n) or a percent ($n\%$) in the TopValues property of the query's property sheet. This type of query returns the top (or bottom) n rows or top (or bottom) *n* percent of rows from a recordset. They're useful when you wish to return only a select proportion of records meeting the query criteria.

Normally, you use top value queries only when you've also chosen sort fields; otherwise you'll be getting a more-or-less random assortment of records. (It's worth noting, however, that this won't be a *true* random sample; instead it will be whatever proportion of records happens to come up first.)

If you use an ascending sort, Access returns the bottom-most records. If you use a descending sort instead, Access returns the top-most records. Nulls are treated as the smallest numeric value, earliest date, or first alphabetically ordered string. Thus, when you know that the Top column may contain nulls, you may wish to explicitly exclude them using criteria.

For example, to display the top 20 percent of the oldest patients, you could create a query like the one shown in Figure 3.18. The dynaset of this query is shown in Figure 3.19.

FIGURE 3.18:

The qryPatientsTop20pct query returns the top 20 percent of the oldest patients because a descending sort on age has been chosen.

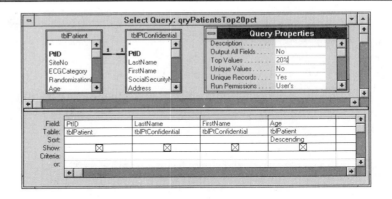

FIGURE 3.19:

The top 20 percent of the oldest patients returned by qryPatientsTop20pct

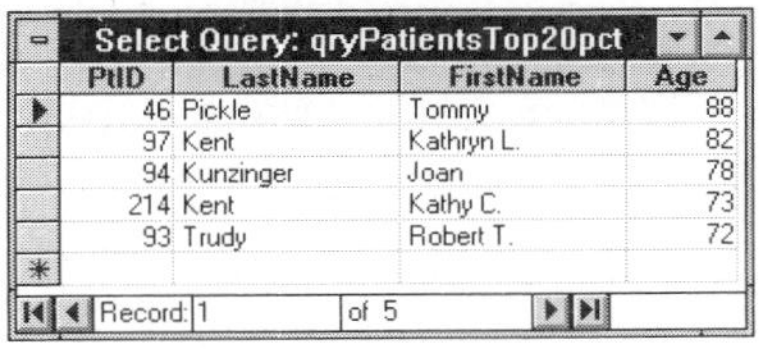

Access processes the TopValues property after all criteria, joins, sorts, and groupings have been applied. When processing percent top values, Access chooses the closest number of records less than or equal to the requested percentage. In the preceding example, Access returned 5 out of 30 rows, or 17 percent of the rows—20 percent had been requested.

Ties are treated as any other row, except when multiple rows qualify as the last selected row. When there is a tie on the last selected row, Access returns *all* rows with the last value. If three rows had been aged 72, then Access would have returned eight rows instead of five in the preceding example. With no sorts defined, Access uses all the query's output columns to decide on ties. Otherwise, Access uses only the sort columns to determine both the ordering of the rows and the resolution of ties.

Using Parameters to Specify Criteria at Run Time

You can create queries that allow the specification of criteria at run time in Access using parameters. Parameters are simply references in criteria or expressions that have not been previously defined. Most often, you will use parameters in query criteria to dynamically change the criteria based on user input.

For example, say you wished to list the patient records for all patients enrolled between two dates but you wanted the user to determine the date range at the time the query was run. You could accomplish this with a parameter query and two parameters, as demonstrated by the query qryPtsRandomizedByDate (*randomization* is a research term to indicate that a patient was enrolled in a study and allocated randomly to one of two or more treatments) shown in design mode in Figure 3.20. The two parameters are found in the Criteria cell for the RandomizationDate field, which looks like this:

```
Between [Beginning Date:] And [Ending Date:]
```

Enclose each parameter in square brackets. After creating a parameter, you need to tell Access the parameter's name and its datatype. Although this step is optional, we strongly recommend it. Choose Query ➤ Parameters to bring up the Query Parameters dialog box (see Figure 3.20). This dialog has two columns, Parameter and

FIGURE 3.20:

The qryPtsRandomizedByDate parameter query. Two parameters have been defined using the Query Parameters dialog box. These parameters are referred to in the criteria for RandomizationDate.

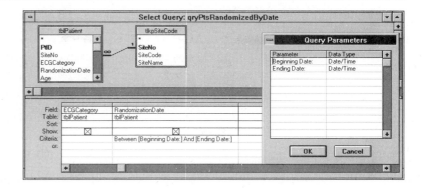

Data Type. In the Parameter column, enter the same parameter name you used in the query criteria row *without* the brackets. Choose a datatype using the pull-down combo box list. The equivalent SQL commands are shown here. (Note the addition of the Parameters statement.)

```
PARAMETERS [Beginning Date:] DateTime, [Ending Date:] DateTime;
SELECT  DISTINCTROW tblPatient.PtID, tlkpSiteCode.SiteName,
tblPatient.ECGCategory, tblPatient.RandomizationDate
FROM tlkpSiteCode
INNER JOIN tblPatient ON tlkpSiteCode.SiteNo = tblPatient.SiteNo
WHERE ((tblPatient.RandomizationDate Between [Beginning Date:]
And [Ending Date:]));
```

TIP

Entering the correct parameter name in the Query Parameters dialog is much easier and less prone to spelling errors if you use the Cut and Paste commands. Before choosing Query ➤ Parameters, select the parameter that you entered into the QBE grid criteria and press Ctrl+C to copy it to the clipboard. Then, when you choose Query ➤ Parameters, you can paste the name into the parameter column using Ctrl+V. The square brackets are optional in the Query Parameters dialog (but not on the QBE grid).

You don't *have* to use the Query Parameters dialog box. Parameter queries will usually run fine without the explicit naming and datatyping of parameters. We recommend using the Query ➤ Parameters command, however, because explicitly typed parameter queries will be faster. In addition, when you use the Query ➤ Parameters command, you can control the order in which Access prompts users for parameters.

When you create parameter queries, Access, by default, prompts the user for unresolved parameters with one or more Enter Parameter Value dialogs. You don't, however, have to use these default dialogs. You may prefer instead to create a form to prompt the user for the parameters and have the query parameters point to these form controls. This works because Access will not prompt the user for parameters that have already been satisfied.

For example, the parameter query qryPtParam uses a form, fdlgPtParam (the "fdlg" tag denotes dialog form), to feed it three parameters. You could use this query to list all women or men with last and first names matching a user-entered wildcard pattern. Each of the three parameters references controls on fdlgPtParam. The fields and their criteria are listed here:

Field	Criteria
First-Name	Like [Forms]![fdlgPtParam]![txtFirstNameSearch] & "*"
Last-Name	Like [Forms]![fdlgPtParam]![txtLastNameSearch] & "*"
Sex	IIf([Forms]![fdlgPtParam]![grpSexSearch]=1,"M","F")

When the check mark button on fdlgPtParam is clicked, the following subprocedure is triggered:

```
Sub cmdOK_Click()

    On Error GoTo cmdOK_ClickErr
```

```
Dim strMsg As String
Dim strProcName As String
Const MB_ICONSTOP = 16
Const MB_OK = O

strProcName = "cmdOK_Click"

Me.Visible = False
DoCmd OpenQuery "qryPtParam"
DoCmd Close A_FORM, Me.FormName

cmdOK_ClickDone:
    Exit Sub

cmdOK_ClickErr:
    Select Case Err
    Case Else
        strMsg = "Error#" & Err & "--" & Error$(Err)
    End Select
    MsgBox strMsg, MB_ICONSTOP + MB_OK,
    ➥ "Procedure " & strProcName
    Resume cmdOK_ClickDone

End Sub
```

The fdlgPtParam form and the datasheet returned by qryPtParam are shown in Figures 3.21 and 3.22, respectively.

FIGURE 3.21:

fdlgPtParam form used to collect the three parameters needed to run the qryPtParam query

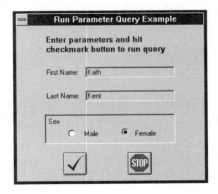

FIGURE 3.22:

Datasheet returned by the qryPtParam parameter query

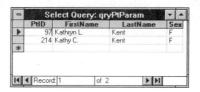

This type of form-driven querying process is often called Query By Form (QBF). A more elaborate and generic QBF system is detailed in Chapter 8.

> **TIP**
>
> When using reports that are driven off parameter queries, you might wish you could refer to the values of the parameters on the report itself. For a report that had parameters for the Start Date and End Date, you'd likely want to print these dates in the report's header. You can refer to a query's parameters from a report by simply referencing the parameter as if it were the name of a control on the report. For example, to refer to the [Enter Start Date] parameter on the underlying query of the rptOverDueOrders report, you would use the expression =Reports!rptOverDueOrders![Enter Start Date]

Parameters in parameter queries can also be set from code using the query's Parameters collection. See Chapter 6 for more details on Parameters collections and Parameter objects.

Query Datasheet Layout

By default, Access determines the width of the output columns based on whether the column is a table field or a calculated field. For *table fields*, Access borrows the column widths from the table's datasheet. If you haven't customized the column widths of your datasheets, Access uses the default width (approximately one screen inch). For *calculated fields*, Access always sets the column width to the default width (again, approximately one screen inch). Just as for table datasheets, you can adjust the column widths and row heights to whatever you like. New to version 2.0, Access now saves query datasheet layout information (column widths and row heights) with the query definitions. You cannot save, however, the widths of the Design view QBE grid columns; they are reset to the default width every time you open the query in Design view.

Dynasets: Updatable Recordsets

Select queries in Access that don't involve the aggregation of data produce dynasets. (Some people refer to the records returned by totals and crosstab queries as dynasets, too, but technically this is incorrect.)

Dynasets and snapshots are both types of *recordsets*. Snapshots are the read-only recordsets produced by totals, crosstabs, and certain nonupdatable select queries. Using Access Basic code you can also force a normally updatable select query to produce a snapshot by using the type argument of the OpenRecordset method. This is discussed in Chapter 6.

Version 1 of Access introduced the concept of the updatable dynaset. As mentioned at the beginning of this chapter, the Access dynaset is a revolutionary concept in desktop databases. Still, although the concept of dynasets is both exciting and powerful, figuring out when a 1.x Access dynaset was updatable was often confusing. Fortunately, Microsoft has reworked this area considerably for version 2.0, and the end result is nothing short of startling: with a few exceptions, almost every field in an Access 2.0 dynaset is updatable! Still, there are a few rules Access follows to determine the *updatability* of a dynaset.

The following queries are *never* updatable:

- Action, crosstab, and aggregate (totals) queries (They don't produce dynasets.)
- Multitable queries joined on non-primary key fields (or fields that don't have unique indexes)

- Multitable queries with no joined fields (This type of query is often referred to as a cartesian product query.)

- Queries with the Unique Values query property set to Yes (SELECT DISTINCT queries)

If a query doesn't fall into one of the preceding categories, the Access query processor determines dynaset behavior using the following rules:

- Calculated fields are never updatable.

- The fields in single-table queries are fully updatable. Records can be deleted. Records can be added as long as the primary key of the table is included in the dynaset.

- Multitable queries with output fields from only one table behave like single-table queries that have been filtered using the second table's records. The fields are updatable, and records can be deleted and added. All changes affect the table with output fields only.

- The fields in two-table queries with one-to-one relationships are updatable. Record deletions affect both tables. You can add records as long as the primary key of one of the tables is included in the dynaset. Added records affect both tables.

- The fields in two-table queries with one-to-many relationships are updatable. Record deletions affect the "many-sided" table only. You can add records, and they will affect both tables as long as the primary key of each is included in the dynaset. If a table's primary key is not included in the dynaset, any record additions will not affect that table. If neither table's primary key is included, record additions are disallowed.

- The fields in three-table many-to-many queries (two one-to-many relationships) are updatable. Record deletions affect the *linking* (middle) table. You can add records, and they will affect each table as long as that table's primary key is included in the dynaset.

- In other multitable queries with three or more tables, use the two-table rules as guidelines. With a few exceptions (noted above), most fields are updatable. Usually there will be one table that is the "most many" of the tables. When fields from more than one table are included in the query, record deletions affect the "most many" table.

- In one-to-many queries with fields from both tables, changes to the foreign key column of the "many-sided" table cause Access to perform a row fix-up operation, requerying the "one" table for data matching the new foreign key value. If the lookup fails because no matching key exists in the "one" table, however, Access disallows the key change.

- In one-to-many queries with fields from both tables, changes to the primary key column of the "one-sided" table are disallowed.

Using Dynasets in Applications

Because the rules for dynaset updatability were more complicated in Access version 1, you had to be very careful about their use in applications. This situation is much simpler with version 2.0. Most dynaset fields are now updatable, and inserts and deletes are more predictable. All this extra power, however, comes at a price: There are some situations in which you don't want users updating certain fields or adding or deleting records.

To control the editing of dynaset data, you need to present the dynaset to the application user with a form. You can control editing by adjusting several properties of the form (DefaultEditing, AllowEditing, and AllowUpdating) or properties of individual controls (Enabled and Locked). In addition, you may wish to attach subprocedures or functions to various events of the form and its controls (for example, On Delete, Before Update, Before Insert, and so on) to control editing behavior even further. The important points to note are that in version 2 of Access, unlike in prior versions, dynaset behavior is much more predictable, and through the use of forms, you now have the control you need to integrate them properly into the application. For further information on the Enabled and Locked properties of controls, see Chapter 7; for further information on the DefaultEditing, AllowEditing, and AllowUpdating properties of forms and form events, see Chapter 8.

Troubleshooting Dynasets

If you create a dynaset whose updatability differs from what you expected, look for one of the following possible causes:

- **Joins on non–primary-key fields:** One non-primary key join will render an entire dynaset read-only. Go back and create primary keys, if possible.

- **Joins to the results of a query with totals:** This situation also renders the dynaset read-only. One work-around you may wish to consider is this: make the totals query into a make-table query, create a primary key on the resulting table, and use that table in the second query instead.

- **Including fields from a table that aren't absolutely needed:** Don't include all the fields from every table just because you might need one of its fields. If you don't need any of the fields from a table in the dynaset, don't include them.

- **Including the wrong copy of a primary/foreign key field that appears in two tables related in a one-to-many relationship:** If you wish to edit fields from the "one" side of the relationship, include its copy of the field. If you wish to edit fields from the "many" side of the relationship (and use the row fix-up feature mentioned earlier), include its copy of the linking field (the foreign key copy) instead.

Summary

Select queries and the updatable dynasets they produce play a central role in most Access applications. They are the building blocks on which you construct the rest of your application. In this chapter, we learned that

- Select queries play a central role in Access applications.

- Access queries are based on a variant of query by example (QBE).

- Queries go hand in hand with Access structured query language (SQL).

- Access offers considerable flexibility in the specification of inexact criteria patterns.

- Query calculations take the place of calculated fields (which Access doesn't support) in tables.

- You should anticipate data with null values using the Is Null operator and IsNull( ) function when necessary.

- Never rely on a table's natural sort order in applications. Use query sorting instead.

- You can use parameter queries to allow the specification of criteria at run time.

- Access 2.0's dynaset behavior is more predictable and powerful than in version 1.x.

- You can restrict the ability of users to update query records by using them in forms and manipulating various control and form properties.

CHAPTER

FOUR

Aggregate and Action Queries

4

- Analyzing your data using crosstab and totals queries

- Taking advantage of the power of action queries

- Creating a transaction-posting system using action queries

- Charting your data using Microsoft Graph

Of all the types of queries that Access supports, you'll probably use select queries the most, but there will also be times when you need to do more than just view data. When you need to aggregate and summarize data, you'll use totals and crosstab queries. And when you need to make global changes in your database, you'll turn to action queries. This chapter focuses on when and how to best use totals, crosstab, and action queries in your applications. All the examples are drawn from a fictitious order-entry database called CH4.MDB for a pizza delivery business.

Aggregate Queries: Totals and Crosstab

You use *aggregate queries* to summarize and analyze data. You can use them to spot trends in your data, to generate summary statistics, and as the source for summary reports and graphs.

Aggregate queries are very different from ordinary select queries because you use them to condense data contained in hundreds, thousands, or even millions of rows into a few screens of useful information. When you execute aggregate queries you'll notice that none of the fields in the query's datasheet are updatable. This occurs because the data has been aggregated or summarized and therefore no longer points back to a single row in the original table.

If you need to analyze the data you collect in your Access databases, you'll find aggregate queries indispensable. The two types of aggregate queries in Access are totals and crosstab queries. The next two sections discuss the details of these queries.

Totals Queries

You change a regular select query to a totals query by choosing View ➤ Totals or by clicking the Sigma icon. The first thing you will notice when you turn on Totals is that a new row, Total, appears in the query grid just above the Sort row.

A totals query is commonly used to summarize the data across multiple records and produce summary statistics. For example, suppose you wanted to count the number of orders by the method the customer used to pay for the order (for example, check, cash, or credit card). You could create a query like qtotPaymentMethod, shown in Design view in Figure 4.1 and in Datasheet view in Figure 4.2. The SQL statement would look like this:

```
SELECT DISTINCTROW tblOrder.PaymentMethod, Count(*) AS Orders
FROM tblOrder
GROUP BY tblOrder.PaymentMethod;
```

Here are the basic steps for creating a totals query:

1. Create a new select query and add any necessary tables.

2. Drag to the query grid any fields that will be used to define the groups.

3. Change the type of query to a totals query. Any columns you added to the query grid should have Group By selected for the Total cell.

FIGURE 4.1:

The qtotPaymentMethod query in design mode. This query counts the number of orders placed using each payment method.

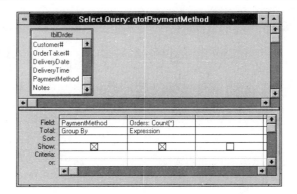

FIGURE 4.2:

The qtotPaymentMethod datasheet. This totals query displays a frequency distribution of a payment method.

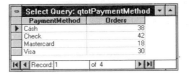

4. Decide what you want to appear in each cell of the query's datasheet. If you want the cell value to be a count of records, create an additional column with the expression*fieldname*:Count(*) in the Field cell and select Expression for the Total cell. If you wish to use an aggregate function instead, choose a column to aggregate on and select the appropriate aggregate function for the Total cell. You can also use a custom expression, in which case you would enter the expression in the Field cell and select Expression for the Total cell.

5. Set any criteria desired and run the query.

TIP The Jet database engine in Access 2.0 has built-in optimizations for aggregate counts of the form Count(*), which counts all rows in the table meeting any optional criteria. Because of these optimizations, queries using this form of Count are significantly faster than those using Count([*column*]). (These two forms of Count yield the same results if there are no nulls in *column*.)

Totals Options

In totals queries, every field in the query grid (table fields and calculated fields) must have a Total row option selected. By default, Access assigns table fields the Group By option and calculated fields the Expression option. The three types of totals options are

- Group By, for defining grouping levels

- Aggregate functions (Count, Sum, Min, Max, First, Last, Avg, StDev, Var, and Expression), for computing summary statistics for each group

- Where, for specifying criteria on fields for which you do not wish to define groups.

Table 4.1 outlines the use of these options.

TABLE 4.1: The Totals Query Options and When to Use Them

Totals Option	When to Use It
Group By	To define the groups for which you wish to calculate totals. If you choose only one Group By field, Access creates a group (a row in the recordset) for each unique value of that field. If you choose multiple Group By fields, a group will be created for each unique combination of values of the grouping fields
Count	To calculate the number of records with non-null values for a group
Sum	To calculate the sum of the values for a field in each group. Null values are not counted
Min	To calculate the smallest value for a field in each group. Null values are not counted
Max	To calculate the largest value for a field in each group. Null values are not counted
First	To calculate the first value for a field in each group. Null values are not counted
Last	To calculate the last value for a field in each group. Null values are not counted
Avg	To calculate the average of the values for a field in each group. The average is a statistical estimate of the center (or the mean) of the distribution of values in a group. Null values are not counted
StDev	To calculate the standard deviation for a field in each group. The standard deviation is a statistical estimate of the dispersion of the distribution of values in a group. Larger values indicate a group with a great variation in values. Null values are not counted
Var	To calculate the variance for a field in each group. The variance is the square of the standard deviation. Null values are not counted
Expression	To calculate a custom aggregate expression. One special case of a custom expression is Count(*), which counts the total number of rows in a group, including rows with null values
Where	To specify criteria that limit the records in the recordset without using the fields to define groups. When you use this option, you must also clear the check box in the Show row

When you use multiple Group By fields without any Sort fields, Access sorts and groups the data in the order in which the fields appear on the query grid (from left to right). If you're using aggregate queries to spot trends in the data, you may wish to try different orderings of the Group By fields. For example, if you wanted to summarize the sales for each employee by month, you could choose to group by month and then employee (see Figure 4.3, qtotSalesByMonth&Employee) or by employee and month (see Figure 4.4, qtotSalesByEmployee&Month). The first option would make it easy to make employee-to-employee sales comparisons for a given month, and the second option would make it easy to track monthly sales growth for each employee. A third option would be to use a crosstab query, as discussed later in the chapter.

FIGURE 4.3:

Because qtotSalesByMonth&Employee groups the data by month first and then employee, you can use it to easily compare different employees' sales for any given month.

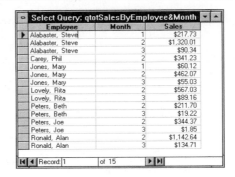

FIGURE 4.4:

Because qtotSalesByEmployee&Month groups the data by employee first and then month, you can use it to show month-to-month sales growth for any given employee.

Access follows these rules when determining how to sort the recordsets for totals queries:

- If you don't specify any sorting, Access sorts Group By fields in ascending order, using a left-to-right precedence when there are multiple Group By fields.

- If you specify sorting on *all* Group By fields, Access sorts them in the chosen order (ascending or descending), again using a left-to-right precedence when there are multiple Group By fields.

- If you specify sorting on *some* but not all Group By fields, on aggregate fields only, or on some combination of Group By fields and aggregate fields, Access sorts only those fields with specified sorts.

TIP You may find it useful to sort by the aggregate fields instead of by the Group By fields. For example, if you calculated total sales, TotalSales, grouped by EmployeeName, you might want to sort by TotalSales in descending order rather than by EmployeeName. This would list employees in order of sales performance rather than alphabetically (which would be the default if no sorting were specified).

Controlling Criteria Timing

In an aggregate query, by changing the placement of your criteria you can control when those criteria are applied. Any criteria placed on fields with the Group By or Where option are applied *prior* to any grouping, whereas criteria placed on aggregate functions (Count, Sum, Min, Max, First, Last, Avg, StDev, Var, and Expression) are applied *after* the aggregation of data.

For example, say you wished to count the total number of pizza orders by employee and type of pizza, but only if an employee sold a given type of pizza more than once. Such a query might be constructed like qtotPizzaSalesByEmployee, which is shown in both Design and Datasheet views in Figure 4.5. The >1 in the aggregate Total Sold column implies that you want Access to group by employee and pizza type and then count the number of pizzas sold, including a group only if the total number of pizzas sold exceeds 1. Criteria used on grouping or aggregate fields are equivalent to using the SQL HAVING clause. Shown here is the SQL for the qtotPizzaSalesByEmployee query:

```
SELECT DISTINCTROW tblEmployee.LastName AS Employee,
tblMenu.MenuDescription AS Item,
Sum(tblOrderDetails.Quantity) AS [Total Sold]
FROM tblMenu INNER JOIN (tblEmployee INNER JOIN
(tblOrder INNER JOIN
tblOrderDetails ON tblOrder.[Order#] =
tblOrderDetails.[Order#])
ON tblEmployee.[Employee#] = tblOrder.[OrderTaker#])
ON tblMenu.[Menu#] = tblOrderDetails.[Menu#]
GROUP BY tblEmployee.LastName, tblMenu.MenuDescription
HAVING ((tblMenu.MenuDescription Like "*Pizza*") AND
((Sum(tblOrderDetails.Quantity))>1));
```

FIGURE 4.5:

The qtotPizzaSalesByEmployee totals the orders for each combination of pizza and employee. A group is included only if the total quantity sold for the entire group is greater than one pizza.

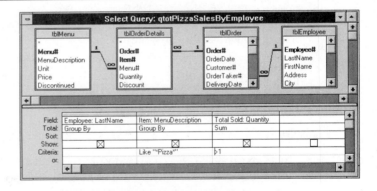

There will also be times where you wish criteria to be applied prior to the aggregation of data. You can use another field with the Where option to force Access to apply criteria prior to aggregation. For example, suppose you created the same query as above but you wished to count individual orders only if more than one pizza was sold *for that order*. A query that does just this, qtotMultPizzaSalesByEmployee, is shown in both Design and Datasheet views in Figure 4.6. This is accomplished by removing the ">1" criterion from under Total Sold and placing it under a nonaggregated copy of Quantity using the Where option. Fields with the Where option selected are used only for applying criteria and will not show up in the query's output. The SQL for this query is shown here:

```
SELECT DISTINCTROW tblEmployee.LastName AS Employee,
tblMenu.MenuDescription AS Item,
Sum(tblOrderDetails.Quantity) AS [Total Sold]
FROM tblMenu INNER JOIN (tblEmployee INNER JOIN
(tblOrder INNER JOIN tblOrderDetails ON tblOrder.[Order#] =
tblOrderDetails.[Order#]) ON
tblEmployee.[Employee#] = tblOrder.[OrderTaker#]) ON
tblMenu.[Menu#] = tblOrderDetails.[Menu#]
WHERE ((tblOrderDetails.Quantity>1))
GROUP BY tblEmployee.LastName, tblMenu.MenuDescription
HAVING ((tblMenu.MenuDescription Like "*Pizza*"));
```

Note that the >1 criterion ends up in the Where clause for this query, meaning that it will be applied prior to any aggregation.

TIP
It might not be obvious how to count the number of Yes or No values in a yes/no column. Since Access stores Yes as –1 and No as 0, you can rely on these facts when creating your query. To count the number of Yes occurrences for a yes/no field, sum the absolute value of the field—for example, Sum(Abs([ReceivedLetter])). To count the number of No values, sum the value plus 1—for example, Sum([ReceivedLetter]+1).

FIGURE 4.6:

The qtotMultPizzaSalesByEmployee query totals the orders for each combination of pizza and employee. An individual order is included for a group only if more than one pizza was sold for that order.

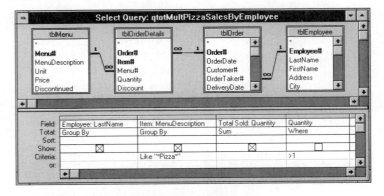

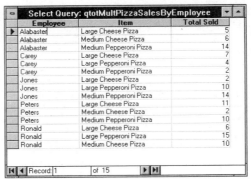

Crosstab Queries

Crosstab queries are closely related to totals queries. Like totals queries, crosstab queries summarize data across records. In fact, you can redefine many crosstab queries as totals queries, and vice versa. Crosstab queries differ from totals queries, however, in how the results are displayed. While totals queries present results in a tabular grid with the groups as rows and the fields as columns, crosstab queries change the grid so that one field's values are the rows and a second field's values are the columns. Recall the pair of nested totals queries presented earlier in this chapter, qtotSalesByEmployee&Month and qtotSalesByMonth&Employee, and the fact that, depending on how you wanted to analyze the data, you needed to choose one query over the other. This situation is a good candidate for a crosstab query because with a single crosstab query, you can analyze the data by both month and employee. The screens in Figure 4.7 show this crosstab query, qxtbSalesByEmployee&Month, in both Design and Datasheet views.

The qxtbSalesByEmployee&Month crosstab query SQL is shown here:

```
TRANSFORM Sum([Quantity]*[Price]*(1-[discount])) AS Sales
SELECT [LastName] & ", " & [FirstName] AS Employee
FROM tblMenu INNER JOIN (tblEmployee INNER JOIN (tblOrder
INNER JOIN tblOrderDetails ON tblOrder.[Order#] =
tblOrderDetails.[Order#]) ON tblEmployee.[Employee#] =
tblOrder.[OrderTaker#]) ON tblMenu.[Menu#] =
tblOrderDetails.[Menu#]
GROUP BY [LastName] & ", " & [FirstName]
PIVOT DatePart("m",[OrderDate]);
```

Here are the basic steps you use to create a crosstab query:

1. Create a new select query and add any necessary tables.

2. Drag to the query grid the two fields that will define the groups. (In the preceding example, we used expressions rather than table fields for the two Group By fields. Either can be used.)

FIGURE 4.7:

The qxtbSalesByEmployee&Month crosstab query makes it easy to analyze either monthly trends by employee or employee trends by month.

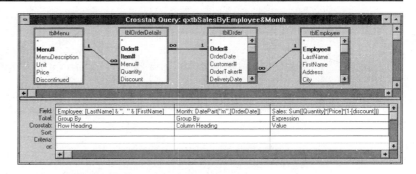

3. Change the type of query to a crosstab query. The two columns you added to the query grid should have Group By selected for the Total cell.

4. Decide which field you want for the rows and which field you want for the columns. For the field you will use for the rows, select Row Heading in the Crosstab cell. Likewise, for the field you will use for the columns, select Column Heading.

5. Decide what you want to appear in each cell of the cross-table. If you want the cell value to be a count of records, create an additional column with the expression *fieldname*:Count(*) in the Field cell, select Expression for the Total cell, and select Value for the Crosstab cell. If you wish to use an aggregate function instead, drag an additional field to the query grid, and select the appropriate aggregate function for the Total cell and Value for the Crosstab cell. You can also use a custom expression like that used in the preceding example.

6. Set any criteria desired and run the query.

Microsoft added the TRANSFORM and PIVOT statements to Access SQL to support crosstabs. Access SQL is discussed in detail in Chapter 5.

Crosstab Options

Crosstab queries have both a Total row (like totals queries) and a Crosstab row. The options for the Total row are the same as for totals queries: Group By for defining grouping levels, aggregate functions (Count, Sum, Min, Max, First, Last, Avg, StDev, Var, and Expression) for computing summary statistics for each group, and Where for specifying criteria on fields for which you do not wish to define groups. The crosstab options are Row Heading, Column Heading, Value, and "(not shown)".

The total and crosstab options are closely related. Table 4.2 details the relationship of the two options.

You may select only one value and one column heading for a crosstab query. You may select multiple row headings, however, just as in totals queries. For example, if you wished to expand qxtbSalesByEmployee&Month so that it also grouped on menu item (in addition to employee and month), you'd have to choose one of the fields as the column heading of the crosstab and the other two as the row headings. Multiple row headings are nested from left to right, just as for multiple GroupBy fields in a totals query.

TABLE 4.2: Relationship between Crosstab and Totals Options in Crosstab Queries

Totals Option	Row Heading	Column Heading	Value	(not shown)
Group By	Yes	Yes	No	No
Aggregate Function	No	No	Yes	No
Where	No	No	No	Yes

Creating Row Totals

You can create an extra row heading for crosstab queries that totals the values for an entire row. You create this special row heading by adding a Row Heading column to the query grid with the same attributes as the Value entry, except that you replace Value with Row Heading and create an alias for the entry, such as Total Orders. (It's simple if you just cut and paste the Value column, change the crosstab cell to Row Heading, and alias the field name.) For example, you could add a totals column to the qxtbSalesByEmployee&Month presented earlier in this chapter. The screens in Figure 4.8 show this new query, qxtbSalesByEmployee&Month&Totals, in both Design and Datasheet views.

Note that this special totals row heading is always positioned by Access to the left of the column headings.

Crosstab Limitations

Crosstab queries and totals queries have many similarities. For example, you can use both of them to analyze data, and both produce read-only recordsets (snapshots). Even though crosstab snapshots appear similar to and behave similarly to totals query snapshots, there are some important differences you need to be aware of.

First, you must recall that the columns in crosstab snapshots are derived from the *values* of the crosstab Column field. This means that the column names will often contain characters that are not legal column names. Access provides some relief here: for real numbers containing decimal places, Access replaces decimal points

The qxtbSalesByEmployee&Month&Totals query displays both monthly and total year-to-date (YTD) sales.

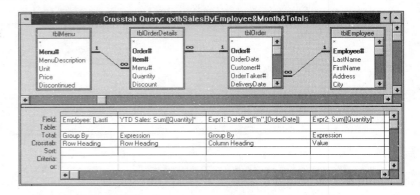

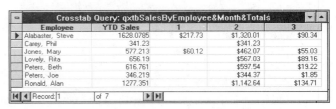

with underscore characters. However, text columns can still produce illegal or reserved names. For example, if you had a two-character text column for State/Province, it might contain the value ON for Ontario, but On is a reserved Access constant. This won't affect your ability to run the crosstab query, but you will encounter difficulties when trying to use the crosstab as a source for a report, a graph, or another query. Usually you can work around this problem by enclosing the illegal column name reference in brackets—for example, [on].

Second, unlike totals queries, in a crosstab query you cannot define criteria on the Value field. Thus, you can't create a crosstab query that is equivalent to the earlier totals query example that grouped by employee and type of pizza and included a group only if the total pizzas sold were greater than 1 (Figure 4.5). That is, you can't do it in one step. You can work around this limitation by first creating a totals query with the desired criteria and then basing a crosstab query on the results of the totals query.

For example, recall the qtotPizzaSalesByEmployee query shown earlier. You wouldn't be able to create the equivalent crosstab query in one step because that query includes criteria on the Value field. If you attempt to run the query, you'll get the alert dialog "Value field can't specify a Criteria clause." The solution is to create a query, qxtbPizzaSalesByEmployee, that uses qtotPizzaSalesByEmployee as its source. The only tricky part is deciding which aggregate function to use for the value column—in this case, the TotalSold column. Since the data has already been aggregated once, you don't want (or need) to further aggregate it, but Access requires you to choose *some* aggregate function. You can choose any aggregate function that will return that value when applied to just one value. Most aggregate functions, including Sum, Avg, Min, Max, First, and Last, will do the trick; we have chosen Sum for qxtbPizzaSalesByEmployee, which is shown in both Design and Datasheet views in Figure 4.9.

Finally, crosstab queries, in contrast to totals queries, cannot contain implicit parameters. An *implicit parameter* is a parameter that has *not* been explicitly defined using the Query ➤ Parameters dialog. The work-around is to explicitly define each parameter used in a crosstab query.

FIGURE 4.9:

The qxtbPizzaSalesByEmployee crosstab query is based on the results of a totals query, qtotPizzaSalesByEmployee.

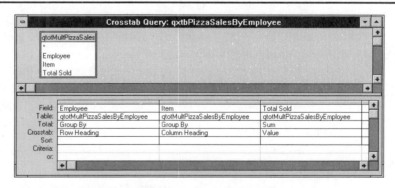

Fixed Column Headings

Crosstab queries have a unique property called *ColumnHeadings* that you can use for several purposes:

- To place the columns in a certain order. If you don't use the ColumnHeadings property, columns will always be ordered alphabetically. Often this is not the desired order, especially when you are dealing with dates.

- To include a certain column, even if it has no values.

- To exclude a column, even if it *does* have values.

Using Fixed Column Headings for Dates

By default, Access arranges column headings in ascending sorted order. Although you can easily change the sort order to descending, sometimes it is more appropriate to order the columns differently. In these cases you can use the ColumnHeadings property to stabilize the headings and get added control over the layout of the columns. For example, in the qxtbSalesByEmployee&Month crosstab query presented earlier, you'd probably prefer to list months as Jan and Feb instead of 1 and 2. You can change this easily by using Format([OrderDate], "mmm") instead of DatePart("m",[OrderDate]) for the Column field. Unfortunately, since the Format() function returns a variant text string, Access orders the Month column alphabetically instead of chronologically. The solution is to use the ColumnHeadings property. For this query, qxtbSalesByEmployee&Month1, you would enter the following in the ColumnHeadings property:

```
"Jan", "Feb", "Mar"
```

The screen in Figure 4.10 shows the result of the revised query.

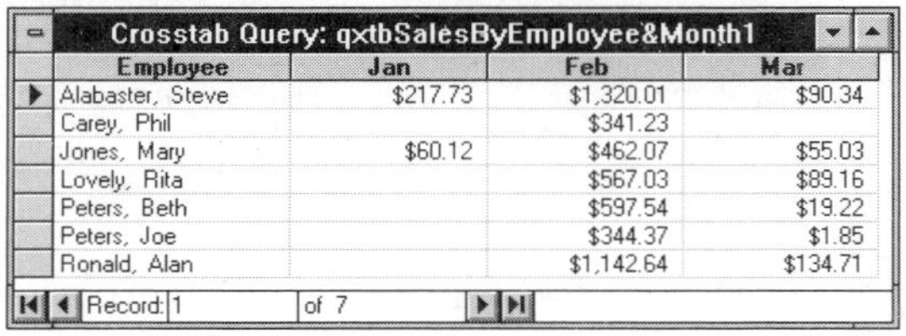

FIGURE 4.10:

This crosstab query shows employee sales by month (as a three-character string). The query was constructed using the Format() function and the ColumnHeadings property.

Employee	Jan	Feb	Mar
Alabaster, Steve	$217.73	$1,320.01	$90.34
Carey, Phil		$341.23	
Jones, Mary	$60.12	$462.07	$55.03
Lovely, Rita		$567.03	$89.16
Peters, Beth		$597.54	$19.22
Peters, Joe		$344.37	$1.85
Ronald, Alan		$1,142.64	$134.71

WARNING Fixed column headings must match the data values *exactly*. When you use the ColumnHeadings property, you can inadvertently hide data that does not match the specified headings. For example, let's say you were looking at 1993 sales by country. If the data values for the Country field were "USA", "Canada", "France", and so on, and you chose fixed headings of United States, Canada, France, and so on, the USA records would not appear in the crosstab and you might wrongly conclude that there were no United States sales in 1993.

Manipulating the ColumnHeadings Property from Code

You cannot access the ColumnHeadings property of crosstab queries directly from code. Instead, ColumnHeadings is part of the SQL property. There are situations in which it would be nice to be able to adjust the column headings in code without having to manually parse out the SQL statement, so we created a set of functions, glrGetColumnHeadings() and glrSetColumnHeadings(), to support direct manipulation of this property. You call the functions using the following syntax:

varColHead = glrGetColumnHeadings (*varSQL, varErr*)

varReturn = glrSetColumnHeadings (*varSQL, varNewColumnHeadings,varErr*)

where *varSQL* contains a valid crosstab SQL statement, which you would normally read in from an existing crosstab QueryDef; *varNewColumnHeadings* contains the new column headings as a variant text string; and *varErr* is a variant to hold any returned error codes.

These functions work by parsing and checking the SQL statement to make sure it is a valid crosstab SQL statement containing a Pivot clause. Both functions call a private function, ParseColumnHeadings(), to do the bulk of the work. The three functions are shown in Listing 4.1.

Listing 4.1

```
Const CH_NO_OLD_COLHEADS = 1
Const CH_NO_PIVOT_CLAUSE = 2
Const CH_NULL_SQL = 3
Const CH_NULL_NEW_COLHEADS = 4

Function glrGetColumnHeadings(ByVal pvarSQL As Variant,
➥ pvarErrReturned As Variant) As Variant

    ' Takes a SQL statement and returns the ColumnHeadings
    ' property.  For crosstab queries only.

    On Error GoTo glrGetColumnHeadingsErr

    Dim varColHeadBegin As Variant

    ' Initialize returned values
    glrGetColumnHeadings = Null
    pvarErrReturned = Null
    varColHeadBegin = Null

    ' Parse the SQL statement to look for existing ColumnHeadings
    glrGetColumnHeadings = ParseColumnHeadings(pvarSQL,
    ➥ pvarErrReturned, varColHeadBegin)

glrGetColumnHeadingsDone:
    On Error GoTo 0
    Exit Function

glrGetColumnHeadingsErr:
    Select Case Err
    Case Else
        MsgBox "App Error # " & Err & "--" & Error$,
        ➥ MB_ICONSTOP + MB_OK, "glrGetColumnHeadings"
    End Select
    Resume glrGetColumnHeadingsDone

End Function


Function glrSetColumnHeadings(pvarSQL As Variant,
➥ pvarNewColHead As Variant, pvarErrReturned As Variant)
➥ As Variant
```

```
' Creates/modifies ColumnHeadings for a crosstab
' query SQL statement.
' Works with crosstab queries only.

On Error GoTo glrSetColumnHeadingsErr

Dim varColHeadBegin As Variant
Dim varColHead As Variant

' Initialize returned values
glrSetColumnHeadings = 0
pvarErrReturned = Null
varColHeadBegin = Null

If IsNull(pvarSQL) Then
    pvarErrReturned = CH_NULL_SQL
ElseIf IsNull(pvarNewColHead) Then
    pvarErrReturned = CH_NULL_NEW_COLHEADS
End If

' Parse the SQL statement to look for existing ColumnHeadings
varColHead = ParseColumnHeadings(pvarSQL, pvarErrReturned,
➥ varColHeadBegin)

If pvarErrReturned > 1 Then
    ' Not valid crosstab query
    GoTo glrSetColumnHeadingsDone
ElseIf pvarErrReturned = CH_NO_OLD_COLHEADS Then
    ' No existing ColumnHeadings, so we will insert new
    ' In clause
    varColHeadBegin = Len(pvarSQL) - 2
    pvarErrReturned = Null
    pvarSQL = Mid$(pvarSQL, 1, varColHeadBegin - 1) &
➥ " In (" & pvarNewColHead & ");"
Else
    ' Replace existing ColumnHeadings
    pvarSQL = Mid$(pvarSQL, 1, varColHeadBegin - 1) &
➥ pvarNewColHead & ");"
End If

glrSetColumnHeadings = -1

glrSetColumnHeadingsDone:
    On Error GoTo 0
    Exit Function
```

```
glrSetColumnHeadingsErr:
    Select Case Err
    Case Else
        MsgBox "App Error # " & Err & "--" & Error$,
        ➥ MB_ICONSTOP + MB_OK, "glrSetColumnHeadings"
    End Select
    Resume glrSetColumnHeadingsDone

End Function

Private Function ParseColumnHeadings(ByVal pvarSQL As Variant,
➥ pvarErrReturned As Variant, pvarColHeadBegin As Variant)

    ' Parses an existing SQL statement to look for ColumnHeadings
    ' which are part of the Pivot clause.

    On Error GoTo ParseColumnHeadingsErr

    Dim strPivotClause As String
    Dim strInClause As String
    Dim strColHead As String
    Dim lngPivotLoc As Long
    Dim lngInLoc As Long
    Dim lngColHeadBegin As Long

    ' Initialize returned values
    ParseColumnHeadings = Null
    pvarErrReturned = Null
    pvarColHeadBegin = Null

    ' Check for non-null SQL statement
    If IsNull(pvarSQL) Then
        pvarErrReturned = CH_NULL_SQL
        GoTo ParseColumnHeadingsDone
    End If

    ' Search for Pivot clause.
    ' Pivot clause is where ColumnHeadings are located.
    lngPivotLoc = InStr(pvarSQL, "Pivot")
    If lngPivotLoc = 0 Then
        pvarErrReturned = CH_NO_PIVOT_CLAUSE
        GoTo ParseColumnHeadingsDone
    End If
```

```
' Search exisiting ColumnHeadings.
strPivotClause = Mid$(pvarSQL, lngPivotLoc)
lngInLoc = InStr(strPivotClause, " In")
If lngInLoc = 0 Then
    pvarErrReturned = CH_NO_OLD_COLHEADS
    GoTo ParseColumnHeadingsDone
End If

' Now parse out the ColumnHeadings
strInClause = Mid$(strPivotClause, lngInLoc)
lngColHeadBegin = InStr(strInClause, "(") + 1
strColHead = Mid$(strInClause, lngColHeadBegin,
➥ Len(RTrim$(Mid$(strInClause, lngColHeadBegin))) - 4)
ParseColumnHeadings = Trim$(strColHead)
pvarColHeadBegin = lngPivotLoc + lngInLoc +
➥ lngColHeadBegin - 2

ParseColumnHeadingsDone:
    On Error GoTo 0
    Exit Function

ParseColumnHeadingsErr:
    Select Case Err
    Case Else
        MsgBox "App Error # " & Err & "--" & Error$,
        ➥ MB_ICONSTOP + MB_OK, "ParseColumnHeadings"
    End Select
    Resume ParseColumnHeadingsDone

End Function
```

Aggregate Query Examples

Totals and crosstab queries make excellent tools for analyzing your data. The following sections present several examples of how to make the most of aggregate queries.

Frequency Distributions

You can use totals queries to create frequency distributions or tallies of your data. A *frequency distribution* is simply an accounting of how many records there are for each unique value for a given field. Frequency distributions help you get a feel for your data.

For example, say you wished to determine the frequency with which each menu item was being ordered. You could create a totals query similar to qtotItemFreq, shown in both Design and Datasheet views in Figure 4.11. Its SQL is shown here:

```
SELECT DISTINCTROW tblMenu.MenuDescription, Count(*) AS Count
FROM tblMenu LEFT JOIN tblOrderDetails ON
tblMenu.[Menu#] = tblOrderDetails.[Menu#]
GROUP BY tblMenu.MenuDescription;
```

FIGURE 4.11:

A simple frequency distribution of menu items. tblMenuDescription is included in the query in order to look up the full menu descriptions.

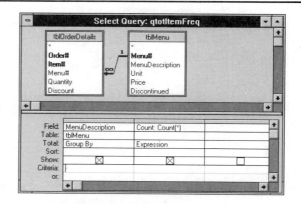

The frequency distribution is especially useful for the analysis of categorical fields. *A categorical field* is usually a text, integer, or byte field that has a limited number of categories, such as sex or country. Frequency distributions are also helpful for looking for anomalies in the data, such as records with a negative age or a sex of 3.

Descriptive Statistics

For *continuous fields*, you may wish to calculate descriptive statistics, such as the average and standard deviation. (A continuous—as opposed to a categorical—field is a real or integer numeric field that can have a continuous range of values, such as age or salary.) For example, say you wanted to calculate basic statistics on the cost of menu items. To get a better picture of the distribution of cost, you may wish to calculate the mean, the standard deviation, the minimum value, the maximum value, and a count of the number of records. Figure 4.12 shows the query, qtotPriceStats, in both Design and Datasheet views. The SQL is shown here:

```
SELECT DISTINCTROW Count(tblMenu.Price) AS CountOfPrice,
Avg(tblMenu.Price) AS AvgOfPrice, StDev(tblMenu.Price)
AS StDevOfPrice,
Min(tblMenu.Price) AS MinOfPrice, Max(tblMenu.Price)
AS MaxOfPrice
FROM tblMenu;
```

FIGURE 4.12:

The qtotPriceStats query, which computes basic statistics for the cost of menu items. Since no groups have been defined, Access computes statistics for the entire tblMenu table.

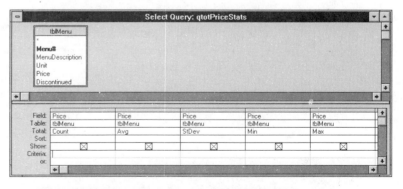

Notice that there are no GroupBy fields in this query. If no groups are chosen, Access computes statistics for all records in the query.

You may also wish to calculate descriptive statistics broken down by one or more categorical fields. For example, you might want to analyze cost by unit (the unit in which the item is sold). You can accomplish this by adding a single Group By field. The results of this query are displayed in the screen in Figure 4.13.

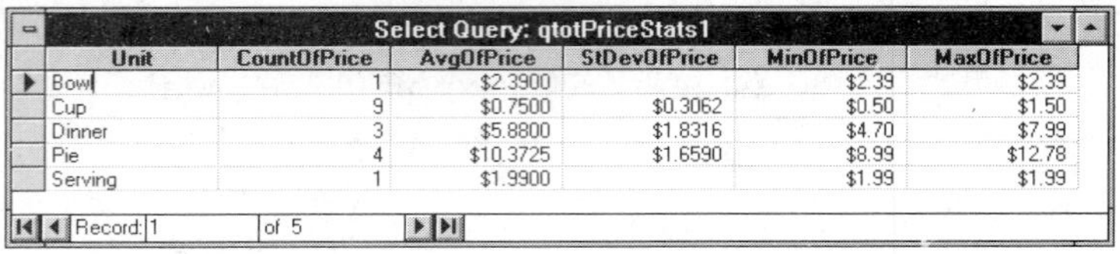

FIGURE 4.13:

The qtotPriceStats1query shows statistics on cost by unit. Items sold by the unit Pie (for example, pizzas) are, on average, the most expensive.

Unit	CountOfPrice	AvgOfPrice	StDevOfPrice	MinOfPrice	MaxOfPrice
Bowl	1	$2.3900		$2.39	$2.39
Cup	9	$0.7500	$0.3062	$0.50	$1.50
Dinner	3	$5.8800	$1.8316	$4.70	$7.99
Pie	4	$10.3725	$1.6590	$8.99	$12.78
Serving	1	$1.9900		$1.99	$1.99

Record: 1 of 5

Creating Both Row and Column Totals in Crosstabs

Although you can easily create a row heading column to total the entries for an entire row, Access provides no mechanism for creating a row that totals the values for an entire column. We've come up with a work-around, however, to create column totals using two queries that are then pasted together using a third union query. (Union queries are covered in more detail in Chapter 5.) We'll illustrate with an example.

Let's say you wish to cross-tabulate sales of dinner menu items by employee and you wish to see both the row (employee) totals and the column (menu item) totals. Here are the steps to produce the desired query:

1. Create a crosstab like that shown in Figure 4.14. Include a totals row, as discussed in the earlier section "Creating Row Totals," and name this row "{Total}". Save the query as qxtbEmployeeDinnerSales.

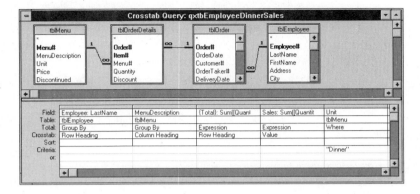

FIGURE 4.14:

The qxtbEmployeeDinnerSales query creates a crosstab that sums sales by employee rows and menu item. The {Total} field creates an extra column that sums the values in each row.

2. Make a copy of this crosstab query. For the copy, change the Employee row heading from

```
Employee: [LastName]
```

to

```
Employee: "{Total}"
```

By changing the RowHeading column to a constant named "{Total}", you force Access to create a single-row crosstab query that will serve as a global column total. Save this query, shown in Figure 4.15, as qxtbTotalDinnerSales.

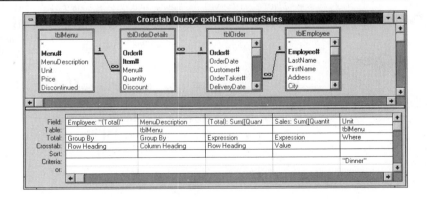

FIGURE 4.15:

The qxtbTotalDinnerSales query creates a single-row crosstab similar to the one in Figure 4.14, but with total sales for *all* rows.

3. Create a SQL-specific union query that simply joins the two queries. Use the following SQL syntax:

   SELECT * FROM qxtbEmployeeDinnerSales

   UNION

   SELECT * FROM qxtbTotalDinnerSales;

   This simple union query pastes together the rows from the two queries, giving you the desired result, which is displayed in Figure 4.16.

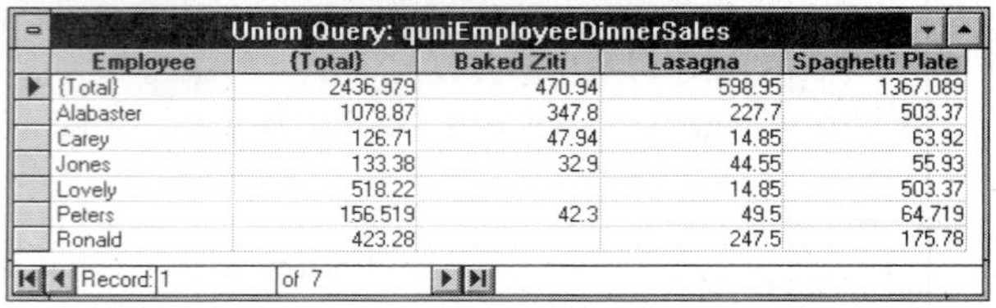

FIGURE 4.16:

The final query, quniEmployeeDinnerSales, pastes together the qxtbEmployeeDinnerSales and qxtbTotalDinnerSales queries using a union query.

Employee	{Total}	Baked Ziti	Lasagna	Spaghetti Plate
{Total}	2436.979	470.94	598.95	1367.089
Alabaster	1078.87	347.8	227.7	503.37
Carey	126.71	47.94	14.85	63.92
Jones	133.38	32.9	44.55	55.93
Lovely	518.22		14.85	503.37
Peters	156.519	42.3	49.5	64.719
Ronald	423.28		247.5	175.78

Union Query: quniEmployeeDinnerSales

Record: 1 of 7

There are a few points worth noting about this approach:

- There's no way to specify formatting of the output of a union query. Thus, the currency values are shown as real numbers with a variable number of decimal places. However, you could have used the Format() function to take care of this.

- There's no way to have the totals rows and columns sort to the outside, although you could always use a report to accomplish this.

- You could also have used a report to create the column totals.

Charting Your Data

Included with Access is a graphing applet called Microsoft Graph. You can create a chart in Access using Microsoft Graph in several ways, including using the Graph

Form Wizard and the Graph Control Wizards found in forms and reports. You can also manually connect an OLE control on a form or report to Graph or even use a third-party graphing tool that supports OLE 2. For the following examples, we use the Graph Control Wizard to embed a graph on a report.

WARNING Microsoft Graph is a resource hog. We recommend not having other applications (besides Access) running when using Graph from within Access since Graph can deplete graphics resources so much as to cause system lockups or General Protection Faults (GPFs) under Windows 3.0 and 3.1. This shouldn't be a problem with Windows 4.0 and Windows NT.

Charts are almost always based on summarized—not raw—data. Thus, it makes sense to use the results of a totals or crosstab query as the record source for a chart. Although Microsoft Graph does provide some limited options for the aggregation of data, you'll usually be better off using aggregate queries for all but the most basic charts.

For example, the totals query shown earlier, qtotItemFreq, which displays a frequency distribution of ordered menu items, would make a good source for a horizontal bar chart. Using the Graph Control Wizard, you can create such a chart quite easily—in fact, almost automatically—since the Wizard makes lots of guesses as to what you want. Probably the only tricky part is answering the question, "How do you want to calculate the totals for each category on your graph?" followed by three choices: sum, average, and count. Since you've already aggregated the data, it would be nice if there were a "No, thank you" choice, but either of the first two choices (see Figure 4.17) should do the job. Actually, the first choice, "Add (sum) the

FIGURE 4.17:

You'll need to answer the question shown here to create your graph with the Graph Wizard. If you've used a totals or crosstab query as your record source, select the first choice.

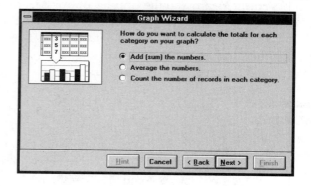

numbers" is probably the better one since summing the data is computationally simpler than averaging the data. (Note that if you *hadn't* already aggregated the data using a totals query, you would have only three choices: sum, average, and count. Now do you see why we suggested aggregating the data first?)

Once the basic graph has been created, you can use Graph to customize things by double-clicking the embedded graph. For example, we've customized the graph shown in Figure 4.18 slightly, changing the type of graph to a horizontal bar chart and enlarging it so all the labels show up.

FIGURE 4.18:

Graph based on the qtotItemFreq totals query

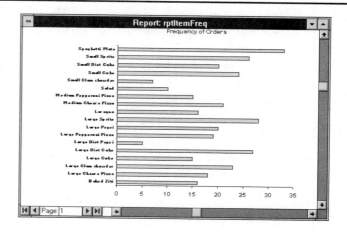

Rebuilding a Corrupted Windows Registration Database

When using Microsoft Graph or other OLE applications, you may occasionally experience problems resulting from a corrupted Windows registration database. (The registration database is a Windows storage area that keeps track of OLE applications.) If you attempt to start Microsoft Graph and you get an error message regarding the registration database, you should be able to rebuild the Graph entry by following these steps: (1) Run Access Setup. Choose the Add/Remove option, and remove Graph. (2) Exit and restart Windows. (3) Run the Registration Editor (REGEDIT.EXE) and check that there are no references to GRAPH5. If there are, select the entries and use the Edit ➤ Delete File Type command. (4) Run Access Setup again. Choose the Add/Remove option and add Graph.

See Chapter 19 for more details on object linking and embedding.

Creating a Two-Level Chart with Date Categories

Creating a chart with two levels—that is, two Group By fields—isn't much more involved than the one-level chart shown in the last example. Creating any graph is essentially a three-step process:

1. Create the necessary aggregate query.

2. Run the Graph Wizard to generate the graph based on this aggregate query.

3. Refine the graph using Microsoft Graph.

For example, say you wished to chart the quantity of orders by day of week (Mon, Tue, and so on) and payment method (such as check or cash). Following the steps listed above, you'd start by creating a query such as the totals query qtotOrderBy-Dow&PayMethod shown in Design view in Figure 4.19. This query uses the following expression for the first Group By column to create a three-character text string representing the day of the week:

```
DayofWeek: Format([OrderDate], "ddd")
```

FIGURE 4.19:

The qtotOrderByDow&PayMethod totals query computes quantity grouped by day of week and payment method.

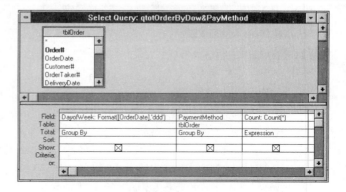

Next, you would create the graph using the Graph Wizard, embedding it in a form or report. If you used the Graph Control Wizard on a report, you'd answer a series of questions:

Q: Where do you want the graph to get its data?

A: The query qtotOrderByDow&PayMethod.

Q: Which fields contain the data you want for your graph?

A: DayofWeek, PaymentMethod, and Count.

Q: Which categories do you want along the graph's axis?

A: DayofWeek.

Q: How do you want to calculate the totals for each category on your graph?

A: Add (sum) the numbers.

Q: Do you want to link the data on your graph to a field on the report?

A: No (the default).

Q: What type of graph do you want? Data Series in Rows or Columns?

A: A column chart (the default) and Columns (the default).

Q: What title do you want on your chart? Do you want the chart to display a legend?

A: "Orders by Day of Week and Payment Method" and Yes (the default).

The resulting graph, shown in Figure 4.20, has one problem: it's sorted alphabetically by day of week instead of in the normal day-to-day sequence we're all used to. Recall that we solved this type of problem in the earlier section "Fixed Column Headings" by using the ColumnHeadings property of a crosstab query. But we based the graph on a totals query, which lacks this property. To solve the problem you need to change the query to a crosstab query analogous to the qtotOrderBy-Dow&PayMethod totals query, with DayofWeek as the column and the following fixed ColumnHeadings:

```
"Sun", "Mon", "Tue", "Wed", "Thu", "Fri", "Sat"
```

This produces the same graph, embedded in the report rptOrdersByDow&PayMethod1, this time with days of the week correctly sorted, as shown in Figure 4.21.

FIGURE 4.20:

The rptOrdersByDow&PayMethod report displays orders by day of week and payment method, but day of week is not sorted correctly.

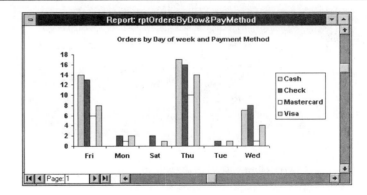

FIGURE 4.21:

Using a crosstab query with fixed column headings, you can construct the same graph as shown in Figure 4.20, but with days of the week now correctly sorted.

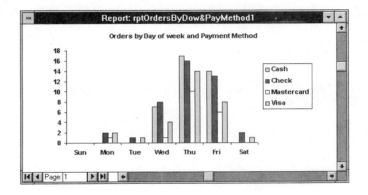

Action Queries

Although the phrase "action query" is something of an oxymoron, action queries are nonetheless a very important aspect of Access. They allow you to efficiently make bulk changes to your tables and move data among them. Although you can do anything an action query can do by defining and stepping through recordsets one row at a time using Access Basic code, you'll find using action queries almost always a simpler and more efficient (faster) way to perform bulk updates to your data. There are times, of course, when you are forced to use procedural code because you just cannot express the operation using an action query. In this case you'll need to use Access Basic and data access objects (see Chapter 6). Note, however, that in many cases an Action query is the better choice for accomplishing a bulk update.

> **TIP**
>
> In version 2.0 you can "try before you buy" an action query (see the rows that will be affected—updated, deleted, or copied to another table—by the action query) by choosing View ➤ Datasheet or clicking the Datasheet icon. In version 1.x these options were grayed out so you had to change the type of the query to a select query to obtain a preview of the results.

The four types of action queries are

Update

Delete

Make-table

Append

> **TIP**
>
> Action queries, like select queries, can contain parameters.

> **WARNING**
>
> Because Access 1.x provided no means to determine programmatically whether an action query failed because of locking conflicts, key violations, or other errors—no trappable run-time error would be triggered—most developers avoided their use in multiuser applications. For version 2.0, Microsoft has improved the situation by adding an option (DB_FAILONERROR) to the Execute method of QueryDefs. Now if an error is encountered you can trap the error, but you still can't determine how many records were prevented from being updated/deleted/appended or which type of error occurred. Thus, you must still use action queries with caution in multiuser applications. See Chapter 11 for more details.

Update Queries

You use update queries to make bulk updates to data in a table. This is usually a far more efficient process than either making the changes through the user interface (using the search and replace dialog) or opening a recordset and "walking the table," updating data one row at a time.

For example, say you wished to change the discount for all items ordered after a certain date to a new formula that was based on quantity sold. The following expression changes the discount to 0, if 5 or less were ordered; (Quantity/1000), if 6–49 were ordered (for example, this would be 0.20, or a 20 percent discount for a quantity of 20); or 0.50, or a 50 percent discount rate if 50 or more were ordered:

```
IIf([Quantity]>5,IIf([Quantity]<50,[Quantity]/1000,.5),0)
```

You could accomplish this using an update query such as qupdDiscount, shown in Design view in Figure 4.22. The equivalent SQL code is shown here:

```
UPDATE DISTINCTROW tblOrderDetailsCopy
SET tblOrderDetailsCopy.Discount =
IIf([Quantity]>5,IIf([Quantity]<50,[Quantity]/1000,0.5),0);
```

You enter the new value in the Update To row. This value can be a constant, the value of another column, or an expression like the one shown in Figure 4.22. For complex scenarios the expression can reference a user-defined function.

FIGURE 4.22:

The update query qupdDiscount changes the discount rate, stored in the field Discount, to a formula based on quantity. Also shown is the optional shadow field, NewDiscount, which can be useful for previewing the effects of the update.

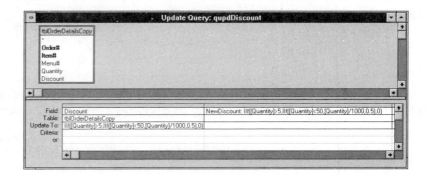

Although you can use the View ➤ Datasheet option mentioned in a tip in the preceding section, it displays the rows that will be affected by the update with only their *existing* values. In most cases you'd also find it useful to preview the change to the data you're about to make. You can do this by following these steps:

1. Construct the update query as desired.

2. Create a *shadow field* for each field to be updated. Simply copy the expression in the Update To cell to the Field cell of an empty column on the query grid. You may find it useful to give the shadow field a descriptive name. For example, for qupdDiscount, you might name the temporary shadow field NewDiscount.

3. Change the type of the query to select. (Don't worry; your Update To row will be preserved.)

4. Run the select query and check the output to make sure it does what you want it to.

5. Change back to Design view and change the type of the query back to update. Delete each of the shadow fields and execute the query. (You don't really need to delete the shadow fields—they won't affect execution and they'll disappear when you save and reopen the query.)

You'll find update queries are good for taking data that you've imported into Access from another source and massaging it into a usable format. Other good uses for update queries include making global changes to tax rates, cascading changes from one table to another, and updating calculated fields in tables.

You can update multiple fields in a single update query, but the fields must all come from the same table. You can use the values in one table, however, to update the values in another. (See the example later in this chapter in the section "Updating Data Across Tables.")

> **WARNING** Records updated using an update query may cause records in other tables to be updated if you've created relationships and have turned on the cascading updates option.

Delete Queries

You use delete queries to delete batches of records from tables. As was the case for update queries, this is usually more efficient than either deleting records through the user interface or walking a table and deleting records one row at a time.

For example, say you wished to delete all the discontinued menu items from tblMenu. You could accomplish this by using the qdelDiscontinuedItems Delete query shown in Figure 4.23. Its SQL is shown here:

```
DELETE DISTINCTROW tblMenu.Discontinued
FROM tblMenu
WHERE ((tblMenu.Discontinued=True));
```

FIGURE 4.23:
The delete query qdelDiscontinuedItems removes all discontinued menu items from tblMenu.

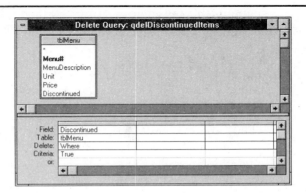

As with other queries, you can refer to multiple tables in a delete query. You indicate which table to delete records from by dragging the * (asterisk) field from that table to the query grid and choosing From in the Delete row. (You can skip this step when you've included only one table in the Delete query.) You can also add other fields to the query grid to restrict which records get deleted. For these fields, select Where in the Delete row.

If two tables are related in a *one-to-one relationship,* you may delete both tables with a single delete query by dragging both asterisk fields to the query grid.

For two tables related in a *one-to-many relationship,* however, you need to run two queries to delete records from both tables. See the example in the section "Deleting Data from Related Records in Multiple Tables" later in this chapter.

WARNING Records deleted using a delete query may cause records in other tables to be deleted when you have created relationships and have turned on the cascading deletes option.

Make-Table Queries

You use make-table queries to create tables from other tables or queries. Make-table queries are useful for creating permanent, temporary, and archive tables. As with append queries (discussed in the next section), you'll find make-table queries very handy for massaging imported data into the proper format. Fields in the new (destination) table can come from existing tables or queries, can be created using an expression, or can be constants.

For example, say you wished to back up all records from tblOrders that occurred before a certain date (02/01/94) to a new backup table, tblOldOrders. You could accomplish this using the qmakOldOrders make-table query shown in Figure 4.24. Its SQL is shown here:

```
SELECT DISTINCTROW tblOrder.[Order#], tblOrder.OrderDate,
tblOrder.[Customer#], tblOrder.[OrderTaker#],
tblOrder.DeliveryDate,
tblOrder.DeliveryTime, tblOrder.PaymentMethod, tblOrder.Notes
```

```
INTO tblOldOrders
FROM tblOrder
WHERE ((tblOrder.OrderDate<#02/1/94#));
```

The qmakOldOrders query will not, of course, delete the records from tblOrder, but you could accomplish this easily by changing qmakOldOrders into a delete query and then executing that query without making any other changes to the design.

When using make-table queries, Access creates a field in the target table for each field on the query grid with its Show check box checked. Access uses the name of the field in the source table for each table-based field or the name you give to any calculated expressions. (It's not a good idea to let Access use default names unless you find Exp1, Exp2, and so forth, to your liking). You can also change the name of any table-based fields by aliasing them. Simply add an alias name, in the format

AliasName: *FieldName*

to the field name in the query grid.

One convenient feature of make-table queries is that you can create the new table in another database (Access, non-native ISAM, or ODBC). This is especially useful for archiving or transferring data to another database without having to export it. For more information, see the section "Action Query Properties" later in this chapter.

FIGURE 4.24:

The make-table query qmakOldOrders backs up older orders (prior to 2/1/94) to the tblOldOrders table.

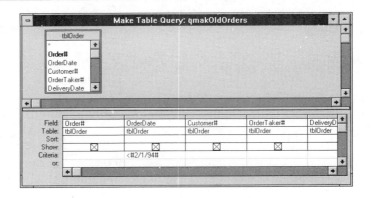

Both make-table and append queries can aggregate data using the View ➤ Totals option. Put another way, you can also use totals queries to create tables or append records to another table. Thus, you can easily make permanent tables to hold the results of a totals query in one step. Just create your totals query as usual and then convert it to a make-table or append query before running it.

Append Queries

Append queries are similar to make-table queries. The difference is that you use an append query to add records to an existing table, whereas make-table queries always create a new table, wiping out any existing table with the same name.

Append queries fail if the target table does not exist. Other than this difference, the two behave very much the same. Append queries are useful for moving data between tables. They often are used (along with an initial make-table query) to populate a table from either multiple sources or the same source at different times.

For example, after running the qmakOldOrders make-table query shown in the preceding section, you might want to run an append query each month that archived orders more than one month old to tblOldOrders. Such a query, qappOldOrders, is shown in Figure 4.25. Its SQL shown here:

```
INSERT INTO tblOldOrders ( [Order#], OrderDate, [Customer#],
[OrderTaker#],
DeliveryDate, DeliveryTime, PaymentMethod, Notes )
SELECT DISTINCTROW tblOrder.[Order#], tblOrder.OrderDate,
tblOrder.[Customer#], tblOrder.[OrderTaker#],
tblOrder.DeliveryDate,
tblOrder.DeliveryTime, tblOrder.PaymentMethod, tblOrder.Notes
FROM tblOrder
WHERE ((tblOrder.OrderDate<DateAdd('m',-1,Date())));
```

Like a make-table query, an append query does not delete the records from the original table. Also like make-table queries, append queries can be used to copy data to tables in other databases.

The append query qappOldOrders archives older orders (those with OrderDates more than one month prior to today) to the tblOldOrders table.

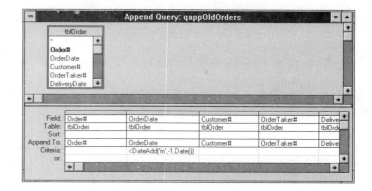

The fields for an append query don't have to match exactly the fields in the target table. By default, Access copies data to fields with the same name, but you can override this behavior simply by adjusting the name of the target field in the Append To cell. You can also use a field to set criteria without sending its data to the target table by blanking out the name of a field in the Append To cell. (This is equivalent to unchecking the Show check box for select queries.)

You must be careful when appending records to a table with a counter column. In this case Access follows these rules:

- If you don't include the counter column in the append query, Access assigns the newly appended record the next available counter value.

- If you include the counter column in the append query and there is an existing record with that value, the append fails with a "key violations" error message.

- If you include the counter column in the append query and the requested value for the appended record is greater than the value for any existing records, Access appends the record using the requested value and changes the next available counter value to the largest of the appended new values plus 1.

- If you include the counter column in the append query and the requested value for the appended record is less than the highest existing counter value but not the same as any existing records, Access appends the record using the requested value, but it also increments the next available counter value by 1. (Thus, in this case Access behaves as if it first adds the record using the next available counter value and then updates the record to use the value requested by the append query.)

Action Query Properties

For many action queries, you'll never need to adjust the properties. In fact, make-table and append queries prompt you for the DestinationTable and DestinationDB properties so you can set these properties without having to open the query's property sheet. In addition to query properties, each source table has a set of field list properties, and each field on the query grid has a set of field properties. (These properties, which are the same as for select queries, are discussed in Chapter 3.) The query properties, however, differ enough from those for select queries that we have summarized them in Table 4.3.

TABLE 4.3: Query Properties for Action Queries

Property	Description	SQL	Default Value
Description	Documents purpose of query	*None*	*None*
OutputAllFields	Places all fields from all tables/queries in dynaset. Equivalent to using * for each table list	*	No
TopValues	Returns only the top *n* or top *n* percent of rows. If you include % after *n* (for example, 75%), Access returns the top percentage. Otherwise it returns the top number of row	TOP *n* or TOP *n* PERCENT	Returns all rows per specified criteria
UniqueValues	When this property is set to Yes, Access returns only unique rows based on a comparison of all outputted fields. This option significantly slows down queries. When this property is set to Yes, UniqueRecrds must be set to No	DISTINCT	No

TABLE 4.3: Query Properties for Action Queries (continued)

Property	Description	SQL	Default Value
UniqueRecords	When this property is set to Yes (the default), the query will return only unique records, based on all fields in the underlying tables, not just those present in the query. Use of this option will *not* significantly affect query performance. When this property is set to Yes, UniqueValues must be set to No	DISTINCTROW	Yes
RunPermissions	Determines whether the query is run with the owner's (the person who created the query) set of permissions or the user's (the person running the query). Note that version 1.x defaulted to using the owner's permissions	*None*	User's
Source-Database	Name of the database that contains the source tables.[1] Use the Source property of each source tables' field list properties to include tables from more than one database	FROM	(current)
Source-ConnectStr	Type of database or ODBC connect string for external source tables[2]	FROM	*None*
Destination-Table	Name of the table that will hold the results of the make-table or append query	INTO for make-table queries; INSERT INTO for append queries	*None*
Destination-Database	The name of the database that will hold the results of the make-table or append query[1]	INTO for make-table queries; INSERT INTO for append queries	(current)

TABLE 4.3: Query Properties for Action Queries (continued)

Property	Description	SQL	Default Value
Destination-ConnectStr	Type of database or ODBC connect string for the database that will hold the results of the make-table or append query[2]	INTO for make-table queries; INSERT INTO for append queries	None
RecordLocks	Type of multiuser record locking to use for the dynaset (All Records, or Edited Record). See Chapter 11 for more details	None	Edited Record
ODBCTimeout	Time in seconds to cancel the query if the ODBC server doesn't respond. Not applicable for non-ODBC tables	None	60

[1]For the current database (or any attached tables in the current database), enter (current); for a different Access database, enter the path and name of the database—for example, C:\ACCESS\DATA\CLIENTS; for non-native ISAM databases, enter the subdirectory in which the database is located—for example, D:\DATA; for ODBC databases, leave blank. Note that when using non-native tables, it's usually more efficient to work with attached tables than to use this property.

[2]For the current database or another Access database (or any attached tables in the current database), leave blank; for non-native ISAM databases, enter a string to indentify the type and version of the product followed by a semicolon—dBASE III;, dBASE IV;, FoxPro 2.0;, FoxPro 2.5;, FoxPro 2.6;, Paradox 3.x;, Paradox 4.x;, or Btrieve;); for ODBC databases you must enter a product-specific connection string—for example, "ODBC;DSN=custdsn;UID=userid;PWD=password;DATABASE=customer;"). Note that, when using non-native tables, it's usually more efficient to work with attached tables than to use this property.

Each type of action query has a different set of properties. Table 4.4 displays the intersection of the property sets.

TABLE 4.4: Properties Sets of Action Queries

Property	Update	Delete	Make-Table	Append
Description	✓	✓	✓	✓
OutputAllFields			✓	✓
TopValues			✓	✓
UniqueValues			✓	✓
UniqueRecords	✓	✓	✓	✓
RunPermissions	✓	✓	✓	✓
SourceDatabase	✓	✓	✓	✓
SourceConnectStr	✓	✓	✓	✓
DestinationTable			✓	✓
DestinationDB			✓	✓
DestConnectStr			✓	✓
Record Locks	✓	✓	✓	✓
ODBC Timeout	✓	✓	✓	✓

Action Queries in Action

You'll find action queries very useful for accomplishing a variety of tasks in Access. As mentioned earlier, they are an efficient mechanism for making bulk changes to your tables and for moving data from one place to another. To give you an idea of their usefulness, we've included in this section several examples.

Removing Duplicates

Have you ever tried to create a primary key for a column with existing duplicate values? This is a common occurrence when you import records from another database program that doesn't support primary keys. Access refuses to create a primary key when duplicate values are present. But how do you quickly and easily locate and eliminate the duplicate records?

We offer two solutions. Both solutions use aggregate action queries. The first—the hand-pruning method—involves the use of an aggregate make-table query and a second select query to create an updatable dynaset of duplicate records that you can then use to browse and prune out the duplicates by hand. The second—the bulk-project method, from Access developer Michael Corning—uses an aggregate append query to project one copy of the duplicate rows to a second table. (A third method that employs subqueries is presented in Chapter 5.)

The basic steps for the *hand-pruning method* are as follows:

1. Create a totals query with a single Group By on the column you wish to become the primary key (the candidate key column). Also, add an expression column to count the number of rows for each group. Add criteria for this column to select only groups in which there are duplicates (Count > 1).

2. Convert this query to a make-table query. By using a make-table rather than a select query, you ensure that the dynaset created in step 3 is updatable.

3. Create a select query joining the original table to the new table made in step 2. Join the two tables on the candidate key column. Include all columns from the original table and none from the new table in the query.

4. Use the select query from step 3 to browse through the duplicate rows. Delete or change the candidate key value for all duplicate rows.

The steps for the *bulk-project method* for removing duplicates are as follows:

1. Use a make-table query (or use the Copy and Paste commands) to make a copy of the structure of the table.

2. Create a totals query that groups by the candidate key column and uses an aggregate function such as First or Last for each remaining column in the table.

3. Convert this query to an append query and append the rows to the copy of the table made in step 1. (If you tried to combine the first three steps into one make-table totals query, you'd find that Access renames all the fields in the new table to something like FirstofFirstName and so forth. This is why we suggest going to the trouble of copying the structure of the table and appending records to the copy instead.) You'll have to match up the columns for the two tables.

4. Delete the original table and rename the copy.

Once you've completed the steps for either method, you'll be able to create the primary key without fear of duplicate values.

The chapter database includes a table called tblImport, which contains duplicate order records that prevent you from designating Order# as the primary key for the table. If you attempt to create a primary key on Order#, Access complains with the dialog shown in Figure 4.26.

Here are the steps for removing the duplicates using the hand-pruning technique from tblImport:

1. Create a totals query based on tblImport. Place Order# on the QBE grid and choose Group By for the Total cell. Create the following new column:

   ```
   RecCount: Count(*)
   ```

   In the Total cell for this column, select Expression. In the Criteria cell for this column, enter the following:

   ```
   >1
   ```

   This restricts the query to only records where a count of Order# is greater than 1 (that is, those with duplicate entries).

2. Execute the query. The resulting recordset should contain a record for each duplicate Order# and a count of the number of duplicates in the CountofOrder# column.

FIGURE 4.26:

Access does not allow you to create a primary key on a column with duplicate values.

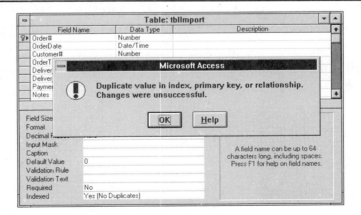

3. Change the query to a make-table query. Name the new table tblImportDups. This query, qmakImportDups, is shown in Design view in Figure 4.27. Its SQL is shown here:

```
SELECT DISTINCTROW tblImport.[Order#],
Count(*) AS RecCount INTO tblImportDups
FROM tblImport
GROUP BY tblImport.[Order#]
HAVING (((Count(*))>1));
```

FIGURE 4.27:

The qmakImportDups query lists all duplicate IDs.

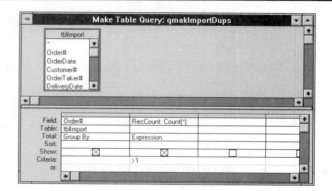

4. Create a select query (without totals) that joins the new table, tblImport-Dups, with the original table, tblImport, on the column Order#. Include all the columns from tblImport in the query grid. Don't include any columns from tblImportDups—you're including this table only to filter the records from tblImport. Sort by Order# so that all duplicate records will be displayed together. Execute the query. You will now have a dynaset that contains all the records with duplicate orders. Since this dynaset is updatable, you can browse through it and prune out the true duplicates. The dynaset for qry-HandPruneDups is shown in Figure 4.28.

Here are the steps for removing the duplicate records from tblImport using the bulk-project method:

1. Create a make-table query (or use the Copy and Paste commands) to make a copy of the structure of tblImport. To use a make-table query, place criteria

FIGURE 4.28:

The qryHandPruneDups query joins tblImportDups to tblImport in a one-to-many relationship. You can use it to interactively browse and prune records with duplicate order numbers.

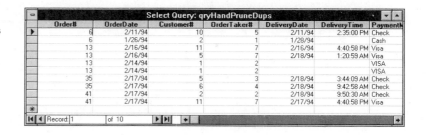

Order#	OrderDate	Customer#	OrderTaker#	DeliveryDate	DeliveryTime	Payment
6	2/11/94	10	5	2/11/94	2:35:00 PM	Check
6	1/26/94	2	1	1/28/94		Cash
13	2/16/94	11	7	2/16/94	4:40:58 PM	Visa
13	2/16/94	5	7	2/18/94	1:20:59 AM	Visa
13	2/14/94	1	2			VISA
13	2/14/94	1	2			VISA
35	2/17/94	5	3	2/18/94	3:44:09 AM	Check
35	2/17/94	6	4	2/18/94	9:42:58 AM	Check
41	2/17/94	2	2	2/18/94	9:50:30 AM	Check
41	2/17/94	11	7	2/17/94	4:40:58 PM	Visa

on one of the columns that will never be true—for example, enter **<0** for Order#. Place all the columns from tblImport on the query grid. This causes the structure, but none of the rows, to be copied. Call the make-table query qmakImportNew and the new table tblImportNew.

2. Create a totals query based on tblImport. Place all the columns from tblImport on the query grid. For Order#, choose Group By in the Total cell. For the remaining columns, select the appropriate aggregate function that will always select the record you wish to *keep*. For example, you might find First, Last, Min, or Max most appropriate. For this example, choose First. Run the query as a select query to make sure the correct records have been selected.

3. Convert this query to an append query. Choose tblImportNew as the target table. Match up the columns for the two tables. Name this query qappBulkProject and execute it. This should populate tblImportNew with only one copy of each order. qappBulkProject is shown in Figure 4.29 in Design view.

4. Check the records in tblImportNew. When you're satisfied that it's correct, delete the original table, tblImport, and rename tblImportNew to tblImport.

One of these two techniques should work in most situations in which you are faced with duplicate records that must be eliminated prior to creating a primary key. The bulk-project method doesn't require any hand-pruning of records, which is both its strong point and its downfall. Use this technique if you don't care which duplicate record is deleted or if you always wish to keep the first (or last) copy of a duplicate set of records. Use the hand-pruning method instead if the occurrence of duplicates is less predictable and requires a case-by-case analysis.

FIGURE 4.29:
The qappBulkProject query projects only one row per Order# to tblImportNew, eliminating any duplicates.

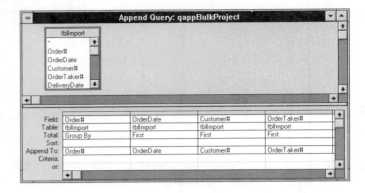

Deleting Data from Related Records in Multiple Tables

If you need to delete two tables that are related in a one-to-one relationship, you can accomplish the delete with a single delete query. Deleting records, however, from both sides of a one-to-many relationship requires at least two queries and careful planning—you'll want to avoid deleting records in step 1 that are needed for the specification of criteria in step 2. The order in which you delete the tables is dictated by the criteria you use to select records to be deleted. The various scenarios are summarized here:

Criteria Based on	Query Order
Linking column (primary key of "one" table) only	Order doesn't matter
Field(s) from "one" table	Delete "many" table first
Field(s) from "many" table	Delete "one" table first
Field(s) from both tables	You'll need to project the primary keys to a temporary table using a make-table query and then link that temporary table back to each of the other tables to perform the deletes (in any order)

This scenario assumes that referential integrity has *not* been enabled. (You'll need to delete only records from the "one" side of the relationship if you've enabled referential integrity and have turned on the cascading deletes option.)

For example, say you wished to delete an entire order (both tblOrder records and tblOrderDetails records) if either the order date was prior to 2/1/94 *or* the order included an order of lasagna. Since you wish to delete records from two tables related in a one-to-many relationship with fields from both tables, you'll need to create a temporary *projection table* (a table that has been projected from another table) that contains the Order# for any orders meeting these criteria. Figure 4.30 shows such a query, qmakDeleteProjection, which creates the temp table tblDeleteProjection.

FIGURE 4.30:

The qmakDeleteProjection make-table query creates a temporary delete projection table you can then use to delete records from both sides of the one-to-many relationship.

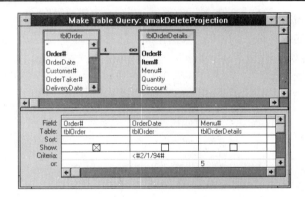

Once you've created the delete projection table, you can create the two delete queries that will delete the records from the two tables. To delete the appropriate records from the orders table, create a delete query that joins tblDeleteProjection to tblOrder by Order# and drag the asterisk field from tblOrder to the query grid. Similarly, to delete the appropriate records from the order details table, create a delete query that joins tblDeleteProjection to tblOrderDetails by Order# and drag the asterisk field from tblOrderDetails to the query grid. An example of this query, qdel1toMOrderDetails, is shown in Figure 4.31.

FIGURE 4.31:

This delete query deletes detail records from tblOrderDetails when the order date was prior to 2/1/94 *or* the order included lasagna using a temporary table, tblDeleteProjection.

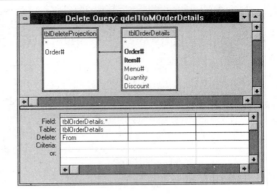

Updating Data across Tables

At times you'll need to update the records in one table based on data from a second table—for example, when you receive records from another office with changes to customer phone numbers. Once the new table is attached or imported, you'll need to find some way to copy the changes from this new table to the regular customer table. Although you might be tempted to accomplish this task by using data access objects and walking the records of the first table and then making changes to the second table, you'll probably find an update query more efficient.

For example, say you have just imported a table named tblCustomerMods that contains the same records as your regular customer table, tblCustomer, except for some changes to phone numbers in five of the records. You could update the phone numbers in tblCustomer using an update query that joined the two tables by Customer# and include one field, Phone# from tblCustomer, on the query grid. You would enter the following in the Update cell of this field to change the value of Phone# in tblCustomer to the value found in tblCustomerMods:

```
[tblCustomerMods].[Phone#]
```

and the following in the Criteria cell for Phone#:

```
<>[tblCustomerMods].[Phone#]
```

These criteria would ensure that you updated only records that needed to be changed. The update query, qupdCustomerPhone, is shown in Figure 4.32.

FIGURE 4.32:

This update query updates the phone number in tblCustomer with the value in tblCustomerMods when the two values are different.

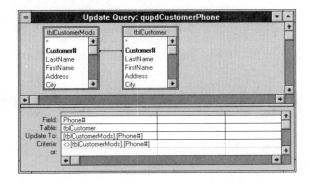

Snapshot Reports

Sometimes you'll find it handy to base reports on snapshots of the database. Snapshot reports are useful in the following situations:

- You wish to create a report at a fixed point in time and preserve the data at that time point in order to maintain an audit trail of the data.

- You've created a report based on a series of complex queries and you find that it takes too long to run.

- You've created a report based on a series of complex queries that will not execute because you've run out of memory.

- Your application is running over a network in either a file-server or client-server environment and the number of records is large.

In these situations you'll want to use a snapshot table as the source of the report instead of a query. To create a snapshot table, simply use a make-table query before running the report that creates the record source for the report. Of course, there are several disadvantages to this approach:

- The snapshot table will take up extra space in the database. You may not have enough free space to accommodate the additional table. This table will have to be re-created every time you need to run the report. If you repeatedly make and delete such a table, you will need to compact the database more frequently to recover space taken up by the deleted copies.

- If you forget to rerun the make-table query before running the report, you risk creating a report that is based on out-of-date data.

- For some reports, using a make-table query may actually take longer than basing the report on a select query.

Creating a Transaction-Posting System

In many accounting, point-of-sale, and banking applications, it's common to want users to enter new records into a transaction table and then post those records to the main data tables in a separate step. Here are some of the reasons for using this type of system:

- Better control over the timing of transactions

- Ability to easily roll back newly entered records

- Better performance for large systems

- Ability to create transactions (for example, take orders) "off line" even when the network or main database is down

- Better control over when records are locked in a multiuser system

You'll find action queries useful for creating transaction posting systems. You can use them to post records, delete records from the transaction table, and maintain an audit trail history table.

For example, in the chapter database we have created two transaction tables, tblPostOrder and tblPostOrderDetails, to hold pizza orders that have been entered using the frmPostOrders data entry form. Records from these tables are then posted to the tblOrder and tblOrderDetails tables using a posting function. The transaction system is driven using a simple switchboard form, fmnuPostingExample; two functions, glrPostOrders and glrUndoOrders; and a series of eight action queries. The elements of the system are summarized in Table 4.5.

TABLE 4.5: Database Objects in the Sample Transaction Posting System

Object Type	Object	Purpose
Table	tblPostOrder	Holds pending transactions for the tblOrder table
	tblPostOrderDetails	Holds pending transactions for the tblOrderDetails table
	tblPostHistory	Maintains an audit trail of all transaction postings
Query	qappPostOrder	Posts records from tblPostOrder to tblOrder
	qappPostOrderHist	Posts an audit trail record to tblPostHistory for each posted order record
	qdelPostOrder	Deletes records from tblPostOrder after they have been posted
	qappUnPostOrderHist	Posts an audit trail record to tblPostHistory whenever an order record is undone
	qappPostDetails	Posts records from tblPostOrderDetails to tblOrderDetails
	qappPostDetailsHist	Posts an audit trail record to tblPostHistory for each posted order detail record
	qdelPostDetails	Deletes records from tblPostOrderDetails after they have been posted
	qappUnPostDetailsHist	Posts an audit trail record to tblPostHistory whenever an order details record is undone

TABLE 4.5: Database Objects in the Sample Transaction Posting System (continued)

Object Type	Object	Purpose
Form	fmnuPostingExample	The switchboard form that runs the example
	frmPostOrders	A simple main/subform data entry form for entering new order transactions
	fsubPostOrderDetails	The subform containing detail records that is embedded in frmPostOrders
Module	basPostingExample	Contains two functions, glrPostOrders and glrUndoOrders, that are called from fmnuPostingExample

The switchboard form that drives the system is shown in Figure 4.33. One of the queries used to maintain an audit trail of transactions is shown in Figure 4.34. Listing 4.2 provides the transaction-posting functions.

FIGURE 4.33:

Switchboard form that drives the transaction-posting example

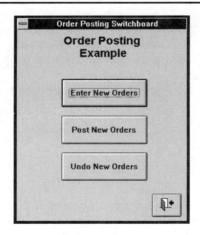

FIGURE 4.34:

The qappPostOrderHist append query creates an audit trail for each transaction posted to the tblOrder table.

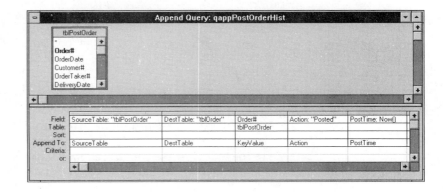

Listing 4.2

```
Function glrPostOrders()

    ' Example of a record posting routine that posts records
    ' from tblPostOrder to tblOrder and tblPostOrderDetails
    ' to tblOrderDetails.

    On Error GoTo glrPostOrdersErr

    Dim wrk As WorkSpace
    Dim db As Database
    Dim qdfAppOrder As QueryDef
    Dim qdfAppOrderHist As QueryDef
    Dim qdfDelOrder As QueryDef
    Dim qdfAppDetails As QueryDef
    Dim qdfAppDetailsHist As QueryDef
    Dim qdfDelDetails As QueryDef
    Dim lngOrderCnt As Long
    Dim lngDetailsCnt As Long
    Dim fTransaction As Integer

    ' Flag to keep track if a transaction is open.
    ' This will be used in the error handler to determine if
    ' we need to rollback a transaction.
    fTransaction = False

    Set wrk = DBEngine.Workspaces(0)
    Set db = wrk.Databases(0)
```

```
lngOrderCnt = DCount("*", "tblPostOrder", "")
lngDetailsCnt = DCount("*", "tblPostOrderDetails", "")

' Posts the data from the order posting table to the
' orders table
Set qdfAppOrder = db.OpenQueryDef("qappPostOrder")
' Creates an audit trail of the posting
Set qdfAppOrderHist = db.OpenQueryDef("qappPostOrderHist")
' Deletes the posted record from the order posting table
Set qdfDelOrder = db.OpenQueryDef("qdelPostOrder")

' Posts data from the details posting table to orders table
Set qdfAppDetails = db.OpenQueryDef("qappPostDetails")
' Creates an audit trail of the posting
Set qdfAppDetailsHist =
➡ db.OpenQueryDef("qappPostDetailsHist")
' Deletes the posted record from the details posting table
Set qdfDelDetails = db.OpenQueryDef("qdelPostDetails")

If lngOrderCnt = 0 And lngDetailsCnt = 0 Then
    MsgBox "No records to post.", MB_OK + MB_ICONSTOP,
    ➡ "Post New Orders"
    GoTo glrPostOrdersDone
End If

' Wrap whole posting within a transaction and use the
' DB_FAILONERROR option of the execute method.
' This ensures that if any one element fails,
' the whole transaction will fail.
wrk.BeginTrans
fTransaction = True

    qdfAppOrder.Execute (DB_FAILONERROR)
    qdfAppOrderHist.Execute (DB_FAILONERROR)
    qdfDelOrder.Execute (DB_FAILONERROR)

    qdfAppDetails.Execute (DB_FAILONERROR)
    qdfAppDetailsHist.Execute (DB_FAILONERROR)
    qdfDelDetails.Execute (DB_FAILONERROR)

wrk.CommitTrans
fTransaction = False
MsgBox "Records successfully posted.", MB_OK +
➡ MB_ICONINFORMATION, "Post New Orders"
```

```
glrPostOrdersDone:

    ' Cleanup time.  If we encounter an error
    ' closing objects, just continue.
    On Error Resume Next

    qdfAppOrder.Close
    qdfAppOrderHist.Close
    qdfDelOrder.Close
    qdfAppDetails.Close
    qdfAppDetailsHist.Close
    qdfDelDetails.Close
    db.Close
    wrk.Close

    On Error GoTo 0
    Exit Function

glrPostOrdersErr:
    Select Case Err
    Case Else
        MsgBox "App Error # " & Err & "--" & Error$,
        ➡ MB_ICONSTOP + MB_OK, "glrPostOrders"
    End Select

    If fTransaction Then
        ' We hit an error, so roll back the entire transaction.
        wrk.Rollback
    End If

    MsgBox "Records Not posted.", MB_OK + MB_ICONSTOP, "Post
    ➡ New Orders"
    Resume glrPostOrdersDone

End Function


Function glrUndoOrders()

    ' Example of a record posting routine that deletes records
    ' from tblPostOrder and tblPostOrderDetails without
    ' posting them.

    On Error GoTo glrUndoOrdersErr
```

```
Dim wrk As WorkSpace
Dim db As Database
Dim qdfAppOrderHist As QueryDef
Dim qdfDelOrder As QueryDef
Dim qdfAppDetailsHist As QueryDef
Dim qdfDelDetails As QueryDef
Dim lngOrderCnt As Long
Dim lngDetailsCnt As Long
Dim fTransaction As Integer

' Flag to keep track if a transaction is open.
' This will be used in the error handler to determine if
' we need to roll back a transaction.
fTransaction = False

Set wrk = DBEngine.Workspaces(0)
Set db = wrk.Databases(0)

lngOrderCnt = DCount("*", "tblPostOrder", "")
lngDetailsCnt = DCount("*", "tblPostOrderDetails", "")

' Creates an audit trail of the non-posting
Set qdfAppOrderHist =
➥ db.OpenQueryDef("qappUnPostOrderHist")
' Deletes the record from the order posting table
Set qdfDelOrder = db.OpenQueryDef("qdelPostOrder")

' Creates an audit trail of the non-posting
Set qdfAppDetailsHist =
➥ db.OpenQueryDef("qappUnPostDetailsHist")
' Deletes the record from the details posting table
Set qdfDelDetails = db.OpenQueryDef("qdelPostDetails")

If lngOrderCnt = 0 And lngDetailsCnt = 0 Then
    MsgBox "No records to undo.", MB_OK + MB_ICONSTOP,
    ➥ "Undo New Orders"
    GoTo glrUndoOrdersDone
End If

' Wrap whole posting within a transaction and use the
' DB_FAILONERROR option of the execute method.
' This ensures that if any one element fails,
' the whole transaction will fail.
```

```
    wrk.BeginTrans
    fTransaction = True

        qdfAppOrderHist.Execute (DB_FAILONERROR)
        qdfDelOrder.Execute (DB_FAILONERROR)

        qdfAppDetailsHist.Execute (DB_FAILONERROR)
        qdfDelDetails.Execute (DB_FAILONERROR)

    wrk.CommitTrans
    fTransaction = False
    MsgBox "Records successfully undone.", MB_OK +
    ➡ MB_ICONINFORMATION, "Undo New Orders"


glrUndoOrdersDone:

    ' Cleanup time.  If we encounter an error
    ' closing objects, just continue.
    On Error Resume Next

    qdfAppOrderHist.Close
    qdfDelOrder.Close
    qdfAppDetailsHist.Close
    qdfDelDetails.Close
    db.Close
    wrk.Close

    On Error GoTo 0
    Exit Function

glrUndoOrdersErr:
    Select Case Err
    Case Else
        MsgBox "App Error # " & Err & "--" & Error$,
        ➡ MB_ICONSTOP + MB_OK, "glrUndoOrders"
    End Select

    If fTransaction Then
        ' We hit an error, so roll back the entire transaction.
        wrk.Rollback
    End If
```

```
MsgBox "Records Not undone.", MB_OK + MB_ICONSTOP,
➡ "Undo New Orders"
Resume glrUndoOrdersDone
```

End Function

Before you can use these functions in your own database, you'll need to import the module basColHead and each of the queries and tables from CH4.MDB.

Here are some interesting points regarding the functions:

- The DB_FAILONERROR option is used when executing the action Query-Defs. This makes it possible to detect whether an error has occurred during the execution of the query.

- Six action queries are executed together within a transaction to post records. If any of the six queries fail, the entire transaction is rolled back.

- A flag variable is used to denote when a transaction has been entered. The error-handling routine uses this to determine whether a transaction needs to be rolled back.

Many elements of this system draw upon parts of Access that are discussed in later chapters, including Chapter 6, Chapter 11, and Chapter 14.

The preceding example is just that: an example. In practice, you'll probably want to extend such a system with these additional features:

- Separate objects into multiple databases to improve performance and allow each user to have his or her own transaction tables. The application and posting tables would be stored on each workstation, and the master tables would be stored in a data database on the file server (or in a client-server back end). See Chapters 11 and 12 for more details on why this is useful and how to do it.

- Move the audit trail table into its own database to provide extra insulation in the event of a system crash.

- Implement security so you can add the name of the user posting the transaction to the audit trail table.

- Create the QueryDefs in code using SQL statements rather then reading in the QueryDefs from saved action queries.

- Create a mechanism to ensure that the Order# for each order is unique across all workstations. This would probably require you to maintain a separate set of order numbers for each workstation or create a custom counter function. (See Chapter 11 for an example of how to do this.)

Summary

In this chapter you've learned how to construct and use aggregate and action queries. Topics that were covered include

- The structure of a totals query
- How to control the timing of criteria in totals queries
- The structure of a crosstab query
- How to add a totals row heading to a crosstab query
- How to get around some of the limitations of crosstabs
- How to analyze and graph your data using totals and crosstab queries
- How to manipulate the ColumnHeadings property of crosstab queries
- How to total both rows and columns in a crosstab query
- The structure of update, delete, make-table, and append queries
- How to manipulate the properties of action queries
- How to remove duplicates using an action query
- How to delete data from multiple tables using a delete query
- How to update data across tables using an update query
- How to create snapshot reports using a make-table query
- How to create a transaction-posting system using action queries

There are, of course, many other uses for aggregate and action queries. This chapter has merely scratched the surface of possibilities.

CHAPTER

FIVE

Access SQL

- Understanding Access SQL

- Learning the differences between Access SQL and ANSI SQL

- Creating tables with DDL SQL

- Using subqueries and union queries

Structured Query Language (or SQL, pronounced both as "ess-cue-ell" and "see-quel"—we prefer the latter pronunciation) is by far the most popular nonprocedural data access language today on computers of all sizes. Access includes support for this pervasive standard, but its implementation is incomplete and diverges from the standard in many places. Just pinning down Access' level of conformance is a chore; while Access SQL supports only a subset of SQL-89, at the same time it supports some elements of the newer SQL-92 standard. Thus, if you're already familiar with SQL, you may find Access' uneven support for the standard confusing. And if you're new to SQL and want to learn Access SQL in detail, you'll find a dearth of documentation on Microsoft's dialect of the standard query language.

A Brief History of SQL

SQL was invented, like many database standards, including the relational model itself and query by example, at an IBM research laboratory in the early 1970s. SQL was first described in a research paper presented at an Association for Computing Machinery (ACM) meeting in 1974. Created to implement E.F. Codd's relational model (originally described in an ACM paper in 1970), it began life as SEQUEL (for Structured English Query Language), briefly becoming SEQUEL/2 and then simply SQL.

Today there are hundreds of databases on platforms ranging from billion-dollar super computers down to thousand-dollar personal computers supporting SQL. This makes it the de facto data access language standard, but at the same time it's also an official standard. There are three American National Standards Institute (ANSI) SQL standards: SQL-86 (the most commonly implemented SQL today), SQL-89 (a minor revision), and the recently published SQL-92 (a major revision).

When most people speak of SQL, they are talking about the SQL-86 or SQL-89 standard, often extended by vendors to make it a more complete language. Only very recently have vendors begun to implement parts of the much more comprehensive SQL-92 standard. It will take years for many vendors (including Microsoft) to fully implement SQL-92.

Fortunately, Access SQL really shines in one crucial area: most of Access SQL directly maps to Access Query By Example (QBE) in both directions. This means you can learn Access SQL by constructing queries using QBE, switching to SQL view to see the equivalent SQL. Conversely, the SQL-savvy developer can skip QBE entirely and directly enter queries using the SQL view. In fact, such developers can use their SQL knowledge to learn Access QBE.

This chapter covers Access SQL in its entirety. It should prove useful to both the SQL-fluent developer coming to Access from other SQL implementations *and* the SQL-naive developer looking to make sense of this strange new language.

Where Can You Use Access SQL?

Unlike most other products that support SQL, Access has no SQL command line or similar facility into which you can directly enter SQL statements and press the ↵ key or click a button to view the results. The closest thing to this in Access is the Access Basic Immediate window, but it doesn't allow you to directly enter SQL statements. Instead, you enter SQL into the SQL view of the Access query facility and switch to Datasheet view when you wish to view the results.

Most of the time you'll find Access' way of doing things preferable to a SQL command-line interface because Access formats the data in a fully forward- and backward-scrollable window. What's more, you can instantly switch among SQL view, where you enter the SQL statements; Query view, where you can compose and view the equivalent query specification using QBE; and Datasheet view, where the results of the query are displayed.

If you find yourself still missing a SQL command-line type facility, you can always create your own using a simple form like the one shown in Figure 5.1. The main advantage of this type of SQL scratchpad form is that you can view the SQL statement and its output simultaneously.

FIGURE 5.1:

Simple SQL scratchpad form for testing SQL statements

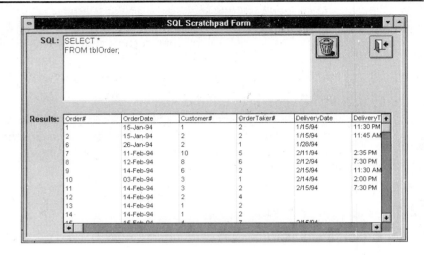

We created this scratchpad form using a text box in which the SQL statement is entered and a list box control in which the results are displayed. An event procedure attached to the AfterUpdate event of the text box changes the RowSource property of the list box to the entered SQL text. The event procedure is shown in Listing 5.1.

Listing 5.1

```
Sub txtSQL_AfterUpdate()

    On Error GoTo txtSQLAfterUpdateErr

    Dim txtSQL As Control
    Dim lboResults As Control
    Dim txtWidth As Control

    Set txtSQL = Me!txtSQL
    Set lboResults = Me!lboResults

    ' Remove the listbox grid if a null entry was made.
    ' Otherwise, make provisions for the maximum number of
    ' columns allowed (255) and turn column headings on.
    If IsNull(txtSQL) Then
        lboResults.ColumnHeads = False
```

```
        lboResults.ColumnCount = 1
        lboResults.RowSource = Null
        lboResults.ColumnWidths = Null
    Else
        lboResults.ColumnHeads = True
        lboResults.ColumnCount = 255
        lboResults.RowSource = txtSQL
        ' This next line causes the horizontal scroll bar to
        ' appear by forcing the width of columns to be
        ' greater than the total width of the control.
        lboResults.ColumnWidths = "1 in;1 in;1 in;1 in;
        ➡ 1 in; 1 in"
    End If

txtSQLAfterUpdateDone:
    On Error GoTo 0
    Exit Sub

txtSQLAfterUpdateErr:
    Select Case Err
    Case Else
        MsgBox "Error #" & Err & Error$, MB_OK +
        ➡ MB_ICONSTOP, "SQL Scratchpad Error"
    End Select
    Resume txtSQLAfterUpdateDone

End Sub
```

No parsing or elaborate error checking of the SQL statement is necessary; the list box control is smart enough (or dumb enough, if you prefer) to ignore an invalid SQL statement without generating an error. Many of the examples in this chapter are shown using this simple SQL scratchpad form.

NOTE The SQL scratchpad form and all the tables and queries used in the examples in this chapter are included in the CH5.MDB database on the companion disk.

In addition to SQL view there are several other places in Access where you can use SQL statements. You can use SQL as the row source for combo box, list box, and embedded graph controls. The SQL scratchpad form takes advantage of the fact that list boxes can be populated by SQL statements. In addition, you can use SQL to create and modify query definitions that are manipulated with Access' Data Access Objects (DAO) language.

Learning Access SQL

Although SQL may seem at first to be daunting in complexity, when it comes right down to it, it's a fairly straightforward language to learn and use. Except for a few additions, Access SQL is pretty much a subset of ANSI SQL-89. The remainder of this chapter describes Access SQL in detail.

The SELECT Statement

The *SELECT statement* is the bread and butter of Access SQL—or any SQL, for that matter. If you learn the SELECT statement and all its clauses, you'll know most of what's to know about SQL. Select queries *select* rows of data and return them as a dynaset recordset.

The basic syntax of the SELECT statement is

SELECT *column-list*

FROM *table-list*

[WHERE *where-clause*]

[ORDER BY *order-by-clause*];

SELECT statements *must* include SELECT and FROM clauses. The WHERE and ORDER BY clauses are optional.

SQL Syntax Conventions

This chapter uses the following conventions for the specification of SQL syntax:

Items in all UPPERCASE indicate keywords you must enter literally. Items in *italicized* mixed case indicate placeholders for specific values you enter.

If the placeholder includes the word *list* or *clause,* this indicates a simplification of a more detailed syntax that will be discussed later in the chapter. For example, "WHERE *where-clause*" is the syntax for a simplified WHERE clause.

Square brackets ([item]) in the syntax diagrams in this chapter denote optional items. For example, "CONSTRAINT [UNIQUE] *index*" indicates that CONSTRAINT is required, that the keyword UNIQUE is optional, and that you must enter the name of an index in place of *index*.

Curly braces combined with vertical bars ({OPTION1 | OPTION2}) are used to denote a choice. In this case you can choose only option1 *or* option2.

An ellipsis (...) combined with the square brackets notation indicates a repeating sequence. For example, "*column1* [,*column2* [, ...]]" indicates that you may include one or more columns.

You customarily start each clause of a SQL statement on a new line, but this is done only for the sake of clarity since you may break the lines wherever you please. Another custom is to enter keywords in all caps, but this is not required. We follow these customs throughout this chapter. You should terminate SQL statements with a semicolon, although Access (but not many other SQL implementations) will still process SQL statements that lack semicolon terminators.

The SELECT Clause

You use the *SELECT clause* to specify which columns to include in the resulting recordset. The column names are analogous to fields dropped onto the QBE grid with the Show box checked. Just as in QBE, you can use an asterisk (*) to indicate all fields from a table. The syntax of the SELECT clause is

SELECT {* | *expression1* [AS *alias1*] [, *expression2* [AS *alias2*] [, ...]]}

The expressions can be simple column names, computed columns, or SQL aggregate functions. For example, you can select all the columns in a table like this:

SELECT *

You indicate a single column—for example, LastName—like this:

SELECT LastName

You choose multiple columns—for example, Customer#, FirstName, and LastName—like this:

SELECT [Customer#], LastName, FirstName

In the preceding example, the Customer# column is enclosed in square brackets because its name contains a special character. You need to use square brackets to delimit all column names that include special characters or spaces. (Don't confuse these *required* brackets with the square brackets used in the syntax diagrams to indicate optional parameters.) At your discretion you may also use brackets to enclose names that don't require them. For example, you could also enter the preceding statement as

SELECT [Customer#], [LastName], [FirstName]

You can change the name of output columns and create computed columns using SQL, just as you can in QBE. To create a computed column, enter an expression instead of a table-based column. To rename a column, add "AS *aliasname*" after the column or expression.

For example, to return Customer#, renamed as "ID", and the concatenation of first and last names, renamed as "Customer Name", you could enter the following:

SELECT [Customer#] AS ID, [FirstName] & " " & [LastName] AS
[Customer Name]

If you include multiple tables (or queries) in the SELECT statement (see the section "Joining Tables" later in this chapter), you will likely need to refer to a particular column that has the same name in more than one table included in the query. In this case you must use the fully qualified version of the column name using this syntax:

table-or-query.column

For example, you could select the column Customer# from table tblOrder using the following:

```
SELECT tblOrder.[Customer#]
```

NOTE   Access QBE *always* generates SQL that uses fully qualified column names, even for single-table queries.

The FROM Clause

You use the *FROM clause* to specify the names of the tables or queries from which to select records. If you use more than one table, you must specify here how the tables are to be joined. See the section "Joining Tables" later in this chapter for more details on multitable queries. For now, here's the simplified single-table syntax:

FROM *table-or-query* [AS *alias*]

For example, you would enter the following SELECT statement to return all columns and all rows from table tblOrder. (This query is shown in Figure 5.1.)

```
SELECT *
FROM tblOrder;
```

If you wished to return only the Order# and OrderDate columns, you could enter the following SELECT statement:

```
SELECT [Order#], [OrderDate]
FROM tblOrder;
```

Like the SELECT clause, where you can alias (temporarily rename) columns, you can also alias table names in the FROM clause. Include the alias, sometimes called a *correlation name,* immediately after the table name, along with the AS keyword. To expand on the last example, you could have renamed tblOrder as Orders Table using the following SELECT statement:

```
SELECT [Order#], [OrderDate]
FROM tblOrder AS [Orders Table];
```

Correlation names are often used for convenience—correlation names such as T1 and T2 (where T1 stands for *table 1*) are often used to reduce typing—but *sometimes* they are required. You must use them for the specification of self joins (see the later section "Self Joins") and certain correlated subqueries (see the later section "Subqueries").

The WHERE Clause

You use the optional *WHERE clause* to restrict or filter the rows returned by a query. The WHERE clause corresponds to the Criteria and Or lines of QBE. Columns referenced in the WHERE clause needn't be included in the SELECT clause column list. (You can accomplish the same end in QBE by unchecking the Show box under a column used to set criteria.) A WHERE clause in Access SQL may contain up to 40 columns or expressions linked by the logical operator AND or OR. You may also use parentheses to group logical conditions.

The syntax of the WHERE clause is as follows:

WHERE *expression1* [{AND | OR} *expression2* [, ...]]

For example, you could restrict the rows returned by the SQL statement presented earlier to only those orders taken by OrderTaker# = 2 with the following SELECT statement:

```
SELECT [Order#], [OrderDate]
FROM tblOrder
WHERE [OrderTaker#] = 2;
```

Figure 5.2 shows the result of this query.

FIGURE 5.2:

Simple select query that displays Order# and OrderDate for all orders taken by OrderTaker #2

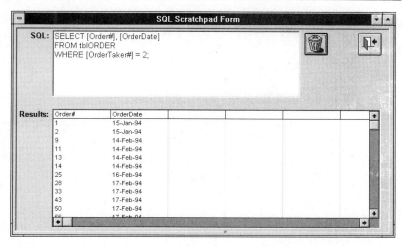

WHERE clause expressions take the same format as expressions in QBE. You may reference columns, built-in and user-defined functions, constants, and operators in each expression. Here are several examples of valid WHERE clauses:

```
WHERE[Customer#] = 4
WHERE Sex = "Female" AND Age BETWEEN 21 AND 29
WHERE LastName IS NOT NULL OR (LastName IS NULL AND
FirstName = "Joe")
WHERE OrderDate > DateAdd("yyyy", -1, Date())
```

Access SQL is less forgiving than Access QBE about the specification of criteria. Keep the following rules in mind when entering expressions:

- Always enclose text strings in quotes; either single or double quotes are fine. For example:

  ```
  Where LastName =  "Jones"
  ```

- Surround dates with the number character (#). For example:

  ```
  Where OrderDate > #4/15/95#
  ```

- Always use the keyword LIKE with wildcard characters when you wish to use inexact pattern-matching criteria. For example:

  ```
  Where FirstName LIKE "P*"
  ```

NOTE ANSI SQL uses double quotes the same way Access SQL uses square brackets. In ANSI SQL, you can only use single quotes for text strings.

The ORDER BY Clause

You use the optional *ORDER BY clause* to sort the rows by one or more columns. You use the ASC or DESC keyword to specify ascending or descending order. Ascending is the default. The ORDER BY clause corresponds to the Sort line in QBE. As with QBE, precedence in sorting is left to right.

NOTE The sort order Access uses is specified at the time you create the database using the View ➤ Options ➤ NewDatabaseSortOrder setting. Once created, sort order cannot be changed unless you compact the database. Access uses the "General" (U.S.) sort order by default. You can change the sort order to other international sort orders.

Just as with the WHERE clause, columns referenced in the ORDER BY clause needn't be included in the SELECT clause column list. You can sort text, numeric, and date/time columns, which will be sorted alphabetically, numerically, and chronologically, respectively, just as you'd expect. Don't include memo- or OLE-object type fields in an ORDER BY clause; you cannot sort on these column types. The ORDER BY syntax is as follows:

ORDER BY *column1* [{ASC | DESC}] [, *column2* [{ASC | DESC}] [,...]]

For example, if you wanted to list your customers alphabetically by last and then first name, you could use the following SQL statement:

```
SELECT *
FROM tblCustomer
ORDER BY LastName, FirstName;
```

Joining Tables

If you've properly normalized your database (see Chapter 2), you'll undoubtedly need to create queries that draw data from more than one table. When you access multiple tables in SQL, just as in Access QBE, you must *join* the tables on one or more columns to produce meaningful results. If you don't join the tables, you'll produce a Cartesian product query, which is usually undesired. (A *Cartesian product* is the arithmetic product of two input tables. For example, two 25-row tables joined this way result in a 625-row recordset.)

There are two ways to join tables in Access SQL (actually, three if you include subselects, which are covered in the section "Subqueries" later in this chapter): in the FROM clause and in the WHERE clause. Joins in the WHERE clause have always been a part of SQL; joins in the FROM clause are a feature that was added to the ANSI standard in SQL-92. Since Access QBE generates SQL statements that use the FROM clause method, we prefer this method even though it is sometimes harder to read.

Using the older SQL-89–compliant syntax, you join tables like this:

SELECT *column-list*

FROM *table1*, *table2*

WHERE *table1.column1* = *table2.column2*;

Note that this syntax makes no provision for outer joins (see Chapter 3 for more information on outer joins), although some vendors have suggested extensions to the standard.

In contrast, the SQL-92–compliant syntax looks like this:

SELECT *column-list*

FROM *table1* {INNER | LEFT [OUTER] | RIGHT [OUTER]} JOIN *table2*

ON *table1.column1* = *table2.column2*;

The keyword OUTER is optional.

The next example contrasts the two join methods. Say you wished to select Order#, Order-Date, and CustomerName for all orders occurring before February 1, 1994. Using the older SQL-89–compliant join syntax, you would enter the SQL statement shown in Figure 5.3. Using the newer syntax, you would enter the equivalent statement shown in Figure 5.4.

FIGURE 5.3:

SELECT statement that joins the tables tblOrder and tblCustomer using SQL-89–compliant join syntax

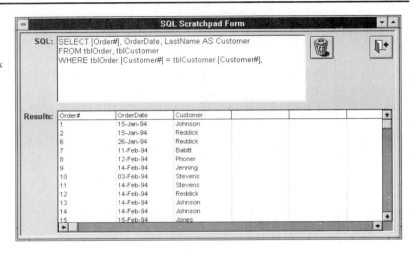

FIGURE 5.4:

SELECT statement that joins the tables tblOrder and tblCustomer using SQL-92–compliant join syntax

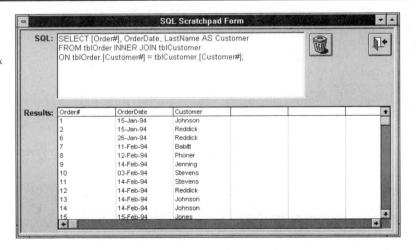

Although it's useful to be familiar with the SQL-89–style join syntax (especially if you will be using other products that are SQL-89 compliant), we recommend using the SQL-92–compliant syntax for joining tables. It's more powerful, and it's consistent with the SQL generated by Access QBE. More important, recordsets produced using the SQL-89 syntax are not updatable.

NOTE Access can also use the non-equality join operators >, >=, <, <=, and <> for joins using either the SQL-89– or SQL-92–style syntax. These types of joins, which are rarely used, are not discussed here.

Multiple Joins

As when using Access QBE (see Chapter 3), you can create SELECT statements that join more than two tables. A simplified syntax for specifying joins of multiple tables in the FROM clause is as follows:

FROM (…(*table1* JOIN *table2* ON *conditionA*) JOIN *table3* ON *conditionB*) JOIN…)

NOTE To simplify the preceding syntax diagram, we've used the word JOIN to indicate *any* type of join. You would, of course, use one of the following instead: INNER JOIN, LEFT OUTER JOIN, or RIGHT OUTER JOIN.

You may find this nested-style syntax a little confusing. It implies a set order in which the joins are performed—for example, "first join table1 to table2 and then join that result to table3 and then…." But the order of joins doesn't really matter in Access. No matter how you specify the order in the FROM clause, the Jet query processor decides on the optimum ordering of joins for the sake of efficiency. This is the way it *should* be in the relational model.

So it would seem that this syntax is counter intuitive. Alas, this type of syntax *is* necessary for the specification of outer joins in the ANSI SQL standard because order *does* matter with outer joins. But there's yet another twist: even though ANSI SQL supports the use of parentheses to allow you to arbitrarily combine outer and inner joins in any order, Access does not. This arises from the fact that the Jet query processor ignores the placement of parentheses when processing queries. Because of this, Access SQL has very specific rules on how outer joins can be combined with inner joins or other outer joins.

NOTE

In a left outer join, the unmatched rows in the table on the left side of the join are *preserved*. In a right outer join, the unmatched rows in the table on the right side of the join are preserved. As Access executes an outer join, it first looks at each row in the preserved table. If a row in the other (non-preserved) table matches a row in the preserved table, Access creates a result row from the two. Otherwise Access creates a result row from the columns in the preserved table and fills the columns from the other (non-preserved) table with nulls. An outer join will always have as many rows as or more rows than the equivalent inner join.

The Jet engine enforces the following rules when combining joins in a single query:

- The non-preserved table in an outer join *cannot* participate in an inner join.
- The non-preserved table in an outer join *cannot* be the non-preserved table of another outer join.

These rules can also be expressed using QBE: A table with an arrow pointing toward it *can't* also be connected to either a line with no arrow or another arrow pointing toward it.

So even though you must use the parentheses, for all practical purposes they are ignored as the Jet query engine processes your query. Instead, you must follow the preceding rules when combining outer joins. If you need to create a query, however, that does not follow these rules, you can usually break it up into multiple stacked queries that Jet *can* handle. For example, say you wished to list all customers and the items they ordered but include customers who made no orders. To solve this problem, you might create a four-table, three-join query that looks like this:

```
SELECT tblCustomer.LastName, tblOrder.OrderDate,
tblOrderDetails.Quantity, tblMenu.MenuDescription
FROM ((tblOrder INNER JOIN tblOrderDetails
ON tblOrder.[Order#] = tblOrderDetails.[Order#])
INNER JOIN tblMenu ON tblOrderDetails.[Menu#] = tblMenu.[Menu#])
RIGHT JOIN tblCustomer ON tblOrder.[Customer#] =
tblCustomer.[Customer#]
ORDER BY tblCustomer.LastName, tblOrder.OrderDate;
```

Unfortunately, the preceding query will not work. If you attempt to execute it, you get the "Query contains ambiguous joins" error message. This is because the non-preserved side of the outer join (in this case, the left side of a right outer join) is combined with several inner joins. The solution to this dilemma is to create the query in two steps:

1. Create a query that joins the tables tblOrder, tblOrderDetails, and tblMenu using inner joins. Save the query, for example, as qryItems.

2. Create a second query that combines the result of qryItems with tblCustomer using an outer join.

The first query's SELECT statement (qryItems) would look like this:

```
SELECT tblOrder.[Customer#], tblOrder.OrderDate,
tblOrderDetails.Quantity, tblMenu.MenuDescription
FROM (tblOrder INNER JOIN tblOrderDetails ON tblOrder.[Order#] =
tblOrderDetails.[Order#])
INNER JOIN tblMenu ON tblOrderDetails.[Menu#] = tblMenu.[Menu#]
ORDER BY tblOrder.OrderDate;
```

The second query would then look like this:

```
SELECT DISTINCTROW tblCustomer.LastName, qryItems.OrderDate,
qryItems.Quantity, qryItems.MenuDescription
FROM tblCustomer LEFT JOIN qryItems ON tblCustomer.[Customer#] =
qryItems.[Customer#]
ORDER BY tblCustomer.LastName, qryItems.OrderDate;
```

You can use these two *stacked* queries, whose datasheet is shown in Figure 5.5, to produce the correct answer.

Self Joins

Self joins are useful for answering certain types of queries when you have recursive relationships or when you wish to pull together and "flatten" multiple rows from a table. For example, if you stored the ID# of supervisors in an employees table, you could join the employees table to itself to display employees and their supervisors on a single row of a report. In a database in which you stored multiple addresses of a customer in separate rows of an address table, you could also use a self join to pull together into a single record both home and work addresses.

FIGURE 5.5:

Customers and their orders, including rows in which no orders were made. (Note the first row.) This query, because it requires combining outer and inner joins with inner joins on the non-preserved side of the outer join, must be created using two stacked queries.

LastName	OrderDate	Quantity	MenuDescription
Ayala			
Babitt	11-Feb-94	45	Large Cheese Pizza
Babitt	17-Feb-94	6	Small Diet Coke
Babitt	17-Feb-94	6	Lasagna
Babitt	17-Feb-94	1	Salad
Babitt	17-Feb-94	1	Large Sprite
Babitt	17-Feb-94	5	Small Sprite
Babitt	17-Feb-94	1	Small Sprite
Fallon	17-Feb-94	1	Large Coke
Fallon	17-Feb-94	3	Lasagna
Fallon	17-Feb-94	8	Small Sprite
Fallon	17-Feb-94	5	Large Diet Pepsi
Fallon	17-Feb-94	10	Small Diet Coke
Fallon	17-Feb-94	9	Large Sprite
Fallon	17-Feb-94	4	Large Pepsi
Fallon	17-Feb-94	1	Medium Pepperoni Pizza
Fallon	17-Feb-94	8	Small Diet Coke
Fallon	17-Feb-94	3	Salad

Select Query: qryCustomerItems2

Record: 1 of 344

The trick to creating self joins in QBE is to alias the second copy of a table so it is treated as if it were a separate table. You use this same trick to create self joins using SQL. For example, the table tblEmployee contains a column, Supervisor#, that uses the same ID number as Employee# to designate an employee's supervisor. Say you wished to view the names of all employees and their supervisors' names, even if an employee lacked a supervisor. This last requirement means that you need to use an outer join to create the desired query. The SELECT statement that accomplishes this is shown in Figure 5.6.

FIGURE 5.6:

This self-join query produces a list of all employees and their supervisors. By using an outer join, you can include the CEO, Mary Jones, even though she has no supervisor.

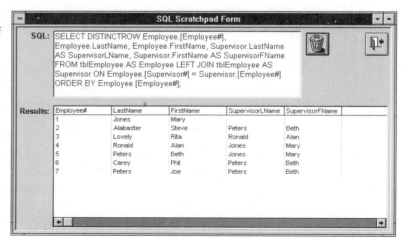

SQL Scratchpad Form

```
SQL: SELECT DISTINCTROW Employee.[Employee#],
     Employee.LastName, Employee.FirstName, Supervisor.LastName
     AS SupervisorLName, Supervisor.FirstName AS SupervisorFName
     FROM tblEmployee AS Employee LEFT JOIN tblEmployee AS
     Supervisor ON Employee.[Supervisor#] = Supervisor.[Employee#]
     ORDER BY Employee.[Employee#];
```

Results:

Employee#	LastName	FirstName	SupervisorLName	SupervisorFName
1	Jones	Mary		
2	Alabaster	Steve	Peters	Beth
3	Lovely	Rita	Ronald	Alan
4	Ronald	Alan	Jones	Mary
5	Peters	Beth	Jones	Mary
6	Carey	Phil	Peters	Beth
7	Peters	Joe	Peters	Beth

The ALL, DISTINCTROW, and DISTINCT Predicates

You can precede the SELECT clause column-name list with one of the mutually exclusive quantifier predicates: ALL, DISTINCTROW, or DISTINCT. (The DISTINCTROW predicate is unique to Access SQL.) These quantifiers control how duplicate values and duplicate records are handled. Here's the basic syntax of the SELECT clause predicates:

SELECT [{ ALL | DISTINCT | DISTINCTROW }] *column-list*

If you use no keyword, ALL is assumed. ALL returns all rows that meet the specified criteria. No special processing of the rows is done to ensure uniqueness. This is equivalent in QBE to setting *both* the UniqueValues and UniqueRecords properties to No.

If you use the keyword DISTINCT, Access eliminates any duplicate rows in the result set *based on the columns contained in the SELECT clause*. If more than one column is specified in the SELECT clause, Access discards duplicates based on the values of them all. When you use DISTINCT, the query's recordset is never updatable and performance may be adversely affected. Thus, use DISTINCT only when necessary. Using the DISTINCT predicate in a SELECT statement is equivalent to setting the UniqueValues property to Yes in QBE.

NOTE When you've included the primary key for a single-table query or each of the primary keys for a multitable query, including the DISTINCT predicate has no effect (other than slowing down execution of the query) because the presence of the primary keys already guarantees uniqueness of the recordset.

If you use the keyword DISTINCTROW, Access eliminates any duplicate rows in the result set *based on all the columns in the source tables*. DISTINCTROW has *no* effect when the query references only one table or returns at least one column from all included tables. In these cases, which include the vast majority of queries, using DISTINCTROW is equivalent to using ALL (or no predicate) and doesn't affect the performance of the query. The DISTINCTROW predicate corresponds to the

183

Unique Records property in QBE (which is the QBE default). The DISTINCTROW predicate is unique to Access SQL.

It's worth noting that for most types of queries for which DISTINCTROW is applicable—queries with multiple tables *and* where at least one table is included in the FROM clause without a corresponding column in the SELECT clause (that is, a table is included without any output columns)—it produces the same result as the DISTINCT predicate, with one significant difference: the query's recordset is updatable.

For example, you might use the following query to list the descriptions of all menu items that have been ordered at least once in the last year:

```
SELECT ALL MenuDescription
FROM (tblMenu INNER JOIN tblOrderDetails ON tblMenu.[Menu#] =
tblOrderDetails.[Menu#])
INNER JOIN tblOrder ON tblOrderDetails.[Order#] =
tblOrder.[Order#]
WHERE ((tblOrder.OrderDate > DateAdd("yyyy",-1,Date())))
ORDER BY MenuDescription;
```

With the ALL predicate, the preceding query returns 343 rows—one row for each Order Detail item. Replacing ALL with DISTINCT returns 18 rows in a nonupdatable recordset—one row for each menu item ordered at least once during the last year. Replacing DISTINCT with DISTINCTROW returns the same 18 rows, but this time the query is updatable. The datasheets returned by the three queries, each using a different predicate, are contrasted in Figure 5.7.

The TOP Predicate

You use the TOP predicate to return the top *n* rows or top *n* percent of rows from a recordset. This is useful when you wish to return only a select proportion of records meeting the query criteria. The TOP predicate is unique to Access SQL and is equivalent to using the TopValues property in QBE.

We recommend using the TOP predicate only *along with* an ORDER BY clause; otherwise you get a more-or-less random assortment of records. (It's worth noting, however, that this *won't* be a true random sample; instead it will be whatever proportion of records happens to come up first.)

If you use an ORDER BY clause with the ASC (or no) keyword, TOP returns the bottommost records. If you use an ORDER BY clause with the DESC keyword, TOP returns the top-most records.

FIGURE 5.7:

Three queries of menu items sold within the last year. The first query uses the ALL predicate, which returns 343 rows, including duplicates. The second query uses DISTINCT and returns 18 rows, but the recordset is read-only. The third query uses DISTINCTROW and also returns 18 rows, but the recordset is updatable. (Note the new row asterisk at the bottom of the datasheet.)

NOTE   Nulls are treated by the TOP predicate as the smallest numeric value, earliest date, or first alphabetical text string. Thus, when you know in advance that the Top column may contain nulls, you may wish to explicitly exclude nulls in the WHERE clause.

There are two forms of TOP: alone and with PERCENT. Either form of TOP can be combined with the ALL, DISTINCT, or DISTINCTROW predicate. The syntax is as follows:

SELECT [{ ALL | DISTINCT | DISTINCTROW }] [TOP *n* [PERCENT]] *column-list*

For example, to return the top five most costly items ever ordered, where cost equals Quantity*Price*(1–Discount), you could use the SELECT statement shown in Figure 5.8.

FIGURE 5.8:

This query returns the top five largest item sales by using the TOP predicate and a descending ORDER BY clause. Note that more than five rows are returned because of a tie for fifth place.

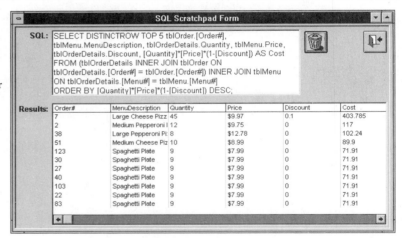

Access processes the TOP predicate after all criteria, joins, sorts, grouping, and other predicates have been applied. Ties are treated as any other row, except when multiple rows qualify as the last selected row—for example, the fifth row for a Top 5 specification (see Figure 5.8). When there is a tie on the last selected row, Access returns *all* rows with equivalent values. With no ORDER BY clause, Access uses all the columns from the SELECT clause to decide on ties. Otherwise Access uses only the columns contained in the ORDER BY clause to determine both the ordering of rows and the resolution of ties, even if some or all of the ORDER BY columns don't appear in the SELECT clause.

The WITH OWNERACCESS
OPTION Declaration

You use the WITH OWNERACCESS OPTION declaration to allow users of a query you have created to inherit your security rights while running the query. This gives the users of a query you've created the ability to run the query, even if they don't have the necessary security permissions to one or more of the underlying tables. When you omit this declaration, the user without proper security clearance to the source tables does not inherit your security and thus cannot run the query. Using the declaration is equivalent to setting the RunPermissions property in QBE to "Owner's". Omitting the declaration is equivalent to setting it to "User's". The syntax for using the WITH OWNERACCESS OPTION declaration is as follows:

SELECT *column-list*

FROM *table-list*

[WHERE *where-clause*]

[ORDER BY *order-by-clause*]

[WITH OWNERACCESS OPTION];

Aggregating Data

Aggregate queries are useful for summarizing data, calculating statistics, spotting bad data, and looking for trends. These types of queries, which produce read-only recordsets, were discussed in detail in Chapter 4 using Access QBE. In this section we outline how they are specified using Access SQL.

You can construct three types of aggregate queries using Access SQL:

- Simple aggregate queries based on a SELECT statement *without* a GROUP BY clause
- GROUP BY queries using a SELECT statement *with* a GROUP BY clause
- Crosstab queries that use the TRANSFORM statement

All these queries have one thing in common: they use at least one aggregate function in the SELECT clause. The valid aggregate functions are detailed in Table 5.1.

TABLE 5.1: The SQL Aggregate Functions and Their Usage

Aggregate Function	Purpose
Avg([column[1]])	Mean or average of non-null values for the column
Count([column])	Count of the number of non-null values for a column
Count(*)	Count of the total number of rows in the result set, including rows with null values
Sum([column])	Sum of the non-null values for the column
Min([column])	Smallest non-null value for the column
Max([column])	Largest non-null value for the column
First([column])	Value of the column in the first row of the result set, which can be null[2]
Last([column])	Value of the column in the last row of the result set, which can be Null[3]
StDev([column])	Sample standard deviation for the column. Null values are not included. This is a measure of the dispersion of values[4]
StDevP([column])	Population standard deviation for the column. Null values are not included. This is a measure of the dispersion of values[4]
Var([column])	Sample variance for the column. Null values are not included. The square of the sample standard deviation[4]
VarP([column])	Population standard deviation for the column. Null values are not included. The square of the population standard deviation[4]

[1]Although [column] is used throughout the table, you can also use expressions instead of columns in each of the aggregate functions.

[2]This may be null and is not the same as Min() unless the query also sorts by the same column in ascending order and there are no null values.

[3]This is not the same as Max() unless the query also sorts by the same column in ascending order and there are no null values.

[4]The sample standard deviation and variance use a denominator of $(n - 1)$, whereas the population aggregate functions use a denominator of (n), where n = the number of records in the result set. For most statistical analyses, the sample aggregate functions are preferable.

You can create expressions made up of a combination of aggregate functions combined mathematically. Aggregate functions can also reference expressions. For example, these aggregate expressions are all valid:

Aggregate Expression	Use
Sum(Abs([Discontinued]))	Calculates the sum of the absolute value of the yes/no column Discontinued, which counts the *number of Yes values*
Sum(Abs([Discontinued]+1))	Calculates the sum of the absolute value of the yes/no column Discontinued plus 1, which counts the *number of No values*
Avg([DeliveryDate])–Avg([OrderDate])	Calculates the difference in the average delivery and order dates

Aggregate Queries without a GROUP BY Clause

You can use an aggregate SELECT statement without a GROUP BY clause to calculate summary statistics on all rows meeting the WHERE clause criteria. This is useful for calculating grand totals for an entire table or a subset of a table. To create this type of aggregate SELECT, you must include aggregate functions and nothing *but* aggregate functions in the SELECT clause of a SELECT statement. (If you try to mix aggregate and non-aggregate expressions without a GROUP BY clause, you get an error and Access refuses to process the query.)

For example, say you wished to count the total number of orders in the tblOrder table and the earliest and latest times an order was taken. You could construct an aggregate query like that shown in Figure 5.9.

FIGURE 5.9:

This simple aggregate query calculates the total number of orders and the earliest and latest delivery times.

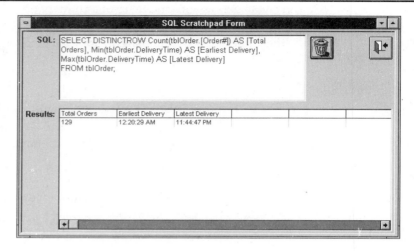

Using a GROUP BY Clause

You use a *GROUP BY clause* to define groups of rows for which you wish to calculate some aggregate function. Here's how the GROUP BY clause (and HAVING clause) fit into the overall SELECT statement syntax:

SELECT *column-list*

FROM *table-list*

[WHERE *where-clause*]

[GROUP BY *group-by-clause*]

[HAVING *having-clause*]

[ORDER BY *order-by-clause*];

The syntax of the GROUP BY clause is

GROUP BY *group-by-expression1* [*,group-by-expression2* [, ...]]

Expressions in the GROUP BY clause can reference table columns, calculated fields, or constants. Calculations cannot include references to aggregate functions. The GROUP BY fields define the groups in the recordset. When you use a GROUP BY clause, all fields in the SELECT clause either must be arguments to an aggregate function or must be present in the GROUP BY clause. In other words, each column included in the resulting recordset must either define a group or compute some summary statistic for one of the groups.

For example, the SQL statement in Figure 5.10 computes the number of orders by customer.

FIGURE 5.10:

This GROUP BY SELECT statement counts the number of orders made by each customer.

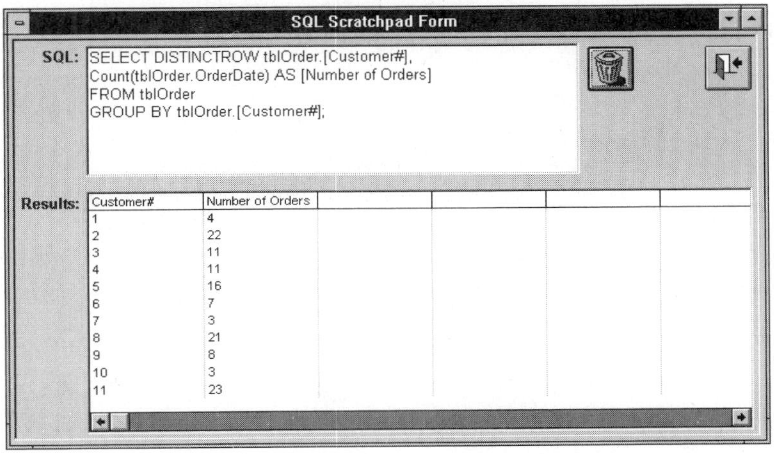

```
SQL Scratchpad Form

SQL:  SELECT DISTINCTROW tblOrder.[Customer#],
      Count(tblOrder.OrderDate) AS [Number of Orders]
      FROM tblOrder
      GROUP BY tblOrder.[Customer#];

Results:  Customer#    Number of Orders
          1            4
          2            22
          3            11
          4            11
          5            16
          6            7
          7            3
          8            21
          9            8
          10           3
          11           23
```

When you use multiple GROUP BY fields, the groups are defined from left to right, just as in an ORDER BY clause. The GROUP BY clause automatically orders values in ascending order without need of an ORDER BY clause (see Figure 5.10). If you wish, however, for the groups to be sorted in descending order, you can reference the same fields in an ORDER BY clause with the keyword DESC.

For example, say you wished to count the number of orders by menu item and date, with menu items sorted alphabetically and dates sorted in descending order so as to show the most recent orders first. This GROUP BY SELECT statement is shown in Figure 5.11.

You may also find it useful to sort by the aggregate column or some other column not contained in the GROUP BY clause. For example, if you calculated total sales grouped by employee, you could sort by total sales in descending order rather than by employee. This would allow you to list out the top-performing employees first.

FIGURE 5.11:

This SELECT statement groups alphabetically by MenuDescription and then in reverse date order to show the total number of orders taken each day for a particular menu item.

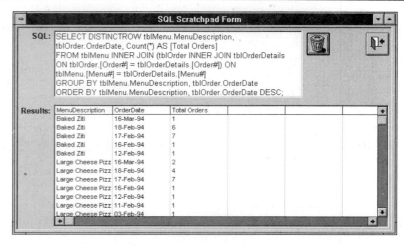

(See the "Totals Options" section in Chapter 4 for more details on how Access handles the sorting of groups under various scenarios.)

You can specify up to ten GROUP BY fields, but be careful about adding unnecessary fields to the GROUP BY clause since each additional field causes the query to execute more slowly.

Using the HAVING Clause

Aggregate select queries may contain a WHERE clause, a *HAVING clause,* or both. Any criteria contained in a WHERE clause is applied *before* the grouping of rows. Thus, you can use WHERE clause criteria to exclude rows you don't want grouped. In contrast, any criteria contained in a HAVING clause is applied *after* grouping. This allows you to filter records based on the summary statistics calculated for each group. The syntax for the HAVING clause is similar to that for the WHERE clause:

HAVING *expression1* [{AND | OR} *expression2* [, …]]

For example, say you wished to calculate the average quantity ordered for each menu item but exclude any individual order from being included in the calculation if less than a quantity of five were ordered. Since this requires the rows with a quantity of five to be excluded prior to grouping, you would use a WHERE clause. The SELECT statement would be constructed as follows.

```
SELECT tblMenu.MenuDescription, Avg(tblOrderDetails.Quantity)
AS AvgOrdered
FROM tblMenu INNER JOIN tblOrderDetails ON tblMenu.[Menu#] =
tblOrderDetails.[Menu#]
WHERE tblOrderDetails.Quantity > 5
GROUP BY tblMenu.MenuDescription;
```

On the other hand, you might want to calculate the same query but eliminate a menu item from the recordset if, *on average,* fewer than five of the items were sold for each order. This type of query requires the criteria to be applied *after* the average quantity has been calculated for each group, so you would use a HAVING clause instead. The SQL statement and result of this query are shown in Figure 5.12.

FIGURE 5.12:

The criteria for this query need to be applied after the grouping of data, so you use a HAVING clause.

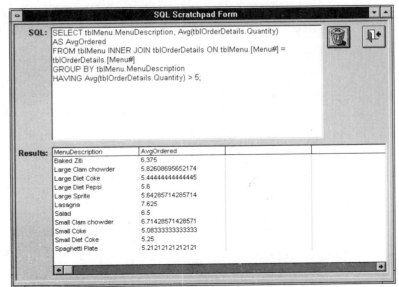

TIP You can also use a HAVING clause without a GROUP BY (see the earlier section "Aggregate Queries without a GROUP BY Clause"). The whole table is treated like a single group for the sake of the HAVING clause.

Creating Crosstab Queries with the TRANSFORM Statement

Microsoft added the *TRANSFORM statement* to Access SQL to support the creation of crosstab queries. Crosstab queries, which were discussed in detail in Chapter 4, are useful for summarizing data in a nice condensed, tabular format.

The basic syntax of the TRANSFORM statement is shown here:

TRANSFORM *aggregate-function*

select-statement

PIVOT *column-headings-field* [IN (*value1*, [*value2*, [, ...]])];

The *aggregate-function* must be one of the SQL aggregate functions discussed earlier in the chapter. This aggregate function is used for the values of each cell of the cross-tab table. The *select-statement* is a slightly modified GROUP BY SELECT statement. The *column-headings-field* is the field that is pivoted to become the column headings. The values in the optional IN clause specify fixed column headings.

Witness the Transformation

The TRANSFORM statement is tricky to construct, especially since it is nonstandard SQL. An easy way to create a TRANSFORM statement is to take an existing GROUP BY SELECT statement and *transform* it (maybe that's why they call it that) into a TRANSFORM statement.

Before you can hope to do this, however, you must have a suitable SELECT statement. It must have at least two GROUP BY fields and no HAVING clause. The TRANSFORM statement doesn't support the use of HAVING clauses. (You can work around this limitation by basing a crosstab query on the results of a totals query that has already applied the needed HAVING clause. There's an example in Chapter 4 that does just this in the "Crosstab Limitations" section.) In addition, you'll want to make sure the column headings field won't have more than 254 values. While this is the theoretical limit, in practice you'll find that crosstab queries are probably inappropriate where the column heading field contains more than 20 or so values. As long as your SELECT statement meets these criteria, you can convert it to a TRANSFORM statement.

An example should help make this clearer. Say you wished to look at the total dinner sales for each dinner menu item by employee. You might start by constructing a GROUP BY query that joined the tables tblMenu, tblEmployee, tblOrder, and tblOrderDetails. The GROUP BY columns would be tblEmployee.LastName and tblMenu.MenuDescription. The query would look like this:

```
SELECT tblEmployee.LastName AS Employee,
tblMenu.MenuDescription, Sum([Quantity]*[Price]*(1-[discount]))
AS Sales
FROM tblMenu INNER JOIN (tblEmployee INNER JOIN
(tblOrder INNER JOIN tblOrderDetails ON tblOrder.[Order#] =
tblOrderDetails.[Order#]) ON tblEmployee.[Employee#] =
tblOrder.[OrderTaker#]) ON tblMenu.[Menu#] =
tblOrderDetails.[Menu#]
WHERE ((tblMenu.Unit="Dinner"))
GROUP BY tblEmployee.LastName, tblMenu.MenuDescription;
```

The datasheet for this query is shown in Figure 5.13.

FIGURE 5.13:

This GROUP BY query computes the total sales of each menu item by employee.

Employee	MenuDescription	Sales
Alabaster	Baked Ziti	$347.80
Alabaster	Lasagna	$227.70
Alabaster	Spaghetti Plate	$503.37
Carey	Baked Ziti	$47.94
Carey	Lasagna	$14.85
Carey	Spaghetti Plate	$63.92
Jones	Baked Ziti	$32.90
Jones	Lasagna	$44.55
Jones	Spaghetti Plate	$55.93
Lovely	Lasagna	$14.85
Lovely	Spaghetti Plate	$503.37
Peters	Baked Ziti	$42.30
Peters	Lasagna	$49.50
Peters	Spaghetti Plate	$64.72
Ronald	Lasagna	$247.50
Ronald	Spaghetti Plate	$175.78

Select Query: qtotEmployeeDinnerSales

Record: 1 of 16

Continuing with this example, say you wanted the result of this query displayed as a crosstab table instead. You could convert the SELECT statement into a TRANSFORM statement using the following steps:

1. Take the existing GROUP BY SELECT statement and plug it into the skeleton of a TRANSFORM statement. That is, insert a line with the word

TRANSFORM before the SELECT statement and a line with the word PIVOT after it. This would give you the following:

```
TRANSFORM
SELECT tblEmployee.LastName AS Employee,
tblMenu.MenuDescription, Sum([Quantity]*[Price]*(1-[discount]))
AS Sales
FROM tblMenu INNER JOIN (tblEmployee INNER JOIN
(tblOrder INNER JOIN tblOrderDetails ON tblOrder.[Order#] =
tblOrderDetails.[Order#]) ON tblEmployee.[Employee#] =
tblOrder.[OrderTaker#]) ON tblMenu.[Menu#] =
tblOrderDetails.[Menu#]
WHERE ((tblMenu.Unit="Dinner"))
GROUP BY tblEmployee.LastName, tblMenu.MenuDescription
PIVOT;
```

2. Move the aggregate function that will define the value of each crosstab cell into the TRANSFORM clause. In this example you would move the expression that calculates sales. Thus, the SQL becomes

```
TRANSFORM Sum([Quantity]*[Price]*(1-[discount])) AS Sales
SELECT tblEmployee.LastName AS Employee,
tblMenu.MenuDescription
FROM tblMenu INNER JOIN (tblEmployee INNER JOIN
(tblOrder INNER JOIN tblOrderDetails ON tblOrder.[Order#] =
tblOrderDetails.[Order#]) ON tblEmployee.[Employee#] =
tblOrder.[OrderTaker#]) ON tblMenu.[Menu#] =
tblOrderDetails.[Menu#]
WHERE ((tblMenu.Unit="Dinner"))
GROUP BY tblEmployee.LastName, tblMenu.MenuDescription
PIVOT;
```

3. Move the field from the GROUP BY clause that will become the column headings to the PIVOT clause. Also delete the reference to this field from the SELECT clause. Thus, you have

```
TRANSFORM Sum([Quantity]*[Price]*(1-[discount])) AS Sales
SELECT tblEmployee.LastName AS Employee
FROM tblMenu INNER JOIN (tblEmployee INNER JOIN
(tblOrder INNER JOIN tblOrderDetails ON tblOrder.[Order#] =
tblOrderDetails.[Order#]) ON tblEmployee.[Employee#] =
tblOrder.[OrderTaker#]) ON tblMenu.[Menu#] =
tblOrderDetails.[Menu#]
```

```
WHERE ((tblMenu.Unit="Dinner"))
GROUP BY tblEmployee.LastName
PIVOT tblMenu.MenuDescription;
```

That's it! The crosstab datasheet produced by the preceding TRANSFORM statement is shown in Figure 5.14.

FIGURE 5.14:

This crosstab query is equivalent to the totals query shown in Figure 5.13. Note that the crosstab statement produces a more compact, readable summarization of the data.

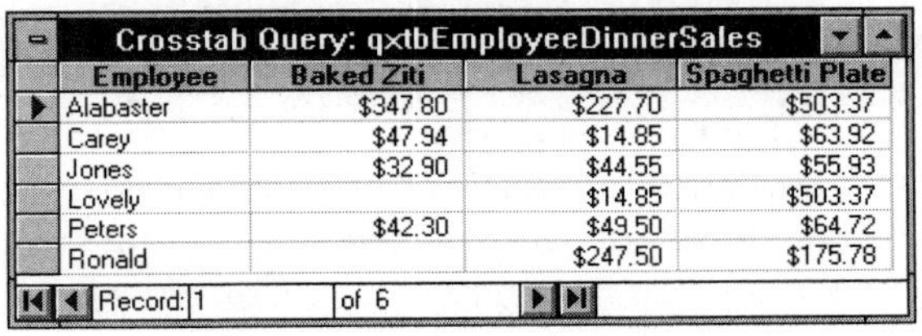

Employee	Baked Ziti	Lasagna	Spaghetti Plate
Alabaster	$347.80	$227.70	$503.37
Carey	$47.94	$14.85	$63.92
Jones	$32.90	$44.55	$55.93
Lovely		$14.85	$503.37
Peters	$42.30	$49.50	$64.72
Ronald		$247.50	$175.78

Crosstab Query: qxtbEmployeeDinnerSales — Record: 1 of 6

To recap the conversion process in more general terms, here are the steps for converting a SELECT statement into a TRANSFORM statement.

1. Ensure that the SELECT statement contains at least two GROUP BY fields, no HAVING clause, and a field suitable to become the column headings. Surround the existing SELECT statement with a Transform "shell" like this:

   TRANSFORM

   select-statement

   PIVOT;

2. Move the aggregate function that will be used for the crosstab cell values up into the TRANSFORM clause. The SQL should now look like this:

   TRANSFORM *aggregate-function*

   select-statement

   PIVOT;

3. Move one of the GROUP BY fields—the one that is to become the column headings—to the PIVOT clause. Delete the reference to this same field from

the SELECT clause. The resulting TRANSFORM statement should now produce a crosstab query:

TRANSFORM *aggregate-function*

select-statement

PIVOT *column-heading-field*;

Multiple Row Headings

TRANSFORM statements can include multiple row headings. You create the additional row headings by adding another GROUP BY field to the embedded SELECT statement. For example, you might wish to break down sales additionally by PaymentMethod. The SQL statement that creates this additional row heading and its output are shown in Figure 5.15. Note that the only differences between the earlier SQL statement and this one are the addition of tblOrder.PaymentMethod to the SELECT and GROUP BY clauses of the embedded SELECT statement.

FIGURE 5.15:
This TRANSFORM statement produces a crosstab table that contains two row headings, Employee and Payment Method.

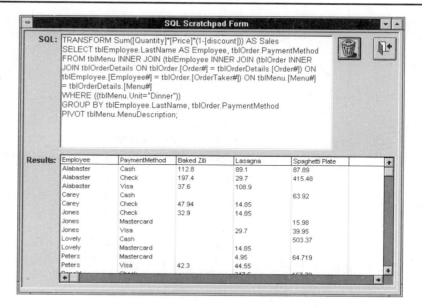

Creating a Totals Column

You can create an additional column to calculate row totals in a crosstab table by adding an additional aggregate field to the SELECT clause of the TRANSFORM statement. Don't include the additional aggregate function anywhere else in the TRANSFORM statement. Any aggregate functions you add to the TRANSFORM statement's SELECT clause will be added to the crosstab between the row headings field(s) and the column headings field. For example, the TRANSFORM statement shown in Figure 5.16 was created by adding the Sum() aggregate function to the SELECT clause.

FIGURE 5.16:

By adding an aggregate function to the SELECT clause, you can create a column that totals the values for each row.

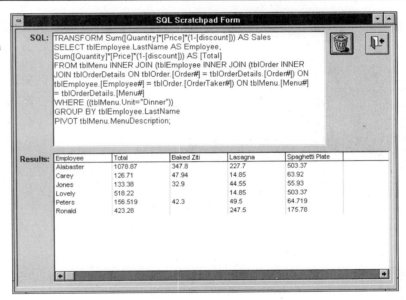

This additional aggregate function isn't limited to totaling the row values; you can use any valid SQL aggregate function here. For example, you could calculate the average sales per order. You can also include multiple aggregate functions in the SELECT clause; each will be displayed between the row headings and column headings fields.

Using the IN Clause to Create Fixed Column Headings

You can create fixed column headings by using the *IN clause*. Place the optional IN clause immediately after the PIVOT clause in a TRANSFORM statement. The syntax is

PIVOT *column-headings-field* [IN (*value1*, [*value2*, [, …]])]

You can use the IN clause to order the values other than alphabetically (this is especially useful for alphanumeric date strings), exclude columns you don't wish to appear in the crosstab table, or include columns that may not exist in the recordset. For example, to create a crosstab table that excluded sales of "Spaghetti Plate" but included "Dinner Salad", even if there weren't any, you would use the following PIVOT and IN clauses:

```
PIVOT tblMenu.MenuDescription IN ("Baked Ziti", "Lasagna",
"Dinner Salad")
```

Union Queries

Union queries are supported in Access using SQL; there is no equivalent QBE method for creating a union query. UNION is not a SQL statement or even a clause. Instead it is an operator you can use to horizontally splice together two or more compatible queries. The basic syntax is as follows:

select-statement1

UNION [ALL]

select-statement2

[UNION [ALL]

select-statement3]

[…]

Union queries produce *read-only* recordsets.

For example, say you wished to create a query that combined the names and addresses of both employees and customers for a mailing you wished to do. You might create a union query like that shown in Figure 5.17.

FIGURE 5.17:

This union query combines the names and addresses from the tblEmployee and tblCustomer tables.

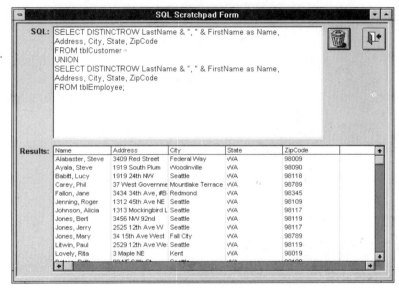

> **WARNING** Although the Design View button is disabled when you create a SQL-specific (union, data definition, or SQL pass-through) query, you can always change the type of the query to a select or action query using the Query menu. Be careful, however, because when you change the query type of a SQL-specific query, your existing SQL statement is erased without so much as a confirming dialog.

Using the TABLE Option

You can use a shortcut syntax when you wish to include all the columns from a table or another query. This syntax employs the TABLE option and allows you to replace any of the SELECT statements with

TABLE *table-or-query*

which is equivalent to the following SELECT statement:

SELECT * FROM *table-or-query*

For example, the following two union queries are equivalent:

```
SELECT * FROM tblOrder
UNION
SELECT * FROM tblBackOrder;
```

and

```
TABLE tblOrder
UNION
TABLE tblBackOrder;
```

The ALL Option

By default, Access eliminates duplicate records for union queries. You can force Access to include duplicates, however, by using the *ALL option* after the UNION operator. Using the ALL option speeds up the execution of union queries even if they don't have any duplicate records because Access can skip the extra comparison step, which can be significant with large recordsets.

Sorting the Results

You can use an ORDER BY clause in the *last* SELECT statement of a union query to order the resulting recordset. If some of the column names differ, you need to reference the name assigned to the column by the *first* SELECT statement. For example, the following union query is valid:

```
SELECT LastName FROM tblNames
UNION
SELECT EmployeeName FROM tblEmployees
ORDER BY LastName;
```

While each SELECT statement in a union query *can* have an ORDER BY clause, all but the last one are ignored.

Compatible Queries

You can string together as many select queries as you like in a union query; you're limited only by the fact that, as for all queries, the entire compiled query definition must fit into a single 64K segment of memory. The queries need to be *compatible*, however, which means they must have the same number of columns. Typically, the column names and datatypes of the two unioned queries would be the same, but this isn't required. If they aren't the same, Access uses the following rules to combine them:

- For columns with *different names*, Access uses the column name from the first query.

- For columns with *different datatypes*, Access converts the columns to a single datatype that is compatible with all the columns' datatypes. For example, Access uses the Long Integer type when you combine an integer column with a long integer column. Similarly, text combined with a number produces a text column, date data combined with a yes/no column produces a text type, and so on.

- Access won't combine a memo- or OLE-type object with another datatype. You can use columns of these datatypes in a union query only when you combine them with like-typed columns.

For example, the query shown in Figure 5.18 is valid syntactically, although it makes little sense.

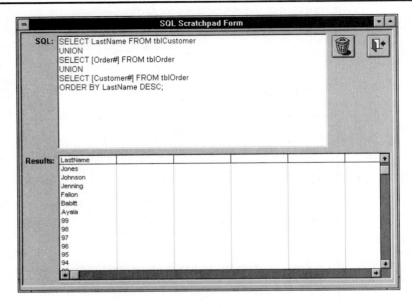

FIGURE 5.18:

This nonsensical but syntactically correct union query combines LastName from tblCustomer with Order# and Customer# from tblCustomer. The datatype of the output column will be text.

Subqueries

Subqueries are a useful part of SQL that allow you to embed SELECT statements within other SELECT statements (or action SQL statements, which are covered later in this chapter in the section "Updating Data with SQL"). Typically, you use subqueries (which are also known as subselects) in the WHERE clause of a SQL statement to filter the query based on the values in another query (the subquery). There are three forms of syntax for subqueries:

- *expression* [NOT] IN (*select-statement*)
- *comparison* [{ANY | SOME | ALL}] (*select-statement*)
- [NOT] EXISTS (*select-statement*)

Subqueries may be nested several levels deep; the actual limits on subquery nesting are undocumented.

We discuss the use of each of the three types of subqueries in the next sections.

Most of the time you can use either a subquery or a join to create equivalent queries. You'll find a subquery is often easier to conceptualize than the same query that employs joins, but it's really a matter of personal preference. It's nice that with version 2.0, you now have a choice.

You can also use subqueries in Access QBE. Their use in QBE is analogous to their use in Access SQL. In QBE you can use subqueries in the Criteria or Field cell of a query.

Checking Values against a Lookup Table

Often you'd like to be able to check the value of a column against some list of values in another table or query. For these situations you would use the IN form of a subquery. For example, say you wished to view the number, name, and price of all menu items that have ever been sold in quantities of ten or more. You could do this with the subquery shown in Figure 5.19.

Alternatively, this query could have been expressed using a join instead of a subquery. The equivalent join query is shown in Figure 5.20.

This form of subquery can return only a single column. If it returns more than one column, Access complains with an error.

Using the NOT operator, you can also use this form of a subquery to look for values that are not contained in the list.

Comparing Values against Other Values

Subqueries also come in handy when you wish to compare a value against rows in another query. You can do this using the second form of the subquery syntax. This form of subquery is also limited to returning a single column. For example, you

FIGURE 5.19:

This select query employs a subquery to find all menu items that have sold in quantities of ten or more.

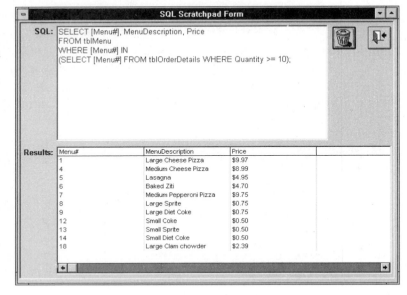

FIGURE 5.20:

This select query uses a join to find all menu items that have sold in quantities of ten or more. This query produces the same result as the query in Figure 5.19.

could use the subquery in Figure 5.21 to list all menu items that are more expensive than "Baked Ziti" (which sells for $4.70).

Note that the subquery in the query in Figure 5.21 returns one value, so you don't need to use the ANY, ALL, or SOME predicate. If it returned more than one row, an error would occur. When the output of the subquery is multiple rows, you must use one of these predicates. The following table outlines the differences of the predicates:

Predicate	Meaning
None	Makes a comparison with a single value
ANY or SOME	Is true if the comparison is true for any row returned by the subquery—in other words, if the comparison is true against the first row *or* the second row *or* the third row, and so on
ALL	Is true if the comparison is true for all rows returned by the subquery—in other words, if the comparison is true against the first row *and* the second row *and* the third row, and so on

FIGURE 5.21:

This query lists all menu items for which the price is higher than the price of baked ziti ($4.70).

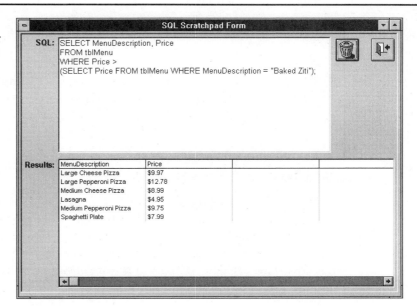

When you don't use the ALL, SOME, or ANY predicate, you must guarantee that at most one value is returned. You can accomplish this by placing criteria on the subquery that selects a row by its primary key value. Another way to accomplish this is to use a SQL aggregate function in the subquery. Finally, you can also use a Top 1 predicate in the SELECT clause of the subquery. For example, the following three comparisons might all be used to ensure that Age is less than the age of the oldest student (assuming, of course that you knew in advance that student number 35 was the oldest):

```
WHERE Age < (SELECT Age FROM tblStudent WHERE StudentId = 35)
WHERE Age < (SELECT Max(Age) FROM tblStudent)
WHERE Age < (SELECT TOP 1 Age FROM tblStudent ORDER BY Age DESC)
```

You can use the ANY or SOME predicate (the two are equivalent) to make a comparison against any of the rows returned or use the ALL predicate to make a comparison against all the rows returned by the subquery. For example, the following comparison would select rows in which Age was less than the age of *any* of the students—in other words, where age was *less than the oldest student*:

```
WHERE Age < ANY (SELECT Age FROM tblStudent)
```

On the other hand, you could use the following comparison to select rows in which Age was less than the age of *all* of the students—in other words, where Age was *less than the youngest student*:

```
WHERE Age < ALL (SELECT Age FROM tblStudent)
```

NOTE The ANY, SOME, and ALL predicates will include rows with null values. This differs from the equivalent statements using the Min() and Max() aggregate functions, which exclude nulls.

Checking for Existence

The last form of a subquery comparison uses the EXISTS predicate to compare values against the existence of one or more rows in the subquery. If the subquery returns any rows, the comparison is True; if it returns no rows, the comparison is False. You can also use NOT EXISTS to get the opposite effect. Since you're checking only for the existence of rows, this form of subquery has no restriction on the number of columns returned.

So far, all the subqueries presented in this chapter have been independent of the *outer* query (the query that contains the subquery). You can also create subqueries that are linked to the outer query. This type of subquery is termed a *correlated subquery* because it references the other query using its correlation name (discussed in the section "The FROM clause" earlier in this chapter). The correlation name can be the same as the table name or it can be a table's alias name.

Each of the three types of subqueries can be correlated, but subqueries that use the EXISTS predicate are almost always correlated. (Otherwise they wouldn't be very useful.)

For example, you might want to find menu items that have never been ordered. You could accomplish this using the NOT EXISTS subquery shown in Figure 5.22. Running this query shows you that large anchovy pizzas have never been ordered.

The subquery in Figure 5.22 is termed a correlated subquery because it references the data in the outer query—the data in tblMenu—in the WHERE clause of the subquery.

FIGURE 5.22:

Using a NOT EXISTS correlated subquery, you can determine that no one has ever ordered a large anchovy pizza.

Using Subqueries in the SELECT Clause

Typically you use subqueries in the WHERE clause of a query, but you may find occasion to also use a subquery that returns a single value in the SELECT clause. For example, say you wished to create a query similar to the one in Figure 5.22 but instead of listing only menu items that have never been ordered, you'd prefer to list all menu items with an additional field that indicates whether they've ever been ordered. You could accomplish this with the query shown in Figure 5.23. This query moves the subquery into the SELECT clause, gives it an alias name, "Ever Ordered?", and formats it using an IIf() function.

FIGURE 5.23:
This query lists each menu item and whether or not it has ever been ordered. It accomplishes this using a correlated subquery in the SELECT clause of a query.

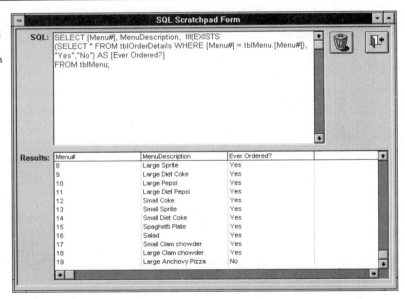

You might also use a subquery in a SELECT clause to list a calculated constant that was used in selecting the rows. For example, you might want to list all menu items with prices higher than the average price, along with the average price as an output column. You could accomplish this with the following subquery:

```
SELECT [Menu#], MenuDescription, Price,
(SELECT Avg(Price) FROM tblMenu)
```

```
AS AveragePrice
FROM tblMenu
WHERE [Price] > (SELECT Avg(Price) FROM tblMenu);
```

Example: Using a Subquery to Find Duplicates

In the "Action Queries in Action" section in Chapter 4 we showed several alternate ways to find and eliminate duplicates using action queries. In that chapter we presented the "hand-pruning" and "bulk-project" methods. Using a subquery, you can create an updatable dynaset of duplicate rows similar to the one produced by the hand-pruning method but with only a single query and no temporary tables.

Recounting the example from Chapter 4, say you have a table called tblImport that contains duplicate order records that prevent you from designating Order# as the primary key for the table. You can identify the duplicates using the following correlated subquery:

```
SELECT *
FROM tblImport
WHERE [Order#] IN (SELECT [Order#] FROM [tblImport]
GROUP BY [Order#] HAVING Count(*)>1 ) ORDER BY [Order#];
```

This subquery produces a dynaset with all the columns in tblImport but only the duplicate records. You can use this dynaset to visually scan through each of the duplicate rows and prune out the true duplicates. This method is how the Find Duplicates Query Wizard works.

There are many uses for subqueries, far more than have been covered in this chapter. As mentioned previously, you can solve most queries as either subqueries or joined queries. Choose the method that makes the most sense for you.

Parameterized SQL

Just as in Access QBE, you can specify *parameters* to be resolved at run time using SQL. To do this, you use the PARAMETERS declaration. The syntax for its usage is as follows:

PARAMETERS *parameter1 datatype1* [, *parameter2 datatype2* [, ...]];

sql-statement;

For example, if you wanted to list the date and Employee# of all items for a particular order but have the user enter the Order# when the query was run, you could construct a SELECT statement with a PARAMETERS declaration like this:

```
PARAMETERS [Enter Customer Number] Long;
SELECT DISTINCTROW OrderDate, [OrderTaker#]
FROM tblOrder
WHERE [Customer#]=[Enter Customer Number]
ORDER BY OrderDate;
```

Using External Data Sources

There are three ways to refer to data sources outside an Access database in a SQL statement:

- Use attached tables.
- Use the IN clause.
- Use direct references to the external tables.

By far the easiest and most efficient way to reference external tables is to use attached tables. Once a table is attached to an Access database, you refer to it in SQL statements exactly the same as you would if it were a native Access table. If, however, you wish to refer to a table located in another Access database, a non-native ISAM database, or an ODBC server database and it is not attached to the current database, you can use either the IN clause or the direct reference technique.

To refer to one or more tables located in the same Access database or ODBC database or the same subdirectory for non-native ISAM databases, it's easier to use the IN clause. The syntax for SELECT statements and the source tables for action queries is as follows:

FROM *tablelist* IN

{*"path"* | *"path"* *"product"* | *""* [*product*; DATABASE = *path*;] |

"ODBC; connect-string;" }

For Access databases you must specify a complete path to the database, including the MDB extension. For external ISAM databases you can use either the *"path"* *"product"* syntax or the *""* [*product*; DATABASE = *path*;] syntax. For ODBC data sources, you need to use a data source–specific connect string.

For non-native ISAM data sources, you must use one of the following product names:

dBASE III

dBASE IV

FoxPro 2.0

FoxPro 2.5

FoxPro 2.6

Paradox 3.x

Paradox 4.x

Btrieve

Similarly, you can use this syntax to refer to the destination table for SELECT INTO and INSERT INTO statements:

INTO table IN

{*path* | *"path"* *"product"* | *""* [*product*; DATABASE = *path*;] |

"ODBC; *connect-string*;*"* }

For example, if you wished to select all the columns from a dBASE database named Cust, you would use a SELECT statement like the one shown in Figure 5.24.

TIP

It is more efficient to use attached tables than the IN clause or direct external table references, although for ISAM data sources the difference in speed may not be noticeable. This is not true for ODBC data sources, however, where the IN clause or direct external table references are very inefficient. You should always use attached tables for ODBC data sources because Jet can then manage the connections more efficiently.

FIGURE 5.24:
This SELECT statement lists all the columns in the Cust dBASE database.

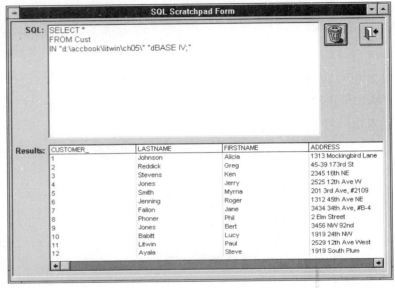

Sometimes you need to refer to multiple external data sources that are located either in different subdirectories/databases or in heterogeneous data sources. For example, you might want to join a table that's stored in dBASE format with a Paradox table. In these cases the IN clause technique will not work, but Access provides another way to refer to these tables: the *direct reference* method. You can use this syntax in a FROM clause like this:

FROM {*path* | "*path*" "*product*" | "" [*product*; DATABASE = *path*;] |

"ODBC; *connect-string*;" }.*filename*

For example, the query shown in Figure 5.25 joins a native Access table, tblOrder-Details, to a Paradox table, Orders, and a dBASE table, Cust, in a single SELECT statement.

FIGURE 5.25:

This SELECT statement performs a heterogeneous join of a native Access table, tblOrderDetails, a Paradox table, Orders, and a dBASE table, Cust.

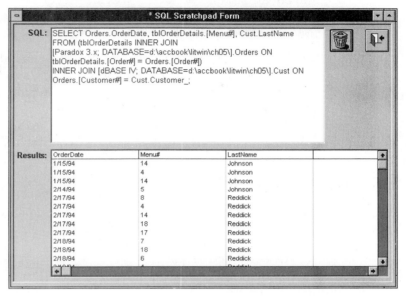

Updating Data with SQL

In addition to querying data, you can use SQL to make changes to data. You can use Access SQL to update records, delete records, or copy records to another table. Using Access SQL to make batch updates is usually more efficient than making row-by-row changes through the user interface. Access SQL has four commands for updating data, all of which have analogous counterparts in Access QBE:

SQL Statement	QBE Query
UPDATE	Update
DELETE	Delete
INSERT INTO	Append
SELECT INTO	Make-table

All but the last one, SELECT INTO, are part of the ANSI SQL standard. (The ANSI standard uses SELECT INTO in a very different way to move a single row of data into a list of variables. The two usages are not equivalent.)

Once you have learned the SELECT statement and all its predicates, declarations, and clauses, you'll find learning the action SQL statements relatively easy. This is because each of these statements is similar syntactically to SELECT. Thus, even though each one includes WHERE clauses, for example, we will not repeat the discussion of WHERE clauses here. We will note, however, where there are differences between clauses in action SQL statements and the SELECT statement.

The UPDATE Statement

You use *update queries* to change values in one or more columns in a table. The syntax is

UPDATE *table-or-query*

SET *column1 = expression1* [, *column2 = expression2*] [, ...]

[WHERE *criteria*];

You can update the values in either a table or a query, but if you use a query it must be updatable. The expressions in the SET clause can be constants or the result of a calculation. For example, to increase the price of all non-pizza menu items by 10 percent, you could use the following update query:

```
UPDATE tblMenu
SET tblMenu.Price = [Price]*1.1
WHERE MenuDescription NOT LIKE "*Pizza*";
```

The ANSI standard supports the use of subqueries in the SET clause, while Access SQL does not. Fortunately, Access SQL supports the use of joins in the UPDATE clause (this is nonstandard SQL), which gives you almost equivalent functionality. The syntax used for joins in the UPDATE clause is the same as the join syntax used for SELECT statements in the FROM clause. For example, to change the phone numbers in the tblCustomer table to new phone numbers stored in another table, tblCustomerMods—which you might have imported from another copy of the database on another machine—you could use the following UPDATE statement:

```
UPDATE tblCustomerMods INNER JOIN tblCustomer ON
tblCustomerMods.[Customer#] = tblCustomer.[Customer#]
```

```
SET tblCustomer.[Phone#] = [tblCustomerMods].[Phone#]
WHERE tblCustomer.[Phone#]<>[tblCustomerMods].[Phone#];
```

This UPDATE statement uses a WHERE clause to limit the updates to records that need only to be modified—those in which the phone numbers are different.

The DELETE Statement

You use the *DELETE statement* to delete rows from Access tables. Its syntax is as follows:

DELETE [*table.**]

FROM *from-clause*

[WHERE *criteria*];

The use of "*table.**" is optional for delete queries that refer to only a single table. (Access also allows you to refer to a single column in the DELETE clause—for example, "DELETE tblOrder.OrderDate". In fact, Access QBE often generates DELETE statements in this misleading style, but don't let this confuse you; the entire record is deleted, not only the values in the column.) For single-table queries, the syntax can be simplified to

DELETE

FROM *table*

[WHERE *criteria*];

For example, to delete all discontinued items from tblMenu, you could use the following DELETE statement:

```
DELETE
FROM tblMenu
WHERE Discontinued = True;
```

You can create DELETE statements that reference multiple tables, but you must follow these rules:

- You can use the data in one table to decide which rows to delete from another related table. You can accomplish this by using a join in the FROM clause or by using a subquery in the WHERE clause. Tables can be related in either a one-to-one or one-to-many relationship. (Note that you may be prevented from deleting rows from a table if referential integrity is turned on.)

- You can delete rows from multiple tables in a single delete query if the tables are related in a one-to-one relationship.

- You can delete rows from multiple tables related in a one-to-many relationship with a series of DELETE statements. See the examples presented in Chapter 4 for details.

NOTE   You may not need to worry about this at all if you've defined a relationship between the two tables and have turned on the cascading deletes option. In this case, if you delete a row from the "one" side of a relationship, Access automatically deletes the related rows in the "many" side table.

For example, to delete all customers from tblCustomer who have not placed an order during the past year, you would create and execute the following DELETE statement, which uses a subquery to find the proper rows:

```
DELETE
FROM tblCustomer
WHERE tblCustomer.[Customer#] NOT IN
(SELECT [Customer#] FROM tblOrder WHERE OrderDate >
DateAdd('yyyy',-1,Date()));
```

Access SQL departs from the ANSI standard by its support for named tables in the DELETE clause and joins in the FROM clause.

If you wish to delete the value in one or more columns but not the entire record, use the UPDATE statement instead of DELETE and set the values to null. For example, you could use the following UPDATE statement to set the LastName and FirstName columns in tblCustomer to null for a particular customer:

```
UPDATE tblCustomer
SET LastName = NULL, FirstName = NULL
WHERE [Customer#] = 4;
```

The INSERT INTO Statement

You use the *INSERT INTO* (or just INSERT) *statement* to copy rows from one table (or query) into another table. You can also use it to add a single row of data to a table using a list of values. The syntax of the first form of the INSERT INTO statement is

INSERT INTO *target-table*

select-statement;

> **TIP**
>
> The *target-table* reference can refer to an external table using the IN predicate or a direct reference. (See the discussion in the section "Using External Data Sources" earlier in this chapter.)

In its simplest form, you can use this form of the INSERT INTO statement to copy the contents of one table to another. For example, to copy all the rows from tblNew-Customers to tblCustomers, you could use the following INSERT INTO statement:

```
INSERT INTO tblCustomers
SELECT * FROM tblNewCustomers;
```

Any valid SELECT statement that produces recordsets, including SELECT statements with GROUP BY clauses, joins, UNION operators, and subqueries can be used. This embedded SELECT statement can also include references to one or more queries. For example, to append records from the SELECT GROUP BY statement presented earlier in the chapter in the section "Creating Crosstab Queries with the TRANSFORM Statement" to a table named tblEmployeeDinnerSales, you could use the following INSERT INTO statement:

```
INSERT INTO tblEmployeeDinnerSales
SELECT tblEmployee.LastName AS Employee,
tblMenu.MenuDescription,
Sum([Quantity]*[Price]*(1-[discount])) AS Sales
FROM tblMenu INNER JOIN (tblEmployee INNER JOIN
(tblOrder INNER JOIN tblOrderDetails ON tblOrder.[Order#] =
tblOrderDetails.[Order#]) ON tblEmployee.[Employee#] =
tblOrder.[OrderTaker#]) ON
tblMenu.[Menu#] = tblOrderDetails.[Menu#]
WHERE ((tblMenu.Unit="Dinner"))
GROUP BY tblEmployee.LastName, tblMenu.MenuDescription;
```

You use the second form of the INSERT INTO statement to create a single new row in a table and populate it with values. It's syntax is

INSERT INTO *target-table* [(*column1* [, *column2* [, …]])]

VALUES (*value1* [, *value2* [, …]])

If you omit the column references in the INSERT INTO clause, you must include a value for each column in the target table in the exact order in which the columns appear in the table definition. If you include the column references, you may omit columns (other than the primary key and other required columns) or change the order in which they appear in the table definition. For example, you could add a new row to tblMenu using the following INSERT INTO statement:

```
INSERT INTO tblMenu ([Menu#], Price, MenuDescription)
VALUES (50, 29.99, "Family Platter")
```

The SELECT INTO Statement

You use the *SELECT INTO statement,* unique to Access SQL, to create a new table from the rows in another table or query. Its syntax is

SELECT *column1* [, *column2* [, …]] INTO *new-table*

FROM *table-list*

[WHERE *where-clause*]

[ORDER BY *order-by-clause*]

For example, you could use the following SELECT INTO statement to copy all purchases made by Customer# = 9 (Bert Jones) from tblOrder to a new table called tblJonesOrders:

```
SELECT [Order#], OrderDate, [Customer#], [OrderTaker#],
DeliveryDate, DeliveryTime, PaymentMethod, Notes
INTO tblJonesOrders
FROM tblOrder
WHERE [Customer#] = 9;
```

Like the INSERT INTO statement, the SELECT INTO statement can include any valid SELECT statement that produces recordsets, including SELECT statements with GROUP BY clauses, joins, UNION operators, and subqueries. The example used in the preceding section could be rephrased as the following SELECT INTO statement:

```
SELECT tblEmployee.LastName, tblMenu.MenuDescription,
Sum([Quantity]*[Price]*(1-[discount])) AS Sales
INTO tblEmployeeDinnerSales
FROM tblMenu INNER JOIN (tblEmployee INNER JOIN
(tblOrder INNER JOIN tblOrderDetails ON tblOrder.[Order#] =
tblOrderDetails.[Order#]) ON tblEmployee.[Employee#] =
tblOrder.[OrderTaker#]) ON
tblMenu.[Menu#] = tblOrderDetails.[Menu#]
WHERE ((tblMenu.Unit = "Dinner"))
GROUP BY tblEmployee.LastName, tblMenu.MenuDescription;
```

> **NOTE** Tables created by SELECT INTO statements will not contain primary keys, indexes, or any column or table properties other than the defaults assigned to any new table.

Data Definition with SQL

Prior to Access version 2.0 you had no way to programmatically create and modify table definitions. Microsoft added two methods for programmatically creating and manipulating table schemas in Access 2.0: Data Access Objects (DAO) and Data Definition Language (DDL) queries. (When it rains, it pours!) In this section we discuss the use of DDL queries. Using DAO to create and modify schemas is covered in Chapter 6.

It's important to note that DDL queries offer only a subset of the schema definition capabilities that either the Access user interface or DAO provides. But DDL queries still have their place. They help bridge the gap between the SQL standard and Access SQL. Furthermore, it's likely that the support for DDL queries will only get better in future versions of Access. In the meantime, there's at least one good reason for using DDL rather than either of the alternatives: it's based on a standard language that has widespread support—SQL. If you already have a fair amount of experience with SQL, using DDL queries will likely seem more natural than the other language-based alternative, DAO. Still, be aware that Access DDL support is incomplete and you may be required to go elsewhere in Access to get the job finished.

Like union queries, you must enter DDL queries using SQL view; there's no QBE counterpart. You can also execute a DDL query by defining and executing a QueryDef much like an action query.

Four DDL statements are supported by Access SQL:

DDL Statement	Purpose
CREATE TABLE	Creates a new table schema
ALTER TABLE	Modifies an existing table schema
CREATE INDEX	Creates a new index
DROP	Deletes a table schema or an index

In addition, you can use the CONSTRAINT clause in either a CREATE TABLE or ALTER TABLE statement to create constraints. (In Access' simplified support of CONSTRAINT, this means the creation of indexes.) Each of these statements and the CONSTRAINT clause are discussed in the next few sections.

The CREATE TABLE Statement

You use the *CREATE TABLE statement* to create a new table. Its syntax is

CREATE TABLE *table*

(*column1 type1* [(*size1*)] [CONSTRAINT *column-constraint1*]

[, *column2 type2* [(*size2*)] [CONSTRAINT *column-constraint2*]

[, ...]]

[CONSTRAINT *table-constraint1* [, *table-constraint2* [, ...]]]);

You specify the datatype of a column using one of the Jet engine SQL datatype identifiers or its synonyms. They are summarized in Table 5.2.

TABLE 5.2: SQL Datatypes and Their Counterparts in Table Design Mode

SQL Datatype and Synonyms	Table Design Field Type
BIT, BOOLEAN, LOGICAL, LOGICAL1, YESNO	Yes/No
BYTE, INTEGER1	Number, Size = Byte
COUNTER, AUTOINCREMENT	Counter
CURRENCY, MONEY	Currency
DATETIME, DATE, TIME	Date/Time
SHORT, INTEGER2, SMALLINT	Number, Size = Integer
LONG, INT, INTEGER, INTEGER4	Number, Size = Long
SINGLE, FLOAT4, IEEESINGLE, REAL	Number, Size = Single
DOUBLE, FLOAT, FLOAT8, IEEEDOUBLE, NUMBER, NUMERIC	Number, Size = Double
TEXT, ALPHANUMERIC, CHAR, CHARACTER, STRING, VARCHAR	Text
LONGTEXT, LONGCHAR, MEMO, NOTE	Memo
LONGBINARY, GENERAL, OLEOBJECT	OLE Object

WARNING The Jet engine SQL datatypes and their synonyms, which are derived from ANSI SQL datatypes, differ from the Access datatypes in several subtle ways. Use care when selecting the correct datatype keyword. Most notably, using the SQL datatype INTEGER produces a Number column with Size = *Long* because INTEGER in ANSI SQL is a 4-byte integer value (which in Access is a Long Integer).

You can use the optional *size* parameter to specify the length of a text column. If *size* is left blank, text columns are assigned a size of 255. Note that this differs from the default column size of 50 assigned when creating new tables with the user interface. Other datatypes do not use this option.

Two types of constraints can be created using a CREATE TABLE statement: single-column indexes and multicolumn (or table) indexes. You specify both of these indexes using the CONSTRAINT clause, which is discussed in the next section.

For example, to create a table tblNewMenu to mimic the schema of the tblMenu table found in the CH5.MDB sample database, you could use the following CREATE TABLE statement:

```
CREATE TABLE tblNewMenu
([Menu#] LONG, MenuDescription TEXT (50), Unit TEXT (50),
Price CURRENCY, Discontinued BIT);
```

The CONSTRAINT Clause

In the SQL-92 standard, *constraints* are used to restrict the values that can be added to a table. You can use constraints in SQL-92 to create primary and foreign keys, constrain columns to be UNIQUE or NOT NULL, and to create validation rules (the CHECK constraint). Access SQL supports each of these uses except for the NOT NULL and CHECK constraints. Since the only constraints currently supported by Access are ones requiring the definition of indexes, you might find it convenient to think of the Access CONSTRAINT clause as being used to create indexes. (Be aware, however, that support for the NOT NULL and CHECK constraints may be added at a later date.)

You use the CONSTRAINT clause in CREATE TABLE and ALTER TABLE statements. There are two forms of the CONSTRAINT syntax. You use the first form for single-column constraints:

CONSTRAINT *name* {PRIMARY KEY | UNIQUE |

REFERENCES *foreign-table* [(*foreign-column*)]}

The multiple-column version of the CONSTRAINT clause is as follows:

CONSTRAINT *name* {PRIMARY KEY (*column1*, [*column2* [, ...]]) |

UNIQUE | REFERENCES *foreign-table* [(*foreign-column1*

[, *foreign-column2* [, ...]])]}

For example, you could use the following CREATE TABLE statement to create the tblNewMenu table and a unique index on the column MenuDescription:

```
CREATE TABLE tblNewMenu
([Menu#] LONG, MenuDescription TEXT CONSTRAINT MenuDescription
UNIQUE, Unit TEXT, Price CURRENCY, Discontinued BIT);
```

TIP Anytime you create an index in Access, even a single-column index, you must assign it a name. Since the Access UI assigns primary key indexes the name PrimaryKey and single-column indexes the same name as the column and there's no good reason to do otherwise, we recommend using these same naming conventions in DDL queries. Less clear is what to name foreign key indexes; we have chosen here to use the naming convention "*referenced-tablename*FK". For example, a foreign key to tblCustomer would be tblCustomerFK. (The Access UI gives less descriptive names of the form *Reference, Reference1,* and so forth.) For non–primary key multicolumn indexes, we again recommend using the same naming convention used by the UI: *index1, index2,* and so on.

As a second example, say you wished to create two tables, tblOrders and tblItems, and relate them in a one-to-many relationship. You need tblOrders to have the following columns: OrderId (the primary key), OrderDate, and CustomerId. Table tblItems should contain OrderId, ItemId, and ItemDescription. For tblItems, OrderId and ItemId will make up the primary key and OrderId will be a foreign key reference to the same-named column in tblOrders. You could use the following two CREATE TABLE statements executed one after the other (you can't place multiple SQL statements in a DDL query) to create the two tables:

```
CREATE TABLE tblOrders
(OrderId LONG CONSTRAINT PrimaryKey PRIMARY KEY,
OrderDate DATETIME, CustomerId LONG );

CREATE TABLE tblItems
(OrderId LONG CONSTRAINT tblOrdersFK REFERENCES
tblOrders, ItemId LONG, ItemDescription TEXT (30),
CONSTRAINT PrimaryKey PRIMARY KEY (OrderId, ItemId) );
```

TIP   For foreign key references you can omit the name of the foreign key column if it is the primary key in the referenced table.

Both forms of CONSTRAINT lack any way to create non-unique indexes within a CREATE TABLE or ALTER TABLE statement. This *is* consistent with the SQL-92 standard. Fortunately, you can use the CREATE INDEX statement, described in the next section, to create this type of index.

The CREATE INDEX Statement

In addition to the CONSTRAINT clause of the CREATE TABLE and ALTER TABLE commands, you can use the *CREATE INDEX statement* to create an index on an existing table. (CREATE INDEX is not a part of the ANSI standard but is usually implemented by most vendors.) The syntax of the CREATE INDEX statement is

CREATE [UNIQUE] INDEX *index*

ON *table* (*column1* [, *column2* [, …]])

[WITH {PRIMARY | DISALLOW NULL | IGNORE NULL}]

If you include the UNIQUE keyword, the index disallows duplicate values. You must give a name to each index, even if it is a single-column index. See the preceding section for suggested index-naming conventions.

You can create a primary key index by using the PRIMARY option in the WITH clause. All primary key indexes are automatically unique indexes, so you needn't (but you can if you insist) use the UNIQUE keyword when you use the PRIMARY option.

You use the IGNORE NULL option to prevent Jet from creating index entries for null values. If the indexed column will contain nulls and there may be many nulls, you can improve the performance of searches on non-null values by using this option. This is equivalent to using the IgnoreNulls property of the index in table design mode.

You can use the DISALLOW NULL option to have the Jet engine prevent the user from entering null values in the column. This is similar to setting the Required property of a column in table design mode to Yes. Choosing this option has the same effect, but this "hidden" feature is maintained by the index, not the column, and has no analogous property in the UI. If you use this option, you won't be able to turn it off through the user interface—the Required property of the underlying column will act independently—unless you delete the index.

You can create a multicolumn index by including more than one column name in the ON clause.

You can create only one index at a time with the CREATE INDEX statement. Also, there's no facility for creating descending-ordered indexes using the CREATE IN-DEX statement; you must use the UI to alter the sort order of any indexes created using DDL queries.

You could use the following CREATE INDEX statement to add a unique index that ignored nulls to the column MenuDescription in tblMenu:

```
CREATE UNIQUE INDEX MenuDescription
ON tblMenu (MenuDescription)
WITH IGNORE NULL;
```

The ALTER TABLE Statement

You can use the *ALTER TABLE statement* to alter the schema of an existing table. With it you can add a new column or constraint or delete a column or constraint. (You can't modify the definition of either.) You can operate on only one field or in-dex with a single ALTER TABLE statement. The ALTER TABLE statement has four forms.

The first form is used to *add a column* to a table:

ALTER TABLE *table* ADD [COLUMN] *column datatype* [(*size*)]

[CONSTRAINT *single-column-constraint*];

The keyword COLUMN is optional. As in the CREATE TABLE statement, you spec-ify the datatype of the new column by using one of the Jet engine SQL datatype identifiers or its synonyms (see Table 5.2 earlier in this chapter). You can use the op-tional SIZE parameter to specify the length of a text column. If *size* is left blank, text columns are assigned a size of 255. You can also specify an optional index for the column using the CONSTRAINT clause. (See the section "The CONSTRAINT Clause" earlier in this chapter.)

For example, you could use the following ALTER TABLE statement to add the integer column, Quantity, to the tblItems table:

```
ALTER TABLE tblItems ADD Quantity SHORT;
```

NOTE One annoying "feature" of ALTER TABLE is that all added columns are inserted at the beginning of the table. Thus, in the preceding example, Quantity becomes the first column in tblItems.

You can use the second form of ALTER TABLE to *add constraints* to a table:

ALTER TABLE *table* ADD CONSTRAINT *constraint*;

For example, you could use the following ALTER TABLE statement to add an index to the new column:

```
ALTER TABLE tblItems ADD CONSTRAINT Quantity UNIQUE (Quantity);
```

As with the CREATE TABLE statement, you are limited to creating indexes that are unique or serve as primary or foreign keys.

You use the third form of ALTER TABLE to *remove a column* from a table:

ALTER TABLE *table* DROP [COLUMN] *column*;

Again, the keyword COLUMN is optional. For example, you could use the following ALTER TABLE statement to remove the ItemDescription column from tblItems:

```
ALTER TABLE tblItems DROP COLUMN ItemDescription;
```

NOTE You can't remove an indexed column from a table without first removing its index.

You use the final form of ALTER TABLE to *remove an index* from a table:

ALTER TABLE *table* DROP CONSTRAINT *index*;

You refer to an index by name. For example, to remove the primary key from tblOrders, you would use the following ALTER TABLE statement:

```
ALTER TABLE tblOrders DROP CONSTRAINT PrimaryKey;
```

> **NOTE** You can't delete an index that is involved in a relationship without first deleting all the relationships in which it participates.

The DROP Statement

You can use the *DROP statement* to remove tables or indexes. It has two forms.

You use the first to *remove a table* from a database:

DROP TABLE *table*;

For example, you could use the following DROP statement to remove the tblItems table from the current database:

```
DROP TABLE tblItems;
```

You use the second form of DROP to *remove an index* from a table:

DROP INDEX *index* ON *table*;

For example, to delete the index named Index1 from tblCustomer, you could use the following DROP statement:

```
DROP INDEX Index1 ON tblCustomer;
```

> **NOTE** To drop an index from a table, you can use either the ALTER TABLE statement or the DROP statement. You must use caution when using DROP because there is no confirming dialog when it is executed.

Differences between Access SQL and SQL-92

Access SQL is a hybrid SQL. It differs considerably from each of the SQL standards and doesn't *completely* support *any* of the ANSI SQL standards. It lacks large chunks of the standards, particularly in the areas of security and cursors. Sometimes it supports the same functionality found in one of the standards, but with a different syntax. For example, the syntax of the UPDATE statement is nonstandard but essentially equivalent to the functionality in the SQL-92 UPDATE statement. In other cases, similar functionality is provided elsewhere in Access. For example, security is handled in Access using either the UI or DAO. Finally, Access SQL has some useful features that are not present in any of the standards. A few of the extensions are dynaset updatability, support for crosstab queries, and the SELECT INTO statement.

The ANSI SQL standards are so varied that it's difficult to pin down all the differences between Access and the various flavors of SQL. Many of these differences have been noted throughout the chapter. Nonetheless, we have attempted to summarize the major differences between Access SQL and SQL-92 in Table 5.3. (Note that this table is not comprehensive; it covers only the major differences.)

TABLE 5.3: Major Differences between Access SQL and ANSI SQL-92

Feature	Supported by SQL-92	Supported by Access SQL	Comments
Security (GRANT, REVOKE, and so on)	Yes	No	Access security system serves the same purpose
Transaction support (COMMIT, ROLL-BACK, and so on)	Yes	No	Access offers a similar facility in DAO
Views (CREATE VIEW statement)	Yes	No	A saved query is equivalent to a view
Temporary tables (in the SQL-92 sense)	Yes	No	All tables are persistent

TABLE 5.3: Major Differences between Access SQL and ANSI SQL-92 (continued)

Feature	Supported by SQL-92	Supported by Access SQL	Comments
Joins in FROM clause	Yes	Yes	Access, however, doesn't support all the variations on the syntax
Joins in UPDATE, DELETE statements	No	Yes	Unique to Access SQL
Support for FULL OUTER JOIN and UNION JOIN	Yes	No	A union join is different from the UNION operator
Full support for mixing heterogeneous joins	Yes	No	Access has limited support for mixing heterogeneous joins
Support for subqueries in SET clause of UPDATE statements	Yes	No	Access offers support for joins instead
Support for multiple tables in DELETE statements	No	Yes	Unique to Access SQL
SELECT DISTINCTROW	No	Yes	Unique to Access SQL
SELECT TOP N	No	Yes	Unique to Access SQL
Cursors (DECLARE CURSOR, FETCH, and so on)	Yes	No	DAO supports the equivalent use of table cursors
Domain support (CREATE DOMAIN, ALTER DOMAIN, and so on)	Yes	No	Access doesn't support domains
Complete support for constraints	Yes	No	Access supports only a subset of constraint functionality
Assertions (CREATE ASSERTION, DROP ASSERTION, and so on)	Yes	No	Access doesn't support system-wide rules

TABLE 5.3: Major Differences between Access SQL and ANSI SQL-92 (continued)

Feature	Supported by SQL-92	Supported by Access SQL	Comments
Row value constructors	Yes	No	Access doesn't support this feature
Case expressions	Yes	No	Similar functionality is found using the IIf() function
Full referential integrity support in CREATE TABLE statement	Yes	No	Access only partially supports this feature in SQL. Cascade support is also provided using the Access UI
Standardized system tables and error codes	Yes	No	Access uses its own system for naming system tables and error codes
Standard datatypes	Yes	Yes	Access supports most but not all the SQL datatypes
Standard string operators	Yes	No	Access provides several alternative string-manipulation functions
Standard wildcard characters	Yes	No	Access uses ? and * instead of the SQL _ and %
Support for Access Basic functions	No	Yes	You can use most ABC functions in Access SQL
Additional aggregate functions	No	Yes	StDev, Var, StDevP, and VarP are unique to Access SQL
TRANSFORM statement	No	Yes	Used to create crosstab queries
Parameters	No	Yes	For defining parameters to be determined at run time
SELECT INTO statement	No	Yes	Unique to Access SQL

Summary

In this chapter we have covered all the components of Access SQL, including

- A brief history of SQL
- The many places where you can use Access SQL
- The SELECT statement and all its clauses, predicates, and variations
- The various types of joins: inner, outer, self
- The ALL, DISTINCT, and DISTINCTROW predicates
- The TOP predicate
- The WITH OWNERACCESS OPTION declaration
- Aggregate queries, including GROUP BY and TRANSFORM (crosstab) queries
- Union queries
- Subqueries and all of their variations
- Parameterized SQL
- Using external data sources
- Action SQL: UPDATE, DELETE, INSERT INTO, and SELECT INTO
- Data Definition Language (DDL) SQL: CREATE TABLE, CONSTRAINT, CREATE INDEX, ALTER TABLE, and DROP
- The differences between ANSI SQL and Access SQL

CHAPTER

SIX

Using Data Access Objects

- Handling Access' objects programmatically

- Creating, deleting, and modifying database objects from Access Basic

- Creating a simple database container replacement

Although Microsoft introduced the Jet engine in Access 1.0, it's been substantially upgraded since then. Between the release of Access 1.0 and Access 2.0, Microsoft released Visual Basic 3.0, WinWord 6.0, and Excel 5.0, all of which shared the Jet engine with Access 1.x. Because of this shared use of the technology, the Jet engine must be application independent. The services it supplies must work with any application that needs those services. Therefore, you'll see thoughout this chapter references to engine-defined properties and application-defined properties. Those things the engine must support need to be generic enough to be used by all the applications that call the engine, requesting data services.

To make the Jet engine more accessible to Access developers, Access 2.0 includes a new feature, data access objects (DAO). DAO allows the Access Basic programmer to interact directly with the Jet engine. You can now create, modify, and delete any of the database objects from your Access Basic code without having to resort to many of the tricks you might have needed to try in Access 1.x. DAO includes hundreds of new objects, methods, and properties. This chapter covers the basics and gets you started in programmatic manipulation of Jet engine objects, using DAO. In addition, the chapter covers some of the Access-specific additions to DAO. These additions make it possible to interact with Access objects as though they were part of the engine-supplied object model.

Introduction to DAO

Data access objects are those objects in Microsoft Access that are created and maintained by the Jet engine. The following lists show the data access objects available using Jet 2 (the version of the Jet engine used in Access 2.0), categorized by type.

- **Engine-level objects:**

DBEngine	Object representing the Jet engine. All references to DAO start with a reference to the DBEngine object. This is the "hook" through which you interact with the Jet engine
Workspace	Object representing an active session of the Jet engine

| Container | Object that contains information about other DAOs |
| Document | Object representing information about non-Jet objects |

- **Database-level objects:**

Database	Object representing an open database
TableDef	Object representing a table saved in a database
QueryDef	Object representing a query saved in a database
Parameter	Object representing a query's parameter
Field	Object representing a field in a table, query, index, recordset, or relation
Index	Object representing a table's index
Relation	Object representing a relationship between table or query fields
Property	Object representing a property of an object
Recordset	Object representing a set of records in a table, dynaset, or snapshot

- **Security objects:**

| Group | Object representing a group in Access Security |
| User | Object representing a user as defined in the Access security model |

Security objects are discussed in Chapter 22.

Collections—Visiting All the Objects

All objects except DBEngine have an associated collection that contains all the objects of the given type. For example, the TableDefs collection contains a TableDef object for each table saved in the database. Collections make it easy to "visit" all the objects of a specific type, looping through all the items in the collection. Since you can refer to all the items in a collection either by name or by position, you have the best of both worlds. If you know the specific object's name, you can find it by name, as in the following code fragment:

```
Dim db As Database
Dim tdf As TableDef

Set db = DBEngine.WorkSpaces(0).Databases(0)
Set tdf = db.TableDefs("tblCompanies")
Debug.Print tdf.Name
```

If you want to refer to an object by number, to loop through all the items in a collection, you can do that, too:

```
Dim db as Database
Dim intI As Integer

Set db = DBEngine.WorkSpaces(0).Databases(0)
' Loop through all the TableDefs
For intI = 0 To db.TableDefs.Count - 1
    ' Print out the name of the selected TableDef object.
    Debug.Print db.TableDefs(intI).Name
Next intI
```

The mechanisms shown here work for all the collections.

Refreshing Collections

When you first open a database and then reference any specific collection of objects, that collection will certainly be up to date. As you create and delete objects, though, Access does not necessarily keep the collections updated. This inconsistency occurs whether you create and delete objects programmatically using DAO or through the user interface. The problem is amplified in a multiuser environment as users create and delete objects in the same database.

To ensure that the collection you are referring to is current, use the *Refresh* method. Each collection of data access objects has a Refresh method that forces Access to re-read objects and fill the collection from beginning to end.

If your application has created a new *persistent object* (one that is saved on disk with the database), like a table or a query, you won't see it immediately in the database container. To force Access to display the new object, you need to move to a different collection in the window and then move back to the original collection. Access updates the database container only when you make a change to the database through the user interface. When you make programmatic changes using DAO, it won't update the window properly until it must.

Understanding the DAO Hierarchy

To be able to use DAO effectively in your applications, you must understand that objects can contain other objects. When you refer to objects, you do so through the hierarchy of containers and containees. All DAO references start with the DBEngine and work down from there. Figure 6.1 displays the hierarchy of objects.

For example, if you wanted to refer to a parameter object, you could follow the diagram to find this path through the hierarchy:

DBEngine → Workspaces → Databases → QueryDefs → Parameters → Your Parameter

As you'll see in following sections, this ordering plays a major part in your being able to manipulate data access objects effectively.

FIGURE 6.1:

Access object hierarchy

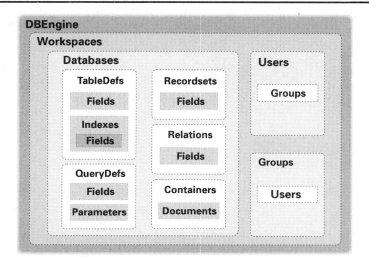

Using Object Variables

Through the course of this book, we make many assumptions about your knowledge of Access and Access Basic. We use standard variable types without explanation, assuming that you'll understand statements like the following:

```
Dim intX as Integer
```

On the other hand, object variables, the basis of all Access Basic code surrounding data access objects, require a little explanation.

When you create a normal variable, you're asking Access to reserve enough space to hold the information whose datatype you've specified. If you don't specify a datatype, Access assumes the most space the variable might need and uses a variant-type variable. When you create an object variable (a variable that will refer to either a user-interface or a data access object), Access creates only a "pointer." That is, the variable it creates only *refers* to a real object; it's not a real object itself.

For example, when you write code like this:

```
Dim db As Database
Dim rst As Recordset
Dim frm As Form
Dim ctl As Control
```

none of those variables actually hold any data, nor do they refer to any real objects at this point. To make an object variable actually refer to a real object, you must use the Set keyword. In every case, you use Set to "point" the variable at a real object (which must already exist). For example, using the variables in the previous example, you might see code like this:

```
Set db = DBEngine.Workspaces(0).Databases(0)
Set rst = db.OpenRecordset("tblCustomers")
Set frm = Forms!frmYourForm
Set ctl = frm(0)
```

In each case you've made the object variable refer to an actual object. Without this step, the object variables are just placeholders, waiting to actually refer to something.

If in the course of your code you point a data access object variable (a TableDef, Recordset, and so on) at an actual object, be sure to close your object before you leave your procedure. Although Access claims to do this for you, it is good programming practice to close anything you open. This same principle doesn't necessarily apply to user-interface objects, such as forms, where the user sees the object you just opened. In cases where your object refers to an open database object—for example, when you have code like this:

```
Set db = DBEngine.Workspaces(0).OpenDatabase(C:\SAMPLE.MDB")
```

closing the object variable does not actually close the real object. Closing the variable releases it from referring to the real object and releases any memory the variable used in setting up its link with the real object. Therefore, code like this:

```
db.Close
```

ensures that Access releases the appropriate memory once you're done using the variable. On the other hand, you should only close objects you've explicitly opened. Never close a database referring to DBEngine. Workspaces(0). Databases(0)—you didn't open it.

Referring to Objects

You refer to data access objects by following the hierarchy presented in the preceding section. Start with the DBEngine object and work your way down from there. The general format for referring to objects is

DBEngine.*ParentCollection.ChildCollection*(*ChildObject*)

To refer to any member of any collection, you can use one of four syntactical constructs. Table 6.1 lists the four methods you can use. (In each example you're attempting to refer to the database named Sales that you'd previously opened as the only database in workspace 0.)

TABLE 6.1: Methods for Referring to Objects

Syntax	Details	Example
collection("name")		DBEngine.Workspaces(0).Databases("Sales")
collection(*var*)	Where *var* is a string or variant variable	strDatabase="Sales" DBEngine.Workspaces(0).Databases(strDatabase)

TABLE 6.1: Methods for Referring to Objects (continued)

Syntax	Details	Example
collection(*ordinal position*)	Where *ordinal position* is the object's position within its collection	DBEngine.Workspaces(0).Databases(0)
collection!*name* collection![*name*]	Brackets are necessary if *name* contains a nonstandard character, such as a space	DBEngine.Workspaces(0).Databases!Sales

The Database Object Problem

In an effort to maintain compatibility with applications written for Access 1.x, the Jet designers were forced to accept a constraint that will affect all the code you write that accesses DAO. The rule is this: You must assign your chosen database object to a database variable before you can reference any objects below it in the hierarchy.

This can cause some confusion when you need to refer to objects in a generic sense. For example, you can refer to a user object directly in your code using the following lines:

```
Dim usr As User
Set usr = DBEngine.Workspaces(0).Users("dan")
Debug.Print usr.Name
```

However, you cannot refer to a table, or any other object below the Databases collection, directly in code. The following reference causes an "Object is no longer valid" (3420) error:

```
Dim tdf As TableDef
Set tdf =  DBEngine.Workspaces(0).Databases(0).
➡ TableDefs("tblCustomers")
```

To make this reference work, you must first assign DBEngine.Workspaces(0).Databases(0) to a database variable and make all subsequent references using that database variable. The following fragment will run without error:

```
Dim tdf As TableDef
Dim db as Database
Set db = DBEngine.Workspaces(0).Databases(0)
Set tdf = db.TableDefs("tblCustomers")
```

Note that you must first assign a database object variable to the current database and then refer to the table through the database object variable.

A Reminder about Syntax

Once you've gotten past the database variable limitation, you'll need to remember all the different syntax options available to you. As a reminder, following are the four ways you could refer to a table named tblContacts in the current database. This particular table is the third table in the TableDefs collection.

- **Using a string literal:**

```
Dim db As Database
Dim tdf As TableDef

Set db = DBEngine.Workspaces(0).Databases(0)
Set tdf = db.TableDefs("tblContacts")
```

- **Using a string variable:**

```
Dim db As Database
Dim tdf As TableDef
Dim strTable As String

strTable = "tblContacts"
Set db = DBEngine.Workspaces(0).Databases(0)
Set tdf = db.TableDefs(strTable)
```

- **Using the position:**

```
Dim db As Database
Dim tdf As TableDef

Set db = DBEngine.Workspaces(0).Databases(0)
' Retrieve the third TableDef. Remember that collections
' are 0-based.
Set tdf = db.TableDefs(2)
```

- **Using the table name directly:**

```
Dim db As Database
Dim tdf As TableDef

Set db = DBEngine.Workspaces(0).Databases(0)
Set tdf = TableDefs![tblContacts]
```

Bang (!) versus Dot (.)

The bang (!) and dot (.) identifier operators help describe the relationships among fields, controls, and properties in an expression. They indicate that one part of an expression belongs to another.

In general, the bang is followed by the name of something you created: a form, report, or control. It also indicates that the item to follow is an element of a collection. You'll usually follow the dot with a property name.

You can also think of the uses this way: a bang separates an object from the collection it's in (a field in a table, a form in the Forms collection, a control on a form), while a dot separates an object from a property of that object.

Ordinal Positions

As you've seen, you can refer to an object by using the ordinal position within its collection. The Jet engine assigns and maintains these ordinal positions, and they always start with position number 0. For the Workspaces and Databases collections, ordinal position 0 always refers to the current workspace and the current database (the one that's open in the user interface). For example, when you start Microsoft Access, it opens a Jet engine session and assigns it to the first ordinal position in the Workspaces collection. When you open a database through the user interface (using the File ➤ Open Database menu item), Access assigns the database to the first ordinal position in the Databases collection.

For objects other than workspaces and databases, an object's ordinal position is dependent on the order in which it was added to its collection. The first table you create will have a lower ordinal position than tables you create later. As you create and delete objects, an object's ordinal position changes within its collection. Additionally, Access creates objects (such as the system tables) that may preclude your objects from starting at ordinal position 0. Because of this, it is not a good idea to refer to a specific object using its ordinal position. You should use the ordinal position of objects only as loop indexes, for iterating through all the objects in a collection.

Using Default Collections

You can see from the previous examples that a simple object reference can result in a long line of code. Fortunately, DAO provides default collections for most object types. You can use the default collection behavior of objects to make your code more compact (but somewhat less readable). The following table lists the default collection within each object type:

Object	Default Collection
Container	Documents
Database	TableDefs
DBEngine	Workspaces
Group	Users
Index	Fields
QueryDef	Parameters
Recordset	Fields
Relation	Fields
TableDef	Fields
User	Groups
Workspace	Databases

Given that the default collection for DBEngine is the Workspaces collection, you can shorten this expression:

```
DBEngine.Workspaces(0)
```

to

```
DBEngine(0)
```

This means "refer to the first open workspace."

Given that the default collection for the workspaces object is the Databases collection, you can shorten this expression:

```
DBEngine.Workspaces(0).Databases(0)
```

to

DBEngine(0)(0)

This means "refer to the first open database in the first open workspace."

You can use similar contractions to simplify your code. Be aware, though, that using default collections to reduce your code also makes it less readable: whoever is reading the code will have to understand the meaning of the expression without any visual clues.

Enumerating through Collections

Since you can access any object in any of the data access object collections by its position in the collection, you can loop through the elements of any collection to look at or modify any object in the collection. Use the Count property of a collection to determine the size of the collection. Remember that the ordinal position of objects within a collection starts at 0, so that if a collection contains three elements, they'll be numbered 0 through 2.

For example, you could use code like this to print out the names of all the tables in your database:

```
Dim db As Database
Dim intI As Integer

Set db = DBEngine.Workspaces(0).Databases(0)
For intI = 0 To db.TableDefs.Count - 1
    Debug.Print db.TableDefs(intI).Name
Next intI
```

Properties

If you have worked with forms, reports, and controls, you are already familiar with referencing properties. (See Chapters 7 through 9 for more information on user-interface objects.) However, data access objects and the interaction between the Jet

Properties and Methods

Data access objects have both properties and methods.

Properties are attributes of objects that can be retrieved and (sometimes) set. For example, most objects have the property Name, which returns the name of the object. You could use the following statement to retrieve the name of a TableDef object referred to by the variable tdf:

```
strName = tdf.Name
```

Properties can be thought of as the adjectives that describe objects.

Methods are actions that can be applied to objects. For example, Recordset objects provide the MoveNext method, which moves the current record pointer to the next record. You could use the following statement to move to the next record of the recordset referred to by the variable rst:

```
rst.MoveNext
```

Methods can be thought of as the verbs that act upon objects.

engine and Microsoft Access introduce new subtleties when you are working with properties.

Properties for data access objects behave somewhat differently from Microsoft Access properties. Each object has a collection of properties. For Access objects (forms and reports, for example), every property that will ever exist for the object exists when you create the object. This is not necessarily the case for data access objects. Properties may not exist in the collection until you set them to a specific value, depending on the specific object. Therefore, it's important that you understand the differences among the different types of properties used in DAO.

Types of Properties

DAO properties can be either built in or user defined.

Built-in properties always exist for an object. They define the basic characteristics of an object and are available to any application that uses the Jet engine (such as

Access or Visual Basic). For example, for Field objects, Name and Type are built-in properties. They define the basic characteristics of a field.

User-defined properties are added to the properties collection of an object. These properties may be added either by Microsoft Access as a client of the Jet engine or by you as an application developer. If Microsoft Access added the property to the object, it's treated as a special case of a user-defined property. Properties added by Access have two distinct characteristics:

- Once Access adds them to the appropriate collection, you can't. You can't, for example, create your own property named Description for a TableDef object once a Description property has already been added.

- The properties Access adds are properties it needs in order to do its job. They can't be provided by the Jet engine since they're specific to Access.

User-defined properties do not exist until they are added to the object's Property collection. While this may seem obvious, it does cause some unexpected behavior. For example, Description is not a built-in property. Even though you can type in a field's description while defining the table, the Jet engine doesn't know about it until you've actually typed it into the properties list for the table. If you try to retrieve the Description property of an object that has not yet had this property set, you will get a trappable run-time error (3265), "Name not found in this collection."

Referring to Data Access Object Properties

As part of every object reference, you need to include a full path from the "head" object, DBEngine, to the object you care about. At each level you need to separate the name of the parent object from the object at the next level down the object hierarchy. And at each level you need to know which separator to use: a bang (!) or a dot (.). When you're just referring to objects, as in the preceding section, "Referring to Objects," there's no question: you either use a bang or you use no separator at all (enclosing a string containing the object name within parentheses).

For properties, though, the syntax gets a bit more complex. In general, you follow the Access 1.x guidelines: if you created the object, use a bang; otherwise, use a dot. This rule may seem a bit ambiguous since it's not always totally clear when *you've* created an object, and it's not always clear who "you" is (you the developer, or Access acting for you). Access lets you choose one of three constructs, depending on the type of property you're referring to:

- To refer to a built-in property, use *object.property*.
- To refer to a user-defined property, *use object.Properties!name*
- To refer to any property, use *object.Properties("propertyname")*

Note that the third item may be the preferable form since you do not need to worry about whether the property is built in or user defined. Also note that unless you are referring to a built-in property, you must refer to it through the Properties collection.

For example, to refer to a TableDef's Name property, you normally use a dot since Name is a built-in property:

```
strName = tdf.Name
```

or

```
strName = tdf.Properties("Name")
```

To refer to the Description property (which is an application-defined property), refer to it as a member of the Properties collection. You can't use an *object.Description* because Description is an application-defined property, which is a special case of a user-defined property. Even though you didn't create the property, it's not a built-in property. In this case Access created the property for you when you entered a value for it into the table's property sheet. You can use either of the following two methods to retrieve the Decription property's value:

```
strDescription = tdf.Properties("Description")
```

or

```
strDescription = tdf.Properties!Description
```

For more information on creating your own properties, see the section "Creating Your Own Properties" later in this chapter.

Enumerating the Properties

Listing 6.1 shows code you could use to print out all the properties of any table:

Listing 6.1

```
Function ListProperties(strTable As String)
    Dim db As Database
    Dim tdf As TableDef
    Dim prp As Property
    Dim intI As Integer

    Set db = DBEngine(0)(0)
    ' You could use the following expression:
    ' Set tdf = db.TableDefs(strTable)
    ' but the TableDefs collection is the default
    ' collection for a database object. Therefore,
    ' its use is unnecessary in the expression.
    Set tdf = db(strTable)

    For intI = 0 To tdf.Properties.Count - 1
        Set prp = tdf.Properties(intI)
        Debug.Print prp.Name, prp.Value
    Next intI
End Function
```

You'll find ListProperties() in basProperties (in CH6.MDB).

The output from the preceding code might look something like this:

Name	tblContacts
Updatable	−1
DateCreated	3/16/94 9:22:37 AM
LastUpdated	3/16/94 5:59:20 PM
Connect	
Attributes	0
SourceTableName	
RecordCount	0
ValidationRule	

ValidationText

Description   My Contacts

Data Definition Using DAO

The previous sections have been using data access objects to refer to existing objects and properties. A large portion of DAO's power, though, lies in its ability to programmatically create and manipulate objects. Using the Create and Append methods, you can create and modify virtually any data access object.

Creating Objects

To create a new object, follow these three steps:

1. Use one of the Create*Object* methods to create the object (CreateTable, CreateIndex, and so on)

2. Define the new object's characteristics by setting its properties. Some properties (such as its name) are essential to its existence and must be specified when you create the object. Others can be specified later.

3. Append the object to its collection to make it a permanent part of your database.

The following example creates a new table called tblOrders and adds two fields to it. You'll find the complete function in Listing 6.2 a little later in this section (and in basCreateTable in CH6.MDB):

```
Function CreateOrdersTable()

    Dim dbCurrent As Database
    Dim tdfOrders As TableDef
    Dim fld1 As Field
    Dim fld2 As Field

    Set dbCurrent = DBEngine(0)(0)
    Set tdfOrders = dbCurrent.CreateTableDef()
    tblOrders.Name = "tblOrders"
```

```
Set fld1 = tdfOrders.CreateField("OrderID", DB_LONG)
Set fld2 = tdfOrders.CreateField("Customer", DB_TEXT, 30)
```

At this point the new table and its two fields exist only in memory. To make the new objects a permanent part of the database, you must use the Append method. If you do not append a new object to a collection, it will not be saved as an object in the database.

NOTE Creating objects and giving them properties is not enough. You must take the step of appending them to the correct collection, or Access will never know of their existence. If your program exits before you've used the Append method to add them to a collection, they will be discarded.

The next lines save the new objects to the database:

```
tdfOrders.Fields.Append fld1
tdfOrders.Fields.Append fld2

dbCurrent.TableDefs.Append tblOrders
```

Finally, you can refresh the TableDefs collection to ensure that the new objects are included in it. In a multiuser environment, the new table may not be immediately available to other users unless you refresh the collection. The following line refreshes the TableDefs collection:

```
dbCurrent.TableDefs.Refresh
```

Even using the Refresh method, Access won't update the Database Container window itself until it must. It will only show the new table you've created once you move to a different collection and then back to the list of tables.

Listing 6.2

```
Function CreateOrdersTable()
    Dim dbCurrent As Database
    Dim tdfOrders As TableDef
    Dim fld1 As Field
    Dim fld2 As Field
```

```
    Set dbCurrent = DBEngine(0)(0)
    Set tdfOrders = dbCurrent.CreateTableDef()
    tdfOrders.Name = "tblOrders"

    Set fld1 = tdfOrders.CreateField("OrderID", DB_LONG)
    Set fld2 = tdfOrders.CreateField("Customer", DB_TEXT, 30)

    ' Now, do all the appending, just as in
    ' the previous example.
    tdfOrders.Fields.Append fld1
    tdfOrders.Fields.Append fld2

    dbCurrent.TableDefs.Append tdfOrders
    dbCurrent.TableDefs.Refresh
End Function
```

Although it's not documented, Access does support the Visual Basic syntax:

Dim objectVar As New Object

This syntax creates the object variable and the object to which it points, both at the same time. Once you've created an object this way (by running the procedure that includes the declaration), you still need to assign the values of the properties of the object, and you need to append it to the appropriate collection.

For example, you could rewrite the preceding function as shown here:

```
Function CreateOrdersTable2()
    Dim dbCurrent As Database
    ' Create the objects RIGHT NOW, as opposed
    ' to creating variables to point to objects that
    ' you'll create later.
    Dim tdfOrders As New TableDef
    Dim fld1 As New Field
    Dim fld2 As New Field

    Set dbCurrent = DBEngine(0)(0)
    ' The tabledef's already created, so
    ' just assign the properties.
    tdfOrders.Name = "tblOrders"

    ' The fields are already created, so just
    ' assign the properties.
    fld1.Type = DB_LONG
    fld1.Name = "OrderID"
```

```
    fld2.Type = DB_TEXT
    fld2.Size = 30
    fld2.Name = "CustomerName"

    ' Now, do all the appending, just as in
    ' the previous example.
    tdfOrders.Fields.Append fld1
    tdfOrders.Fields.Append fld2

    dbCurrent.TableDefs.Append tdfOrders
    dbCurrent.TableDefs.Refresh
End Function
```

Since this syntax isn't documented in Access, we strongly suggest that you avoid it when writing new code. If you're importing existing Visual Basic code it will help, but you'll probably be better off avoiding it in new code.

The CreateObject Methods

Each data access object, with the exception of DBEngine, has an associated *Create* method. Table 6.2 summarizes the methods and their syntax.

TABLE 6.2: Object Creation Methods

Object	Method	Arguments	Datatype	Description
Table	Create-TableDef	Name	String	Name of the new table
		Attributes	Integer	Settings for attached, system, and hidden tables
		Source	String	An attached table's base table type information
		Connect	String	An attached table's base table path and file name
Field	Create-Field	Name	String	Name of the new field
		Type	Integer	Datatype of the new field
		Size	Integer	Size of the field if it is a text field
Index	Create-Index	Name	String	Name of the new index

TABLE 6.2: Object Creation Methods (continued)

Object	Method	Arguments	Datatype	Description
Query	Create-QueryDef	Name	String	Name of the new query
		SQL	String	Valid SQL string that defines the new query
Relation	Create-Relation	Name	String	Name of the new relation
		Table	String	Name of the relation's primary table
		ForeignTable	String	Name of the relation's foreign table
		Attributes	Integer	Settings for relationship type, enforce referential integrity, and cascaded updates and deletes
Workspace	CreateWorkspace	Name	String	Name of the new workspace
		User	String	Name of an existing user. This user will become the owner of the new workspace object. For code that references the new workspace object, *User* will, in effect, be the user executing the code
Database	Create-Database	DatabaseName	String	Name of the file that contains the database
		Locale	String	Collating order of the database
		Options	Integer	Options for the new database. You can specify whether or not the database is to be encrypted and which version (1.0, 1.1, or 2.0) of the file format to use when saving the database
Group	Create-Group	Name	String	Name of the new group
		PID	String	Personal identifier for the new group

TABLE 6.2: Object Creation Methods (continued)

Object	Method	Arguments	Datatype	Description
User	CreateUser	Name	String	Name of the new user
		PID	String	Personal identifier for the new user

Creating an Index

As part of your applications, you may need to create an index programmatically. To create the index you use the CreateIndex method of a TableDef object. Once you've used this method to create the index object, you need to set the properties of the index. You also need to create field objects and append them to the Fields collection of the index object, indicating to the index which fields it will need to maintain. Finally, you use the Append method to append the new index to the Indexes collection of the table.

Follow these steps to create a new index:

1. Use the CreateIndex method of a TableDef object to create the index object, and set its Name property (either in the function call itself or by assigning a value to the Name property sometime before you append the index to the Indexes collection).

2. Assign values to the new index's properties, as appropriate. All the properties are read/write for an index object that hasn't yet been appended to the Indexes collection but are read-only once that has occurred. The ones you'll most likely be interested in are the Name, Primary, Unique, and Required properties.

3. Use the CreateField method to create a field object for each field that makes up part of the index, and append each to the index's Fields collection. This collection of fields indicates to the index which fields it must maintain values for in order to keep itself current.

4. Use the Append method of the original TableDef object to append the index object to its Indexes collection.

NOTE Since all the properties of an index object are read-only once the object has been appended to its collection, if you need to modify a property of an index once it's been created, you must delete the object and then create a new one.

TIP In Access 2.0, using DAO, you can name your indexes any way you wish. If you're using code, however, that counts on your primary key being named PrimaryKey (and almost anyplace you're using the Seek method in your code, it will be), you must ensure that your primary keys are named the standard value, PrimaryKey. Otherwise, existing code might break.

The CreatePrimaryKey() function in Listing 6.3 creates the primary key for any specified table. You pass to this function the name of the table, the name of the primary key, and an array of field names to use as part of the primary key. Along the way, CreatePrimaryKey() calls the FindPrimaryKey() function, which returns the name of the primary key if it exists or Null if it doesn't. If a primary key already exists, CreatePrimaryKey() deletes the primary key so it can create a new one. We've also included a test procedure, TestCreatePK, to test the functionality. You'll find all these examples in the module basPK in CH6.MDB.

Listing 6.3

```
Function FindPrimaryKey(tdf As TableDef) As Variant
    ' Given a particular tabledef, find the primary key name,
    ' if it exists.

    Dim idx As Index
    Dim intI As Integer

    For intI = 0 To tdf.Indexes.Count - 1
        Set idx = tdf.Indexes(intI)
        If idx.Primary Then
            FindPrimaryKey = idx.Name
            Exit Function
        End If
```

```
    Next intI
    FindPrimaryKey = Null
End Function

Function CreatePrimaryKey(strTableName As String,
➡ strKeyName As String, astrIdxFields() As String) As Integer
    Dim idx As Index
    Dim tdf As TableDef
    Dim db As Database
    Dim fld As Field
    Dim intI As Integer
    Dim varPK As Variant
    Dim intRetval as Integer

    On Error GoTo CreatePrimaryKey_Err

    Set db = DBEngine.WorkSpaces(0).Databases(0)
    Set tdf = db.TableDefs(strTableName)

    ' Find out if the table currently has a primary key.
    ' If so, delete it now.
    varPK = FindPrimaryKey(tdf)
    If Not IsNull(varPK) Then
        tdf.Indexes.Delete varPK
    End If
    ' Create the new index object.
    Set idx = tdf.CreateIndex(strKeyName)

    ' Set the new index up as the primary key.
    ' This will also set:
    '    IgnoreNulls property to False,
    '    Required property to True,
    '    Unique property to True.
    idx.Primary = True

    ' Now create the fields that make up the index, and append
    ' each to the collection of fields.

    ' Loop through all the elements in the
    ' astrIdxFields() array.
    For intI = LBound(astrIdxFields) To UBound(astrIdxFields)
        If Len(astrIdxFields(intI)) > 0 Then
            Set fld = idx.CreateField(astrIdxFields(intI))
            idx.Fields.Append fld
        End If
```

```
        Next intI
        tdf.Indexes.Append idx
        intRetval = True

CreatePrimaryKey_Exit:
    Exit Function

CreatePrimaryKey_Err:
    MsgBox "Error: " & Error & " (" & Err & ")"
    intRetval = False
    Resume CreatePrimaryKey_Exit
End Function

Sub TestCreatePK()

    ' Build a single-field primary key for tblCustomers.

    ReDim astrIdxFields(0) As String
    Dim fOK As Integer

    astrIdxFields(0) = "Customer ID"
    astrIdFields(1) = "Company Name"
    fOK = CreatePrimaryKey("tblCustomers", "PrimaryKey",
    ➡ astrIdxFields())
End Sub
```

Creating Relationships

To create a relationship you use the CreateRelation method of a database object. Once you've used this method, you must set the properties of the relation, including the names of the two tables or queries involved. You must also create a field object for each field involved in the relationship and append each of those to the relation's Fields collection. Finally, you append the relation to the database's Relations collection.

Follow these steps to create a new relation:

1. Open the database that will be the basis for your relation.

2. Verify that the referenced table (the primary table in the relation) has a primary key in place.

3. Use the CreateRelation method of the database to create the relation object. Either set the relation's properties when you create it or set the properties one by one after the fact. These properties include the Table, ForeignTable, and Attributes properties.

4. Create a field object for each primary key field from the primary table involved in the relationship. For each field object, supply the ForeignName property, which corresponds to the name of the matching key field in the secondary table. Append each new field object to the relationship's Fields collection.

5. Use the Append method to append the new relation object to the database's Relations collection.

The following table lists all the possible values for the Attributes property of a relation object:

Constant	Description
DB_RELATIONUNIQUE	Relationship is one-to-one
DB_RELATIONDONTENFORCE	Relationship isn't enforced (no referential integrity)
DB_RELATIONINHERITED	Relationship exists in the database that contains the two attached tables
DB_RELATIONLEFT	The relationship is a left outer join
DB_RELATIONRIGHT	The relationship is a right outer join
DB_RELATIONUPDATECASCADE	Updates will cascade
DB_RELATIONDELETECASCADE	Deletions will cascade

Set the property to be one or the sum of more than one of these constants. If you set no value for the Attributes property, Access attempts to create a one-to-many inner joined relationship with referential integrity enabled.

Listing 6.4 demonstrates, in the simplest case, the steps involved in creating a relationship. This function (from basRelations in CH6.MDB) creates a left outer join between tblCustomers and tblItems and enables cascading updates.

Listing 6.4

```
Function CreateRelationship()
    ' Create a relationship between tblCustomers and tblItems.
    ' The relation will be a left outer join, with cascading
    ' updates enabled.

    Dim db As Database
    Dim rel As Relation
    Dim fld As Field

    On Error GoTo CreateRelationship_Err

    Set db = DBEngine.WorkSpaces(0).Databases(0)

    ' Create the new relation object.
    Set rel = db.CreateRelation()

    ' Set the relation's properties.
    rel.Name = "Relation1"
    rel.Table = "tblCustomers"
    rel.ForeignTable = "tblItems"
    ' Create a left outer join containing tblCustomers
    ' and tblItems, with cascading updates enabled.
    rel.Attributes = DB_RELATIONLEFT Or
➡ DB_RELATIONUPDATECASCADE
    ' Or, you could set all the properties when you create
    ' the object:
    ' Set rel = db.CreateRelation("Relation1", "tblCustomers",
    ' tblItems", DB_RELATIONLEFT Or DB_RELATIONUPDATECASCADE)

    ' Set the relation's field collection.
    Set fld = rel.CreateField("Customer ID")
    fld.ForeignName = "Customer ID"
    rel.Fields.Append fld
    ' You could append more fields, if you needed to.

    ' Append the relation to the database's relations
    ' collection.
    db.Relations.Append rel
```

```
CreateRelationship_Exit:
    Exit Function

CreateRelationship_Err:
    MsgBox "Error: " & Error & " (" & Err & ")"
    Resume CreateRelationship_Exit
End Function
```

Creating Your Own Properties

Access' support for DAO makes it possible for you to create your own properties and append them to the Properties collection for an object. For example, you might like to add a LastUpdated property to a table to keep track of the last time the table was touched by a user. Just as for adding an object of any other type, you take three steps:

1. Use the CreateProperty() method to create the new property.
2. Define the new property's characteristics by setting its properties. (You may have done this in step 1.)
3. Append the object to the Properties collection to make it a permanent part of your database.

The code in Listing 6.5 creates LastChanged and LastUser properties and appends them to the tblContacts table. (You can find the function in basAddProps in CH6.MDB.) The following paragraphs go through the function in detail.

The function's caller has passed in the name of the table to operate on, so the first step is to set up references to the current database and to the correct TableDef object:

```
Dim DB As Database
Dim tdf As TableDef

Set DB = DBEngine.Workspaces(0).Databases(0)
Set tdf = DB.TableDefs(strName)
```

Then you need to create the new property objects. When you call CreateProperty(), you may supply the property's name, type, and initial value. You can also set those properties later, before you append the property to the table's Properties collection. In this case it's simpler just to do it all in the call to CreateProperty(). You set the

LastChanged property to contain the current time and the LastUser property to contain the current user ("Admin", unless you've logged in as someone else). (This step corresponds to steps 1 and 2 in the previous list of steps necessary to create new properties.)

```
Set prpLastChanged =
➡ tdf.CreateProperty("LastChanged", DB_DATE, Now)
Set prpLastUser =
➡ tdf.CreateProperty("LastUser", DB_TEXT, CurrentUser())
```

Use the Append method to add the properties to the table so that they become persistent. Since the Append method triggers a run-time error if you've already appended the properties, you can avoid the problem by turning off error checking while appending:

```
On Error Resume Next
tdf.Properties.Append prpLastChanged
tdf.Properties.Append prpLastUser
On Error GoTo 0
```

To list the properties, you can loop through the Properties collection:

```
Dim intI As Integer
Dim prp As Property
For intI = 0 To tdf.Properties.Count - 1
    Set prp = tdf.Properties(intI)
    Debug.Print prp.Name, prp.Value
Next intI
```

To modify the LastChanged property, use one of the two possible syntax variations:

tdf.Properties!LastChanged = Now

or

tdf.Properties("LastChanged") = Now

Listing 6.5

```
Function AddProps (strName As String)
    ' An example function:
    ' 1. Create two new properties for any table:
    '        LastChanged - date of last change to data in table.
    '        LastUser - the last person who used this table.
    ' 2. List out all the properties of the TableDef object.
```

```
' 3. Change the LastChanged property value to reflect the
' current time.

Dim db As Database
Dim tdf As TableDef
Dim prpLastChanged As Property
Dim prpLastUser As Property

' Get references to the current database and the
' correct table.
Set db = DBEngine.Workspaces(0).Databases(0)
Set tdf = db.TableDefs(strName)

' Create the two new properties.
Set prpLastChanged =
➡ tdf.CreateProperty("LastChanged", DB_DATE, Now)
Set prpLastUser =
➡ tdf.CreateProperty("LastUser", DB_TEXT, CurrentUser())

' This code will fail if the properties have already
' been added, so just let the errors occur,
' and keep on going.
On Error Resume Next
tdf.Properties.Append prpLastChanged
tdf.Properties.Append prpLastUser
On Error GoTo 0

' Now list out all the properties.
Dim intI As Integer
Dim prp As Property
For intI = 0 To tdf.Properties.Count - 1
    ' This syntax works, no matter whether
    ' the property is built-in or user-defined.
    Set prp = tdf.Properties(intI)
    Debug.Print prp.Name, prp.Value
Next intI

' Reset the LastChanged property, just to show how:
tdf.Properties!LastChanged = Now
' or:
' tdf.Properties("LastChanged") = Now
End Function
```

Modifying Objects

You can modify existing objects using DAO methods and properties without having to open the object in design mode. There are, however, other restrictions to keep in mind when setting properties of data access objects. Some properties can be set only when the object is created. They cannot be changed after the object has been appended to its collection. An example of this restriction is the Attributes property of TableDef objects. You cannot change the Attributes property of an existing TableDef object but must set this value when you first create the object. If you must alter the Attributes property for a given tabledef, you need to create a new one, copy in all the information from the existing one, and set the Attributes property before you use the Append method to add the tabledef to your database. Also, you need to be aware that some properties do not exist for a data access object until they have been set to a value. (See the section "Types of Properties" earlier in this chapter for a reminder about this limitation.)

Connecting and Reconnecting Attached Tables

The Connect property of TableDef objects gives you control over attached tables. Using this property in conjunction with the SourceTableName property and the RefreshLink method, you can alter the location of the table feeding data to Access. In Access 1.x this was an arduous process, involving the TransferTable action. Now it's simply a matter of modifying a few properties.

The Connect Property

Every TableDef object has a Connect property—a string that identifies the type of attached table and its location in the system's file structure. It does not specify the particular table (or file name, in the case of many of the external datatypes). The SourceTableName property contains the actual file name. Table 6.3 lists all the possible connection types, the necessary Connect string, and an example. (For local native Access tables the Connect property is a zero-length string [""]).

TABLE 6.3: Connection Strings for Various Connection Types

Connection Type	Connect String	Example
Microsoft Access Database	;DATABASE=*drive*:*path**filename*	;DATABASE=C:\DATA\MYDB.MDB
dBASE III	dBASE III;DATABASE=*drive*:*path*	dBASE III;DATABASE=C:\DBASE
dBASE IV	dBASE IV;DATABASE=*drive*:*path*	dBASE IV;DATABASE=C:\DBASE
Paradox 3.x	Paradox 3.x; DATABASE=*drive*:*path*	Paradox 3.x; DATABASE=C:\PDOXDATA
Paradox 4.x	Paradox 4.x; DATABASE=*drive*:*path*	Paradox 4.x; DATABASE=C:\PDOXDATA
Btrieve	Btrieve; DATABASE=*drive*:*path*\FILE.DDF	Btrieve;DATABASE= C:\MYAPP\MYCUST.DDF
FoxPro 2.0	FoxPro 2.0;*drive*:*path*	FoxPro 2.0; DATABASE=C:\FOXDATA
FoxPro 2.5	FoxPro 2.5;*drive*:*path*	FoxPro 2.5; DATABASE=C:\FOXDATA
ODBC	ODBC; DATABASE=defaultdatabase; UID=*username*;PWD=*password*; DSN=*datasourcename*	ODBC; DATABASE=mycust;UID=dan; PWD=Secret;DSN=CustTable

In general, the Connect string names the database that contains the table you want to connect to. Notice that in Table 6.3 the database is the actual .MDB file for Access tables. For other datatypes, use the directory that contains the table as the database. This makes sense here since other DBMS programs, such as Paradox and FoxPro, use the DOS directory structure as the database; there is no single central file as with Access.

Creating an Attached Access Table

The function in Listing 6.6 creates an attached table in the current database, pulling in data from a different .MDB file. To use it, you might try this:

```
fSuccess = CreateAttached("AttachedTable",
➡ "C:\AppPath\MDBFile.MDB", "tblContacts")
```

To create a new attached table, you must follow the same steps that have been covered already: create the object, set its properties, and then append it to the parent collection. CreateAttached() first creates the new TableDef object:

```
Dim db As Database
Dim tdf As TableDef

Set db = DBEngine.Workspaces(0).Databases(0)
Set tdf = db.CreateTableDef(strTable)
```

Then the function must set the appropriate properties. For an attached table, you need to set the Connect and SourceTableName properties. Since you're attaching a native Access table, the Connect string doesn't specify a data source; it just describes the path to the .MDB file:

```
tdf.Connect = ";DATABASE=" & strPath
tdf.SourceTableName = strBaseTable
```

Finally, the code must append the new TableDef object to the TableDefs collection:

```
db.TableDefs.Append tdf
```

In addition, the function adds some error handling. For example, you might already have created a TableDef object with a particular name, or you might try to attach data from an .MDB file that doesn't exist. In either case, the error handler pops up a message box and causes the function to return a False value (instead of the True value it returns if it succeeds in creating the new TableDef object). You'll find CreateAttached() in the module basAttach in CH6.MDB.

Listing 6.6

```
Function CreateAttached(strTable As String, strPath As String,
➡ strBaseTable As String) As Integer
    ' Create an attached table in the current database,
    ' from a table in a different MDB file.

    ' In:
    '    strTable - name of table to create
    '    strPath - path and name of MDB containing the table
    '    strBaseTable - name of table in strPath MDB
    ' Out:
    '    Return value: True/False, indicating success
    ' Modifies:
    '    Nothing, but adds a new table.
    '
```

```
        Dim db As Database
        Dim tdf As TableDef
        Dim strConnect As String
        Dim intRetval As Integer

        On Error GoTo CreateAttachedError

        Set db = DBEngine.Workspaces(0).Databases(0)
        Set tdf = db.CreateTableDef(strTable)

        ' Set up the tabledef's properties.
        ' Set the path to the MDB file.
        tdf.Connect = ";DATABASE=" & strPath
        ' Set the source table name.
        tdf.SourceTableName = strBaseTable

        ' Append the new tabledef to the TableDefs collection.
        db.TableDefs.Append tdf
        intRetval = True

CreateAttachedExit:
        CreateAttached = intRetval
        Exit Function

CreateAttachedError:
        MsgBox "Error: " & Error & " (" & Err & ")"
        intRetval = False
        Resume CreateAttachedExit
End Function
```

Modifying an Existing Attached Table

As users work with your application, sooner or later its attached tables will need to be moved to a new location in the system's file structure. Your application will trigger a run-time error when it later tries to access the moved table. To take care of this problem, you can write a function that checks attached tables and then reconnects them if necessary. The function CheckAttachedTable(), in Listing 6.7, tests an attached table and makes sure it's still where Access thinks it is. ReattachTable(), also in Listing 6.7, reattaches the table if necessary. Its code is very similar to that in CreateAttached() (in Listing 6.6). You'll find both functions in basAttach in CH6.MDB.

After setting up the requisite database and tabledef object variables, the code in Re-AttachTable() checks the Connect property for the particular tabledef. If it's a zero-length string, the table is a native table, and there's nothing to be done. Otherwise it builds up the new connection string and assigns it to the Connect property of the TableDef object:

```
If Len(tdf.Connect) > 0 Then
    tdf.Connect = ";DATABASE=" & strNewPath
    '
    '
End If
```

The code's next step is to attempt to refresh the link between the local Access database and the foreign data. The function uses the tabledef's RefreshLink method to do this. If the link isn't valid, this RefreshLink fails and the error-handling code posts a message and returns a False value from the function. If it succeeds, the function returns a True value, indicating its success:

```
On Error Resume Next
tdf.RefreshLink
ReAttachTable = (Err = 0)
```

Armed with a function to reattach tables if necessary, you can attack the problem of checking to make sure your tables are correctly attached, reattaching them if necessary. CheckAttachedTable() does this work for you.

The majority of the code in CheckAttachedTable() can be summarized in a few steps:

1. Turn on inline error handling (On Error Resume Next).

2. Attempt to create a recordset based on the requested table.

3. If the attempt fails, call ReattachTable() to attempt to reattach it. If that fails, post a failure message and return False.

4. If the recordset creation succeeded, just close the recordset and return a True value from the function.

Listing 6.7

```
Function CheckAttachedTable (strTable As String,
➡ strNewPath As String) As Integer

    ' Checks the named table and attempts to reattach it if
    ' it's not attached properly.
    '
    ' In:
    '     strTable - table to check
    '     strNewPath - path to connect to if test fails
    ' Out:
    '     Return Value - True if successful, False otherwise.

    Dim db As Database
    Dim rst As Recordset

    Set db = DBEngine.Workspaces(0).Databases(0)

    On Error Resume Next
    Set rst = db.OpenRecordset(strTable, DB_OPEN_DYNASET)

    ' Check for failure.  If the OpenRecordset failed, then
    ' attempt to reattach the table.
    If Err <> 0 Then
        If Not ReAttachTable(strTable, strNewPath) Then
            MsgBox "Could not reattach table '" &
            ➡ strTable & "'"
            CheckAttachedTable = False
        End If
    Else
        rst.Close
        CheckAttachedTable = True
    End If
    On Error Goto 0
End Function

Private Function ReAttachTable (strTable As String,
➡ strNewPath As String) As Integer

    ' Reattaches the named table to the named path
    ' In:
    '     strTable - table to reattach
    '     strNewPath - path to attach to
```

```
' Out:
'      Return value: True if successful, False otherwise

Dim db As Database
Dim tdf As TableDef

' Assume success.
ReAttachTable = True

Set db = DBEngine.Workspaces(0).Databases(0)
Set tdf = db.TableDefs(strTable)

' If Connect is blank, it's not an attached table
If Len(tdf.Connect) > 0 Then
    tdf.Connect = ";DATABASE=" & strNewPath

    ' The RefreshLink might fail if the new path
    ' isn't OK. So trap errors inline.
    On Error Resume Next
    tdf.RefreshLink
    ReAttachTable = (Err = 0)
    On Error Goto 0
End If
End Function
```

Working with Non-Native Attached Tables

The previous examples all deal with Access tables. You can also create attached tables based on other data sources. When dealing with external data sources, you use the Connect property to specify the directory in which the file exists (its "database") and the SourceTableName property to specify the actual table. The example in Listing 6.8 creates an attached Paradox table in the current database. (Look in basAttach in CH6.MDB for CreatePDX3Attached().)

Two features that distinguish this function from the previous examples that created attached tables are centered around the Connect string itself. First of all, the information you need to attach a foreign table is different than with a native table. For Access tables you need to supply the new table name, the path and file name of the foreign MDB file, and the table within that database you'd like to attach. For other data sources you'll need to supply the new table name, the DOS path or database name that contains the external data, and the name of the table containing the data you'd like to attach. Second, as you can see in the following code fragment, the Connect property itself must indicate the data source for all but Access native tables:

```
tdf.Connect = "Paradox 3.x;DATABASE=" & strPath
tdf.SourceTableName = strBaseTable
```

WARNING Although the code in Listing 6.8 does successfully attach the table if all goes well, in real-world use you *must* include error-handling code with any procedures that access any data, and especially those that deal with file manipulations. Although we've left out the error handling here for the sake of clarity, understand that this is not code you can use for applications. Without robust error handling in code that's used to handle attachments, you're just begging for trouble. Too many things can go wrong at run time!

Listing 6.8

```
Function CreatePDX3Attached(strTable As String,
➡ strPath As String, strBaseTable As String)
    '
    ' Create attached Paradox 3.0 table in current database
    '
    ' In:
    '   strTable - name of the table to create
    '   strPath - path where the Paradox file "lives"
    '   strBaseTable - name of the Paradox table
    ' Out:
    '   Return value: True/False, indicating success
    ' Modifies:
    '   Nothing, but adds a new table.
    ' Comments:
    '   Before using a function like this, you'd need to
    '   add some serious error handling.
    '
    Dim db As Database
    Dim tdf As TableDef

    Set db = DBEngine.Workspaces(0).Databases(0)
    Set tdf = db.CreateTableDef(strTable)
```

```
' Set the tabledef's properties and append it
' to the TableDefs collection.
tdf.Connect = "Paradox 3.x;DATABASE=" & strPath
tdf.SourceTableName = strBaseTable
db.TableDefs.Append tdf

CreatePDX3Attached = True
End Function
```

Knowing Your Limitations

Access cannot allow you to change the data source type of an existing attached table; nor can you change the name of the base table. For example, you cannot change an attached Paradox table into an attached dBASE III table, and you cannot change an attachment based on MYCUST.DBF into one based on MY-CUST2.DBF. You can change only the path of an existing attached table.

If you need to change the type or base table name of an existing attached table, you must first delete the attached table and then re-create it. Note that deleting an attached table does not delete the underlying table, only the Access link to that table.

Determining the Type of an Attached Table

When you examine an attached table, you may want to know its type. The function in Listing 6.9 (from basAttach in CH6.MDB) returns the type of an attached table, returning a string representing the portion of the Connect string that indicates the attachment type.

The logic behind the function is very simple. It takes four steps to determine the attachment type, attempting to be as "smart" about it as possible. It first compares the Attributes property of the table in question against the intrinsic constant, DB_AT-TACHEDODBC. If this comparison returns a non-zero value, you're assured that the table is an ODBC table, and the function returns "ODBC".

The rest of the tests count on the tabledef's Connect property. If the string is zero-length, the table must be native (nonattached). If the first character is a semicolon, the table must be an attached Access table. Otherwise the function returns the portion of the Connect property that falls before the first semicolon in the string.

Listing 6.9

```
Function GetTableType(strTableName As String) As String

    Dim dbSource As Database
    Dim strTableType As String
    Dim strConnect As String
    Dim tdf As TableDef
    Dim lngAttributes As Long
    Dim strConnectType As String
    Dim intPos As Integer

    Set dbSource = DBEngine.Workspaces(0).Databases(0)
    Set tdf = dbSource.TableDefs(strTableName)
    lngAttributes = tdf.Attributes

    If (lngAttributes And DB_ATTACHEDODBC) Then
        strTableType = "ODBC"
    Else
        strConnect = tdf.Connect
        If Len(strConnect) = 0 Then
            strTableType = "Access Native"
        ElseIf Left$(strConnect, 1) = ";" Then
            strTableType = "Access Attached"
        Else
            intPos = InStr(strConnect, ";")
            If intPos > 0 Then
                strTableType = Left$(strConnect, intPos - 1)
            Else
                strTableType = "Unknown"
            End if
        End If
    End If
    GetTableType = strTableType
End Function
```

Working with Recordsets

In almost any Access application, sooner or later you'll need to manipulate data from Access Basic. Access provides a rich set of data access objects to allow you to view, edit, add, and delete fields, rows, and tables. In its attempt to be as flexible as possible, Access provides three separate means of working with data: tables, dynasets, and snapshots. Each has its own uses and capabilities. The following sections discuss these issues.

Meet the Recordsets

Although Access provides three types of Recordset objects, the one you use in any given situation depends on the source of the data being referenced and the methods you need to use to access the data. Table 6.4 lists each recordset type along with its benefits and drawbacks.

TABLE 6.4: Recordset Types and Their Benefits/Drawbacks

Recordset Type	Description	Benefits	Drawbacks
Table	Set of records in a table in a database	Can use indexes for quick searches. Data can be edited	Works only for local Access tables, not attached tables
Dynaset	Set of pointers (bookmarks) referring to data in tables or queries in a database	Can include data from multiple tables, either local or attached. Can be based on SQL string. Data can be edited in most cases	Some dynasets may not be editable. Cannot perform indexed searches using the faster Seek method
Snapshot	Copy of a set of records as it exists at the time the snapshot is created	Can optionally be set to scroll forward only, allowing faster operations	Data cannot be edited. All records in Recordset's data source are read before control is returned to the program. Doesn't reflect changes to data made in a multiuser environment. A snapshot is a picture of the data at the time the snapshot is created, and no updates will be reflected in its set of rows. Cannot perform indexed searches using the faster Seek method

In Access 1.x you were forced to treat the three different Recordset objects (tables, dynasets, and snapshots) differently. Since each recordset type had its own object variable type, you needed different code to deal with each type.

The Recordset object in Access 2.0 merges tables, dynasets, and snapshots into a single unified object type. This removes the need for different properties, methods, and syntax for accessing records. You use a single method for opening any of the three types of recordsets, and you use a consistent set of methods and properties when dealing with the data. This removes a great deal of the confusion involved with manipulating recordsets in Access 1.x. Although Access 2.0 retains the 1.x methods and properties for backward compatibility, using the new recordset datatype will make your code easier to maintain and troubleshoot.

Creating a Recordset

You use an expression like one of the following to create a recordset:

    Dim rst As Recordset

    Set rst = db.OpenRecordset(*Source* [, *Type* [, *Options*]])

or

    Set rst = *object*.OpenRecordset([*Type* [, *Options*]])

(Parameters enclosed in square brackets are optional.)

In the first example you're creating a new recordset based on something in the database referred to by the database variable db. The *Source* parameter indicates where the data will come from and must be one of the following:

- An existing table
- An existing query that returns rows
- A SQL statement that returns rows

In the second example *object* can be any previously opened database object, such as a table, a query, or even another recordset variable. Since you've already specified the source of the data, you needn't specify it again when creating a recordset based on an existing object.

In both cases the *Type* parameter specifies the type of the recordset. It should be one of the following built-in constant values:

- DB_OPEN_TABLE, to open a table recordset
- DB_OPEN_DYNASET, to open a dynaset recordset
- DB_OPEN_SNAPSHOT, to open a snapshot recordset

If you don't specify a type, Access automatically chooses the type it can open most quickly for the given *Source*. For example, if you create a recordset based on a table in the current database and don't specify *Type*, Access automatically opens a table recordset. Likewise, if *Source* is an attached table, a query, or a SQL string and you've not specified the *Type* parameter, Access automatically opens a dynaset recordset. In addition, you cannot specify DB_OPEN_TABLE if the *Source* parameter is a SQL expression or a tabledef that refers to an attached table. If you do, Access triggers a trappable error (3011), "Couldn't find object...," for SQL expressions or (3219), "Invalid operation," for attached tables.

The *Options* parameter controls the multiuser access behavior of the recordset. It can be one of the following values:

Constant	Description
DB_DENYWRITE	Other users can't modify or add records. This effectively write-locks the recordset's underlying data source(s). Note that when you lock a dynaset recordset, you are locking all the underlying tables
DB_DENYREAD	Other users can't view records. This option applies only to table recordsets. By setting this option you are completely locking other users out of viewing the table

Constant	Description
DB_READONLY	You can only view records; other users can modify them. This is a useful safeguard that can keep your code from inadvertently modifying data
DB_APPENDONLY	You can only append new records. This option applies only to dynaset recordsets
DB_INCONSISTENT	Inconsistent updates are allowed. This option is for dynaset recordsets only
DB_CONSISTENT	Only consistent updates are allowed. This option is for dynaset recordsets only
DB_FORWARDONLY	The recordset is a forward-scrolling snapshot. Use this type of recordset when you are making only one pass through the records. Since a forward-only snapshot does not copy data into a scrollable buffer, it can run much more quickly

Consistent versus Inconsistent Updates

When you create a Recordset object based on more than one table, Access by default allows you to make changes only to the "many" side of a join. This is known as a consistent update. At times you may want to update both sides of join. To do this, set the DB_INCONSISTENT option. This allows you to update fields in both sides of the join. Note that this may violate the relationships between tables that your application needs. It is up to you to provide the necessary code to ensure that any "implied" referential integrity is maintained.

If you've turned on referential integrity for a relationship and if you've enabled cascading updates, the DB_INCONSISTENT and DB_CONSISTENT options will cause identical behavior. In this case the referential integrity takes control, and the cascading updates will update the "many" side of the relationship when you update the "one" side.

Creating Recordset Objects

The following examples show a number of ways you can create Recordset objects. This list isn't exhaustive, but it does show some representative cases.

- **To create a recordset based on a table or a saved query:**

```
Dim dbSales As Database
Dim rstCustomers As Recordset
Dim rstSales As Recordset

Set dbSales = DBEngine.Workspaces(0).Databases(0)
' This will create a table-type Recordset.
Set rstCustomers = dbSales.OpenRecordset("tblCustomers")
' These will create a dynaset-type Recordset.
Set rstSales = dbSales.OpenRecordset("qrySales")
Set rstCustomers = dbSales.OpenRecordset(
➥ "tblCustomers", DB_OPEN_DYNASET)
```

- **To create a dynaset-type recordset based on a SQL string:**

```
Dim dbSales As Database
Dim rstCustomers As Recordset
Dim strSQL As String

Set dbSales = DBEngine.Workspaces(0).Databases(0)
Set rstCustomers =
➥ dbSales.OpenRecordset("SELECT * FROM CUSTOMERS;")
```

or

```
strSQL="SELECT * FROM CUSTOMERS;"
Set rstCustomers = dbSales.OpenRecordset(strSQL)
```

- **To create a table-type recordset that locks other users out of the source's records:**

```
Dim dbSales As Database
Dim rstCustomers As Recordset

Set dbSales = DBEngine.Workspaces(0).Databases(0)
Set rstCustomers = dbSales.OpenRecordset(
➥ "tblCustomers", DB_OPEN_TABLE, DB_DENYREAD)
```

- **To create a snapshot-type recordset based on a table:**

```
Dim dbSales As Database
Dim rstCustomers As Recordset

Set dbSales = DBEngine.Workspaces(0).Databases(0)
Set rstCustomers = dbSales.OpenRecordset(
➡ "tblCustomers", DB_OPEN_SNAPSHOT)
```

Moving through a Recordset

Once you've created a recordset, Access provides a variety of methods for navigating through the rows: MoveFirst, MoveLast, MovePrevious, and MoveNext. Each of these works in the manner you would expect, based on the name. In addition, Access provides the Move method, which can move a specified number of rows forward or backward, either from the current row or from a stored bookmark. If the object is a table-type recordset, the movement follows the order of the active index, which you can set using the Index property of the recordset. If you have not specified the index for table-type recordsets, the row order is unknown.

Using the Move Method

Although the actions of the other preceding methods are obvious, based on their names, the Move method is a bit more ambiguous. The Move method of a recordset accepts one or two parameters:

rst.Move *rows*[, *start*]

The *rows* parameter indicates the number of rows to move (greater than 0 for forward, less than 0 for backwards), and the optional *start* parameter can contain a saved bookmark. If you supply the value for the bookmark, Access starts there and moves the appropriate number of rows from that spot. If you don't specify the start location, Access assumes you want to start moving from the current row.

Finding the Number of Rows in a Recordset

Unlike any implication made by its name, the RecordCount property of recordsets does not return the actual number of rows in a given recordset. It actually returns the number of rows *accessed so far* in the recordset if the recordset is not a table-type recordset. This very common misconception leads to a lot of confusion. To find the actual number of rows in a recordset, you must first use the MoveLast method (and then move somewhere else, if you like) before checking the value of the Record-Count property. If you don't move to the last row, the RecordCount property returns either 0 (if there are no rows) or 1 (if there is one or more rows) when you first create the recordset. (Table-type recordsets maintain their RecordCount property without moving to the last row.)

In a single-user environment, the RecordCount property always correctly returns the number of rows in the recordset, once you've let Access calculate how many there are by moving to the last row. If you delete a row, either through the user interface or through Access Basic code, the RecordCount property stays in sync. In a multiuser environment things are a bit more complex. If you're sharing data with another user and you both have a recordset open that's based on the same data, deletions made on the other machine won't immediately show up on your machine. Access won't update the RecordCount value until the code actually accesses the deleted row. Then Access decrements the RecordCount. Therefore, in a multiuser environment, if you must know exactly how many rows are currently in the recordset, you should take the following steps:

1. Use the Requery method on the Recordset object.
2. Use the MoveLast method to move to the end of the recordset.
3. Check RecordCount for the current value.

You could use the function in Listing 6.10 as a simple example. (You'll find GetRecordCount() in basRecordset in CH6.MDB.) It uses the Restartable property of the recordset to make sure it can requery the recordset and just returns –1 if it can't. In that case the caller would know that the GetRecordCount() function wasn't able to requery the recordset and that it needs to find a less-generic means of solving the problem. Once GetRecordCount() knows that it can requery the recordset, it follows the steps outlined above, preserving and resetting the position in the recordset using the recordset's Bookmark property. (See the section "Using Bookmarks" later in this chapter for more information). This function is actually useful only for dynaset-type recordsets since table-type recordsets can't be requeried and snapshot-type recordsets don't need to be requeried. Since a snapshot-type recordset won't reflect any changes made by other users, its RecordCount property won't change once it's created.

Listing 6.10

```
Function GetRecordCount(rst As Recordset)

    ' Return the current record count for a Recordset.
    ' If the Recordset isn't Restartable (and table-type
    ' Recordsets aren't) then just return -1, indicating
    ' that the caller needs to reopen the Recordset in order
    ' to pick up any foreign changes.

    ' In:
    '       rst:  the previously opened Recordset object
    ' Out:
    '       Return Value: the number of rows in rst if
    '                     rst was restartable; -1, otherwise.

    Dim strBM As String

    If rst.Restartable Then
        rst.Requery
        If rst.Bookmarkable Then
            strBM = rst.Bookmark
        End If
        rst.MoveLast
        GetRecordCount = rst.RecordCount
        If rst.Bookmarkable Then
            rst.Bookmark = strBM
        End If
    Else
        GetRecordCount = -1
    End If
End Function
```

Testing for Boundaries

Every recordset supports two properties, BOF and EOF, that indicate whether the current row is at the end of the recordset (EOF) or at the beginning of the recordset (BOF):

- If you use MovePrevious while the first row is current, BOF becomes True and there is no current row.
- If you use MovePrevious again, BOF stays True but a run-time error occurs.
- If you use MoveNext while the last row is current, EOF becomes True and there is no current row.
- If you use MoveNext again, EOF stays True but a run-time error occurs.

Testing for an Empty Recordset

Often when you create a recordset you want to know immediately whether or not that recordset actually contains any rows. It's quite possible to create a recordset that doesn't return any rows, and you might need to take different steps based on whether or not the result contained any rows.

There are a number of ways to test for an empty recordset, but the two methods that follow ought to serve your needs. The following expression:

```
If rst.EOF and rst.BOF Then
```

checks to see whether both the EOF and BOF properties for the recordset are True. If so, there must *not* be any rows, since that's the only way the current position could be both at the beginning and the end of the recordset. In addition, you can use the following expression:

```
If rst.RecordCount = 0 Then
```

Either of these expressions returns a True value if the recordset contains no rows when it's created.

Looping through All the Rows

Although you're likely to have less reason than you'd think to loop through all the rows of a recordset (that's what action queries are for!), the syntax is quite simple. Listing 6.11 walks through a recordset backwards, from the end to the beginning, and if there are any records to be had, prints out one of the fields in the underlying data. (Look in basRecordset in CH6.MDB for ListNames().)

Listing 6.11

```
Function ListNames()
    Dim db As Database
    Dim rst As Recordset

    Set db = DBEngine.Workspaces(0).Databases(0)
    Set rst = db.OpenRecordset("tblCustomers")
    ' Check first to see if there are any rows.
    If rst.RecordCount > 0 Then
        ' Move to the end.
        rst.MoveLast
        ' Loop back towards the beginning.
        Do Until rst.BOF
            Debug.Print rst![Contact Name]
            rst.MovePrevious
        Loop
    End If
    rst.Close
End Function
```

Creating a Recordset Based on a QueryDef

If you need to create a recordset based on any select query (about which you might know nothing at all until your program is running), you must supply the recordset with all the parameters the querydef requires. Without DAO, doing so required knowing in advance what the parameters were and supplying their values in your code. With the addition of DAO you can loop through all the parameters of your querydef and evaluate the necessary parameters.

A problem occurs because Access cannot fill in the parameters' values when you're creating a recordset based on a querydef. It's up to you to supply those values for the querydef before you attempt to create the recordset.

Your query won't be able to run at all unless all the necessary parameters are available. If your query uses form objects as parameters, for example, you need to make sure the appropriate form is open and running, with appropriate values filled in, before you attempt to run a query based on those parameters.

The following code works with any QueryDef object that represents a select query:

```
Dim intI As Integer
Dim qdf As QueryDef
Dim prm As Parameter
Dim rst As Recordset

For intI = 0 To qdf.Parameters.Count - 1
    Set prm = qdf.Parameters(intI)
    prm.Value = Eval(prm.Name)
Next intI
Set rst = qdf.OpenRecordset(DB_OPEN_DYNASET)
```

It loops through all the parameters of the object (and there may be none, in which case the loop won't ever execute), pointing a Parameter variable at each of the parameters for the querydef, one at a time. For each parameter the code evaluates the Name property using the Eval() function and assigns the return value to the Value property of the parameter. This retrieves the value of each parameter, without your having to know in advance where the parameter is getting its value.

For example, if your query has a single parameter, on the City field:

```
Forms!frmInfo!CityField
```

the QueryDef container contains a single parameter object, whose Name property is Forms!frmInfo!CityField. Through the use of the Eval() function, the code in Listing 6.11 retrieves the value that's stored in that field and assigns it to the *Value* property of the specific parameter object. This satisfies the needs of the QueryDef object, and you'll be able to create the recordset you need, based on that querydef. The Incremental Search example in Chapter 7 uses this mechanism to allow the underlying code to create a recordset on almost any select query, whether or not it requires parameter values.

Finding Specific Records

You handle the task of finding specific data in a recordset differently, depending on the type of the recordset. Table-type recordsets can use an indexed search to find data, but dynaset- and snapshot-type recordsets cannot.

Finding Data in Table-Type Recordsets

If you've created a table-type Recordset object, you can use the fast Seek method to locate specific rows. (Attempting to use the Seek method with any recordset other than a table-type recordset results in a run-time error (3219), "Invalid Operation.") You must take two specific steps to use the Seek method to find data:

1. Set the recordset's Index property. This tells Access which index you'd like it to search through. If you want to use the primary key for searching, you must know the name of the primary key. (It's usually PrimaryKey, unless your application has changed it).

2. Use the Seek method to find the value you want, given a search operator and one or more values to search for. The search operator must be one of the following:

   <

   <=

   =

   >=

   >

   indicating how you want Access to search. If the operator is =, >=, or >, Access searches from the beginning of the recordset. Otherwise it starts at the end and works its way backward. To indicate to Access what it needs to search for, you supply one or more values, corresponding to the keys in the index you selected. If you based your index on one value, you need to supply only one value here. If your index includes multiple columns, you must supply all the values unless your search operator is something other than =.

For example, if your database contained an index named OrderIndex containing three columns—OrderNumber, OrderItem, and OrderDate—and you wanted to find the first item for order number 3, order item 17, for any date, the following fragment could get you to the correct row:

```
rst.Index = "OrderIndex"
rst.Seek ">=", 3, 17
```

The values you send to the Seek method must match the datatypes of the values in the index. In this case the values were numeric. Had they been strings or dates, you would have needed to use matching datatypes in the call to the Seek method.

Once you've used the Seek method to find a row, you must, *without fail*, use the recordset's NoMatch property to check that you actually found a row. The following code expands on the previous fragment, handling the success or failure of the seek:

```
rst.Index = "OrderIndex"
rst.Seek ">=", 3, 17
If rst.NoMatch Then
    MsgBox "Unable to find a match!"
Else
    MsgBox "For the selected row, the item name was: " &
➡ rst!ItemName
End If
```

TIP The Seek method always starts at the beginning (or end) of the recordset when it searches. Therefore, using Seek inside a loop, searching for subsequent rows that match the criteria, is generally fruitless. Unless you modify the value once you find it so that further searches no longer find a match on that row, your loop will continually find the same row.

Finding Data in Dynaset- and Snapshot-Type Recordsets

Unlike table-type recordsets, dynaset- and snapshot-type recordsets cannot use the Seek method for finding data. Because they might well be based on ordered subsets of the original data, Access can't always use an index to speed up the search.

Therefore, any search involving dynasets or snapshots might be a linear search, visiting every row in the recordset until it finds a match. Access will use an index if it can.

On a bright note, however, Access provides much greater flexibility in dynaset/snapshot searches. The four different methods (FindFirst, FindNext, FindPrevious, and FindLast) allow you to optimize the search so it has to look through the smallest number of rows to find the data it needs. Since you can use FindNext with these searches, you won't need to start back at the beginning of the recordset to find subsequent matches. In addition, you can use loops to walk your way through the records since you can restart the search without going back to the first row.

You use the same syntax for each of these methods:

Recordset.{FindFirst | FindPrevious | FindNext | FindLast} *criteria*

where *Recordset* is an open dynaset- or snapshot-type recordset variable and *criteria* is a WHERE clause formatted as if in a SQL expression, without the word *WHERE*. For example, the following fragment searches for a last name of "Smith":

```
rst.FindFirst "[LastName] = 'Smith'"
```

Just as with the Seek method, you must follow every call to a Find method with a check of the recordset's NoMatch property. If that property is True there is no current row, and the search fails. Often, when performing some operation that requires looping through all the rows that match some criteria, you can use code like this:

```
strCriteria = "[LastName] = 'Smith'"
rst.FindFirst strCriteria
Do While Not rst.NoMatch
    ' Since you know you found a match,
    ' do something with the current row.
    Debug.Print rst![FirstName]
    rst.FindNext strCriteria
Loop
' When you get here, you know that rst.NoMatch is True.
```

Of course, many such loops can be replaced with action queries, which are almost always a better solution to the given progamming problem.

Using Quotes in Strings

In building criteria for Find methods and in several other places in Access Basic (when calling domain functions and when creating SQL strings, for example), you often need to embed variable values into a string. Because the Jet engine has no way of finding the value of Access Basic variables, you need to supply their values before you ask it to do any work for you. This can cause trouble because Access requires delimiters (quotes for strings, # for dates) around those values, but they aren't part of the variables themselves. This causes many Access developers, experienced and neophyte alike, a great deal of anguish.

For example, imagine you have a variable named strName that contains the name you'd like to match in your call to the FindFirst method (for the sake of simplicity here, "Smith"). You need to build a string that represents the required WHERE clause:

```
[LastName] = 'Smith'
```

As a first attempt, you might try this:

```
strCriteria = "[LastName] = strName"
```

But when you attempt to run the search, Access complains with a run-time error, "Can't Bind Name 'strName'." The problem is that the expression in strCriteria was this:

```
[LastName] = strName
```

Most likely, no one in your table has that particular last name.

As a second attempt, you might try a new approach:

```
strCriteria = "[LastName] = " & strName
```

When you attempt to run the search this time, Access again complains with a run-time error, "Can't Bind Name 'Smith'." In this case it was using the value

```
[LastName] = Smith
```

which won't work because Access expects string values to be enclosed in quotes.

It should be clear by now that you need to get the quotes into that string. Access provides no less than three solutions to this problem.

All the solutions need to arrive at a value for strCriteria that looks like this:

```
[LastName] = "Smith"
```

or like this:

```
[LastName] = 'Smith'
```

Following are a number of solutions to this particular problem. These exercises are actually simpler to envision if you do the work in reverse order.

The first solution is based on the fact that Access treats two quote characters side-by-side inside a string as representing one quote character. Remembering that every string expression must be enclosed in a pair of quotes, the first step in the first solution involves enclosing the final expression in those quotes. When enclosed in quotes, each internal quote needs to be replaced with two. The expression then becomes

```
"[LastName] = ""Smith"""
```

With the name separated out, the expression becomes

```
"[LastName] = """ & "Smith" & """"
```

Finally, with the constant replaced with the variable, the expression becomes

```
"[LastName] = """ & strName & """"
```

This last expression is the one you'd use with the FindFirst method.

You could also replace each quote with its ANSI representation, CHR$(34). If you go to the Immediate window and ask Access to print out the value

```
? CHR$(34)
```

it responds by printing a double-quote symbol. Therefore, again working backward:

```
[LastName] = "Smith"
```

becomes

```
"[LastName] = " & Chr$(34) & "Smith" & Chr$(34)
```

which becomes

```
"[LastName] = " & Chr$(34) & strName & Chr$(34)
```

If you create a string variable (perhaps named strQuote) and assign to it the value Chr$(34), you can use this expression:

```
"[LastName] = " & strQuote & strName & strQuote
```

You can also create a constant and assign to it a value that will resolve to be the string that is just a quotation mark. You can't use the Chr$() function when creating a constant, so this is the only way to create a constant value that does what you need.

```
Const QUOTE = """"
```

This might be the most straightforward solution to the problem.

The third solution involves replacing each internal quote with an apostrophe. That is, following the same backward steps:

```
[LastName] = "Smith"
```

becomes

```
[LastName] = 'Smith'
```

which becomes

```
"[LastName] = 'Smith'"
```

which becomes

```
"[LastName] = '" & "Smith" & "'"
```

which becomes (finally)

```
"[LastName] = '" & strName & "'"
```

The main problem with this solution (which many developers use) is that the value stored in strName cannot contain a single-quote symbol. If it did, you'd end up with an apostrophe embedded within a string that's enclosed in apostrophes. That's not allowed in Access' syntax. Therefore, you can use this method only when strName contains a value that could never contain an apostrophe.

To summarize, when building a string expression in Access that needs to contain a variable that represents a string, you must ensure that the final expression includes the quotes that enclose that string variable. The three suggested solutions are

```
Const QUOTE = """"
"[LastName] = """ & strName & """"
"[LastName] = " & QUOTE & strName & QUOTE
"[LastName] = '" & strName & "'"
```

To complicate issues, date variables need to be delimited with #, not quotes, in an expression. Following the steps presented above, the solution for the date problem would be

```
"[DateField] = #" & varDate & "#"
```

That's a lot simpler than the string case.

Finally, numeric values require no delimiters at all, and you can simply represent a string variable using an expression like this:

```
"[NumericField] = " & intNumber
```

In each case the important issue is that you place the value of the variable into the string being sent off to FindFirst, rather than the name of the variable. The Jet engine (which ultimately receives the request to find a row) has no clue what to do with an Access Basic variable. It's up to your code to supply the value before requesting help from the Jet engine.

Using Bookmarks

One of the primary functions needed in any database product is the ability to move quickly to a specified row. Access provides a number of ways to move about in recordsets, as seen in the earlier section, "Moving Through a Recordset." In addition to the methods presented there, Access provides, for most recordsets, the Bookmark property.

What Is a Bookmark?

Every active recordset maintains a single current row. To retrieve a reference to that row, you can store the bookmark for that row. The bookmark itself is a string, the exact value of which is of no particular importance to you. Access uses the value, but under no circumstances can you use the value in any sort of calculation. You can perform two basic operations with bookmarks:

- Retrieve the value of the bookmark, in order to store it for later retrieval

- Set the value of the bookmark to a previously stored value, effectively setting the current row to be the row where you were when you originally saved the bookmark

You can retrieve and store as many bookmarks for a given recordset as you care to maintain. Manipulating bookmarks in Access is the fastest way to maneuver through rows. For example, if you need to move from the current row and then move back to it, you can use one of two methods:

- **Store the primary key value:** Move from the row, and use the Seek or Find-First method to move back to the original row, using the saved primary key value to find the row.

- **Store the bookmark:** Move from the row, and then use the bookmark to move back to the original row.

The second method, using the bookmark, is much faster than the first. The code to do this might look something like the following example:

```
Dim strBM as String

strBM = rst.Bookmark
' Move to the first row.
rst.MoveFirst
'
' Now do whatever you moved from the current row to do.
'
' Then move back to the original row.
rst.Bookmark = strBM
```

Bookmarks and Record Numbers

If you're moving to Access from an Xbase environment, you might be tempted to think of bookmarks as a replacement for record numbers. In reality, that's not the case. Since Access is set based, record numbers really have no validity here. Access neither stores nor maintains a record number in its data, and you can't count on a bookmark to act as a permanent locator for any given row. Once you close a recordset, the bookmark value is no longer valid. In addition, you cannot use bookmarks as locators across different recordsets, even though the recordsets might be based on the same data and might contain the same rows in the same order. On the other hand, as stated in the preceding section, bookmarks provide an excellent means of moving about in an open recordset.

To Bookmark or Not to Bookmark

Not all recordsets in Access support the Bookmark property. Some data sources make it impossible for Access to maintain bookmarks, so it is your responsibility as a developer to check the Bookmarkable property of a recordset before attempting to use bookmarks with that recordset. Any recordset based on native Access data always supports bookmarks, but external data may not. If the recordset does not support bookmarks, attempting to use the Bookmark property results in a trappable error (3159), "Not a valid bookmark."

Also be aware that there is no valid bookmark when you've positioned the current row to be the "new" row in a recordset. That is, the following code will trigger a run-time error (3021), "No Current Record":

```
rst.MoveLast
' Move to the "new" row.
rst.MoveNext
strBM = rst.Bookmark
```

We've used this fact several times throughout this book to find out whether the current row is, in fact, the "new" row. If an attempt to retrieve the bookmark fails, you know you're on the "new" row. For more information, see the section "At the New Record?" in Chapter 8.

> **TIP**
>
> Access 2.0 treats the new row differently than did Access 1.x. Previously Access did not create the bookmark for the new row until you saved it. Now Access creates the bookmark as soon as you add data to the row. Therefore, if you have code in your old applications that counts on the absence of a bookmark for the new row in any event besides a form's Current event, you may find that that code no longer handles the new row properly.

The Clone Method

Every recordset maintains a single "current" row, or *cursor*. For bookmarkable recordsets, you can use the Bookmark property to set and retrieve a marker for this row. If you need to refer to the same recordset in two different ways, with two different cursors, you can use the Clone method to create a clone of a recordset. With a clone of the original recordset, you can effectively maintain two separate "current" rows. This way you can compare the values in two of the rows in the recordset, for example.

You might be tempted to ask, "Why use the Clone method instead of just creating a new recordset based on the same source?" The answer is clear: creating a recordset clone is faster, in most cases, than creating a new Recordset object. When the source of the data is a querydef, the difference can be enormous. Rather than reexecuting the entire query to produce the new recordset, the Clone method just points a separate object variable at the original set of rows. This effectively gives you two current rows and two bookmarks, based on the same data. You can also assign the bookmark from one recordset to its clone since they really are the same recordset.

Be aware of these two issues:

- A recordset created with the Clone method does not have a current row. To set a specific row as being the current row, use any of the Find or Move methods (FirstFirst, MoveFirst, and so on) or set the recordset's Bookmark property with a value retrieved from the original recordset. Remember that bookmark assignments work only when applied to identical recordsets (which the original and its clone are).

- Using the Close method on either the original recordset or its clone doesn't affect the other recordset.

As an example of using the Clone method, imagine the following situation: you'd like to create a function to compare certain columns in the current row to see whether they have the same value as the same columns in the previous row. You could use the Clone method to handle this problem, as you'll see in Listing 6.12. In this case you just check the value in the Country field. This example also uses the form's RecordsetClone property to retrieve the underlying recordset, which is covered in the next section. The sample form, frmLookup in CH6.MDB, uses this function in the Current event of the form to display or hide a label if the current Country field has the same value as the field in the previous row. Figure 6.2 shows this form in action.

frmLookup displays or hides a label, based on the comparison of the current and previous values in the Country field.

Listing 6.12

```
Function CheckPreviousRow(frm As Form, strFieldName As String)
    Dim rst As Recordset
    Dim rstClone As Recordset

    ' Set rst to refer to the form's Recordset,
    ' and set its bookmark to match the form's.
    Set rst = frm.RecordSetClone
    rst.Bookmark = frm.Bookmark

    ' Now create the Recordset clone, and make it
    ' refer to the same row as rst, which is on the same
    ' row as the form.
    Set rstClone = rst.Clone()
    rstClone.Bookmark = rst.Bookmark

    ' Move the clone Recordset to the previous row.
    ' If this puts us at the BOF, then the result has to be
    ' FALSE, and leave the function.
    rstClone.MovePrevious
    If rstClone.BOF Then
        CheckPreviousRow = False
    Else
        ' If you're not at BOF, then retrieve
        ' the necessary info.
        CheckPreviousRow =
    ➡ (rst(strFieldName) = rstClone(strFieldName))
    End If
```

```
      rstClone.Close
End Function
```

The RecordsetClone Property

You use the RecordsetClone property to retrieve a reference to a form's recordset. Any bound form maintains its own recordset, the set of rows onto which the form provides a window. You'll often need to manipulate that set of rows without showing your work on the visible form. To do this you create a recordset based on the form's recordset and do your manipulations there. For example, the code in Listing 6.13, called from the AfterUpdate event of a combo box, searches for a specific company name on a form and sets the form to show the correct row once it finds a match. To see this form in action, try out frmLookup in CH6.MDB. Figure 6.3 shows this form in use.

FIGURE 6.3:

Choosing a name from the combo box forces the code in Listing 6.13 to locate the correct row.

Listing 6.13

```
Const QUOTE = """"
Sub cboCompany_AfterUpdate()
    Dim rst As Recordset

    Set rst = Me.RecordSetClone
    rst.FindFirst "[Company Name] = " & QUOTE &
    ➥ Me!cboCompany &QUOTE
    If rst.NoMatch Then
        MsgBox "No match was found. Something is REALLY wrong!"
    Else
```

```
        Me.Bookmark = rst.Bookmark
    End If
    rst.Close
End Sub
```

NOTE

Creating recordsets using the RecordsetClone property is the only place in Access Basic where you create a Recordset object without using the standard syntax (DBEngine.Workspaces(0).Databases(0), and so on). Because you're retrieving the record source from a form, Access treats this case a bit differently. The results are almost the same, though: you end up with a Recordset object variable referring to a recordset. The recordset you retrieve, however, doesn't support all the same properties as a real recordset. You can't set a form recordset's Filter or Sort property, for example.

Sorting Recordsets

When using recordsets as part of your applications, you'll often need to present the rows in a specific order. Again, Access treats table-type recordsets differently from dynaset and snapshot-type recordsets. For all objects, however, remember that unless you specify a sorting order, Access uses an unpredictable sorting order for the rows.

Sorting Table-Type Recordsets

For table-type recordsets you can specify the ordering by setting the Index property. (Access does not allow you to set the Index property of any other type of recordset. Attempting to do so will only get you a run-time error [3219], "Invalid Operation.") As soon as you set that property, the rows appear in their new ordering. After applying an index, Access appears to leave the current row at the same relative location in the recordset. That is, if you had moved to the first row before setting the Index property, the first row would still be current afterward. This behavior is not documented, however, and you would be wise to explicitly set the current row after setting the Index property.

Listing 6.14 shows a function that lists the first field in the index, in index order, for each index in a specified table. ListIndexFields() does its work by looping through the TableDef object's collection of indexes. For each index in the collection, it gathers up the index name and the first field's name and uses them to set the index and to print out the value of that field for each row in the recordset. To test ListIndexFields() you might want to create a table with just a few rows and create an index for a few of the columns. Then, in the Immediate window, enter

> ? ListIndexFields(*"YourTableName"*)

replacing *YourTableName* with the name of your table. This should show all the indexes in your table, with the first indexed field in indexed order. (Look for ListIndexFields() in basRecordset in CH6.MDB.)

Listing 6.14

```
Function ListIndexFields(strTable As String)
    Dim rst As Recordset
    Dim db As Database
    Dim tdf As TableDef
    Dim strField As String
    Dim idx As Index
    Dim intI as Integer

    Set db = DbEngine.Workspaces(0).Databases(0)
    Set tdf = db.TableDefs(strTable)
    Set rst = db.OpenRecordset(strTable, DB_OPEN_TABLE)
    ' List values for each index in the collection.
    For intI = 0 To tdf.Indexes.Count - 1
        Set idx = tdf.Indexes(intI)
        rst.Index = idx.Name
        ' The index object contains a collection of fields,
        ' one for each field the index contains.  This
        ' example will only show the first field in the index.
        strField = idx.Fields(0).Name
        Debug.Print
        Debug.Print "Index is: " & rst.Index
        Debug.Print "==========================="
        ' Move through the whole Recordset, in index order,
        ' printing out the first index field.
        rst.MoveFirst
        Do While Not rst.EOF
            Debug.Print rst(strField)
```

```
            rst.MoveNext
        Loop
     Next intI
     rst.Close
End Function
```

Sorting Dynaset and Snapshot-Type Recordsets

Just as with table-type recordsets, unless you specify a sorting order for dynaset and snapshot-type recordsets, the rows will show up in an indeterminate order. The natural order for these derived recordsets is a bit more complex since it might depend on more than one table. In any case, if you need a specific ordering, you must set up that ordering yourself. Don't rely on natural ordering at any time in Access—it is not reliable for all circumstances.

To create sorted dynaset or snapshot-type recordsets, you have two choices, outlined in the next two sections.

Using a SQL ORDER BY Clause

You can create a Recordset object using a SQL statement including an ORDER BY clause. To do so, specify the SQL expression as the row source for the OpenRecordset() method. For example, this fragment:

```
Set db = DBEngine.Workspaces(0).Databases(0)
Set rstSorted = db.OpenRecordset(
➡ "SELECT * FROM tblCustomers ORDER BY [LastName];")
```

creates a recordset based on tblCustomers, including all the columns, sorted by the LastName column. You can base a recordset on a SQL string only when creating recordsets based on a database object (as opposed to other uses of OpenRecordset(), which can be based on tables, queries, or other recordsets). Attempting to do so will get you a run-time error (3001), "Invalid Argument." Creating a recordset using a SQL expression creates a dynaset-type recordset.

Using the Sort Property

You can set the Sort property of any non–table-based recordset to change its sort order. The Sort property must be a string, in the same style as the ORDER BY clause of a SQL expression. You must specify the column on which to sort and, optionally, the ordering. The next time you create a recordset based on this recordset, the new sort order will take effect. (This is different from the way table-type recordset sorting works; there, the sorting takes effect immediately.) The following fragments show how to set the Sort property:

```
rst.Sort = "[LastName]"          ' Defaults to ascending
rst.Sort = "[LastName] Asc"      ' Ascending sort
rst.Sort = "[LastName] Desc"     ' Descending sort
```

Here are some things to remember when using the Sort property:

- The new sort order doesn't take effect until you create a new recordset, based on the old one.

- The Sort property doesn't apply to table-type recordsets. Use the Index property for them.

- It might be faster to open a new recordset based on a SQL expression than to use the Sort property.

The following code shows two methods for creating a sorted dynaset-type recordset:

```
Dim db As Database
Dim rst As Recordset
Dim rstSorted1 As Recordset
Dim rstSorted2 As Recordset

Set db = DBEngine.Workspaces(0).Databases(0)
' Create a sorted Recordset using SQL.
Set rstSorted1 = db.OpenRecordset(
➡ "SELECT * FROM tblCustomers ORDER BY [LastName];")
' Create a sorted Recordset based on an existing Recordset.
Set rst = db.OpenRecordset("tblCustomers" DB_OPEN_DYNASET)
rst.Sort = "[LastName]"
Set rstSorted2 = rst.OpenRecordset()
'
' Do whatever you need to do here with the sorted recordsets
'
rst.Close
rstSorted1.Close
rstSorted2.Close
```

Filtering Non-Table Recordsets

Just as with sorting a recordset, you have two choices if you want to create a filtered subset of rows. These choices are outlined in the next two sections. You'll need to decide which method to use based on the circumstances of your application.

Using a SQL WHERE Clause

You can create a recordset by using a SQL statement including a WHERE clause. To do so, specify the SQL expression as the row source for the OpenRecordset method. For example, this fragment:

```
Set db = DBEngine.Workspaces(0).Databases(0)
Set rstSorted=db.OpenRecordset(
➡ "SELECT * FROM tblCustomers WHERE [ZipCode] = '90210';")
```

creates a recordset based on all the columns in tblCustomers, including only the rows where the ZipCode field is "90210". You can use this method only when creating recordsets based on a database object (as opposed to other uses of OpenRecordset(), which can be based on tables, queries, or other recordsets). Attempting to do otherwise will get you a run-time error (3001), "Invalid Argument."

Using the Filter Property

You can also set the Filter property of any non-table recordset to change the set of rows it contains. The Filter property must be a string, in the same style as the WHERE clause of a SQL expression. The next time you create a recordset based on this recordset, the new filtering will take effect. For example, you generally use the Filter property like this:

```
' rst is an existing recordset.
rst.Filter = "[Age] > 35"
Set rstFiltered = rst.OpenRecordset()
' Now rstFiltered contains all the rows from rst that
' have an [Age] field greater than 35.
```

Here are some things to remember when using the Filter property:

- The new filtering doesn't take effect until you create a new recordset, based on the old one.

- The Filter property doesn't apply to table-type recordsets.

- It might be faster to open a new recordset based on a SQL expression than to use the Filter property.

The following code shows two methods for creating a filtered dynaset-type recordset:

```
Dim db As Database
Dim rst As Recordset
Dim rstSQL as Recordset
Dim rstFiltered As Recordset

Set db = DBEngine.Workspaces(0).Databases(0)
Set rstSQL = db.OpenRecordset(
➡ "SELECT * FROM tblCustomers WHERE [ZipCode] = '90210';")
Set rst = db.OpenRecordset("tblCustomers" DB_OPEN_DYNASET)
rst.Filter= "[ZipCode] = '90210'"
Set rstFiltered = rst.OpenRecordset()
```

Editing Data in a Recordset Object

Of course, any database application needs to be able to add, update, and delete data. Access provides methods to accomplish each of these tasks. The next few sections discuss the various data-manipulation methods that Access supports.

When Is a Recordset Modifiable?

You can modify data, of course, only if you have permission to do so. When you open a recordset, you may be able to retrieve the data for viewing only. If so, your attempts to modify the data will result in a run-time trappable error. You can always edit table-type recordsets unless someone else has placed a lock on that table (opened it exclusively or created a recordset based on it with an option that precludes others from changing its data). You can edit dynaset-type recordsets unless locks have been placed by other users, just as with table-type recordsets. In addition, join rules may prevent editing of certain fields. (For more information on join-based editing rules, see Chapter 3.) Snapshot-type recordsets are never modifiable since they're read-only by definition.

Changing Data in a Recordset

To change the data in any recordset from Access Basic (assuming that the recordset is updatable), take the following steps:

1. Move to the desired row.

2. Use the Edit method to put the current row in edit mode.

3. Make changes.

4. Use the Update method to save the edits.

Skipping any of these steps will lead to undesirable results. The most important step, however, is the final one. If you make changes to the row but forget to use the Update method to commit those changes, Access treats the row as if you'd never made any changes at all.

The following code finds the first row in the dynaset-type recordset in which the LastName field contains "Smith" and changes it to "Smythe":

```
rst.FindFirst "[LastName] = 'Smith'"
If rst.NoMatch Then
    MsgBox "No Match was Found!"
Else
    rst.Edit
        rst![LastName] = "Smythe"
    rst.Update
End If
```

Adding New Records to a Recordset

To add new rows to a recordset from Access Basic (assuming that neither updatability nor security keeps you from doing so), follow these steps:

1. Use the AddNew method to add a new row. (All fields will be set to Null.)

2. Fill in fields as needed.

3. Use the Update method to save the new row.

As in the preceding section, if you neglect to call the Update method before you leave the current row, Access discards any changes you've made and does not add the new row.

When you use the AddNew method, the current row remains the row that was current before you added the new row. If you want to make the new row be the current row, use the Move method, using as its parameter the bookmark returned from the LastModified property of the recordset.

The following example adds a new row to the recordset and fills in a few of the fields. Once it's done, it makes the new row the current row:

```
rst.AddNew
    rst![LastName] = "Smith"
    rst![FirstName] = "Tommy"
rst.Update
rst.Move 0, rst.LastModified
```

Dynaset-type recordsets treat new rows a bit differently than do table-type recordsets. For a dynaset-type Recordset object, Access always places the new row at the end of the recordset. For table-type recordsets, if you've set the Index property, Access places the row at its correct spot in the index. For dynaset-type recordsets, Access adds the new row to the underlying table. If you're working with a table-type recordset, though, new rows added to the table won't be seen by users who've based a recordset on that table until they refresh their rows.

In a multiuser situation, attempting to add a new row might cause a locking error. In terms of locking issues, when you use the AddNew method and Access must create a new page to hold the new record, page locking is pessimistic. If the new record will fit in an existing page, page locking is optimistic. If the final row has been locked by another user adding a row, you'll get an error (3186), "Couldn't save; currently locked by user...." To take care of this error, set an error handler that will deal with error 3186 by trying to save the record again. You can do this in a loop, with a finite number of attempts. Handle other errors as necessary. For more information on locking mechanisms, see Chapter 11.

Deleting Data from a Recordset

To delete a row from a recordset, follow these steps:

1. Move to the desired row.

2. Use the Delete method to delete it.

> **TIP**
>
> Unlike the other methods of modifying rows, you don't need to use the Update methods when deleting a row. Once you delete it, it's gone—unless, of course, you wrapped the entire thing in a transaction. In that case you can roll back the transaction to retrieve the deleted row.

> **TIP**
>
> After you delete a record, it is still the current record. The previous row is still the previous row, and the next row is still the next row. Use MoveNext to move to the next row, if that's where you'd like to be.

The code in Listing 6.15 deletes all the rows from a table, although it is, of course, the slowest way to do so. In reality, you'd use a delete query to do the work. To try this function out, check in basRecordset in CH6.MDB.

Listing 6.15

```
Function ZapTable (strTable As String)
    Dim rst As Recordset
    Dim db As Database
    Dim wrk As WorkSpace
```

```
        Set wrk = DBEngine.WorkSpaces(0)
        Set db = wrk.Databases(0)
        Set rst = db.OpenRecordset(strTable)
        ' See the next section for more information on using
        ' transactions to speed updates, edits, and deletes.
        wrk.BeginTrans
        rst.MoveFirst
        Do
            rst.Delete
            ' Without this MoveNext, Access would continually try
            ' to delete the same row, the first one.
            rst.MoveNext
        Loop Until rst.EOF
        wrk.CommitTrans
        rst.Close
End Function
```

Using Transactions to Speed Recordset Operations

Any recordset operations that change data can benefit dramatically from using transactions. Transactions are primarily intended for allowing rollbacks and commits of bulk data changes (see Chapter 11 for more details on transactions), but since transactions buffer data reads and writes, you can use them to speed up update, edit, and delete operations. Begin a transaction after opening the recordset but before you make any changes. Commit the transaction after you've made the last change but before you close the recordset.

Listing 6.15 uses this technique to speed the row deletions. It starts a transaction before the first row change and commits it after the final change.

Before using transactions in this way, there are some things you should know:

- Access 1.x benefitted from transactions to speed access only when you didn't open a database for exclusive use. Access 2.0 benefits from transactions regardless of how you open the database.

- Always be sure to close all your object variables before you leave each procedure. Under normal circumstances this is just good programming practice. In procedures that you call from within a transaction, however, failure to do so can lead to problems and erroneous error messages.

Using Containers to Handle Saved Documents

A *container* object contains information about saved database objects. Some of the containers are provided by the Jet engine and some by the application. Table 6.5 lists the containers, the parent for each container, and what each contains.

Each container object contains a collection of documents, each of which is an object in the database. A container object containing the tables, however, doesn't contain the data that's in those tables. It just contains information about the particular saved objects that exist inside the database. For example, you could retrieve the permissions, the date of creation, and the owner of particular documents by perusing a container object.

Each container object acts like a bag that holds non-engine objects. The Jet engine can get very limited information about them, such as their creator and creation time, through DAO. This allows the engine to know, in a limited sense, about the objects that are application specific. The main significance of containers is that they

- Give you information about the live Access objects; that is, they give you a mechanism you can use to walk through collections of non-DAO objects

- Provide the only method for retrieving information about your saved macros, modules, reports, and forms

- Let you treat non-engine objects as if they were data access objects instead of application-provided objects; that is, they let you use the set of DAO rules and tools with non-DAO objects

Since security is provided at the engine level, Jet has to know about non-DAO objects so it can handle their security. For more information on this topic, see Chapter 22.

To refer to a particular container, use the syntax

Containers("*name*")

where *name* is one of the items in the first column from Table 6.5.

TABLE 6.5: Containers and Their Parents

Container	Parent	Contains Information about
Databases	Jet database engine	Containing database
Tables	Jet database engine	Saved tables and queries
Relationships	Jet database engine	Saved relationships
Forms	Microsoft Access	Saved forms
Reports	Microsoft Access	Saved reports
Scripts	Microsoft Access	Saved macros
Modules	Microsoft Access	Saved modules

NOTE   The Forms and Reports containers are very different from the Forms and Reports collections. Using the containers, you can work with any forms or reports in the database. Using the collections, you can refer only to currently opened forms and reports.

A Case Study: Using DAO

As an example of using DAO as part of an application, we've provided a simple replacement for the database container (see Figure 6.4) that you can import into any application. You can use it directly as is, or you can modify it to add new functionality. You might want to remove some of the objects for your own applications. For example, you might like to provide users with a list of only certain tables and queries. Perhaps you don't want to show your users a list of macros or modules. Given frmDBC as a starting place, you can make as many changes as you like to fit your own needs. The point of the sample is to demonstrate the use of DAO when dealing with table and query objects and the Access-specific code to deal with the other database objects: forms, reports, macros, and modules.

The sample database container is simpler than the one you'll find in Access 2.0, but it provides many of the same features.

Designing frmDBC

The design considerations for frmDBC were to

- Provide a list of all the tables, queries, forms, reports, macros, and modules in the current database
- Provide the same functionality as the Access database container
- Allow resizing of the list to match the size of the form
- Allow for customization

The following sections discuss the form itself and how it does its work.

Choosing an Object Type and an Action

The buttons on the left side of frmDBC are part of an option group (grpObjects). When you click one of the buttons, the code attached to the option group's AfterUpdate event refills the list box (lstObjects) that displays the list of objects. The particular list that lstObjects displays depends, of course, on the value of grpObjects.

To make the code as simple as possible, we've used the intrinsic Access Basic constants A_TABLE, A_QUERY, A_FORM, A_REPORT, A_MACRO, and A_MODULE wherever possible. These constants provide the values for the buttons in the option group and make up the choices available in all the Select Case statements within the code. Whenever possible, use the Access-defined constants in your code.

Once you've chosen an object type (and forced the list box to refill itself) and once you've selected an object from the list, you can select one of the action buttons at the top of the form (New, Open, or Design). Depending on the circumstances, one or more of those buttons might have a different caption and might be disabled.

Visual Effects and Speed (or Lack Thereof)

We attempted to make the faux-database container as similar as possible to the real one to give you a recognizable starting point. Although it would be possible to emulate the "tabbed" look of the Access 2.0 database container, we decided that time would be better spent on the workings of the form than on the look of the buttons.

On the other hand, the list box does resize to fit the form, no matter what size you choose for the form itself. This trick can be performed because of the modifiability of control characteristics at run time. Everytime the form fires off its Resize event, the code figures out the current form size and resizes the list box inside the form accordingly. For more information on modifying controls and their sizes based on the size of the parent form, see Chapter 8.

NOTE   Everytime you resize a list box, Access forces it to requery its record source. In this case you'll find this requery totally unnecessary, and it occurs several times for each resize. Therefore, we've played a little trick. Before the code actually performs the resize, it stores the list box's RowSourceType property. (The list box is filled from a list-filling function, so the information is stored in the RowSourceType property.) After it's done resizing the control, it resets the RowSourceType property. Of course, this forces one requery, but at least it's only one, and not three or more. You may want to try this mechanism yourself whenever you need to modify the properties of a list or combo box and find that it's taking longer than you'd like.

Finally, you'll probably notice that filling the list using frmDBC takes significantly longer than the corresponding action using the real database container. This shouldn't be surprising; Access keeps this information internally and uses a low-level language to fill the list. FrmDBC must enumerate through the database's DAO and then must use slow Access Basic to fill the list. If this weren't a chapter on DAO, however, we might have used a different method to fill the list. The system table, MSysObjects, maintains a complete set of information about every object in the database. The Type column contains an integer describing each object, and the types are listed in the following table. You could query the information in this table to fill the list.

Object	Type Value in MsysObjects
Table	1
Query	5
Form	−32768
Report	−32764
Macro	−32761
Module	−32766

Any and/or all of these values could change at any time. Since this information is not documented and since Microsoft continues to dissuade developers from counting on any specific information in the system tables, any reliance you make on this information is strictly at your own risk. On the other hand, reading information from MSysObjects (which is read-only, by the way) is certainly faster than enumerating through DAO. If you feel you must, you could alter the FillList() function in frmDBC to use the information in the system tables, rather than calling GetObjectList().

Displaying the Object List

For this example you use a list-filling callback function to fill the list of objects. For more information on the mechanics of writing and using these functions, see Chapter 7. For now, the important issue is filling an array with a list of all the objects of a particular type. Access calls the function ListObjects(), in frmDBC's module, when it needs to fill the list. The most important piece of ListObjects() is the call to GetObjectList(), which fills in a dynamic array (astrObjects()) with a list of all the objects of the type specified by grpObjects (the option group on the form).

```
Set DB = DBEngine.Workspaces(0).Databases(0)
intCount = GetObjectList(DB, grpObjects, astrObjects( ), False,
➡ QRY_ANYTYPE, False)
```

The function GetObjectList() takes six parameters, described in the following table, and returns the number of objects it found. Once ListObjects() gets the list it needs from GetObjectList(), it can display it in the list box.

Parameter	Datatype	Description
DB	Database	A reference to the current database
intType	Integer	One of A_TABLE, A_QUERY, and so on

Parameter	Datatype	Description
astrList()	String array (dynamic)	Array to hold the returned list
fIncSysObjs	Integer	Include the system objects in the list?
fIncThisForm	Integer	Include the current form in the list?

Filling the Object List

The function GetObjectList() is the heart of this entire form. Given a reference to the current database and a value indicating which object type it should check on, it fills the array it's been passed with a list of all the items of the requested type. Listing 6.16 shows the entire function, and the following paragraphs go through the code, one bit at a time.

Listing 6.16

```
Function GetObjectList(DB As Database, intType As Integer,
➡ astrList() As String, fIncSysObjs As Integer,
➡ lngFlags As Long, fIncThisForm As Integer)

    ' Fill an array with a list of objects of a given type.
    ' Parameters:
    '  DB -- a database reference
    '  intType -- one of A_TABLE, A_QUERY, A_FORM,
    '             A_REPORT, A_MACRO or A_MODULE
    '  astrList() -- the dynamic string array to be filled in
    '  fIncSysObjs -- Include System objects (Yes/No)
    '  lngFlags -- special flags about the list (for example,
    '              you could specify the query type here)
    '  fIncThisForm -- Show the current form name? (Yes/No)
    '
    ' Fills in astrList() with the list of object names.
    ' Returns the number of objects added to the list.
```

```
Dim intCount As Integer
Dim intNumObjs As Integer
Dim intI As Integer
Dim fSystemObj As Integer
Dim ctr As Container
Dim strName As String

Const OBJ_HIDDEN = &H1

intCount = 0

On Error GoTo GetObjectListError
DoCmd Hourglass True
Select Case intType
    Case A_TABLE
        DB.TableDefs.Refresh
        ' Get the number of tables and
        ' make the array that size.
        intNumObjs = DB.TableDefs.Count
        ReDim astrList(intNumObjs)

        Dim tbl As TableDef
        For intI = 0 To intNumObjs - 1
            Set tbl = DB.TableDefs(intI)
            ' Check and see if this is a system object.
            fSystemObj = isSystemObject(A_TABLE,
        ➥ tbl.Name, tbl.Attributes)
            ' Unless this is a system object and you're not
            ' showing system objects, or this table has its
            ' hidden bit set, add it to the list.
            If (fSystemObj Imp fIncSysObjs) And
        ➥ ((tbl.Attributes And OBJ_HIDDEN) = 0) Then
                astrList(intCount) = tbl.Name
                intCount = intCount + 1
            End If
        Next intI
    Case A_QUERY
        DB.QueryDefs.Refresh
        ' Get the number of queries and
        ' make the array that size.
        intNumObjs = DB.QueryDefs.Count
        ReDim astrList(intNumObjs)
```

```
            Dim qry As QueryDef
            For intI = 0 To intNumObjs - 1
                Set qry = DB.QueryDefs(intI)
                ' Check and see if this is a system object.
                fSystemObj = isSystemObject(
              ➥ A_QUERY, qry.Name, 0)
                ' Unless this is a system object and you're not
                ' showing system objects, or it's the wrong
                ' query type, add it to the list.
                If (fSystemObj Imp fIncSysObjs) Then
                    If ((qry.Type = lngFlags) Or
                  ➥ (lngFlags = QRY_ANYTYPE)) Then
                        astrList(intCount) = qry.Name
                        intCount = intCount + 1
                    End If
                End If
            Next intI
        Case A_FORM
            Set ctr = DB.Containers("Forms")
        Case A_REPORT
            Set ctr = DB.Containers("Reports")
        Case A_MACRO
            Set ctr = DB.Containers("Scripts")
        Case A_MODULE
            Set ctr = DB.Containers("Modules")
    End Select
    Select Case intType
        Case A_FORM, A_REPORT, A_MACRO, A_MODULE
            ctr.Documents.Refresh
            intNumObjs = ctr.Documents.Count

            ReDim astrList(intNumObjs)
            For intI = 0 To intNumObjs - 1
                strName = ctr.Documents(intI).Name
                fSystemObj = isSystemObject(
              ➥ intType, strName, 0)
                ' Unless this is a system object and you're not
                ' showing system objects add it to the list.
                If (fSystemObj Imp fIncSysObjs) Then
                        ' If it's not true that you're to skip
                        ' this form and you've hit this form in the
                        ' container, add the item to the list.
                        If Not (Not fIncThisForm And
                      ➥ (intType = A_FORM) And
                      ➥(strName = Me.Name)) And
```

```
              ➥ Not isDeleted(strName) Then
                  astrList(intCount) =
                  ➥ ctr.Documents(intI).Name
                  intCount = intCount + 1
              End If
          End If
      Next intI
  End Select
GetObjectListExit:
  DoCmd Hourglass False
  GetObjectList = intCount
  Exit Function

GetObjectListError:
  HandleErrors Err, "GetObjectList"
  ' If there was an error, better reset
  ' the count of objects back to 0.
  intCount = 0
  Resume GetObjectListExit
End Function
```

The main body of GetObjectList(), once it's initialized local variables and set up the environment by turning on the hourglass cursor, consists of a Select Case statement with one case for each of the possible object types. For tables and queries, the code uses DAO methods to compile the list. For forms, report, macros, and modules, the code uses Access' version of DAO, its containers, to iterate through the different objects.

Creating a List of Tables

The first step in compiling the list of tables is to refresh the TableDefs collection. This ensures that the collection is completely current and contains the entire list. Then you can retrieve the count of objects in the collection and resize the passed-in dynamic array so it's large enough to hold the entire list of items:

```
DB.TableDefs.Refresh
' Get the number of tables and make the array that size.
intNumObjs = DB.TableDefs.Count
ReDim astrList(intNumObjs)
```

Once you know the number of tables in the collection, you can loop through each of the tabledefs, assigning the variable tdf to refer to each, in turn:

```
Dim tdf As TableDef
For intI = 0 To intNumObjs - 1
    Set tdf = DB.TableDefs(intI)
    '
    '
Next intI
```

Deciding Whether to Add a Table

For each particular tabledef, you may or may not want to add it to the output array. If you have not requested that the function include system tables and the current table is a system table, you'll want to skip it and not add it to the output array. In any case, skip tables that have their hidden attribute set.

```
fSystemObj = isSystemObject(A_TABLE, tdf.Name, tdf.Attributes)
' Unless this is a system object and you're not showing system
' objects, or this table has its hidden bit set,
' add it to the list.
If (fSystemObj Imp fIncSysObjs) And Not
➥ (tdf.Attributes And OBJ_HIDDEN) Then
    astrList(intCount) = tdf.Name
    intCount = intCount + 1
End If
```

Checking for System Objects

The first step in the preceding code was to determine whether or not the current table is a system object. To determine this you can call the function isSystemObject():

```
Function isSystemObject(intType As Integer,
➥ ByVal strName As String, ByVal lngAttribs As Long)

    If (strName Like "USys*") Then
        isSystemObject = True
    Else
        isSystemObject = ((intType = A_TABLE) And
        ➥ ((lngAttribs And DB_SYSTEMOBJECT) <> 0))
    End If
End Function
```

In two instances the current object could be treated as a system object:

- The name of the object is Usys followed by any text. This naming convention allows the user to create objects that Access will display, in the database container, only when the Show System Objects option is set to Yes.

- The object is a table, and its Attribute field has its DB_SYSTEMOBJECT bit set.

Using "Like" in Access Basic

Unlike Access 1.x, Access 2.0 allows the use of the Like operator in Access Basic. Thus, you can now use expressions like

```
If (strName Like "USys*") Then
```

This does not extend to the In or Between operator, however.

Using Bitwise Operators to Check Attributes

Checking to see whether a particular attribute has been set for an object requires you to use the bitwise And operator. The And operator returns a nonzero value if the value you're checking and the appropriate intrinsic constant (DB_SYSTEMOBJECT, in this case) have at least one bit set in the same positions. Therefore, to check whether a particular object is a system table, you can use the following expression:

```
isSystemObject = ((intType = A_TABLE) And
➥ ((lngAttribs And DB_SYSTEMOBJECT) <> 0))
```

This expression returns a True value if both parts of the expression are True; that is, if the type is A_TABLE and the bitwise comparison of the object's attribute and DB_SYSTEMOBJECT isn't 0.

Checking for Inclusion

You'll want to include the table in your list unless one of the following situations exists:

- Its attribute includes the bit that indicates that the table is to be hidden.
- You've asked to not include system tables, and this table is a system table.

To check whether the table's attribute includes the Hidden bit, you need to check the return value from ANDing it with OBJ_HIDDEN (1). If

```
tdf.Attributes AND OBJ_HIDDEN
```

returns a non-zero value, the matching bit is set in both values.

You also need to check whether or not to include a table, based on whether you've requested to include system tables and whether this particular table is a system table. Based on these two conditions, you have four possible outcomes, as shown in Table 6.6.

TABLE 6.6: Decision Table for System Table Inclusion

System Table?	Include System Tables?	Include This Table?
Yes	Yes	Yes
Yes	No	No
No	Yes	Yes
No	No	Yes

As you can see in Table 6.6, you'll want to include the current table in the output array unless the current table is a system table and you've elected not to include system tables. You could build a complex logical expression to indicate this information to Access, but Access makes this a bit simpler by providing a single logical operator that works exactly as you need.

The IMP (implication) operator takes two values and returns a True value *unless* the first operand is True and the second is False. This exactly matches the truth table shown in Table 6.6. Given that the variable fSystemObj indicates whether or not the current table is a system object and the variable fIncSysObjs indicates whether or not you want to include system objects, you can use the expression

```
fSystemObj IMP fIncSysObjs
```

to know whether to exclude the table based on whether or not it's a system table. Therefore, to check both criteria for inclusion, you can use the following expression:

```
If (fSystemObj Imp fIncSysObjs) And
➥ Not(tdf.Attributes And OBJ_HIDDEN)
➥ Then
```

This expression returns a True value if both parts return a True value.

Adding the Table

Once you've decided that a particular table is to be added to the list of tables, you'll want to place the Name property of the current tabledef to the output array and then increment the count of objects:

```
astrList(intCount) = tdf.Name
intCount = intCount + 1
```

When the loop is done, the output array, astrList(), will contain one item for each acceptable table in the database.

Creating a List of Queries

To create a list of queries, the steps are almost completely parallel to the steps necessary to create a list of tables. The following sections discuss the few differences.

Using Different Datatypes

To manipulate queries rather than tables, you need to use querydef variables instead of tabledef variables. Therefore, the initialization code, when you are building the query list, looks like this:

```
DB.QueryDefs.Refresh
' Get the number of queries and
' make the array that size.
intNumObjs = DB.QueryDefs.Count
ReDim astrList(intNumObjs)
```

```
Dim qry As QueryDef
For intI = 0 To intNumObjs - 1
    Set qry = DB.QueryDefs(intI)
    '
    '
Next intI
```

Besides the changes from tabledef to querydef references, the code is identical to the code dealing with tables.

Checking for System Objects

Since queries can't be system objects in the normal sense, the only way isSystemObject() will return True is if the query has a name that starts with *Usys*. Therefore, in the call to isSystemObject(), there's no point in passing in the object's attribute since you aren't really interested in checking the attribute to see whether the query is a system object. The function call is

```
fSystemObj = isSystemObject(A_QUERY, qry.Name, 0)
```

The third parameter, the object's attributes value, could actually be anything since isSystemObject() looks at the attribute only if the object happens to be a table.

Checking the Query Type

The fifth parameter to GetObjectList(), lngFlags, allows you to indicate exactly which type of queries you'd like to find in the output array. If you pass a specific query type, the code returns only queries of that type. If you pass in the constant QRY_ANYTYPE, the function returns queries of any type. The following code shows these steps:

```
' Unless this is a system object and you're not showing system
' objects, or it's the wrong query type, add it to the list.
If (fSystemObj Imp fIncSysObjs) Then
    If ((qry.Type = lngFlags) Or (lngFlags = QRY_ANYTYPE)) Then
```

In summary, aside from the differences noted, gathering a list of queries is just like gathering a list of tables. Both use DAO to enumerate the collections, and both use Jet engine-provided properties to know whether or not to include the object in the output array.

Gathering Lists of Access Objects

Although the lists of objects in your Access database besides tables and queries aren't handled by the Jet engine and aren't technically part of data access objects, we discuss them here just to complete the description of the replacement database container. From the users' point of view, there's no difference between Jet objects and Access objects, but from the developer's point of view, they're really separate entities.

Finding a Container

If you've asked GetObjectList() to retrieve a list of the available forms, reports, macros, or modules, you won't be enumerating through a Jet collection. Instead, you'll be looping through one of four different Access containers. Since one container can be treated like any other, your first step is to create a variable of type Container to refer to the correct Access container. The following is the code from GetObjectList() that performs this task:

```
Case A_FORM
    Set ctr = DB.Containers("Forms")
Case A_REPORT
    Set ctr = DB.Containers("Reports")
Case A_MACRO
    Set ctr = DB.Containers("Scripts")
Case A_MODULE
    Set ctr = DB.Containers("Modules")
```

Looping Through the Containers

Once you've pointed the variable ctr at a particular container, the code to loop through all the elements of the container should look very familiar. Once you've determined that the current object matches the caller's interest in system objects, you have two new problems to handle:

- If this object is a form, should you list the current form?

- Is this object deleted? Access doesn't immediately remove deleted objects from the containers, and you won't want to display these objects in the list.

One of the parameters you passed to GetObjectList(), fIncThisForm, indicates whether or not you want to include the current form in the list. Therefore, the following line of code excludes the current form name from the list, as well as any deleted objects:

```
If Not (Not fIncThisForm And (intType = A_FORM) And
➥ (strName = Me.Name)) And Not isDeleted(strName) Then
```

The isDeleted() function takes a very low-tech approach to checking for deleted objects:

```
Private Function isDeleted (ByVal strName As String)
    isDeleted = (strName Like "~TMP*")
End Function
```

It just looks for object names that start with ~TMP, which is how Access renames deleted objects.

Finishing It Up

Finally, once you've filled in the array of items, GetObjectList() returns the count of items in the array that it's filled in. The calling function, ListObjects(), uses that count to know how many items to display.

Using frmDBC in Your Own Application

To use frmDBC in your own applications, just import it. Since all the code it needs to run is encapsulated in its module, there's nothing else you need. You might want to consider, however, making various alterations to it. For example, you might want to add some columns or remove some of the toggle buttons that appear along the left side of the form. In any case, the sample form was left simple so you can modify it for your own needs. Probably the only serious complication you will run across is the resizing of the list box. You'll need to decide for yourself how resizing the form will affect the resizing of individual columns.

Undocumented Object Syntax

Digging through the Access 2.0 Wizards, you'll come across some interesting syntax and DLL calls that aren't documented in the *Language Reference* manual. Although Microsoft neither supports nor condones the use of undocumented features, if they're used in the Wizards you can feel relatively safe that they're going to be around for a while. If the Wizard developers need the features, they're likely to survive and remain supported by Access. Although the syntax demonstrated in this section isn't officially documented, the Wizards do use it and Visual Basic uses it, as does VBA in Excel. This section examines the undocumented object syntax, and Chapter 21 covers the undocumented DLL calls.

Comparing Two Object References

You may need at some point to know whether two object variables refer to the same object. To compare two simple variables, you can just check their equality:

```
If intX = intY Then ...
```

If you try the same syntax with object variables, Access complains at compile-time that the variables have no value and that you can't compare them. It's true—they have no real value. They're just references to objects. If you were programming in C, you could just compare the values of the pointers to see whether they were pointing to the same location. In BASIC, however, you can't do that.

To solve this problem, BASIC uses the Is operator. The only documented uses of Is in Access are these:

If TypeOf *control* Is *someType* Then...

and

Select Case *someVar*

    Case 1,2,3, Is > 10

and

If *someValue* Is Null Then...

You actually can compare two object variables using the syntax

If *objectVar1* Is *objectVar2* Then...

This expression will be True if both *objectVar1* and *objectVar2* point to the same object. To check the opposite case, use an expression like this:

If Not *objectVar1* Is *objectVar2* Then…

For example, suppose you need to write a function that compares all the data in two recordsets and returns a True or False value, depending on whether all the data is the same. If the two recordset variables that get passed to this function actually refer to the same object, then there's nothing to do, and your function should just return a True value.

You should note in these examples that calling the OpenRecordset method twice and assigning the return value to the two variables does *not* create two references to the same object. Those two calls to OpenRecordset() create two separate objects. They refer to the same data, but the objects themselves are distinct. To end up with two object variables that refer to the same object, you must either assign them to refer to the same persistent object (such as a tabledef or querydef) or assign one to point to an object you create and then assign a second to refer to the first, as in this fragment:

```
Set rst1 = db.OpenRecordset("tblCustomers")
Set rst2 = rst1
```

In this fragment both rst1 and rst2 will refer to the same object: the recordset created by the call to OpenRecordset(). In the next fragment qdf1 and qdf2 will refer to the same object since the assigned object is a single persistent querydef:

```
Set qdf1 = db.QueryDefs("qryCustomers")
Set qdf2 = db.QueryDefs("qryCustomers")
' The next line prints -1 (TRUE) in the immediate window.
Debug.Print qdf1 Is qdf2
```

The two code fragments that follow show the skeleton of the data comparison function and a test routine to give it a try. In TestIt(), the first call to CompareData() will return False since it's comparing two different references to the same data. The second call will return True since it passes two identical object variables.

```
Function CompareData(rst1 As Recordset, rst2 As Recordset)
    If rst1 Is rst2 Then
        CompareData = True
    Else
        ' Now do the real comparisons
        '
```

```
            ' For now, let's just return False
            CompareData = False
        End If
End Function

Function TestIt()
    Dim rst1 As Recordset
    Dim rst2 As Recordset
    Dim db As Database

    Set db = DBEngine.Workspaces(0).Databases(0)
    Set rst1 = db.OpenRecordset("tblCustomers")
    Set rst2 = db.OpenRecordset("tblCustomers")
    ' This will return FALSE for now,
    ' since rst1 and rst2 do not point to the same
    ' exact object.
    Debug.Print CompareData(rst1, rst2)

    Set rst2 = rst1
    ' This will return TRUE, since rst1 and rst2
    ' point to the exact same object.
    Debug.Print CompareData(rst1, rst2)
    rst1.Close
    ' Not only is there no need to close rst2, you can't do it.
    ' Since rst1 and rst2 refer to the exact same object,
    ' once you close rst1, you can't even use rst2 in your
    ' code, since the object to which it points no longer
    ' exists.
End Function
```

NOTE   For some reason Access does not support the *"objectVar1* Is *object-Var2"* syntax for Document objects. We've tested it with all the other object types, but Access will not compile code that attempts to use this syntax to compare two document objects. As with any other undocumented technology, the reason behind this is, "It does what it does."

Using Nothing

When a variant-type variable has not yet been initialized, its value is Empty. You can use the IsEmpty() function to see whether the variant has ever had a value assigned to it. This concept is available for object variables, too, although this functionality isn't documented. This operation uses the built-in value Nothing (a built-in constant like Null). The next two sections cover the use of Nothing.

Checking for Nothing

If you want to check a variant variable to see whether or not it's currently empty, you can use the IsEmpty() function. With object variables, however, there's no function to test for this. When using object variables, your only recourse has been to enable an error trap, attempt to use the variable, and see whether it fails. To take care of this problem, you can use the syntax

If *objectVar* Is Nothing Then...

This expression returns a True value if the object variable in the expression has not been assigned to point to an actual object or if it's been reset to point to Nothing (see the next section). This check can be useful to your functions if you want to ensure that an object variable you're using definitely points to something before you begin working with it. You might preface such a function with code like this:

```
Function DoSomething(rst As Recordset)
    If rst Is Nothing Then
        DoSomething = Null
        Exit Function
    Else
        ' Go on about your business...
    End If
End Function
```

Assigning Nothing

When using variant variables, you can reset the value of the variable to be empty using the value of another empty variable. There's no documented way to reset an object variable to point to nothing. By now, you've probably surmised that you can use the Nothing keyword to perform this task. For example, the following fragment resets the object variable to again point to no object:

```
Dim rst As Recordset
Set rst = db.OpenRecordset("tblCustomers")
'
' Do stuff with rst...
'
rst.Close
Set rst = Nothing
```

Since you're assigning a value to an object variable, the "Set" is required in the last statement above. Note that setting an object variable to be Nothing does not close the object to which it points. You must explicitly close the object and then set it to Nothing. The main advantage of setting an object variable to Nothing is that you can then check the variable with

```
If rst Is Nothing Then...
```

and react accordingly. Just closing the object that a variable points to will not reset the value of the variable to Nothing, and future comparisons to Nothing will return False unless you explicitly set the variable to Nothing.

Summary

This chapter has presented a broad overview of Access' object model. Although we've made attempts to bring our own personal perspectives into this chapter, a full understanding of this material requires far more depth than we can cover here. Because of the similarities between the object models in Access, Visual Basic, and Excel, you would be well-served to spend as much time as possible "digging in" to this material since this is clearly the way future Microsoft products will be going.

This chapter covered these major topics:

- Access' support for DAO
- Objects that Access provides
- Referring to objects
- Iterating through collections
- Using properties

- Data definition using DAO
- Working with Access' recordsets
- Using Access' application-supplied containers
- Undocumented object syntax

There's much, much more to know. As a start, Chapter 22, focusing on Access Security, covers (among other things) programmatic control over security features using DAO.

PART III

User Interface

CHAPTER
SEVEN

Controlling Controls

- Using the form and report controls

- Understanding control events and properties

- Using the Tag property in a standardized way

- Combining controls to work together

- Creating forms and controls programmatically

7

In this chapter you'll learn about each of the different Access controls, and you'll find some hints on deciding which control is best for a given datatype or situation, along with examples of many of the control types. In addition, you'll find a number of reusable solutions to common challenges you'll confront when designing your user interfaces.

Controls and Their Uses

Controls are the workhorses of Access applications. You can use them for inputting and outputting data, as well as displaying static information. In addition, you can use controls as global variables, to calculate intermediate values, or to add aesthetic interest to your forms. Forms and reports share most of the same controls. (You can put a button on a report, for example, but it doesn't really make much sense to do so.) The focus of this chapter is on controls for forms.

You can think of controls in Access as being windows, just as all the other elements of a Windows application are windows. As with any window, a control can receive information from the user only when it has input focus. To allow a user to be able to enter text into a text box or to check an item in a check box, that control must first have been selected, either by the user or under your program's control.

Controls have *values*, supplied by you at design time, by the data the control is being fed from, or by the user at run time. The value of the control is the value you see displayed in that control. For a text box the value is obviously the text displayed inside the box. For a list box the value of the control is the chosen item (or Null, if no item is chosen). For an OLE object the value of the control is the object (whether it be a *Paintbrush* bitmap, a *Draw* drawing, an *Excel* spreadsheet, or a *Word* document).

Controls also have *properties* that your application can set and change. This chapter touches on the useful, pertinent, and difficult properties throughout its discussion of the various controls. If you're upgrading to Access 2.0 from an earlier version, you may want to revise your coding style. In earlier versions only the Locked, Enabled, and Visible properties were modifiable at run time. Now, almost all the control properties can be modified at any point, making it much easier to create professional-looking applications.

Code-Behind-Forms

With the release of Access 2.0, Microsoft added support for Code-Behind-Forms (CBF). CBF allows you to easily attach Access Basic code to any event property for any control. This new feature is discussed in greater depth in Chapter 8, but be aware that when this chapter refers to attaching code to a given control or to a property of a control, it is talking about creating event procedure functions and subroutines that are stored with the form itself. You can gain access to the code behind forms by clicking the "…" button next to the specific event on the property sheet and choosing Code Builder from the Choose Builder dialog box. (You can also reverse the order. If you choose [Event Procedure] from the row's drop-down list, you can then click the Build (…) button, and Access will take you directly to the CBF.) You can also choose the Code button on the toolbar to access this code. Figures 7.1 and 7.2 show the property sheet and dialog box in action.

FIGURE 7.1:
Click the "…" button for access to the Code-Behind-Forms.

FIGURE 7.2:
Choose the Code Builder item to edit Access Basic code attached to the chosen event.

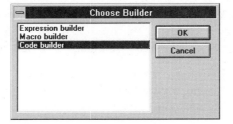

Some Standard Control Properties

Before we launch into a discussion of all the different controls and their various properties and events, this seems like a good time to discuss some of the standard properties and events that most controls share. Later in the chapter we'll discuss individual controls with their unique properties and events.

Using the Tag Property to Create Your Own Properties

Access provides the general-purpose Tag property, which allows you to specify and store any information (up to 2048 characters) about a given control. Access never notices what's stored in this property, so it makes a perfect place to store information about a control that is pertinent to your application. You might find it tempting to place arbitrary values in this unused slot, but it's a good idea to avoid this urge. If you adopt a standard method of storing values in the Tag property, you can actually create your own user-defined properties for controls. We would like to propose a standard at this point.

DOS stores values in its environment space using a very structured format:

Name1=Value1;Name2=Value2;Name3=Value3;

We suggest just such a format for using the Tag property to contain user-defined information. Using this format guarantees that various pieces of your application won't overwrite information stored in the Tag property of a given control. If all access to the Tag property goes through a set of functions that set and get the specific values by their names, you have a very ordered and safe way to store and retrieve values. Using this method allows you to store multiple bits of information about a control and retrieve those bits when necessary.

Imagine a situation in which you want to change a group of text box controls so that they are no longer bound to table fields (so Access will not keep them updated with data as you move from record to record), but you do want to know which field is associated with that control. This might be useful in preparing a query-by-form querying tool, where you want to gather unbound information but use it to filter specific fields. In this case you might find it useful to take the information that *was* in the ControlSource property and store that information in the Tag property. The Tag property might look like this:

Name1=Value1;ControlSource=[LastName];*Name3=Value3;*

Then, when you need to find out the field associated with this control, you can call the appropriate function to retrieve just that one piece of information.

To implement this functionality we've provided a set of functions you can include in any of your applications. (To use the functions, import the module basTags from CH7.MDB.) The set of functions includes glrPutTag(), which puts a tag name and its value into the Tag property for a specific control, and glrGetTag(), which retrieves a specific tag value from the Tag property of a specific control. These two functions, described below, should provide the flexibility you need to use the Tag property to its fullest advantage. Figure 7.3 shows the glrPutTag() and glrGetTag() functions setting and retrieving the tag value, TimeModified.

FIGURE 7.3:

Use the glrPutTag() and glrGetTag() functions to place and retrieve values from the Tag property of a control.

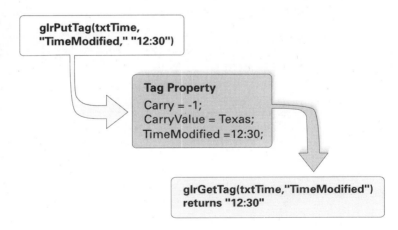

In addition, to make this interface as simple as possible, we've made the rules for the structure of the Tag property string a bit more stringent than those controlling the DOS environment. In particular, the syntax for the Tag property is as follows:

TagName1=TagValue1;TagName2=TagValue2;...;TagNameN=TagValueN;

To use glrGetTag() and glrPutTag(), follow these rules:

- Each tag name and value pair must be separated by an equal sign (=).
- Each pair must be followed by a semicolon (;), although you can change this particular separator by modifying the SEPARATOR constant in the code.
- The separator character (;) cannot appear in the tag value.

If you use the provided functions to place values into the Tag property, these rules won't be a concern since the code will follow them. The only problem occurs when you place values into the Tag property at design time. In that case, be careful to follow the rules exactly since the provided functions may not work otherwise. The functions are declared as follows:

```
Function glrPutTag(ctl as Control, strTagName as String,
➡ varTagValue as Variant)
Function glrGetTag(ctl As Control, strTagName As String)
```

The following list describes the parameters for each of the functions:

Argument	Description
ctl	Control whose Tag property you want to manipulate
strTagName	String expression resulting in the name you want associated with the piece of data stored in the Tag property
varTagValue	Variant expression resulting in the value you want to have stored in the Tag property of the specified control

TIP

To include the functionality as described here in your own applications, include the basTags module from CH7.MDB.

NOTE

Access never records any property changes your running application makes in the form's design. Just as with any other property, changes made to the Tag property with glrPutTag() will not appear in the property sheet. If you want to make persistent changes to any property, you need to make them when your form is in design mode.

Using the TabStop and TabIndex Properties

The TabIndex property allows you to control the order in which users will arrive at controls as they use the Tab or ↵ key to move from control to control on your form. The TabIndex property lets you assign an ordinal value (zero-based) to each control on your form, specifying how you want the user to move between controls. Access maintains the list, ensuring that no value is used twice and that no value is skipped. You can also use the Edit ➤ Tab Order menu item to edit the TabStop properties in a more visual environment.

The TabStop property (Yes/No) can remove a control from the form's tab list. Normally, if you press the Tab key to move from control to control on a form, the focus moves in tab order through the controls. If you set a control's TabStop property to No, Access skips that particular control. Controls that have their TabStop property set to No will still appear in the Edit ➤ Tab Order dialog box, however.

You can use the TabStop and TabIndex properties to gain complete control over the flow of your application's forms. You could, for example, change the tab order of fields based on a choice the user had made. The example form, frmTabOrder (in CH7.MDB), changes the tab order from row-first to column-first, based on a choice made by the user (see Figure 7.4).

FIGURE 7.4:

You can control the tab order programmatically, allowing users to choose the order in which they'd like to fill out a form.

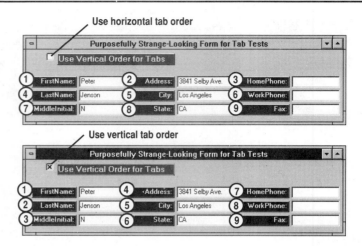

The code required to change the tab order at run time is quite simple. This code example was attached to the AfterUpdate event of the chkTabOrder control. All it needs to do is check the state of the check box and set the tab order accordingly.

```
Sub chkTabOrder_AfterUpdate()
    If chkTabOrder Then
        ' Use a column-wise ordering.
        txtFirstName.TabIndex = 1
        txtLastName.TabIndex = 2
        .
        .
        .
        txtFax.TabIndex = 9
    Else
        ' Use the AutoOrder ordering.
        txtFirstName.TabIndex = 1
        txtAddress.TabIndex = 2
        .
        .
        .
        txtFax.TabIndex = 9
    End If
End Sub
```

Using the DisplayWhen Property

On forms, you can control when Access will display a control. (Report controls don't include the DisplayWhen property but must use the Visible setting instead.) If you want the control to appear only when you print the form, set the Display-When property to Print Only (1). To make the control appear at all times, select Always (0), and to make it display only on screen and not at print time, choose Screen Only (2). This functionality allows you to create forms that can also be used to print out a specific record. You set the DisplayWhen property to Screen Only for all the controls you want displayed only when the user is looking at the form on screen.

Tools in the Toolbox

You select a tool from the toolbox by first choosing the control type you want. Note that once you've chosen a control type, if you pass the mouse cursor over the form you're working on, you'll see the cursor change to represent the control you've chosen. If you want an unbound control, just click on your form where you want the control to be. The crosshair indicates where the upper left-hand corner of the control will go. If you want to create a bound control, choose a field from the fields list and drag it down into the form. Once you've anchored the upper-left corner, you can drag while holding down the left mouse button to size the control as you want.

NOTE   Several of the standard controls do not need much resizing. The check box, the option button, and the page break will most likely never need to be (or can't be) resized. Resizing the combo box helps only to a certain extent since its height should never exceed the maximum size of the drop-down button (the button to the right of the drop-down list). All the other controls can and will need to be resized to fit your needs.

Using Labels

Labels are the simplest of all non-graphic Access controls. A label presents *static* text on a form or report. That is, it doesn't change as you move from record to record. Labels can never receive input focus and thus can never be used to input data. They are skipped over in the form's tab order. Labels, then, are best for displaying information on forms you never want your users to be able to change, such as data-gathering instructions or your company's name. Generally, you also use labels to display the field names for bound controls. Unless told otherwise, Access creates a label control to accompany any bound control you create, including the field name and a colon.

NOTE   You cannot create a label without text. That sounds obvious, but it's very disconcerting when you accidentally try to do it! If you size a label just right but then click some other control before entering a caption value, Access just removes the label as though you had never created it. You can delete the text once you've created it, however, but a label without text isn't very useful.

You can change the color, font name, font size, and text alignment for text in a label. You can also change the Color and SpecialEffect properties of the label itself. It's best to standardize the appearance of the field labels in your application, and you'll find that the control default properties can help you out. See the section "Using Default Control Properties to Your Advantage" later in this chapter for more information.

Once you've changed the font (name or size) for a particular label, you may find that the text no longer fits inside the label. Double-clicking any of the control *handles* (the little black boxes that surround the control frame) causes Access to resize the control for best fit—that is, Access resizes the control so it's just big enough for your text. This can be useful if you're trying out different font sizes. This is equivalent to choosing the Format ➤ Size to Fit menu item. Figure 7.5 shows this auto-sizing in action.

You may be tempted to create labels with lots of different styles and attributes. If so, remember that end users generally appreciate and benefit from consistency in

FIGURE 7.5:

Double-clicking a sizing handle chooses the best-fit size for your labels.

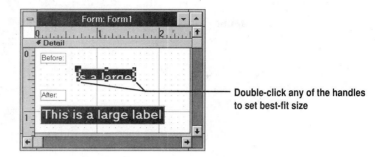

Double-click any of the handles to set best-fit size

appearance and functionality. The following sections outline some ideas for standardizing your use of labels. (Although all the concepts here apply equally to other controls, labels are prime candidates for artistic misuse). See chapter 13 for a more thorough discussion of user interface design issues.

Special Effects   Users may find your forms clearer if controls that are raised always act as a receiver of the focus. If something appears raised on the screen, users will attempt to click it. Clicking bound field labels sends focus to the attached field. Therefore, making field labels raised makes sense—clicking them moves the focus to the field. On the other hand, making an informational label raised might not make sense since you won't ever be transferring focus when you click that label.

Colors   Pick a uniform color scheme across your form. Labels with bold characters in bright yellow on a dark blue background are very visible on most monitors. Bold characters in bright yellow on a bright red background work equally well for important messages. If you are in a whimsical mood, you might try bright yellow on violet. Although this odd combination might not have occurred to you, it is used to eye-catching effect on the road signs surrounding Disney World and works well on informal Access applications, as well.

On the other hand, be aware that these bright colors may not be appropriate in many business situations. You may find that subdued colors (black, gray, and white) work best for your serious applications. Use the colors that work best for the particular application, but be consistent.

Fonts   Pick a font that fits your application. (Script fonts are *never* appropriate in a business application, as far as we can tell.) You should, unless you are certain of your target, avoid selecting fonts that might not exist on your users' machines. Windows makes substitutions for TrueType fonts that your users don't have, but the effect is often not pretty. Sticking with the standards (System and MS Sans Serif) is usually safe, although almost all users of Windows 3.1 and higher can be counted on to have Arial and Times New Roman fonts on their systems, too. In addition, Windows 3.1 users will also have the Wingdings font—a very useful source for symbols.

Using Text Boxes

While labels are the simplest of all Access controls, text boxes are the most ubiquitous. You can use text boxes to display data, as well as to capture it. They can be single- or multiple-lined. They can display scroll bars if you want them to. Text boxes can contain any amount of textual information, up to approximately 32,000 characters (although in reality this will probably be less, depending on your particular circumstances).

You can think of a text box as a mini-notepad, allowing you to enter free-form text. If you think your data entry will require more than one line or if you are using a text box to display information from a memo field, your best bet is to enable scroll bars. (Set the ScrollBars property to Vertical rather than None.)

> **TIP**
>
> As is the Windows standard, the ⏎ key does not cause Access to insert a carriage return/line feed in your text box but rather to move to the next control. To move to a new line, you must press Shift+Enter. To make the ⏎ key insert a carriage return/line feed, set the EnterKey-Behavior property of the text box to New Line in Field. This makes the text box work more like what you might expect but less like the rest of Windows.

If you are using text boxes for data entry on a form (and chances are that you are), you should strongly consider displaying a label control for each text box you use, making clear to the user the purpose of that particular text box. That's the default behavior in Access, and you probably are better off sticking with it unless you have a specific reason not to.

Just as with label controls, your applications will be more coherent if you adopt a standard format for your data input and form display. If you use the Forms Wizards to create your forms, you know that one "look" for a form can be very attractive. Once you've set a standard for your forms, stick with it. You may find that adhering to the concept, "If it's raised I can click it; if it's sunken I can type into it" helps your design process. You might also consider color schemes to indicate fields the user cannot change as opposed to those that need user input. A darker background for read-only fields (the BackColor property) might be useful. Figure 7.6 shows different ways you might want to use text boxes on a form.

> **NOTE** At this point Access text boxes can support only a single font and a single text attribute (bold, italic, or underline). Until the advent of an OCX custom control that supports text attributes (a little word processor, in essence), you will need to either forego fonts and formatting within text boxes or embed a foreign document in your form or table.

FIGURE 7.6:
Sample text boxes: raised, lowered, and normal

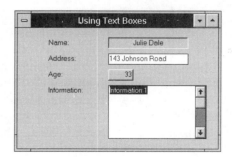

The Misunderstood DefaultValue Property

The DefaultValue property provides a default value when you create a new record. That's the only time it does any work! Many developers confuse this property with one (which doesn't exist) that would place a default value into a control if you left it empty and moved on to the next record.

To use the DefaultValue property, you can place an expression (or in this instance, an Access Basic function that returns a value) in the property sheet. Access places the result of the expression or Access Basic function in the control each time you create a new record. For example, were you to place the expression

```
=GetDefault(Form)
```

in the property sheet and create this function in a module:

```
Function GetDefault(frm as Form)
    GetDefault = frm!Caption
End Function
```

then, each time you created a new record, Access would place the form's caption in the text box.

On the other hand, to place a value into a control when you leave it blank, you need to provide some Access Basic code attached to the BeforeUpdate event of the form:

```
Sub Form_BeforeUpdate(Cancel As integer)
    If IsNull(Me![Action]) Then
        frm!Action = "(Nothing Assigned)"
    Endif
End Sub
```

Note that Access will execute this code only if you've changed some field in the record since Access fires off the BeforeUpdate event only if there is something to update in the underlying recordset. Also, since the DefaultValue property takes effect only when you're adding new rows, if you change the DefaultValue property once there are existing rows of data, you have to go back and modify the values for those preexisting rows.

Carrying Values Forward into New Records

In some instances your application may require the ability to carry forward values into the new row when your user adds a new row using a form. Access does not provide this ability on its own, but it's not difficult to implement it in Access Basic. This functionality requires storing away field values as Access writes the current record to the underlying table and then, when the new record becomes current, copying the saved data into the correct fields.

This is a perfect case for using the Tag property, as described in the earlier section "Using the Tag Property to Create Your Own Properties." All this requires, then, is copying the current data to the Tag property in the AfterUpdate event of the form and copying that data back into the control in the form's Current event, if the current record is the New record. To control which fields get carried over into the new record, you must place a tag value in the Tag property (Carry=−1, in this example). If the code finds this tag value in the Tag property, it knows to carry forward the value in that particular field. Figure 7.7 shows the form frmCarryTest (from CH7.MDB), which demonstrates these ideas.

Listings 7.1 and 7.2 contain all the code necessary to implement the carry functionality. These listings consist of both the code that must be attached to your form and the supporting routines that you will find in the module basCarry.

FIGURE 7.7:
City and State values are carried over from record to record as you add new records.

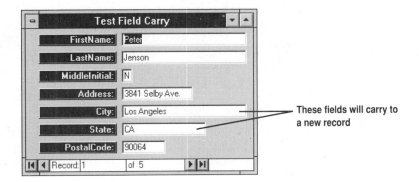

These fields will carry to a new record

The glrSweep supporting routine requires special mention here. This subroutine accepts two parameters, the name of the form to operate on, and a command to execute for each control on that form that has the Carry tag value in its Tag property. This subroutine loops through each control on the form, and for each one that passes its test it calls the Access Eval() function to execute the function whose name is passed as a parameter, passing it information about the current control. This mechanism was used here since both the RestoreValues() and StoreValues() functions need to act on all the controls on the form that are to be carried. Rather than writing the looping and checking code twice (and maintaining it twice), we localized the looping and checking code to one location and just called the appropriate function from within the loop. There are, of course, other ways to accomplish the same end result: you could pass in a constant indicating which function to call, for example. This seemed like a good opportunity to show off the powerful Eval() function, which is often forgotten in application development.

For the carrying code to work, your form must contain code attached to several form events. In the form's Load event you need code that places the Carry tag value into the Tag property and places the first record's values into the Tag property for the fields you're interested in carrying over. You could also place the value

```
Carry=-1;
```

into the Tag properties for the selected controls at design time and not worry about doing it when the form loads. If you have a large number of fields to carry over, this method may result in better performance since there's less code to run at form load time. A sample Form_Load event procedure might look like this:

```
Sub Form_Load()
    Dim varOK As Variant
    ' Replace these two lines with calls to glrPutTag()
    ' for each field on your form for which you want to
    ' carry values.
    varOK = glrPutTag(City, "Carry", True)
    varOK = glrPutTag(State, "Carry", True)
    glrSweep Me, "glrStoreValues"
End Sub
```

After you enter data into the new record, you'll want to store it away to be used in creating the next new record. To do this, attach code to the AfterUpdate event of the form to walk through all the controls on the form and copy the values for "tagged" fields into the Tag property:

```
Sub Form_AfterUpdate( )
    glrSweep Me, "glrStoreValues"
End Sub
```

Finally, when you move to the new record, you'll need to place the appropriate information on the form. Attach code to the form's Current event to walk through all the controls on the form, copying the values for "tagged" fields from the Tag property onto the form. Of course, you want this behavior only if you're on the new record (you don't want changes carried back to previous records), so you need to make sure you're on the new record before moving the data onto the form. To do that, you need to call glrAtNew(), which returns True if you're on the new record. The glrAtNew() function counts on the fact that attempting to retrieve a bookmark for the new record will trigger an error. If that error occurs, you're at the new record.

```
Function glrAtNew (frm As Form)
Const ERR_NO_CURRENT_ROW = 3021
    Dim strTemp As String

    On Error Resume Next
    strTemp = frm.BookMark
    glrAtNew = (Err = ERR_NO_CURRENT_ROW)
End Function

Sub Form_Current ()
    If glrAtNew(Me) Then
        glrSweep Me, "glrRestoreValues"
    End If
End Sub
```

The two functions that actually do the work, RestoreValues() and StoreValues(), are quite similar. Each gets the control on which to act, based on the form and control name passed in, and then either gets or sets the value of the control to or from the Tag property (using glrGetTag() or PutTag()).

One interesting item to note about these two functions (shown completely in Listing 7.2) is their use of a rather odd syntax:

```
Set ctl = Forms(strForm)(strControl)
```

In this case strForm and strControl are both string variables. If you knew the names of these two objects, you could use the standard syntax

Set ctl = *Forms!YourForm!YourControl*

Since you know neither of these values until run time, you can use the variable syntax instead. This syntax can save you a few lines of code each time you use it. That is, the alternative is to use something like this:

```
Dim frm As Form
Set frm = Forms(strForm)
Set ctl = frm(strControl)
```

To use basCarry in your own applications, follow these steps:

1. Import the basCarry module from CH7.MDB.

2. Import the basTags module from CH7.MDB.

3. Attach code, as mentioned above, to your form's Open, Current, and AfterUpdate events.

Listing 7.1

```
Sub Form_AfterUpdate()
    ' Go through all the fields on the form, storing away the
    ' value for which the tag value "Carry=-1" is set in the
    ' Tag property.

    glrSweep Me, "glrStoreValues"
End Sub

Sub Form_Current ()
    ' If currently at the New record, restore the values stored
    ' away to be carried forward.

    If glrAtNew(Me) Then
        glrSweep Me, "glrRestoreValues"
    End If
End Sub

Sub Form_Load()
    ' At form load time, prepare the fields you want to
    ' carry forward by setting the flag in the Tag property.
    ' You could also just set these at design time.
```

```
' Also, you need to prime the stored values, so the call to
' StoreValues here will save away the values for the very
' first record.

Dim varOK As Variant

varOK = glrPutTag(City, "Carry", True)
varOK = glrPutTag(State, "Carry", True)
glrSweep Me, "glrStoreValues"
End Sub
```

Listing 7.2

```
Function glrAtNew(frm As Form)
    ' Check to see if the current record is the New record.
    ' Returns True/False.

    ' This function is based on the concept that you can't
    ' retrieve a bookmark for the New record, so Access flags
    ' the error. This function returns True if the error
    ' is non-zero, which it will be if the New record is
    ' current.

Const ERR_NO_CURRENT_ROW = 3021

    Dim strTemp As String

    On Error Resume Next
    strTemp = frm.BookMark
    glrAtNew = (Err = ERR_NO_CURRENT_ROW)
    On Error Goto 0
End Function

Function glrRestoreValues(strForm As String, strControl As String)
    Dim varTemp As Variant
    Dim ctl As Control

    ' Deal with the error that might occur when trying
    ' to access the control name passed in.
    On Error Resume Next

    Set ctl = Forms(strForm)(strControl)
    If Err = 0 Then
        If IsNull(ctl) Then
```

```
              ' If glrGetTag() can't find the tag value it needs,
              ' it'll just return Null. And that will be fine
              ' in this case.
              ctl = glrGetTag(ctl, "CarryValue")
         End If
     End If
RestoreValuesExit:
    On Error Goto 0
    Exit Function

RestoreValuesErr:
    MsgBox Error & " (" & Err & ")"
    Resume RestoreValuesExit

End Function

Function glrStoreValues(strForm As String, strControl As String)
    Dim varTemp As Variant
    Dim ctl As Control

    ' Deal with the error that might occur when trying
    ' to access the control name passed in.
    On Error GoTo StoreValuesErr
    Set ctl = Forms(strForm)(strControl)
    If Err = 0 Then
        varTemp = glrPutTag(ctl, "CarryValue", ctl)
    End If

StoreValuesExit:
    Exit Function

StoreValuesErr:
    MsgBox Error & " (" & Err & ")"
    Resume StoreValuesExit
End Function

Sub glrSweep(frm As Form, strCommand As String)
    ' Walk through all the controls on the form, looking in the
    ' Tag property for the Carry tag value. If it's there and
    ' it's True, then execute the command passed into this
    ' function.

Const QUOTE = """"
    Dim IntI As Integer
```

```
    Dim varTemp As Variant

    For IntI = 0 To frm.Count - 1
        If glrGetTag(frm(IntI), "Carry") Then
            varTemp = strCommand & "(" & QUOTE & frm.Name &
          ➡ QUOTE & "," & QUOTE & frm(IntI).Name & QUOTE & ")"
            varTemp = Eval(varTemp)
        End If
    Next IntI
End Sub
```

Using the Eval() Function

You can use the Eval() function in Access to evaluate an expression and return its value. It provides a mechanism for emulating other languages' (such as C/C++) support for function pointers. This extremely powerful concept is one of the bases of object-oriented languages.

Access Basic cannot do all that C/C++ can, nor does it attempt to. But the Eval() function can give you some very powerful capabilities. As described in the on-line Help, the Eval() function "Evaluates an expression and returns its value." What Help doesn't state is that the expression can be just about anything!

To use Eval() to execute functions, you just need to build a string expression that, when evaluated, creates the function call you want. Since the Eval() function must retrieve a value and return it, the expression you build must either return a value itself or call a function that returns a value. (Subroutines are not allowed.) In addition, any functions you call must be global in scope. (You won't be able to call any functions that are attached directly to a form).

As a very simple example, suppose you have a generic error-handling function that needs to handle messages differently, depending on whether or not you're in debugging mode. In debugging mode you want to have error messages brought to your attention with MsgBox() calls, but in real use you just want them logged to a table. You could, of course, check to see whether you were debugging each and every time you called the error-handling function and decide what to do at that point. On the other hand, you could set a global variable that indicated which of two functions to call, Debug() or Log(), depending on whether or not you were debugging. You could then call the correct function, passing in the error message:

```
Dim strFunc as String
Function frmYourForm_OnOpen()
    ' Set strFunc to point to the right function to call.
    strFunc = IIf(Debugging, "Debug", "Log")
    ' Now do whatever else you need...
End Function

Function ErrorHandler(strError as String)
    Dim varTemp as Variant
    ' Call the correct function to handle this
    ' error message.
    varTemp = Eval(strFunc & "(""" & strError & """)")
    ' Do whatever else you need to do...
End Function
```

For example, calling the function

```
varTemp = ErrorHandler("This is a test")
```

passes the string "This is a test" to the ErrorHandler() function, removing the quotes on the way. ErrorHandler() will need to put the quotes back in so it can pass the string down to the correct function (either Debug() or Log()) to handle, via the Eval() function. Notice the multiple quotes inside the Eval() function. These are necessary to build up the correct expression to be passed to the called function.

The string passed to Eval() must evaluate as the exact expression you want to have Access evaluate. You may find it useful to rewrite the ErrorHandler() function like this:

```
Function ErrorHandler(strError as String)
    Dim varTemp as Variant
    Dim strTemp as String

    strTemp = strFunc & "(""" & strError & """)"
    MsgBox strTemp
    ' Call the correct function to handle this error message.
    varTemp = Eval(strTemp)
    ' Do whatever else you need to do...
End Function
```

until you get the syntax correct in your own function. This displays the expression that's about to be evaluated before Access gets it.

You may work with Access for a long time before you find a situation for which Eval() is uniquely suited. When you do, however, its availability will make your code much tighter and easier to maintain.

Using the InputMask Property to Control Input

The InputMask property allows you to control, down to the level of specific characters, the values users enter into text boxes. You can specify whether the user can enter digits, alphabetic characters, or both and whether or not those characters are required. In addition, you can force conversion of any and/or all characters to upper- or lowercase. You can specify static characters that are unchangeable and appear in every record, and you can control whether or not those characters are actually stored with the data (such as the "( ) - " characters you might use when prompting for a telephone number).

The InputMask property consists of three parts, separated by semicolons. Each of the pieces is described in Table 7.1.

TABLE 7.1: The Three Sections of the InputMask Property String

Section	Description	Example
1	The input mask itself	00000\-#### (zip code with optional four extra digits)
2	0 = Access stores the mask characters with the data	If 0, 12345-6789 would be stored in the underlying table
	1 = Access uses the mask characters for display only	If 1, 123456789 would be stored in the underlying table
3	The character used as a prompt character. Use a space in quotes (" ") for a blank	If the mask were 00000\-####;1;#, you would see #####-#### in the input field, waiting for input

Table 7.2 explains how Access interprets characters in the input mask. Note that Access does not support input functions. That is, you must specify an input character in the mask for each character you might need to input. Access will accept only as many characters as you specify in the input mask.

TABLE 7.2: Input Mask Characters

Template Character	Allowed Replacement	Entry Required
0	Digit (0–9)	Yes
#	Digit or space	No (blank positions converted to spaces)
L	Letter (A–Z)	Yes
?	Letter	No
A	Letter or digit (A–Z, 0–9)	Yes
a	Letter or digit	No
&	Any character or space	Yes
C	Any character or space	No
. , : ; -, /	Decimal point, thousands, date, and time separators (the characters will depend on International settings in the Windows Control Panel)	N/A
<	Force characters to the right to be converted to lowercase	N/A
>	Force characters to the right to be converted to uppercase	N/A
!	Fill the mask from right to left (rather than left to right) if there are optional characters to the left of the mask. The exclamation point can be anywhere in the mask	N/A
\	Display the next character as a literal (\D is displayed as D)	N/A

To create text in which the first character is uppercase and the rest is lowercase, use an input mask like this:

>&<&&&&&&&&&&&

This forces the string into the format you want, but there are two caveats. First of all, you must enter a mask character for each character in the longest text value you'll need (perhaps the same as the width of the field). Second, this works only for single-word entries. To convert multiple-word text to "proper" case, you need to do the conversion in code attached to the AfterUpdate event of the text box.

TIP Unless you're using monospaced fonts, when you choose the third portion of the input mask, think about the width of the "space" character as opposed to the width of the characters you'll be accepting into those spaces. For example, using ! as the prompt character when you're expecting numeric digits as input values is visually jarring. The thin ! characters get pushed aside as more and more digits are entered. Very wide characters (like @) take up far more space than most of the normal characters. The underscore character (_) makes a good prompt character in most cases and makes it clear to the user that you're waiting for input.

TIP You can trap the error that occurs when your user attempts to leave a text box before satisfactorily completing the input mask requirements by attaching code to the form's Error event. For more information, see the section "Form-Level Error Handling" in Chapter 8.

Presto! Turn a Text Box into a Label

Normally, you can select text boxes on forms and type data into them. In some cases you may want to *freeze* the contents of a text box—that is, make it impossible to select the text box—but without altering its appearance. Setting the Enabled property to No makes it impossible to select the control, but it also dims the contents. If you also set the Locked property to Yes, the control will appear normal, but it will be locked out from user intervention. You won't be able to select it, and Access will remove it from the tab order. (If you set just the Locked property to Yes, leaving the Enabled property as Yes, you can select the text box, but you can't type anything into it.) Figure 7.8 demonstrates all the possibilities for combining the Enabled and Locked properties.

FIGURE 7.8:

All four possible combinations of the Locked and Enabled properties

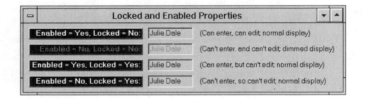

The ControlSource Property and Calculated Controls

Access developers often use text boxes to display calculated values. Figure 7.9 shows a form with a DueDate field, drawing its data from a table, and two text boxes displaying the number of days overdue for this payment. To create a calculated control, you have two choices:

- Use an expression.

- Use a user-defined Access Basic function.

The second and third text boxes on the sample form use one of the preceding methods for calculating the number of days late.

FIGURE 7.9:
Using calculated controls on a form. Note that both methods (using an expression and using Access Basic) return the same value.

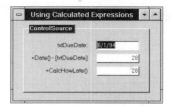

In either case you must precede the value in the property sheet with an equal sign (=), which indicates to Access that this is more than just an ordinary field name.

To create an expression that will be evaluated when the control gets recalculated—for example, to calculate the past due amount—use the expression

```
=Date() - txtDueDate
```

This simple expression calculates the number of days since the due date and displays it. Figure 7.9 shows this example in action.

Your other option is to create an Access Basic function that places a value in the text box.

> **NOTE**
>
> In general, if you want a specific event to place a value into a control on a form, it is not enough to specify a function call in the property sheet. Your function must explicitly place its value into the control. In most properties, Access completely disregards the return value from the function. Combined with the fact that Access can call only functions (which must return values), not subroutines (which do not return values), from the property sheet, it's easy to get confused. On top of that, Access is inconsistent as to how it treats function calls from the property sheet. The DefaultValue and ControlSource properties, for example, pass the return value from a function call on to the text box. All event properties disregard the return value.

TIP

Access provides three properties of the Screen object: ActiveControl, ActiveForm, and ActiveReport. Screen.ActiveControl returns the currently active control, Screen.ActiveForm returns the currently active form, and Screen.ActiveReport returns the currently active report. You might be tempted to count on these properties to allow you to write generic Access Basic functions to be called from forms. In several cases these are helpful, but for the most part you're better off passing the Form property (from the property sheet) or the Me object (from CBF) down to functions called in global modules. The main problem is that often in the Access environment there is actually no current form or control. Attempting to access one of these properties at those times causes a run-time error. This makes it particularly difficult to debug Access Basic code that contains these objects.

Using the same example as above, you could create an Access Basic function:

```
Function CalcHowLate()
    CalcHowLate = Date() - frm!txtDueDate
End Function
```

To use an Access Basic function to supply the ControlSource value, precede its name with an equal (=) sign. That is, use =CalcHowLate() in this example. Figure 7.9 shows this form in action.

Using Two-State Controls (the Yes/No Crowd)

All the controls described in the following sections (toggle button, option button, and check box) can represent data that has two states when used alone on a form. (When grouped in an option group, they can represent more information.). Therefore, they all represent reasonable ways to present yes/no data to the user for acceptance. Each represents its two states differently, and you can use these differences to your advantage.

The Toggle Button

The toggle button has two states—up and down. Its "up" state represents the False/No condition (unselected), and its "down" state represents the True/Yes condition (selected). It can display either text or a picture (but, unfortunately, not both). Access creates a dithered version of the picture on the button for its depressed state, relieving you from having to supply two separate bitmaps, one for the "up" state and one for the "down" state.

Using toggle buttons to represent yes/no information to the user can make your forms more visually appealing than using simple check boxes, but they make sense in only a limited number of situations. If your user is inputting information that answers a simple yes/no question, toggle buttons aren't as clear as check boxes. On the other hand, if you are gathering other two-state information (alive or deceased, U.S. citizen or not), toggle buttons often are quite useful. Here's the real test: if you're tempted to use a toggle button alone on a form with a text description, use a check box instead. If you need a group of check boxes or if you can use a picture instead of text, consider using toggle buttons.

The Option Button

Option buttons do represent two states, but common usage suggests that you use them most often in option groups to allow selection of a single item from the group. In that situation the two states can be thought of as "selected" and "not selected." For that reason programmers often refer to option buttons as *radio buttons*, harkening back to the automobile radios of yesteryear with mechanical buttons that you could depress only one at a time to select a station and pressing one "unpressed" the rest.

When representing yes/no data, the option button displays a filled circle when it's in the True/Yes state. When displaying the False/No state, it displays just an empty ring.

Avoid using single option buttons on forms. You should limit their usage to the radio button image in option groups. If you need a single option button, use a check box instead.

The Check Box

The check box is the standard two-state control. When in the Yes (True) state, it displays an *X* inside a box. When in the No (False) state, it displays just an empty box. Check boxes commonly stand alone or are used in groups to select multiple options. You can use check boxes in option groups, but common usage suggests that you avoid this situation. Using check boxes in an option group allows you to choose only a single value, and this spoils the imagery of check boxes—allowing multiple choices. If you want to make a group of check boxes *look* like an option group, you can enclose them within a rectangle, as described in the section "Rectangles As Option Groups" later in this chapter.

The check box control actually can represent a third state that neither the option button nor the toggle button can display. If you bind the check box to a Yes/No field and create a new record, the current value is unknown (actually, Null), and the check box displays a gray-filled box. Figure 7.10 shows all three types of two-state controls, with all their possible values. (Note the Null value in the check boxes.)

FIGURE 7.10:
All the two-state controls

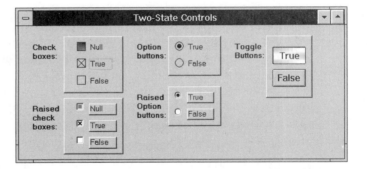

Using Option Groups—Controls inside Controls

The option group is a one-of-a-kind control in Access. It allows you to group multiple controls (toggle buttons, option buttons, or check boxes) for the purpose of choosing a single value. Each subcontrol has its own value (set in the OptionValue property), and when it's chosen it assigns that value to the option group. Usually an option group consists of multiples of a single type of control. Figure 7.11 shows three different option groups, one for each type of subcontrol. In addition, this figure includes an option group composed of various subcontrols. Although there's no reason why you can't create an option group combining different subcontrols, it's a good idea to avoid doing so since it's confusing and serves no real purpose.

FIGURE 7.11:
Four option group examples. We don't recommend creating option groups composed of different subcontrols.

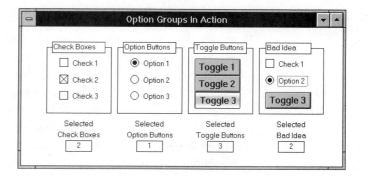

There's nothing keeping you from assigning the same OptionValue property to multiple subcontrols. As a matter of fact, if you copy a control within an option group, Access assigns the new control the same option value as the original control. This can be confusing since choosing one subcontrol will simultaneously select all subcontrols with the same OptionValue property. On the other hand, there's nothing keeping you from skipping option values. They need not be contiguous. The only limitation is that they must be integer values.

TIP.

In the interest of preserving screen real-estate and simplifying your input forms, consider using a combo box if you find that your option group includes more than five items. Option groups take up a great deal of space on the screen, and with more than five subcontrols in the group it becomes difficult to choose the correct item.

The value of an option group can be only a single numeric value. No matter how much you'd like an option group to return a string or any other datatype, it is limited to representing a single integer. This means that the option value of each internal subcontrol is also limited to being an integer. If you must use text values, for example, you can create an array of strings in your application and use the value returned from the option group as an index into your array. See the section "Returning 'Real' Information from Option Groups" later in this chapter for information on returning string values.

TIP

Since option groups can return only a single value, you are limited to making only one choice from the group of subcontrols inside it. This design indicates that you would be better off using only toggle buttons or option buttons in an option group since each of those is suited for making a single choice. If you need an option group that contains check boxes, allowing you to choose several items, consider creating a "faux" option group. To do this, enclose your check boxes within a rectangle (rather than within an option group). This way they'll look as though they are part of an option group but will allow multiple selections. Note, though, that you will have to examine each check box separately to find which ones you have selected. If you have controls inside an option group, you don't need to examine each separately, since all you care about is the single control you've selected, and Access assigns that value to the option group.

Access treats the option group, once it's populated with subcontrols, as a single control; when you select the container and move it, all the internal controls move, too. When you delete the container, Access deletes all the internal controls. Unless you're aware that this will happen, it can cause havoc in your development. Make sure you really intend to delete all the internal controls before you delete an option group!

Moving Controls to a New Neighborhood

You'll find that moving a currently existing control into an option group does not work. Although the subcontrol will appear to be inside the option group, they will not function together. To add items to an option group, use either of the following two methods:

- **Create a new control:** Select the option group and then choose your subcontrol from the toolbar and place it in the option group. Note that when you move the cursor to drop a subcontrol, the option group becomes highlighted as you pass the cursor over it. This visual prompt indicates that the option group is ready to receive a subcontrol.

- **Cut and paste an existing control:** Once you've used the Edit ➤ Cut menu item to cut the control, select the option group. With the option group selected, choose Edit ➤ Paste. Access places the control inside the option group as a real, active subcontrol.

NOTE Controls in an option group lose their properties that deal with the underlying data, such as the ControlSource and ValidationRule properties, since they are no longer independent representations of data from the underlying record source. On the other hand, they gain the OptionValue property since you must assign each a unique value. This is the value the control will return to the option group once you've made a choice. Therefore, you'll note that the property sheet for an independent control is a bit different from the property sheet for an identical control in an option group.

Assigning and Retrieving Values

Because the option group's value is the value of the chosen subcontrol, you can assign a value to the option group by making an assignment to the option group name. For example, the following Access Basic code assigns the value 3 to the option group grpTestGroup:

```
grpTestGroup = 3
```

Access would select the subcontrol in grpTestGroup that had the OptionValue of 3.

Likewise, you can retrieve the value of the option group just by referencing its name. The expression

```
varNewValue = grpTestGroup
```

assigns the value chosen in grpTestGroup to the variant variable varNewValue.

To be completely clear, the reason the previous assignment works is that you're actually assigning the Value property of grpTestGroup to varNewValue. Since the Value property of a control is its default property, Access knows that that's what you meant when you specified no property at all.

NOTE   The option group's value is Null when there are no items chosen. Therefore, just as with any other form control, consider retrieving its value into a variant-type variable that can handle the possible Null return value.

Returning "Real" Information from Option Groups

Although option groups can return only integral values, you can easily work around this problem if you want an option group to gather and show information from a text field that has only a limited number of possible values. It may be that you're sharing data with other applications or that you just aren't able to change the field format to meet Access' requirements. In that case you'll need a few tricks to use option groups to represent textual information.

TIP

If at all possible, try to reorganize your tables in such a way that limited-option fields can be stored as integers. Not only does this make it simple to use an option group to show the data, it cuts down on memory usage. Imagine that you have 1000 records, each with one of the words "Overnight", "2nd Day Air", or "Ground" in the Delivery field. Not only is this field prone to data entry problems, it's using a lot more disk/memory space than necessary. If you were to create a small table with those three values and an integer attached to each, you could just store the integers in your main table. Data entry would be simpler, you'd be using less memory, and everyone involved would be happier.

To bind the option group to text values rather than integer values, you need to create an extra text box on your form. Normally you would make this text box invisible (set its Visible property to No), but for this example it will stay visible. Figure 7.12 shows the finished form (frmDelivery in CH7.MDB). For the purposes of this example, the option group's name is grpDelivery and the text box's name is txtDelivery. The text box is bound to the field containing the text, and the option group is unbound; the text box is the control that will send and receive data to and from the underlying table, and the option group will be used just to collect and display that data.

FIGURE 7.12:

Binding an option group to a text value. Note the bound text box, which normally would be invisible.

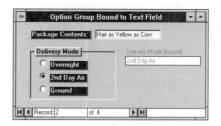

Once you have the bound text box on the form, you need to solve two problems:

- As you move from record to record, how do you get the right option in the option group to be chosen?
- As you make a choice in the option group, how do you get its value written out to the underlying data, if it's not bound?

To answer the first question you need to attach code to the form's Current event. Access fires off this event each time it makes a record current and allows you to set the value of the option group for each record. For this simple case you can use the Switch() function, which returns the value corresponding to the first true statement it finds in its parameters:

```
grpDelivery = Switch(txtDelivery = "Overnight", 1,
➡ txtDelivery = "2nd Day Air", 2, txtDelivery = "Ground",
➡ 3, True, Null)
```

Using the Switch() Function

You can use Switch() to take the place of nested If...Then...Else...End If statements. Its general syntax is

retval = Switch(*expr1, var1* [, *expr2, var2*...[, *expr7, var7*]])

where *expr1* through *expr7* are expressions that return either True (–1) or False (0) and *var1* through *var7* are the values to be returned if the corresponding expression is True. Switch() returns the value corresponding to the first expression it finds in its list that returns True.

For example, the Switch() function call in the previous example:

```
grpDelivery = Switch(txtDelivery = "Overnight", 1,
➡ txtDelivery = "2nd Day Air", 2, txtDelivery = "Ground",
➡ 3, True, Null)
```

could have been written as

```
If txtDelivery = "Overnight" Then
    grpDelivery = 1
ElseIf txtDelivery = "2nd Day Air" Then
    grpDelivery = 2
```

```
ElseIf txtDelivery = "Ground" Then
     grpDelivery = 3
End If
```

Be aware of a few issues that arise when you use Switch():

- You can include up to seven expression/value pairs. To check more than seven different expressions, you need to use some other control structure—most likely a Select Case structure.

- Switch() returns null if either none of the expressions return a True value or if the value associated with the first True expression is null.

- Although only one of the expressions may be True, Access will evaluate every one of the expressions. This can lead to undesirable side effects. For example, if you try this:

```
varValue = Switch(x = 0 Or y = 0, 0, x >= y, x/y, x < y, y/x)
```

you will inevitably end up with an Overflow error since, if either x or y is 0, you end up dividing by 0 even though it appears that you've checked for that in the first expression.

To answer the second question, you need to attach code to the AfterUpdate event of the option group. This code will place the correct value into the bound txtDelivery text box, which will, in turn, send it to the underlying data source. For this example, you should use code like this:

```
txtDelivery = Choose(grpDelivery, "Overnight",
➡ "2nd Day Air", "Ground")
```

Using the Choose() Function

Like the Switch() function, the Choose() function is yet another replacement for nested If…Then…Else…End If statements. It takes an integer between 1 and 13 as its first parameter and then a list of up to 13 parameters from which to choose. Access returns the value corresponding, in position, to the index you passed as the first parameter. Its general syntax is

Choose(intIndex, *expr1* [, *expr2*]…)

Be aware of the following issues that arise when you use Choose():

- You can include only 13 possible return values. To include more you need to use some other control structure—most likely a Select Case structure.

- The index value can only be a value between 1 and 13, inclusive. If you pass a floating-point value, Access converts it to an integer following the same rules it does for the Fix() function.

- Although Choose() returns only one of the values, it evaluates them all. Beware of possible side effects. If you call a function in one or more expressions, each of those functions will be called. For example, if each of your expressions called the InputBox() function, each and every one of the expressions would get evaluated, causing the InputBox() dialog box to pop up multiple times as Access evaluated the list of expressions.

Using List and Combo Boxes

List boxes and combo boxes (otherwise known as drop-down list boxes) share many similar properties and uses. Combo boxes combine a text box and a list box in one control. Both list and combo boxes present a list of values, allowing you to choose a single item. They can present multiple columns of data, and you can use them as full data structures, with hidden columns that can contain data.

Differences between List and Combo Boxes

Although list and combo boxes share many of the same properties, events, and uses, several of their specific details are unique to their particular control type. Table 7.3 lists those idiosyncrasies.

TABLE 7.3: Differences between List and Combo Boxes

Item	List Box	Combo Box
Item choices	Allows you to choose only from the items already in the list	Allows you either to choose from the values in the list or to add new ones. This actually depends on the LimitToList property and also on which column is bound to the underlying field. For more information, see the section "The LimitToList Problem" later in this chapter
Screen real estate	Takes up as much space as you assign it. Works best when as many items as possible are immediately visible	Takes up the space of a single text box when it doesn't have the input focus and as many lines as you specify (in the ListRows property) when it has the focus.
Keyboard handling	Matches only the first character of items in its list against letters you press. Pressing an *M* matches the first item that starts with *M*. Pressing it again finds the next, and so on. Pressing a different letter finds the first item that starts with that letter	Performs an incremental search as you type. That is, if you press *M* it scrolls to find the first item that begins with *M*. If you then press *i,* it finds the first item that begins with *Mi* and scrolls to that item. Pressing Backspace returns the selection to the previous item you chose. In addition, if you've set the AutoExpand property to Yes, as you type, Access automatically finds and displays the first underlying data element that matches the number of characters you've typed so far. This auto-fill feature, similar to that found in several popular financial packages, is extremely useful, especially when combined with the LimitToList property

Important Properties of List and Combo Boxes

Access' Control Wizards can perform most of the work of creating list and combo boxes on your forms. At times, though, you might want to create the combo or list box from scratch, when you find that you don't get the flexibility you need when using the Wizard. List and combo boxes provide great flexibility in how they allow you, as a programmer, to display information to the user while controlling the input. Unfortunately, with this degree of flexibility, the plethora of options can be daunting. Many of the properties are interrelated and collectively affect how the control operates. The following sections detail some of the properties you need to understand to get the full benefit from these controls.

The ControlName Property

The ControlName property specifies the internal reference name for the control. The actual value of this property has no real significance, except as a convenience for the programmer.

> **TIP**
>
> Many beginning Access programmers confuse the ControlName property with the ControlSource property. The control name specifies only the name by which you, the programmer, will refer to the control. It has nothing to do with the underlying data, while the control source is actually linked with the data.

The ControlSource Property

The ControlSource property links the control with the underlying data. Specifying a field name tells Access where to retrieve the value of the control and where to place the value returned from the control once you select an item. The control returns the value from the column set in the BoundColumn property. With other controls, you can enter an expression preceded by an equal (=) sign for the ControlSource property. With list and combo boxes, this option only succeeds in making the control read-only.

The RowSourceType Property

The RowSourceType property specifies where to retrieve the rows of data the control displays. The options are

- **Table/Query:** The data comes from a table or query or from a SQL expression. In any case, the RowSource property specifies the table/query name or the SQL expression that will retrieve the data set.

- **Value List:** The data comes from a list that you specify explicitly in the RowSource property.

- **Field List:** The data will consist of a list of fields from the table or query specified in the RowSource property.

- **(User-Defined):** If you specify a function name with no equal sign and no trailing parentheses, Access calls it to fill the list or combo box. See the section "Filling a List or Combo Box Programmatically" later in this chapter for more information.

The RowSource Property

The RowSource property specifies which data to retrieve for presentation in the list or combo box. Its syntax depends on the RowSourceType property. Figure 7.13 (frmLists from CH7.MDB) demonstrates some of the methods of filling a list box via

FIGURE 7.13:
One form showing some of the various methods of filling a list or combo box via the property sheet

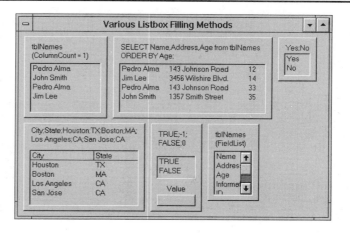

the property sheet. The following sections detail the information you need to supply for the RowSource property, based on your choice in the RowSourceType property.

Table/Query   Enter the name of a table, query, or SQL expression that will retrieve the data you wish to display. Here are some examples:

- **tblNames:** Retrieves as many columns from the table named tblNames as the ColumnCount property specifies.

- **SELECT Name, Address, Age FROM tblNames ORDER BY Age:** Retrieves a maximum of three columns from tblNames, ordered by age. If the number in the ColumnCount property is less than the requested number of columns in the RowSource, the ColumnCount property controls the number of columns Access displays.

Value List   Enter a list of values, separated by semicolons, one row at a time. If the ColumnHeads property is Yes, the first row of data will go into the column headings in the control. If you set the ColumnCount property incorrectly, the data will not go into the columns and rows as you had planned. Figure 7.13 shows the examples in action. Here are some examples:

- **Yes;No:** Displays just the two values Yes and No. Note that the display is also tied to the ColumnCount property. If the ColumnCount is 1, Yes and No each appears in its own row. If the ColumnCount is 2 or higher, Yes and No both appear on the first row of the control.

- **City;State;Houston;TX;Boston;MA;Los Angeles;CA;San Jose;CA:** Displays a two-column list with four rows of data, assuming these properties:

     ColumnCount = 2

     ColumnHeads = Yes

- **True;-1;False;0:** Displays just the two values True and False and stores a Yes/No value back to the underlying field, given these properties:

     ColumnCount = 2

     ColumnWidths = ;0

     BoundColumn = 2

     ControlSource = a Yes/No field from the underlying data source

Field List Enter the name of a table or query from the form's RecordSource. The fields will be listed in their physical order in the table or in the order in which they were placed into the query. There is no way to alphabetize the list. Here is an example:

- **tblNames:** Displays a list of the fields in the table tblNames, assuming that tblNames is a table in the current database.

The ColumnCount Property

The ColumnCount property controls the number of columns of data Access will store in the control's data area. The actual number of displayed columns can be no more than the number specified in this property, but it might be less, depending on the contents of the ColumnWidths property. Even if you render some of the data invisible (by using a ColumnWidth setting of 0), it's still loaded into the control, and you can retrieve it by using the Column(n) property.

Set the ColumnCount property with a number or a numeric value. Access rounds nonintegral values to the nearest whole number.

The ColumnWidths Property

The ColumnWidths property sets the widths of the columns in the control and should be filled with a semicolon-delimited list of integers, one per column. The default width is approximately 1 inch or 3 centimeters, depending on the unit of measurement. Leaving a value out of the list accepts the default width. A setting of 0 hides a column. If the physical area dedicated to the control is not wide enough to display all the columns, Access truncates the right-most column, and the control displays horizontal scroll bars. Note that a single-column control will never have horizontal scroll bars, no matter how wide that single column is.

For each of the examples, the control contains four columns and is 5 inches wide. All measurements are in inches. Figure 7.14 shows these example list boxes (frmListWidths from CH7.MDB).

- **2;2;2;2:** Each column is 2 inches wide. Since this is 3 inches wider than the control, Access provides horizontal scroll bars.

- **2:** The first column is 2 inches wide, and the rest assume the default width (1 inch).

- **2;0;3;0:** The first and third columns are displayed. The second and fourth are hidden.

- **(Blank):** All four columns are evenly spaced over the width of the control since the control is wider than the sum of the default widths. If it were narrower than the total widths, the first three columns would each be 1 inch wide (the default width) and the last column would use the rest of the space (2 inches).

FIGURE 7.14:

Various ColumnWidths settings

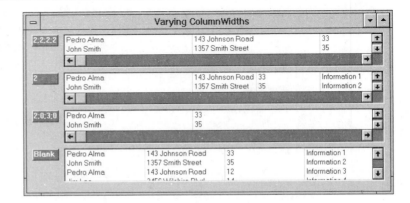

The ColumnHeads Property

The ColumnHeads property indicates whether or not Access should display a single row of column headings at the top of the control. (For combo boxes, Access displays this heading row only when you've asked it to expose the drop-down list.) When the RowSourceType property is ValueList, the first row of data goes into the header. If the RowSourceType is FieldList, the first field in the list goes into the header row. You should therefore not use the FieldList row source type when displaying column headers. If you do, Access displays the field names in the header row.

The BoundColumn Property

The BoundColumn property indicates which of the columns in the control will actually be returned when you've made a selection from the list. This means that the control returns the value from this column when you assign its value to a variable, for example.

Normal Operation   You must set the BoundColumn property as an integer between 0 and the number stored in the ColumnCount property.

To retrieve the value from the control, use varMyVariable = cboTestCombo. The variable varMyVariable receives the value from the chosen row in cboTestCombo, from the column specified in its BoundColumn property.

To set the value of the control, use cboTestCombo = varMyVariable. This code selects the first row in cboTestCombo in which the value in the column specified in the BoundColumn property matches the value stored in varMyVariable. If Access can't find a match, the control value will be null.

The Special Case   If you set the BoundColumn property to 0, Access returns the selected row number in the control; the value of the control will be the row number of the selected row. Although this isn't very useful for bound controls—the chosen row number won't mean much when stored in a database—it can be very useful if you need to select a particular row in the control.

Suppose, for example, that you want to make sure you've selected the first row of an unbound list box for each record, before the user even gets a chance to make a choice. Normally, to specify the row of the control you want selected, you would just assign a value to the control.

Unfortunately, in some cases (for example, when the RowSource of the control is a SQL query), you don't know the value of the bound field in the first row. To get around this problem, set the BoundColumn property to 0. Once you've done this, you can just assign the control the value 0, which will select the first row (the row values are zero-based). To retrieve values from a control with the BoundColumn set to 0, use the Column property, discussed in the next section. To see an example of setting the BoundColumn property to 0, see the section "Creating a Multi-Pick List Box" later in this chapter.

The Column Property

The Column property of list and combo boxes is not available at design time but figures prominently at run time. It allows you access to data in any of the columns of the control. Use 0 to refer to the first column, 1 for the second, and so on. (In a fit of nonstandardization, Access uses zero-based numbers for the columns. This means that when you set the BoundColumn property to 1, you use Column(0) to retrieve the value stored there.)

For example, to retrieve the data stored in the second column of cboTestCombo, use

```
varTestVariable = cboTestCombo.Column(1)
```

Present a Name, Store an ID

Given these facts:

- A list/combo box can contain more than one column (ColumnCount > 0).
- The first visible column is the one Access displays in the text box portion of the combo box.
- Any column in the list/combo box can be bound to the underlying data (BoundColumn).
- You can set the width of any column to 0, rendering it invisible (ColumnWidths).
- List/combo boxes have their own separate source of data (RowSource).

it's easy to create a list or combo box that displays user-friendly information (like a name) but stores information the user doesn't normally care to see (like a counter value). Figure 7.15 shows such a combo box in action. In this example you're filling in a shipping form and want to choose the delivery method from a combo box. The delivery method is stored as an integer, but you can't expect users to remember the integer associated with each carrier. Therefore, you can use a query (qryDelivery-Method) to feed the data for the combo's RowSource property. The second column in the combo has been made invisible (ColumnWidths set to ";0"), and the combo box will store the chosen value in its second column, the ID, to the underlying data (BoundColumn = 2, ControlSource = *DeliveryMethod*). You should be able to apply this same method to any situation in which you want to present the user with one piece of information but store a different, related piece of information.

FIGURE 7.15:

Display text, but store an ID to the underlying data.

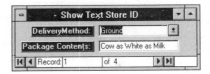

 When your combo box is bound to a numeric field (as it is in the previous example), you need to set the TextAlign property yourself. Since Access thinks you're really displaying a numeric value, it aligns the text to the right (which is how it treats numeric values). Set the TextAlign property manually to display the text the way you want it aligned.

The LimitToList Problem

The LimitToList property indicates to Access whether or not to allow you to enter new values into a combo box. Setting this property to Yes allows you to disregard the current list of values and enter a new one, and setting it to No forces you to choose a value from the current list. If you set your combo box's BoundColumn property to any column besides the first visible column, Access will (and must) set the LimitToList property to Yes.

You may not, at first thought, agree with this design decision. Imagine, though, for a moment, what's really going on here. Access displays and lets you enter values for the first visible column in the combo box. Therefore, if the control's Bound-Column property is set to 1, Access can take whatever it is you type and store it in the underlying data, even if it's not currently in the list. On the other hand, if the BoundColumn property is greater than 1 and you enter a value that's not already part of the list, Access needs to be able to store a value it doesn't have. Therefore, Access has no choice but to disallow new entries into combo boxes where the first column isn't displaying the bound field. Figure 7.16 shows, in pictorial form, why Access must make this limitation.

Combo boxes don't always do exactly what you might expect in terms of string matching. For example, if the LimitToList property is set to Yes, you might think that typing enough characters to find a match at all would be sufficient for Access

FIGURE 7.16:

LimitToList must be set to Yes if you've bound your combo box to a column other than the first column.

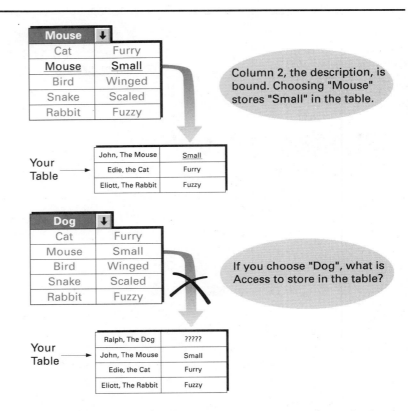

to accept the selected value. That is not the case. You must type enough characters to indicate a *unique* match before Access will accept your value and let you leave the field. This can be frustrating for users who will type some characters, see the match in the combo box, and attempt to accept that value by pressing ↵. Unless the characters they've typed so far constitute a unique match, they'll need to keep typing. Combining the LimitToList property with the AutoExpand property, though, will make many users happy. If you set both LimitToList and AutoExpand to Yes, your users can leave the combo box as soon as Access has found any matching value in the list.

In addition, null values are always a problem. If the LimitToList property is Yes and you type a value into a combo box and then delete it by backspacing over all the characters, the value now will not match any value in your list (unless you happen to have an empty value in your list). You will not be able to leave the combo box.

An easy way out is to press the Esc key, which undoes your change and lets you leave the control.

Taming the NotInList Event

Access 2.0 adds a new event for combo boxes that gives your application more control over how and when it adds new items to the data underlying the combo box. When a user attempts to enter an item into a combo box (whose LimitToList property is set to Yes) that doesn't match one of the existing items in list, Access triggers the NotInList event. If you have code in the form's module reacting to that event, you can take one of three actions, depending on how you fill in the Response argument that Access passes to the subroutine:

- If you place the value DATA_ERRDISPLAY in Response, Access displays its standard error message.

- If you place DATA_ERRCONTINUE in Response, Access doesn't display its error message, giving you the chance to display your own. If you use this option, make sure you really do display your own error message. Users will be rather confused, otherwise.

- If you place DATA_ERRADDED in Response, you must add the item to the underlying record source, and then Access requeries the combo box for you, effectively adding it to the list.

Since the third option is the most interesting (and the on-line Help topic for this event is rather misleading), this is where we'll focus.

Access passes your procedure two parameters: NewData contains the current text in the combo box, and Response allows you to send back the results of your subroutine.

The following simple case, from frmNotInList in CH7.MDB, just asks the user whether or not to add the new item to the list:

```
Sub cboTest_NotInList (NewData As String, Response As Integer)
    Dim strMsg As String
    Dim rst As Recordset
    Dim db As Database
```

```
Const MB_YESNO = 4
Const MB_QUESTION = 32
Const IDNO = 7

    strMsg = "'" & NewData & "' is not in the list. "
    strMsg = strMsg & "Would you like to add it?"
    If MsgBox(strMsg, MB_YESNO + MB_QUESTION, "New Company") =
➡ IDNO Then
        Response = DATA_ERRDISPLAY
    Else
        Set db = DBEngine.Workspaces(0).Databases(0)
        Set rst = db.OpenRecordset("tblCompanies")
        rst.AddNew
            rst("Company") = NewData
        rst.Update
        Response = DATA_ERRADDED
    End If
End Sub
```

The code first pops up a message box, asking the user whether to add the new value. If the user consents, the procedure runs code to add the new value and then tells Access to requery the combo box. By passing back DATA_ERRADDED in the Response parameter, you're telling Access that it should requery the combo and then try again to verify that the item exists in the list. If the item still isn't in the list for some reason (the sample code doesn't deal with errors, and it ought to), you'll still see the default error message from Access.

In general, your situations won't be this simple. Most likely, you'll need to gather some information from the user before adding a new row to the table. In that case you'll probably want to pop up a form, gather the information, add it to the table, and then send the DATA_ERRADDED back to Access to indicate that you've added the new row.

The BeforeUpdate and AfterUpdate Events

Just as with the other controls, Access fires off the BeforeUpdate event just before it attempts to update the underlying record set, and the AfterUpdate event occurs just after. You can attach code to either of these events to trap the selection event in either a list or a combo box.

Even more interesting is the ability to trap *movement* in a list box. Access triggers both the BeforeUpdate and the AfterUpdate events everytime you move the selection bar in a list box. Access must do this because, were you to leave the list box with a Tab or Shift+Tab key at any point, the currently selected item would become the value of the control. This doesn't occur in a combo box, though, since Access won't write any value to the recordset until you've made a selection by clicking, pressing ↵, or leaving the combo. Since you can attach code to the Before/AfterUpdate events in a list box, you can make changes to other controls on your form based on the current value in the list box. Thus, you have the choice of using a "push" method for filling unbound controls on your form (that is, you *push* values into them) in addition to the simpler "pull" method, where the controls use expressions to pull in their values from other sources.

Using Combo and List Boxes to Fill In Other Controls

Access provides several methods by which you can choose a value and have the corresponding data from other fields filled in for you on a form. The method you choose depends on whether or not the controls to be filled in are bound and how many controls you want filled in.

Data Filled In for Free: Using Row Fixup

Row Fixup is a very misunderstood and under-utilized feature. It comes into play anytime you have a one-to-many query, your form is set up to allow editing to "Default Tables" (or you're in Datasheet view), and you make a change to the "many" side of the one-to-many query. If the field you change on the "many" side is the linking value between the two tables, Access knows that there can be only one set of data that matches that value and fills in all the new data, based on the changed value. (For an example of this specific behavior, see the Orders form in NWIND.MDB, which ships with Access.) Row Fixup is really of value only when you're looking up some information for part of a larger form, as in an address on a shipping form, since the lookup must take place in a one-to-many query. If you just want to use a combo box to choose a name and have that person's information show up in text boxes, you should look at the other lookup techniques provided here.

Pulling versus Pushing Data into Controls

Imagine that you want to provide a combo box from which the user can choose a value. Once a value has been chosen, you want to fill in various other controls on the form with data found in the row that corresponds to the value the user just chose. The methods for doing this are different, depending on whether or not those other fields are bound. If the other controls are bound, you must "push" data into them; otherwise, they can "pull" the new data in themselves. You might think of the pull method as being *passive*, since the data just flows in, and the push method as being *active*, since you must provide code to copy the data from the list or combo box. For examples of each type of mechanism, you can investigate frmPullTest and frmPushTest in CH7.MDB. Figure 7.17 shows frmPullTest in action, and Figure 7.18 shows frmPushTest.

FIGURE 7.17:

frmPullTest uses the Column() property in each of its text boxes to retrieve the values from the current row.

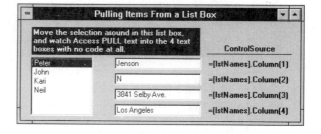

FIGURE 7.18:

frmPushTest uses a small Access Basic function to copy values from lstNames to each of the text boxes.

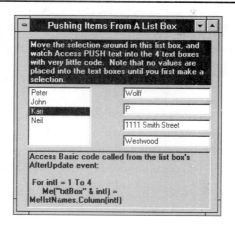

Pulling Data into Unbound Controls

If the controls to be filled in are unbound, their ControlSource property is empty and you can use an expression to pull in data from the combo box where the user just made a choice. All references in this example work equally well for list boxes and combo boxes.

To make this happen, just follow these steps:

1. **Fill the combo:** Create a query (or use an existing table) that contains the data you want to present to the user, plus any other fields you want filled in automatically once the user makes a choice. Later steps will be simpler if you make sure the value to be displayed in the combo is the first field in the table or query, but that isn't imperative.

2. **Prepare the combo:** Set the ColumnWidths property so that the correct column is visible and the other columns are invisible. If the first column is the one you want displayed and you have five columns total, your Column-Widths setting would be

   ;0;0;0;0

   This tells Access to use the default width for the first column and 0 width (hidden) for the next four columns.

3. **Prepare the other controls:** Set the ControlSource property for each of the controls into which you want data pulled. In each case, set the ControlSource property to

   =*YourCombo*.Column(n)

   where *YourCombo* is the ControlName of the combo and n is the column number (starting at 0) you want pulled into the control.

Once you've set up the form, Access takes care of the rest. Anytime the combo box changes, the other controls on the form will recalculate and pull the value they need from the combo box. If you're pulling information from a list box, the information will be updated each time you move the selection bar in the list box. This is a convenient way to browse items as your user moves through the list box using the arrow keys. It takes absolutely no Access Basic to accomplish a great deal!

> **TIP**
>
> Since the controls must have a calculated ControlSource for this method to work (and are therefore read-only), you might find it useful to also set the Locked property to Yes and the Enabled property to No. This way they look normal, but your user can't make changes.

Pushing Data into Bound Controls

If you need to fill in controls that are bound, their ControlSource property is not empty and you can't use the "pull" method as described in the previous section. In this case you'll need to push data into them once you've made a choice from the combo or list box. This is simple, also, but requires a bit of code.

The steps you follow to implement this method are just the same as they were for the "pull" method. In this case, though, you need to leave the ControlSource property of the text boxes alone. The assumption is that you're using this method because those controls are bound to data fields. To apply the "push" method, you attach code to the AfterUpdate event of the combo or list box, which will fill the appropriate controls. In the example form, frmPushText, the code just loops through all the columns and sends out data to each of the four conveniently named text boxes:

```
Dim intI As Integer
For intI = 1 To 4
    Me("txtBox" & intI) = lstNames.Column(intI)
Next intI
```

Filling a List or Combo Box Programmatically

Access provides you with many ways to get data into a list box without programming at all. You can supply a table or query name, a list of items, or a SQL string. With the new functionality added in version 2.0, you have even fewer limitations than you did in previous versions since you can now change the RowSource property of the list box while your program is running.

There is still at least one case in which you'll need to write Access Basic code to fill a list box: if you need to fill the list box with values from an array, you must write code to do it. We suggest two such methods, but creative programmers can probably come up with others. You can either manipulate the RowSource property directly, providing a semicolon-delimited list of values, or write an Access Basic callback function to provide Access with the needed values.

Changing the RowSource Property

Imagine a situation in which you have two buttons on your form. Choosing one of those buttons fills a list box with values from one specific field, and choosing the other fills the list box with values from a different field. Figure 7.19 shows a form like this in action (frmFillTest in CH7.MDB).

FIGURE 7.19:
Click the Show Locations button to see a list of locations or the Show Products button to see a list of products.

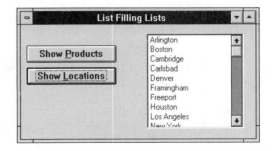

The following method creates a semicolon-delimited list of items for the list box (which must have its RowSourceType property set to Value List) based on the recordset chosen by the user.

```
Set rst = db.OpenRecordset("Select [" & strField & " From "] &
➡ strTable & " Order by [" & strField & "]",
➡ DB_OPEN_DYNASET)
Do Until rst.EOF
    strFill = strFill & rst(strField) & ";"
    rst.MoveNext
Loop
frm!lstShowList.RowSource = strFill
rst.Close
```

This code creates the Recordset object and walks through that object, building up a string in the format:

Item1;Item2;Item3;Item4;...ItemN;

and then places that string in the list box's RowSource property. Since the RowSource property can contain only 2048 characters, however, you're limited to small recordsets when you use this method.

Listing 7.3 shows the entire function. Interestingly, we performed some simple timing tests. Compared to the more obvious method, which is to set the RowSource-Type to Table/Query and the RowSource to a SQL string describing the list, this method performed favorably for small lists. For larger lists, you'll have to try both and convince yourself.

Listing 7.3

```
Const SHOW_PRODUCTS = 1
Const SHOW_LOCATIONS = 2

Function SetListBoxContents(frm As Form, intFlag As Integer)
    ' Example function to show a method of filling lists using
    ' Access Basic.

    Dim db As Database
    Dim rst As Recordset
    Dim strField As String
    Dim strTable As String
    Dim strFill As String

    Set db = DBEngine.WorkSpaces(0).Databases(0)

    Select Case intFlag
        Case SHOW_PRODUCTS
            strField = "Products"
            strTable = "tblProducts"
        Case SHOW_LOCATIONS
            strField = "Locations"
            strTable = "tblLocations"
        Case Else
            Exit Function
    End Select
```

```
      Set rst = db.OpenRecordset("Select [" & strField & "] From
      ➡ " & strTable & " Order by [" & strField & "]",
      ➡ DB_OPEN_DYNASET)
      Do Until rst.EOF
          strFill = strFill & rst(strField) & ";"
          rst.MoveNext
      Loop
      frm!lstShowList.RowSource = strFill
      rst.Close
      db.Close
End Function
```

Using a Callback Function to Fill the List Box

To fill a list or combo box with an array of values or display information from an internal Access data structure, your best alternative is to use a list-filling function. Access allows you to supply a function that tells it all about the list or combo box you want displayed. You tell Access how many columns, how many rows, the formatting for individual elements, and the actual data elements themselves. This is the only case in which Access directly calls a user-created function and uses the information it receives back from that function. This is, in effect, what makes your function a *callback* function—you are supplying information Access needs to do its job.

All this flexibility comes at a price, however. For Access to be able to communicate with your function, it needs to have a very specific interface and it must respond in expected ways when Access requests information from it. Access calls your function at various times as it's filling the list box and indicates to your function exactly which piece of information it requires at that moment by providing an action code as one of the parameters. Metaphorically, everytime Access calls this function, it's asking a question. It's up to your function to supply the answer. The question might be, "How many columns are there?" or "What value do you want displayed in row 1, column 2?" In any case Access supplies all the information you need to retrieve or calculate the necessary answer. The return value from the function returns the question's answer to Access.

To attach your function to the list/combo box on a form, type its name (*without* a leading equal sign and *without* trailing parentheses) in the RowSourceType on the property sheet. This break in the normal syntax for the property sheet tells Access that you're specifying a callback function. Figure 7.20 shows the property sheet set up to use a callback function.

FIGURE 7.20:

Note the syntax of using a callback function: no leading equal sign, no trailing parentheses.

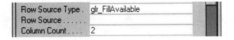

Row Source Type .	glr_FillAvailable
Row Source	
Column Count	2

Setting Up Your Callback Function

Any function that will be used as a list-filling callback function must accept exactly five parameters, the first declared As Control and the rest As Variant. The following table lists the various parameters and their descriptions:

Parameter	Description
ctlField	Control-type variable that refers to the list box or combo box being filled
varID	Unique value that identifies the control being filled; you may find it more useful to check the ctlField.Name if you need to differentiate between controls using this code
varRow	Row being filled in (zero-based)
varCol	Column being filled in (zero-based)
varCode	The "question" Access is asking your function; its value indicates what action your function should take

A typical function declaration looks like this:

```
Function FillList(ctlField as Control, varID as Variant,
➡ varRow as Variant, varCol as Variant, varCode as Variant)
```

Your function reacts to each of the values in varCode, returning the information Access requests. Table 7.4 lists the possible values for varCode, their constant names as defined by Access, and the information Access is requesting when it sends you each of the constants.

TABLE 7.4: The LB_ Constants and Their Uses in Filling a List or Combo Box Programmatically

varCode	Constant	Meaning	Return Value
0	LB_INITIALIZE	Initialize	Non-zero if your function can successfully fill the list; 0 or Null otherwise
1	LB_OPEN	Open	Non-zero ID value if function can successfully fill the list; 0 or Null otherwise. Many functions use the return value from the Timer() function to get a unique value
2	Not used		Not used, although Access does call the function with this value. Its use is not documented
3	LB_GETROWCOUNT	Number of rows	Number of rows in the list (can be 0); −1 if unknown. If you specify −1, Access calls the function to retrieve values (LB_GETVAL) until you return a Null value
4	LB_GETCOLUMNCOUNT	Number of columns	Number of columns in the list (can't be 0); should match the value in the property sheet. You can, of course, just pass back ctlField.ColumnCount
5	LB_GETCOLUMNWIDTH	Column width	Width of the column specified in the varCol parameter (can be 0), measured in twips (1/1440 inch). Specify −1 to use the property sheet values
6	LB_GETVALUE	Value	Value to be displayed at row varRow and column varCol
7	LB_GETFORMAT	Format string	Format string to be used in displaying the value at row varRow and column varCol. Specify −1 to use the default format

TABLE 7.4: The LB_ Constants and Their Uses in Filling a List or Combo Box Programmatically (continued)

varCode	Constant	Meaning	Return Value
8	LB_CLOSE	Not used	Not used, so no return value. Access does call your function with this value, though. Its use is not documented
9	LB_END	End	Returns nothing. Used when you close the form or requery the control. Use this portion of your function to release memory or clean up as necessary

When Access requests values for the list (LB_GETVALUE), it supplies a row and a column number, implying that you need to have random access to your data. Filling a list box from a recordset, then, is a tricky issue since you don't really have random access to Recordset objects in Access. You can emulate random access, however, using the Move method for Recordset objects. We present both methods of solving this problem. The first solution here suggests copying data from your recordset into an array, so you actually *can* access specific rows at will, but this method becomes quite slow when your datasets are large. The second solution uses the Move method to get to the exact record you need, based on the most recent record you were on and the new row number you need to get to. This method starts up more quickly since it's not copying data into an array, but it's slower in execution since it must refer to actual data on disk to display its contents.

In general, your callback function will probably look something like the code in Listing 7.4. It needn't be terribly complex, and once you've written a few of them, you should be able to cut and paste a new one in seconds.

Listing 7.4

```
Function FillList(ctlField as Control, varId as Variant,
➥ varRow as Variant, varCol as Variant, varCode as Variant)

    Dim varRetval as Variant
    Dim intRows as Integer
```

```
Dim intCols as Integer
Static aData() as Variant

Select Case varCode
    Case LB_INITIALIZE
        ' Initialization code
        ' Figure out how many rows and columns there are
        ' to be, and ReDim the array to hold them.
        ReDim aData(intRows, intCols)
        ' Code to fill the array would go here.
        varRetval = True
    Case LB_OPEN
        ' Return a Unique ID code. The built-in Timer
        ' function works well.
        varRetval = Timer
    Case LB_GETROWCOUNT
        ' Return number of rows
        varRetval = intRows
    Case LB_GETCOLUMNCOUNT
        ' Return number of columns
        varRetval = intCols
    Case LB_GETCOLUMNWIDTH
        ' Return the column widths. If you return -1
        ' from this call, Access will use the default
        ' width for the specific column. That way,
        ' you can use the property sheet to supply the
        ' column widths.
        Select Case varCol
            Case 0
                ' Handle the first column
                varRetval = 1440
            Case 1
                ' Handle the second column
                ' and so on.
                varRetval = -1
        End Select
    Case LB_GETVALUE
        ' Return actual data.
        ' This example returns an element of the
        ' array filled in case LB_INITIALIZE.
        varRetval = aData(varRow, varCol)
    Case LB_GETFORMAT
        ' Return the formatting info for a given row
```

```
                    ' and column. This feature did not work in
                    ' Access 1.x, by the way.
                    varRetval = Null
             Case LB_END
                    ' Clean up
                    Erase aData
             End Select
             FillList = varRetval
      End Function
```

Using a Callback Function

Displaying a list of table and/or query names is a prime candidate for using a call-back function. Since you can get such a list only by enumerating Access objects, the callback function provides the most reasonable way to get the values into a list box. (You could, of course, base your list box on a query that pulls values directly from the undocumented MSysObjects table. Since that method is not supported by Microsoft, we're going to persue the documented, but more complex, solution.) This example makes heavy use of data access objects to do its work. (See Chapter 6 for more information on the object collections.) The full code for this example can be found in Listing 7.5. Figure 7.21 shows the example form (frmListTables from CH7.MDB) in use.

In the LB_INITIALIZE case your goal is to set up the array to be used for later retrieval in the LB_GETVALUE case. In this example you need to find out how many tables and queries there are and store that value away. If there are no tables or queries (an unlikely event since every database has at least the system tables), return a False value, telling Access your function is unable to initialize the list box.

FIGURE 7.21:
Choose Tables, Queries, or Both to
display a list of the selected items.

```
Set db = DBEngine.Workspaces(0).Databases(0)
' Figure out the greatest number of entries
' there might be.
intItems = db.TableDefs.Count + db.QueryDefs.Count
If intItems = 0 Then
    varRetval = False
Else
.
.
.
```

Once you've found that there are some tables or queries to display, your next step in the initialization case is to build up the array you will send to Access in the LB_GETVALUE case. Based on choices you've made on the form, the function will pull in different items for the list. For example, to get a list of queries, the code looks like this:

```
If ShowQueries() Then
    For intLoop = 0 To db.QueryDefs.Count - 1
        Set qry = db.QueryDefs(intLoop)
        astrTableName(intInc) = qry.Name
        intInc = intInc + 1
    Next intLoop
End If
```

The variable intInc will indicate the number of elements in the list box once you've finished all the looping, and this is the value you pass back to Access in the LB_GETROWCOUNT case.

The rest of the code closely follows the skeleton example. It uses the default column widths and doesn't even bother dealing with the LB_GETFORMAT case since it's just using the default formats. When asked to supply a value (in the LB_GETVALUE case), it just returns the value for the given row from the array it built in the LB_INITIALIZE case. Finally, when the Access shuts down the list box, the LB_END case uses the Erase command to release the memory used by the array.

Listing 7.5

```
Const SHOW_TABLES = 1
Const SHOW_QUERIES = 2
Const SHOW_BOTH = 3
Function FillTableOrQueryList(ctlField As Control,
```

```
➥ varID As Variant, varRow As Variant,
➥ varCol As Variant, varCode As Variant)
    ' Fill a combo or list box with a list of
    ' tables or queries.

    ' These variables "hang around" between
    ' calls to this function.
    Static astrTableName() As String
    Static intInc As Integer

    Dim db As Database
    Dim intCount As Integer
    Dim varRetval As Variant
    Dim intLoop As Integer
    Dim intItems As Integer
    Dim tdf As TableDef
    Dim qdf As QueryDef

    varRetval = Null
    Select Case varCode
        ' Initialize
        Case LB_INITIALIZE
            Set db = DBEngine.Workspaces(0).Databases(0)
            ' Figure out the greatest number of entries
            ' there might be.
            intItems = db.TableDefs.Count + db.QueryDefs.Count
            If intItems = 0 Then
                varRetval = False
            Else
                ' Set up the array to hold names.
                ReDim astrTableName(intItems)
                ' Set up variable to hold the number of names.
                intInc = 0

                ' If the "Show Tables" or "Show Both" option
                ' button is selected, gather up table names.
                If ShowTables() Then
                    For intLoop = 0 To db.TableDefs.Count - 1
                        Set tdf = db.TableDefs(intLoop)
                        ' The Imp operator returns TRUE except
                        ' when the first condition is True and
                        ' the second is False. That is, it will
                        ' return True unless this is a system
```

```
                                ' table and system tables are not
                                ' being shown.
                                If isSystem(tdf.Attributes) Imp
                              ➡ ShowSystem() Then
                                    astrTableName(intInc) = tdf.Name
                                    intInc = intInc + 1
                                End If
                            Next intLoop
                        End If
                        ' If the "Show Queries" or "Show Both" option
                        ' button is selected, gather up query names.
                        If ShowQueries() Then
                            For intLoop = 0 To db.QueryDefs.Count - 1
                                Set qdf = db.QueryDefs(intLoop)
                                astrTableName(intInc) = qdf.Name
                                intInc = intInc + 1
                            Next intLoop
                        End If

                        ' Tell Access that the list box is OK, so far.
                        varRetval = True
                    End If
            Case LB_OPEN
                ' Get a Unique ID number for control.
                varRetval = Timer
            Case LB_GETROWCOUNT
                ' Get the Number of rows.
                varRetval = intInc
            Case LB_GETCOLUMNCOUNT
                ' Get the Number of columns.
                varRetval = 1
            Case LB_GETCOLUMNWIDTH
                ' Get the Column width.
                ' Use default width.
                varRetval = -1
            Case LB_GETVALUE
                ' Get the actual data for the row.
                varRetval = astrTableName(varRow)
            Case LB_END
                ' Clean up (release memory)
                Erase astrTableName
        End Select
        FillTableOrQueryList = varRetval
End Function
```

```
Function InitForm(frm As Form)
    frm!grpChooseGroup.SetFocus
    frm!grpChooseGroup = 1
    frm!chkShowSystem = False
    frm!lstTables.Requery
End Function

Function isSystem(varAttr As Variant)
    isSystem = ((varAttr And DB_SYSTEMOBJECT) <> 0)
End Function

Function ShowQueries ()
    Dim ctl As Control
    ' Make the decision based on what's checked on the form.
    Set ctl = Forms!frmListTables!grpChooseGroup
    ShowQueries = (ctl = SHOW_QUERIES Or ctl = SHOW_BOTH)
End Function

Function ShowSystem()
    ShowSystem = Forms![frmListTables]!chkShowSystem
End Function

Function ShowTables()
    Dim frm As Form
    Dim ctl As Control

    ' Make the decision based on what's checked on the form.
    Set ctl = Forms!frmListTables!grpChooseGroup
    ShowTables = (ctl = SHOW_TABLES Or ctl = SHOW_BOTH)
End Function
```

To include this form in your own application, follow these steps:

1. Import the module basListTables from CH7.MDB into your application.

2. Import the form frmListTables from CH7.MDB into your application.

3. Modify the AfterUpdate event of the list box lstTables to *do* something with the user's choice. Perhaps you'll want to place it into a global variable for later use.

Using the Move Method to Access Data

With the addition of the Move method in Access 2.0, you now have another choice when filling list and combo boxes programmatically. The syntax of the Move method is this:

Recordset.Move *lngRows*[, *strBookMark*]

where *lngRows* specifies the number of rows to move and *strBookMark* specifies an optional bookmark from which to start. In this example, which fills a list box without using an array (as opposed to the previous example), you keep track of the last row request from Access, as well as the previous bookmark for the recordset. That way, when Access requests that you retrieve the data for a specific row in the list box, you can easily move to the same row in the recordset and retrieve the correct data. Note that this isn't as easy as complete random access, in which you could just move to a specific row in the recordset, but it's awfully close.

The form frmFillMoveList, in CH7.MDB, demonstrates a simple use of this method. The list box, lstCompanies, uses the function FillMoveList() to fill itself. You can find the entire function in the module basFillMoveList in CH7.MDB.

In the LB_INITIALIZE case the function opens the recordset, storing a reference to it in the static variable, rst. FillMoveList() then stores away, for later use, a bookmark for the current record, varBM. In addition, it initializes the static variable, lngRow, that will keep track of the most recently accessed row.

```
Set db = DBEngine.Workspaces(0).Databases(0)
Set rst = db.OpenRecordset("qryCompanies", DB_OPEN_DYNASET)
varBM = rst.BookMark
lngRow = 0
FillMoveList = True
```

TIP

As mentioned in Chapter 6, it's not enough to create a static recordset variable. Once the database variable it's based on goes out of scope, the recordset variable does, too. The solution is to make sure that both the database variable and the recordset variable are declared using the Static keyword. This way they'll both be available for the lifetime of the function.

To speed up the form-loading process, you tell Access to figure out for itself how many rows there are in this recordset. By returning a −1 value in the LB_GETROW-COUNT case, you can avoid the slow process of loading the entire recordset, which is the only way to get to the end of the recordset to find the number of rows.

```
Case LB_GETROWCOUNT
    FillMoveList = -1
```

The only other interesting case, LB_GETVALUE, does most of the work. It must first calculate the difference between the row it's been requested to retrieve data for, Row, and the last row in the recordset it accessed, lngRow. This difference tells the Move method the number of rows it will need to move the record pointer. Then it can just use the Move method to move the correct number of rows, store away the new bookmark and row number, and send back the correct data to Access.

To tell Access that it's reached the end of the recordset and it should stop trying to request data, you must pass a Null value back to Access. When Access has asked your code for data in a row that doesn't exist, your attempt to store the bookmark will fail since there is no active record. At that point you can check to see whether the value of Err is 0. If it is not, an error has occurred and you can send back null. Otherwise, just return the data as requested.

```
On Error Resume Next
lngMove = Row - lngRow
rst.Move lngMove, varBM
varBM = rst.BookMark
If Err = 0 Then
    lngRow = Row
    FillMoveList = rst!Company
Else
```

```
     FillMoveList = Null
End If
On Error GoTo 0
```

You'll need to decide for yourself which of these two methods to use when writing a list-filling callback function. If you can pull data from a single record source, you're better off using the Move method, as in the second example. If you're filling the list from an array or are using multiple recordsets, as in the first example, use an array to fill your list. At least, with the addition of the new Move method, you have a choice.

> **NOTE** You probably wouldn't use a list-filling callback function in a case as simple as the second example here. If you could specify a single query as your record source, you'd just set the RowSource property for the list box and write no code at all. But there will be times when you need to fill a list or combo box with a callback function, and in those situations you must choose which method is best for you. Note that in some cases using a list-filling function will actually execute more quickly than supplying the recordset name in the RowSource property. You'll need to experiment when working with large datasets.

Emulating a Permanently Open Combo Box

Access does not supply a drop-down list box control, and there will be times when you must have the list portion of a combo-like control permanently open. You can emulate this arrangement, however, with the pairing of a list box and a text box. The issue, of course, is performing the incremental search as you type into the text box, finding the matching elements of the list box as you type. Because Access 2.0 provides the Change event, you can attach code to this event property that finds the first entry in the list box that matches the text you currently have in the text box. This functionality looks and feels just like the search capability in Windows Help and should fit well into many applications. Figure 7.22 shows a sample form, frmTestIncSrch from CH7.MDB, in action.

FIGURE 7.22:
Typing into the text box will find the first matching value in the list box.

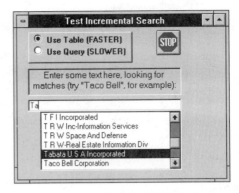

The drawbacks to this pairing, however, are somewhat serious. Because Access must do a lookup in the underlying data source for every change you make in the text box, response time can be slow in certain cases. On the other hand, if you can bind the list box to a table and use an index for lookups, the speed is quite reasonable even for large lists.

The sequence of steps necessary to accomplish this hybrid control is quite simple. Everytime Access fires off the Change event for the text box, it calls the glrIncSrch() function. This function tries to find the first entry in the list box's underlying recordset that matches the text currently in the text box. If the list box is bound to a table, the function uses the PrimaryKey index with the Seek method to find the first match. This method is quite fast. If the list box is bound to a query (and it must be bound to either a table or a query for this code to work at all), it uses the FindFirst method of the recordset to find the first match. This method is, unfortunately, much slower. If there's any way you can bind the list box to a table, we recommend that approach. The lookup times are much faster when using the Seek method on a table-type recordset rather than using the FindFirst method on a dynaset-type recordset.

The function grlIncSrch() uses some interesting techniques. (See Listing 7.6 for the complete code for this example.) First of all, rather than opening and closing a Recordset object for every lookup, it maintains a global recordset variable. The first time you try to perform a lookup, the attempt to access the recordset will fail, triggering an error condition. The error handler first needs to figure out whether the row source for the list box is a query or a table (since the function needs to treat these differently), calling the GetType() function to get this information. GetType()

assumes that the object is a table and, if it fails to find an object by that name in the TableDefs collection, decides that the object must be a query.

Listing 7.6

```
Const OBJ_TABLE = 1
Const OBJ_QUERY = 2

Const ERR_OBJECT_VAR_NOT_SET = 91
Const ERR_OBJECT_NOT_VALID = 3420
Const ERR_ILLEGAL_OP = 3219
Const ERR_NO_OBJECT = 3011

Dim mdb As Database
Dim mrst As Recordset

Private Function GetType(pdb As Database, strObject As String)
    ' Determine whether the object passed in is a query or
    ' a table. To do this, attempt to access the item in
    ' the TableDefs collection.  If that fails, well, then
    ' it must be a query.

    Dim strTemp As String

    On Error Resume Next
    GetType = OBJ_TABLE
    strTemp = pdb.TableDefs(strObject).name
    If Err <> 0 Then
        GetType = OBJ_QUERY
    Else
        ' The SourceTableName property is non-null for
        ' attached tables, so that appears to be an easy
        ' way to check for that.
        If Not Len(pdb.TableDefs(strObject).SourceTableName)
    ➥ = 0 Then
            GetType = OBJ_QUERY
        End If
    End If
    On Error GoTo 0
End Function

Function glrIncSearch (ctlTextBox As Control, ctlListBox
➥ As Control, strField As String)
```

```
' Perform the incremental search in ctlListBox, looking
' for what's been typed in ctlTextBox so far.  This routine
' opens the RecordSet variable mrst if it's not already
' set up.  If mrst is a table, it'll use the Seek method,
' otherwise, it'll use the FindFirst (much slower!) method.
'
' This method assumes that the field you're searching on
' is a TEXT field. If not you'll need to change the
' line dealing with mrst.FindFirst (only if you're using
' a query, rather than a table).

Dim varValue As Variant
Static intType As Integer

On Error GoTo glrDoIncSearchErr
varValue = ctlTextBox.Text

LookItUp:
    If intType = OBJ_TABLE Then
        mrst.Seek ">=", varValue
    Else
        mrst.FindFirst strField & " >= """ & varValue & """"
    End If
    If Not mrst.NoMatch Then
        ctlListBox = mrst(strField)
    Else
        MsgBox "No Match!"
    End If

glrDoIncSearchExit:
    Exit Function

glrDoIncSearchErr:
    If Err = ERR_OBJECT_VAR_NOT_SET Or Err =
➡ ERR_OBJECT_NOT_VALID Then
        ' If you got here, it's because the lookup failed
        ' because the object variable, mrst, hasn't been set yet.

        ' Get the current database.
        Set mdb = DBEngine.WorkSpaces(0).Databases(0)

        ' Figure out if the RowSource for the list box
        ' is a table or a query, since you must treat them
        ' differently when searching.
        intType = GetType(mdb, (ctlListBox.RowSource))
```

```
            ' If the source is a table, open up a Table
            ' Recordset object. Otherwise, open up a Dynaset object.
            If intType = OBJ_TABLE Then
                Set mrst = mdb.OpenRecordset(ctlListBox.RowSource,
                ➡ DB_OPEN_TABLE)
                mrst.Index = "PrimaryKey"
            Else
                SetRS ctlListBox.RowSource
            End If
            ' Now go back and attempt the lookup again.
            Resume LookItUp
        Else
            ' If it was some other error, just get out of here!
            GoTo glrDoIncSearchExit
        End If
End Function

Sub glrIncSrchEnd()
    ' Close the form's Record set variable.  If,
    ' for some reason, this causes an error,
    ' just disregard it.

    On Error Resume Next
    mrst.Close
    On Error Goto 0
End Sub

Function glrUpdateSearch(ctlTextBox As Control,
➡ ctlListBox As Control)

    ' Set the value of the text box to match
    ' that in the list box.

    ctlTextBox = ctlListBox
End Function

Private Sub SetRS(varRowSource As Variant)
    Dim qdf As QueryDef
    Dim intI As Integer
    Dim strName As String
    Dim prm As Parameter

    Set mdb = DBEngine.WorkSpaces(0).Databases(0)
```

```
      mdb.QueryDefs.Refresh

      On Error Resume Next
      Set qdf = mdb.OpenQueryDef(varRowSource)
      If Err = ERR_ILLEGAL_OP Or Err = ERR_NO_OBJECT Then
]           ' This must mean that you've attempted to
            ' open a querydef that is a table or a SQL string.  In
            ' that case, just open the Recordset and leave.
          Set mrst = mdb.OpenRecordset(varRowSource,
➡ DB_OPEN_DYNASET)
      Else
          For intI = 0 To qdf.Parameters.Count - 1
              Set prm = qdf.Parameters(intI)
              prm.Value = Eval(prm.name)
          Next intI
          Set mrst = qdf.OpenRecordset(DB_OPEN_DYNASET)
      End If
      On Error GoTo 0
  End Sub
```

If it finds that the row source is a table, it opens a table-type Recordset object based on the same data as the list box. Otherwise it opens a dynaset-type Recordset object. In either case the global variable mrst ends up pointing to the Recordset object, and the recordset will remain open until you close the form. (The code attached to the form's Close event closes the recordset.) Once everything's opened up, the function resumes back at the top, where it can now successfully do its work. The following code fragment shows the error-handling code in glrIncSrch():

```
varValue = ctlTextBox.Text
Set db = DBEngine.WorkSpaces(0).Databases(0)
intType = GetType(db, (ctlListBox.RowSource))
If intType = OBJ_TABLE Then
    Set mrst = db.OpenRecordset(ctlListBox.RowSource,
    ➡ DB_OPEN_TABLE)
    mrst.Index = "PrimaryKey"
Else
            SetRS ctlListBox.RowSource
End If
Resume LookItUp
```

Rather than just opening the Recordset object directly, glrIncSrch() calls the SetRS procedure to handle this case. To be as flexible as possible, SetRS attempts to resolve any parameters involved with the Querydef. By walking through the Parameters collection, it can supply all the values for the query, as long as the values are available. Listing 7.6 shows the code for SetRS.

You should notice that the assignment

```
varValue = ctlTextBox.Text
```

uses the Text property rather than the Value property, which is the default property for text boxes. Since the value in the text box has not yet been committed at the point at which the function needs to access its contents, the Value property has not yet been updated. The Text property is always current while the control is active, but the Value property is not.

Doing the work is really quite simple. If the list box is bound to a table, the function uses the Seek method to find the first value greater than or equal to the value in the text box. If the list box is bound to a query, the function builds a string expression to be used as the criteria for the FindFirst method and uses it to search for the first match. In either case, if the NoMatch property is Yes after the search, there's not much the function can do (especially since the search really can't fail unless something is seriously wrong with the data), and it just displays a message box and quits:

```
If intType = OBJ_TABLE Then
    mrst.Seek ">=", varValue
Else
    mrst.FindFirst strField & " >= """ & varValue & """"
End If
If Not mrst.NoMatch Then
    ctlListBox = mrst(strField)
Else
    MsgBox "No Match!"
End If
```

You might also notice that we've included code to fill in the text box with the currently selected value from the list box if you either click it in the list box or leave the text box at any point. This seems like reasonable and helpful behavior, similar to the way the AutoExpand property for combo boxes works.

In summary, the issues surrounding the use of this code are as follows:

- The list box's ControlSource must be either a table or a query.
- If the ControlSource is a table, the field you display must be the primary key (although you could change this in the code if you needed to).

- Using a query as the ControlSource is far more flexible, but it's much slower than using a table. This issue is far less important on small datasets. In simple timing tests, the hybrid control was approximately 50 percent slower in response to keystrokes than a similarly set up combo box, with a dataset of approximately 2000 items.

- Because the code uses a global variable to refer to the list box's underlying recordset, you cannot use this code for more than one pair of controls at the same time.

To include this functionality in your own application, follow these steps:

- Import the basIncSrch module from CH7.MDB.

- Create the text box and the list box.

- Attach code to the events as shown in Figure 7.23, replacing the control names and the field name with your own.

FIGURE 7.23:
Attach function calls to these events to implement the hybrid control on your own forms.

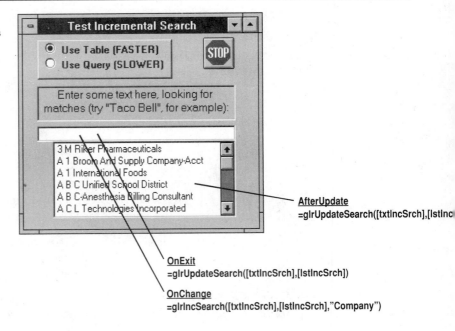

AfterUpdate
=glrUpdateSearch([txtIncSrch],[lstInc

OnExit
=glrUpdateSearch([txtIncSrch],[lstIncSrch])

OnChange
=glrIncSearch([txtIncSrch],[lstIncSrch],"Company")

Making Multiple Selections in a List Box

Access list boxes allow only a single selection. This limitation is quite a drawback when you need to supply your user with a list from which to choose a number of items. Fortunately, you can code around this problem by showing the user two list boxes, one representing available items and the other representing selected items. By moving items from one list to the other, your users can select a group of items on which to work. Figure 7.24 shows a sample multi-pick list box (frmMultiPik from CH7.MDB) in action.

By clicking the buttons (or double-clicking the list boxes), the user can select a group of items.

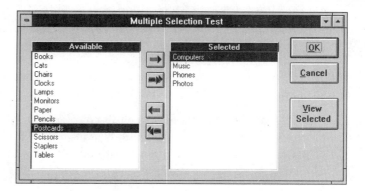

> **TIP**
>
> Microsoft has released a multiple-selection list box as an OLE custom control, available on CompuServe. Check the MSACCESS forum on CompuServe to pick up a copy of this custom control.

There are several ways to accomplish this goal using Access Basic, and we've chosen a method that allows you some flexibility. By using the code presented here you'll be able to base your multiple-pick hybrid control on a recordset (either a table or a query) or on two arrays of values, one representing the available list and one representing the selected list. You might want to open frmMultiPik in CH7.MDB and experiment a bit while reading the following sections.

Our implementation of multiple-pick lists uses three arrays: one master array and two subsidiary arrays that keep pointers to the rows in the master array that are available and those that are selected. The master array stores the data to display, along with the selection status of that particular piece of data. This array (aFull-Array() in the code) is based on this structure:

```
Type typeDataRow
    varData As Variant
    fSelected As Integer
End Type
```

The two subsidiary integer arrays, aAvailable() and aSelected(), do no more than store the index numbers of the available and selected items. When the code needs to fill in the Available or Selected list, it uses list-filling callback functions. (See the section "Using a Callback Function to Fill the List Box" earlier in this chapter.) In each case the callback function walks through each element of the available or selected array and fills the appropriate list box with the data from the master array. Given that varRow represents an index in the Selected list box, the item displayed in the list box will be aFullArray(aSelected(varRow)).varData. Figure 7.25 diagrams the relationships between the arrays and list boxes.

Like many other examples in this chapter, multiple-pick lists can be easily incorporated into your own applications. Rather than dissecting the full code for multiple-pick lists here, refer to basMultiPik in CH7.MDB. There are some points worth discussing here, though.

Filling the Two List Boxes

Unlike most other examples in this book, the two list boxes in this example have their BoundColumn property set to 0. As mentioned in the section "The Special Case" earlier in this chapter, setting the BoundColumn property to 0 effectively binds the list box to the selected row number, starting with 0. If the list box had a ControlSource (which these don't), you'd end up storing the chosen row number in the underlying data. In this case set the BoundColumn property to 0 so you can both retrieve the selected row and specify the particular row to select, programmatically.

In addition, these list boxes contain two columns. The first, visible, column contains the data from the master array. The second, hidden, column contains the master array index from which this particular piece of data came. Therefore, it takes two

FIGURE 7.25:

The two subsidiary arrays point to the available and selected items in the master array.

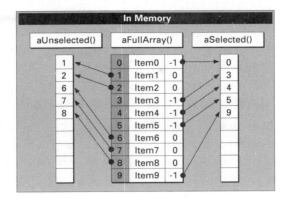

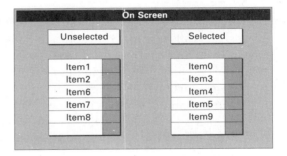

passes through the callback function to fill both columns. In one call to the function, when varCol is 0, Access retrieves the value for the first column. Access retrieves the value for the second column in a second call to the list-filling function:

```
Case LB_GETVALUE
    ' Get the data for each of the two columns.
    If varCol = 0 Then
        varRetval = aFullArray(aSelected(varRow)).varData
    Else
        varRetval = aSelected(varRow)
    End If
```

Using the Eqv Operator

To fill each of the two subsidiary arrays, basMultiPik walks through the master array, copying all the selected or available rows to the appropriate array. The list-filling functions call the function that does this, passing in an integer parameter indicating whether it should return all the available or all the selected rows. Therefore, the function should return any row in which the master array's fSelected value is the same as the requested value and return a True value when both values are True or both values are False. You could code this:

```
If (aFullArray(intLoop).fSelected AND fSelected) OR
➡ (NOT aFullArray(intLoop).fSelected AND NOT fSelected) Then ...
```

but Access provides a better way. The *Eqv* operator compares two integer values and returns a True value if they have the same "truth" value and False otherwise. Therefore, you can rewrite the previous attempt as:

```
If aFullArray(intLoop).fSelected Eqv fSelected Then
```

One Callback or Two?

It's true that Access does pass your callback function a unique identifier for each control that calls into that function, and it also passes a handle to the control being filled. Given that information, it would seem that you could write a single function to fill the two list boxes used in this example. Actually, it turns out that combining these two functions, glrFillSelected() and glrFillAvailable(), into one function is more work than it's worth. The problem is, we found, that the two list boxes get filled in bits and pieces, overlapping in time. Although they could physically be combined, the resulting code would be so convoluted and difficult to maintain that it made more sense to separate them.

Retrieving the Selected List

This hybrid control, the pairing of two different list boxes, wouldn't do you much good if you couldn't easily find out which items had been selected by the user. Therefore, the module basMultiPik includes a function your application can call to retrieve an array containing the list of selected items. The sample form (frmMulti-Pik) displays the list in a message box when you click the button labeled View Selected. To retrieve the list for your own use, call the function glrGetSelectedItems(), passing in a reference to the active form and a dynamic array that the function can fill in with the selected items. For example, in the sample form, the Click event of the View Selected button executes this code:

```
Sub cmdChosen_Click()
    Dim intI As Integer
```

```
    Dim aSelected() As Variant
    Dim strShowIt As String

    ' Get an array filled with the selected items.
    glrGetSelectedItems Me, aSelected()
    For intI = 0 To UBound(aSelected) - 1
        strShowIt = strShowIt & aSelected(intI) & Chr$(13) &
        ➡ Chr$(10)
    Next intI
    MsgBox strShowIt, 0, "Multiple Pick Test"
End Sub
```

Issues to Consider

The implementation of multiple-pick lists presented here is not completely generic. There are several issues of which you should be aware before you attempt to use this hybrid control in your own applications:

- The code is non-reentrant—you can't have multiple forms with multiple-pick lists on them at the same time.

- The data must come from either a table or query or from an array. To use a recordset variable to fill the list, you need to create an array and fill it with the appropriate data in the Sub SetupArrays().

- Think twice before using this method with large lists (more than 1000 data elements or so). It can take a long time to fill the arrays when you have many elements.

- Multiple-pick lists make sense only when the data elements you present to the user are unique. You may need to concatenate multiple fields in a query, creating a list of unique values. Once you have that unique list, you can present it to the user.

To include multiple-pick lists in your own applications, follow these steps:

1. Import the module basMultiPik from CH7.MDB.

2. Create your form, including two lists boxes and four data movement buttons. You may find it easiest to just copy the six controls from frmMultiPik in CH7.MDB by first importing frmMultiPik, then copying the appropriate controls, and then deleting frmMultiPik from your database.

3. Set the properties of the two list boxes, as shown in Figure 7.26. You must set the ColumnCount to 2 and the BoundColumn to 0. The other two settings (ColumnHeads and ColumnWidths) presented in Figure 7.26 are suggestions only.

FIGURE 7.26:

Attach the appropriate event code to your controls to implement multiple-pick lists.

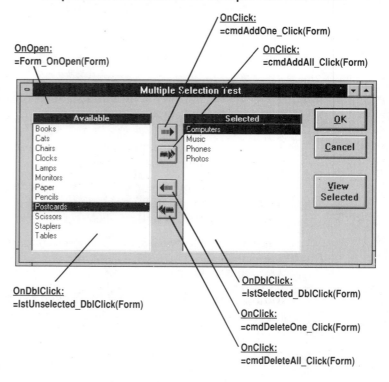

Required Event Handlers for Multiple-Pick List Boxes

OnClick:
=cmdAddOne_Click(Form)

OnClick:
=cmdAddAll_Click(Form)

OnOpen:
=Form_OnOpen(Form)

OnDblClick:
=lstUnselected_DblClick(Form)

OnDblClick:
=lstSelected_DblClick(Form)

OnClick:
=cmdDeleteOne_Click(Form)

OnClick:
=cmdDeleteAll_Click(Form)

4. Attach the event code as shown in Figure 7.27. If you copied the controls as suggested in step 2, this step isn't necessary.

5. In the declarations section in your copy of basMultiPik, change the values of the constants ADD_ONE_BUTTON through DELETE_ALL_BUTTON. Again, if you copied the controls from the sample form, there's no need to change the names.

FIGURE 7.27:

Set the list boxes' properties
correctly to create multiple-pick lists.

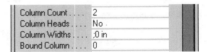

Column Count	2
Column Heads	No .
Column Widths	;0 in
Bound Column	0

6. Modify the subroutine SetupArrays to fill in the data as necessary. The
   example SetupArrays will not work in most cases, so this alteration is
   imperative. You'll want to choose to fill the lists either from arrays (using
   DoMultiPikArray) or from a field (using DoMultiPikField). Following the
   example SetupArrays, call either of the two subroutines from your own
   SetupArrays() function.

How and When to Use Subforms

To display data from more than one table in any but a one-to-one relationship (a
single form based on a query will handle the simple one-to-one case), you need to
investigate subforms. Although you can use subforms in the one-to-one case, they
are not required. A subform is nothing more than a related form displayed within
a form: it can be displayed in Datasheet or Form view, and it can, in turn, contain
another subform. Access allows nesting subforms two deep so that you can display
data in a one-to-many-to-many relationship. In addition, subforms have a bit of an
identity crisis: from their own point of view, they're forms. From the point of view
of their parent form, they're controls, just like any other control.

Why Use a Subform at All?

You may work with Access for quite a while without hitting the need for a subform.
Often, subforms are a "solution in search of a problem." The next two sections discuss two of the most obvious uses of subforms.

Displaying a One-to-Many Relationship

A subform can be useful for displaying the records that are linked to the current record on the main form. This usage corresponds to the standard one-to-many relationship. Think, for example, of a lawyer on the main form and her project list on the subform or, perhaps, a teacher on the main form and his students on the subform. Since you can display the subform in either Form or Datasheet view (and can switch back and forth at run time unless you set the properties of the subform otherwise at design time), you have maximum flexibility in how you view the data.

Displaying a Consistent Background Form with Same-Sized Smaller Forms Displayed within It

At some point you may need to gather a great deal of information from a user (a setup program, for instance) and won't care to gather it all on one single form. One way to handle this would be to create a single main form with push buttons indicating the categories of information. Then, create subforms, one for each category, and place them all on the main form at the same location. Set all their visible properties to False, and in the Click event of each button, set the appropriate subform's Visible property to Yes. This is a very effective way of emulating OS/2 2.x's Notebooks.

Creating a Subform

You first need to create the form you wish to use as a subform. It needs no special handling at all and can be any form you happen to have created. Remember that you will need to modify any special form-level properties for the subform on the form itself (not as a subform on some other form). You can make those changes at any point, though. The DefaultView, ViewsAllowed, and ScrollBars are important properties to consider when designing your subforms. If you save the form that will become the subform without scroll bars and in a particular view, that's how Access will display it on the main form.

Drag and Drop

The easiest way to create a subform is to select and drag an existing form from the database container to your main form. Access will understand that you intend to create a subform and do the work for you. In addition, if you have created any default relationships between the tables on which you've based the form and subform, Access will fill in the LinkChildFields and LinkMasterFields properties for you. Note that this subform is not a copy of the original form, but just a reference to it. That is, if you make changes to the original form that is now a subform, closing and reopening the main form will update all the information stored in the main form, and the subform will reflect any changes you've made.

NOTE If your main form has its DefaultView property set to Continuous Forms (the Access default for new forms) and you place a new subform control on that form, Access warns you via a dialog box that it will change the form to single-form mode. Access cannot display subforms on continuous forms.

Choosing a Control from the Toolbox

You can create a subform by choosing the Subform control from the toolbox. Once you place your control on the form, you can specify the source object, which tells Access where to retrieve the form at display time. Access provides you with a list of possible objects, which, in this case, will be a list of the currently defined forms in your database. In addition, you can change the SourceObject property while your form is in use. That is, when you change the SourceObject property for the subform control, Access pulls in different forms as you make the change.

Relating the Parent to the Child

The LinkChildFields and the LinkMasterFields properties control how the main form and the subform relate and interact. Once these properties have been correctly set, record pointer movement in the master form will trigger appropriate movement in the child form. This way the records displaying in the child form should always match the record displaying in the master form.

Allowable Settings

The LinkChildFields property applies to the subform, and the LinkMasterFields property applies to the main form. In each case, you can enter one of the following:

- A field name from the underlying recordset (a table or a query), identified in the RecordSource property
- A list of fields, separated by semicolons

The number of fields you enter must match exactly in both property settings. Although the field names can match, there is no reason why they must. As long as the datatypes match and the data is related, this connection should work.

Setting the Values Automatically

Under either of the following two conditions, Access fills in the LinkChildFields and the LinkMasterFields properties automatically:

- Both forms are based on tables, and the Edit ➤ Relationships menu item has been used to create default relationships between the two tables.
- Both forms contain fields of the same name and datatype, and the field on the main form is the primary key of the underlying table.

Always check the validity of the supplied links since Access might make some incorrect assumptions. Unless one of the preceding conditions is true, Access cannot make a determination of how to link the forms and leaves the properties empty.

Retrieving Calculated Values from Subforms

You may find it useful to employ subforms to display detail records and report on the total of some value displayed there on the main form. The Access *User's Guide* explains this process, but it skimps on one important issue: how do you retrieve values from subforms, back on the main form?

The complete syntax is rather complex and not at all obvious:

Forms![*Your Form Name*]![*SubForm Name*].Form![*Your Control Name*]

The important issue here is that you must use the Form property to access properties of the subform. To explore this syntax you might take a look at the properties available when you have selected your subform in design mode. You'll notice that none of the actual form properties are available at this point. Therefore, were you to use the syntax

Forms![*Your Form Name*]![*SubForm Name*]

you'd have access only to those properties that you see in the property sheet. For example, you could set the Visible property of the subform:

Forms![*Your Form Name*]![*SubForm Name*].Visible = True

but you couldn't get access to any of the controls on the subform. The Form property effectively gives you access to all the controls on the subform itself. You must include the ".Form" to be able to set or retrieve control properties for controls on the subform. That is, to make a control on the subform invisible, you would use code like this:

Forms![*Your Form Name*]![*SubForm Name*].Form!

➡ [*Your Control Name*].Visible = FALSE

Going All the Way

Access allows you to nest subforms three deep. That is, you can place a form that itself contains a subform as a subform on a form. This usage can be quite useful if you want to represent a one-to-many-to-many relationship on a form. For example, your client, a law office, might need to display information about each lawyer, the lawyer's clients, and billing information for each client. By nesting subforms you could create a form that allowed your client to page through each lawyer and, for each, view each client. For each client, a third form could display the billable events for that client. Figure 7.28 shows a very simple form with two nested subforms.

Since most of the interesting things you can do with subforms involve their acting as real forms, we cover subforms in detail in Chapter 8.

FIGURE 7.28:

The main form represents a lawyer, the first subform represents one of the lawyer's clients, and the second subform represents the billable activities for that client.

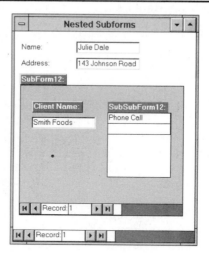

Graphical Controls

The two graphical controls, line and rectangle, have several properties and no methods. The rectangle can react only to mouse events (Click, DblClick, Mouse-Down, MouseUp, and MouseMove), and the line control has no event properties. Both are provided mostly for aesthetics, although the rectangle can imitate other controls. For example, a rectangle and a label make a convincing replica of an option group. You can use this fake option group when multiple choices are necessary. You can use the line for separating areas of a form and use the rectangle to group controls on a form and to create borders.

The Line Control

The line control has only a few interesting properties. Several of them deal with the sizing box surrounding the line, where the line goes from either the upper-left corner to the lower-right corner or from the lower-left corner to the upper-right corner.

The LineSlant Property

The LineSlant property applies only to the line control. Its value is either / (a forward slash) or \ (a backward slash), indicating which way the line slants within its surrounding box.

The Width/Height Properties

The Width and Height properties apply to the box surrounding the line, and their quotient determines the mathematical slope of the line. If you need to ensure that a line control on a form is either horizontal or vertical, you can set its height or width to 0 in the property sheet.

The BorderStyle Property

The BorderStyle property is not very useful when applied to a line since a line is *all* border. Changing the BorderStyle property to Clear (0) essentially makes the line invisible.

The Rectangle Control

Like the line control, the rectangle has few interesting properties, no methods, and only a few pertinent events. The issues raised here apply to many different controls but have a great impact on rectangles, where you're most likely to use these options.

The Format ➤ Send to Back menu item becomes important as you work with rectangles. For the purposes of form design, it helps if you visualize your forms as layers of transparent plastic, like cartoon cels, with controls painted on them: sending a control to the back is like moving that control's layer of plastic to the back of the stack of cels that make up a form. Unless you send your rectangles to the back of your forms, they will overlay controls you attempt to place within them. You could set the BackStyle property to Clear (0), but that would only allow you to create rectangles with the same color as the background of the form they're on. If you want rectangles of varying colors to be behind other controls, you need to use the Format ➤ Send to Back menu command.

Because a rectangle can change its look so easily, you can use it to emulate other controls, in situations where those other controls won't work as you want. Changing the SpecialEffect and BackColor properties can make rectangles look like buttons and/or option groups, for example.

Rectangles As Buttons

In your application you may want buttons with colored faces on your forms. Normally, command button controls can appear only as gray and raised. For a red button, you can use a rectangle and attach code to its Click event. Although this pairing will not emulate the "pushed in" button state, it will do in most cases, and you could programmatically create the pushed-in look if you needed it.

Rectangles As Option Groups

Option groups normally allow you to make only a single choice from the available radio buttons, check boxes, or toggle buttons. On some occasions, though, you may need to provide an option group–like container that allows more than one choice. To create this sort of object, you can use a rectangle and a label control. This combination looks exactly like an option group, but that's as far as it goes. Several important characteristics pertinent to option groups are conspicuously absent:

- Option groups return a value, but rectangles cannot. You must examine controls inside a rectangle to determine which you have chosen.

- Controls inside an option group move with the option group when you move it. To move a rectangle and any controls inside it, you need to actively select them all (click on the form and drag to surround the entire rectangle) before attempting to move the rectangle.

Rectangles As 3D Frames and Chiseled Lines

If you've played with the Forms Wizard supplied with Access, you've probably noticed some of the interesting effects you can create with raised and sunken rectangles. Figure 7.29 shows two of these. If you create a rectangle with a very small height (about 0.3 to 0.5 inches) and make it raised or sunken, you achieve the "chiseled" look used in the Forms Wizard. (See examples 1 and 2 in Figure 7.29.) If

FIGURE 7.29:
Examples of rectangles as 3D frames and chiseled lines

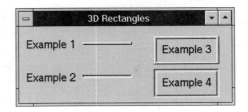

you nest one rectangle inside another and play with the SpecialEffects property, you can create some interesting frames, as you can see in examples 3 and 4 in Figure 7.29. Unless you turn off the Format ➤ Snap to Grid menu item or make the grid granularity very small, you have to size and place the rectangles by changing values in the property sheet. You can also use the Shift+arrow or Ctrl+arrow key, which size or move the control in small increments.

> **NOTE**
> If you try to combine the SpecialEffects properties of controls (Raised, Lowered) with other visible effects, you will invariably fail. The Special-Effect property controls whether or not the following properties apply at all: BorderStyle, BorderColor, and BorderWidth. If you set the SpecialEffect property to either Raised (1) or Sunken (2), Access ignores these properties. If you set the SpecialEffect property to Normal (0), Access acknowledges all these properties.

The Page Break Control

You can use the page break control on forms in a different manner than you might on a report. On a report, a page break control determines where a user-inserted page break goes. On a form, a page break control determines where Access will position the top of the form when the user presses the Pg Up or Pg Dn key. On a report, modifying the Visible property of the page break control makes common sense: if you want the page break to appear in the output, you make it visible; if you don't, you make it invisible. On a form, though, the Visible property isn't nearly as useful. Making the page break control invisible on a form would only alter which page of the form would become visible when the user pressed one of the paging keys. Modifying this might confuse the user. We cover the use of page break controls and their functionality in multipage forms in the next chapter.

Using Command Buttons

Command buttons are most often associated with actions. Their most common use is with a macro or Access Basic code attached to their Click event. They have several interesting and useful properties and events, as described in the following sections.

Macros to Buttons, Automagically

Knowing that many people are likely to create macros and then assign them to command buttons on forms, Access allows you to select a macro name in the Database Container window and drag it onto a form. Doing this creates a command button for you, with the Caption property set to be the name of the macro. This feature is of limited value if you store more than one macro in a given macro group, but if you store one macro per group, it's a nice feature. As a developer you're more likely to be writing Access Basic modules than writing macros, so there's not much point dwelling on this feature.

Command Button Properties

Some of the properties associated with command buttons are different from those for all other controls, so it's worth a moment to go over the unique properties here.

The Picture Property

Unlike any other control, a command button can display either a bitmapped image or a text caption on its surface. (It would be nice if you could mix both on the button, but that option is not currently available.) You can specify either a bitmap or an icon file to be placed on the surface of the button. Access displays your chosen picture centered and clipped on the button. In addition, Access attempts to display the *center* of your image in the center of the button; this way, if you shrink the button size so it's smaller than the picture, the center of the picture will still show. To simulate the button being depressed, Access shifts the bitmap to the right and down about 1 or 2 pixels. For this reason very large bitmaps look rather strange when you click the button. You might consider sticking with icon-sized bitmaps for your buttons.

TIP

Access stores only the bitmap image, not a pathname reference to that image, in the button's properties. Therefore, if you change your mind about the image or just want to find out which file is currently being displayed in the button's picture, you're out of luck. There's really no way to retrieve this information. The PictureData property can tell you the bit-level image of the picture, but that's probably not going to help you much. On the other hand, you can use the Picture-Data property of a button to set the picture on a button. The simplest use for this is to copy a picture from one button to another by assigning a PictureData property from one to the other. See Chapter 21 for more information on using the PictureData property.

The Transparent Property

The command button's Transparent property turns off all display attributes but leaves the button active. This property allows you to overlay a button on another control that might not normally be able to receive focus or fire off events. For example, you could place a transparent command button on top of a line and assign an action to its Click event. To the user it would appear as if the line were reacting to the mouse click! You can also overlay transparent command buttons on bitmaps on forms, allowing various pieces of the bitmap to react to mouse clicks. Imagine a bitmap of the United States, with each state's name printed on the state. With a transparent button overlaid on the state's name, you could allow users to click on the image of the state and have Access react to the click.

In Access 1.x, transparent buttons were easy to lose on a form in design mode. Many developers complained that they couldn't remember where they left them. In Access 2.0, transparent buttons appear on the form, in design mode, with a thin border. That way they're still visible. If you have overlaid transparent buttons on other controls, you need to move the top layer (the transparent buttons) out of the way to access the underlying controls.

> **NOTE**
> Do not confuse the Transparent property with the Visible property. When you set a control's Visible property to No, you completely disable that control. Not only is it invisible, but Access removes it from the form's tab order, and it can never receive focus. When the Transparent property is Yes, on the other hand, Access turns off only the display attributes for the button. All the other attributes still apply. You can reach it by tabbing to it or clicking it. All its events are active.

The AutoRepeat Property

The AutoRepeat property determines whether Access will repeat the code attached to the Click event for a button while you hold down the button. Access fixes the initial repeat to be 0.5 second after the first repetition. Subsequent repeats occur each 0.25 second or at the duration of the macro, whichever is longer.

> **NOTE**
> The AutoRepeat property has no effect if the code attached to the button causes record movement on the form. Moving from row to row cancels any automatic repetitions.

One use for the AutoRepeat property is to simulate a spin-button control. In this sort of arrangement you create a text box and two little buttons, usually one with an up arrow and one with a down arrow. As you press the up-arrow button some value in the text box increases, and as you press the down-arrow button the value decreases. One issue to consider when doing this, though, is that Access performs the repeat without consideration for Windows' screen-painting needs. Therefore, it's probable that your code will get far ahead of Windows' ability to repaint the text box. Anytime you cause screen activity using an auto-repeat button, you need to use the DoEvents action to allow Windows time to catch up.

Example: Simulating Spin-Button Controls

Spin buttons provide one way to both control the values your users input and make it simpler for them to change numeric and date values. Access does not include this control as part of its toolbox, but you can simulate it using a text box and two buttons. The basic concept should be familiar—two buttons, one pointing up and the other pointing down, "attached" to a text box. Pressing the up button increments the value in the text box, and pressing the down button decrements the value. Although you could theoretically use this mechanism for text values, it's not often used that way. For the most part, spin buttons are restricted to date and integer entry.

In Listing 7.7 you'll find Access Basic code that allows you to use spin-button controls in your own projects. We've provided two versions of the code—one for the simple case in which you just want to allow the spin buttons to cause the text box to go up or down in value, and one for the case in which you want to provide minimum and maximum values. This advanced version also allows for value-wrapping at either end of the range or at both ends and also works with dates. Figure 7.30 shows the two spin-buttons in action, along with text boxes displaying the function calls necessary to make them work. The sample form is frmSpinTest in CH7.MDB.

FIGURE 7.30:
Examples of spin-buttons. Note that the advanced example can spin through dates as well as through numeric values.

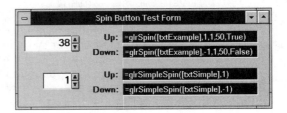

The simple case, in which the code doesn't limit the range your user can spin through, just pulls the current value from the attached text box, increments or decrements it, and then assigns it back to the text box. This code is in the function glrSimpleSpin() in Listing 7.7. Of course, this action can cause an error since the user could have entered a non-numeric value into the text box. The code disregards errors (using On Error Resume Next) so that the buttons do nothing if they find an invalid value in the text box. If no error has occurred, the code uses DoEvents to allow Windows to repaint the screen as necessary to keep up with the changing values.

Listing 7.7

```
Const BOUND_NONE = 0
Const BOUND_MIN = 1
Const BOUND_MAX = 2
Const BOUND_BOTH = BOUND_MIN + BOUND_MAX

Const TYPE_NULL = 0
Const TYPE_DATE = 1
Const TYPE_NUMBER = 2
Const TYPE_STRING = 3

Const KEY_GREYMINUS = 45
Const KEY_GREYPLUS = 43

Private Sub DoProperty(varProperty As Variant)
    ' Attempt to fire off the control's Before and AfterUpdate
    ' events. If they're stored as Event Procedures, then it's
    ' not going to happen, since you can't execute that code.
    ' It's private.

    Dim varTemp As Variant

    On Error GoTo DoPropertyErr
    If Not IsNull(varProperty) Then
        If varProperty = "[Event Procedure]" Then
            ' Do Nothing, because you can't.
        ElseIf Left$(varProperty, 1) = "=" Then
            varTemp = Eval(Mid$(varProperty, 2))
        Else
            DoCmd RunMacro varProperty
        End If
    End If
DoPropertyErr:
    Exit Sub
End Sub
```

```
Private Function GetType(varValue As Variant)
    If IsNull(varValue) Then
        GetType = TYPE_NULL
    ElseIf IsDate(varValue) Then
        GetType = TYPE_DATE
    ElseIf IsNumeric(varValue) Then
        GetType = TYPE_NUMBER
    Else
        GetType = TYPE_STRING
    End If
End Function

Sub glrHandlePlusMinusKeys(ctl As Control, intKey As Integer)
    Dim varRetval As Variant
    Dim intDataType As Integer

    ' All the references to ctl use the .Text property to
    ' retrieve the current value.  Since the control is
    ' still active, its value has not been committed,
    ' and, as such, the .Value property is not yet available.

    If IsNull(ctl.Text) Or (intKey <> KEY_GREYMINUS And
    ➡ intKey <> KEY_GREYPLUS) Then
        ' Do nothing.  Let Access handle this key.
    Else
        ' Figure out whether this value is a date, a number,
        ' or neither.
        intDataType = GetType(ctl.Text)
        If intDataType = TYPE_DATE Or
        ➡ intDataType = TYPE_NUMBER Then
            If intKey = KEY_GREYPLUS Then
                ' The SetType() call is only required for
                ' date types, really.
                ctl = SetType(ctl.Text, intDataType) + 1
            ElseIf intKey = KEY_GREYMINUS Then
                ctl = SetType(ctl.Text, intDataType) - 1
            End If
        End If
        intKey = 0
    End If
End Sub
```

```
Function glrSimpleSpin(ctl As Control, intInterval As Integer)

    ' This is the simple case. Just increment or decrement
    ' the value in the control that's passed in. Disregard
    ' any errors that might occur, since none can really be
    ' fatal.

    On Error Resume Next

    ctl = ctl + intInterval
    If Err = 0 Then
        DoEvents
        HandleProperties ctl
    End If
    On Error Goto 0
End Function

Function glrSpin(ctl As Control, intInterval As Integer,
➡ varMin As Variant, varMax As Variant, fAllowWrap As Integer)

    ' Handle updating and calculating the values for
    ' spin buttons.

    Dim varNewValue As Variant
    Dim intBoundaries As Integer
    Dim intDataType As Integer

    ' Get the data's datatype.  Only spin if this is a date
    ' or a number.
    intDataType = GetType(ctl)
    If intDataType <> TYPE_NUMBER And intDataType <> TYPE_DATE
➡ Then
        Exit Function
    End If

    ' Check the boundaries.  Assume that the user didn't pass
    ' in any boundaries.
    intBoundaries = BOUND_NONE

    ' If the boundary isn't null and if its datatype matches
    ' that of the control's data, then use it as a boundary.
    ' Repeat for both the max and the min value.
    If Not IsNull(varMin) And GetType(varMin) = intDataType Then
        intBoundaries = intBoundaries + BOUND_MIN
    End If
```

```
    If Not IsNull(varMax) And GetType(varMax) = intDataType Then
        intBoundaries = intBoundaries + BOUND_MAX
    End If

    ' Calculate what the new value ought to be.
    varNewValue = SetType(ctl, intDataType) + intInterval

    ' Now compare that new value against the boundary values,
    ' and force the value to be a specific bound value if
    ' necessary.

    If intBoundaries And BOUND_MIN Then
        If varNewValue < varMin Then
            varNewValue = IIf(fAllowWrap, varMax, varMin)
        End If
    End If
    If intBoundaries And BOUND_MAX Then
        If varNewValue > varMax Then
            varNewValue = IIf(fAllowWrap, varMin, varMax)
        End If
    End If

    ctl = varNewValue
        DoEvents
    HandleProperties ctl
End Function

Private Sub HandleProperties(ctl As Control)
    Dim varProp As Variant

    DoProperty (ctl.BeforeUpdate)
    DoProperty (ctl.AfterUpdate)
End Sub

Private Function SetType(varValue As Variant,
➨ intDataType As Integer)

    ' Handle the conversion of the value retrieved from the
    ' control.  If it's a date, convert it into a REAL date
    ' (a variant of type 7) so Access can use it as a date.
    ' Otherwise, leave it alone.

    SetType = IIf(intDataType = TYPE_DATE, CVDate(varValue),
➨ varValue)
End Function
```

To use the glrSimpleSpin() function, call it from the Click event of the buttons you want to use to control the text box. That is, use something like this:

=glrSimpleSpin([*txtYourTextBox*], *increment*)

where [*txtYourTextBox*] is the name of the text box containing the value your buttons are going to alter and *increment* is the amount to add to the value in the text box each time the button is pressed. (Generally, use +1 to go up and −1 to go down). Figure 7.30 shows this function call in use.

The more complex case, in which you can control the minimum and maximum values allowed in the text box, is contained in the function glrSpin() in Listing 7.7. This function allows you to specify the control to manipulate, the increment (either positive or negative), the minimum and maximum values, and a True/False value indicating whether or not to allow wrapping. If you allow wrapping the value will go from the maximum value back to the minimum value when moving up and from the minimum to the maximum when moving down. If you don't allow wrapping no further movement will be allowed once the user reaches an end point (either the maximum or the minimum value). Since you call this function from the Click event of both the spin-buttons, there's nothing stopping you from putting in different parameters for the up button than for the down button. In some cases this makes sense. For example, if you want the user to be able to wrap back to the lowest value after reaching the highest value when moving up but not to be able to wrap after reaching the lowest value when moving down, you can do that.

To use the glrSpin() function, attach a call to it from the Click event of your spin buttons:

=glrSpin([*txtYourTextBox*], *increment*, *min*, *max*, *allow wrap?*)

where [*txtYourTextBox*] is the name of the text box containing the value your buttons are going to alter and *increment* is the amount to add to the value in the text box each time the button is pressed. (Generally, use +1 to go up and −1 to go down). The value *min* specifies the minimum value, and *max* specifies the maximum value. If you don't wish to specify a minimum or maximum value, send Null instead of an integer. In addition, if you specify both a minimum and a maximum value, you can enable wrapping by sending True as the final parameter. If you don't send both a minimum and a maximum value or if you send False for the final parameter, the function will not wrap as you move up or down with the spin-buttons.

Once you have the correct function call attached to the Click event of the button, you must make sure the AutoRepeat property is set to Yes. This ensures that the action will repeat as you hold down the button.

How the glrSpin() Function Works

The glrSpin() function is much more complicated than the glrSimpleSpin() function since it's attempting to do a great deal more work. The steps it goes through are outlined in the next few paragraphs.

First, check the datatype of the value that's currently in the text box control. If it's anything except a number or a date, just leave the function now. This will keep the function from attempting to modify text values. This check calls the function Get-Type() (see Listing 7.7), which just calls the internal isNull, isDate(), and isNumeric() functions:

```
intDataType = GetType(ctl)
If intDataType <> TYPE_NUMBER And intDataType <> TYPE_DATE Then
    Exit Function
End If
```

Next, find the specified boundaries for the up and down motions. First, assume that there are no boundaries specified. Check the existence and types of the *min* and *max* parameters. If either of them is both non-null and of the same datatype as the text box's contents, store that information away for later.

This code maintains a single variable, intBoundaries, to keep track of the existence of the boundary settings. If neither boundary value is set, the value of intBoundaries will be BOUND_NONE. If you provide only a minimum setting, its value will be BOUND_MIN. If you provide only a maximum setting, its value will be BOUND_MAX. If you provide both, its value will be BOUND_BOTH.

The following code fragment shows the code from glrSpin() that calculates the value of intBoundaries:

```
intBoundaries = BOUND_NONE
If Not IsNull(varMin) And GetType(varMin) = intDataType Then
    intBoundaries = intBoundaries + BOUND_MIN
End If
If Not IsNull(varMax) And GetType(varMax) = intDataType Then
    intBoundaries = intBoundaries + BOUND_MAX
End If
```

Next, calculate the new value, based on the datatype of the current value and the *increment* parameter. This expression calls the user-defined SetType() function (as opposed to just adding the value to ctl directly) specifically to deal with date datatypes (see Listing 7.7):

```
varNewValue = SetType(ctl, intDataType) + intInterval
```

If you've specified a lower boundary and the newly calculated value for the control is less than the minimum value, set the value to be either the minimum value (if wrapping is not allowed) or the maximum value (if wrapping is allowed). The same logic applies to the upper boundary:

```
If intBoundaries And BOUND_MIN Then
    If varNewValue < varMin Then
        varNewValue = IIf(fAllowWrap, varMax, varMin)
    End If
End If
If intBoundaries And BOUND_MAX Then
    If varNewValue > varMax Then
        varNewValue = IIf(fAllowWrap, varMin, varMax)
    End If
End If
```

Finally, set the text box's value to be the newly calculated value and give Windows some time to catch up. (If you're not sure why the DoEvents is necessary here, try the example without it. You'll see that the numbers don't get repainted for every change.)

```
ctl = varNewValue
DoEvents
```

There's one more area of concern here: when you change the value of a control through Access Basic, Access does not fire off that control's Before or AfterUpdate event. To get around this problem, both glrSimpleSpin() and glrSpin() call the subroutine HandleProperties once they're done. This subroutine attempts to call the code that the Before/AfterUpdate events would have called. To do so, HandleProperties gathers up the string found in the control's property settings and sends that string to the DoProperty subroutine:

```
Private Sub DoProperty (varProperty As Variant)
    Dim varTemp As Variant

    On Error GoTo DoPropertyErr
    If Not IsNull(varProperty) Then
```

```
        If varProperty = "[Event Procedure]" Then
        ElseIf Left$(varProperty, 1) = "=" Then
            varTemp = Eval(Mid$(varProperty, 2))
        Else
            DoCmd RunMacro varProperty
        End If
    End If
DoPropertyErr:
    Exit Sub
End Sub
```

DoProperty looks at the property string and, depending on what it finds there, either calls the Eval() function to execute Access Basic code or runs the attached macro. Unfortunately, if you've attached Access Basic code directly to the event (using Code-Behind-Forms), there's no way this function can execute that code. Therefore, if you want some action to occur in the Before/AfterUpdate event for the text box you're using as part of your spin-button trio, you need to place that action in either a macro or a module, but not in CBF.

The Default/Cancel Properties

Every form can have exactly one button that acts as the default button (its Click event gets triggered when you press ↵ on the form) and exactly one button that acts as the Cancel button (its Click event gets fired off when you press Esc on the form). A button with its Default property set to Yes acts as the form's default, and a button with its Cancel property set to Yes acts as the form's cancel button. Note that each form can have at most one of each of these, and setting a button's Default or Cancel property to Yes sets any other button's matching property to No.

You might think, as do many developers, that setting a button's Cancel property actually causes something to happen, perhaps closing the form. This is simply not true. All that happens as a result of a button's Default or Cancel property being set to Yes is that that button receives focus and Access fires off its Click event when you click the correct key.

Give the assignment of Default and Cancel properties some serious thought. For situations in which something destructive might happen at the click of a button, make the Cancel button the default button. To do so, set both the Default and the Cancel properties to Yes.

The Visible Property

Unlike the Transparent property, setting the Visible property to Off for a button actually disables a button completely. This is the same behavior as with other controls, but it can be confusing for command buttons.

The DisplayWhen Property

If you are inclined to print single records from your form, you will find the Display-When property indispensable. Since you probably will not care to print the buttons on the form with the data, set the DisplayWhen property for the buttons to ScreenOnly (2). This way, when you print the form, the buttons won't print along with the data.

Enabled

In modern, user-driven applications, it's important to make sure users can't make choices that shouldn't be available. It may have been reasonable at one point for a user to click a button only to be confronted with a dialog box that shouted, "This option is not currently available!" The reasonable way to handle this situation is for you to disable the button when the option isn't available so the user can't click it in the first place. Set the Enabled property to No when you want the button to be unavailable. Set it to Yes when you want the user to be able to press the button. You may be tempted to make unavailable buttons invisible, but many people find this distracting since they tend to think, "I saw that option a minute ago; where did it go?"

Command Button Events

Command buttons provide the same events as other controls, but you're likely to use just two of them, Click and DblClick. Access fires off the Click event when you click a button and the DblClick event when you click twice within the double-click time interval (as defined through the Windows Control Panel). You can assign any macro or Access Basic function to either of these events.

You might be tempted to assign different actions to the Click and the DblClick events. Don't bother. Access can't possibly differentiate between the two events and will always attempt to fire off the Click event before the DblClick event. This functionality can be useful to you at times, though. When you want the DblClick event to add to the Click event, it works to your advantage. In general, if you want to attach code to both events, make sure the code attached to the DblClick event extends the action done in the Click event. In actuality, you won't want to use the DblClick event for buttons very often.

Using Default Control Properties to Your Advantage

Access stores default settings for each type of control with each form. To describe the settings for individual controls on the form, Access stores just the settings that *differ* from the default settings. Therefore, if a control has the same settings as the form defaults, Access won't need to store settings for that control. This affects only the stored image of the form; the comparison to the default values is only a save/load issue. All settings for all controls are available once Access loads the form (so there's no actual run-time memory savings).

You can change the default settings for a specific control in two ways. The first involves setting the properties before you actually create the control. The second lets you create the control, specify all its settings, and then tell Access to make those settings the default settings for that type of control.

Either way, when you specify the default settings, other controls of that type you create will inherit the default settings. Previously created controls won't be affected by changes to the default settings.

To set the default settings for a specific type of control before creating one, click that control in the toolbox. Notice that the title for the property sheet has changed to indicate that you're now setting properties for the *default* version of the control. Make whatever changes you want.

To set the default settings based on a specific control you've already created, create your control and set the properties you want. Once you're satisfied, choose the Layout ➤ Change Default menu option. This stores the settings used in the selected control in the form's default settings for that type of control.

Either way you do it, once you've set the default properties, any controls of that type that you create from then on, on the current form, will inherit those properties. When you save the form, Access will save only the properties for each control that differ from the default values. Judicious use of default properties can speed up your development time, as well as make forms smaller and therefore speed their load time.

Creating Controls Programmatically

Access provides functions to create forms and reports, and the controls on these objects, programmatically. This is, of course, how all the Access Wizards work. They gather information from you about how you want the form or report to look, and then they go through their code and create the requested form or report. Chapter 20 covers in detail how you can create your own Wizards, but there are other uses for those functions. Specifically, if you want to create a form or report with many similar controls that can be easily described in a programmatic manner, you may be able to use one or more of these functions.

Functions That Create Forms and Controls

CreateForm() and CreateReport() create a form or report and return that object as the return value of the function:

CreateForm([*database* [, *formtemplate*]])

CreateReport([*database* [, *reporttemplate*]])

The following table describes the parameters for these two functions:

Argument	Description
database	String expression representing the database in which to place the new form or report. To use the current database, use a zero-length string here ("")
template	String expression representing the form or report template to use in creating the new form or report. Use the word *Normal* to use the standard template. To use the template specified in the View ➤ Options menu, use a zero-length string ("")

The following fragment will create a new form, with the caption "My New Form":

```
Dim frm As Form
Set frm = CreateForm( "", "" )
frm.Caption = "My New Form"
```

Use CreateControl() and CreateReportControl() to create new controls on forms and reports, respectively. The following fragment details the parameters you use when calling CreateControl() and CreateReportControl():

```
CreateControl(formname As String, controltype As Integer [,
➡ sectionnumber As Integer [, parent As String [, fieldname As
➡ String [, left As Integer [, top As Integer [, width As
➡ Integer [, height As Integer]]]]]]] )
CreateReportControl(reportname As String, controltype As Integer
➡ [, sectionnumber As Integer [, parent As String [, fieldname
➡ As String]]] )
```

Table 7.5 lists the parameters for the two functions, along with the possible values for those parameters.

An Example Using CreateForm() and CreateControl()

As part of a project, you need to create a form with 42 similar command buttons, numbered 1 through 42, in 6 rows of 7 buttons each. You could do this by hand, spending a while getting all the controls just right. You could also do this with the CreateForm() and CreateControl() functions. Listing 7.8 contains the entire function you can use to create the form, as shown in Figure 7.31.

TABLE 7.5: Parameters for CreateControl() and CreateReportControl()

Argument	Description
formname, reportname	String expression identifying the name of the open form or report on which you want to create the control. If you've just created a form using CreateForm() and have assigned the return value of that function to a variable (frmNewForm, for example), you can reference that form's FormName property here (frmNewForm.FormName)
controltype	Integer identifying the type of control you want to create:

Integer	Control Type
100	Label
101	Rectangle
102	Line
104	Command button
105	Option button
106	Check box
107	Option group
108	Bound object frame
109	Text box
110	List box
111	Combo box
112	Subform/subreport
114	Unbound object frame
118	Page break
122	Toggle button

section	Integer identifying the section that will contain the new control:

Integer	Section
0	(Default) Detail section
1	Form or report header section
2	Form or report footer section
3	Form or report page header section

TABLE 7.5: Parameters for CreateControl() and CreateReportControl() (continued)

Argument	Description
	Integer Section
	4 Form or report page footer section
	5 Group-level 1 header section (reports only)
	6 Group-level 1 footer section (reports only)
	7 Group level 2 header section (reports only)
	8 Group level 2 footer section (reports only)
	If a report has additional group level sections, the header/footer pairs are numbered consecutively beginning with 9
parent	String expression identifying the name of the parent control. If you don't wish to specify the parent control, use ""
boundFieldName	String expression identifying the name of the field to which the new control should be bound. If you specify the boundFieldName, not only does it fill in the ControlSource property, it inherits the table properties, such as the Format and ValidationRule properties
left, top	Integer expressions indicating the coordinates for the upper-left corner of the control
width, height	Integer expressions indicating the width and height of the control

FIGURE 7.31:

The Calendar form in design mode, after all the buttons have been created by the CreateCalendar() function

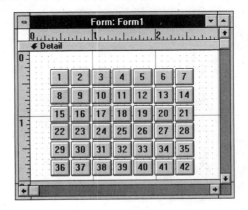

CreateCalendar() creates the form by calling the CreateForm() function. Since it specifies a zero-length string for both the database and the template, it will create the form in the current database and use the template specified in the View ➤ Options settings:

```
Set frm = CreateForm("", "")
frm.Caption = "Calendar"
```

All measurements specified for CreateControl() must be in twips ($\frac{1}{1440}$ of an inch), so you need to convert all your values into twips before calling the function. These controls are to be 0.25 inch in height and 0.30 inch in width, with a 0.03 inch gap between them.

```
intHeight = .25 * 1440
intWidth = .30 * 1440
intGap = .03 * 1440
```

CreateCalendar() loops through 6 rows of 7 command buttons, creating each control with a call to CreateControl(). It uses the width and height values to figure where to place the buttons and then sets the Width, Height, and Caption properties of the button it has just created. Note that this call to CreateControl() uses the FormName property of the newly created form to reference the form, creates a control of type 104 (command button) in section 0 (detail section), and specifies no parent or bound field name.

Listing 7.8

```
Function CreateCalendar()
    Dim frm As Form
    Dim ctl As Control

    Dim intI As Integer
    Dim intJ As Integer

    Dim intHeight As Integer
    Dim intWidth As Integer
    Dim intGap As Integer

    Dim intCols As Integer
    Dim intRows As Integer

    intCols = 7
    intRows = 6
```

```
Set frm = CreateForm("", "")
frm.Caption = "Calendar"

' Measurement properties are specified in TWIPS from
' Access Basic. So we need to convert all values from
' inches to twips, by multiplying by 1440.
intHeight = .25 * 1440
intWidth = .30 * 1440
intGap = .03 * 1440

For intI = 1 To intRows
    For intJ = 1 To intCols
        Set ctl = CreateControl(frm.Name, 104, 0, "",
        ➡ "", intJ * (intWidth + intGap), intI * (intHeight +
        ➡ intGap))
        ctl.Width = intWidth
        ctl.Height = intHeight
        ctl.Caption = 7 * (intI - 1) + intJ
    Next intJ
Next intI
End Function
```

Summary

This chapter has introduced each of the control types (except OLE controls, which are covered in Chapter 19). We've attempted to cover the nonintuitive properties and events and have suggested solutions to some common Access problems. In general, we covered the following topics:

- Access controls and their properties, events, and methods make up the bulk of your user interface.

- Using Access Basic and the Tag property, you can emulate the creation of user-defined properties.

- Using Access Basic in combination with controls, you can emulate several hybrid controls that are not intrinsic to Access.

- You can use a control's default properties to ease the development burden.

- You can create controls and forms programmatically, leading to a more uniform layout.

CHAPTER

EIGHT

Topics in Form Design and Usage

- Understanding the appearance and operation of forms

- Building form-based encapsulated tools

- Resizing forms to match screen resolution

- Creating a generic query by form mechanism

- Understanding form events

If your applications are like many of the Access applications in use, a large majority of their functionality is centered around forms. Most likely, from the user's perspective, your application *is* just a set of forms. In this chapter you'll find insights into using and creating forms in ways you might not otherwise have considered. This chapter doesn't attempt to show you how to create or design forms, but rather how to use the forms you've created in original and interesting ways.

NOTE   Although you won't find a complete discussion of using the Windows API (Application Programmer's Interface) until Chapter 17, some of the examples in this chapter rely heavily on API calls. If you find yourself buried too deeply in the details, you may want to skip ahead to Chapter 17 and peruse the information there concurrently with this chapter.

Introduction to CBF

Access 2.0 includes a new feature, Code-Behind-Forms, that allows you to store program code and a form in one neat package. This means that now, as in Visual Basic, choosing an event from the property list takes you directly to a subroutine that is tied to that particular event. The event procedures are subroutines named controlName_eventName, and their scope is private to the form. In several cases Access passes parameters to these procedures that provide information about the circumstances of the particular event. For example, mouse events receive information about the mouse location and clicked buttons, and key events receive information about the particular key that was pressed. This encapsulation makes it very easy to create forms that perform a single purpose, which you can reuse in various applications.

To get to a form's module, you have several choices:

- From the Database Container window, once you're showing the list of forms, you can click the Code button on the toolbar.

- In form design mode, click the same toolbar button.
- From the form's property sheet, for any event property, you can click the ... button, which takes you to the particular event procedure for this control.
- In form design mode, right-click any control and choose the Build Event menu item.

NOTE You can't pass your own parameters to CBF event procedures. To pass a parameter to the procedure, you have to use a function attached to the event instead.

One of the most important issues involving CBF is that the code attached to a given form is not loaded into memory until that form is loaded. Therefore, if your application is large and involves many forms, no memory is used for the code that resides in those forms until you actually use them. For library databases you'll find this to be a real memory savings. The Wizards that ship with Access, for example, use CBF extensively in an attempt to use as little of your memory as possible until it's absolutely necessary.

A common misconception about controls and their attached event procedures causes new Access programmers a great deal of trouble. Most beginners assume that copying a control from one form to another also copies the control's event procedures to the new form. But this is not so, unfortunately. Copying a control copies only the control and its properties. You must manually copy its event procedures from one form's module to the other's.

Many of the forms demonstrated in this chapter rely heavily on CBF to maintain their reusability. By keeping all their code in CBF, these forms become encapsulated entities that you can import directly into your own applications. On the other hand, code stored in CBF can be hard to study since it's not loaded into memory until the form is loaded, and attempts to use Access' Search functionality won't find any matches in a form's CBF if that form isn't loaded. (Chapter 15 suggests a possible solution to this problem.) In addition, you may find that in our attempt to modularize the examples in this chapter, some procedures occur in multiple forms' CBF.

If you import more than one of the forms from this chapter into your own applications, you might want to take a few minutes and peruse the imported forms' CBF. You will probably find some general-purpose procedures duplicated. We've attempted to point these out to you along the way. Moving those routines to global modules can save you some memory overhead.

Controlling the Look of Your Forms

The basic Access form consists of several pieces of built-in functionality, some or all of which you might like to remove or modify for your applications. Figure 8.1 points out the built-in parts of forms that Access allows you to control. By changing properties of the form, you can remove or change any of these features.

FIGURE 8.1:

Each of the pieces of an Access form can be changed, removed, or included at any time.

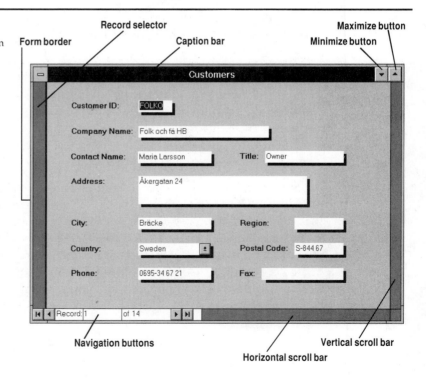

Using Properties to Control the Look of Your Form

You can use certain properties, in various groups or singularly, to control your form's appearance. Several of these properties are interrelated, and changing one may affect others. For example, if you set the BorderStyle property to None, it doesn't matter what you have set for the MinButton or MaxButton property. In this case those features will be invisible. Table 8.1 shows the form properties you can use to modify the appearance of the form's border.

TABLE 8.1: Form Appearance Properties

Property	Determines	Possible Values
BorderStyle	Type of border and various border elements	None, Thin, Sizable, Dialog
MinButton	Whether the minimize button is visible	Yes, No
MaxButton	Whether the maximize button is visible	Yes, No
ControlBox	Whether the control box (menu) is visible	Yes, No
NavigationButtons	Whether the record number indicator and navigation buttons are visible	Yes, No
ScrollBars	Which of the scroll bars are visible	None, Horizontal Only, Vertical Only, Both
RecordSelectors	Whether the record selector bar is visible	Yes, No
AutoResize	Whether Access resizes the form to show complete rows	Yes, No
PopUp	Whether your form stays on top of all other forms	Yes, No
Modal	Whether you can switch to other forms while this form is loaded	Yes, No

Windows Handles, Classes, Access Forms, and MDI

To make the best use of the different types of forms in Access, you must first have a basic understanding of Windows handles, classes, and parent-child relationships. These concepts will play a large part in your understanding the different form types in Access. You'll also use this information in the section "Using Forms as Toolboxes" later in this chapter to create floating toolbars.

The Windows Handle (or hWnd)

In Windows, almost every object you see on the screen is an object with properties and events, just as in Access. Every button, scroll bar, dialog box, and status bar is a window. To keep all these windows straight, Windows assigns to each a unique window *handle*—a unique integer—through which it can refer to the specific window. This window handle is generally referred to as the window's *hwnd* (handle to a *window*). Access makes this value available to you, for every form, in that form's hWnd property. (Like many other properties, the hWnd property is available only at run time and therefore can't be found in the form's property sheet.)

Windows Classes

In addition, every window is a member of a window *class*. Window classes share events and code, so windows of the same class can react the same way to outside stimuli. For example, all scroll bars are either part of the class SCROLLBAR or part of a class derived from the SCROLLBAR class. (Actually, not all scroll bars are based on this class since a programmer can create a scroll bar from scratch. It's just a combination of bitmaps and code. But almost no one does it that way since Windows provides this standard class with little effort on your part.) Every window type in Access has its own class name. You'll find some of these classes listed in Table 8.2, along with the parent for that window type (which will be important in the next section). Figure 8.2 shows a simple class hierarchy diagram for these Access window classes.

TABLE 8.2: Sample Access Window Classes and Their Parents

Class Name	Description	Parent
OMain	Main Access window	
MDICLIENT	Access desktop	Main Access window
ODb	Database container	MDIClient window
OForm	Normal form frame	MDIClient window
OFormPopup	Popup form frame	Main Access window
OFormSub	Access form (the area that contains other controls)	Any normal or popup form window

FIGURE 8.2:

Small sample of the Access window class hierarchy

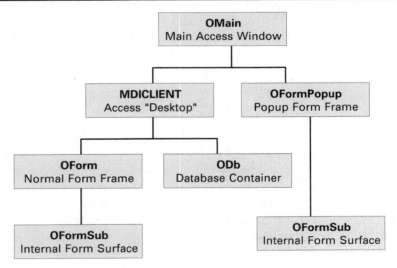

Multiple Document Interface (MDI)

The Multiple Document Interface (MDI) presents a standard way of writing applications for Windows in which one main window can contain many subordinate, child windows. Access is such an application, as is Excel, among many others. In MDI applications, the child windows minimize within the bounds of the parent's window and show an icon when minimized. You can't size or drag child windows beyond the borders of their parent. The hierarchical organization of every MDI application is basically the same: you have a main window containing a special window—the MDI client—and within that window you have multiple child windows. In Access the MDI client window's class is MDICLIENT and the main Access window's class is OMain. As you'll note in Table 8.2, the MDI client's parent is the main Access window, whose window class is OMain. It is actually the window that's situated within the Access main window; it contains all the other Access windows, including the design surfaces and running applications. This window normally extends from the bottom of the docked toolbars to the top of the status bar and from the left to the right of the main Access window.

Normal, Popup, and Modal Forms

The Access terms *Normal*, *Popup*, and *Modal* describe a form's interaction with other forms and with the Access main window. You can control these attributes with the Popup and Modal properties at design time or with the OpenForm action at run time.

A *normal* form allows other forms in Access to both overlay it and take the focus away from it. Unless you specify otherwise this is the standard behavior for every form you create. Normal forms are children of the MDI client window; therefore, you can't size or drag them outside the Access window's boundaries.

A *popup* form (one that either has its Popup property set to Yes or has been loaded by the OpenForm action with the dialog attribute set) floats above all other Access windows. These forms aren't children of the MDI client window at all; they have the Access main window as their parent. Therefore, they aren't limited to the Access window's area. You can drag them outside the Access window's borders or size them larger than the Access main window. Since they are children of the main Access window, however, if you minimize Access you minimize all its child windows, including popup forms.

A *modal* form (whether or not it's a popup form) retains the focus until you either close or hide it (by setting its Visible property to No). No matter how much you click on other areas of the program, Access ignores those mouse clicks until the modal form lets go of the focus.

Making Your Form System Modal

Setting a form's Modal property makes it modal within Access, but you can still switch away from the form to other Windows applications. If you need to make Access system modal so your users won't be able to switch to any other application, you can do so. Only one application can be system modal at a time, of course. The code to do this, though, is quite simple and requires only two calls into the Windows API. The first function call, glrFindAccessHWnd(), tries to retrieve the window handle for the main Access window. Once it finds that window, it calls SetSysModalWindow() (aliased as glr_apiSetSysModalWindow() in the code) to set that window as the system modal window. Once the window is system modal, you won't be able to move or resize it, so you need to take care of those operations before you call the function that makes Access "king." Although it's not documented, calling SetSysModalWindow() with a value of 0 sets no window to be system modal. The following listing shows the code you need to make Access system modal and to make it no longer system modal. (You can find it in basSysModal in CH8.MDB.) To use this code in your own application, import the modules basSysModal and basFormGlobal.

```
Declare Function glr_apiSetSysModalWindow Lib "USER" Alias
➡ "SetSysModalWindow" (ByVal hWnd As Integer) As Integer

Function glrSetSystemModal (fTurnOn As Integer)

    ' Make the Access window the system modal window, returning
    ' the handle of the previous system modal window, if any.

    ' If fTurnOn is True, set Access to be system modal.
    ' If fTurnOn is False, set Access NOT to be system modal.

    Dim hWnd As Integer
```

```
    If fTurnOn Then
        hWnd = glrFindAccessHWnd()
        If hWnd = 0 Then Exit Function
    Else
        hWnd = 0
    End If
    glrSetSystemModal = glr_apiSetSysModalWindow(hWnd)
End Function
```

Before you can decide how you want your form to look, you must decide how you want to use it. In some uses you'll want all the form's features available, but in others you'll want to remove some or all of the trappings. The following sections ask some questions and provide simple answers for the most general cases.

Is Your Form Unbound?   Does your form display rows from a recordset, allowing the user to scroll through them? If so, it's bound, and if not, it's unbound. If it's unbound you don't have any use for the navigation buttons, so set the NavigationButtons property to No. In addition, you won't need the record selector bar, so you should remove it, also, by setting the RecordSelectors property to No.

Does Your Form Need to Scroll?   Is the viewing surface of your form larger than the window area? If so, you need to use either or both of the scroll bars. If not, you can remove them by setting the ScrollBars property to Horizontal Only, Vertical Only, or None.

Is Your Form a Custom Dialog?   If your form is a custom dialog box, you probably don't want your users to resize or maximize it. In this case you'll want to remove the maximize button and perhaps remove the control box, too. If you remove the control box, though, remember that you must provide a means to close the form. Although you can use the Alt+F4 key to close popup forms and Ctrl+F4 to close other forms, most users don't know that. Removing the control box and not providing some other means of closing the form will confuse users. On the other hand, removing the control menu is not enough to deter users from closing forms when you don't want them to. See the section "Controlled Closing" a little later in this chapter.

Is Your Form a Popup? If your form is intended to float on top of all the other Access windows, it's considered a popup form. If that's the case you'll most likely want to set the Popup property to Yes and the BorderStyle property to Dialog, which produces a thick border that can't be resized. Most applications use this thick border as a visual indicator to the user that the form will float. If you also want your form to grab the focus and retain it until the user is done working with the form, set the Modal property to Yes.

Understanding the BorderStyle Property

The BorderStyle property is the most complex of the properties affecting the appearance of your forms. It offers only four options (None, Thin, Sizable, and Dialog), but these options are tied to the Popup and Modal properties, as well as to the MinButton, MaxButton, and ControlBox properties. Table 8.3 lists the different BorderStyle property settings.

TABLE 8.3: BorderStyle Setting Options

BorderStyle Setting	Description
None	No border. The form also has none of the other border elements; the MinButton, MaxButton, and ControlBox properties are ignored and treated as if they were all No
Thin	Thin border. The form can include any combination of the MinButton, MaxButton, or ControlBox properties. The Size option on the control menu is disabled, and you can't resize the form by any means. You'll often use this setting for popup forms
Sizable	The default, sizable border
Dialog	If the Popup property is Yes, the form has a thick border. If the Popup property is No, the form has a thin border. In either case it includes only a control box and a title bar (It can't be maximized, minimized, or resized.)

As you can see, the setting for the BorderStyle property, in combination with the Popup property, can affect other properties, as well. Table 8.4 summarizes the effects the BorderStyle and Popup properties have on other properties.

TABLE 8.4: Effects of Combinations of BorderStyle and Popup Properties

Border-Style	Popup	Resizing Allowed?	Minimize Button?	Maximize Button?	Control Box?	Border Width
Dialog	Yes	No	No	No	Yes	Thick
Dialog	No	No	No	No	Yes	Thin
None		No	No	No	No	None
Sizable		Yes	Yes	Yes	Yes	Standard
Thin		No	Yes	Yes	Yes	Thin

Switching Modes

If you've set the BorderStyle property to anything but Sizable, you won't be able to switch directly among design, datasheet, and form modes. You'll need to close the form between mode changes. This was a design decision brought about by the fact that using any border style besides Sizable requires re-creating the form window when you switch modes.

Controlled Closing

You can remove the control box and provide your own Close button in an attempt to control the way users close your forms, but there is still at least one more way to close the form: users can use the Ctrl+F4 key (for normal forms) or the Alt+F4 key(for popup forms) to bypass your own form-closing mechanism. If you want complete control over your forms, you need to plug this one last hole. You may also want to leave the control box visible so your users can use the Move, Size, and Restore commands found there. You might just want to disable the Close command on that menu. In many cases you'll want to combine both methods, disabling the menu item and disallowing the keystrokes to unload the form. The following sections cover both of these techniques.

Disabling the Close Menu Item

Like all the other components of Windows, every menu can be identified by its handle. Once you have that handle you can modify the menu, adding or deleting items or perhaps making items checked or disabled. (For more information on modifying menu components, see Chapter 10.) Windows conveniently provides a mechanism for retrieving the handle of a form's control menu (often called its system menu); you can use the GetSystemMenu() API function to retrieve the menu handle you need. Once you have that handle you can use the EnableMenuItem() API function to enable or disable items on the control menu.

Because the items you'll find on system menus throughout Windows are relatively standard, the Windows API provides a group of command constants that Windows understands when you tell it to modify a menu item. Listing 8.1 includes the constants from the group that apply to Access as predefined constants. When you tell Windows which item on the menu you want to enable or disable, you specify either a position or a command by "name" (actually, by its value). In this case, since you can't be sure exactly where on the system menu you'll find the Close menu item, you use the SC_CLOSE constant. Listing 8.1 shows the entire set of code you need to disable and reenable the Close item on the system menu.

Listing 8.1

```
Declare Function glr_apiGetSystemMenu Lib "USER" Alias
➡ "GetSystemMenu"(ByVal hWnd As Integer,
➡ ByVal fRevert As Integer) As Integer
Declare Function glr_apiEnableMenuItem Lib "USER" Alias
➡ "EnableMenuItem" (ByVal hMenu As Integer,
➡ ByVal intIDEnableItem As Integer,
➡ ByVal fEnable As Integer) As Integer

Global Const MF_BYCOMMAND = &H0

' Action constants
Global Const MF_DISABLED = &H2
Global Const MF_ENABLED = &H0
Global Const MF_GRAYED = &H1

' Menu item name constants
Const SC_SIZE = &HF000
Const SC_MOVE = &HF010
Const SC_MINIMIZE = &HF020
Const SC_MAXIMIZE = &HF030
Const SC_NEXTWINDOW = &HF040
Const SC_CLOSE = &HF060
Const SC_RESTORE = &HF120
```

```
Function glrEnableControlMenuItem(frm As Form,
➡ intItem As Integer, fEnable As Integer)

    ' Enable or disable items on the control menu for a
    ' form, depending on the fEnable parameter passed in.
    '
    ' intItem can be one of:
    ' SC_MOVE
    ' SC_SIZE
    ' SC_MINIMIZE
    ' SC_MAXIMIZE
    ' SC_NEXT
    ' SC_CLOSE
    ' SC_RESTORE

    Dim intRetval As Integer
    Dim intMenu As Integer
    Dim intAction As Integer

    If frm.ControlBox Then
        intMenu = glr_apiGetSystemMenu(frm.hWnd, False)
    Else
        intMenu = 0
    End If
    intRetval = 0

    ' If you got a menu handle, then do the work.
    If intMenu <> 0 Then
        If fEnable Then
            intAction = MF_BYCOMMAND + MF_ENABLED
        Else
            intAction = MF_BYCOMMAND + MF_DISABLED +
            ➡ MF_GRAYED
        End If
        intRetval = glr_apiEnableMenuItem(intMenu,
        ➡ intItem, intAction)
    End If

    glrEnableControlMenuItem = intRetval
End Function
```

Disregarding the Alt+F4/Ctrl+F4 Keys

To close the final loophole allowing users to close your forms behind your back, you must restrict the use of the Alt+F4 and Ctrl+F4 keys. Fortunately, you can accomplish this without having to check whether the user pressed either Alt+F4 or Ctrl+F4 to close your form. For this method to work, your form must include some method of allowing the user to close it, usually using a command button. It involves these four simple steps:

1. In your form's CBF, in the Declarations area, define an integer variable (fOKToClose, for this example).

2. In your form's Open event set the value of fOKToClose to False. You might also want to call glrEnableControlMenuItem(), disabling the Close item on the control menu.

3. In the code attached to the Click event of the button used to close your form, set fOKToClose to True.

4. In your form's OnUnLoad event, check the value of fOKToClose. If it's False set the Cancel variable to True, halting the form's closing.

That's all there is to it. Unless your user clicks your button, there's no way this form is going to close. Listing 8.2 shows the minimal CBF your form might contain to implement this method. You can investigate frmCloseTest in CH8.MDB to see this in action.

Listing 8.2

```
' Variable to control when the form can be closed.
Dim fOKToClose As Integer

Sub cmdClose_Click()
    ' If you click the Close button, set the variable
    ' so the OnUnload event will let you out.
    fOKToClose = True

    ' Now that you've cleared the way, close the form.
    DoCmd Close
End Sub
```

```
Sub Form_Open(Cancel As Integer)
    Dim varTemp As Variant

    ' Set the trap, so no one can close the form without
    ' pressing the Close button.
    fOKToClose = False

    ' Disable the Close item on the system menu, just
    ' to be polite, since it wouldn't do anything, anyway.
    varTemp = glrEnableControlMenuItem(Me, SC_CLOSE, False)
End Sub

Sub Form_Unload (Cancel As Integer)
    If Not fOKToClose Then
        Cancel = True
    End If
End Sub
```

If you really care to control when and how your form can be closed by your users, you'll want to incorporate a combination of the suggestions discussed here. You might want to remove the control menu altogether or just disable the Close menu item. In either case you'll probably want to set the Cancel variable in the UnLoad event so users can't close the form with an unanticipated keystroke. Although there's no real need to disable the Close menu item if you're using the Cancel method, it's a user-friendly thing to do. Your users would be awfully confused by their attempts to use the Close menu item if it did absolutely nothing.

To disable or enable items on the control menu, you need to import the basControlMenu and basFormGlobal modules from CH8.MDB. The glrEnableControlMenuItem() function has the following syntax:

intRetval = glrEnableControlMenuItem (*formObject*, *MenuItem*, *fEnable*)

where *formObject* is a form reference, *MenuItem* is a constant from the list in basControlMenu indicating which menu item to work on, and *fEnable* is either True (enable) or False (disable).

Removing a Form's Caption Bar

As part of an application you may need to remove a form's caption bar. Although Access allows you to remove the entire border, this may not be what you need for a particular look. Removing the control menu and the minimize/maximize buttons and setting the form's caption to a single space will almost work, but it still leaves the thick bar above the form. Figure 8.3 shows a sample form (frmNoCaptionBar from CH8.MDB) with its caption bar removed. The code in this section is based on code originally created by Tad Orman of Microsoft Product Support Services.

FIGURE 8.3:
Removing a form's caption bar
leaves it with a sizable border,
but you can't move the form by
any means.

Removing the form's caption bar relies on changes to the form's window style. When any application creates a new window, it sets up some information about the style of that window. The Windows API provides functions to retrieve and set the style information, and you can change many of the window styles even after the window has been created. The presence or absence of the caption bar is one of those modifiable styles, and the code in Listing 8.3 (the glrRemoveCaptionBar() function) works by changing the form's window style when called from the form's Open event.

Changing the Window Style

To change the window's style, follow these steps:

1. Retrieve the current window style (a long integer).

2. Turn off the particular bit in the value that controls whether or not the window has a caption bar.

3. Set the style for the window with the newly altered style value.

To retrieve and set the style value, you can call the Windows API functions GetWindowLong() (aliased as glr_apiGetWindowLong()) and SetWindowLong() (aliased as glr_apiSetWindowLong()). In each case you tell Windows which particular value you're getting or setting by passing the constant GWL_STYLE (aliased as glrGWL_STYLE).

To tell Windows to turn off the caption bar, you need to change the value returned from the call to GetWindowLong(). Windows treats the 32-bit value as a set of 32 binary flags, each controlling one attribute of the window, where each can have a value of 0 (False) or 1 (True). For example, the window style value contains a bit controlling the display of the caption bar, the minimize and maximize buttons, and the control menu. The only one of these that Access doesn't give you control over is the display of the caption bar.

To change one of the settings you use either the And or the Or bitwise operator. The And operator takes any two values and returns 1 in any of the positions that were non-zero in both values and 0 in any of the positions where either or both were 0. The Or operator sets any position to 1 if either of the corresponding positions is 1, and 0 otherwise. Therefore, to force a specific bit to be on, you use the Or operator with a number that has all zeros except in the particular bit you care about, where you have a 1. (This works because any value Ored with 0 isn't changed, but any value Ored with 1 is set to 1.) To force a bit to be off, you use the And operator with 1's in all the bits except the one you care about, where you have a 0. (This works because any value Anded with 1 isn't changed, but any value Anded with 0 is set to 0.) To control whether you're turning bits on or off, you can use the Not logical operator, which flips all the bits of a value from 0 to 1 or from 1 to 0.

Therefore, given that the constant WS_CAPTION (aliased as glrWS_CAPTION here) contains the correct bit settings to turn on the display of the caption bar, you could Or it with the value returned from GetWindowLong() to force the display on. To turn it off, you And it with NOT WS_CAPTION. This leaves all the bits alone except the one controlling the caption bar display, which is set to 0. When you make this change and call SetWindowLong(), Windows redisplays the window without the caption bar.

The following three lines of code execute the steps necessary to retrieve and set the window style value:

```
lngOldStyle = glr_apiGetWindowLong(frm.hwnd, glrGWL_STYLE)
lngNewStyle = lngOldStyle And Not glrWS_CAPTION
```

```
lngOldStyle = glr_apiSetWindowLong(frm.hwnd, glrGWL_STYLE,
➡ lngNewStyle)
```

Resizing the Window

Unless you do a little more work, the form will look rather odd at this point. Since you haven't told Windows to redraw the form (and Access knows nothing about the work you've been doing behind its back), there is now a see-through region where the caption used to be. You now must resize the form without the caption bar.

This section of code requires three Windows API functions:

- GetWindowRect() (aliased here as glr_apiGetWindowRect()) fills a user-defined datatype, a variable of type glrTypeRECT, with the current coordinates of the form.

- GetSystemMetrics() (aliased here as glr_apiGetSystemMetrics()) tells you the height of the caption bar that was just removed. When you pass in the SM_CYCAPTION constant (aliased here as glrSM_CYCAPTION), Windows returns to you the height of the caption bar.

- MoveWindow() (aliased here as glr_apiMoveWindow()) moves the window. (Actually, it won't be moved; you'll just call MoveWindow() in order to resize it. Other Windows API functions are available to resize windows, but this one is the easiest to call, given the coordinate information you'll know at this point.)

This code requires some brute-force calculations—figuring out the height of the old caption and subtracting that from the current height of the window. Subtracting the height of the caption bar from the current height of the form should leave you with a form that's the correct height. See Listing 8.3 for the exact details.

Listing 8.3

```
Function glrRemoveCaptionBar(frm As Form)
    ' Remove a form's caption bar
    glrRemoveWindowCaptionBar frm.hWnd
End Function
```

```
Sub glrRemoveWindowCaptionBar(ByVal hWnd As Integer)

    ' Remove a window's caption bar, given its hWnd.

    ' You can use this code, modified from the Access
    ' Knowledge Base, to remove the caption bar from
    ' your forms.  See frmNoCaptionBar.

    ' If you want to use this code in your own app, include
    ' this module and basFormGlobal.

    Dim lngOldStyle As Long
    Dim lngNewStyle As Long
    Dim rct As glrTypeRECT
    Dim intRetVal As Integer
    Dim intDX As Integer, intDY As Integer

    ' Get the current window style of the form.
    lngOldStyle = glr_apiGetWindowLong(hWnd,
    ➥ glrGWL_STYLE)

    ' Turn off the bit that enables the caption.
    lngNewStyle = lngOldStyle And Not glrWS_CAPTION

    ' Set the new window style.
    lngOldStyle = glr_apiSetWindowLong(hWnd,
    ➥ glrGWL_STYLE, lngNewStyle)

    ' The caption's been removed, but now resize
    ' the whole window to match the size of the interior.

    ' Get the current size, including the caption.
    glr_apiGetWindowRect hWnd, rct

    ' Calculate the new width and height.
    intDX = rct.intX2 - rct.intX1
    intDY = rct.intY2 - rct.intY1 -
    ➥ glr_apiGetSystemMetrics(glrSM_CYCAPTION)

    ' Move the window to the same left and top,
    ' but with new width and height.
    ' This will make the new form appear
    ' a little lower than the original.
```

```
        intRetVal = glr_apiMoveWindow(hWnd, rct.intX1,
     ➡ rct.intY1, intDX, intDY, True)
End Sub
```

Using glrRemoveCaptionBar() in Your Own Applications

To use glrRemoveCaptionBar() in your own applications, follow these steps:

1. Import both the modules basCaption and basFormGlobal from CH8.MDB into your own database.

2. Call glrRemoveCaptionBar() from your form's Open event. You'll need either to place a call to it directly from the property sheet (placing "=glrRemoveCaptionBar(Form)" in the property sheet) or to call it from the code you have currently attached to your Open event.

Note that once you've removed a form's caption bar, Access never puts it back for you. If you want to use the form in design mode once you've removed the caption bar, you must close the form and reopen it in design mode. Since Access has no way of knowing that you've removed the caption bar, it can't know that it needs to put one on the form in design mode.

Retrieving and Saving Information about Forms

You may find in your applications that you need more information about your forms than Access can give you. You may need to discern whether your user has positioned the current record at the "new" record. Or you may just want to be able to tell whether or not a specific form is open. You might, for example, need to save and restore your forms' locations from one session to the next. If your users can resize and move forms, this is especially important. (See the section "Screen Resolution and Distributing Forms" later in this chapter for more information on scaling forms as they're resized.) You'll find the solutions to these problems in the sections that follow.

Which Form Is This?

If you write Access Basic code attached to controls or sections on a form, you'll often need to pass to that code an object that refers to the current form. Many beginning developers count on the Screen.ActiveForm object to get this information. You should avoid this method if at all possible since Screen.ActiveForm often returns a reference to a different form than the one you'd intended. If you're working with a popup form, for example, and the current form is a different form altogether, you don't want code attached to the popup form to attempt to work on the other loaded form.

Access provides a simple solution to this problem. From anywhere on the form's design surface, you can retrieve and pass to Access Basic code any of the form's properties. One of these properties is the form's Form property, which is a reference to the form itself. You can pass this property as a parameter to any function you call from the property sheet so the function can know which form it should be concerned with. For example, if your form calls a function named FormOnCurrent() from its Current event, you could place this expression:

```
=FormOnCurrent(Form)
```

in the property sheet to pass a reference to the current form to the function. The function declaration would be something like this:

```
Function FormOnCurrent(frm as Form)
```

On the other hand, if your code exists in the form's CBF (Code-Behind-Forms) you can use "Me" to refer to the current form. That is, in the external function declared above, you could retrieve the form's caption with this expression:

```
strCaption = frm.Caption
```

but in CBF, you could use this expression:

```
strCaption = Me.Caption
```

without explicitly defining Me. It always contains a reference to the current form. If you need to create global procedures that can be called from multiple forms, you can still call these from CBF. Just pass the Me object to those functions as a parameter from the form's event procedure. For example, to call the previously mentioned FormOnCurrent() function from a form's module, use this:

```
intRetval = FormOnCurrent(Me)
```

At the New Record?

It is sometimes vitally important for your application to be able to sense whether or not your user has moved to the "new" record (the extra record at the end of editable recordsets). Access does not provide a built-in test for this, so testing for it requires a bit of thought. The best solution we've come up with is to use an error condition. That is, because a certain action triggers an error condition only if you're at the new record, you can use that fact to detect that you're at the new record. (The uses of error handlers are covered in more detail in Chapter 14.)

Using Errors for Good

Access maintains a bookmark for each row in a recordset. This bookmark is a unique, randomly created string whose actual value is unimportant and that can't be counted on to be any specific value. (Experimentation shows that the bookmark value, a string, is actually a binary-coded long integer. You may find some use for the specific value stored in a bookmark, but the value was not intended to be used in this way.) Not all recordsets support bookmarks, but all bound forms do. Therefore, you can safely use the technique described here on any form, no matter what the source of the data.

NOTE   The Access documentation states that many different record sources do not support bookmarks. This may be the case, although we haven't found this to be true for forms. Experimentation has shown that any bound form supports bookmarks, as does the recordset retrieved from the form's RecordSetClone property. This may not be true in every single case, so check this fact carefully before using it in your own application.

An attempt to retrieve the new record's bookmark triggers a run-time error in Access since the new record doesn't yet *have* a bookmark. Therefore, you can use this very simple function to test whether you're currently positioned on the new record:

```
Function AtNewRecord(frm As Form)

    ' Check to see if the form's current
    ' record is the New record.

    Dim varTemp As Variant

Const ERR_NO_CURRENT_ROW = 3021

    On Error Resume Next
    varTemp = frm.BookMark
    AtNewRecord = (Err = ERR_NO_CURRENT_ROW)
    On Error GoTo 0
End Function
```

The AtNewRecord() function attempts to retrieve the current bookmark for the form. If it fails it can only be because you've positioned the form so that it's displaying the new record. Since the function sets up an error handler to let errors pass ("On Error Resume Next"), you can just check the state of the Err function after the attempt to retrieve the bookmark. If it's ERR_NO_CURRENT_ROW you know that you are at the new record.

Is a Specific Form Loaded?

In Access 1.x if you needed to know whether a specific form were currently loaded into memory, you could use a method similar to that used in the previous example. That is, attempting to retrieve information about the form would trigger a run-time error if the form weren't loaded, so you could base your decision on the occurrence of that run-time error.

In Access 2.0 there's a simpler way to detect whether or not a specific form (or any other object) is loaded into memory. The trick is to use the SysCmd() function, which returns information about any object. If you call SysCmd(), passing to it the constant SYSCMD_GETOBJECTSTATE, along with the name of your object and a constant indicating the object type (one of A_FORM, A_REPORT, and so on), it returns an integer indicating the current state of that object. As long as the return value is non-zero, you know that the object is open.

```
Function isOpen(strName As String, intObjectType as Integer)
    ' Returns True if strName is open, False otherwise.
    isOpen = (SysCmd(SYSCMD_GETOBJECTSTATE, intObjectType,
    ➡ strName) <> 0)
End Function
```

(The sample form, frmCreateQBF in CH8.MDB, uses isOpen(). Look in its module for the FixUpForm() function to see isOpen() in use.)

Saving and Restoring Form Locations

Many Windows applications save information about the size and location of their internal forms (or windows) from one invocation to the next. That way, when the user starts the program, the application is laid out just as it was when it was last used. Although you can save an Access form's location by explicitly saving it, you may not want (or be able) to save a form in order to preserve its size and location.

Most applications that save their state do so in a standardized text file—a Windows .INI file. (Take a look at WIN.INI in your Windows directory for an example. Although your application could write directly to WIN.INI, it's usually a good idea to use your own private .INI file.) The Windows API provides functions that make it simple to read and write information to and from such a file. Since you can call these API functions from Access and since you can call a function when a form loads and when it closes, you can read the information from the file when your form opens and write it back out when the form closes.

An .INI file usually consists of sections delimited with section headers. Since your application may already use its own .INI file (especially if it's distributed with the Access run-time version), the routines that save and restore form dimensions must work with your existing .INI file. The procedures you'll use store the information in a section titled [WindowCoords], with one row for each form you track. A sample section in the file might look like this:

```
[WindowCoords]
Form1=1,1,100,200
Form2=1,1,300,450
```

The individual rows store the coordinates of the upper-left and lower-right corners of your form. The goal, then, of the necessary functions is to read the data from the .INI file every time you load the form and to move the form to the correct size and location at that point. Then, when closing the form, you call a function to write the coordinates back out to the .INI file. You can find the necessary functions in the bas-SaveSize module in CH8.MDB.

Reading and Writing .INI Files

Although the code presented here is geared toward saving and restoring screen co-ordinates, you should be able to use the API function declarations to read and write any information you want to a private .INI file. This is an easy way to store information about your application's environment and users.

> **NOTE**
>
> Access complains if it finds multiple external function declarations with the same name anywhere within any of the loaded modules or libraries. This is why all the API declarations we use throughout this book include an alias (they're always prefixed with "glr_api"). If you ever find yourself in a situation where you can't compile a module because of external function name collisions, you'll need to remove one of the Declare statements that's duplicated. The examples for this chapter and Chapter 10 include many overlapping declarations. To make it simpler to use modules from both chapters, we've grouped the overlapping declarations in each chapter's code so they're easier to find. If you receive "Duplicate Procedure Name" errors from Access when you attempt to run your code, find the appropriate section in the code and comment out the redundant procedure declaration.

To use the API functions you must include declarations for the functions you need, chosen from the following list, in a module in your application:

```
' Get an integer from a private .INI file
' Returns either the integer it found, or the value
' sent in intDefault.
Declare Function glr_apiGetPrivateProfileInt Lib "KERNEL" Alias
➥ "GetPrivateProfileInt"(ByVal strAppName As String,
➥ ByVal strKeyName As String, ByVal intDefault As Integer,
➥ ByVal strFileName As String) As Integer
```

```
' Get a string from a private ..INI file
' Returns the number of bytes copied into strReturned, not
' including the trailing null.
Declare Function glr_apiGetPrivateProfileString Lib "KERNEL"
➡ Alias "GetPrivateProfileString"(ByVal strAppName As String,
➡ ByVal strKeyName As String, ByVal strDefault As String,
➡ ByVal strReturned As String, ByVal intSize As Integer,
➡ ByVal strFileName As String) As Integer

' Get a string from WIN.INI
' Returns the number of bytes copied into strReturned, not
' including the trailing null.
Declare Function glr_apiGetProfileString Lib "KERNEL" Alias
➡ "GetProfileString"(ByVal strAppName As String,
➡ ByVal strKeyName As String, ByVal strDefault As String,
➡ ByVal strReturned As String, ByVal intSize As Integer)
➡ As Integer

' Get an integer from WIN.INI
' Returns either the integer it found, or the value
' sent in intDefault.
Declare Function glr_apiGetProfileInt Lib "KERNEL" Alias
➡ "GetProfileInt"(ByVal strAppName as String,
➡ ByVal strKeyName As String, ByVal intDefault As Integer)
➡ As Integer

' Write a string to a private .INI file
' Returns a non-zero value if successful, otherwise
' it returns a 0.
Declare Function glr_apiWritePrivateProfileString Lib "KERNEL"
➡ Alias "WritePrivateProfileString"(ByVal strAppName As
➡ String, ByVal strKeyName As String,
➡ ByVal strValue As String, ByVal strFileName As String)
➡ As Integer

' Write a string to WIN.INI
' Returns a non-zero value if successful, otherwise
' it returns a 0.
Declare Function glr_apiWriteProfileString Lib "KERNEL" Alias
➡ "WriteProfileString" (ByVal strAppName As String,
➡ ByVal strKeyName As String, ByVal strValue As String)
➡ As Integer
```

The GetProfileString(), GetProfileInt(), and WriteProfileString() functions work with the Windows .INI file, WIN.INI. The others work with a specified, private .INI file. For more information on declaring external functions, see Chapter 17.

Table 8.5 describes each of the parameters.

TABLE 8.5: Parameters for the Windows Profile Reading/Writing Functions

Parameter	Description	Example
strAppName	Name of the section	WindowCoords
strKeyName	Entry whose value is to be written or retrieved	Form1
intDefault	Integer value to use if strKeyName is not found in the .INI file	(any integer)
strDefault	String value to use if strKeyName is not found in the .INI file	(any string)
strValue	String to be written out to the .INI file	(any string)
intSize	Size, in characters, of the buffer created to hold the return string from the .INI file	(any integer)
strReturned	String buffer to hold the value found in the .INI file. Must be made large enough to hold intSize characters	Space(intSize)

TIP

Whenever you call an API function, you're going outside of Access' "world," and it can't protect you from errors. If you make a mistake you can easily crash Access, Windows, or your entire computer. Make sure you've saved any work in all open applications before running any Access application that uses API calls for the first time.

Here are some points to note:

- If you write to an .INI file that doesn't exist, Windows creates it. If you attempt to write to a section that doesn't exist within the .INI file, Windows creates the section.

- The only difference between the pairs of functions GetProfileInt()/GetPrivateProfileInt(), GetProfileString()/GetPrivateProfileString(), and WriteProfileString()/WritePrivateProfileString() is the addition of the file name parameter in the private .INI functions.

- There is no WriteProfileInt() or WritePrivateProfileInt() function, so you need to use the WriteProfileString() and WritePrivateProfileString() functions anytime you need to write to your .INI file.

- The strings you pass to receive the returned information (strReturned) must be explicitly sized to contain enough space for the response before you call the API function.

- Strings returned from API calls are null terminated and are not ready for use in Access without some manipulation. The simplest solution is to use the Left() function with the return value from GetProfileString()/GetPrivateProfileString() and peel off the part you're interested in.

Here are two examples of setting and retrieving information from .INI files:

- **Example 1:** Retrieve the short date format from WIN.INI.

```
Function GetShortDate()
    Dim strBuffer As String * 128
    Dim intChars As Integer

    intChars = glr_apiGetProfileString("intl", "sShortDate",
    ➡ "", strBuffer, 128)
    GetShortDate = Left(strBuffer, intChars)
End Function
```

- **Example 2:** Write the string "Form1=1,1,12,30" to MyApp.INI, in the WindowCoords section.

```
intRetval = glr_apiWritePrivateProfileString("WindowCoords",
➡ "Form1", "1,1,12,30", "MyApp.INI")
```

Putting It All Together

Once you know how to read and write information in .INI files, you still need to know how to retrieve and set the form's size and location. These steps require yet three more Windows API function calls:

```
Declare Sub glr_apiGetWindowRect Lib "USER" Alias
➡ "GetWindowRect"(ByVal hWnd As Integer,
➡ rectangle As typeRect)
Declare Sub glr_apiMoveWindow Lib "USER" Alias "MoveWindow"
➡ (ByVal hWnd As Integer, ByVal X As Integer,
➡ ByVal Y As Integer, ByVal nWidth As Integer,
➡ ByVal nHeight As Integer, ByVal bRepaint As Integer)
Declare Function glr_apiGetParent Lib "USER" Alias "GetParent"
➡ (ByVal hWnd As Integer) As Integer
```

Retrieving Window Coordinates

The GetWindowRect() subroutine fills in a user-defined type with a window's current coordinates relative to the edge of the screen. MoveWindow() moves and sizes a window relative to the window's parent (which in this case is most likely the Access main window). Therefore, when you retrieve a form's coordinates, you must make them relative to its parent's coordinates. To get information about the form's parent you need the GetParent() function. All three of these functions require a window handle, but this isn't a problem since every form in Access provides its own handle through its hWnd property.

NOTE   Although Access provides the MoveSize macro action, it's not really appropriate in all circumstances. Since it works only with the current form, it requires you to select a form before running the action. For the purposes of this example, this requires setting the focus to the form before changing its position. Even with screen display turned off, it is quite ugly. In addition, using MoveSize requires you to specify coordinates in twips, not in pixels. This requires some extra calculations to convert the retrieved screen location values from twips into pixels.

Given this information you'll find it easy to retrieve a form's coordinates. This function by itself might be useful to you elsewhere since, although forms provide read-only WindowWidth and WindowHeight properties, they don't provide a Top or Left property. You can use the GetFormSize subroutine (Listing 8.4) in your own applications, filling in a typeRect variable with the coordinates of a form relative to its parent. The parent, by the way, will be either the Access MDI client window (for normal forms) or the Access main window (for modal forms).

Listing 8.4

```
' Store rectangle coordinates.
Type typeRect
    intX1 As Integer
    intY1 As Integer
    intX2 As Integer
    intY2 As Integer
End Type

Private Sub GetFormSize(frm As Form, rctR As typeRect)

    ' Fill in rctR with the coordinates of the window.

    Dim hwndParent As Integer
    Dim rctParent As typeRect

    ' Find the position of the window in question, in
    ' relation to its parent window (the Access desktop).
    hwndParent = glr_apiGetParent(frm.hWnd)

    ' Get the coordinates of the current window and
    ' its parent.
    glr_apiGetWindowRect frm.hWnd, rctR
    glr_apiGetWindowRect hwndParent, rctParent

    ' Subtract off the left and top parent coordinates,
    ' since you need coordinates relative to the parent for
    ' the glr_apiMoveWindow() function call.
    rctR.intX1 = rctR.intX1 - rctParent.intX1
    rctR.intY1 = rctR.intY1 - rctParent.intY1
    rctR.intX2 = rctR.intX2 - rctParent.intX1
    rctR.intY2 = rctR.intY2 - rctParent.intY1
End Sub
```

This procedure, given a form object and a rectangle structure to fill in, first finds the parent of the form. It then finds the window coordinates of the two windows (the form and its parent) and calculates the coordinates of the child form as compared to the upper-left coordinates of the parent window.

Moving Windows

When it comes time to place the form at a specific size and location, use the MoveWindow() API function. This function needs the window handle, the upper-left corner's coordinates, the width and height of the window, and information regarding whether or not to repaint the window immediately. The coordinates of the upper-left corner must be relative to the form's parent. Since you previously retrieved this information using the GetFormSize subroutine above, this step should be simple.

The SetFormSize subroutine (Listing 8.5) takes a window handle and a rectangle structure filled with the new coordinates of that window, calculates the width and height based on the coordinates in the rectangle structure, and calls MoveWindow() to move the form.

Listing 8.5

```
Private Sub SetFormSize(frm As Form, rctR As typeRect)

    Dim intWidth As Integer
    Dim intHeight As Integer

    intWidth = (rctR.intX2 - rctR.intX1)
    intHeight = (rctR.intY2 - rctR.intY1)

' No sense even trying if either is less than 0.
    If (intWidth > 0) And (intHeight > 0) Then
        ' You would think the MoveSize action would work
        ' here, but that requires actually SELECTING the
        ' window first. That seemed like too much work,
        ' when this procedure will move/size ANY window.
        glr_apiMoveWindow frm.hWnd, rctR.intX1, rctR.intY1,
        ➥ intWidth, intHeight, True
    End If
End Sub
```

The Final Steps

Once you know how to save and restore the information from the .INI file and how to retrieve and set the window size, the only step left is to actually move the information to and from the .INI file. For the most part this work is just brute force, and you can study the code in basSaveSize if it interests you.

The GetToken() Function

There is one additional general-purpose routine in basSaveSize that you might find useful in other applications. Once you've gathered the information about the form's size and location, the application stores that information as a comma-delimited list in the .INI file. When you retrieve that information, you need to break it back out into the separate pieces. (This is normally referred to as *parsing the string*.) The GetToken() function in basSaveSize does this for you—it pulls a piece from a string, given a specific delimiter and the numbered item from the string that you want. For example:

```
GetToken("1,1,100,200", 3, ",")
```

returns "100" since it's the third token in the list separated with commas. That's how the function is used in this example. On the other hand, you could also use it to retrieve words a sentence. This example:

```
GetToken("This is a test of how this works", 5, " ")
```

returns "of" since that's the fifth token in the space-delimited list. Listing 8.6 shows the entire GetToken() function.

Listing 8.6

```
Private Function GetToken(strFrom As String,
➡ intWhich As Integer, strSeparator As String)

    ' Pull the requested token from strFrom, delimited by
    ' strSeparator.
    ' Example:  GetToken("23,34,45,56,67", 3, ",")
    ' would return "45"
    ' Example:
    '   GetToken("This is a test of how this works", 4, " ")
    ' would return "test"
    '
```

```
        Dim intPos As Integer
        Dim intPos1 As Integer
        Dim intCount As Integer

        intPos = 0
        For intCount = 0 To intWhich - 1
            intPos1 = InStr(intPos + 1, strFrom, strSeparator)
            If intPos1 = 0 Then
                intPos1 = Len(strFrom) + 1
            End If
            If intCount <> intWhich - 1 Then
                intPos = intPos1
            End If
        Next intCount
        If intPos1 > intPos Then
            GetToken = Mid$(strFrom, intPos + 1, intPos1 -
        ➥ intPos - 1)
        Else
            GetToken = Null
        End If
    End Function
```

Using glrGetFormInfo() and glrSaveFormInfo() in Your Own Applications

To use the glrGetFormInfo() and glrSaveFormInfo() functionality in your own applications, follow these steps:

1. Import the modules basSaveSize and basFormGlobal from CH8.MDB into your application.

2. Add a call to glrGetFormInfo() to your form's Open event. Either add it to the code you already call or just call it directly. In either case pass it the current form's Form property.

3. Add a call to glrSaveFormInfo() to your form's Close event. Either add it to the code you already call or just call it directly. In either case, pass it the current form's Form property.

4. Modify the constants INI_FILE and INI_SECTION in basSaveSize to meet your own needs. The values originally stored there are for demonstration purposes only.

When you open the form, the code attached to the Open event calls the glrGet-FormInfo() function and sizes and positions the form correctly. When you close the form, the Close event code stores away the current size and position information into your own .INI file.

Retrieving the Interior Coordinates of a Form

If you allow your users to resize your forms while your application is running, you may at some point need to know the dimensions of the interior portion of your form. This information will be used extensively in the section "Screen Resolution and Distributing Forms" later in this chapter. Besides issues of screen resolution, though, you might want to move or resize controls on your form based on the form's size. The example in this section maintains a single button on a form, half the width and half the height, centered on the form, no matter how you resize it. Figure 8.4 shows three instances of the same form, sized differently. In each case the code attached to the form's Resize event has calculated the current dimensions of the form and has reset the size and position of the button accordingly.

FIGURE 8.4:
The width and height of the form's border control the size and positioning of the button on the form.

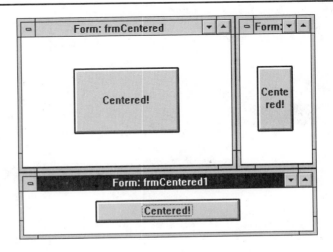

Access maintains the dimensions of the interior of a form separately from the dimensions of the containing frame. This way your forms can scroll horizontally and vertically. This flexibility makes things complicated, though, when you want to use the border size to control what happens inside your form. To make the form's surface the same size as the form border, for example, you need to set the form's Width property and the Detail sections' Height property, neither of which need to have anything to do with the actual dimensions of the form's border. And if you have more than one section, the issues get quite complex. (The code in the section "Screen Resolution and Distibuting Forms" deals with these concepts. For now we look at the simple (but common) example of a form with a single section.)

Units of measurement can also cause problems. Access measures its sizes in twips ($\frac{1}{1440}$ inch). Windows returns values in logical screen measurements (pixels), not physical measurements like twips or inches, when you ask it for the dimensions of the interior of a window. To retrieve the interior dimensions of a window, you call GetClientRect(), which retrieves the interior dimensions of a window, as opposed to GetWindowRect(), which retrieves the dimensions of the entire window. Luckily, Windows also provides a mechanism for retrieving the relationship between pixels and twips for a given display driver: the GetDeviceCaps() function.

There are two basic steps involved in resizing a form's interior to match its border size. You must first get the information from Windows about the current size of the form's border. Once you have that information and have converted it to twips, you can set the form's interior components to be the same size (Form.Width and Section.Height) as the border. We'll bypass detailed discussion of the glrGetSize() function shown in Listing 8.7 since these are the same issues covered in greater detail later in the chapter, when we cover form scaling. Listing 8.8, taken from frmCentered in CH8.MDB, shows how you might use the dimensions retrieved with glrGetSize() to resize the button on the example form.

> **TIP**
>
> To use the glrGetSize() function in your own application, import the modules basFormGlobal and basFormSize from CH8.MDB into your own application. To retrieve the form's dimensions, call glrGetSize(), passing to it a form object and two integer variables, which glrGetSize() will fill in with the width and height of the form (in twips) (see Listing 8.7).

Listing 8.7

```
Type typeRect
    intX1 As Integer
    intY1 As Integer
    intX2 As Integer
    intY2 As Integer
End Type

Declare Function glr_apiCreateIC Lib "GDI" Alias "CreateIC"
➥ (ByVal strDriverName As String, ByVal lpDeviceName As
➥ Any, ByVal lpOutput As Any, ByVal lpInitData As Any) As
➥ Integer
Declare Function glr_apiDeleteDC Lib "GDI" Alias "DeleteDC"
➥ (ByVal intDC As Integer) As Integer
Declare Function glr_apiGetDeviceCaps Lib "GDI" Alias
➥ "GetDeviceCaps"(ByVal hDC As Integer, ByVal nIndex As
➥ Integer) As Integer
Declare Sub glr_apiGetClientRect Lib "USER" Alias
➥ "GetClientRect"(ByVal hWnd As Integer, rct As typeRect)

' Windows API Constants
Const TWIPS_PER_INCH = 1440

Sub glrGetSize (frm As Form, intWidth As Integer,
➥ intHeight As Integer)

    ' Get the size of the current form. On the
    ' first pass, get necessary info from Windows
    ' about the screen resolution. Otherwise, just
    ' call the Windows API to get the current form size.

    Dim rct As typeRect
    Dim intIC As Integer

    ' Store away the screen resolution. Don't bother
    ' gathering that info if it's already been gathered.
    Static intTwipsPerPixelX As Integer
    Static intTwipsPerPixelY As Integer

    ' First time through here, call Windows and find out
    ' information about the screen display.
```

```
    If intTwipsPerPixelX = 0 Then
        intIC = glr_apiCreateIC("DISPLAY", glrAPINULL,
        ➥ glrAPINULL, glrAPINULL)
        If intIC <> 0 Then
            ' Find the number of twips per pixel in both
            ' directions.
            intTwipsPerPixelX = glrTWIPS_PER_INCH /
            ➥ glr_apiGetDeviceCaps(intIC, glrLOGPIXELSX)
            intTwipsPerPixelY = glrTWIPS_PER_INCH /
            ➥ glr_apiGetDeviceCaps(intIC, glrLOGPIXELSY)
            intIC = glr_apiDeleteDC(intIC)
        End If
    End If
    glr_apiGetClientRect frm.hWnd, rct
    intWidth = (rct.intX2 - rct.intX1) * intTwipsPerPixelX
    intHeight = (rct.intY2 - rct.intY1) * intTwipsPerPixelY
End Sub
```

Listing 8.8

```
Sub Form_Resize ()
    Dim intWidth As Integer
    Dim intHeight As Integer
    Dim ctl As Control

    ' Get the current coordinates
    glrGetSize Me, intWidth, intHeight

    ' Set the form width
    Me.Width = intWidth

    ' Set the detail section height
    Me.Section(0).Height = intHeight

    ' Get a reference to the single control.
    Set ctl = Me!cmdCentered

    ' Set the coordinates of the button so that
    ' it's centered.
    ctl.Width = intWidth / 2
    ctl.Height = intHeight / 2
    ctl.Left = (intWidth - ctl.Width) / 2
    ctl.Top = (intHeight - ctl.Height) / 2
End Sub
```

Using Forms as Toolboxes

By setting the right combination of properties, you can make a form that you create look and act like a standard toolbox. (Although the terms *toolbar* and *toolbox* are often used interchangeably, we think of a toolbar as a group of buttons fixed to the application window, usually right below the menu bar, and a toolbox as a free-floating collection of buttons.) Generally, most application toolboxes have these characteristics in common:

- They float above all other forms in your application.

- They have a control menu but neither a minimize nor a maximize button.

- They have a double-thick, nonsizable border.

- They consist of buttons with pictures indicating actions, perhaps with a status-bar label.

Toolboxes usually provide generic buttons that work with any window your user might have loaded. For example, you might want to provide a record navigation toolbar that would allow your users to move from row to row in a form and would reflect the state of the form the user had most recently chosen. Toolbars are also very useful when working with forms in design mode. Although Access provides a wide range of development tools, you might want to augment these with your own. The simple example you'll find here provides buttons to align groups of controls, as well as to center controls horizontally or vertically. Figure 8.5 shows the sample toolbox, frmToolbox from CH8.MDB, in action. You should be able to take the example you see here and modify it for your own purposes.

FIGURE 8.5:
This sample toolbox allows you to align groups of controls with each other or to center them horizontally or vertically.

Creating Your Toolbox

You'll want your toolbox to float above all the other windows in your Access application. To make this happen you need to set the form's Popup property to Yes. In addition, you need to set other properties to make the form act like a standard popup toolbox. Table 8.6 lists all the properties you'll need to set. Some of these property values are the Access default values, but make sure they're set correctly, in any case.

TABLE 8.6: Toolbox Form Properties

Property	Value
Popup	Yes
BorderStyle	Dialog
ViewsAllowed	Form
ShortcutMenu	No
DefaultView	Single Form
Scrollbars	Neither
RecordSelectors	No
NavigationButtons	No
AutoResize	Yes
AutoCenter	No

The Popup Property

As you read earlier in this chapter, a form that has its Popup property set to Yes has a different parent than a normal window. Normal forms have the Access MDI client window as their parent (and can't be moved outside that window), but popup forms have the Access window itself as their parent. In addition, their Windows class is different, granting them different properties. Therefore, you can move popup windows anywhere on the Windows desktop, and they stay "above" all the other, normal Access forms. Setting the Popup property to Yes, then, is crucial in order to allow your popup toolbox to function correctly since the code that locates the active form will rely on the fact that your toolbox has a different parent than the other forms.

The AutoResize Property

Although setting the AutoResize property to Yes isn't imperative, it certainly makes the design process simpler for you. Normally Access saves the dimensions and location of a form with the form when you save it. In design mode, though, Access always displays the horizontal and vertical scroll bars on a form. Since you're using your toolbox form without scroll bars, you'll want it just the right size to include the controls you've placed on it. Setting the AutoResize property to Yes causes Access to resize the form to the correct size to just contain the internal design surface when it loads the form. If you want an exercise in design frustration, turn this property to No and try to get your form sized correctly.

The BorderStyle Property

Setting the BorderStyle property to Dialog is an important step in creating a toolbox. By doing so you ensure that the form isn't sizable and that it's surrounded by a double thick, solid border. One item to keep in mind: once you've changed the BorderStyle property to anything but Sizable, you can no longer go directly from design to form mode again (until you change it back to Sizable, of course). Unless you remember this you might be surprised when your popup toolbox doesn't work as you intended. When you switch directly from Design to Form view, Access treats your toolbox form just like any other form: its parent is the MDI client window, and it won't float above other forms.

Placing Objects on the Form

The sample toolbox form consists of command buttons and a label control. You'll want to choose buttons whose pictures are familiar to your users and whose actions are clearly related to the pictures. For the example, we've chosen to use the alignment pictures Access itself uses for the align Top/Left/Right/Bottom buttons and similar pictures for the Center Horizontal/Vertical buttons. In this case we've also added a simple status bar in the toolbox that updates to describe the current button as you move the mouse over the buttons or as you move from button to button with the keyboard. There's no reason why you can't include other control types in your own toolboxes, but this sample was meant to be simple.

Updating the Status Label

If you're creating your own toolbox, this might be a good time to activate the status bar. That is, once you've created the form, including all the buttons and with all the necessary properties set, you can test it out. It won't actually do anything yet, of course, but this is a good time to add the descriptive text in the status bar label control. (You can, of course, use the SysCmd() function to place text in the normal Access status bar. Our experience has shown that many users never notice text that's placed there. For toolboxes, which might be positioned far from the status bar, a separate status indicator can be very useful.)

Since you want the text updated everytime the mouse enters each button and you also want it updated as buttons each get the focus, you need code attached to both the OnMouseMove and OnEnter events. To keep from duplicating text on each place, we've used a common procedure, DisplayText, that takes as a parameters an integer describing the button in question. These constants:

```
Const ALIGN_LEFT = 0
Const ALIGN_RIGHT = 1
Const ALIGN_TOP = 2
Const ALIGN_BOTTOM = 3
Const CENTER_VERT = 4
Const CENTER_HORIZ = 5
```

are used throughout the code to indicate which button is current. Then, from both the MouseMove and Enter events, the attached code calls DisplayText, passing the appropriate constant for each button.

The DisplayText procedure in the following listing can react to the parameter, placing the correct text into lblStatus:

```
Sub DisplayText(intWhich As Integer)
    Dim strText As String

    Select Case intWhich
        Case ALIGN_TOP
            strText = "Align Top"
        Case ALIGN_BOTTOM
            strText = "Align Bottom"
        Case ALIGN_LEFT
            strText = "Align Left"
        Case ALIGN_RIGHT
            strText = "Align Right"
```

```
        Case CENTER_HORIZ
            strText = "Center Horizontal"
        Case CENTER_VERT
            strText = "Center Vertical"
    End Select

    If lblStatus.Caption <> strText Then
        lblStatus.Caption = strText
    End If
End Sub
```

Note that the code updates lblStatus only if the text to be placed there is different than the text that's already there. This reduces the flickering effect you'd see otherwise. Since Access fires off the MouseMove event everytime the mouse moves even a tiny amount, this procedure would otherwise be updating the label for each move. This way it updates the label's caption only when there's new text to be placed there. You might find it interesting to try this function without checking the current text, comparing the way the status label looks in either case. You'll probably agree that the extra processing required to check the text first is worth the time it takes, based on the improvement in the screen display.

Beyond the Basics

Once you have your toolbox performing the basic functions (that is, appearing correctly and updating the status bar), you need to perform the following actions for each button:

- Determine the previous active window.
- Return to that window.
- Take the appropriate action.

Finding the Active Window

Once you've created your toolbox form and its buttons and status bar, you need to make it actually *do* something. If you're intention is to have it take some action on the form where you were prior to clicking one of its buttons, it will need some way to figure out what the last active object was. To find this information you will rely on the fact that Access uses the MDI model for its workspace. Open forms and reports are all children of the same MDI client window, while popup forms are children of the Access window itself. Luckily, the Windows API function GetWindow(), when asked to retrieve information about children of a particular window, finds the top-most child window first. Since the active window is always the top-most window, you can get a handle to the window you want to find.

Listing 8.9 shows the functions you need in order to find the most recently active child of Access' MDI client window. To use them you must have a list of the Windows class names for the objects you might need to find from your own toolboxes. Table 8.7 lists several objects and their "official" class names.

TABLE 8.7: Sample Access Objects and Their Class Names

Object	Class Name	Comment
Database Container	ODb	There is only one database container, so finding the first object with this class type is always sufficient
Form	OForm	All forms are of the same class
Report	OReport	All reports are of the same class
Floating Access Toolbar	OTBDock	Contains a window of class OToolbar, which is the actual toolbar
Access Toolbar	OToolbar	All toolbars are of this class. Floating, undocked toolbars are encased in a window of class OTBDock
Macro Design Window	OScript	
Module Design Window	OModule	
Table	OTable	Whether the table is in Design or Datasheet view, the internal display is a window of the class OGrid
Query	OQry	

TIP

Table 8.7 lists just a few of the many window classes Access creates. If you want to explore on your own, you need a tool that can examine windows and tell you information about them. One such tool is SPY.EXE, which ships with Microsoft's Visual C++ Compiler. That's the tool we used to gather the class name information you see here. You can also find freeware tools that provide similar functionality. SUPERSPY.EXE, from SoftBlox Inc., is available on this book's companion disk.

To find the first occurrence of a particular child class, you call glrGetAccessChild() (see Listing 8.9) with the appropriate class name. For example,

```
hWnd = glrGetAccessChild("ODb")
```

returns to you the handle of the Database Container window. Calling the function as

```
hWnd = glrGetAccessChild("OForm")
```

returns to you the handle of the active standard form. It won't find popup forms since it only looks through the children of the MDI client window.

The more general-purpose function glrFindChildClass() takes two parameters: the handle of a window through which to look for children and the class of the child you're interested in. Using this function, given that you know the Access main window's handle, you could find the MDIClient window's handle by calling the function like this:

```
hWnd = glrFindChildClass(hWndAccess, "MDIClient")
```

How the Functions Work

glrGetAccessChild() starts by asking Windows for the handle of the main Access window. The API function, GetParent(), does the work here, in the function glrFind-AccessHWnd(). It looks at the parent of the current window, then at that window's parent, and so on, until it finds a window whose class name indicates it's the Access main window. If it can't find that handle, of course, all bets are off and the function must give up. Once glrGetAccessChild() has the handle for the Access window, it calls the glrFindChildClass() function, requesting Access' child window of the MDIClient class. Once it finds this handle it can call glrFindChildClass() once more, requesting the necessary child of the MDIClient window.

glrFindChildClass() uses the Windows API function GetWindow(), which can iterate through all the children of a window, looking for a specific class type. You can call it once with the GW_CHILD flag, in which case it finds the window's first child. Calling it subsequently, with the handle of that child and the GW_HWNDNEXT flag, finds siblings of that child. If glrFindChildClass() looks through all the children and doesn't find one of the right type, it just returns 0, indicating failure. The loop boils down to these lines of code, iterating through all the children of the window whose handle is hWnd:

```
hWndCurrent = GetWindow(hWnd, GW_CHILD)
Do While hWndCurrent <> 0
    intClassLen = GetClassName(hWndCurrent, strClassName,
    ➥ MAX_LEN - 1)
    If Left(strClassName, intClassLen) = strClassNameToMatch
    ➥ Then
        fFound = True
        Exit Do
    End If
    hWndTemp = GetNextWindow(hWndCurrent, GW_HWNDNEXT)
    hWndCurrent = hWndTemp
Loop
```

Armed with glrFindChildClass() and some program like Microsoft's SPY.EXE, you should be able to find a handle to any child window for any application, should the need arise.

Listing 8.9

```
Function glrFindAccessHWnd()
    Dim hWnd As Integer
    Dim strBuff As String
    Dim intCount As Integer

Const MAX_SIZE = 255

    hWnd = glr_apiGetActiveWindow()

    ' Walk the parent tree, looking for the main Access
    ' window.
    Do
        strBuff = Space(MAX_SIZE)
        intCount = glr_apiGetClassName(hWnd, strBuff,
        ➥ MAX_SIZE)
        strBuff = Left(strBuff, intCount)
```

```
        ' If the class name indicates the main Access
        ' window, you're done.
        If strBuff = glrACCESS_CLASS Then
            Exit Do
        End If

        ' Get the current window's parent.
        hWnd = glr_apiGetParent(hWnd)

        ' If the attempt failed, you're out of luck!
        If hWnd = 0 Then
            Exit Do
        End If
    Loop
    glrFindAccessHWnd = hWnd
End Function

Function glrFindChildClass(hWnd As Integer,
➥ strClassNameToMatch As String) As Integer

    ' Locate a specific child of the window represented by
    ' the passed-in Window handle. This code assumes that
    ' for a specific parent, you only care about the first
    ' child found that matches the class name.

Const MAX_LEN = 255

    Dim hWndCurrent As Integer
    Dim hWndTemp As Integer
    Dim strClassName As String * MAX_LEN
    Dim fFound As Integer
    Dim intClassLen As Integer

    ' Get the handle to the first child of window in
    ' question.
    hWndCurrent = glr_apiGetWindow(hWnd, glrGW_CHILD)
    ' Assume you didn't find the window you want.
    fFound = False

    ' Loop through all the child windows, looking for the
    ' one with the right class name.
```

```
        Do While hWndCurrent <> 0
            ' Get the class name of the current child window.
            intClassLen = glr_apiGetClassName(hWndCurrent,
        ➡ strClassName, MAX_LEN - 1)
            ' Does it match the one you're looking for?
            'If so, get out of this loop.
            If Left(strClassName, intClassLen) =
        ➡ strClassNameToMatch Then
                fFound = True
                Exit Do
            End If
            ' If the current child is not the one you want,
            ' go on to the next one.
            hWndTemp = glr_apiGetNextWindow(hWndCurrent,
        ➡ glrGW_HWNDNEXT)
            hWndCurrent = hWndTemp
        Loop
        ' If a match was found, return its hWnd.  Otherwise,
        ' return 0.
        glrFindChildClass = IIf(fFound, hWndCurrent, 0)
End Function

Function glrGetAccessChild(strClass As String) As Integer

    ' Find the handle to the requested child window. It
    ' first finds the handle to the Access main window
    ' (class "OMain").  If it finds this window, then it
    ' looks through that window's children for the main MDI
    ' client window (class "MDIClient").  If it finds that
    ' window (and it BETTER!), it looks through that
    ' window's children for the first window of the
    ' specified class.  If it finds it, it will return the
    ' hWnd.  If not, it'll return NULL.

    Dim hWnd As Integer

    hWnd = glrFindAccessHWnd()
    ' If we can't find the Access window, something is
    ' terribly wrong!
    If hWnd = 0 Then
        GoTo glrGetAccessChildError
    End If
    ' Going into this function, hWnd is the handle for the
    ' main Access window. The return value is either the
    ' main MDI client window handle, or Null.
```

```
    hWnd = glrFindChildClass(hWnd,
    ➥ glrACCESS_MDI_CLIENT_CLASS)
    If hWnd = 0 Then
        GoTo glrGetAccessChildError
    Else
        ' Going into this function, hWnd is the handle for
        ' the main MDI client window. The return value is
        ' either the handle for the database container, or
        ' Null.
        hWnd = glrFindChildClass(hWnd, strClass)
    End If
    glrGetAccessChild = hWnd
glrGetAccessChildExit:
    Exit Function

glrGetAccessChildError:
    ' Only get here if an error has occurred -- couldn't
    ' find a necessary window handle.
    glrGetAccessChild = 0
    GoTo glrGetAccessChildExit
End Function

Function glrGetClassName(hWnd As Integer)

    ' Given a window's handle, retrieve the class
    ' name associated with that window.

Const MAX_SIZE = 255

    Dim strClass As String * MAX_SIZE
    Dim intChars As Integer

    If hWnd = 0 Then
        strClass = ""
    Else
        intChars = glr_apiGetClassName(hWnd, strClass,
        ➥ MAX_SIZE)
        strClass = Left$(strClass, intChars)
    End If

    glrGetClassName = strClass
End Function
```

Making the Previous Form Current

Once you know the handle of the last-active form, you'll want to make it the current window again. That was the point of all this code. Unfortunately, Access provides no method for activating a window based on its handle. To do that you need one more Windows API function, SetFocus(). Given a window handle, SetFocus() makes the appropriate window active.

For the example toolbox you'll find in CH8.MDB, all the actions are appropriate only if the active form is in Design view. Therefore, the function you call that returns you to the previously active form must also check the mode of the form. It returns a True value if the form is opened in design mode (the CurrentView property is 0) and a False value otherwise. Listing 8.10 shows the GetToForm() function, which the sample toolbox uses to return to the form that was active before you clicked a button on the toolbox. Each button's Click event code checks the return value of GetToForm() before it takes any action. If the function returned a False value, each button does nothing at all.

Listing 8.10

```
Const glrACCESS_CLASS = "OMain"
Const glrACCESS_MDI_CLIENT_CLASS = "MDICLIENT"
Const glrACCESS_FORM_CLASS = "OForm"

Function GetToForm( )
    ' Move back to the first active form.

    Dim hWnd As Integer
    Dim varTemp As Variant

Const DESIGNVIEW = 0

    GetToForm = False

    ' Attempt to find the active form.
    hWnd = GetAccessChild(glrACCESS_FORM_CLASS)
```

```
        ' If you found a form, then go to it.
        If hWnd <> 0 Then
            ' Set the focus to the selected form.
            varTemp = glr_apiSetFocus(hWnd)

            ' The form's hWnd better match the active
            ' form's hWnd!
            Set gFrm = Screen.ActiveForm
            If gFrm.hWnd = hWnd Then
                If gFrm.CurrentView <> DESIGNVIEW Then
                    MsgBox "This command is available only in
                    ➡ design view!"
                End If
            Else
                ' If the active form's hWnd doesn't match the
                ' one you just set the focus to, then something
                ' very strange is going on.
                MsgBox "An unknown error has occurred."
            End If
            GetToForm = True
        End If
End Function
```

Taking Action

By checking the return value from GetToForm() in each button's Click event code, you can be assured you won't perform an action that isn't reasonable for the form. If your toolbox is to perform actions that make sense in other contexts, you'll want to modify GetToForm() to check that the object is opened in the appropriate context for your actions. In this case the four buttons that align groups of controls do nothing more than replicate menu items. A sample event code procedure might look like this:

```
Sub btnAlignTop_Click()
    If GetToForm() Then
        On Error Resume Next
        DoCmd DoMenuItem 3, 3, 5, 2, A_MENU_VER20
    End If
End Sub
```

To maintain compatibility with Access 1.x applications, the folks at Microsoft devised a clever "hack" to indicate to Access Basic that you're referring to the Access 2.0 menu tree when you're using DoMenuItem. By adding a fifth parameter, the version number, they made it possible for existing Access Basic code to work correctly as long as no one tries to use any of the new menu items. In this case the alignment menu items are all new and are counting on the specific locations in the Access 2.0 menus. Therefore, to make this code work correctly, you must include the version number, using the Access constant A_MENU_VER20.

The two buttons that center controls require more code since there are no built-in menu items to do that job. They both use the InSelection property, checking for inclusion in the selected group of controls. For any control in the selection, the code takes the appropriate action. (The gFrm variable is global to the form, filled in by the GetToForm() function. This saves every single event code procedure needing to retrieve the form reference.) The following listing shows a function to center controls horizontally:

```
Sub btnCenterHorizontal_Click()
    Dim intI As Integer
    Dim ctl As Control
    Dim intWidth As Integer

    If GetToForm() Then
        intWidth = gFrm.Width

        For intI = 0 To gFrm.Count - 1
            Set ctl = gFrm(intI)
            If ctl.InSelection Then
                ctl.Left = (intWidth - ctl.Width) / 2
            End If
        Next intI
    End If
End Sub
```

Using frmToolbox in Your Own Applications

We've designed frmToolbox so you can just import it from CH8.MDB into your own application database (along with basFormGlobal and basWindowRelationships), open it in form mode, and use it while you're designing forms. You can use it, as is, as a development tool.

More likely, though, you'll want to take the concepts involved in frmToolbox and create your own toolboxes. If you're interested in using the underlying code but not the exact functionality, consider removing some of the code that's stored with the form. If you're going to use frmToolbox as part of your own application or library database, import it into your database. We've included the functions you'll need, along with the necessary declarations, in basWindowRelationships and basFormGlobal in CH8.MDB. To include those functions, just import those particular modules into your application.

Creating Self-Disabling Navigation Buttons

Access provides several methods for your users to move from one row of data on a form to another. You can use the standard form navigation buttons, but they provide absolutely no flexibility to you as a developer. You can also use the Button Wizard to create the navigation buttons for you on your form. In each case the solutions lack one feature that many clients request: they'd like buttons that don't do anything to be disabled. That is, if you're already at the last row in the recordset, the button that takes you to the last row ought to be disabled. If you're on the new row, the button that takes you there ought not be available. Few things are more frustrating to the end user than clicking a button and having nothing happen or, worse, clicking a button and finding out that the action isn't available.

You can easily create your own buttons that replace the functionality Access provides and additionally give you the functionality described above. As an example you can look at frmNavigate in CH8.MDB. This form includes buttons you can copy onto your own forms that handle form navigation for you. Figure 8.6 shows frmNavigate positioned at the last row in the underlying recordset. Note that the buttons that would move you to the next and last rows are currently disabled.

FIGURE 8.6:
Since the current row is the last row in the recordset, the Next and Last buttons are disabled.

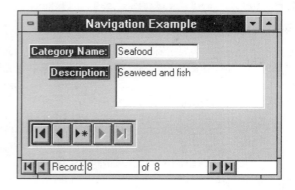

Forms and Their Data

Every bound form acts as a moving "window" for the form's underlying data. At any given time your form can display one or more rows from that dataset, and your Access Basic code can also manipulate that dataset. You can create a Recordset variable and assign to it the value of the form's RecordSetClone property. In this manner Access allows you to view and modify the same set of data that the user sees on the form. Since Access maintains two completely separate record pointers for the form and its underlying recordset, you can move around freely in the recordset, while the form's displayed record doesn't change at all.

In addition, forms maintain a unique bookmark for each row in the underlying data, separate from the bookmark Access maintains for the recordset itself. In this way you can save and retrieve the form's bookmark independently of the form's recordset bookmark. When you first retrieve a copy of the form's recordset (using the RecordSetClone property), your position in the recordset is officially undefined, and you'll need to position yourself on a particular row. You can use any of the MoveXXXX (MoveFirst, MoveLast, MoveNext, MovePrevious) methods to position the record pointer, or you can equate the recordset and the form's Bookmark properties. Doing so sets the current row in your recordset to be the same as the row currently shown on the form. Code to do this might look like the following:

```
Dim rst as RecordSet
Set rst = frm.RecordSetClone
rst.Bookmark = frm.Bookmark
```

You may be confused by the use of the Set keyword. The rules for its use are quite simple, though. The only basic concept to remember is that some datatypes are simple (for example: integer, double, and variant) and some are objects (for example: Form, Control, Recordset, and Index). All object variables, when created, are just references. They aren't objects but are rather pointers to objects. You must "point" them at a real object before you can use them for anything. There are three ways to join an object variable with a real object:

- Use the Set keyword to point a variable at an object.
- Use the "Dim x as New y" syntax, which is neither documented nor supported. This works only for certain objects (not recordsets or controls) and is not recommended.
- Use the CreateXXX() methods, such as CreateReport(), CreateRelation(), CreateIndex(), and so on. In this case you first DIM the variable and then assign it the return value from one of these functions.

In any case, attempting to use an object variable without first attaching it to a real object will get you nothing except the error message, "Object doesn't have a value." For more information on object variables, see the section "Using Object Variables" in Chapter 6.

Controlling Row Movement

Two issues are involved in controlling the row movement programmatically:

- Moving from row to row
- Disabling the correct buttons at the correct time

The issues involved in moving from row to row are simple. Each button calls, from its Click event, a distinct procedure in basNavigate. Each of these procedures calls into a common procedure, NavMove, which performs the action. For example, the Last button calls this procedure:

```
Function glrNavLast(frm As Form)
    NavMove frm, A_LAST
End Function
```

(The constants A_FIRST, A_PREV, A_NEW, A_NEXT, and A_LAST are all defined by Access.) You might be tempted, if writing this procedure yourself, to use the

GotoRecord macro action to perform the necessary movement here. If you do, however, you'll be limiting the functionality of these buttons. Since GotoRecord can act only on the current form, you'd never be able to use these buttons to cause record movement on a different form. To avoid this problem, NavMove (Listing 8.11) uses the MoveXXXX methods of the form's recordset to move about.

Listing 8.11

```
Private Sub NavMove (frm As Form, intWhere As Integer)
    '
    ' Move to the correct row in the form's recordset,
    ' depending on which button was pushed.  This code
    ' doesn't really need to check for errors, since the
    ' buttons that would cause errors have been disabled
    ' already.
    Dim rst As Recordset
    Dim fAtNew As Integer

Const ERR_NO_CURRENT_RECORD = 3021

    On Error GoTo NavMoveError
    If intWhere = A_NEWREC Then
        DoCmd GoToRecord A_FORM, frm.Name, A_NEWREC
    Else
        fAtNew = AtNewRecord(frm)
        Set rst = frm.RecordSetClone
        rst.BookMark = frm.BookMark
        Select Case intWhere
            Case A_FIRST:
                rst.MoveFirst
            Case A_PREVIOUS:
                If fAtNew Then
                    rst.MoveLast
                Else
                    rst.MovePrevious
                End If
            Case A_NEXT:
                rst.MoveNext
            Case A_LAST:
                rst.MoveLast
        End Select
        frm.BookMark = rst.BookMark
    End If
```

```
NavMoveExit:
    Exit Sub

NavMoveError:
    If Err = ERR_NO_CURRENT_RECORD And AtNewRecord(frm) Then
        Resume Next
    Else
        MsgBox Error$ & " (" & Err & ")"
        Resume NavMoveExit
    End If
    Resume NavMoveExit
End Sub
```

In theory this should be all you need to move around in your recordset. There are two problems, though. This code won't handle the disabling of unavailable buttons. It also causes an error condition (3205) when you try to move past the last row or before the first row: "Can't go to specified record."

Disabling Buttons

To correctly enable and disable navigation buttons, you need to be able to retrieve the current row location. That is, if you're currently on the first row, you need to know that as soon as you get there so the appropriate buttons (Previous and First) can be disabled. If you're on the last row you'll want the Next and Last buttons to be disabled. If you're on the New row you'll want the New, Next, and Last buttons disabled. Access doesn't include functionality to inquire about the current row location, so you have to do some work behind the scenes to figure this out, as described in the following sections.

Checking the Current Location

You can use the form's recordset and its Bookmark property to check the current row's location within its recordset. For example, you could take these steps to check whether the current displayed row in the form was the first row:

1. Retrieve a copy of the form's recordset using the RecordSetClone property.

2. Set the location in the recordset to be the same as that displayed on the form, using the Bookmark property.

3. In the recordset, move to the previous record, using the MovePrevious method. If the recordset's BOF property is now True, you must have been on the first row.

If you want to write a function that just checks to see whether you're on the first row, here's one way to do it:

```
Function AtFirstRow(frm As Form)
    ' Return True if at first row, False otherwise.
    Dim rst as RecordSet
    Set rst = frm.RecordSetClone
    rst.Bookmark = frm.Bookmark
    rst.MovePrevious
    AtFirstRow = rst.BOF
    rst.Close
End Function
```

You could apply the same logic to check whether you were at the last row. In the section "At the New Record?" earlier in this chapter, we discussed a method to check whether you're on the new record. Armed with the knowledge assembled here, you should now be able to write a single function that checks all these states and disables the correct buttons.

There's one more issue, though. Some forms are not updatable at all. If they're based on non-updatable queries or tables, if you've set the AllowUpdating property for the form to "No Tables", or if you've set the DefaultEditing property for the form to "Read Only" or "Can't Add Records", you can't add a new row. In that case you also need to disable the New button.

The function you want should execute the following steps to determine which buttons are available as you move from row to row on the form:

1. Check the updatability of the form and its recordset, and set the New button's availability based on that information. Also, if you're on the new row, disable the button, since you can't go there if you're already there.

2. If you're on the new row already, enable the First and Previous buttons if there's any data in the recordset (disable them otherwise), and disable the Next and Last buttons.

3. If you're not on the new row, check for the beginning and end of recordset cases, as discussed above.

You'll find the procedure you need in Listing 8.12. glrEnableButtons() takes a form reference as a parameter and enables and disables the navigation buttons on the form according to your location within the form's recordset. To use it you must call it from the Current event of your form. Note that the code is dependent on the specific names for buttons (cmdFirst, cmdPrev, cmdNew, cmdNext, cmdLast). Make sure your buttons have the correct name before attempting to use this code.

Listing 8.12

```
Function glrEnableButtons(frm As Form)
    '
    ' Attached to the specified form's Current event.
    '
    ' This function enables and disables buttons as
    ' necessary, depending on the current record on the
    ' form.
    '
    ' This function counts on buttons named cmdFirst,
    ' cmdPrev, cmdNext, cmdLast and cmdNew.  One
    ' could code around this, but it seemed like
    ' overkill for this example.
    '
    Dim rst As Recordset
    Dim fAtNew As Integer
    Dim fUpdateable As Integer

    Set rst = frm.RecordSetClone

    ' Check to see if you're on the new record or not.
    fAtNew = AtNewRecord(frm)

    ' If the form isn't updatable, then you sure
    ' can't go to the new record!  If it is, then
    ' the button should be enabled unless you're already
    ' on the new record.
    fUpdateable = rst.Updatable And (frm.DefaultEditing <= 2)
    frm!cmdNew.Enabled = IIf(fUpdateable, Not fAtNew, False)

    If fAtNew Then
        frm!cmdNext.Enabled = False
        frm!cmdLast.Enabled = False
        frm!cmdFirst.Enabled = (rst.RecordCount > 0)
        frm!cmdPrev.Enabled = (rst.RecordCount > 0)
```

```
    Else
        ' Sync the recordset's bookmark with
        ' the form's bookmark.
        rst.BookMark = frm.BookMark

        ' Move backwards to check for BOF.
        rst.MovePrevious
        frm!cmdFirst.Enabled = Not rst.BOF
        frm!cmdPrev.Enabled = Not rst.BOF

        ' Get back to where you started.
        rst.BookMark = frm.BookMark

        ' Move forward to check for EOF.
        rst.MoveNext
        frm!cmdNext.Enabled = Not (rst.EOF Or fAtNew)
        frm!cmdLast.Enabled = Not (rst.EOF Or fAtNew)
    End If
End Function
```

Creating Your Own Navigation Buttons

You can easily create your own navigation buttons. To do so, just follow these steps:

1. Import the module basNavigate from CH8.MDB.

2. Create five command buttons or copy the five buttons from frmNavigate in CH8.MDB. They must be named cmdFirst, cmdPrev, cmdNew, cmdNext, and cmdLast.

3. From your form's Current event, call the glrEnableButtons() function. If this is the only item in the form's Current event, you can call it directly from the property sheet, using the expression

```
=glrEnableButtons(Form)
```

If you already have code attached to your Current event, just call the function, passing it the form reference. That is, if you're calling it from CBF, you can use a statement like this:

```
varRetval = glrEnableButtons(Me)
```

4. From each button's Click event, call the appropriate glrNavXXXX() function. For the cmdFirst button, for example, use

```
=glrNavFirst(Form)
```

The functions to call are glrNavFirst(), glrNavPrev(), glrNavNew(), glrNav Next(), and glrNavLast().

Once you've set up the buttons and the event procedures, you should be able to open the form in form mode and use the navigation buttons to move about in your form's data.

We've also included a popup toolbox record navigation tool in CH8.MDB. You can use it as part of your own applications, and you might want to take the time to pick it apart since it uses some interesting design techniques. To use it, follow these steps:

1. Import the form frmRecNavPopup into your application from CH8.MDB.

2. Import the modules basFormGlobal and basWindowRelationships from CH8.MDB.

3. Import the module basPopup. (This step is optional.)

4. For any form you want to use with frmRecNavPopup, add a function call to the form's Current and Activate events. You'll need to call the Handle-Popup() function, passing a reference to the current form. See the forms Categories and Customers in CH8.MDB for examples. (This step is optional.)

To use the popup toolbox, open a form and then open the toolbox. Clicking the various buttons on the toolbox should navigate through the rows on the form. To fully appreciate the toolbox, though, you should also follow steps 3 and 4 above. If you add the function calls to your form's Current and Activate events, your forms can tell the popup toolbox what they're doing and where they are. This allows frmRec-NavPopup to track row changes when the user uses other methods besides the toolbox to change rows, and it makes it possible for the toolbox to know exactly which form is the current form. If you're writing applications and want to use frmRec-NavPopup, we strongly suggest you set up your forms to call HandlePopup().

Why Create Your Own Toolbox

You could create a new toolbar, using the tools that Access provides, to control record navigation. However, if you create a toolbox from scratch (like frmRecNavPopup), you can include these features:

- You can maintain the current row number for the selected form.

- You can supply your own bitmaps. On Access' toolbars, you're limited to the images they supply.

- By creating your own toolbox you'll have complete control over the actions your toolbox takes. Using Access' toolbars, you have no control over the action of each button.

On the other hand, your own toolbox cannot dock itself like Access' toolbars can. In addition, creating your own toolbox requires a great deal of handwritten code. Using Access' toolbars requires none.

Screen Resolution and Distributing Forms

When you set up Windows to run on your computer, you must choose a screen driver for use with your hardware. Your choice of screen driver forces your monitor to display a specific screen resolution, usually one of 640x480 (standard VGA), 800x600 (Super VGA), 1024x768 (Super VGA or 8514/a), or 1280x1024. These numbers refer to the number of picture elements (*pixels*) in the horizontal and vertical directions. If you create forms that look fine on your screen running at 1024x768, those same forms may be far too large to be displayed by a user who's working at 640x480 (still the most popular screen resolution since it's the resolution supported by most laptop and portable computers). Similarly, if you create forms at 640x480, someone who's working at 1280x1024 will see them as very small forms. (A full-screen form created at 640x480 takes up about a quarter of the screen at 1280x1024—although this is not necessarily something your users will want to change. Many people who use large displays and high-resolution adapters appreciate the fact that they can see not only a full-screen form, but a great many other Access objects at the same time.)

One unattractive solution to this problem is to create multiple versions of your forms, one for each screen resolution that you care to support. This, of course, requires maintaining each of those forms individually if you make changes to the form. The following sections deal directly with the resolution issue. We present code you can use to scale your forms as they load, allowing them to look reasonable at almost any screen resolution. In addition, we include code you can attach to the Resize event of a form, allowing users to resize a form and all its controls at run time.

Understanding Screen Resolutions

Before you can understand the solution to the screen resolution issue, you must understand the problem. Figure 8.7 shows a scale image of the four standard Windows screen resolutions, superimposed. As you can see, a form that appears full-screen at 640x480 will take up only a small portion of a 1280x1024 screen, and a full-screen form at 1024x768 will be too large for a screen at 800x600. The difference in the number of pixels is only one of two issues you need to consider in scaling forms. You must also think about the size of the pixels—the number of pixels per logical inch of screen space. Each screen driver individually controls how large each pixel is in relation to what Windows thinks an "inch" is. Windows provides API calls to gather all this information, which we'll need later in this section. For now, the

FIGURE 8.7:

All four standard VGA screen resolutions, superimposed

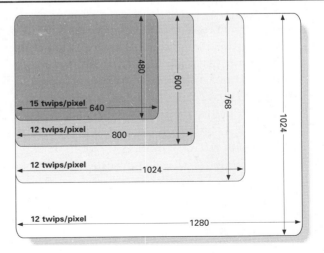

information of concern is the number of twips per pixel. (A twip is equivalent to $\frac{1}{1440}$ inch.) Practical experience shows that screens at 640x480 use 15 twips per pixel, and all other VGA screen resolutions use 12 twips per pixel. That means that at low resolution VGA, 100 pixels take up 1500 twips (a little more than one logical inch), while at higher resolutions, 100 pixels take up 1200 twips (a little less than one logical inch). Therefore, to correctly scale your forms for different resolutions, you need to take both ratios into account. You need to compare, for both the screen on which the form was prepared and the screen on which it will be displayed, the pixels used and the twips-per-pixel value. The ratios of these values control how you scale the form.

Listing 8.13 includes the portions of the code necessary to scale your forms at load time and to allow resizing by users at run time. (The full module is too long to print here. To study it, look at basFormScale in CH8.MDB.) This code makes extensive use of Windows API calls to retrieve information about the current display and the sizes of forms. For more information about the Windows API and calling DLLs, see Chapter 17.

Scaling Forms as They Load

To solve the problem of displaying forms so that they take up the same proportion of the screen real estate on different screen resolutions, it would seem that all you need do is calculate the ratio of the original screen dimensions to the current screen dimensions and scale the form accordingly. Unfortunately, the calculation is further complicated by the twips-per-pixel issue, discussed earlier in this chapter. Since different screen resolutions use a different number of twips for each pixel, you must also take this into account when calculating the new size for the form. The x-axis sizing ratio, when moving from 640x480 to 1024x768, is not just 1024/640. You must multiply that value by the ratio of the twips-per-pixel values, 12/15. (Think of it this way: as far as Windows is concerned, pixels are "bigger" at 640x480, taking 15 twips. At higher resolution, a pixel takes up only 12 twips.) Therefore, the correct ratio is 1024/640 * 12/15, or 1.28. Figure 8.8 shows a single form, 400x120 pixels, created in 640x480 resolution, as it would display on a screen in 1024x768 resolution. The first example shows it unscaled, and the second example shows it scaled.

FIGURE 8.8:

Scaling a form causes it to appear approximately the same on screens with different resolutions.

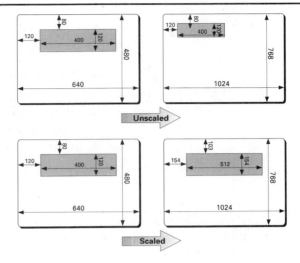

Retrieving Display Information

To scale your forms you must first retrieve information about the current display driver. To do this, you must use a Windows *device context*, a data structure that provides a link between the Windows API and the device driver. Actually, for this example, you can use an *information context*, which is a lower-powered device context, unable to write information back to the driver. Any calls to the Windows API dealing with the display driver must pass an information context or display context handle as the first parameter. To get the information context handle, use the following code. (glrAPINULL is a constant defined as 0&.)

```
intIC = CreateIC("DISPLAY", glrAPINULL, glrAPINULL, glrAPINULL)
```

Once you have the information context handle, intIC, you can obtain the information you need about the current display driver. First of all you must retrieve the pixel resolutions of the current display driver. You can use the Windows API function GetDeviceCaps() to obtain this information:

```
intScreenX = GetDeviceCaps(intIC, glrHORZRES)
intScreenY = GetDeviceCaps(intIC, glrVERTRES)
```

Next, you must find out the number of pixels per logical inch in both the horizontal (X) and vertical (Y) directions. Once you have those values, divide them into the number of twips per inch (TWIPS_PER_INCH = 1440) to find the number of twips per pixel. You can again use the Windows API function GetDeviceCaps() to retrieve this information:

```
intTwipsPerPixelX = TWIPS_PER_INCH / GetDeviceCaps(intIC,
➡ LOGPIXELSX)
intTwipsPerPixelY = TWIPS_PER_INCH / GetDeviceCaps(intIC,
➡ LOGPIXELSY)
```

Now you can calculate the ratio of the current screen resolution to the resolution that was active when the form was created. The original values will have been passed in to this function in the parameters intX and intY:

```
sglFactorX = intScreenX / intX
sglFactorY = intScreenY / intY
```

But as mentioned before, this isn't accurate enough. You need to take into account the differences in the number of twips per pixel between different display adapters. To do this you scale the scaling factors by the ratio of the twips-per-pixel value for the original display, as compared to the value for the current display. (GetTwips() is a local function that attempts to determine the twips-per-pixel value for the original display, given the horizontal resolution of that display.)

```
sglFactorX = sglFactorX * (intTwipsPerPixelX / GetTwips(intX,
➡ X_AXIS))
sglFactorY = sglFactorY * (intTwipsPerPixelY / GetTwips(intX,
➡ Y_AXIS))
```

Armed with the values for sglFactorX and sglFactorY, you have the information you need to correctly scale the form as you open it in the new display resolution. You should be able to just multiply the form's width, height, and position of the upper-left corner by that scaling factor and end up with the form in a relative position on the screen with the new width and height. Figure 8.8 demonstrates this calculation.

Scaling the Form's Contents

Scaling the form is only part of the problem, however. Just changing the size of the container won't help much if you can't see all the controls inside it. Therefore, you need a way to change the size of all the controls inside the form, as well. The function glrScaleForm(), called from your form's Open event, calls the glrResizeForm() function to resize all the controls. You can also call this subroutine directly from your form's Resize event, allowing you to dynamically resize all the controls on the form every time the user resizes the form. This can be a striking feature, allowing the user to make a form take up less screen real estate but still be available for use. Figure 8.9 shows a form both full size and scaled down to a smaller size.

To accomplish this visual feat you can attach a call to glrResizeForm() to your form's Resize event. The glrResizeForm() function loops through all the controls on the form, scaling them by the ratio between the previous size of the form and the current size of the form. Note that in this situation you don't care about any screen resolution issues; you're just comparing the current size of the form to the previous size of the form to find the sizing ratio.

The function first checks to make sure the user has not sized the form to its minimum size, with no space inside the form. In that case Access acts as if there were no active form, so the code cannot go any further. The code calls the GetClientRect() API function to find the form's height and just returns if the height is 0:

```
glr_apiGetClientRect frm.hWnd, rctNew
intHeight = (rctNew.intY2 - rctNew.intY1)
If intHeight = 0 Then
    Exit Function
End If
```

FIGURE 8.9:

Two copies of the same form, one at full size and one scaled to a smaller size

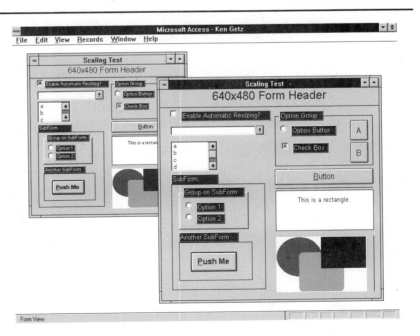

Once the function has found the dimensions for the current form, it calculates the current width. Then it can calculate and store the scaling factors, based on the previous sizes stored in rctOriginal:

```
intWidth = (rctNew.intX2 - rctNew.intX1)

sglFactorX = intWidth / (rctOriginal.intX2 - rctOriginal.intX1)
sglFactorY = intHeight / (rctOriginal.intY2 - rctOriginal.intY1)
```

Finally, it stores away the current form sizes so it will have them available on the next pass through here:

```
rctOriginal.intX1 = rctNew.intX1
rctOriginal.intX2 = rctNew.intX2
rctOriginal.intY1 = rctNew.intY1
rctOriginal.intY2 = rctNew.intY2
```

Once all the preliminary work has been done, if there's resizing to be done the function now calls the workhorse function, SetFormSize().

Scaling the Controls

In theory SetFormSize() does nothing more than just loop through all the controls on the form, scaling their locations and sizes by the scaling factors calculated in the calling function. In practice there are a number of details that aren't, at first, obvious, such as the following:

- The order of events is important. If your form is growing, you must expand the section heights before you allow the controls to expand. Otherwise the expanding controls will push out the boundaries of the sections and make the scaling invalid. The opposite holds true if your form is shrinking. In that case you cannot shrink the section heights until after you've sized all the controls. Otherwise you risk artificially compressing the control locations.

- You must deal carefully with controls that contain other controls. A group can contain toggle buttons, option buttons, and check boxes. A subform can contain any control and possibly yet another subform (nested, at most, two deep). To maintain the correct scaling you need to walk through all the controls on the form, build an array containing information about all the container controls, scale all the controls on the form, and then scale the containers. In addition, if you run across a subform you must recursively call the function again, scaling all the controls on that subform. If that subform contains a subform you must call the function once more to handle that final subform. Once the function has handled all the controls on the form, it loops through the array of containers and scales them correctly.

- Some controls don't need their height or font scaled. For example, you can't really change the height of a check box. (You can try, but it won't look very good.) Several controls don't even own a FontName property. The Set-FormSize subroutine calls the ChangeHeight() and ChangeFont() functions to find out whether it should bother trying to change the particular property at all.

- You want to *move* forms only when they're first loaded. After that, it should be up to the user. Therefore, the code that positions the form itself should be called only if the subroutine was called from glrScaleForm().

You should be able to follow all these design decisions in Listing 8.13, which includes the full source to the SetFormSize subroutine. If you want to study the complete workings of form scaling, look in the module basFormScale in CH8.MDB.

Steps to Successful Scaling

Due to limitations of the technology, the methodology presented here is far from perfect. Each time Access fires off the Resize event, the function calculates the current control or font size based on the previous size. This recursive calculation inevitably leads to roundoff errors. Once your user compresses the form down beyond readability, attempts to expand it will often result in an unreadable mess. One alternative method would have been to store away the original size of each control on the form. Then, at each resize attempt you could have compared the current size of the form to the original size, scaling each control accordingly. This method might have been more accurate but would have slowed down the process; in the trade-off of speed against accuracy, speed won again.

In any case, there are some rules you must follow to make it possible for this code to work:

- Use TrueType fonts for each control you will scale. This code will scale only the fonts in labels, buttons, text, and combo and list boxes. Unfortunately, the default font used in all controls is not scalable. You must either modify your form defaults or select all the controls and change the font once you're finished designing. On the other hand, beware of using fonts that won't be available on your users' machines. All copies of Windows 3.1 ship with Arial and Times Roman fonts; choosing one of these for your buttons, labels, and list, combo, and text boxes guarantees a certain level of success.

- Do not design forms at 1280x1024 and expect them to look good at 640x480. By the time forms get scaled that far down, they're very hard to read. Certainly, using 800x600 or 1024x768 for development should provide forms that look reasonable at all resolutions.

- The current implementation of this code does not handle subforms shown as datasheets. Although it may be possible to make this work, at this point you should avoid datasheets if you want to resize forms.

- Do not attempt to mix the AutoCenter property with a call to glrScaleForm() called from the Open event. The AutoCenter property will attempt to center the form before it's resized and will cause Access to place the form somewhere you don't expect it to be.

- The code that handles the form resizing is not meant to work with more than one form at a time. Since it maintains the previous size of the form in a global structure, it can handle only one form at a time. If your application needs to have multiple scalable forms open at the same time, you must modify the code to handle multiple storage structures. You could rewrite the global code and place a copy in each form's private module to work around this limitation.

To include this functionality in your own applications, follow these steps:

1. Include the modules basFormScale and basFormGlobal from CH8.MDB in your database.

2. Ensure that all the fonts on your form are scalable. (Use TrueType fonts if possible, since they're all scalable.)

3. To scale the form to fit the current resolution when it loads, attach a call to glrScaleForm() to your form's Open event. Pass to the function a reference to your form and the x and y resolutions of the screen for which it was designed:

```
glrScaleForm Me, 1024, 768
```

4. To allow dynamic resizing of the form's controls, attach a call to glrResize-Form() to your form's Resize event. The first parameter to glrResizeForm() is a reference to your form, and the second parameter tells the subroutine whether

or not to actually do the resize. If this value is True the subroutine changes all the controls. If it's False it just resets the storage of the form's current size:

```
glrResizeForm Me, (Me!chkEnableResize)
```

Because your form always calls the function from the Resize event, the function always knows the form's previous size. That way, if you decide to allow resizing, it will work correctly. The example forms base this decision on a check box on the form itself.

Listing 8.13

```
Private Sub GetScreenScale(intX As Integer,
➡ intY As Integer, sglFactorX As Single,
➡ sglFactorY As Single)

    ' In:  intX, intY:  x and y screen resolutions
    '                   when the form was created.
    ' Out: sglFactorX, sglFactorY:  scaling factors for
    '                   the x and y directions.

    Dim intScreenX As Integer
    Dim intScreenY As Integer

    Dim intTwipsPerPixelX As Integer
    Dim intTwipsPerPixelY As Integer

    Dim intIC As Integer

    On Error GoTo GetScreenScaleError

    ' Get the information context you need to find the
    ' screen info.
    intIC = glr_apiCreateIC("DISPLAY", glrAPINULL,
    ➡ glrAPINULL, glrAPINULL)

    ' If the call to CreateIC didn't fail, then get the
    ' info.
    If intIC <> 0 Then
        ' Find the number of pixels in both directions on
        ' the screen, (640x480, 800x600, 1024x768,
        ' 1280x1024?)
        intScreenX = glr_apiGetDeviceCaps(intIC, glrHORZRES)
        intScreenY = glr_apiGetDeviceCaps(intIC, glrVERTRES)
```

```
        ' Find the number of twips per pixel in both
        ' directions.
        intTwipsPerPixelX = glrTWIPS_PER_INCH /
        ➥ glr_apiGetDeviceCaps(intIC, glrLOGPIXELSX)
        intTwipsPerPixelY = glrTWIPS_PER_INCH /
        ➥ glr_apiGetDeviceCaps(intIC, glrLOGPIXELSY)

        ' Release the information context.
        intIC = glr_apiDeleteDC(intIC)

        ' Get the ratio of the current screen size to the
        ' design-time screen size.

        sglFactorX = intScreenX / intX
        sglFactorY = intScreenY / intY

        ' Finally, take into account the differences in the
        ' display resolutions.  At 640x480, you get more
        ' twips per pixel (15) as opposed to 12 at higher
        ' resolutions.
        ' Note:  GetTwips always takes the X RESOLUTION as
        ' its first parameter.
        sglFactorX = sglFactorX * (intTwipsPerPixelX /
        ➥ GetTwips(intX, X_AXIS))
        sglFactorY = sglFactorY * (intTwipsPerPixelY /
        ➥ GetTwips(intX, Y_AXIS))
    End If

GetScreenScaleExit:
    Exit Sub

GetScreenScaleError:
    HandleError "GetScreenScale", Err, Error
    Resume GetScreenScaleExit
End Sub

Private Sub GetFormSize(frm As Form, rctR As glrTypeRect)

    ' Fill in rctR with the coordinates of the window.

    Dim hwndDesk As Integer
    Dim rctDesk As glrTypeRect
```

```
' Find the position of the window in question, in
' relation to its parent window (the Access desktop).
hwndDesk = glr_apiGetParent(frm.hWnd)

' Get the coordinates of the current window and its
' parent.
glr_apiGetWindowRect frm.hWnd, rctR
glr_apiGetWindowRect hwndDesk, rctDesk

' Subtract off the left and top parent coordinates,
' since you need coordinates relative to the parent for
' the grl_MoveWindow() function call.
rctR.intX1 = rctR.intX1 - rctDesk.intX1
rctR.intY1 = rctR.intY1 - rctDesk.intY1
rctR.intX2 = rctR.intX2 - rctDesk.intX1
rctR.intY2 = rctR.intY2 - rctDesk.intY1
End Sub
```

Using Query by Form to Create a SQL Expression

As part of almost any application, you'll be called upon to allow your users to choose a subset of rows from a table or query. Access' Filter and Query Builders, though straightforward, are far more complex than many users need and are capable of handling. In addition, you have very little programmatic control over what users do once you place them in the Query Builder. For many users, a simple form into which they could supply values they'd like to have matched in the output set would do fine. In this section we present some standard methods you can use to create the necessary forms and to retrieve the filtering information from your users.

The concept is simple: you call the glrDoQBF() function, specifying the form you want to use. The glrDoQBF() function pops up a modal form, with one control per field from the underlying dataset. You can enter text into those controls, make choices from list boxes, or click check boxes just as though entering data. Once you've indicated that you're finished, the code goes through each control on the form. The contents of controls that have been specially prepared and have values in them get added to a SQL expression, which gets returned to your code. At this point you can do whatever you like with that SQL expression: you can use it to create a filter on a different form or create a new table, or you can save it for later.

The code that walks through all the controls attempts to be somewhat intelligent. In tandem with the information about the underlying field's datatype, it adds the appropriate quote or # marks for strings and dates. It also assumes you want string expressions treated as though you had entered an asterisk at the end of the text so you can enter a single letter and get all values that start with that letter. (You can change that behavior by changing some comments in the code.) Finally, it attempts to determine whether you've entered an operator (<, >, =, Like, Not, In) and if so leaves the value untouched. This capability allows some flexibility but brings with it some responsibility. If you enter

```
In (CA, TX, MI)
```

into the control tied to the State field, the resulting SQL expression will contain the clause

```
[State] In (CA, TX, MI)
```

which the Access engine won't be very happy about. You could, of course, write code to parse out the user's expression and make sure it's syntactically correct.

At this point, if your users want to explore functionality beyond simply entering a value to be matched, you need to train them in the intricacies of Access expression syntax. Figure 8.10 shows a sample QBF form in action. As the form is currently filled in, the SQL Builder returns the string

```
((([LastName] Like "M*") And ([State] Like "CA*"))
```

The QBF Ground Rules

For the SQL-building code presented here to work, you must follow some rules in creating your QBF forms. If you like you can just run the tool we've provided (frmCreateQBF in CH8.MDB) to help create the form. If you want to create your own, though, here are the rules:

- All the controls on the form must be unbound. That is, their ControlSource property should be empty.

- In the Tag property for each control into which you want to allow the user to supply a filtering value, you must place the following two values:

    qbfField=*strFieldName*;qbfType=*intType*;

FIGURE 8.10:
A partially filled-in QBF form that
returns a SQL string that should find
all customers in California whose
last names start with *M*.

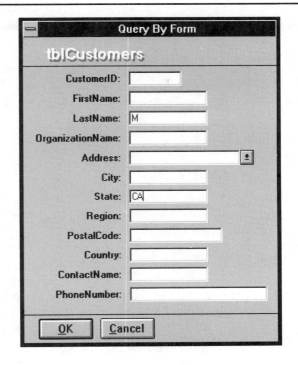

where *strFieldName* is the field name whose value you want filtered by this
control and *intType* is the field type, chosen from this list:

Boolean	1
Byte	2
Integer	3
Long	4
Currency	5
Single	6
Double	7
Date	8
Text	10
LongBinary	11
Memo	12

For example, the Tag property for a text control based on a text field called LastName in the underlying data might look like this:

```
qbfField=LastName;qbfType=10;
```

- Somewhere on the form, place two command buttons. One of these buttons will accept the values the user has entered, and the other will cancel and disregard the values. Attach this code to the Click event of the "accept" button:

```
=glrQBF_DoHide(Form)
```

Attach this code to the Click event of the Cancel button:

```
=glrQBF_Close()
```

To avoid all of these issues you can use the form included in CH8.MDB, frmCreateQBF. This form, when run, presents you with a list of the forms in your database, allowing you to create a QBF form based on any of them. In addition, you can use frmCreateQBF to test out your QBF forms. Choosing the Test button will bring up your form in QBF mode. Once you've clicked the OK or Cancel button, you see a message box showing the SQL expression representing your choices. Figure 8.11 shows frmCreateQBF in action. The form frmCreateQBF contains all the code it uses (except for the code dealing with the tag property in the module basTags and the SQL string builder in basBuildSQL) in its own code space, so importing this form and the modules basTags and basBuildSQL should be all you need to do to use the form.

FIGURE 8.11:
You can use frmCreateQBF to help you create your QBF forms, based on your current input forms.

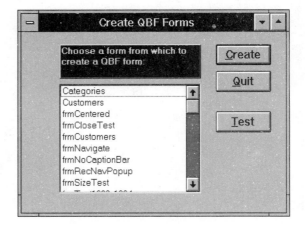

> **TIP**
>
> If you use frmCreateQBF to create your QBF forms, you will end up with filtering forms that are almost identical to your data entry forms. Users often find this similarity comforting. You might consider changing the background color of one of the two forms so that visual clues make it clear to users that they're not entering data but searching for it.

Building the Input Form

Most of the work done by frmCreateQBF happens in the CreateQBF() function in frmCreateQBF's module. This function goes through a series of steps for each form you create:

1. It creates a copy of your original form and fixes up all its properties so it will function correctly as a QBF form. The function sets every event property to null and removes the navigation buttons, scroll bars, and record selector. (FixUpForm() in frmCreateQBF)

2. It walks through each control on the new form, fixing up the Tag property to contain the information necessary to build the SQL expression. For each control on the form, FixTags() stores the ControlSource property as a string in the Tag property, attempts to retrieve the field type from the form's record source, and then stores that value in the Tag property, too. The function also removes any event properties for the controls. (FixTags() in frmCreateQBF)

3. It deletes extraneous controls, like command buttons, subforms, and calculated controls. Since these can't be used to gather information on a QBF form, they would just be in the way. (DeleteExtraControls in frmCreateQBF)

4. It creates a form footer or appends to an existing form footer. FixTags() adds OK and Cancel buttons to the form. Clicking the OK button hides the form and clicking the Cancel button closes the form. The glrDoQBF() function will use the status of the form to decide what to return to your function. (Create-Footer in frmCreateQBF)

5. It sizes the new form correctly, saves it, and puts it away.

Saving the State of the Original Form

As part of the process of building the new form, FixUpForm tries to preserve the state of the original form. It tries to leave the form open and in design mode if it had originally been open and in design mode. This code does the work:

```
fWasDesign = False
fWasOpen = isFormOpen(strFormName)
If fWasOpen Then
    fWasDesign = isFormDesign(Forms(strFormName))
End If
```

At the end, the subroutine executes the following code, which should put the form back in its original state. Since it's currently open and in design mode, all the code must check for is whether it should be closed or whether it needs to be left in design mode:

```
If fWasOpen Then
    If Not fWasDesign Then
        DoCmd OpenForm strFormName, A_NORMAL
    End If
Else
    ' If it wasn't open, close it.
    DoCmd Close A_FORM, strFormName
End If
```

Access 2.0 provides a new method of testing whether or not a particular object is currently open: SysCmd(), passed SYSCMD_GETOBJECTSTATE as its first parameter, returns a non-zero value if the object is open. It also returns other information about the state of the object, but that information is superfluous when it's just checking to see whether or not the object is open. You can use the following function to check whether any particular object is open. The intObjectType parameter must be one of the six standard intrinsic object constants: A_TABLE, A_QUERY, A_FORM, A_REPORT, A_MACRO, or A_MODULE.

```
Function isOpen(strName As String, intObjectType as Integer)
    isFormOpen = (SysCmd(SYSCMD_GETOBJECTSTATE, intObjectType,
    ➡ strName) <> 0)
End Function
```

Using the Status Bar As a Progress Meter

While creating the QBF Form, CreateQBF() keeps you informed of its progress by updating a meter bar on the status bar. This functionality is neatly hidden in the "grab-bag" SysCmd() function. Although SysCmd() is not new in Access 2.0, its use was undocumented in Access 1.0 and kept very quiet in Access 1.1. SysCmd() now appears in the manual and on-line help. The SysCmd() function has ten documented entry points, but to create a moving status indicator you need only three of these. To create a progress meter you need to call SysCmd() at least three times: once to initialize the meter, at least once to update the meter, and once to close the meter and clear the status bar. Figure 8.12 shows the progress meter in action.

FIGURE 8.12:

You can use SysCmd() to create a moving progress meter on the status bar.

Initializing the Progress Meter

To initialize the progress meter you must call the SysCmd() function with the following syntax:

varRetval = SysCmd(SYSCMD_INITMETER, *strPromptText*, *intMaxValue*)

You replace *strPromptText* with the text you want to have displayed on the status bar ("Creating QBF Form:" in Figure 8.12) and *intMaxValue* with the numeric value that will scale to 100 percent of the meter. In the calls you make to update the meter, you pass to SysCmd() the current value you want displayed. If intMaxValue were 4, you could pass values from 0 through 4 when you updated the meter. A value of 1 would fill 25 percent of the meter, 2 would fill 50 percent, and so on. CreateQBF() uses a value of 100, so the values it uses to update the meter are the same as the percentage SysCmd() displays on the status bar.

Updating the Progress Meter

To update the progress meter, call SysCmd() with the following syntax:

varRetval = SysCmd(SYSCMD_UPDATEMETER, *intCurrentValue*)

You could call SysCmd() multiple times as your function progresses, each time passing in a value that is less than or equal to the value *intMaxValue* that you used when you initialized the meter. It's up to you to decide how often and with which values to update the meter. Access does not make any changes to the length of the status bar unless you specifically call SysCmd().

NOTE There is only one progress meter to be had. If, as part of your application, you initiate some internal operation that requires Access to use the progress meter, it will take control. Access will preserve the state of the meter, however, so that your application will again find the meter just where it was when Access took over. Unfortunately, this can make for some very strange-looking applications as the progress meter flies from one end to the other.

TIP

Although it makes sense to update the status bar after you've accomplished the task you're reporting on, the status bar actually looks better if you update it first. That is, suppose you're about to embark on a specific task you've figured will take 10 percent of the calculation time for your application. If you update the progress meter once you're done with this task, the meter sits at 0 percent while that is happening. What's more, when you're done with your tasks and update the progress meter to 100 percent, the user will never see it get there because you're likely to clear out the status bar soon after. If you update the status bar before you execute each task, it no longer sits at 0 percent during the first portion, and it gets to 100 percent as you perform the last chunk of work instead of after you're done.

CreateQBF() performs only a few discrete tasks and so breaks up the progress meter into ten pieces. Some very rudimentary timings on large forms gave us some idea of how long each process took, and we assigned arbitrary values to use when updating the meter. The longer a task appeared to take, the more length we gave it on the meter. Listing 8.14 shows CreateQBF(), including calls to update the progress meter:

Listing 8.14

```
Function CreateQBF(strFormName As String)
    DoCmd Echo False
    StatusOpen "Creating QBF Form:", 100

    ' FixUpForm() leaves the form open in design mode.
    StatusUpdate 30
    varTemp = FixUpForm(strFormName)
    If IsNull(varTemp) Then
        GoTo CreateQBFExit
    End If
    strFormName = CStr(varTemp)

    ' Now set frm to be the new form.
    Set frm = Forms(strFormName)
    StatusUpdate 70
```

```
    If Not FixTags(frm) Then
        GoTo CreateQBFExit
    End If

    StatusUpdate 80
    DeleteExtraControls frm
    StatusUpdate 90
    CreateFooter frm
    DoCmd OpenForm strFormName, A_NORMAL
    varTemp = strFormName

    StatusUpdate 100
    ' Window-Size To Fit
    DoCmd DoMenuItem A_FORMBAR, 4, 5
    DoCmd DoMenuItem A_FORMBAR, A_FILE, A_SAVEFORM
    DoCmd Close A_FORM, strFormname
    StatusClose
    CreateQBF = varTemp
CreateQBFExit:
    DoCmd Echo True
    Exit Function

CreateQBFError:
    CreateQBF = Null
    StatusClose
    HandleErrors Err, "CreateQBF()"
    Resume CreateQBFExit
End Function
```

StatusOpen, StatusUpdate, and StatusClose are subroutines defined in frm-CreateQBF(), simplifying the interface to SysCmd():

```
Sub StatusOpen(strPrompt as String, intMax as Integer)
    varTemp = SysCmd(SYSCMD_INITMETER, strPrompt, intMax)
End Sub

Sub StatusUpdate(intTemp As Integer)
    varTemp = SysCmd(SYSCMD_UPDATEMETER, intTemp)
End Sub

Sub StatusClose()
    varTemp = SysCmd(SYSCMD_REMOVEMETER)
End Sub
```

Displaying Text on the Status Bar

To display text on the status bar, you need to call SysCmd() twice: once to place the text and once to remove it. Once you've placed text on the status bar, it becomes the default text. Anytime Access needs to write something to the status bar, it does so. Once a few seconds go by, though, it redisplays your text.

To display text, call SysCmd() with this syntax:

varRetval = SysCmd(SYSCMD_SETSTATUS, *strYourText*)

replacing *strYourText* with the actual text to be displayed.

To remove your text, call SysCmd() again:

```
varRetval = SysCmd(SYSCMD_CLEARSTATUS)
```

WARNING Do not attempt to mix the two uses of SysCmd() (status meter and status text). If you're in the middle of displaying a status meter and you insert a call to display status text, you'll overwrite the meter with the text, and the next time you attempt to update the meter you'll trigger a run-time error. If you must flip between displaying text and displaying the meter, you must reinitialize and reset the meter after each text display.

Building the SQL Expression

The goal of creating the QBF form is to allow a user to type in example values and have the form return to your application a SQL expression representing the choices made. For example, imagine that the user has entered "**M**" into the Lastname field and "**CA**" into the State field. Here is the expression you would get back from the form:

```
((([Lastname] Like "M*") And ([State] Like "CA*"))
```

To accomplish this goal, you need some code that loops through every control on the QBF form, checking for values and building up the SQL expression as it goes. The function BuildWhereClause() (in basBuildSQL) in CH8.MDB does the looping work, calling BuildSQLString() to build each component piece.

One Piece at a Time

BuildSQLString() takes the field name, its value, and its datatype and returns a chunk of a SQL expression. Given the following call to BuildSQLString():

```
strChunk = BuildSQLString("StartDate", "11/12/93", 8)
```

the variable strChunk would contain the string

```
([StartDate] = #11/12/93#)
```

on return from the function. BuildSQLString() attempts to format the expression correctly, based on the datatype. It also tries to recognize whether or not the user has supplied an operator as part of the expression. If so, the function doesn't change the value at all, assuming that if the user supplied an operator, the formatting is correct, too. Therefore, the expression

```
strChunk = BuildSQLString("StartDate", "> #1/1/94#", 8)
```

would place the value

```
([StartDate] > #1/1/94#)
```

in strChunk. To determine whether or not the expression contains an operator, BuildSQLString() calls the isOperator() function (Listing 8.15).

Listing 8.15

```
Private Function isOperator(varValue As Variant)

    ' Return a logical value indicating whether a
    ' value passed in is an operator or not.
    ' This is NOT infallible.

    Dim varTemp As Variant

    varTemp = Trim(UCase(varValue))
    isOperator = False

    ' Check first character for <,>, or =
    If InStr("<>=", Left(varTemp, 1)) > 0 Then
        isOperator = True
    ' Check for IN (x,y,z)
```

```
      ElseIf ((Left(varTemp, 4) = "IN (")
      ➡ And (Right(varTemp, 1) = ")")) Then
          isOperator = True
      ' Check for BETWEEN ... AND ...
      ElseIf ((Left(varTemp, 8) = "BETWEEN ") And (InStr(varTemp,
      ➡" AND ") > 0)) Then
          isOperator = True
      ' Check for NOT xxx
      ElseIf (Left(varTemp, 4) = "NOT ") Then
          isOperator = True
      ' Check for LIKE xxx
      ElseIf (Left(varTemp, 5) = "LIKE ") Then
          isOperator = True
      End If
End Function
```

This low-tech solution is far from infallible (it would fail on a text expression such as "Like Wow, Man!", assuming that the "Like" was an operator), but it does handle most of the simple cases.

After deciding whether or not to modify the field value, BuildSQLString() (Listing 8.16) makes the appropriate changes to format the expression for Access SQL. It converts True/False values to –1/0, adds quotes around text values, adds # signs around date values, and leaves numeric values alone. The function skips binary data since it cannot be used as part of a SQL expression.

Listing 8.16

```
const QUOTE = """"

Private Function BuildSQLString(strFieldName As String,
➡ varFieldValue As Variant, intFieldType As Integer)

    ' Build string that can be used as part of a
    ' SQL WHERE clause. This function looks at
    ' the field type for the specified table field,
    ' and constructs the expression accordingly.

    Dim strTemp As String

    strTemp = "[" & strFieldName & "]"
    ' If the first part of the value indicates that it's
    ' to be left as is, leave it alone. Otherwise,
    ' modify the value as necessary.
```

```
    If isOperator(varFieldValue) Then
      strTemp = strTemp & " " & varFieldValue
    Else
        Select Case intFieldType
            Case DB_BOOLEAN
                ' Convert to TRUE/FALSE
                strTemp = strTemp & " = " &
              ➥ IIf(varFieldValue, "-1", "0")
            Case DB_TEXT, DB_MEMO
                ' Assume we're looking for anything that STARTS
                ' with the text we got. This is probably a LOT
                ' slower. If you want direct matches instead,
                ' use the commented-out line.
                ' strTemp = strTemp & " = " & QUOTE &
              ➥ varFieldValue & QUOTE
                strTemp = strTemp & " LIKE " & QUOTE &
              ➥ varFieldValue & "*" & QUOTE
            Case DB_BYTE, DB_INTEGER, DB_LONG, DB_CURRENCY,
          ➥ DB_SINGLE, DB_DOUBLE
                ' Convert to straight numeric representation.
                strTemp = strTemp & " = " & varFieldValue
            Case DB_DATE
                ' Convert to #date# format.
                strTemp = strTemp & " = " & "#" &
              ➥ varFieldValue & "#"
            Case Else
                ' This function really can't handle any of
                ' the other data types (DB_BINARY?)
                strTemp = ""
        End Select
    End If
    BuildSQLString = strTemp
End Function
```

Stringing the Pieces Together

To build the required SQL expression, BuildWhereClause() loops through all the controls on the form. For each control it attempts to retrieve the value of the original ControlSource property for the control by retrieving the qbfField expression from the Tag property. If that fails it moves on to the next control. Otherwise, armed with the data field with which this control is linked, it checks for the value the user might have entered into the control. If the user entered something (that is, if the value isn't null), the function tries to retrieve the original field datatype that was stored in the control's Tag property. Finally, with the data field and datatype it can call BuildSQLString() to create the chunk of the WHERE clause that applies to this field and append it to the end of the complete expression. (To review the glrPutTag() and glrGetTag() functions, see Chapter 7.) The following listing shows the loop that constructs the WHERE clause:

```
For intI = 0 To frm.Count - 1
    Set ctl = frm(intI)
    ' Get the original control source.
    varControlSource = glrGetTag(ctl, "qbfField")
    If Not IsNull(varControlSource) Then
        ' If the value of the control isn't null...
        If Not IsNull(ctl) Then
            ' then get the value.
            varDataType = glrGetTag(ctl, "qbfType")
            If Not IsNull(varDataType) Then
                strTemp = "(" & BuildSQLString(CStr(
                ➡ varControlSource), ctl,
                ➡ CInt(varDataType)) & ")"
                strLocalSQL = strLocalSQL & IIf(Len(strLocalSQL)
                ➡ = 0, strTemp, " AND " & strTemp)
            End If
        End If
        On Error GoTo 0
    End If
Next intI
If Len(strLocalSQL)  0 Then strLocalSQL =
➡ "(" & strLocalSQL & ")"
BuildWHEREClause = strLocalSQL
```

Using QBF in Your Own Applications

To include QBF functionality in your own applications, follow these steps:

1. From CH8.MDB, include the form frmCreateQBF and the modules bas-BuildSQL and basTags (if your database doesn't already include this module).

2. Create your QBF forms either by running frmCreateQBF or on your own.

3. Before you distribute your database, delete the form frmCreateQBF since you won't be using that as part of your application.

When you're ready to pop up the QBF form and retrieve the information from the user, call the glrDoQBF() function using the following syntax:

strSQL = glrDoQBF(*strFormName, fCloseForm*)

The first parameter to glrDoQBF is a string that contains the name of the form to be opened. The second parameter is a True/False value that tells glrDoQBF() whether or not to close the form once it's done. No matter how you've set this flag, the function call leaves the QBF form hidden, but if you plan to make further calls to glrDoQBF(), the form will pop up more quickly if it's already loaded. The function returns the SQL WHERE clause that it built from the user's input.

Using Popup Forms in Your Applications

The structure of the glrDoQBF() function is very similar to others you'll see in the next few sections. The QBF form, as well as the calendar and calculator (frmCalendar and frmCalc), all pop up as modal forms, waiting until the user has finished with whatever needs to be done with the form. By opening it with the A_DIALOG flag, Access waits until the form has been closed before continuing with the function. The form must have been designed such that if the user wants a value returned to the caller, the form is hidden. If the user wants to cancel any changes, the form must be closed. Therefore, once the calling function regains control, it can check to see whether or not the form is loaded. If it is, that indicates that the user wants to retain the changes made, and the function returns those changes to your application. If not, the function returns null. By creating tools this way, you can encapsulate almost all of the code in the form itself, making it simple to add the tools to your applications. The following listing shows the glrDoQBF() function, a sample for many popup applications:

```
Function glrDoQBF(strFormName As String, fCloseIt As Integer)
    Dim strSQL As String
    DoCmd OpenForm strFormName, , , , , A_DIALOG
```

```
' You won't get to here until the user closes or hides
' the form.
If IsFormLoaded(strFormName) Then
    strSQL = BuildWHEREClause(Forms(strFormName))
    If fCloseIt Then
        DoCmd Close A_FORM, strFormName
    End If
End If
glrDoQBF = strSQL
End Function
```

What you do with the returned SQL expression is up to you. You could filter a form, create a query, or pop up a datasheet showing just the records that matched the criteria provided by the user. By providing you with just the SQL WHERE clause, we've made it possible to use glrCreateQBF() in many different situations.

Using Other Popup Tools

We've provided two other popup tools, a calendar and a calculator, that fit into your application in very much the same manner as the QBF form. In both cases you make a single function call, which returns to your application the value returned from the popup form. In the case of the calendar the return value will be the chosen date (or null, if none was chosen). For the calculator the function will return the result of the user's calculations. The inner workings of these tools aren't the issue here, but rather their interface to your application. Once you've seen how these forms work, you should be able to use the techniques to create your own popup tools.

The concept is simple. Here are the steps for creating a popup form tool:

1. Include a method to close the form or to hide it. The calculator uses buttons, and the calendar uses either double-click or the ↵ key to hide the form or the Esc key to close it. Closing the form causes the calling code to disregard changes made to the form. Hiding your form allows the calling code to retrieve the necessary information from it and then close it.

2. Use the OpenForm macro action with the A_DIALOG flag to open the form as a dialog box.

3. Your function will regain control once the user closes or hides the popup form. At that point check to see whether the form is still loaded. If so, retrieve the necessary information and return that as the function's value. Otherwise, return null.

The following is the code for the glrDoCalc() function:

```
Function glrDoCalc()
    DoCmd OpenForm "frmCalc", , , , , A_DIALOG
    If isFormLoaded("frmCalc") Then
        glrDoCalc = Forms!frmCalc!lblReadOut.Caption
        DoCmd Close A_FORM, "frmCalc"
    Else
        glrDoCalc = Null
    End If
End Function
```

The code used to pop up the calendar is very similar:

```
Function glrDoCalendar(varPassedDate As Variant) As Variant
    Dim frmCal As Form

    varStartDate = IIf(IsNull(varPassedDate), Date,
    ➥ varPassedDate)
    DoCmd OpenForm CALENDAR_FORM, , , , , A_DIALOG

    If isFormLoaded(CALENDAR_FORM) Then
        Set frmCal = Forms(CALENDAR_FORM)
        glrDoCalendar = DateSerial(frmCal!Year,
        ➥ frmCal!Month, frmCal!Day)
        DoCmd Close A_FORM, CALENDAR_FORM
    Else
        glrDoCalendar = Null
    End If
End Function
```

In this case you can pass to the function the date you want to have displayed on the calendar when it first appears. You can also pass a null value to have it use the current date.

TIP

If you include more than one module from this book in your own application, you may find duplicated private functions or subroutines. For example, the isFormLoaded() function appears in many of the modules. Since we can't guarantee which combinations of modules and forms you'll want to include in your own applications, we've placed these small helper functions in the particular modules where they're needed. You may want to remove the Private keyword from one such instance and delete the others. There's no need to carry around multiple copies of the same function.

You can easily include either or both the popup calendar and calculator in your own applications. Follow these steps to include one or both:

1. From CH8.MDB, include the module basCalc or basCalendar.

2. Include the form frmCalc or frmCalendar.

3. When you want to pop up the calendar, call it with code like this:

   ```
   varDate = glrDoCalendar(varStartDate)
   ```

   where varStartDate is either null or a specific date/time value. The function returns the date the user selected either by double-clicking or pressing ↵ (see Figure 8.13).

FIGURE 8.13:
Calendar (frmCalendar), called from frmTestPopup (also in CH8.MDB)

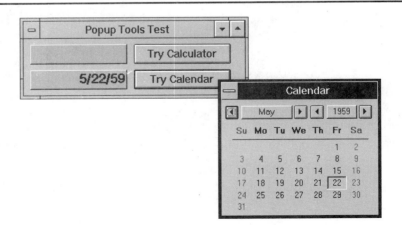

4. When you want to pop up the calculator, call it with code like this:

```
varValue = glrDoCalc()
```

The function returns the result of the user's calculations (see Figure 8.14).

FIGURE 8.14:
Popup calculator (frmCalc) in action

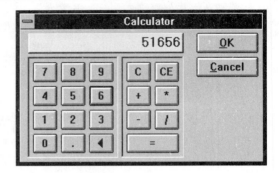

Form-Level Error Handling

Many errors can occur while your form is active. Some of these are standard runtime errors: perhaps a file is missing, a query your form expects to find isn't actually there, or the user does something you hadn't expected. Other errors are errors in the Access engine itself, and they can't be caught with normal error trapping. (For information on handling run-time errors, see Chapter 14.) You may find that you want to replace the standard Access behavior when these errors occur with behavior that is a little friendlier toward the user.

Access provides a form event to handle these engine errors. If you attach code to the Error event of a form, your procedure will be called whenever a trappable error occurs while the form is running. If you place your code in the CBF, you're sent two parameters from Access. The syntax for the call is

Sub Form_Error (*DataErr* As Integer, *Response* As Integer)

The value *DataErr* will contain the error number for the error that just occurred, and *Response* allows you to specify how you want Access to handle the error. If your code handles the error to your satisfaction and you don't want Access to intervene or display its own message, place the value DATA_ERRCONTINUE in *Response*. If you want Access to display its own error message, place DATA_ERRDISPLAY in *Response*. You can, of course, use the built-in Error() function to display the Access error message that corresponds to *DataErr*, or you can devise your own error message.

The sample Form_Error() subroutine shown in Listing 8.17 traps four errors that might pop up. In each case the procedure replaces the standard Access error message with its own. If an error occurs that it hadn't planned on, it just passes the responsibility back to Access. The form frmErrorSample in CH8.MDB includes this particular error handler. In this example the following special conditions occur:

- The State field has a table-level validation rule. (Only "TX" will be allowed as the state.)
- The Age field is set up to accept numeric input only, between 0 and 255.
- The LastName field is set up as the key field.

The error-handling procedure reacts to any of the following events:

- The user enters a state other than "TX" in the State field.
- The user enters a non-numeric value in the Age field or a value out of range.
- The user creates or modifies a record such that the LastName field is empty.
- The user creates or modifies a record such that the LastName field (the primary key) is not unique.

In any of these cases the error-handling procedure takes over and displays the prepared message. If any other engine-level error occurs, Access' own error handling prevails.

NOTE If any Access Basic error occurs within the Form_Error() subroutine, Access just disregards the procedure and handles any engine-level errors itself. That is, you won't get any error messages dealing with your coding error, but your procedure just won't get called.

Chances are that you'll find a number of uses for form-level error handling. You can trap errors here that would have been impossible to trap in earlier versions of Access. You could replace the error handling for these and other engine errors with your own, more personal, error handler. For one reason or another, however, the Error event is not as powerful as it might be in that it does not, in general, allow you to handle multiuser errors. Access 2.0 always handles those itself. For more information, see Chapter 11.

> **NOTE** The form error handler will not trap Access Basic run-time errors. If your code causes an error to occur or if the user is executing your code when an error occurs, your code should deal with those errors. The form-level error handler is meant to deal with errors that occur while the form has control and you're just waiting for the user to choose some action that will place your code into action again.

Listing 8.17

```
Sub Form_Error(DataErr As Integer, Response As Integer)

Const ERR_DATA_VALIDATION = 3318
Const ERR_DATA_TYPE = 2113
Const ERR_DUPLICATE_KEY = 3022
Const ERR_NULL_KEY = 3058

Const MB_ICONEXCLAMATION = 48

    Dim strCRLF As String
    Dim strMsg As String

    strCRLF = Chr$(13) & Chr$(10)

    Select Case DataErr
        Case ERR_DATA_VALIDATION, ERR_DATA_TYPE
            strMsg = "The data you entered does not fit the
        ➥ requirements for this field."
```

```
                strMsg = strMsg & strCRLF & "Please try again,
              ➡ or press Escape to undo your entry."
                MsgBox strMsg, MB_ICONEXCLAMATION
                Response = DATA_ERRCONTINUE
            Case ERR_DUPLICATE_KEY
                strMsg = "You've attempted to add a record which
              ➡ duplicates an existing key value."
                strMsg = strMsg & strCRLF & "Please try again,
              ➡ or press Escape to undo your entry."
                MsgBox strMsg, MB_ICONEXCLAMATION
                Response = DATA_ERRCONTINUE
            Case ERR_NULL_KEY
                strMsg = "You've attempted to add a new record
              ➡ with an empty key value."
                strMsg = strMsg & strCRLF & "Please supply a key
              ➡ value, or press Escape to undo your entry."
                MsgBox strMsg, MB_ICONEXCLAMATION
                Response = DATA_ERRCONTINUE
                ' You can even place them on the right field!
                Me!txtLastName.SetFocus
            Case Else
                ' It's an unexpected error.
                ' Let Access handle it.
                Response = DATA_ERRDISPLAY
        End Select
End Sub
```

Using Subforms in Your Applications

Subforms are useful for at least two unrelated purposes: they are perfect for displaying data from one-to-many relationships, and you can use them to group together otherwise disparate groups of controls on a form. Both of these uses have some facets that aren't usually discussed, so the next few sections deal with areas of subform use that may be giving you difficulty.

Nested Subforms versus Separate, Synchronized Subforms

As long as you're interested in displaying one-to-many relationships, you'll find it quite simple to drag and drop a form onto another form. If you've defined relationships for the tables involved, it becomes even easier since Access fills in the ChildLinkFields and MasterLinkFields properties for you.

This method has its good and bad sides, however. If you nest subforms you're limited to having at most three levels of data: the main form plus two levels of nested subforms. On the other hand, forms involving nested subforms are simple to set up. Figure 8.15 shows an example from CH8.MDB, frmNestedMain, which draws on

FIGURE 8.15:

Access makes it simple to create a form with two nested subforms, as long as you need only three levels and don't need to display any but the lowest-level forms in Form view.

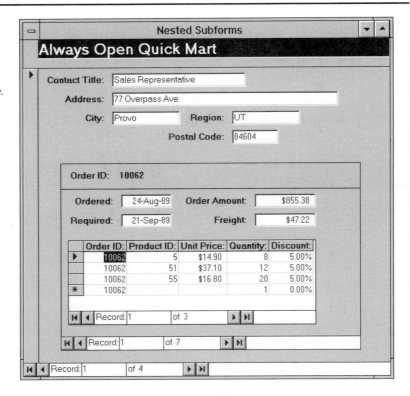

frmNestedOrders, which in turn includes frmNestedOrderDetail. The two inner forms are linked on OrderId, and the two outer forms are linked on CustomerID. This example requires no macros or Access Basic code.

Although you'll find it easy to create examples like frmNestedOrders, you'll also run into some limitations if you want the form to look much different than the example. You can't, for example, make any form except the lowest-level form appear in Datasheet or Continuous Forms view, and you can't use more than two subforms. If you want any of the intermediate forms to appear in Datasheet or Continuous Forms view or if you need more than three levels of data displayed, you'll have to consider some other method.

As a reminder, the syntax for retrieving values from subforms from somewhere off the subform can be daunting. For example, to retrieve a value from txtName on the subform whose ControlName property is frmSub1, which lives on frmMain, you'd use the syntax

Forms!frmMain!frmSub1.Form!*txtName*

The reference to frmSub1 takes you to the control that contains the subform. The ".Form" gets you to the actual form property of that control, from which you can access anything on the form.

Referencing controls on nested subforms follows the same pattern. To reference a check box named chkAlive on frmSub2, which is a control on frmSub1, which is a control on frmMain, you'd use the syntax

Forms!frmMain!frmSub1.Form!frmSub2.Form!chkAlive

Finally, the expression might be shorter, depending on the current scope when you need to retrieve the value. For example, if you were trying to retrieve the value on frmSub2 as part of the ControlSource expression for a text box on frmSub1, you'd only need to refer to

frmSub2.Form!chkAlive

since you're already on the form contained in frmSub1.

The Access Expression Builder can help you create these complex references. Once in the Expression Builder, if you double-click the Forms item in the first list box, then double-click on Loaded Forms, and then double-click again on the name of your main form, you should see the subform name. Double-click that subform name and you see the name of the nested subform, if there is one. Once you've navigated to the form you want to reference, choose the appropriate control or property, and the Expression Builder builds up the necessary reference for you.

Using Synchronized Subforms

Creating synchronized subforms in Access 1.x was a complicated process, due to some strange interactions between events on the different forms. In Access 2.0 the process is more straightforward. Figure 8.16 shows frmSynchMain with its included subforms, frmSynchOrders and frmNestedOrderDetail. Instead of nesting

FIGURE 8.16:

frmSynchMain with its included subforms

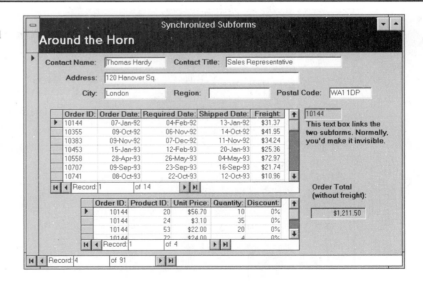

the two subforms, frmSynchMain synchronizes the two subforms. The mechanism is quite simple: in the "primary" subform's Current event, fill in a (normally) hidden text box. The code might look something like this:

```
Sub Form_Current()
    ' Disregard errors that would occur if you opened this
    ' subform as a normal form, without a parent property or
    ' without a textbox named txtLink.
    On Error Resume Next
    ' Using the Parent property allows this form to be used
    ' as a subform on any form which happens to use a textbox
    ' named txtLink to link it with other subforms.
    Me.Parent!txtLink = Me![Order ID]
End Sub
```

The error handler takes care of the case in which you might try to open the form on its own (without its being a subform of a form that contains a linking text box named txtLink).

The "secondary" subform's MasterLinkFields property is set to that same text box, with its ChildLinkFields property set to the control name of the text box ([Order ID] in this example). Therefore, as the user moves from row to row in frmSynchOrders, frmNestedOrderDetail will show only the orders with the same Order ID field as the chosen row in frmSynchOrders. This concept could be extended even further. If there were a one-to-many relationship starting from frmNestedOrderDetail, its Current event could fill in a text box to which yet another form could be linked with its LinkMasterFields property.

Using Subforms to Replace Multiple-Page Forms

If you've used correct versions of Microsoft Word for Windows or Excel, you must have noticed the tabbed dialog forms they use. Although Access doesn't directly support this look, you can emulate its most important features: you provide a series of buttons, each of which displays a different page, or subform, loaded with other controls. (You will find a technique for creating tabbed dialog boxes, like those in Word and Excel, in Chapter 20.) Figure 8.17 shows an example of a multipage form in design mode (frmOptionsMultiPage from CH8.MDB). Many programmers use

FIGURE 8.17:

The first two pages of a multipage example (frmOptionsMultiPage) in design mode

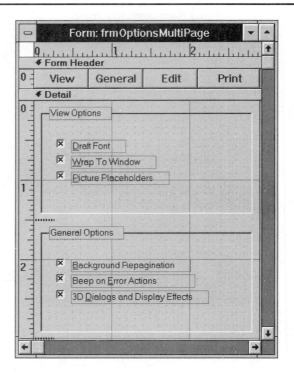

multipage forms for this purpose (as do the Access Wizards, for the most part), but you'll find several drawbacks to using multipage forms:

- Multipage forms can be difficult to handle in design mode since you end up with a form that you must scroll vertically to view.

- You're limited to a maximum of 22 inches for the Detail section. This may just not be enough for your application.

- Buttons that apply to the entire form must be in either the form header or the footer. This may not match the style of other forms in your application.

- Unless you load your form using the A_DIALOG option for the OpenForm macro action, Access provides no way for you to keep your users on a specific page. They can always use the PgUp and PgDn keys to move from page to page unless you've used the A_DIALOG option. In addition, unless you take some extra care, you have no way of keeping your users from using the Tab and Shift+Tab keys to move from the end of one page onto the next or previous page.

Replacing multipage forms with a single main form and multiple subforms will alleviate most of these problems. Figure 8.18 shows two of the example subforms in design mode. On the other hand, this method has its drawbacks, too:

- Using subforms, you'll find it more difficult to track data from one page to the next. On a single form with multiple pages, all the controls have the same scope. On multiple subforms the code necessary to access each control becomes more complicated.

- Designing the separate forms that will become the subforms can be complex since it's more difficult to display them all at once than if you're just changing pieces of one big form.

- Sizing and placing the forms exactly requires more patience than with multipage forms.

For your own application you must decide which is the better alternative. If you need more than 22 inches of form space, you have no choice; you'll need to opt for

FIGURE 8.18:

Two subforms, destined to appear in frmOptionsSubForms in CH8.MDB

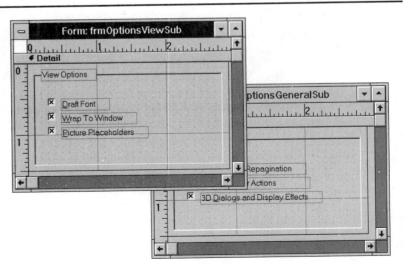

multiple subforms. Otherwise, make your choice after studying the examples in the next few sections. (If you opt for the synthesized tabbed dialogs as discussed in Chapter 20, you'll most likely decide on the multiple-subform method since that's how the examples in that chapter work.)

Creating Multipage Forms

If your form contains one or more evenly spaced page-break controls and if you either set the form's AutoSize property to Yes or set the form's size to show just one of those pages, you need a multipage form. Your users can easily move from page to page, either using the PgUp and PgDn keys or by clicking the buttons you provide to move them from page to page (using the GotoPage method). As mentioned earlier, the total length of the Detail section can be no more than 22 inches (due to limitations of the 16-bit integers that Access uses to store positions). The example form, frmOptionsMultiPage in CH8.MDB, places four buttons in the form's header, all part of an option group named grpButtons. The AfterUpdate event for the option group contains just a single line of code:

```
Me.GotoPage grpButtons
```

which sets the current page to match the value of the button the user just pushed. Notice that since the whole Detail section moves from page to page, you must place any form-wide buttons (the option group and the OK and Cancel buttons) in either the form header or the footer.

TIP

To keep the user from moving from page to page using the PgUp and PgDn keys, you need to open your multipage form as a dialog box. That is, it's not enough to set its Popup property to Yes. You must actually use the OpenForm macro action, setting the sixth parameter to Dialog (or A_DIALOG, if called from Access Basic).

Setting the Tab Order

When you create your multipage form, don't forget to check the tab order of the controls. Use the Edit ➤ Tab Order menu item to set the order such that a control on the first page is first in the tab order. Otherwise, when you first open the form, Access scrolls the first control in the tab order into view. This may make your form display rather oddly.

Creating Multi-Subform Forms

If your form requires more than 22 inches for the Detail section or if you find managing a very long form intimidating, you might find the multiple-subform method a useful change. To make the multiple subforms work correctly, you attach code to the AfterUpdate event of the option group containing the page-selection buttons that will make the correct subform visible and the rest invisible. The code used in frmOptionsSubForms looks like this:

```
Me!frmOptionsViewSub.Visible = (Me!grpButtons = 1)
Me!frmOptionsGeneralSub.Visible = (Me!grpButtons = 2)
Me!frmOptionsEditSub.Visible = (Me!grpButtons = 3)
Me!frmOptionsPrintSub.Visible = (Me!grpButtons = 4)
```

The expression on the right side of each equal sign will evaluate to either True or False, causing each subform to be made visible or invisible, depending on the button you've pressed. Figure 8.19 shows frmOptionsSubForm in action.

FIGURE 8.19:
Choosing a button in the option group causes Access to display the correct subform.

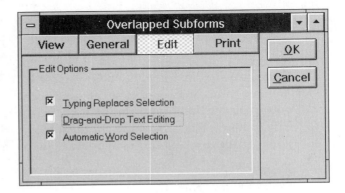

You prepare the subforms just as you would the separate pages for a multipage form. Try to lay out each subform with major controls in the same location (the group boxes on these forms all have the same upper-left corner), and clearly label each "page" so the user understands which page is current. When you design the container form (frmOptionsSubForms), make sure you assign a default value to the option group containing the buttons, set the matching subform's Visible property to Yes, and set the rest of the subforms' Visible properties to No. This ensures that Access displays the correct page when you first open the main form.

Compare and Decide

Neither method is perfect, and both have inherent limitations. Play with the two examples (frmOptionsSubForms and frmOptionsMultiPage in CH8.MDB) and decide for yourself which method will work best in your application. Remember that multipage forms have a limited page length, while multiple subforms are, for all intents and purposes, limited only by the maximum number of controls you can place on a form. Neither method will replace the built-in tabbed dialogs you'll find in other Microsoft products, but they provide a similar metaphor for your own Access applications.

Deciphering Events

Programming in Access boils down to basically one activity: reacting to events. Although this basic paradigm hasn't changed with Access 2.0, the event model certainly has. Not only does Access 2.0 expose many more events to the Access programmer, but many of the events are interrelated and can seem somewhat daunting to the beginner.

To make it simpler for you to follow the order of events that occur when you manipulate forms and controls at run time, we've concocted a mechanism by which you can watch the events firing off for a specific form. In addition, it would be quite easy to mimic this behavior in a form of your own. That way you could add a few lines of code to an existing form to watch its events as they occur.

Figure 8.20 shows the event-debugging facility at work. (Yes, we know that NWIND.MDB includes its own Show Events form, but it's somewhat limited. Our example provides you with a great deal more flexibility and allows you to hook the tests into your own forms.)

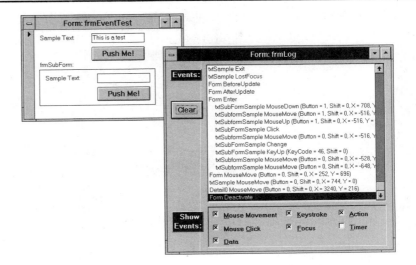

FIGURE 8.20:

Each and every event that occurs while frmEventTest is active gets registered on frmLog.

For this mechanism to be of much use you must trap each event as it occurs, logging the event to frmLog. Figure 8.21 shows the form in design mode, alongside the property sheet, with each event trapped with its own event procedure. You'll find both forms in CH8.MDB. To test them out, first run frmLog and then frmEventTest. If you load them in this order, you'll get to see the form-loading events logged as frmLog loads itself.

What's Going On?

Every event procedure in frmEventTest (and frmSubForm, the subform inside frmEventTest) calls the same procedure to handle the event: LogEvent (in basEvents in CH8.MDB). LogEvent takes two parameters: a string to display in the list box on frmLog and an integer flag indicating the specific type of event. Using these flags, LogEvent can determine whether or not to display the particular event, based on the event-type choices you've made on frmLog. A call to LogEvent might look something like this:

```
Sub cmdPushMe_Click()
    LogEvent "cmdPushMe Click", glrEVENT_MOUSECLICK
End Sub
```

In design mode each event shows its own event procedure.

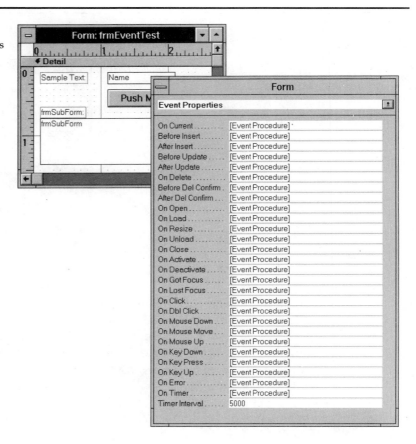

if you wanted to display only the control name and the event. You could also pass in more information, like this:

```
Sub txtSample_MouseUp(Button As Integer, Shift As Integer,
➡ X As Single, Y As Single)
    LogEvent "txtSample MouseUp (Button = " & Button &
    ➡ ", Shift = " & Shift & ", X = " & X & ", Y = " & Y & ")",
    ➡ glrEVENT_MOUSECLICK
End Sub
```

This example displays all the information that Access passes in to the event procedure. As you experiment with frmEventTest, you'll see both kinds of expressions.

The module basEvents includes constant declarations for each of the seven types of events that this mechanism traps. Table 8.8 shows the constants and how they're used.

TABLE 8.8: Event Types for frmLog

Constant	Value	Events
glrEVENT_MOUSEMOVEMENT	1	MouseMove
glrEVENT_FOCUS	2	Activate, Deactive, Enter, Exit, GotFocus, LostFocus
glrEVENT_KEY	3	KeyDown, KeyPress, KeyUp
glrEVENT_ACTION	4	Close, Error, Load, Open, Resize
glrEVENT_MOUSECLICK	5	Click, DblClick, MouseDown, MouseUp
glrEVENT_TIMER	6	Timer
glrEVENT_DATA	7	AfterDelConfirm, AfterInsert, AfterUpdate, BeforeDelConfirm, BeforeInsert, BeforeUpdate, Change, Current, Delete

As each event occurs, the code in LogEvent sends the text you passed to it to the logging form and requeries the list box on that form. It will post the event only if the appropriate check box has been selected on the logging form. Listing 8.18 shows the code for LogEvent.

Listing 8.18

```
Sub LogEvent(strEvent As String, intEventType As Integer)
    On Error GoTo LogEventErr

    Dim fShowIt As Integer
    Dim ctl As Control

    Dim frm As Form
    Set frm = Forms(LOG_FORM)

    fShowIt = True
    Select Case intEventType
        Case glrEVENT_MOUSEMOVEMENT
            fShowIt = frm!chkMouseMovement
```

```
        Case glrEVENT_MOUSECLICK
            fShowIt = frm!chkMouseClick
        Case glrEVENT_KEY
            fShowIt = frm!chkKeystroke
        Case glrEVENT_FOCUS
            fShowIt = frm!chkFocus
        Case glrEVENT_ACTION
            fShowIt = frm!chkAction
        Case glrEVENT_TIMER
            fShowIt = frm!chkTimer
        Case glrEVENT_DATA
            fShowIt = frm!chkData
    End Select

    If fShowIt Then
        frm!txtNewItem = strEvent
        frm!lstLog.Requery
    End If

LogEventErr:
    Exit Sub
End Sub
```

How frmLog Works

The logging form, frmLog, consists of a few check boxes indicating to you which type of events to track and a list box listing the events as they occur. Since the code that controls frmLog is all private (it "lives" in the CBF), there's no direct way to call into it; adding a new item to the list box requires some special effort. To make this happen, the final lines of LogEvent (in Listing 8.18) place the text to be added to the list box into a hidden text box on frmLog (txtNewItem) and then force the list box to be requeried. Requerying the list box, which uses a list-filling callback function to fill itself, causes the called function to add the text it finds in txtNewItem to a global array of event messages and then places the new value into the list box. Listing 8.19 shows the callback function. It's a very typical callback function, filling the list box with items from mastrLogItems(), the array holding all the text that's been sent from the LogEvent procedure. Obviously, since this mechanism stores all the items in an array (this allows you to scroll about in the list box), there's a physical limit to the number of items you'll want to track. The events add up fast! Use the Clear button occasionally to empty the list.

Listing 8.19

```
Function FillLog(ctl As Control, lngID As Long,
➥ lngRow As Long, lngCol As Long, intCode As Integer)
➥ As Variant
    Select Case intCode
        Case LB_INITIALIZE
            ' If the array size is 0 (and this'll only
            ' happen the first time around), set up the
            ' array.
            If mlngSize = 0 Then
                InitArray
            End If

            ' Add the current item in the text box
            ' to the list.
            AddItemToList

            ' Set the value of the list box, which
            ' is bound to column 0, to be the most recently
            ' added row. This makes the most current row
            ' visible.
            ctl = mlngItems - 1
            FillLog = True

        Case LB_OPEN
            FillLog = Timer

        Case LB_GETROWCOUNT
            FillLog = mlngItems

        Case LB_GETCOLUMNCOUNT
            FillLog = 1

        Case LB_GETCOLUMNWIDTH
            FillLog = -1

        Case LB_GETVALUE
            FillLog = astrLogItems(lngRow)

    End Select
End Function
```

The only complications in this mechanism are in adding items to the list and managing the size of the list. The code handles both these problems in the AddItemToList subroutine, shown in Listing 8.20. First off, if there's nothing in txtNewItem but this function has been invoked anyway, it just exits:

```
If IsNull(Me!txtNewItem) Then Exit Sub
```

To maximize the speed of the mechanism, AddItemToList doesn't add a new row to the array each time an event occurs. Calling ReDim Preserve for each item would really place a drag on performance. Instead, AddItemToList increases the size of the array only when it needs to, adding groups of rows, CHUNK_SIZE at a time. (CHUNK_SIZE is a constant defined in the module's Declarations area.) The procedure uses the module global variable mlngItems to know how many items are currently in the array of events:

```
' An error will occur when the array overflows.
' In that case, go to AddChunk, to add more space.
On Error GoTo AddChunk
mastrLogItems(mlngItems) = Me!txtNewItem
Me!txtNewItem = Null
mlngItems = mlngItems + 1
```

If an error occurs while AddItemToList is adding a row to the array, the code needs to add another chunk of rows to the array. The code in the error-handling portion of the routine does just that. It first tells Access to disregard errors and then attempts to retrieve the largest element of the array. If this fails, it must be because there are no rows at all in the array so far, and the code resets the value of mlngSize to 0. It then just adds CHUNK_SIZE to the number of elements and uses the ReDim Preserve command to set the new size of the array:

```
On Error Resume Next
mlngSize = UBound(mastrLogItems)
' If there's error, that means the
' array currently has no elements at all.
' This only happens the first time through here.
If Err <> 0 Then
    mlngSize = 0
End If
mlngSize = mlngSize + CHUNK_SIZE
ReDim Preserve mastrLogItems(mlngSize)
On Error GoTo AddChunk
Resume
```

Listing 8.20

```
Sub AddItemToList()
    ' If there's no new item to add to the list,
    ' then just get out of here.
    If IsNull(Me!txtNewItem) Then Exit Sub

    ' An error will occur when the array overflows.
    ' In that case, go to AddChunk, to add more space.
    On Error GoTo AddChunk
    mastrLogItems(mlngItems) = Me!txtNewItem
    Me!txtNewItem = Null
    mlngItems = mlngItems + 1
    Exit Sub

AddChunk:
    ' You get here if the array fills up.

    On Error Resume Next
    ' Get the upper bound of the array.
    mlngSize = UBound(mastrLogItems)
    ' If there's error, that means the
    ' array currently has no elements at all.
    ' This only happens the first time through here.
    If Err <> 0 Then
        mlngSize = 0
    End If

    ' Increase the array size by CHUNK_SIZE rows.
    mlngSize = mlngSize + CHUNK_SIZE
    ' Redim the array to be the new size, preserving
    ' the old info.
    ReDim Preserve mastrLogItems(mlngSize)
    ' Reset the error handler.
    On Error GoTo AddChunk
    ' Go back to the line that caused the error.
    Resume
End Sub
```

Using This Mechanism with Your Own Forms

To use this event-viewing mechanism with your own forms, take the following steps:

1. Import the form frmLog into your own application.

2. Import the module basEvents.

3. Make a working copy of any form you want to enable for event tracking. You definitely don't want to make all the changes to a "real" copy of your form.

4. Add calls to LogEvent to each event you wish to track. For each event procedure, be sure to pass the subroutine the appropriate parameters. Use Table 8.8 to help decide which events should go with which action types.

Once you've taken these steps (and step 4 can take a *long* time to prepare), you can track any events of importance to you. If you're confused about the order of events (Load/Open, GotFocus/LostFocus, and so on), there's no better way to test things out.

Summary

Through the use of Windows API calls and Access Basic code, you can exact a great deal of control over the appearance and actions of your forms. In particular, you can control

- The border controls, individually or collectively
- The modality of the form
- When or whether your form gets closed
- The size and position of forms from one Access session to the next
- Form-level error handling

You've learned to create various Access tools, including

- Toolboxes
- Popup utilities
- Auto-sizing forms
- Self-disabling navigation buttons
- Query by form SQL Builders
- Multipage and multi-subform forms, emulating tabbed dialogs

And finally, along the way, you've encountered some useful tidbits, such as

- Reading and writing Windows .INI files
- Access window classes and their relationships
- Using the RecordSetClone property of bookmarks and forms
- Determining whether a specific form is loaded
- Detecting record position states
- Moving and sizing windows
- Enabling/disabling control menu items
- Resizing forms for various screen resolutions
- Using SysCmd() to create a status meter

CHAPTER

NINE

Topics in Report Design and Printing

- Using report and section events and properties

- Controlling sorting and grouping programmatically

- Altering the report layout programmatically

- Retrieving information about your printer

- Creating a list of available output devices

- Using the Windows printing mechanisms to control printed output

Designing reports ought to be a simple task. In theory, you never have to worry about data input, validation, movement from field to field, or capturing an endless number of different fields on the same form. On the other hand, designing a report that is both functional and aesthetically pleasing can be difficult. You may be attempting to simulate an existing report from some other database system, or you may be designing your own reports. In this chapter we cover some of the basics involved in designing creative reports, focusing on the issues that elude or confuse many developers: report and section events, sorting and grouping options, and handling printer devices. You won't find many Windows API calls in this chapter since they won't normally help much when you're creating reports. Access gives you all the flexibility you need.

Learning to harness that flexibility is the challenge you face when you create reports. This chapter assumes that you've already managed to create simple reports and now need to work with the various events and properties to add functionality. In addition, the chapter covers some common problem areas and suggests interesting solutions to those problems. The second half of the chapter details some of the more esoteric areas of reports in Access: controlling your print destination, print output, and margin settings programmatically. All the other documentation available on these topics is geared toward C and Windows SDK programmers, as opposed to Access developers. The material in this chapter will make it possible for you to completely control your users' printing environment.

Reports versus Forms

As you have discovered, designing effective reports is a very different task than designing forms. A given form may contain various sections, like a report, but unlike reports, most forms are not geared toward repetitive, front-to-back processing. Forms are most often oriented toward presenting and retrieving information from a user in an interactive environment, while reports generally leave the user out of the process. As a matter of fact, your entire mind-set must be different when preparing reports and when dealing with report events and methods. You might imagine the Access formatting engine walking forward through your report design, formatting sections, pulling in data, formatting the data, and retreating as it discovers that the section won't fit on a page, always moving on a forward roll. It's this forward motion that propels the Access report engine: there's no going back as Access lays out and prints your reports.

In general, your whole interaction with reports is different than it is with forms. For example, you need never be concerned with user input when designing a report, but you will be concerned with undoing actions taken by the steam roller–like reporting engine. When creating a form, you might have placed some initialization code in the form's Open event. This won't work for reports, as you'll see, because the user might open the report in preview mode and want to restart the report several times, moving back to the first page. Understanding the conglomerate of report events, methods, and properties and how these differ from the corresponding elements of forms, then, will allow you to tame the Access report engine.

Controlling Sorting and Grouping

After layout of the controls on the report, the highest-level control you have over the results from a report are the sorting/groupings. It's impossible to completely separate these two issues since grouping is so dependent on the sort order. Figure 9.1 shows a typical report layout, with groups set up based on the Company-Name and ContactName fields. If you've created any reports up to this point, you're probably well aware of the possibilities involved with using group headers and footers. What you might not have noticed is that group headers and footers, as well as every other section on the report, supply event hooks; you can use the "break" in the processing as a signal to your program code, which might need to react to the new group that is about to be printed or has just been printed. (We discuss report and section events throughout this chapter.)

You also may be unaware that you can control the sorting and grouping properties of reports programmatically. You can create new reports or modify existing ones, creating new sections as necessary, and can modify the sort information, as well. The next few sections suggest methods for controlling the sorting and grouping characteristics of your reports from your Access Basic code.

FIGURE 9.1:
The sample report is grouped on the CompanyName and ContactName fields.

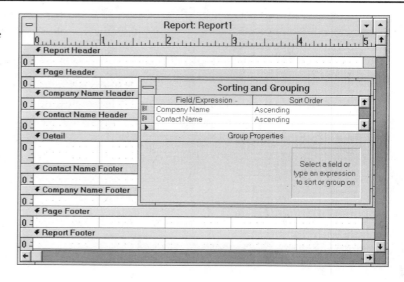

The Section Property

Forms, reports, and all controls expose the Section property. For controls, it's just an indication of which section of the parent form or report it appears on, and this isn't the issue here (although the value returned from a control's Section property corresponds with the numbers used in specifying a form or report's section). For forms and reports the Section property provides an array of all the sections contained on the given object, referred to by number, as shown in Table 9.1. To refer to any specific section, you treat it as an element from an array of sections, as in the following:

```
Forms!frmExample.Section(1).Visible = False
```

which makes the Form Header section invisible for frmExample.

Here are two more items to remember about sections:

- Besides the sections listed in Table 9.1, additional group-level section headers and footers are numbered consecutively starting with 9.

- Forms never contain more than five sections (numbered 0 through 4).

TABLE 9.1: Section Numbers and Their Descriptions

Setting	Description
0	Detail section
1	Form or Report Header section
2	Form or Report Footer section
3	Form or Report Page Header section
4	Form or Report Page Footer section
5	Group-level 1 Header section (reports only)
6	Group-level 1 Footer section (reports only)
7	Group-level 2 Header section (reports only)
8	Group-level 2 Footer section (reports only)

There's not much you can do with the Section property on its own; anytime you deal with the Section property, you'll be interested in the properties of that particular section. Unlike other property arrays in Access (the Column property, for example), the Section property does not ever return a value on its own.

Setting Physical Characteristics Using the Section Property

Besides setting the visibility of a specific section, you often need to set the height of a section. For an example, the frmCreateQBF form discussed in Chapter 8 creates a Footer section on a form, if one doesn't already exist, and sets its height. (Although this example pertains to a specific form, all the code works just as well with reports.) The code fragment in Listing 9.1 makes sure the Form Footer section is visible. To do this, it checks to see whether the form is already showing a Footer section and if not, creates one, setting the height of both the header and footer to 0. Code later in the function sets the particular height for the footer. Note that if you create a footer, you also create a header. This code sets the height of the header to 0 and sets its Visible property to False, ensuring that it won't be visible in the running form. This code fragment calls the isFooterSection() function, which is discussed in the following section.

Listing 9.1

```
' If there isn't already a footer, turn on headers
' and footers, and then turn off the header.
Const SECTION_HEADER = 1
Const SECTION_FOOTER = 2
If Not isFooterSection(frm) Then
    ' Form Design, Format, Form Header/Footer
    DoCmd DoMenuItem A_FORMDS, 3, 10
    frm.Section(SECTION_HEADER).Visible = False
    frm.Section(SECTION_HEADER).Height = 0
    frm.Section(SECTION_FOOTER).Height = 0
End If

' Make SURE the footer is visible.
frm.Section(SECTION_FOOTER).Visible = True
```

TIP

If you want a section to be as short as possible (just tall enough to include the controls inside it, with no extra vertical space), set the height to 0. A section can never obscure controls it contains, and setting its height to 0 is the quick and easy way to make the section just big enough.

Determining Whether a Particular Section Exists

Access provides no simple way of determining whether a given section has been created on a form or report. The following function (from frmCreateQBF in CH8.MDB) demonstrates one method: it attempts to retrieve the height of the section in question. If this attempt doesn't trigger a run-time error, the section must have existed. You could, of course, extend this to work with any section.

```
Function isFooterSection(frm As Form)
    ' Returns TRUE if there currently is a footer
    ' section on the form, FALSE otherwise.
    Dim varTemp as Variant
```

```
      On Error Resume Next
      varTemp = frm.Section(SECTION_FOOTER).Height
      isFooterSection = (Err = 0)
End Function
```

Determining How Many Sections Exist

Forms are guaranteed to have no more than 5 sections but may have less. Reports may have up to 25 sections (5 standard, plus up to 10 groups with both a header and a footer). Access provides no built-in way to determine how many sections an object contains, and you may need to know this information. The following function demonstrates one solution to this problem: loop through the report, retrieving section heights and counting all the sections for which you don't trigger a run-time error. Since no report can contain more than 25 sections, that's as far as you need to look. You're also guaranteed that every form or report contains at least one section, Section(0) (the Detail section). You use that fact, in the function shown in Listing 9.2, to verify that the requested form is, in fact, loaded at the time you call the function.

> **NOTE** It was tempting, when trying to optimize this function, to make assumptions about the existence of sections. Unfortunately, all the sections besides the paired page header/footer and report header/footer are individually selectable. This means you really do need to check out every section from 0 through 25.

Listing 9.2

```
Function CountSections(rpt As Report)

' There are 5 fixed sections, plus a possible 10*2 for
' groupings.
Const MAX_SECTIONS = 25

    Dim intCount As Integer
    Dim intI As Integer
    Dim intHeight As Integer
```

```
On Error Resume Next
intCount = 0

' First check and make sure that the report exists.
' Checking the height of the detail section
' is as good a test as any!
intHeight = rpt.Section(0).Height

' If the report's not here, just quit,
' returning 0.
If Err <> 0 Then
    GoTo CountSectionsExit
End If

' Now loop through all the sections,
' counting up the ones that exist.
For intI = 0 To MAX_SECTIONS - 1
    Err = 0
    intHeight = rpt.Section(intI).Height
    If Err = 0 Then
        intCount = intCount + 1
    End If
Next intI
CountSectionsExit:
    CountSections = intCount
End Function
```

Creating New Report Sections

Besides the method included in Listing 9.1 (using DoMenuItem), Access doesn't provide a method for creating Page or Report Header or Footer sections. For creating group headers and footers, though, Access provides the CreateGroupLevel() function. Since sections beyond the Detail section and the page and report headers and footers are all manifestations of groupings, this function allows you to create all sections except the standard five (Detail, Report Header, Report Footer, Page Header, and Page Footer). This function takes four parameters:

intLevel = CreateGroupLevel(*strReport*, *strExpr*, *fHeader*, *fFooter*)

The following list describes the parameters:

- *strReport* is a string expression containing the name of the report on which to create the group.

- *strExpr* is the expression to use as the group-level expression.

- *fHeader* and *fFooter* indicate whether or not to create sections for the header and/or footer. Use True (–1) to create the section, False (0) otherwise.

The function returns an index into the array of group levels on your report. (See the next section for more information.) Access 2.0 supports no more than ten group levels, so a run-time error (2153), "Maximum number of group levels exceeded," occurs if you attempt to create more groups than that.

Accessing Group Levels

Access treats group levels in the same manner as sections: it maintains an array of group levels, which you access like this:

```
intVar = Reports!Report1.GroupLevel(0).SortOrder
```

Just as with the array of sections, you cannot access the GroupLevel array directly; rather, you must access one of its properties. The expression

```
varTemp = Reports!Report1.GroupLevel(0)
```

generates a compile-time error since you've attempted to retrieve information about the GroupLevel itself rather than one of its properties. Just as with sections, Access externalizes no information about the number of GroupLevels. To enumerate them you need a function similar to that found in Listing 9.2 to count or walk through the array of GroupLevels. See Listing 9.3 for such a function. Note that this function is much simpler than the similar one in Listing 9.2 since groups must be consecutively numbered. Removing a section bumps all the sections that follow it up the list. The functions in both Listing 9.2 and Listing 9.3 can be found in basSections in CH9.MDB.

Listing 9.3

```
' Count the number of groups in a report.
Function CountGroups (rpt As Report)

    Dim intI As Integer
    Dim intOrder As Integer
```

```
      On Error Resume Next
      For intI = 0 To MAX_GROUPS - 1
          intOrder = rpt.GroupLevel(intI).SortOrder
          If Err <> 0 Then
              Exit For
          End If
      Next intI
      CountGroups = intI
End Function
```

GroupLevel Properties

Just as with sections, you can access only properties of group levels, not the group levels themselves. To that end the GroupLevel array exposes these properties: GroupFooter, GroupHeader, GroupInterval, GroupOn, KeepTogether, SortOrder, and ControlSource. The following sections describe these parameters and their uses.

GroupHeader and GroupFooter Properties

The GroupHeader and GroupFooter properties tell you whether or not a specific group level shows a Header and/or Footer section. In either case the property returns True (−1) if the section exists and False (0) otherwise. The property is read-only from Access Basic, so you can't use it to create new Header/Footer sections. You must use the CreateGroupLevel() function mentioned earlier in this chapter to create new sections.

This code fragment determines whether or not there is a group header for group 0:

```
If Reports!rptTest1.GroupLevel(0).GroupHeader Then
    ' Do something
End If
```

The GroupOn Property

The GroupOn property specifies how data is to be grouped in a report. The values for the property depend on the datatype of the field or expression on which the GroupLevel is grouped. None of the settings except 0 (Each Value) is meaningful unless you have a group header or group footer selected for the group.

TIP
The Access on-line Help states that these values aren't available if you haven't created a group header or footer. That doesn't appear to be true; you can select a value for the GroupOn property other than 0 regardless of whether you've set up a header or footer. It just doesn't make any difference. Since you're not breaking the data into visible groups, it doesn't matter what you're grouping on. All the groupings look the same when you're not grouping.

Table 9.2 displays all the possible values for the GroupOn property.

TABLE 9.2: Possible Values for the GroupLevel's GroupOn Property

Setting	Value
Each Value	0
Prefix Characters	1
Year	2
Qtr	3
Month	4
Week	5
Day	6
Hour	7
Minute	8
Interval	9 (see the GroupInterval property)

The GroupInterval Property

The GroupInterval property defines an interval that is valid for the field or expression on which you're grouping. You can set the property only when the report is in Design view, and its value is dependent on the value of the GroupOn property. As with the GroupOn property, the Access documentation states that you must have created a group header or footer before setting the value of this property to anything other than its default value (1). Actually, you can change it if you like, but unless you have a group header or footer created, it just won't have any effect. If the GroupOn value is 0 (Each Value), the GroupInterval property is treated as if it were 1, no matter what its value.

Set the GroupInterval property to a value that makes sense for the field or expression on which you're grouping. If you're grouping on text the GroupInterval property defines how many characters on which to group. If you're grouping on dates and you set the GroupOn property to 5 (grouping on weeks), setting the GroupInterval property specifies how many weeks to group together.

The following example creates a group, grouping on a date/time field, breaking every five minutes:

```
Dim intLevel As Integer
Dim rpt As Report

intLevel = CreateGroupLevel("rptTest", "DateField", True, False)
Set rpt = Reports!rptTest
rpt.GroupLevel(intLevel).GroupOn = 8
rpt.GroupLevel(intLevel).GroupInterval = 5
```

The KeepTogether Property

The KeepTogether property specifies whether the data in the group level is to be kept together when printed. You can set the property only when the report is in Design view. As with the GroupOn property, the Access documentation states that you must have created a group header or footer before setting the value of this property to anything other than its default value (0). Actually, you can change it if you like, but unless you have a group header or footer created, it just won't have any effect. The possible values for the KeepTogether property are shown in Table 9.3.

TABLE 9.3: Possible Values for the GroupLevel's KeepTogether Property

Setting	Value	Description
No	0	Makes no attempt to keep the header, detail, and footer on the same page
Whole Group	1	Attempts to print the header, detail, and footer all on the same page
With First Detail	2	Attempts to print the header and the first detail row on the same page

Under some circumstances Access is forced to ignore this setting. For example, if you've specified "Whole Group " (1 in Access Basic), Access attempts to print the Group Header, Detail, and Footer sections on the same page. If that combination will not fit on a single page, Access is forced to ignore the setting and print it as best it can. The same concept can hold true if you've chosen "With First Detail" (2 in Access Basic). In that case Access attempts to place the group header and the first detail row on the same page. If the combination of the two is larger than a single page, all bets are off and Access prints as best it can.

As with all the rest of the GroupLevel properties, you set the KeepTogether property through the GroupLevel array. For example, the following code fragment asks Access to attempt to print all of GroupLevel 0 on the same page:

```
Reports!rptTest1.GroupLevel(0).KeepTogether = 2
```

NOTE   As useful as it would be, Access does not provide a method for preventing a group footer from being the first line on a page. There is no With Last Detail setting for footer sections, just With First Detail for headers.

The ControlSource and SortOrder Properties

The ControlSource property of a group level specifies the field or expression on which the group is to be grouped and/or sorted. By default the ControlSource property matches the value you used to create the group level and should be identical to the second parameter you passed to the CreateGroupLevel() function. Although you cannot use CreateGroupLevel() to alter the field on which a group is based, you can change the group's ControlSource property. Like all the rest of the group-level properties, you change the ControlSource and SortOrder properties only when the report is in Design view.

Use the SortOrder property to set the sorting order of rows in the Detail section of a group level. Table 9.4 shows the possible values for the SortOrder property.

You use the SortOrder property in combination with the ControlSource property to define the sorting characteristics of the group.

TABLE 9.4: Possible Values for the GroupLevel's SortOrder Property

Setting	Value	Description
Ascending	0	Sorts values in ascending order (0–9, A–Z) (default)
Descending	−1	Sorts values in descending order (9–0, Z–A)

Using the GroupLevel Properties

In your application you may need to change the GroupLevel properties of an existing report. For example, you might want to allow the user to choose the field that's displayed on your report, from a choice of two or more fields, and still group correctly on the chosen field. CH9.MDB contains such an example, frmSortOrder and rptPhoneBook. Figure 9.2 shows the form and report in action.

In this example frmSortOrder loads rptPhoneBook. Depending on which of the option buttons you've selected, it sets up the report to group on either CompanyName or ContactName, setting the header information appropriately. The code in Listing 9.4 does the work.

FIGURE 9.2:
Changing the sort order requires changing the GroupLevel's ControlSource property.

Listing 9.4

```
Sub cmdPreview_Click()
On Error GoTo Err_cmdPreview_Click

    Dim DocName As String

    DocName = "rptPhoneBook"
    Reports(DocName).Painting = False
    ' You must open the report in design mode to change its
    ' GroupLevel properties.
    DoCmd OpenReport DocName, A_DESIGN
    ResetSort DocName, IIf(Me!grpSort = 1, "Company Name",
    ➡ "Contact Name")
    DoCmd OpenReport DocName, A_PREVIEW

Exit_cmdPreview_Click:
    Reports(DocName).Painting = True
    Exit Sub

Err_cmdPreview_Click:
    MsgBox Error$
    Resume Exit_cmdPreview_Click

End Sub

Sub ResetSort(strDocName As String, strField As String)
    Dim rpt As Report
    Set rpt = Reports(strDocName)
    rpt!txtName.ControlSource = strField
    rpt!txtLetter.ControlSource = "=Left([" & strField & "], 1)"
    rpt.GroupLevel(0).ControlSource = strField
    rpt.GroupLevel(1).ControlSource = strField
    rpt.GroupLevel(0).SortOrder = Me!chkDescending
    rpt.GroupLevel(1).SortOrder = Me!chkDescending
End Sub

Sub Form_Open(Cancel As Integer)
    Dim intSortOrder As Integer
    Dim strControlSource As String
    Dim rpt As Report

    On Error Resume Next
    DoCmd OpenReport "rptPhoneBook", A_PREVIEW
    If Err <> 0 Then
```

```
        MsgBox "Unable to open 'rptPhoneBook'"
        Exit Sub
    End If

    ' Set the controls on the form to match the report
    ' itself, as it was last saved.
    Set rpt = Reports!rptPhoneBook
    intSortOrder = rpt.GroupLevel(0).SortOrder
    strControlSource = rpt.GroupLevel(0).ControlSource
    Me!grpSort = IIf(strControlSource = "Company Name", 1, 2)
    Me!chkDescending = intSortOrder
End Sub
```

CmdPreview_Click() either opens the report (if it isn't already open) or switches it to Design view and then calls the ResetSort procedure to change the grouping and sorting expressions and the sort order. In addition, Listing 9.4 includes the form's OnOpen code, which not only opens the report but retrieves the current Group-Level settings from the report so it can set its own controls accordingly.

NOTE   Since the example changes properties of the report in Design view, Access prompts you to save changes when you close the report.

Events of Reports and Their Sections

As in all the other areas of Access, it's the events that drive the application. As your users interact with Access' user interface, it's up to your application to react to the events that Access fires off. Reports themselves support only load/unload events (Open, Activate, Close, Deactivate, and Error), but their sections react to events that occur as Access prints each record.

Report Events

Table 9.5 lists the events that reports can initiate. As indicated in the table, when you open a report, Access fires off the Open and then the Activate event. When you close the report Access executes the Close and then the Deactivate event.

TABLE 9.5: Report Event Properties

Event	Event Property	Occurs When
Open	OnOpen	You open a report but before the report starts printing or becomes visible (before the Activate event)
Activate	OnActivate	The report becomes the active window or starts printing (after the Open event)
Deactivate	OnDeactivate	You move to another Access window or close the report (after the Close event)
Close	OnClose	You close the report (before the Deactivate event)
Error	OnError	A Microsoft Access Jet engine error occurs while the report has the focus

Activation versus Deactivation

When you switch from one report to another (in preview mode), the report you're switching away from executes its Deactivate event before the new report executes its Activate event. If you switch to any other Access window from a report, the report's Deactivate event still executes. If you switch to a different application or to a popup window within Access, the Deactivate event does not fire; that is, the Deactivate event fires off only when you switch to another window whose parent is also the Access MDI Client window. (See Chapter 8 for more information on the MDI Client window.) This makes sense; the main reason you use the OnActivate/OnDeactivate events is to set up menus and toolbars for the specific report, as opposed to any other Access window. Since popup Access windows do not have their own menus or toolbars, you don't need to execute the event code.

Using the Open and Activate Events

When Access first opens a report, it runs the code attached to the report's Open event before it runs the query that supplies the data for the report. Given this fact you can supply parameters to that query from the report's Open event. You might, for example, pop up a form that requests starting and ending dates or any other information your query might need. To see this in action, open rptPhoneBookParam in CH9.MDB. (See Figure 9.3, although this figure is somewhat misleading—the form and the report would never actually be visible at the same time.)

FIGURE 9.3:
The report's OnOpen event loads the parameter-gathering form, which, in turn, provides a parameter for the report's underlying query.

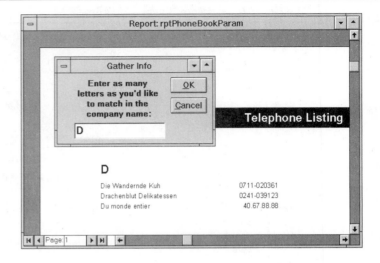

In this example rptPhoneBookParam's Open event executes the code found in Listing 9.5.

Listing 9.5

```
Sub Report_Open(Cancel As Integer)

    ' Set the global variable.
    strForm = "frmParam"

    DoCmd OpenForm strForm, , , , , A_DIALOG
    ' Set the cancel flag if the parameter form isn't
    ' still open.
    Cancel = Not IsFormOpen(strForm)
End Sub

Sub Report_Activate()
    If isFormOpen(strForm) Then
        DoCmd Close A_FORM, strForm
    End If
End Sub
```

This code first opens frmParam modally so that code execution halts until you either hide or close the form. Just as described in Chapter 8, the OK button hides the form and the Cancel button closes the form altogether. On return from the OpenForm action, the code checks to see whether the form is still open, and if not it uses the Cancel parameter to indicate that Access should abort the attempt to load the report.

Once Access has executed the Open event, it can go ahead and load the data that's going to populate the report. Since Access wouldn't be at this point for this report unless the parameter-providing form were still open (but hidden), you're assured that Access will be able to find the form it needs in order to supply the parameter for qryCustomerNameParam. The query uses the expression

```
Like Forms!frmParam!txtName & "*"
```

to filter its rows.

Finally, once the report executes its Activate event, the query no longer needs the form, and the code attached to the Activate event can close the form.

Avoiding Empty Reports

There's nothing stopping you from choosing a filter for a report that returns no rows at all. In that case the report prints "#Error" in the Detail section. If you want to avoid this problem, you can add code to the Open event of your report that checks the number of rows in the report's underlying record source and sets the Cancel flag if there is none. Unfortunately, the only realistic way to solve this problem involves using DCount(), which means that if there is a large number of rows returned, it could slow down your report's startup.

```
If DCount("*", Me.RecordSource) = 0 Then
    Cancel = True
End If
```

Using the Error Event

Access triggers a report's Error event when an error occurs in the Access Jet engine while the report is either formatting or printing. Although this eventuality is less likely with a report than it might be for a form, it still can occur. For example, if a table is opened exclusively by some user or a report is bound to a recordset that doesn't exist, Access triggers this error.

As with most other form and report events, you're far better off using the built-in module (CBF) to handle the Error event. In this case Access provides two parameters to your event handler, allowing you functionality you'd be missing if you called a macro or an external routine to handle this event. By using CBF you can control how Access handles the error once you've investigated it.

When an error occurs during the formatting or printing of your report, Access calls the code attached to the Error event, passing two parameters:

- **DataErr:** An integer containing the same value as the Err() function would return. You can use the DataErr value with the Error$() function to display the exact error message matching the current error condition.

- **Response:** An integer into which you can place a value telling Access what it should do once your event handler has finished its work. The following table lists the possible values for Response:

Constant	Description
DATA_ERRCONTINUE	Access ignores the error and continues without displaying its normal error message. If you've displayed your own message, choose this option
DATA_ERRDISPLAY	Access displays its error message (default)

Listing 9.6 shows a simple error-handling routine. Although this example does little more than display a message box in response to the error that can occur when a user has removed the query or table to which a report has been bound, it should provide a starting place for your own error handlers.

NOTE

The Error$0 function won't always do exactly what you want. Many of the error messages include replaceable parameters (usually stored internally as the | character). When Access displays these messages itself, it replaces the | with the name of an appropriate object. The example in Listing 9.6 traps such an error, and it must handle the message box text itself.

Listing 9.6

```
Sub Report_Error(DataErr As Integer, Response As Integer)

Const ERR_NO_RECORD_SOURCE = 2580

    Select Case DataErr
        Case ERR_NO_RECORD_SOURCE
            MsgBox "This report is bound to a table or query
            ➡ that doesn't exist: '" & Me.RecordSource & "'"
        Case Else
            MsgBox Error$(DataErr)
    End Select
    Response = DATA_ERRCONTINUE
End Sub
```

Section Events

Just as report events focus mainly on loading and unloading the report itself and on setting up the overall data that will populate the report, section events deal with the actual formatting and printing of that data. The following table lists the three events that apply to report sections:

Event	Event Property	Occurs When
Format	OnFormat	Access has selected the data to go in this section but before it formats or prints the data
Print	OnPrint	Access has formatted the data for printing (or previewing) but before it prints or shows the data

Event	Event Property	Occurs When
Retreat	OnRetreat	Access needs to move to a previous section while formatting the report

The Format Event

Access executes the code attached to a section's OnFormat property once it has selected the data to be printed in the section but before it actually prints it. This allows you to alter the layout of the report or to perform calculations based on the data in the section at this particular time.

For a report's Detail section Access calls your code just before it actually lays out the data to be printed. Your code has access to the data in the current row and can react to that data, perhaps making certain controls visible or invisible. See the example in the section "Altering Your Report's Layout Programmatically" later in this chapter for more information on this technique.

For group headers the Format event occurs for each new group. Within the event procedure, your code has access to data in the group header and in the first row of data in the group. For group footers the event occurs for each new group, and your code has access to data in the group footer and in the last row of data in the group. For an example of using this information, see the "Sales Report" example later in this chapter.

For actions that don't affect the page layout or for calculations that absolutely must not occur until the section is printed, use the Print event. For example, if you're calculating a running total, place the calculation in the Print event since this avoids any ambiguities about when or whether the section actually printed.

If you've placed code for the Format event in the report's code module, Access passes you two parameters: FormatCount and Cancel. The FormatCount value corresponds to the section's FormatCount property. The Cancel parameter allows you to cancel the formatting of the current section and move on to the next by setting its value to True. This parameter corresponds to using

```
DoCmd CancelEvent
```

from within your code.

The Print Event

Access executes the code attached to a section's OnPrint property once it has formatted the data to be printed in the section but before it actually prints it. For a report's Detail section, Access calls your code just before it actually prints the data. Your code has access to the data in the current row. For group headers the Print event occurs for each new group. Within the event procedure, your code has access to data in the group header and in the first row of data in the group. For group footers the event occurs for each new group, and your code has access to data in the group footer and in the last row of data in the group.

For actions that require changing the report's layout, use the Format event. Once you've reached the Print event, it's too late to change the report's layout.

Just as it does for the Format event, Access passes two parameters to your code for the Print event if you place your code in the report's module. The PrintCount parameter corresponds to the section's PrintCount property. The Cancel parameter allows you to cancel the printing of the current section and move on to the next by setting its value to True. This parameter corresponds to using

```
DoCmd CancelEvent
```

from within your code.

The Retreat Event

Sometimes Access needs to move back to a previous section while it's formatting your report. For example, if your group level's KeepTogether property is set to "With First Detail Row", Access formats the group header and then the first row and checks to make sure they'll both fit in the space available on the current page. Once it has formatted the two, it retreats from those two sections, executing the Retreat event for each. Then it again formats the sections and finally prints them.

If you've made any changes during the Format event, you may wish to undo them during the Retreat event. Since you really can't know during the Retreat event whether the current section will actually be printed on the current page, you should undo any layout changes made during the Format event.

Counting rows from the Format event makes a very simple example. If you include code attached to a section's Format event procedure that increments a counter for each row, include code in the Retreat event that decrements the counter. Otherwise the Format event may be fired multiple times for a given row, and the count will be incorrect. (Of course, there are several other ways to take care of this problem, including checking the FormatCount property. This example is intended only to explain why you might need to use the Retreat event.)

TIP

Access triggers the Retreat event in two very predictable places, among others. If you've created a group and set its KeepTogether property to "With First Detail", Access triggers the Format event, then the Retreat event, and then the Format and Print events for the first row in the group as it attempts to fit the header and the first row on the same page. The same concept applies to groups in which you've set the KeepTogether property to "All Rows", in which case Access formats each row, retreats from each row, and then formats the ones that will fit on the current page. Although there are many other circumstances in which Access will fire off the Retreat event, you can be assured that setting the group's KeepTogether property will force it.

Section Design-Time Properties

Report sections maintain a set of properties different from any other Access objects. Table 9.6 lists those properties, and the following sections discuss some of them and give examples and hints for their use in designing your reports. Each of the properties in Table 9.6 applies to all report sections except the Page Header and Footer.

TABLE 9.6: Report Section Properties

Property	Description	Settings
CanGrow	Determines whether the size of a section will increase vertically so Access can print all its data	Yes (−1); No (0)
CanShrink	Determines whether the size of a section will shrink vertically to avoid wasting space if there is no more data to print	Yes (−1);No (0)

TABLE 9.6: Report Section Properties (continued)

Property	Description	Settings
NewRowOrCol	Specifies whether Access always starts printing a section in a multicolumn layout at the start of a new row (Horizontal layout) or column (Vertical Layout)	None (0); Before Section (1); After Section (2); Before & After (3)
ForceNewPage	Determines whether Access prints a section on the current page or at the top of a new page	None (0); Before Section (1); After Section(2); Before & After (3)
KeepTogether	Determines whether Access attempts to print an entire section on a single page	Yes (−1); No (0)

The CanGrow/CanShrink Properties

Setting either the CanGrow or CanShrink property causes other controls on the report to move vertically to adjust for changes in the sections' heights. Sections can grow or shrink only across their whole widths, so they must account for the maximum size needed within themselves. If you have a text box horizontally aligned with an OLE object that cannot shrink, the section will not shrink, no matter how little text there is in the text box. If you set a control's CanGrow property to Yes, Access sets the CanGrow property for the control's section to Yes, also. You can override this by changing the section's CanGrow property back to No if you need to do so.

Why CanShrink Doesn't and CanGrow Won't

Microsoft Product Support Services suggests the following reasons why the CanGrow and CanShrink properties might not always do what you think they ought:

- Overlapping controls will not shrink, even when you've set the CanShrink property to Yes. If two controls touch at all, even by the smallest amount, they won't grow or shrink correctly.

- Controls shrink line by line (vertically). This means, for example, that if there is a group of controls placed on the left side of a page and a large control (for example, an OLE picture) on the right side of the page, the controls on the left side will not shrink unless the picture is blank and hidden.

- Space between controls is not affected by the CanShrink or CanGrow property.

- Controls located in the page header or page footer will grow to, at most, the height of the section. Neither the Header nor the Footer section itself can grow or shrink.

> **TIP**
>
> Under some circumstances you may find that no matter what you do, your controls just will not grow or shrink correctly. If all else fails, you might try deleting and re-creating those particular controls. There have been cases reported in which this has helped.

The NewRowOrCol Property

The NewRowOrCol property applies only when your report uses multiple columns for its display. When you choose to use multiple columns in the Print Setup dialog (selecting the More options button), you can select either Horizontal or Vertical layout for your items. Choosing Vertical prints items down the first column, then down the second, and so on. Choosing Horizontal prints across the first row, in the first column, the second column, and so on, and then goes on to the second row, printing in each column. You might use the Vertical layout for printing phone book listings and the Horizontal layout for printing mailing labels.

The NewRowOrCol property allows you to maintain fine control over how the Detail section of your report prints when it's using multiple columns. Table 9.7 describes each of the property's possible settings and how you can use them to control the layout of your report.

You'll want to experiment with the NewRowOrCol property if you're working with multicolumn reports. You can find an example of its use in the section "Company, Contacts, and Hardware" later in this chapter.

TABLE 9.7: NewRowOrCol Property Settings

Setting	Value	Description
None	0	Row and column breaks occur naturally, based on the settings in the Print Setup dialog and on the layout of the current page so far (default)
Before Section	1	The current section is printed in a new row or column. The next section is printed in the same row or column
After Section	2	The current section is printed in the same row or column as the previous section. The next section is printed in a new row or column
Before & After	3	The current section is printed in a new row or column. The next section is also printed starting in a new row or column

The ForceNewPage Property

The ForceNewPage property allows you to control page breaks in relation to your report sections. Table 9.8 details the four options that are available for this property. Since you can control this option while the report is printing, you can, for example, decide, based on a piece of data in a particular row, to start the section printing on a new page. You can accomplish the same effect, although not quite as elegantly, by including a Page Break control on your report and setting its Visible property to Yes or No, depending on the data in the current row.

TABLE 9.8: ForceNewPage Property Settings

Setting	Value	Description
None	0	Access starts printing the current section on the current page (default)
Before Section	1	Access starts printing the current section at the top of a new page
After Section	2	Access starts printing the next section at the top of a new page
Before & After	3	Access starts printing the current section at the top of a new page and prints the next section starting on a new page, too

The KeepTogether Property

The KeepTogether property simply asks Access to try to print a given section all on one page. If it won't fit on the current page, Access starts a new page and tries printing it there. Of course, if it can't fit on one page, Access must continue printing on the next page, no matter how the property is set.

The KeepTogether property for sections is much simpler than the KeepTogether property for groups. The Section property doesn't attempt to keep together different sections, as does the GroupLevel property. It just refers to the "togetherness" of each individual section.

Section Run-Time Properties

Some section events occur only while Access is formatting or printing the report (for example, the Format and Print events, discussed earlier in this chapter). Table 9.9 lists the run-time properties, and the following sections present more information and suggestions for their effective use.

TABLE 9.9: Section Run-Time Properties

Property	Description	Settings
MoveLayout	Specifies whether Access should move to the next printing location on the page	True (−1): the section's Left and Top properties are advanced to the next print location; False (0): the Left and Top properties are unchanged
NextRecord	Specifies whether a section should advance to the next record	True: advance to the next record; False: stay on the same record
PrintSection	Specifies whether a section should be printed	True: the section is printed; False: the section isn't printed
FormatCount	Indicates the number of times the OnFormat event has occurred for the current section	Read-only while the report is being formatted; not available in design mode
PrintCount	Indicates the number of times the OnPrint event has occurred for the current section	Read-only while the report is printing; not available in design mode

MoveLayout, NextRecord, and PrintSection Properties

The MoveLayout, NextRecord, and PrintSection properties, when combined, control exactly how Access moves from row to row in the underlying data and whether or not the current row will be printed. Table 9.10 presents all the possible combinations of the three properties and how they interact. By combining these three layout properties, you'll have a great deal of flexibility in how you lay out your reports. The examples "Printing Multiple Labels" and "Inserting Blank Lines" later in this chapter demonstrate the use of these properties.

TABLE 9.10: The Section Run-Time Properties and Their Interactions

MoveLayout	NextRecord	PrintSection	Results
True	True	True	Move to the next print location, move to the next row, and then print the row (default)
True	True	False	Move to a new row and move to the next print location, but don't print the row (leaves a blank space where the row would have printed)
True	False	True	Move to the next print location, stay on the same row, and print the data
True	False	False	Move to the next print location, but don't skip a row and don't print any data. This effectively leaves a blank space on the paper without moving to a new row in the data
False	True	True	Don't move the print location, but print the next row right on top of the previous one. This allows you to overlay one row of data on another
False	True	False	Don't move the print location and don't print anything, but skip a row in the data. This allows you to skip a row without leaving any blank space on the page
False	False	True	Not allowed
False	False	False	Not allowed

The FormatCount Property

Access increments a section's FormatCount property each time it executes the Format event for that section. Once it moves to the next section, it resets the FormatCount property to 1.

In some circumstances Access must format a section more than once. For example, as Access reaches the end of a page, it's possible that the current section won't fit. Access attempts to format the section and, if it doesn't fit, formats it again on the next page. It calls the OnFormat event code twice, first with a FormatCount property of 1 and then with a FormatCount property of 2.

If you're performing some calculation or action from your OnFormat event code, pay careful attention to the FormatCount value. For example, you want to increment counters only if the FormatCount value is 1. If you normally take an action in the OnFormat event code, you must skip the action if the FormatCount value is greater than 1.

The PrintCount Property

Access increments a section's PrintCount property each time it executes the Print event for that section. Once it moves on the next section, it resets the PrintCount property to 0.

Access attempts to print a section more than once when that section spans more than one page. For example, if a section requires more than a single page for its output, Access calls the OnPrint event code once for each page, incrementing the PrintCount property. If you're attempting to maintain running totals, adding in an amount each time a report section prints, you need to check the PrintCount property and add in the value only once. The following code might be used in a section's OnPrint event code. (If you place the code in the report's attached module, Access passes the PrintCount property to the code as a parameter. If not, you need to refer to the PrintCount property using the standard syntax.)

```
If PrintCount = 1 Then
    lngRunningTotal = lngRunningTotal + Me!OrderAmount
End If
```

Examples Using Report and Section Events and Properties

The following sections contain examples and solutions to some common problems. Each example here refers to a specific report or form in CH9.MDB. In each case you might find it useful to open the specific report in design mode and follow along with the description you find here. Change properties and see what happens. Experimentation is the best way to find out how each of the report and section properties affects the printed output.

Printing Multiple Labels

Printing multiple labels based on a count stored with the label data makes a perfect example of the use of the MoveLayout, NextRecord, and PrintSection properties. In this example the user has stored, in the LabelCount column of a table, the number of copies of the row to be printed. Listing 9.7, which would be attached to the On-Print property of the Detail section containing the label, shows the code necessary to print the correct number of labels. (See rptMultiLabel in CH9.MDB to test this example.) Given the data shown in Figure 9.4, the design surface shown in Figure 9.5 creates the labels shown in Figure 9.6.

FIGURE 9.4:

Each row in the table contains a column indicating the number of labels to be printed.

FIGURE 9.5:

The report design includes a visible control containing the LabelCount column. In your labels, this could be made invisible.

FIGURE 9.6:
The labels will contain as many multiples as you requested in your table.

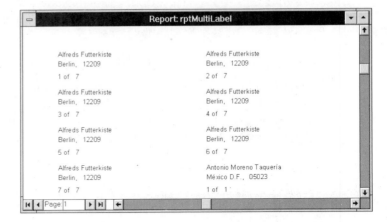

Listing 9.7

```
Sub Detail1_Print(Cancel As Integer, PrintCount As Integer)
    If Me!txtLabelCount = 0 Then
        Me.NextRecord = True
        Me.MoveLayout = False
        Me.PrintSection = False
    Else
        If PrintCount < Me!txtLabelCount Then
            Me.NextRecord = False
        End If
    End If
End Sub
```

To make this technique work you must create a text box on your report for the field that contains the count. You can make it invisible, but it has to be on the report for the code to be able to get to it. (In this example the text box control is named txtLabelCount.) Unlike forms, reports must contain a control bound to any column they reference. Forms can reference any column in the underlying data without actually having to contain a control bound to that field.

This example does its work quite simply. If the user has requested no labels at all for the particular row, the code tells Access to move to the next record (NextRecord = True) but not to move to the next print position (MoveLayout = False) and not to print anything at all (PrintSection = False). Otherwise, if the PrintCount value is less than the number of labels to be printed (Me!txtLabelCount), don't move to the next record (NextRecord = False), but use the default value for the other properties. This causes Access to print the data from the current row and move to the next print location.

Although you might be tempted to attach this code to the OnFormat event, it won't work correctly. Since Access must decide at format time how to lay out the labels on the page, the FormatCount value to which the OnFormat event has access won't always be correct, especially when you've filled a page without completing the run of a particular row.

Handling Odd and Even Pages

Perhaps you print your reports double sided (either on a duplex printer or by using a printing utility such as *Click*Book, from BookMaker Corporation). In general, given that the first page of a document prints on the front of a piece of paper, odd-numbered pages appear on the right and even-numbered pages appear on the left when you bind the document. Quite often, in published documents, you'll want the page numbers to appear flush right on odd-numbered pages and flush left for even-numbered pages. Although Access doesn't provide a built-in method to accomplish this, it's actually quite easy to do.

To alternate left and right alignment for alternating pages, take these two steps:

1. Create your Page Footer control so that it spans the entire width of your report (see Figure 9.7). Enter the ControlSource value you'd like.

2. Attach the code in Listing 9.8 to the Format event of the Page Footer section. This handles setting the TextAlign property for the Footer section as each page gets printed. For every page, the code checks the page number MOD 2 (the remainder when you divide the page number by 2, which is 0 for even pages and 1 for odd pages). It sets the TextAlign property to ALIGN_RIGHT for odd pages and ALIGN_LEFT for even pages.

FIGURE 9.7:

Your footer can alternate alignments easily if it spans the entire page.

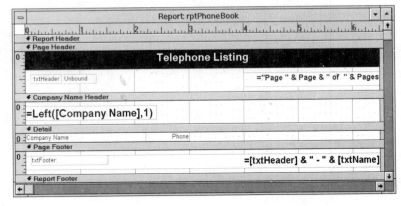

Listing 9.8

```
Sub PageFooter2_Format(Cancel As Integer, FormatCount
➦ As Integer)

Const ALIGN_LEFT = 1
Const ALIGN_RIGHT = 3

    Me!txtFooter.TextAlign = IIf(Me.Page Mod 2 <> 0,
    ➦ ALIGN_RIGHT, ALIGN_LEFT)
End Sub
```

Controlling the Starting Page Number

Every report supports a read/write property that indicates and/or sets the current page number. By inspecting the Page property of the current report, you can determine which page is currently active. You can also set the Page property, effectively resetting Access' understanding of the current page number. You could, if you had a reason to, set the Page property to 1 in the page header's Format event. Then, every time Access formatted a page header (once per page), it would reset the report's Page property to 1.

A more useful trick involving the Page property is the ability to set the starting page number to some value other than 1. This is especially useful if you need to chain reports or number chapters with a page number including the chapter number, with each chapter starting at page 1. Your only issue here is deciding when to reset the page number. If you want to print an entire report, starting at a particular page number, set the Page property in the report header's Format event. If you need to set the Page property based on data that could occur at the top of any given page, set the value in the page header's Format event.

For an example, see rptSales in CH9.MDB. This report sets the first page number to 6 in the report header's Format event. Numbers increase consecutively from there. The code to make this change is minimal, of course:

```
Sub ReportHeader0_Format(Cancel As Integer,
➡ FormatCount As Integer)
    Me.Page = 6
End Sub
```

Since the report's Open event occurs before any of the formatting events, you could also use that hook to retrieve the starting page number, storing it in a variable, and then apply that variable to the Page property in the report header's Format event. (We discuss the other interesting features of this report, including the alternate gray bars, in the section "Sales Report" later in this chapter.)

Numbering Items on a Report

Access makes it simple to number rows on a report. By changing two properties of a text box, you can create a row counter that will count rows either over the total report or just within a group. The report rptNumberRows in CH9.MDB demonstrates both types of row counters, as you can see in Figure 9.8.

To create a row counter on a report, set a text box's properties as follows:

Property	Setting
RunningSum	Over Group (1) or Over All (2)
ControlSource	=1

FIGURE 9.8:

Use the RunningSum property to create a row counter in a report.

Numbering Rows Report

A. 1	1	Ana Trujillo Emparedados y helados	L. 6	46	LILA-Supermercado
A. 2	2	Antonio Moreno Taquería	L. 7	47	LINO-Delicateses
A. 3	3	Around the Horn	L. 8	48	Lonesome Pine Restaurant
A. 4	4	Alfreds Futterkiste	L. 9	49	Lehmanns Marktstand
B. 1	5	Berglunds snabbköp	M. 1	50	Magazzini Alimentari Riuniti
B. 2	6	Blauer See Delikatessen	M. 2	51	Maison Dewey
B. 3	7	Blondel père et fils	M. 3	52	Mère Paillarde
B. 4	8	Bólido Comidas preparadas	M. 4	53	Morgenstern Gesundkost
B. 5	9	Bon app'	N. 1	54	North/South
B. 6	10	Bottom-Dollar Markets	O. 1	55	Ottilies Käseladen
B. 7	11	B's Beverages	O. 2	56	Océano Atlántico Ltda.
C. 1	12	Cactus Comidas para llevar	O. 3	57	Old World Delicatessen
C. 2	13	Consolidated Holdings	P. 1	58	Princesa Isabel Vinhos
C. 3	14	Comércio Mineiro	P. 2	59	Piccolo und mehr
C. 4	15	Centro comercial Moctezuma	P. 3	60	Paris spécialités
C. 5	16	Chop-suey Chinese	P. 4	61	Pericles Comidas clásicas
D. 1	17	Drachenblut Delikatessen	Q. 1	62	Que Delícia
D. 2	18	Du monde entier	Q. 2	63	Queen Cozinha
D. 3	19	Die Wandernde Kuh	Q. 3	64	QUICK-Stop
E. 1	20	Eastern Connection	R. 1	65	Ricardo Adocicados
E. 2	21	Ernst Handel	R. 2	66	Richter Supermarkt
F. 1	22	France restauration	R. 3	67	Romero y tomillo
F. 2	23	Folies gourmandes	R. 4	68	Rattlesnake Canyon Grocery
F. 3	24	Furia Bacalhau e Frutos do Mar	R. 5	69	Rancho grande
F. 4	25	Franchi S.p.A.	R. 6	70	Reggiani Caseifici
F. 5	26	Folk och fä HB	S. 1	71	Save-a-lot Markets
F. 6	27	Familia Arquibaldo	S. 2	72	Seven Seas Imports
F. 7	28	FISSA Fabrica Inter. Salchichas S.A.	S. 3	73	Simons bistro
F. 8	29	Frankenversand	S. 4	74	Spécialités du monde
G. 1	30	Galería del gastrónomo	S. 5	75	Split Rail Beer & Ale
G. 2	31	Godos Cocina Típica	S. 6	76	Suprêmes délices
G. 3	32	Gourmet Lanchonetes	S. 7	77	Santé Gourmet
G. 4	33	Great Lakes Food Market	T. 1	78	Toms Spezialitäten
G. 5	34	GROSELLA-Restaurante	T. 2	79	Trail's Head Gourmet Provisioners
H. 1	35	HILARIÓN-Abastos	T. 3	80	Tortuga Restaurante
H. 2	36	Hungry Coyote Import Store	T. 4	81	The Cracker Box
H. 3	37	Hanari Carnes	T. 5	82	The Big Cheese
H. 4	38	Hungry Owl All-Night Grocers	T. 6	83	Tradição Hipermercados
I. 1	39	Island Trading	V. 1	84	Vaffeljernet
K. 1	40	Königlich Essen	V. 2	85	Victuailles en stock
L. 1	41	Let's Stop N Shop	V. 3	86	Vins et alcools Chevalier
L. 2	42	La corne d'abondance	W. 1	87	Wolski Zajazd
L. 3	43	La maison d'Asie	W. 2	88	Wartian Herkku
L. 4	44	Laughing Bacchus Wine Cellars	W. 3	89	Wellington Importadora
L. 5	45	Lazy K Kountry Store	W. 4	90	White Clover Markets
			W. 5	91	Wilman Kala

This technique takes advantage of the fact that setting the RunningSum property causes the current row's value to be the sum of all the previous rows' values plus the current row's value. Since the current row's value in this case is always 1, the running sum just increments by 1. You could, of course, place some other value in the ControlSource property to force it to increment by a different value.

You can examine rptNumberRows to see how it works, but the most important setting is that for the RunningSum property of the text boxes. If set to Over Group, it continues to sum only over the current group. Everytime Access starts a new group, its value gets reset to 0. If set to Over All, the value gets reset only at the beginning of the report and continues to increment for the rest of the report.

Inserting Blank Lines

If your report consists of a long list of values, you may want to insert a blank line at regular intervals. Figure 9.9 shows such a report, with a blank line inserted after each group of five rows.

This technique again involves the NextRecord and PrintSection properties. The code in Listing 9.9 does the work for you, and you can copy it into any of your own report's modules (look in rptBlankEveryNLines in CH9.MDB). It does its work by counting up the lines that have been printed so far on each page; when the number is an even multiple of the group size plus 1 (that is, if you're breaking after five lines, you'll be looking for lines that are a multiple of 6), the report skips to the next print location but does not move to the next record (NextRecord = False) and doesn't print anything (PrintSection = False). This inserts a blank row.

> **NOTE**
>
> The HandleLine subroutine checks each control's Visible property before it sets it visible or invisible. Although this may seem redundant, it might actually speed up the report. Since checking a control's state is faster than actually setting a property for the control, checking first saves some property setting if the control is already in the right state.

HandleLine uses the MOD operator to figure out when to insert a blank line. If you haven't used the MOD operator, this might appear confusing. The MOD operator returns the remainder you get when you divide the first operand by the second. That is, if you have

```
? 5 MOD 2
```

FIGURE 9.9:

Insert a blank line to separate large groups into readable chunks.

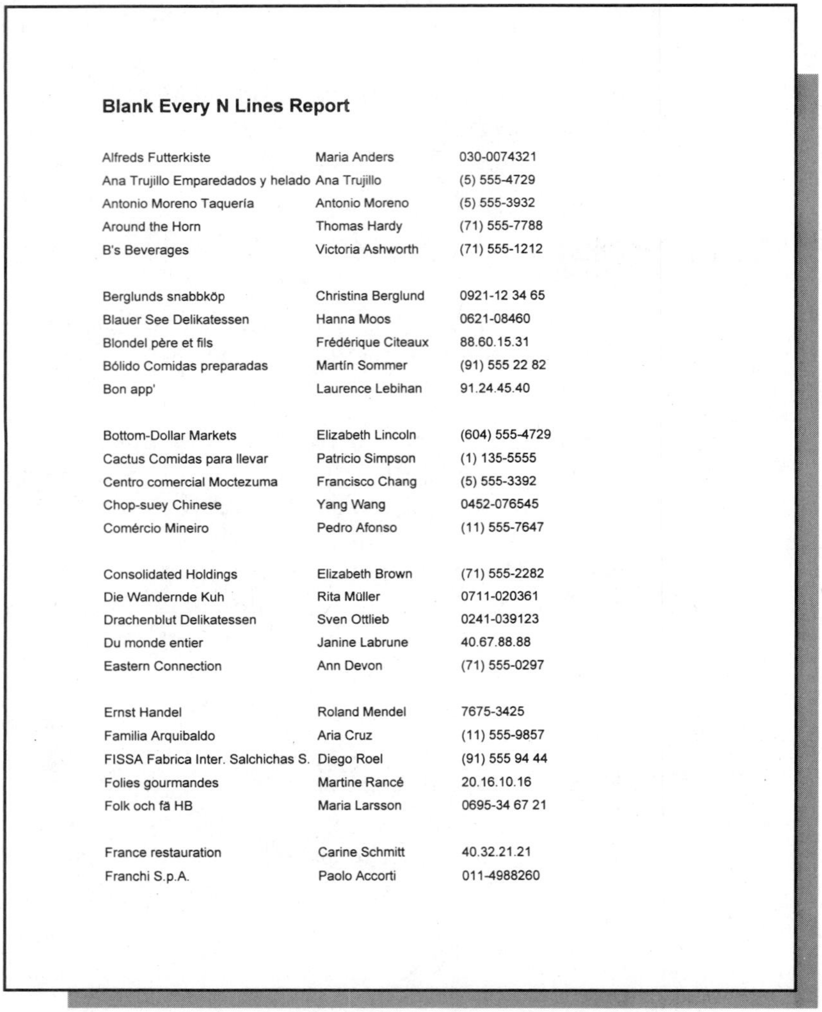

Blank Every N Lines Report

Alfreds Futterkiste	Maria Anders	030-0074321
Ana Trujillo Emparedados y helado	Ana Trujillo	(5) 555-4729
Antonio Moreno Taquería	Antonio Moreno	(5) 555-3932
Around the Horn	Thomas Hardy	(71) 555-7788
B's Beverages	Victoria Ashworth	(71) 555-1212
Berglunds snabbköp	Christina Berglund	0921-12 34 65
Blauer See Delikatessen	Hanna Moos	0621-08460
Blondel père et fils	Frédérique Citeaux	88.60.15.31
Bólido Comidas preparadas	Martín Sommer	(91) 555 22 82
Bon app'	Laurence Lebihan	91.24.45.40
Bottom-Dollar Markets	Elizabeth Lincoln	(604) 555-4729
Cactus Comidas para llevar	Patricio Simpson	(1) 135-5555
Centro comercial Moctezuma	Francisco Chang	(5) 555-3392
Chop-suey Chinese	Yang Wang	0452-076545
Comércio Mineiro	Pedro Afonso	(11) 555-7647
Consolidated Holdings	Elizabeth Brown	(71) 555-2282
Die Wandernde Kuh	Rita Müller	0711-020361
Drachenblut Delikatessen	Sven Ottlieb	0241-039123
Du monde entier	Janine Labrune	40.67.88.88
Eastern Connection	Ann Devon	(71) 555-0297
Ernst Handel	Roland Mendel	7675-3425
Familia Arquibaldo	Aria Cruz	(11) 555-9857
FISSA Fabrica Inter. Salchichas S.	Diego Roel	(91) 555 94 44
Folies gourmandes	Martine Rancé	20.16.10.16
Folk och fä HB	Maria Larsson	0695-34 67 21
France restauration	Carine Schmitt	40.32.21.21
Franchi S.p.A.	Paolo Accorti	011-4988260

the result would be 1 since the remainder when you divide 5 by 2 is 1. The MOD operator is most useful for determining whether one number is a multiple of another since if it is, the result will be 0. To tell whether a number is even, you can use the expression

```
If x MOD 2 = 0 Then ...
```

Listing 9.9

```
Sub HandleLine()
    Dim fShowLine As Integer
    Dim intI As Integer
    Dim ctl As Control

Const BREAK_COUNT = 5

    fShowLine = ((intLineCount Mod (BREAK_COUNT + 1)) <> 0)

    For intI = 0 To Me.Count - 1
        ' Walk through all the controls
        ' in the detail section, setting
        ' them all either visible or invisible.
        Set ctl = Me(intI)
        If ctl.Section = 0 Then
            ' It's always faster to check first, then
            ' set a property, since there's nothing slower
            ' than setting a property.
            If ctl.Visible <> fShowLine Then
                ctl.Visible = fShowLine
            End If
        End If
    Next intI

    If Not fShowLine Then
        ' If you're not showing the current
        ' row, then don't move to the next record,
        ' and don't print the section.
        Me.NextRecord = False
        Me.PrintSection = False
        intLineCount = 0
    End If
    intLineCount = intLineCount + 1
End Sub
```

> **TIP**
>
> If you just want to insert a blank line between your groups and don't care about breaking specific-sized groups, you can set up a group footer that's blank (with its CanShrink property set to No). Then, when the group breaks, Access inserts a blank space between groups.

Some Simple Sample Reports

The following three reports show off some of the effects various properties can make on the printed output of an Access report. Each was designed to show off specific techniques.

- **Sales report:** Alternating gray bars, displaying report properties on the report, creating page totals
- **Telephone book:** Using multiple columns with full-page-width title, section titles, and footer page-range listing
- **Companies, contacts, and hardware:** Using multiple subreports and report properties to link separate reports

The Sales Report

The sales report (see Figure 9.10) lists companies in reverse order of sales and, within sets of equal sales, in alphabetical order by company name. For visibility, every other line is printed in gray, and each page contains a total sales of the companies printed on that page.

We'll take this in steps:

1. Create the basic report, with no gray and no totals.
2. Add the page totals (using the OnPrint event).
3. Add the alternate gray lines (using the OnFormat event).

FIGURE 9.10:

Company names in decreasing order of sales, with added alternate gray bars

COMPUTER SURVEY DATA

COMPANY NAMES IN DECREASING ORDER OF REVENUE
(Actual values have been altered to protect confidentiality)

COMPANY NAME	SALES (In Millions of $'s)
Bottom-Dollar Markets	4654
QUICK-Stop	675
Old World Delicatessen	454
Berglunds snabbköp	434
Galería del gastrónomo	356
GROSELLA-Restaurante	356
Hungry Coyote Import Store	356
Split Rail Beer & Ale	356
North/South	68
Morgenstern Gesundkost	57
Mère Paillarde	56
Océano Atlántico Ltda.	56
Suprêmes délices	56
Trail's Head Gourmet Provisioners	56
Bon app'	54
Que Delícia	54
Spécialités du monde	54
La maison d'Asie	46
B's Beverages	45
France restauration	45
La corne d'abondance	45
Laughing Bacchus Wine Cellars	45
Rancho grande	43
LINO-Delicateses	36
Maison Dewey	36
Magazzini Alimentari Riuniti	35
Blauer See Delikatessen	34
Cactus Comidas para llevar	34
FISSA Fabrica Inter. Salchichas S.A.	34

Report: rptSales (tblCustomers)   Page Total: 8630   Page 6

Step 1: Create the Basic Report—No Gray, No Totals

Figure 9.11 shows the design surface for the basic, no-frills sales report. The sorting and grouping have already been performed, using the setup shown in Figure 9.12.

For this report Access prints information from the Report Header section once, on the first page. It prints the information in the Page Header and Page Footer sections once on each page and prints the Detail section once for each row of data.

FIGURE 9.11:

Plain sales report's design surface

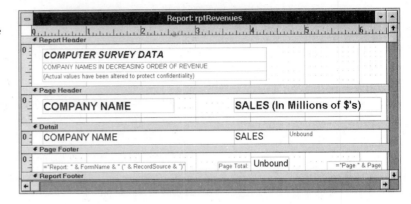

FIGURE 9.12:

Sorting and Grouping dialog for the sales report

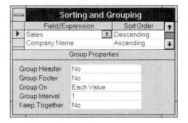

A Reminder: Using Expressions in Reports

Remember that you can place an expression as the ControlSource for any control on a report, as long as you follow these rules:

- Precede it with an equal sign (=).
- Build up your expression using the concatenation operator (&).
- Place literals inside quotes: "Page ".
- Place control names inside square brackets ([ ]).

For example, the expression

```
="Report: " & Name & " (" & RecordSource & ")"
```

builds an expression that will appear like this on the printed report:

```
Report: rptSales (qryBanks)
```

At this point perhaps you're wondering where the Name and RecordSource variables came from. See the next section for an answer.

Using Report Properties

If you look carefully at the Page Footer section of the report, you'll notice that it's using some of the report's properties—Name, RecordSource, and Page—as values that are shown on the report. You can use any of the report's properties as built-in variables on the report printout.

Step 2: Adding Page Totals

Unlike the Report and Group Header/Footer sections, Page Header/Footer sections don't support aggregate functions, so you have to "fake out" Access in order to create page totals. Our solution (only one of many possible solutions) has two parts. Each of these refers to a control in the page footer, necessary for accumulating the running total. In this sample report (rptSales), that text box is named txtPage-Total.

1. As each page header is printed, reset the running total to 0 in preparation for accumulating the value for the current page.

2. As each row is printed, accumulate the running total in a control in the page footer.

Because you surely do not want a value added into the running total unless that particular row has been slated to be printed on the current page, you should attach the code that updates the totals to the section's Print event. (If you insisted on using the Format event, you would need to add code to the matching Retreat event that would back out of the addition if the row were not to be printed.) In this simple example there's no chance that the Print and Format events could be fired off independently (since there's only one printed row per row in the data), but you need to think about the differences between the Print and Format events when deciding how to attach actions to events. Access fires off the Format event when it's formatting a section but isn't yet sure whether or not it will get printed. It fires off the Print event only when it's about to actually print the row.

Resetting the Total for Each Page

In the Page Header's Format event (which occurs only as each page starts its formatting process), you call the following code:

```
Me!txtPageTotal = 0
```

This resets the text box in the page footer that will accumulate the total for each page.

Accumulating the Sales As You Go

In the Detail section's Print event, you call the following code:

```
Me!txtPageTotal = Me!txtPageTotal + NullToZero(Me!txtSales)
```

where the NullToZero() function is as follows:

```
Function NullToZero(ByVal varValue as Variant)
    NullToZero = Iif(IsNull(varValue), 0, varValue)
End Function
```

This adds the current row's sales value to the current page total. Remember that the only event code that can access each and every row's data is the OnPrint and OnFormat handlers. It's here that you need to place any code that must react to each row as it gets printed or formatted. When each page is finally pushed out of the printer, this total will be correct since you've been maintaining it as Access has printed each row.

Step 3: Alternating White and Gray Bars

Although this sort of maneuver was quite tricky in previous versions of Access, in Access 2.0 you can easily create alternate gray and white bars. We've even taken some pains to ensure that you can use this routine in any of your reports. You can find the procedure AlternateGray (Listing 9.10) in CH9.MDB, in the report module for rptSales. It does its work by walking through all the controls on the report. If they're in the Detail section, AlternateGray sets their background colors to either white or gray, depending on what was used for the previous row. The following code performs that work:

```
For intI = 0 To Me.Count - 1
    Set ctl = Me(intI)
    ' The Detail section is section 0.
    If ctl.Section = 0 Then
        ctl.BackColor = intColor
    End If
Next intI
```

The routine uses a module global variable, fGray, to keep track of whether or not the current row should be printed. The procedure AlternateGray() switches it between True and False using this code:

```
fGray = Not fGray
```

If you want to ensure that the first row on each page is printed in white, set the value of fGray to False in the page header's Format event code.

Listing 9.10

```
Sub AlternateGray()

Const COLOR_GRAY = &HCOCOCO
Const COLOR_WHITE = &HFFFFFF

    Dim intColor As Long
    Dim ctl As Control
    Dim intI As Integer

    intColor = IIf(fGray, COLOR_GRAY, COLOR_WHITE)

    For intI = 0 To Me.Count - 1
        ' Walk through all the controls
        ' in the detail section, setting
        ' them all either one color or the other.
        Set ctl = Me(intI)
        If ctl.Section = 0 Then
            ctl.BackColor = intColor
        End If
    Next intI
    fGray = Not fGray
End Sub
```

TIP

To include this functionality in your own reports, copy the subroutine named AlternateGray from rptSales to your own report, declare the fGray integer variable in your module's declarations area, and add the necessary call to AlternateGray to the Format event of the Detail section. You might also set the value of fGray to False (or True) in the page header's Format event handler (to reset the first row on each page to a known color).

Using Rules to Speed Up Printing

If you've set the FastLaserPrinting property for a form or report, Access attempts to use rules when printing the graphics. Rules are a special optimization available on LaserJet printers that implement the Hewlett-Packard Printing Control Language (HPPCL). Most HP LaserJet and compatible printers can use rules. (Post-Script printers, however, are an entirely different animal, and the FastLaserPrinting property will have no effect when printing to these printers. The same is true for dot matrix printers.)

Rules are regions on the page that are filled, gray-scale, and rectangular. The most common use of a rule is as a horizontal or vertical line since lines are actually very thin rectangles. The border around a text box is another prime example. To be treated as a rule, the region must be gray scaled; colors aren't allowed.

Printing rules is fast because rules print as text, in the text band. A printer that supports HPPCL has two kinds of bands: text and graphics. Text bands accept text and rules and print relatively quickly. Graphics bands print more slowly and accept everything, including text and rules, but the printer ignores nongraphics information.

When you print to an HPPCL printer, a conversation is set up between the program (Access) and the printer:

1. Access tells the printer, "I want to print a page."

2. The printer tells Access, "Fine, I've got a text band that I need you to fill. The text band is the size of the entire page."

3. Access fills the text band with all the text and rules on the page.

4. The printer says, "Okay, now it's time to print the graphics. I've only got 1MB of memory installed, so I probably can't handle all the graphics on the page at once. Let's break the page down into smaller chunks, about a third of the page at a time. Give me the info for the first graphics band, the top third of the page."

Note that the more memory you have installed in the printer, the larger and fewer the bands. Also note that the printer is only guessing as to how much information can fit in a band. If the program sends more than will fit in the printer's memory, it reports a memory overflow. This can happen if your output contains a lot of graphics information.

5. Access looks through what it has to print and sends information from the top third of the page to the printer.

Note that entire objects that intersect with the band are printed, even if only one pixel falls within the band. The printer clips everything that falls outside the band. This means, of course, that if an object overlaps more than one band, it's sent to the printer once for each band. The printer doesn't print the part that falls outside the band that's currently printing, but the information is sent to the printer once for each band that contains part of the image.

6. Steps 4 and 5 are repeated for the second and third bands.
7. The printer tells Access, "I'm done asking for bands."
8. Access tells the printer, "Go print the page."

In the previous example Access has to process the page four times before it can be printed: once for the text band and three times for the graphics bands. If Access does not have anything to go into a graphics band, it can tell the printer to skip asking for graphics bands and proceed directly to printing the page. If you use Fast-LaserPrinting and include only rectangular objects that can be printed as rules on your form or report, Access takes approximately one fourth the time before it returns control to your application because it sends the entire job to the Print Manager. Furthermore, the actual print run will take less time because a LaserJet prints text much more quickly than graphics. So if you can arrange to have only text and rules on your printouts, your reports will print much more quickly than if you add a single graphics element. Even if you have a graphics element, your printouts will be faster with rules (since they print more quickly than the equivalent in the graphics band), but the speed increase will not be nearly as dramatic.

Rules are different than normal lines in one important way: they don't hide what is underneath them. Normally, when you print a line or box on a page, the printer performs clipping to avoid having the bottom object show through if another object on the page is "underneath" it. For example, if you put a small black square on a page and then put a larger white square over the top of it, you will not normally see the black square when printing. However, if FastLaserPrinting is turned on (so the printer uses rules to print the rectangles), the black square shows through. A good rule of thumb is to never overlap objects on a form or report that uses rules.

If you print reports containing text and line graphics on a printer that supports HPPCL, rules can vastly speed up printing.

Using Report-Drawing Methods

There is a somewhat simpler solution to the alternating gray bar report. Although the methods used in this solution are beyond the scope of this book (we are not covering the report-drawing methods here), you may find this elegant solution worthwhile.

Rather than changing the background colors of each control, this solution just draws a gray rectangle over the entire Detail section area for every other row. The alternating mechanism works just the same as in the original solution, but there is no need to loop through controls when using the drawing methods.

The replacement procedure, FillGray (rptSales in CH9.MDB), first sets the scaling mode for the report to twips so it matches screen measurements. Then it sets the drawing mode to create a box with an invisible border. Finally, it draws a rectangle from the upper-left corner of the section to the lower-right corner, in gray. It does this only on the rows that need to be gray. For the alternate rows, it does nothing at all.

```
Sub FillGray()

Const COLOR_GRAY = &HC0C0C0
Const SM_TWIPS = 0
Const DS_INVISIBLE = 5
```

```
' If the current section is to be printed in gray, then
' just draw a rectangle covering the entire section area.
If fGray Then
    ' Measure in twips.
    Me.ScaleMode = SM_TWIPS
    Me.DrawStyle = DS_INVISIBLE

    ' Draw the line.
    Me.Line (0, 0)-(Me.ScaleWidth, Me.ScaleHeight),
    ➡ COLOR_GRAY, BF
End If
' Next time, do it the opposite of the way you did it
' this time.
fGray = Not fGray
End Sub
```

If you find this solution more to your liking, replace the calls to AlternateGray with calls to FillGray. The output should be exactly the same, either way.

The Phone Book

Many people use Access to maintain their phone books and address lists. The report you'll see in this section creates a phone book–like listing of names and telephone numbers and adds a few twists. It incorporates large group separators, prints in three vertical columns, and puts a "names on this page" indicator at the bottom of the page. Figure 9.13 shows the layout of the first page of rptPhoneBook, in CH9.MDB.

Again, we'll take this in steps:

1. Create a basic list, sorted and grouped on Company Name, with a page number on each page.

2. Print the list in three columns, with a full-span page header and page footer.

3. Add the "names on this page" indicator with alternating alignment, and hide the page number on the first page.

FIGURE 9.13:

Multicolumn, grouped phone book

Telephone Listing			
A		**G**	
Alfreds Futterkiste	030-0074321	Galería del gastrónomo	(93) 203 4560
Ana Trujillo Emparedados y helados	(5) 555-4729	Godos Cocina Típica	(95) 555 82 82
Antonio Moreno Taquería	(5) 555-3932	Gourmet Lanchonetes	(11) 555-9482
Around the Horn	(71) 555-7788	Great Lakes Food Market	(503) 555-7555
B		GROSELLA-Restaurante	(2) 283-2951
B's Beverages	(71) 555-1212	**H**	
Berglunds snabbköp	0921-12 34 65	Hanari Carnes	(21) 555-0091
Blauer See Delikatessen	0621-08460	HILARIÓN-Abastos	(5) 555-1340
Blondel père et fils	88.60.15.31	Hungry Coyote Import Store	(503) 555-6874
Bólido Comidas preparadas	(91) 555 22 82	Hungry Owl All-Night Grocers	2967 542
Bon app'	91.24.45.40	**I**	
Bottom-Dollar Markets	(604) 555-4729	Island Trading	(24) 555-8888
C		**K**	
Cactus Comidas para llevar	(1) 135-5555	Königlich Essen	0555-09876
Centro comercial Moctezuma	(5) 555-3392	**L**	
Chop-suey Chinese	0452-076545	La corne d'abondance	30.59.84.10
Comércio Mineiro	(11) 555-7647	La maison d'Asie	61.77.61.10
Consolidated Holdings	(71) 555-2282	Laughing Bacchus Wine Cellars	(604) 555-3392
D		Lazy K Kountry Store	(509) 555-7969
Die Wandernde Kuh	0711-020361	Lehmanns Marktstand	069-0245984
Drachenblut Delikatessen	0241-039123	Let's Stop N Shop	(415) 555-5938
Du monde entier	40.67.88.88	LILA-Supermercado	(9) 331-6954
E		LINO-Delicateses	(8) 34-56-12
Eastern Connection	(71) 555-0297	Lonesome Pine Restaurant	(503) 555-9573
Ernst Handel	7675-3425	**M**	
F		Magazzini Alimentari Riuniti	035-640230
Familia Arquibaldo	(11) 555-9857	Maison Dewey	(02) 201 24 67
FISSA Fabrica Inter. Salchichas S.A.	(91) 555 94 44	Mère Paillarde	(514) 555-8054
Folies gourmandes	20.16.10.16	Morgenstern Gesundkost	0342-023176
Folk och fä HB	0695-34 67 21	**N**	
France restauration	40.32.21.21	North/South	(71) 555-7733
Franchi S.p.A.	011-4988260		
Frankenversand	089-0877310		
Furia Bacalhau e Frutos do Mar	(1) 354-2534		

Alfreds Futterkiste - North/South

Step 1: Creating the Basic List

Since reports do their own sorting, based on the choices made in the Sorting and Grouping dialog box, this report is based on a table rather than on a query. If you look at the report design (Figure 9.14), you'll notice that the list is grouped on [Company Name] (prefix characters:1), which means that Access will start a new group every time the first letter of the last name changes. When that happens, it prints out the current value's group footer and the next value's group header. To get Access to sort the companies within the group, you must add [Company Name] to the Sorting and Grouping dialog again.

FIGURE 9.14:

Phone book's design surface

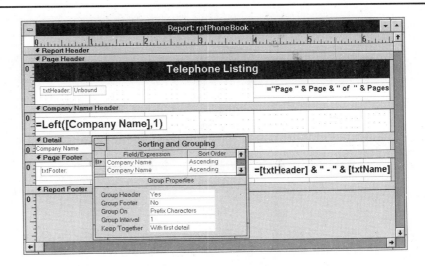

FIGURE 9.14:

Phone book's design surface

Each time Access starts a new group, it prints out the Company Name Header section, which consists of a large copy of the first letter of the company name at that moment. (Remember that the group header has access to the data from the first row of its section and the group footer has access to the last row of data in the section.)

Step 2: Printing the Multicolumn Report

Setting up reports to print in multiple columns requires digging around in a dialog box buried in the Print Setup dialog. By pressing the More >> button you get some added options that control the number and type of columns you use in your report. Figure 9.15 shows the Print Setup dialog.

Table 9.11 shows the items you'll be concerned with when creating a multicolumn report.

FIGURE 9.15:

By pressing the More >> button on the Print Setup dialog, you get the extra options shown at the bottom here.

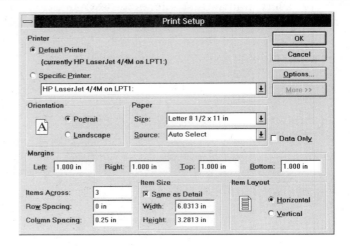

TABLE 9.11: Multicolumn Report Option Settings

Item	Description	Setting for the Phone Book
Items Across	Number of columns	3
Same as Detail	Is each column the same width as the Detail section in the report design?	No (unchecked)
Width	Width of each column	2.3
Item Layout	Do you want your columns to go across (Horizontal) or up and down (Vertical)?	Vertical

Making the changes outlined in the table should transform your report from a boring one-column list to an exciting phone book–style layout.

One important point: if you want the header and footer to span the entire report (as you do in this case), you must set the report design surface width to the width of the entire report. Then, place controls in the Detail section (and its Header/Footer sections) only as wide as your columns will be. Finally, make sure the Same as Detail option is unchecked, with the Width option set to the width that each column will fill. This way, the report's width determines the width of the Report Header and Footer sections, but the Width setting in the Print Setup dialog controls the width of each column.

You might also find it interesting to try setting the Item Layout property to Horizontal instead of Vertical. In that case Access prints each row and then moves horizontally to the next print location. When all the columns are full across the page, it moves to the next row. You'll most likely want to try setting the NewRowOrColumn property for the group header to Before & After Section. This places each section header on a new row, by itself, with the data beginning on the following row. Figure 9.16 shows the horizontally arranged phone book.

FIGURE 9.16:

Setting the Item Layout property to Horizontal changes the look of the phone book.

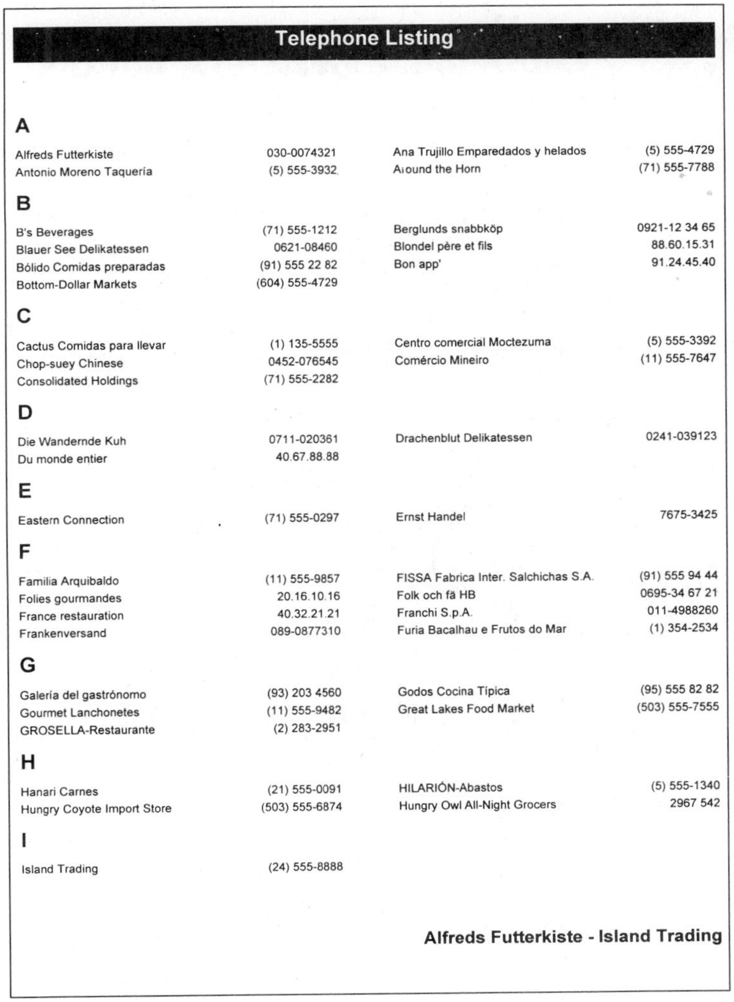

Telephone Listing

A

Alfreds Futterkiste	030-0074321	Ana Trujillo Emparedados y helados	(5) 555-4729
Antonio Moreno Taquería	(5) 555-3932	Around the Horn	(71) 555-7788

B

B's Beverages	(71) 555-1212	Berglunds snabbköp	0921-12 34 65
Blauer See Delikatessen	0621-08460	Blondel père et fils	88.60.15.31
Bólido Comidas preparadas	(91) 555 22 82	Bon app'	91.24.45.40
Bottom-Dollar Markets	(604) 555-4729		

C

Cactus Comidas para llevar	(1) 135-5555	Centro comercial Moctezuma	(5) 555-3392
Chop-suey Chinese	0452-076545	Comércio Mineiro	(11) 555-7647
Consolidated Holdings	(71) 555-2282		

D

Die Wandernde Kuh	0711-020361	Drachenblut Delikatessen	0241-039123
Du monde entier	40.67.88.88		

E

Eastern Connection	(71) 555-0297	Ernst Handel	7675-3425

F

Familia Arquibaldo	(11) 555-9857	FISSA Fabrica Inter. Salchichas S.A.	(91) 555 94 44
Folies gourmandes	20.16.10.16	Folk och fä HB	0695-34 67 21
France restauration	40.32.21.21	Franchi S.p.A.	011-4988260
Frankenversand	089-0877310	Furia Bacalhau e Frutos do Mar	(1) 354-2534

G

Galería del gastrónomo	(93) 203 4560	Godos Cocina Típica	(95) 555 82 82
Gourmet Lanchonetes	(11) 555-9482	Great Lakes Food Market	(503) 555-7555
GROSELLA-Restaurante	(2) 283-2951		

H

Hanari Carnes	(21) 555-0091	HILARIÓN-Abastos	(5) 555-1340
Hungry Coyote Import Store	(503) 555-6874	Hungry Owl All-Night Grocers	2967 542

I

Island Trading	(24) 555-8888		

Alfreds Futterkiste - Island Trading

Step 3: Indicating the Group Names and Hiding the First-Page Page Number

You have two final challenges in creating this report:

- Provide an indication of the group of names that are shown on the current page.

- Hide the page number on the first page.

Gathering Information, but Only in the Footer

To create a text box that displays the range of names on the current page, you need a bit more trickery. By the time Access formats the page footer, it has access to only the current row, which is the last row to be printed on the page. But you need to know the *first* name on the page, also. The trick here is to store away the first name when you can get it—when Access is formatting the page header. The easiest way to use it is to place it in a hidden text box in the report's page header during the page header's Format event. Then, as the control source for a text box on the page footer, the first name can be retrieved from its storage place and concatenated to the current (last) name. This works fine, except for one small problem: it can work only from the page footer. Since Access formats the page in a linear fashion (from top section to bottom), your names will be off by one page, one way or another, if you try this in any other sequence.

Therefore, in the report's Page Header section, call the following code from the Format event. In this example, the text box txtName contains the current row's [Company Name] field, and txtHeader is the text box in the page header that's used for storage.

```
Me![txtHeader] = Me![txtName]
```

Then, as the ControlSource for a control in the page footer, use this expression:

```
=[txtHeader] & " - " & [txtName]
```

This concatenates the stored first name and current final name in the control.

Printing the Page Range Anywhere

The Solutions database that ships with Access 2.0 suggests an alternate method for gathering and printing the page range information, but it's quite complex and works only if you follow their rules exactly. On the other hand, it does allow you to print the information anywhere you like on the page.

The suggested solution requires that you use the Pages property somewhere on the report, which forces Access to make two passes through the report. Once you've done that you can calculate, during the first pass, the name ranges for each page and store them in an array. Then, on the second pass, you can retrieve the values in the array and use them on the report. If you absolutely must place the page range somewhere besides the page footer, this may be the best solution. See Solution.MDB (shipped with Microsoft Access 2.0) for more information.

Hiding the Page Number

Hiding the page number on the first page requires a single step: if the current page is page 1, set the Visible property of the text box that contains the page number to False. The following line of code, placed in the report Page Header section's Format event handler, should do the trick:

```
Me![txtPage].Visible = (Me.Page <> 1)
```

The preceding single-line assignment works the same as this code block:

```
If Me.Page <> 1 Then
    Me![txtPage].Visible = True
Else
    Me![txtPage].Visible = False
End If
```

The expression

```
(Me.Page <> 1)
```

will either be True or False, depending on whether or not Me.Page equals 1. The Visible property of a text box must either be True or False, so you just assign the value of the preceding expression to the property. Although the assignment may at first appear complex, it's really quite simple, and you can use the same mechanism anytime you need to assign a logical value based on a logical condition.

Combining the previous two steps—building the page range and hiding the page number on the first page—the report Page Header's Format event handler looks like this:

```
Sub PageHeader0_Format(Cancel As Integer,
➡ FormatCount As Integer)
    ' Store away the first row's [Company Name] field.
    Me![txtHeader] = Me![txtName]

    ' Set the page number visible on all but the first page.
    Me![txtPage].Visible = (Me.Page <> 1)
End Sub
```

Avoiding Widows

Although Access does provide a mechanism for ensuring that group headers don't get separated from their group (the KeepTogether property in the Group Header section), this mechanism is unaware of column breaks. Unless you take some steps, you'll find that group headings can easily be pulled apart from their groups across columns, leaving you with the group header at the bottom of one column and the associated data at the top of the next.

To avoid this problem you use a little trickery. The generally accepted solution involves deciding on a threshold of separation—that is, deciding how far down the page you can be and still allow Access to print the group header. You can place code in the Group Header's Print event handler that will decide whether or not to print the header in the current location. The code in Listing 9.11 checks to see whether the Top property of the Group Header section is past 8.75 inches down the page. If so, it tells Access to move to the next print location but not to print anything. Although the value of 8.75 inches is arbitrary, it does work well for this particular report. You may need to alter the value for your own reports.

Listing 9.11

```
Sub GroupHeader2_Print(Cancel As Integer, PrintCount
➡ As Integer)

Const NEW_GROUP_LIMIT = 8.75
Const TWIPS_PER_INCH = 1440
```

```
        ' Don't forget to convert to twips (multiply by 1440)
        If Me.Top > NEW_GROUP_LIMIT * TWIPS_PER_INCH Then
            Me.MoveLayout = True
            Me.NextRecord = False
            Me.PrintSection = False
        End If
End Sub
```

Companies, Contacts, and Hardware

Sometimes you'll find that one complex report really requires several smaller, linked reports. The report in Figure 9.17 is one such report. It shows a single company site, the listed contacts for that site, and the computer hardware and software the company uses at that site. The data comes from three different tables:

- A list of companies' sites (with siteID as the primary key)
- A list of names, with each row also containing a siteID field—a foreign key from the site table
- A list of hardware and software items, one row per item, again with a siteID field as a foreign key from the site table.

Figure 9.17 shows the required output, created with almost no code at all.

Designing the Report

Looking at the report, you see three distinct sections: the site information, the contact information, and the hardware/software list. Since there isn't any way to create those three different sections within the confines of a single report, this situation is a perfect candidate for using subreports. You create this report in three steps, by creating three separate reports and then combining them:

1. Contact Information
2. Hardware/Software List
3. Site Information (the main report)

FIGURE 9.17:
Subreports make this complex report possible.

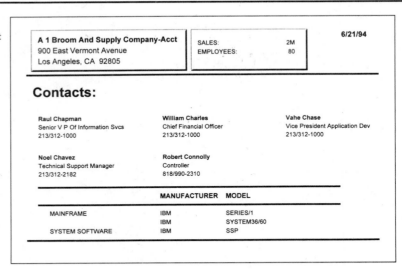

The main report will contain the site information, and its siteID will link it with the two subreports. As the report prints, moving from siteID to siteID, Access will display only the contacts and hardware/software for the specific siteID. You should be able to create each of the subreports independently, as long as you plan ahead and include the linking field, siteID, somewhere on the report surface (and it can be invisible, of course). Although the final report is rather complex, each piece is simple.

The Multicolumn Contact List

After building the phone book list in the previous example, creating the multicolumn contact list should be trivial. The only differences in this case are that the items are to increment horizontally rather than vertically and that each item is in a vertical clump of data rather than a horizontal one. Figure 9.18 shows the design surface for this report (rptBankInfoSub1 in CH9.MDB).

Design surface for the three-column
contact list

Pertinent Properties

To get the report just right, you set the properties for the Header section as follows:

Property	Value
NewRowOrCol	After Section
ForceNewPage	BeforeSection (only necessary when the report is not used as a subform)

You set the Sorting and Grouping dialog so that the report is sorted/grouped on Company, then Last, and then First, with the properties on the first grouping as shown here:

Property	Value
GroupHeader	Yes
GroupFooter	No
GroupOn	Each Value
GroupInterval	1

Finally, you open the Print Setup dialog and set the properties there, as shown in the following table, so the report will print in three columns:

Property	Value
ItemsAcross	3
SameAsDetail	Yes (checked)
ItemLayout	Horizontal

As you set these properties, try variations and run the report. The best way to learn what each property does is to play with an existing report, changing properties and seeing how the output changes. Use Print Preview, of course, to save a few trees.

Hardware/Software List

The hardware/software report should seem simple compared with the other reports you've been creating. Figure 9.19 shows the design surface for this simple report (rptBankInfoSub2 in CH9.MDB).

FIGURE 9.19:

Design surface for the simple list of hardware and software

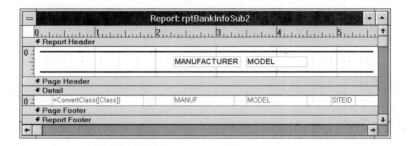

The only interesting feature of this report is its use of a simple Access Basic function to convert the code representing the class type into an English word for that class. You can call any Access Basic function to provide the contents of a report control: just assign the function you want placed in the control as the return value from the function. In the property sheet entry for the ControlSource property, enter

```
=ConvertClass([Class])
```

Access calls the ConvertClass() function shown in Listing 9.12 and places the return value from the function in the text box. The function itself can reside in either the report's module or a stand-alone module.

Listing 9.12

```
Function ConvertClass(varClass As Variant)
    Select Case varClass
        Case "CPU"
            ConvertClass = "MAINFRAME"
        Case "OPR"
            ConvertClass = "SYSTEM SOFTWARE"
```

```
        Case "PRG"
                ConvertClass = "APPLICATION SOFTWARE"
        Case Else
                ConvertClass = "UNKNOWN"
    End Select
End Function
```

The Main Report

The main report consists of little more than a few fields showing information about the particular site, and the two subreports you've just created (rptBankInfo in CH9.MDB). Figure 9.20 shows the design surface for the main report.

The simplest way to create a report with subreports is to make the report design surface and the Database Container window visible at the same time. To do so, drag the subreport from the Database Container window directly onto the report. In this case you want to remove the labels Access attaches to the subreports.

FIGURE 9.20:

Design surface for the main report

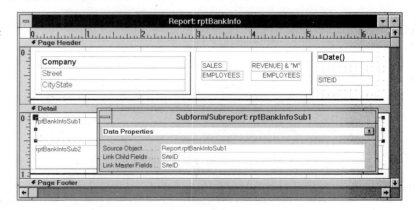

619

> **TIP**
>
> Although it is not necessary for this report, you may sometimes need to embed an existing form in a report. Access allows this, treating the form as if it were a subreport. You can drag a form from the database container onto the report's surface to create a subreport just as easily as you can drag a report.

Linking It All Up

Once you've created the main report, the only job left is to link it all up. To do this you set some properties for the newly created subreports. From the main report's point of view (and that's where you are now—on the main report), these subreports are just controls, like any other report control. They have properties just like all other controls. In Figure 9.20 you can see the property sheet for the first subform, showing just the data properties for the subform.

To link the master and child reports, Access uses the LinkMasterFields and LinkChildFields properties in the subreport control. The LinkMasterFields property tells Access the name of the field(s) from the main report that must match the value(s) of the field(s) specified in the LinkChildFields property. In this case, as the report moves from siteID to siteID, you want to display just the rows in the two subreports whose siteID fields match the current siteID on the main report. It's important to remember that Access needs the actual name of the field, not the name of the control that displays that field, in the LinkChildFields property. Control names are acceptable in the LinkMasterFields property.

For more information on subforms and subreports and how Access links them with their parents, see the section "How and When to Use Subforms" in Chapter 7.

Other Important Properties

Before leaving this report, you need to concern yourself with a few other properties, as described in the following sections.

The CanGrow Property

In this example there's no way to know ahead of time how much vertical space the two subreports will require. Access provides the CanGrow property so you can decide whether or not to allow the Subreport control to grow as necessary. Sometimes you'll want a fixed-size subreport. Here, though, you set the CanGrow property to Yes so all the information will be visible.

CanShrink Property

Some of the sites might not list any contacts. In that case you'll want the contacts subreport to take up no space at all. To make that happen you set the CanShrink property for the subreport control to Yes. For specific details about when Access restricts the functionality of the CanShrink (and CanGrow) property, see the section entitled "Why CanShrink Doesn't and CanGrow Won't" earlier in this chapter.

Altering Your Report's Layout Programmatically

In some instances you may need to alter the complete layout of the Report Detail section on a row-by-row basis. Imagine, for example, that you're printing a questionnaire and that each question can be a yes/no, multiple-choice, write-in, or 1-through-10 type question. Your table containing the questions includes a column that indicates which question type to use on the report. RptQuestions in CH9.MDB is such a report; it makes different controls visible, depending on which question type is currently being printed. Figure 9.21 shows the printed report.

FIGURE 9.21:

The printed survey shows different controls, depending on the question type.

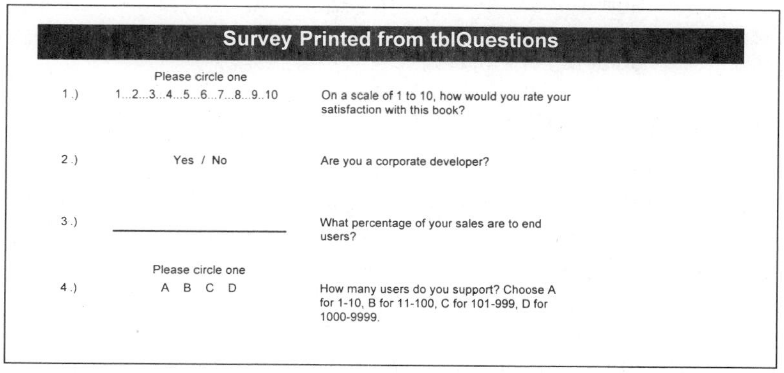

Survey Printed from tblQuestions		
	Please circle one	
1.)	1...2...3...4...5...6...7...8...9..10	On a scale of 1 to 10, how would you rate your satisfaction with this book?
2.)	Yes / No	Are you a corporate developer?
3.)	_____	What percentage of your sales are to end users?
	Please circle one	
4.)	A B C D	How many users do you support? Choose A for 1-10, B for 11-100, C for 101-999, D for 1000-9999.

The concept here is simple. The report has several controls that always show up: dsptxtQuestion, dsptxtCount, and dsplblCount. (We're using the "dsp" prefix to indicate that these controls display for each row.) In addition it contains five controls (four text boxes and a line) that Access displays or hides, depending on the question type. Figure 9.22 shows the design surface, with the controls spread out. Normally, all the user-response controls overlay one another. To make them easier to see, we've spread them out vertically.

FIGURE 9.22:

Design surface for the questionnaire

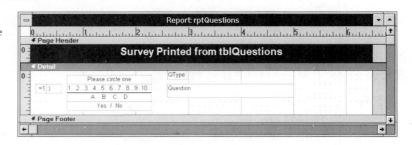

Listing 9.13 contains the Access Basic code that controls which of the user-response controls are visible in each printed row. Since Access calls this code for each row in the Detail section, it must first hide all the user-response controls and then enable the ones that apply to this particular row. Once it's hidden all the nonessential controls, it shows the controls that are necessary for this particular question type.

Listing 9.13

```
Sub Detail0_Format(Cancel As Integer, FormatCount As Integer)

Const TYPE_FILLIN = 1
Const TYPE_1To10 = 2
Const TYPE_ABCD = 3
Const TYPE_YESNO = 4

    Dim intI As Integer
    Dim ctl As Control
```

```
' Turn off all the controls in the detail section,
' except the question and its counter, which never go away.
For intI = 0 To Me.Count - 1
    Set ctl = Me(intI)
    If ctl.Section = 0 Then
        If Left(ctl.Name, 3) <> "dsp" Then
            If ctl.Visible Then
                ctl.Visible = False
            End If
        End If
    End If
Next intI

Select Case Me!QType
    Case TYPE_1To10
        Me!lbl1To10.Visible = True
        Me!lblCircleOne.Visible = True

    Case TYPE_ABCD
        Me!lblABCD.Visible = True
        Me!lblCircleOne.Visible = True

    Case TYPE_YESNO
        Me!lblYesNo.Visible = True

    Case TYPE_FILLIN
        Me!linFillIn.Visible = True

    Case Else

End Select
End Sub
```

Of course, this isn't the only solution to this problem. If you knew that the user-response controls could all be labels, you could just as easily change the Caption property of the labels, based on the question type. In this case, though, since one of the controls is a line, that method isn't workable.

> **TIP**
>
> The code in Listing 9.13, in its attempt to hide all the Detail section controls, checks to see whether a control is visible before making it invisible. You might think this is redundant; after all, regardless of whether the control is visible, setting its Visible property to False definitely makes it invisible. That's true, but it's very slow to set a control property, in comparison to the time it takes to *check* that property. If you can avoid setting properties, your application will run more quickly. In this case, since there are so few controls, it won't make any measurable difference. If, on the other hand, you had a large number of controls in the Detail section, this could save some considerable time and effort.

If you expand on the "questionnaire" method you can create very complex reports that, in design mode, take up just a very small amount of space. This can be particularly useful when you remember that your reports are limited to 22 inches of design space! Rather than iterating through your questions by hand, create a report to create the questionnaire for you.

Controlling Print Setup Information

Although Access provides a standardized Print Setup dialog box, programmatically controlling the values you'll find is difficult using the standard means. You might be tempted to try using SendKeys to control the print settings, but you'll run into obstacles quickly when you try to control specific printer settings, such as paper size, for which each printer driver provides a list. Even worse, every printer's Options dialog box is different, making the control of that portion completely impossible with SendKeys.

Luckily, Windows provides a standardized mechanism for conversing with the printer driver to retrieve and set information. The Windows API defines two user-defined types, generally referred to as the DEVMODE and DEVNAMES structures by the Windows SDK documentation. Listing 9.14 shows the Access Basic type declarations for appropriate user-defined types to contain the information stored in the DEVMODE and DEVNAMES structures, as well as the Access-defined prtMip information, defined later in this section. You can find all these declarations in basPrtGlobal, in CH9.MDB.

Access makes all this information available to you, so you can retrieve and change very specific printer settings. All reports—and forms in Form view, as well as tables and queries in Datasheet view—provide three properties: prtDevMode (associated printer-specific settings), prtDevNames (associated with the specific chosen printer), and prtMip (defined only in Access to support margin settings and page layout information). Later in this chapter we discuss methods for retrieving all the information, setting new values, and replacing the values in the properties. Listing 9.14 shows the user-defined data structures we use throughout this chapter when we refer to each of the different prtX (prtDevMode, prtDevNames, and prtMip) properties.

> **NOTE**
>
> The Access Wizards use structures very similar to those shown in Listing 9.14. We could have used those exact structures throughout the book and not have bothered to create our own. Since you can't distribute the Wizard code with applications you create with the run-time version of Access, however, we wanted to enable you to write code you could distribute. If you use the declarations and examples from this chapter, there's no limitation on distribution.

Listing 9.14

```
' Structure for prtDevMode
Type glr_tagDevMode
    strDeviceName As String * 32
    intSpecVersion As Integer
    intDriverVersion As Integer
    intSize As Integer
    intDriverExtra As Integer
    lngFields As Long
    intOrientation As Integer
    intPaperSize As Integer
    intPaperLength As Integer
    intPaperWidth As Integer
```

```
        intScale As Integer
        intCopies As Integer
        intDefaultSource As Integer
        intPrintQuality As Integer
        intColor As Integer
        intDuplex As Integer
        intYResolution As Integer
        intTTOption As Integer
End Type

' Structure for prtDevNames
Type glr_tagDevNames
        intDriverPos As Integer
        intDevicePos As Integer
        intOutputPos As Integer
        intDefault As Integer
End Type

' Structure for prtMip
Type glr_tagMarginInfo
        intLeft As Integer
        intTop As Integer
        intRight As Integer
        intBottom As Integer
        intDataOnly As Integer
        intWidth As Integer
        intHeight As Integer
        intDefaultSize As Integer
        intItemsAcross As Integer
        intRowSpacing As Integer
        intColumnSpacing As Integer
        intItemLayout As Integer
End Type
```

Introducing the prtDevMode property

The prtDevMode property, which applies to reports and forms, contains information about the printing device that prints the object. It contains, among other things, the name of the device, information about the driver, the number of copies to print, the orientation of the printout, the paper tray to use when printing, and the print quality to use. All this information corresponds directly with Windows'

DEVMODE structure, used by every single Windows program that ever intends to do any printing.

Although Access makes all this information available to you so you can retrieve and set print properties for reports and forms, it doesn't make it easy. The prtDevMode property is nothing more than a text string with all the information from the DEVMODE structure strung together. It's up to your code to pick apart the text string, make changes as necessary, and reassign the property. And unlike almost every other property in Access 2.0, the prtDevMode property is only read/write when the report or form is in design mode. You won't be able to make changes to the prtDevMode property while running the report—which makes sense since you really can't be changing things like the printer name or margins while printing the report. Table 9.12 lists each field in the DEVMODE structure, its datatype, and a short description. Some of the fields contain enumerated data, and the choices for those items are listed in Tables 9.13 through 9.17 in this chapter.

We'll show how to retrieve and modify the prtDevMode property in the next section. For now, here are some ideas to keep in mind as you peruse the tables that describe the DEVMODE information:

- Not all printer drivers support the DEVMODE structure. Drivers that work only in Windows 3.0 do not, and some current drivers also do not. If you find that your printer driver does not support this information (if you retrieve a null value for the prtDevMode property of a form or report), contact the printer manufacturer and see if there is a more current driver available.

- Before providing a list of choices to your user (paper sizes, TrueType options, and so on), check the capabilities of the current device and limit your choices to options the device supports. Although Access does not provide this capability and you cannot access this information directly through Windows API calls from Access, we've provided a DLL that allows you to retrieve this information. We cover this functionality (calling the DeviceCapabilities() function) in the section "Retrieving Printer Capabilities" later in this chapter.

- Many printer drivers store additional information immediately following the DEVMODE structure. Therefore, when retrieving and setting the prtDevMode property, be aware that most often it will require more than the documented 68 bytes. Plan on 512 bytes or more, and check the intDriverSize and intExtraSize fields when manipulating the values. (The sum of those two fields gives you the total size used by the prtDevMode property.)

TABLE 9.12: prtDevMode Fields and Their Contents

Setting	Datatype	Description
Device Name*	32-character string	Name of the device supported by the driver: "HP LaserJet 4/4M", for example
Specification Version*	Integer	The version number of the DEVMODE structure in the Windows SDK. For Windows 3.1 this ought to be 778 (&H30A)
Driver Version*	Integer	Driver version number assigned by the driver developer
Size*	Integer	Size, in bytes, of the DEVMODE structure
Driver Extra*	Integer	Size, in bytes, of the optional driver-specific data, which can follow this structure
Fields	Long	Specifies a set of flags that indicate which of the members of the DEVMODE structure have been initialized. It can be 0 or more of the values in Table 9.13, added together. See tblFields in CH9.MDB, which contains a lookup table for each of the values that can be part of this member
Orientation	Integer	Paper orientation. It can be either 1 (Portrait) or 2 (Landscape)
Paper Size	Integer	Size of the paper to print on. The value can be chosen from Table 9.14. If you choose 256 (User-Defined, Size), the length and width of the paper are specified in the Paper Length and Paper Width members
Paper Length	Integer	Paper length in tenths of a millimeter. Overrides the setting in the Paper Size member (limited by data storage to 328 centimeters)
Paper Width	Integer	Paper width in tenths of a millimeter. Overrides the setting in the Paper Size member (limited by data storage to 328 centimeters)
Scale	Integer	Factor by which the printed output is to be scaled. The apparent page size is scaled from the physical page size by a factor of Scale/100
Copies	Integer	Number of copies printed if the printing device supports multiple-page copies
Default Source	Integer	Default bin from which paper is fed. See Table 9.15 for a list of possible values

TABLE 9.12: prtDevMode Fields and Their Contents (continued)

Setting	Datatype	Description
Print Quality	Integer	Printer resolution. See Table 9.16 for a list of device-independent_values. If you specify a positive value it's treated as the x-resolution, in dots per inch (DPI), and is not device independent. In this case the Y-Resolution field must contain the y-resolution in DPI
Color	Integer	Specifies Color (1) or Monochrome (2) printing if the device supports color printing
Duplex	Integer	Specifies Simplex (1), Horizontal (2), or Vertical (3) print mode for printers that support duplex printing
Y-Resolution	Integer	Specifies the y-resolution for the printer, in dots per inch (DPI). If this value is specified you must also specify the x-resolution in the Print Quality member. These values are device specific
True Type Option	Integer	Specifies how TrueType fonts should be printed. See Table 9.17 for a list of possible values

*Read-only for any specific printer.

TABLE 9.13: Initialized Field Flags for prtDevMode

Constant	Value
DM_ORIENTATION	&H0000001
DM_PAPERSIZE	&H0000002
DM_PAPERLENGTH	&H0000004
DM_PAPERWIDTH	&H0000008
DM_SCALE	&H0000010
DM_COPIES	&H0000100
DM_DEFAULTSOURCE	&H0000200
DM_PRINTQUALITY	&H0000400
DM_COLOR	&H0000800
DM_DUPLEX	&H0001000
DM_YRESOLUTION	&H0002000
DM_TTOPTION	&H0004000

TABLE 9.14: Available prtDevMode Paper Sizes

Value	Paper Size
1	Letter (8.5 × 11 in.)
2	Letter Small (8.5 × 11 in.)
3	Tabloid (11 × 17 in.)
4	Ledger (17 × 11 in.)
5	Legal (8.5 × 14 in.)
6	Statement (5.5 × 8.5 in.)
7	Executive (7.25 × 10.5 in.)
8	A3 (297 × 420 mm)
9	A4 (210 × 297 mm)
10	A4 Small (210 × 297 mm)
11	A5 (148 × 210 mm)
12	B4 (250 × 354)
13	B5 (182 × 257 mm)
14	Folio (8.5 × 13 in.)
15	Quarto (215 × 275 mm)
16	11 × 17 in.
18	Note (8.5 × 11 in.)
19	Envelope #9 (3.875 × 8.875 in.)
20	Envelope #10 (4.125 × 9.5 in.)
21	Envelope #11 (4.5 × 10.375 in.)
22	Envelope #12 (4.25 × 11 in.)
23	Envelope #14 (5 × 11.5 in.)
24	C size sheet
25	D size sheet
26	E size sheet
27	Envelope DL (110 × 220 mm)
28	Envelope C5 (162 × 229 mm)
29	Envelope C3 (324 × 458 mm)
30	Envelope C4 (229 × 324 mm)

TABLE 9.14: Available prtDevMode Paper Sizes (continued)

Value	Paper Size
31	Envelope C6 (114 × 162 mm)
32	Envelope C65 (114 × 229 mm)
33	Envelope B4 (250 × 353 mm)
34	Envelope B5 (176 × 250 mm
35	Envelope B6 (176 × 125 mm)
36	Envelope (110 × 230 mm)
37	Envelope Monarch (3.875 × 7.5 in.)
38	6-3/4 Envelope (3.625 × 6.5 in.)
39	US Std Fanfold (14.875 × 11 in.)
40	German Std Fanfold (8.5 × 12 in.)
41	German Legal Fanfold (8.5 × 13 in.)
256	User-defined

TABLE 9.15: Available Paper Source Values for prtDevMode

Value	Paper Source
1	Upper or only one bin
2	Lower bin
3	Middle bin
4	Manual bin
5	Envelope bin
6	Envelope manual bin
7	Automatic bin
8	Tractor bin
9	Small-format bin
10	Large-format bin
11	Large-capacity bin
14	Cassette bin
256	Device-specific bins start here

TABLE 9.16: Available Print Quality Values for prtDevMode

Value	Print Quality
−4	High
−3	Medium
−2	Low
−1	Draft

TABLE 9.17: Available True Type Options for prtDevMode

Value	True Type Option
1	Print TrueType fonts as graphics. This is the default for dot matrix printers
2	Download TrueType fonts as soft fonts. This is the default for Hewlett-Packard printers that use Printer Control Language (PCL)
3	Substitute device fonts for TrueType fonts. This is the default for PostScript printers

Retrieving the prtDevMode Information

Actually retrieving the prtDevMode information is, of course, trivial. Since prtDevMode is a property of forms and reports, you can retrieve the information by simply copying it from the object into a string variable. Once it's there, though, you must somehow get it into a structure with the appropriate fields set up for you. The glr_tagDevMode structure shown here is what you need:

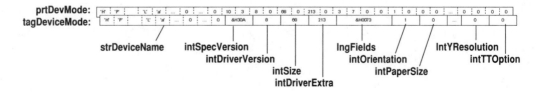

However, you also need a method for getting the string you've read directly from the object's property into the structure. The answer is Access Basic's LSet statement.

Access' LSet statement allows you to copy bytes of data from one variable to another, even if they're of different datatypes. Normally, Access allows you to copy information between two variables of the same datatype. In this case you need to copy data from a string datatype to a variable of type glr_tagDevMode. The value returned by the prtDevMode property is laid out perfectly, so performing a byte-by-byte copy into the glr_tagDevMode structure fills in all the fields correctly. The graphic on the previous page shows this "overlay" in progress. In the graphic, the top row represents the prtDevMode string, and the bottom row represents the variable of type glr_tagDevMode into which you've copied that data. The LSet command makes it easy to perform this operation, although there are a few issues you need to understand first, as described in the following sections.

Using LSet to Copy Unformatted Data

The LSet command actually has two variations. In one context LSet allows you to left-align text within a string variable type, padding the extra room with spaces. In a different context LSet overlays the data stored in one user-defined type into a variable of a different user-defined type. This is the functionality you'll need. Note, however, the use of the term *user-defined*. Both variables must be of a user-defined type. Since your goal here is to move data from a string variable (the data retrieved directly from the object's prtDevMode property) into a user-defined variable, you must first take one intermediate step: place the data into a user-defined type that is nothing more than a fixed-length string:

```
' Temp structure for prtDevMode info.
Type glr_tagDevModeStr
    ' The 512 is arbitrary, and just has to be large enough
    ' for the largest DevMode structure.
    strDevMode As String * 512
End Type
```

Given a type declaration for such a datatype, you could retrieve the prtDevMode property and assign it to a variable of type glr_tagDevMode, as in the following code fragment:

```
Dim DM as glr_tagDevMode
Dim DMStr as glr_tagDevModeStr

DMStr.strDevMode = Reports!Report1.prtDevMode
LSet DM = DMStr
```

That code overlays the value retrieved from the prtDevMode property of Report1 into the glr_tagDevMode variable, DM. You should now be able to access any member of DM, just as you would with any other user-defined type. For example,

```
Debug.Print DM.strDeviceName
```

should print the name of the printer assigned to print this particular report.

Using LSet to Replace the Data

Once you've made the necessary changes to the glr_tagDevMode structure, you'll want to replace the value of the prtDevMode property. To do so, use the LSet command again:

```
Dim DM as glr_tagDevMode
Dim DMStr as glr_tagDevModeStr

DMStr.strDevMode = Reports!Report1.prtDevMode
LSet DM = DMStr
'
' Do work here, manipulating DM.
'
LSet DMStr = DM
Reports!Report1.prtDevMode = DMStr.strDevMode
```

A Simple Example Using prtDevMode

Anytime you want to manipulate the values in the prtDevMode property, follow these steps:

1. Declare variables of type glr_tagDevMode and glr_tagDevModeStr.

2. Copy the prtDevMode property from the report or form into the glr_tagDevModeStr variable.

3. Use LSet to copy the bytes into the glr_tagDevMode variable.

4. Make whatever changes you like.

5. Use LSet to copy the bytes back into the glr_tagDevModeStr variable.

6. Replace the value of the prtDevMode property for the form or report from the glr_tagDevModeStr variable.

For example, Listing 9.15 demonstrates changing the number of copies to be printed of a given report. (Look in basSetCopies in CH9.MDB for SetCopies() and SetCopies2(), presented in the next section.)

Listing 9.15

```
Function SetCopies(strName As String, intCopies As Integer)

    ' This simple function would require
    ' error checking for real use.  In addition,
    ' it requires that the report in question be
    ' already open in design mode (you can't set the
    ' prtDevMode property in Report mode).

    Dim rpt As Report

    ' 1.  Declare variables of type glr_tagDevMode and
    '        glr_tagDevModeStr.
    Dim DM As glr_tagDevMode
    Dim DMStr As glr_tagDevModeStr

    Set rpt = Reports(strName)
    ' Some reports might not support the
    ' prtDevMode property, because the printer
    ' they're to be sent to doesn't support it.
    If Not IsNull(rpt.prtDevMode) Then

        ' 2.  Copy the prtDevMode property from the
        '        report or form into the
        '        glr_tagDevModeStr variable.
        DMStr.strDevMode = rpt.prtDevMode

        ' 3.  Use LSet to copy the bytes into the
        '        glr_tagDevMode variable.
        LSet DM = DMStr

        ' 4.  Make whatever changes you like, and set
        '        the lngFields entry accordingly.
        DM.intCopies = intCopies
        DM.lngFields = DM_COPIES

        ' 5.  Use LSet to copy the bytes back into the
        '        glr_tagDevModeStr variable.
        LSet DMStr = DM
```

```
      ' 6.  Replace the value of the prtDevMode
      '     property for the form or report from the
      '     glr_tagDevModeStr variable.
      rpt.prtDevMode = DMStr.strDevMode
   End If
End Function
```

And a Bit Simpler

To make it a bit easier for you to retrieve and set values in the prtDevMode property, we've provided functions in basDevMode (in CH9.MDB), glrRetrieveDevMode() and glrSetDevMode(). Each takes three parameters:

- The name of the form or report to use
- The type of the object (A_FORM or A_REPORT)
- A variable of type glr_tagDevMode (glrRetrieveDevMode() will fill this in from the object's prtDevMode property, and glrSetDevMode() will place its value into the object's prtDevMode property.)

Each function returns either True or False, indicating the success of the operation.

Using these functions you could rewrite SetCopies as follows:

```
Function SetCopies2(strName As String, intCopies As Integer)
   Dim DM As glr_tagDevMode
   Dim fSuccess As Integer

   If glrRetrieveDevMode(strName, A_REPORT, DM) Then
      DM.intCopies = intCopies
      DM.lngFields = DM_COPIES
      fSuccess = glrSetDevMode(strName, A_REPORT, DM)
   End If
End Function
```

An Important Reminder

Remember, all the properties mentioned in this section (prtDevMode, prtDevNames, prtMip) are available only in *design mode*. You must make sure your report or form is open in design mode before attempting to set any of these properties. (You can *retrieve* the properties, of course, no matter what the mode.)

Changing Paper Size

Contrary to the information presented above, many printers do not allow you to specify a user-defined page size. Those that do tend to be dot matrix printers, and not all of them support the feature. In addition, some printers use a page size of 0 to indicate a user-defined size, and some use 256. You need to retrieve information about the specific printer (see the section "Retrieving Printer Capabilities" later in this chapter for information on this) before trying to set a specific nonstandard page size.

If you find that you can change the size, you must change a number of fields in the prtDevMode string. You not only need to inform the printer that you're setting a user-defined size, you need to send the coordinates. The code listed here changes the paper size to 1000×1000 units (10 cm $\times$ 10 cm):

```
DM.intPaperSize = 256
DM.intPaperLength = 1000
DM.intPaperWidth = 1000
DM.lngFields = DM_PAPERSIZE Or DM_PAPERLENGTH Or
➥ DM_PAPERWIDTH
```

You must set the lngFields value so that the driver knows you've changed the paper size values.

Using the prtDevMode Property in Your Applications

If you want to use any of the procedures discussed in the preceding sections in your own applications, you should import both basPrtGlobal and basDevMode from CH9.MDB. Once you have those modules in your application, you should be able to call the functions you need in order to manipulate the prtDevMode property effectively.

Controlling Print Layout Information

Access makes the print layout information for a given report or form available to you through the object's prtMip property. This information includes margin settings, number of columns, spacing between columns, and the layout (horizontal or vertical) of those columns. Just as with the prtDevMode property, Access provides this information as a single string value, which you must pick apart yourself. Table 9.18 shows the elements of this property and their possible values. Listing 9.14, presented earlier in this chapter, shows an Access user-defined type you can use to extract and set information in the prtMip property.

TABLE 9.18: prtMip Fields and Their Contents

Setting	glr_tagMarginInfo Field	Description	Possible Values
Left	intLeft	Left margin, in twips ($1/1440$ inch)	1 to 32767 (22.75 inches)
Top	intTop	Top margin, in twips	1 to 32767
Right	intRight	Right margin, in twips	1 to 32767
Bottom	intBottom	Bottom margin, in twips	1 to 32767
Data Only	intDataOnly	Print only the data, without gridlines, borders, or graphics	True (−1) or False (0)
Item Size Width	intWidth	Width, in twips, for each column	1 to 32767
Item Size Height	intHeight	Height, in twips, for each column	1 to 32767
Default Size	intDefaultSize	Specifies whether each column should be the same size as the Detail section or use the Width and Height settings	True (−1), use the width of the Detail section; or False (0), use the Width and Height settings
Items Across	intItemsAcross	Number of columns across for multicolumn reports or forms	1 to 32767 (Of course, that doesn't make 32767 a reasonable value!)

TABLE 9.18: prtMip Fields and Their Contents (continued)

Setting	glr_tagMarginInfo Field	Description	Possible Values
Row Spacing	intRowSpacing	Space between detail rows, in twips	1 to 32767
Column Spacing	intColumnSpacing	Space between detail columns, in twips	1 to 32767
Item Layout	intItemLayout	Specifies vertical or horizontal layout	1953 for Horizontal, 1954 for Vertical

Just as with the prtDevMode property, the steps you use when modifying one or more prtMip options are as follows:

1. Declare variables of type glr_tagMarginInfo and glr_tagMarginInfoStr.

2. Copy the prtMip property from the report or form into the glr_tagMarginInfoStr variable.

3. Use LSet to copy the bytes into the glr_tagMarginInfo variable.

4. Make whatever changes you like.

5. Use LSet to copy the bytes back into the glr_tagMarginInfoStr variable.

6. Replace the value of the prtMip property for the form or report from the glr_tagMarginInfoStr variable.

For example, Listing 9.16 demonstrates changing the number of columns and the column width for a given report. (Look in basSetColumns in CH9.MDB for Set-Columns() and SetColumns2(), presented in the next section.)

Listing 9.16

```
Sub SetColumns(strName As String, intCols As Integer,
➡ sglWidth As Single)
    ' Set the number of columns for a specified
    ' report. Pass in the name of the report, the
    ' number of columns to print, and the width of
    ' each, in inches.
```

```
' To keep this example simple, all error checking
' has been removed.

' 1.   Declare variables of type glr_tagMarginInfo
'      and glr_tagMarginInfoStr.
Dim mip As glr_tagMarginInfo
Dim mipTemp As glr_tagMarginInfoStr

' 2.   Copy the prtMip property from the report or
'      form into the glr_tagMarginInfoStr variable.
mipTemp.strMip = Reports(strName).prtMip

' 3.   Use LSet to copy the bytes into the
'      glr_tagMarginInfo variable.
LSet mip = mipTemp

' 4.   Make whatever changes you like.
mip.intItemsAcross = intCols
' Convert inches to twips.
mip.intWidth = glrTWIPS_PER_INCH * sglWidth
' Tell the report not to use the detail section
' width.
mip.intDefaultSize = False

' 5.   Use LSet to copy the bytes back into the
'      glr_tagMarginInfoStr variable.
LSet mipTemp = mip

' 6.   Replace the value of the prtMip property for
'      the form or report from the
'      glr_tagMarginInfoStr variable.
Reports(strName).prtMip = mipTemp.strMip
End Sub
```

Making It a Bit Simpler

To simplify your interactions with the prtMip property, we've supplied the glrRetrieveMIP() and glrSetMIP() functions, in basPrtMip (CH9.MDB). These two functions operate exactly like the glrRetrieveDevMode() and glrSetDevMode() functions described earlier in this chapter. You pass in an object name, its type (A_FORM or A_REPORT), and an appropriate structure to fill in. In this case you'll pass a glr_tagMarginInfo structure. Using these two functions, you could rewrite the procedure SetColumns like this:

```
Sub SetColumns2(strName As String, intCols As Integer,
➡ sglWidth As Single)
    Dim fSuccess As Integer
    Dim MIP As glr_tagMarginInfo

    If glrRetrieveMIP(strName, A_REPORT, MIP) Then
        MIP.intItemsAcross = intCols
        MIP.intWidth = glrTWIPS_PER_INCH * sglWidth
        MIP.intDefaultSize = False
        fSuccess = glrSetMip(strName, A_REPORT, MIP)
    End If
End Sub
```

Using these functions relieves you of dealing with LSet or the intermediate glr_tag-MarginInfoStr structure.

Using prtMip in Your Own Applications

To retrieve or modify settings in an object's prtMip property, you need to import the basPrtMip and basPrtGlobal modules from CH9.MDB. Once you have that code in your application, you should be able to use the functions there to manipulate all the margin settings you need.

Introducing the prtDevNames Property

Both reports and forms support a property, previously undocumented, that contains information about the current output device associated with that form or report. That is, if you use the Print Setup menu option to select a specific printer for a form or report, that information is stored with the object. When you print the form or report, Access attempts to send the printout to the specified device, based on what it finds in the prtDevNames property of the object. To momentarily change the output device (to send the report to the fax instead of to the printer, for example), you need to retrieve the prtDevNames property, set it to the fax device, print the document, and then set it back.

The prtDevNames property stores three pieces of information about the specific output device in a manner that's convenient for programmers working in C or C++ (the standard Windows programming languages) but not as convenient for Access programmers. The property itself is just an exact copy of the DEVNAMES structure that's used as part of the Windows SDK. The DEVNAMES structure contains the device name, the driver, and the output port in a variable-length string, with each piece of information followed by a null character (CHR$(0)). In addition, the property starts out with a group of four integers. Each of the first three integers contains the offset of one of the three strings that follow, and the fourth contains a 0 or a 1, depending on whether the current device is the Windows default output device. Table 9.19 lists the members of the DEVNAMES structure, stored in the prtDevNames property. The order of the three strings in the structure is not important, as long as the offsets are consistent with that ordering. In the examples you'll find the device name, then the driver name, and finally, the output port. You'll find that the three pieces of information the prtDevNames structures needs are the same three pieces of information we'll gather from WIN.INI in the section "Controlling Your Destination" later in this chapter. Therefore, it should be simple to build up a new prtDevNames property based on the user's choice from the list of possible output devices. Here is an example prtDevNames string, using the Generic/Text Only driver:

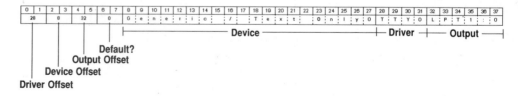

Using the prtDevNames property

To use the prtDevNames property, you must be able to perform two basic manipulations: build up the string and break it apart. The module basPrtNames in CH9.MDB contains two functions that perform these tasks. The function glrBuildDevNames() takes as a parameter a structure of type glr_tagDeviceRec, containing the device name, the driver name, and the output location, and builds up an appropriate string. This function just takes the three strings, concatenates them with Chr$(0) inserted between them and at the end, and calculates the offsets for each.

TABLE 9.19: prtDevNames Fields and Their Contents

Member	Description
Driver Offset	Offset from the beginning of the structure to a null-terminated string that specifies the file name (without the extension) of the device driver
Device Offset	Offset from the beginning of the structure to a null-terminated string that specifies the name of the device
Output Offset	Offset from the beginning of the structure to a null-terminated string that specifies the MS-DOS device name for the physical output port
Default	Specifies whether the strings in this structure identify the default Windows printer (1 if True, 0 if False)
Device Name	Specified device name. It cannot be longer than 32 characters (including the trailing null) and must match one of the items from WIN.INI in the [devices] section
Driver Name	Specified driver name. It cannot be longer than nine characters (including the trailing null)
Output Name	Specified output port. It cannot be longer than 9 characters (including the trailing null)—for example, "LPT1:"

To store away the offsets, you'll find it easiest to store them as integers in a user-defined type with four elements:

```
Type glr_tagDevNames
    intDriverPos As Integer
    intDevicePos As Integer
    intOutputPos As Integer
    intDefault As Integer
End Type
```

Once you've filled in all the values, you can use the LSet command to copy the structure, byte by byte, into a string-type variable. Once you have the four integers in the string variable, you can concatenate the list of three strings onto the end of the string variable. Just as before, you must create a simple user-defined type, consisting of just the string you want, into which you can LSet the values in the glr_tag-DevNames structure. That is, given the user-defined type

```
Type glr_tagDevOffsets
    strDevInfo As String * 8
End Type
```

you can use the LSet command to copy the 8 bytes of information into that string. The code might look like this:

```
Dim devNames As glr_tagDevNames
Dim devStr As glr_tagDevOffsets
.
. ' Fill the values in devNames here
.
LSet devStr = devNames
```

Listing 9.17 contains the glrBuildDevNames() function, which creates the prtDevNames string, given the three pieces of information it needs.

Listing 9.17

```
Function glrBuildDevNames(dr As glr_tagDeviceRec)

    Dim devNames As glr_tagDevNames
    Dim devStr As glr_tagDevOffsets

    ' Check for maximum length for the device name
    ' (leaving room for the null terminator)
    If Len(dr.strDeviceName) > MAX_DEVICE - 1 Then
        MsgBox "Invalid Device Name!", 16, "glrBuildDevNames()"
        Exit Function
    End If

    ' The first offset is always offset 8
    devNames.intDevicePos = 8
    devNames.intDriverPos = devNames.intDevicePos +
    ➥ Len(dr.strDeviceName) + 1
    devNames.intOutputPos = devNames.intDriverPos +
    ➥ Len(dr.strDriverName) + 1
    ' Since you're forcing a new printer setting, tell
    ' Windows that it's not the default printer.
    devNames.intDefault = 0

    ' Both sides of the LSet need to be user-defined types,
    ' so use devStr (of type glr_tagDevOffsets) instead of
    ' just a plain ol' string.
    LSet devStr = devNames
    glrBuildDevNames = devStr.strDevInfo & dr.strDeviceName &
    ➥ Chr$(0) & dr.strDriverName & Chr$(0) & dr.strPort &
    ➥ Chr$(0)
End Function
```

Pulling apart the pieces of the prtDevNames property is even easier. The function glrParseDevNames() (in basDevNames in CH9.MDB) takes in a prtDevNames string and fills in the appropriate pieces of the glr_tagDeviceRec structure. In addition, the function returns the value 1 if the selected device is the default Windows output device and 0 otherwise. Once the function has used LSet to copy the four integer values into the glr_tagDevNames structure, it can use the offsets in the structure to pull apart the pieces. Note that the function uses the glrTrimNull() function to get rid of everything past the first null character in the string that's past the beginning of the output port string. Listing 9.18 shows the entire glrParseDevNames() function.

> **NOTE**
>
> Access is not neat about the value returned in the prtDevNames property. It will often have trailing "junk" after the information you're interested in. Since you can't count on its length, you must be careful to copy out only the parts that are of interest to you. When you're retrieving the property from a form or a report, be sure to throw away all but the first 58 characters of the string. (That gives you room for 8 bytes of offsets, 32 bytes for the device, and 9 bytes each for the port and the driver name.) In the sample application, you'll find the constant MAX_DEVNAME defined as 58.

Listing 9.18

```
Function glrParseDevNames(strPrtDevNames As String,
➡ dr As glr_tagDeviceRec)

    Dim DN As glr_tagDevNames
    Dim temp As glr_tagDevOffsets

    ' To use LSet, both sides must be user-defined types.
    ' Therefore, copy the string into a temporary
    ' structure, so you can LSet it into dn.
    temp.strDevInfo = Left(strPrtDevNames, 8)
    LSet DN = temp
```

```
      dr.strDeviceName = Mid(strPrtDevNames, DN.intDevicePos + 1,
      ➡ DN.intDriverPos - DN.intDevicePos - 1)
      dr.strDriverName = Mid(strPrtDevNames, DN.intDriverPos + 1,
      ➡ DN.intOutputPos - DN.intDriverPos - 1)
      dr.strPort = glrTrimNull(Mid(strPrtDevNames,
      ➡ DN.intOutputPos + 1))
      glrParseDevNames = DN.intDefault
End Function
```

Controlling Your Destination

Windows allows you to print a document to any of the installed printer devices just by changing the current printer selection, using the Print Setup dialog. You can install a fax printer driver that will intercept your printing and send your document out the fax modem, for example, or just have multiple printer choices installed for various printing jobs.

Almost every Windows application uses the standard Print Setup dialog provided with Windows 3.1. This works fine in an interactive environment. But under program control you must find some other way to specify a list of possible devices and provide a method for the user to choose a new output destination. Then, once you've changed the document's destination and told your application to send the document to that device, you need to set things back the way they were.

CH9.MDB contains a form demonstrating the use of the prtDevNames (and prtDevMode) property, allowing you to choose a form or report from your database and print it to any of the installed print devices. The form, zfrmPrintDest, displays a list of all the forms and reports and a list of the installed printer devices (see Figure 9.23 later in the chapter). Once you select an object and an output device, you can print either to the original device or to the chosen device. The code in zfrmPrintDest accomplishes this goal by changing the value of the prtDevNames property for the chosen object, and it changes it back once it's been printed.

WARNING It is imperative that you set the prtDevMode property at the same time you set the prtDevNames property if you are changing the output destination. Changing just the prtDevNames property will cause your system to crash unless you happen to be very lucky. In the examples that follow, you'll see that before you change the prtDevNames property, you should request the default DevMode structure from the printer driver, perhaps copy over the current user settings, and set the object's prtDevMode property before changing the prtDevNames property. Failure to follow these steps will, sooner or later, cause Windows to crash.

The problem of providing your users a means of selecting a specific output device and sending the current document to that device has two parts. First of all, you must be able to build a list of all the installed output devices. Then, once your user has chosen one from the provided list, you must be able to use the prtDevNames property to control the destination of the particular document. Neither of these steps is terribly difficult, once you know the tricks.

Providing a List of Output Devices

Windows maintains a list of all the installed output devices in WIN.INI, under the "[devices]" heading. For example, the [devices] section in your WIN.INI might look like this:

```
[devices]
Generic / Text Only=TTY,LPT1:
HP LaserJet 4/4M=HPPCL5E,LPT1:
HP LaserJet III=HPPCL5MS,LPT1:,LPT2:
HP LaserJet Series II=HPPCL,LPT1:
WINFAX=WINFAX,COM3:
```

Each line represents one device, and the syntax of each line can be represented as

Device Name=Driver,Output1[,Output2[,Output3]]

To provide your users a list of devices, you need to read all the items from WIN.INI and create an array of these items in Access. Luckily, Windows provides a mechanism for reading all the items within a section at once. The Windows API call GetProfileString() can retrieve either a single line from an .INI file or a whole section, depending on how the parameters to the function are filled in. In general, the syntax for GetProfileString() is this:

int GetProfileString(*strSection*, *strEntry*, *strDefault*,

➡ *strReturnBuffer*, *intReturnBufferSize*)

where the following is true:

- *strSection* is the name of the section in WIN.INI from which to read. In this case the section will be "devices".

- *strEntry* is the item within the section to retrieve. If the value is null (0&), Windows fills the buffer (strReturnBuffer) with all the items in the section. Each item will be terminated with a single null value (CHR$(0)), and the entire string will end with two nulls. If you pass a specific value to GetProfileString(), Windows places the portion of the matching entry to the right of the equal sign in *strReturnBuffer*.

- *strDefault* is the value to return in *strReturnBuffer* if no match can be found. This value must never be null. You know that your search didn't find any matches if *strReturnBuffer* is the same as *strDefault* after the function call.

- *strReturnBuffer* is the string buffer into which Windows will place the text found by the function call. If *strEntry* is a single item, *strReturnBuffer* will contain either the portion of that specified entry to the right of the equal sign (if it's found) or the string in *strDefault* (if it's not).

- *intReturnBufferSize* is the size, in characters, of *strReturnBuffer*. As with many Windows API calls, you must specify the width of the buffer before passing it to the Windows DLL. For example, to create a 1024-character buffer, you can use either

```
Dim strReturnBuffer as String * 1024
```

or

```
Dim strReturnBuffer as String
strReturnBuffer = Space$(1024)
```

The function returns the number of characters returned in *strReturnBuffer*.

Therefore, to get a string containing all the different installed output devices, you could make this single call to Windows:

```
Dim strMatchStr as String * 255
varTemp = GetProfileString("devices", O&, "Default",
➥ strMatchStr, 255)
```

You'd then need code to pull apart this string, breaking it at each null value and placing the values into an array. You can find the code to do this in the function glrGetRawDevices() (in basSetPrinter in CH9.MDB). glrGetRawDevices() fills the array passed to it with each of the devices found in WIN.INI using the brute-force method of walking through the string returned from GetProfileString(), pulling off pieces until it runs out of characters.

Unfortunately, the situation is a bit more complicated than it would at first appear. As shown in the sample "[devices]" section earlier in this section, a single device can be configured to run from more than one specific port. For example, in the sample section the HP LaserJet III is set up to work with either LPT1: or LPT2:. Therefore, to present your user with a complete list of choices, you need to take this raw list of devices and prepare a complete list, one for each port.

Your final goal, then, is to create an array of information about output devices. Each element of this array will contain a specific output device name, its driver name, and a specific output port. The user-defined type used as the basis for this array is declared in the module basPrtGlobal—the glr_tagDeviceRec:

```
Type glr_tagDeviceRec
    strDeviceName As String
    strDriverName As String
    strPort As String
End Type
```

The module basSetPrinter contains a function, glrFillDeviceArray(), that takes the raw array of strings and creates the necessary array of structures. The code itself isn't terribly enlightening, although you might find it instructive to work through it. Perhaps you'll even be able to find a faster way to pull apart the pieces! On return from this function, the application will have a global array of structures, each containing a specific pairing of device and port.

Armed with this array, you now have all the information you need. Given an array that you want to present to the user as a list or combo box, your best solution in

Access is to write a list-filling callback function in Access Basic. The function glrFillDeviceList() calls the functions mentioned above to fill the array in its initialization case and then uses the values from that array when asked to provide data. Figure 9.23 shows the sample form in use with the list of devices visible. You should be able to easily use the code provided in basSetPrinter in your own applications by just importing the entire module. Listing 9.19 shows the function that fills the list of devices. You can call this function directly from your own applications once you've imported basPrtGlobal and basSetPrinter.

FIGURE 9.23:

The sample form, zfrmPrintDest, shows the list of all available output devices and their ports.

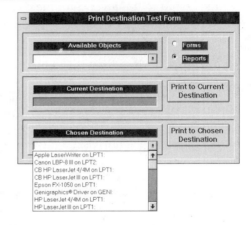

Listing 9.19

```
Function glrFillDeviceList(ctlField As Control,
➡ varID As Variant, varRow As Variant, varCol As Variant,
➡ varCode As Variant)
    Static intCount As Integer
    Dim varRetval As Variant

    Select Case varCode
        Case LB_INITIALIZE
            ' Fill the array aDevList() with all the devices.
            intCount = glrGetDevices(aDevList())
            varRetval = (intCount > 0)
        Case LB_OPEN
            varRetval = Timer
```

```
        Case LB_GETROWCOUNT
            varRetval = intCount
        Case LB_GETCOLUMNCOUNT
            varRetval = 1
        Case LB_GETCOLUMNWIDTH
            varRetval = -1
        Case LB_GETVALUE
            varRetval = aDevList(varRow).strDeviceName &
        ➥ " on " & aDevList(varRow).strPort
    Case LB_END
            Erase aDevList
    End Select
    glrFillDeviceList = varRetval
End Function
```

Providing a List of Reports or Forms

Although it's not a primary concern of this example, you'll also find a list of available forms or reports on the sample form. This allows your users to choose an object from the existing items in the Database Container window. You could use DAO to retrieve this information (see Chapter 6), but it's simpler to retrieve it by delving into the undocumented system tables. (To view the system tables, choose View ➤ Options ➤ Show System Objects. If you set this value to Yes, Access makes the system tables visible in the Database Container window). The MSysObjects table maintains an active list of all the objects in the database, including a column that keeps track of each object's type. If you open MSysObjects, you'll see that the last column consists of an integer value. Experience shows that all forms have the value –32768 and all reports have the value –32764 in the Type column. Therefore, you can create a SQL expression that returns just a list of forms or a list of reports.

To create such a list, you can use an expression like this:

```
Select Name from MSysObjects Where (Left(Name, 4) <> 'zFrm'
➥ And Type = IIF([grpListType]=2, -32768, -32764))
➥ Order by Name;
```

This expression looks at the group box, grpListType, allowing the user to choose either forms or reports (see Figure 9.24) by pulling the object type (2 for forms and 3 for reports, which matches the A_FORM and A_REPORT constants) from the value of the group box. In addition, this particular example skips any form with a

FIGURE 9.24:
The Available Objects combo box
uses the system tables to provide the
user with a list of objects.

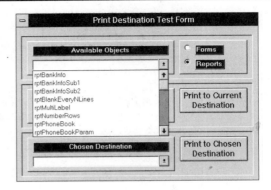

name beginning with "zFrm", avoiding the problem of allowing you, as part of this example, to attempt to load the form that's currently running.

Retrieving the Default DevMode Structure

Before you attempt to change the values stored in the prtDevNames property, you must also be able to retrieve a particular printing device's default DEVMODE structure. This really has nothing to do with Access, but rather with the fact that Access has exposed some rather low-level functionality. If you change the prtDevNames settings, you're in effect telling Access to use a different printing device. If you don't also change the prtDevMode property to match that new device, it's guaranteed that the two properties will collide. (Remember, the prtDevMode property also contains the name of the printing device.) In many cases this isn't catastrophic, and you'll never notice the difference. Switching between some pairs of printers, on the other hand, can be detrimental to the health of your application, Windows, and any other applications that are currently running. The GPF (General Protection Fault) caused by this error is generally fatal, and you'll usually end up quitting Windows or rebooting your computer.

Every printer that supports the DEVMODE structure maintains default values for each of the fields, and you can retrieve the default DEVMODE from the driver, calling the driver's ExtDeviceMode() function. Once you have the default values, you can copy the user-modifiable values from your form or report's prtDevMode property into your copy of the default DEVMODE structure. Then you can use this new combined DEVMODE structure as the prtDevMode property for your object. The read-only fields (device name, DEVMODE size and extra size, and so on) must not be changed, however.

Unfortunately, it's not possible to retrieve printer driver information directly from Access. Although the printer driver is a DLL just like all the other libraries you can access from Basic, unlike other Windows DLLs the name of the library to load isn't known until run time. Since Basic's Declare statement requires that you know the name of the library you're going to call when you write the code, you're out of luck. To call a function in the printer driver, you need to be able to find the address of the particular function and call it through that address. This mechanism just isn't available in Basic, so we've provided our own DLL, ACCPRINT.DLL, to accomplish this task. (This DLL is also used later in the chapter, in the section "Retrieving Printer Capabilities.")

Accessing the Printer Driver

To call functions in a printer driver, your Access code must load the printer driver DLL into memory, retrieve a handle to that library, and then call ACCPRINT.DLL with that handle. The Windows API provides a simple function you can use—Load-Library() (aliased as glr_apiLoadLibrary() in the example code). Once you've finished using the DLL, you must unload it, using the Windows API function FreeLibrary() (aliased as glr_apiFreeLibrary() in the code). Actually, you won't personally need to worry about loading and freeing the printer driver since we've provided a function to retrieve the default DEVMODE structure for you. The function glrGetDefaultDM() takes as a parameter a variable of type glr_tagDeviceRec (containing the printer driver name, the device name, and the port). It loads the driver, retrieves the default DEVMODE structure, frees the library, and returns the DEVMODE structure as a string (just as though it had been retrieved from an object's prtDevMode property). Listing 9.20 shows the glrGetDefaultDM() function.

To perform the task of retrieving the default DEVMODE structure yourself, glrGet-DefaultDM() calls the glrGetDM() function that resides in ACCPRINT.DLL. It's declared in basPrtGlobal in these ways:

```
Declare Function glrGetDMLng Lib "ACCPRINT.DLL" Alias "glrGetDM"
➡ (ByVal hLib As Integer, ByVal strDevice As String,
➡ ByVal strPort As String, ByVal lngDM As Long,
➡ ByVal intMode As Integer) As Integer
Declare Function glrGetDMStr Lib "ACCPRINT.DLL" Alias "glrGetDM"
➡ (ByVal hLib As Integer, ByVal strDevice As String,
➡ ByVal strPort As String, ByVal dm As String,
➡ ByVal intMode As Integer) As Integer
```

The function requires five parameters:

- The handle to a previously loaded printer driver library

- A string containing the name of the print device ("HP LaserJet 4/4M", for example)

- A string containing the name of the output port ("LPT1:", for example)

- The address of a string in which to place the results, or a null value when retrieving the DEVMODE size

- The mode to use, either DM_SIZE (0) to retrieve the size of the structure or DM_COPY (2) to retrieve a copy of the default structure

You call the function once (as glrGetDMLng()) to retrieve the size of the printer driver's DEVMODE structure. Once you know the size, you allocate enough space in your output string to contain the whole thing. Then you call grlGetDM() again (this time as glrGetDMStr()) to retrieve the actual DEVMODE structure.

> **NOTE**
>
> This may be the first time you've encountered a single DLL function aliased two different ways. To be able to pass a string's address to the DLL, you normally declare the parameter ByVal, As String. In this case, though, you also need to pass a null value (0&) as the address when you're trying to retrieve the size of the DEVMODE structure. To avoid the type conflicts that would otherwise arise, we just declared the function twice, passing a string in one version and passing a Long in the other. The DLL gets a Long value either way—either a null value or the address of a string buffer—but Basic isn't that forgiving about different variable types. Providing two different declarations for the same function gets around this difference between C and Basic.

Listing 9.20

```
Function glrGetDefaultDM(dr As glr_tagDeviceRec)
    Dim strBuff As String
    Dim intRetval As Integer

    If Not LoadTheDriver(dr) Then Exit Function
    ' Get the DEVMODE structure size, or -1 on
    ' failure.
    intRetval = glrGetDMLng(hLib, dr.strDeviceName, dr.strPort,
    ➡ 0, 0)
    If intRetval > -1 Then
        ' Allocate enough space for the DEVMODE
        ' structure.
        strBuff = Space(intRetval)
        ' Retrieve the driver's DEVMODE structure.
        intRetval = glrGetDMStr(hLib, dr.strDeviceName,
        ➡ dr.strPort, strBuff, 2)
    End If
    glrUnloadDriver
    glrGetDefaultDM = strBuff
End Function
```

Copying Values from One DEVMODE to Another

Once you've retrieved the printer driver's default DEVMODE structure, you copy the settings for the current document that apply to the new printer into that DEVMODE structure. We've provided a function in basDevMode, glrCopyDMValues(), that does the work for you. It looks at each bit in the lngFields member of the structure, and for each field that has been initialized by the new driver, it copies the data from the original prtDevMode property. Listing 9.21 shows the entire function.

Listing 9.21

```
Sub glrCopyDMValues(strOldDM As String, strNewDM As String)

    Dim dmOld As glr_tagDevMode
    Dim dmNew As glr_tagDevMode
    Dim dmTemp As glr_tagDevModeStr

    ' Copy the string into a structure, using
    ' LSet. Since both sides of LSet must be user-
    ' defined types, copy the string into a temporary
    ' structure first.
    dmTemp.strDevMode = strOldDM
    LSet dmOld = dmTemp
    dmTemp.strDevMode = strNewDM
    LSet dmNew = dmTemp

    ' Copy all the old settings.
    ' Some of these may not apply to the newly chosen
    ' printer. Check the flags, so only applicable
    ' ones get copied over.
    If dmNew.lngFields And DM_ORIENTATION Then
        dmNew.intOrientation = dmOld.intOrientation
    End If
    If dmNew.lngFields And DM_PAPERSIZE Then
        dmNew.intPaperSize = dmOld.intPaperSize
    End If
    If dmNew.lngFields And DM_PAPERLENGTH Then
        dmNew.intPaperLength = dmOld.intPaperLength
    End If
```

```
      If dmNew.lngFields And DM_PAPERWIDTH Then
          dmNew.intPaperWidth = dmOld.intPaperWidth
      End If
      If dmNew.lngFields And DM_SCALE Then
          dmNew.intScale = dmOld.intScale
      End If
      If dmNew.lngFields And DM_COPIES Then
          dmNew.intCopies = dmOld.intCopies
      End If
      If dmNew.lngFields And DM_DEFAULTSOURCE Then
          dmNew.intDefaultSource = dmOld.intDefaultSource
      End If
      If dmNew.lngFields And DM_PRINTQUALITY Then
          dmNew.intPrintQuality = dmOld.intPrintQuality
      End If
      If dmNew.lngFields And DM_COLOR Then
          dmNew.intColor = dmOld.intColor
      End If
      If dmNew.lngFields And DM_DUPLEX Then
          dmNew.intDuplex = dmOld.intDuplex
      End If
      If dmNew.lngFields And DM_YRESOLUTION Then
          dmNew.intYResolution = dmOld.intYResolution
      End If
      If dmNew.lngFields And DM_TTOPTION Then
          dmNew.intTTOption = dmOld.intTTOption
      End If
      ' Copy the value back into a string.  Again,
      ' this must go through the temp structure, since
      ' that's the only way LSet can work.
      LSet dmTemp = dmNew

      ' Since the structure dmTemp is set up to hold 512
      ' characters, but there's not that much stuff in
      ' the devMode structure, trim off all but the
      ' necessary bytes.
      dmTemp.strDevMode = Left(dmTemp.strDevMode, dmNew.intSize +
      ➥ dmNew.intDriverExtra)
      strNewDM = dmTemp.strDevMode
End Sub
```

> **TIP**
>
> Manually changing printer drivers, using Access' Print Setup dialog, doesn't preserve settings like the glrCopyDMValues0 procedure does. If, for example, you had set up your report to print in landscape mode and then changed printer drivers manually, that value would be reset to the new driver's default orientation. This is yet another reason to use the functionality demonstrated here rather than using SendKeys to do the work.

Saving, Printing, and Restoring

Once you know how to put together and break apart the prtDevNames string and how to retrieve the default DEVMODE structure for the new driver, you're ready to control print destinations for forms and reports. The code to do this is embedded in the cmdChosen_Click() procedure in the form module attached to zfrmPrintDest, and it breaks down into seven steps:

1. Get the old prtDevNames and prtDevMode properties.
2. Create the new prtDevNames string, based on the chosen output device.
3. Retrieve the default prtDevMode string for the newly selected printer.
4. Copy the current printer settings into the new prtDevMode string.
5. Set the new prtDevNames and prtDevMode strings for the report/form.
6. Print the form or report.
7. Replace the old prtDevNames string. (If you're not planning on saving your changes, this step is unnecessary.) Also, replace the original prtDevMode string.

Retrieving the Old Properties

To retrieve the old prtDevNames property, the sample application calls the glrRetrieveDevNames() function, passing to it an object name and that object's type (A_FORM for forms or A_REPORT for reports). The glrRetrieveDevNames() function attempts to open the appropriate object, retrieves its prtDevNames property, and leaves the object open in design mode so later code can alter its properties. It also fills in the strOldDM variable so you can both replace the value of the prtDevMode property when you're done and copy values from it to the new DEVMODE structure you'll retrieve from the new output device:

```
strOldDevName = glrRetrieveDevNames(strName, intType, strOldDM)
```

Creating the New prtDevNames String

Before you can print to a new destination, you must have chosen an item from the list of output devices. Since the combo box showing the list of devices, cboDestination, has its BoundColumn property set to 0, the value of the control is the index of the chosen item. That number corresponds to an element in the array that filled the combo. So, given the value of the control, your code knows the specific device that was chosen. Passing the chosen item number to glrFillStructure fills the passed-in glr_tagDeviceRec structure with the information from the array of installed output devices. Once you have the glr_tagDeviceRec structure filled in, you can call glrBuildDevNames() to build the appropriate value to be used as a new prtDevNames string:

```
glrFillStructure CInt(ctl), dr
strNewDevName = glrBuildDevNames(dr)
```

Retrieving the Default DEVMODE Structure for the New Printer

As mentioned earlier, before you can change the output device you need to have the default DEVMODE structure for the new device you're switching to. You can call the glrGetDefaultDM() function to retrieve that information. You can then use the glrCopyDMValues procedure to copy the values from the current DEVMODE structure to the new one.

```
strDM = glrGetDefaultDM(dr)
glrCopyDMValues strOldDM, strDM
```

Setting the New Properties

To set the new prtDevNames string, your application must open the form or report in design mode and assign the newly created string to its prtDevNames property. (Remember that none of the prtDevMode, prtDevName, or prtMip properties are modifiable at run time.) To avoid problems when switching printer drivers, you must also assign the new printer's DEVMODE structure to the object's prtDevMode property at this point.

The simple matter of assigning the prtDevNames and prtDevMode properties is complicated in this application only because the object to be printed can be either a form or a report. The subroutine glrSetDevName (in basPrtDest) does the work for you in this case:

```
glrSetDevName strName, intType, strNewDevName, strDM
```

Listing 9.22 shows the glrSetDevName subroutine.

Listing 9.22

```
Sub glrSetDevName(strName As String, intType As Integer,
➡ strDevName As String, strDevMode As String)
    If intType = A_FORM Then
        DoCmd OpenForm strName, A_DESIGN
        Forms(strName).prtDevMode = strDevMode
        Forms(strName).prtDevNames = strDevName
    ElseIf intType = A_REPORT Then
        DoCmd OpenReport strName, A_DESIGN
        Reports(strName).prtDevMode = strDevMode
        Reports(strName).prtDevNames = strDevName
    Else
        MsgBox "Invalid Object Type!", 16, "glrSetDevName()"
    End If
End Sub
```

Printing the Object (Finally!)

To print the object you can use the Print macro action. You'll probably want to switch to Normal view (instead of Design view) for printing. In addition, you may or may not want to close the object when you're done printing. (If you do close it without saving, you needn't worry about resetting the prtDevNames and prtDevMode properties.) The DoPrint subroutine in the basFormEvents module takes care of the printing and closing details for you. It opens the object in an appropriate view for printing, does the printing, and then either puts it back into design mode so the caller can restore its state or closes it. If you asked DoPrint to close the object, it calls the DoClose subroutine to do the work. (You'll find both procedures in the module attached to zfrmPrintDest.) This subroutine makes sure the warnings have been turned off (SetWarnings False) so Access won't complain about the form or report's being changed. It also resets some objects on the main example form, cleaning up after the print job.

Replacing the Old Properties

Finally, to reset the prtDevNames property to its original state, you can call the glrSetDevName subroutine again, this time passing the old prtDevNames value. This restores the original state of the form or report's prtDevNames and prtDevMode properties, allowing you to print to the originally chosen device:

```
glrSetDevName strName, intType, strOldDevName, strOldDM
```

All the rest of the code in the sample application deals with manipulating the form or report object you've selected to print and with the user interface of the application itself. You may find it useful to study the code in the application, but in any case you should be able to adopt it to your own needs quite easily.

Retrieving Printer Capabilities

To use the prtDevMode property to its fullest, you'll want to provide a means of allowing your users to make choices about their printed output. You might want to allow them to programmatically choose a particular page size, the number of copies, or the paper source. Access, though, does not provide a means of determining your printer's capabilities. Windows, of course, does provide just such a mechanism, although it does so in a second-hand manner.

When Access (or any other Windows application) presents you with a Printer Setup dialog box, it has requested information from the printer driver to know which options to make available to you. Windows itself doesn't know what each printer can do; it's up to the individual drivers to make that information available. Therefore, every printer driver must contain a specific function, DeviceCapabilities(), that other Windows programs can call to retrieve information about what the printer can do.

Just as with the glrGetDefaultDM() function presented earlier, you can't call directly into the printer driver from Access. Since Basic requires that you know the name of the DLL into which you're calling at the time you write your code, unless you provide different DECLARE statements for each and every printer driver you'll ever want to access, you need to use our ACCPRINT.DLL to retrieve information from the printer driver. We first describe the DeviceCapabilities() function as the driver implements it and then discuss how you can use it in your own applications. You have choices here: you can call the lower-level functions we've provided, which call directly into our DLL, which calls the driver. See Table 9.20 for a list of all the options when calling our DLL.

You could also just call the higher-level functions, which shield you from having to worry about many of the details involved in calling the DLL. We strongly recommend that you use the higher-level functions since they make your use of this information much, much simpler. Table 9.21 lists all the high-level functions, the parameters to each, and the return values.

TABLE 9.20: Options Available When Calling ACCPRINT.DLL

Value	High-Level Function in basPrintCap	Meaning
DC_BINNAMES	glrGetBinNames()	Copies an array containing a list of the names of the paper bins into the strOutput parameter. To find the number of entries in the array, call glrDeviceCapabilitiesLng with the lngOutput parameter set to 0; the return value is the number of bin entries required. (Each bin name can be up to 24 (BINNAME_SIZE) bytes long.) This allows you to make sure your output string is long enough to hold all the entries. Otherwise the return value is the number of bins copied
DC_BINS	glrGetBins()	Retrieves a list of available bins. The function copies the list to lngOutput as an array of integers. If you call glrDeviceCapabilities with lngOutput set to 0, the function returns the number of supported bins, allowing you to allocate a buffer with the correct size. See the description in Table 9.12 of the intDefaultSource member of the DEVMODE structure for information on these values
DC_COPIES	glrGetCopies()	Returns the maximum number of copies the device can produce
DC_DRIVER	glrGetDriverVersion()	Returns the printer-driver version number
DC_DUPLEX	glrGetDuplex()	Returns the level of duplex support. The function returns 1 if the printer is capable of duplex printing. Otherwise the return value is 0

TABLE 9.20: Options Available When Calling ACCPRINT.DLL (continued)

Value	High-Level Function in basPrintCap	Meaning
DC_ENUM-RESOLUTIONS	glrGetEnumResolutions()	Returns a list of available resolutions. If lngOutput is 0 the function returns the number of available resolution configurations. Resolutions are represented by pairs of long integers representing the horizontal and vertical resolutions
DC_EXTRA	glrGetExtraSize()	Returns the number of bytes required for the device-specific portion of the DEVMODE structure for the printer driver
DC_FIELDS	glrGetFields()	Returns the lngFields member of the printer driver's DEVMODE data structure. The lngFields member indicates which members in the device-independent portion of the structure are supported by the printer driver
DC_FILEDE-PENDENCIES	glrGetFileDependencies()	Returns a list of files that also need to be loaded when a driver is installed. Call glrDeviceCapabilitiesLng() with lngOutput set to 0 to return the number of files. Call glrDeviceCapabilities() to fill a string buffer with an array of file names. Each element in the array is exactly 64 (FILEDEPENDENCY_SIZE) characters long
DC_MAX-EXTENT	glrGetMaxExtent()	Returns a typePOINT_INT variable containing the maximum paper size the intPaperLength and intPaperWidth members of the printer driver's DEVMODE structure can specify
DC_MIN-EXTENT	glrGetMinExtent()	Returns a typePOINT_INT variable containing the minimum paper size the intPaperLength and intPaperWidth members of the printer driver's DEVMODE structure can specify
DC_ORIENTA-TION	glrGetOrientation()	Retrieves the relationship between portrait and landscape orientations in terms of the number of degrees portrait orientation is to be rotated counterclockwise to get landscape orientation. It can be one of the following values: 0 (no landscape orientation); 90 (portrait is rotated 90 degrees to produce landscapes—for example, PCL); 270 (Portrait is rotated 270 degrees to produce landscape—for example, dot matrix printers)

TABLE 9.20: Options Available When Calling ACCPRINT.DLL

Value	High-Level Function in basPrintCap	Meaning
DC_PAPER-NAMES	glrGetPaperNames()	Retrieves a list of the paper names supported by the model. To find the number of entries in the array, call glrDeviceCapabilitiesLng() with the lngOutput parameter set to 0: the return value is the number of paper sizes required (each paper size name can be up to 64 (PAPERNAME_SIZE) bytes long). This allows you to make sure your output string is long enough to hold all the entries. Otherwise, the return value is the number of paper names
DC_PAPERS	glrGetPapers()	Retrieves a list of supported paper sizes. The function copies the list to lngOutput as an array of integers and returns the number of entries in the array. If you call glrDeviceCapabilitiesLng() with lngOutput set to 0, the function returns the number of supported paper sizes. This allows you to allocate a buffer with the correct size. See the description in Table 9.12 of the intPaperSize member of the DEVMODE data structure for information on these values
DC_PAPERSIZE	glrGetPaperSize()	Copies the dimensions of supported paper sizes in tenths of a millimeter to an array of typePOINT_INT structures pointed to by lngOutput. This allows an application to obtain information about nonstandard paper sizes
DC_SIZE	glrGetDMSize()	Returns the intSize member of the printer driver's DEVMODE data structure
DC_TRUETYPE	glrGetTrueType()	Retrieves the driver's capabilities with regard to printing TrueType fonts. The return value can be one or more of the following capability_flags: DCTT_BITMAP (1): device is capable of printing TrueType fonts as graphics; DCTT_DOWNLOAD (2): device is capable of downloading TrueType fonts; DCTT_SUBDEV (4): Device is capable of substituting device fonts for TrueType. In this case the strOutput parameter should be 0
DC_VERSION	glrGetSpecVersion()	Returns the specification version to which the printer driver conforms

TABLE 9.21: High-Level Functions for Retrieving Printer Driver Capabilities

Function Name	Parameters	Return Values
glrGetBinNames()	dr As glr_tagDeviceRec, astrBinNames() As String	Fills in astrBinNames(), returns the number of bins
glrGetBins()	dr As glr_tagDeviceRec, aintList() As Integer	Fills in aintList(), returns the number of bins
glrGetCopies()	dr As glr_tagDeviceRec	Returns the number of copies
glrGetDriverVersion()	dr As glr_tagDeviceRec	Returns the driver version number
glrGetDuplex()	dr As glr_tagDeviceRec	Returns 1 if duplex allowed, otherwise 0
glrGetEnumResolutions()	dr As glr_tagDeviceRec, aptlngList() As typePOINT_LONG	Fills in aptlngList(), returns the number of resolutions
glrGetExtraSize()	dr As glr_tagDeviceRec	Returns the "extra" size of the DEVMODE
glrGetFields()	dr As glr_tagDeviceRec	Returns the DEVMODE lngFields value
glrGetFileDependencies()	dr As glr_tagDeviceRec, astrList() As String	Fills in astrList(), returns the number of file dependencies
glrGetMaxExtent()	dr As glr_tagDeviceRec, ptValue As typePOINT_INT	Fills in ptValue with the max X and Y dimensions
glrGetMinExtent()	dr As glr_tagDeviceRec, ptValue As typePOINT_INT	Fills in ptValue with the min X and Y dimensions
glrGetOrientation()	dr As glr_tagDeviceRec	Returns the orientation (see Table 9.20)
glrGetPaperNames()	dr As glr_tagDeviceRec, astrNames() As String	Fills in astrNames(), returns the number of paper names
glrGetPapers()	dr As glr_tagDeviceRec, aintList() As Integer	Fills in aintList(), returns the number of papers
glrGetPaperSize()	dr As glr_tagDeviceRec, aptList() As typePOINT_INT	Fills in aptList(), returns the number of paper sizes
glrGetDMSize()	dr As glr_tagDeviceRec	Returns the size of the DEVMODE structure
glrGetTrueType()	dr As glr_tagDeviceRec	Returns the TrueType flag (see Table 9.20)
glrGetSpecVersion()	dr As glr_tagDeviceRec	Returns the driver spec version

The Printer Driver's DeviceCapabilities() Function

To request information about the capabilities of the printer driver, you call the DeviceCapabilities() function exported by each driver. To access this particular function we've provided a function in ACCPRINT.DLL, glrDeviceCapabilities(), that you can call from Access. In Listing 9.23 you'll find two Declare statements for the function. Just as with the glrGetDM() function mentioned earlier, you need to call glrDeviceCapabilities() in two different ways. If you pass 0 for the fifth parameter, the driver returns the number of items in the array you're requesting. If you pass it the address of a string buffer in the fifth parameter, it returns the actual data. To make it possible to call the function both ways, we've provided two ways of calling it. If you call glrDeviceCapabilitiesLng(), you pass a long integer in the fifth parameter. If you call glrDeviceCapabilities(), you pass the address of a string buffer in the fifth parameter. This difference in calling conventions points out one more reason why you'd be better served in using the high-level functions discussed below.

Listing 9.23

```
Declare Function glrDeviceCapabilitiesLng Lib "ACCPRINT.DLL"
➥ (ByVal hLib As Integer, ByVal strDevice As String,
➥ ByVal strPort As String, ByVal intCapability As Integer,
➥ ByVal lngOutput As Long, ByVal lngDevMode As Long) As Long
Declare Function glrDeviceCapabilities Lib "ACCPRINT.DLL"
➥ (ByVal hLib As Integer, ByVal strDevice As String,
➥ ByVal strPort As String, ByVal intCapability As Integer,
➥ ByVal strOutput As String, ByVal lngDevMode As Long) As Long
```

No matter which way you call glrDeviceCapabilities(), it requires six parameters. The following table lists those parameters and gives information about each:

Parameter	Description
hLib	The handle to a printer driver DLL, previously loaded with a call to glrLoadLibrary() or the equivalent
strDevice	The device name, as listed in Win.INI ("HPLaserJet 4/4M")

Parameter	Description
strPort	The output port, as listed in Win.INI ("LPT1")
intCapability	An item chosen from the first column of Table 9.20, indicating the capability about which to inquire
strOutput or lngOutput	Either a string buffer to be filled or 0 to indicate that you're requesting the number of elements the function will return
lngDevMode	The address of a glr_tagDeviceMode variable, 0 for your purposes

An Example of Calling glrDevice-Capabilities() Directly

This example calls glrDeviceCapabilities() directly. You will most likely find it easier to call the high-level functions (listed in the second column of Table 9.20) than to use this example's code directly. We started out using code like this but quickly realized that much of the code was the same among the different capabilities. Although you might never use this code, it does demonstrate how to use glrDeviceCapabilities() in case you need it for purposes we haven't considered.

Retrieving a List of Paper Names

The code in Listing 9.24 requests a list of the supported paper names from a specific printer driver. You pass to it a filled-in glr_tagDeviceRec variable, along with a dynamic array that it can fill with the list of names. It returns the total number of items it received from the driver. The function that called GetPaperNames() would need to fill in the glr_tagDeviceRec structure, create the dynamic array, and then call the function (see Listing 9.24).

GetPaperNames() first attempts to load the requested printer driver into memory, using the LoadLibrary() function (aliased as glr_apiLoadLibrary()). If it fails, the function returns a value between 0 and 32. You need to check for this error anytime you call LoadLibrary() directly.

```
hLib = glr_apiLoadLibrary(dr.strDriverName & ".DRV")
' hLib values between 0 and HINSTANCE_ERROR signify an error.
If hLib >= 0 And hLib <= HINSTANCE_ERROR Then
    hLib = 0
    MsgBox "Unable to load requested driver (" & dr.strDriverName
    ➥ & " (" & hLib & "))"
    varTemp = 0
    GoTo GetPaperNamesExit
End If
```

You must retrieve from the driver the number of items in the array it will be return-ing so you can allocate enough space in the string buffer it will fill in. To do this you call glrDeviceCapabilitiesLng(), passing a 0 in the fifth parameter and the capability ID in the fourth parameter. If this call succeeds, it returns to you the number of ele-ments in the array of names.

```
' Find out how many items there are in the list.
lngItemCount = glrDeviceCapabilitiesLng(hLib, dr.strDeviceName,
➥ dr.strPort, DC_PAPERNAMES, 0, 0)
' glrDeviceCapabilities() will return -1 if there's an error.
If lngItemCount = -1 Then
    lngItemCount = 0
    GoTo GetPaperNamesExit
End If
```

Once you know how many elements there will be, you can use ReDim to resize the output array to fit them all. Given a known size for each element you'll be retrieving from the driver (PAPERNAME_SIZE, in this case), you can use Access' String() function to make sure the string buffer is large enough. Failure to execute this step will surely cause Windows to crash since it might very well overwrite Access code or data with the output values when you call DeviceCapabilities(). Finally, you can call grlDeviceCapabilities() to retrieve the necessary string buffer full of informa-tion from the driver:

```
' Reset the size of the array to fit all the items.
ReDim astrList(lngItemCount - 1)

' The size of each element you'll be reading from the string.
intItemSize = PAPERNAME_SIZE

' Clear out the string buffer you'll use to retrieve
' info from the driver, or you'll be sorry!
strItemName = String(intItemSize * lngItemCount, 0)
```

```
' Retrieve the info, in strItemName.
varTemp = glrDeviceCapabilities(hLib, dr.strDeviceName,
➡ dr.strPort, DC_PAPERNAMES, strItemName, 0)
```

You're still missing the final step at this point, though. You need to pull apart the pieces of the array. (They're stored in one big, continuous stream in strItemName.) This is simple enough, of course, since you know the length of each piece. It's just a matter of pulling out each piece with the Mid() function, trimming off trailing nulls (using the glrTrimNull() function), and assigning the substring to the current row in astrList().

```
' The driver will return -1 if there was an error.
If varTemp <> -1 Then
    ' Go through the string, picking apart the pieces,
    ' breaking every PAPERNAME_SIZE chars.
    For intI = 0 To lngItemCount - 1
        astrList(intI) = glrTrimNull(Mid(strItemName,
        ➡ intI * intItemSize + 1, intItemSize))
    Next intI
End If
```

As you'll see in the next section, we've done all this work for you. You should be able to retrieve any of the printer's capabilities easily with the high-level functions listed in the second column of Table 9.20.

Listing 9.24

```
Function GetPaperNames(dr As glr_tagDeviceRec, astrList()
➡ As String)
    Dim lngItemCount As Long
    Dim strItemName As String
    Dim varTemp As Variant
    Dim intI As Integer
    Dim strDevice As String
    Dim strOut As String
    Dim intItemSize As Integer

Const HINSTANCE_ERROR = 32

    ' Load the driver DLL.
    hLib = glr_apiLoadLibrary(dr.strDriverName & .DRV")
    ' hLib values between 0 and HINSTANCE_ERROR signify an
    ' error.
    If hLib >= 0 And hLib <= HINSTANCE_ERROR Then
        hLib = 0
```

```
        MsgBox "Unable to load requested driver (" &
        ➥ dr.strDriverName & " (" & hLib & "))"
        varTemp = 0
        GoTo GetPaperNamesExit
    End If

    ' Find out how many items there are in the list.
    lngItemCount = glrDeviceCapabilitiesLng(hLib,
    ➥ dr.strDeviceName, dr.strPort, DC_PAPERNAMES, 0, 0)
    ' glrDeviceCapabilities() will return -1 if there's
    ' an error.
    If lngItemCount = -1 Then
        lngItemCount = 0
        GoTo GetPaperNamesExit
    End If

    ' If there aren't any items, it's time to quit.
    If lngItemCount = 0 Then
        GoTo GetPaperNamesExit
        Erase astrList
    End If

' Reset the size of the array to fit all the items.
    ReDim astrList(lngItemCount - 1)

    ' The size of each element you'll be reading from
    ' the string.
    intItemSize = PAPERNAME_SIZE

    ' Clear out the string buffer you'll use to retrieve
    ' info from the driver, or you'll be sorry!
    strItemName = String(intItemSize * lngItemCount, 0)

    ' Retrieve the info, in strItemName.
    varTemp = glrDeviceCapabilities(hLib, dr.strDeviceName,
    ➥ dr.strPort, DC_PAPERNAMES, strItemName, 0)

' The driver will return -1 if there was an error.
    If varTemp <> -1 Then
        ' Go through the string,picking apart the pieces,
        ' breaking every PAPERNAME_SIZE chars.
        For intI = 0 To lngItemCount - 1
            astrList(intI) = glrTrimNull(Mid(strItemName,
            ➥ intI * intItemSize + 1, intItemSize))
```

```
        Next intI
    End If
GetPaperNamesExit:
    ' Set the return value now (either 0 or the number
    ' of items).
    GetPaperNames = IIf(varTemp = -1, 0, lngItemCount)
End Function
```

Saving Effort by Calling the High-Level Interfaces

To save you some time (and us as well), we've provided a high-level interface to each of the printer capabilities. The name of each of these functions is listed in Table 9.21. The second column of this table lists the parameters you need to pass to each function, and the third column lists the return values. You'll probably find it much simpler to call these functions directly since they perform for you almost all the work shown in Listing 9.24. The code in Listing 9.25 is quite similar to the code you'd need to retrieve any of the printer's capabilities.

GetPaperNameList(), in Listing 9.25, first fills in a glr_tagDeviceRec structure. This example pulls its information from the default printer listed in WIN.INI, using the glrGetCurrentDevice() function (see basSetPrinter in CH9.MDB):

```
' Set up the device rec.
If Not glrGetCurrentDevice(dr, ",") Then
    Exit Function
End If
```

Once GetPaperNameList() has the device information, it can call glrGetPaperNames() directly. This fills in the dynamic array, astrSizes(), and returns the number of elements in the array:

```
' Get the list of paper sizes.
intCount = glrGetPaperNames(dr, astrSizes())
```

Finally, once you have the array of paper names, you can use it however you like. This simple example just displays the list in the Immediate window:

```
' You might use astrNames() to fill a list box, for example.
For intI = 0 To intCount - 1
    Debug.Print astrNames(intI)
Next intI
```

Listing 9.25

```
Function GetPaperNameList()
    Dim dr As glr_tagDeviceRec
    Dim astrNames() As String
    Dim intCount As Integer
    Dim intI As Integer

    ' Set up the device rec.
    If Not glrGetCurrentDevice(dr, ",") Then
        Exit Function
    End If

    ' Get the list of paper sizes.
    intCount = glrGetPaperNames(dr, astrNames())

    ' You might use astrNames() to fill a list box, for example.
    For intI = 0 To intCount - 1
        Debug.Print astrNames(intI)
    Next intI
End Function
```

A Major Example

To see an example of all this technology in action, check out frmDevCaps in CH9.MDB (see Figure 9.25). This form displays all the information it can retrieve from the printer driver you select from the list of installed drivers. The code you'll find in the form module deals mostly with displaying the information, but in it you'll find lots of calls to the functions listed in Table 9.21. Although it's doubtful you'll need all this information in any of your applications, you may well need one or more of the items from frmDevCaps when you present lists of formatting options to your users.

Summary

In this chapter we've taken a look at reports and printing from several angles. We covered these issues:

- Report and section events and properties

- A series of sample reports, using events and properties
- Undocumented details of printing, including the prtDevMode, prtDevNames, and prtMip properties

We've worked through some problematic issues in report design, but we've barely scratched the surface. Report design is even more complex than forms design. As long as you keep forward motion of the report engine in mind, you can control the flow of events on your reports.

As for the printing issues, although the information presented here is relevant to all of Windows, Access is alone in the manner in which it presents this information (unlike Word, Excel, or any of the other Microsoft products). Getting at and changing printer characteristics isn't easy with Access, but you have enough generic routines under your belt now to at least make it possible. You should be able to use the prtDevMode, prtDevNames, and prtMip properties in your own applications, given the sample routines in this chapter.

FIGURE 9.25:

The form frmPrtCaps demonstrates all the values available by calling glrDeviceCapabilities().

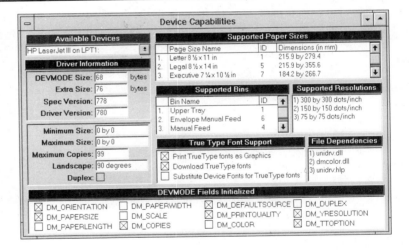

CHAPTER

TEN

Menus, Toolbars, and User-Interface Macros

- Knowing how and when to use macros

- Using Access' toolbars

- Manipulating Access' menus programmatically

- Reacting to mouse clicks with a popup menu

- Setting and retrieving global options

10

This chapter covers areas of Access that require you to use macros and areas that concern themselves with macros. You'll learn about menus and toolbars, as well as the AutoKeys and AutoExec macros. We discuss reasons for using macros as opposed to using Access Basic. In addition, we cover the entire Windows API dealing with menus, as it applies to your Access applications. Also, since you'll be modifying global options settings in this chapter, we cover the Application.GetOption() and SetOption methods.

Just as a point of reference, macros in Access work differently than macros in any other Microsoft product: unlike the macros of Word or Excel, they're not recordable and they don't create Access Basic code. They do provide a simple front end to programming for novice users and, as this chapter outlines, are required for some operations in Access.

To Macro or Not to Macro

When creating Access applications, you usually have a choice as to the method you employ when automating actions. Access supplies a group of more than 40 macro actions, from which you can create simple (and perhaps not-so-simple) applications without writing any Access Basic code at all. In their attempt to provide a database program "for the masses," the Access development team has done an excellent job. With the addition of new macro actions in Access 2.0, you really can do a great deal using only macros.

But it should be clear from the preceding chapters that the authors of this book do not subscribe to the "macros only" school of application development. The following lists show our reasons why you should choose Access Basic over macros for a given project.

Choose macros if you

- Need to prototype your application quickly. Since macros make it simple to open, close, and manipulate forms and reports, you'll find it easy to mock up the flow of an application using macros.

- Don't really care about complete bullet-proofing. Since macros can't trap for errors, Access itself handles any run-time errors that occur while your application is running. If you're providing an application for your own purposes or for in-house use, then perhaps it's not worth the time trapping for errors.

- Need to use user-defined menus, trap keystrokes, or provide a macro that runs automatically, without any command-line interference. Each of these actions requires a macro.

Otherwise, use Access Basic. Since you can more easily comment, document, and control Access Basic code, it seems the wiser choice for large applications. You must use Access Basic if you need to

- Call functions in DLLs, including all the Windows API functions
- Control transaction processing (allowing rollbacks of partially completed sets of actions)
- Use scoped variables (variables that are visible only from specific areas of your application)
- Provide commented printouts of your application code (Although you can print macros, it's much more difficult to document them carefully than it is to document Access Basic code.)

Actually, most applications use a combination of Access Basic and macros. Since menus, key trapping, and auto-execution require macros, these macros are a part of almost every application. You may also find that some actions are just easier using macros and that their use doesn't compromise the robustness of your application. You need to make these decisions yourself, based on your own needs.

In addition, you'll find that your Access Basic programming will be enhanced if you completely understand all the macro actions. Since there are some operations in Access that require macro actions (opening and closing forms, for example), you need to know which of the hundreds of Access operations supported by Access Basic require macro actions (and the DoCmd keyword) and which are directly supported by Access Basic. It's to your benefit to experiment with macros first, learning their capabilities, before moving on to Access Basic.

The following sections detail the three areas of Access that require macros:

- Trapping keystrokes globally
- Providing user-defined menus
- Executing a macro from the command line or automatically at startup

In addition, we cover the use of toolbars since they fit so neatly into this group of topics.

The AutoKeys Macro

You may find in some instances that your application would work better if certain keystrokes could be mapped to actions of your choosing. Access provides a global key-remapping interface, centered around the AutoKeys macro. The next few sections discuss how and why you'd use this special macro.

Choosing Your Name

By default, Access looks for a macro named AutoKeys to control the global key mappings. You can change the name of this macro to be any macro you like, using the View ➤ Options menu/dialog. Figure 10.1 shows the dialog in action. By specifying a name here you're instructing Access to look in this macro for actions to take

---

FIGURE 10.1:
Choose a name (AutoKeys is the default) to specify the name of your key-mapping macro.

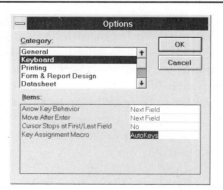

when any key is pressed. (For the sake of simplicity, the rest of this chapter refers to whatever macro you've assigned in the View ➤ Options menu as the AutoKeys macro.)

Creating Your Key Actions

To create your key mappings, you need to create a new macro. In design mode, make sure the macro names are visible by either clicking the "macro names" button on the toolbar or choosing the View ➤ Macro Names menu option. Enter a key name formatted like the examples in the first column of Table 10.1 into the Macro Name column of the design grid. Enter an action to take when that key is pressed in the Action column of the design grid. Just as with any other macro you create, the Action column can contain any of the standard macro actions and can use the RunCode action to run Access Basic code.

TABLE 10.1: AutoKeys Macro Names Syntax

SendKeys Syntax	Key Combinations
^A or ^2	Ctrl + any letter or number
{F11}	Any function key, 1 through 12
^{F11}	Ctrl + any function key
+{F11)	Shift + any function key
^+{F11}	Ctrl + Shift + any function key
{Insert}	Ins
^{Insert}	Ctrl+Ins
+{Insert}	Shift+Ins
^+{Insert}	Ctrl+Shift+Ins
{Delete} or {Del}	Del
^{Delete} or ^{Del}	Ctrl+Del
+{Delete} or +{Del}	Shift+Del
^+{Delete} or ^+{Del}	Ctrl+Shift+Del

To separate your key mappings, just place a new macro name (actually, the key name to map) on a new row. Access stops playing back each macro when it runs across a new name in the macro group. You might want to separate each macro from the next with a blank line and perhaps some comments.

Figure 10.2 shows the macro editor in use, with two key mappings already laid out. In this case if the user presses the Ctrl+S key and if the current object is a form (see the section "Restricting Key Playback to the Desired Environment" later in this chapter), Access puts up a message box followed by an extra beep. If the user presses Shift+Ins, Access performs the Edit ➤ Cut menu item (just a little practical joke, since the user is probably expecting this combination to paste the contents of the clipboard instead).

FIGURE 10.2:

The macro editor in action, modifying the AutoKeys macro

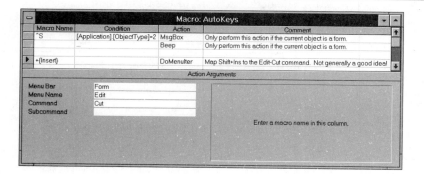

Not All Keystrokes Are Created Alike

Table 10.1 lists the only keystrokes that are valid within your AutoKeys macro. Access really must restrict the values to those in this list; think what would happen if you reassigned the A key, for example, in your AutoKeys macro! On the other hand, it would be nice if Access made it possible to trap certain untrappable keys, like the PgUp and PgDn keys, as well as the Esc key. If you use any keys not listed in this table, Access gives you a warning message when you attempt to save the macro.

The following key combinations are noticeably absent from the list in Table 10.1:

- Alt+function keys
- Alt+Ins
- Alt+Del
- Esc
- Cursor movement keys (in any combination with Ctrl, Shift, or Alt)
- Alt+A through Alt+Z (reserved for hot-key usage)

Hierarchy of AutoKeys Mappings

Access always looks in the AutoKeys macro first, before looking into its own internal key mappings. That is, if you have a standard Access key remapped, your mapping will take precedence. If you've remapped Shift+Ins in your AutoKeys macro, the standard Access use of this key (to paste text from the clipboard) will no longer work. Your macro could, of course, trap these built-in keys for their own use and then perform the standard action when they were done.

WARNING Do not attempt to trap a standard keystroke, performing some action when you press that particular key, followed by a call to SendKeys to perform the original keystroke. Once Access has remapped the key it's completely remapped, and using SendKeys will cause an infinite loop. You can use Ctrl+Break to get out of the loop, but it certainly won't do what you'd expect. Instead of using SendKeys to perform the original keystroke, use DoMenuItem, if possible.

Restricting Key Playback to the Desired Environment

Although keys assigned in the AutoKeys macro normally take effect anyplace in the Access environment, you can limit that. If you set a condition in the macro sheet's Condition column, the macro attached to the particular keystroke will be played out only if the condition is met. For example, see Figure 10.2. In that example the macro attached to Ctrl+S will be skipped unless the current object is a form. If you press the key combination anywhere else, Access will see that the condition isn't met and just skip the action.

You can also skip the action from Access Basic code that the macro calls (using the RunCode macro action). Once your code gets control, it can check the necessary condition. If that condition isn't met, it can either use the DoCmd CancelEvent action or just exit the current function. To match the macro condition in Figure 10.2, you need code like that shown in Listing 10.1.

Listing 10.1

```
Function DoMsgBox()
    If Application.CurrentObjectType = A_FORM Then
        MsgBox "AutoKeys got you here!"
        DoCmd Beep
    End If
End Function
```

Allowing for Multiple AutoKeys "Sets"

Access makes it simple for you to change the current key assignment macro. Although it assumes you want to use a macro named AutoKeys unless you've told it otherwise, your application can change that value at run time. You can use the GetOption() and SetOption methods of the application object to retrieve and set the name of the macro. (See the section "Controlling Global Options" later in this chapter for more information on the GetOption() and SetOption methods.) To change the current key assignment macro, use this code:

```
Application.SetOption "Key Assignment Macro", "YourNewMacroName"
```

To retrieve the current setting (so you can store away its value to reset later, perhaps), use this code:

```
strOldMacroName = Application.GetOption("Key Assignment Macro")
```

In CH10.MDB you'll find the example form frmAutokeys, which demonstrates the method of changing the key assignment macro while your application is running.

Although it might not at first be completely obvious why you'd need to change key assignments midstream, think about the following scenario. Imagine that your application consists of several completely distinct portions, each with its own set of tables and activities. You'd like to supply consistent key mappings for all the pieces, but the actions those keystrokes must produce are very different, depending on the section of the application that's currently active. Your macros could, of course, detect the current portion of the application that's running and react differently in each instance. Since complex macros are very difficult to maintain and debug, a better solution would be to use separate key assignment macros for each section of your application. The macros are global throughout Access, and you can have only one loaded at a time, so you need to use Application.GetOption() to retrieve the current macro setting, store it away, set your new value with Application.SetOption (which takes effect immediately), and restore the old value when you leave.

AutoKeys versus Keypress Events

Although the use of AutoKeys macros and Keypress events (KeyPress, KeyDown, and KeyUp) might seem somewhat overlapping, they really are designed for different uses altogether. Table 10.2 lists some comparisons between the two.

TABLE 10.2: Comparing Autokeys and KeyPress Events

Feature	AutoKeys	Keypress Events
Scope	Global throughout Access	Local to the specific control (or form)
Keystroke Trapping	Limited to very specific keys	Can trap any key on the keyboard (KeyDown/KeyUp)
Precedence	Take precedence over Access' built-in keystrokes	Take precedence over *all* keystrokes (including Autokeys')

You use AutoKeys mappings when you want to supply a quick way to activate some action in your applications. That is, if you want Ctrl+B to start a backup, you could assign the Ctrl+B key mapping to perform the necessary action. Unless your macro restricted the use of the key, you'd be able to press Ctrl+B anywhere while your application was running and have the action take place.

You use KeyDown/KeyUp/KeyPress events when you need to react to a key the user has pressed while interacting with a particular control. Rather than causing some action to take place, the KeyPress events can be used to react to each keystroke in a stream of keystrokes. You can trigger other events, depending on the keystroke that's been pressed; convert the keystroke to a different keystroke; or even disregard the keystroke.

The interaction between the KeyDown event and the mappings in the AutoKeys macro is somewhat difficult to pin down. The sample form, frmKeyDownTest in CH10.MDB (see Figure 10.3) helps demonstrate that interaction. Following the directions on that form will show that the Ctrl+Z keystroke mapping in the AutoKeys macro takes precedence over the key trapping in the KeyDown event.

AutoKeys mapping and the use of the KeyPress event are complementary: the KeyPress event can trap and react only to "typable" characters, and AutoKeys can trap and react only to characters that KeyPress skips. For example, if a control has code that reacts to the KeyPress event and the application has an AutoKeys macro that traps for Ctrl+Z, the KeyPress event code won't even notice that particular keystroke. Since the KeyPress event can trap only keys that have corresponding ASCII values (A–Z, a–z, 0–9, and Backspace), it will live harmoniously with any settings you've made in your AutoKeys macro.

FIGURE 10.3:
frmKeyDownTest proves that AutoKeys mappings take precedence over the KeyDown event.

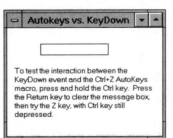

AutoKeys in Competition with SendKeys

Be very careful when mixing SendKeys actions with AutoKeys key mappings. Unless you keep careful track of the keys you're trapping with AutoKeys mappings, you can find things not going the way you'd planned. Since SendKeys sends its keystrokes through Access' key handler as though the user had typed them from the keyboard, the AutoKeys mappings intercept and alter them as it's been told. This is especially important when your code resides in a library database that needs to work with various user databases. Since there's no way you can know how the user has remapped the keyboards with the AutoKeys macro, you should never use SendKeys in a library database except for keys that cannot be remapped using the AutoKeys macro.

Running a Macro Automatically

For most applications you want Access to take a specific action automatically every time a user loads your application. Although it would be nice if Access provided a facility for executing a procedure at startup, it does not. Instead, you must use a macro. If your application contains a macro named Autoexec, Access executes that macro after it loads the database. Because of the limitations of macros, we suggest that this macro do nothing more than use the RunCode action to execute an Access Basic procedure.

Other Macros Allowed, Too

If you'd like to be able to specify a particular macro to be run when your application loads, you have another choice. You may have a particular application that you use for varying circumstances. In one instance you'd like to start it and run Macro1. In other instances you'd like to start it and run a different macro, Macro2. To make this happen you need to tell Access, from the command line, which macro to run. You can specify both a database and a startup macro from the command line, as in:

MSACCESS *YourApp*.MDB /x*YourMacro*

Access will run the macro name that follows the /x (with or without a separating space) as soon as it loads the application. By setting up different icons that run Access with various startup macros, you can control exactly which portion of your application gets executed when the user clicks a given icon.

> **WARNING** If your application includes an Autoxec macro and your command line tells Access to run a different macro when it loads your application (using the /x option), Access first runs the Autoxec macro and then your specified macro. This certainly isn't a bug, but it is something to be aware of.

Skipping the Autoexec Macro

If you have a macro running automatically everytime you start your application, sooner or later you're going to want to run the application *without* running that macro. To bypass the Autoexec macro, you press and hold the Shift key when you load the database. This is a standard keypress, used in (at least) Access, Word, and Excel to bypass auto-executing code.

If your application is running in the Access run-time environment, your users won't be able to bypass the Autoexec (or the command line–specified) macro at all. The run-time environment disregards the Shift key at load time.

Using Custom Toolbars in Your Application

Toolbars provide another means of communication between your application and its users. By providing carefully planned toolbars you can make your application far easier for your users to work with and to find their way through. As we discuss in Chapter 13, a well-designed application provides an explicit means to accomplish every action that will occur often. Although you might allow a double-click on a control to start an action, this isn't an explicit action; the user has to know about the double-click. You might include a menu item to start the same action, but the user must still search through the menus to find the item. A better alternative would be to provide a toolbar button for each commonly used activity.

Access provides two types of toolbars: built-in and custom. Access itself ships with 18 toolbars, 2 of which are left empty for your use. In addition, you can create as many toolbars as you like for each application. The discussion in the following sections focuses on using toolbars in your applications.

Using Your Own Toolbars with Forms

To use custom toolbars in your application, you take two steps:

1. Turn off the standard toolbars, if you don't want them to be visible.

2. Turn on your own custom toolbars.

To perform these actions you use the ShowToolbar macro action. The Access Basic syntax for the action is

DoCmd ShowToolbar *strToolbarName*[, *fShow*]

where *strToolbarName* is the actual name of the toolbar to act upon and *fShow* is one of the following:

```
A_TOOLBAR_YES
A_TOOLBAR_NO
A_TOOLBAR_WHERE_APPROP
```

If you leave off the *fShow* argument, Access assumes you want to turn off the toolbar (A_TOOLBAR_NO).

Using the ShowToolbar macro action is similar to choosing the View ➤ Toolbars dialog, except that by using the macro action you can specify whether to display a toolbar in all views, as opposed to only the view in which it's appropriate. You could, if you liked, use the following code to make the form design toolbar visible, no matter what you were doing in Access:

```
DoCmd ShowToolbar "Form Design", A_TOOLBAR_YES
```

Therefore, you could create a function like this one, which turns on or off the specified toolbar and does the opposite with the standard Form view toolbar.

```
Sub ShowYourToolbar(strToolbar As String, fTurnOn as Integer)
    DoCmd ShowToolbar strToolbar, Iif(fTurnOn, A_TOOLBAR_YES,
    ➡ A_TOOLBAR_NO)
    DoCmd ShowToolbar "Form View", Iif(fTurnOn, A_TOOLBAR_NO,
    ➡ A_TOOLBAR_WHERE_APPROP)
End Sub
```

If you want to display only a single toolbar for every form in your application, the steps are simple: as part of the Autoexec macro, call the ShowToolbar macro actions to set the visibility of the appropriate toolbars. If you want different forms to display different toolbar configurations, call ShowYourToolbar("YourToolbar", True) from your form's Activate event handler, and call ShowToolBar("YourToolbar", False) from your form's Deactive event handler. The form frmTestToolbar in CH10.MDB demonstrates these concepts. Figure 10.4 shows frmTestToolbar in action.

FIGURE 10.4:

You can load a toolbar in your form's Activate event and hide it in the Deactivate event.

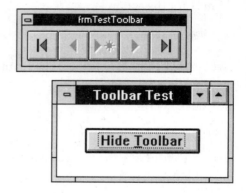

Allowing Users to Change Toolbars

You can use the global option setting Can Customize Toolbars to control whether or not your users can change the toolbars. If this option is set to Yes, users can add or delete toolbar buttons. If it's set to No, they won't be able to make changes to the toolbars. In either case they'll be able to move, size, hide, or show them. To change the value you can use the SetOption method of the Application object, along with the voCUSTOMIZE_TOOLBARS constant. (See the section "Controlling Global Options" later in this chapter for more information.)

Where Are Those Toolbar Changes?

If you allow your users to change the toolbars, you need to be aware of where those changes are stored. Changes to the appearance of a toolbar (where it's located and its size and position) are stored in the system database (SYSTEM.MDA, by default). Each logged-in user maintains a different group of settings for toolbars in the system database. As long as each user logs in under a unique name, each can have a distinct workspace environment.

Changes to the content of the toolbars (the buttons displayed on the toolbar) are stored in one of two places, depending on whether the toolbar is built in or custom. Content changes for built-in toolbars are stored in the system database, under the name of the user who made the change. Again, as long as users log in using unique names, they should each see their own toolbars. Content changes for custom toolbars, however, are stored with the particular application that contains the toolbar. If you want your users to be able to change your custom toolbars, make sure each user owns a copy of the application database locally. Otherwise, each person's changes would overwrite other changes that had been previously made.

Moving Toolbars Around

Access stores information about your custom toolbars in one of its system tables, MSysToolbars. (To display the system tables, set the View ➤ Options menu item Show System Tables to Yes.) Although Microsoft neither documents nor supports the modification of Access' system tables, you can use the MSysToolbars table to move toolbars from one database to another. Unlike most of the other system tables, MSysToolbars is not read-only. This means you can rename and delete toolbars directly in MSysToolbars. In addition, you can append toolbars from one database into another, and if the destination database doesn't yet have any toolbars, you can just copy the entire MSysToolbars table from one database to another. This can save you work since you won't have to rebuild all your toolbars as you move from one application to another.

You can use the sample subroutine glrCopyToolBars in Listing 10.2 to copy the entire MSysToolbars table if the output database doesn't yet contain toolbars or just append the current set of toolbars if it does. Note that this procedure contains no error checking. If you were to use this for any reason besides helping your development process, you'd need to add some serious error handling to deal with all the errors that might come up. In addition, this code doesn't deal with the problems involved with duplicate toolbar names. Since this isn't an issue for Access, just for your users, you'll want to manually resolve the multiple name issues yourself.

Listing 10.2

```
Sub glrCopyToolbars(strOutput As String)
    Dim strSQL As String
    Dim db As Database
    Dim rst As Recordset

    Set db = OpenDatabase(strOutput)
    ' Opening the record set based on MSysToolbars might fail,
    ' so set the error trap.
    On Error Resume Next
    Set rst = db.OpenRecordset("MSysToolbars", DB_OPEN_TABLE)
    If Err <> 0 Then
        ' If the OpenRecordSet() failed, just export the table.
        DoCmd TransferDatabase A_EXPORT, "Microsoft Access",
        ➥ strOutput, A_TABLE, "MSysToolbars", "MSysToolbars"
    Else
        ' If MSysToolbars already existed, then just run
        ' an append query to tack these onto the end. It'll be
        ' up to you to rename them if there are name conflicts.
        strSQL = "INSERT INTO MSysToolbars (Grptbcd, TbName)
        ➥ IN '" & strOutput & "'"
        strSQL = strSQL & " SELECT DISTINCTROW
        ➥ MSysToolbars.Grptbcd, MsysToolbars.TbName"
        strSQL = strSQL & " FROM MsysToolbars"
        DoCmd SetWarnings False
        DoCmd RunSQL strSQL
        DoCmd SetWarnings True
    End If
    rst.Close
    db.Close
End Function
```

Be aware that the methods described here are not documented, nor are they supported by Microsoft. You can use these methods because they currently work, but they aren't guaranteed to work in any other version of Access. If you want to count on programmatic control of the toolbars, here are some traps to watch out for:

- Access reads in the list of available toolbars only when it loads the database. Therefore, if you modify MSysToolbars by hand, you must reload the database to see your changes take effect in the toolbars' user interface.

- Nothing keeps you from creating two toolbars with the same name when you create them programmatically. Access itself, through its user interface, doesn't allow you to do this. If you create two toolbars with the same name, Access' user interface behavior will be unpredictable. Therefore, if you copy toolbars from one database to another, be sure to rectify any name conflicts yourself.

- Depending on your permissions, you may or may not be able to write to MSysToolbars.

Based on all these possible problems, we suggest you modify MSysToolbars only when your application is under development. If you try to copy or append toolbar data from a running application, you're asking for trouble unless you've kept very tight reins over the user's interactions with the toolbars.

Using Toolbars in the Run-Time Environment

The Access run-time executable does not support Access' built-in toolbars. If you're developing an application that will be distributed with the run-time version of Access, you must supply your own set of toolbars for every circumstance in which you'd like your users to see a toolbar. In addition, the run-time version does not automatically display the toolbars based on the current context. You must explicitly use the ShowToolbar macro action each time you want to show or hide a particular toolbar. The run-time version turns off all toolbars, by default. If you want a toolbar visible when your application starts up, you must place a call to the ShowToolbar macro action in your Autoexec macro.

Don't Try This at Home—What You Can't Do with Access Toolbars

Although the toolbar support in Access 2.0 is phenomenal when compared with that in Access 1.1, there are still quite a few "holes." To keep you from spending time trying to find these features, here's a list of things you *can't* do with Access toolbars:

- You can't add your own bitmaps. Access stores the entire range of toolbar bitmaps in one clump in MSAIN200.DLL. There are two copies of the set, one for large buttons and one for small. The resources are numbered 326 and 327 in the DLL (use a resource editor like APSTUDIO.EXE, which is part of Microsoft Visual C++, to examine them). Although you could, of course, modify the bitmap in MSAIN200.DLL, this is neither supported nor condoned by Microsoft. Although it won't break your copy of Access (unless you do something wrong with the bitmap), you don't have the legal rights to distribute altered copies of that DLL. We provide this information here only for interest's sake.

- You can't modify the functionality of the buttons Access does provide. Although you can attach a button to a toolbar that calls your own code, you can't change what the built-in buttons do when they're pressed.

- You can't modify toolbars programmatically. There's no interface for adding or deleting buttons from your applications' code.

- You can't dock/undock or move toolbars from within your applications.

- You can't provide custom help topics for your toolbars.

- You can't call functions stored in a form's module. Since they're encapsulated in the form, there's no way to get at them externally.

- You can't trap any events that occur because of the user's interactions with toolbars. That is, you won't know when they've opened, closed, clicked, docked, or hidden your toolbar.

We all hope that future versions of Access give us more programmatic control over the toolbars.

Menus in Access

In Access, as in all other Windows programs, menus are resources (just like icons and bitmaps). As such, there are limits to the number and size of menus you can have loaded at any given time, just as there's a limit to the number of graphics elements that Windows can have loaded at once. Since menu items are normally text, however, this limit is usually not a problem. Access ships with a number of prebuilt menu layouts, and you can create your own. Unlike most of the other Windows desktop applications from Microsoft, however, you cannot add items to the existing menu structures in Access. All menus in Access are either prebuilt or user defined. You must use Access' macros to create your own menus, and if you want to modify an existing menu tree, you need to re-create all the pieces of it yourself, adding or removing the items you need.

The following sections discuss how you can create, modify, and use user-defined menus in Access. In addition, we provide examples and code for using the Windows API to manipulate the menus in ways that most Access users wouldn't even imagine. You'll be able to modify text on menus, place or remove a check mark next to menu items, disable and enable specific menu items or entire pull-down menus, all while your application is running. In addition, you'll be able to supply your own menu when your user clicks the right mouse button, instead of its pulling down the standard Access context-sensitive menus. (This technique is available only in the standard version of Access. In the run-time version, the right mouse button is disabled.)

Creating Menus

Access provides only a single menu at any given time. Unlike other MDI applications (such as Visual Basic), you cannot attach a menu to a specific form. All menus are attached to the main Access window, and their parent is the running instance of Access itself. (You can, of course, have each form *invoke* a different set of menu items. Using the form MenuBar property you can have Access display a specific menu for each form in your application.) In addition, Access maintains only a single instance of each menu layout. If you make changes using the Windows API to a menu layout (modifying text, for example), everyplace in Access where that layout might be used will also see your changes. Your changes will also be persistent thoughout your Access session until you either change them back or restart Access. None of your changes to Access menus, using the API, will remain across sessions.

WARNING   Each of Access' built-in menu layouts is stored in MSAIN200.DLL, and Access reads them in from that library each time it starts up. If you have a resource editor like APSTUDIO.EXE (part of Visual C++), you can look through MSAIN200.DLL to see all the different menu layouts. Never make any changes to the menu structures in MSAIN200.DLL. If you do, it's guaranteed that Access will not run correctly. Although it's instructive to dig through the DLL to see how the Access resources are stored, you should never make any changes to this file.

Since Access provides no mechanism at all for modifying the built-in menus, you must create an entirely new replacement menu system if you need to change or remove even a single menu item from the standard menus. Luckily, Access 2.0 includes a Menu Builder that makes it slightly easier than it was in previous versions to create your own menus. We first discuss creating menus using the Menu Builder and then examine the steps necessary to create your own or modify previously created menus by hand.

TIP   If you're going to create a new menu system, your best bet is to base it on an existing menu tree. The Menu Builder Wizard provides a list of all the existing menus. You'll find it much simpler to choose one of these and remove or modify items than to start from scratch and build your own. If you must create a new menu system from scratch, plan it carefully before starting. Windows provides a standard way of using menus. (See Chapter 13 for more information on Windows standards.)

TIP

Using the Windows API, you can remove menu items manually from the standard Access menus rather than having to create a whole new menu system. Although removing menu items using the API is too much work if you need to remove many of them, for just a few it works well. You can easily remove menu items at startup and replace them when you're done. See the sections later in this chapter, starting with "Manipulating Menus," covering modifications to the menu structure using Windows API calls.

Using the Menu Builder Wizard

In this exercise we walk through the steps for modifying the Form menu bar (the standard menu) to remove the New ➤ Module menu item, and we add a new item to the File menu to run your (imaginary) Access Basic function, ZipItUp(). To get started, choose File ➤ Add-Ins ➤ Menu Builder. You are given four choices: Edit, New, Delete, and Cancel. For this exercise, choose New. Figure 10.5 shows the list of available menu bars.

FIGURE 10.5:

When creating a new menu, start by selecting an existing menu on which to base it.

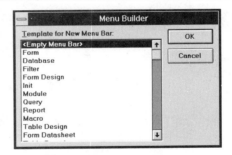

Since you want to modify the standard Form menu bar, choose that option. Once you do you see a dialog box like the one in Figure 10.6. Your first step is to remove the New ➤ Module menu item. To do so, select that item and click the Delete button. Your new menu system will not include that particular menu item. Figure 10.7 shows this action.

FIGURE 10.6:

The Menu Builder allows you to visually create your menu trees.

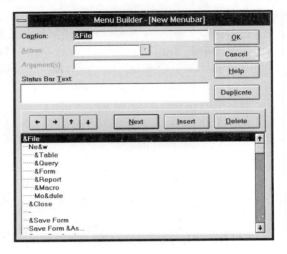

FIGURE 10.7:

You delete a menu item by selecting it and then deleting it. The New ➤ Module menu item in this example is now deleted.

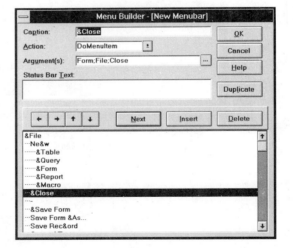

Next, to add the Zip It Up menu item right above the Exit menu item, scroll down until you've highlighted the Exit menu item. Click the Insert button (which inserts a new row above the current cursor location) and enter the new command, &Zip It Up, filling in the Action item by selecting RunCode. (The Menu Builder supports only RunCode, RunMacro, and DoMenuItem actions.) Finally, enter the name of the Access Basic procedure (ZipItUp()) to execute when you choose the menu item, and fill in the status bar text. You've now added the new menu item you needed, and the dialog should look like the one in Figure 10.8.

FIGURE 10.8:

The Menu Builder after you've added your new items

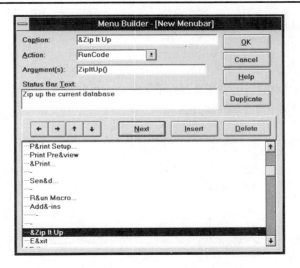

Once you're satisfied with your modified menu, click the OK button on the Menu Builder. This saves your modified menu tree, with one macro group per main menu item or submenu. Access requests a name for the group of menus. For this example, choose Sample_MenuBar. The Menu Builder will create all the macros for you. Figure 10.9 shows the macro list after you've created the menu system in this example.

You can modify your menu system at any time. Just choose Menu Builder from the File ➤ Add-Ins menu, and when it requests the name of the menu to modify, choose your top-level menu (Sample_MenuBar in this case). The Menu Builder goes through all the menus and submenus and presents them to you in the same editing form, for modification.

The macro list after you've created
your menu bar

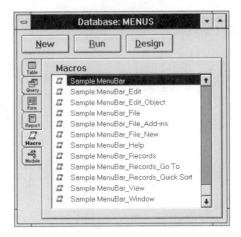

Situations the Menu Builder Can't Handle

If you modify your menu macros manually between sessions with the Menu Builder, you might add some functionality that the Menu Builder just can't handle. There are two possible outcomes: the Menu Builder won't be able to load your macros at all, or it will warn you that it has to lose some of your changes.

The Menu Builder won't be able to open your macros if

- You've added rows to the menu bar macro that contain actions besides AddMenu.
- You've used actions other than DoMenuItem, RunCode, or RunMacro for any row in any of the menu macros.

The Menu Builder warns you, when it attempts to load the menu structure, that it will delete any of the following characteristics when it saves your menu macros:

- Blank rows, or rows with comments only
- Names that don't follow the Menu Builder's naming conventions (Don't rename the macros!)
- Expressions in the Conditions column in a menu bar macro

NOTE You can use a condition in any menu macro, on the line that contains the AddMenu action. The decision to show or not show the menu item is checked only when the form in question is loaded. (That is, you can't use the condition to dynamically add or remove the menu item.) You cannot use a condition on the macro that actually performs the action for the specific menu item.

Some Tips on Using the Menu Builder

The following group of tips will help you in your Menu Builder menu creations:

- You can't fill in Action or Arguments for any menu item that has menu items indented beneath it. If you change a menu item from a "child" item to a "parent" item, the Menu Builder removes the Action and Arguments fields for that item.

- Since the Menu Builder can edit only menus whose macro action is DoMenuItem, RunCode, or RunMacro, if you have any menus built that run other actions, you won't be able to edit that menu tree with the Menu Builder. For example, if your menu contains the Close macro action, the Menu Builder will refuse to load your menu tree.

- Remember that inserting a new item inserts it above the current cursor location. To change the level of the chosen item, use the arrow buttons. Access allows you to indent a menu to any level you like, but when it tries to save the menu, it complains and refuses to save if you've skipped a level.

- If you want to use DoMenuItem as the action for a menu item, be sure to use the builder provided to supply the arguments. Click the "..." button to the right of the text box, and Access provides an easy means for you to fill in the required list of arguments.

Examining Menu Macros

Whether you create menus using the Menu Builder or by hand, you need to understand how Access uses and stores menu macros. The top-level menu bar, each item on the main menu, and each submenu exists in its own macro group. Within that group you'll find an entry for each menu item that appears on the specific menu. For menus attached to the given item, Access uses the AddMenu macro action to specify the menu to pop up if you choose the particular item. For menu items that perform an action, the macro specifies the action to take when the user clicks the item.

For example, frmModifyMenuItems in CH10.MDB uses a sample menu layout. This menu tree includes three top-level menu items, each with a pull-down menu. The File ➤ New item includes a submenu. The final top-level menu has no name and so displays no text on the menu bar. Although this may seem silly at this point, it becomes important when you are creating menus to attach to the right mouse button click, as described later in this chapter. (See the section "Attaching User-Defined Menus to the Right Mouse Button Click.") Since this example shares the menu structure with that one, it will still show up as part of this set of macros. (To see this menu in action, run frmModifyMenuItems in CH10.MDB and choose the Use Custom Menu Bar button.)

In Outline view, the menus lay out as shown in Table 10.3.

TABLE 10.3: The Menu in Outline View

File	New	Form
		Module
		Query
	Close	
Utilities	Run NotePad	
	Run Calculator	

	Save Settings	
(Hidden)	Form Popup	Form Item 1
		Form Item 2
		Form Item 3
	Listbox Popup	ListBox Item 1
		ListBox Item 2
		ListBox Item 3

TABLE 10.3: The Menu in Outline View(continued)

Label Popup	Label Item 1
	Label Item 2
	Label Item 3
Button Popup	Button Item 1
	Button Item 2
	Button Item 3

Although not a perfect representation, Figure 10.10 shows a schematic diagram of how the simple menu lays out. The macro mcrNewMenu is the top-level menu and points to mcrNewMenu_File, mcrNewMenu_Utilities, and mcrNewMenu_Hidden. The one menu item that loads a submenu, the File ➤ New item, points to the mcrNewMenu_File_New macro.

FIGURE 10.10:

Schematic diagram of the menu

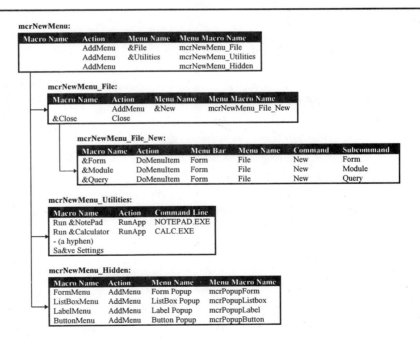

At each level Access uses the AddMenu macro action to add a new menu item. For these actions you must specify the AddMenu action in the Action field, telling Access to add a new menu item here. You must also specify the Macro Name parameter. Its exact value doesn't really matter since the Menu Name parameter tells Access the name to display on the menu. If you leave the Menu Name field blank, Access does not display the menu item. You must also specify the Menu Macro Name parameter, which tells Access which macro to look in for the next menu level. If you leave this item blank, Access disregards the menu item altogether.

If your macro describes an action instead of a submenu, you must specify the menu text (in the Macro Name field), the action to take (in the Action field), and the specific parameters describing that action (which are different for each of the actions). Although the menu item is not very useful if you don't specify an action, you needn't. The menu will display correctly, but it won't do anything.

Attaching the Menu to a Form

Once you've created your menu structure, you need some way to attach it to a form. To do this you specify the name of the main, top-level menu macro in the form's MenuBar property (in the Other Properties group on the property sheet). If you leave this property blank, the form displays either the Access default menu bar or the application's global menu bar, if you've assigned one. (See the section "The Global Menu Bar" later in this chapter.) In addition, your application can easily change the menu bar your form uses. The code in Listing 10.3 shows a way to attach a different menu bar while your application is running. This code is from frmModifyMenuItems in CH10.MDB. You'll also see examples later in the chapter of using the Windows API to modify existing menus at run time.

Listing 10.3 changes the MenuBar property of the current form from a user-defined menu bar back to the default menu bar by setting the MenuBar property to a macro name or to null. Setting the property to to null causes the form to use the Access default or application global menu bar.

Listing 10.3

```
Sub cmdCustomMenuBar_Click()

Const TEXT_CUSTOM = "Use &Custom Menu Bar"
Const TEXT_STANDARD = "Use &Standard Menu Bar"
```

```
    If IsNull(Me.MenuBar) Then
        Me.MenuBar = "mcrNewMenu"
        Me!cmdCustomMenuBar.Caption = TEXT_STANDARD
    Else
        Me.MenuBar = Null
        Me!cmdCustomMenuBar.Caption = TEXT_CUSTOM
    End If
' Re-fill the list box showing the top-level menus.
FillTopLevelList
End Sub
```

Menu Tips

Keep the following tips in mind when creating your menus:

- You can nest menus as deeply as you like, although nesting more than two levels deep is probably not a very good idea; it makes it difficult for users to find the menu items they need. To nest menus, just add an AddMenu action within your menu macro.

- To add a menu hot key (an underlined character in the text, providing access via the Alt key and the specified letter), place an ampersand (&) in front of the character you want to have underlined. To actually place an ampersand in your menu item, use two together (&&). Figures 10.6, 10.7, and 10.8 show the menu builder in action, with ampersands included in each menu item.

- To place a menu divider in your menu, use a single hyphen in the Macro Name column. (See the representation of mcrNewMenu_Utilities in Figure 10.10 earlier in this chapter.)

The Global Menu Bar

In addition to the specific Form and Report menu bars, you can specify a menu bar that Access will display for all windows. Access allows you to specify a single menu bar that can be used globally, such as when you're in the database container, in query design mode, or in macro design mode. Any form or report's specifically designated menu bar always takes precedence over the global menu bar, and setting a form or report's MenuBar property to null causes it to display the application global menu bar, if one exists. Therefore, the default Access menu bar has the lowest priority for display. The application global menu bar has a higher priority and displays for all areas of Access that don't maintain their own user-defined menus. Finally, forms or reports for which you've specified a macro in the MenuBar property always display their own menus, independent of the global settings.

To assign the global menu bar, set the Application object's MenuBar property to the name of the macro that defines the menu bar you'd like to make global. Most often you do this in Access Basic code called from your Autoexec macro. This fragment sets the Application menu bar to be mcrYourGlobalMenu:

```
Application.MenuBar = "mcrYourGlobalMenu"
```

Your application can change the global menu at any time, of course, by just resetting the application's MenuBar property. If you watch Access' menus carefully, you'll see that's exactly what it does: it changes the menu tree based on the current context. Your applications can do that, too, by changing the Application.MenuBar property to a macro that contains the menu you'd like to have displayed in the current situation.

Manipulating Menus

Access' Menu Builder makes it moderately easy to create your own sets of menus. What Access lacks, though, is any mechanism for modifying, manipulating, or otherwise controlling user-defined menus while your application is running. Many applications require the ability to programmatically enable and disable, check and uncheck, or hide and restore menu items. Although Access itself doesn't provide these capabilities, the Windows API can give you the control you need.

Providing a Simpler Interface

Windows provides many functions you can use to set and retrieve information about menus. To make it simpler for you to use these functions, we've provided a set of "wrapper" functions. You can find these Access Basic functions in bas-MenuHandling in CH10.MDB. You'll need to import this module into any application you write that includes any of the menu-handling functionality. Table 10.4 lists all the public procedures in that module, along with a short description of each. The discussions in the following sections refer to procedures in this table instead of using the Windows API functions directly. You can peruse basMenuHandling for the intimate details of calling each function. The rest of this chapter covers how to use most of them.

TABLE 10.4: Windows API Menu-Handling Wrapper Procedures

Procedure Name	Description
glrCheckMenuItem()	Places or removes a check mark before a specific menu item, given the top-level menu number and the item number within that menu
glrCheckSubMenuItem()	Places or removes a check mark before a menu item, given the menu handle and the ordinal menu item number
glrEnableMenuBarItem()	Enables or disables a menu item on the menu bar
glrFindAccessHWnd()	Retrieves the window handle for the main Access Window
glrGetMenuBar()	Retrieves the menu handle for the main Access menu bar
glrGetMenuBarText()	Retrieves the menu text from any of the menu bar items
glrGetMenuBarTitles()	Fills a passed-in array with all the menu text on the menu bar
glrGetMenuHandles()	Retrieves the menu handle for the menu bar and a specific submenu (attached to the main menu bar)
glrGetMenuText()	Retrieves the menu text from any menu item, given the menu handle and the ordinal menu item number
glrGetMenuTitles()	Fills a passed-in array with all the menu text on any menu, given the menu handle
glrGetSystemMenu()	Retrieves the menu handle of the system menu for a given window
glrGrayMenuItem()	Enables or grays a user-defined menu item on any menu attached to the menu bar
glrGraySubMenuItem()	Enables or grays a user-defined menu item on any menu, given a menu handle and the ordinal menu item number

TABLE 10.4: Windows API Menu-Handling Wrapper Procedures (continued)

Procedure Name	Description
glrHandlePopup	Uses the right mouse button to pop up a user-defined menu
glrHiliteMenuBarItem()	Highlights a specific menu bar item (not terribly useful, really)
glrInsertMenuBarItem()	Inserts a menu item in the menu bar at a specific location
glrInsertMenuItem()	Inserts a menu item in any menu at a specified location
glrIsItemChecked()	Determines whether an item on a top-level menu is grayed
glrIsItemDisabled()	Determines whether an item on a top-level menu is disabled
glrIsItemGrayed()	Determines whether an item on a top-level menu is grayed
glrIsMenuBarItemDisabled()	Determines whether a menu bar item is disabled
glrIsSubItemChecked()	Determines whether an item on any menu is grayed, given a menu handle and the ordinal menu item number
glrIsSubItemDisabled()	Determines whether an item on any menu is disabled, given the menu handle and the ordinal menu item number
glrIsSubItemGrayed()	Determines whether an item on any menu is grayed, given a menu handle and the ordinal menu item number
glrRemoveMenuBarItem()	Removes an item from the main menu bar
glrRemoveMenuItem()	Removes an item from any menu, given a menu handle and the ordinal menu item number
glrResetSystemMenu()	Resets the system menu back to the Windows default for a given window
glrSetMenuBarText()	Sets the text of any menu bar item
glrSetMenuText()	Sets the text of any menu item, given a menu handle and the ordinal menu item number

In this chapter we shield you from needing to know how the API calls work. You are welcome to load up basMenuHandling and study the calls to the API, but you can do a great deal of work without ever digging very deeply. The layer we've provided makes it simple to do the work you need without your having to know anything about the details of the API calls themselves.

> **NOTE**
>
> Some of the API functions declared in basMenuHandling are so seldom used that we didn't provide interfaces for them. We discuss them as needed throughout the rest of the chapter. In addition, some added functionality is available if you want to push the API just a little harder. You can, for example, change a horizontal dividing line into a vertical dividing line, giving you a two-columned menu, using the glr_apiModifyMenu() function, but we leave this esoteric functionality for the reader to explore.

Knowing Your Limitations

Although the Windows API provides all the control you could possibly want, Access limits that control by grabbing some of its own. For any built-in menu item or any user-defined menu item whose macro action is DoMenuItem, Access maintains strict control over the status of the menu item. At the time you pull down a menu, Access decides whether each item in the menu is to be available and whether it's to be checked. No matter what you did while the menu was closed, Access controls how it looks once it's dropped down.

This scenario becomes clearer if you envision the menus as a large data structure in memory. This data structure contains information about the menu hierarchy, the text of each item, a command ID or a submenu handle, and the state of each item. When you ask the Windows API to enable or disable a particular item, for example, you're storing specific information in that data structure in memory. When Access displays one of its own menus, it decides, just before it shows you the menu, what the status of each item in the menu ought to be. It might check to see whether you've done anything that might require undoing or whether you've displayed the Immediate window. In any case, no matter how you've changed that data structure in memory, Access can and does override your changes with its own decisions about how those menus ought to appear. Given this information, there's no way you can, for example, make the Edit ➤ Undo menu item available if Access has decided it should be grayed. In addition, if you perform some action and then use the Windows API to inquire whether or not the Edit ➤ Undo menu item is grayed out, you will not receive current information. Since Access doesn't bother updating the menu data structure until it's just about to display the menu, you'll retrieve out-of-date information.

User-defined menus, however, don't normally have these limitations. If the menus you create don't call the DoMenuItem action, you can control their state completely using API calls. Since Access doesn't care about your menus, it won't interfere with their availability or checked state. If your user-defined menus call the DoMenuItem action, however, Access will control their state as if they were built-in menu items.

If you're determined to retrieve information from the Access built-in menus, we've provided an interface to a function from the Windows API that will help you. To retrieve the state of an internal menu, you first pull down the menu and then retrieve its state. This will be ugly in your application since there's no way to hide that menu's flopping down. Windows does provide a method, the LockWindowUpdate() function, for turning off all screen updates. Therefore, you can turn off the screen updating, pull down the necessary menu, turn screen updating back on, and then go about your business, retrieving the state of the menu item you care about.

You can use the subroutine glrEchoOff in basMenuHandling (CH10.MDB) to control the screen updating. Pass it True to turn off the Access screen updating and False to turn it back on. You can use it with a SendKeys action to turn off the display, pull down the necessary menu that needs to have its states set by Access, and then turn it back on.

For example, if you need to know whether or not the Edit ➤ Undo menu item is currently available, you could use code like this:

```
glrEchoOff True
SendKeys "%E{Esc 2}"
glrEchoOff False
```

to turn off the screen display, pull down the menu and immediately close it up, and then turn on the screen display again. After that you can call glrIsItemGrayed() (see the section "Retrieving Top-Level Information" later in this chapter) to check the state of the menu item.

API or Not?

With many menu issues you don't have much choice as to whether or not to use the Windows API. If you want to programmatically gray out, check, or disable a menu item, you have to use the Windows API. On the other hand, if you want to create a menu tree that replicates the entire Access menu tree, with just a few items missing, you have a choice. You can use the Menu Builder to create the macros for you since it's so easy to duplicate an entire menu system using that tool. You may find it easier, though, if you're just going to change or remove a few of the standard Access menu items, to modify the existing menus rather than create your own full set with macros. There are some caveats to this method, of course, since Access doesn't know about or support changes made to its menus with the Windows API. In any case, if you're careful about controlling the menus, you should be able to do a great deal using the rich set of menu-manipulation functions included in the Windows API.

Running the Example

The menu state example form, frmModifyMenuItems, demonstrates many of the topics covered in the following sections. It shows how to retrieve a list of menu items; modify a menu item's text; disable, gray, and check a menu item; retrieve the state of a given menu item; and change a form's menu while the form is running. If you play with the form, you'll notice that you don't get much control over the standard menu items. You can tell the form to make a specific item grayed, but once you pull down the menu it still appears normal. This is just the way Access handles menus. You'll get a better response if you switch to the custom menu bar. Using the custom menu bar you should be able to modify any menu item any way you like. Figure 10.11 shows the sample form in action. In this case the user has disabled the File menu and has tried to pull down the File pull-down menu. Note that in this case the File menu is highlighted, but there's no pull-down portion. Because the item has been disabled, you can't pull down the menu.

Getting a Handle on Menus

Like almost every other data structure in Windows, to manipulate a menu you must have some way to address it. To do so, you must know the handle for that menu. A *handle* is simply a unique number (an unsigned integer) you use to refer to a Windows object—in this case, a menu. In many ways a handle is analogous to a primary key of type Counter in an Access table. The number itself has no significance, but you can use its value in order to refer to a row in an Access table. In the

frmModifyMenuItems in action. The File menu has been disabled.

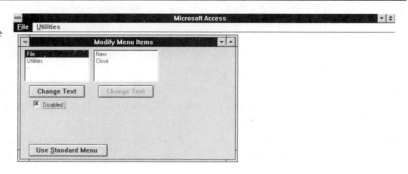

same way, you don't really care what the value of the menu handle is; you just need to know it to refer to a particular menu.

You need a menu handle to be able to use Windows API procedures with any menu. To retrieve a menu handle, you have three choices:

- You can call glrGetMenuBar(), which returns the handle of the main Access menu bar.

```
hMenuBar = glrGetMenuBar()
```

- You can call glrGetMenuHandles (which itself calls glrGetMenuBar()), which fills in the handle of the main menu bar in addition to the handle of a specific menu attached to the menu bar:

```
Dim hMenuBar as Integer
Dim hMenu as Integer
Dim intSubMenu as Integer
```

```
intSubMenu = 1
' Get the handle to the menu bar and the 2nd menu
' (since the menus start counting at 0).
glrGetMenuHandles intSubMenu, hMenuBar, hMenu
```

- You can call glrGetSystemMenu(), which returns a handle to a system menu:

```
' Retrieve a handle for the current form's System Menu.
hSystemMenu = glrGetSystemMenu(Screen.ActiveForm.hWnd)
```

To obtain the handle to a specific submenu, you need to call the API directly. The following example retrieves the menu handle of the menu attached to the fourth menu item on the menu referred to by hSubMenu:

```
newHandle = glr_apiGetSubMenu(hSubMenu, 3)
```

Once you know the handle for a specific menu, you can retrieve the handle to any menu attached to that menu by calling the glr_apiGetSubMenu() function.

Handling the System Menu

The system menu (sometimes called the control menu) is a standard piece of the Windows 3.x window interface. Unless you specifically remove the system menu, it's always there, in the upper-left corner of each window. Figure 10.12 shows a standard form with its system menu opened.

FIGURE 10.12:
Access forms use the standard system menu.

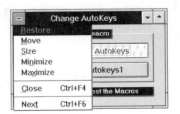

The system menu is, for your purposes, a normal menu that just happens to be attached to each and every form. You can retrieve its menu handle by calling glrGetSystemMenu(). Once you have that handle, you can treat it just like any other menu, following the techniques outlined in the rest of this chapter. The major difference you'll find when dealing with the system menu is that Windows knows the default state of the menu. If you make changes to the system menu on any form (or on the main Access window itself), you can reset it to its original state by calling glrResetSystemMenu().

In addition, you most often refer to items on the system menu differently than you might on normal menus. When working with most menus you refer to menu items by their position in the menu. Starting with 0, you count from the top of the pull-down menu (including the menu dividing lines) to refer to any specific menu item. On the system menu, however, you often refer to menu items by their action instead of their position. Since all the items on the system menu are standard, Windows provides built-in values that refer to their functionality as opposed to their position. See Listing 8.1 in Chapter 8 for more information on modifying the system menu.

Retrieving and Setting Menu Item Status

A specific menu item may be in one of a number of different states at any given time. It can be disabled, in which case it looks normal, but it can't be selected. It can be grayed, in which case it both looks disabled and can't be chosen. Finally, Windows can place or remove a check mark next to the menu item. The functions presented in the following sections will help you control all these states.

Retrieving the Current Status

To retrieve the current state of a menu item, you can call one of seven functions from basMenuHandling. You decide which function to use based on the location of the item and which state you want to retrieve.

Retrieving Top-Level Information

The functions glrIsItemChecked(), glrIsItemDisabled(), and glrIsItemGrayed() all work in the same way, returning a True/False value indicating whether or not the specified menu item is checked, disabled, or grayed:

```
fChecked = glrIsItemChecked(2, 6)
```

After this function call, fChecked will contain True or False, depending on the state of the seventh item on the third pull-down menu. (All menu items start counting at 0 and include any menu dividers in the count.)

Each of these functions uses the ordinal menu item number (the first parameter) to retrieve the handle for the correct menu. They use the second parameter to indicate which item on the menu you're interested in. This makes these functions simple to use as long as you care only about items on the first level of menus.

Retrieving Any Level Information

To inquire about the state of any arbitrary menu item, on any level, you must supply the menu handle yourself. The module basMenuHandling also includes the functions you use to retrieve the handle, so this shouldn't be a real drawback. You can use glrIsSubItemChecked(), glrIsSubItemDisabled(), and glrIsSubItemGrayed() to check the state of any arbitrary menu item. You could always use these functions in place of the corresponding glrIsItem…() functions, but the other functions are simpler to use when dealing with top-level menus.

These functions expect to receive a menu handle and an item number within the menu as parameters. Given those items, the functions can retrieve the information you need from the specific item on the specific menu.

Imagine you want to check the disabled state of the fourth menu item on the submenu attached to the third menu item on the submenu attached to the second item on the menu bar. You could use code similar to this:

```
Dim hMenuBar As Integer
Dim hSubMenu As Integer
Dim hSubSubMenu As Integer
Dim fIsDisabled As Integer

' Get the handles to the menu bar and the 2nd pull-down menu
glrGetMenuHandles 1, hMenuBar, hSubMenu
' Get the handle to the third item on the 3rd sub menu.
hSubSubMenu = glr_apiGetSubMenu(hSubMenu, 2)
' Get the information about the 4th menu item.
fIsDisabled = glrIsSubItemDisabled(hSubSubMenu, 3)
```

Retrieving Menu Bar Information

Unlike normal menu items, menu bar items can be neither checked nor grayed. The only allowed attribute change for them is to be disabled. To make it as simple as possible to inquire about this state, you can use the glrIsMenuBarItemDisabled() function. It takes one parameter, the ordinal value of the menu item to check. To see whether the fourth menu bar item is disabled, you could use this code:

```
fIsDisabled = glrIsMenuBarItemDisabled(3)
```

One More Reminder

It never hurts to reiterate this issue: you really can't retrieve current information about the Access built-in menus using these tools (unless you go through the hoops mentioned above, pulling down the menus first). Since Access doesn't ensure that the menus are current until you pull them down, the states you retrieve with these function calls may or may not be current. For values that can change only because the user pulled down the menu and made a choice, you can safely retrieve the state. For values that might change because of something the user has done in the user interface, the menus are destined to be out of sync.

Setting the Status

Just as you can retrieve information about a menu's state, you can set the state of many menu items. You can set the grayed, enabled, and/or checked status of items on submenus. (You can set only the enabled status of menu bar items.) You must keep in mind that since Access controls its own menu items, your attempts to set the state of most of the Access menu items will appear to succeed, but your changes will be overridden when Access needs to redisplay the particular menu. You'll have more success setting the status of your own menu items.

To get a feel for how these status settings work, try out frmModifyMenuItems. It allows you to change the enabled state of menu bar items and the checked/grayed state of first-level submenu items.

Setting Top-Level Menu Status

You can use the functions glrCheckMenuItem() and glrGrayMenuItem() to set the state of a menu item in a top-level menu. These functions return the previous state of the menu item. Using glrCheckMenuItem() is an example:

```
fChecked = glrCheckMenuItem(2, 6, True)
```

After this function call, fChecked will contain True or False, depending on the previous state of the seventh item on the third pull-down menu (all menu items start counting at 0), and the menu item will currently be checked.

Setting Any Level Menu Status

To set the state of any arbitrary menu item, on any level, you must supply the menu handle yourself. You can use glrCheckSubItem() and glrGraySubItem() to set the state of any arbitrary menu item. There's no reason not to use these functions in every case, in place of the corresponding glrCheckMenuItem() and glrGrayMenuItem() functions, but the other functions are simpler to use when you're dealing with top-level menu items.

Each of the two functions grlCheckSubItem() and glrGraySubItem() accepts a menu handle, an item number within that menu on which to act, and a logical value, telling the function whether to set the state or clear it. You use the glrGetMenuHandles and glr_apiGetSubMenu() procedures to retrieve the appropriate menu handles before you can call these functions.

Imagine you want to set the fourth menu item on the submenu attached to the third menu item on the submenu attached to the second item on the menu bar to be grayed out. You could use code similar to this:

```
Dim hMenuBar As Integer
Dim hSubMenu As Integer
Dim hSubSubMenu As Integer
Dim fWasGrayed As Integer

' Get the handles to the menu bar and the 2nd menu item.
glrGetMenuHandles 1, hMenuBar, hSubMenu
' Get the handle to the third item on the 3rd sub menu.
hSubSubMenu = glr_apiGetSubMenu(hSubMenu, 2)
' Set the state of the 4th menu item.
fWasGrayed = glrGraySubItem(hSubSubMenu, 3, True)
```

Setting the Menu Bar Status

Although you can theoretically disable submenu items, your users won't be very happy if you do. Your applications will be much clearer if you gray out items instead. There's little more frustrating than clicking a menu item that looks perfectly normal but does nothing. On the menu bar itself, you have no choice. Windows doesn't allow you to gray out items there, so your only choice is to disable items. This is why we've included a function, glrEnableMenuBarItem(), that works on menu bar items but not a corresponding function for other menu items.

To use the glrEnableMenuBarItem() function, you pass it two pieces of information: it expects to receive the menu item number (starting with 0) and a logical value indicating whether to enable (True) or disable (False) the menu item. For example, to disable the File menu item while a form is active, you would use this:

```
fSuccess = glrEnableMenuBarItem(0, False)
```

When you've disabled a menu bar item, it looks normal until you click it. At that point Access highlights the menu bar item, but it doesn't drop down the attached menu. You've effectively blocked the user from choosing that menu item. Figure 10.11, presented earlier in this chapter, shows frmModifyMenuItems just after it's disabled the File menu and you've attempted to choose that menu item.

Retrieving Menu States

All the functions in basMenuHandling that retrieve information about a specific menu item's state go through a single utility function, GetSpecificItemState() (see Listing 10.4). The function is very simple. It just calls the Windows API function GetMenuState(), passing in the menu handle and the position of the menu item on that menu you're interested in.

GetMenuState() (aliased here as glr_apiGetMenuState()) returns an integer, with different pieces of information coded into each of its 16 bits. To retrieve just one piece of information, you can perform a bitwise And of the returned value with a predefined constant. (In this case the calling function passes that constant down to GetSpecificItemState().) Perform the bitwise comparison using the following syntax:

fTrueOrFalse = ((*CodedInteger* And *Constant*) = *Constant*)

If the bit of interest is set (equal to 1), fTrueOrFalse will be non-zero. In GetSpecific-ItemState() it's the last line that does this test for you. The function returns True if the bitwise comparison returns a non-zero value and False otherwise.

Listing 10.4

```
Private Function GetSpecificItemState(hMenu As Integer,
➡ intItem As Integer, intFlag As Integer)


    Dim intTemp As Integer

    intTemp = glr_apiGetMenuState(hMenu, intItem, MF_BYPOSITION)
    GetSpecificItemState = ((intTemp And intFlag) = intFlag)
End Function
```

Understanding the Low-Level Activity

As part of our interface between your application and the Windows API functions that deal with menus, we've provided functions to set the checked and/or grayed status of any menu item. The functions are glrCheckMenuItem(), glrCheckSub-MenuItem(), glrGrayMenuItem(), and glrGraySubMenuItem(). All four functions work in basically the same manner. Windows provides a function to set or clear the check, (CheckMenuItem()) and a function to gray or enable a menu item (Enable-MenuItem()). In either case the function accepts a handle to a menu structure, an ordinal number representing the position of the item in question on that menu, and a flag telling Windows what action to take. The choice of whether you call glrCheckMenuItem() or glrCheckSubMenuItem() is dictated by whether or not you care to find the menu handle yourself. If you call glrCheckMenuItem() or glrGray-MenuItem(), the function finds the menu handle but can do so only for top-level menus. If you call glrCheckSubMenuItem() or glrGraySubMenuItem(), you can work with any menu item on any menu, but you'll need to find the menu handle yourself, using the glr_apiGetSubMenu() function.

To illustrate, look at the two functions glrGrayMenuItem() and glrGraySub-MenuItem() in Listing 10.5. Notice that the only difference between them is that glrGrayMenuItem() calls glrGetMenuHandles() first, to retrieve the handle to the requested submenu. From that point on, they do the exact same work. (The corresponding functions, glrCheckMenuItem() and glrCheckSubMenuItem(), work in exactly the same manner.)

Both functions call glr_apiEnableMenuItem() to gray or enable a menu item. This function takes the menu handle, the item number on that menu, and a flag telling the function what to do. In this case you pass to it either the MF_GRAYED or MF_ENABLED constant (defined by the Windows API). In addition, you need to tell Windows whether you're referring to the menu item by position or by menu ID. Every menu item has a menu ID associated with it, assigned at the time the program is written. When you're referring to menu items from code, you can either refer to them by their position (in which case the API call must know the exact menu handle for the menu that contains the item) or by command (in which case Windows searches the menu whose handle you pass to the API call and descends into all subordinate menus). For your purposes, since you have no way of knowing the menu IDs, you'll almost always want to refer to menu items by position. To tell that to Windows, you add in the MF_BYPOSITION constant every time you're telling Windows what to do with your menu items. If you call our middle-level functions in basMenuHandling, you won't have to worry about this. If you modify those functions or need to add some more of your own, this will be a concern. If you're working with the system menu, by the way, you'll want to use the MF_BYCOM-MAND flag since in that case you do know the menu IDs. See the section "Disabling the Close Menu Item" in Chapter 8 for more information.

Finally, each function returns the previous state of the menu item. That is, if you're attempting to set an item to gray, glrGrayMenuItem() will return True if it was previously grayed or False if it wasn't. Since the API function EnableMenuItem() returns the previous status of the menu item, it's a simple task to check the particular bit in the status that you care about (see the preceding section) and return True or False.

Listing 10.5

```
Function glrGrayMenuItem(intSubMenu As Integer,
➡  intItem As Integer, fEnableIt As Integer) As Integer
```

```
        Dim intOldState As Integer
        Dim hSubMenu As Integer
        Dim hTopMenu As Integer

        glrGetMenuHandles intSubMenu, hTopMenu, hSubMenu
        intOldState = glr_apiEnableMenuItem(hSubMenu, intItem,
    ➥ IIf(fEnableIt, MF_ENABLED, MF_GRAYED) Or MF_BYPOSITION)
        glrGrayMenuItem = Not ((intOldState And MF_GRAYED) =
    ➥ MF_GRAYED)
End Function

Function glrGraySubMenuItem hMenu As Integer,
➥ intItem As Integer, fEnableIt As Integer)

        Dim intOldState As Integer

        intOldState = glr_apiEnableMenuItem(hMenu, intItem,
    ➥ IIf(fEnableIt, MF_ENABLED, MF_GRAYED) Or MF_BYPOSITION)
        glrGraySubMenuItem = Not ((intOldState And MF_GRAYED) =
    ➥ MF_GRAYED)
End Function
```

Retrieving or Modifying Menu Text

In addition to being able to retrieve or modify the state of any menu item, you can retrieve or modify the actual text of any menu item. Access uses this trick when it changes the Edit ➤ Undo menu item to Can't Undo when there's nothing to undo. You can use this same principle in your own applications, changing menu items to match the current situation. In basMenuHandling, we've included functions to retrieve a single menu item (glrGetMenuBarText() and glrGetMenuText()), to retrieve all the menu text in a specific menu into an array of strings (glrGetMenuBarTitles() and glrGetMenuTitles()), and to set a specific menu item's text (glrSetMenuBarText() and glrSetMenuText()).

You've probably noticed that many menu items in Windows have a hot-key name on the right side of the menu item. For example, the File ➤ Save Form menu item has Ctrl+S on the right side. You can reproduce this effect, although you'll need to go outside Access to do it. In a text editor (like Notepad), enter the name you want, followed by a tab character and then the text you want on the right side of the menu item. Copy that to the clipboard (using the Edit ➤ Copy menu in Notepad), and paste it into your macro definition in Access. (You'll see a vertical bar where the Tab character is). It's the Tab character that tells Windows to display the following text to the right in the menu, and the Access macro editor won't allow you to enter a Tab character. This still leaves the problem, however, of reacting to the keystroke you specify. Unless you choose a keystroke that Access already traps, you must supply an AutoKeys macro to trap the keystroke. Using the AutoKeys macro is the closest you can come, but AutoKeys can't trap Ctrl+letter keys.

Retrieving Menu Item Text

To retrieve a single menu item's text, you can call glrGetMenuBarText(), passing it an ordinal number, starting with 0, that represents the position of the item on the menu bar. Or you can call glrGetMenuText(), passing it a menu handle for the menu in question and the ordinal position of the menu item whose text you want to retrieve. For example, the following code retrieves the text from the third item on the second menu hanging off the menu bar:

```
Dim hTopMenu As Integer
Dim hSubMenu As Integer
Dim strText As String

glrGetMenuHandles 1, hTopMenu, hSubMenu
strText = glrGetMenuText(hSubMenu, 2)
```

Retrieving the Number of Menu Items

To retrieve the number of menu items, you can call the Windows API function glr_apiGetMenuItemCount(), passing to it the handle of the menu. All the API wrapper functions in this chapter assume that you know how many menu items there are and won't pass a value that's outside the reasonable range. If you aren't sure, check first. The following code retrieves the number of menu items in the third submenu and prints out their text:

```
Dim hTopMenu As Integer
Dim hSubMenu As Integer
Dim intCount As Integer
Dim intI As Integer

glrGetMenuHandles 2, hTopMenu, hSubMenu
intCount = glr_apiGetMenuItemCount(hSubMenu)
For intI = 0 To intCount - 1
    Debug.Print glrGetMenuText(hSubMenu, intI)
Next intI
```

Retrieving All the Text from a Menu

Sometimes you want to retrieve all the items from a menu in one function call. Although the Windows API doesn't support this directly, we've provided two functions to make this simple for you. You can call glrGetMenuBarTitles() or glrGetMenuTitles() to fill an array with all the items on a specific menu. Your only obligation is to provide a dynamic array for the function to resize and fill in.

For example, the following code retrieves all the items from the File menu and prints them to the Debug window.

```
Dim astrMenuItems() as String
Dim hTopMenu As Integer
Dim hSubMenu As Integer
Dim intCount As Integer
Dim intI As Integer

glrGetMenuHandles 0, hTopMenu, hSubMenu
intCount = glrGetMenuTitles(hSubMenu, astrMenuItems())
For intI = 0 To intCount - 1
    Debug.Print astrMenuItems(intI)
Next intI
```

The sample form, frmModifyMenuItems, uses this technique to show all the menu items in a list box.

Changing Menu Item Text

Changing the text of a menu item is no more difficult than retrieving it. You can call glrSetMenuBarText(), passing to it the position to change and the new text, to change an item on the menu bar. Or you can call glrSetMenuText(), passing in a menu handle, the position of the menu item you want changed, and the new text. In either case Windows takes care of the details, and you end up with a changed menu item. If you're working with the standard Access menus, you'll want to use one of the functions in the preceding sections to retrieve the menu items before you change them so you can change them back when you're done. Remember that Access maintains only one copy of each of its menu bars and associated menu items, so if you change the text of an item on the Forms menu bar, every other form (unless it has its own menu bar defined) will also see the same change. Even after your application is finished, any other application opening a form will see your changes. So, as in so many other areas of programming, *if you change a menu item, put it back the way it was.*

The following code retrieves the text from the fourth item on the Edit menu and replaces it with "My Access Application":

```
Dim strOldText As String
Dim hTopMenu As Integer
Dim hSubMenu As Integer
Dim fSuccess As Integer

' Get the menu handle for the Edit menu.
glrGetMenuHandles 1, hTopMenu, hSubMenu
' Get the previous text in the fourth slot on the Edit menu.
strOldText = glrGetMenuText(hSubMenu, 3)
fSuccess = glrSetMenuText(hSubMenu, 0, "My Access Application")
```

The sample form, frmModifyMenuItems, uses this same method when it allows you to modify menu items. Figure 10.13 shows the menus altered as in the previous example. (Remember that menu items start numbering at 0, and dividers are included in the count. Thus, the fourth menu item in Figure 10.13 has an ordinal position number of 3.)

NOTE

You won't be able to use this method to alter the text of user-defined menu items. Access must correlate the menu text with the matching macro item, and altering the menu text will confuse Access. This technique works fine for user-defined menus but not for the action items *on* those menus.

FIGURE 10.13:

The text of the fourth item on the Edit menu has been changed.

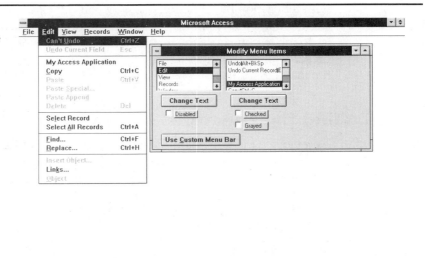

Removing Menu Items

Many Access applications' menuing systems consist mainly of the standard Access menus, with some items removed. Even removing a single menu item, using the standard Access menu macros, requires you to create the full Access menuing system in macros, minus the single item you don't want on your menus. You can use the functions from basMenuHandling, glrRemoveMenuBarItem(), and glrRemove-MenuItem() to remove menu items, instead.

Preserving Information

Every menu item carries around with it information about what to do when you se-lect that item. If choosing the item causes another menu to be displayed, the item you chose stores the handle for that menu. If choosing the item causes an action to occur, the item stores an action ID. (The program you're running knows what to do with that action ID. This explains why you can't add a completely new menu item from within your running Access application. Access wouldn't have any idea what to do when you chose the item.) When you remove a menu item, it's up to you to preserve those pieces of information so you can put them back when you restore the menu item. The functions in basMenuHandling help you with this process.

Calling the Functions

To remove a menu item on the menu bar, you call glrRemoveMenuBarItem(). You pass it three parameters: the item number to remove, a variable in which to store the handle to the submenu attached to it, and a variable to hold the text of the item. The function fills in the last two parameters, so your code can preserve them and later restore them. For example, the following code removes the Edit menu from the Access menu bar:

```
Dim hSubMenu As Integer
Dim strMenuText As String
Dim fSuccess As Integer

fSuccess = glrRemoveMenuBarItem(1, hSubMenu, strMenuText)
MsgBox "You removed the '" & strMenuText &
➡ "' menu (its submenu handle was: " & hSubMenu & ")"
```

To call glrRemoveMenuItem() you must also pass in the handle to a menu as the first parameter. In addition, since a submenu item might have either an action ID or a menu handle (but not both), you pass in a variable for each. On return, one will be 0 and one will contain a value. For example, to remove the Undo item on the Edit menu, you could use this code:

```
Dim hSubMenu As Integer
Dim hTopMenu As Integer
```

```
Dim hSubSubMenu As Integer
Dim intActionID As Integer
Dim strMenuText As String
Dim fSuccess As Integer
Dim strText As String

' Get a handle to the Edit menu.
glrGetMenuHandles 1, hTopMenu, hSubMenu
' Remove the first item.
fSuccess = glrRemoveMenuItem(hSubMenu, 0, intActionID,
➡ hSubSubMenu, strMenuText)
strText = "You removed the '" & strMenuText & "' menu "
If intActionID > 0 Then
    strText = strText & "(its action ID was: " &
    ➡ intActionID & ")"
Else
    strText = strText & "(its handle was: " & hSubMenu & ")"
End If
MsgBox strText
```

Later, when you needed to restore the menu item, you could use the values stored in intActionID, hSubSubMenu, and strMenuText to set everything back the way it was originally.

The Good, the Bad, and the Ugly— Removing Menu Items

The good part of removing menus in code (rather than by creating an entire set of macros to replace part of the standard Access menuing scheme) is that it requires a lot less overhead both in preparation and in objects your application must carry around. Rather than having one macro for each menu bar, you can use a single module to manipulate your menus directly. In addition, Access appears to be able to use DoMenuItem to access the menu items you've removed, even though they're no longer visible. On the other hand, using SendKeys to access the menu items will no longer work. (This isn't a terrible loss since you ought to avoid using SendKeys to access menu items at all costs. It makes your code nearly impossible to read and, even worse, makes it impossible to run in versions of Access translated to other languages.)

The bad part of removing menus in code is that you're ultimately responsible for undoing everything you do. If you create menus using macros, Access takes care of all the details for you. If you remove a top-level menu item, for example, it's up to your application to put it back when it's done. Generally, you'll want to remove menu items in the Activate event and replace them in the Deactivate event for forms. This way you're guaranteed that whenever focus moves away from the particular form, the menus revert to their normal state.

The ugly part of removing menus in code is that Access doesn't have a clue as to what you're doing "behind its back." You're treading on very thin ice when you change Access' menu structure using Windows API calls. Be very careful, and test your work strenuously before handing it out to end users. Make sure all the remaining menus work correctly and any DoMenuItem calls you make from your code still work as designed.

TIP

Access maintains only a single copy of its own menu bars. That is, each different state in Access has its own menu bar and only one copy of that menu bar. If your code changes an Access menu bar, every other instance in Access that shares that menu bar sees the change as well. For instance, if you remove a menu item from a running form's menu bar, any other running form that doesn't maintain its own menu bar will see the same change. Therefore, if your code makes changes to any built-in menu bar, you absolutely must undo your changes, normally in the form's OnDeactivate event. Then reset the changes in the form's OnActivate event.

TIP

As you remove items from menu bars, the ordinal position value of the following menu items moves up to fill the space you just created. Therefore, if you're deleting more than one menu item, you may be better served by deleting from the bottom up. Otherwise, as you delete, the positions of the items you need to delete later change. This can make the process somewhat confusing (to say the least). And remember: if you delete a menu item, you need to put it back later.

Inserting Menu Items

Although you can insert your own menu items into the Access menu bars at run time, doing so is generally a waste of time. Since you have no way to attach an action ID to the new menu that means anything to Access, any newly created menu items wouldn't be able to actually do anything. The only useful purpose we can find for inserting new menu items is to replace menu items you've previously removed. If you store away the text, the ID, and/or the submenu handle for a given menu item, you can easily place that menu item back where it came from on the menus. In fact, this action is imperative if you intend to allow your users to go back to the standard Access menus after you've modified any of those menu bars. It would be rude, indeed, to modify the Access menu bars and leave them modified when your application exits.

We've provided two functions to handle inserting menu items: glrInsertMenuBarItem() and glrInsertMenuItem(). To insert an item into the menu bar, use glrInsertMenu-BarItem(), passing to it the position in which to insert the item, the handle to the pull-down menu for this item, and the text to use. Remember that every item on the menu bar must drop down a menu when it's selected, so you need to supply a menu handle. The following code demonstrates how you might use this function. It removes the Edit menu and then later restores it:

```
Dim hSubMenu As Integer
Dim hTopMenu As Integer
Dim strMenuText As String
Dim fSuccess As Integer

' Fill in hSubMenu and strMenuText
fSuccess = glrRemoveMenuBarItem(1, hSubMenu, strMenuText)
' Now the menu's gone.  Do whatever your application requires
' here.
'
'
' Now put the menu back.
fSuccess = glrInsertMenubarItem(1, hSubMenu, strMenuText)
```

To insert a menu item on a pull-down menu, you must provide the same information as before, but now you also need to provide an action ID, which might be 0 (if the menu item has a submenu attached). You also need to supply the handle to the menu on which the item is to be inserted. The following code removes the Toolbars item from the View menu (when you have a form loaded) and later restores it. In this case the hSubSubMenu variable will always be 0 since this particular item has an action ID, not a submenu.

```
Dim hTopMenu As Integer
Dim hSubMenu As Integer
Dim hSubSubMenu As Integer
Dim intActionID as Integer
Dim strMenuText As String
Dim fSuccess As Integer

' Get a handle to the View menu.
glrGetMenuHandles 2, hTopMenu, hSubMenu
' Remove the 6th item (Toolbars) from the View menu.
fSuccess = glrRemoveMenuItem(hSubMenu, 5, intActionID,
➡ hSubSubMenu, strMenuText)
' Now the menu item's gone.  Do whatever your application
' requires here.
'

'
' Now put the menu back.
fSuccess = glrInsertMenuItem(hSubMenu, 5, intActionID,
➡ hSubSubMenu, strMenuText)
```

Highlighting a Menu Bar Item

Although we haven't found a good use for this functionality, Windows does provide a method of highlighting a particular menu bar item. Since it's your imagination doing the driving here, we've included a function you can call that highlights an item on the menu bar. The example form frmTestPopup demonstrates this functionality. Figure 10.14 shows this form in action.

To use the function glrHiliteMenuBarItem(), you need only pass to it a menu bar item number and a logical value indicating whether to turn the highlight on or off. For example, the following code highlights the Edit menu bar item, allows you to take some actions, and then turns off the highlight:

```
Dim fSuccess As Integer

fSuccess = glrHiliteMenuBarItem(1, True)
'
' Do whatever your application requires here.
'
' Then turn off the highlight.
fSuccess = glrHiliteMenuBarItem(1, False)
```

FIGURE 10.14:

Highlighting a menu item makes it appear that the user has chosen the item and that it's disabled.

Attaching User-Defined Menus to the Right Mouse Button Click

Access 2.0 has added a popular feature—popping up a context-sensitive menu when the user clicks the right mouse button. Unfortunately, Microsoft didn't make this feature available to your applications as well. Although it requires a bit of trickery, you can provide your own application-specific right mouse button menus. The functionality is based on the following factors:

- You can easily trap the right mouse click on any object and fire off code in reaction to the click.

- Windows provides an API function, TrackPopupMenu() (aliased as glr_apiTrackPopupMenu()), that allows you to pop up a menu at the mouse position, provided you have a handle to a menu and a position.

- You can retrieve the handle to an existing menu, using the glr_apiGetSubMenu() API function.

- The MouseDown event tells you where the mouse click occurred, but it's given with respect to the upper-left corner of the control itself or the upper-left corner of the form (if you clicked on the form). TrackPopupMenu() expects its coordinates to be relative to the upper-left corner of the screen. You can use various Windows API functions to calculate the mouse click coordinate with respect to the screen.

- You must have a menu handle for TrackPopupMenu(). If you don't want the user to see that menu on the menu bar, you can create a menu with no title and then disable it. It won't appear on the menu bar, and users won't be able to drop down the menu, although if they click the menu's position on the menu bar they'll see a little dark spot.

The following sections examine each of these factors, in reverse order, demonstrating how you can create your own context-sensitive menus that pop up wherever the user clicks the right mouse button. The sample form frmTestPopup demonstrates this functionality, as shown in Figure 10.15.

Creating a Hidden Menu

If you want a right mouse button click to pop up an existing menu, you can skip the technique described in this section. The next section shows how to retrieve the handle for the menu in question. If you want a right mouse button click to pop up a menu that doesn't appear on the menu bar, you have to take this extra step.

FIGURE 10.15:

FIGURE 10.15:

frmTestPopup can show any of the existing menus when you click the right mouse button.

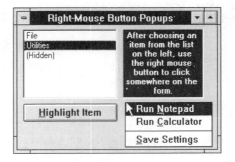

When you create your menu bar, you create an AddMenu action for each menu attached to the menu bar. For each menu item you tell Access the menu name, the menu macro name, and perhaps the status bar text. Although Access claims that the Menu Name field is required, that's not necessarily true. The field is required if you want the menu to show up on the menu bar. Since that's exactly what you *don't* want, you just leave the Menu Name field blank. Of course, this is really useful only for the right-most menu items on the menu bar. If you use this technique for items in the middle of the bar, you'll find unsightly holes in your menu. Figure 10.16 shows an example menu bar macro with the Menu Name field left blank.

FIGURE 10.16:

Leave the Menu Name field blank to place a null value in the menu bar.

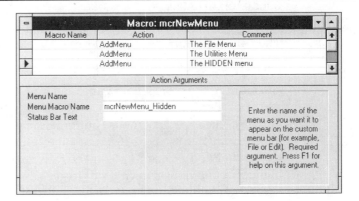

Although nothing keeps you from using this same trick on menus other than the menu bar, it's not very useful. Supplying blank menu items on pull-down menus is not going to endear you to your users, and there's nothing you can do to hide the fact that the blank item is there in the menu.

Handling Multiple Popup Menus

If you need several different popup menus, you might consider creating a single menu on the menu bar containing menu items, each of which points to one of your popup menus. That is, move everything down one level. You'll still have a hidden menu hanging off the menu bar, but each of your right mouse button popup menus will be a submenu of that hidden menu. The sample form, frmTestPopup, uses this technique for its hidden menu. The intent was to pop up a different menu for each of the different control types on the form.

In the declarations area, the following constants keep track of the type of item you clicked over:

```
Const ITEM_FORM = 0
Const ITEM_LISTBOX = 1
Const ITEM_LABEL = 2
Const ITEM_BUTTON = 3
```

Then, in each control's MouseDown event, the event procedure makes this call:

```
HandleMouseDown Me!cmdHilite, ITEM_BUTTON, Button, X, Y
```

substituting the correct item name and item type for the first and second parameters. HandleMouseDown, also in the form's module, first checks to make sure you've clicked the right mouse button. If so, it checks to see which menu you've selected from the list box. If it's not the hidden menu, HandleMouseDown uses glrHandlePopup to show the menu you've chosen. If you've chosen the hidden menu, HandleMouseDown needs to get a handle to the correct submenu by calling GetHiddenMenu(), as shown in Listing 10.6.

Listing 10.6

```
Sub HandleMouseDown (ctl As Control, intType As Integer,
➡ intButton As Integer, X As Single, Y As Single)
    Dim hMenu As Integer

    If intButton = RIGHT_BUTTON Then
        ' If you call HandlePopup from a control, you need to
        ' add to the X and Y coordinates the position of the
        ' control, since all the mouse coordinates
        ' must be relative to the window's upper left corner.
        If intMenuNumber <> intHidden Then
            glrHandlePopup Me, intMenuNumber, X + ctl.Left,
            ➡ Y + ctl.Top
        Else
            hMenu = GetHiddenMenu(intType)
            glrTrackPopup Me, hMenu, X + ctl.Left, Y + ctl.Top
        End If
        DoCmd CancelEvent
    End If
End Sub
```

Once it has a handle to the menu, it calls glrTrackPopup to pop up the menu. (The other procedure, glrHandlePopup, ends up calling glrTrackPopup, too. It just finds the menu handle for you before calling it.) Note that since the X and Y values passed to the Event procedure are relative to the upper-left corner of the control, you need to add to those values the Left and Top properties of the control so that the coordinates are relative to the form. That's the way glrTrackPopup and glrHandlePopup expect to receive them.

The GetHiddenMenu() function presents one more example of calling Windows API menu functions to walk through the menu tree. It first retrieves the menu bar handle (glrGetMenuBar()) and then finds out how many items there are on the menu bar (glr_apiGetMenuItemCount()). Since you know the hidden menu is the last item on the menu bar, you can use glr_apiGetSubMenu() to get a handle to the hidden pull-down menu. Once you have that handle, you call glr_apiGetSub-Menu() again to retrieve the handle to the correct submenu of the hidden menu, corresponding to the intItem parameter. The following code demonstrates this technique:

```
Function GetHiddenMenu (intItem As Integer)
    Dim hTopMenu As Integer
    Dim hSubMenu As Integer
```

```
    Dim intCount As Integer

    ' Get the handle to the menu bar.
    hTopMenu = glrGetMenuBar()
    ' Find out how many items there are on the menu bar.
    intCount = glr_apiGetMenuItemCount(hTopMenu)
    ' Get a handle to the hidden submenu.
    hSubMenu = glr_apiGetSubMenu(hTopMenu, intCount - 1)
    ' Get the handle to the correct submenu of the hidden menu.
    GetHiddenMenu = glr_apiGetSubMenu(hSubMenu, intItem)
End Function
```

Disabling the Hidden Menu

Although you've made the hidden menu invisible on the menu bar by not supply-ing a Menu Name field for the macro, the user can still pull it down by clicking on the correct region on the menu bar. To keep this from happening you must dis-able the menu. We've supplied a function that makes this simple: glrEnable-MenuBarItem(). You can call this function from your form's Load event (assuming your hidden menu is the third menu bar item):

```
fSuccess = glrEnableMenubarItem(2, False)
```

There's really no need to reenable the item since it's part of a user-defined menu bar and the user should never be able to pull it down. If you have more than one hidden menu, just call the function for each menu bar item.

Popping Up the Menu

Once you've reacted to the mouse click and gotten the handle to the correct menu, you can call glrTrackPopup (if you know the menu handle) or glrHandlePopup (which works only with top-level menus and ends up calling glrTrackPopup, too). The glrTrackPopup procedure takes care of all the details involved in displaying the menu. Most of its energy is spent figuring out the coordinates of the mouse click, in terms of the whole screen, since that's what the TrackPopupMenu() API call ex-pects. Once it knows those coordinates, it can call TrackPopupMenu() directly, and Windows displays the menu corresponding to the passed-in menu handle at the lo-cation where you clicked. If you're interested, you can study the code in glrTrack-Popup to see how to find the coordinates of the mouse click in terms of the full screen. Listing 10.6 shows the code from frmTestPopup that pops up the menu when you click a control.

Using glrTrackPopup from Your Own Apps

You should be able to easily transfer this right mouse button menu technology to your own applications. You must decide whether you need just one or two different popup menus or many. If you need just a few, you can hang them directly off the menu bar and call glrHandlePopup to display them. To do that you call glrHandlePopup, passing to it a reference to the form in question, the position of the menu to pop up on the menu bar, and the X and Y coordinates (relative to the form) of the mouse cursor where you clicked.

If you need more than one or two different popup menus, consider the second alternative, placing your menus as submenus of a single hidden main menu. In that case you call glrTrackPopup, passing to it a reference to the form, the menu handle of the menu you want displayed, and the X and Y coordinates of the mouse (relative to the form).

Study the code in frmTestPopup for more ideas. The code you'll find there is specific to that particular form, but the concepts should be readily applicable to any form to which you'd like to apply this functionality.

Controlling Global Options

In Access 1.x you were required to go through some pretty serious gyrations to change settings in the View ➤ Options menu. At best, you'd have to use SendKeys to drop down the menu, using the Tab key to get to the option in question and other keys to change the value.

Access 2.0 provides two methods of the application object, GetOption() (a function) and SetOption (a subroutine), that can set and retrieve global options. The syntax necessary to call them is

Application.SetObject *optionName*, *Setting*

Setting = Application.GetObject(*optionName*)

The only catch is that the *optionName* values must be the exact text you see in the View ➤ Options menu. Table 10.5 lists all the possible optionName values in its first column. You must enter the values exactly as shown here. (Misspellings and abbreviations will fail.) If you're writing applications to be used in other countries, you'll want to make some provision for altering the strings in your code since they'll be different for each country. The next section suggests a method for making this translation process work a little more smoothly.

NOTE Although it doesn't appear to be documented, translated (non-English) versions of Access will understand the English values for SetOption and GetOption().

TABLE 10.5: Application.GetObject/SetObject Options and Constants

General		
Menu Option	**Constant**	**Allowable Values**
Show Status Bar	voSHOW_STATUS_BAR	−1 (Yes); 0 (No)
Show System Objects	voSHOW_SYSTEM_OBJECTS	Yes; No
OLE/DDE Timeout (sec)	voOLE_DDE_TIMEOUT	0 through 300
Built-In Toolbars Available	voBUILT_IN_TOOLBARS	Yes; No
Confirm Document Deletions	voCONFIRM_DELETIONS	Yes; No
Confirm Action Queries	voCONFIRM_QUERIES	Yes; No
New Database Sort Order	voSORT_ORDER	0 (General); 1 (Traditional Spanish); 2 (Dutch); 3 (Swedish/Finnish); 4 (Norwegian/Danish); 5 (Icelandic); 6 (Czech); 7 (Hungarian); 8 (Polish); 9 (Russian); 10 (Turkish); 11 (Arabic); 12 (Hebrew); 13 (Greek)

TABLE 10.5: Application.GetObject/SetObject Options and Constants (continued)

General

Menu Option	Constant	Allowable Values
Ignore DDE Requests	voIGNORE_DDE	Yes; No
Default Find/Replace Behavior	voFIND_REPLACE	0 (Fast Search); 1 (General Search)
Default Database Directory	voDEFAULT_DIRECTORY	(Any valid path)
Confirm Record Changes	voCONFIRM_CHANGES	Yes; No
Can Customize Toolbars	voCUSTOMIZE_TOOLBARS	Yes; No
Enable DDE Refresh	voENABLE_DDE_REFRESH	Yes; No
First Weekday	voFIRST_WEEKDAY	0 (Sunday); 1 (Monday); 2 (Tuesday); 3 (Wednesday); 4 (Thursday); 5 (Friday); 6 (Saturday) (conflicts with every other use of week days in Access!)
First Week	voFIRST_WEEK	0 (starts on Jan. 1); 1 (first four-day week); 2 (first full week)
Show Tooltips	voSHOW_TOOLTIPS	Yes; No
Color Buttons on Toolbars	voCOLOR_BUTTONS	Yes; No
Large Toolbar Buttons	voLARGE_BUTTONS	Yes; No

Keyboard

Menu Option	Constant	Allowable Values
Arrow Key Behavior	voARROW_KEYS	0 (Next Field); 1 (Next Character)
Move After Enter	voMOVE_AFTER_ENTER	0 (No); 1 (Next Field); 2 (Next Record)
Cursor Stops at First/ Last Field	voCURSOR_STOPS	Yes; No
Key Assignment Macro	voKEY_ASSIGNMENT	(Any valid macro name)

TABLE 10.5: Application.GetObject/SetObject Options and Constants (continued)

Printing

Menu Option	Constant	Allowable Values
Left Margin	voLEFT_MARGIN	0 to the width of the printed page
Right Margin	voRIGHT_MARGIN	0 to the width of the printed page
Top Margin	voTOP_MARGIN	0 to the height of the printed page
Bottom Margin	voBOTTOM_MARGIN	0 to the height of the printed page

Form & Report Design

Menu Option	Constant	Allowable Values
Form Template	voFORM_TEMPLATE	(Name of any form in the current database)
Report Template	voREPORT_TEMPLATE	(Name of any report in the current database)
Objects Snap To Grid	voSNAP_TO_GRID	Yes; No
Show Grid	voSHOW_GRID	Yes; No
Selection Behavior	voSELECTION_BEHAVIOR	0 (Partially Enclosed); 1 (Fully Enclosed)
Show Ruler	voSHOW_RULER	Yes; No
Move Enclosed Controls	voMOVE_ENCLOSED	Yes; No
Control Wizards	voCONTROL_WIZARDS	Yes; No

TABLE 10.5: Application.GetObject/SetObject Options and Constants (continued)

Datasheet

Menu Option	Constant	Allowable Values
Default Gridlines Behavior	voGRIDLINES	On (−1); Off(0)
Default Column Width	voCOLUMN_WIDTH	0 to 22.75 in (0 to 32767 twips)
Default Font Name	voFONT_NAME	(Name of any installed font)
Default Font Size	voFONT_SIZE	(Depends on the chosen font)
Default Font Weight	voFONT_WEIGHT	0 (Extra Light); 1 (Light); 2 (Normal); 3 (Bold); 4 (Extra Bold); 5 (Heavy)
Default Font Italic	voFONT_ITALIC	Yes; No
Default Font Underline	voFONT_UNDERLINE	Yes; No

Query Design

Menu Option	Constant	Allowable Values
Output All Fields	voOUTPUT_ALL_FIELDS	Yes; No
Run Permissions	voRUN_PERMISSIONS	0 (User's); 1 (Owner's)
Show Table Names	voSHOW_TABLE_NAMES	Yes; No

Macro Design

Menu Option	Constant	Allowable Values
Show Macro Names Column	voMACRO_NAMES	Yes; No
Show Conditions Column	voMACRO_CONDITIONS	Yes; No

TABLE 10.5: Application.GetObject/SetObject Options and Constants (continued)

Module Design

Menu Option	Constant	Allowable Values
Syntax Checking	voSYNTAX_CHECKING	Yes; No
Tab Stop Width	voTAB_STOP	1 to 30

Multiuser/ODBC

Menu Option	Constant	Allowable Values
Default Record Locking	voRECORD_LOCKING	0 (No Locks); 1 (All Records); 2 (Edited Record)
Default Open Mode for Databases	voOPEN_MODE	0 (Exclusive); 1 (Shared)
Refresh Interval (sec)	voREFRESH_INTERVAL	1 to 32,766
Update Retry Interval (msec)	voRETRY_INTERVAL	0 to 1000
Number of Update Retries	voRETRY_COUNT	0 to 10
ODBC Refresh Interval (sec)	voODBC_REFRESH	1 to 3600

Remember that the options settings are both global and persistent. If you make a change, be sure to set it back. Certainly, if you change any settings using Application.SetObject, you must make an effort to reset the values when your application exits. Whether your user exits through an error handler or through the normal shut-down procedures, you should reset any options your application changed. That is, your application might contain code to set the value for the OLE/DDE Timeout to be 100 seconds. In the application's startup routine you might include code like this (the variable intTimeOut is global):

```
intTimeOut = Application.GetOption("OLE/DDE TimeOut (sec)")
Application.SetOption "OLE/DDE TimeOut (sec)", 100
```

Then, in the code that's executed when your application shuts down, include a statement like this:

```
Application.SetOption "OLE/DDE TimeOut (sec), intTimeOut
```

If you don't reset the value when your application shuts down, your user will find the settings as your application left them the next time Access starts up.

Making It a Bit Simpler

To make it a bit simpler for you to use the GetOption() and SetOption methods, we've supplied a module containing all the possible options, with associated constants. This way, rather than using the exact strings each time you set or retrieve options, you can use the constants. This saves your typing the strings, which can introduce errors. Instead of using this expression:

```
Application.SetOption "Update Retry Interval (msec)", 100
```

you can use

```
Application.SetOption voRETRY_INTERVAL, 100
```

Table 10.5 includes a list of all the menu options, their associated constants, and the allowed values for each. To use these in your own applications, import basView-Opts from CH10.MDB.

Summary

Although you won't be using macros for a large part of your applications, they do have their uses. Since you must use macros to create menus, trap global keystrokes, and auto-execute code, they do have their place in your database. They can't, however, replace carefully written, error-trapped Access Basic code. You'll need to use macros:

- To automatically start up execution when your application is loaded
- To trap keystrokes and react to them globally
- To create menus

In addition, the standard Access menu engine gives you very little control over your menus. We've presented a number of uses for the Windows API, in terms of manipulating, modifying, and controlling your user-defined menus. Armed with the Access Basic routines covered in this chapter, you should be able to do most of what you need to do with menus. You can

- Remove and insert menu items
- Gray and ungray menu items
- Disable and reenable menu items
- Change the text of menu items
- Retrieve the number of menu items
- Retrieve an array filled with menu text
- Pop up a menu in response to a mouse click

Access toolbars provide a nice medium for simplifying your applications, although their lack of programmatic control can make them difficult to manage. If you don't need to modify or move them under program control or add your own button images, Access 2.0 provides all the tools you need.

Throughout this part of the book, we've focused on the user-interface elements in Access—controls, forms, reports, and user-interface macros. Armed with your basic knowledge and the tricks you've found here, you should be set to create some inventive interfaces for your applications.

PART IV

Multiuser Development

CHAPTER

ELEVEN

Developing Multiuser Applications

- Using record-locking options

- Designing multiuser applications

- Splitting a database to improve performance

- Implementing a custom record-locking strategy

Does either of these stories sound familiar to you?

- **Developer A:** Making my application multiuser is a no-brainer. All I need to do is flip the multiuser switch. Now where is that darn thing in Access? Oh, here it is; all I need to do is uncheck the Exclusive check box in the Open Database dialog.

- **Developer B:** No way! You have to be a certified engineer or something like that. I'll have to hire someone else to make the conversion.

The truth of the matter lies somewhere in between these two extremes. Developing Access applications for multiuser systems requires extra planning and a shift from single-user application thinking, but it's not especially difficult to learn. In this chapter we explore the behavior of networked applications in Access. We don't cover network hardware or operating systems—except for very briefly—but the good news is that you don't need to become a network administrator or a specialist in cabling and hubs to develop multiuser applications. Let your network administrator or hardware specialist worry about those aspects. (Of course, it can't hurt to communicate with this person and learn a bit about network hardware and operating systems over time.) We do discuss, however, how to *plan* and *think* multiuser and how to avoid the common pitfalls of multiuser development.

> **NOTE**   Access works well with most of the networking software on the market today, including Windows NT, Windows for Workgroups, NetWare, and LANtastic.

Setup on a Network

Before installing Access on a network, you need to decide whether Access will be installed only on the file server or on each workstation.

The first option, installing Access on the file server *only*, has several advantages:

- The network administrator has central control of the executables, minimizing maintenance chores.

- Hard-disk space usage is kept to a minimum on workstations.
- Users with diskless workstations can run Access.

But this scenario also has several disadvantages:

- Each time a workstation runs Access, the Access .EXE, DLLs, and other files are sent over the network cable to each workstation. Since Access is much more than a single executable (it may call over 20 DLLs during execution, swapping portions of itself to and from memory), network traffic will be very high.
- Performance can vary from acceptable to abysmal.

A better alternative is to install a copy of Access on each workstation on the network. The major advantage of this scenario is performance. Access startup and execution will be significantly faster. Of course, this scenario does carry with it a disadvantage when compared with the file-server–only scenario: you (or the network administrator) will have to maintain multiple copies of Access rather than just one. Still, we feel strongly that any added maintenance burden under this scenario is greatly overshadowed by the substantial increase in performance.

TIP   With a workstation-install strategy, you must make a further decision: where to locate your SystemDB file (by default, named SYSTEM.MDA). This file contains a number of global Access settings, including the options set with the View ➤ Options command, the list of most recently used files, and User and Group membership information (see Chapter 22). If you are not using Access security with your applications, we recommend that you keep a copy of SystemDB on each workstation to improve performance and to allow users to customize their own working environments. If you are implementing security, you can still make local copies of SystemDB, but you must remember to update every local copy whenever you make a change in User or Group membership. In this situation, however, you may find the performance improvement of having multiple copies of the SystemDB is greatly overshadowed by the increased maintenance burden.

Access Locking and Novell NetWare 3.11

When using data from a server back end, Access uses the locking facilities provided by that back end. There is a bug in NetWare 3.11 TTS (Transaction Tracking System) that can result in a server's abending when running certain Access queries or otherwise requesting a large number of locks. Each page of records Access locks uses one or more locks from the NetWare TTS. The defaults in NetWare allow a single workstation to have 500 locks at any given time. This results in a limit of 1MB of data that Access can deal with in a single transaction. Since Access tries to lock every record involved in either an update or a delete query before actually carrying out the update or delete, it is quite possible to bump into this limit on a moderately large database.

The problem is that NetWare 3.11 reacts rather poorly to having its lock limit exceeded. It appears to count a lock violation every time it looks at the connection in question, which is still trying to lock more records. Eventually (in about 3–5 minutes) some internal table overflows, and the entire server goes down, with a frightening message that instructs you to cycle the power. There are two things you can do if this happens to you. The first is to increase the number of locks available, and the second is to apply the NetWare patch that prevents the abend of the server. (Very large queries can still fail, but at least the server doesn't fail along with them.) To increase the number of locks available, enter the following commands at the file server console or in your AUTOEXEC.NCF file:

```
set maximum record locks per connection = 10000
set maximum record locks = 200000
```

The first parameter is the most locks any single connection can have, and the second is the most the entire server can keep track of. These values (10,000 and 200,000) are the maximums that NetWare 3.11 can accommodate. By setting the maximum record locks per connection to 10,000, Access can handle a transaction up to 20MB. To fix the server abend problem, you need to download the latest NetWare 3.11 patch file. It can be found on CompuServe in the NOVFILES section; as of this writing, the current version is 311PTD.ZIP.

You will need to load two of the NLMs from this file, either directly from the server console or in your AUTOEXEC.NCF file:

```
load patchman.nlm
load ttsfix.nlm
```

This problem is specific to NetWare version 3.11 and has been fixed in later versions of NetWare.

Installing the Network Administrator Version of Access

Access has an option to install a special administrator version on the file server you can then use to install individual copies of Access on each workstation. Using this install technique, you need to use the diskettes only once, and the installation process is much faster.

To install the special administrator version of Access on the file server, use the /a option when running Setup. You invoke this option, which copies the Access files to a subdirectory of your choice on the file server, using the following syntax:

    a:\setup /a

Once you've done this, you can put away your disks and install Access on each workstation *automatically* using the following syntax:

    u:path\setup /q

where *u:path* is the path to the special administrator installation on the file server. This installs a *typical* (as defined by the Access Setup program) installation on the workstation without any user interaction. Access determines what goes into a typical installation by using the default settings found in the setup script file,

SETUP.STF. /q is the quiet switch, which suppresses all user interaction and presents just a single dialog box at the end of Setup telling you whether or not Setup completed successfully. If you'd like to skip this final dialog box also, use the /q1 switch instead. Alternatively, you can leave off both switches, in which case the user is prompted for installation information and SETUP.STF is ignored.

If you would prefer more control over the type of installation performed, you can edit the setup script file (SETUP.STF) that is found in the *u:path* subdirectory on the file server. (We suggest editing a copy of this file.) It's easiest to edit this oddly formatted, multicolumn, tab-delimited text file using a spreadsheet program. To change which type of install is performed (Typical, Complete/Custom, Laptop [Minimum], or Workstation), you need to change the Yes to the left of "&Typical" to No and change one of the No values next to the other three options to Yes. Make sure only one of these four options is set to Yes. When you've finished editing the setup script file, run Setup using this syntax:

u:path\setup /t *scriptname* /n *username* /q

where *u:path* is the path to the special administrator installation on the file server, *scriptname* is the name of the script file (for example, NEWSCR.STF), and *username* is the name of the desired registration name (for example, "Mary Jones"). You *must* enter the quotes. To have the Setup program use the workstation name (the one specified in the DefName topic of the [MS User Info] section of the user's WIN.INI file), use " " for the *username*.

For additional information on modifying SETUP.STF, refer to the Help file ACREADME.HLP that was installed in your Access subdirectory.

Multiuser Settings

Several options and settings in Access affect how your applications behave in a multiuser environment. Before you can create multiuser applications, you need to be aware of these settings, which are described in the following sections.

Database Open Modes

There are three ways to affect how a database is opened in Access:

- When you start Access you can include a database name on the command line and either the /Excl or /Ro parameter to open that database in exclusive or read-only mode, respectively.

- You can check or uncheck the equivalent check boxes when using the File ➤ Open Database dialog box.

- You can change the default database open mode using the View ➤ Options command, changing the Default Open Mode for Databases setting under the Multiuser/ODBC options. The setting can be Exclusive for single-user access or Shared for multiuser access to the database.

TIP In Access 1.x, changing the View ➤ Options setting to forbid exclusive opening sets only the default behavior, which the user can still override. With the introduction of Access 2.0 you can prevent a user from opening a database in exclusive mode by using the Security ➤ Permissions command to uncheck the OpenExclusive permission of the database.

The Refresh Interval

Using the View ➤ Options command, you can also set the refresh interval. Access automatically checks the recordsets of open forms and datasheets to see whether changes have occurred at the frequency set by the refresh interval. The default refresh interval is 60 seconds, which may be too long for some applications. If you set the refresh interval to too small a value, however, you may create excessive network traffic. Finding the proper setting for your application may require some experimentation. In general, the smaller the network, the smaller you can set the refresh interval without adverse effect.

You can override the default refresh interval in your applications by using the Refresh method, the Requery method, or the Requery action. Record *refreshes*—either automatic refreshes by Access using the refresh interval or manual refreshes using the Refresh method—are faster than requeries. New records added by other users, however, appear only during a requery, and records deleted by other users vanish from your copy only after a requery. (All the values in the fields of deleted records, however, are replaced with the string "#DELETED" when the record is refreshed.)

Given the choice, you should use the Requery *method* rather than the almost-equivalent Requery *action.* The method reruns the query that's already in memory, while the action reloads it from disk. The exception to this rule is when you have used DAO to modify the underlying query definition. You should then use the re-query action to reload the querydef from disk.

> **TIP** Even if you leave the refresh interval very high, Access automatically refreshes the current record whenever a user attempts to edit it. The benefit of a shorter refresh interval lies chiefly in giving quicker visual feedback that someone else has locked or changed a record while you are viewing it.

Locking Options

To provide concurrent access to records by multiple users, Access locks records. But unlike some other databases, Access doesn't lock individual records; instead it locks a 2K (2048 bytes) page of records. The advantage of page locking is that there's less overhead and thus generally better performance over true record locking. Unfortunately, this also means that Access usually locks more records than you would like. This is especially an issue when you employ pessimistic locking (defined later in this section) since this type of record locking allows users to keep records locked for long periods of time.

In a multiuser environment you can open recordsets in one of three modes:

- **No Locks:** This is often called *optimistic locking* and is the default setting. With the No Locks setting, the page of records that contains the currently edited record is locked only during the instant when the record is being saved—not during the editing process. This allows for concurrent editing of records with fewer locking conflicts.

- **Edited Record**: As soon as a user begins to edit a record, the page containing the currently edited record is locked until the changes are saved. This is known as *pessimistic locking*.

- **All Records:** This setting causes all the records in the entire recordset to be locked at once. You won't find this option very useful except when doing batch updates or performing administrative maintenance on tables.

You can adjust locking options for database objects that manipulate recordsets. Table 11.1 shows which locking options (No Locks, Edited Record, or All Records) are available for each database object. The point at which records are actually locked is also shown in Table 11.1. The default RecordLocks setting for most of these objects is taken from the Default Record Locking option established using the View ➤ Options Multiuser/ODBC command.

TABLE 11.1 : Available RecordLocks Settings for Various Access Objects

Access Object	No Locks	Edited Record	All Records	Default	When Records Are Locked
Table datasheets	Yes[1]	Yes[1]	Yes[1]	DRL	Datasheet editing
Select query datasheets	Yes	Yes	Yes	DRL	Datasheet editing
Crosstab query datasheets	Yes	Yes	Yes	DRL	Query execution
Union query datasheets	Yes	Yes	Yes	DRL	Query execution
Update and delete queries	No	Yes	Yes	DRL	Query execution
Make-table and append queries	No	Yes	Yes	DRL	Query execution[2]
Data definition queries	No	No	Yes	All Records[3]	Query execution
Forms	Yes	Yes	Yes	DRL	Form and datasheet modes

TABLE 11.1: Available RecordLocks Settings for Various Access Objects (continued)

Access Object	No Locks	Edited Record	All Records	Default	When Records Are Locked
Reports	Yes	No	Yes	DRL	Report execution, preview, and printing
OpenRecordset	Yes	Yes	Yes	Edited Record[4]	Between Edit and Update methods

Yes = available option

No = option not available for this object

DRL = Default Record Locking option setting for the database

[1] There is no RecordLocks property for table datasheets. Datasheets use the Default Record Locking option setting for the database.

[2] For make-table and append queries, the target tables are locked.

[3] There is no RecordLocks property for data definition queries. Access locks the entire table.

[4] Changed using the LockEdits property of recordsets. Edited Record is the default unless you use the DB_DENYWRITE or DB_DENYREAD option of the OpenRecordset method, in which case the entire table is locked.

The Default Record Locking option is ignored when you open recordsets of type table or dynaset in Access Basic using the OpenRecordset method. In this case Access employs pessimistic locking (Edited Record) unless you either set the option of the OpenRecordset method to DB_DENYWRITE or DB_DENYREAD or alter the LockEdits property. As you might expect from the name, you can use the DB_DENYWRITE option to lock all records for updates. You can go one step further and deny write *and* read access to table-type recordsets (only) by using the more restrictive DB_DENYREAD option.

No record locking is performed for snapshot-type recordsets since they are read-only.

If you haven't used either the DB_DENYWRITE or DB_DENYREAD constant when opening the recordset, you can use the LockEdits property of dynaset and table recordsets to specify the type of locking to be used. The default of −1 (True) uses pessimistic (Edited Record) locking. You can force optimistic (No Locks) record locking by setting this property to 0 or False.

Access automatically creates an .LDB file of the same name as the database whenever it finds that one does not exist. This file keeps track of record locks. If you experience a GPF (General Protection Fault), power failure, or reboot while a record is locked, the .LDB file will be left in a state that reports which records were locked at the time of the problem. Since this lock would now have no owner, the effect is a permanent lock of the record. The solution to this problem is to close the database (in a multiuser environment, all users must close it) and delete the .LDB file. Microsoft Access creates a new .LDB file whenever none is found. On the other hand, there's no reason to delete the .LDB file if you've shut down Access through the normal means.

Forcing Access to Lock Records

You can force Access to lock individual records by creating record sizes that are larger than half a page—that is, larger than 1024 bytes. This works because Access won't begin storing a new record on a partially filled page if it can't fit the entire record on that page. You can estimate the size of your records by using the following table and summing the size of each column:

Column Datatype	Storage Size
Byte	1 byte
Integer	2 bytes

Column Datatype	Storage Size
Long Integer	4 bytes
Single	4 bytes
Double	8 bytes
Currency	8 bytes
Counter	4 bytes
Yes/no	1 bit
Date/time	8 bytes
Text	*variable*
Memo	14 bytes
OLE	14 bytes

The contents of memo and OLE-type columns are stored elsewhere in the .MDB file, so you only need to count the overhead for their address pointers. Text columns present the greatest problem for estimating record size because they're variable-length fields—Access uses 1 byte per actual stored character. (Zero-length strings use 1 byte; null strings use 0 bytes.)

You also have to account for overhead, which includes the following:

- Seven bytes per record for record overhead
- One byte variable-length column overhead for each text, memo, and OLE column
- One additional byte for every 256 bytes of the total space occupied by all text, memo, and OLE datatype columns
- One byte fixed-column overhead for each yes/no, byte, integer, single, double, and date/time column

The easiest way to pad a record to exceed 1024 bytes is to create four dummy text columns in the table with default values that are 255 characters long. For example, fill the default value of each of the dummy columns with 255 x's. Don't place these dummy columns on your forms. Then, whenever a new record is created, Access will automatically create a record with the four x-filled dummy fields, which forces it into record-locking mode. For larger tables, you won't need to use so many dummy fields. Create as many as you need to make the size of the table exceed 1024 bytes.

The CH11.MDB database includes a simple table named tblForceRecordLocking and an accompanying form, frmForceRecordLocking, that uses this technique. Try it out with two machines on a network (or two instances of Access on a single machine) and you will notice that Access only locks each individual record—even when it's at a new record at the end of the table.

And now for the main caveat: this strategy wastes a lot of disk space and increases network traffic. Still, if you decide to use pessimistic locking and absolutely must have record locking, you may wish to consider this technique.

Bug Alert: Write Conflicts and Referential Integrity Don't Mix

There's a bug in Access 2.0 that may cause problems when you use referential integrity and optimistic locking. The bug occurs under the following circumstances:

- You have a one-to-many relationship defined for two tables *without* cascading updates turned on

and

- You attempt to save changes to any field—other than the primary key field—for a record on the "one" side of the relationship

and

- Someone else has saved changes to the record since you began editing it.

As to be expected, you will get the Write Conflict dialog (see Figure 11.3 later in this chapter), which gives you three options:

- Save Record
- Copy to Clipboard
- Drop Changes

The bug occurs when you choose the first option. Access complains with the error message shown in Figure 11.1. But this error message is spurious, because you haven't edited the primary key field. You can work around this bug by setting updates *on*, which should correct the problem.

Spurious error message that occurs with optimistic locking and referential integrity

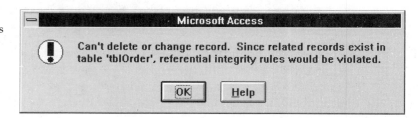

Transaction Processing

Transaction processing is a database term that refers to the process of grouping together changes to your data into batches that are treated as a single atomic unit. Either the entire batch of *transactions* succeeds or they all fail. For example, when updating hospital admission records, you'd want to consider both the patient's checkout and bill as part of a single transaction. If the patient's room is marked as vacant but the billing table fails to get updated, the patient gets a free hospital stay; if the bill goes out but the room records aren't changed, there is an empty space that the hospital's computer will never find.

Transaction processing is useful in any application where one action *must* occur in concert with one or more other actions. Transaction processing is commonly required in banking and accounting applications, as well as in many others.

Transaction-Processing Basics

Access supports transaction processing with the BeginTrans, CommitTrans, and Rollback methods of the Workspace object. BeginTrans allows you to mark the start of a series of operations that should be considered as a unit. CommitTrans takes everything since the most recent BeginTrans and writes it to disk. Rollback is the opposite of CommitTrans; it undoes all your changes back to the last CommitTrans. In skeletal form, transaction processing usually looks something like this:

```
On Error GoTo Err_Handler
'  ...
    Dim wrkCurrent As WorkSpace
    Set wrkCurrent = DBEngine.Workspaces(0)
'  ...
    wrkCurrent.BeginTrans
        ' (Any series of data changes here)
    wrkCurrent.CommitTrans

Err_Handler:
    wrkCurrent.Rollback
    ' (further error processing)
```

NOTE   In Access 1.x you can use the BeginTrans, CommitTrans, and Rollback *statements,* which differ from the *methods* of the same name. The transaction statements always work in the default workspace—Workspaces(0). Although the transaction statements are still supported in Access 2.0, Microsoft recommends that you modify your code to use the corresponding methods instead.

Here are some issues you need to be aware of when performing transaction processing:

- Not all recordsets support transaction processing, particularly those involving non-Access attached tables. None of the non-native ISAM formats support transactions, but most ODBC data sources do. You can check the Transactions property of a Recordset object to see whether it supports transaction processing.

- Transactions affect *all* changes to data in the workspace. Everything you do after a BeginTrans method is committed or rolled back as a single unit. This applies even to changes across multiple databases open within a single workspace.

- You can nest transactions in Access databases up to five levels deep. Inner transactions must be committed or rolled back before the surrounding ones. You cannot nest transactions on attached server tables.

- If you close a workspace without explicitly committing its transactions, all pending transactions are automatically rolled back.

- Access handles its own transaction processing on bound forms. You cannot use transaction processing in Code-Behind-Forms procedures to group together changes made via bound forms. You can, however, perform transactions on recordsets unrelated to the record source.

Transaction Processing in a Multiuser Setting

Transaction processing has extra importance in multiuser applications. When more than one user is modifying the database, you can no longer depend on the results of one change being present when you start another unless you wrap the pair of updates in a BeginTrans/CommitTrans structure. Thus, you'll want to use transactions often in a multiuser setting.

When you use transaction processing in a multiuser setting, Access treats the entire transaction as a single disk write but otherwise respects your specified locking setting. Thus, if you're using pessimistic locking (LockEdits = True), Access locks a record when an Edit or AddNew method is encountered. If you're instead using optimistic locking (LockEdits = False), Access doesn't lock the record until it encounters an Update method. Within the confines of a transaction, however, Access accumulates these locks without releasing them until the entire transaction has been either committed or rolled back.

If Access encounters a locked record within a transaction, the standard set of trappable errors occurs. For example, if a record needed by a transaction is locked by another user when the transaction process attempts to lock the record, the transaction fails with a 3260 error, "Couldn't update; currently locked by user *username* on machine *machinename*." In this case you need to either obtain the necessary lock or roll back the transaction.

Multiuser Action Queries

Access 1.x provided no means to determine programmatically whether an action query failed. If any records failed to be updated because of locking conflicts or other errors, no trappable run-time error was triggered. This meant that in a multiuser environment, you had to basically run action queries with a blindfold on unless you managed to hack together some scheme for detecting whether the action query had indeed worked. Thus, many developers avoided their use in multiuser applications.

For version 2.0 Microsoft has improved the situation by adding an option (DB_FAILONERROR) to the Execute method of querydefs. Now if an error is encountered you can trap the error, but you still can't determine how many records were prevented from being updated, deleted, or appended or which type of error (locking conflict, key violation, or other) occurred.

Listing 11.1 shows an example of using the DB_FAILONERROR option.

Listing 11.1

```
Function ActionQueryExample()

    On Error GoTo ActionQueryExampleErr

    Dim db As Database
    Dim qdf As QueryDef

    ActionQueryExample = False

    Set db = DBEngine.Workspaces(0).Databases(0)

    Set qdf = db.OpenQueryDef("qdelOrders")

    qdf.Execute (DB_FAILONERROR)

    ActionQueryExample = True

ActionQueryExampleDone:
    If qdf Is Nothing Then qdf.Close
    Exit Function
```

```
ActionQueryExampleErr:
    MsgBox "Error occurred. Rolled back.", , "ActionQueryExample"
    Resume ActionQueryExampleDone

End Function
```

If an error occurs when the DB_FAILONERROR option is used, you can't stop Access from rolling back the transaction—it's automatic—whether or not you wrap the query in a transaction. If Access encounters any error during the execution of the action query, the entire query is stopped and no changes are made. In other words, it's all or nothing. Either you use the default Execute method option and let the query run to completion without any idea of how many records were actually updated or you use the DB_FAILONERROR option, which stops the query dead if *any* error is encountered.

> **NOTE** While we certainly appreciate Microsoft's adding the DB_FAILONERROR option to Access 2.0, the situation has been only half fixed. We need better information and finer control. When an error is encountered as Access attempts to execute an action query and before execution, Access should report how many records would be updated and how many (and which ones and why) would not be updated because of locking or other problems. This isn't asking for a lot, since this information is already reported to Access by the Jet engine—that's how the Access UI is able to report these numbers when the query is run interactively—but there's no way to get at this information programmatically.

It's ultimately your choice whether you use action queries in a multiuser setting. There may still be situations in which either you don't need to ensure that all records were changed or you can build in a retry loop.

Designing Multiuser Applications

When you design multiuser applications everything gets magnified in size. Problems that were just minor annoyances in your single-user applications suddenly become *big-time* problems. The problems that arise generally fall into three categories:

- Locking and error-trapping issues
- Performance issues
- Security issues

In the next few sections we discuss various traps to avoid and the techniques and strategies you can apply to help minimize the problems. If alternative strategies exist, we've tried to mention them all so you can decide which one is best for your application. We also share with you our biases and concerns. Much of the time there's no right answer; you'll have to weigh the trade-offs with which each possible solution comes. Still, just knowing the problem is half the battle.

Choosing a Locking Strategy That Works

Although we briefly described Access' locking options earlier in the chapter, we failed to mention how you decide which one is best for you or your particular application. In this section we compare the standard optimistic and pessimistic locking options and several nonstandard alternatives that require additional work to implement.

Standard Locking Options

The advantages and disadvantages of the two standard locking strategies are contrasted in this section.

The *advantages* of *pessimistic* locking are as follows:

- It is simple for the developer.
- It prevents users from overwriting each other's work.
- It may be less confusing to the user than optimistic locking.
- It works well for small workgroups or where users are not likely to be editing the same record.

The *disadvantages* of *pessimistic* locking are as follows:

- It will usually lock multiple records. (How many depends on the size of the records.)
- When a user is at the end of a table (and thus has locked the last page), other users may be prevented from adding new records.
- It is not recommended where lots of users will be editing the same records or where lots of users will be adding new records at the same time.

The *advantages* of using *optimistic* locking are as follows:

- It is simple to use.
- It allows more than one user to edit the same record at the same time. (Some may consider this a disadvantage.)
- It is less likely to lock other users out of records.
- It provides better performance than pessimistic locking.

The *disadvantages* of using *optimistic* locking are as follows:

- It may be confusing to the user when there's a write conflict.
- Users can overwrite each other's edits.

Unless you have a compelling reason to use pessimistic locking, we strongly recommend that you consider optimistic locking. In most applications you don't want your users prevented from being able to edit or—even worse—add new records for potentially long periods of time. When using bound forms, you must also balance whether you would rather teach your users to recognize and deal with locked records (see Figure 11.2) or teach them how to deal with the Write Conflict dialog (see Figure 11.3). Both situations may cause confusion to the untrained.

FIGURE 11.2:

Under pessimistic locking, users are locked out of being able to change a record that is on the same page as a record being edited by another user. (Note the slashed-O icon in the record selector.)

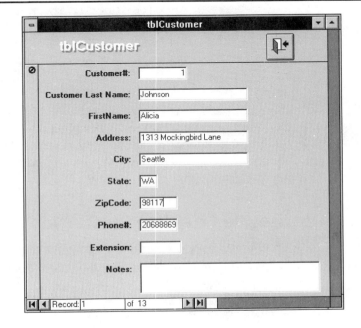

FIGURE 11.3:

Under optimistic locking, users may encounter the Write Conflict dialog when attempting to save a record that has been changed by another user.

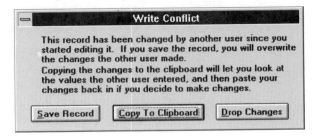

> **TIP**
>
> If you have set the RecordSelector property of a form to No, the slashed-O icon does not appear when a record is pessimistically locked. Access beeps at the user, but other than this audible signal users won't have any clue as to why they can't edit the values in the record. No trappable error is generated, either. Thus, it's important to leave the RecordSelector property set to Yes when using pessimistic locking with bound forms.

In some applications you may need to use both strategies on different forms. For example, in an inventory application you must ensure that the QuantityOnHand column is pessimistically locked so that salespeople don't try to post a sale beyond QOH without invoking back-order processing. On the other hand, you might use optimistic locking on a vendor address form since it's unlikely that two change-of-address requests for the same vendor will be given to two different users for posting at the same time.

Alternative Locking Strategies

If you're not happy using either optimistic or pessimistic locking for your forms in Access, you can choose from one of three alternative strategies:

- Use unbound forms to collect data and then handle the updating of records, using data access object commands behind the scenes.

- Use forms bound to temporary transaction tables that are used to collect data off line. Then create a system for posting transactions to the master data tables. There's an example of this strategy in Chapter 4, using a series of action queries to perform the posting activities.

- Use hybrid forms that you switch between being bound to the master data tables and to temporary transaction tables. In this scenario a user would open a form in read-only browse mode with the form bound to the master data table. After the user clicked the Edit button, the current record would be copied to a transaction table, the record source would be switched to the temporary table, and the user would edit a temporary copy of the record. When the user clicked Save, the record would be posted back to the master data table and the record source of the form would then be switched back to the master table.

Each of these strategies works best when you've split your database into data and application databases. (See the section "Splitting Databases" later in this chapter.) Then you can create the temporary tables in the application database without having to worry about one user's temp tables colliding with another's.

All these strategies also require you to trap for and handle locking conflicts when the data is posted to the master data tables.

The *advantages* of using any of these alternative strategies are as follows:

- You have more control than when you use bound forms.
- More than one user can edit the same record.
- You receive better performance than with pessimistic locking.

The *disadvantages* of using these strategies are as follows:

- They are time consuming to implement and maintain.
- You have to handle all the things that Access would normally handle (for example, reading records, navigating, writing records, and so on) and trap for and handle all the possible errors that might occur (both locking and other kinds of errors).

Not Recommended: Home-Grown Locking

You might also consider a more radical alternative: abandon Access' locking schemes and maintain your own record-locking system. This strategy would require you to maintain a series of locking tables—probably one per database table—that you would use to set and release record locks. Although this strategy may seem tempting, we think this is the *wrong* way to create applications for several reasons. First of all, it requires considerably more work than any of the other schemes. Second, your application will be more difficult to maintain since only you will be familiar with the locking system. Third, you'll still have to allow for and handle record-locking conflicts in updating *your* record lock tables. Finally, if the database is to be shared by other Access or Visual Basic applications, you'll have to duplicate your locking system in each of these applications, making the maintenance burden even worse.

Error Handling and the Broken On Error Event

All professional applications should employ error handling (see Chapter 14), but in a multiuser environment proper error-handling is *critical*. You need to trap for and handle all the things that can (and will) go wrong whenever you read or write rows of data. Since you can't trap for errors using macros, it's a given that multiuser applications should *always* be developed using Access Basic rather than macros.

Several error messages can occur in various multiuser situations, but the three most common are summarized in Table 11.2.

TABLE 11.2: Common Multiuser Error Codes

Error Code	Error Message	Comment
3186	Couldn't save; currently locked by user *username* on machine *machinename*	Usually occurs when you use the Update method with optimistic locking
3197	Data has changed; operation stopped	Usually occurs when you use the Edit or Update method with optimistic locking and another user changed the record while you were editing it. Following this message you get the Write Conflict dialog
3260	Couldn't update; currently locked by user *username* on machine *machinename*	Usually occurs when you attempt to use the Update method on a record that has been locked. This is most commonly encountered using pessimistic locking but may also occur with optimistic locking

When manipulating recordsets, you'll need to anticpate and handle each of the errors found in Table 11.2. To handle locked records, you probably will want to include some form of a retry loop. You would include such a loop within an error handler to make several attempts at gaining access to locked records. There's a good example of how to do this later in the chapter in the section "Using Counter Fields in a Multiuser Setting."

Microsoft added the On Error event to forms in version 2.0 with the intention of allowing the developer to trap for and handle data errors—including multiuser locking and overwrite errors—that occur within bound forms. (The On Error event is discussed in Chapters 8 and 14.) Had this been implemented as originally intended by Microsoft, we would have considerable flexibility in handling record-locking errors without having to resort to using unbound forms. (See "Alternative Locking Strategies" earlier in this chapter.) Unfortunately, for some unknown reason, the On Error event does not get locking or overwrite conflict errors passed to it. Microsoft has indentified this as a problem and has promised to fix it in a future release of the product. In the meantime, if you decide to use bound forms you're stuck with the Access UI handling all locking conflicts for you.

Splitting Databases

No matter which locking scheme you employ, you are still left with the fact that Access puts everything (that is, data, forms, reports, queries, macros, and code) in a single database by default. Performance can suffer considerably because every time an object (for example, a form) is used it must be sent across the network to the user. In a production setting, where nothing but the data stored in tables is being changed, much of this network traffic is unnecessary.

You can eliminate this unnecessary traffic by splitting the database into an *application database* and a *data database*. Install the data database (with tables only) on the file server and a copy of the application database (containing all other objects) on each workstation. From each copy of the application database, use the File ➤ Attach command to attach to the set of tables in the data database.

There are several advantages and disadvantages to splitting your databases.

The *advantages* are as follows:

- Performance (especially user-interface performance) is improved considerably.

- You can create temporary tables on each workstation and not worry about naming and locking conflicts for temporary objects.

- Splitting the database makes the updating of applications easier since the data and application are kept separate. Changes to the application can be made off site and easily merged back into the application database without disturbing the data.

The *disadvantages* are as follows:

- Access ignores referential integrity between local and remote tables. Fortunately, Access enforces any referential integrity constraints you've established between individual tables in the remote database. (And with the introduction of version 2.0, Access now draws the lines between related attached tables in the QBE Design window and the Relationships window.)

- Access hard-codes the paths to attached tables. This means that if you move the data database, you have to delete and reattach all attached tables.

Managing Attached Tables

Since Access hard-codes attached table paths, their use requires extra maintenance for you. If you move the data database with attached tables, you have to delete and reattach all attachments. Doing this by hand can be a tedious process, but fortunately you can employ DAO to automate the process. Using DAO to manage attachments is discussed in detail in Chapter 6.

One of the authors of this book has created an Access add-in for managing attachments called Attachment Initializer (ATTINI.MDA). This add-in library works by storing the paths and file names of attached tables in an .INI file. It works with both Access and non-Access attached tables and can be found on the disk that comes with this book.

NOTE   Access 2.0 includes its own Attachment Manager, which you can start from the File ➤ Add-Ins menu. However, this built-in utility is suitable only for extremely simple cases since it is neither especially easy to use nor very flexible. For example, it provides no means for detaching and reattaching a table in order to use a different copy. For serious use you'll want to implement one of the alternative methods presented here.

Integrating Attached Tables into Your Applications

When you split an existing single-database application into data and application databases, you may be required to alter some of your Access Basic code. You can't use table-type recordsets or the Seek method on attached tables. You can, however, use one of two alternative methods instead:

- Create dynaset-type recordsets and use the (slower) FindFirst method.
- Use the OpenDatabase method to open the data database directly. This requires that you know the exact path of the database. Then you can create table-type recordsets and use the Seek method just as if the tables were local.

Whichever method you choose, you'll almost definitely have to make changes to your application code.

Splitting a Database in Two

To create a new application using data and application databases, just create two databases. One database will hold all the tables; the other will hold everything else. Attach to the data database's tables from the application database. Run the application from the application database. (Of course, you might decide to use multiple data databases if certain lookup data tables, for example, are shared among multiple application databases.)

If you need to split an existing single-database application into two databases, follow these steps:

1. Make a backup copy of your existing database.

2. Create a new empty database to hold the data tables.

3. Import all the data tables from the original database into the new (data) database.

4. Delete these same tables from the original (now to become the application) database.

5. Compact the application database at this point to recover the space previously occupied by the tables.

6. From the application database, attach to each of the tables in the data database.

7. Rewrite any code that makes use of table-type recordsets. Test all existing code to make sure it works.

8. Create a routine for managing attachment paths (or use the Attachment Initializer add-in on the book disk).

Put the data database on the file server. Put a copy of the application database on each workstation. If different workstations use different network paths, you'll need to customize the attachment paths for each copy.

Using Counter Fields in a Multiuser Setting

While counters are a handy datatype for the primary key of a table in a single-user database, there are times when they won't quite work in a multiuser situation. If you're working in a straight Access environment on a network, you'll typically have your data in a shared file on your file server. Each time it needs to assign a counter value, Access must ensure that its own internal record of the last counter value for this table is briefly locked so that no one else is assigned the same counter.

In version 1.x of Access, there were occasional reports of missing or duplicate counters in networked databases, which may have resulted from overloading the counter assignment process. With the introduction of version 2.0, Microsoft made several improvements to this process that minimize the potential for overloading, but it remains a possibility. By implementing your own counters and explicitly handling locking conflicts in your code, you can avoid any problems, especially if you're developing an application that will be used simultaneously by many users adding new records.

Access counters are also limited to being a sequential series of long integers. While the counter datatype guarantees that your counter values will be unique, they will not necessarily be sequential—Access won't reuse values when a record is created but not saved. Nor can you use the built-in counter to assign, say, part numbers that follow a pattern of AA000 through ZZ999. To implement a patterned counter or make sure no values in the counter are ever skipped, you can write your own counter function and substitute it for the built-in one.

NOTE Things get even more complex when your data back end is not Access but SQL Server, dBASE, or some other database. These other databases do not support a native counter datatype, or they supply counters in ways Access can't handle. For example, you can simulate a counter in a SQL Server table with a trigger that assigns the value after the record is saved. Access 1.x requires the primary key to be present before the record is saved, so this method won't work. With Access 2.0 this problem has been solved; Access can now maintain a link to a new record even if the primary key is assigned at save time by the SQL back end. But you might still want to do your counter maintenance in Access, if it's your only tool for adding new records, to keep your code all in a single product.

Custom Counter Basics

You can implement your own custom counters for an Access database by maintaining a separate table to hold the next counter value. This table takes the place of the system table where Access would store the next counter value itself. You must still lock the table when you need a counter value, but by doing so under Access Basic control you can control the locking (and trap for errors) yourself, rather than depending on Access to do so. You can also improve upon the native Access abilities by maintaining one table for each counter. This way, a lock against one counter field has no chance of blocking another counter field (because of page locking).

For maximum flexibility in multiuser situations in which you may be using many front-end databases to maintain the same back-end data, you should maintain the counter tables in a separate database. If users are adding records from two distinct front ends, this technique still allows them to share a counter table without the overhead of maintaining different versions of code.

Implementing a Custom Counter

We have split the activity of obtaining a new counter into two parts. A low-level routine handles the counter increment or returns −1 if there is an error and a counter value cannot be retrieved. A high-level routine handles the assignment of this counter to a new record and determines what to do about any errors. Both routines are contained in the module basCounter in the CH11.MDB database.

glrGetNextCounter() is the low-level routine that interfaces directly with the counter database. It takes a single parameter—the name of the table that will use the counter value. In tables with _ID appended to the base table name, the counters themselves are stored in a separate database identified by the global constant COUNTER_DB (by default, CH11CNT.MDB). For example, the counter for tblDog is stored in tblDog_ID. This counter table has a simple structure: it consists of a single Long Integer column with the name NextCounter. glrGetNextCounter() can be found in Listing 11.2.

Listing 11.2

```
Function glrGetNextCounter(ByVal strTableName As String) As Long

' Return next counter value for a particular table. Counters are
' stored in the COUNTER_DB in tables with _ID appended to the
' table name they are the counter for.  Returns -1 if a valid
' counter value cannot be retrieved due to locking problems.

    On Error GoTo glrGetNextCounter_Err
```

```
    Dim wrkCurrent As WorkSpace
    Dim dbCounter As Database
    Dim recCounter As Recordset
    Dim lngNextCounter As Long
    Dim lngWait As Long
    Dim lngX As Long
    Dim intLockCount As Integer
    DoCmd Hourglass True

    intLockCount = 0

    ' Open a recordset on the appropriate table in the counter's
    ' database, denying all reads to others while it is open
    Set wrkCurrent = DBEngine.Workspaces(0)
    Set dbCounter = wrkCurrent.OpenDatabase(strCounterDbName,
    ➥ False)
    Set recCounter = dbCounter.OpenRecordset(strTableName &
    ➥ "_ID", DB_OPEN_TABLE, DB_DENYREAD)

    ' Increment and return the counter value
    recCounter.MoveFirst
    recCounter.Edit
        lngNextCounter = recCounter![NextCounter]
        recCounter![NextCounter] = lngNextCounter + 1
    recCounter.Update

    glrGetNextCounter = lngNextCounter

    recCounter.Close
    dbCounter.Close

glrGetNextCounter_Exit:
    DoCmd Hourglass False
    Exit Function

glrGetNextCounter_Err:
    ' Table locked by another user
    If Err = CNT_ERR_RESERVED Or Err = CNT_ERR_COULDNT_UPDATE
    ➥ Or Err = CNT_ERR_OTHER Then
        intLockCount = intLockCount + 1
        ' Tried too many times, give up
        If intLockCount > MAX_RETRIES Then
            glrGetNextCounter = -1
            Resume glrGetNextCounter_Exit
        ' Otherwise, let Windows process and try again
```

```
        Else
            ' Let windows catch up
            DoEvents
            ' Let the Jet engine catch up and free any pending
            ' read locks that it hasn't had the idle time to free
            DBEngine.Idle DB_FREELOCKS
            lngWait = intLockCount ^ 2 * Int(Rnd * 20 + 5)
            ' Waste time, but let Windows multitask during this
            ' dead time
            For lngX = 1 To lngWait
                DoEvents
            Next lngX
            Resume
        End If
    ' Unexpected error
    Else
        MsgBox "Error " & Err & ": " & Error$, MB_OK +
        ➡ MB_ICONSTOP + MB_DEFBUTTON1, "glrGetNextCounter"
        glrGetNextCounter = -1
        Resume glrGetNextCounter_Exit
    End If

End Function
```

When there is no contention for counters, glrGetNextCounter() does its work by simply retrieving and incrementing the NextCounter column. In a multiuser situation, however, it is possible for one user to try to get a counter while another user already has the table locked. In this case you can use error-trapping code to wait a moment and try again. The first part of the error handler in glrGetNextCounter() looks like this:

```
intLockCount = intLockCount + 1
' Tried too many times, give up
If intLockCount > MAX_RETRIES Then
    glrGetNextCounter = -1
    Resume glrGetNextCounter_Exit
' Otherwise, let Windows process and try again
Else
    ' ...
End If
```

You'll need to set MAX_RETRIES to balance between potential failure and potential delays to the user. Depending on your network, you may find a value between 3 and 20 is appropriate. If the table is not free after a number of retries, it generally means that someone else has it locked open for a reason not related to assigning counters (for example, as a side effect of a GPF encountered when assigning a counter).

The second part of the preceding If...Then...Else statement contains the code that forces the retry of the operation that encountered the lock. It's shown here:

```
Else
    ' Let windows catch up
    DoEvents
    ' Let the Jet engine catch up and free any pending
    ' read locks that it hasn't had the idle time to free
    DBEngine.Idle DB_FREELOCKS
    lngWait = intLockCount ^ 2 * Int(Rnd * 20 + 5)
    ' Waste time, but let Windows multitask during this
    ' dead time
    For lngX = 1 To lngWait
        DoEvents
    Next lngX
    Resume
End If
```

Rather than just immediately retrying to obtain the lock, glrGetNextCounter() includes some time-wasting logic. It's useful to review this logic since it's likely you'll want to include similar code in all your routines that may experience locking conflicts. The first two statements in the Else clause are there to waste time and free up any pending locks that might just need a little more time to be released.

Next, a long integer, lngWait, is calculated based on a formula that squares the number of retries and multiplies the result by a random number between 5 and 25. Then a For...Next loop is executed for lngWait iterations to waste time. The inclusion of the DoEvents statement ensures that any other Windows tasks are given processor time during this "dead" period. By including a random number and squaring the time for each retry, glrGetNextCounter() is attempting to separate out any users who were requesting locks at the same point in time.

If this doesn't make sense, think of an analogy: have you ever gotten disconnected when talking to someone over a telephone and both of you started redialing at the same time, repeatedly getting busy signals? If only one of you would just wait a little, the other could get through. This is exactly what the function is trying to do by making the waiting period a function of the number of retries and a random number: prevent two or more users from repeatedly retrying to obtain the lock at the same instant in time.

After the For...Next loop, the actual retry is accomplished with the Resume statement.

The function glrAssignID() handles the high-level counter assignment. It is called from the BeforeInsert event of the form and is passed three parameters: the Form object, the name of the underlying table that holds the custom-counter field, and the name of the custom-counter field (which is of datatype Long Integer). glrAssignID() deletes any record that cannot be assigned a counter. Depending on your particular circumstances, you may need a more sophisticated high-level control routine. For example, you might want to save records that couldn't be assigned an ID to a temporary local table rather than discard them entirely. glrAssignID() is shown in Listing 11.3.

Listing 11.3

```
Function glrAssignID(frm as Form, ByVal strTableName As String,
➥ ByVal strCounterField As String) As Variant

' Runs from BeforeInsert when new record is added to a table
' Assumes that the table has a field called ID available
' Removes any record that cannot be saved

    On Error GoTo glrAssignID_Err

    Dim lngNewID As Long

    lngNewID = glrGetNextCounter(strTableName)

    If lngNewID <> -1 Then
        frm(strCounterField) = lngNewID
    Else
        MsgBox "Can't Add Record; Counter Not Available",
        ➥ MB_OK + MB_ICONSTOP + MB_DEFBUTTON1, "Error
        ➥ Saving Record"
        SendKeys "{ESC}{ESC}"
    End If

glrAssignID_Exit:
    Exit Function
```

```
glrAssignID_Err:
    SendKeys "{ESC}{ESC}"
    MsgBox "Error " & Err & ": " & Error$, MB_OK + MB_ICONSTOP
    ➥ + MB_DEFBUTTON1, "glrAssignID"
    Resume glrAssignID_Exit

End Function
```

One final thought about custom counter functions: you can also use them to assign a counter that is a datatype other than a monotonically increasing long integer. For example, if your company uses numbers of the form "AAA111" for part numbers, you could modify the glrGetNextCounter() function to return a counter in this custom format.

Security

Although security is not really a multiuser-specific concern, it certainly becomes more necessary in a multiuser environment. As the number of workstations running your application increases, the more likely it is you'll want to prevent unauthorized users from gaining access to either the data *or* the application.

Using security also allows Access to accurately inform you as to who has locked a record in its error messages. Even if you intercept Access' built-in locking-error messages, you still may want to parse out the user name and use it in any custom error messages. But if you don't use security, every user will be named Admin.

As mentioned earlier in this chapter, you can also use security to prevent users from opening a database in exclusive mode and intentionally or unintentionally locking other users out. (See Chapter 22 for more on security.)

The Wire

When moving from single-user to multiuser applications, you need to start thinking about potential data bottlenecks. Remember that every time your application requests data, it is sent over the network (also know as *the wire*) to the workstation. Thus, you'll want to minimize sending large amounts of data over the wire, for both the sake of the user requesting the data and the overall performance of the network. This is especially critical in wide area networks where the wire might be a slower telephone line rather than an Ethernet cable—although even Ethernet is much slower than the internal operations of your computer.

One Record at a Time

One area that demands special attention is how *much* of a recordset you give your users in a form. Although Access makes it very easy to bind a form to an entire table or query, letting users navigate to their heart's content, you'll quickly find this doesn't work well with even moderately large tables (more than a thousand rows) on a network. You're better off presenting each user with a single record at a time and programmatically changing the record source of the form rather than using the FindFirst method to move to a specific record. In version 1.x you could change the record source of a form by using the ApplyFilter action. In version 2.0 you can directly change the form's RecordSource property at run time.

The frmChngRecSrc Sample Form

In CH11.MDB we created a form, frmChngRecSrc, that demonstrates the technique of displaying only one record at a time to minimize network traffic. The form (see Figure 11.4), which would be used to enter customer orders for a business, draws its records from tblOrder. It also contains a subform, fsuborderDetails, for the editing of detail information. frmChngRecSrc includes these features:

- It's bound to a SQL statement that returns the first record in the table using a top 1 query. It's SQL is

```
SELECT Top 1 * FROM tblOrder Order By tblOrder.[Order#]=1;
```

- The user navigates to another order by entering a different order number in a text box control, txtGotoOrder, located in the form header. (This could also have been implemented using a combo box control.) This triggers an event procedure attached to the AfterUpdate event of txtGotoOrder. The event procedure builds a new SQL statement based on the value entered into the text box and changes the record source accordingly.

- The form toggles among three modes (Browse, Edit, and AddNew); the current mode is indicated in the form's caption. Users switch among modes

FIGURE 11.4:
The frmChngRecSrc is used to browse or edit a single record at a time. It opens initially in Browse mode, which is indicated in the form's caption.

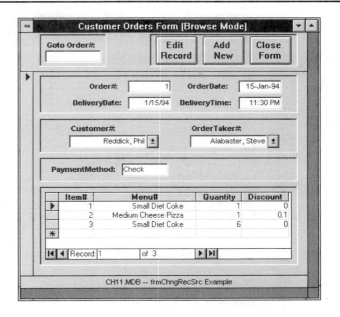

using buttons located in the header. The form opens in Browse mode to minimize inadvertent changes to the data.

- When the user switches to Edit mode or AddNew mode, the Edit Record and Add New button captions change to Save Record and Cancel, respectively, and the navigation text box and Close Form button are made invisible.

The AfterUpdate event procedure attached to txtGotoOrder is shown in Listing 11.4.

Listing 11.4

```
Sub txtGotoOrder_AfterUpdate()

    On Error GoTo txtGotoOrderAfterUpdateErr

    Dim strProcName As String
    Dim strSQL As String
    Dim ctlId As Control
    Dim strMsg As String
    Dim varRows As Variant
```

```
    strProcName = "txtGotoOrder_AfterUpdate"

    Set ctlId = Me!txtGotoOrder

    ' Exit if the text box is null
    If IsNull(ctlId) Then
        GoTo txtGotoOrderAfterUpdateDone
    End If

    ' Check if the entered Order# matches any existing records
    varRows = DCount("*", "tblOrder", "tblOrder.[Order#]= "
    ➡ & ctlId)
    If varRows = 0 Then
        strMsg = "There is no existing Order# " & ctlId & "."
        MsgBox strMsg, MB_ICONEXCLAMATION + MB_OK,
        ➡"Procedure " & strProcName
        GoTo txtGotoOrderAfterUpdateDone
    End If

    ' Build Select string
    strSQL = "SELECT DISTINCTROW * "
    strSQL = strSQL & "FROM tblOrder "
    strSQL = strSQL & "WHERE tblOrder.[Order#]= " & ctlId & ";"

    ' Change the form's RecordSource
    ' Access will automatically do a requery
    Me.RecordSource = strSQL

txtGotoOrderAfterUpdateDone:
    ' Null out value
    ctlId = Null
    On Error GoTo 0
    Exit Sub

txtGotoOrderAfterUpdateErr:
    Select Case Err
    Case Else
        strMsg = "Error#" & Err & "--" & Error$(Err)
    End Select
    MsgBox strMsg, MB_ICONSTOP + MB_OK,
    ➡ "Procedure " & strProcName
    Resume txtGotoOrderAfterUpdateDone

End Sub
```

The subroutine in Listing 11.5 is called from the header buttons to toggle the Locked property of each of the controls on the Detail section of the form.

Listing 11.5

```
Sub ToggleEditMode(fEdit As Integer)

    ' Toggle edit mode for each appropriate control
    ' in the detail section of the current form
    ' by setting the controls' locked properties.
    ' If fEdit = True, then set locked to False
    ' If fEdit = False, then set locked to True

    ' Skip any controls whose locked property can't be set
    On Error Resume Next

    Dim intI As Integer
    Const SECTION_DETAIL = 0

    For intI = 0 To Me.Count - 1
        'Only disable controls in detail section
        If Me(intI).Section = SECTION_DETAIL Then
            Me(intI).Locked = Not fEdit
        End If
    Next intI

End Sub
```

All the Access Basic code used in frmChngRecSrc, including additional event procedures not shown here, has been implemented using Code-Behind-Forms.

Test, Test, Test!

You need to test your applications more thoroughly if they are to be used on a network. The rule to remember here is, "If something can go wrong, it will." This means that you must set aside a significant amount of time for testing and debugging your multiuser applications.

One advantage of developing in the Windows environment is that you can develop, test, and debug multiuser applications on a single machine by starting two instances of Access and switching back and forth between the two instances. While this should allow you to test for and fix most potential problems, you'll still need to test the application on the target network under a typical load of users to find problems that might be masked by the round-robin nature of Windows' built-in multitasking. In other words, there's no substitute for the real thing.

Hardware

At the beginning of the chapter, we stated that you didn't need to be a network hardware or operating system expert to develop solid multiuser applications. On the other hand, don't completely ignore these issues. You could develop the best multiuser application ever, but if the network employs a slow file server hard drive, cheap network interface cards, bad wiring, and a poorly configured network operating system, it's the application that will look bad to your users. When it comes down to it, users don't care whether it's a hardware or software problem; they just want it to work—and in real time.

When you're looking to optimize performance on a network, you need to start by looking at the same factors you consider when optimizing single-user systems. For example, you may wish to increase the memory, hard disk space, size of the Windows swap file, and processor speed for each workstation. (See Chapter 16 for more details on performance tuning.) In addition, you may wish to consider the following network hardware issues:

- Consider upgrading the file server in the areas of speed and memory.

- Consider replacing older, cheaper, 16-bit network interface cards (NICs) with good-quality 32-bit cards.

- Consider using some sort of RAID (Redundant Array of Inexpensive Drives) technology on your file server.

- For larger Novell NetWare–based networks that appear to be maxing out the capacity of the file server, consider using multiple segments. This means installing multiple NICs on the file server to *segment* the network into smaller chunks.

- Consider upgrading to faster wiring.

If you don't want to get down and dirty with networking operating systems and hardware—and we don't blame you—you may want to hook up with a networking specialist to help you tune things up.

Summary

The important point to remember when writing multiuser applications is to anticipate problems. Multiuser applications need to handle (that is, recover from) the errors that occur when locks are placed on pages of records. In general, there is no set of perfect answers that applies to all multiuser applications. You'll have to develop the appropriate solution for your particular database and consider each of the following:

- Balance network security and maintenance against efficiency and speed when choosing whether to install Access on each workstation.

- Adjust your multiuser settings to achieve optimum performance for your particular application.

- Balance ease of use, data integrity, and ease of programming in developing your locking strategy and counter routines.

- Be aware of the errors that can occur when sharing data among multiple users.

- Split your database into separate data and application databases for increased performance.

- Use transactions to ensure the integrity of your data when multiple operations must occur in concert.

- Minimize data going across the network wire.

- Don't forget to adequately test your applications.

- Don't completely ignore hardware and operating system issues, especially if you're not getting the performance you'd like.

CHAPTER
TWELVE

Developing Client-Server Applications

- Using Access as a client

- Setting up and controlling ODBC

- Using ODBC data efficiently

- Managing connections to your server

- Controlling the flow of data

The term *client-server* has come to mean many different types of processing. Some of the original client-server work used servers to provide graphics processing for simple client workstations that did not have enough processing power. Others provided access to scarce resources, such as document printers. In a distributed computing environment, servers often execute entire business transactions for a client or perform other complex processing. Within the database market, most client-server work focuses on the use of database servers, usually SQL based. These servers provide database access and management services for client programs or workstations. Clients and servers can also communicate via several different methods, such as remote procedure calls (RPC), ODBC, Network DDE, and in the future, remote OLE automation.

In this chapter we discuss the use of Access as a front end to SQL-based database management servers. We focus on the use of ODBC as the method of communication between Access and the database server.

The Difference between File-Server and Client-Server

When you first look at using Access in a client-server system, you'll probably think it's an easy task. After all, if you bought this book, you've probably developed in Access for a while now. Migrating to client-server should just mean loading your data tables onto the server and changing the attachments, right?

Wrong. Client-server systems are a completely different architecture from native Access. Migrating from one to the other often requires many changes in the design, implementation, and support of your application. Before you convert your application, you should understand the differences and the impact they will have on your application.

Most applications built with Access support multiple users all at the same time, with little attention spent on this during development. Most of the differences between Access multiuser processing in file-server mode and client-server mode come from differences in the fetching and updating of data.

When several users are running a multiuser Access application in file-server mode, each of them is running a full copy of the Access database engine (Jet). Each copy of Jet is independently managing the physical files used to store the application. The only link between these independently executing engines is the .LDB file for each of the .MDB files used by the application. Most often, only the "data" .MDB is actually being shared. (See Chapter 11 for details on splitting databases into "application" and "data" databases.)

Each instance of Jet manages its own cache of physical pages from the file, updates the pages on each client's machine, and sends the updated physical pages back over the network. Each copy of Jet performs the index updating, system table maintenance, and other database management functions required to process your application's work.

In marked contrast to this, when you use Access as a front-end application and the database resides on a database server, the server provides all the data management functions for the application. Only the *server* updates the physical file and sees the physical pages in the database. Each user's copy of Access sends requests to the server and gets data, or pointers to the data, back from the server.

You might think that the issue of where the database is managed has little impact on you or your applications. That's, of course, the story you're likely to get from the vendors. Unfortunately, it simply isn't true with today's products. All of today's server products have their roots in a very different world from today's distributed processing, desktop-oriented environment that you have grown to appreciate using Access. These servers are all products from the mainframe and UNIX world and were developed around the concepts of processing using low-cost, low-capacity clients and having skilled support staffs and highly skilled administrators. As a result of their roots, none of these servers will readily take advantage of a product like Access as a client. It is *your* job as a developer to implement a system that takes advantage of both Access *and* the server.

Table 12.1 shows the key differences in processing between an Access-only multiuser application and a client-server application using Access and a database server.

TABLE 12.1: Key Differences between File-Server and Client-Server Access Applications

Process	Native Access (File-Server) Processing	Client-Server Access Processing
Updating data	Each user's machine fetches the physical pages over the network, updates them, and writes them back to the shared drive. Because of this, a failure on any client machine has a good chance of corrupting the database and requiring a shutdown and repair	The server database engine manages all updates of the physical database. Because of this, management problems with the network and individual machine failures are greatly reduced
Security	The Access security model covers all portions of a multiuser Access application	The Access security model is applied to the Access application portions of the application (forms, reports, modules, and macros). The security system of the database server controls accessing and updating the actual data. You still use Access security for forms, reports, modules, and queries, so both security systems must be kept current
Validation rules	Validation rules are part of native Access and the data engine	Validation rules and triggers must be defined at the server. They will not display the Access-defined error message when triggered. Your application will need to handle notifying the user appropriately
Support for special datatypes	Supports Counter, OLE, and Memo datatypes	Server dependent
Referential integrity	Defined within Access	RI must be defined directly at the server if the server supports it. You cannot establish referential integrity rules across servers or between server data and Access stored data
Updatable queries/views	Access allows update of almost any type of join. Access allows update of both sides of a one-to-many join	Most servers prohibit updates to joined queries. Access will update a view (at all) only if you specifically define it

Why Use Client-Server?

By this point you are probably wondering whether client-server is such a good idea after all. This is a good frame of mind from which to approach the native-Access versus client-server decision because moving to a client-server implementation requires learning a new approach to application programming. It also requires giving up many of your familiar tools and losing some of the strong integration that you find in Access. There are, however, several compelling reasons why you should choose to use a database server as a back end to Access applications:

- Reliability
- Transaction and data integrity
- Performance
- Cost of total system
- Improved management

> **NOTE** Each of the preceding reasons assumes that you have a choice as to where to store the data. But often you will consider using Access in a client-server environment simply because the data already resides on a database server and you wish to use Access to gain access to the data while continuing to keep the data on the server to support existing applications.

Reliability and Data Protection

Access runs a copy of the database engine on every client machine and has no synchronized transaction log or distributed transaction commit system. A failure of any single client machine or network component therefore has the potential to corrupt the entire database. Usually the database can be fixed, but repairing an Access database requires all users to log off the database. Repair of a large database can take several hours, and no user can be using the database during the repair. On the other hand, since all updating and data management on a server occur at the *server,* failures on the network or client machines rarely affect the database. Also, most servers have fast and robust recovery facilities.

Transaction Processing and Data Integrity

The transaction support built into Jet has access to the data only for its own current session. It cannot resolve problems left from a previous failed session or from another copy of Jet that failed somewhere else on the network. The transaction support built into Jet also does not have full protection for the database if a failure occurs while Jet is committing a transaction. In addition, the current implementation of Jet can leave locks orphaned in the .LDB file, requiring a shutdown and purge of the .LDB file before anyone can access or repair the data. As a result of this, failures that occur while a copy of Access is committing a transaction can result in data loss, data lockout, or database corruption. The windows are small, but they may be sufficient to cause you to seriously consider client-server if you are implementing systems that, for example, process real funds transactions. In this case, money will not be properly transferred or accounted for if the transaction partially commits.

Performance Considerations

Performance is another important reason to consider client-server, but one that is often misrepresented. Unlike the reliability issues, there are many approaches to providing good performance from a native Access multiuser system. On the other hand, there are cases in which a server is the only way to achieve appropriate performance.

If your application performs tasks similar to those listed in Table 12.2, you are a prime candidate for performance improvements from client-server. If your application has performance problems but does not match these types of processing, you may want to review the application and try to correct the performance without converting to client-server. You may still benefit from moving some or all of your tables to a server, but often processing-intensive applications, such as data analysis, cross-tab reporting, and data modeling, work best on individual workstations. (You might wish to consider moving the main data to a server and set up downloads for your application rather than converting your application to actually use the data on the server.)

TABLE 12.2: Applications That Will Likely Benefit from Client-Server Implementations

Processing Type	Benefit of Server Processing
High-volume transaction processing	Minimizes network traffic since only requests flow over the network. Faster response time for the same hardware cost. Better lock management reduces contention
Processing long-running queries against shared data	Servers are designed to manage different priority accesses. Lower network traffic since only query results go over the network
Updating single fields in large records	Much lower network traffic since only the updated fields have to be sent

Total System Cost

Related to performance is the total system cost. You need to have more power at each workstation in a file-server–based environment and generally need a faster network. Because of these factors, for large systems, client-server is usually cheaper than file-server if the workstations are dedicated devices. Of course, as more group-ware systems are introduced, each workstation will need more power, so this may end up a false economy.

System Management

One often overlooked area in client-server is overall system management and administration. Windows for Workgroups and the Access Workgroup Manager program offer only very limited management services compared to a Windows NT Advanced Server or a UNIX server machine.

Role of Access in Distributed Applications

Because Access is a full database management product, you have a great deal of flexibility in establishing the role of Access in your distributed application. The three main approaches we cover are

- Using Access as a true front-end process
- Using Access with both Jet tables and attached server tables
- Using Access as a store-and-forward application

NOTE You can also use ODBC to import data into an Access system and use the system as though there were no attachment to an outside data source. While we do not cover this approach in the chapter, it is often useful for data analysis and some decision-support systems. It allows the use of outside data with the least impact on your Access development style.

Using Access as a True Front-End Process

You can implement a pure client-server application using Access as a front-end process, storing all data on the server and implementing all queries so that they run using the server's SQL engine. By doing this you centralize all the data administration functions on the server. All table maintenance and associated work are done in a single environment. You can implement this approach by using SQL pass-through (SPT) for all your queries, an approach we cover in the section "Query Parsing" later in this chapter.

The biggest downside to this approach is performance. Access is a complete database product. You cannot really disable all the database-related processing and have only a forms and reports engine, so you are paying for a lot of overhead from which you get no benefit. Another downside is the loss of all of Access' native processing capabilities. You may be better off using an application development tool such as Visual Basic if you are planning to build a system using this approach where the desktop portion of the application does no data management.

Using Access with Both Jet Tables and Attached Server Tables

The most common approach to client-server with Access is to have a mix of local (Access-owned) and server-based data. The local data may be copies of relatively static data from the server, or it may be data that no one outside your workgroup needs to access. Common techniques that fall under this general approach are

- Downloading lookup tables to each client machine at login time
- Maintaining custom or auxiliary data in local databases
- Downloading bulk data to client machines for processing a series of reports or performing extended interactive analysis

Each of these areas is covered in more detail in the section "Partitioning Work between Client and Server" later in this chapter.

Using Access as a Store-and-Forward Application

An approach related to the preceding one is using Access to perform store-and-forward processing to a server. In store-and-forward processing, Access is acting as a full database product for the user and then turning around and acting as a client to the database server to update the shared database. This approach is useful if your server is over a wide area network (WAN) rather than a high-speed local area network (LAN) but may be useful in some cases even for local (non-WAN) processing.

One example of store-and-forward is an order entry application. In a pure client-server system, every detail item goes back to the server, perhaps multiple times, to validate and enter the item. In a store-and-forward approach, you use a set of local Access data tables to store the detail data as the order is entered and initial validation is done. After Access captures the entire order, it sends it to the server in a single transaction for final validation and loading into the shared database.

Understanding ODBC

Access uses the Open DataBase Connectivity (ODBC) standard to connect to servers. ODBC is a common language definition and a set of protocols that allow a client to interactively determine a server's capabilities and adapt the processing to work within the functions supported by the server. ODBC is implemented using components within Access, on each client machine running separately from Access, and on the database server machine. Figure 12.1 shows the overall processing structure that ODBC processing adds to your environment. To use ODBC to connect from Access to a back-end database, you need three things:

- A network that allows communications between the client machine and the machine that holds the back-end database
- The ODBC driver manager that comes with Access
- An ODBC driver that can work with your back-end database

There are many sources for ODBC-compliant drivers. Many database and hardware vendors now provide them, and there are several third-party sources for drivers.

FIGURE 12.1:
ODBC processing architecture

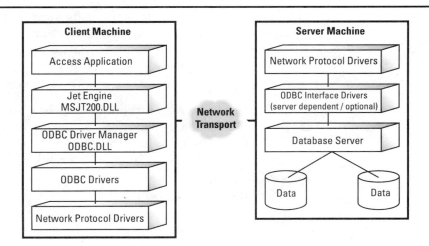

ODBC processing consists of three major activities:

- Establishing connections
- Parsing queries
- Managing record sources

The key to getting reliable performance lies in understanding all three of these areas and how your specific ODBC driver and back-end server handle each.

Establishing Connections

ODBC processing revolves around *connections*. When a client needs access to data on a server, the ODBC software at the client end (in the case of Access, Jet and the underlying ODBC drivers) performs several steps to establish a connection:

1. Find the system and path information for the appropriate connection.
2. Connect over the appropriate network(s) to the database server.
3. Check for a stored login for the database.
4. Prompt the user (if required) for login and password information.
5. Gather information about the capabilities of the server.
6. Gather information about the capabilities of the ODBC driver.
7. Gather information about the table(s) that are being connected.

Jet uses all this information to determine the best way to process your query using the server's SQL engine. This information comes from the Connect string of the attached table and from the ODBC.INI file.

Because of the cost of performing this work, you generally want to make connections only once for each session. This is what happens when you use attached tables, because Access caches connection information for attached tables locally. This in turn allows Jet to connect to the table when you reference it without all the overhead of a dynamic connection. When converting your application, try to remove all uses of the OpenDatabase() function or method and open recordsets only against queries or attached tables.

Query Parsing

Jet handles a query for an ODBC connection in one of two ways. You can use either of the following:

- A regular Jet-optimized Access query
- A SQL pass-through (SPT) query

If you use an SPT query, Access does no parsing of the query and passes the SQL string directly to the database server for processing. It is your responsibility to ensure that the string is a valid SQL statement. On the other hand, you can also use a regular Access query, whereupon Jet interprets and optimizes the query locally, determining the best execution path. During the optimization step, Jet partitions the query execution into a Jet-executed component and a server-executed component.

When you use SPT queries, there is minimal overhead introduced on the Access side, but there is also minimal control and no assistance from Access. SQL pass-through works best for the following activities:

- Performing data definition language (DDL) operations or other administrative actions on the server
- Executing SQL when the SQL syntax is not supported by Access
- Executing very short SQL actions, such as single row fetches or updates
- Processing SQL statements that join tables in two databases on the same server
- Processing SQL updates when you need to check on the number of rows updated
- Processing large action queries within transactions

Except in these cases it is usually more efficient to use Jet-optimized Access queries. Only convert to pass-through queries if you encounter a significant performance problem, such as a query that Jet fails to optimize properly. The normal SQL parsing for ODBC processing is similar to the Jet processing for native Access tables. The major difference is that once the Jet engine has isolated the commands that need to be processed at the server, it generates a SQL string in the common ODBC SQL dialect, which is in turn translated by your server-specific ODBC driver into your server's

SQL dialect. When Jet executes the query, it executes all the portions of a query that are local and sends the translated SQL strings to the server for processing.

Managing Record Sources

When you convert to ODBC from native Access, you may find that complex forms open slowly compared to other forms. When you built your forms in native Access, you probably did not worry about how many different sources of data the form used since it all came from one place anyway. When you use ODBC you need to limit the number of different record sources on a form to ensure reasonable performance and usability.

As mentioned earlier in this chapter, ODBC uses connections to talk to the server. Depending on the server, there may be a single physical connection opened or there may be a separate physical connection for each active recordset. In some cases, such as with Microsoft/Sybase SQL Server, there can be two connections for a single recordset (except when there are fewer than 100 records when only one connection is used). Whether they are actual physical links or logical links over a shared path, all connections use memory and use up processing resources to manage. Thus, you need to be careful about the number of active recordsets your application uses in order to work efficiently under ODBC. Each row source on your form is a separate connection. Each bound subform will have one or more connections. A connection is in use

- Until all associated data has been returned from the server
- While any transactions are outstanding

Jet may cache a connection, once made, to avoid the cost of reestablishing the connection the next time it requires data. You can control this caching process by way of parameters in the ODBC section of your .INI file.

Configuring ODBC for Your System

Access provides a wide range of configuration options for controlling ODBC. It is important to review all of these and match them to your planned use of the system, your company's network, and the configuration of the server.

Table 12.3 contains descriptions of each configuration option and points out some potential settings for various conditions.

TABLE 12.3: Settings in MSACC20.INI

Parameter	Value	Use
TraceSQLMode (or SQLTraceMode)	0	Turns off tracing of the Jet to server SQL dialog (default)
	1	Traces all dialog of SQL between Jet and the ODBC interface. The output will be in a file named SQLOUT.TXT
TraceODBCAPI	0	Disables tracing the ODBC API-level interface (default)
	1	Traces ODBC API calls into file ODBCAPI.TXT. You would use this only for debugging an ODBC driver or resolving a problem when working with a vendor. Normally, for working on your application's performance or debugging your SQL, you should use a SQL trace instead
DisableAsync	0	Allows Access to continue processing while the server processes an ODBC request (default)
	1	Forces Access to wait for each ODBC request to complete before proceeding. You should set this only for debugging purposes since it can have severe performance problems
LoginTimeout	s	Aborts a login attempt if the server has not responded in s seconds (default: 20; range: not documented [appears to be 1–32767])
QueryTimeout	s	Provides a default value for query processing timeouts in seconds. Individual queries can override this with the Timeout property (default: 60; range: not documented [appears to be 1–32767])
ConnectionTimeout	s	Sets the length of time in seconds during which Jet will maintain an inactive connection before releasing it. If your server is not licensed on a per-connection basis, setting this higher may improve response time. If you frequently run out of connections, lower this value (default: 600; range: not documented [appears to be 1–32767])

TABLE 12.3: Settings in MSACC20.INI (continued)

Parameter	Value	Use
AsyncRetryInterval	*m*	Sets the length of time in milliseconds. Jet waits each time it checks on the progress of an async query (default: 500; range: not documented [appears to be 1–32767])
AttachCaseSensitive	0	Does not use case when matching table names (default)
	1	Performs a case-sensitive search when opening tables
SnapshotOnly	0	Allows processing that uses updatable recordsets (default)
	1	Forces the use of read-only Snapshot recordsets
AttachableObjects	*string*	Includes the server's system objects in the selection list for attaching tables. *string* is a list of all the system objects to include in the selection list (default: 'Table', 'View', 'System Table', 'Alias', and 'Synonym')
TryJetAuth	1	Try Jet Userid & Password before prompting the user for a different ID and password (default). You can use this setting if you keep IDs and passwords in sync between Access and the server
	0	Prompts the user for a different ID and password. Use this setting if your Access IDs are not kept in sync with the server
PreparedInsert	0	Generates data-specific inserts that reflect only the supplied columns (default). You should normally use this setting
	1	Uses a predefined INSERT that uses all columns in the table
PreparedUpdate	0	Generates data-specific updates that reflect only the supplied columns (default). You should normally use this setting
	1	Uses a predefined UPDATE that updates all columns

You can provide additional information Access uses to manage your server connections in an optional table, MSysConf. You must add this table to each *server* database. It provides Access-specific information to assist in managing connections. Table 12.4 describes each of the settings for the MSysConf table.

TABLE 12.4: Settings in Your MSysConf Table

Parameter	Value	Use
101	0	Does not store user IDs and passwords for attached tables. This value prompts the user for ID and password information each time the tables are attached
	1	Stores the user ID and password information with the connect string information for attached tables (default)
102	d	Sets the data fetch delay time. Jet will delay d seconds between each fetch of a block of rows from the server (default: 10; range: not documented [appears to be 1–32767])
103	n	Sets the number of rows to fetch from the server at each interval. You use these two settings (102 and 103) to control the rate at which data is brought from a server to Access during idle time (default: 100; range: not documented [appears to be 1–32767])

Mapping ODBC and Access Datatypes

ANSI SQL standards define datatypes differently from Access. You need to understand how ODBC maps datatypes, both from the server to Access and from Access tables to the server. You can find datatype mappings from ODBC to Access in Table 12.5 and mappings from Access to ODBC in Table 12.6. You need to verify which datatypes your specific server supports.

TABLE 12.5: ODBC Datatypes and Their Mapping to Access

ODBC Datatype	Microsoft Access Datatype
SQL_BIT	Yes/No
SQL_TINYINT	
SQL_SMALLINT	Number—Size: Integer
SQL_INTEGER	Number—Size: Long Integer
SQL_REAL	Number—Size: Single
SQL_FLOAT	Number—Size: Double

TABLE 12.5: Settings in Your MSysConf Table (continued)

ODBC Datatype	Microsoft Access Datatype
SQL_DOUBLE	
SQL_TIMESTAMP	DateTime
SQL_DATE	
SQL_TIME	Text
SQL_CHAR	if <= 255, then Text (Field Size = lPrecision); if > 255, then Memo
SQL_VARCHAR	
SQL_BINARY	if <= 255, then Binary (Field Size = lPrecision); if > 255, then OLE Object
SQL_VARBINARY	
SQL_LONGVARBINARY	OLE Object
SQL_LONGVARCHAR	Memo
All Others	TEXT, length = 255

Note: Precision is the maximum number of digits used by the datatype of the column.

TABLE 12.6: Access Datatypes and Their Mapping to ODBC and Servers

Microsoft Access Datatype	ODBC Datatype
Yes/No	SQL_BIT, if supported; otherwise SQL_SMALLINT, if supported; otherwise SQL_INTEGER, if supported; otherwise SQL_VARCHAR(5)
Number—Size: Byte	SQL_SMALLINT, if supported; otherwise SQL_INTEGER, if supported; otherwise SQL_VARCHAR(10)
Number—Size:Integer	
Number—Size: Long Integer	SQL_INTEGER, if supported; otherwise SQL_VARCHAR(20)
Currency	SQL_DECIMAL(19,4), if SQL Server/Sybase; otherwise SQL_FLOAT, if supported; otherwise SQL_VARCHAR(30)
Number—Size:Single	SQL_REAL, if supported; otherwise SQL_FLOAT, if supported; otherwise SQL_VARCHAR(30)
Number—Size:Double	SQL_FLOAT, if supported; otherwise SQL_VARCHAR(40)
DateTime	SQL_TIMESTAMP, if supported; otherwise SQL_VARCHAR(40)
Text(Field Size)	SQL_VARCHAR(MIN(Field Size, ServerMax))

TABLE 12.6: Access Datatypes and Their Mapping to ODBC and Servers (continued)

Microsoft Access Datatype	ODBC Datatype
Binary(Field Size)	SQL_VARBINARY(MIN(Field Size,ServerMax)), if supported; otherwise query fails
Memo	SQL_LONGVARCHAR(ServerMax), if supported; otherwise SQL_VARCHAR(2000), if ServerMax >= 2000; otherwise query fails
OLE Object	SQL_LONGVARBINARY(ServerMax), if supported; otherwise SQL_VARBINARY(2000), if ServerMax >= 2000; otherwise query fails

Tables 12.5 and 12.6 define the mapping used by Access and ODBC drivers to map datatypes. You must use caution when using any of the datatypes that do not have an exact mapping, such as Decimal (on the server) or Currency or Datetime (in Access). Different servers, and even different ODBC drivers, can result in slight variations in the handling of these datatypes. Some ODBC drivers will produce errors when dealing with decimal numeric data or will map it only to a text field in Access. Datetime processing will vary depending on the server you use, so carefully review your processing needs for this type of data.

Understanding Your Server

Part of the promise of ODBC is that you can develop applications that are server independent. It turns out, though, that while ODBC certainly makes it easier to move from server to server, it is still important to write your application with the target server in mind. Both the server and the connecting software will affect the processing of your SQL. The SQL language used in Access is quite far from any specific ANSI standard. (Chapter 5 outlines most of the differences.) Access has several features not supported by most servers and lacks features present in some servers.

Some important areas to check for different servers are security, counter fields or their equivalent, joins, support for the use of multiple indexes within a single query, and transaction processing support. The level of transaction support is a function of both the server and the ODBC driver. You need to match the features of your server with the features of Access that your application uses. If your application functionality is dependent on features your server does not support, you should look at a different server, rework your application, or consider not migrating the application.

You need to consider the following server characteristics when picking a server and developing your Access applications:

- Does the server support SQL-92 Join syntax?
- What Join syntax is supported?
  - Inner joins only
  - Outer joins
  - Nested inner and outer joins (Note that this would require SPT queries.)
- Does the server support subqueries?
- Does the server support auto-incrementing or identity fields (counters)?
- Does the server support referential integrity?
- Does the server allow updates on any joined queries? If so, which updates and deletes are supported?
- Does the server support stored procedures or triggers?
- Does the server support cascading updates or deletes?
- Which built-in functions does the server support?
- Which date/time functions does the server support?

Defining an Efficient Client-Server Design

When implementing client-server systems, you need to address several design areas that you typically do not need to deal with in a stand-alone Access application. The next few sections cover each of these design areas in detail.

Establishing Rules for Transactions

You must clearly define and document all your data activity that is to be grouped together so that the transaction protection and recovery features of your server can work correctly.

Jet applies the following rules regarding transactions when processing against an ODBC data source:

- Forms must use optimistic locking.
- Recordsets must use optimistic locking.
- Only the outermost transaction is used if nested transactions are encountered.
- Only a single workspace is used for an ODBC connection. Multiple workspaces are consolidated.
- Action queries are processed in a single transaction.
- Recordsets created inside an Access Basic transaction are processed under that transaction.

Because of the limitations of locking choices and lack of control over transactions (see Chapter 11), bound forms are usually not useful if you are doing standard client-server processing with Access. On the other hand, you can use bound forms in store-and-forward implementations or against downloaded data with good results. In addition, you may be able to successfully use bound forms directly against server tables or views in the following circumstances:

- When the form is based on a single table
- When the system is coded to handle update contention that will occur from optimistic locking
- When the data being updated does not need to be kept private while a set of changes is completed

Forms that will usually meet these criteria include

- Inquiry-only forms (based on read-only recordsets)
- Master table maintenance forms

Processing that generally does *not* work well using bound forms in the client-server setup includes

- Updates or inserts of master/detail combinations such as orders
- Updates in which multiple rows of a table must be changed at once

Establishing Data Concurrency Requirements

Review each major data component in your application to determine how current the data needs to be. Data concurrency defines how frequently data stored on the client machine must be refreshed from the server in order to ensure that any changes are reflected on each client. For data with very high concurrency requirements, the client must always retrieve the data from the server and not cache or store it locally. On the other hand, data that changes via nightly batch loads from a mainframe can be downloaded overnight by means of batch jobs or at startup and remain on the client throughout the day. Most data will fall somewhere in between these two extremes.

Understanding the Client-Server Conversation

You must understand which messages will flow between your client and server machines to process particular requests. You can use the trace functions listed in Table 12.3 to capture the message stream. Here are some important points to remember about connections and threads (multiple conversations over a single connection):

- Many servers can support only a single active thread over a connection, so one client may tie up a large number of connections if they are allowed to have a number of active recordsets at once.
- There is a significant overhead in first establishing a connection for a particular table because the ODBC layer has to get all the table, field, and index properties. You should try to use attached tables where possible. If you cannot attach to tables for some reason, consider using pass-through SQL.

Creating Efficient Client-Server Applications

Creating efficient client-server applications requires that you follow certain principles:

- Try to move data only once.
- Make sure the server gives you only what you need.
- Minimize contention with other users.

Each of these priniciples is discussed in the next few sections.

Try to Move Data Only Once

Access has a penchant for allowing the user to view data in several formats, views, and orders. It is very costly to reload the data to the client when processing in a client-server environment. In situations in which a dataset will be used for analysis, you should consider downloading the data into working tables on the client.

Make Sure the Server Gives You Only What You Need

It is important to avoid recordsets based on all fields and all rows of a table. If you really need this level of data, consider importing or downloading the data from the server instead of attaching to it. You can always refresh the data from the server by dropping your local table and re-importing. For forms, always define a query for the record source, and always include a WHERE clause that is as restrictive as possible—one row is usually best. Avoid the use of the all-fields identifier (*) in your queries. Create form-specific queries that contain only the fields required for that form.

For reports, consider defining the base data for the report as a table and running an append query to load it from the server. This avoids many of the pitfalls you will find when trying to interpret all the data access requirements of a report.

Minimize Contention with Other Users

The most common reason given for implementing a client-server system is its great multiuser performance. You must make sure, however, that your design builds on the strength of that performance and does not restrict or limit it. A major area in which Access-based systems tend to limit the performance of servers is logical data contention and locking. Since Access hides most of the transaction management from you if you use bound forms, it is critical that you understand what Access does on your behalf. It is also important to match your data requests to your locking approach to ensure that data locks occur at the appropriate level.

For example, in a problem management system, if users leave a lock on the "outstanding problem queue" while they update a problem in the queue, other users will not be able to pick up new work. On shared-control oriented tables, you need to make sure the updates to these tables are in separate, short-lived transactions.

Partitioning Work between Client and Server

Some of your most critical decisions during the design process will be splitting, or partitioning, the work between Access and the server. When using Access as a front end, you need to use client hardware that has almost as much memory and processing power as a machine used for stand-alone Access. Access differs from many front-end clients (for example, PowerBuilder and ObjectView) in this respect because Access *always* creates an entire application. To end up with an efficient client-server system, you must leave appropriate portions of the application in native Access.

Taking Advantage of Access

When splitting the workload between Access and server, always remember that Access is a complete database system. You can take advantage of this by caching data locally on each client machine as it is first used or even at login time. By doing this you can reduce both network traffic and the load on your server, allowing you to support many more concurrent users on the same server and network. This is especially easy to implement if you are converting an existing application since you already have the native Access processing coded.

Review all your data requirements and identify the data that matches the following conditions:

- Data is static or relatively static.
- Users do not need to see each other's changes immediately.
- Data is always used together as a set, with each set needing to be used together exclusively.

Also, review your processing requirements to look for the following situations:

- Data entry systems in which several detail records are entered to build a complete transaction. This may be an order, an invoice, a parts list, or one of several other cases matching the traditional header-detail data pairing.
- Reports showing several aspects of the same data.
- Reports that do a great deal of data consolidation.

When you have processing needs matching the above types, you can benefit by downloading the data onto the client machine for processing or, when going the other way, by capturing the user's activity locally and uploading data to the server only when the user's session or activity is complete.

If your application uses a number of lookup tables, set up your system to load these at startup time. You can then design your forms and reports to use the local data in pick lists, in combo boxes, or when displaying descriptive lookup text instead of codes.

If your users typically work on a particular set of data for an extended period and other users should not work on this same data concurrently, you have a prime candidate for downloading the data and processing it locally. An example of this might be a problem management system or an order processing system.

Data Entry Systems

Many data entry systems feature an operator doing heads-down, high-speed entry of a lot of detail data for an order and then committing the entire order to the system.

The partial order is of no use to others in the system. In fact, you do not want other groups to see a partially entered order because it could skew results of their work. Thus, it makes sense in these cases to use local Access tables to capture the order and then upload the data to the server only when the entire order is complete.

Reporting Systems

Reporting itself is rarely a good reason for considering a move to client-server. Often it is the hardest part to convert. Usually, the most flexible way to implement reporting in a client-server environment is to either download the data used by reports to local tables on which the reports are then based or to base reports on stacked queries. With stacked queries, the report's query uses a query based on the server's tables rather than directly referencing the tables. This helps avoid problems where Jet is unable to produce an efficient partitioning of work, particularly for reports using crosstabs or extensive aggregate processing. Initially, you should probably just download temporary tables for your reports. Convert reports to server-based record sources only if you encounter severe performance problems downloading the data.

Identifying Data Sources on Your Server

If you are implementing a new client application that uses existing server-resident data in a corporation, you need to research which data is available to you. You may also need to understand your organization's rules regarding access to and updates of the data. Most corporations with existing server systems also have rules about using the data, as well as design, documentation, and reporting rules for the applications that use the data, that you will need to follow.

It is important to identify all the data sources your system will use and verify where the data resides. If your data sources are spread across multiple server, make sure you get the mapping, and make sure the administrator of the system knows you are a user. Access can handle retrieving data from multiple back-end sources, but it is best for performance to control the number of sources in a single query. Once you have identified all the sources, make sure you create explicit connect strings for each data source so that searches of distributed network directories are not needed at attachment or table open time.

A useful habit to get into when using shared data servers is to create a copy of each table locally in Access and populate this table with sample data. This way you can refine your programs against local data without affecting the whole user base while you work out the best queries and reports. Once you have your queries refined, just replace the local tables with attached server tables and, during a quiet time on the network, test your application against the server.

> **TIP**
>
> If you are planning on doing client-server development, consider acquiring a developer's version of one of the server products. Microsoft and Oracle both offer these, as do Watcom and IBM. They range in price from $500 to around $1000, but the investment is well worth it if you develop many client-server applications.

Mapping Data to Your Interface Components

Mapping your data and documenting your data requirements for each user interface component are good ideas for *any* Access system. They are critical, however, for creating a client-server system with predictable performance. Since each connection to a server is somewhat costly, it is important to track the number of active connections your application will need. This is especially important with products such as SQL Server, where the server cannot maintain multiple active recordsets across the same connection.

For each form or report, you need to identify the primary data source. This is usually a query based on attached tables from the server. Next, you need to identify the subforms, controls, and Access basic functions used by the form and list all their data requirements. As you're mapping the data, you must evaluate exactly how much data will be returned for each component. After you do this, make sure you set up criteria that restrict the data returned from the server to only what is needed at any given time.

TIP You can use the Access 2.0 Database Documentor add-in to produce a listing of all the queries, record sources, row sources, and control sources for your forms and reports.

After you have defined your criteria, review these against the server database to make sure appropriate indexes exist.

As you map data to your application's components, you'll need to

- Identify your record sources
- Identify criteria and parameters
- Identify the data source of controls
- Define all expressions

Identify Your Record Sources

For each form and report you have defined, create a working table or query that will act as its record source. Be sure to identify where each field will come from. If the data is coming from multiple sources, such as multiple servers or both client and server, consider splitting the query into components. Then stack the queries into the final record source. This approach helps the Jet optimizer control multiple varying data sources.

Identify Criteria and Parameters

As mentioned earlier in this chapter, it is important to restrict data that's retrieved by the client. Always review the criteria for each data source used by a form or report (or any other recordsets). If you are using unbound fields on your forms as criteria for queries, be sure to match datatypes carefully. You should always explicitly define your parameters for any query that goes against a server. Defining the parameters is required by most servers, and Access will have to retrieve the entire table and process the criteria locally if it cannot specify the datatype to the server. Jet attempts to do this for you if you have not defined your parameters, so explicit definition is safest.

Identify the Data Source of Controls

In addition to the main data source for a bound form or report, there are often controls bound to other sources. You must analyze the data source of each control that has a separate row source. In a client-server system, it is best not to have many controls that separately fetch data from the server. Try either to use locally cached data or to add the data to the main query.

Define All Expressions

The proper handling of expressions, particularly expressions that perform aggregate functions such as totals or averages, makes a big difference in the performance of a client-server application. Including an expression that needs to be evaluated before the result set is determined may result in every row of the underlying tables being passed from the server back to your client machine. You need to

- Ensure that expressions in queries are calculated only for outputted records
- Avoid column-based expressions in the criteria
- Avoid performing GROUP BYs and ORDER BYs on expressions
- Avoid domain functions within queries

Building Your Queries and Local Data Tables

After you have defined your user interface and identified all the data sources on your server, you need to define your local tables and all the queries your system will use. You can use a make-table query against your server to create any local work tables that are based on server tables or queries.

Designing queries in a client-server system is more complicated than in a native Access environment. As mentioned earlier in this chapter in the section "Understanding ODBC," there are two main ways Jet handles queries: SQL pass-through and Jet-controlled. The following sections cover how and when to use each approach.

Using Pass-Through

SQL pass-through (SPT) queries are a tool that allows you to bypass the Jet database engine and send your predefined SQL strings to the server. Some cases require you to use SPT—for these cases you have no option. There are also cases in which SPT may be the easier way to accomplish something or in which SPT provides the best performance. Situations requiring the use of SPT were outlined earlier in this chapter in the section "Query Parsing."

When using "regular" (non-SPT) Access queries, there are many things to keep in mind. The key point is to make sure that as much processing as possible is transferred to the server. To do this you need to have gathered the information from the section "Understanding Your Server" earlier in this chapter to know what can be processed there. You also need to understand which types of query processing Access will never attempt to send to a server.

Server-Supported Functions

At a maximum, only the functions listed in Table 12.7 are passed to a server. If your SQL uses any other functions or any user-defined functions, the part of the query containing those functions will be processed on the client. Some servers may not support all these functions. Refer to the data you gathered about your server for specifics.

TABLE 12.7: Server-Supported Operators and Functions

Type	Operator or Function
General operators	=, <>, <, <=, >, >=, AND, OR, NOT, LIKE, IS NULL, IS NOT NULL, IN, &, +, −, *, /, IDIV, MOD
Numeric functions	ABS(), ATN(), COS(), EXP(), FIX(), INT(), LOG(), RND(), SGN(), SIN(), SQR(), TAN()
String functions	ASC(), CHR(), INTR(), LCASE(), LTRIM(), LEFT(), LEN(), MID(), RTRIM(), RIGHT(), SPACE(), STR(), STRING(), TRIM(), UCASE()
Aggregate functions	MIN(), MAX(), AVG(), COUNT(), SUM()
Date/time functions	DATE(), NOW(), TIME(), SECOND(), MINUTE(), HOUR(), WEEKDAY(), DAY(), MONTH(), YEAR(), DATEPART('ddd'), DATEPART('www'), DATEPART('yyy'), DATEPART('mmm'), DATEPART('qqq'), DATEPART('hhh'), DATEPART('nnn'), DATEPART('sss'), DATEPART('ww'), DATEPART('yyyy')
Conversion functions	CInt(), CLng(), CSng(), CDbl(), CCur(), CStr(), CVDate()

In addition to functions that cannot be performed at the server, several other conditions will result in a query's being performed either entirely or partially on the client:

- Multiple-level GROUP BYs
- GROUP BYs including DISTINCT
- Joins over GROUP BYs
- Joins over DISTINCT clauses
- Certain combinations of outer and inner joins
- Queries stacked on unions
- Subqueries that include data from more than one source

You should consider crosstab queries a special case when developing queries. While no server supports crosstabs directly, most servers will process the underlying aggregate query if the following conditions are met:

- Row and column headers may not contain aggregates.
- The value field must contain only one aggregate.
- There can be no user-defined ORDER BY clause.

If you meet these conditions, your crosstab query will be processed on the server, and the local Jet engine will have to do only the final formatting to present the crosstab.

Building Your Forms

Building forms for client-server applications requires some special considerations beyond those covered in Chapter 8. You must pay special attention to how your searching and navigation processes work. You must also be closely aware of your data sources. The following sections cover each of these subjects in detail.

Choosing Bound and Unbound Fields

After you have identified all the data requirements and data sources for your forms, you need to create the forms and link all the fields to their data sources. Whenever possible, link bound fields to a field from the record source of the form rather than creating a separate row source for each control. In a client-server environment each row source will result in a separate connection to the server.

If you do use controls bound to separate data sources (including subforms), make sure either that they are set to be hidden when the form opens or that the fields used to link to them or provide criteria for them are filled in during the form's Open event. Firing off the query for a subform with null criteria can create a major, unneeded workload for your network. This is especially important for subforms since they tend to be more complex than list boxes or combo boxes.

Choosing an Appropriate Design for Your Forms

Often an Access form allows a user both to navigate to a specific record and to then perform detailed work on the record. Several approaches to form design provide good performance for these situations. The goal of each approach is to present the user with a small subset of the fields to use to select the records they need and a separate recordset for the detail. The form should be set up to fill the detail recordset only *after* the criteria are selected by the user.

Using an Unbound Main Form and a Subform for Detail

One of the simplest approaches you can use for search and edit forms is to create your edit form as though it would be used directly and then embed it as a subform on an unbound form. You can set the record source of the subform based on a query that references fields on the unbound main form rather than using the master and child linking fields. On the main form, create the controls users will use to establish the criteria for their final recordset. You should set the default value on each of the criteria fields to a value that will cause the subform to return no rows when the form is first opened. If you use a combo box, list box, or other pick-list mechanism to allow the user to find records, you should use a hidden field to hold the criteria and fill it in the AfterUpdate event procedure of the pick-list type control. Provide a command button, toolbar button, or menu selection for users to indicate that they are finished setting criteria. An example of this approach is shown in Figure 12.2.

FIGURE 12.2:
After indicating that you're done specifying criteria, the form retrieves the requested rows.

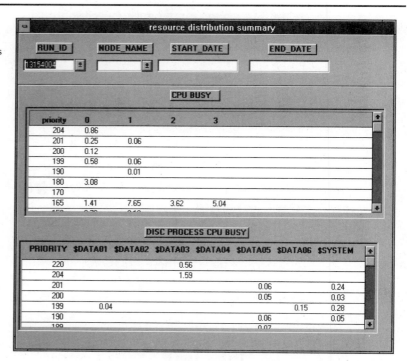

If the pick lists are based on fairly static data, such as order types, lists of valid codes, or processing status codes, this data should be downloaded to the client at startup. For more volatile data, you should accept the overhead of fetching it from the server each time the form is opened to ensure that users receive the most current data.

Using a Dynamic Record Source

You can provide more flexibility by using a modified version of the form/subform model presented in the preceding section. Create the SQL for the detail form dynamically based on the values filled in on the unbound main form. This eliminates the need for the hidden fields for criteria and helps ensure that the most efficient SQL can be used for each alternative set of criteria. You must use dynamic SQL instead of a fixed query with parameters if you are using LIKE in your criteria and appending wildcard characters to the user's selections. If you use fixed criteria, you will end up with a full table scan since the optimizer cannot predict how to use the indexes. You should also use dynamic SQL instead of a fixed query if your table has multiple indexes but your server can use only a single index for each table in a query. By building the SQL based on the fields selected by the user, you have the best chance of using the most restrictive index each time.

Using Unbound Controls in the Header or Footer

You can use a variation on the approach just described on a single form. Place the unbound controls that are used for criteria entry in the header or footer and, at run time, either filter the form using the ApplyFilter action or reset the form's record source using the form's RecordSource property. (An example of this technique is discussed in Chapter 11 in the section "The Wire.") This has the advantage of using only a single bound form, but it offers fewer user interface design alternatives since the header and footer must always appear at a specific location.

Using FindFirst

One approach to record navigation and searching that works much better in client-server than in native Access is the FindFirst method. In Access this always results in a scan, but with servers, Jet will often use a new query, and the server can process an efficient search. You can take advantage of this by placing your search criteria in the header or footer area of a form and using FindFirst to move the Detail section to the desired data.

Making the Best Use of Controls

The next few sections describe some specific areas to review in your forms' use of controls.

Basing Controls on Controls

Instead of using expressions based on the underlying queries or tables, base expressions on the values of other controls on the form when you can. This keeps the query as simple and clean as possible. It is very important from a user's perceived performance perspective to put lookup functions at the form level instead of at the query level. If Access does not realize that your lookup function is required only for data display, it will process the lookup for *all* the rows of your recordset before opening the form.

Combo and List Boxes

Make sure the queries that provide data for your combo and list boxes are as restrictive as possible. Avoid opening a combo box against an entire table unless it is a small lookup table. If you are planning to use a combo box on a form as a pick list to supply criteria, download the data for the pick list into a work table on the client so that each use of the combo box does not go back to the server. You can usually improve the performance of a form by using *unbound* combo and list boxes. Modify either the RecordSource or Filter property of the affected form or subform to reposition the current record to the selected data instead of binding a column from the control to the underlying data.

You should consider these guidelines when implementing combo and list boxes:

- The displayed field should be a text field.

- The control should be based on as few columns as possible.

- Combo boxes that are driven off the server will perform better with the Auto-Expand property set to No.

- Combo and list boxes with binary bound columns from a server will show extremely poor performance.

Subforms

Subforms can greatly improve how your user views the performance of your application, or they can kill it. For client-server systems you must first decide whether a subform is appropriate or whether the data could be presented by using the header and detail areas of a single form. Each active subform on a form uses another active connection, so you must use them sparingly.

Make sure the linking fields for your subforms contain appropriate data when the main form is initially opened. In native Access you may leave the LinkMasterFields property without default values, which can cause a major slowdown when opening the form.

You should try to link forms and subforms for the client-server environment by basing the subform on a parameter query that uses fields from the main form rather than by filling in the master and child link properties. You will get more control by using a parameter query instead of allowing Access to rebuild the subform's SQL based on the master and child link properties. This will often allow Jet and your server to process more efficiently.

Deciding How to Open Your Form

When possible, open your form either by explicitly setting the RecordSource property before opening the form or by using a parameter query as the base of the form and providing the parameter values when opening the form. You can also use the Where parameter of the OpenForm action, but this is less efficient than directly restricting the form's record source. Avoid opening a form against an unrestricted record source since this often creates a very large recordset.

Building Reports

Reports often cause problems for client-server work in Access. Access has a powerful reporting module that offers many data analysis tools. Most of these tools assume that the data they are working with is local and that fetching the data multiple times will not cause unacceptable overhead.

You may find that the easiest solution is to split your report processing into two parts. First, set up a query that extracts all the required data from your server. While building this query, do not worry about obtaining totals, grouping, or other reporting requirements. After you have isolated the data for the report, build the query or queries used by the report based on the server query. When you need to run multiple reports from a single data source, you should download the data into local Access tables and base the reports on these temporary tables.

Exceptions to this general approach are

- Generating a summary report from a very large database
- Generating a report using statistics (such as median) that are supported by your server directly but are not supported in Access

Effects of Grouping and Sorting

Access cannot send multiple-level GROUP BYs directly to servers. If you do not download the data into an Access table with indexes that support the GROUP BYs, the recordset is sorted on the client machine. The grouping and sorting in the report design will override the grouping and sorting in a query, so do not use grouping and sorting in the query when you are grouping and sorting data within the report.

Selecting Data Sources for Fields

All the points about data sources raised for forms apply equally to reports. Since reports represent a read-only snapshot of a database, there are more cases in which downloaded data can be used than there are for forms. Applying all formatting on the report fields instead of the query fields also helps with query optimization.

Creating Header and Footer Fields and Expressions

You should try to base the summary fields in your headers and footers on fields from the Detail sections of your reports instead of on expressions against the tables.

Graphs

When including graphs in a report, you must pay close attention to the data source and the location of the OLE server. You usually use a separate record source for each chart on a report. Make sure the record source is restricted to exactly what should be graphed. Do not use the query to add formatting or titles or to provide anything other than the raw data for the graph. Provide all legends, titles, and formatting by means of OLE Automation. Allowing the server to do what it does best—providing data from its tables—should keep your reports working smoothly.

Common Client-Server Migration Problems

It's likely you will encounter problems when moving existing file-server applications to a client-server environment. While much of this chapter has provided useful information for this process, this section offers additional troubleshooting assistance.

In your applications, look for the troublespots described in the following sections.

Non-Updatable Queries

One of the first problems you may run into is that queries (or views) that are updatable in Access will be read-only on your server. In these cases Jet processes the join operation locally and manages the fetches and updates to the server's tables on the client side. This is not as efficient as handling the updates solely on the server, and it may also introduce increased contention problems, depending on how Access and your server define the transactions for these updates. You may want to consider redesigning your system to avoid doing updates on joined data. Typically, as long as your network is well designed, the server will be fast enough to allow the split in updating that Jet produces. The major problem comes with the increased network load that sometimes occurs with this type of system.

Converting Validation Rules

Validation rules are another area that requires special consideration during migration. Access-defined validation rules cannot be used by any current server. If your server supports triggers and stored procedures, you should be able to convert most Access rules to server-based triggers. If you do this, you will need to add in your own error handling to replace the validation text and error trapping you had in your native Access application. You will need to test your specific server to determine the error processing related to stored procedures and triggers. Take extra care when converting table-level validation rules and validation rules that use Access functions. Most servers will not have the same set of predefined functions as Access, so you may need to have stored procedures written to replace them. In some cases you may need to do the validation locally in Access Basic before the data is sent to the server.

User-Defined Functions

Special attention is also required for any queries that use user-defined functions or built-in Access functions. Since the server will not support them, Jet returns them to your application to perform locally. This may not be too bad if the functions are only on the final output since they will be applied only as the data is sent from the server to the client. You will experience severe performance problems, however, if they are part of query criteria, order by, group by, or aggregate expressions. If you have any of these cases, look at converting the functions to stored procedures on the server. You could also split your query to allow all the server processing that doesn't involve the Access function to occur in one server query, returning a record-set that is then processed locally.

Counter, OLE, and Memo Fields

The presence of counter fields in your database requires the use of a stored procedure on many servers to provide a similar function. Most servers now support equivalents of OLE and memo fields, but if you use either of these, make sure you understand exactly *how* the server supports them.

Combo and List Boxes

Combo and list boxes that reference large numbers of server rows will be a problem. You get much better performance if you either cache the data locally or use appropriate criteria to restrict the list to a small number of entries.

Summary

In this chapter we have covered the basics of implementing a client-server system using Access. We introduced the major areas to consider when planning a client-server system or planning a migration to client-server. More specifically, we covered these issues:

- Selecting a server to match your processing needs
- Understanding the mechanics of ODBC processing

- Configuring Access for ODBC
- Mapping your transactions in client-server systems
- Taking advantage of Access' strengths in creating client-server applications
- Choosing the best form and control design for efficient processing
- Building efficient reports
- Identifying problem areas when migrating an application to client-server

By following the guidelines laid out in this chapter, it's possible to use Access as an effective client-server front end. Properly done, this approach can extend the capacity of an interactive Access application well into the tens or even low hundreds of active users. By taking advantage of the native processing power of Access, you can retain many of the benefits of an Access application while gaining the reliability, protection, and interactive transaction performance of a client-server system.

Resources

This chapter has merely scratched the surface on the issues involved in client-server development. Several other excellent sources of information may help further in this process. The version 2.0 Access Developer's Toolkit comes with the *Advanced Topics* manual, which includes chapters on ODBC and client-server applications. There are also many Microsoft knowledge-base articles available from Microsoft on specific issues, problems, and work-arounds for both ODBC and client-server. Microsoft's *Jet Database Engine ODBC Connectivity* white paper also contains excellent information on using Access in a client-server environment.(You can access knowledge-base articles and the white paper on CompuServe, the MSDN, and TechNet CD's and through Microsoft's download services.) Your ODBC driver vendor and your database server vendor should be able to supply help in configuring the server and getting the ODBC links running properly.

PART · V

Building Applications

CHAPTER

THIRTEEN

Providing an Elegant Interface

- Designing consistent, user-aware applications

- Using the Windows interface to your advantage

- Saving and restoring application color values

- Creating a simple/advanced two-state dialog box

When you have your application running perfectly on the computer on your desk, you're still a long way from being finished. Most programmers put together the functionality first and worry about the interface last, if at all. If you just create a switchboard form and throw on a few buttons to launch other forms and reports, you're not doing your users much of a service. You need to take time up front to think about user interface design. Your goal should be to come up with a design that is useful and elegant and that empowers users to get the most out of your application. This chapter focuses on some principles of user-interface design that may help your applications meet these goals.

Designing for the User, Not for the Programmer

There's a difference between "useful and elegant" and "clever and unique." You may have revolutionary ideas for reworking the way Windows applications are presented to the user. In the real world of useful applications, though, cleverness is far less important than ease of use. The flashiest interface in the world is worthless if it forces users to learn new techniques for skills they already have. Use the Windows interface and the Windows way of doing things, even if you think you might have a better way. This means, for example, that accelerator keys should be indicated by underlining, that important actions shouldn't be hidden behind double-clicking fields, and that lists should be presented in a scrolling vertical column.

While Windows may evolve as future products in the family are delivered by Microsoft, there are already 40 million desktops running the standard Windows interface. The more your products conform to this interface, the better off you'll be. There's time enough to write to revolutionary new interfaces as they appear on the market.

Learning from the Pros

When designing your own applications, take hints from the folks who write the tools you use to create applications. Although they bend the rules for their own use, all the Microsoft Office products (Access, Word, Excel, and Powerpoint) contain excellent examples of how to design an interface. For an example of how you can capitalize on the standard Windows metaphors, take a look at the opening moments of any of the Office applications. You'll see that they provide instant feedback for the user by putting up a "splash screen," hiding the fact that there's a lot of activity going on behind the scenes as they initialize data structures and load their graphical elements. You can do the same in your products by providing a nicely centered splash screen in Access and user feedback as your application initializes. You can either specify a bitmap file as your splash screen and have it automatically displayed at run time or add a bitmap to a form and have that form be the first one opened. It can even close itself with the aid of a simple DoCmd Close action in an On Timer event procedure.

Using Your AutoExec Macro Wisely

The first chance you get to interact with your users is in your AutoExec macro, which runs whenever your database is opened. To avoid potential error-trapping problems, keep your Autoexec macro as simple as possible. In fact, one line will do, with the express purpose of throwing further execution to Access Basic. Figure 13.1 shows a sample Autoexec macro that does nothing more than transfer its execution to an Access Basic function.

FIGURE 13.1:
Use the AutoExec macro to run an extended AutoExec() function.

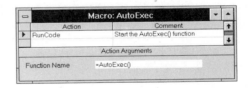

The AutoExec() function can then proceed with the task of initializing your user environment, as well as your data structures. Listing 13.1 shows an AutoExec() that starts by giving the user some immediate feedback and then proceeds to load forms and initialize variables "behind the scenes." By preloading forms in this fashion with the A_HIDDEN attribute, you can trade off a slightly longer initialization period for snappier operation later in the application. Users generally notice one lengthy delay less than a series of small but annoying ones.

Listing 13.1

```
Function AutoExec()

    ' Runs at database initialization only. Called directly
    ' from the AutoExec macro in order to transfer processing
    ' immediately into Access Basic.

' Make up some menu constants...
Const A_WINDOWMENU = 4
Const A_HIDE = 3

    On Error GoTo AutoExec_Err

    Dim dbCurrent As Database
    Dim rstPreload As Recordset
    Dim intPreload As Integer
    Dim varRet As Variant

    DoCmd Hourglass True

    ' If not running under the Access runtime,
    ' hide the database window and provide a splash form.
    ' If you're using the runtime, specify a bitmap
    ' to be used as a splash screen in the INI file.
    If Not SysCmd(SYSCMD_RUNTIME) Then
        DoCmd SelectObject A_MACRO, "AutoExec", True
        DoCmd DoMenuItem A_FORMBAR, A_WINDOWMENU, A_HIDE
        DoCmd OpenForm "frmSplash"
        DoEvents
    End If

    ' Remove the toolbar to keep users out of mischief
    Application.SetOption "Built-In Toolbars Available", False

    ' Now get the list of forms to preload
    Set dbCurrent = DBEngine.Workspaces(0).Databases(0)
    Set rstPreload = dbCurrent.OpenRecordset("qryPreload",
    ➡ DB_OPEN_SNAPSHOT)
```

```
        ' Initialize the status bar
        rstPreload.MoveLast
        intPreload = rstPreload.RecordCount
        varRet = SysCmd(SYSCMD_INITMETER, "Initializing...",
    ➡ intPreload)
        intPreload = 1

        ' Open all the forms in the list.
        ' This example assumes a field named FormName which
        ' contains the names of the forms to load.
        rstPreload.MoveFirst
        Do Until rstPreload.EOF
            DoCmd OpenForm rstPreload![FormName], , , , , A_HIDDEN
            varRet = SysCmd(SYSCMD_UPDATEMETER, intPreload)
            intPreload = intPreload + 1
            rstPreload.MoveNext
        Loop

        ' Open the switchboard as a visible form
        DoCmd OpenForm "frmSwitchboard"

        ' And apply the user's saved colors.  See the examples
        ' later in the chapter for more info on glrApplyColors.
        Call glrApplyColors

AutoExec_Exit:
        ' Clean up and exit
        rstPreload.Close
        varRet = SysCmd(SYSCMD_REMOVEMETER)
        DoCmd Hourglass False
        Exit Function

AutoExec_Err:
        MsgBox "Error " & Err & ": " & Error$, 0, "AutoExec"
        Resume AutoExec_Exit

End Function
```

You'll store the list of forms to be opened in tblPreload, but you can use qryPreload to reorder this table to include an explicit load order. This allows for dependencies between forms; for example, if you design one form to retrieve information from an .INI file, it is critical that you load it before any of the forms that depend on it.

Placing Your User in Control

One of the biggest gains in the shift to using a graphical user interface (GUI) is the change from straightforward code-driven programming to event-driven programming. Rather than acting on data and requiring users to follow the lead of the program, your Access application must react to mouse clicks and keyboard events and follow the lead of the user. As part of this paradigm, the control of the interaction must shift to the user. If users don't feel in control, they'll look for another application to use instead of yours.

Providing Multiple Access Methods

As part of the notion of user control, it's important to provide multiple ways to get to any particular activity. For example, if you have a form for entering new complications in a medical procedure, it's not enough to provide a command button on your switchboard to open the form. Different users think in different ways. Some like to choose items from menus, while others look only for buttons. Your program must accommodate all the various standard ways to perform actions in Windows.

Also be sure that the different interfaces are consistent. If you have a command button for an action, you should also have an accelerator key for that command button, a menu item that performs the same action, a toolbar button that also performs the action (if you've implemented custom toolbars), a status bar that indicates which operation will be performed in response to any of these actions, and a Help file topic offering further information. Yes, it's a lot of work, but work spent here in bulletproofing the user interface is just as important as work spent bulletproofing your code.

Using Standard Menu Items

Experienced users will expect to find certain standard menus and items in your application. Be sure to implement these standard items unless there is a very good reason not to. (For example, in an accounting application you might be tempted to leave out Print Preview at times when a report is required, although even then you should show the Print Preview menu item but disable it.) At an absolute minimum you should have a File ➤ Close or File ➤ Exit and a Help choice on every form's custom menus. Microsoft defines a set of 17 standard menu items that Windows applications should implement (see Table 13.1), although many of them do not apply well to Access forms. You need to decide which of these to implement in your Access applications. If you use any of the items in Table 13.1, though, you should take the effort to ensure that each appears in the specific recommended menu. For example, make sure you don't place the Copy menu item in the File menu. Users will find this confusing since the standard dictates that the Cut, Copy, and Paste menu items all appear in the Edit menu.

TABLE 13.1: Standard Windows Menu Items and Their Use

Menu	Item	Function
File	New	Creates a new document with a default name
	Open	Opens an existing document via the common file dialog
	Save	Saves the active document
	Save As	Saves the active document, assigning a new name via the common file dialog
	Print	Prints the active dialog
	Print Setup	Sets up the printer via the common dialog
	Exit	Terminates the application
Edit	Undo	Reverses the last editing action
	Cut	Transfers selected data to the clipboard and removes it from the current field
	Copy	Transfers selected data to the clipboard
	Paste	Transfers data from the clipboard, replacing the current selection (if any)
	Paste Link	Creates a link to the data on the clipboard
	Links	Displays the standard Links dialog
Help	Contents	Opens the Help window at the main topic list
	Search for Help On...	Opens the Help window and displays the standard search dialog
	How to Use Help	Opens the Help window and displays instructions for its use
	About...	Displays a standard dialog box of information about the application

Using Carefully Planned Shortcut Keys

You should also follow Windows standards when assigning shortcut keys. In general:

- Use single keys for frequently performed tasks. (For example, F6 in Access switches panes in a view.) Access uses most function key assignments itself, and you should avoid reassigning these keys in case you end up dealing with a sophisticated user who already knows the Access interface. F10 is available, and F11 and F12 are not likely to be noticed by end users and may normally be safely reassigned.

- Use Shift+key combinations for actions that extend or are complementary to their unshifted counterparts. For example, in Access, F7 opens the Find dialog box and Shift+F7 opens the Replace dialog box.

- Use Ctrl+key combinations for larger-scale analogs of their unshifted counterparts. For example, with F6 used to cycle through the parts of an individual window, Ctrl+F6 can cycle among different windows in the same application. Shift+Ctrl+F6 might cycle through windows but in reverse order.

- Use Alt+key combinations as mnemonic accelerator keys (for example, Alt+F,S for File ➤ Save) or reserve them for system use (for example, Alt+Tab, which Windows uses to cycle through all the active applications).

Planning for All Your Users

Microsoft provides suggested guidelines to make your application friendly to disabled users. These are the major points to consider:

- Don't rely on sound alone for any situation that requires attracting the user's attention.

- Don't rely on color to convey information. (A significant proportion of the male population is color-blind.)

- Don't require rapid response to a prompt. Wait for confirmation even on default choices.

- Don't use rapidly flashing design elements, which can cause seizures in some users.

Note that there are also hardware-based reasons that make some of these important design considerations for all users. For example, if you rely on color to convey information, your application won't work well on a monochrome monitor.

Allowing for Nonlinear Use

Don't expect or try to force linear movement through your application. You have to remember that this is *Windows,* and your users are for the most part going to be armed with mice. Even if your application itself has a straightforward linear flow, users will step outside it to other running applications—to cut and paste data (incidentally destroying anything you might have stored on the clipboard), click everywhere, and in general make a nuisance of themselves.

Very few applications have a linear flow (although many programmers seem happiest thinking in linear terms). Almost any application has multiple actions that could be performed all at once—editing a lookup table to bring a new choice into a combo box, putting up a report in print preview mode and then hopping back to data entry without closing it, and so on. Make sure users can jump around and have multiple parts of your application open at once. This is more consistent with the way the real world works, in all its wonderful confusion; more important, it's consistent with the way the rest of the Windows world works.

Supporting Multiple Data Interaction Modes

You may find that you need two different data entry forms for each table of your application to accommodate the two typical ways that users work with data. In general, you'll find that there is both a data entry mode and a data browsing mode and that working with both on the same form is difficult unless you're prepared to manipulate the visible properties of many controls.

Data entry mode allows users to fill tables with little hand-holding. The goal is simply to get the new data in quickly. You must allow for verification and easy changes, but in data entry mode you don't have to deal with searching and sorting the data. Forms designed for data entry mode typically rely heavily on input masking, tab order, defaults, and status bar messages to move the experienced user through quickly. Whenever possible, data entry mode forms should do immediate data validation on a field rather than on a record basis and offer auditory feedback for users who may be working in a "heads-down" fashion.

Data browsing mode is often used by less sophisticated users who need to look things up and work with them but don't do any heavy data entry. Data browsing forms tend to feature combo boxes for selecting records quickly from a list already prepared by the application. On-screen help may need to be more detailed. If the primary use of your data browsing forms is for extracting information from your application, the data needs to be protected from casual changes. Often, such browsing forms will be opened in a read-only mode or with most of their controls locked and disabled, perhaps with an Edit button to enable editing for those users who are allowed to do so.

Your design decisions are even more complicated than this because there are different classes of data entry persons and data browsers. For example, data entry runs the gamut of users, from the legendary heads-down data entry person to the person taking orders over the phone, with every level in between. The person taking orders over the phone will probably appreciate the days you spent getting the look and feel of that form just right. Give that same form to heads-down data entry operators and they will immediately complain that your pretty form is getting in the way of the job. Similarly, you would probably design a form to be used occasionally by executives to look up data differently than one used daily by an analyst. The key point is to get to know who your users are and how they will be using the program. By using Access' security system, you can easily detect the class of user and change the user interface accordingly.

Using the Correct Controls

From a data entry standpoint there's not much difference between a text box, a combo box, and an option group; for your users, though, they have very different implications. A text box suggests free-form data entry, while a combo box or an option group suggests choosing from a list. While it is possible to allow free entry through a combo box, your users may not realize this option is present if they're conditioned to the way such controls are used in other Windows programs.

Choosing the correct control contributes to the perceived "directness" of your application. As computers and GUIs evolve, it becomes easier and easier to work with an object/action paradigm, in which you select an object and then carry out some action on it. This is most obvious with command buttons and selection controls: you select an object from a list and then choose a command button (or menu item) to perform some action on it. Buttons and menu items are most commonly used for actions, so you should use them this way as well. Don't, for example, assign an important action to the double-click event of a text box unless you quite clearly tell your users that you've done so. Even then, you should rethink your event model to avoid such "hidden" actions (or provide the double-click event as a shortcut to using a command button).

Being Consistent

Your application's controls should be visually consistent. You need to consider three main areas of consistency:

- Internal consistency
- Suite consistency
- Environmental consistency

Internal consistency refers to consistency within your application. If you use shadowed text boxes for data entry on one form, you should use shadowed text boxes for data entry on all the others, or at least all others of the same class. (Perhaps entry and review forms might subscribe to different control conventions as visual cues for their different uses.)

Suite consistency refers to consistency among all applications you deliver, at least to a particular client. If you produce an Accounts Payable database and a Payroll database, by using the same control conventions in both you make it easier for users to move from one to the other. Your applications also begin to develop a personal look and feel that your clients will identify with you, which can help in marketing.

Environmental consistency refers to consistency with the rest of Windows. Of course, not all Windows applications follow the exact same path, but there are certain broad conventions you should respect. For example, people expect to be able to click controls that look like command buttons and have something happen. Although it's possible to make a text box look like a command button in Access by setting its properties so that it appears raised, with a gray background and black text, it's just not a good idea. Since it will look like a button, users will expect it to *act* like a button. Changing the user's expectation will violate consistency with the rest of your Windows applications.

In general, in the Windows interface, raised items suggest action and moving of the focus, sunken controls are used for data entry, and flat-surface controls are good for relaying information. If you're going to deviate from this model, do so with a good reason and do it consistently throughout your application.

Toggle buttons, radio buttons, and check boxes can all be used to choose from a small number of alternatives, but they say very different things to the user. Toggle buttons normally indicate a mutually exclusive selection. Radio buttons are also mutually exclusive, but they are not as good as an immediate visible clue—although they have the advantage of being a much more familiar Windows control for most people. You should reserve check boxes for alternatives that are *not* mutually exclusive (and therefore should be used only outside an option group since Access restricts the items in an option group to be mutually exclusive) because this is the way they work in other Windows applications. You can place check boxes in a rectangle control to emulate an option group in appearance, but make sure it's clear that users can select more than one option. If your users become accustomed to the idea that option groups can allow only a single value, they may not understand that this "fake" option group allows multiple selections.

Using Colors, Fonts, and Pictures Thoughtfully

Access makes it easy to change the look of your application. With one click you can turn the background of your form from green to purple. With another few mouse-clicks you can change a font from 10-point MS Sans Serif to 42-point Palm Springs italic. Click here, click there, and fields change from raised to sunken or grow thick orange borders. This flexibility is one of the greatest strengths and, at the same time, one of the greatest weaknesses of Access. It's far too easy to design garish, jarring, and generally unusable forms. Figure 13.2 shows such a form, pulled from an actual, working Access application.

FIGURE 13.2:

An Access form gone bad

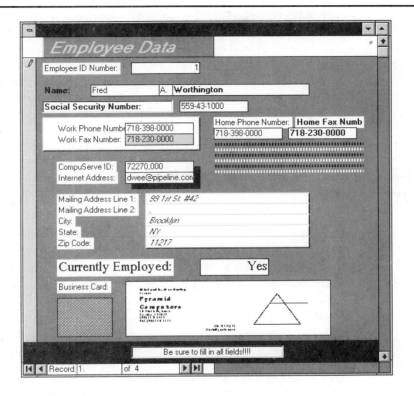

Just as you shouldn't immediately take a new car out on the freeway and floor the accelerator, you should restrain your Access customization. Remember the importance of clarity and consistency, and strive for a simple elegance. Your users and your reputation will thank you.

You should also restrain any tendency to clutter your form with little pictures and icons. If you must use icons to indicate actions, try to be clear, which means being standard yet again. The world doesn't need yet another set of icons for cut/copy/paste; choose the standard set you like best and propagate it throughout your application. Use the standard set of bitmaps that Access provides in order to promote consistency. This isn't to say there's no room for individuality and creativity in form design, but if there's an existing image in the product, you might do well to use it.

Remember that fonts don't ship with your application. Unless you have control of the target system, you have no choice but to stick with the standard fonts. MS Serif, MS Sans Serif, and System are safe. Arial, Courier New, and Times New Roman are reasonably safe—you're unlikely to be running Access on a system without Windows 3.1 anyway. Beyond that, you'll have to make arrangements for distribution with the font vendor, require your users to purchase the same fonts you have, or design your own font with one of the font-creation packages on the market.

Dealing with Different System Hardware

In some cases you may be able to completely ignore hardware issues. If you are installing a custom application to a small base of computers and you have access to all of them, you can survey the hardware installed and act accordingly. However, if you gain any significant market penetration, you need either to specify precisely the requirements for your package or to deal with differing hardware on differing systems. You need to consider, in particular, the screens, mice, and printers you are likely to run into.

Screen Design Issues

Screen issues revolve around size and color depth. As we discussed in Chapter 8, you can retrieve the screen dimensions via the Windows API and resize your forms dynamically, depending on the ratio between your current screen size and design screen size. This technique allows you to fill your customers' screens properly despite hardware differences between their systems and your own.

To add to the video confusion, users employ different Windows video drivers. If you prosper in your work you may well be running the latest 16-million-color driver on your system. Before you release your forms with the colors lovingly tweaked for your system, investigate their look in 256-, 16-, and 2-color mode, for customers who may be a bit more hardware impaired than you. Use the DOS-mode Windows setup to temporarily install the standard VGA and LCD screen drivers and see how your masterpiece looks with them. You may discover a sudden need to redesign if green on blue turns into amber on amber.

Also be aware of the position of your forms when you distribute your applications. If you use the AutoCenter property of the form and if it fits on your users' screens, you'll do fine. If you don't have Access position the form for you and you've done your development work on a different resolution driver than your users use to run the application, you may have a problem with forms appearing off the edge of your users' screens. Either use AutoCenter or make sure the forms appear in the upper left-hand corner of your screen when you save them.

Life without a Mouse

Hard though you may find it to believe, not everyone has (or wants to use) a mouse. Be sure your application is friendly to keyboard users as well as mouse users:

- Use accelerator keys liberally.
- Make sure your menus have all the options your forms do.
- Check your tab order after every form redesign.

Don't assume that built-in properties in Access will take care of you; Access itself is guilty of not allowing all actions to be performed without a mouse. (Try editing relationships without a mouse, for example.) Also, remember your left-handed users, and in your Help file consider referring to your mouse's Primary and Secondary buttons, or Button 1 and Button 2, rather than the left and right mouse buttons.

Different Printers for Different Clients

The final critical piece of hardware you need to deal with is your user's printer. Chapter 9 discusses the techniques involved in switching printers at run time and allowing users to choose a printer for each report as they print it. To maintain flexibility and compatibility with other Windows products, you should implement these techniques in your own applications.

Planning for Ease of Use

If there's one thing to keep in mind for successful user interface design, it's ease of use. The easier you make the application to use, the more users will enjoy it, and the more likely they are to order more work from you. A number of things add up to ease of use; although individually they are small things, implementing most or all of them can add up to a substantially better impression.

Using Sensible Default Values

Be sure to use sensible defaults in your application. This applies not only to default data (for example, supplying the state name that's the most likely when making a choice in the customer list) but to default actions. You should make it very easy to do the things the user most often wants to do. That is, if a user is entering a new record, make saving the new row be the default action by setting the Default property of your Save command button to True. Users can always remove the record or undo the change later. By making Save the default, you guarantee that most of the time users can accomplish the work they need with a single keystroke. Of course, you should still make it possible, but not the default, to perform other actions that are not the most likely.

Allowing Users to Set Their Environment

No matter how carefully you consider color, size, and other design elements of your forms, some users will decide they want something different. Even though you like the soothing colors of the Ocean color scheme, there will be some users who prefer Hot Dog Stand. Your default environment settings should work on any machine, but if you have time, implement ways for users to change these. Not only will such customization make your application look more professional, but the ability to implement changes will help your users feel more in control.

Using the Color Chooser to Set Colors

The Color Chooser form (frmColorChooser), in the sample database CH13.MDB, demonstrates one method you can use to put your application's colors under user control. Color choices are stored in an .INI file and are thus persistent from session to session. The user's choices apply globally to all open forms in your application, but you can mark specific elements to protect them from user changes. Figure 13.3 shows the Color Chooser form in action.

FIGURE 13.3:
Use frmColorChooser in your applications to allow users to select their own colors.

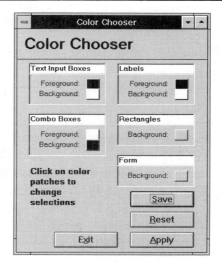

Storing Global Values

The Color Chooser application uses a second form, frmScratchpad, to hold the actual numeric values of the colors it changes. This secondary form, which you would ordinarily open as a hidden form, provides a handy place for globally accessible values. In a full-scale application you could use it to store many things besides color values. (You could also use global variables to store this information, but by placing it on a form you can access the values from anyplace in Access: queries, macros, or Access Basic.) The logic for frmScratchpad is entirely within event procedures. In the Open event it calls the Windows API GetPrivateProfileString() function repeatedly to get the most recently saved color scheme; in the Unload event it

saves the current scheme to the same file with calls to WritePrivateProfileString().
If you were to use this form within your own application, you'd want to expand the
Form_Open procedure to handle whatever information you needed to load from
your .INI file. It assumes an .INI file with the same name as the database file itself,
stored in the same directory as the database. Figure 13.4 shows the scratchpad form
as it would appear if it were opened as a normal (unhidden) form.

FIGURE 13.4:

frmScratchPad stores globally
accessible values.

The Color Chooser works by first initializing its own storage and display of colors
to the values loaded from the .INI file onto the frmScratchpad form. The form initializes its colors in the Open event, so that by the time the form is visible it is already displaying the correct colors. The color patches do double duty, as a display
and an input device for colors and as a storage medium. The code in Listing 13.2
shows the actions taken by the form as it loads. It first makes sure the scratchpad
form has already been opened. Once it knows that the scratchpad is open, it can call
the CopyColors subroutine to copy the colors from the scratchpad (which come directly from the .INI file) into its own controls. Listing 13.3 shows the CopyColors
subroutine.

Listing 13.2

```
Sub Form_Open(Cancel As Integer)

    Dim frmScratch As Form

Const SCRATCHPAD = "frmScratchPad"

    On Error Resume Next
    Set frmScratch = Forms(SCRATCHPAD)
    If Err <> 0 Then
```

```
        Err = 0
        DoCmd OpenForm SCRATCHPAD
        Set frmScratch = Forms(SCRATCHPAD)
        If Err <> 0 Then
            MsgBox "Unable to open scratchpad form!"
            Cancel = True
        End If
    End If

    If Err = 0 Then
        CopyColors Me, frmScratch
    End If
End Sub
```

Listing 13.3

```
Sub CopyColors(frm As Form, frmScratch As Form)

    frm![shpTextForeground].BackColor =
    ➡ frmScratch![txtTextForeground]
    frm![shpTextBackground].BackColor =
    ➡ frmScratch![txtTextBackground]
    frm![shpLabelForeground].BackColor =
    ➡ frmScratch![txtLabelForeground]
    frm![shpLabelBackground].BackColor =
    ➡ frmScratch![txtLabelBackground]
    frm![shpComboForeground].BackColor =
    ➡ frmScratch![txtComboForeground]
    frm![shpComboBackground].BackColor =
    ➡ frmScratch![txtComboBackground]
    frm![shpShapeBackground].BackColor =
    ➡ frmScratch![txtShapeBackground]
    frm![shpFormBackground].BackColor =
    ➡ frmScratch![txtFormBackground]
    ' Walk through all the controls on all the forms, and apply
    ' the selected colors.
    Call glrApplyColors
End Sub
```

Selecting New Colors

Each of the color patches on the Color Chooser form reacts to the Click event. When the user clicks one of these, Access calls the code in the form's module to invoke the PickNewColor subroutine, passing to it a reference to the current control and the name of the control on the scratchpad form to update. Listing 13.4 shows the code to choose one color and the common PickColor procedure, which all the color patches call to select a color.

Listing 13.4

```
Sub shpTextForeground_Click()
    Call PickColor(Me!shpTextForeground, "txtTextForeground")
End Sub

Sub PickColor (ctl As Control, strScratchControl As String)

    Dim lngNewColor As Long

    lngNewColor = PickNewColor(CLng(ctl.BackColor))
    If lngNewColor <> -1 Then
        Forms![frmScratchPad](strScratchControl) = lngNewColor
        ctl.BackColor = lngNewColor
    End If
End Sub
```

PickColor ends up calling the PickNewColor procedure, which you'll find in the basUtilities module. It works by calling the common Windows dialog function to choose a color. Although you can't call this dialog directly from Access Basic, the Access development team has thoughtfully provided interfaces to many Windows functions that aren't normally available in Access. The functions themselves exist in MSAU200.DLL and are normally called through wrapper functions in WZBUILDER or WZLIB.MDA. (Chapter 21 covers this otherwise undocumented DLL.) If you purchase the Access Developer's Toolkit you'll get commented copies of these libraries. The copies that ship with the retail version of Access 2.0 have had their comments removed, and you'll find studying the commented versions to be much simpler than trying to wade through mountains of uncommented code. One issue still remains: when you ship an application with the run-time module, you do not have a license to ship the Access libraries with your application, making it impossible to call the wrapper functions from an application that will be distributed this way. To avoid this issue, we've copied and renamed the necessary declarations and datatypes so you can use the code in the Color Chooser without having to have any of the Wizards loaded. By using the standard Windows interface, you not only avoid all the work of implementing your own interface, you avoid the confusion of having multiple methods of choosing colors, one in your Access application and another in other Windows applications. Listing 13.5 shows the PickNewColor procedure.

Listing 13.5

```
' Structure passed to WLIB_GetColor
Type glr_msauUIGetColorInfo
    hWndOwner As Integer
    rgbResult As Long
    Flags As Long
    rgCustColors(16) As Long
End Type

Declare Function glr_msauUIGetColor Lib "MSAU200.DLL" Alias
➥ "#3"(gci As glr_msauUIGetColorInfo) As Long
Global Const glrCC_RGBINIT = &H1
Global Const glrCC_FULLOPEN = &H2
Global Const glrCC_PREVENTFULLOPEN = &H4
Global Const glrCC_SHOWHELP = &H8

Function PickNewColor(lngCurrentColor As Long) As Long

    Static gci As glr_msauUIGetColorInfo
    Dim lngRetval As Long

    gci.rgbResult = lngCurrentColor
    gci.hWndOwner = glr_apiUIGetActiveWindow()
    gci.Flags = glrCC_RGBINIT
    lngRetval = glr_msauUIGetColor(gci)
    glrPickNewColor = IIf(lngRetval = 0, gci.rgbResult, -1)
End Function
```

Applying the New Colors

The Apply button takes the chosen colors and applies them to all open forms (which, if you're following the strategy of preloading forms, will be all of them). This routine could be extended to open and modify closed forms as well. The function takes advantage of the new Tag property of controls in Access 2.0 to flag controls whose colors should not be altered; it skips over any control whose Tag property includes "Protect=-1;". You need to manually set that value in the Tag property when you create your forms. Using the standard functions to retrieve part of a tag setting (glrGetTag() and glrPutTag(), introduced in Chapter 7), you can just add the setting to any other values you already have stored in your Tag property for any control. Listing 13.6 shows the code that applies the colors to each control and form.

Listing 13.6

```
Sub glrApplyColors()

    ' Read the user color choices from frmColorChooser and apply
    ' them throughout the application

Const MAX_SECTIONS = 5
Const ERR_INVALID_SECTION = 2462

    Dim frmChange As Form
    Dim frmColors As Form
    Dim varTag As Variant
    Dim intFormCount As Integer

    Dim ctlChange As Control
    Dim intForm As Integer
    Dim intItem As Integer
    Dim lngTextForeColor As Long
    Dim lngTextBackColor As Long
    Dim lngLabelForeColor As Long
    Dim lngLabelBackColor As Long
    Dim lngComboForeColor As Long
    Dim lngComboBackColor As Long
    Dim lngShapeForeColor As Long
    Dim lngShapeBackColor As Long
    Dim lngFormBackColor As Long

    Dim lngNewForeColor As Long
    Dim lngNewBackColor As Long
    Dim varRetval As Variant

    On Error GoTo glrApplyColors_Err

    DoCmd Hourglass True

    Set frmColors = Forms!frmScratchPad
    ' Preload all the colors from the scratchpad, to
    ' avoid form references in the loop that follows.
    lngTextForeColor = frmColors![txtTextForeground]
    lngTextBackColor = frmColors![txtTextBackground]
```

```
        lngLabelForeColor = frmColors![txtLabelForeground]
        lngLabelBackColor = frmColors![txtLabelBackground]
        lngComboForeColor = frmColors![txtComboForeground]
        lngComboBackColor = frmColors![txtComboBackground]
        lngShapeBackColor = frmColors![txtShapeBackground]
        lngFormBackColor = frmColors![txtFormBackground]

        intFormCount = Forms.Count
        varRetval = SysCmd(SYSCMD_INITMETER, "Applying colors...",
        ➡ intFormCount)
        For intForm = 0 To intFormCount - 1
            varRetval = SysCmd(SYSCMD_UPDATEMETER, intForm + 1)
            Set frmChange = Forms(intForm)
            For intItem = 0 To MAX_SECTIONS - 1
                frmChange.Section(intItem).BackColor =
                ➡ lngFormBackColor
            Next intItem
            For intItem = 0 To frmChange.Count - 1
                Set ctlChange = frmChange(intItem)
                varTag = glrGetTag(ctlChange, "Protect")
                If IsNull(varTag) Or Not varTag Then
                    If TypeOf ctlChange Is textbox Then
                        lngNewForeColor = lngTextForeColor
                        lngNewBackColor = lngTextBackColor
                    ElseIf TypeOf ctlChange Is Label Then
                        lngNewForeColor = lngLabelForeColor
                        lngNewBackColor = lngLabelBackColor
                    ElseIf TypeOf ctlChange Is ComboBox Then
                        lngNewForeColor = lngComboForeColor
                        lngNewBackColor = lngComboBackColor
                    ElseIf TypeOf ctlChange Is ListBox Then
                        lngNewForeColor = lngComboForeColor
                        lngNewBackColor = lngComboBackColor
                    ElseIf TypeOf ctlChange Is Rectangle Then
                        lngNewBackColor = lngShapeBackColor
                    End If
                    SetColor ctlChange, lngNewForeColor,
                    ➡ lngNewBackColor
                End If
            Next intItem
        Next intForm

glrApplyColors_Exit:
    varRetval = SysCmd(SYSCMD_REMOVEMETER)
```

```
    DoCmd Hourglass False
    Exit Sub

glrApplyColors_Err:
    If Err = ERR_INVALID_SECTION Then
        Resume Next
    Else
        MsgBox "Error " & Err & ": " & Error$, 0,
        ➥ "glrApplyColors"
        Resume glrApplyColors_Exit
    End If
End Sub
```

Resetting and Saving the Stored Colors

The Reset button on the Color Chooser form reloads the values from the .INI file and resets all the colors appropriately. This button will be useful if you play with the colors to the point that they become unacceptable and you just want to start over. The Save button saves the current settings to the .INI file, so further attempts to reset the colors will retrieve the most recently saved set.

Generally, you'll use a scenario as presented in the section "Using Your Autoexec Macro Wisely" earlier in this chapter. In that section we suggest that you preload all your forms, if possible, and set their colors at that point by calling the glrApply-Colors procedure. The success of this action will depend on your having previously loaded the frmScratchPad form. Once that's done, though, the call to glrApplyColors should affect all the loaded forms, hidden or not. You can, of course, call glrApplyColors at any point while your application is running. And you can load frmColorChooser at any time to allow the user to reset colors.

Including the Color Chooser

To include the Color Chooser in your own applications, follow these steps:

1. Import both frmColorChooser and frmScratchPad into your application.

2. Import the three modules basGlobals, basUtilities, and basTags into your application.

3. Set the Tag property for any controls whose color you don't want to have reset by the Color Chooser to include "Protect=-1;".

Then, when you want to use the Color Chooser, just open the form. If the scratch-pad form isn't open, the Color Chooser form will open it as a hidden form, and the scratchpad form will be left open. When you choose the Apply button, the form will apply the chosen colors to all the objects on all the open forms.

Providing Ample Feedback

Your users deserve plenty of feedback in your application. Anytime your application is going to take over the screen for two seconds or more, you should turn on the hourglass cursor and, if necessary, provide other feedback. If the operation will take more than a few seconds, use the SysCmd() function to provide visual cues as to how much longer the user will have to wait. Although the glrApplyColors procedure doesn't actually take very long to do its work, we've included calls to SysCmd() to update the status bar as it handles each of the forms. You can also customize your feedback through custom error handling so that any error messages your users see are tailored to your own application (see Chapter 14).

Be sure to use the status bar property on your controls. It's a simple-to-implement solution to providing front-line help for users. Although this is an easy point to skip, it's worth the care it takes to set the StatusBarText property for each and every control. By implementing complete status bar messages, you move your applications one step closer to matching the polish shown in mainstream applications. In cases in which your users might not be interacting directly with forms and controls, you can write custom messages to the status bar with the SysCmd() function.

Being Forgiving

Build in forgiveness for risky actions. The single level of undo available in Access is sometimes not enough to ensure robustness in your applications. You should consider implementing multiple-level undo in your own code or saving backup copies of tables that are about to undergo massive changes.

Simple Is Better

When you get deeply familiar with Access, you have to constantly fight the temptation to show off. It's so simple to toggle visible properties, move data hither and thither, display totals, and even make things flash on and off that it's hard to resist the temptation. You should avoid overly complex forms because human beings are basically simple creatures. We can instantaneously grasp only about 7 things at once—maybe 5, maybe 9, but certainly not 20. If your interface requires the user to choose from 20 different command buttons, it's just not simple enough.

Divide and Conquer

Often, the problem is just insufficient depth of choices. By organizing your action choices into a logical "tree" with multiple levels, you can keep the number of choices at each level to a minimum. For example, Figure 13.5 shows a very "busy" form switchboard.

FIGURE 13.5:
Too many buttons on a single switchboard can lead to severe end-user overload.

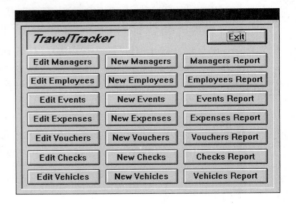

Notice that there are logical groupings here that the developer is not taking advantage of. The several "edit" buttons all go together, as do the "new" buttons and the "print" buttons. With a little work, you can turn this interface into a much simpler one that allows the user to first make a major choice and then a minor one. Figure 13.6 shows the simpler interface in action.

Another solution to this same problem is to use tabbed dialog boxes, like those found in current versions of Microsoft Word and Excel. Although Access doesn't support this specific look directly, you can emulate it in a number of different ways.

FIGURE 13.6:
Dividing tasks into different levels
can simplify the user interface.

Chapter 8 showed one technique, using buttons and hidden subforms. In Chapter 20 you'll find yet another solution. The Tabbed Dialog Wizard there can help you set up tabbed dialogs using line controls to build the tabs.

Avoiding Overly Complex Dialogs

You'll want to carefully examine dialog boxes for extraneous complexity. There is a constant tension between keeping things simple enough for beginning users and providing a rich set of choices for advanced users. One way to handle this is to use an unfolding dialog box, similar to Access' own Print Setup dialog. Figure 13.7 shows a sample dialog box in its initial state. Figure 13.8 shows it in its expanded state.

FIGURE 13.7:
Dialog box in its initial state

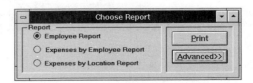

The technique makes use of Windows API functions to determine the characteristics of the form and then the Access MoveSize macro action to change its size. The entire form is actually present at all times, as you can see, in Figure 13.9. The code resizes the form as necessary, depending on its current state.

You'll find the form and the code to drive it in CH13.MDB. The basGlobals module contains the necessary Windows API function declarations. You use GetSystem-Metrics() to inquire about the size of system elements such as caption bars and the

FIGURE 13.8:

Dialog box in its expanded state

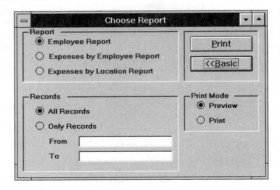

FIGURE 13.9:

Expanding dialog box in design mode

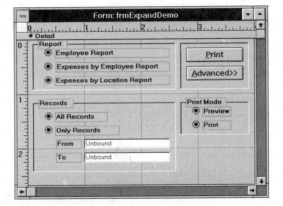

other three functions to give you access to information about device capabilities. You use them to retrieve information about the number of pixels per inch so you'll be able to specify sizes in inches rather than in pixels or twips.

In the Form_Open event procedure you call these API functions to perform the necessary calculations, storing the results in module global variables. This way the necessary values will be available when you need to resize the form later in the application. By knowing the size of the caption and borders, you can allow for them when you resize the form in response to a button click. Listing 13.7 shows the form's Open event procedure and the form module's Declarations section. This procedure gathers the size of the caption bar and the form borders, stores them away, and then sets the size of the form to the "basic" form size (the smaller of the two sizes).

Listing 13.7

```
' General Constants
Const TWIPS_PER_INCH = 1440

Dim sngCaptionHeight As Single
Dim sngBorderWidth As Single

' Keep track of current form state.
Dim intAdvanced As Integer

Const CMD_ADVANCED = "&Advanced>"
Const CMD_BASIC = "<&Basic"

' Sizes, in inches, of the form dimensions.
Const HEIGHT_BASIC = 1
Const HEIGHT_ADVANCED = 2.5
Const WIDTH_FORM = 4

Sub Form_Open (Cancel As Integer)

    Dim intPixelsX As Integer
    Dim intPixelsY As Integer
    Dim intIC As Integer

Const APINULL = O&

' GetDeviceCaps Constants
Const WU_LOGPIXELSX = 88
Const WU_LOGPIXELSY = 90

' GetSystemMetrics Constants
Const SM_CYCAPTION = 4
Const SM_CXFRAME = 32
Const SM_CYFRAME = 33

    ' Determine number of pixels per inch in each direction
    ' on this screen
    intIC = glr_apiUICreateIC("DISPLAY", APINULL, APINULL,
    ➥ APINULL)
```

```
intPixelsX = glr_apiUIGetDeviceCaps(intIC, WU_LOGPIXELSX)
intPixelsY = glr_apiUIGetDeviceCaps(intIC, WU_LOGPIXELSY)

' Store the caption height and border width in controls on
' the form. This makes for faster access, since we will be
' using them repeatedly as we work
sngCaptionHeight =
➡ ((glr_apiUIGetSystemMetrics(SM_CYCAPTION) +
➡ (2 * glr_apiUIGetSystemMetrics(SM_CYFRAME)))
➡  / intPixelsY) * TWIPS_PER_INCH
sngBorderWidth = ((2 *
➡ glr_apiUIGetSystemMetrics(SM_CXFRAME))
➡ / intPixelsX) * TWIPS_PER_INCH

' Resize the form to WIDTH_FORM inches by HEIGHT_BASIC
' inches, allowing for borders and caption.
DoCmd MoveSize , ,
➡ (TWIPS_PER_INCH * WIDTH_FORM) + sngBorderWidth,
➡ (TWIPS_PER_INCH * HEIGHT_BASIC) + sngCaptionHeight

' Clean up before exiting
intIC = glr_apiUIReleaseDC(0, intIC)
intAdvanced = False
End Sub
```

Expanding and Contracting the Form

Once you have the numbers describing the dimensions of the form and its borders in hand, it's trivial to resize the form in response to a button click. Listing 13.8 shows the code you use to switch the size, based on the current state of the form. This code checks the value stored in the intAdvanced module variable, and if it's True the code knows to switch into "basic" mode. If not, it switches into advanced mode. Switching modes involves a call to the MoveSize macro action, leaving the top and left coordinates blank. This way Access sizes the form but does not move it. In addition, the sample form shares a single button for switching modes. The code changes the caption on the button, depending on the current state.

Listing 13.8

```
Sub cmdSwitchMode_Click()
    Dim sngHeight As Single
    Dim sngWidth As Single
```

```
    Dim lngWidth As Long
    Dim lngHeight As Long

    ' Set the width and height variables, and set the
    ' button caption.
    If intAdvanced Then
        sngWidth = WIDTH_FORM
        sngHeight = HEIGHT_BASIC
        Me!cmdSwitchMode.Caption = CMD_ADVANCED
    Else
        sngWidth = WIDTH_FORM
        sngHeight = HEIGHT_ADVANCED
        Me!cmdSwitchMode.Caption = CMD_BASIC
    End If
    lngWidth = CLng(TWIPS_PER_INCH * sngWidth + sngBorderWidth)
    lngHeight = CLng(TWIPS_PER_INCH * sngHeight +
➡ sngCaptionHeight)
    DoCmd MoveSize , , lngWidth, lngHeight
    intAdvanced = Not intAdvanced
End Sub
```

Creating Expanding Forms

You should be able to emulate this type of form in your own applications. To do so, follow these steps:

1. Import the basGlobals module from CH13.MDB.

2. Create your own form, sizing the form to be the largest of the two sizes. Make a clear horizontal dividing line on the form. (We used rectangles for this purpose in the sample form.)

3. Use the rulers on the form to decide how large you'll want the form to be in both the basic and advanced modes.

4. Create the button on your form that will switch modes. It will be simpler if the button's Name property is set to cmdSwitchMode so it matches the code example.

5. Copy and paste the code from frmExpandDemo's module (the Declarations section, the Form_Open procedure, and the cmdSwitchMode_Click procedure).

6. In design mode, select the mode-switching command button, and on its property sheet, select the Click event. From the drop-down list, choose Event Procedure. This hooks up the event procedure stored in the form's module.

7. Change the constants in the form module's declarations area to match your specific situation.

Once you follow those steps you should be able to use your double-mode form within your application.

Summary

User interface design is far from being an exact science. All we can really do is offer general guidelines, but *you* need to think about your particular situation and users to decide the best method for designing a useful, workable user interface. You'll need to ask yourself a series of questions:

- Is your initial load process clean and fast? Does it provide the user with some feedback or something to look at while you load forms?

- Is the user in control of your program rather than the other way around?

- Are your menus, command buttons, accelerator keys, toolbar buttons, status bars, and Help files all working together? Can both mouse- and keyboard-oriented users use your application?

- Do you accommodate fast, heads-down data entry?

- Do you accommodate safe and easy data browsing?

- Do your controls make sense for what they're doing? Do they match the Windows defaults?

- Is your application internally consistent? Does it use a single metaphor throughout?

- Is your application suite consistent? Does it encourage users to think of your work as an integrated whole?

- Is your application environmentally consistent? Does it work the way Windows applications normally work?

- Are your forms restrained and elegant?
- Are your fonts available to your end users?
- Will your application work in different video resolutions? With and without a mouse? With different printers?
- Are your defaults sensible? Can users change the defaults to match their own preferences?
- Do you provide feedback for all lengthy processes?
- Do you allow users to retract or undo risky actions?
- Is your interface simple and easy to use?

Perhaps the best way to check for good design in your interface is to actually test-drive it. Sit down with your application for half a day. Enter and edit data. Print reports. Search for records. Put the whole thing through its paces with an eye toward a realistic working session. The aim here is not to check that all of your code works as it should; you should have already established that with test cases as you went along. What you want to know now is whether a human being can work with your design for any substantial period of time. If you get bored and frustrated, imagine how the end user will feel.

When you think you're done, you need to do one final thing in the user interface area: bring the users back in. Make time to sit with the end users for a few hours when you have your first release ready and see how they actually use the application. You might be surprised at how much they can tell you about making your interface better, if you have the patience and humility to listen to them.

CHAPTER

FOURTEEN

Handling Errors

- The syntax and construction of error handlers

- Using the OnError property of forms

- Implementing a Call Stack

- Creating a standard error handler

- Using Assertions

Three kinds of errors can occur in your Access Basic code:

- Compile-time errors
- Logic errors
- Run-time errors

Compile-time errors occur when you have incorrect syntax in your code. The compiler requires that these errors be fixed before the code will run. Depending on the state of the Syntax Checking Module Design option, Access flags the error either when you enter the improper syntax or when the code is compiled.

Logic errors occur when your code doesn't do what you intended because of improper logic, a misunderstanding of how certain statements and functions work, or outright mistakes. For example, if you use a less-than operator (<) when you mean to have a less-than or equal-to operator (<=), you have a logic error.

Run-time errors occur when some condition makes your code invalid. For example, code that opens a table works fine unless the table doesn't exist. Then Access generates a run-time error (because the table must exist to be opened) and displays an alert that contains the error message, stopping the code at that point. This can be disastrous for your applications.

Fortunately, run-time errors can be handled in Access Basic. Access provides a mechanism using the On Error statement that allows you to trap a run-time error and handle the problem. One of the main reasons for using Access Basic instead of macros is that Access Basic can trap run-time errors. When a macro receives a run-time error, it stops with an alert. In Access Basic, you can write an error handler to prevent alerts from reaching the user and produce more robust code.

Error handlers offer a way to recover gracefully from most problems your application meets. The effective use of error handlers is the mark of a professional application that handles all the oddball cases that arise rather than putting up nasty alerts and halting unexpectedly.

The On Error Statement

You invoke an error handler with the On Error statement, which comes in several varieties, as described in the following sections. Each procedure can have as many On Error statements as you like. However, only the most recently executed On Error statement remains in force.

The On Error GoTo Label Statement

The first variety of error handler is the On Error GoTo *Label* statement. When an error occurs after an On Error GoTo *Label* statement, control passes to the assigned label. Listing 14.1 shows the most common format for an error handler.

Listing 14.1

```
Sub glrGenericSubWithHandler()
    ' Stub showing standard way to construct an error handler

    On Error GoTo glrGenericSubWithHandlerError

    ' Some code that might generate a run-time error

Exit Sub
glrGenericSubWithHandlerError:
    ' Error Handler
Exit Sub
End Sub
```

When an error occurs, control immediately passes to the label specified in the On Error GoTo *Label* statement. The label must appear in the same procedure as the On Error GoTo *Label* statement. By convention, the error handler appears at the end of the procedure.

Access requires that label names be unique across the entire module. Labels in Code-Behind-Forms (CBF) must be unique for the entire form. If you add the function name to the text for the label, you are guaranteed a unique label.

Use an Exit Sub or Exit Function statement to keep the normal flow of control from passing into the error handler. In addition, you must exit your error handler with an explicit Resume (described in the section "Using Resume Statements" later in this chapter) or Exit Sub/Function. You cannot just "fall out" of an error handler at the end of the function.

The On Error Resume Next Statement

Creating an error handler with the On Error GoTo *Label* statement can require quite a few lines of code. Sometimes you want to ignore errors. Other times you know exactly which error to expect and want to handle it without having to write a full error handler. The On Error Resume Next statement informs Access that you want control to resume at the statement immediately after the statement that generated the error, without any visible intervention from Access. For example, if you are at-tempting to open a database and don't care if the database actually exists, you might have some code like that shown in Listing 14.2.

Listing 14.2

```
Global db As Database
Sub glrOpenDB (ByVal strFileName As String)
    ' Example showing an On Error Resume Next
    '   Sets global variable db to be the database
    '   if it succeeds.

    On Error Resume Next

    Set db = DbEngine.Workspaces(0).OpenDatabase(strFileName)
End Sub
```

In this example, if the database doesn't exist or if there is some other error opening the database, control passes to the next statement (in this case, the End Sub statement).

A slightly more complex example is shown in Listing 14.3.

Listing 14.3

```
Sub glrSetControlColors (frm As Form, ByVal lngColor As Long)
    ' Changes the color of all the controls on the
    ' form to the color specified by lngColor

    Dim i As Integer
```

```
On Error Resume Next

For i = 0 To frm.count - 1
    frm(i).BackColor = lngColor
Next i
End Sub
```

This procedure loops through all the controls on a form specified by a form variable and changes the BackColor property of the controls to the value specified by the lngColor argument. Some controls, such as command buttons, do not have a Back-Color property. When these controls are reached, a run-time error normally is generated. The On Error Resume Next statement lets the program ignore the error and continue.

The On Error GoTo 0 Statement

When you use an On Error GoTo *Label* or On Error Resume Next statement, it remains in effect until the procedure is exited, another error handler is declared, or the error handler is canceled. The On Error GoTo 0 statement cancels the error handler. Subsequent errors are again trapped by Access (or an error handler in a calling procedure, as described in the section "Hierarchy of Error Handlers" later in this chapter). This statement also resets the value of the Err() function to 0, so if you need that value you must cache it in a variable.

Although it isn't required, you might find it a good programming practice to use an On Error GoTo 0 statement when exiting from procedures that set up an error handler. This makes explicit the range that is covered by the error handler.

Handling Errors

After trapping an error with the On Error GoTo *Label* statement, you will want to take some action. What you do depends on your application. If you are trying to open a table and the table doesn't exist, you might want to report an error to the user. On the other hand, you might decide instead to go ahead and create the table by executing a make-table query.

Determining Which Error Has Occurred

Three useful predefined functions help with the process of determining which error has occurred and how to handle it: Err(), Error(), and its variation, Error$(). The Err() function returns an integer that uniquely identifies the error. The Error() function returns a variant that contains a message describing the error. Error$() is the same as Error() except that it returns a string describing the message instead of a variant. You should use Error$() instead of Error() anytime the code is expecting a string (which is most of the time) since Access has to perform a conversion operation from a variant if you use Error().

NOTE

As Microsoft releases new versions of Access, the Err( ) function usually returns the same value it does in previous versions. This isn't the case with the Error( ) and Error$( ) functions; the messages are quite likely to change from version to version. For example, in Access 1.x, Error$(2049) returns "Name '|' contains invalid characters." In Access version 2.0, the same error number returns "Name '|' contains invalid characters or is too long." As you can see, Microsoft expanded the error message to explain another reason why this error might occur. If you are programming for an international market, versions of Access localized to other languages will return messages in the localized language. Doing a string comparison of the return value of the Error( ) function almost certainly won't work for some versions of Access. Comparing strings isn't as fast as comparing numbers, either. For these reasons, it is always better to compare error numbers.

If you are using a full error handler at the bottom of the procedure, you can use the general construction shown in Listing 14.4.

Listing 14.4

```
Sub glrTypicalErrorHandlerSub()
    ' Example showing the construction of a procedure with an
    ' error handler.
```

```
    Dim db As Database
    Dim tbl As Recordset

    On Error GoTo glrTypicalErrorHandlerSubError

    ' Some code that might generate a run-time error
    Set db = DBEngine.Workspaces(0).Databases(0)
    Set tbl = db.OpenRecordset("tblTable", DB_OPEN_TABLE)

    ' You would do some processing with tbl here

glrTypicalErrorHandlerSubDone:
    On Error Resume Next
    tbl.Close
Exit Sub
glrTypicalErrorHandlerSubError:
    Select Case Err
    Case 3011    ' Cannot find object
        MsgBox "tblTable doesn't exist. Call the database
        ➥ administrator."
    Case Else
        MsgBox "The application encountered unexpected error #"
        ➥ & Err & " with message string '" & Error & "'",
        ➥ MB_OK Or MB_ICONEXCLAMATION Or MB_DEFBUTTON1 Or
        ➥ MB_APPLMODAL, "glrTypicalErrorHandlerSub"
    End Select
    Resume glrTypicalErrorHandlerSubDone
End Sub
```

The Select Case statement uses the Err() function to determine which error has occurred. It is a good idea to use a Select Case statement even if you have only one case you want to handle since this makes it easy for you to add other cases later just by inserting another Case statement. Always use a Case Else to trap unexpected errors. You can use a MsgBox statement in the Case Else, an Error statement, or an error-reporting routine, as shown in the section "Creating an Error-Reporting Routine" later in this chapter.

It is important to realize that two or more statements in your main code can generate the same error. If you want different things to happen in your error handler for each of those statements, you must set a flag in your main code and use If statements within the Case statement in your error handler. A more complicated method would define several different error handlers with On Error statements as you reached different parts of your code. Fortunately, most code doesn't require this complexity. If it does, it might be time to consider splitting the procedure into several smaller procedures.

An example of the use of flags is shown in Listing 14.5.

Listing 14.5

```
Sub glrAddLineNumbers()
    ' Opens C:\FILE1.TXT and writes a new file C:\FILE2.TXT.
    ' Reports any errors opening the file
    '
    Dim fState As Integer
    Dim strInput As String
    Dim lngLineNumber As Long

    Const FSTATEOPENINGFILE1 = 1
    Const FSTATEOPENINGFILE2 = 2

    On Error GoTo glrAddLineNumbersError

    fState = FSTATEOPENINGFILE1
    Open "c:\file1.txt" For Input As #1

    fState = FSTATEOPENINGFILE2
    Open "c:\file2.txt" For Output As #2

    lngLineNumber = 1
    Do Until EOF(1)
        Input #1, strInput
        Print #2, lngLineNumber, strInput
        lngLineNumber = lngLineNumber + 1
    Loop
    Close #2
glrAddLineNumbersCloseFile1:
    Close #1
glrAddLineNumbersDone:
Exit Sub
glrAddLineNumbersError:
    Select Case Err
    Case 70, 75 ' Permission denied or Path/File access error
        Select Case fState
        Case FSTATEOPENINGFILE1
            MsgBox "Could not open 'c:\file1.txt'. Something
            ➡ probably has the file locked.", MB_OK Or
            ➡ MB_ICONEXCLAMATION Or MB_DEFBUTTON1 Or
```

```
      ➥ MB_APPLMODAL, "glrAddLineNumbers"
        Resume glrAddLineNumbersDone
    Case FSTATEOPENINGFILE2
        MsgBox "Could not open 'c:\file2.txt'. The file may
      ➥ be write protected or locked.", MB_OK Or
      ➥ MB_ICONEXCLAMATION Or MB_DEFBUTTON1 Or
      ➥ MB_APPLMODAL, "glrAddLineNumbers"
        Resume glrAddLineNumbersCloseFile1
    End Select
  Case Else
    MsgBox "Unexpected error.", MB_OK Or MB_ICONEXCLAMATION
      ➥ Or MB_DEFBUTTON1 Or MB_APPLMODAL, "Add Line Numbers"
  End Select
Resume glrAddLineNumbersDone
End Sub
```

This listing shows a procedure that opens an ASCII file named C:\FILE1.TXT. It reads each line, adds a line number to the beginning of the line, and writes a new file, C:\FILE2.TXT, with the changes. There are two Open statements in the procedure that can fail, and you want to show two different error messages to the user, depending on which one failed. Also, if opening the second one fails, you need to close the first one before exiting the procedure. The variable fState holds a flag indicating which open statement is being processed. When an error occurs, this variable is checked to determine which error message to display. Using the constants FSTATEOPENINGFILE1 and FSTATEOPENINGFILE2 instead of just the numbers 1 and 2 makes the meaning of the current value of fState more explicit.

The Resume Statement

To return to the main part of the procedure from the error handler, you use a Resume statement. The Resume statement has three forms:

- Resume
- Resume Next
- Resume *Label*

They are described in the following sections.

Resume   Resume by itself returns control to the statement that caused the error. Use the Resume statement when the error handler fixes the problem that caused the error and you want to continue from the place where you encountered the problem. In the example shown in Listing 14.4, if the error handler ran a make-table query that created tblTable, you would use a Resume statement. Note, however, that if you didn't fix the problem that caused the error, an endless loop occurs when the original statement fails again. Use this form of Resume with extreme caution.

Resume Next Use the Resume Next statement inside an error handler when you want to ignore the statement that caused the error. Control returns to the statement following the one that caused the error, similar to the On Error Resume Next statement. Use Resume Next when you have fixed the problem that caused the error from within the error handler or when you can safely ignore the error.

Resume Label Use the Resume *Label* statement when you want to return to a line other than the one causing the error or the following line. Resume *Label* is similar to a GoTo statement except that you can use it only from inside an error handler. The example in Listing 14.4 shows this use of the Resume statement to jump to the label glrTypicalErrorHandlerSubDone.

The Error Statement

Sometimes in an error handler you want Access to act as though there were no error handler in place, such as in the Case Else part of the error handler. Use the Error statement to generate an error. The Error statement differs from the Error() function. The statement takes an argument of an error number and causes Access to generate that particular error. You normally use it with the Err() function to generate the error that would have occurred had no error handler been in place, as in Error Err.

You can use the Error statement in your main code during debugging to test an error handler. Thus, if you insert Error 44 in your main code, Access acts as though error 44 had occurred and generates a run-time error. Control then passes to your error handler, if you have one in place.

Using Err() with On Error Resume Next

If you have only one statement in a piece of code that can fail, you might not want to write a full error handler. The Err() function with the On Error Resume Next statement can catch errors in your main code. Lay out your code like that in Listing 14.6.

Listing 14.6

```
Sub glrOnErrorResumeNextExample()
    ' Example showing the use of On Error Resume Next
    '
    Dim db As Database
    Dim tbl As Recordset
    Dim intErr As Integer

    ' Some code that might generate a run-time error
    ' for example
    Set db = DBEngine.Workspaces(0).Databases(0)

    On Error Resume Next
    Set tbl = db.OpenRecordset("tblTable", DB_OPEN_TABLE)
    intErr = Err     ' Get error (if any) now and store it away
    On Error GoTo 0
    Select Case intErr
        Case 0        ' No Error
            ' Do nothing
        Case 3011   'Can't find object
            MsgBox "tblTable doesn't exist. Call the database
            ➥ administrator."
            GoTo SubNameDone
        Case Else
            Error intErr     ' Stop here with error message
    End Select

    ' Do some processing with tbl

    tbl.Close
SubNameDone:
End Sub
```

Note that as soon as you have two different statements that can cause a run-time error, it is usually more efficient to write an error handler using the On Error GoTo

Label syntax since the overhead of constructing the error handler is encountered only once. If you use Err() with On Error Resume Next, always use a Select Case statement with a Case Else clause. Otherwise, error numbers you don't have Case statements for may produce unexpected results.

Hierarchy of Error Handlers

Access behaves in a somewhat unexpected manner, in terms of error handlers, when one procedure calls another. If the called procedure generates an error that isn't handled within the procedure, the calling procedure receives the error. Access acts as though the procedure call itself generated the error.

> **TIP**
>
> If you have any calls to user-defined functions or subs in your code, you need to be very aware of this feature of Access's error handlers; it can cause control to unexpectedly jump into your calling procedure's error handler. It is advisable to include an error handler in every procedure in your application.

To demonstrate the hierarchy of error handlers, glrFunctionA() calls glrSubB in Listing 14.7.

Listing 14.7

```
Function glrFunctionA()
    ' Sample function to show the hierarchy of
    ' error handlers.
    '

    On Error GoTo glrFunctionAError

    Call glrSubB

    MsgBox "You might expect to get to here, but you don't."
glrFunctionADone:
Exit Function
glrFunctionAError:
```

```
        Select Case Err
        Case 1
            MsgBox "You got here from glrSubB"
            Resume glrFunctionADone
        Case Else
            Error Err
        End Select
Exit Function
End Function

Sub glrSubB()
    ' Stub procedure. Generates an error, but doesn't
    ' handle it.
    '

    ' Cause an error in this Sub. There is no error handler.
    Error 1
End Sub
```

Access generates an error when it executes the Error 1 statement in glrSubB. Since glrSubB doesn't contain an error handler, control immediately passes back to glrFunctionA(). glrFunctionA() does contain an error handler, so it processes the error. If glrFunctionA() didn't contain an error handler, control would pass to the procedure (if any) that called glrFunctionA(). If Access gets to the top of the call stack without finding an error handler, it puts up an alert.

Access acts as though the Call statement itself generates the error. The Resume Next in glrFunctionA() returns control to the statement following the Call statement; control doesn't return to glrSubB. If you use a Resume statement instead of a Resume Next in glrFunctionA(), the Resume statement returns control to the Call statement in glrFunctionA(). This calls glrSubB again, which in this case puts you into an endless loop as the error repeats.

The OnError Property

When you are using a form or report, under the covers Access is using Jet for all data access. Anytime Access has to populate the fields on a bound form or fill a list box, it is making calls to Jet. Any of these calls might fail. In Access version 1.x, an error resulted in an alert being reported to the user. Access version 2.0 gives you a way to trap those errors through the use of the OnError property.

The property sheet of a form or report shows a property called OnError. When the Code Builder is invoked on this property, you see a shell that looks like the following:

Sub Form_Error(*DataErr* As Integer, *Response* As Integer)

End Sub

DataErr is the value that would be returned by the Err() function had the error occurred in Access Basic. *Response* is a value you fill in before the procedure terminates. It tells Access whether or not it should report the error to the user. *DataErr* and *Response* are the variable names proposed by the Access Code Builder, but you can rename them to any variable names. Listing 14.8 shows an example of a routine to handle the error event.

Listing 14.8

```
Sub Form_Error(DataErr As Integer, Response As Integer)
    ' Reports errors for the form, attached to OnError property
    '
    ' In:
    '    DateErr Error number of error
    '
    ' Out:
    '    Response    DATA_ERRCONTINUE or DATA_ERRDISPLAY
    '
    ' History:
    '    Created 4/22/94 GRR; Last Modified 4/22/94 GRR
    Select Case DataErr
    Case 2279    ' The value you entered isn't appropriate for the
                 ' input mask '¦' specified for this field. Press
                 ' Esc to cancel your changes.
        MsgBox "You need to fix the value in this field"
    Case 3314    ' Field '¦' can't contain a null value.
        MsgBox "You left a required field blank"
    Case 3022    ' Duplicate value in index, primary key, or
                 ' relationship. Changes were unsuccessful.
        MsgBox "You already have one of these"
    Case Else
        Call glrErrorOutput(DataErr, Error(DataErr))
    End Select
    Response = DATA_ERRCONTINUE
```

End Sub

The variable Response can receive one of two values: DATA_ERRCONTINUE or DATA_ERRDISPLAY. The value DATA_ERRDISPLAY causes Access to display the error message that would have appeared if you hadn't had an error handler attached to the form. DATA_ERRCONTINUE causes this error message to be suppressed.

The function Error(DataErr) returns the Jet error string associated with the error.

Unfortunately, the OnError property does not let you trap multiuser locking problems.

For more information on the Form and Report Error events, see Chapter 8.

Creating an Error-Reporting Subroutine

You can create a generic subroutine that reports errors like those found in Listing 14.9. You can then use "ErrorOutput Err, Error" in the Case Else statement of your error handlers. This provides a standard way of documenting unexpected errors.

Listing 14.9

```
Global Const FDEBUG = True
Const GLR_STRERRORFILE = "c:\accerr.txt"
Sub glrErrorOutput(ByVal intErr As Integer, ByVal varError As
➡ Variant)
    ' Reports an error to the screen, via a message box, to
    ' the immediate window, and to the file specified by the
    ' GLR_STRERRORFILE constant.
    Dim db As Database
    Dim iastrProcNames As Integer

    Set db = DBEngine.Workspaces(0).Databases(0)
    MsgBox "The application encountered an unexpected error.",
    ➡ MB_OK Or MB_ICONEXCLAMATION Or MB_DEFBUTTON1 Or
    ➡ MB_APPLMODAL
    Open GLR_STRERRORFILE For Append As #1
    Print #1, Format(Now, "mm/dd/yy hh:nn") & " " & db.name & " "
    ➡ & CurrentUser() & " Error #" & intErr & " " & varError
```

```
        Close #1
        If FDEBUG Then
            Debug.Print "The database name is: "; db.name
            Debug.Print "The current user is: "; CurrentUser()
            Debug.Print "The Error # is: "; intErr
            Debug.Print "The Error statement is: "; varError ·
            Stop
        End If
End Sub
```

The FDEBUG global constant determines whether the information within the If statement prints to the Immediate window when an error occurs. You can use this information to add the unexpected error to the Select Case statement in the error handler. Set the FDEBUG flag to False before releasing your code to your client or user.

The constant GLR_STRERRORFILE names a text file that will have a summary of all errors written to it. This is useful for determining information about an error when you are debugging the application over the phone. For more information on creating activity logs, see Chapter 15.

The Stop statement acts as a breakpoint. You can then use the View Calls feature of Access to see where the error occurred.

Implementing a Call Stack

When you are at any breakpoint, you can select View ➤ Calls to see which function caused the error. Unfortunately, Access doesn't provide any method for retrieving this information from your code. When you get an unexpected error, it's useful to know what code is being executed. Since Access provides no way to get at the information it keeps internally (that is, the name of the currently executing procedure), you must maintain the information yourself if you need it. The three procedures shown in Listing 14.10 will help with this process. See the next section for information on the glrAssert() function used in this example.

Listing 14.10

```
Global Const GLR_IASTRPROCNAMESMAX = 16
Global glr_astrProcNames(GLR_IASTRPROCNAMESMAX) As String
Global glr_iastrProcNames As Integer
```

```
Sub glrEnterProcedure (ByVal strProcName As String)
    ' Places the procedure name specified by strProcName
    ' on the stack, which is the glr_astrProcNames()
    ' array. Cannot be nested more than
    ' GLR_IASTRPROCNAMESMAX levels deep.
    '

    ' If this assertion is violated, you probably need to
    ' increase the value of GLR_IASTRPROCNAMESMAX. You might
    ' also have a problem with infinite recursion.
    Call glrAssert(glr_iastrProcNames < GLR_IASTRPROCNAMESMAX)

    glr_iastrProcNames = glr_iastrProcNames + 1
    glr_astrProcNames(glr_iastrProcNames) = strProcName
End Sub

Sub glrExitProcedure (ByVal strProcName As String)
    ' Removes the procedure name specified by the strProcName
    ' variable from the procedure stack, glr_astrProcNames.
    ' Checks to make sure that the procname passed in is the
    ' same as the top of the stack.
    '

    ' Assert that the top of the stack is the same as the
    ' procedure name passed in. Usually this assertion fails
    ' if someone missed doing a glrEnterProcedure or
    ' glrExitProcedure in some other procedure.
    Call glrAssert(strProcName =
    ➥ glr_astrProcNames(glr_iastrProcNames))

    ' Do not underflow the stack
    Call glrAssert(glr_iastrProcNames > 0)

    glr_astrProcNames(glr_iastrProcNames) = ""
    glr_iastrProcNames = glr_iastrProcNames - 1
End Sub

Sub glrAssert (ByVal f As Long)
    ' Asserts that the expression f is True, if not reports
    ' an error.
    If Not f Then
        Call glrErrorOutput(32767, "Assertion Failed")
    End If
End Sub
```

These procedures create a global array, glr_astrProcNames. This array is populated with the name of the current procedure. When one procedure calls another, the index glr_iastrProcNames is incremented so that a stack of procedure names is maintained. The constant GLR_IASTRPROCNAMESMAX determines the maximum depth of the call stack and can be set as large or small as your code requires. When a procedure is exited, the name is removed from the stack and glr_iastrProc-Names is decremented.

To get any useful information from these functions, you must rigorously use the glrEnterProcedure and glrExitProcedure calls at the entry point and exit point of every procedure. Listing 14.11 shows an example of how to use these functions.

Listing 14.11

```
Sub glrEnterAndExitExample()
    ' An example block of code showing how glrEnterProcedure
    ' and glrExitProcedure should be used.
    On Error GoTo glrEnterAndExitExampleError
    Call glrEnterProcedure("glrEnterAndExitExample")

    ' Some code that might fail in an unexpected way

glrEnterAndExitExampleDone:
    Call glrExitProcedure("glrEnterAndExitExample")
Exit Sub
glrEnterAndExitExampleError:
    Select Case Err
    Case Else
        Call glrErrorOutput(Err, Error$)
    End Select
    Resume glrEnterAndExitExampleDone
End Sub
```

The code in Listing 14.9 would then be rewritten as shown in Listing 14.12 to show the call stack.

Listing 14.12

```
Sub glrErrorOutput(ByVal intErr As Integer, ByVal varError As
➡ Variant)
    ' Reports an error to the screen, via a message box, to the
    ' immediate window, and to the file specified by the
    ' GLR_STRERRORFILE constant.
```

```
Dim db As Database
Dim iastrProcNames As Integer

Set db = DBEngine.Workspaces(0).Databases(0)
MsgBox "The application encountered an unexpected error.",
➥ MB_OK Or MB_ICONEXCLAMATION Or MB_DEFBUTTON1 Or
➥ MB_APPLMODAL
Open GLR_STRERRORFILE For Append As #1
Print #1, Format(Now, "mm/dd/yy hh:nn") & " " & db.name & " "
➥ & CurrentUser() & " Error #" & intErr & " " & varError
Print #1, "Calls:"
For iastrProcNames = glr_iastrProcNames To 0 Step -1
    Print #1, glr_astrProcNames(iastrProcNames)
Next iastrProcNames
Close #1
If FDEBUG Then
    Debug.Print "The database name is: "; db.name
    Debug.Print "The current user is: "; CurrentUser()
    Debug.Print "The Error # is: "; intErr
    Debug.Print "The Error statement is: "; varError
    Stop
End If
End Sub
```

The payoff for adding this code to your functions comes when you have delivered your application to a client and are debugging it by phone. When the client opens the file C:\ACCERR.TXT, the output will look like this:

```
04/09/95 12:00 C:\DATA\MDB\APPLICAT.MDB Admin Error #5 Illegal
➥ function call
Calls:
glrEnterAndExitExample
OverallGlobalModule
```

The output shows you the entire call stack from when the error occurred, including the name of the procedure that caused the error.

Finding Logic Errors

As stated at the beginning of this chapter, the three kinds of errors are compile-time errors, logic errors, and run-time errors. Access points out any compile-time errors anytime you use Run ➤ Compile Loaded Modules. Error handlers handle run-time errors. But what can you do about logic errors? If you were a perfect programmer, you would probably never have any logic errors because you'd never make mistakes, you'd always know exactly how Access works, and all your assumptions would always hold true. Professional programmers can't count on perfection. Instead, they're better off using assertions to verify the state of their code at various points.

An *assertion* is a statement that says that at a certain point the code should be in a certain state. If the code isn't in the expected state, an error message is reported.

Listing 14.10, which was presented earlier in this chapter, shows several examples of assertions. One such assertion is that the code isn't going to exceed the amount of space allocated for the array. An assumption is made that the code will never be nested more than 16 levels deep. The following line appears in the code:

```
Call glrAssert(glr_iastrProcNames < GLR_IASTRPROCNAMESMAX)
```

This line asserts that the current index into the array is less than the maximum index you specified in the GLR_IASTRPROCNAMESMAX constant, which was defined to be 16. If the value in glr_iastrProcNames is more than that, an error message is reported. The procedure glrAssert is shown again in Listing 14.13.

Listing 14.13

```
Sub glrAssert(ByVal f As Long)
    ' Asserts that the expression f is True, if not reports
    ' an error.
    If Not f Then
        Call glrErrorOutput(32767, "Assertion Failed")
    End If
End Sub
```

The code in glrAssert simply says that if the value passed is False, then report an error. The value passed in is usually the evaluation of a comparison expression.

For this routine we invented an error number to represent the Assertion Failed error. We selected 32767 because it is the largest error number that can be used. The largest error number Access 2.0 uses is 7951. When you create your own error numbers, you should start with 32767 and work backward toward 1 since this reduces the chance of overlapping error numbers in future versions of Access.

For another example of using assertions, suppose you have the routine shown in Listing 14.14.

Listing 14.14

```
Function glrBackupTape(ByVal lngMonth As Long) As String
    ' Part of a tape backup scheme. Reports a color of
    ' tape to use in rotation based on the month number
    ' passed in.
    '
    ' The constant INTTAPESPERYEAR indicates how many
    ' tapes are used in the rotation cycle.
    '
    ' In:
    '    lngMonth    A number between 1 and 12
    '
    ' Out:
    '    A string with the color tape to use in the backup
    '
    ' Example:
    '    MsgBox "Use the " & glrBackupTape(Month(Now)) & " backup
    '    tape"
    Dim strBackup As String
    Const INTTAPESPERYEAR = 4

    On Error GoTo glrBackupTapeError
    Call glrEnterProcedure("glrBackupTape")

    ' Assert that the month number is valid
    Call glrAssert(lngMonth >= 1 And lngMonth <= 12)

    ' Select a backup tape based on the month
    Select Case (lngMonth - 1) Mod INTTAPESPERYEAR
    Case 0 ' January, May, September
        strBackup = "black"
    Case 1 ' February, June, October
        strBackup = "red"
    Case 2 ' March, July, November
        strBackup = "blue"
    Case 3 ' April, August, December
        strBackup = "green"
    Case Else
        ' We shouldn't ever reach here
        Call glrAssert(False)
    End Select
    glrBackupTape = strBackup
glrBackupTapeDone:
    Call glrExitProcedure("glrBackupTape")
```

```
Exit Function
glrBackupTapeError:
    Select Case Err
    Case Else
        Call glrErrorOutput(Err, Error$)
    End Select
    Resume glrBackupTapeDone
End Function
```

The function glrBackupTape() determines a backup tape to use based on the month passed in, rotating among four colored tapes during the year. An assumption is made that the month number is between 1 and 12. Suppose the code that calls the function does something like this:

```
MsgBox "Use the " & glrBackupTape(Now) & "backup tape."
```

The Access function Now() returns the number of days since December 30th, 1899. This is clearly not a number between 1 and 12. The assertion that the month number is to be between 1 and 12, using the line "Call glrAssert(lngMonth >= 1 And lngMonth <= 12)", means that the code would stop immediately upon executing the statement. If the assertion is not there, the large number is subjected to the Mod operator, forcing it within the range of 0 to 3, which is a valid month number. The code would operate but not give the expected result. This could be a hard bug to track down if the assertion were not there.

Assertions put assumptions about your code into the code itself rather than relying on the programmer to always apply the assumption. Assertions are especially important when multiple programmers are working on a project because the other programmers on the project probably won't know the assumptions the person writing the code has made unless they are explicit in the code or comments. Assertions are like comments with the force of the compiler behind them.

In the Case Else statement of the previous example, the following code appeared:

```
' We shouldn't ever reach here
Call glrAssert(False)
```

Since an assertion of the value False always fails, this is a way of reporting an error about what should be unreachable code. This is useful to put in Case Else statements to trap for values that are unacceptable. As written, the code with this example will never be reached. But suppose someone changed the value of the constant INTTAPESPERYEAR from 4 to 6. Then the assertion would fail because there are no Case statements for the values 4 and 5 in the Select Case block.

You should precede most assertions with a comment that describes why the assertion might fail: the month is out of range, the procedure name is not the same as the top of the stack, the code should never be reached, and so on. In some cases the comment might suggest how to fix the assertion. For example, it might suggest increasing the INTTAPESPERYEAR constant and adding more Case statements to the case block.

Liberal use of assertions in your code will help in finding many logic errors. The trade-off is that they add slightly to the size and reduce the speed of your code.

Summary

This chapter has covered the following issues:

- Creating run-time error handlers
- Using the On Error Goto *Label*, On Error Resume Next, and On Error Goto 0 statements
- Determining which error occurred using the Err(), Error(), and Error$() functions
- Recovering from errors using the Resume, Resume Next, and Resume *Label* statements
- Understanding the hierarchy of error handlers
- Implementing a call stack to help with the debugging of unexpected errors
- Using assertions to locate logic errors

By using these techniques you can create code that will stand up to the beating your users will give it. If your code does fail, you can quickly locate the problem and resolve it with minimum effort.

CHAPTER

FIFTEEN

Debugging Applications

- Avoiding bugs in the first place

- Using the Immediate window

- Creating and maintaining activity logs

- Avoiding debugging pitfalls

There's no question as to where bugs in code come from. Bugs come from programming. Worse yet, bugs come from fixing other bugs. Writing bug-free code is as unlikely as typing a novel with no typographical errors in it; if you write code, you'll write buggy code. Finding and fixing bugs is the subject of this chapter. Fortunately, programmers with a strategy for fixing bugs and experience in applying it fix bugs more quickly and introduce fewer new bugs when they are debugging. You should aspire to be one of these debugging pros, and in this chapter we give you a few hints on how to get there.

Avoiding Bugs

Although you'll never write code with no bugs, certain strategies can help you avoid inserting unnecessary bugs. You should develop the necessary discipline to use these strategies whenever you write code, even if you think you're writing a function to use only in testing or for your own internal application. Good habits are hard to develop but are also hard to lose once you develop them. The next few sections describe how you can avoid letting bugs slip into your Access Basic code by following these rules:

- Fix bugs as they appear.
- Use comments.
- Organize your code.
- Modularize your code.
- Use Option Explicit.
- Avoid variants if at all possible.
- Use explicit conversion functions.
- Beware the simple Dim statement.
- Group your Dim statements.
- Use the tightest possible scoping.
- Watch out for "hidden" modules.
- Use consistent naming conventions.

Internalizing these suggestions will help you develop a good mind-set for avoiding bugs and for removing the ones that inevitably creep into your code.

As a single rule of thumb, the best bug-avoidance strategy is to take your time and to avoid the urge to make your code "cleverer" than necessary. At times you simply must use the newest, most complex features of any programming language, but in general, the simpler way is the better way. With this strategy in mind, there are some specific tactics that work well in Access coding to help avoid bugs.

Fixing Bugs as They Appear

It's critical to fix bugs as they reveal themselves, rather than wait until you have more features implemented; hurried cleanup at the end of a project will pressure you to apply band-aids instead of real fixes. If your application is failing when the invoice amount is exactly $33.00, don't just patch the procedure like this:

```
If intInvoiceAmt=33 Then
     MyFunction = intTheCorrectValue
Else...
```

Instead, you must figure out *why* the call is failing and fix its cause instead of the apparent symptom. This requires steady and systematic testing, which is something programmers tend to avoid. Would you rather write 500 lines of code or try 50 test cases on existing code? Most of us would choose the former since writing code is fun and testing is boring. But if you keep in mind how little fun you'll have if your application doesn't work when it's shipped, you'll buckle down and do the boring testing work, too.

Using Comments

Old code is harder to debug than new code because it is less fresh in your mind. For most people, old code is any code that's more than two days old. One way to help keep your code from aging rapidly is to insert comments. There's an art to sensible commenting; it depends on inserting just enough to tell you what's going on without going overboard and cluttering up your code. Generally, one comment for 10 to 20 lines of code, combined with variable naming that follows a standard and a structured layout, is about right. Novice programmers have a tendency to go overboard, as in this example:

```
' Make sure the numbers in the combo box and the text box add up
' to less than the acceptable total
If cboStartTime + CInt(txtSlots) > MAX_SLOTS Then
    ' If not, put up an error message...
    MsgBox "Not enough time in day", MB_ICON_STOP, "Schedule
    ➥ Error"
    ' ...and exit the application
    GoTo cmdSchedule_Click_Exit
End If
' Find the last slot that needs to be modified
intSlotLast = cboStartTime + CInt(txtSlots) - 1

' Set an object to the current database
Set dbCurrent = DBEngine.Workspaces(0).Databases(0)
' Open a querydef object with the Prospective schedule query
' loaded
Set qdfSchedule =
➥ dbCurrent.OpenQueryDef("qryScheduleProspective")
' Get the first query parameter from the Installer combo box
qdfSchedule.Parameters(0) = cboInstaller
' Get the second query parameter from the Date combo box
qdfSchedule.Parameters(1) = cboDate
```

Reading through code like this is like trying to understand a telephone conversation with a bad echo on the line. By trimming down the number of comments to a more sensible level, you can highlight the overall structure of the code and note any particularly tricky spots for future programmers, including yourself. Remember, if you've named your variables correctly, their names will act as little mini-comments in the code itself:

```
' Check to see that we have enough hours left in the day
If cboStartTime + CInt(txtSlots) > MAX_SLOTS Then
    MsgBox "Not enough time in day", MB_ICON_STOP, "Schedule
    ➥ Error"
    GoTo cmdSchedule_Click_Exit
End If
intSlotLast = cboStartTime + CInt(txtSlots) - 1

' Get a list of open timeslots to check
Set dbCurrent = DBEngine.Workspaces(0).Databases(0)
Set qdfSchedule =
➥ dbCurrent.OpenQueryDef("qryScheduleProspective")
qdfSchedule.Parameters(0) = cboInstaller
```

```
qdfSchedule.Parameters(1) = cboDate
Set rstSchedule = qdfSchedule.OpenRecordset(DB_OPEN_DYNASET)
```

To Strip or Not to Strip

Another reason for keeping the number of comments to a reasonable level is that comments do take up space in memory while your database is loaded. Some programmers go so far as to encourage comment stripping, the practice of removing all comments from production code. We don't recommend this, except under the most dire circumstances, since it requires you to maintain a commented version to work on and an uncommented version to ship, and it increases the chance that you will introduce errors by failing to keep the two versions in perfect synchronization.

Organizing Your Code

In addition to commenting your code, you should do whatever you can to keep it organized. This means, in part, using tabs to indicate the flow of code and, in part, splitting procedures into smaller procedures. The basic notion of using tabs is that statements that "go together" should be at the same tab level, and statements that are subordinate to others should be indented one more tab stop. While there is room for disagreement, most Access programmers lay out their code something like this:

```
' Initialize the array that governs visibility and set up records
For intI = 1 To intTotalTabs
    intShow(intI) = False
    rstLoggedData.AddNew
        rstLoggedData![State] = False
    rstLoggedDate.Update
Next intI
intShow(intTabNumber) = True
```

In Access Basic many programmers prefer to use indentation not just to match up traditional control structures (For…Next, If…Then…Else, Do…Loop, While…Wend) but also to indicate levels of data access object activity (BeginTrans/CommitTrans, AddNew/Update, and so on).

Modularizing Your Code

Modularization is a fancy term for a simple idea: you should break up your code into a series of relatively small procedures instead of just a few mammoth ones. There are several key benefits to writing code this way:

- You make it easier to understand each procedure. Code that is easier to understand is easier to maintain and to keep bug free.

- You can localize errors to a smaller section of the total code. If a variable is used only in one ten-line function, any error messages referring to that variable are most likely generated within that function.

- You can lessen the dangers of side effects caused by too-wide scoping of variables. If you use a variable at the top of a 500-line function and again at the bottom for a different loop, you may well forget to reinitialize it.

Using Option Explicit

When you create a new module, Access puts a single statement at the top—Option Compare Database—which controls the sort order used in that module. You should get into the habit of immediately adding, on the next line, the Option Explicit statement. This statement forces you to declare all your variables before referring to them in your code. This may seem like a nuisance, but it will prevent some hard-to-find errors from cropping up in your code. Without Option Explicit, Access allows you to use any syntactically correct variable in your code, regardless of whether you declare it, but any variable you forget to declare will be initialized to a variant and given the value Null at the point where you first use it.

You must add the Option Explicit statement to each and every module in your application, as well as to each form or report module. Why Access doesn't make it possible to set this option once and forget about it is a mystery, but take the time to insert it yourself. The hours you save in debugging time will make it well worth the effort.

Using Option Explicit is an easy way to avoid errors such as the one you'll find in the following code fragment. Errors like this one are almost impossible to catch late in the development cycle since they're buried in existing code. Don't feel bad if you don't immediately see the error in the fragment; it's difficult to find. That's why you'll want to use Option Explicit—to avoid just this sort of error.

```
Function UpdateLog(intSeverity As Integer, strProcedure As
➥ String, strTracking As String) As Integer

    Dim dbCurrent As Database
```

```
Dim rstUsageLog As Recordset
Dim intFull As Integer
Dim qryArchive As QueryDef

' Don't log activities that aren't severe enough to
' bother with
If intSeverity < intMinSeverity Then
    Exit Function
End If

DoCmd SetWarnings False

' Append a new record to the usage log
Set dbCurrent = dbEngine.Workspaces(0).Databases(0)
Set rstUsageLog =
➡ dbCurrent.OpenRecordset("zstblUsageLog",
➡ DB_OPEN_DYNASET)
rstUsageLog.AddNew
    rstUsageLog![Severity] = intSeverty
    If Err Then
        rstUsageLog![ErrorCode] = Err
        rstUsageLog![ErrorText] = Error$
    End If
    rstUsageLog![User] = CurrentUser()
    rstUsageLog![Date] = Now
```

In case you missed it, the error occurred on this line of code:

```
rstUsageLog![Severity] = intSeverty
```

A small spelling error like this would cause only zeros to be stored in the Severity field and could cause you several hours of debugging time.

Avoid Variants if at All Possible

The Variant datatype is convenient, but it's not always the best choice. It's tempting to declare all your variables as variants so you don't have to worry about what's in them. The Access design team did not put in explicit types to make your life difficult; they put them in because they're useful. If you think something will always be an integer, dimension it as an integer. If you get an error message later because you've attempted to assign an invalid value to that variable, the error message will point straight to the problem area of your code and give you a good idea of what went wrong. Variants are also slower than explicitly dimensioned variables for the same operations since they have the overhead of tracking which type of data they are holding at any given time. In addition, variants are larger than almost any other datatype and so take longer to move around in memory. If for nothing else, these last two reasons should be enough to make you reconsider using variants whenever possible.

> **TIP**
>
> In some instances you have no choice about your datatypes. If you're assigning values to variables that might at some point need to contain a null value, you need to use the Variant datatype. This is the only datatype that can contain a null value, and attempting to assign a null value to a nonvariant variable triggers a run-time error. The same goes for function return values. If a function might need to return a null value, the return value for that function must be a variant.

This same advice applies to choosing functions. If you know that a function can return only a string and never a null value, use the string version. For example, Left$() is often preferable to Left() since the former returns a string and the latter returns a variant. Using the variant versions of the string functions also encourages you to be sloppy since you don't have to think about whether or not you can use the string version. If you take the time to consider which is the better function for your situation, you're more likely to end up with code that works the first time.

Using Explicit Conversion Functions

There will be times in your applications when you need to convert variables from one datatype to another. Access is forgiving about these conversions and most often does the work for you. For example, the following code fragment works without any intervention on your part:

```
Dim strState as String
Dim varState as Variant

varState = "CA"
strState = varState
```

As a matter of fact, you probably write code that does this sort of thing without even thinking about it. In fact, whenever you assign a value of one datatype to a variable of a different datatype, Access has to do some type conversion. You can avoid some hard-to-find bugs by always using explicit conversion functions when converting datatypes.

For example, in the following code fragment, Access blithely copies the value from varY into intX, but in doing so it truncates the value of the number:

```
Dim intX As Integer
Dim varY As Variant

varY = 123.456
intX = varY
' Now intX = 123 and varY = 123.456
```

If your intent is to move the value from varY into an integer variable, your code will be more explicit in its intent if you use the CInt() function. If your intent is to maintain the floating-point value, you should use the CSng() function. If you do that, however, Access won't compile the code, since this assignment is illegal:

```
intX = CSng(varY)
```

At least you would know about it before your program ran!

Beware the Simple Dim Statement

Even the simple Dim statement can introduce subtle bugs into your code. Consider this statement:

```
Dim strFirst, strLast As String
```

The intent here is clearly to define two string variables on one line. However, this is not the way Access Basic works. The As clause applies only to the variable it immediately follows, not to all variables on the line. The result of the preceding declaration is that strLast is a string variable but strFirst is a variant variable, with slightly different behavior. For example, strFirst will be initialized to Empty and strLast to a zero-length string. You must explicitly define the type of every single variable in Access basic. The simplest way to ensure this is to get into the habit of declaring only one variable per statement.

Grouping Your Dim Statements

You can declare your variables anywhere in your procedures, as long you declare them before they are actually used, and Access will understand and accept the declarations. For the sake of easier debugging, though, you should get into the habit of declaring variables at the top of your procedures. This makes it easy to see exactly what a particular procedure is referring to and to find the declarations when you are in the midst of debugging.

Using the Tightest Possible Scoping

Always use the tightest possible scoping for your variables. Some beginning programmers discover global variables and promptly declare all their variables as global to avoid the issue of scoping altogether. This is a sloppy practice that will backfire the first time you have two procedures, both of which change the same global variable's value. If a variable is used solely in a single procedure, declare it there. If it is used only by procedures in a single module, declare it with module scope. Save global scope for only those few variables you truly need to refer to from widely scattered parts of your code.

If you need a variable to be available globally but want to restrict the scope of procedures that can change that value, you might consider "hiding" it from the rest of your application. To do so, create the variable as a module global variable in a specific module. In that module, place any function that needs to modify the value of the variable. In addition, add one extra function that you'll use to retrieve the value from outside the module. If you want to be able to assign a new value to the variable from a different module, you can also include a procedure that will do that for you. In any case, no procedure in any other module will be able to modify the value of this variable. By hiding the variable in this manner, you can be assured that no other procedures in any other modules can possibly modify your variable without going through your procedures. Listing 15.1 shows a simple case of this mechanism.

Listing 15.1

```
Dim intCurrentValue As Integer

Sub SetCurrentValue(intNewValue As Integer)
    intCurrentValue = intNewValue
```

```
End Sub

Function GetCurrentValue()
    GetCurrentValue = intCurrentValue
End Function
```

Given the code in Listing 15.1, any procedure in any module can retrieve the value of intCurrentValue (by calling the GetCurrentValue() function) and can set the value (by calling SetCurrentValue). If you made SetCurrentValue private, however, no procedure outside the current module could change the value of intCurrent-Value. By protecting your *faux*-global variables in this manner, you can avoid errors that can easily occur in multiple-module applications, especially ones written by multiple programmers.

Watching Out for "Hidden" Modules

Although Access 2.0's new Code-Behind-Forms doesn't add any new wrinkles to the debugging process, it definitely adds one to the process of avoiding bugs. Modules attached to forms or reports aren't loaded into memory unless their form or report is, too. When you perform a Search operation (perhaps to rename an object), Access does not look through modules attached to forms and reports that aren't currently loaded. This means that you quite possibly might have mismatched object names between global modules and those that are attached to forms or reports.

To avoid this problem you need to either manually open each form or report module and perform your search or use some Access Basic code to loop through all the existing forms and reports and open each one for you. If you do this, of course, you'll want to have a matching routine to close them all up for you, once you're done searching. The code in Listing 15.2 takes care of this problem. (You'll find the code in basOpenAll in CH15.MDB. CH15.MDB has the OpenAll code attached to the Ctrl+O key in its AutoKeys macro and the CloseAll code attached to the Ctrl+L key.) One word of warning: if you have many complex forms or reports, you can easily run out of resources before the code manages to open all the objects. If so, it'll just stop loading, and you'll need to handle the rest manually.

Listing 15.2

```
Function glrOpenAll()
```

```
        Dim db As Database
        Dim ctr As Container
        Dim intForms As Integer
        Dim intReports As Integer
        Dim strMsg As String
        Dim strLastForm As String
        Dim strLastReport As String
        Dim fDoingReports As Integer

        On Error GoTo glrOpenAll_Err

        Set db = DBEngine.Workspaces(0).Databases(0)

        fDoingReports = False
        Set ctr = db.Containers("Forms")
        For intForms = 0 To ctr.Documents.Count - 1
            strLastForm = ctr.Documents(intForms).Name
            DoCmd OpenForm strLastForm, A_DESIGN, , , , A_ICON
        Next intForms

        fDoingReports = True
        Set ctr = db.Containers("Reports")
        For intReports = 0 To ctr.Documents.Count - 1
            strLastReport = ctr.Documents(intReports).Name
            DoCmd OpenReport strLastReport, A_DESIGN
            DoCmd Minimize
        Next intReports

glrOpenAll_Exit:
        glrOpenAll = intForms + intReports
        On Error Goto 0
        Exit Function

glrOpenAll_Err:
        strMsg = "Error: " & Error & " (" & Err & ").  "
        If fDoingReports Then
            strMsg = strMsg & "The last report opened was: " &
            ➥ strLastReport & "."
        Else
            strMsg = strMsg & "The last form opened was:
            ➥ " &strLastForm & "."
        End If
        MsgBox strMsg
        Resume glrOpenAll_Exit
End Function
```

```
Function glrCloseAll()

    Dim intI As Integer

    For intI = 0 To Forms.Count - 1
        DoCmd Close A_FORM, Forms(0).Name
    Next intI
    For intI = 0 To Reports.Count - 1
        DoCmd Close A_REPORT, Reports(0).Name
    Next intI
End Function
```

Using Consistent Naming Conventions

In addition to the conventions discussed here that help structure your code, you should consider adopting a consistent naming convention for objects and variables in your code. We (along with many other programmers) have standardized on the naming conventions you'll find in Appendix A of this book. A consistent naming standard can make it simple for you to find errors lurking in your programs, in addition to making them simpler for multiple programmers to maintain.

For example, say you need to add together two numeric values. You'd like their result to be stored with the appropriate precision. If you write code like this:

```
Dim number1 As Integer
Dim number2 As Double
.
.
.
number2 = 12.345
number1 = number2 + 23.456
```

Access assigns the sum to number1, but because number1 is declared to be an integer, Access truncates the value. If you used the Leszynski/Reddick naming convention, as we have throughout this book, your code would look something like this:

```
Dim intNumber1 As Integer
Dim dblNumber2 As Double
.
.
.
```

```
dblNumber2 = 12.345
intNumber1 = dblNumber2 + 23.456
```

Given those names, it's clear that you're assigning the value from a double-precision number into an integer and that some truncation is about to happen. With careful use of a naming convention, you can avoid just this sort of hidden bug.

The Limited Set of Available Tools

Access includes a very limited set of tools for debugging your Access Basic procedures. These include the Immediate window, breakpoints, Step Over and Step Into, and the call stack. In addition, Access 2.0 adds the ability to debug library code. (Debugging library code was virtually impossible in Access 1.x.)

The Immediate window (Figure 15.1) gives you a place to investigate the effects of Access Basic code directly, without the intervention of macros, forms, or other methods of running the code. You open the Immediate window by clicking the

FIGURE 15.1:
Immediate window

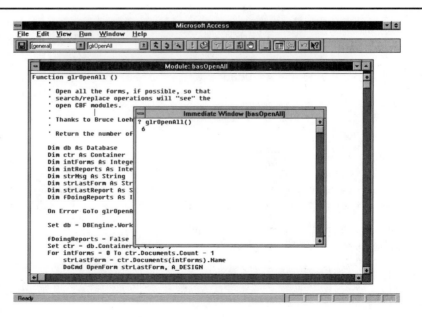

Immediate Window button on the toolbar or selecting View ➤ Immediate Window. Access makes the choices available only when you are working in a module. The Immediate window vanishes whenever you switch the focus away from Access Basic, but it returns when you go back to a module. Immediate window contents are preserved as long as you are in a single session of Access, even if you close one database and open another.

Breakpoints allow you to set locations in your code at which Access will temporarily halt in its execution of your code. Figure 15.2 shows Access Basic code halted at a breakpoint. Once Access stops at a breakpoint, you can use the Immediate window to probe what's going on within Access Basic, checking the value of variables and confirming that your code is doing what you expect it to do. You can also use the Step Into and Step Over functionality (using either the toolbar buttons or the F8/Shift+F8 keys) to move through your code statement by statement so you can watch it execute in slow motion.

In Access 2.0 you can now debug code in libraries as well as code in your own modules. (For more information on creating libraries, see Chapter 20.) This capability wasn't present in Access 1.x, and it is not enabled by default. To enable library

FIGURE 15.2:

Access Basic code halted at a breakpoint

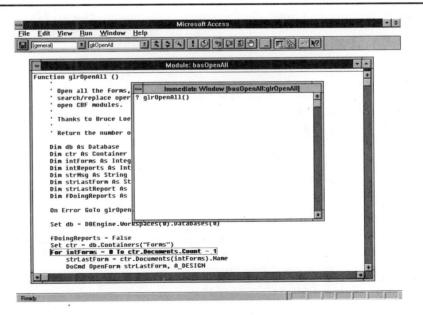

debugging, open your MSACC20.INI file in a text editor and add the following line to the [Options] section:

```
DebugLibraries=True
```

Now when you start Access, you can treat modules in libraries just like any other module. Pressing F2 while any module is open on screen brings up an enhanced selection dialog, which allows you to specify which procedure in which function in which database to investigate. Figure 15.3 shows the enhanced selection dialog.

FIGURE 15.3:

Enhanced procedure selection dialog

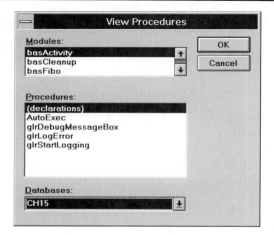

Access 2.0 also adds the ability to display the call stack when a function is paused at a breakpoint. The call stack lists each active function, with the current function at the top of the list, the one that called it next on the list, and so on. If the function was originally called from the Immediate window, this is noted at the end of the list. If the function is called from elsewhere in Access (for example, directly from a Click event or from a RunCode macro action), there is no way to know from where it was called. Figure 15.4 shows the call stack as it might appear at a breakpoint in your code.

Access 2.0 still does not offer the ability to set Watch variables. In a full implementation of Visual Basic for Applications, as in Microsoft Excel, you can define an expression as a Watch variable, and the debugging environment will automatically present you with its value whenever you halt your function at a breakpoint.

FIGURE 15.4:

Access call stack

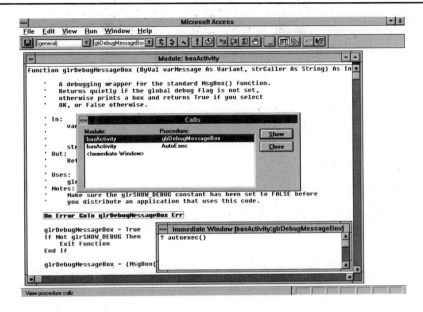

In Access, the best you can do is enter the expression you want evaluated in the Immediate window when you encounter a breakpoint.

TIP If you are going to be evaluating the same complex expression many times, you may wish to assign an AutoKeys macro to send it to the Immediate window via a SendKeys action.

The Immediate window displays the last 100 lines of output at all times. As more output is appended to the end, older lines disappear from the top of the list. With the capability to scroll back the Immediate window, you can position the cursor on an evaluation line and press ↵, and Access will recalculate the expression and display its value. If you want to remove the lines in the Immediate window above your current location, use Shift+Ctrl+Home to select them all, and then press Del. To remove lines below your current location, select them with Shift+Ctrl+End first.

> **TIP**
>
> The Immediate window places a blank line after each result it prints. To make it easier to "replay" the evaluation of expressions that already appear in the Immediate window, be sure to add an extra blank line between your evaluation attempts. Then, when you move up to an existing expression and press ↵, the output won't overwrite the following expression.

Debugging with the Immediate Window

You can use the Immediate window to test the results of any Access Basic code you write. Formally, the Immediate window is named the Debug object from within Access Basic. As an object it's rather limited since its only method is the Print method. Using Debug.Print from Access Basic requests the Immediate window to print the value that follows the command. From within the Immediate window itself, you needn't specify the object since it's the current object and just the Print command will do.

> **TIP**
>
> Access Basic provides a shortcut for the Print method, as have most previous versions of Basic. When in the Immediate window, you can just use the ? symbol to replace the word "Print". All our examples use this shortcut.

Running Code from the Immediate Window

You can easily run any function or procedure that's in scope from the Immediate window. For example, if you enter this expression:

```
? MyFunction()
```

in the Immediate window, Access attempts to print out the return value from the function named MyFunction(), which it can do only by executing the function. To execute a subroutine, just call it directly from the Immediate window:

```
Call MySub
```

At any time you can also check the value of a variable by entering

```
? intSomeVariable
```

in the Immediate window.

Scoping rules apply as in normal Basic. That is, variables are available from the Immediate window only if they're currently in scope. You can tell what the current scope is by looking at the Immediate window's title bar. It always reflects what it sees as the current scope. If you're in the middle of debugging a particular procedure, that procedure's name appears in the title bar. If not, only the module's name appears. At any point, only variables and procedures that are available in the current scope are available to you in the Immediate window.

Creating New Code in the Immediate Window

You can also execute code while in the Immediate window. For example, you can set the value of the variable intMyVar by typing

```
intMyVar=5
```

in the Immediate window and pressing ↵. Of course, the variable must already be dimensioned elsewhere in your code and must be in scope at the time. This prevents you from assigning a value to a local variable unless you are halted at a breakpoint in its home procedure. You cannot enter a Dim statement (or any of its cousins, including ReDim, Global, and Const) in the Immediate window.

Any statement you enter for direct execution in the Immediate window must fit on a single line. You cannot, for example, enter a multi-line If...Then...Else for evaluation in the Immediate window, although you can execute a single-line If...Then statement. To get around this limitation, you can use the : (colon) character to separate multiple Access Basic statements on the same line.

For example, the following code could run a loop for you, given that you had previously defined the variable intCount somewhere in your code and that it was currently in scope:

```
For intCount = 0 To 10:Debug.Print intCount:Next intCount
```

Using the Immediate Window to Track Running Code

You can use the Immediate window as a way of tracking a running procedure. As mentioned earlier in this chapter, you can use the Print method of the Debug object (the Immediate window) to display any expression from within your running code. For example, running the function in Listing 15.3 (from basFibo in CH15.MDB) produces the output shown in Figure 15.5.

Listing 15.3

```
Function Fibo(intMembers As Integer)
    ' Print the requested number of elements of the
    ' standard Fibonacci series (s(n) = s(n-2) + s(n-1))
    ' to the Immediate Window.

    Dim intI As Integer
    Dim intCurrent As Integer
    Dim intPrevious As Integer
    Dim intTwoPrevious As Integer

    intPrevious = 1
    intTwoPrevious = 1

    Debug.Print intPrevious
    Debug.Print intTwoPrevious

    For intI = 3 To intMembers
        intCurrent = intPrevious + intTwoPrevious
        Debug.Print intCurrent
        intTwoPrevious = intPrevious
        intPrevious = intCurrent
    Next intI

End Function
```

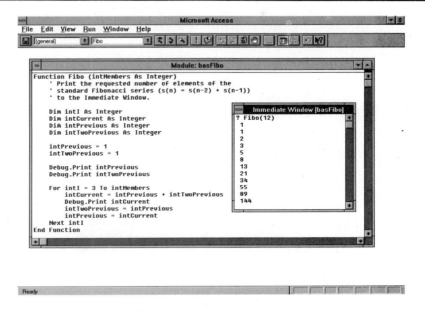

FIGURE 15.5:
Output from running Fibo()

Handling Remnant Debug Code

You can safely leave Debug.Print lines in your shipping code if you wish. As long as the user does not for some reason have a module open in Design view with the Immediate window displayed, these lines will have no visible effect and only a slight performance penalty. If you're concerned about even this slight performance degradation, and especially if you're using Debug.Print inside a loop, then by all means remove or comment out—by placing an apostrophe (') character at the beginning of the line—any Debug.Print statements before delivering your application.

Using Breakpoints

Using a breakpoint is the equivalent of putting a roadblock in your code. When you set a breakpoint, you tell Access to stop executing your code in a particular spot but to keep the system state in memory. This means that all the variables the function was dealing with are available for your inspection in the Immediate window.

Access provides a toolbar, with appropriate breakpoint buttons, to aid in your debugging efforts. Figure 15.6 shows the debugging toolbar, with each of the pertinent buttons labeled.

FIGURE 15.6:

Debugging toolbar

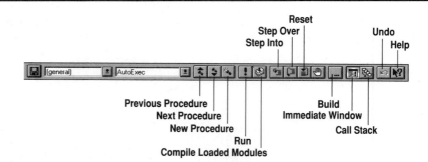

To set a breakpoint on a particular line of code, place your cursor anywhere on the line and do one of the following: click the Breakpoint button on the toolbar, choose Run ➤ Toggle Breakpoint, or press the F9 key. Access displays the chosen line in boldface type in the Module window. When you're executing code and you hit a breakpoint, the focus switches to the window with the breakpoint showing, and a dashed box surrounds the statement where execution is halted. Access suspends execution *before* it executes the particular statement. This way you can check or set the value of variables in your code before executing the chosen line of code.

Access does not save breakpoints with your code. If you close a module and reopen it, any breakpoints you have set in it vanish. If you need to preserve your breakpoints across sessions, you can use the Stop statement, which acts as a permanent breakpoint and is saved with your module. Just as with a breakpoint, Access pauses the execution of your code as soon as it encounters the Stop statement. Of course, you'll need to remove Stop statements from your code before you distribute your application since they will stop the execution of your running code in any environment.

You can also reset breakpoints manually with the Run ➤ Toggle Breakpoint command, the F9 key, or the Breakpoint button on the toolbar. You can also clear all breakpoints you have set with the Run ➤ Clear All Breakpoints item. This resets every breakpoint you have set, including those in global modules and those in CBF.

When Access halts your Access Basic code at a breakpoint, you may choose where to continue execution. Placing the insertion point on any statement in the procedure that is halted and choosing Run ➤ Set Next Statement causes execution to begin at that statement when you continue the function. You cannot skip to another procedure in this fashion, though. If you are wading through several open code windows, the Run ➤ Show Next Statement item brings you back to the one where execution is paused.

When done with a particular debugging session, you can click the Reset button from the toolbar or choose Run ➤ Reset. This halts the execution of all suspended procedures and reinitializes all variables. This clears the status of the currently running code so that there will no longer be a current line of code, there will be no current procedure, and all global variables will have been reset.

Step Into versus Step Over

When a breakpoint has halted the execution of your function, you can continue to execute it in "slow motion" in two different ways:

- Choosing Run ➤ Step Into, pressing the F8 key, or clicking the Step Into toolbar button causes your code to execute one statement at a time. If you're stepping through your code in this fashion and the current line of code is a call to a user-defined procedure, Access opens that procedure's code on screen, and debugging proceeds there.

- Choosing Run ➤ Step Over, pressing Shift+F8, or clicking the Step Over toolbar button also executes code one line at a time, but only within the context of the current procedure. Calls to other procedures are considered atomic by the Step Over action; it executes the entire procedure at once. This is especially useful if your code calls Access Basic code that you've previously debugged. Rather than taking the time to walk through the other procedures, which you're confident are in working order, you can use the Step Over functionality to execute them at full speed while you're debugging.

TIP

If you have more than one statement on a line in your code, stepping through the code executes each of them in turn. The dashed box outline moves along each statement as it is executed.

NOTE

Neither Step Over nor Step Into will continue execution into library code, whether it be Access code in an MDA library or other code in an external DLL.

Your Friend, the MsgBox() Function

As an alternative to setting breakpoints, you can use the MsgBox() function to indicate your program's state. With this strategy you decide what you would like to monitor and add calls to the MsgBox() function to return the particular information when you want to see it. You can enhance this technique by writing a wrapper for the MsgBox() function so that these messages are posted only when you have a global variable set to indicate that you want to see debugging messages. The sample function in Listing 15.4 uses the global constant glrSHOW_DEBUG for this purpose. This flag controls whether the glrDebugMessageBox() function should in fact interrupt execution of your code or whether it should just quietly return to the calling procedure. You'll find this function in basActivity in CH15.MDB. To use it in your own applications, import the module, and call glrDebugMessageBox() as described in the following paragraphs.

Listing 15.4

```
Function glrDebugMessageBox(ByVal varMessage As Variant,
➡ strCaller As String) As Integer

    On Error GoTo glrDebugMessageBox_Err

    glrDebugMessageBox = True
    If Not glrSHOW_DEBUG Then
```

```
        Exit Function
    End If

    glrDebugMessageBox = (MsgBox(CStr(varMessage),
➥ MB_OKCANCEL + MB_ICONQUESTION, "Debug: " &
➥ strCaller) = IDOK)

glrDebugMessageBox_Exit:
    Exit Function

glrDebugMessageBox_Err:
    MsgBox "Error " & Err & ": " & Error$, 16,
➥ "glrDebugMessageBox"
    Resume glrDebugMessageBox_Exit
End Function
```

You can sprinkle as many calls to glrDebugMessageBox() as you like into your code and make them all active or inactive at once by changing the value of the glrSHOW_DEBUG constant. Typically, you can use these message boxes to return news on the state of the program's execution. For example, here's a possible code fragment from your application's AutoExec() function (called from the Autoexec macro):

```
If Not glrDebugMessageBox("About to Start Logging",
➥ "AutoExec") Then
    Stop
End If

varRet = StartLogging()

If Not glrDebugMessageBox("StartLogging returned " & varRet,
➥ "AutoExec") Then
    Stop
End If
```

Each call to glrDebugMessageBox() first checks to see whether the global debugging constant glrSHOW_DEBUG is True. If not, it just returns True, and your code can just continue. If you are in debug mode instead, the function displays whatever you pass to it (see Figure 15.7).

If you click OK, the function returns a True value. If you click Cancel or press the Esc key, the function returns False, which in turn should halt your program execution back at the point where you called the glrDebugMessageBox() function.

FIGURE 15.7:

glrDebugMessageBox() displays anything you send it to aid in the debugging process.

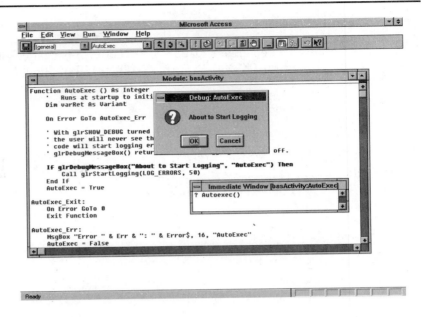

Techniques and Strategies for Debugging

The most common debugging strategy for beginning application developers is to have no strategy at all. Perhaps this occurs because so many developers these days started as users, became power users, and then started writing code without ever having had a structured introduction to a formal programming language.

You can start developing a strategy by understanding that bugs, despite the name, are not cute little things that scurry around in your code. Bugs are mistakes, pure and simple. And they're *your* mistakes; the program didn't put them there, and the end user didn't put them there. Removing these mistakes gives you an opportunity to become a better programmer.

Systematic Debugging

Systematic debugging is a matter of rigorously following five procedures:

- Gather data about the effects of the bug.
- Develop test cases to isolate the bug into a smaller section of your code.
- Confirm your diagnosis before you try to fix it.
- Change code only with a reason.
- Make only one change at a time.

As the first step in debugging you must identify the bug you're looking for. Often this is the 10 percent of the work that takes 90 percent of the time; once you've isolated a bug, fixing it is usually straightforward. How you go about identifying the bug depends on how you decide it's there. If you are getting an error message from your application, you need to consider all the possible sources of the messages. If you're getting vague feedback from your users, you need to step carefully with them through what they're doing until you actually see the failure yourself.

As you gather data about the nature of the bug, you'll be developing test cases that point to the specific actions that cause it to become obvious. If double-clicking in a particular combo box is the original suspect, you need to try the same action with a greater or lesser number of records available to the box, with different records showing on the underlying form, and so on. Perhaps it is just double-clicking in the combo box when on the new record and before the record is saved that causes your code to crash. Ideally, you want a set of actions that always reproduces the bug and another set just different enough that the bug doesn't show up.

Before you start fixing code, make sure you understand the nature of the problem. A common error occurs when you declare Access Basic variables to be of a specific simple datatype (Integer, Long, String, and so on) and, as part of your application, copy data from a table into these variables. In your own testing, everything works fine. At the client's site your client receives "Invalid Use of Null" messages all the time.

There are two solutions to this problem, and each requires some understanding of the particular application. Clearly, you cannot place null values into Integer, Long, or String variables, so you might consider changing them all to variants. On the other hand, perhaps the solution is to disallow null entries into those particular fields in the table. Your decision on the solution needs to take into account the particular situation.

It seems obvious that you should change code only with a reason, but surprisingly, many programmers ignore this principle. "Experience" often masquerades as a reason when it is really a synonym for "wild guess." Don't just change your loop from

```
For intI = 0 To intCount - 1
```

to

```
For intI = 1 To intCount
```

until and unless you can point to your code and show exactly where and how the off-by-one error is occurring. Take the time to thoroughly understand the bug before you try fixing it. Otherwise, you never know what you're fixing, and the bug will surely crop up somewhere else.

Finally, no matter how good you are and how sure you are of your work, make only one change to your code at a time, and then test it again. It's all too easy to fall into the trap of making multiple fixes without keeping records and then having to junk the current version and reload from a backup because you have no idea which things worked and which only made things worse. Take baby steps, and you'll get there faster.

There are two more bits of debugging strategy you might want to consider. Many programmers find "confessional debugging" to be one of the most useful techniques around. Confessional debugging works something like this: you grab your printouts and go into the next cubicle, interrupt the programmer working there, and say "Hey, sorry to bother you, but I've got this Access Basic function that keeps crashing. See, I pass in the name of a form here and then declare a form variable and then—oh, wait, that's not the form itself but the form's name. Never mind; thanks for your help." When you get good at it, you can indulge in this sort of debugging with non-programmers as the audience or even (in times of desperation) by talking things through with your dog or a sympathetic (but bored) loved one.

If all else seems to be failing, take a break. It's easy to get stuck in a mental loop in which you try the same things over and over, even though they haven't worked at all yet. Take a walk. Have lunch. Your mind's background processing can solve many bugs while the foreground processes are thinking about something else altogether. Many programmers have told stories of waking up in the middle of the night, having just dreamed about a bug they weren't even aware existed until then, along with its solution. Having written down the information during the night, they've gone into work, found the previously unspotted bug, and fixed it on the spot.

Creating and Maintaining Activity Logs

Even after you've sent your application off to the end users, it will likely still harbor a few bugs. Perhaps there are input conditions you forgot to test, or perhaps the clients forgot to tell you about a particular set of data they try to store. Sooner or later, though, you're likely to get a call from the client complaining about a program crash. Such calls tend to be frustrating. Rare indeed is the programmer who has never heard, "Oh, there was an error message, but I didn't write it down."

Fortunately, you can have Access write down the errors for you. It's fairly easy to have your application keep a log of errors and activity that you can inspect when you have the chance to go out on site and continue debugging. With the new capabilities of Access 2.0, you can get even fancier if the circumstances dictate. For example, if you are connected to your client by electronic mail, you can write a function that uses the SendObject action to automatically mail you the error log when it hits a certain number of entries.

The sample module basActivity (in CH15.MDB) contains basic error-logging functionality designed to meet several requirements:

- It stores only a limited number of errors to avoid grabbing huge chunks of your client's hard drive in case some error recurs frequently.
- It can be set to a variety of sensitivity levels.
- It stores as much information as possible about the state of your program when it is called.

The module basActivity starts off by declaring several module global variables:

```
'    0 = No logging
'    1 = Log only untrapped errors
'    2 = Log all errors
'    3 = Log all activity
```

```
Const LOG_NONE = 0
Const LOG_UNTRAPPED = 1
Const LOG_ERRORS = 2
Const LOG_ALL = 3

' mintDetail controls the level of logging
Dim mintDetail As Integer

' mintMaxLoggedErrors controls the number of log records to
' keep active
Dim mintMaxLoggedErrors As Integer
```

In the implementation in the sample code, these global variables are initialized in a simple subroutine meant to be called from your application's AutoExec() function. See Listing 15.5 for the code. You pass to this procedure the detail level to be logged (0 through 3) and the maximum number of rows to be maintained in the error log.

Listing 15.5

```
Sub glrStartLogging(pintDetailLevel As Integer,
➡ pintMaxErrors As Integer)

    ' Initialize the module variables used by the error
    ' logging routines.
    ' You must call this routine before using the logging
    ' functionality.
    '
    ' In:
    '       pintDetailLevel: the level for logging. One of 0,
    '       1, 2, 3, where -1 = Leave the value unchanged
    '         0 = No logging (LOG_NONE)
    '         1 = Log only untrapped errors (LOG_UNTRAPPED)
    '         2 = Log all errors (LOG_ERRORS)
    '         3 = Log all activity (LOG_ALL)
    '       pintMaxErrors: the number of errors to maintain in
    '       the log, or
    '                       -1 to leave the value unchanged.

    If pintDetailLevel >= 0 Then
        mintDetail = pintDetailLevel
    End If
```

```
    If pintMaxErrors >= 0 Then
        mintMaxLoggedErrors = pintMaxErrors
    End If
End Sub
```

The actual work of logging errors and activity is done in a second function, glrLog-Error() (see Listing 15.6), which can be called in a variety of ways. glrLogError() takes three parameters:

- **intErrorNumber:** The Err value from the calling function, or 0 if there was no error
- **strCalledFrom:** The name of the calling procedure or form
- **fTrapped:** True if the error was explicitly trapped, False if it was unexpected

To log errors in your applications, first import zstblActivity from CH15.MDB, and then call glrLogError() from any place you'd like to log the current activity. It will write an entry to zstblActivity each time you call it.

With these choices for calling glrLogError(), you can use it for tracking many things. For example, if you'd like to monitor the way in which your users interact with your application, you can add a standard call to the Open event procedure of each form you design:

```
varRet = glrLogError(0, Me.Name, True)
```

and set the mintDetail variable to LOG_ALL. This gives you a running log of exactly which forms are opened in sequence.

You can also track errors in your functions and even adjust the level of tracking, depending on the circumstances. For example, you might ordinarily keep a log of only severe errors by setting mintDetail to LOG_UNTRAPPED, but when such an error occurs adjust the logging level so that you track all activity and so get more context if the error continues to happen:

```
ApplyColors_Err:
    If Err = ERR_INVALID_SECTION Then
        varRet = glrLogError(Err, "ApplyColors", True)
        Resume Next
    Else
        Call glrStartLogging(LOG_ALL, -1)
        varRet = glrLogError(Err, "ApplyColors", False)
```

```
        Resume ApplyColors_Exit
    End If
End Function
```

Listing 15.6

```
Const MB_ICONSTOP = 16
Const ERROR_TABLE = "zstblActivity"

Function glrLogError(intErrorNumber As Integer,
➥ strCalledFrom As String, fTrapped As Integer) As Integer

    ' Log an error or activity to the ERROR_TABLE table

    On Error GoTo glrLogError_Err

' Error levels for tracking in the table:
'    0 for non-error activity
'    1 for expected errors
'    2 for unexpected errors
Const ERRLEVEL_NONE = 0
Const ERRLEVEL_EXPECTED = 1
Const ERRLEVEL_UNEXPECTED = 2

    Dim db As Database
    Dim rst As Recordset
    Dim intErrLevel As Integer

    ' Check to see whether logging is turned on at all, and
    ' if so whether the current situation is severe enough
    ' to log
    If intErrorNumber = 0 Then
        intErrLevel = ERRLEVEL_NONE
    Else
        intErrLevel = IIf(fTrapped, ERRLEVEL_EXPECTED,
        ➥ ERRLEVEL_UNEXPECTED)
    End If
    Select Case mintDetail
        Case LOG_NONE            ' No logging
            GoTo glrLogError_Exit

        Case LOG_UNTRAPPED       ' Untrapped errors only
            If intErrLevel = ERRLEVEL_NONE Or fTrapped Then
                GoTo glrLogError_Exit
            End If
```

```
      Case LOG_ERRORS         ' All errors
          If intErrLevel = ERRLEVEL_NONE Then
              GoTo glrLogError_Exit
          End If

      Case Else       ' All activity
          ' Don't do anything special.
End Select

' If you get this far, then log the error.
Set db = DBEngine.Workspaces(0).Databases(0)
Set rst = db.OpenRecordset("SELECT * FROM " &
➡ ERROR_TABLE & " ORDER BY [Date];", DB_OPEN_DYNASET)

rst.AddNew
    rst![Level] = intErrLevel
    rst![User] = CurrentUser()
    rst![Date] = Now

    ' Ignore any errors generated by lack of active objects
    On Error Resume Next
    rst![ActiveForm] = Screen.ActiveForm.Name
    rst![ActiveReport] = Screen.ActiveReport.Name
    rst![ActiveControl] = Screen.ActiveControl.Name
    On Error GoTo glrLogError_Err

    rst![Procedure] = strCalledFrom
    rst![ErrorCode] = intErrorNumber
    If intErrLevel > ERRLEVEL_NONE Then
        rst![ErrorText] = Error$(intErrorNumber)
    End If
    If glrSHOW_DEBUG And intErrLevel > ERRLEVEL_NONE Then
        rst![Explanation] = InputBox$("An Error has been
        ➡ detected.  Please describe your current activity
        ➡ below.", "Error Logging")
    End If
rst.Update

' Discard oldest record if the table is full
rst.MoveLast
If rst.Recordcount >= mintMaxLoggedErrors Then
    rst.MoveFirst
    rst.Delete
End If
```

```
    rst.Close
    glrLogError = True

glrLogError_Exit:
    Exit Function

glrLogError_Err:
    ' If you ever hit this point, do NOT log the error
    ' to avoid endless recursion.
    MsgBox "Error " & Err & ": " & Error$, MB_ICONSTOP,
    ➥ "glrLogError"
    glrLogError = False
    Resume glrLogError_Exit
End Function
```

Debugging Difficulties

As you debug, you'll come across some particular problems you'll need to watch out for. Most of them equate to the software version of the Heisenberg Uncertainty Principle: Stopping code to investigate it can change the state of your program, either introducing spurious bugs or (perhaps worse) hiding actual bugs. Unfortunately, there isn't much you can do about most of these problems other than know that they exist.

Resetting the Stopped State

If you set up a function to present a particular environment to the user and then stop it midstream, the application often won't be in the proper environment for you to proceed with your debugging. For example, you may have left screen echo off, warnings off, or the hourglass cursor on. You may also be shipping code with the toolbars turned off and yet want them handy when you're debugging things. The simplest solution to this problem is to have a utility function available, either in your production database or loaded in a library, to reset the environment to a more hospitable state. Listing 15.7 shows a function (from basCleanUp in CH15.MDB) you could possibly attach to a keystroke, using an Autokeys macro that will reset most of your environment. Once you've assigned this function to a keystroke, it's just a simple matter of pressing one key combination whenever you stop the code and can't quite see what you're doing.

Listing 15.7

```
Function glrCleanUp()

    ' Return the application to normal programming mode.
    ' Reinstate screen updating,
    ' reset the cursor to its normal state, and reset warnings.

Const MB_ICONSTOP = 16

    On Error GoTo glrCleanUp_Err

    Application.Echo True
    DoCmd Hourglass False
    DoCmd SetWarnings True
    Application.SetOption "Built-In Toolbars Available", True

glrCleanUp_Exit:
    On Error GoTo 0
    Exit Function

glrCleanUp_Err:
    MsgBox "Error " & Err & ": " & Error$, MB_ICONSTOP,
    ➡ "glrCleanUp"
    Resume glrCleanUp_Exit
End Function
```

Handling Modal Forms

If you have a modal form on screen when an error occurs in your code, that's too bad; the focus will stay with the form. You'll have to close the form before you can check the error, which of course introduces many chances for the state of the system to change. For example, any event procedure tied to the OnClose property of the modal form will immediately be activated, possibly removing the very values that are causing the problem. If the form was modal just to control the user's actions, you can temporarily make it a normal form, but if it was modal to stop code from executing, there's nothing you can do about it. In that case you need to rely on MsgBox() calls to track down errors (perhaps using the glrDebugMessageBox() function).

Avoiding Screen.ActiveForm and Screen.ActiveControl if Possible

Code that refers to Screen.ActiveForm or Screen.ActiveControl won't work properly when called from the Immediate window. When the Immediate window has the focus there is no active form or active control. Any attempt to access Screen.ActiveForm or Screen.ActiveControl from your code while debugging will result in an error. In event procedures you can work around this limitation by using the Me object instead of Screen.ActiveForm.

Problems with Focus Events

If you are debugging forms that have event procedures tied to their GotFocus or LostFocus event, those events will be triggered as you move away from the form to the Immediate window and back. If you are trying to debug such events, or other low-level events such as KeyDown or MouseMove, you can't use any of the standard debugging tools. Instead, think about sprinkling glrDebugMessageBox() calls into your code or even having the function dump status information continuously into a table for later inspection.

Summary

If you are serious about Access application development, you're going to write code, and if you write code, you're going to have to debug code. It makes sense to do whatever you can to make this process easier and faster. As you write code, you should always strive consciously to write robust and easily maintainable code:

- Plan your code in advance.
- Don't get too "clever."
- Structure and comment your code.
- Use indentation and naming conventions.
- Modularize your code.
- Use Option Explicit.
- Minimize your use of variants.

- Use the tightest scoping possible.

When bug avoidance fails, make sure you use a systematic and structured approach to bug removal:

- Gather data about the effects of the bug.
- Develop test cases to isolate the bug into a smaller section of your code.
- Confirm your diagnosis before you try to fix it.
- Change code only with a reason.
- Make only one change at a time.

The temptation is always present to attempt a quick-and-dirty fix rather than plod along with the systematic approach. Don't let yourself fall prey to this temptation. It usually wastes much more time than it saves, muddying the waters before it forces you back to the approach outlined in this chapter.

CHAPTER

SIXTEEN

The Jet Engine and Application Optimization

- How the Jet engine processes and optimizes queries

- How to make your applications run more quickly

- How to take advantage of Rushmore to make your queries fly

The Jet database engine (or simply Jet) handles all the database processing for Access (and Visual Basic). Jet is an advanced relational database engine. Figure 16.1 shows how Jet fits into the Access architecture.

FIGURE 16.1:

Access and Jet

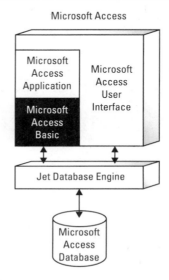

What Is a Database Engine?

Database management systems (DBMS) are programs that manage data. DBMS programs consist of many components, not the least of which are the user interface and the database engine. The user interface handles all the interactions between the user and the DBMS program, including data viewing and editing through forms, reports, and so forth. The database engine, on the other hand, is the part that links the DBMS program and the data.

Some DBMS programs have simple database engines that are nothing more than routines for reading and writing records of data. These DBMS programs lack support for security, referential integrity, transaction processing, remote data, and other advanced features that more modern engines provide.

Advanced database engines supply most or all of these critical features, as well as providing a single entry point for all users of a database. This ensures that all users—even if the user is another program—are using the data stored in the database in a manner consistent with the rules of the business. The advanced database engine built into Access—the Jet database engine—offers all these features.

The Jet Engine Architecture

The Jet engine is composed of a series of Dynamic Link Libraries (DLLs). These DLLs can be thought of as distinct but interconnected programs, all working together under the "hood" of the Jet engine. They are the

- Jet DLL
- Data Access Objects DLL
- External ISAM DLLs
- ODBC Driver Manager DLL

Figure 16.2 shows how these components interrelate.

The Jet DLL

The Jet DLL (MSAJT200.DLL) is the main Jet engine program, which evaluates and executes requests for data. If the request is for native Jet data—data stored in the Access Database (.MDB) format—the Jet DLL also handles reading and writing

FIGURE 16.2:

Microsoft Jet database engine architecture

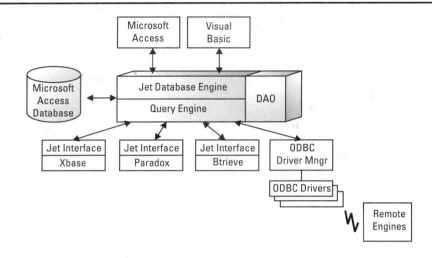

the data. If, on the other hand, the request involves non-native data, the Jet DLL makes calls to either the ODBC Driver Manager DLL or one of the external ISAM DLLs.

The Data Access Objects DLL

The Data Access Objects DLL (DAO2016.DLL) is the Jet component that provides the programmer interface to the Jet engine. Data access objects (DAO) are the part of Access Basic (and Visual Basic) that you use to programmatically manipulate Jet data. Future versions of Microsoft's Visual C++ and Visual Basic for Applications (VBA) are also likely to include support for this data-manipulation language. DAO is discussed in detail in Chapter 6.

External ISAM DLLs

Jet provides access to several external Indexed Sequential Access Method (ISAM) format files using a series of installable .DLL files. The Jet engine supports three external ISAM formats: Xbase (XBS200.DLL), Paradox (PDX200.DLL), and Btrieve

(BTRV200.DLL). These DLLs handle the reading and writing of data stored in multiple versions of dBASE, FoxPro, Paradox, and Btrieve file formats.

> **NOTE** Indexed Sequential Access Method (ISAM) is a physical method for storing data in a database. The term is also commonly used to refer to non-server databases.

The ODBC Driver Manager DLL

The Open Database Connectivity (ODBC) standard is a Microsoft-sponsored industry standard for accessing client-server data. When Jet needs to access data stored in an ODBC-supported data source, such as Microsoft/Sybase SQL Server or Oracle, it calls the ODBC Driver Manager (ODBC.DLL). The Driver Manager—which technically is not part of Jet—then calls the host database program using the appropriate ODBC driver.

You can also gain access to Jet (Access) databases using the *Access* ODBC driver. This allows users to get at Jet data from Microsoft Word for Windows, Excel, and other ODBC-compliant clients. ODBC is discussed in detail in Chapter 12.

> **NOTE** The Microsoft Access 2.0 ODBC driver that ships with Access (ODBCJT16.DLL) is a temporary driver limited to working only with other Microsoft Office products. At the time of this writing, Microsoft had announced that it was working on a more full-featured, robust Jet driver that would provide both 16- and 32-bit ODBC access to native Jet (Access) data, as well as non-native ISAM file formats supported by Jet.

The Jet Expression Evaluator

Jet has its own expression evaluator, separate from Access Basic's, that is used to evaluate expressions such as "(intValue1 + 2) > intValue2". Having two different expression evaluators in Access has subtle repercussions because they work slightly differently. The Jet expression evaluator is used in WHERE clauses (criteria) in queries and validation rules. The Access Basic expression evaluator is used in all Access Basic code, including user-defined functions called from a query's WHERE clause.

One difference between the two expression evaluators is that the Access Basic expression evaluator treats logical operators, such as And, on a bit level, whereas the Jet expression evaluator operates on an integer level. Thus "1 And 2" evaluates to False in Access Basic (since the binary representations of 1 and 2 have no bits in common) but to True in Jet (since they're both True expressions, as far as Jet is concerned; remember, any non-zero quantity is treated as True). For example, suppose you have a query like the following, which is attempting to return only rows in which the value in intColumn1 is odd. (Odd numbers all have their least-significant bit set.)

```
SELECT tblTable1.intColumn1
FROM tblTable1
WHERE (tblTable1.intColumn1 And 1);
```

The result will not be what you might expect. Jet's expression evaluator operates on integers instead of bits; the 1 is treated as the value True. Since any value Anded with True returns the truth value of the original value, the "And 1" becomes superfluous in this case. The WHERE clause always evaluates to True unless intColumn1 contains 0. Thus, the query returns the records in which intColumn1 contains non-zero numbers.

In contrast, suppose you rewrote the query so it looked like this:

```
SELECT tblTable1.intColumn1
FROM tblTable1
WHERE PerformAnd(tblTable1.intColumn1, 1);
```

using the function PerformAnd(), which looked like this:

```
Function PerformAnd(intValue1 As Integer, intValue2 As Integer)
➡ As Integer
    PerformAnd = intValue1 And intValue2
End Function
```

Since Access Basic performs logical operations on a bit level, the function returns True only if the low-order bit is 1. Only odd numbers have the low-order bit set to 1, so the query returns the rows in which intColumn1 contains odd numbers. Therefore, this version of the query will satisfy your original goal of showing rows in which intColumn1 contains odd values.

These differences do not show up often, but you should be aware of them.

The Jet Query Engine

The Jet query engine is responsible for the interpretation and execution of queries. Jet processes queries in four steps:

1. Definition
2. Compilation
3. Optimization
4. Execution

This process is shown in Figure 16.3.

Query Definition

You can define queries using one of several mechanisms: QBE, SQL, or DAO. Whichever method you use to create the query definition, the query eventually gets converted to SQL, and it is passed to the Jet query optimizer, which then compiles and optimizes the query.

FIGURE 16.3:

The Jet query engine compiles, optimizes, and executes a query definition to produce a recordset.

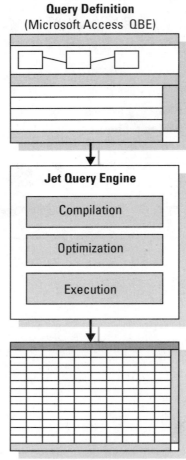

Query Definition
(Microsoft Access QBE)

Jet Query Engine

Compilation

Optimization

Execution

Query Result Set
(Microsoft Access Datasheet)

Query Compilation

Before Jet can optimize a query, it must parse the SQL statement that defines the query and bind the names referenced in the query to columns in the underlying tables. The Jet query engine compiles the SQL string into an internal query object definition format, replacing common parts of the query string with tokens. The internal format can be likened to an inverted tree: the query's result set sits at the top of the tree (the tree's root) and the base tables are at the bottom (the leaves). The query compilation step is depicted in Figure 16.4.

FIGURE 16.4:

During query compilation, Jet parses the SQL and compiles it into a query tree.

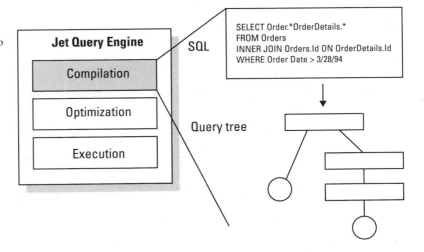

Query definitions are parsed into distinct elements when compiled. These elements include the

- Base tables
- Output columns (the columns that will appear in the query's result set)
- Restrictions (in QBE, the criteria; in SQL, WHERE clause elements)
- Join columns (in QBE, the lines connecting two tables; in SQL, the columns in the JOIN clause)

- Sort columns (in QBE, sort columns; in SQL, the columns in the ORDER BY clause)

Each of these elements comes into play as the query optimizer considers different execution strategies, as described in the following sections.

Query Optimization

The query optimizer is the most complex component of Jet. It's responsible for choosing the optimum query execution strategy for the compiled query tree. The Jet query engine uses a cost-based algorithm, costing and comparing each potential execution strategy and choosing the one that's fastest. Jet calculates the cost for two major operations in the execution of queries: base table accesses and joins.

Base Table Access Plans

For each table in the query, the Jet query optimizer must choose a base table access plan. The three ways of accessing the rows in a table are

- **Table scan:** Scanning a table record by record without use of an index. This may be necessary if a restriction column is not indexed or if the restriction is not very selective (a large percentage of the base table rows are being requested). Each data page is read only once for a table scan.

- **Index range:** Reading records in a table using an index over one of the single-table restrictions (query criteria). A data page may be read more than once for an index range.

- **Rushmore restriction:** A Rushmore restriction is used when there are restrictions on multiple indexed columns. By using multiple indexes, Jet is able to reduce considerably the number of data pages it needs to read. In many cases Rushmore queries can be executed by Jet without its reading any data pages. (Of course, Jet still has to read index pages, but reading index pages only is almost always more efficient.)

Rushmore Query Optimizations

Jet 2.0 includes support for Rushmore query optimizations. In Jet 1.x, Jet could use only one index for a base table access. Using techniques borrowed from FoxPro, Jet 2.0 can now use more than one index to restrict records. Rushmore-based query optimization is used on queries involving restrictions on multiple indexed columns of the following types:

- **Index Intersection:** The two indexes are intersected with And. Used on restrictions of the form

    " WHERE Company = 'Ford' And CarType = 'Sedan' "

- **Index Union:** The two indexes are unioned with Or. Used on restrictions of the form

    " WHERE CarType = 'Wagon' Or Year = '1994' "

- **Index Counts:** Queries that return record counts only. Used for queries of the form

    " SELECT Count(*) FROM Autos WHERE Company = 'Dodge' And

    ➡ CarType='Truck'; "

You can execute many queries much more quickly using the Rushmore query optimizer. Rushmore can't work, however, if you don't build multiple indexes for each table.

Rushmore Benchmarks

To give you an idea of what Rushmore means, we ran some informal benchmarks. We created several single-table queries from a randomly populated 61,000-record table that references two relatively unselective, non-unique, indexed columns: Quantity and Item. Table 16.1 summarizes the results that compared version 1.1 (without Rushmore) to version 2.0 (with Rushmore):

TABLE 16.1: Results Comparing Version 1.1 (without Rushmore) to Version 2.0 (with Rushmore)

Restrictions	Returned Records	Version 1.1 Time (secs)	Version 2.0 Time (secs)	Ratio of times (2.0 / 1.1)
SELECT *...WHERE Quantity = 13	5	1.4	0.4	3.5
SELECT *...WHERE Quantity = 13 And Item = 2	3	8.1	0.6	13.5

TABLE 16.1: Results Comparing Version 1.1 (without Rushmore) to Version 2.0 (with Rushmore) (continued)

Restrictions	Returned Records	Version 1.1 Time (secs)	Version 2.0 Time (secs)	Ratio of times (2.0 / 1.1)
SELECT *...WHERE Quantity = 13 Or Item = 25	11	33.1	0.4	82.8
SELECT Count(*)...WHERE Quantity = 5 And Item = 10	293	8.8	0.8	11.0

Most strikingly, index union queries (SELECT *...WHERE Quantity = 13 Or Item = 25) appear to receive the biggest performance gain in version 2.0, running in the benchmarks over 80 times more quickly than the equivalent version 1.1 queries. Even the single-restriction query that should not have benefited from Rushmore optimization (SELECT *...WHERE Quantity = 13) ran more quickly in 2.0, pointing to non-Rushmore improvements in the query optimizer.

NOTE These informal benchmarks don't cover all possible query scenarios. Queries involving multiple tables, queries with more selective indexes or GROUP BY clauses, and queries returning a different percentage of records will achieve different performance ratios.

Join Strategies

For queries involving more than one table, the optimizer must consider the cost of joins, choosing from the following five join types:

- Nested iteration join
- Index join
- Lookup join
- Merge join
- Index-merge join

The Jet query optimizer uses statistics about the tables in the query (discussed in the next section) to determine which join strategy to use. Each possible join combination is considered to determine which will yield the least costly query execution plan. The five join strategies are contrasted in Table 16.2.

TABLE 16.2: Contrasting Jet Join Strategies

Join Strategy	Description	When Used
Nested iteration join	"Brute-force" iteration through the rows in both tables	Only as a last-ditch effort. May be used when there are few records or no indexes
Index join	Scans rows in the first table and looks up matching rows in the second table using an index	When the rows in the second table are small (or no data needs to be retrieved from this table) or when the rows in the first table are small or highly restrictive
Lookup join	Similar to the index join except that a projection and sort on the second table are done prior to the join	When rows in the second table are small but not indexed by the join column
Merge join	Sorts rows in the two tables by the join columns and combines the two tables by scanning down both tables simultaneously	When the two tables are large and the result set needs to be ordered on the join column
Index-merge join	Similar to a merge join, except that indexes are used to order the two tables	Instead of a merge join when each input is a table in native Jet database format. Each input must have an index over its join column, and at least one of the indexes must not allow nulls if there is more than one join column

Query Statistics

When evaluating various base table access plans and join strategies, the Jet query optimizer looks at the following statistics for each base table:

- Number of records in the base table.

- Number of data pages occupied by the base table. The more data pages need to be read, the more costly the query.

- Location of the table. Is the table in a local ISAM format or is it from an ODBC database?

- Indexes on the table. When looking at indexes, the optimizer is concerned with

  - **Selectivity:** How "unique" is the index? Does the index allow for duplicates? A unique index is the most highly selective index available since every value is distinct.

  - **Number of index pages:** As with data pages, the more index pages, the more costly the query.

  - **Whether nulls are allowed in the index:** Nulls in an index may rule out the usage of an index-merge join (see the preceding section).

Putting It All Together

In determining the optimum query execution plan, the Jet query optimizer iterates through the various combinations of base table access plans and join strategies. Before choosing a join strategy, the optimizer selects a base table access plan. The optimizer then stores the estimated number of records returned and a cost indicating how expensive it would be to read the table. Next, the optimizer generates all combinations of pairs of tables and costs each join strategy. Finally, the optimizer adds tables to the joins and continues to calculate statistics until it finds the cheapest overall execution plan.

The query optimizer also considers the type of result set when costing various join strategies. When returning a dynaset (as opposed to a snapshot), Jet often favors join strategies that are efficient at returning the first page of records quickly, even if the chosen execution strategy is slower at returning the complete result set. For dynasets, this tends to rule out joins that require sorting, such as lookup joins and merge joins.

For queries based on many tables, the time spent estimating the cost of all potential join combinations could easily exceed the time spent executing any given execution strategy. Because of this, the query optimizer reduces the potential number of joins it needs to consider by using the following rule: Consider joining only the results of a join to a base table. The query optimizer will never consider joining the results of one join to the results of another. This considerably reduces the potential number of joins Jet needs to look at. The optimization steps are depicted in Figure 16.5.

After a query has been compiled and optimized by the Jet query optimizer, two additional steps are taken prior to the execution of the query.

For queries involving ODBC data sources, the remote post-processor determines how much of a query can be sent to the back end for processing by the database server application. The goal here is to send as much of the query as possible to the server, taking advantage of the server's abilities in executing queries involving server tables. This reduces the number of records that need be sent across the network wire to Jet. The remote post processor identifies those parts of the query tree that can be satisfied by server queries and generates the server SQL strings for each remote query. (This partitioning of ODBC queries is discussed in more detail in Chapter 12.)

FIGURE 16.5:
The query optimizer determines the cost of various execution plans and chooses the best (the least costly plan as measured by estimated execution time).

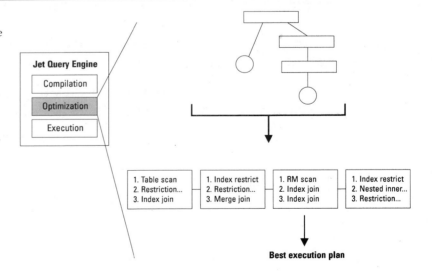

Finally, the post processor takes the compiled query tree and moves it to a new, cleaner, and smaller execution segment. This is the final step prior to query execution.

Query Execution

Once the optimizer has determined the optimum query execution plan, the query engine runs through the final query tree and executes each step to return the recordset.

You can direct Jet to create dynasets or snapshots. When Jet runs a dynaset-based query, it creates a set of unique key values (sometimes called a *keyset*) in memory that points back to the rows in the underlying tables. This keyset-driven cursor model is very efficient since Jet needs to read only these key values and store them in memory (overflowing to disk if necessary). The values of the other columns in the dynaset aren't read until needed (such as when a user scrolls the datasheet to that screen of dynaset rows), minimizing the time needed to execute the query.

For snapshot-based queries, Jet must run the query to completion and extract all the query's columns into the snapshot. When the query contains many columns, it's likely that Jet won't be able to fit the entire snapshot into memory, requiring Jet to overflow the result set to disk, substantially slowing the query. Since Jet reads only the key values of dynasets into memory, the same dynaset-based query might fit entirely in memory, resulting in a significant performance boost.

Forcing Jet to Recompile and Optimize a Query

Queries are compiled and optimized the first time you run a query. They are not recompiled until you resave and rerun the query. Make sure you run all queries at least once before delivering an application to users. This will eliminate subsequent compilations. Don't save the query after running it, or it may be saved in an uncompiled state.

Since Jet makes optimization decisions based on the size of source tables when you compiled the query, it's a good idea to force Jet to recompile a query after you've altered indexes or significantly changed the schema or number of rows in the tables.

Taking Advantage of Rushmore

There is no way to turn Rushmore on or off. Jet takes advantage of Rushmore optimizations anytime you have criteria that reference multiple indexed columns from the same table. If you have queries that *don't* include multiple restrictions or that contain restrictions on columns for which you haven't created indexes, Rushmore won't be used. Thus, it's important to create indexes on all columns that are used in query restrictions.

> **NOTE**   You won't notice much difference in execution speed between versions 1.1 and 2.0 for queries with single-column restrictions or no restrictions.

Rushmore works for both native and attached Access tables, as well as for attached FoxPro and dBASE tables. Queries involving ODBC, Btrieve, or Paradox tables do not benefit from Rushmore.

Keeping Statistics Accurate

The costing algorithms the query optimizer uses are dependent on the accuracy of the statistics provided by the underlying engine. Statistics for non-native tables will, in general, be less accurate than for native Access tables. For ODBC queries in which the whole query is sent to the server for processing, however, this is irrelevant since the server will be optimizing and executing the entire query.

For native Access tables, statistics may be inaccurate if many transactions are rolled back. Statistics can also be wrong if Jet (or the database application calling Jet) terminates abnormally without being able to update statistics to disk.

> **TIP**
>
> To force Jet to update the statistics in a Jet database, you should regularly compact the database. Compacting the database may also speed up queries because it writes all the data in a table to contiguous pages. This makes scanning sequential pages much faster than when the database is fragmented. Before compacting a database, you should also run a disk defrag utility so that Jet can store the newly compacted database in contiguous space on the disk.

Tuning Your Application's Performance

The faster your application and each of its components perform, the more usable it will be. No user (or developer) likes a slow application. But getting extra performance sometimes requires you to make trade-offs and may affect other aspects of the application's usability, stability, and maintainability. Thus, it's important to keep these other issues in mind as you tune your applications for speed.

Some of the many aspects of performance tuning are outlined here:

- Hardware and memory
- DOS and Windows configuration
- Access configuration
- Database design
- Query design
- Forms design
- Reports design
- Single-user versus multiuser, file-server versus client-server application design
- Access Basic coding

To create applications that perform well you will have to address many if not all of these areas. Depending on the design of your application, some issues will be less important than others. For example, an application that has only one or two simple reports may not need much attention paid to this component. On the other hand, the same application may need a lot of attention paid in the areas of query and form tuning. The remainder of this chapter addresses performance tuning, looking at each of the areas listed above.

NOTE   Although some limited multiuser and client-server performance tips are given in this chapter, additional performance suggestions can be found in Chapters 11 and 12.

Speeding Up Access

Access is a complex piece of software made up of many components running on top of another complex piece of software—Windows. But it's even more complicated than that since Windows is really a whole family of operating systems: Windows, Windows for Workgroups, and Windows NT. Hardware, of course, will also have a major impact on the speed of Windows.

Hardware and Windows Issues

Like most Windows-based programs, Access runs more quickly on a faster machine. Microsoft recommends at a minimum a 386SX-based PC with at least 6MB of RAM. This is really the *barest* of minimums, and you and your users will likely be dissatisfied with workstations of this nature. More realistically, the target machine should have

- At least a fast 386DX-based processor
- 8MB or more of RAM
- VGA or better video resolution
- A 60MB or larger hard drive with 20ms or faster access time

If you have to decide whether to get more RAM or a faster processor, we suggest you choose more RAM. For example, a 25MHz 486-based PC with 12MB of RAM will likely execute your applications more quickly than a 33MHz 486-based PC with 8MB of RAM.

For all installations you should consider doing the following:

- Create a permanent Windows swap file on a noncompressed disk partition.
- If using Windows for Workgroups, enable 32-bit disk access if you have a hard disk controller that supports 32-bit disk access.
- If you can use Windows for Workgroups' 32-bit disk access, use its 32-bit file access cache *instead* of SmartDrive. Remove SmartDrive since it isn't needed and will just waste memory when using the 32-bit file access cache.
- Eliminate RAM drives. The memory devoted to RAM drives is usually better spent elsewhere.
- Eliminate disk-compression software, or at least consider placing your databases on noncompressed partitions. Access databases perform significantly more slowly on compressed partitions.
- Use a defrag utility regularly on your hard disks.

Configuring Low-Memory Machines

The more RAM you can free up for Access and your application, the better. This means that when you are working with less than about 12MB of RAM, you should consider some or all of the following:

- Reduce the number of DOS terminate-and-stay resident (TSR) utilities you load.
- Eliminate wallpaper.
- Eliminate screen savers, especially elaborate ones.
- Don't use SmartDrive's double buffering unless it's needed. (See your DOS manual for more details.)
- Reduce the size of your disk cache.

- Eliminate unneeded Windows applets, calendars, and memory-hungry utilities.
- Shut down your e-mail application during Access sessions.

Some of these recommendations are even helpful if you think you have plenty of RAM, especially if you plan to use DDE or OLE with other applications.

Here are our recommendations for the amount of RAM to devote to a SmartDrive (or a similar disk-cache program) cache when using Access in various configurations:

System RAM	Amount to Devote to a Disk Cache
< 8MB	0–128K
8–12MB	128K–256K
13MB–15MB	512K–1MB
16MB–32MB	1MB–4MB

We recommend disabling delayed-write (also termed write-behind or lazy-write) caches on the disk that holds your .MDB databases, especially in a multiuser environment. Any extra performance you get using a delayed-write cache is overshadowed by the increased danger of a power failure's corrupting your database.

Anything else you can do to increase the amount of available memory, reduce the amount of system resources used, or increase the performance of Windows will likely result in a speedup of your Access applications.

Configuring Access

You can adjust several global Access settings to improve application performance. Our recommendations include the following:

- Don't install unnecessary add-ins. Use the File ➤ Add-Ins ➤ Add-In Manager to review and remove installed add-ins. This frees up memory that would otherwise be occupied.
- Remove Access' built-in Wizards, especially if users will never be creating objects outside the confines of your application. This frees up memory for your applications.

- Regularly compact your database. This efficiently arranges the data in the .MDB file. Run a hard disk defrag utility before compacting. This ensures that your .MDB file is stored on disk in one contiguous file rather than a series of file fragments (which makes database operations less efficient).

- If an application is being used in single-user mode only, open it exclusively.

You can adjust two settings in the [ISAM] section of MSACC20.INI to improve performance: MaxBufferSize and ReadAheadPages. You can adjust MaxBufferSize to control the size of the internal cache that Jet maintains for reading records. Unless you have a large amount of RAM (24MB or more), it's better to take away memory from any generic disk caches (such as SmartDrive) and allocate it instead to *Jet's* cache since for data operations, Jet's internal cache will be "smarter" than any generic cache. You can also adjust the number of pages of records that Jet reads ahead when sequentially reading through a table. The default and range of settings are summarized in the following table:

Setting	Default	Range
MaxBufferSize	512	18–4096
ReadAheadPages	16	0–31

In low-memory situations, you may wish to reduce the default settings. In high-memory situations, increase these settings.

Speeding Up Queries

With Jet's sophisticated query optimizer, discussed earlier in the chapter, you don't have to be concerned about the order of columns and tables in queries. The Jet query optimizer decides on the most efficient query strategy and reorders the query's tables and columns to best optimize the query. You can, however, help the optimizer by following these simple guidelines:

- Create indexes on all columns used in query joins, restrictions, and sorts.

- Use primary keys instead of unique indexes whenever possible. Primary key indexes disallow nulls, giving the Jet query optimizer additional join choices.

- Use unique indexes instead of non-unique indexes whenever possible. Jet can then better optimize queries because statistics on unique indexes are more accurate.

- Include as few columns as needed in the result set. The fewer columns returned, the faster the query, especially if you can completely eliminate columns from a table that is necessary only for restricting records.

- Refrain from using complex expressions, such as those involving the IIf() function, in queries. If using nested queries (queries based on the results of other queries), try to move up any expressions to the highest (last) query.

- Use Count(*) instead of Count([*column*]). Jet has built-in optimizations that make Count(*) much faster than column-based counts.

- Use the Between operator in restriction clauses rather than open-ended >, >=, <, and <= restrictions. This returns fewer rows. For example, use "Age Between 35 and 50" rather than "Age >= 35".

- When creating restrictions on join columns that are present in both tables in a one-to-many join, it is sometimes more efficient to place the restriction on the "one" side of the join. Other times it might be more efficient to place the restriction on the "many" side. You'll have to test which is more efficient for each query since the ratio of the sizes of the tables and the number and type of restrictions used determine which is more efficient.

- Normalize your tables, decomposing large non-normalized tables into smaller normalized ones. Since this reduces the size of tables (and therefore the number of pages required to hold tables), it causes join strategies that involve table scans to execute more quickly.

- In some instances, it might also help to *denormalize* databases to reduce the number of joins needed to run frequently used queries. (See Chapter 2 for additional design details.)

When in doubt, experiment! Don't assume one way to do it is faster just because it *should* be.

Avoiding "Query Too Complex" Errors

When compiling queries, the Jet query engine must fit the entire compiled query into a single 64K segment because of the 16-bit architecture of Jet. Because of this segment size limitation, Jet may be unable to compile certain very large queries. The most common manifestation of this limit is the "Query Too Complex" error message. (The message was "Out of Memory" in Access 1.x.) When this error occurs, you may be able to create an equivalent query that uses less memory by following these guidelines:

- Reduce the number of output columns in the query. Don't include columns that aren't absolutely needed.

- Refrain from using complex expressions, such as those involving the IIf() function, in queries. If using nested queries, try to move up any expressions to the highest (last) query.

- If you must use them, replace complex expressions with user-defined functions that perform the equivalent functionality.

- Use shorter table and field names.

Speeding Up Forms

Most Access applications revolve around forms, so it goes without saying that any improvements to the performance of forms will realize large gains in the usability of your applications. The following sections detail several areas to consider when optimizing your forms.

Limiting a Form's RecordSource with Large Recordsets

It's tempting to create forms in Access that are based on a huge recordset of tens or hundreds of thousands of records. But you will quickly discover a severe performance penalty when starting up such forms or attempting to navigate to a different record using the FindFirst method. The problems are exacerbated when you attempt to use these types of forms in a networked file-server or client-server environment.

The solution is simple. Rather than giving users *all* the records and navigating around the form's dynaset, set up the form to serve up a single record at a time. Then, instead of using the FindFirst method to move to a different record, change the form's RecordSource property. Chapter 11 includes an example of this technique in the section "The Wire."

Speeding up Combo Boxes with Many Rows

Microsoft made some major changes to combo box behavior with version 2.0. Many of the changes improved the usability of combo boxes for row sources with a small number of rows. At the same time, these changes have also severely affected the performance of combo boxes with row sources with a moderate to large number of rows. The performance degradation is especially severe for combo boxes meeting all of the following criteria:

- The combo box's control source is bound.
- A hidden column is the bound column.
- A non-text column is the bound column.
- There are over several hundred rows in the combo box's row source.

Unfortunately, these settings are very common. There is no simple solution for all situations, but the following remedies may help:

- Consider reworking the form so that the combo box is not grabbing so many rows. You might use other controls on the form to refine the search and reduce the number of rows in the combo box's row source. For example, have the user enter an employee's territory into a territory control to reduce the number of entries in an EmployeeId combo box.
- Change the bound row source column from a numeric to a text field. Surprisingly, this may have a dramatic effect on performance since much of the performance degradation appears to be in converting numbers into a string so that Access can do comparisons of each entered character.

- Don't hide the bound combo box column.

- Reduce the number of columns in the combo box's row source.

- Unbind the combo box control source. Use a hidden text box that is bound to the column on the form's record source. Use an event procedure attached to the Current event of the form to update the combo box to the value of the hidden text box. Use a second event procedure attached to the AfterUpdate event of the combo box to update the value of the hidden text box and keep the two controls in sync with each other.

- Set the AutoExpand property of the combo box to False. (If necessary, you could add an event procedure to the combo box's NotInList event that set AutoExpand to True when the user entered a value that wasn't in the combo box list. Reset AutoExpand to False using an event procedure attached to the combo box's AfterUpdate event.)

The best solution is to rework the form so that the combo box is never looking up more than a few hundred rows. If you absolutely need a combo box with thousands of rows, however, you'll have to try some of the other suggestions.

NOTE   Versions of Access after 2.0 may have solved some of these combo box performance problems.

Other Form Speed-Up Tricks

Other things you can do to speed up your forms or reduce their memory usage include the following:

- Instead of opening and closing forms, load often-used forms hidden and make them visible and invisible. This uses up more memory and system resources, so you have to balance this technique against memory considerations.

- Reduce the complexity of forms. Break complex forms into multiple pages or multiple forms.

- Consider the trade-offs of using Code-Behind-Forms (CBF) versus global modules. Using CBF reduces the amount of memory used since the code is only loaded with the form. (Global modules are always loaded into memory when either the database is opened or, for add-ins, at Access startup.) Using CBF, however, also increases the load time for each form. CBF is especially recommended for add-ins since most add-ins are only occasionally used and therefore the startup time is not so critical. (See Chapter 20 for more details on add-ins.)

- Place controls containing memo and bound OLE objects on pages of a form other than the first or on ancillary forms that can be popped up using a command button. This allows users to browse quickly through records when they don't need to view these complex objects.

- Convert linked unbound OLE objects to unlinked pictures. This makes the objects uneditable, but usually this is acceptable since users can't edit unbound objects at run time anyway. Use Edit ➤ Object ➤ Change to Picture to convert the object into a bitmap picture.

Speeding Up Reports

If you're creating complex reports, you may find yourself faced with the dreaded Out of Memory dialog or reports that take hours to print. One cause for this is that Access creates a separate query for each section of the report. The total space occupied by each of these queries, once compiled into an internal format, must fit within a single 64K segment. Many of the suggestions found under the sections "Speeding Up Queries" and "Avoiding 'Query Too Complex' Errors" earlier in this chapter also apply here since this is often more of an issue for the underlying queries. In addition, you can try the following:

- Move query expressions onto the report.

- Avoid situations in which one query pulls the data from tables and a second query just filters the data. The more information you can pull together into one query, the better. One query uses less memory.

- Avoid including fields in the query that aren't used in the final output of the report.

- If you're using subreports, look at the queries they're based on. Generally, subreports should not be based on the same query as the main report. If they are, try rethinking your design so you can work without the subreport.

- Add subreports to replace multiple expressions that call domain functions like DLookup() or DSum(). By using a subreport, you can often get the same functionality as you get with the slower domain functions, without using any expressions.

Speeding Up Access Basic: A Baker's Dozen of Access Basic Optimizations

As in any programming language, there are often many ways to accomplish the same task in Access Basic. Since you're dealing not only with a language but also with the interface and the underlying data, all tied together in the language, the choices are often even more complicated than with other, more standard languages. The following sections propose a baker's dozen of optimizations, some more potent than others. Probably no single application will be able to use each of these, but you can add them to your "bag of tricks" as you program in Access. You'll also find a method for timing those optimizations, so you can create your own test cases.

Creating an Access Basic Stopwatch

Although you could use the Access Basic Timer() function to calculate the time a specific process requires, it's probably not the wisest choice. Since it measures time in seconds since midnight, it's not terribly accurate. Even though you'll most likely be timing intervals larger than a single second, you'll want a bit more accuracy than the Timer() function can provide. The Windows API provides the GetTickCount() function (aliased as glr_apiGetTickCount() in the sample code), which returns to you the number of milliseconds that have passed since Windows was started. (Not that it matters for testing purposes, but Timer() "rolls over" every 24 hours. Get-TickCount() keeps on ticking for up to 49 days before it resets the returned tick count to 0. Most likely, if you're timing something that runs for 49 days, you're not terribly interested in milliseconds, but that's what you get.)

To test each of the proposed optimizations, you need some mechanism for starting and stopping the clock. The subroutine glrStartTimer stores the current return value from glr_apiGetTickCount() into a global variable, lngStartTime. You must call this subroutine directly before any code you want to have timed. When you're done with the critical section of code, you'll want to call the function glrEndTimer(), which returns to you the difference between the current time and the time when you called glrStartTimer, or the elapsed time. Listing 16.1 shows the declarations and code for the timer functions.

Listing 16.1

```
Declare Function glr_apiGetTickCount Lib "USER" Alias
➡ "GetTickCount"() As Long
Dim lngStartTime As Long

Sub glrStartTimer()
    lngStartTime = glr_apiGetTickCount()
End Sub

Function EndTimer()
    EndTimer = glr_apiGetTickCount() - lngStartTime
End Function
```

Getting Reasonable Results

You will find that running any given test only once doesn't provide reliable results. There are just too many external forces in play when you're running under Windows. To get a reasonable idea of the benefit of a given optimization test, you need to run the test code many times within the given test case and then run the test case many times, averaging the results. For simplicity, each of the tests in this chapter takes as its only parameter a Long value indicating the number of times you want to run the test. The functions loop the specified number of times with the clock running and return the elapsed time as the return value of the function.

If you want to add your own tests to this test mechanism, you must follow those constraints when planning your tests. In addition, for each test case, you need two versions: a "slow" version (labeled as "Test1a()" in this example) and a "fast" version (labeled as "Test1b()" in this example). Once you've provided the two functions, you can call the function glrRunTests(), which, in turn, calls both functions the specified number of times. glrRunTests() averages the elapsed times returned as the results from the functions and reports on the comparative speed of the two functions. Listing 16.2 shows the glrRunTests() function. Notice that glrRunTests() takes four parameters, as shown in Table 16.3. glrRunTests() returns a string in this format:

Results: Test1a() is about *nn*% faster (or slower) than Test1b()

TABLE 16.3: The glrRunTests() Parameters

Parameter	Description	Datatype
strFunc1	Name of the "slow" function to test	String expression
strFunc2	Name of the "fast" function to test	String expression
varReptFunc	Number of times to repeat the function call	Variant
varReptOp	Number of times to repeat the operation in the function	Variant

For example, to call glrRunTests() to test functions Testa() and Testb(), running each function 10 times to average the results and having each function loop internally 10,000 times, call glrRunTests() like this:

```
strResult = glrRunTests("Testa", "Testb", 10, 10000)
```

Listing 16.2

```
Function glrRunTests(strFunc1 As String, strFunc2 As
➥ String, varReptFunc As Variant, varReptOp As Variant)

    ' The assumption is that strFunc1 will be slower
    ' than strFunc2.

    Const MB_ICONSTOP = 16

    Dim varI As Variant
    Dim varResults1 As Variant
    Dim varResults2 As Variant
    Dim varDiff As Variant
```

```
Dim intAmount As Integer
Dim strResult As String
Dim varTemp As Variant

For varI = 0 To varReptFunc - 1
    varTemp = SysCmd(SYSCMD_SETSTATUS, "Running " &
    ➡ strFunc1 & "() Pass " & varI)
    varResults1 = varResults1 + Eval(strFunc1 & "(" &
    ➡ varReptOp & ")")
Next varI

For varI = 0 To varReptFunc - 1
    varTemp = SysCmd(SYSCMD_SETSTATUS, "Running " &
    ➡ strFunc2 & "() Pass " & varI)
    varResults2 = varResults2 + Eval(strFunc2 & "(" &
    ➡ varReptOp & ")")
Next varI
varResults1 = varResults1 / varReptFunc
varResults2 = varResults2 / varReptFunc
Debug.Print varResults1, varResults2


varDiff = varResults1 - varResults2
If Abs(varDiff) < .005 Then varDiff = 0

' Better check for division by 0 and overflow
' which both can occur from a very small value in
' varResults1.
On Error GoTo RunTestsError
intAmount = Abs(Int((varResults1 - varResults2) /
➡ varResults2 * 100))
strResult = strFunc2 & "() is about "
Select Case Sgn(varDiff)
    Case 0
        strResult = strResult & " the same speed as "
    Case 1
        strResult = strResult & intAmount & "% faster than "
    Case -1
        strResult = strResult & intAmount & "% slower than "
End Select
strResult = strResult & strFunc1 & "()"
glrRunTests = "Results: " & strResult
```

```
RunTestsExit:
    ' Clear the status line.
    varTemp = SysCmd(SYSCMD_CLEARSTATUS)
    Exit Function

RunTestsError:
    MsgBox Error, MB_ICONSTOP, "RunTests()"
    glrRunTests = ""
    Resume RunTestsExit
End Function
```

Using the Eval() Function

glrRunTests() uses the Eval() function to execute each of the two tests. (See Chapter 7 for more information on the Eval() function.) As a reminder, the Eval() function takes as a parameter a string containing code you want Access to execute. If you intend to use Eval() to execute functions, you should be aware of the various limitations involved in using this technique:

- Access performs no error checking on the string you send to Eval(). If it works, great. If not, you get, at best, a "User Defined Error" message. At worst, you crash (and lose data). You would be wise to check the string you're about to send to Eval() by using MsgBox or Debug.Print to display the string before its execution. This way you can verify that the string to be executed is, in fact, laid out exactly as you think it ought to be.

- Scoping rules are always an issue. Eval() cannot interpret any local variables, nor can it handle private functions. You can remember the rules this way: any object you want to send to Eval() must also work in macros. Just as Access Basic variables aren't available in macros, they aren't available once Eval() gets hold of the string to be executed. glrRunTests() uses local variables, but they become part of the string passed to Eval() and are passed as values, not as variable names.

- The string you pass to Eval() must represent a function, returning a value of some sort. That value will be the return value from the call to Eval(). Neither subroutines nor expressions are allowed.

NOTE
The effectiveness of each of the optimizations that follow depends on many factors, including the actual code in use at the time, the relative speed of your hard disk versus the processor in your computer, and other programs currently using Windows' memory and resources. The timing results presented here are for comparison only. You'll need to decide for yourself in some of the marginal cases whether or not the optimization will really help. Therefore, a word of warning: take any suggestions of optimizations with a grain of salt. Try them out in your own applications before swearing by them. As they say in the auto industry, "These numbers are for comparison only. Your mileage may vary."

The Optimizations

We present these suggested optimizations in no particular order. In some cases we've listed two separate copies of the code, once for the slow test and once for the fast one. If possible, we've folded the two together, indicating the slow and fast differences with comments. In each case the significant difference between the two test methods is set in *italics*. CH16.MDB includes the full source for both versions of each test, so you can try them out yourself.

To simplify your experiments with the test cases we present here, you can use frmRunTests from CH16.MDB. Figure 16.6 shows this form in use. It includes a combo box from which you can choose the specific test case to run and spin buttons allowing you to specify how many loops to execute inside the routine, as well as how many times to call each routine. (See Chapter 7 for more information on creating your own spin buttons.) The View Slower and View Faster buttons pop up forms that pull the source code for the functions from memo fields in the underlying table, so you can look at the code as you test. Finally, the clock button starts the test, running the slow version as many times as you've requested and then running the faster version the same number of times.

Clearly, this method of testing is far from perfect. The order in which you run the tests might make a difference, and if you have a disk cache installed, that might make a difference, too. In our informal testing (and that's all this can be—measurements of relative differences), neither factor made much difference. Reversing the order of the tests made almost no difference, nor did removing the disk cache.

FIGURE 16.6:

frmRunTests allows you to choose a specific test and run it, resulting in a comparison between the slow and fast versions.

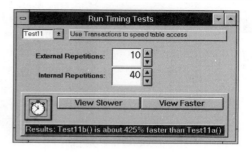

Remember, the goal of these tests is to determine which of two methods is the faster, not to gather exact timings. In each case we ran the tests on a 486/66 with 32MB of memory. (It's possible that some of the differences will disappear or reverse in low-memory situations as things are swapped back and forth from your Windows swap file.) The percentage differences we found depend totally on the specific tests we ran and the setup of our system, but we've tried to make them representative of the kinds of improvements you'd see, too.

The results of our performance tests are summarized in Table 16.4.

TABLE 16.4: Summary of the Results of the Access Basic Performance Tests

Test Number	Optimization	Range of Speedup[1]
1	Integer variables instead of variants	35–40%
2	Integer division instead of real division	30–40%
3	Logical assignments instead of If … Then	5–15%
4	Len() for testing for zero-length strings	45–55%
5	"Not var" to toggle True/False	15–25%
6	GetTickCount() instead of Timer()	750%
7	Use object variables	105–110%
8	Use implicit logical comparisons	5–10%
9	Refer to controls by number in loops	15–20%
10	IsCharAlphaNumeric instead of Asc()	35–45%

TABLE 16.5: Summary of the Results of the Access Basic Performance Tests (continued)

Test Number	Optimization	Range of Speedup[1]
11	Transactions	220–250%
12	If…Then…Else instead of IIf()	90–100%
13	CreateQueryDef() instead of RunSQL	25–35%

[1] The range of improvement using the test functions, number of function calls, and number of repetitions as specified in tblTests

Some of the comparisons are more dependent than others on the assumptions made. For example, Test2, which evaluates the difference between using integer and real division, couldn't be constructed in too many different ways. It's doubtful you'd get results differing much from those in Table 16.4 by rewriting the code. On the other hand, Test11, which compares making updates to a table with and without using transactions, will give widely differing results depending on the number of columns and rows updated within the transaction. Thus, it's important to be aware of the assumptions made for each test when interpreting the results.

Use Integers Instead of Variants Whenever Possible

Unless you specify otherwise, Access creates all variables using its default type, the Variant datatype. In order to be able to hold data of any simple type, variants must be at least as big and complex as any of the types they can contain. "Big and complex" equates with "slower," so you should avoid variants if at all possible. Of course, there will be many times when you can't avoid them, but if you're just ill informed or being lazy, your code will suffer. Listing 16.3 shows two test cases, the only difference being the declaration of the variant varX in Test1a() versus the integer intX in Test1b().

Listing 16.3

```
Function Test1a(lngRepeats As Long)
    Dim varX As Variant

    glrStartTimer
    Do While lngRepeats > 0
        varX = varX + 1
        varX = varX - 1
        lngRepeats = lngRepeats - 1
    Loop
    Test1a = glrEndTimer()
End Function

Function Test1b(lngRepeats As Long)
    Dim intX As Integer

    glrStartTimer
    Do While lngRepeats > 0
        intX = intX + 1
        intX = intX - 1
        lngRepeats = lngRepeats - 1
    Loop
    Test1b = glrEndTimer()
End Function
```

In our tests we found the use of integers to be, on average, 35 to 45 percent faster than using variants.

Use Integer Division Whenever Possible

Access provides two division operators, the / (floating-point division) and \ (integer division) operators. In order to perform floating-point division, Access must convert the operands to floating-point values. This takes time. If you don't care about the fractional portion of the result, you can save a substantial amount of time by using the integer division operator instead. Listing 16.4 shows the two examples used to test this difference; they differ only in the operator used to perform the division.

Listing 16.4

```
Function Test2a/b(lngRepeats As Long)
    Dim varX As Variant

    glrStartTimer
    Do While lngRepeats > 0
        ' Use the following line for Test2a
        varX = 1000 / 1
        ' Use the following line for Test2b
        ' varX = 1000 | 1
        lngRepeats = lngRepeats - 1
    Loop
    Test2a = glrEndTimer()
End Function
```

In our tests we found the use of integer division to be, on average, 30 to 40 percent faster than using floating-point division.

Use Logical Assignments When Possible

Like many other languages, Access handles logical values as integers. In addition, Access performs right-to-left expression evaluation. The combination of these two features allows you to make logical assignments directly as part of an expression. For example, many people write code like this:

```
If x = 5 Then
    y = True
Else
    y = False
End If
```

This code is wordier than it need be. The intent is to set the variable y to True if x is equal to 5 and False otherwise. The expression (x = 5) has a truth value of its own—that is, it's either True or False. You can assign that value directly to y in a single statement:

```
y = (x = 5)
```

Although it may look confusing, Access Basic (along with many other programming languages) will interpret it correctly. Starting from the right, Access will calculate the value of the expression x = 5 (either True or False) and assign that value to the variable y. Other languages, including C and Pascal, use distinct assignment and equality operators, making this a little clearer. In C, for example, the statement would read

```
y = (x == 5)
```

with the "=" performing the assignment and the "==" checking the equality.

Anyplace you use an expression like the If...Then... End If statement above, you should be able to replace it with a single assignment statement. Listing 16.5 shows the two routines used to compare the speed of these two methods.

Listing 16.5

```
Function Test3a/b(lngRepeats As Long)
    Dim intI As Integer
    Dim fEven As Integer

    glrStartTimer
    Do While lngRepeats > 0
        ' Use the following block for Test3a
        If lngRepeats Mod 2 = 0 Then
            fEven = True
        Else
            fEven = False
        End If
        ' Use the following block for Test3b
        ' fEven = (lngRepeats Mod 2 = 0)
        lngRepeats = lngRepeats - 1
    Loop
    Test3a = glrEndTimer()
End Function
```

If you find these logical assignments hard to read, you may choose to skip using them, since the improvement in performance is slight. (In our tests they were 5 to 15 percent faster.) If, however, logical assignments seem natural to use and read, then by all means use them.

Use Len() to Test for Zero-Length Strings

There are several ways you can check to see whether the length of a particular string is 0 in Access Basic. One method is to compare the string to " ", and another is to compare the length of the string to 0. Comparing the results of the Len() function to 0 is measurably faster. Listing 16.6 shows the two routines used to test this optimization.

Listing 16.6

```
Function Test4a/b(lngRepeats As Long)
    Dim strTest As String
    Dim fEmpty As Integer

    glrStartTimer
    strTest = "x"
    Do While lngRepeats > 0
        ' Use this line for Test4a
        fEmpty = (strTest = "")
        ' Use this line for Test4b
        ' fEmpty = (Len(strTest) = 0)
        lngRepeats = lngRepeats - 1
    Loop
    Test4a = glrEndTimer()
End Function
```

In our tests we found the use of Len() to be, on average, 45 to 55 percent faster than comparing the string against " ".

Use "Var = Not Var" to Toggle True/False

In many circumstances you need to toggle the state of a variable between True and False. You might be tempted to write code like this:

```
If x = True Then
    x = False
Else
    x = True
End If
```

You might think that either of the following solutions would be an improvement over the original:

```
If x Then
    x = False
Else
    x = True
End If
```

or

```
x = IIf(x, False, True)
```

Testing shows that neither is as good as the original expression (and the IIf() solution is much slower). But the best solution is to use the following expression:

```
x = Not x
```

That way, if x is currently True, it will become False. If it's False, it will become True. Listing 16.7 shows the two functions used to test this optimization.

Listing 16.7

```
Function Test5a/b(lngRepeats As Long)
    Dim fTest As Integer

    glrStartTimer
    Do While lngRepeats > 0
        ' Use this line for Test5a.
        If fTest = True Then
            fTest = False
        Else
            fTest = True
        End If
        ' Use this line for Test5b
        ' fTest = Not fTest
        lngRepeats = lngRepeats - 1
    Loop
    Test5a = glrEndTimer()
End Function
```

In our tests we found the use of "var = Not var" to be, on average, 45 to 55 percent faster than the fastest If...Then...Else test.

Use GetTickCount() Rather Than Timer()

As mentioned earlier in this chapter, the Windows API function GetTickCount() (aliased as glr_apiGetTickCount() in the examples) returns the number of milliseconds that have elapsed since you started the current Windows session. The Access Basic function Timer() returns the number of seconds that have elapsed since midnight. If you're interested in measuring elapsed times, you're far better off using GetTickCount(), for three reasons:

- GetTickCount() is more accurate (milliseconds rather than seconds).
- GetTickCount() runs longer without "rolling over."
- Calling GetTickCount() is significantly faster.

Calling GetTickCount() is no more complex than calling Timer(), once you've included the proper API declaration for it. In the Declarations section of any module in your application, you'll need to include the statement

```
Declare Function glr_apiGetTickCount Lib "USER" Alias
➡ "GetTickCount"()As Long
```

With that declaration in place, you can call it from any module in your application, just as though it were an internal Access Basic function. Listing 16.8 shows the functions used to test Timer() versus glr_apiGetTickCount().

Listing 16.8

```
Function Test6a/b(lngRepeats As Long)
    Dim varTime As Variant

    glrStartTimer
    Do While lngRepeats > 0
        ' Use this line for Test6a.
        varTime = Timer
        ' Use this line for Test6b.
        ' varTime = glr_apiGetTickCount()
        lngRepeats = lngRepeats - 1
    Loop
    Test6a = glrEndTimer()
End Function
```

In our tests we found the use of GetTickCount() to be, on average, 750 percent faster than using Timer().

Cache Object References

In writing Access Basic code, you often need to retrieve or set properties of the various forms, reports, and controls in your application. Generally, you refer to these objects with statements like this:

```
strCaption = Forms!frmTest!lblTest.Caption
```

For a single reference to an object, there's not much you can to do speed up the reference. If, on the other hand, you're going to be referring to many of the properties of that object or using that object in a loop of some sort, you can achieve a substantial speed increase by pointing an object variable at that object and using that variable to reference the object.

For example, if you were going to reference all of a specific control's properties, you would be well served to use code like this, rather than referring to the control with the full syntax each time:

```
Dim ctl as Control
Set ctl = Forms!YourForm!YourControl

Debug.Print ctl.ControlName
Debug.Print ctl.Width
' etc...
```

Listing 16.9 shows the two routines used to test the differences between direct and indirect referencing.

Listing 16.9

```
Function Test7a(lngRepeats As Long)
    Dim strCaption As String

    DoCmd OpenForm "frmTest", , , , , A_HIDDEN
    glrStartTimer
    Do While lngRepeats > 0
        strCaption = Forms!frmTest!lblTest.Caption
        lngRepeats = lngRepeats - 1
    Loop
    Test7a = glrEndTimer()
    DoCmd Close A_FORM, "frmTest"
End Function

Function Test7b(lngRepeats As Long)
    Dim strCaption As String
    Dim ctl As Control
```

```
    DoCmd OpenForm "frmTest", , , , , A_HIDDEN
    Set ctl = Forms!frmTest!lblTest

    glrStartTimer
    Do While lngRepeats > 0
        strCaption = ctl.Caption
        lngRepeats = lngRepeats - 1
    Loop
    Test7b = glrEndTimer()
    DoCmd Close A_FORM, "frmTest"
End Function
```

In our tests we found the use of object variables to be, on average, 105 to 110 percent faster than using explicit control references.

Don't Use Explicit Logical Comparisons

When testing for the truth value of an expression in an IIf() expression or an If ...Then...Else statement, there is no point in actually comparing the condition to the value True. That is, these two expressions are completely equivalent:

```
If x = True Then
```

and

```
If x Then
```

Leaving out the explicit comparison will make a small difference in the speed of your code. You'd have to use this construct many, many times before this optimization made any measurable difference in the speed of your code, but every little bit helps! Listing 16.10 shows the code used to test this minor optimization.

Listing 16.10

```
Function Test8a/b(lngRepeats As Long)
    Dim fTest As Integer

    fTest = True
    glrStartTimer
    Do While lngRepeats > 0
        ' Use this line for Test8a.
        If fTest = True Then
```

```
        ' Use this line for Test8b.
        ' If fTest Then
            fTest = Not fTest
        End If
        lngRepeats = lngRepeats - 1
    Loop
    Test8a = glrEndTimer()
End Function
```

In our tests we found the use of implied logical comparisons to be, on average, 5 to 10 percent faster than explicit comparisons.

Refer to Controls by Number If Possible

Access Basic gives you several choices when you're referring to controls on a form. For example, given a form with 16 command buttons, you could refer to the first button (cmdButton1) in your code several ways (assuming that cmdButton1 was the first control to be placed on the form):

```
Dim ctl as Control
Set ctl = Forms!frmTest1!cmdButton1
Set ctl = Forms!frmTest1("cmdButton1")
Set ctl = Forms!frmTest1(0)
```

If you intend to loop through all the controls on the form, you have fewer choices. You can either build up a string expression that contains the name of the control (as in function Test9a()) or you can use an integer variable to refer to the specific control (as in Test9b()). The latter method is measurably faster but you should use it only where you are looping through controls. Listing 16.11 shows the two methods in action.

Listing 16.11

```
Function Test9a/b(lngRepeats As Long)
    Dim intI As Integer
    Dim strCaption As String
    Dim frm As Form

    DoCmd OpenForm "frmTest1", , , , , A_HIDDEN
    Set frm = Forms!frmTest1
    glrStartTimer
    Do While lngRepeats > 0
        For intI = 1 To 16
```

```
                  ' Use the next line for the slow version
                  strCaption = frm("cmdButton" & intI).Caption
                  ' Uncomment this for faster test.
                  ' strCaption = frm(intI - 1).Caption
           Next intI
           lngRepeats = lngRepeats - 1
       Loop
       Test9a = glrEndTimer()
       DoCmd Close A_FORM, "frmTest"
End Function
```

In our tests we found that referencing controls by number, to be, on average, 15 to 20 percent faster than using a string expression.

Use IsCharAlphaNumeric()

You may find yourself needing to find out whether or not a particular character is an alphanumeric character (that is, checking to see whether it falls in the range of characters from A–Z, a–z, or 0–9). One standard method for doing this in Access Basic is to compare the Asc(UCase(*character*)) to the ANSI values for the ranges. The Windows API provides a function specifically for this purpose, IsCharAlphaNumeric() (aliased as glr_apiIsCharAlphaNumeric() in the examples). In addition, you can use a similar API function, IsCharAlpha(), to check a character to see whether it's between A and Z. An added bonus of using the Windows API functions is that they're internationalized. Many characters outside the normal A–Z range are considered legal text characters in other countries. The brute-force, comparison method would fail on such characters. To top it all off, the API method is significantly faster than performing the comparisons yourself.

To use IsCharAlphaNumeric(), you need to include the following declaration in any module in your application:

```
Declare Function glr_apiIsCharAlphaNumeric Lib "USER" Alias
➥ "IsCharAlphaNumeric"(ByVal intChar As Integer) As Integer
```

Listing 16.12 shows two functions you can use to compare the speeds of the two methods.

Listing 16.12

```
Function Test10a/b(lngRepeats As Long)
    Dim intC As Integer
    Dim strC As String
    Dim lngX As Long

    Const FIRST_CHAR = 65
    Const LAST_CHAR = 90
    Const FIRST_DIGIT = 48
    Const LAST_DIGIT = 57

    strC = "x"
    glrStartTimer
    Do While lngRepeats > 0
        intC = Asc(UCase(strC))
        ' Use this line for Test10a
        If (intC >= FIRST_CHAR And intC <= LAST_CHAR) Or
     ➥  (intC >= FIRST_DIGIT and intC <= LAST_DIGIT) Then
        ' Use this line for Test10b
        ' If glr_apiIsCharAlphaNumeric(Asc(strC)) Then
            lngX = lngX + 1
        End If
        lngRepeats = lngRepeats - 1
    Loop
    Test10a = glrEndTimer()
End Function
```

In our tests we found the use of IsCharAlphaNumeric() to be, on average, 35 to 45 percent faster than using Asc().

Wrap Table Updates/Appends in Transactions

Surrounding programmatic updates/appends in a BeginTrans/CommitTrans pair speeds up the operation. Transactions speed up database updates because Access stores all the updates within a transaction in an internal buffer (in memory, spilling over to disk) and writes them all to disk at once when the transaction is committed. As you might imagine, this can have a considerable impact on your application speed, especially if it is updating many records within a loop. Many factors affect how much of a performance boost you will realize when using transactions, including

- The setting of MaxBufferSize in MSACCESS.INI
- Disk-caching software
- The size of the row being added
- The number of columns in the row that are updated
- The number of rows being updated

Any of these factors (or others) may affect this optimization, but you will more than likely find that a well-placed BeginTrans/CommitTrans pair can help considerably in your applications.

Listing 16.13 shows the routine used to test this optimization. (Uncomment the transaction statements to convert from Test11a() to Test11b().)

Listing 16.13

```
Function Test11a/b(lngRepeats As Long)
    Dim DB As Database
    Dim tbl As Table
    Dim strSQL As String

    Set DB = CurrentDB()
    Set tbl = DB.OpenTable("tblContacts")
    glrStartTimer
            ' Uncomment the next line for Test11b.
            ' BeginTrans
            Do While lngRepeats > 0
                tbl.AddNew
                    tbl!Company = "LMH Consulting"
                    tbl!Street = "2840 Colby Ave"
                    tbl!City = "Los Angeles"
                    tbl!State = "CA"
                    tbl!Country = "USA"
                    tbl!RegionCode = "90064-4226"
                    tbl!Phone = "310-836-5406"
                    tbl!First = "Louis"
                    tbl!Last = "Harris"
                    tbl!Title = "Owner"
```

```
                    tbl.Update
                    lngRepeats = lngRepeats - 1
              Loop
              ' Uncomment the next line for Test 11b.
              ' CommitTrans
       tbl.Close
       Test11a = glrEndTimer()
       DoCmd SetWarnings False
       strSQL = "DELETE * FROM tblContacts"
       DoCmd RunSQL strSQL
       DoCmd SetWarnings True
End Function
```

In our tests we found the use of transactions to be 220 to 250 percent faster for our particular update scenario. Your applications may realize even greater improvements if more updates are performed within a transaction.

Watch Out for Slow IIf() Components

Shorter code isn't necessarily faster. Although this fact is documented both in the Access on-line help and in the manuals, it's easy to miss: in the IIf(), Choose(), and Select() functions, Access Basic evaluates any and all expressions it finds, regardless of whether they actually need to be evaluated from a logical point of view. Given an expression like this:

```
varValue = IIf(fFlag, Function1(), Function2())
```

Access Basic will call both Function1() and Function2(). Not only can this lead to undesired side effects, it can just plain slow down your program. In a case like this you're better off using the standard If...Then...End If construct, which will execute only the portions of the statement that fall within the appropriate clause. Given the statement

```
If fFlag Then
    varValue = Function1()
Else
    varValue = Function2()
End If
```

you can be assured that only Function1() *or* Function2() will end up being called. The same concepts apply for the Choose() and Select() functions. If you plan on calling functions from any of these functions, you may be better served by using an If...Then... End If or a Select Case statement.

Beyond any optimization considerations, IIf() is very dangerous when dealing with numeric values and division. If this was your expression:

```
intNew = IIf(intY = 0, 0, intX/intY)
```

it would appear that you had appropriately covered your bases. Your code checks to make sure that intY isn't 0 and returns an appropriate value if it is, rather than attempting to divide by 0. Unfortunately, if y is 0 this statement will still cause a run-time error. Since Access will evaluate both portions of the IIf() expression, the division by 0 will occur and will trigger an error. In this case you need to either trap for the error or use the If...Then...Else statement.

Listing 16.14 shows the two functions used to test this optimization. Note that any speed increase noted in this test is dependent on the actual functions called, so it's up to you to test your own applications and determine any speed increases.

Listing 16.14

```
Function Test12a(lngRepeats As Long)
    Dim varRetval As Variant

    glrStartTimer
    Do While lngRepeats > 0
        ' Use this line for Test12a.
        varRetval = IIf(1 = 1, DummyFunc(1), DummyFunc(1))
        ' Use the following block for Test12b.
        ' If 1 = 1 Then
        '     varRetval = DummyFunc(1)
        ' Else
        '     varRetval = DummyFunc(1)
        ' End If
        lngRepeats = lngRepeats - 1
    Loop
    Test12a = glrEndTimer()
End Function

Function Test12b(lngRepeats As Long)
    Dim varRetval As Variant

    glrStartTimer
    Do While lngRepeats > 0
If 1 = 1 Then
        varRetval = DummyFunc(1)
```

```
        Else
            varRetval = DummyFunc(1)
        End If
lngRepeats = lngRepeats - 1
    Loop
    Test12b = glrEndTimer()
End Function
```

In our particular tests we found the use of If...Then...Else to be, on average, 90 to 100 percent faster than using the equivalent IIf() function. Note that any speed increase noted in this test is dependent on the actual functions called.

Use CreateQueryDef() instead of RunSQL

When running an action query from your Access Basic code, you have two choices: either you can use the RunSQL macro action or you can create a QueryDef object and then use its Execute method. When using the RunSQL action, you're limited to a 255-character SQL string, so this in itself may make your decision for you. On the other hand, given a choice of using either method, you'll find that creating a Query-Def object is almost always faster.

Using Temporary QueryDefs

Access 2.0 provides a useful mechanism for creating temporary QueryDef objects: just don't provide a name! If you use a zero-length string for the name parameter of the CreateQueryDef() method, Access creates a temporary "in-memory" query. You no longer have to worry about the proliferation of querydefs and name collisions, and since Access doesn't write temporary querydefs to disk, they're a lot faster, too. Another plus: you don't have to delete temporary querydefs—they automatically disappear when the Query-Def object goes out of scope. For example, you can use code like this to create a temporary querydef:

```
Dim db As Database
Dim qdf As QueryDef
Set db = DBEngine.Workspaces(0).Databases(0)
Set qdf = db.CreateQueryDef("", "SELECT * FROM tblCustomers
➡ WHERE Age > 30;")
```

Listing 16.15 shows two ways to accomplish the same goal—deleting all the rows from tblContacts. With the slower method you could use the RunSQL action to run the SQL string "DELETE * From tblContacts". The faster method, using the in-memory querydef, sets the SQL property of the querydef to be that same SQL string and then executes the querydef.

Listing 16.15

```
Function Test13a(lngRepeats As Long)

    ' Use CreateQueryDef/Execute rather than RunSQL

    glrStartTimer
    DoCmd SetWarnings False
    Do While lngRepeats > 0
        DoCmd RunSQL "DELETE * From tblContacts"
        lngRepeats = lngRepeats - 1
    Loop
    Test13a = glrEndTimer()
    DoCmd SetWarnings True
End Function

Function Test13b(lngRepeats As Long)

    ' Use CreateQueryDef/Execute rather than RunSQL

    Dim db As Database
    Dim qdf As QueryDef

    Set db = dbEngine.WorkSpaces(0).Databases(0)
    glrStartTimer
    Do While lngRepeats > 0
        Set qdf = db.CreateQueryDef("", "DELETE * From
        ➥ tblContacts")
        qdf.Execute
        lngRepeats = lngRepeats - 1
    Loop
    Test13b = glrEndTimer()
End Function
```

In our tests we found the use of CreateQueryDef() to be, on average, 25 to 35 percent faster than using the equivalent RunSQL action.

Summary

This chapter has described the architecture of the Jet database engine in detail and presented a variety of suggestions for improving the performance of your Access applications. We covered the following topics:

- The parts of the Jet database engine and how they relate to each other
- The steps for processing a query: definition, compilation, optimization, execution
- How queries are optimized
- How and when Rushmore works
- How to force Jet to recompile a query
- How to keep Jet's statistics accurate
- How application performance is affected by hardware and operating system settings
- How to best configure low-memory machines
- How to optimize queries and avoid "Query too complex" errors
- How to speed up forms
- How to improve the performance of reports
- Thirteen ways to optimize your Access Basic code
- How to test your own optimization ideas

While we attempted to cover the major areas of optimization, this chapter is not meant to be comprehensive, but it makes for a good start.

At every point in designing any application, you're faced with choices. These choices affect how well your application will work, and you need to be informed about the trade-offs in order to best make these choices. This chapter focused on the major areas in which you can improve the performance of your applications.

PART VI

Interoperability

CHAPTER

SEVENTEEN

Accessing DLLs and the Windows API

- Declaring DLL procedures in Access Basic

- Using "by value" and "by reference" to place items on the stack

- Converting C datatypes to Access Basic declarations

- Calling the Windows API

This chapter discusses one of the most powerful features of Access: the ability to call Dynamic Link Libraries (DLLs) from Access Basic procedures. DLLs are written in C or C++. Calling a DLL provides a method of performing tasks that is not permitted by standard Access Basic functions and statements. For example, Access has no intrinsic functions to read and write to an .INI file, but you can do so easily with a DLL call.

Even if you are not proficient in C or C++, you can use DLLs written by someone else. The GLR.DLL file on this book's companion disk, for example, allows you to perform tasks such as closing a program given its instance handle. In addition, every machine that runs Windows automatically has a number of DLLs with hundreds of useful functions. These functions are collectively called the Windows Application Programming Interface (API). Windows programs use these functions to manipulate Windows. The Windows API lets you perform many tasks that are impossible through Access Basic itself, such as reading and writing .INI files and finding out which programs besides Access are currently running.

Learning how to call the Windows API and DLLs in general allows you to vastly extend your ability to manipulate Access and Windows.

Introducing Dynamic Link Libraries

With most compiled programming languages, you can repeatedly use libraries that contain useful functions. In standard C used from DOS, you call functions from the C run-time library to read a string from a file, get a character from the keyboard, or get the current time. These libraries are *statically linked* to the program, meaning that the code is included in the executable that is created. The problem with this is that if you have 200 programs that all write a string to the screen with the printf() function, the code for the printf() function is reproduced 200 times on your disk.

Windows uses a different approach: libraries are usually *dynamically linked* to the program. This means that if you have 200 Windows programs that all write a string to a window, only one copy of the ExtTextOut() code resides on your hard disk. Only a very small amount of overhead is included in each program to call this common code because these common routines reside in a Dynamic Link Library.

Dynamic Link Libraries normally have the extension .DLL and are stored in the Windows\System directory if they are used by more than one program.

When a Windows program runs, tasks that manipulate the operating system call Windows functions. These functions provide facilities to create a window, change its size, read and write .INI file entries, manipulate a file, and so on. Windows stores most of these functions in three DLLs: USER.EXE, GDI.EXE, and KRNL386.EXE (or KRNL286.EXE, if you're running in standard mode instead of enhanced mode). These names are exceptions to the .DLL naming convention of Dynamic Link Libraries.

To use a DLL you generally need documentation that describes the procedures in it and the arguments that they take. The Windows functions are well documented (as described in the section "The Windows API" later in this chapter), but other DLLs often have little or no documentation. Sometimes you can find code that calls these DLLs and adapt the calls to your use. Otherwise, unless you are extremely proficient with a debugger and in reading assembly language, you cannot figure out the arguments to procedures in the DLL.

How to Declare a DLL Function from Access Basic

When you want to use a function in a DLL, you need to tell Access Basic some things about the function:

- The name of the function as you want to call it in your code
- The name of the containing DLL
- The name of the function in the DLL
- The number and datatypes of the arguments to the function
- The datatype of the return value of the function

Given this information, Access Basic knows how to locate the function on the hard disk and how to arrange the arguments on the stack so they are acceptable to the

DLL. The *stack* is a special segment of memory that programs use for storing temporary information. Arguments are pushed onto the stack by Access Basic and manipulated by the DLL, and then the return value is placed on the stack for Access Basic to return to your program.

The Access Basic Declare statement defines the size of the arguments to a DLL function and what the arguments mean. It is *crucial* that the declaration be exactly what the DLL expects. Otherwise, you may be giving the DLL bogus information. In addition, you may often be giving the DLL information in an invalid segment of memory. This results in a General Protection Fault (GP fault), also known as a User Application Error. If you get a GP fault, Access often crashes without giving you a chance to save objects that need to be saved.

Sometimes you can click Ignore in the GP Fault dialog and get back to a stable state. After doing that, you need to save your work, exit Access and Windows, and reboot your machine. Any GP fault can leave Windows in an unstable condition.

WARNING   Because you *will* eventually make a mistake and cause a GP fault, it is important to save all objects that need to be saved before running any code that calls a DLL. This is especially true the first time you attempt to call any given DLL function or when you make a change to a Declare statement. In addition, the DLL may have a bug. Either a bad declaration or a bug in the DLL can cause a GP fault and crash Access. You may even crash Windows, so you should save any objects in other programs running under Windows, too. Keep recent backups of your database, just to cover the slight possibility that it becomes corrupt when Access crashes. DLLs are powerful, but the protection against mistakes normally provided by Access is not available.

Defining the Access Basic Declare statement is similar to defining any other sub or function, except that there is no body to the procedure. Once you have declared a DLL function, you can call it just as though the code were part of Access Basic. You must define Declare statements at the global level; you cannot define them inside a procedure. The Declare statement takes one of two forms, depending on whether the DLL function being called returns a value:

Declare Sub *globalname* Lib *libname* [Alias *aliasname*]

➡ [([*argumentlist*])]

or

Declare Function *globalname* Lib *libname* [Alias *aliasname*]

➡ [([*argumentlist*])] [As *type*]

Here is an example of a Declare statement:

```
Declare Function FindWindow Lib "User"(ByVal lpClassName As Any,
➡ ByVal lpWindowName As Any) As Integer
```

If the function returns no value (that is, it is declared with the return type *void* in the C programming language), you use the Declare Sub format of the Declare statement. If the function returns a value, you use the Declare Function format. It is also possible to use the Declare Sub format of the Declare statement if the function returns a value, but your code *never* uses the return value. Since it is always a good idea to check to see whether the function failed, using Declare Sub with a function that returns a value is not recommended.

Specifying the Lib

The Lib part of the declaration tells Access Basic the DLL's name and also, potentially, its location. The Lib name is enclosed in quotes and is not case sensitive. If the function you are declaring is in one of the three main Windows DLLs, you should just use "User", "GDI", or "Kernel", which Windows translates to the actual DLL names.

If you do not include the path on the DLL name, Windows uses this order to search for the DLL:

1. The current directory

2. The Windows directory

3. The Windows\System directory

4. If you are using Windows 3.1 or later, the Access directory (that is, the directory that contains MSACCESS.EXE)

5. The directories listed in the PATH environment variable

6. The directories mapped to a network drive

This order can cause some confusion. If you put a DLL in the Windows\System directory but there is an older version of the DLL in the Windows directory, the older version will get called. Since this causes lots of problems, there are general conventions as to where to store DLLs:

- If the DLL is called by only one application (for example, only by Access), store the DLL in the directory containing the executable file for the current task (for example, MSACCESS.EXE).

- If the DLL is called by more than one application (for example, something besides Access), store the DLL in the Windows\System directory.

NOTE   In Access versions 1.0 and 1.1, the base part of a DLL's file name had to be the same as the name declared on the Library line in the .DEF file when the file was linked. For example, if the Library line in the file had the value MADH, the name of the .DLL would have to be MADH.DLL. If not, you would get an error message, "Error in Loading DLL," when a function in the DLL was called. You can find the library name of a DLL for which you do not have the .DEF file by using EXEHDR.EXE, which is included with the Microsoft C languages. In version 2.0 of Access, this requirement no longer applies.

A Word of Warning about COMMDLG.DLL

The setup programs of some Windows applications have not followed the conventions as to where to place DLLs, and that has wrought havoc on applications other than their own. One of the most common offenders is COMMDLG.DLL, a DLL supplemental to Windows that contains the most commonly used dialogs (Open, Save As, Color, Print, Print Setup, Find, and Replace). It is included as part of Windows 3.1 but not Windows 3.0. Because of this, programs intended to work with Windows 3.0 must install this DLL.

The programs that install COMMDLG.DLL have not been consistent in terms of placement. Some have placed it in their program directory, some in the Windows directory, and others in the Windows\System directory. Various versions of COMMDLG.DLL are not equal. Later versions have bug fixes that Access needs. If you have an older version of COMMDLG.DLL without the bug fixes in the Windows directory when the correct version is in the Windows\System directory, Access will not work correctly.

You can solve this problem by searching your entire hard disk for COMMDLG.DLL. Move the one with the most recent date to the Windows\System directory, and then delete all other versions. This should not have any impact on other programs since newer versions should always be backward compatible.

Specifying the Alias

The alias part of the declaration is important because it allows you to change the name of the function as it was declared in the DLL to a different name in Access Basic. There are several reasons why you might use the alias:

- To change the name in the DLL to one allowed by Access Basic
- To set the name to a DLL function that is only exposed by ordinal
- To have a unique name for your function in an Access Basic library

Each of these is described in the following sections.

Changing the Name in the DLL to One Allowed by Access Basic

The names that C allows for function names are different from those allowed by Access Basic. Access Basic function names must consist of alphanumeric or underscore characters and begin with a letter. C function names often begin with an underscore. The function name you specify in the Declare statement must be valid in Access Basic. If the name in the DLL doesn't match the Access Basic naming rules, you must use an alias. The name in the DLL might also be a reserved word in Access Basic, or it might be the name of an existing global variable or function, and in these cases, too, you must use an alias.

For example, Access Basic does not allow function names with a leading underscore. If the name in the DLL is _lwrite, you might declare the function as

```
Declare Function lwrite Lib "Kernel" Alias "_lwrite"
➡ (ByVal hFile As Integer, ByVal lpBuffer As String,
➡ ByVal intBytes As Integer) As Integer
```

This defines the function name lwrite() as the _lwrite() function in the Kernel Dynamic Link Library.

Setting the Name That Is Exposed by Ordinal

Every function in a DLL is assigned a number, called its *ordinal*. Every function in a DLL *may* expose its name but is not required to do so. (The programmer writing a DLL chooses which procedures within the DLL can be called from code existing outside the DLL; these functions are *exposed*.) When the DLL is linked, the .DEF file defines whether or not the function name is exposed. If you use the NONAME modifier, the linker does not include the name of the function in a table in the DLL. Not exposing the name has several consequences:

- The DLL is smaller because the string of characters for the name is not included in a table in the DLL.

- Calling the DLL by ordinal number is slightly faster because the name does not have to be looked up in the name table.

- The DLL is slightly more secure from users trying to determine the purpose of the exposed functions since there is no name to help them reverse-engineer the API to the DLL.

If you wish to call a function by ordinal, you must know the ordinal number for the function. You can find this information in the documentation for the DLL (if any) or in the .DEF file for the DLL. You can also use a program called EXEHDR.EXE, included with the Microsoft C languages, to examine a DLL. Whichever way you derive the ordinal, you specify #*ordinalnumber* for the alias name—that is, a pound sign followed by the decimal number of the ordinal. For example, the same lwrite declaration presented earlier might be declared as

```
Declare Function lwrite Lib "Kernel" Alias "#86"
➡ (ByVal hFile As Integer, ByVal lpBuffer As String,
➡ ByVal intBytes As Integer) As Integer
```

You may declare any Access Basic function to use the ordinal in the DLL, but if the name is exported, we recommend you use the name. This is especially true if you do not maintain the DLL. The DLL developer may assume that people will not call a function by ordinal if it is exported by name. Later versions of the DLL may not keep the same ordinal number for the functions in it but will most likely keep the same name.

Having a Unique Name for Your Function in an Access Basic Library

Each declared function in Access Basic must have a unique name. Normally, this doesn't have huge implications since you are not likely to give two different functions the same name or declare the same function twice in your own code. But if you are developing a library that might be included on different systems and that library calls a DLL (including Windows), this issue becomes important. Suppose your library calls the GetPrivateProfileString() Windows function. If you declare the function in the library without an alias, the name GetPrivateProfileString() is used by Access Basic. If users then decide to use GetPrivateProfileString() in their own code and declare it, the name in their code conflicts with the name in your library. Or worse, it might conflict with another library the user has installed since the user has no control over those names. For these reasons, declarations in a library should always use an alias. Thus, you might declare GetPrivateProfileString() in a library as:

```
Declare Function MYLB_GetPrivateProfileString Lib "Kernel"
➡ Alias "GetPrivateProfileString"(ByVal strApplicationName
➡ As String, strKeyName As Any, ByVal strDefault As String,
➡ ByVal strReturnedString As String, ByVal intSize As
➡ Integer, ByVal strFileName As String) As Integer
```

When you used the function in the library, you would then use MYLB_GetPrivateProfileString() as the function name. If another library were included, it might declare the same function using YRLB_GetPrivateProfileString(), but no conflict would occur since YRLB_GetPrivateProfileString() and MYLB_GetPrivateProfileString() are two different functions, as far as Access Basic is concerned.

> **NOTE**
> All the public DLL declarations in this book have been aliased using the prefix "glr_api".

Specifying the Arguments

The arguments to a DLL are passed to it on the stack. The DLL expects those arguments to be placed in a particular order and to have a certain size on the stack. When Access Basic places arguments on the stack, it looks to the Declare statement for direction. Correctly declaring arguments is the trickiest part of using a DLL from Access Basic. This subject is discussed in the following sections.

Understanding By Value and By Reference

You can pass an argument on the stack to a DLL in one of two ways: by value or by reference. *By value* means that the actual value of what is being passed is pushed onto the stack. *By reference* means that the address of what is being passed is pushed onto the stack. Unless you tell it otherwise, Access Basic passes all arguments by reference. On the other hand, most DLLs are written in C, and unless you tell the C compiler otherwise (by passing an address), C passes all arguments by value. The Access Basic declaration must be set up correctly to pass arguments the way the DLL expects them to be passed.

The semantic difference between passing by value and by reference is this:

- When you pass by value, a copy of the value is placed on the stack. Any changes to the value inside the DLL have an effect only on the copy and do not change the value for the calling code.

- When you pass by reference, the address of the value is placed on the stack. If the DLL makes changes to the value, the calling code will be able to see those changes.

A simple DLL might expect to have an integer passed by value as its argument. The C prototype for the function might look like the following. (Statements inside the /* and */ characters in C are comments.)

```
/* Function with integer passed by value */
void FunctionByValue (int w);
```

If the number 6 is to be passed to the function, then when the stack is arranged, the DLL expects to have the stack conceptually look like what is shown in Figure 17.1.

FIGURE 17.1:
Conceptual picture of stack when called by FunctionByValue(6). The value 6 is actually placed on the stack.

Stack

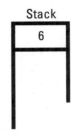

For this function the 6 is placed directly on the stack since the function expects the 6 to be passed by value. A different function might expect to have an integer passed by reference. The C prototype for this function might look like this:

```
/* Function with integer passed by reference */
/* i.e. function expects pointer to integer */
void FunctionByReference (int *pw);
```

If the number 6 is to be passed to the function, then when the stack is arranged, the DLL expects to have the stack conceptually look like what is shown in Figure 17.2.

For this function, the 6 is stored somewhere else in memory and a pointer to the memory where the 6 is stored is placed on the stack.

FIGURE 17.2:

Conceptual picture of stack when called by FunctionByReference(6). A pointer to the value 6 is placed on the stack.

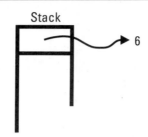

Stack

6

Using By Value and By Reference from Access Basic

From Access Basic, you would declare the two functions described in the previous section in two different ways. The declaration would tell Access Basic that it should arrange the stack the way the DLL wants it. The two declarations would be

```
Declare Sub FunctionByValue Lib "SomeLib.DLL"
➥ (ByVal intValue As Integer)
```

and

```
Declare Sub FunctionByReference Lib "SomeLib.DLL"
➥ (intValue As Integer)
```

Notice the keyword ByVal in the first declaration. After declaring these functions, you could call the functions without having to know whether the value should be passed by value or by reference. For example:

```
Call FunctionByValue(6)
Call FunctionByReference(6)
```

Since the declaration specifies how the stack is to be arranged, you do not need to be concerned with how the DLL expects the arguments when you are *calling* the function. You need to be concerned only when you are *declaring* the function. The exception to this rule is the Any datatype, described in the section "Using the Any Datatype" later in this chapter.

Converting C Parameters into Access Basic Declarations

Most DLLs are written in C. The documentation is usually in the form of a C header file (.h file) that provides the type and number of the arguments to the functions in the DLL. Based on the datatype required, you will need to convert it to an equivalent Access Basic datatype. Table 17.1 shows how to convert various C datatypes to Access Basic.

TABLE 17.1 : Conversions between C Datatypes and Access Datatypes

C Datatype	Access Basic Datatype
ATOM	ByVal atom As Integer
BOOL	ByVal fValue As Integer
BYTE	ByVal intValue As Integer
BYTE *	ByVal lpByte As Any
CALLBACK	ByVal lngAddr As Long
char	ByVal intValue As Integer
char _huge *	strValue As Any
char FAR *	strValue As Any
char NEAR *	ByVal lpNear As Integer
DWORD	ByVal lngValue As Long
FARPROC	ByVal lngAddress As Long
HACCEL	ByVal hAccel As Integer
HANDLE	ByVal h As Integer
HBITMAP	ByVal hBitmap As Integer
HBRUSH	ByVal hBrush As Integer
HCURSOR	ByVal hCursor As Integer
HDC	ByVal hDC As Integer
HDRVR	ByVal hDrvr As Integer
HDWP	ByVal hDWP As Integer
HFILE	ByVal hFile As Integer
HFONT	ByVal hFont As Integer

TABLE 17.1: Conversions between C Datatypes and Access Datatypes (continued)

C Datatype	Access Basic Datatype
HGDIOBJ	ByVal hGDIObj As Integer
HGLOBAL	ByVal hGlobal As Integer
HICON	ByVal hIcon As Integer
HINSTANCE	ByVal hInstance As Integer
HLOCAL	ByVal hLocal As Integer
HMENU	ByVal hMenu As Integer
HMETAFILE	ByVal hMetafile As Integer
HMODULE	ByVal hModule As Integer
HPALETTE	ByVal hPalette As Integer
HPEN	ByVal hPen As Integer
HRGN	ByVal hRgn As Integer
HRSRC	ByVal hRsrc As Integer
HTASK	ByVal hTask As Integer
HWND	ByVal hWnd As Integer
int	ByVal intValue As Integer
int FAR *	intValue As Integer
LONG	ByVal lngValue As Long
long	ByVal lngValue As Long
LPARAM	ByVal lngParam As Long
LPCSTR	ByVal strValue As String
LPSTR	ByVal strValue As String
LPVOID	varValue As Any
LRESULT	ByVal lngResult As Long
UINT	ByVal intValue As Integer
UINT FAR *	intValue As Integer
void _huge *	strValue As Any
void FAR *	strValue As Any
WORD	ByVal intValue As Integer
WPARAM	ByVal intValue As Integer

Using Callback Functions

Some Windows functions require a callback function. A *callback* is a procedure that *you* provide for *Windows* to call. Often the callback is called multiple times by Windows, passing arguments for each object in a Windows internal data structure. For example, a call to the EnumWindows() function requires a callback. The callback is called for each top-level window currently open and is passed a handle to it until they have all been enumerated. In the C declaration, the argument where you indicate the address of the callback has the datatype FARPROC or CALLBACK.

The callback function cannot be implemented in Access Basic. It must reside in a DLL. However, the Windows function that calls the callback can be called from Access Basic. To do so, you need to pass the address of the callback function, which you can retrieve with the GetProcAddress() Windows function. The GetProcAddress() function's two arguments are a handle to the DLL and the name of the function. The handle to the DLL must be retrieved with LoadLibrary and later freed with FreeLibrary.

For example, the code shown in Listing 17.1 starts up an instance of Notepad and then closes it again using the callback function GLR_WndEnumProc() in GLR.DLL. The callback function is shown in Listing 17.2 and works by looking for a window with the instance handle passed in and sending that Window a WM_CLOSE message. If the application is correctly implemented (and Notepad is), it will process the WM_CLOSE message and close itself.

Listing 17.1

```
Declare Function EnumWindows Lib "User"(ByVal WndEnumProc
➡ As Long, ByVal wApp As Long) As Integer
Declare Function GetProcAddress Lib "Kernel" (ByVal hinst As
➡ Integer, ByVal lpszProcName As String) As Long
Declare Function LoadLibrary Lib "Kernel" (ByVal lpLibFileName
➡ As String) As Integer
Declare Sub FreeLibrary Lib "Kernel" (ByVal hLibModule As
➡ Integer)

Sub CallBackDemo()
    Dim intRet As Integer
    Dim hinstLibrary As Integer
    Dim lngAddrLibrary As Long
    Dim hinstApp As Integer
```

```
' Start notepad
hinstApp = Shell("notepad.exe")

' Give the application enough time to start
intRet = DoEvents()

' Load the library
hinstLibrary = LoadLibrary("glr.dll")

If hinstLibrary > 32 Then
    ' Get the address of the GLR_WndEnumProc routine
    lngAddrLibrary = GetProcAddress(hinstLibrary,
    ➥ "GLR_glrWndEnumProc")

    If lngAddrLibrary <> 0 Then
        ' Pass the address of the GLR_WndEnumProc routine to
        ' EnumWindows
        ' with the hinstApp that we want to close
        intRet = EnumWindows(lngAddrLibrary, CLng(hinstApp))
    End If

    ' Free the library
    FreeLibrary (hinstLibrary)
End If
End Sub
```

Listing 17.2

```c
/*================================================================
GLR_glrWndEnumProc
================================================================*/
BOOL __export CALLBACK GLR_glrWndEnumProc
(
HWND hwnd,
LPARAM wApp
)
    {
    if (GetWindowWord(hwnd, GWW_HINSTANCE) == (WORD) wApp)
        if (GetParent(hwnd) == hwndNil)
            {
            PostMessage(hwnd, WM_CLOSE, 0, 0);
            return 0;
            }
    return 1;
    }
```

Instead of doing the LoadLibrary, GetProcAddress, and FreeLibrary calls, you will often find it more efficient to create another function in the DLL that contains the callback function to do the calling of the Windows function. This allows you to use the normal Declare statement to call the function that does the actual work. Chapter 18 shows a function called GLR_CloseApp() that does just this.

Returning Strings from a DLL

Normally, DLLs cannot create Access Basic strings. Access Basic has its own method of storing strings, which is different from the way DLLs store strings. DLLs have no way of creating or extending the size of those strings unless they can understand Access Basic's string descriptors. However, DLLs can change the contents of Access Basic strings that already exist.

Since the stack is a small temporary storage area and a string can be 32K long, strings cannot be passed by value because they could overflow the stack. For this reason, all strings are passed by reference. The ByVal reserved word, when referring to a string, does not mean *by value*, despite its name. When referring to a string, it tells Access Basic that you wish to pass a null-terminated string to the DLL. A *null-terminated string* is a set of characters followed by a null character (ANSI value 0). When the function is called, Access Basic appends a null character to the end of the string and passes a long pointer to the string. If the ByVal is not used, Access Basic passes a string descriptor, which is Access Basic's internal handle to the string. Unless the DLL is prepared to handle Access Basic string descriptors, the ByVal reserved word must be used.

A library included with the Visual Basic 3.0 Professional Edition called VBAPI.LIB allows you to manipulate Access Basic string descriptors from a DLL. With these routines you can create strings in a DLL or change their length. These routines just happen to work on Access strings because of the similarity between Access Basic and Visual Basic, but Microsoft currently makes no guarantees about compatibility in the future. In most cases you will pass information back and forth to a DLL using null-terminated strings.

The GetPrivateProfileString() function is an example of a Windows function that returns a string. When it is called, it looks in an .INI file for a key and in places associated with that key. This is a Declare statement for that function:

```
Declare Function GetPrivateProfileString Lib "Kernel"
➡ (ByVal strApplicationName As String, ByVal strKeyName As
➡ String, ByVal strDefault As String, ByVal
➡ strReturnedString As String, ByVal intSize As Integer,
➡ ByVal strFileName As String) As Integer
```

When the function is called, the Windows Kernel DLL changes the string in the strReturnedString variable. You need to make the string long enough to contain the return value. This is typically done with the String() function, which creates a string with a given size of the specified character. For example:

```
Dim strReturnedString As String
Dim intRet As Integer

' Allocate enough space for the return value.
strReturnedString = String(255, " ")
intRet = GetPrivateProfileString("Options", "SystemDB",
➡ "None", strReturnedString, Len(strReturnedString),
➡ "MSACCESS.INI")
strReturnedString = Left$(strReturnedString, intRet)
```

You can also do this with the Space$() function.

In this case, 255 characters were allocated for the GetPrivateProfileString() function to fill in the return value. After Access Basic calls the function in the DLL, the string is still 255 characters, but they are no longer all spaces; the GetPrivateProfileString() function has changed some of them. After the function call you will want to remove the extra padding characters at the end of the string. You can do this with the Left$() function since the GetPrivateProfileString() function returns the length of the string. Since strings in C are terminated with a null character (ANSI value 0), you can also search for the null character to determine how long the string should be. The Instr() function combined with the Left$() function does the job.

When this function is called, you can picture the stack along the lines of what is shown in Figure 17.3.

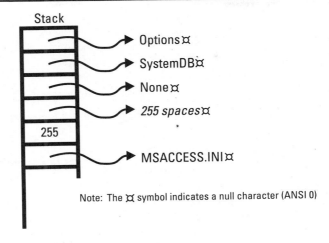

FIGURE 17.3:
Conceptual picture of the stack when calling GetPrivateProfileString()

Note: The ¤ symbol indicates a null character (ANSI 0)

Using the Any Datatype

There is another way you can call the GetPrivateProfileString() function: you can pass a null pointer as the strKeyName argument. If you do this, Windows returns all the keys in the entire section to the string passed in, each key separated by null characters. To get this functionality, you want the stack to look like what is shown in Figure 17.4.

How can you pass a null pointer? You cannot pass an empty string because that would pass a pointer to the empty string. (Remember that strings are passed by reference.) Passing an empty string would result in a stack like the one shown in Figure 17.5.

You will notice that Figures 17.4 and 17.5 are not the same thing. The stack in Figure 17.4 passes a null pointer, and the stack in Figure 17.5 passes a pointer to a null character. So how do you pass a null pointer? The answer is to change the declaration from being a string, which is always passed by reference, to a special datatype called *Any*. The declaration would now appear as

```
Declare Function GetPrivateProfileString Lib "Kernel"
➡ (ByVal strApplicationName As String, strKeyName
➡ As Any, ByVal strDefault As String, ByVal
➡ strReturnedString As String, ByVal intSize As Integer,
➡ ByVal strFileName As String) As Integer
```

FIGURE 17.4:

Conceptual picture of
the stack when calling
GetPrivateProfileString()
with a null pointer

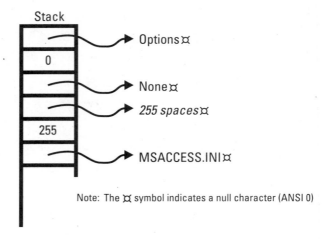

FIGURE 17.5:

Conceptual picture of
the stack when calling
GetPrivateProfileString() with
a pointer to a null character

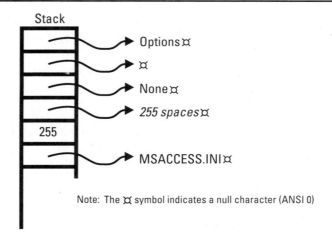

Notice that the ByVal was removed from the strKeyName declaration and the datatype was changed to Any. The Any datatype means that you cannot decide which datatype to use at the time the function is declared; you want to make that decision at the time the function is called. When you call the function, you may still pass the string, or you may pass a null pointer. To pass the string you would call it as you did before, but you must indicate that the string needs to be changed to a null-terminated string by using the ByVal reserved word when the function is called. You would now use this format to call the function:

```
intRet = GetPrivateProfileString("Options", ByVal "SystemDB",
➡ "None", strReturnedString, Len(strReturnedString),
➡ "MSACCESS.INI")
```

If you wanted to pass a null pointer, you would put a 0 on the stack. To do so, you would pass the 0 using ByVal when you call the function, so it would look like this:

```
intRet = GetPrivateProfileString("Options", ByVal O&,
➡ "None", strReturnedString, Len(strReturnedString),
➡ "MSACCESS.INI")
```

Notice that the 0 is followed by an ampersand (&). This means that the 0 constant value should be treated as a long instead of an integer. This puts 4 bytes (the length of a long) on the stack instead of 2 bytes for the default integer. Since a far pointer, which is what the function expects, is 4 bytes, the ampersand is required.

Passing a User-Defined Type to a DLL

Sometimes you will want to pass a user-defined type to a DLL. For example, many of the Windows functions expect a RECT structure, which is a user-defined type, as opposed to one that is supported implicitly by the C language. To do so, you need to define an equivalent type in Access Basic. Here is the definition of a RECT in C:

```
typedef struct tagRECT
{
    int left;
    int top;
    int right;
    int bottom;
} RECT;
```

The equivalent structure in Access Basic is

```
Type RECT
    left As Integer
    top As Integer
    right As Integer
    bottom As Integer
End Type
```

You must pass a structure by reference. The declaration of a function that takes a RECT as an argument might be

```
Declare Sub InvalidateRect Lib "User"(ByVal hWnd As Integer,
➥ lpRect As RECT, ByVal fErase As Integer)
```

Passing an Array

You can pass individual elements of an array like any other variable. If aintValue is an array of integers, calling a DLL with

```
Call FunctionByValue(ByVal aintValue(6))
```

is the same as

```
intTemp = aintValue(6)
Call FunctionByValue(intTemp)
```

Sometimes, though, you'll want to pass an entire array to a DLL. You may do this—but only for numeric arrays, not for strings or user-defined ones. (The reason has to do with how Access Basic stores the array in memory.) To do so, you pass the first element of the array by reference. For example:

```
Call ArrayFunction(aintValue(0), UBound(aintValue))
```

When passing an array to a DLL function, you must give the function some indication of the size of the array. The best way to do this is to have another argument in which you pass the size of the array, as shown in the above call to ArrayFunction(). Otherwise, the DLL cannot determine how large the array is and can go beyond the end of the array. Trying to use a value beyond the end of an array can cause a GP fault.

The Windows API

The Windows API includes about 400 functions. Describing them all is beyond the scope of this book, but they are documented in the Microsoft Windows SDK (Software Development Kit) and Microsoft Visual C++. Even more useful than paper documentation is a Help file, WIN31WH.HLP, that describes each of the functions. This Help file is included as part of the Visual Basic Professional Edition, Visual C++, the Windows SDK, the Microsoft Developer Network CD-ROM, and other

Microsoft products (although the file name changes from product to product). The Access Developer's Toolkit has a different Help file, WIN31API.HLP, that provides just the Windows API declarations and structures. This Help file does not describe each of the arguments to the API functions.

Using WIN30API.TXT and WIN31EXT.TXT

Included in the Access Developer's Toolkit you will find files called WIN30API.TXT and WIN31EXT.TXT. These files contain declarations for each of the approximately 400 Windows functions, plus many Windows constants and structures. It is not a good idea to load these entire files into modules in your database because you will most likely use only a handful of the declarations, and the other declarations eat an enormous amount of resources every time you open your database.

The best way to use these files is to cut and paste just the declarations you use into a module. These files also relieve you of the problem of trying to figure out which Windows DLL a given Windows function resides in. The function can reside in User, GDI, Kernel, or several supplemental DLLs, but you won't be able to tell which from the name of the function, the printed documentation, or the Help file. Since the text files contain the proper declarations, you do not have to guess.

Summary

This chapter has covered the following topics:

- Declaring DLL functions
- Specifying the DLL library name
- Using aliases
- Specifying the DLL arguments
- Understanding by value, by reference, and the stack
- Using callback functions

- Returning strings from a DLL
- Using the Any datatype
- Passing user-defined types to a DLL
- Passing arrays to a DLL
- Using the Windows API
- Using WIN31API.TXT and WIN31EXT.TXT

The chapter discussed how to declare and call a DLL function. DLLs are one of the three ways by which you can reach outside the bounds of Access into other Windows programs, the other two being DDE (see Chapter 18) and OLE (see Chapter 19). The DLL interface allows you to manipulate Windows directly through the Windows API, as well as to call your own DLLs. Combined with a C or C++ compiler and the appropriate knowledge, DLLs allow you to do virtually anything that is possible with Windows. But even without the use of C or C++, the ability to call the Windows API vastly extends the power of Access.

CHAPTER

EIGHTEEN

Using DDE

- What DDE clients and servers are

- Dynamics of a DDE conversation

- Topics and Items

- Properties of each of the DDE commands

- Closing a DDE server

- Using Access as a DDE server

Dynamic Data Exchange (DDE) is a Windows protocol and Application Programming Interface (API) that allows one Windows program to exchange data with another or causes one program to trigger functionality in the other. With DDE, you can extract data from a spreadsheet in Excel, manipulate a Word for Windows document, or control your own Visual Basic program. From other programs you can extract data from an Access database, run a macro, or get a list of existing tables. DDE is a general language protocol for manipulating programs programmatically. This protocol is different from OLE, but there is some overlap of functionality. In the long run, DDE will probably be replaced entirely by OLE when all major applications support OLE Automation. For programs that don't support OLE Automation, you must use DDE. You must also use DDE for controlling programs across a network because OLE Automation cannot currently do that.

Clients and Servers

To be able to use DDE, a Windows program must support the DDE API. A Windows program can support two kinds of DDE functionality:

- Client
- Server

The *client* is the program doing the controlling; the *server* is the program being controlled. A Windows program can support neither, either, or both of these. Microsoft Access supports both. To establish a conversation between two programs using DDE, one program must be acting as a DDE client, the other as a server.

As a DDE client, Access can retrieve information from another program. For example, it can retrieve information from an Excel spreadsheet. When Access is a DDE server, another program can retrieve information from Access. For example, a C program can retrieve information from an Access query.

Dynamics of a DDE Conversation

Figure 18.1 shows an example of a DDE conversation. As you can see, a handshaking operation is going on between the two programs. The client requests something to be done on the server. When the server has completed the task, it acknowledges this by sending either some data or an acknowledgment.

If the acknowledgment is not received within a certain amount of time, Access Basic assumes that the server is not responding and reports a run-time error. The amount of time Access Basic waits before reporting an error is controlled by the View ➤ Options ➤ OLE/DDE Timeout option.

Servers, Topics, and Items

When a DDE client wishes to retrieve some information from a running DDE server, it must know three pieces of information:

- A server name for the DDE server
- The topic
- The specific item of information to retrieved

Each of these is described in the following sections.

DDE Server Names   The DDE server name is a name the DDE server registers with Windows when it starts. Often a server will register more than one name. Access, for example, registers MSAccess, MSACCESS.EXE, MSAccess*InstanceNumber* (for example: MSAccess3246), and Microsoft Access. All of the registered names are valid server names.

Topics   When you establish a conversation between a client and a server, you have to state what you want to talk about. Each server has a list of topics it is

FIGURE 18.1:

Example DDE conversion

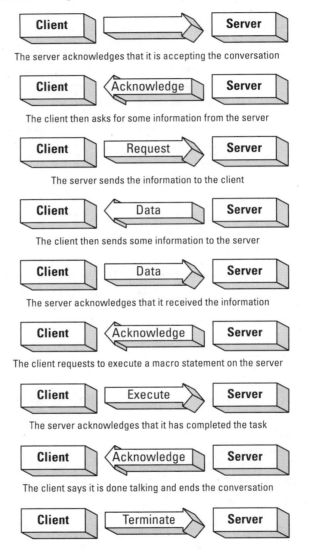

A DDE Conversation begins with the client initiating the conversation with the server

The server acknowledges that it is accepting the conversation

The client then asks for some information from the server

The server sends the information to the client

The client then sends some information to the server

The server acknowledges that it received the information

The client requests to execute a macro statement on the server

The server acknowledges that it has completed the task

The client says it is done talking and ends the conversation

prepared to discuss, and the client must select one of them. These topics vary in scope in different servers. For example, Access is prepared to discuss the following topics:

- Information about the state of Access—whether it is ready to accept DDE commands, which system items it can accept, which clipboard formats it supports, and which topics it can handle
- Information about an open database—which tables, queries, forms, reports, macros, and modules the database contains
- Information from any table in the database—the column names, datatypes, and number of columns in the table; and the data from the table
- Information from any query in the database—the column names, datatypes, and number of columns in the result set of the query; and the data from the query
- Information from any Access SQL statement—the columns names, datatypes, and number of columns in the result set of the SQL statement; and the data the SQL statement returns

For each conversation you must choose one, and only one, topic. You may have multiple DDE conversations going on at once, but each one uses a separate topic.

Items   Items are used once a conversation is established to request information about the topic. For example, if the server is Excel, the topic might be the spreadsheet Sheet1. The item might request information about what is contained in R1C1 on Sheet1. Or if Access is acting as the server and the topic is a SQL query, the item might ask for the next row in the rowset.

Interacting with Other Applications Using DDE Functions

With Access acting as a client, you can connect to any DDE server. To do so, you use the DDE functions in Access Basic. Each DDE client provides more or less the same functionality as Access, but the syntax varies among clients. DDE client operations are performed with the six low-level functions and statements and two high-level functions shown in Table 18.1.

TABLE 18.1: DDE Functions

Function	Purpose	Level
DDEInitiate()	Initiates a DDE conversation between Access and a DDE server	Low
DDETerminate()	Ends a DDE conversation between Access and a DDE server	Low
DDEExecute()	Executes an operation in the DDE server's macro language	Low
DDEPoke()	Sends data to the DDE server	Low
DDERequest()	Retrieves data from the DDE server	Low
DDETerminateAll()	Ends conversations with all DDE servers	Low
DDE()	Initiates a conversation, retrieves some data, and ends the conversation with a DDE server. Valid only on forms in the ControlSource property of text boxes, option groups, check boxes, and combo boxes	High
DDESend()	Initiates a conversation, sends some data, and ends the conversation with a DDE server. Valid only on forms in the ControlSource property of text boxes, option groups, check boxes, and combo boxes	High

The DDE Channel

When the DDEInitiate() function succeeds in connecting a client to a server, Windows creates a channel between them. Conceptually, the channel is a pathway between the client and server where all data between them flows.

Internally, Windows allocates a block of memory that contains the information about the channel. The number that references that block of memory is called a *channel number*. Each of the low-level DDE functions uses that channel number as one of the arguments to the function.

> **TIP**
>
> Because Windows has allocated memory, it is important that you always use the DDETerminate or DDETerminateAll statement when you finish the conversation with the DDE server; otherwise you will have lost some memory to Windows. For example, if you had a DDEInitiate() executed every time you refreshed a form but did not do a DDETerminate, eventually you would run out of memory. A few DDE servers, such as Excel version 3.0, have memory leaks in some cases, which means that you may lose resources even if you terminate properly. You need to watch your resources to make sure you don't eventually run out of memory. The latest releases of programs should have these memory leaks fixed.

DDE Functions and Statements

The following sections describe each of the DDE functions and statements. These statements start a conversation, read data, write data, execute macros, and terminate conversations with a server.

The DDEInitiate() Function

The DDEInitiate() function establishes the conversation between a client and a server. The syntax for the function in Access Basic is

$varChannelNumber$ = DDEInitiate($strApplication$, $strTopic$)

The arguments to the DDEInitiate() function are the name of the application you want to connect to and the topic you wish to discuss.

DDEInitiate() uses the server name to establish a connection with a server that is currently running. Often, an application with which you wish to make a DDE connection is not running. If that is the case, Access looks at the server name you used. If the server name is eight characters or less and is a valid file name, Access assumes that the application name argument must be the file name of an application it should run. Access then tries to execute the application using the WinExec() Windows function. If this succeeds, Access tries again to establish the connection. For this to work the server must register a server name with Windows that is the same as the base part of its executable name. If the application is named WINWORD.EXE, the server must register WINWORD as a server name.

For example, if an Access application is trying to establish a connection with Excel, it might execute the following code:

```
varChannelNumber = DDEInitiate("Excel", "System")
```

If Excel is not running, Access performs a WinExec() of "Excel". The Windows WinExec() function searches directories in this order:

1. The current directory

2. The Windows directory

3. The Windows\System directory

4. In Windows 3.1, the directory containing the executable file for the current task (MSACCESS.EXE, if Access is the DDE client)

5. The directories listed in the PATH environment variable

6. The directories mapped to a network drive

If EXCEL.EXE is not in one of these directories, Access cannot find Excel and generates a run-time error. Otherwise Excel starts and registers the name "Excel" with Windows. Access again tries to establish a conversation with a server that has registered the name "Excel". This still might fail if Windows does not have enough memory or if an Excel option has been set to "Ignore Remote Requests." If the conversation is established, the DDEInitiate() function returns a channel number. Note that if Access fails to make the connection now, Excel is still left running.

The *strApplication* argument of DDEInitiate() performs two operations: starting the application and connecting to the DDE server. Often it is better to break apart those operations. Suppose that Excel is not on the path and is not running. The following code does not work:

```
' Doesn't work
varChannelNumber = DDEInitiate("c:\excel\excel.exe", "system")
```

The reason is that Access tries to use "c:\excel\excel.exe" as the server name. No server has this server name registered with Windows, so Access looks to see whether the server name is eight characters or less and a valid base part of a file name. Since it is not, Access returns a run-time error. To perform a DDE connection with a program that is not in one of the standard places, you start the application yourself with the Shell() function, as shown in the following code:

```
intInstance = Shell("c:\excel\excel.exe", 2)
varChannelNumber = DDEInitiate("Excel", "System")
```

This raises several issues. The first is that several programs or instances of programs can have the same application name registered with Windows. If you have two instances of Excel running, each instance of Excel registers the name "Excel" with Windows as a valid server name. This can happen if an instance of Excel was already running when you executed the Shell statement. When you do a DDEInitiate(), how can you tell whether you are communicating with the instance you just started with the Shell() function? The answer is that you can't if you use the DDE server name "Excel". If you use a server name that is used by more than one server, Windows chooses an instance for the connection. You have no control over which instance Windows chooses.

Fortunately, Excel, Access, and many other DDE servers register several different names with Windows for each instance. One of the names they register is their server name with a unique number of their instance appended to the end. When you execute the Shell() function from Access, the number returned is this unique number. From this you could expect the following to work:

```
' Almost works
intInstance = Shell("c:\excel\excel.exe", 2)
varChannelNumber = DDEInitiate("Excel" & intInstance, "System")
```

However, the instance number Excel registers is unsigned (in the range 0 to 65535), but intInstance is signed (in the range −32768 to 32767). More than half the time, the code works since Windows usually assigns low numbers first. But eventually Windows starts a task with an instance number greater than 32767, the highest signed integer. When this happens, the DDEInitiate() fails because the number stored in intInstance is negative and the number in the topic registered by Excel is positive. To convert the signed instance number returned by the Shell() function to an unsigned long, you can use the following Access Basic function:

```
Function glrUIntFromInt(intSigned As Integer) As Long
    ' This routine takes a signed integer and returns
    ' a long that is the unsigned equivalent

    If intSigned < 0 Then
        ' First convert it to a long
        ' Then mask off any high order bits
        glrUIntFromInt = CLng(intSigned) And &HFFFF&
    Else
        glrUIntFromInt = CLng(intSigned)
    End If
End Function
```

The function works by converting the number to a long. If the number is negative, the high-order bits are masked off using the And operator to result in a positive number. The long return value from this function is appended to the word *Excel* to form the proper server name, allowing Access Basic to convert it to the String datatype in the process:

```
' Works
intInstance = Shell("c:\excel\excel.exe", 2)
varChannelNumber = DDEInitiate("Excel" &
    ➡ UIntFromInt(intInstance), "System")
```

To find the available DDE server names, you can use the DDESpy utility included with the Windows SDK and various other Microsoft applications. However, be warned that this utility shows only servers that use DDEML.DLL, a Windows library that makes DDE operations easier for C programmers. Servers that use an older method of doing DDE through Windows, such as Excel version 4.0, are not shown by this utility.

The DDERequest() Function

The DDERequest() function requests information from the DDE server. The syntax for the DDERequest function is

varRequestedInformation = DDERequest(*intChannelNumber, strItem*)

The arguments to the DDERequest() function are the channel number returned by the DDEInitiate() function and the item you are requesting. For each topic a server understands, you can request certain items of information. You must read the server's documentation to find out which items a server supports for each topic; there is no way to determine this information from the server itself. Unfortunately, it is often difficult to find the section on DDE within most documentation.

For example, on an Excel spreadsheet using the topic "Sheet1", the Excel documentation shows than an item you might request is the value of cell R2C4. This would be expressed as

varValue = DDERequest(varChannelNumber, "R2C4")

DDE Datatypes

DDEInitiate() returns a variable of type variant, but DDERequest() expects an integer. Access coerces the value of the variant into an integer before the call is made. If you wanted, you could use

```
varValue = DDERequest(CInt(varChannelNumber), "R2C4")
```

Using the CInt() function to make the conversion is more explicit, but it is not required since Access will do the conversion for you.

The DDETerminate and DDETerminateAll Statements

When you have completed all DDE operations, you must call DDETerminate or DDETerminateAll to free the channel and release the memory that Windows has allocated to keep information for the channel. The syntax for the DDETerminate statement in Access Basic is

> DDETerminate *intChannelNumber*

The argument is the channel number returned by the DDEInitiate() function.

The DDETerminateAll statement closes all open DDE channels. The syntax is

> DDETerminateAll

Don't rely on Access or Windows to ever reclaim the memory it allocates with a DDEInitiate() if you don't execute one of these two terminating functions. When you are debugging Access Basic code that deals with DDE, it is a good idea to sometimes execute a DDETerminateAll statement in the Immediate window just to have Access clean up any open connections.

The DDEExecute Statement

The DDEExecute statement allows you to run functionality in another program. The syntax for the DDEExecute statement is

> DDEExecute *intChannelNumber*, *strCommand*

What the DDEExecute statement can perform depends on what the server program allows. You must read the documentation for the server program to see the format of the *strCommand* argument. Excel allows you to execute any command-equivalent macro function. The sub shown in Listing 18.1 starts up Excel and then uses a DDEExecute statement to open the spreadsheet C:\DATA\XLS\AMORT.XLS.

Listing 18.1

```
Sub DDETest1()
    Dim varChannelNumber As Variant
    Dim intTaskID As Integer
```

```
    intInstance = Shell("c:\excel\excel.exe", 2)
    varChannelNumber = DDEInitiate("Excel" &
        ➡ UIntFromInt(intInstance), "System")
    DDEExecute CInt(varChannelNumber),
        ➡ "[Open(""c:\data\xls\amort.xls"")]"
    DDETerminate CInt(varChannelNumber)
End Sub
```

NOTE In Access 1.0 and 1.1 you could not use Access as both the client and the server at the same time when doing a DDEExecute. In other words, an Access Basic routine could not perform a DDEExecute statement that ran against the same instance of Access that was running the DDEExecute statement. This was a deliberate limitation of Access to prevent reentrancy problems, where the code that gets executed by the DDEExecute might interfere with the Access Basic routine that is performing the DDEExecute. For version 2.0, this limitiation no longer applies.

The DDEPoke Statement

The DDEPoke statement inserts data into another application. The Access Basic syntax is

DDEPoke *intChannelNumber*, *strItem*, *strData*

To put information into a specific cell in an Excel spreadsheet, you would use

```
DDEPoke varChannelNumber, "R1C2", "1234.56"
```

The DDE() Function

The DDE() function is the high-level version of DDERequest(). You can use it only in the ControlSource property of text boxes, option groups, check boxes, and combo boxes. It performs the tasks of DDEInitiate(), DDERequest(), and DDETerminate() rolled into one function. The syntax is

=DDE(*strApplication, strTopic, strItem*)

For example, if you create a text box on a form and insert the following line into the ControlSource property, the text box is loaded from R1C1 on the Excel spreadsheet Sheet1:

```
=DDE("Excel","Sheet1","R1C1")
```

The DDESend() Function

DDESend() is the high-level version of DDEPoke(). It also can be used only in the ControlSource property of text boxes, option groups, check boxes, and combo boxes. It performs the tasks of DDEInitiate(), DDEPoke(), and DDETerminate() rolled into one function. The syntax is

=DDESend(*strApplication, strTopic, strItem, strItem*)

The return value from the DDESend() function is null if the DDESend() succeeded. If it failed, it returns an error. For example, you might create a text box on a form with this text in the ControlSource property:

```
=DDESend("Excel","Sheet1","R1C2",[txtData])
```

Then you could create another text box on the form with the name txtData. Anytime the data in the txtData control is changed and a requery is issued (using the F9 key), the R1C2 cell on the Excel spreadsheet Sheet1 is updated with the contents of txtData.

Creating Robust DDE Code

DDE requires the DDE server to be running. Since many things (like running out of resources or a user's closing the application) can keep the server from being there, you must always be prepared to handle the fact that any DDE statement can fail. Just because a DDEInitiate() succeeded doesn't mean you can count on the server's being there for any subsequent DDE functions. This means that every routine that calls DDE functions should have an error handler to catch such events (see Chapter 14). The error handler can then clean up gracefully or try to reestablish the connection. Preparing to handle DDE failures requires many lines of error-handling code and also requires spending lots of time testing your code. Making an application that uses DDE robust (able to recover from errors) is a difficult and time-consuming task.

Closing a Shelled Program

The Shell() function is great for starting an instance of a DDE server, but how do you close that server when you are done with it? One way would be to use DDEExecute to execute a macro statement that closes the application you started. Some applications, however, don't implement DDEExecute. Also, you should not shut down a server involved in an active DDE conversation. Doing so can cause memory leaks, GP Faults, or other nasty problems because most DDE servers have bugs when using obscure features. Using DDEExecute to close the server while it is processing the DDEExecute is asking for trouble.

A better method is to close the conversation and then close the application. But how do you close the application? There is no Access Basic function or statement to do it. Nor is there a simple Windows call to close an application given its instance number. We wrote a routine in C called GLR_glrCloseApp, included in the GLR.DLL on the companion disk for this book, that closes the application based on its instance number. Listing 18.2 shows the C code that makes up the routine in the DLL. The code simply enumerates all the running applications in Windows (using an EnumWindows call and the GLR_glrWndEnumProc callback described in Chapter 17) until it finds the one with the proper instance number. It then sends a WM_CLOSE message to the application. If the server is implemented correctly, it is closed after prompting the user to save any objects that need to be saved. Since EnumWindows requires a callback function, you cannot implement the callback within Access.

Listing 18.2

```
/*================================================================
CloseApp

This function closes the app started with WinExec (or Shell in
application programs.
================================================================*/
BOOL __export WINAPI GLR_glrCloseApp
(
UINT wApp  /* the number returned by WinExec to close */
)
    {
    if (wApp >= 32)
        return EnumWindows((WNDENUMPROC) GLR_glrWndEnumProc,
        ➡ (LPARAM) wApp);
    else
        return FALSE;
    }


/*================================================================
WndEnumProc
================================================================*/
BOOL __export CALLBACK GLR_glrWndEnumProc
(
HWND hwnd,
LPARAM wApp
)
    {
    if (GetWindowWord(hwnd, GWW_HINSTANCE) == (WORD) wApp)
        if (GetParent(hwnd) == hwndNil)
            {
            PostMessage(hwnd, WM_CLOSE, 0, 0);
            return 0;
            }
    return 1;
    }
```

The next section gives an example of GLR_CloseApp in use.

Putting It Together

The subroutine shown in Listing 18.3 shows a complete example that

1. Starts an instance of Excel

2. Opens a spreadsheet called C:\DATA\XLS\AMORT.XLS

3. Reads the information in cell R3C6

4. Multiplies it by 10

5. Pokes the result back in the same cell

6. Closes Excel

Listing 18.3

```
Sub DDETest2()
    Dim varChannelNumber As Variant
    Dim intTaskID As Integer
    Dim varValue As Variant
    Dim intRet As Integer

    intTaskID = Shell("c:\excel\excel.exe", 2)
    varChannelNumber = DDEInitiate("excel" &
        ➥ UIntFromInt(intTaskID), "System")
    DDEExecute varChannelNumber,
        ➥ "[Open(""c:\data\xls\amort.xls"")]"
    DDETerminate varChannelNumber
    varChannelNumber = DDEInitiate("excel" &
        ➥ UIntFromInt(intTaskID), "amort.xls")
    varValue = DDERequest(varChannelNumber, "R3C6")
    varValue = varValue * 10
    DDEPoke varChannelNumber, "R3C6", varValue
    DDETerminate varChannelNumber
    intRet = DoEvents()
    intRet = MADH_CloseApp(intTaskID)
End Sub
```

Using DDE Topics and Items

Each DDE server understands various DDE topics. You can identify the topics that a server understands in two ways:

- Read the documentation for the server application.
- Do a DDERequest() of the system topic of the server with the system topic.

Most DDE servers have a topic called *system*. Under the system topic is an item called *topics*. If the server you are connecting to supports this topic and item, the code shown in Listing 18.4 displays the list of topics available to the server named in the strServerName constant (MSAccess) to the Immediate window.

Listing 18.4

```
Sub DDETopics()
    Dim varChannelNumber As Variant
    Const strServerName = "MSAccess"

    varChannelNumber = DDEInitiate(strServerName, "system")
    Debug.Print DDERequest(varChannelNumber, "topics")
    DDETerminate varChannelNumber
End Sub
```

The topics shown for Access are the system topic plus all the databases Access has open. Access doesn't qualify which types the various databases are. There is the system database, which contains security and preference information; the various libraries, including the Wizard library; and the currently open database in the Access user interface. The currently open database always appears last in the list of topics. This particular order is important since DDE is the only way in Access 1.0 and 1.1 to retrieve the name of the currently open database.

Under the system topic are items that tell you information about the server. Replace the word *topics* in Listing 18.4 with the word *sysitems* and you are shown the items the Access system topic supports. The Access system topics supports four items, as described in the following list. Most other DDE servers also support at least these four.

SysItems	List of items supported by the system topic in Microsoft Access
Format	List of the formats Access can copy onto the clipboard
Status	"Busy" or "Ready"
Topics	List of all topics Access DDE supports

Using Access as a DDE Server

Access has a fairly reasonable set of server capabilities, allowing a DDE client to retrieve data in various ways and execute actions or macros. There is only one major feature missing: you cannot change the data directly via DDE using DDEPoke.

The Access system topics and system items were discussed in the preceding section of this chapter. But what can you do with the databases listed? You can

- Retrieve a list of the current tables, queries, forms, reports, macros, or modules
- Retrieve records from a table or select query
- Use a SQL query on any table or query in the database

To retrieve a list of objects, you use the open database name (without the extension) as the DDE topic and the word TableList, QueryList, FormList, ReportList, MacroList, or ModuleList as the DDE item. The DDERequest() returns the names of all objects of the requested type separated by tabs (ANSI code 9).

To retrieve records from a table, select query, or SQL statement, you can construct the DDE topic in one of these forms:

dbName; TABLE *tblTablename*

dbName; QUERY *qryQueryname*

dbName; SQL *strSQLString*

dbName; SQL

If the last form, with just SQL, is used, you can construct the SQL in pieces using the DDEPoke statement. An example is shown in Listing 18.5.

Listing 18.5

```
varChannelNumber = DDEInitiate("MSAccess", "NWIND; SQL")
DDEPoke varChannelNumber, "SELECT *"
DDEPoke varChannelNumber, " FROM Orders"
DDEPoke varChannelNumber, " WHERE [Order Amount] > 500;"
strRequest = DDERequest$(varChannelNumber, "All")
DDETerminate varChannelNumber
```

When your code retrieves information from a table, query, or SQL statement, the DDE item is one of the keywords shown in Table 18.2.

TABLE 18.2: Access Server Item Keywords

Item	Meaning
All	All the data in the table, including field names
Data	All rows of data without field names
FieldNames	Single-row list of field names
FieldNames;T	Two-row list of field names (first row) and their datatypes (second row)
NextRow	Next row in the table or query. When you first open a channel, NextRow returns the first row. If the current row is the last record and you execute NextRow, the request fails
PrevRow	Previous row in the table or query. If PrevRow is the first request over a new channel, the last row of the table or query is returned. If the first record is the current row, the request for PrevRow fails
FirstRow	Data in the first row of the table or query
LastRow	Data in the last row of the table or query
FieldCount	Number of fields in the table or query
SQLText	SQL statement representing the table or query
SQLText;n	SQL statement, in n-character chunks, representing the table or query, where n is an integer up to 255

If you use the item "FieldNames;T", the second line is a list of numbers corresponding to the field names listed in the first line returned (lines are separated by an ANSI code 13). The data numbers correspond to the datatypes shown in Table 18.3.

TABLE 18.3: Datatype Numbers

Number	Datatype
0	Invalid
1	True/False (non-null)
2	Unsigned byte (Byte)
3	2-byte signed integer (Integer)
4	4-byte signed integer (Long)
5	8-byte signed integer (Currency)
6	4-byte single-precision floating-point (Single)
7	8-byte double-precision floating-point (Double)
8	Date/Time (integral date, fractional time)
9	Binary data, 255 bytes maximum
10	ANSI text, case insensitive, 255 bytes maximum (Text)
11	Long binary (OLE Object)
12	Long text (Memo)

NOTE

You cannot specify a field of type 9 through the Access table design mode. Access sometimes creates a field of that type for you if you attach a table to a database that uses that type. "FieldName;T" as an item was implemented for Access version 1.1, so it can't be used with Access 1.0.

When you specify SQLText, the SQL equivalent of the table or query is returned. For a table, this is returned as "SELECT * FROM table;". For a query, it returns the appropriate SQL text. If you use the format SQLText;n, where n is a number between 1 and 255, Access returns the SQL SELECT statement broken into n character chunks, with a line break (ANSI code 13) every n characters.

The NextRow Trap

A common task in DDE is to retrieve the first row of a table with the FirstRow item and then use the NextRow item repeatedly to retrieve each row in the table. There is a problem with this, though: DDE can tell you only whether some task succeeded or failed. It cannot tell you why the task failed. This becomes important when you get an error from the NextRow command. The error may be telling you that you reached the end of the table, or it might be telling you that it received some other problem, such as someone's closing Access while the DDERequest was being processed. If it is important to you to get the complete table, you should follow these steps when retrieving every record in a table:

1. Get the last row using the LastRow item. Store this in a string variable.

2. Get the first row using the FirstRow item.

3. Get each succeeding row with the NextRow item.

4. When you get an error from the DDERequest() with the NextRow item, compare the last row retrieved with the row stored away in item 1. If they match, assume that you have retrieved the entire table. If they don't, you received an error.

Even this method cannot tell you whether you retrieved the entire table. The problem occurs when you are retrieving a table without a primary key. Tables without primary keys can have duplicate records—that is, every field in two different records can be the same. If the last record in the table or query has a duplicate, you may run into the problem. If you retrieve the duplicate record and the next record you request returns an error, you assume that you retrieved the last record, when you really didn't. There is no solution to this problem.

Summary

This chapter has covered the following issues:

- . What DDE clients and servers are
- Dynamics of a DDE conversation

- Topics and items
- Properties of each of the DDE commands
- Closing a DDE server
- Using Access as a DDE server
- The problem with NextRow

The chapter discussed the details of using Dynamic Data Exchange (DDE) from the standpoint of Access as a DDE client and as a server. DDE is one of the three ways of manipulating other Windows programs from Access. The other two are DLLs (see Chapter 17) and OLE (see Chapter 19).

By using DDE, you can combine Access with other applications. For example, you might have an application that constructs a Word for Windows document based on boilerplate text in a database and customer information. Or you might retrieve information from a spreadsheet that is created every month in an accounting department to be included in a sales database.

CHAPTER

NINETEEN

Harnessing the Power of OLE

- Using linking and embedding

- Manipulating OLE bound objects

- Using graphs on your forms

- Expanding Access with OLE custom controls

- Controlling other applications with OLE automation

- Using Regedit

OLE stands for Object Linking and Embedding. While OLE is certainly used for linking and embedding objects (such as bitmaps) in other objects (such as Access forms), it has been expanded to do much more. On a fundamental level, OLE is a protocol and set of function calls provided by Windows that allow programs to communicate with each other. In this chapter we discuss how to use OLE to link and embed objects in Access, how to use OLE from Access Basic to drive another program, and how to use OLE custom controls.

Using OLE to Communicate between Applications

To use OLE to communicate between applications, both applications must support it. The program that starts the conversation between the programs is called the *container application*, or *client*, and the program that responds is called the *object application*, or *server*. We use both sets of terms and have tried to avoid the term *object application* when the word *object* would be confusing.

Since OLE is evolving and since it supports several different ways of interacting, you are limited to the features of OLE the client and server mutually support. For example, Access acts as a client for OLE but not as a server. Other programs, such as Graph, act only as a server. On the other hand, Visio (from Shapeware) is designed to work as both a client and a server. For example, a Visio drawing cannot be embedded in Graph because Graph acts only as a server, but a Graph object can be embedded in Visio. OLE objects can be nested, so the Visio drawing with the Graph object can then be embedded in an Access form.

Access Basic supports OLE automation to drive an OLE automation server, such as Visio or Excel. However, Access is not itself an OLE automation server, so you cannot use the OLE automation features of Visual Basic for Applications (VBA) in Excel to manipulate Access.

A Word about Objects

The word *object* is perhaps the most overused word in computer lingo today. You have object-oriented languages, object-oriented databases, object this, and object that. Within Access, you have objects placed on forms and objects in Access Basic. Add to this Object Linking and Embedding. Because everyone else is loose with the term *object,* applying it to a number of different things, we're going to have to make it work overtime, too. The context surrounding it should tell you which definition of *object* we are referring to. You might want to replace the word *object* in your thinking with the word *thing*. An object is just a "thing" you can interact with. From the Access perspective it boils down to this: the ways you can manipulate an object (thing) are its - *methods;* how it looks and feels are its *properties;* and how it reacts to being manipulated are its *events*.

Linking and Embedding

OLE is most frequently used to *link* or *embed* objects within Access forms. This creates a compound document. In a *compound document*, one document—in Access this would be a form or report—can contain one or more other documents, such as a Word for Windows document, an Excel spreadsheet, or a Visio drawing. These in turn can also be compound documents—the Visio drawing you embed might have a bitmap embedded in it. *Document* is a generic term that can also include things without visual representations, such as recorded sounds.

There are two ways to create an Access compound document: linking and embedding. Embedding includes the entire server document within the Access database. Linking includes a presentation of the data in the database but only the only name of the file needed to retrieve the data that creates that presentation. The presentation is in the form of a Windows metafile that Access can display very quickly on the screen.

Embedding an Object

When you embed an object, the OLE server sends two things to Access:

- The native data
- The presentation

The native data is the information the server needs to create the presentation. For an Excel spreadsheet, this is the data contained in the .XLS file. When the user opens the form or report, the presentation is displayed as a bitmap or Windows metafile. Figure 19.1 shows a form with an embedded spreadsheet.

While browsing the form, the user can modify the native data by opening the OLE server (provided the form's Locked property is set to No and the Enabled property set to Yes).

FIGURE 19.1:

Access form with an embedded Excel spreadsheet

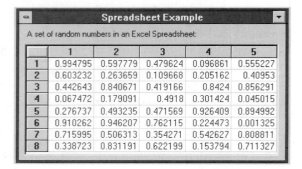

Linking an Object

When you link an object rather than embed it, the presentation bitmap or metafile is stored within the database but the native data is stored in the original file. This means that the presentation data of a linked bitmap is simply a duplicate of the native bitmap data. However, the bitmap presentation of a linked spreadsheet can be considerably smaller than the native spreadsheet data.

OLE keeps the presentation separate from the native data for speed. If it did not, every time the object was displayed, OLE would have to restart the server. This would be slow! Because Access stores the presentation in the database, it can be displayed quickly.

In-Place Editing of Embedded Objects

OLE has two ways of displaying embedded objects. The older convention (OLE version 1) presents the OLE object as a separate application, with its own main window, title, menu, and toolbars. The newer convention (allowed in OLE version 2) is called *in-place editing* or *in situ* editing. When the embedded object is made active, the OLE object application takes over the Access menu and toolbars. For example, when you activate a Word for Windows object embedded in a form, the menu and toolbars switch to Word for Windows, even though you are still technically in Access. When you click outside the bounds of the embedded object, Access resumes control of the menu and toolbars. Figure 19.2 shows an Access form with an embedded Word for Windows document that is activated with in-place editing. There is

FIGURE 19.2:

Word For Windows activated in Access with in-place editing

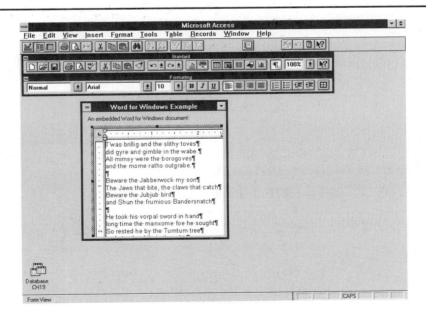

one difference beween the normal Access toolbars and the toolbars of a server activated with in-place editing: the server's toolbars cannot be "docked" underneath the menu bar.

Because writing an object application that supports in-place editing is difficult and the technology is relatively new, there are few servers with in-place editing functionality at this point. To complicate matters, Access 2.0 cannot use in-place editing in some object applications even though the applications themselves support it. For example, Visio version 2.0 supports in-place editing, but because of the way Access and Visio are implemented, Access must open a Visio document in a separate window. Visio Express, a pared-down form of Visio that supports only embedding, does not have this interaction problem.

In-place editing occurs only under limited circumstances:

- If the form is in form mode, not design mode
- If the object application supports it
- If the way the object application supports it works for Access
- If you have the Locked property set to No and the Enabled property set to Yes
- If you are editing an embedded object, not a linked one

If all of these conditions are not met, the document is opened in its own window.

When a document is activated with in-place editing, it may require extra space around it. For example, when Word for Windows is activated, the rulers appear outside the bounding box of the object frame. You will have to take this into account when you design your forms.

Inserting an Unbound OLE Object into an Object Frame

To insert (embed or link) an OLE object into a form or report, select the Object Frame tool and click on the form. When you do this, the dialog shown in Figure 19.3 appears.

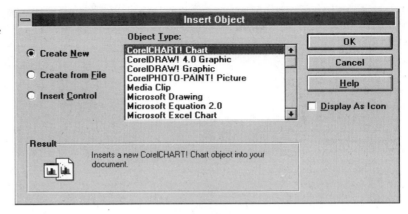

Insert Object dialog with the Create
New option button selected

Note that this procedure stores the same OLE object for every record in the database. If you want to store a different OLE object for every record in the database, see the section "Inserting an OLE Object in a Bound Object Frame" later in this chapter.

Embedding the Object in the Object Frame

To embed a new object, such as a new Word for Windows document, select the object type from the list box and click the OK button. Word for Windows then starts from within Access and you can type the text you want to appear in the OLE frame.

To embed an existing object, select Edit ➤ Insert Object ➤ Create from File. Do not check the Link check box in this dialog.

When an embedded OLE object is opened in a separate window, the server program replaces some of the menu items on the File menu with items relevant to the embedding situation. For example, File ➤ Save becomes File ➤ Update Item, and File ➤ Close becomes File ➤ Close and Return to Form: *formname*. The title bar for the document also changes to show the embedded object. Figure 19.4 shows Word for Windows editing an embedded object. When the object is updated, both the native data and the presentation are embedded in the Access form.

FIGURE 19.4:

Word for Windows editing an
embedded object

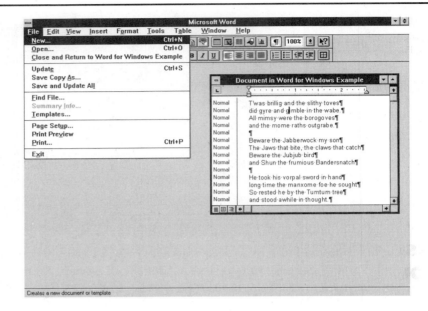

If the Display as Icon check box is selected in the Insert Object dialog box, an icon replaces the normal presentation. This reduces the size of the embedded object, since an icon takes very little space. Select this option if you always expect the user to open the server to see or manipulate the data. Certain objects, such as sounds, don't have visual presentations. These objects are always displayed as icons regardless of whether you check the Display as Icon check box.

Linking an OLE Object in the Object Frame

When you link an object, it must already exist. For example, if you are linking an Excel spreadsheet, the .XLS file must be on the disk. You link an object by selecting "Create from File" from the Insert Object dialog box. The dialog then changes to the one shown in Figure 19.5. The file name of the existing file is specified. Be sure to check the Link check box; otherwise the object is embedded rather than linked.

FIGURE 19.5:
Insert Object dialog with the Create from File option button selected

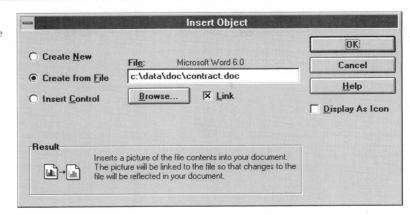

FIGURE 19.5:
Insert Object dialog with the Create from File option button selected

Inserting an OLE Object in a Bound Object Frame

When you use the Object Frame control discussed earlier in this chapter to place an OLE object on a form, the same object is shown for every record in the database. There will be times when you want to store a different OLE object for every record in the database, such as storing a picture of the house for every record describing a house in a real estate application. To do this, use the Bound Object Frame control. The difference between the object frame and the bound object frame is that the bound object frame can be bound to an OLE object field in a table. When this is done, you can insert a different OLE object into each record. Thus, the object frame is *bound* to the OLE object field in the table.

OLE objects are stored in different places, depending on whether they are bound or unbound. If they are bound, they are stored in an OLE Object column in a table. If they are unbound, they are stored as part of the form or report.

The easiest way to insert a bound object frame is to follow these steps:

1. Add a column with the OLE Object datatype to a table.

2. Open a form and bind it to the table with the OLE Object column.

3. Select the Bound Object Frame tool in the toolbox. (When you select the Bound Object Frame tool from the toolbox before dragging the field to the form, the field is created using a bound object frame rather than a text box.)

4. Open the Field List by clicking the Field List icon in the toolbar.

5. Drag the OLE object field to the form.

To insert an OLE object into the bound object frame, you must be in form mode. Then click on the bound object frame and select Edit ➤ Insert Object. The Insert Object dialog appears, just as it did for the (unbound) object frame. The object can now be embedded or linked, as described earlier in this chapter. Since this object frame is bound, the OLE object for only the single record changes. You can then move to the next record and insert a different OLE object into it.

Inserting Graphs

You can use Microsoft Graph version 5.0 to add graphs to your forms and reports. The Graph objects can get data either from the database or from an outside source, such as an Excel spreadsheet. With an outside source, you use an object frame (either bound or unbound) just like any other OLE object and simply select Microsoft Graph 5.0 Chart from the Object Type list.

Access has the Graph tool for creating graphs from data in the current database. The Graph tool in the toolbox always presents a Wizard, regardless of whether you have Control Wizards turned on. The Wizard leads you through a series of questions as to how to link the data to the Graph object. The Wizard is meant to be self documenting—there is no documentation in the manuals or Help system—but the questions could use some further elaboration.

The Wizard sometimes cannot produce the information you want to graph. In this case you have to adjust the SQL in the RowSource property after the Wizard finishes. In most cases, the graph will not look the way you want, so you will have to use the Graph server to adjust properties such as the font and orientation of the text on the X axis.

The "pages" of the dialog that the Wizard visits are determined by your answers. For example, if you don't select a date field, the Wizard does not ask you about dates.

TIP

The Form and Report Wizards library (WZFRMRPT.MDA) contains the Graph Wizard. Open the form "ChartWizard" and examine the code behind the form. You will have to use the Add-in Manager to uninstall the Wizard before you can open the database. See Chapter 20 for information about the Add-in Manager.

The first and most important step of creating a graph is to create a select or crosstab query that results in exactly the data you wish to graph. Use the query datasheet to view the query to make sure the data is what you want.

The first page of the Graph Wizard is shown in Figure 19.6. It asks, "Where do you want your graph to get its data?" You can select any table or query, including the table or query bound to the current form. Select the query that you created.

The next page of the Wizard asks, "Which fields contain the data you want for your graph?" If your graph is a bar chart, each item selected here produces its own bar.

If one of the fields selected is a date field, the Wizard asks for information on how you want the date information grouped before continuing.

After you select fields, if your form is bound, the Wizard asks, "Do you want to link the data in your graph to a field on the form?" If you answer no to this question, the same graph appears on every record that is displayed. If you answer yes

FIGURE 19.6: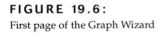
First page of the Graph Wizard

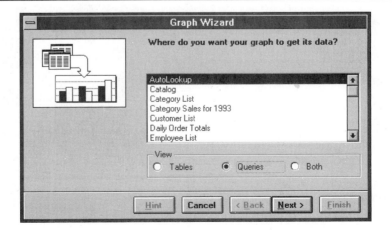

you may specify information to have the graph change for every record that is displayed. It does this through the page shown in Figure 19.7.

FIGURE 19.7:

Link page of the Graph Wizard

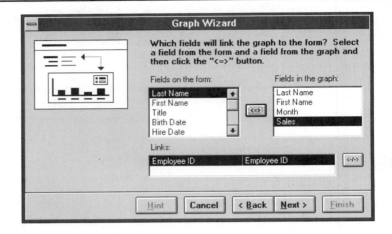

You then select the type of graph you want displayed. The screen in Figure 19.8 shows the types offered on this page. The Data Series question determines what is graphed and what appears on the X axis of the graph.

FIGURE 19.8:

Type page of the Graph Wizard

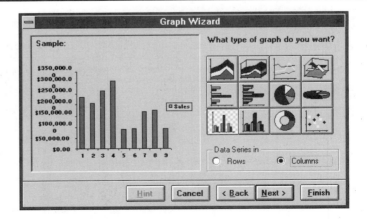

The final page in the graph asks, "What title do you want on your chart?" and "Do you want the chart to display a legend?" After answering these questions, you click the Finish button to have the Wizard put the Graph object on the form or report.

After creating the chart, examine the SQL in the RowSource. Does this produce the information you need? Next, double-click the Graph object. The graph server opens, showing the data. Change any of the size, color, font, legend, or other properties of the chart until it meets your satisfaction. Often the text on the graph is not displayed readably. Changing the font size to a smaller size or changing the text alignment to vertical may help. See Chapter 4 for several examples of using the Graph Wizard to graph data from totals and crosstab queries.

OLE Properties

Certain properties on a properties sheet are unique to, or have special meaning to, OLE objects. These are documented fully in the Help file, but a brief overview is included in Table 19.1.

TABLE 19.1: OLE-Specific Form Properties

Property	Meaning
Data Properties	
OLEClass	Displays a description of the kind of object contained in an OLE field. This information is set by the OLE server
RowSourceType	Some OLE servers, such as Microsoft Graph, understand data sent to them by Access. This property sets the type of data to be sent to the server
RowSource	Data to be sent to the server
LinkChildFields	With servers that send data to the OLE object, LinkChildFields specifies the fields within the RowSource that are restricted to those that match the LinkMasterFields entries
LinkMasterFields	Specifies fields on the form that match, one for one, with fields in the LinkChildFields property
DisplayType	Specifies whether the OLE object should display a regular presentation or just an icon

TABLE 19.1: OLE-Specific Form Properties (continued)

Property	Meaning
Update Options	When a linked object is changed, the presentation within Access changes automatically if the UpdateOptions property is set to Automatic. If it is set to Manual, you must use the Edit ➤ Links option to update the link.
OLEType	Specifies whether the object is linked, embedded, or neither
OLETypeAllowed	Specifies whether the object can be linked, embedded, or both
Class	The OLE class, retrieved from the OLE registration database
SourceDoc	If the data is linked, this specifies the file name of the linked object. For an embedded object this file name is used as a template
SourceItem	If the data is linked, this property specifies the data within the file to be linked. For example, you might just link a specific range in an Excel spreadsheet
ColumnCount	Specifies the number of columns of the RowData sent to the OLE object, such as a graph .
Enabled	Must be set to True for the user to be able to edit an OLE object. Also, the Locked property must be set to False

Layout Properties

Property	Meaning
SizeMode	Either Clip, Stretch, or Zoom. Clip displays the object as its actual size in the original; if the boundaries of the control are smaller than that, the excess is clipped. Stretch sizes the object to the size of the control, distorting the object to make it fit. Zoom sizes the object to the size of the control, but the aspect ratio of the control is maintained
ColumnHeads	Sends column headings to the OLE server

Event Properties

Property	Meaning
OnUpdated	The Updated event occurs when an OLE object's data is modified

Other Properties

Property	Meaning
AutoActivate	Controls how the user can activate an OLE object. If this property is set to Double-Click, the user double-clicks the object to activate it (either in place or in a separate window, depending on the server). If set to GetFocus, the object merely has to get the focus to activate it. If set to manual, the object is activated only by code setting the Action property to OLE_ACTIVATE

TABLE 19.1: OLE-Specific Form Properties (continued)

Property	Meaning
Verb	Specifies an integer that controls what happens when the object is activated. The verbs for a server are specified in the Registration database. The most common verbs are to edit and open the server object. You can also specify a negative number, which activates the object in different ways. See the Access documentation or Help file for more information
Locked	Must be set to False for the user to be able to modify an object. The control must also be enabled

OLE Custom Controls

Have you ever designed a form in Access and said to yourself, "This is a place where I need a multi-select list box?" Have you ever made a list box very small to simulate a text box connected to a spin control? Have you worked around the fact that you can't put text and a bitmap on the same button unless you modify a bitmap to add the text? OLE custom controls can solve these problems. Collectively called OCXs because of their .OCX file extensions, these custom controls allow you to infinitely extend the control set provided by Access. Very few are available as this book goes to press. (The Calendar control, Scroll Bar control, and Data Outline control come with the Access Developers Toolkit (ADT), and a Multi-Select List Box control is now available in the Access Forum on CompuServe.) OCX controls are a new format, and Access 2.0 is the first container to support them. Visual Basic has supported custom controls with the .VBX extension for years. OCXs are similar in purpose to VBXs, but they are *not* compatible. Many of the vendors who make VBXs will port their custom controls to OCXs. Many other OCXs will undoubtedly be published soon by Microsoft or third-party developers. The following sections assume you have an OCX.

Inserting OLE Custom Controls

You place OLE custom controls on forms by inserting them into an object frame. You create an object frame just as you do for an unbound object; however, this time you click the Insert Control option button in the Insert Object dialog. When you click this option button, the dialog looks like the one in Figure 19.9.

FIGURE 19.9:

Insert Object dialog with the Insert
Control option button selected

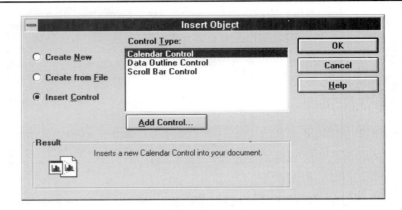

The Control Type list box lists the controls that are available. To add a control to the list, click the Add Control button and specify the file name. To insert the control, select the control name from the list and click the OK button.

Modifying Custom Control Properties

Because OCXs are extensions of the Access feature set, the special properties of the control do not appear in the standard property sheet. For example, if you insert the Scrollbar control on a form, the property that selects which orientation—horizontal or vertical—the control takes does not appear on the property sheet. When you select the scrollbar on the form, the Edit menu has a new entry called Scroll Bar Control Object. When you select this option, a hierarchical menu appears with three options: Edit, Properties, and Change to Picture (see Figure 19.10). Selecting the Properties item from the menu causes the properties page for the custom control to appear.

The Properties Page dialog box allows you to change the properties of the object. Figure 19.11 shows the Scroll Bar Control Properties page.

Some properties may not be available through the user interface. For example, the font properties of the calendar OCX can be manipulated only through code.

The other two options on the hierarchical menu are much less useful than the Properties option. The Edit option opens the custom control in a separate window.

FIGURE 19.10:

Edit menu for editing scrollbar properties

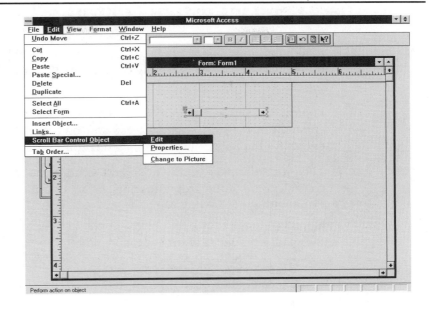

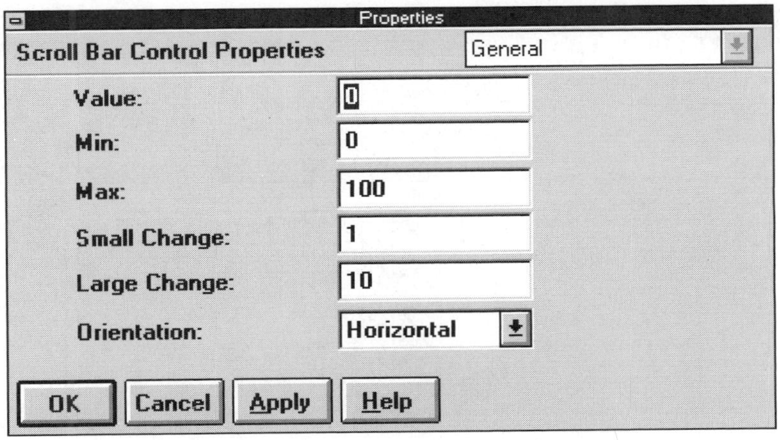

FIGURE 19.11:

Scroll Bar Control Properties page

The Change to Picture option converts the control into a Windows metafile that contains a picture of the custom control. The metafile can be manipulated only as an image from that point on—it is no longer a custom control.

The Calendar Custom Control

The calendar OCX comes in the Access Developer's Toolkit. As described earlier in this chapter, you insert it on a form by drawing an object frame, clicking the Insert Control option button, selecting the Calendar Control from the list box, and clicking OK.

Figure 19.12 shows a simple Personal Information Manager (PIM) based on the calendar OCX. It allows you to select a date on the calendar on the left and show the events for the date in a subform on the right.

The properties page for the calendar OCX does not show all the properties for the control. Some of the properties must be set in code. You do this in the Form Load event with the following code:

```
Sub Form_Load
    oleCalendar.object.value = Now
    oleCalendar.object.font.name = "Arial"
    oleCalendar.object.font.size = 12
    oleCalendar.object.font.bold = True
End Sub
```

FIGURE 19.12:

Simple Personal Information Manager form

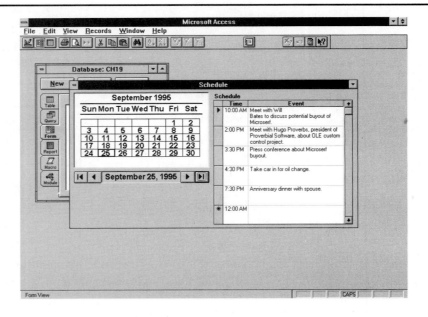

We named the OLE Frame control in which the calendar was placed oleCalendar. To get at the calendar-specific properties, you use the property "object" followed by the property name you wish to access. The Value property of the Calendar control contains the date that is currently selected. By writing some code to set it to the date returned by the Now() function, you set the date displayed by the calendar control to today's date. The other three properties set the typeface shown in the calendar control to 12-point Arial bold.

The buttons below the calendar change the set date by months or years. They call four methods implemented by the Calendar control: PreviousYear, PreviousMonth, NextMonth, and NextYear. You hook these methods to the OnClick events of the four buttons as shown here:

```
Sub cmdNextMonth_Click()
    oleCalendar.object.NextMonth
Sub End

Sub cmdNextYear_Click()
    oleCalendar.object.NextYear
Sub End

Sub cmdPreviousMonth_Click()
    oleCalendar.object.PreviousMonth
Sub End

Sub cmdPreviousYear_Click()
    oleCalendar.object.PreviousYear
Sub End
```

Each of these methods changes the Value property of the control. Anytime the value property changes, BeforeUpdate and AfterUpdate events occur. In the AfterUpdate event of the control, the date in the text box between the buttons is changed to reflect the current date. Also, a requery method is executed on the subform to show the events associated with the newly selected date. The code is shown here:

```
Sub oleCalendar_AfterUpdate()
    txtDate = oleCalendar.object.Value
    subSchedule.Requery
End Sub
```

The PIM example is included on the companion disk for the book, but you will need the calendar OCX from the ADT to be able to run it. Also, to use any OCX control you need a DLL named OC1016.DLL. This DLL comes with the ADT, and you can also find it on CompuServe in the Access forum as OC1016.ZIP.

OLE Automation

OLE Automation is the protocol designed to replace DDE as the standard interprocess communication mechanism in Windows. In order for you to use OLE Automation, the OLE server must support it and the OLE client must have a language that can manipulate the server. Manipulating OLE Automation is similar to manipulating DAO. You follow a hierarchy of objects until you get to the object you want. After you get to the object, you manipulate it with methods and properties.

The following sections describe an extensive demonstration of OLE Automation using the Visio 2.0 product from Shapeware. (It is likely that future versions of Visio will require minor changes to the code.) Visio is a drawing package that uses predefined shapes to create drawings. Even if you don't have Visio, you can run the demonstration code. It just reports an error when it attempts to start Visio. The sample application uses Visio as a specialized kind of report writer to create a project chart from information collected from an Access form.

The Visio Project Wizard

You can find the Visio Project Wizard on the companion disk for this book. Follow the directions in the README.TXT file as to where to place the files on your hard disk. If you like, you can rename the database from VISIO.MDB to VISIO.MDA and install it using the Add-in Manager so that it always appears on the Add-in menu. In the following discussion we go over the important portions of this Wizard in detail, covering the main points of OLE Automation as we go.

When the database is opened, the switchboard form shown in Figure 19.13 is displayed. Clicking the Run the Project Wizard button starts the Wizard. The main part of the Wizard is a form, frmProject, containing five "pages." The Next and Back buttons move through these five pages once a project name is specified. The first page is shown in Figure 19.14. Before you run the Wizard for the first time, you must set it up. Clicking the Set Up Wizard button opens a second form, frmCustomize, shown in Figure 19.15.

FIGURE 19.13:

VISIO.MDB switchboard form

FIGURE 19.14:

Page one of the Visio Project Wizard

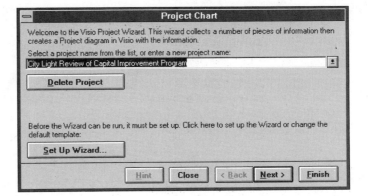

FIGURE 19.15:

Visio Project Wizard Configure dialog

The Configure Wizard Dialog

On the Configure Wizard form, you must indicate where you placed the Visio template file on your hard disk. You must then load the styles available in that template into an Access table so the Wizard can use them later. The code that loads the styles is presented in Listing 19.1.

Listing 19.1

```
Sub cmdLoadStyles_Click()
    Dim db As Database
    Dim rst As Recordset
    Dim oleVisio As Object
    Dim doc As Object
    Dim docs As Object
    Dim styles As Object
    Dim i As Integer

    Call glrEnterProcedure("cmdLoadStyles_Click")
    On Error GoTo cmdLoadStylesClickError

    DoCmd Hourglass True

    ' First clear the existing styles table
    Set db = CodeDB()
    Set rst = db.OpenRecordset("tblStyles", DB_OPEN_TABLE)
    If Not rst.eof Then
        rst.MoveFirst
        Do Until rst.eof
            rst.Delete
            rst.MoveNext
        Loop
    End If

    Set oleVisio = CreateObject("visio.application")
    Set docs = oleVisio.[Documents]
    Set doc = docs.[open](txtTemplate)
    Set styles = doc.styles
    For i = 1 To styles.count
        rst.AddNew
        rst!StyleId = i
        rst!Style = styles(i).Name
        rst.Update
```

```
        Next i
        doc.[close]
        Set doc = Nothing

cmdLoadStylesClickDone:
        On Error Resume Next
        oleVisio.[quit]
        Set styles = Nothing
        Set doc = Nothing
        Set docs = Nothing
        Set oleVisio = Nothing
        rst.Close
        db.Close
        DoCmd Hourglass False
        Call glrExitProcedure("cmdLoadStyles_Click")
Exit Sub
cmdLoadStylesClickError:
        Select Case Err
        Case 2763
            Select Case glrOLEErr(Error$)
            Case 1   ' File not found.
                MsgBox STRERRORTEMPLATENOTFOUND, MB_OK Or
                ➡ MB_ICONEXCLAMATION Or MB_DEFBUTTON1 Or
                ➡ MB_APPLMODAL, Me.caption
            Case Else
                Call glrErrorOutput(Err, Error$)
            End Select
        Case Else
            Call glrErrorOutput(Err, Error$)
        End Select
        Resume cmdLoadStylesClickDone
End Sub
```

To open an OLE Automation server, you use the CreateObject() function. This function opens a new instance of the application specified as the argument. This argument is a string that varies from application to application and is listed in the documentation for the application. You can also find the string in the Windows Registration database, as described in the section "Using RegEdit" later in this chapter. The string for Visio is "visio.application". The return value is set to a variable with the type "object". When the CreateObject() function is called, Windows opens the OLE Automation server.

After getting the visio.application object, you can use it to get to any of the other objects in Visio. The class hierarchy is shown in Figure 19.16.

FIGURE 19.16:

Visio class hierarchy

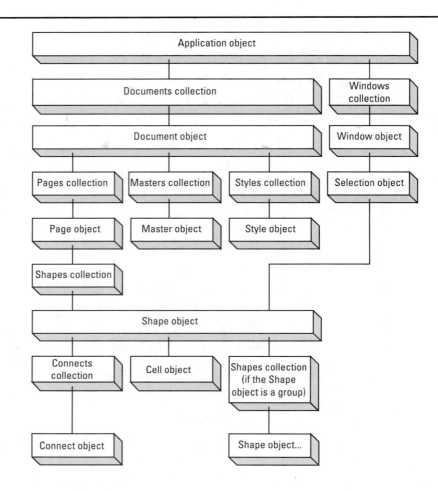

The next statement sets the Docs object to the Documents class under the application object:

```
Set docs = oleVisio.[Documents]
```

Note that we enclosed the class name in square brackets. While in this case it is not strictly required, it is always a good idea. If you don't use the square brackets and the object property or method name conflicts with an Access Basic reserved word, you will get an odd error message based on the improper use of the reserved word.

For example, if you use doc.close instead of doc.[close], you get the error message, "Method not applicable for this object" when you try to compile the code.

The next line of code sets the doc variable to the result of opening a new document using the template specified in the text box on the form:

```
Set doc = docs.[open](txtTemplate)
```

The next line sets the Styles object to the Styles collection. Looking at the Visio class hierarchy shown in Figure 19.16, note how these Set statements move through it.

```
Set styles = doc.[styles]
```

The next steps iterate over the Styles collection. The Styles collection has a property that is the count of items in the collection. The retrieved style names are added to the tblStyles recordset.

```
    For i = 1 To styles.[count]
        rst.AddNew
        rst!StyleId = i
        rst!Style = styles(i).[name]
        rst.Update
    Next i
```

Then the document is closed:

```
doc.[close]
Set doc = Nothing
```

The object an object variable points to is released when the object goes out of scope or is specifically set to Nothing. *Nothing* means that the variable is no longer pointing at an object. When an object variable is declared, it has the value Nothing until it is assigned a value. When a procedure exits, all local variables go out of scope and the objects are released. You might want to specifically set your objects to Nothing to make apparent what is going on. Nothing frees memory back to Windows the moment the object is released, so if the procedure continues past the last usage of an object variable, it is always a good idea to set the object to Nothing.

Finally, Visio is closed and the remaining cleanup work is done:

```
oleVisio.[quit]
    .
    .
    .
```

This activates the Quit method on the oleVisio object.

When you click the OK button in the Configure dialog, the current record is saved. Since the text box is bound to a field in the tblWizard table, the current file location is stored. This information is used later in the code when you click the Finish button on the Wizard.

OLE Automation Errors

In the error handler (see Chapter 14), note that *all OLE Automation errors map to error number 2763*. The return value of the Error$() function, however, reflects the actual error. This is an unsatisfactory feature of Access because it means that to trap specific OLE Automation errors, you'd have to compare the Error$ to string constants all over your code. If Shapeware decided to change the text of an error message by even one character, all your error handling of that statement would be rendered inoperable and you would have to find all those string comparisons to make changes. Also, in an international environment, you would have to translate these strings throughout your code. And you cannot use const declarations to define the error message strings because the error message sent back from the OLE server typically has an ANSI value 10 embedded to create a blank line. You cannot insert nonprinting characters into an Access Basic string constant.

To reduce the impact of this problem, we created the routine glrOLEErr. This function takes as an argument the error string and returns an arbitrary number that can be used in your error handler to differentiate the errors. Then, if the error messages need to change, you need to change just this one routine. You can add to the glrOLEErr() function as you see fit.

The format of the error message returned for an OLE error is

ApplicationName returned the following error: *ApplicationSpecificErrorMessage*

The glrOLEErr() function, shown in Listing 19.2, parses the string to separate the two variable sections and then performs a Case statement to assign an arbitrary unique number to each error.

Listing 19.2

```
Function glrOLEErr(ByVal strError As String) As Integer
    Dim istrErrorReturned As Integer
    Dim istrErrorErr As Integer
    Dim strReturned As String
```

```
    Dim strApp As String
    Dim strOLEErr As String
    Dim intRet As Integer

    Call glrEnterProcedure("glrOLEErr")
    On Error GoTo glrOLEErrError

    intRet = 0

    strReturned = Mid$(Error$(2763), 3, Len(Error$(2763)) - 4)
    istrErrorReturned = InStr(1, strError, strReturned)
    istrErrorErr = istrErrorReturned + Len(strReturned)
    strApp = Left$(strError, istrErrorReturned - 1)
    strOLEErr = Right$(strError, Len(strError) - istrErrorErr
➡ + 1)
    Do While Left$(strOLEErr, 1) = Chr$(10)
        strOLEErr = Right$(strOLEErr, Len(strOLEErr) - 1)
    Loop
    Select Case strApp
    Case "VISIO"
        Select Case strOLEErr
        Case "File not found."
            intRet = 1
        Case "Object name not found."
            intRet = 2
        Case "Invalid document index."
            intRet = 3
        Case "Path not found."
            intRet = 4
        Case Else
            ' Unknown OLE Error
            Call glrAssert(False)
        End Select
    Case Else
        ' Unknown OLE Server
        Call glrAssert(False)
    End Select
glrOLEErrDone:
    glrOLEErr = intRet
    Call glrExitProcedure("glrOLEErr")
Exit Function
glrOLEErrError:
    Select Case Err
    Case Else
        Call glrErrorOutput(Err, Error$)
```

```
      End Select
      Resume glrOLEErrDone
End Function
```

You can also create Case statements for any other OLE servers you deal with here.

The Visio Project Wizard
Finish Button

The main code to create the project chart in Visio is in the Code-Behind-Forms attached to the Click event of the Finish button. This code starts with getting the name of the template that was stored in tblWizard table. Then, using the Dir$ command, it verifies that the file names specified in the dialog exist. If everything checks out, the Wizard begins the drawing code. This starts similarly to the code that loaded the styles into a table described in the section "The Configure Wizard Dialog" earlier in this chapter.

```
' ADDHERE: Add new drawing code in this section

Set oleVisio = CreateObject("visio.application")
Set docs = oleVisio.[documents]
Set doc = docs.[add](strTemplateName)
```

The first statement here is a comment. This points out a useful tip. There is a string, "ADDHERE", that is searchable in the text. You may find it useful to put in this string for the interesting points in your code that you continually revisit. Then you can search for the text rather than continually having to find the point through the menus. You just open the Code-Behind-Form from the toolbar and then press F3 or Ctrl+F to find "ADDHERE".

The rest of the text is similar to the code described for loading the styles, except that the document is added to the Docs collection with the [add] method rather than the [open] method used previously.

The next section of code verifies that the shapes needed to draw the chart exist on the template. If the user specified a template that doesn't have the shapes, an error occurs.

```
' Check to make sure our master objects are present on
' the stencil
Set docSS = docs(2)
Call glrAssert(Right$(docSS.Name, 4) = ".vss")
```

```
Set msts = docSS.[masters]
Set shp = msts(SHPTASK)
Set shp = msts(SHPRUNNINGTITLE)
Set shp = msts(SHPMAINTITLE)
Set shp = msts(SHPSUBTITLE)
Set shp = msts(SHPTOPTOBOTTOM)
```

The code then proceeds to get the page that is currently loaded from the Pages collection, titles it "Background", and calls a separate procedure, SetupPage, that sets up the page correctly for this drawing based on information in the Wizard dialogs:

```
' Write background
Set pages = doc.[pages]
Set backpage = pages(1)
backpage.[Name] = "Background"
Call SetupPage(backpage)
```

Next, the code moves the page to be a background page in Visio containing objects you probably don't want to change if you tweak the document, and it stores the dimensions of the margins in the typMargin structure. It does this by retrieving information from the Cells collection to retrieve the page height and width. If the user wants a border around the page, it draws the border:

```
backpage.[background] = True
typMargin.dblLeft = txtLeftMargin
typMargin.dblTop = backpage.shapes("ThePage")
➡ [cells]("PageHeight").[result] ("IN") - txtTopMargin
typMargin.dblRight = backpage.shapes("ThePage")
➡ [cells]("PageWidth").[result]("IN") - txtRightMargin
typMargin.dblBottom = txtBottomMargin
If chkBorderBox Then
    Set shp =
➡ backpage.drawrectangle(typMargin.dblLeft - txtBorderBoxMargin,
➡ typMargin.dblBottom - txtBorderBoxMargin,
➡ typMargin.dblRight + txtBorderBoxMargin,
➡ typMargin.dblTop + txtBorderBoxMargin)
End If
```

Limitations of OLE Automation

The next section in the code deals with a problem in OLE Automation. If the OLE server does not specifically expose an object to do what you want, you are stuck. You cannot use OLE Automation. Visio does not expose any method to import a graphic into a drawing. It certainly allows it through the user interface, but there is no OLE Automation method that performs the operation. In OLE Automation, you are limited by which features the product exposes.

To get around this limitation, the code uses SendKeys to import the graphic. The limitations of SendKeys are numerous. No application should use SendKeys if it can possibly avoid it. As this code was being developed, a bug became apparent because Visio 2.0 has two different menu structures, short and full. With Short Menus on, the program crashed because it could not find the menu item it was looking for. If you do use SendKeys, try to verify that you got the expected result. The Windows API FindWindow() function is useful here since it allows you to verify that a particular window currently exists on the system.

The particular case in which SendKeys is used calls for opening the Import dialog and specifying the file name you want to import. Then the code tries to open the Special dialog. If this fails (no dialog is found by FindWindow()), it assumes that Short Menus must be on, tries setting Full Menus on, and then tries again. In the Special dialog, the object just imported is given a name. By referring to this name, we can again use OLE Automation to manipulate the object. Specifically, it is positioned in the correct place on the page using the OLE Automation in the function PositionBitmap(). The pertinent code in this function is shown in Listing 19.3.

Listing 19.3

```
' There is no way through OLE Automation to place a bitmap
' on a drawing. Use SendKeys instead.
' First get the handle of instance of Visio that we started
' and make sure it has the focus.
intRet = glr_apiSetActiveWindow(oleVisio.[WindowHandle])

If txtCompanyBmpFilename <> "" Then
    ' Import the company bitmap
    SendKeys "%FI", True
    If glr_apiFindWindow("AxonDlgCls", "Import") = 0 Then
        Call glrAssert(False)
    End If
    SendKeys txtCompanyBmpFilename & "{Enter}", True
    If glr_apiFindWindow("#32770", 0&) = False Then
        SendKeys "{Enter}", True
    End If

    ' Set the shape name to a name we can recognize from OLE
    ' automation
```

```
SendKeys "%TE", True
If glr_apiFindWindow("AxonDlgCls", "Special") = O Then
    ' Short menus are probably on, try again with long menus
    SendKeys "%WM", True
    SendKeys "%TE", True
    If glr_apiFindWindow("AxonDlgCls", "Special") = O Then
        Call glrAssert(False)
    End If
End If
SendKeys COMPANYBITMAP & "{Enter}", True

' Position the bitmaps on the page using OLE Automation
Call PositionBitmap(backpage.[shapes](COMPANYBITMAP),
➡ cboCompanyBmpLocation, typMargin)
End If
```

Understanding DrawDiagram()

The next section of code in the Wizard writes the running title, main title, and subtitle on the page. This is followed by a call to DrawDiagram. This procedure does the actual drawing of the boxes on the chart and connects them. It takes eight arguments, which are described in Table 19.2.

TABLE 19.2: Parameters for the DrawDiagram Procedure

Argument	Meaning
msts	Collection of master objects on the Visio stencil
page	Visio page object to be drawn to
lngProjectId	Number of the current project
lngParentTaskId	TaskId of the parent of the current object. When first called, this should be 0
shpParent	Object handle for the current shape object. When first called, this should be set to "nothing"
dblTop	How far down from the top margin objects on this level should be drawn
dblLeft	Farthest left objects on this level can be drawn
dblRight	Farthest right objects on this level can be drawn

The trick of this routine is that it uses recursion. *Recursion* is a programming term for a function that calls itself. This process repeats for as many levels as it takes. It's a bit of a black art. (Someone once said that if recursion had been practiced in the Middle Ages, the practitioners would have been burned at the stake.) The procedure opens a recordset to find all the children of the parent Task Id passed in. It draws the first one (by using the "drop" method), fills in the name, and populates it with people. It draws the line to the parent box (if any). It then calls DrawDiagram() with new values for the lngParentTaskId, shpParent, dblTop, dblLeft, and dblRight arguments. The current state of the DrawDiagram() function is left on the Access Basic stack and a new instance is created with new local variables. DrawDiagram() repeats this procedure until all the children of the current box are drawn. When there are no more children to be drawn, DrawDiagram() exits the procedure and control returns to the previous instance of DrawDiagram().

You must be careful when using recursion. In every recursive procedure, there must be some situation in which the recursion does not call itself, and this situation must eventually be met. In DrawDiagram(), this situation occurs when the current object doesn't have any children (that is, the query results in an empty recordset). If the recursive procedure does not have a terminating situation, you get what is known as infinite recursion. The result is an "Out of Stack Space" error when the entire stack is filled with local variables and parameters.

The final result of the Visio Project Wizard is shown in Figure 19.17.

Using Regedit

Windows maintains a file called REG.DAT in the WINDOWS directory to store information about all the OLE servers on a system. When you install a program, the program is registered in the Registration database. If anything happens to the Registration database, such as your accidentally deleting it, OLE will not work. Re-creating a missing or damaged Registration database is a chore. Different programs have different ways of reregistering. Some programs check to see whether the proper registration information is in the database anytime they are run, and if they are not registered, they register themselves. Other programs, such as Visio, require you to put a specific switch on the command line to reregister. For Visio this is /r. And many other programs require you to load a file by hand into the Registration database. Usually OLE registration is poorly documented, if it is documented at all.

FIGURE 19.17:

Result of the Visio Project Wizard

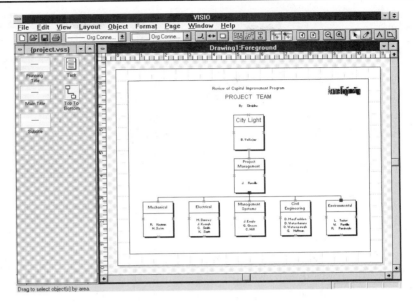

The Registration database is edited by the program REGEDIT.EXE, which is part of Windows and located in your WINDOWS directory. Regedit really is two separate programs located in one executable. There are two interfaces, depending on whether you start Regedit with the /v switch on the command line.

We recommend that in Program Manager, you create two new icons. One icon should have just "REGEDIT.EXE" on the command line. The other should have "REGEDIT.EXE /v" on the command line. These icons let you look at and edit the Registration database. If you use OLE, these will come in handy.

Regedit without the /v option opens a window that looks like the one shown in Figure 19.18. The main reason to use this version of Regedit is to merge a .REG file into REG.DAT. Many programs come with a file, such as WINWORD6.REG, that contains the registration information for the program. By using the File ➤ Merge Registration File option of Regedit, you can merge this file into the REG.DAT Registration database.

One way of re-creating the entries in REG.DAT for programs you cannot find any other way is to set up the program again.

FIGURE 19.18:

Regedit without the /v switch

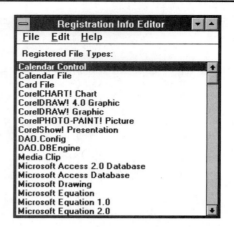

Regedit with the /v option opens a window that looks like the one in Figure 19.19. This window is considerably more complicated that the window without the /v switch. It contains all sorts of information about the registered applications. Among the pieces of information contained are

- Whether the application appears when you use the Insert Object command from the Access menus (controlled by the Insertable keyword)

- The name of the OLE class

- Which extensions are attached to which executables by File Manager

- What happens when you double-click on an embedded application

Some of the pieces of information are application specific. Changing anything in this database is not advisable unless you have a backup file of REG.DAT, since it can make OLE totally inoperable.

For an example of how you might use this database, suppose you had forgotten the object name argument for the CreateObject command for Visio. You could look in REG.DAT and find "visio.application" as a key name in the database.

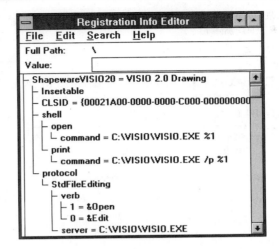

Parsing Bound OLE Object Columns

When a bound OLE object is stored in a table, Access uses a special binary format. This format is the same in both Access 1.0 and 2.0 but could change in future versions of Access.

The format for the data is as follows:

- An object header, describing the data.
- The binary data returned by the OleSaveToStream() Windows API function.
- A footer, which stores a checksum. The checksum confirms that the data is correctly stored.

The object header is a variable-length field. The C structure for the object header is

```
struct OBJECTHEADER
{
WORD type;
WORD cbHdr;
LONG lobjType;
WORD cchName;
WORD cchClass;
```

```
WORD ibName;
WORD ibClass;
POINT ptSize;
char rgch[];
};
```

The fields in the structure are defined in Table 19.3.

TABLE 19.3: Members for the OBJECTHEADER Structure

Structure Member	Meaning
type	Must be loaded with the type signature 0x1c15
cbHdr	sizeof(struct OBJECTHEADER) + cchName + cchClass
lobjType	One of the OLE object type codes OT_STATIC, OT_LINKED, or OT_EMBEDDED
cchName	Count of characters in object name (sizeof(szName) + 1)
cchClass	Count of characters in class name (sizeof(szClass) + 1)
ibName	Offset of object name in structure (sizeof(OBJECTHEADER))
ibClass	Offset of object class in structure (ibName + cchName)
ptSize	Original size of object. The code to set this is shown in Listing 19.4
rgch	Name and class of object, (szName\0szClass\0)

The ptSize of the object is constructed with the code in Listing 19.4.

Listing 19.4

```
if (OleQueryBounds(lpoleobject, (LPRECT) &rc) == OLE_OK)
    {
    ptSize.x = rc.right - rc.left;
    ptSize.y = rc.top - rc.bottom;
    }
```

Following the last byte of the class of the object, OLE writes the result of the Ole-SaveToStream() function. After all the data is written, a checksum is performed on the data. The checksum is computed with the C function shown in Listing 19.5.

Listing 19.5

```
void ComputeObjChecksum()
(
LPBYTE lpb,      // far pointer to the checksum byte
BYTE _huge * hpb,     //huge pointer to saved OLE object
LONG lcbbuf     // number of bytes in saved OLE object
)
    {
    BYTE bChecksum = *lpb

    while (lpbbuf-- > OL)
        bChecksum ^= *hpb++;
    // save the value ORed with a constant
    *lpb = bChecksum | 0xFE05AD00L;
    }
```

If the information in the header or the checksum is not in the expected format, the OLE object is not loaded.

By parsing the information in the OLE object fields yourself, you could potentially perform Windows API calls on the OLE object.

OLE and Resources

Windows 3.1 has two 64K segments of memory to contain system resources. Each program running under Windows eats some part of these 64K segments, usually 10 to 20 percent of the total. When this memory is gone, applications start putting up "Out of Memory" errors or fail to start, despite the fact that you may have 16 megabytes or more of memory on your system.

Because OLE starts at least one server program, this may deplete the available system resources. To reduce the problem, you should monitor your system resources carefully when using OLE. Most copyright notice dialogs in programs will show you the amount of free resources. The SysInfo application available from the About Microsoft Access dialog reports the amount as percentages in the User and GDI memory-available entries. There are also a large number of shareware and freeware applications, as well as commercial applications, that report this information continuously.

The "Chicago" version of Windows (Version 4.0) is reported to change the way system resources are managed and will supposedly fix this problem. In the meantime, monitor your system resources, close unnecessary applications, and be prepared to trap "Out of Memory" errors in your code when you use OLE.

Summary

This chapter has covered the following issues:

- Linking and embedding
- In-place editing of objects
- Using bound OLE objects
- Inserting graphs into your forms
- Setting OLE properties
- Expanding Access with OLE custom controls
- Controlling other applications with OLE Automation
- Using Regedit
- Parsing bound object columns in tables

OLE is the third of three methods to expand the bounds of Access. The other two are DLL calls and DDE, covered in Chapters 17 and 18. This chapter has examined OLE in its various permutations: linking and embedding, custom controls, and OLE Automation. Using these allows you to extend the functionality of Access. With linking and embedding, you can construct compound documents. With OLE custom controls, you can add to the controls provided in the toolbox. With these controls, you can create interfaces that simplify input for your users. OLE Automation allows you to construct applications that span more than one program. You can use OLE Automation to drive another program to provide solutions to your users that would otherwise be beyond the capability of Access. All of these belong in any Access developer's toolbox.

PART VII

Advanced Topics

CHAPTER

TWENTY

Creating Libraries, Wizards, Builders, and Menu Add-Ins

- Writing libraries

- Installing libraries, Wizards, builders, and menu add-ins

- In-depth analysis of the Tabbed Dialog Wizard

- A look at the L/R Naming Builder

- Tips and tricks

An *add-in* is a tool written in Access Basic to enhance or extend the basic functionality of Access. There are three types of add-ins: Wizards, builders, and menu add-ins. All three categories can call the same procedures; it is the user interface implementation that dictates their categorization. A Wizard, such as the Form Wizard, is usually a multipage form that leads the user through a series of questions and then creates an Access table, query, form, report, or control. A builder, such as the Color Builder, is typically a single-page form that collects information and sets a single property on a property sheet. A menu add-in, such as the Database Documentor, is a general-purpose utility that doesn't fit nicely into the other two categories.

Wizards, Builders, and Menu Add-Ins Included with Access 2.0

Table 20.1 lists all the Wizards, builders, and menu add-ins that are included with Access 2.0, as well as their purposes.

TABLE 20.1: Access 2.0 Wizards, Builders, and Menu Add-Ins

Wizard/ Builder/Add-In	Purpose	Where Activated
Add-in Manager add-in	Allows you to quickly and easily install or remove Wizards, builders, and add-ins	From a hierarchical menu on the Access File menu. Can be accessed only with a database open
Archive Query Wizard	Helps you create a query that effectively archives specified records by copying them from an existing table to a new backup table	From the Database window, select New ➤ Query Wizard
Attachment Manager add-in	Allows you to maintain the links to attached tables	From a menu on the File menu
AutoDialer	Allows Access to dial a phone number using an attached modem	Add the AutoDialer button to a form's toolbar, have a field containing a valid phone number selected, and click the AutoDialer button

TABLE 20.1: Access 2.0 Wizards, Builders, and Menu Add-Ins (continued)

Wizard/ Builder/Add-In	Purpose	Where Activated
AutoForm	Creates a form in one step	Highlight a table or query in the Database window and click the AutoForm button
AutoReport	Creates a report in one step	Highlight a table or query in the Database window and click the AutoReport button
Code Builder	Creates an event procedure in the Code-Behind-Forms of a form or report	In the property sheet, click the Builder button, or select a valid item, click the right mouse button, and select Code Builder
Color Builder	Allows you to create custom colors visually for form and report objects	Select the Builder button next to the ForeColor, BackColor, or BorderColor property
Combo Box Wizard	Helps you create a combo box	Make sure View ➤ Command Wizards is checked (or use the toolbox). When you drop a combo box on a form or report, the Wizard is invoked
Command Button Wizard	Helps you create a command button	Make sure View ➤ Command Wizards is checked (or use the toolbox). When you drop a command button on a form or report, the Wizard is invoked
Crosstab Query Wizard	Helps you create a query that summarizes data in a row-and-column format	In the Database window, with the Queries group showing, select New ➤ Crosstab Query
Database Documentor add-in	A revamped version of the Access 1.x Analyzer. It allows you to document your database objects (including module code and security)	Open the database you want to document and select File ➤ Add-Ins ➤ Database Documentor
Expression Builder	Helps you write complex expressions by providing a list of valid Access commands and procedures loaded in the current database	You can access the Expression Builder in most places where you need to build an expression, such as module windows, the Query design window, and the Macro design window

TABLE 20.1: Access 2.0 Wizards, Builders, and Menu Add-Ins (continued)

Wizard/ Builder/Add-In	Purpose	Where Activated
Field Builder	Adds a new field to a table	Use the Shortcut ➤ Build option when the insertion point is in the Field Name column of a table's Design view or click the Builder button on the toolbar
Find Duplicates Query Wizard	Assists you while creating a query that will find duplicate records in a table or query	From the Database window, with the Queries group showing, select New ➤ Find Duplicates Query
Find Unmatched Query Wizard	Creates a query that finds all the records in one table that do not have a match in another table	From the Database window, with the Queries group showing, select New ➤ Find Unmatched Query
Graph Wizard	Guides you through the process of creating a form with an embedded graph (You must have installed Graph 5 with Access for this to Wizard to work.)	With the Form group showing, select New ➤ Graph
Groups/Totals Report Wizard	Helps you create a report that groups data and displays it in a tabular format	From the Database window, select the Report group and then select New ➤ Groups/Total
Import Database add-in	Imports all objects (except relationships) from a specified database (Access 1.0, 1.1, and 2.0) into the current database	From the File Add-ins menu, select Import Database
Input Mask Wizard	Assists you in creating a data entry input mask to make entry more accurate. You can select one of Access's predefined formats or create your own	In the Input Mask property of a field, select the Builder button
List Box Wizard	Helps you create a list box	Make sure Command Wizards is checked via the View menu (or use the toolbox). When you drop a list box on a form or report, the Wizard is invoked

TABLE 20.1: Access 2.0 Wizards, Builders, and Menu Add-Ins (continued)

Wizard/ Builder/Add-In	Purpose	Where Activated
Macro Builder	Helps you create macros for event procedures	From the Event property of a valid Access object, select Builder ➤ Macro Builder
Mailing Label Report Wizard	Assists in the creation of a report that prints mailing labels	With the Report group showing, select New ➤ Mailing Label
Main/Subform Wizard	Helps you create a form that contains an embedded subform	In the Database window, select the Form group and then select New ➤ Main/Subform
Menu Builder add-in	Guides you as you create custom menus	Select Add-ins ➤ Menu Builder from the Access File menu
Microsoft Word Mail Merge Wizard	Helps you create a mail merge between Access and Microsoft Word 6.0 for Windows	From the Database window, select the table or query containing the data you want to merge and select the Mail Merge To Word button on the toolbar
ODBC Connection String Builder	Helps you create an ODBC connection string for a SQL pass-through query	In the SQL Specific Pass-through property sheet, select the Build button next to the ODBCConnectStr property box
Option Group Wizard	This Wizard helps you create option groups on your form or report	Make sure Command Wizards is checked via the View menu (or use the toolbox). When you drop an option group on a form or report, the Wizard is invoked
Picture Builder	Helps you add a picture to a toggle or command button	Select the Builder button that appears next to the Picture Property box in the property sheet

TABLE 20.1: Access 2.0 Wizards, Builders, and Menu Add-Ins (continued)

Wizard/ Builder/Add-In	Purpose	Where Activated
Query Builder	Assists you in the creation of the RecordSource properties for forms, reports, or unbound object frames or the RowSource property of combo and list boxes by letting you use the query builder to create the SQL	Select the Builder button next to the Property box of either the RowSource or the RecordSource in the property sheet
Single-Column Form Wizard	Guides you as you create a form with all fields listed in a single column	With the Forms group showing in the Database window, choose New ➤ Single-Column
Single-Column Report Wizard	Helps you build a form with all fields listed in a single column	Choose New ➤ Single-Column in the Database window with the Report group showing
Summary Report Wizard	Helps you create a summary report with groups and totals	Open the Report Wizard from the Database window and select the Summary Report option
Table Wizard	Guides you through the process of creating a custom table; alternatively, you can choose one of the over 40 predefined ones offered by Access	From the Database window, select the Table tab and then select New ➤ Table Wizard
Tabular Form Wizard	Builds a form that lists fields across the form, with each row representing a new record	Select the Form tab on the Database window and select New ➤ Form Wizards ➤ Tabular Form
Tabular Report Wizard	Builds a report that lists fields across the form, with each row representing a new record	Select the Report tab in the Database window and select New ➤ Report Wizards ➤ Tabular Form

TABLE 20.1: Access 2.0 Wizards, Builders, and Menu Add-Ins (continued)

Wizard/ Builder/Add-In	Purpose	Where Activated
Wizards Customizer	You can customize many of the new Wizards, builders, and menu add-ins included with Access via the Customize option of the Add-in Manager	Start the Add-in Manager. Select a library from the list. If its Wizards can be customized, the Customize command button becomes available. Click and continue. If the button is not enabled, you'll need to manually modify the library by loading it as a database

You're free to peruse the Wizard library code that ships with Access, but you may find the commented version of this code that's part of the Access Developer's Toolkit more useful for determining how these Wizards work.

Libraries

Libraries are databases containing information that is always accessible from Access, regardless of which database is open in the main window. Access 2.0's standard add-ins are stored in five libraries in your ACCESS directory. Library databases usually contain procedures that help the user perform repetitive tasks; they might be used to enter header information into an Access Basic function or help you create an Access object, such as a table. Table 20.2 lists the standard Access 2.0 libraries and their contents.

TABLE 20.2: Access 2.0 Standard Library Databases

File	Purpose
SYSTEM.MDA	Contains information about user operating preferences, security information, and user Access toolbars
UTILITY.MDA	Contains various tables and modules used by Access, as well as the zoom box

TABLE 20.2: Access 2.0 Standard Library Databases (continued)

File	Purpose
WZBLDR.MDA	Stores the standard Command Wizards and builders
WZFRMRPT.MDA	Stores the standard Form and Report Wizards
WZLIB.MDA	Stores the generic library functions and menu add-ins. Must be loaded for any of the other standard Access libraries to operate properly
WZOUTL.MDA	This library is installed if you have the Access Developer's Toolkit. You use it to help you embed Data Outline controls in your application

You can open these libraries to look at their contents, but you should develop your own libraries to store add-ins that *you* create. To look at the Wizard databases, you must first uninstall them using the Add-in Manager.

To look inside UTILITY.MDA, you need to "fake out" Access since you can't open a database if it's loaded as a library, and Access requires some database to be loaded as its utility database. The trick is to create an empty database and modify the UtilityDB setting in the Options section of MSACC20.INI to refer to your empty database. Then you can load UTILITY.MDA and look at any of the items it contains. Make a backup of UTILITY.MDA before changing its contents.

The Access System Libraries

Access 2.0 is a complicated program and requires many pieces to operate correctly. Besides the main executable (MSACCESS.EXE) and its supporting DLLs, Access must have two library files in order to run: SYSTEM.MDA and UTILITY.MDA. These files have two particular roles in running Access.

SYSTEM.MDA maintains user-specific information, including user operating preferences, toolbars, and security information. Because this file contains security information necessary to gain complete access to a secured database, it's a good idea to make regular backups of your SYSTEM.MDA. Note that you can have more than one SYSTEM.MDA file on your system if you have created additional workgroup files using the Workgroup Administration utility, but only one is active at any one time. Your SYSTEM.MDA file is specified in your MSACC20.INI file in the [Options] section.

UTILITY.MDA is just what its name implies: a utility library. This library contains four tables that the Expression Builder uses. In addition, this library contains five forms, one of which is named ZoomForm. This form is what Access displays when you press the Shift+F2 key combination in an Access field or property window. You can edit this form, changing the font size, enlarging the text box, or even enlarging the form itself. UTILITY.MDA also stores various modules needed to perform the Save Output To operations. It also includes two modules that contain all the currently defined Access Basic and DAO constants. Table 20.3 lists the contents of UTILITY.MDA.

NOTE   SYSTEM.MDA and UTILITY.MDA are the default names for these libraries, but you can change the names as long as you adjust the appropriate entries in MSACC20.INI.

TABLE 20.3: Objects in UTILITY.MDA

Object	Type	Purpose
EBFuncNames	Table	Used by the Expression Builder
ExpFunctions	Table	Used by the Expression Builder; stores the name of Access Basic functions
ExpOperators	Table	Used by the Expression Builder; stores the name of Access Basic operators
ExpParams	Table	Used by the Expression Builder; stores the name of Access Basic function parameters
IMEXSpec	Form	Used by the Import Export Specification function of Access
IMEXSubform	Form	Subform for IMEXSpec
Normal	Form	Template to use when you create your own forms or reports
Picture	Form	Use unknown
ZoomForm	Form	Zoom box (Shift+F2)
AbcConstants	Module	Stores Access Basic constants

TABLE 20.3: Objects in UTILITY.MDA (continued)

Object	Type	Purpose
DataConstants	Module	Stores Access Basic constants used for DAO functions
SOA_Ascii	Module	Stores procedures that perform Save Output As ASCII functions
SOA_Biff	Module	Stores procedures that perform the Save Output As Biff (Microsoft Excel Binary Interchange File Format) functions
SOA_RTF	Module	Stores procedures that perform the Save Output As RTF (Rich Text Format) functions
Utils	Module	Stores the zoom box functions, as well various financial functions

When to Use a Library

When you store a module in a normal Access database, it's available only to that particular application. When you store a module in a library database, it is available to all databases because Access loads libraries into memory when it starts up. Thus, library databases are where you store your add-ins. Most of the Wizards, builders, and menu add-ins included in Access 2.0 are implemented in Access Basic and stored in library databases. You should use a library anytime you want a specific procedure made available to multiple databases.

File Name Extensions

Access libraries, by convention, are assigned the MS-DOS file extension .MDA. You can give them any extension you want; however, the Access Add-in Manager will see only libraries with the standard .MDA extension. By default, Access displays databases with the .MDB extension only in the File Open dialog box, which makes it less likely that users will try to open your library. This is desirable because a library database cannot be opened while it is installed in the MSACC20.INI file as a library. During development, you can use the .MDB extension until your application is completely debugged and then rename it to .MDA and install it as a library.

Do's and Don'ts of Implementing Libraries

Implementing an Access add-in library can be complex. The following do's and don'ts will help simplify the process of creating add-ins.

Define an Item's Purpose   When creating an item for a library database, start by specifying its purpose: What will it do and which user interface is appropriate? For example, will it be a Wizard used to create an object or a builder used to set a property? If you can't narrow the purpose to one sentence, such as "My Wizard will create an Access form that acts like a Windows tabbed dialog box," you should rethink your add-in.

Use Unique Names   Access maintains an area reserved for Access Basic global procedure names, variables, and constants. If you have two procedures with the same name, an error will occur when you attempt to load the offending procedure.

Load the database As a Library   Because Access allows the user to open only one database at a time, you need to install your database as a library so that its functions are available while a user's database is open.

Don't Use Macros   Although you can call macros from a library, we highly recommend that you don't. Access macros do not provide any means of error handling; if an error occurs in a library, the user will get an unprofessional-looking message box like the one shown in Figure 20.1.

FIGURE 20.1:
A run-time error in a macro or module without error handling can be disastrous in a library.

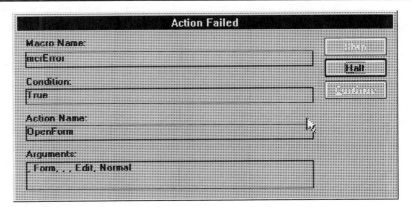

Write Generic Functions   If possible, create generic procedures you can use in multiple databases. Generic procedures rely upon passed parameters and variables rather than hard-coded object names and references.

Use Code-Behind-Forms   Using Code-Behind-Forms allows you to store your Wizard code with the form. This code is not loaded until the form is loaded, thus reducing the memory overhead of your library.

Use Private Procedures   If you are using global modules in your add-in, make your procedures private to the module by adding the Access Basic keyword Private to the Function/Sub statement. This reduces the number of procedure names and the likelihood of duplicate names.

Don't Use Domain Functions   Because domain functions such as DLookup() and DSum() always refer to data in the current (user) database, do not use them in a library database unless you intend to refer to the user's data. If the data source is not a valid domain in the current user database, a trappable Access Basic error (3078) occurs: "Couldn't find input table or query ' | '."

Use Option Explicit   Make sure you have Option Explicit in the Declaration section of all your Access Basic modules. Make sure it is the Declaration section of your Code-Behind-Forms, too.

Compile All Your Access Basic Modules and Compact Your Database   Before you package up your library, compile all your Access Basic modules (including your Code-Behind-Forms). This will decrease the user's initial load time of your library. Also, compact and repair the database to make sure your .MDA file is as small as possible.

Variable Scoping and Libraries

When writing code for your Wizards, you must understand how Access scopes variables and procedures. In Access Basic you can define a variable that has three different levels of scope: global, module, and procedure. Global items are available to all procedures in all modules, including Code-Behind-Forms. Module-level items are available only to procedures in the module in which the item is declared. Procedure-level items are available only to the procedure in which they are defined.

This becomes interesting when you throw libraries into the mix. Here are the basic rules of global variables and libraries:

- Your application database can read and set global values in attached library databases.

- Library databases can read global values of other attached library databases.

- Library databases can read global values of the application database if the code is running from Code-Behind-Forms. Functions stored in global library modules cannot read global values in the application database.

Normally, this wouldn't be an issue. However, because a library can load with compile-time errors in Code-Behind-Forms caused by variables not being defined, you need to be careful about the internal naming structure for global variables in your library. Your Code-Behind-Forms in your library can read global variables in a user's database, but its global procedures cannot.

Installing and Maintaining a Library

Your library database is made available to Access applications through settings in the MSACC20.INI initialization file, which is located in your Windows subdirectory.

There are three ways to install your add-in library:

- Use the Add-in Manager (the preferred method).

- Using a text editor, modify MSACC20.INI.

- Write your own Access Basic installation utility.

Each option has advantages and disadvantages, as listed in the following table:

Option	Advantage	Disadvantage
Add-in Manager	Comes with Access 2.0	Can't be used with run-time applications

Option	Advantage	Disadvantage
Manual Installation	No coding involved	Error prone
Write your own	Your only solution if you are using the Access run-time version	Another piece of code to write

The Access 2.0 Add-in Manager makes it easy for you and your users to install and manage your libraries, as described in the following sections.

Using the Add-In Manager to Administer Access Libraries

The Access 2.0 Add-in Manager is a great tool for administering Access libraries. Although it's called the Add-in Manager, it lets you maintain Wizards and builders as well as menu add-ins. Figure 20.2 shows the Add-in Manager in action.

FIGURE 20.2:

Use the Add-in Manager to control Wizards, builders, and add-ins.

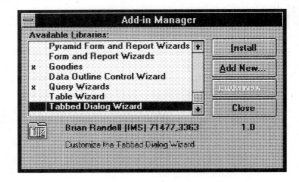

To use the Add-in Manager, follow these steps:

1. Start Access and open an Access database. Access does not allow any Access Basic functionality unless a user database is open, so no add-ins are available if there's no user database open.

2. Select File ➤ Add-ins ➤ Add-in Manager.

The Add-in Manager then displays all currently installed libraries, as well any files with the MS-DOS extension .MDA that are located in your Access directory.

Once in the Add-in Manager, you can install or uninstall any of the libraries listed. An *x* to the left of the library name (or the lack thereof) denotes whether or not the library is already installed. Also, if the library has add-ins that can be customized, the Customize command button is enabled. If you click the button, one of two things happens. If the library contains only one add-in with customizable options, its form appears. If more than one item can be modified, such as the builders in WZBLDR.MDA, the Customize Add-in dialog appears. Figure 20.3 shows the Customize Add-in dialog box.

FIGURE 20.3:
Use the Customize Add-in dialog to select an add-in to customize.

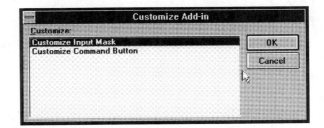

When your library modifications are complete, you must exit and restart Access for your changes to take effect.

If you wish to disable the Add-in Manager, you can do so in one of two ways:

- **To disable only the Add-in Manager:** Use a text editor, such as Notepad, to edit the MSACC20.INI file. In the [Menu Add-Ins] section, insert a semicolon before the line that begins with "&Add-in Manager".

- **To disable all add-ins (including the Add-in Manager):** Use a semicolon before each of the entries in the [Libraries] and [Menu Add-Ins] sections.

When you are editing the text of your MSACC20.INI file, it's always a good idea to make a backup copy first.

Writing Your Own Add-In Manager

The Microsoft licensing agreement for Access and the Access Developer's Toolkit prohibit you from distributing any of the Wizards, builders, and menu add-ins that come with Access. One important add-in you cannot distribute is the Add-in Manager. If this functionality is important for your users, you will need to write your own Add-in Manager. You can look at the functionality of the current Add-in Manager and replace it with one that is functionally equivalent.

Entry-Point Functions of Wizards, Builders, and Add-Ins

Each Wizard, builder, and menu add-in must have one global function that is the entry point. When the user activates the Wizard, builder, or menu add-in, Access calls this entry-point function using a standard set of parameters. The type and number of arguments the function takes change, depending on the type of add-in. Context information is passed to the function in the arguments. Although all the entry point procedures must be functions, the return value is not meaningful.

A *Table or Query Wizard* takes no arguments.

A *Form or Report Wizard* takes two arguments. The first argument is a string telling the Wizard the name of the table or query to which the form or report is bound. The second argument is optional. If it is specified, it contains a unique number identifying the Wizard. You can use this number to have one entry point for two separate Wizards. For example, the Single-Column and Tabular Wizards that Access installs both have the same entry point, but they operate differently, based on the value of the argument.

A *Control Wizard* takes two arguments. The first argument is the name of the control that triggered the Wizard. The second argument is the name of the label attached to the control.

A *builder* takes the same arguments as a Control Wizard.

A *menu add-in* takes no arguments.

Installing Add-Ins, Wizards, and Builders by Hand

When you install add-ins by hand, you must first list each database in the [Libraries] section of the .INI file. The library name must appear on the left side of the equal sign, followed by an *r* or *rw*. For example:

```
wzTable.mda=rw
```

The *r* or *rw* indicates whether the library database itself should be read-only or read/write, respectively. This entry makes the functions available to Access. However, you must make another entry to tell Access when to use the function. You do this in the Wizards sections of the MSACC20.INI file.

Table Wizards must have an entry in the [Table Wizards] section of the .INI file. The entry must have the format

DisplayName=FunctionName,,{StatusbarText}

DisplayName is the name to appear in the Access UI. *FunctionName* is the name of the entry-point function, without parentheses. The *StatusBarText* appears on the status bar when the Wizard is selected. For example:

```
Table=TW_Entry,,{This Wizard creates a new table to store data.}
```

The entries for Query Wizards have the same syntax as Table Wizards except that they appear in the [Query Wizards] section of the .INI file.

The entries for Form Wizards appear in the [Form Wizards] section of the .INI file. The entry must have the format

DisplayName=FunctionName, WizardId, {StatusbarText}

WizardId is the unique number passed into the entry point in the second argument. For example:

```
Single-Column=zwForm, 1,{This Wizard creates a form that displays
➥ fields in a single column.}
```

The entries for Report Wizards have the same syntax as for Form Wizards except that they appear in the [Report Wizards] section of the .INI file.

Control Wizards must have an entry in the [Control Wizards] section of the .INI file. The information for this entry is incorrectly documented in Chapter 5 of the *Advanced Topics* book in the Access Developer's Toolkit. The correct format of the entry is

UniqueName= BuilderType, DisplayName, FunctionName, w

UniqueName is an entry that uniquely identifies the control builder. The *BuilderType* must be one of the following strings. (It appears impossible to add Control Builders to labels or graphs.)

TextBox

OptionGroup

ToggleButton

OptionButton

CheckBox

ComboBox

Listbox

SubformSubreport

ObjectFrame

BoundObjectFrame

Line

Rectangle

PageBreak

CommandButton

For example:

```
MSListBoxWizard=ListBox, List Box Builder, LST_ENTRY,w
```

The entries for builders have the same syntax as for Control Wizards except that they appear in the [Property Wizards] section of the .INI file and the *BuilderType* is replaced by the property name the builder is supposed to affect. The last entry may be *w* or *rw*. If it is *w*, the builder can only write the property. If it is *rw*, the builder can change an existing property.

TIP

An undocumented feature in Access allows you to create Module Builders. To do so, simply create a builder entry in the Property Wizards section, where the *BuilderType* is the word *Module*. Then, when the user right-clicks on a module and selects Build from the popup menu, Access shows a dialog that lists your Module Builder, as well as the default Expression Builder.

Menu add-ins must have an entry in the [Menu Add-Ins] section of the MSAC-CESS.INI file. The format for the entry is

DisplayName=MacroName

or

DisplayName==FunctionName()

Note that the function name is preceded by two equal signs. The *DisplayName* may have an ampersand (&) preceding a character that becomes the shortcut key on the menu. For example:

```
&Menu Builder==CustomMenuBuilder()
```

Using the Add-In Manager to Install Add-Ins

The Add-in Manager uses a table called USysAddIns to determine the properties of an add-in database. Access treats any table that begins with USys or MSys specially, such that it will not appear in the Database window unless the Show Systems Objects option is set to Yes. You will want to turn on this option while working with the USysAddIns table. The easiest way to create the table is to import an existing USysAddIns table from one of the Access Wizards into the current database. You can then modify this table to show the information necessary.

The USysAddIns table contains records that describe information about the add-in database, such as the company name of the author, the version number of the add-in, a description, a logo, and so forth. Each record contains one PropertyName column and nine Val columns. What goes into the Val columns depends on the contents of the PropertyName column. Table 20.4 describes the USysAddIns table properties.

TABLE 20.4: USysAddIns Table Properties

Property	Purpose	Values
AddInVersion	Version number of the library	Val1 = Version Number
CompanyName	Company name of the add-in's developer	Val1 = Company Name
Description	Description of the add-in	Val1 = Description
DisplayName	Name to appear in the Add-in Manager's list	Val1 = Add-in name
Logo	Logo to appear in the Add-in Manager. You cannot use 256-color bitmaps in version 2.0. Their use will cause "Out of memory" error messages. Use 16-color bitmaps or icons instead	Val9 = logo
FunctionToCallOn-Customize	There can be multiple records for this property. If only one appears, the function is called automatically when the user clicks the Customize button in the Add-in Manager. If more than one record appears, a dialog shows up allowing users to select the ones they want	Val1 = Description string to appear in the Selection dialog Val2 = Name of the function followed by parentheses
IniFileEntry	There can be multiple records for this property. It creates entries in the MSACC20.INI file	Val1 = name of the section in which to put the entry Val2 = entry name Val3 = value the entry receives

Wizards

In essence, Wizards, builders, and menu add-ins are all well-thought-out Access applications that can be called from other databases.

Creating a Wizard

There are four steps to designing a Wizard:

1. Define its purpose.

2. Come up with a list of questions for the user. These questions are the foundation of your Wizard; without the answers, your Wizard cannot continue or properly complete its task.

3. Decide which options to provide the user when running your Wizard. For example, these options might include items that affect how a form looks or the number of tabs to place on a tabbed dialog.

4. Decide how the user will call your Wizard. This determines its class—either an Object Wizard that creates Access container objects, such as tables and forms, or a Control Wizard that creates controls for forms and reports.

Designing Your Wizard's User Interface

The success and acceptance of Wizards is largely due to the fact that Wizards let the average user perform complex operations in a few simple steps. The key to a well-written Wizard is a clean and simple user interface with a minimal amount of user intervention. Your Wizard's user interface is one of its most important features and can make or break your tool.

Consistency

One of the key selling points of Microsoft Windows is the consistent user interface. A user interface inconsistent with Windows and Access will frustrate your users. If you model your Wizard after the ones included with Access, users and developers will be familiar with the look and feel of your tool, thereby increasing the likelihood of its success.

Simplicity

Wizards perform their magic by asking a few questions of the user and then invoking some Access Basic to present a finished object. The Access form is your window to the user. Creating a simple-to-use form is easy if you order your questions and group them into one- or two-page categories. It's a good idea to limit your groupings to a maximum of three questions per page in your form. This design will keep the user from being inundated with a form full of text boxes, labels, and other controls.

User Interface Design Tips

You can enhance your Wizard's UI in a number of ways:

- Place controls in the same location on each page. For example, you might always place pictures 0.1 inches from the left and 0.2 inches from the top of the page and place questions 0.2 inches down and 2 inches from the left. Consistency makes your Wizard look professional. Also, consistent placement of controls reduces screen "flashing."

- Keep all the pages the same size. (The Microsoft Wizards are 2.4375 inches high, plus a 0.4167-inch footer.)

- Design your Wizard so it can be displayed on the lowest screen resolution your users might have. If you want to make your Wizard universal, don't make the form larger than 480 x 480 pixels.

- Use color consistently and tastefully, avoiding stark contrasts and garish combinations.

- Stick with the fonts that come with Windows 3.1: Arial, Courier, Courier New, Modern, MS Sans Serif, MS Serif, Plotter, Roman, Script, Symbol, Times New Roman, and WingDings. If your Wizard also has to run under Windows 3.0, you must be even more restrictive in your font choice, eliminating the TrueType fonts.

- When your form opens, make sure it centers on the screen (by using the AutoCenter property) and is sized to fit, showing only one page of your Wizard.

- Place any controls you want available on every page, such as paging command buttons, in the Footer section of the Wizard. You can keep the Header section, or you can hide it by setting the height property to 0.

Controlling Movement

Users should not be able to move to a different page in a Wizard until all the questions on the current page are answered. Therefore, you must control the user's movement in two ways. First, you need to provide a way for the user to move from control to control without leaving the page. Second, you need to provide a way for the user to move to each page.

The standard way to move from item to item on a page is to use the Tab key. The standard way to move to a different page is to use the page control buttons.

Moving Around the Page

A problem arises with multipage forms: if users press the Tab key, they are taken to the next control in the tab order even if it is not on the current page. This allows users to circumvent your flow of control through the Wizard. It also looks tacky. There are several ways to prevent this. One way is to disable every control on the form except those on the current page. A second way is to set the TabStop property to No.

A third way is to add two hidden text boxes on each page of your form. You can place them anywhere in the Detail section of the form. However, we recommend that you place them in the same location on each page, such as the bottom of the Detail section. Figure 20.4 shows a form from the Tabbed Dialog Wizard with tab control text boxes.

Next, arrange the tab order of your controls so that one of the hidden text boxes is always the first tab on a page and the other is last. For example, if you have six controls on page 1, the order would be txtTabStop1First, lblQuestion1, txtAnswer1, lblQuestion2, txtAnswer2, txtTabStop1Last. If you are consistent in naming the hidden controls, they are easier to work with. Figure 20.5 shows how you set the order in the Access Tabbed Order dialog.

After setting the tab order, you need one generic function in your Code-Behind-Forms that will be called by the OnEnter event of the hidden text boxes. The following procedure comes from the Tabbed Dialog Wizard:

```
Function SetCtlFocus(pstrCtlName As String) As Integer
    On Error Resume Next
    DoCmd GoToControl pstrCtlName
End Function
```

FIGURE 20.4:

Tabbed Dialog Wizard's tab control text boxes in Design view

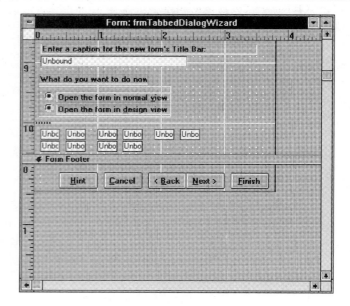

FIGURE 20.5:

Access Tab Order dialog box for the Tabbed Dialog Wizard

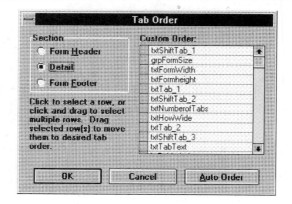

Whenever a user tabs into one of the hidden controls, the procedure moves the cursor to the proper control. To call the function, put the following in the OnEnter property box:

=SetCtlFocus("*ControlName*")

The *ControlName* will be the first control or the last control on the page that can receive focus. In our example above, the control name is txtAnswer in txtTabStop1First's OnEnter event and txtAnswer2 in txtTabStop1Last's. This prevents users from moving to a control on another page using the tab key.

Moving to a Different Page

To control movement from page to page, you also need to disable the PgUp and PgDn keys. This ensures that the only way to move to a different page is with your own control buttons. Disabling the PgUp and PgDn keys is simple, although not well documented. You must open the form using the A_DIALOG flag, as shown here:

DoCmd OpenForm "*YourFormName*", , , , , A_DIALOG

Simply setting the form's properties to Popup and Dialog will *not* disable the paging keys. Using A_DIALOG is a much simpler alternative than trapping keystrokes with the KeyPress events.

You need to track the current page for users to move to a different page. Access does not provide a property to do this. However, you can track it with only three lines of code, as follows:

- In the Declarations section of your form's Code-Behind-Forms, create a module-level variable, such as mintCurrentPage.
- In the form's Load event, add a line of code that sets mintCurrentPage to 1.
- Whenever you change a page, update this variable.

Creating a Sample Wizard

Creating a Wizard can involve just as much work as creating a small application. The next few sections discuss in detail how to build a sample Form Wizard.

The purpose of the Tabbed Dialog Box sample Wizard is to build forms that resemble the tabbed dialog boxes in Excel 5.0 and Word for Windows 6.0. Table 20.5 lists all the Access objects in the Tabbed Dialog Box Wizard (TabWiz) and their purposes.

TABLE 20.5: Objects in TABWIZ.MDA

Object	Purpose
tblFormControls	Contains all the basic controls to create a one-tabbed dialog box. Used to create all dialog boxes
tblTabLabels	Used by the Wizard to build a list of labels that appear on the tabs
tblUserDefaults	Stores the default settings for the Wizard, as selected by the user
tblWizardHints	Stores the text of the Wizard hints
USysAddIns	Installs and customizes the Wizard using the Add-in Manager
USysFormControls	Backup table of tblFormControls (You can use it to restore default settings.)
USysWizardDefaults	Stores the standard defaults for the Wizard
frmTabbedDialogWizard	Main Wizard form
frmTabbedDialogWizardCustomize	Sets the defaults for the Wizard, using a tabbed dialog
frmUserDefaultsSub1	First tab of the Customize dialog
frmUserDefaultsSub2	Second tab of the Customize dialog
frmUserDefaultsSub3	Third tab of the Customize dialog
frmWizardHint	Hint dialog
basTWZGlobal	Stores all global variables, constants, and any API calls
basTWZUtility	Stores entry-point procedures, the global error handler, and utility procedures

Support Objects

When designing a Wizard, you must map out the necessary support objects. TabWiz uses several tables and two global modules. Each object either supports a form or is called by one of the Access Basic procedures used in the Wizard.

The Global Modules basTWZGlobal and basTWZUtility

It is a good idea to decide ahead of time which code can be stored in Code-Behind-Forms and which code must be contained in global modules. For TabWiz, there are two global modules. The module basTWZGlobal does not contain any functions or subs; it only stores the global variables and constants.

The basTWZUtility module contains generic functions, such as the global error handler, some string-management procedures, and the entry-point functions for TabWiz and the TabWiz Customize option.

glrTWZEntry

Each Wizard you write requires a code entry point. The procedure glrTWZEntry is the entry point that starts TabWiz. Since we are creating a Form Wizard, glrTWZEntry accepts the table/query name as a passed-in parameter. The function begins by opening the Wizard form with the A_DIALOG switch. It sets a global variable, declared earlier in basTWZGlobal with the passed-in object name, and then exits. Listing 20.1 shows the glrTWZEntry() function.

Listing 20.1

```
Function glrTWZEntry(pstrTableName As String) As Integer
  On Error GoTo glrTWZEntry_Err

  DoCmd OpenForm "frmTabbedDialogWizard", A_NORMAL, , , ,
  ➥ A_DIALOG

  glr_twzgstrTableName = pstrTableName

  glrTWZEntry = True

glrTWZEntry_Exit:
  On Error GoTo 0
  Exit Function

glrTWZEntry_Err:
  Call glrTWZErrorProc(Err, Error$, "glrTWZEntry",
  ➥ "glr_basTabWizardSupport")
  Resume glrTWZEntry_Exit

End Function
```

glrTWZErrorProc

You need to provide error handling for all procedures you include in your Wizards. Neglecting to trap errors will lead to a confusing dialog if a run-time error occurs. Figure 20.6 shows the dialog you'll see if an untrapped error occurs in your add-in.

The glrTWZErrorProc procedure handles the errors for TabWiz and requires four passed-in arguments:

- The Access error number as an integer
- The Access error message as a string
- The procedure name where the error occurred as a string
- The module name where the procedure is stored as a string

The procedure tells the user what happened and then logs the error to a disk file located in the user's Access subdirectory. Note that glrTWZErrorProc has its own unexpected error handler. This error handler is called by almost every procedure in the entire Wizard. Listing 20.2 shows the complete glrTWZErrorProc.

Listing 20.2

```
Sub glrTWZErrorProc(pintErr As Integer, pstrError As String,
➡ pstrProc As String, pstrMod As String)
On Error GoTo glrTWZErrorProc_Err
  ' Dimension variables
  Dim strFileName As String
  Dim intFreeFile As Integer
```

```
' Initialize variables
twz_NL = Chr$(13) & Chr$(10)
strFileName = SysCmd(SYSCMD_ACCESSDIR) & "TWZ_ERR.TXT"
intFreeFile = FreeFile
Set twz_db = dbengine(0)(0)

' Inform the user what happened.
twz_strMsg = TWZ_TITLE & " encountered an unexpected error." &
➥ twz_NL
twz_strMsg = twz_strMsg & "Access returned error number " &
➥ pintErr & "." & twz_NL
twz_strMsg = twz_strMsg & pstrError

MsgBox twz_strMsg, TWZ_MB_STOP, TWZ_TITLE

' Now log the error to a disk file in the user's Access 2.0
' home directory.
Open strFileName For Append As #intFreeFile
    Print #intFreeFile, "*
    ➥ ************************************************* *"
    Print #intFreeFile, TWZ_TITLE & " encountered an unexpected
    ➥ error"
    Print #intFreeFile, "Access returned error number " & pintErr
    ➥ & "."
    Print #intFreeFile, "Error text: " & pstrError & "."
    Print #intFreeFile, "Date: " & Format$(Now, "mm/dd/yy") & "."
    Print #intFreeFile, "Time: " & Format$(Now, "hh:nn") & "."
    Print #intFreeFile, "Active database: " & twz_db.Name
    Print #intFreeFile, "Active procedure: " & pstrProc & "."
    Print #intFreeFile, "Active module: " & pstrMod & "."
    Print #intFreeFile, "Current user: " & CurrentUser() & "."
Close #intFreeFile
twz_db.Close

glrTWZErrorProc_Exit:
  On Error GoTo 0
  Exit Sub

glrTWZErrorProc_Err:
  twz_strMsg = TWZ_TITLE & " encountered an unexpected error" &
  ➥ twz_NL
  twz_strMsg = twz_strMsg & " in the System Error handler" &
  ➥ twz_NL
```

```
twz_strMsg = twz_strMsg & "Access returned error number " &
➥ pintErr & "." & twz_NL
twz_strMsg = twz_strMsg & pstrError

Beep
MsgBox twz_strMsg, TWZ_MB_STOP, TWZ_TITLE

Resume glrTWZErrorProc_Exit

End Sub
```

The Forms

The forms in TabWiz (see Table 20.5) create the user interface for the Wizard. Included among them is the Customize dialog, which is itself a tabbed dialog. By examining the way this dialog is constructed, you can see how to put the finishing touches on your own dialogs.

frmTabbedDialogWizard   The main form, frmTabbedDialogWizard, is five pages long and contains the controls that collect the data TabWiz needs to work. This form asks a series of questions, such as "How big do you want your form?" Every control on the form has some form of code attached. The following sections discuss the most significant procedures.

Listing 20.3 shows the Declarations area from frmTabbedDialogWizard, which contains the constants it uses to constrain the user input, along with API declarations used in calculating the tabs' text width.

Listing 20.3

```
' Use database order for string comparisons
Option Compare Database
' Dimension all variables
Option Explicit

' *** DoMenuItem Consts ***
Const A_WINDOW = 4
Const A_SIZETOFIT_FORM = 5
Const A_LOADTEXT = 3
Const A_CLOSEMOD = 1
```

```
' *** Error # Consts ***
' No Current Record Error
Const ERR_NOCURRENTREC = 3021

' *** Windows API Calls and Consts for GetTextWidth() ***
Const FONT_NAME = "MS Sans Serif"
Const FONT_SIZE = 8
Const FONT_BOLD = 700
Const FONT_NORMAL = 400
Const API_NULL = 0&
Const MM_TWIPS = 6

Declare Function GetDC% Lib "USER" (ByVal hWnd%)
Declare Function CreateFont% Lib "GDI" (ByVal H%, ByVal W%, ByVal
➡ E%, ByVal O%, ByVal W%, ByVal I%, ByVal U%, ByVal S%,
➡ ByVal C%, ByVal OP%, ByVal CP%, ByVal Q%, ByVal PAF%,
➡ ByVal F$)
Declare Function SetMapMode% Lib "GDI" (ByVal hDC%, ByVal
➡ nMapMode%)
Declare Function GetTextExtent Lib "GDI" (ByVal hDC%, ByVal
➡ lpString$, ByVal nCount%) As Long
Declare Function SelectObject% Lib "GDI" (ByVal hDC%, ByVal
➡ hObject%)
Declare Function DeleteObject% Lib "GDI" (ByVal hObject%)
Declare Function CreateDC% Lib "GDI" (ByVal lpDriverName$, ByVal
➡ lpDeviceName$, ByVal lpOutput$, ByVal lpInitData$)
Declare Function DeleteDC% Lib "GDI" (ByVal hDC%)

' *** General variables and consts ***
' Used for integer return values from Functions
Dim mintRetval As Integer

' What is the current page
Dim mintCurrentPage As Integer

' New Line variable
Dim NL As String

' SysCmd Variables
Dim varSysCmdRetVal As Variant
Dim mintSysCmdSteps As Integer
Dim mintSysCmdStep As Integer
Const SYSCMD_STD = 100
```

```
' *** BuildCmdButtons ***
Dim frmWiz As Form
Dim mintWhichButtons(4) As Integer
Dim mvarButtonLabels(4) As Variant
Const DETAIL_SEC = 0
Const CMD_BUTTON = 104


' *** BuildCode ***
Dim mintNumTabs As Integer

' *** BuildControls ***
Dim msngTabX As Single
Dim msngFormX As Single
Dim msngFormY As Single
Dim mstrTabLabels() As String
Const STD_WIDTH = 4.6
Const STD_HEIGTH = 3
Const EVNT_PROC = "[Event Procedure]"

' *** BuildForm ***
Dim mstrFormCaption As String

'*** LoadDefaults ***
' The option group value for user-defined size.
Const USER_DEFINED_SIZE = 4

' *** IniVariables ***
Dim mintHowToOpen As Integer

' *** cmdNext_Click ***
Dim mintTabs As Integer
```

Form_Load   The Form_Load event procedure initializes the necessary form variables. In addition, it sets control values and puts the user on the correct page and on the correct first control. Listing 20.4 shows the code for the Form_Load event procedure.

Listing 20.4

```
Sub Form_Load()
  On Error Resume Next
  Dim intX As Integer
```

```
NL = Chr$(13) & Chr$(10)

' Move to the correct first control
Me!grpFormSize.SetFocus

' Set the current Page
mintCurrentPage = 1

' Turn off certain controls
Me!cmdBack.Enabled = False

ClearListBox
LoadDefaults

' Requery List box so it doesn't show #Deleted!#
Me!lstTabLabels.Requery
End Sub
```

cmdHint_Click and glrGetWizardHintText   When you click the Hints button, the cmdHint_Click event procedure calls a global function, glrGetWizardHintText(), which gets the hint from a table, tblWizardHints. This function is passed the current page number, stored in mintCurrentPage. If the function finds the text, it stores it to a global variable. Then cmdHint_Click opens frmWizardHint and displays the hint. Listing 20.5 shows these procedures

Listing 20.5

```
Sub cmdHint_Click()
  If glrGetWizardHintText(mintCurrentPage) Then
    DoCmd OpenForm "frmWizardHint", A_NORMAL, , , , A_DIALOG
  Else
    twz_strMsg = "Unable to get hints!" & NL

    Beep
    MsgBox twz_strMsg, twz_MB_WARN, TWZ_TITLE
  End If
End Sub

Function glrGetWizardHintText(pintWhatPage As Integer) As
➡ Integer
  On Error GoTo glrGetWizardHintText_Err
```

```
Set twz_db = CodeDB()
Set TWZ_rec = twz_db.OpenRecordset("tblWizardHints",
➡ DB_OPEN_TABLE)

TWZ_rec.Index = "PrimaryKey"
TWZ_rec.Seek "=", pintWhatPage
twz_gstrWizardHint = TWZ_rec!HintText
TWZ_rec.Close
twz_db.Close

glrGetWizardHintText = True

glrGetWizardHintText_Exit:
  On Error GoTo 0
  Exit Function

glrGetWizardHintText_Err:
  MsgBox Error$
  Resume glrGetWizardHintText_Exit
End Function
```

Moving from Page to Page   The two command buttons, cmdBack_Click and cmdNext_Click, control movement from page to page. Both functions change mintCurrentPage appropriately and then use the GotoPage action to move to the correct page. In addition, they disable themselves if they happen to be on the first or last page.

cmdNext_Click also performs validation on pages 1 and 2. If users have not entered information, they cannot go on to the next page. Pages 3 and 4 contain optional information, so there is no validation done. Listing 20.6 shows these procedures.

Listing 20.6

```
Sub cmdBack_Click()
    On Error Resume Next
    mintCurrentPage = mintCurrentPage - 1
    DoCmd GoToPage mintCurrentPage
    Me!cmdBack.Enabled = (mintCurrentPage <> 1)
    Me!cmdNext.Enabled = True
End Sub

Sub cmdNext_Click()
  On Error GoTo cmdNext_Click_Err
```

```
' Check the current page and then test if the user can continue
Select Case mintCurrentPage
   Case 1
      If IsNull(Me!grpFormSize) Or ((Me!grpFormSize =
      ➡ USER_DEFINED_SIZE) And (IsNull(Me!txtFormWidth) Or
      ➡ IsNull(Me!txtFormHeight))) Then
         twz_strMsg = "Please select either a predefined form
         ➡ size" & NL
         twz_strMsg = twz_strMsg & "or enter a form width and
         ➡ height in the" & NL
         twz_strMsg = twz_strMsg & "proper fields before
         ➡ continuing."

         Beep
         MsgBox twz_strMsg, twz_MB_WARN, TWZ_TITLE

         If Me!grpFormSize = USER_DEFINED_SIZE Then
            Me!txtFormWidth.SetFocus
         Else
            Me!grpFormSize.SetFocus
         End If
         GoTo cmdNext_Click_Exit
      End If
   Case 2
      If IsNull(Me!txtHowWide) Or IsNull(Me!txtNumberOfTabs) Then
         twz_strMsg = "Please enter both the tab width and" & NL
         twz_strMsg = twz_strMsg & "the number of tabs you want" &
         ➡ NL
         twz_strMsg = twz_strMsg & "before continuing."

         MsgBox twz_strMsg, twz_MB_WARN, TWZ_TITLE
         Me!txtNumberOfTabs.SetFocus
         GoTo cmdNext_Click_Exit
      Else
         If CInt(Me!txtNumberOfTabs) > GetMaxTabs() Then
            twz_strMsg = "You've selected too many tabs, or the
            ➡ tabs are too wide" & NL
            twz_strMsg = twz_strMsg & "for this form. You'll either
            ➡ need to change the number" & NL
            twz_strMsg = twz_strMsg & "of tabs, or their
            ➡ widths." & NL
```

```
        Me!txtNumberOfTabs.SetFocus
        MsgBox twz_strMsg, twz_MB_WARN, TWZ_TITLE
        GoTo cmdNext_Click_Exit
      End If
    End If
  End Select

  ' Moving from the 2nd to the 3rd page?  Create the default tabs
  ' first.
  If mintCurrentPage = 1 Then
    Me!txtNumberOfTabs = GetMaxTabs()
  End If
  If mintCurrentPage = 2 Then
    If Me!txtNumberOfTabs <> mintTabs Then CreateDefaultTabs
    Me!txtTabText = Me!lstTabLabels.Column(1)
    mintTabs = Me!txtNumberOfTabs
  End If
  mintCurrentPage = mintCurrentPage + 1
  DoCmd GoToPage mintCurrentPage

  Me!cmdNext.Enabled = (mintCurrentPage <> 5)
  Me!cmdBack.Enabled = True

cmdNext_Click_Exit:
  On Error GoTo 0
  Exit Sub

cmdNext_Click_Err:
  glrTWZErrorProc Err, Error, "cmdNext_Click",
  ➥ "Form.frmTabbedDialogWizard"
  Resume cmdNext_Click_Exit
End Sub
```

txtFormWidth_BeforeUpdate() and txtFormHeight_BeforeUpdate()

The txtFormWidth_BeforeUpdate() and txtFormHeight_BeforeUpdate() functions validate the width and height measurements the user enters when specifying custom measurements for a form. We use functions because while Input mask and validation rules are nice, they are somewhat inflexible. However, the more significant problem is that if the user inserts invalid text, Access pops up a validation error alert. The alert has a Help button that shows Access help rather than your own custom help.

txtHowWide_AfterUpdate() and txtNumberofTabs_BeforeUpdate()

The txtHowWide_AfterUpdate() and txtNumberofTabs_BeforeUpdate() functions are concerned with how wide the user's tabs will be and how many can be built on the form without overrunning the borders. If the user enters a number in txtHow-Wide, it is validated against the rules of the module constants. If, however, the user skips this field and just enters a number in the txtNumberofTabs field, the system will calculate the correct tab width for the number of tabs requested. If the number of tabs requested can be built, the txtNumberofTabs_BeforeUpdate event builds a list of dummy tab labels and places them in the list box on page 3. In addition, it resizes txtTabText so that it is just the width of the tabs.

Listing 20.7 shows these procedures.

Listing 20.7

```
Sub txtNumberofTabs_BeforeUpdate(Cancel As Integer)
  On Error GoTo txtNumberofTabs_BeforeUpdate_Err

  Dim intMaxTabs As Integer
  Dim intChosenTabs As Integer
  Const MIN_TABS = 2

  If IsNull(Me!txtNumberOfTabs) Then Exit Sub

  intMaxTabs = GetMaxTabs()
  intChosenTabs = CInt(Me!txtNumberOfTabs)

  If Not (intChosenTabs >= MIN_TABS And intChosenTabs <=
➥ intMaxTabs) Then
    If intMaxTabs = MIN_TABS Then
      twz_strMsg = "Only " & MIN_TABS & " tabs will fit on this
      ➥ form."
    Else
      twz_strMsg = "Please select a number of tabs between " &
      ➥ MIN_TABS & " and " & intMaxTabs & "."
    End If

    MsgBox twz_strMsg, twz_MB_WARN, TWZ_TITLE
    Cancel = True
  End If
```

```
txtNumberofTabs_BeforeUpdate_Exit:
  On Error GoTo 0
  Exit Sub

txtNumberofTabs_BeforeUpdate_Err:
  glrTWZErrorProc Err, Error, "txtNumberofTabs_BeforeUpdate",
  ➡ "Form.frmTabbedDialogWizard"
  Resume txtNumberofTabs_BeforeUpdate_Exit
End Sub

Sub txtHowWide_AfterUpdate()
  On Error GoTo txtHowWide_AfterUpdate_Err

  ' Set the width of the input box for the tab labels
  ' so it approximates the actual width.
  Me!txtTabText.Width = (Me!txtHowWide * twz_TWIPS_PER_INCH)
  CreateDefaultTabs

txtHowWide_AfterUpdate_Exit:
  On Error GoTo 0
  Exit Sub

txtHowWide_AfterUpdate_Err:
  glrTWZErrorProc Err, Error, "txtHowWide_AfterUpdate",
  ➡ "Form.frmTabbedDialogWizard"
  Resume txtHowWide_AfterUpdate_Exit

End Sub
```

txtTabText_BeforeUpdate and TextFits()   Page 3 allows users to choose the text for each tab label. The code in txtTabText_BeforeUpdate allows labels between 2 and 15 characters and calls the TextFits() function to determine whether the selected text will fit in the available space. (You may find the GetTextWidth() function interesting in that it uses the Windows API to calculate the exact width of a given piece of text in a specific font.)

SetButtonText   SetButtonText sets the command buttons so the user can see what it will look like on the new form. Listing 20.8 shows the code for this function. The argument acts as though it were an index into the array of text boxes and buttons.

Listing 20.8

```
Sub SetButtonText(pintWhichOne As Integer)
  Dim ctl As Control

  Set ctl = Me("cmd" & pintWhichOne)
  On Error Resume Next

  ctl.Caption = Me("txtButton" & pintWhichOne)
  ctl.Visible = (Not IsNull(ctl.Caption))

  On Error GoTo 0
End Sub
```

cmdFinish_Click   Once the Wizard has received all the necessary information from the user, it can finish up and build a new dialog box with the tabs that have been specified. The Wizard is built so that it has a default set of values for the new dialog boxes. If the user does not enter any values, the Wizard uses the defaults. However, there is one required piece of information before it can continue: the user must provide a valid form name for the new form. When a user clicks the Finish button, the Wizard checks to see whether that user has entered a value in txtUser-FormName. If so, the Wizard continues; if not, it alerts the user with a message box, moves to page 5, and puts the focus on the text box.

Once the Wizard confirms that the form has been named, the cmdFinish_Click event procedure begins to build the form. Listing 20.9 shows the cmdFinished_Click procedure.

Listing 20.9

```
Sub cmdFinish_Click()
  Dim strMsg As String

  On Error GoTo cmdFinish_Click_Err

  Application.Echo False
  DoCmd Hourglass True
```

```
If IsNull(Me!txtUserFormName) Then
  DoCmd GoToPage 5
  Me!txtUserFormName.SetFocus
  mintCurrentPage = 5
  Me!cmdNext.Enabled = False
  Me!cmdBack.Enabled = True

  twz_strMsg = "You must name your form before you can" & NL
  twz_strMsg = twz_strMsg & "finish this Wizard."

  Beep
  MsgBox twz_strMsg, twz_MB_STOP, TWZ_TITLE

  GoTo cmdFinish_Click_Exit
End If

varSysCmdRetVal = SysCmd(SYSCMD_INITMETER, "Building form,
➥ please wait", SYSCMD_STD)

' Initialize variables
mintRetval = IniVariables()
mintSysCmdStep = 1
mintSysCmdSteps = (mintNumTabs * 10) + 11

varSysCmdRetVal = SysCmd(SYSCMD_UPDATEMETER,
➥ CInt(mintSysCmdStep / mintSysCmdSteps * SYSCMD_STD))
' Build Form
mintRetval = BuildForm()
mintSysCmdStep = mintSysCmdStep + 1
varSysCmdRetVal = SysCmd(SYSCMD_UPDATEMETER,
➥ CInt(mintSysCmdStep / mintSysCmdSteps * SYSCMD_STD))

' Save Form
mintRetval = SaveForm()
mintSysCmdStep = mintSysCmdStep + 1
varSysCmdRetVal = SysCmd(SYSCMD_UPDATEMETER,
➥ CInt(mintSysCmdStep / mintSysCmdSteps * SYSCMD_STD))

' Add Controls to the Form
mintRetval = BuildControls()

' Add Code to form
mintRetval = BuildCode()
```

```
' Add Command Buttons
mintRetval = BuildCmdButtons()
mintSysCmdStep = mintSysCmdStep + 1
varSysCmdRetVal = SysCmd(SYSCMD_UPDATEMETER,
➥ CInt(mintSysCmdStep / mintSysCmdSteps * SYSCMD_STD))

Dim strFormName As String
strFormName = frmWiz.FormName

' Cleanup
' For now, mintHowToOpen will always
' be 2, since we can't open the form
' in Form mode at this point.
If mintHowToOpen = 1 Then
  DoCmd OpenForm frmWiz.FormName, A_NORMAL
  DoCmd SelectObject A_FORM, frmWiz.FormName, False
  DoCmd DoMenuItem A_FORMBAR, A_WINDOW, A_SIZETOFIT_FORM
Else
  strMsg = ""
  strMsg = strMsg & "To complete the creation of your tabbed
➥ dialog, " & NL
  strMsg = strMsg & "open the form's module in design mode,
➥ and remove the " & NL
  strMsg = strMsg & "apostrophe commenting out the DLL
➥ declaration:" & NL & NL
  strMsg = strMsg & "'Declare Function GetSystemMetrics Lib
➥ ""User"" (ByVal intIndex As Integer) As Integer" &
➥ NL & NL
  strMsg = strMsg & "Once you've done that, save the form and
➥ its module."
  MsgBox strMsg, TWZ_MB_WARN, TWZ_TITLE
  DoCmd OpenForm frmWiz.FormName, A_DESIGN
End If

' Save the form one last time
DoCmd DoMenuItem A_FORMDS, A_FILE, A_SAVEFORM

mintSysCmdStep = mintSysCmdStep + 1
varSysCmdRetVal = SysCmd(SYSCMD_UPDATEMETER,
➥ CInt(mintSysCmdStep / mintSysCmdSteps * SYSCMD_STD))

varSysCmdRetVal = SysCmd(SYSCMD_REMOVEMETER)

DoCmd Close A_FORM, Me.FormName
```

```
   DoCmd SelectObject A_FORM, frmWiz.FormName, False
cmdFinish_Click_Exit:
   Application.Echo True
   DoCmd Hourglass False

   On Error GoTo 0
   Exit Sub

cmdFinish_Click_Err:
   glrTWZErrorProc Err, Error, "cmdFinish_Click",
   ➡ "Form.frmTabbedDialogWizard"
   Resume cmdFinish_Click_Exit
End Sub
```

After the form is created, the user must perform one step that the Wizard cannot. The Wizard creates some code that looks like this:

```
' NOTE: Remove the leading apostrophe ("'") from the
' following line:
' Declare Function GetSystemMetrics Lib "User"(ByVal intIndex As
➡ Integer) As Integer
```

Because of an Access bug, the Wizard cannot insert a Declare statement. Instead it inserts a comment, and the user must remove the apostrophe to activate the statement.

IniVariables()   The IniVariables() function checks to see what information the user has entered on the form. If a specific item has not been entered, its default value is loaded from the table tblUserDefaults. Listing 20.10 shows this function.

Listing 20.10

```
Function IniVariables() As Integer
   On Error GoTo IniVariables_Err

   ' Declare variables
   Dim twz_rec1 As Recordset
   Dim intLoop As Integer
   Dim ctl  As Control
   Dim strCtlName As String
   Dim strFieldName As String

   Const MAX_BUTTONS = 4
```

```
' Set database/recordset variables
Set twz_db = CodeDB()

Set twz_rec = twz_db.OpenRecordset("tblUserDefaults",
➥ DB_OPEN_TABLE)
Set twz_rec1 = twz_db.OpenRecordset("tblTabLabels",
➥ DB_OPEN_TABLE)

' Make the current record current
twz_rec.MoveFirst

' Set the new form's Caption variable
mstrFormCaption = IIf(IsNull(Me!txtFormTitle),
➥ twz_rec!FormCaption, Me!txtFormTitle)

' Set the number of tabs variable
mintNumTabs = IIf(IsNull(Me!txtNumberOfTabs),
➥ twz_rec!NumberTabs, Me!txtNumberOfTabs)

' Set tab width
msngTabX = IIf(IsNull(Me!txtHowWide), twz_rec!TabWidth,
➥ Me!txtHowWide) * twz_TWIPS_PER_INCH

' Get form's dimensions
If Not IsNull(grpFormSize) Then
  Select Case grpFormSize
    Case 1
      msngFormX = 5.7
      msngFormY = 3.3
    Case 2
      msngFormX = STD_WIDTH
      msngFormY = STD_HEIGTH
    Case 3
      msngFormX = 3.5
      msngFormY = 2.6
    Case 4
      msngFormX = CSng(Me!txtFormWidth)
      msngFormY = CSng(Me!txtFormHeight)
  End Select
Else
  msngFormX = twz_rec!FormWidth
  msngFormY = twz_rec!FormHeight
End If
```

```
' Get which command buttons are on
For intLoop = 1 To MAX_BUTTONS
  ' The procedure LoadDefaults filled out the buttons back at
  ' load-time.
  mintWhichButtons(intLoop) = Not IsNull(Me("txtButton" &
➥ intLoop))
  mvarButtonLabels(intLoop) = Me("txtButton" & intLoop).Value
Next intLoop

' Now Get Tab labels
ReDim mstrTabLabels(mintNumTabs)

On Error Resume Next
twz_rec1.MoveFirst
twz_rec1.MoveLast

On Error GoTo IniVariables_Err

If twz_rec1.RecordCount = 0 Then
  For intLoop = 1 To mintNumTabs
    mstrTabLabels(intLoop) = "Tab " & (intLoop - 1)
  Next
Else
  twz_rec1.MoveFirst
  For intLoop = 1 To mintNumTabs
    mstrTabLabels(intLoop) = twz_rec1!TabText
    twz_rec1.MoveNext
  Next
End If

' Determine how the user wants to open the form when built
If IsNull(grpWhatToDo) Then
  mintHowToOpen = twz_rec!HowToOpen
Else
  mintHowToOpen = Me!grpWhatToDo
End If

IniVariables = True

IniVariables_exit:

  ' Close recordset and database variables out.
  twz_rec.Close
  twz_rec1.Close
```

```
    twz_db.Close

    On Error GoTo 0
    Exit Function

IniVariables_Err:
    glrTWZErrorProc Err, Error, "IniVariables",
    ➥ "Form.frmTabbedDialogWizard"
    Resume IniVariables_exit

End Function
```

BuildForm()   Once the IniVariables procedure has initialized all the module variables, the Wizard can build the form. First, it calls the Access CreateForm() function to build a new form. It assigns this form to a module-level control variable, frmWiz. After that, it sets all the necessary form properties, including the record source the user selected when invoking the Form Wizards, as well as the form's height, width, and caption. Listing 20.11 shows the BuildForm() function.

Listing 20.11

```
Function BuildForm() As Integer
    On Error GoTo BuildForm_Err
    ' Form Const
    Const SGL_FORM = 0
    Const NO_SBARS = 0
    Const DIALOG_FORM = 3
    Const GRID_X = 12
    Const GRID_Y = 12
    Const ALLOW_EDITS = 2

    ' Section Consts
    Const SEC_NAME = "secDetail"
    Const DISPLAY_ALWAYS = 0
    Const LTGRAY = 12632256
    Const NORMAL = 0

    ' Create New Form
    Set frmWiz = CreateForm("", "")

    ' Set Form Values
    ' Data Values
    frmWiz.RecordSource = glr_twzgstrTableName
```

```
' Layout Values
frmWiz.Caption = mstrFormCaption
frmWiz.DefaultView = SGL_FORM
frmWiz.ScrollBars = NO_SBARS
frmWiz.Recordselectors = False
frmWiz.NavigationButtons = False
frmWiz.AutoResize = True
frmWiz.AutoCenter = True
frmWiz.BorderStyle = DIALOG_FORM
frmWiz.MinButton = False
frmWiz.MaxButton = False
frmWiz.Width = (msngFormX * twz_TWIPS_PER_INCH)
frmWiz.GridX = GRID_X
frmWiz.GridY = GRID_Y

' Events
frmWiz.OnLoad = EVNT_PROC

' Other
frmWiz.ViewsAllowed = SGL_FORM
frmWiz.DefaultEditing = ALLOW_EDITS
frmWiz.ShortcutMenu = False
frmWiz.PopUp = True
frmWiz.Modal = True

' Section Detail Section Values
frmWiz.Section(0).Name = SEC_NAME
frmWiz.Section(0).DisplayWhen = DISPLAY_ALWAYS
frmWiz.Section(0).CanGrow = False
frmWiz.Section(0).CanShrink = False
frmWiz.Section(0).Visible = True
frmWiz.Section(0).Height = (msngFormY * twz_TWIPS_PER_INCH)
frmWiz.Section(0).BackColor = LTGRAY
frmWiz.Section(0).SpecialEffect = NORMAL

    BuildForm = True

BuildForm_Exit:
  On Error GoTo 0
  Exit Function

BuildForm_Err:
  glrTWZErrorProc Err, Error, "BuildForm",
```

```
   ➥ "Form.frmTabbedDialogWizard"
     Resume BuildForm_Exit

End Function
```

BuildControls()   The BuildControls() function is the key function of the Wizard. It actually builds the tabs on the form. While we were designing the Wizard, we had to make some compromises to achieve the best look. You can continue to tweak the design if you want a slightly different look. Each tab in the dialog box is actually ten Access line controls: five black, three white, and two dark gray. In addition, six other lines are used to create the base of the tab. Information about the optimal display of these lines is stored in the table tblFormControls. Basically, the BuildControls procedure reads through the table, gets the "standard" settings, and then adjusts for the user's preferences.

The Wizard must accommodate multiple tabs of varying sizes. The key to making this work was a standard naming convention for the line controls. Each line control has four parts. The first three characters are the Leszynski/Reddick naming convention (see Appendix A) tag, lin. The next character is either an *I* to designate inside line or an *O* to designate outside line. The next character is a number, 1 to 5, to specify which line is being worked on, with 1 being the far-left vertical line, 2 being the far-left slant, 3 being the horizontal top of the tab, and so on. The next character is an underscore (_). The character after that indicates where the tab number will be placed by the Wizard. The procedure increments this character. The last two characters are an underscore and the number 1. If you enhanced the Wizard to support multiple rows, you would use a different number for each row.

Once the recordset is loaded, the Wizard loops through the recordset until EOF is reached. This loop repeats until the number of tabs requested has been reached. The TabObject field is True if it is one of the ten line characters. If it is not, the Wizard builds a control.

After setting the variables for the control top, left, width, and height, the Wizard creates the control with the Access CreateControl command. Once the control has been built, the Wizard names and sets such properties as color and border width. If it just built the first inner line of any tab (linI1xxxxx), then it creates the tab's label and command button. To make the tabs selectable by both keyboard and mouse and make it a valid control with a tab order, the Wizard needs to create first a label control and then a transparent command button. Once it has completed these steps for every tab, it exits the function. Listing 20.12 shows the BuildControls() function.

Listing 20.12

```
Function BuildControls() As Integer
  On Error GoTo BuildControls_Err

  Dim intTabCount As Integer
  Dim sngCtlX As Single
  Dim sngCtlY As Single
  Dim sngCtlW As Single
  Dim sngCtlH As Single
  Dim ctl As Control
  Dim intRowCount As Integer

  Const GRAY_LINE = "linBox1CTR_02"
  Const DRGRAY_LINE_RT = "linBox1RSR_01"
  Const WHITE_LINE = "linBox1CBR"
  Const TAB_VAR = .1
  Const TAB_STD_WIDTH = 1.1
  Const ALIGN_CENTER = 2
  Const TABNAME = "cmdTab"
  Const LBL_CTL = 100
  Const SHP_CTL = 101
  Const LINE_CTL = 102

  intRowCount = 1

  ' Read through Control Table
  Set twz_db = CodeDB()
  Set twz_rec = twz_db.OpenRecordset("tblFormControls",
➡ DB_OPEN_DYNASET)

Do Until twz_rec.Eof

  intTabCount = 0
  Do Until intTabCount >= mintNumTabs

    If twz_rec.TabObject Then

      Select Case CInt(Mid(twz_rec.ControlName, 5, 1))
        Case 1, 2
          sngCtlX = (twz_rec.CtlLeft * twz_TWIPS_PER_INCH) +
          ➡ (msngTabX * intTabCount)
          sngCtlY = (twz_rec.CtlTop * twz_TWIPS_PER_INCH)
          sngCtlW = (twz_rec.CtlWidth * twz_TWIPS_PER_INCH)
          sngCtlH = (twz_rec.CtlHeight * twz_TWIPS_PER_INCH)
```

```
    Case 3
      sngCtlX = (twz_rec.CtlLeft * twz_TWIPS_PER_INCH) +
      ➡ (msngTabX * intTabCount)
      sngCtlY = (twz_rec.CtlTop * twz_TWIPS_PER_INCH)
      sngCtlW = msngTabX - (TAB_VAR * twz_TWIPS_PER_INCH)
      sngCtlH = (twz_rec.CtlHeight * twz_TWIPS_PER_INCH)

    Case 4, 5
      sngCtlX = (twz_rec.CtlLeft * twz_TWIPS_PER_INCH) +
      ➡ (msngTabX * intTabCount) + (msngTabX -
      ➡ (TAB_STD_WIDTH * twz_TWIPS_PER_INCH))
      sngCtlY = (twz_rec.CtlTop * twz_TWIPS_PER_INCH)
      sngCtlW = (twz_rec.CtlWidth * twz_TWIPS_PER_INCH)
      sngCtlH = (twz_rec.CtlHeight * twz_TWIPS_PER_INCH)
  End Select

Else
  intTabCount = mintNumTabs

  If CStr(twz_rec.ControlName) = GRAY_LINE Then
    sngCtlX = (twz_rec.CtlLeft * twz_TWIPS_PER_INCH)
    sngCtlY = (twz_rec.CtlTop * twz_TWIPS_PER_INCH)
    sngCtlW = (twz_rec.CtlWidth * twz_TWIPS_PER_INCH) +
    ➡ (msngTabX - (TAB_STD_WIDTH * twz_TWIPS_PER_INCH))
    sngCtlH = (twz_rec.CtlHeight * twz_TWIPS_PER_INCH)
  Else
    If CStr(twz_rec.ControlName) = DRGRAY_LINE_RT Then
      sngCtlX = (twz_rec.CtlLeft * twz_TWIPS_PER_INCH) +
      ➡ ((msngFormX - STD_WIDTH) * twz_TWIPS_PER_INCH)
    Else
      sngCtlX = twz_rec.CtlLeft * twz_TWIPS_PER_INCH
    End If

    If CStr(twz_rec.ControlName) = WHITE_LINE Then
      sngCtlY = (twz_rec.CtlTop * twz_TWIPS_PER_INCH) +
      ➡ ((msngFormY - STD_HEIGTH) * twz_TWIPS_PER_INCH)
    Else
      sngCtlY = (twz_rec.CtlTop * twz_TWIPS_PER_INCH)
    End If

    If twz_rec.CtlWidth < 1 Then
      sngCtlW = (twz_rec.CtlWidth * twz_TWIPS_PER_INCH)
```

```
      Else
        sngCtlW = (twz_rec.CtlWidth * twz_TWIPS_PER_INCH) +
        ➡ ((msngFormX - STD_WIDTH) * twz_TWIPS_PER_INCH)
      End If
      If twz_rec.CtlHeight = 0 Then
        sngCtlH = (twz_rec.CtlHeight * twz_TWIPS_PER_INCH)
      Else
        sngCtlH = (twz_rec.CtlHeight * twz_TWIPS_PER_INCH) +
        ➡ ((msngFormY - STD_HEIGTH) * twz_TWIPS_PER_INCH)
      End If
    End If
  End If
End If

  Set ctl = CreateControl(frmWiz.Name, twz_rec.ControlType,
  ➡ DETAIL_SEC, "", "", sngCtlX, sngCtlY, sngCtlW, sngCtlH)

  If twz_rec.TabObject Then
    If intTabCount = 0 Then
      ctl.Name = twz_rec.ControlName
    Else
      ctl.Name = Left$(twz_rec.ControlName, 6) & (intTabCount
      ➡ + 1) & "_" & intRowCount
    End If
  Else
    ctl.Name = twz_rec.ControlName
  End If

  ctl.Visible = twz_rec.Visible

  If twz_rec.ControlType = LINE_CTL Then
    ctl.LineSlant = twz_rec.LineSlant
  End If

  ctl.DisplayWhen = 0
  ctl.BorderStyle = twz_rec.CtlBorderStyle
  ctl.BorderLineStyle = twz_rec.CtlBorderLineStyle
  ctl.BorderColor = twz_rec.CtlBorderColor

  If twz_rec.TabObject Then
    If intTabCount = 0 Then
      ctl.BorderWidth = twz_rec.CtlBorderWidth
    Else
      If Left$(twz_rec.ControlName, 4) = "linI" Then
        ctl.BorderWidth = 0
```

```
      Else
        ctl.BorderWidth = twz_rec.CtlBorderWidth
      End If
    End If
Else
  ctl.BorderWidth = twz_rec.CtlBorderWidth
End If

If twz_rec.ControlType = SHP_CTL Then
  ctl.BackStyle = 0
End If

' Now Build labels
If Left$(twz_rec.ControlName, 5) = "linI1" Then
  Set ctl = CreateControl(frmWiz.Name, LBL_CTL, DETAIL_SEC,
  ➡ "", "", sngCtlX, sngCtlY, msngTabX, (.2 *
  ➡ twz_TWIPS_PER_INCH))
  ctl.Caption = mstrTabLabels(intTabCount + 1)
  ctl.Name = "lbl" & (intTabCount + 1)

  ctl.BackStyle = 0
  ctl.FontName = FONT_NAME
  ctl.FontSize = FONT_SIZE

  If intTabCount = 0 Then
    ctl.FontWeight = FONT_BOLD
  Else
    ctl.FontWeight = FONT_NORMAL
  End If

  ctl.TextAlign = ALIGN_CENTER
End If

' Now build command buttons
If Left$(twz_rec.ControlName, 5) = "linI1" Then
  Set ctl = CreateControl(frmWiz.Name, CMD_BUTTON,
  ➡ DETAIL_SEC, "", "", sngCtlX, sngCtlY, msngTabX,
  ➡ (.2 * twz_TWIPS_PER_INCH))
  ctl.Caption = mstrTabLabels(intTabCount + 1)
  ctl.Name = TABNAME & (intTabCount + 1)
  ctl.Transparent = True
  ctl.FontName = FONT_NAME
  ctl.FontSize = FONT_SIZE
  ctl.OnClick = EVNT_PROC
End If
```

```
        intTabCount = intTabCount + 1
        mintSysCmdStep = mintSysCmdStep + 1
        varSysCmdRetVal = SysCmd(SYSCMD_UPDATEMETER,
        ➥ CInt(mintSysCmdStep / mintSysCmdSteps * SYSCMD_STD))

    Loop

    intTabCount = 0
    twz_rec.MoveNext

  Loop

  twz_rec.Close

  'DoCmd Restore

  BuildControls = True

BuildControls_Exit:
  On Error GoTo 0
  Exit Function

BuildControls_Err:
  glrTWZErrorProc Err, Error, "BuildControls",
  ➥ "Form.frmTabbedDialogWizard"
  Resume BuildControls_Exit

End Function
```

BuildCode()   Now that the form is built and saved and all the necessary controls are created, the Wizard needs to attach the code to the form so that when a tab is clicked, the tabs appear to move. There are four parts to the function that does this. Part one inserts code into the Declarations section of the module. The actual code to be inserted comes from constants in the Declarations section of the Tab-Wiz's Code-Behind-Forms. The Wizard inserts a carriage return/line feed between each line as it builds the code. Listing 20.13 shows the BuildCode() function.

Listing 20.13

```
Function BuildCode() As Integer
  On Error GoTo BuildCode_Err
  Dim strWholeProc As String
```

```
Dim intLoop As Integer
Const LINE_1 = "Option Explicit"
Const LINE_2 = "Dim mintCurrentTab as Integer"
Const LINE_3 = "'Declare Function GetSystemMetrics Lib ""User""
➡ (ByVal intIndex As Integer) As Integer"
Const LINE_4 = "Sub Form_Load ()"
Const LINE_5 = "  mintCurrentTab = 1"
Const LINE_6 = "End Sub"
Const LINE_7 = "Function GetScreenRes () As Integer"
Const LINE_8 = "  On Error GoTo GetScreenRes_Err"
Const LINE_9 = "  Dim intWidth As Integer"
Const LINE_10 = " Const SM_CXSCREEN = 0"
Const LINE_11 = ""
Const LINE_12 = "  Select Case GetSystemMetrics(SM_CXSCREEN)"
Const LINE_13 = "    Case 640"
Const LINE_14 = "      GetScreenRes = 1"
Const LINE_15 = "    Case 800"
Const LINE_16 = "      GetScreenRes = 2"
Const LINE_17 = "    Case 1024"
Const LINE_18 = "      GetScreenRes = 3"
Const LINE_19 = "    Case Else"
Const LINE_20 = "      GetScreenRes = 3"
Const LINE_21 = "  End Select"
Const LINE_22 = ""
Const LINE_23 = "  Exit Function"
Const LINE_24 = ""
Const LINE_25 = "GetScreenRes_Err:"
Const LINE_26 = "  GetScreenRes = False"
Const LINE_27 = "  Exit Function"
Const LINE_28 = ""
Const LINE_29 = "End Function"
Const LINE_30 = "Sub TabPushed (intTabNum As Integer)"
Const LINE_31 = "  On Error Resume Next"
Const LINE_32 = "  Dim strCtlName As String, intCtlNum As
➡ Integer"
Const LINE_33 = "  Dim ctl As Control, intLoop As Integer"
Const LINE_34 = "  Dim strCName As String, strCName2 As String"
Const LINE_35 = "  Dim intResAdj As Integer"
Const LINE_36 = "  Dim intTabPushAdj As Integer"
Const LINE_37 = "  Dim intTabNorm As Integer"
Const LINE_38 = ""
Const LINE_39 = "  intTabNorm = 288"
Const LINE_40 = "  strCName = ""linI1_"" & intTabNum & ""_1"""
Const LINE_41 = "  strCName2 = ""linI5_"" & intTabNum & ""_1"""
Const LINE_42 = ""
```

```
Const LINE_43 = "   Select Case GetScreenRes()"
Const LINE_44 = "     Case 1"
Const LINE_45 = "        intResAdj = 30"
Const LINE_46 = "        intTabPushAdj = 360"
Const LINE_47 = "     Case 2"
Const LINE_48 = "        intResAdj = 26"
Const LINE_49 = "        intTabPushAdj = 349"
Const LINE_50 = "     Case Else"
Const LINE_51 = "        intResAdj = 22"
Const LINE_52 = "        intTabPushAdj = 338"
Const LINE_53 = "   End Select"
Const LINE_54 = ""
Const LINE_55 = "   For intLoop = 1 To 5"
Const LINE_56 = "     strCtlName = ""linI"" & intLoop & ""_"" &
➥ intTabNum & ""_1"""
Const LINE_57 = "     Me(strCtlName).BorderWidth = 2"
Const LINE_58 = "     If strCtlName = strCName Then"
Const LINE_59 = "       Me!linBox1CTR_02.Left =
➥ Me(strCtlName).Left + intResAdj"
Const LINE_60 = "       Me(strCtlName).Height = intTabPushAdj"
Const LINE_61 = "     End If"
Const LINE_62 = "     If strCtlName = strCName2 Then"
Const LINE_63 = "       Me(strCtlName).Height = intTabPushAdj"
Const LINE_64 = "     End If"
Const LINE_65 = "   Next intLoop"
Const LINE_66 = ""
Const LINE_67 = "   strCName = ""linI1_"" & mintCurrentTab &
➥ ""_1"""
Const LINE_68 = "   strCName2 = ""linI5_"" & mintCurrentTab &
➥ ""_1"""
Const LINE_69 = ""
Const LINE_70 = "   For intLoop = 1 To 5"
Const LINE_71 = "     strCtlName = ""linI"" & intLoop & ""_"" &
➥ mintCurrentTab & ""_1"""
Const LINE_72 = "     Me(strCtlName).BorderWidth = 0"
Const LINE_73 = "     If strCtlName = strCName Then"
Const LINE_74 = "       Me(strCtlName).Height = intTabNorm"
Const LINE_75 = "     End If"
Const LINE_76 = "     If strCtlName = strCName2 Then"
Const LINE_77 = "       Me(strCtlName).Height = intTabNorm"
Const LINE_78 = "     End If"
Const LINE_79 = "   Next intLoop"
Const LINE_80 = ""
Const LINE_81 = "   Me(""lbl"" & intTabNum).FontWeight = 700"
```

```
Const LINE_82 = "  Me(""lbl"" & mintCurrentTab).FontWeight =
➡ 400"
Const LINE_83 = ""
Const LINE_84 = "  mintCurrentTab = intTabNum"
Const LINE_85 = "End Sub"

' Insert Declarations Sections
strWholeProc = LINE_1 & NL & LINE_2 & NL & LINE_3 & NL
frmWiz.Module.InsertText strWholeProc

' Insert FormLoad Sub
strWholeProc = LINE_4 & NL & LINE_5 & NL & LINE_6 & NL
frmWiz.Module.InsertText strWholeProc

' Insert GetScreenRes Function
strWholeProc = LINE_7 & NL & LINE_8 & NL & LINE_9 & NL &
➡ LINE_10 & NL
strWholeProc = strWholeProc & LINE_11 & NL & LINE_12 & NL &
➡ LINE_13 & NL & LINE_14 & NL
strWholeProc = strWholeProc & LINE_15 & NL & LINE_16 & NL &
➡ LINE_17 & NL & LINE_18 & NL
strWholeProc = strWholeProc & LINE_19 & NL & LINE_20 & NL &
➡ LINE_21 & NL & LINE_22 & NL
strWholeProc = strWholeProc & LINE_23 & NL & LINE_24 & NL &
➡ LINE_25 & NL & LINE_26 & NL
strWholeProc = strWholeProc & LINE_27 & NL & LINE_28 & NL &
➡ LINE_29 & NL
frmWiz.Module.InsertText strWholeProc

' Insert TabPushed Sub
strWholeProc = LINE_30 & NL & LINE_31 & NL & LINE_32 & NL &
➡ LINE_33 & NL & LINE_34 & NL
strWholeProc = strWholeProc & LINE_35 & NL & LINE_36 & NL &
➡ LINE_37 & NL & LINE_38 & NL
strWholeProc = strWholeProc & LINE_39 & NL & LINE_40 & NL &
➡ LINE_41 & NL & LINE_42 & NL
strWholeProc = strWholeProc & LINE_43 & NL & LINE_44 & NL &
➡ LINE_45 & NL & LINE_46 & NL
strWholeProc = strWholeProc & LINE_47 & NL & LINE_48 & NL &
➡ LINE_49 & NL & LINE_50 & NL
strWholeProc = strWholeProc & LINE_51 & NL & LINE_52 & NL &
➡ LINE_53 & NL & LINE_54 & NL
strWholeProc = strWholeProc & LINE_55 & NL & LINE_56 & NL &
➡ LINE_57 & NL & LINE_58 & NL
strWholeProc = strWholeProc & LINE_59 & NL & LINE_60 & NL &
```

```
➥ LINE_61 & NL & LINE_62 & NL
strWholeProc = strWholeProc & LINE_63 & NL & LINE_64 & NL &
➥ LINE_65 & NL & LINE_66 & NL
strWholeProc = strWholeProc & LINE_67 & NL & LINE_68 & NL &
➥ LINE_69 & NL & LINE_70 & NL
strWholeProc = strWholeProc & LINE_71 & NL & LINE_72 & NL &
➥ LINE_73 & NL & LINE_74 & NL
strWholeProc = strWholeProc & LINE_75 & NL & LINE_76 & NL &
➥ LINE_77 & NL & LINE_78 & NL
strWholeProc = strWholeProc & LINE_79 & NL & LINE_80 & NL &
➥ LINE_81 & NL & LINE_82 & NL
strWholeProc = strWholeProc & LINE_83 & NL & LINE_84 & NL &
➥ LINE_85 & NL
frmWiz.Module.InsertText strWholeProc

  ' Insert one sub for every tab created.
  For intLoop = 1 To mintNumTabs
    strWholeProc = "Sub cmdTab" & intLoop & "_Click()" & NL
    strWholeProc = strWholeProc & "  If Not mintCurrentTab = " &
➥ intLoop & " Then" & NL
    strWholeProc = strWholeProc & "    Call TabPushed(" & intLoop
➥ & ")" & NL
    strWholeProc = strWholeProc & "  End If" & NL
    strWholeProc = strWholeProc & "End Sub" & NL
    frmWiz.Module.InsertText strWholeProc
  Next intLoop

  BuildCode = True

BuildCode_Exit:
  On Error GoTo 0
  Exit Function

BuildCode_Err:
  glrTWZErrorProc Err, Error, "BuildCode",
➥ "Form.frmTabbedDialogWizard"
  Resume BuildCode_Exit

End Function
```

SaveForm()   Once you've built the form, you need to save it. The reason is that later the Wizard will insert some predefined code into the new form's

Code-Behind-Forms, and to use the InsertText method, you must save the form. This procedure is something of a kludge because the Wizard must resort to Send-Keys. Listing 20.14 shows the SaveForm() function.

Listing 20.14

```
Function SaveForm( ) As Integer
  On Error GoTo SaveForm_Err

  ' SendKeys Constant
  Const TWZ_ENTER = "{Enter}"

  Dim strUserFormName As String
  Dim strCurrentFormName As String

  strCurrentFormName = frmWiz.Name
  strUserFormName = Me!txtUserFormName

  DoCmd SelectObject A_FORM, strCurrentFormName

  SendKeys strUserFormName & TWZ_ENTER
  DoCmd DoMenuItem A_FORMDS, A_FILE, A_SAVEFORM
  DoEvents

  Set frmWiz = Forms(strUserFormName)

  SaveForm = True

SaveForm_Exit:
  On Error GoTo 0
  Exit Function

SaveForm_Err:
  glrTWZErrorProc Err, Error, "SaveForm",
  ➡ "Form.frmTabbedDialogWizard"
  Resume SaveForm_Exit

End Function
```

BuildCmdButtons()   The BuildCmdButtons procedure builds the command buttons used to control the new form. By default, it creates OK and Cancel command buttons similar to the Microsoft dialog boxes. The function checks to see which buttons the user wants and then places them on the form. If you have standard code for each button, you could place this function before BuildCode() and then have BuildCode() attach your custom procedures. This function also calls glrTWZRemoveSpecialChr so the command buttons can be named correctly. Listing 20.15 shows the BuildCmdButtons() function and Listing 20.16 shows the glrTWZRemoveSpecialChr() function.

Listing 20.15

```
Function BuildCmdButtons() As Integer
  On Error GoTo BuildCmdButtons_Err

  Dim intLoop As Integer
  Dim sngCtlTop As Single
  Dim sngCtlLeft As Single
  Dim sngCtlSpace As Single
  Dim sngCtlX As Single
  Dim sngCtlY As Single
  Dim ctl As Control
  Const BUTTON = "cmd"
  Const BUTTON_FONT = "System"
  Const BUTTON_FONT_SIZE = 8

  sngCtlTop = .5 * twz_TWIPS_PER_INCH
  sngCtlLeft = (msngFormX - 1.2) * twz_TWIPS_PER_INCH
  sngCtlX = twz_TWIPS_PER_INCH
  sngCtlY = .25 * twz_TWIPS_PER_INCH
  sngCtlSpace = .05 * twz_TWIPS_PER_INCH

  For intLoop = 1 To 4
    If mintWhichButtons(intLoop) Then
      Set ctl = CreateControl(frmWiz.Name, CMD_BUTTON,
      ➥ DETAIL_SEC, "", "", sngCtlLeft, sngCtlTop,
      ➥ sngCtlX, sngCtlY)
      ctl.Caption = mvarButtonLabels(intLoop)
      ctl.Name = BUTTON &
      ➥ glrTWZRemoveSpecialChr(CStr(mvarButtonLabels(intLoop)))
      ctl.Transparent = False
      ctl.FontName = BUTTON_FONT
      ctl.FontSize = BUTTON_FONT_SIZE
    End If
    sngCtlTop = sngCtlTop + sngCtlY + sngCtlSpace
  Next
```

```
   BuildCmdButtons = True

BuildCmdButtons_Exit:
  On Error GoTo 0
  Exit Function

BuildCmdButtons_Err:
  glrTWZErrorProc Err, Error, "BuildCmdButtons",
  ➥ "Form.frmTabbedDialogWizard"
  Resume BuildCmdButtons_Exit
End Function
```

Listing 20.16

```
Function glrTWZRemoveSpecialChr(pstrText As String) As String
On Error GoTo glrTWZRemoveSpecialChr_Err

   Dim intX As Integer
   Dim strNewText As String
   strNewText = ""


   If Len(pstrText) = 0 Then
     ' if a null string is passed in return null
     glrTWZRemoveSpecialChr = "None"
   Else
     ' loop through every character in the string and remove
     ' invalid characters. This does not check for low order
     ' characters.
     For intX = 1 To Len(pstrText)
       If InStr(" &';:.,<>/?=-_+\¦[]{}!@#$%^&*()'""",
       ➥ Mid$(pstrText, intX, 1)) = 0 Then
         strNewText = strNewText & Mid$(pstrText, intX, 1)
       End If
     Next
     glrTWZRemoveSpecialChr = strNewText
   End If

glrTWZRemoveSpecialChr_Exit:
  On Error GoTo 0
  Exit Function

glrTWZRemoveSpecialChr_Err:
```

```
Call glrTWZErrorProc(Err, Error$, "glrTWZRemoveSpecialChr",
➥ "glr_basTabWizardSupport")
glrTWZRemoveSpecialChr = "None"
Resume glrTWZRemoveSpecialChr_Exit

End Function
```

Part two of the four parts that build the form inserts the code that controls the actual tab movement. The function is passed an integer telling it which tab the user has pressed. Then the form code created by the Wizard resizes the lines of the current tab and selected tab, and a gray bar is moved to make it look like the tabs have changed. Also, the Wizard must change the font weight of the tabs. Some additional code turns controls on and off for the dialog box.

Part three simply creates a form-load procedure that sets the current tab. You could enhance the code to remember the last tab the user chose by storing the index of the selected tab in the Tag property of the form and then retrieve that information and set the appropriate tab here.

Finally, part four builds an OnClick event for each tab command button. These subs all call TabPushed, passing it their tab number.

Once all the code has been inserted, the function exits.

Figure 20.7 shows the result of the Tabbed Dialog Wizard.

FIGURE 20.7:
Result of the Tabbed Dialog Wizard

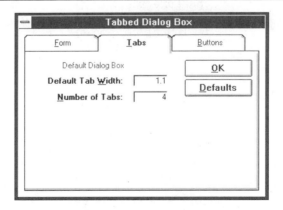

After the form has been created, the creator of the form must add to the TabPushed procedure in the Code-Behind-Forms of the new form to show the appropriate information on the form when the user pushes a button. Probably the best way is to create a series of subforms that you display when any given tab is pressed. Examine the code in the TabPushed procedure for the frmTabbedDialogWizardCustomize form in the Tabbed Dialog Wizard itself for an example.

Builders

The primary purpose of the builders is to help the user set complicated properties or modify existing ones. Microsoft has provided entry points for just about every control property on the property sheet.

Creating a Builder

Creating a builder is just like creating a Wizard, except that it is not as large in scope. You will generally have a form on which the user can set options and then continue. Builders are usually single-form items that perform a single task.

Installing Builders

Builders are installed just like Wizards. You must install the library first and then add a proper entry under the proper section heading. The proper heading for builders is [Property Wizards]. The L/R Builder has a USysAddIns table so you can use the Add-in Manager to add the builder.

The L/R Naming Builder

The L/R Naming Builder demonstrates how a builder works. When a user clicks the Builder button next to the name property of a control on a form or report, the L/R Naming Builder automatically adds the correct tag using the Leszynski/Reddick naming convention (see Appendix A) to the front of the name. If the control hasn't yet been named, it searches valid properties for the control and creates a name. Table 20.6 lists the objects in the LRNAME.MDA library.

TABLE 20.6: Objects in LRNAME.MDA

Object	Purpose
tblControlTypes	Contains the Access Form/Report control types, both number and name; their L/R Naming tag; and unknown text value
USysAddIns	Installs and customizes the Wizard using the Add-in Manager
frmLRNamingOptions	Customizes the tag and unknown text values used by the LR Naming Builder
basLRName	Contains global utility procedures, as well as the LR Naming entry point

Table 20.7 lists the procedures in the basLRName.

TABLE 20.7: Procedures in LRNAME.MDA

Procedure	Purpose
cmd_Close	Closes the form when the user is done
Form_Open	Sets up the form. Calls lsttblControlTypes_AfterUpdate
lsttblControlTypes_AfterUpdate	Places the current tag and unknown text value in the list box in the appropriate text boxes on the form
txtTagValue_AfterUpdate	Updates the tag value shown in the list box with one just entered by the user
txtUnknown_AfterUpdate	Updates the unknown text value shown in the list box with one just entered by the user

glrLRNamerEntry()

The glrLRNamerEntry() function is what Access calls when you click the Builder button. Access automatically passes three parameters to builders whenever they are called:

- A string containing the name of the object on which the control resides
- A string containing the current name of the control
- The current value of the property from which the builder was called

Listing 20.17 shows the glrLRNamerEntry() function.

Listing 20.17

```
Function glrLRNamerEntry(pstrObjectName As String, pstrCtlName
➡ As String, pstrCurrVal As String) As Integer
  On Error GoTo glrLRNamerEntry_Err

  ' Diminsion variables
  Dim intControlType As Integer
  Dim intX As Integer
  Dim varSysCmdRet As Variant

  ' initialize varialbes
  lrn_NL = Chr$(13) & Chr$(10)

  intControlType = WhatKindAmI(pstrObjectName, pstrCtlName)

  If intControlType = SEC Then
    ' Ask whether the user really wants to change ALL the
    ' properties
    lrn_strMsg = "The LR Naming Builder is about to change" &
    ➡ lrn_NL
    lrn_strMsg = lrn_strMsg & "all of your control names." &
    ➡ lrn_NL
    lrn_strMsg = lrn_strMsg & "Do you wish to continue?"

    Beep
    If MsgBox(lrn_strMsg, LRN_MB_QUERY + LRN_MB_YES_NO +
    ➡ LRN_MB_DEFAULT2, LRN_TITLE) = 7 Then
      Exit Function
    End If

    ' Check first to see if you are setting a Form or Report
    ' property
    Select Case (Application.CurrentObjectType)
      Case A_FORM
        varSysCmdRet = SysCmd(SYSCMD_INITMETER, "Changing control
        ➡ names, please wait", 100)
        For intX = 0 To Forms(pstrObjectName).Count - 1
          lrn_intRetVal = SetControlName(pstrObjectName,
          ➡ CStr(Forms(pstrObjectName)(intX).ControlName), -1)
          varSysCmdRet = SysCmd(SYSCMD_UPDATEMETER, CInt((intX +
          ➡ 1) / Forms(pstrObjectName).Count * 100))
        Next
        varSysCmdRet = SysCmd(SYSCMD_REMOVEMETER)
```

```
        Case A_REPORT
          varSysCmdRet = SysCmd(SYSCMD_INITMETER, "Changing control
          ➥ names, please wait", 100)
          For intX = 0 To Reports(pstrObjectName).Count - 1
            lrn_intRetVal = SetControlName(pstrObjectName,
            ➥ CStr(Reports(pstrObjectName)(intX).ControlName), 0)
            varSysCmdRet = SysCmd(SYSCMD_UPDATEMETER, CInt((intX +
            ➥ 1) / Reports(pstrObjectName).Count * 100))
          Next
          varSysCmdRet = SysCmd(SYSCMD_REMOVEMETER)
      End Select

    Else
      Select Case (Application.CurrentObjectType)
        Case A_FORM
          lrn_intRetVal = SetControlName(pstrObjectName,
          ➥ pstrCtlName, -1)

        Case A_REPORT
          lrn_intRetVal = SetControlName(pstrObjectName,
          ➥ pstrCtlName, 0)

      End Select

    End If

    glrLRNamerEntry = True

glrLRNamerEntry_Exit:

    On Error GoTo 0
    Exit Function

glrLRNamerEntry_Err:

    Call glrLRNErrorProc(Err, Error$, "glrLRNamerEntry",
    ➥ "basLRName")
    Resume glrLRNamerEntry_Exit

End Function
```

The first thing the builder needs to do is check which kind of control it is trying to name. To do this it calls the private function WhatKindAmI().

WhatKindAmI()

The WhatKindAmI() function uses TypeOf to test which type of control is being passed. If an error occurs, the focus is on a section name property and it returns SEC, which is a module constant. This tells the entry function how to continue. Listing 20.18 shows the function.

Listing 20.18

```
Private Function WhatKindAmI(pstrObjName As String, pstrCtlName
➡ As String) As Integer

   On Error GoTo WhatKindAmI_Err

   ' Dimension Variables
   Dim frm As Form
   Dim rpt As Report
   Dim ctl As Control
   Dim intCtlType As Integer

   ' Check first to see if you are setting a Form or Report
   ' property
   Select Case (Application.CurrentObjectType)
      Case A_FORM
         Set frm = Forms(pstrObjName)
         Set ctl = frm(pstrCtlName)
      Case A_REPORT
         Set rpt = Reports(pstrObjName)
         Set ctl = rpt(pstrCtlName)
   End Select

   ' Check Control Type and return number
   If TypeOf ctl Is BoundObjectFrame Then
      intCtlType = FRA
   ElseIf TypeOf ctl Is CheckBox Then
      intCtlType = CHK
   ElseIf TypeOf ctl Is ComboBox Then
      intCtlType = CBO
   ElseIf TypeOf ctl Is CommandButton Then
      intCtlType = CMD
   ElseIf TypeOf ctl Is Label Then
      intCtlType = LBL
   ElseIf TypeOf ctl Is Line Then
      intCtlType = LIN
```

```
      ElseIf TypeOf ctl Is ListBox Then
        intCtlType = LST
      ElseIf TypeOf ctl Is ObjectFrame Then
        intCtlType = FRA
      ElseIf TypeOf ctl Is OptionButton Then
        intCtlType = OPT
      ElseIf TypeOf ctl Is OptionGroup Then
        intCtlType = GRP
      ElseIf TypeOf ctl Is PageBreak Then
        intCtlType = BRK
      ElseIf TypeOf ctl Is Rectangle Then
        intCtlType = SHP
      ElseIf TypeOf ctl Is SubForm Then
        intCtlType = LR_SUB
      ElseIf TypeOf ctl Is SubReport Then
        intCtlType = LR_SUB
      ElseIf TypeOf ctl Is TextBox Then
        intCtlType = TXT
      ElseIf TypeOf ctl Is ToggleButton Then
        intCtlType = TGL
      Else
        intCtlType = GRA
      End If

      WhatKindAmI = intCtlType

WhatKindAmI_Exit:
   On Error GoTo 0
   Exit Function

WhatKindAmI_Err:

   Select Case Err
     Case ERR_INVALIDFIELDREF
       WhatKindAmI = SEC
     Case Else
       Call glrLRNErrorProc(Err, Error$, "WhatKindAmI", _
       ➥ "basLRName")
       WhatKindAmI = SEC
   End Select

   Resume WhatKindAmI_Exit

End Function
```

Once the builder knows what kind of control it is setting, it has two branches. If it is on a section, it asks whether the user wants to rename all the controls on the form. If so, the builder loops through all the controls and renames them; if not, it exits. If it is on a single control, it calls SetControlName().

SetControlName()

The SetControlName() function actually renames the control. First, the builder checks the passed-in parameter pintFormOrReport to see whether it is working on a form or a report. Second, it uses a Select Case statement to see what type of control it is working on and sets a variable to the new name. Then, if it sees that the control has a valid L/R tag in front, it asks users if they want to rename the control. Listing 20.19 shows the SetControlName() function.

Listing 20.19

```
Private Function SetControlName(pstrObjectName As String,
➥ pstrCtlName As String, pintFormOrReport As Integer)
➥ As Integer

  On Error GoTo SetControlName_Err

  ' Dimension Variables
  Dim intControlType As Integer
  Dim strTag As String
  Dim intCtlCount As Integer
  Dim strNewCtlName As String
  Dim strNull As String
  Dim intValue As Integer
  Dim strValue As String
  Dim ctl As Control
  Dim strWrkngCtName As String

  ' Initialize Variables
  lrn_NL = Chr$(13) & Chr$(10)
  intCtlCount = 1
  intControlType = WhatKindAmI(pstrObjectName, pstrCtlName)
  Set lrn_db = CodeDB()
  Set lrn_rec = lrn_db.OpenRecordset("tblControlTypes",
➥ DB_OPEN_TABLE)
```

```
lrn_rec.Index = "PrimaryKey"
lrn_rec.Seek "=", intControlType
  strTag = lrn_rec![PreferredTag]
  strNull = lrn_rec![UnknownText]
lrn_rec.Close
lrn_db.Close

strWrkngCtName = pstrCtlName

If Left$(strWrkngCtName, 3) = strTag Then
  strWrkngCtName = Right$(strWrkngCtName, Len(strWrkngCtName) -
  ➡ 3)
End If

strNewCtlName = strTag & RemoveSpecialChr(strNull)

If pintFormOrReport Then
  Set ctl = Forms(pstrObjectName)(pstrCtlName)
Else
  Set ctl = Reports(pstrObjectName)(pstrCtlName)
End If


Select Case intControlType
  Case LBL
    ' Set Control Name using Caption
    If Not Left$(ctl.Name, 4) = "Text" Then
      strNewCtlName = strTag &
      ➡ RemoveSpecialChr(CStr(strWrkngCtName))
    ElseIf Not Left$(ctl.Caption, 5) = "Field" Then
      strNewCtlName = strTag & RemoveSpecialChr(ctl.Caption)
    End If

  Case CMD
    If Not Left$(ctl.Name, 6) = "Button" Then
      strNewCtlName = strTag &
      ➡ RemoveSpecialChr(CStr(strWrkngCtName))
    ElseIf Not Left$(ctl.Caption, 6) = "Button" Then
      strNewCtlName = strTag & RemoveSpecialChr(ctl.Caption)
    End If

  Case GRP, TXT
    If Not Left$(ctl.Name, 5) = "Field" Then
      strNewCtlName = strTag &
      ➡ RemoveSpecialChr(CStr(strWrkngCtName))
```

```
    ElseIf Not IsNull(ctl.ControlSource) Then
    ' Set Control Name Using ControlSource
      strNewCtlName = strTag &
      ➡ RemoveSpecialChr(CStr(ctl.ControlSource))
    End If

Case CBO, LST
  If Not Left$(ctl.Name, 5) = "Field" Then
    strNewCtlName = strTag &
    ➡ RemoveSpecialChr(CStr(strWrkngCtName))
    ' Set Control Name Using ControlSource
  ElseIf Not IsNull(ctl.ControlSource) Then
    strNewCtlName = strTag &
    ➡ RemoveSpecialChr(CStr(ctl.ControlSource))
  End If

Case FRA
  If Not Left$(ctl.Name, 8) = "Embedded" Then
    strNewCtlName = strTag &
    ➡ RemoveSpecialChr(CStr(strWrkngCtName))
  Else
    ' Set Control Name based upon OLE Class
    On Error Resume Next
      strValue = ctl.ControlSource
    On Error GoTo SetControlName_Err
      ' Faster
    If Len(strValue) > 0 Then
      strNewCtlName = strTag &
      ➡ RemoveSpecialChr(CStr(ctl.ControlSource))
    ElseIf Not IsNull(ctl.Class) Then
      strNewCtlName = strTag &
      ➡ RemoveSpecialChr(CStr(ctl.Class))
    End If
  End If

Case GRA
  If Not Left$(ctl.Name, 8) = "Embedded" Then
    strNewCtlName = strTag &
    ➡ RemoveSpecialChr(CStr(strWrkngCtName))
  ElseIf Not IsNull(ctl.Class) Then
    ' Set Control Name based upon OLE Class
    strNewCtlName = strTag &
    ➡ RemoveSpecialChr(CStr(ctl.Class))
  End If
```

```
Case OPT, CHK
  If Not Left$(ctl.Name, 5) = "Field" Then
    strNewCtlName = strTag &
    ➥ RemoveSpecialChr(CStr(strWrkngCtName))
  Else
    ' If this object is in a frame, use the number else
    ' use the Control Source
    On Error Resume Next
      intValue = ctl.OptionValue
    On Error GoTo SetControlName_Err

    If Not intValue = 0 Then
      ' Set Control Name using OptionValue
      strNewCtlName = strNewCtlName & CStr(ctl.OptionValue)
    ElseIf Not IsNull(ctl.ControlSource) Then
      ' Set Control Name Using ControlSource
      strNewCtlName = strTag &
      ➥ RemoveSpecialChr(CStr(ctl.ControlSource))
    End If
  End If

Case TGL
  ' This is a toggle button which can have a Caption
  ' Set Control Name Using ControlSource
  If Not Left$(ctl.Name, 5) = "Field" Then
    strNewCtlName = strTag &
    ➥ RemoveSpecialChr(CStr(strWrkngCtName))
  Else
    On Error Resume Next
      intValue = ctl.OptionValue
    On Error GoTo SetControlName_Err

    If intValue = 0 Then
      ' The toggle button is NOT in an option group
      If Not IsNull(ctl.Caption) Then
        ' if the Caption is not blank then use it.
        strNewCtlName = strTag &
        ➥ RemoveSpecialChr(ctl.Caption)
      ElseIf Not IsNull(ctl.ControlSource) Then
        ' Set the Control name using the Control Source if
        ' it's not null
        strNewCtlName = strTag &
        ➥ RemoveSpecialChr(CStr(ctl.ControlSource))
      End If
```

```
        ElseIf Not IsNull(ctl.Caption) Then
           ' If the caption is not null then use the caption
           strNewCtlName = strTag &
         ➡ RemoveSpecialChr(ctl.Caption)
        Else
           ' Set Control Name using OptionValue
           strNewCtlName = strNewCtlName & CStr(ctl.OptionValue)
        End If
     End If

  Case LR_SUB
     ' Set Control name based upon SourceObject
     If Not Left$(ctl.Name, 8) = "Embedded" Then
        strNewCtlName = strTag &
      ➡ RemoveSpecialChr(CStr(strWrkngCtName))
     ElseIf Not IsNull(ctl.SourceObject) Then
        strNewCtlName = strTag &
      ➡ RemoveSpecialChr(CStr(ctl.SourceObject))
     End If

  Case SHP, LIN, BRK
     ' Use whatever the user has chosen

  Case Else
     ' If we don't know what control type it is then
     strNewCtlName = strTag & "UnknownControlType"

  End Select

' Check right away if the control is already named correctly.
' If so, then ask the user if he wants to rename it.

' Check and make sure the control name is not too long (64 char
' max)
If Len(strNewCtlName) > 60 Then
  strNewCtlName = Mid$(strNewCtlName, 1, 60)
End If

If Left$(pstrCtlName, 3) = strTag And Not intControlType = LIN
➡ Then
  lrn_strMsg = "'" & pstrCtlName & "' appears to be named
  ➡ correctly already." & lrn_NL
```

```
    lrn_strMsg = lrn_strMsg & "Do you want it renamed to:" &
    ➥ lrn_NL
    lrn_strMsg = lrn_strMsg & "'" & strNewCtlName & "'"

    Beep
    If MsgBox(lrn_strMsg, LRN_MB_QUERY + LRN_MB_YES_NO +
    ➥ LRN_MB_DEFAULT2, LRN_TITLE) = 7 Then
      SetControlName = CTL_SKIPPED
      GoTo SetControlName_Exit
    End If
  End If

  ctl.Name = strNewCtlName

  SetControlName = True

SetControlName_Exit:
  On Error GoTo 0
  Exit Function

SetControlName_Err:
  Select Case Err
    Case ERR_NAMECONFLICT
      If Len(strNewCtlName) > 60 Then
        strNewCtlName = Mid$(strNewCtlName, 1, 58)
      End If
      If intCtlCount > 1 Then
        strNewCtlName = Left$(strNewCtlName, Len(strNewCtlName) -
        ➥ 3)
      End If
      strNewCtlName = strNewCtlName & Right$("00" & intCtlCount,
      ➥ 3)
      intCtlCount = intCtlCount + 1
      Resume

    Case Else
      Call glrLRNErrorProc(Err, Error$, "SetControlName",
      ➥ "basLRName")
      Resume SetControlName_Exit

  End Select

End Function
```

Summary

This chapter has covered the following topics:

- Creating and installing a library
- Contents of the Access system libraries
- Entry points for Wizards, builders, and menu add-ins
- In-depth analysis of the Tabbed Dialog Wizard
- A look at the L/R Naming Builder
- Tips and tricks

You saw how libraries, Wizards, and builders work and learned what a library is and how to install one. In addition, this chapter walked you through creating a Wizard and a builder.

CHAPTER

TWENTY-ONE

MSAU200.DLL, the Undocumented Library

- File-handling functions

- Interfaces to Windows' common dialogs

- Font-handling functions

- Miscellaneous functions

To make it possible for the Access Wizards to perform some of their wizardry, Access ships with a special DLL named MSAU200.DLL. The functions that "live" in this library are meant to be called from Access Basic (since, of course, the Wizards are all written in Access Basic), and you can use them, too, in your own applications. The library includes 14 functions, of varying interest to you as an application developer, that break down into four basic categories:

- **File-handling functions:** Copy files, check for file existence, split file name components
- **Interfaces to Windows' common dialogs:** File Open/Close, Font and Color Choosers
- **Font-handling functions:** List available fonts and their sizes
- **Miscellaneous functions:** Use Access' bitmaps, check for existing CBF procedure, call WinWord help

This chapter discusses each of the functions from MSAU200.DLL in detail.

To use MSAU200.DLL in your own applications, you need to ensure that the library exists in the current directory, the Access directory, the Windows directory, the Windows\System directory, or your DOS path. Access places it in the directory that includes MSACCESS.EXE, by default. If you're shipping an application using the Access run-time version and you need to use MSAU200.DLL, you must be sure to place it somewhere where Windows will be able to find it.

WARNING None of the material in this chapter has been documented by Microsoft. That means that *any* of it can change at any time. Since the Access Wizards use everything in this chapter at one time or another, though, we feel strongly that you're also safe in using the functions from MSAU200.DLL.

Using MSAU200.DLL

To use the functions in MSAU200.DLL, you need to have the *Declare* statements for the functions available to your application. In addition, many of the functions require specific user-defined datatypes. The function declarations and datatype definitions are scattered throughout various Wizards and library databases. Although you needn't really do anything special to use these functions and datatypes as they're declared in the Access Wizards, if you write applications to be distributed with the Access run-time version, you can't distribute the Wizard databases with your application. Therefore, you'll need some method of reproducing those declarations and datatypes in your own applications.

To make things as simple as possible, we've created a single module including all the function declarations and datatype definitions you'll need. Import basMSAU200 (from CH21.MDB) into your application, and you'll be able to call any of the functions in MSAU200.DLL. We've aliased each of the functions and datatypes so they won't conflict with the corresponding declarations in the Wizards and libraries, if they're loaded.

NOTE All the external procedure declarations in this chapter use numeric aliases. In Windows, when declaring the external procedure, you can refer to the item either by name or by ordinal number within the DLL. Using the number is actually a tiny bit faster, and it protects you in case the author changes the name of the procedure in a future revision. Mostly, we did this because that's the way the Wizards have these functions declared. Since they're protected from future name changes, we thought it important that our code take the same precautions.

File-Handling Functions

MSAU200.DLL includes four file-handling functions, each of which performs one of the following activities:

- Checks for the existence of a file
- Splits a full path reference into its component pieces
- Gets the full path associated with a file
- Copies a file from one location to another

The next four sections deal with each of these functions individually.

Checking for the Existence of a File

You can check for the existence of a file by calling the glr_msauFileExists() function. To call it, use syntax like this:

intRetval = glr_msauFileExists(*strFileName*)

This function returns 1 if the file exists or 0 otherwise.

For example, to check for the existence of "C:\AUTOEXEC.BAT", you could use the following code:

```
If glr_msauFileExists("C:\AUTOEXEC.BAT") Then
    ' Do something
End If
```

To use glr_msauFileExists() you need to include the following declaration. You can either enter this line into your own module or include basMSAU200 from CH21.MDB.

```
Declare Function glr_msauFileExists Lib "MSAU200.DLL" Alias
➡ "#5"(ByVal strSrc As String) As Integer
```

Splitting a Full Path Reference into Components

As part of many applications, you'll need to take a full path reference, in the format

Drive:\Path\FileName.Ext

and retrieve any one of the single parts of the name (the drive, the path, the file name, or the extension) as a separate piece. The glrSplitPath subroutine (which calls the library function glr_msauSplitPath()) will do the work for you, filling in each of the various pieces.

For example, running the code in Listing 21.1 produces the output shown in Figure 21.1:

Listing 21.1

```
Function TestSplitPath()
    Dim strDrive As String
    Dim strPath As String
    Dim strFileName As String
    Dim strExt As String

    glrSplitPath "C:\Windows\System\MSACC20.INI", strDrive,
    ➥ strPath, strFileName, strExt
    Debug.Print "===================================="
    Debug.Print "Full : " & "C:\Windows\System\MSACC20.INI"
    Debug.Print "===================================="
    Debug.Print "Drive: " & strDrive
    Debug.Print "Path : " & strPath
    Debug.Print "File : " & strFileName
    Debug.Print "Ext  : " & strExt
    glrSplitPath "C:\", strDrive, strPath, strFileName, strExt
    Debug.Print "===================================="
    Debug.Print "Full : " & "C:\"
    Debug.Print "===================================="
    Debug.Print "Drive: " & strDrive
    Debug.Print "Path : " & strPath
    Debug.Print "File : " & strFileName
    Debug.Print "Ext  : " & strExt
End Function
```

FIGURE 21.1:

The glrSplitPath procedure breaks a full path name into its components.

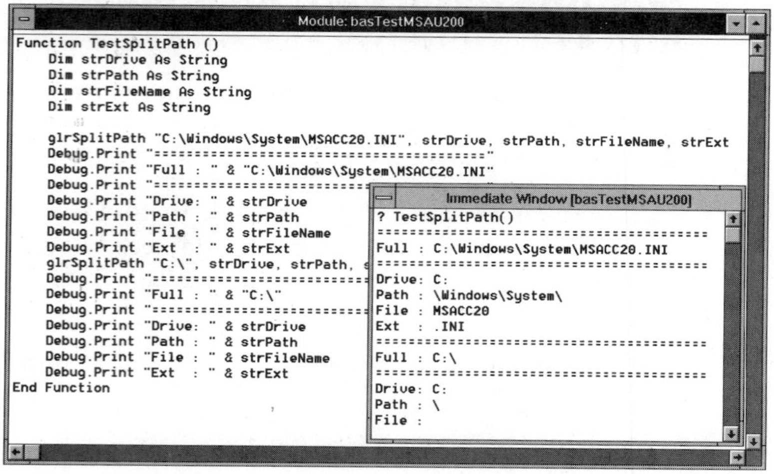

To use glrSplitPath you need to include basMSAU200 from CH21.MDB in your own application. Because the actual function in the DLL requires the strings to be set up in a special fashion, you'll need to call this wrapper routine rather than the actual DLL function itself. You could also just copy the glrSplitPath subroutine into your application and add the declaration for glr_msauSplitPath to your Declarations section:

```
Declare Sub glr_msauSplitPath Lib "MSAU200.DLL" Alias "#7"
➥ (ByVal strPath As String, ByVal strDrive As String,
➥ ByVal strDir As String, ByVal strFName As String,
➥ ByVal strExt As String)
```

Getting the Full Path for a File

You can use the glrFullPath() function (which calls the glr_msauFullPath() routine in MSAU200.DLL) to retrieve the full path for a file, based on a relative path. For example, if the current directory were the \Windows directory,

```
glrFullPath("..\ACCESS2\MSACCESS.EXE")
```

would return the value "C:\ACCESS2\MSACCESS.EXE", a fully qualified path name for the file. If you pass an invalid path to glrFullPath(), it returns a zero-length string.

Because the glr_msauFullPath() function requires a small wrapper function to make it easy to call from Access Basic, we've provided the glrFullPath() function for you to call directly. To use it you must import the basMSAU200 module from CH21.MDB into your own application. You could also copy the glrFullPath() function into your application and add the declaration for glr_msauFullPath() directly to your Declarations section:

```
Declare Function glr_msauFullPath Lib "MSAU200.DLL" Alias
➡ "#6"(ByVal strAbsPath As String, ByVal strFullPath As
➡ String, ByVal intFullPathMax As Integer) As Integer
```

Copying a File

The function glr_msauCopyFile() allows you to copy a file from one location to another. It's a very simple function to use:

```
intRetval = glr_msauCopyFile(strSourceFileName, strDestFileName)
```

If the function succeeds, it will have copied the file from the source location to the destination. The return value indicates the success or failure of the operation. Table 21.1 lists the possible return values and their meanings. (Note that a return value of 0 indicates success for this function. This is different from the way many other Access functions work.)

TABLE 21.1: Possible Return Values from glr_msauCopyFile()

Return Value	Meaning
0	File successfully copied
−101	Can't find the source file
−102	Can't open the destination file (Perhaps it already exists as a read-only file.)
−103	An error occurred while reading from the source file
−104	An error occurred while writing to the destination file
−105	Not enough memory to copy the file
−106	Length of one of the file names was too long

For example, the following fragment copies the file C:\AUTOEXEC.BAT to a file named C:\XXX.XXX:

```
intRetval = glr_msauCopyFile("C:\AUTOEXEC.BAT", "C:\XXX.XXX")
```

To use glr_msauCopyFile you need to include the appropriate external declaration (either by entering this line into your code or by including the module basMSAU200 from CH21.MDB):

```
Declare Function glr_msauCopyFile Lib "MSAU200.DLL" Alias
➥ "#4"(ByVal strSourceFile As String, ByVal strDestFile As
➥ String) As Long
```

Using the Windows Common Dialogs

To standardize specific often-needed dialogs, Windows provides a series of common dialogs that all applications can use. Access uses its own Print Setup dialog (one of the standard dialogs) but provides no mechanism for you to get to any of the others for your own applications. The code in MSAU200.DLL provides a simple interface to the File Open/Save dialog and the Color and Font Select dialogs. The following sections discuss how you can use the code in MSAU200.DLL along with the wrapper functions in basMSAU200 (in CH21.MDB) to make it simple for you to use these common dialogs in your own applications.

Using the File Open/File Save Common Dialog

You cannot have used Windows for long without noticing the standard File Open and File Save dialogs that most applications use. Windows provides them both, and MSAU200.DLL makes it easy for you to use these yourself. In general, in both cases you need to create a variable of the glr_msauGetFileNameInfo datatype. (We've defined this structure for you in basMSAU200.) You fill out certain fields in the structure and then send it off to the glrGetFileName() function. This function either requests a file to open or a name under which to save (depending on the value in one of its parameters) and returns the structure back to you, all filled out with the information the user chose from the dialog.

The structure of the user-defined type, glr_msauGetFileNameInfo, was set by the designers of MSAU200.DLL. If you were to call the common Windows dialog functions yourself—from C/C++ or Pascal, for instance—you'd use structures defined as part of the Windows SDK, which contain a few more fields and many more options. Because you're using MSAU200.DLL to interface to the real library (COMMDLG.DLL), the available options are a bit limited. Table 21.2 lists all the fields in the structure, along with information on using those fields. Table 21.3 lists the possible values for the Flags field in this structure.

TABLE 21.2: Fields in the glr_msauGetFileNameInfo Structure

Field Name	Datatype	Description
hwndOwner	Integer	Handle of the window that is to act as the parent of the dialog. You can use a null value (0&) if you don't want an owner, but this won't normally be the case. Either retrieve the Access handle (if you want the dialog to be modal) or the handle of a form (if you don't). You can use a form's hWnd property to retrieve its handle
szFilter	String * 255	String listing the available file filters. Leave it blank if you don't want to specify any. If you do specify values, use the standard format, Description1|FileSpec1|Description2|FileSpec2|, placing a vertical bar (|) after each item. The items must be in pairs (description, filespec). See TestGetFileName() in Listing 21.2 for more information
szCustomFilter	String * 255	Either an empty string or a list of two items as described in the szFilter item, above. This item provides the chosen filter when the dialog first opens, if it's not empty
nFilterIndex	Long	Number of the file-selection filter pair to use when the dialog first opens. The first pair is numbered 1. If you set this value to 0, Windows uses the selection pair listed in szCustomFilter instead
szFile	String * 255	The file name to use when the dialog is first displayed. After you close the dialog, this field contains the name of the file that was chosen
szFileTitle	String * 255	On output, the file name that was selected, without the drive and path information
szInitialDir	String * 255	Initial directory that the dialog should use

TABLE 21.2: Fields in the glr_msauGetFileNameInfo Structure (continued)

Field Name	Datatype	Description
szTitle	String * 255	Title for the File Open/Save dialog box
Flags	Long	Combination of 0 or more flags from Table 21.3 that control the operation of the dialog box. Combine them using the Or operator
nFileOffset	Integer	Number of characters from the start of the string in szFile to the location where the file name actually starts. The previous characters will contain the drive/path information
nFileExtension	Integer	Number of characters from the start of the string in szFile to the location where the file extension starts
szDefExt	String * 255	Default file extension to be appended to the file name if the user doesn't supply one. Don't include a period in the string

TABLE 21.3: Possible Values for the Flags Field in the glr_msauGetFileNameInfo Structure

Constant Name	Value	Description
glrOFN_READONLY	&H1	If set before calling the dialog box, forces the Read Only check box to be checked. After the dialog is closed, this flag will be set if the user checked that check box
glrOFN_OVERWRITEPROMPT	&H2	The dialog will issue a warning message if the user selects an existing file for a File Save As operation
glrOFN_HIDEREADONLY	&H4	Hides the Read Only check box from the dialog box
glrOFN_NOCHANGEDIR	&H8	Prohibits the user from changing directories
glrOFN_SHOWHELP	&H10	Shows a Help button on the dialog. Although this option works, the button will not, so its use in Access is limited
glrOFN_NOVALIDATE	&H100	Disables file name validation. Normally, COMMDLG.DLL checks the chosen file name to make sure it's a valid name

TABLE 21.3: Possible Values for the Flags Field in the glr_msauGetFileNameInfo Structure (continued)

Constant Name	Value	Description
glrOFN_ALLOWMULTISELECT	&H200	Allows the user to select more than one file name. If more than one is selected, after the dialog returns the buffer szFile will contain the chosen path followed by all the files within that path that were chosen, separated with spaces—for example, C:\ FILE1.TXT FILE2.TXT
glrOFN_EXTENSIONDIFFERENT	&H400	Used on return only, this flag will be set if the chosen file name has a different extension than that supplied in the szDefExt field
glrOFN_PATHMUSTEXIST	&H800	Forces the user to supply only valid path names
glrOFN_FILEMUSTEXIST	&H1000	Forces the user to supply only existing file names
glrOFN_CREATEPROMPT	&H2000	The dialog prompts users if the selected file doesn't exist, allowing them to go on or make a different choice
glrOFN_SHAREAWARE	&H4000	Ignores sharing violations. Since Access code cannot handle the errors that occur when sharing violations occur in this code, you should not set this flag
glrOFN_NOREADONLYRETURN	&H8000	Forces the user to select files that aren't read-only and directories that aren't write-protected
glrOFN_NOTESTFILECREATE	&H10000	Normally, COMMDLG.DLL tests to make sure you'll be able to create the file when you choose a file name for saving. If this flag is set, it doesn't test, providing no protection against common disk errors

To call the function, you needn't supply values for all these fields. Listing 21.2 shows a simple case of using the common dialogs to retrieve a file name to open. Figure 21.2 shows the dialog box this function pops up.

Listing 21.2

```
Function TestGetFileName()
    Dim gfni As glr_msauGetFileNameInfo

    gfni.szInitialDir = "C:\"
    gfni.szTitle = "Choose A File"
    gfni.szFilter = "All Files (*.*)|*.*|Access files
➡  (*.mdb,*.mda)|*.mdb;*.mda|"
    If glrGetFileName(gfni, True) = 0 Then
        MsgBox Trim(gfni.szFile)
        If gfni.Flags And glrOFN_READONLY Then
            MsgBox "You opened the file read-only!"
        End If
    End If
End Function
```

FIGURE 21.2:
The code in Listing 21.2 causes this dialog to pop up.

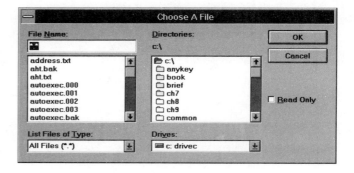

There are a few items to note about this function:

- Since all the strings in the datatype are fixed-length strings, you need to use the Trim() function to remove trailing spaces when you want to use the data that's in those strings.

- You can use several of the values in the Flags field to determine information about how the user opened the file (glrOF_READONLY, glrOF_EXTENSION-DIFFERENT, and so on). Check their state using the And operator, as shown in Listing 21.2.

- Most likely, you'll want to at least supply values for the fields used in Listing 21.2: szInitialDir, szTitle, and szFilter. You can, of course, supply other values, but those will be the most useful ones. Note that you must end each entry in the szFilter field with a vertical bar and that each entry must consist of two values: the text description of the filter item and the filespec that will select that group. In addition, if you want to use two different filespecs within a group (as we did in Listing 21.2), separate them with a semicolon (;) in the second portion of the group.

To choose a file name for saving, just set the second parameter to glrGetFileName() to False. That way, you've indicated to MSAU200.DLL that you're trying to save a file rather than load it.

To use glrGetFileName() in your own applications, you need to import basMSAU200 from CH21.MDB. Since it uses its own datatype and many flags, you're better off just importing the entire module (as you will be for any of the common dialog wrappers covered in this chapter).

Selecting Colors

If you need to allow your users to choose colors within your application, your easiest solution is to use the Windows common dialog Color Chooser. Figure 21.3 shows the Color dialog in action.

Just as with the file name–choosing dialog, MSAU200.DLL makes it simple for you to use this dialog. All you need to do is call glrPickNewColor(), passing to it the color you'd like to have selected as a default. This wrapper function sets up the call to glr_msauGetColor() and returns the user's color choice to the calling procedure.

Unlike the File Open/Save dialog, there are few options you can change when dealing with the Color dialog. Therefore, to simplify its use, we've set up glrPickNewColor() to accept only one parameter; you'll send to it the default color to use when the user first sees the dialog. Table 21.4 lists all the fields in the glr_msauGetColorInfo data structure. You most likely won't ever need to interact with any of them. Table 21.5 lists all the options you can use in the Flags field of the structure.

FIGURE 21.3:

Windows color-choosing common dialog

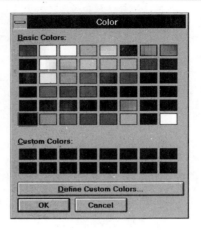

TABLE 21.4: Fields in the glr_msauGetColorInfo Structure

Field Name	Datatype	Description
hWndOwner	Integer	Handle of the window that is to act as the parent of the dialog. You can use a null value (0&) if you don't want an owner, but this won't normally be the case. Either retrieve the Access handle (if you want the dialog to be modal) or the handle of a form (if you don't)
rgbResult	Long	Contains the user's color selection after the user has dismissed the dialog. If the glrCC_RGBINIT flag is also set in the Flags field, you can place the initial color setting in this field, also
Flags	Long	A combination of 0 or more flags from Table 21.5 that control the operation of the dialog box. Combine them using the Or operator
rgCustColors(16)	Long	Storage for 16 custom colors, as defined by the user. Make the data structure STATIC if you want these preserved between calls to the function. If you want to preserve the colors between invocations of your program, you need to store the 16 colors in an .INI file and retrieve them at program startup

TABLE 21.5: Possible Values for the Flags Field in the glr_msauGetColorInfo Structure

Constant Name	Value	Description
glrCC_RGBINIT	&H1	Uses the color in the rgbResult field to initialize the dialog box
glrCC_FULLOPEN	&H2	Opens the full dialog box, including the custom color portion, when the dialog first appears
glrCC_PREVENTFULL-OPEN	&H4	Only the left side of the dialog will be available

To use glrPickNewColor() from your own applications, you must import basMSAU200 from CH21.MDB into your application. Once it's there you can call glrPickNewColor(), passing to it a default color number. Listing 21.3 shows an example of a use for glrPickNewColor().

Listing 21.3

```
Function testPickNewColor()

    ' A test case for glrPickNewColor().
    ' Loop until the user chooses the Cancel button.

    Dim lngColor As Long
    Do
        lngColor = glrPickNewColor(lngColor)
        Debug.Print "Color: " & lngColor
    Loop Until lngColor = -1
End Function
```

Selecting Fonts

Anytime you choose a new font, in most applications you'll be using the standard Windows font selection dialog to make your choice. You can use the same dialog from your Access applications, using a function in MSAU200.DLL. Just as with the file-choosing dialogs, you need to create and fill in a user-defined datatype, glr_msauGetFontInfo, and then pass that data structure to the glrGetFont() function, which, in turn, calls the glr_msauGetFont() function that resides in

MSAU200.DLL. You need the wrapper function in this case to do some string conversions, to and from the format the DLL expects. Once the user has dismissed the dialog box, glrGetFont() returns to you the data structure filled in with the choices the user made. Table 21.6 describes the fields that make up the glr_msauGetFontInfo structure. Table 21.7 lists all the possible values for the Flags field in the glr_msauGetFontInfo data structure, and Table 21.8 lists the possible font types that might be returned in the nFontType member of the structure.

TABLE 21.6: Fields in the glr_msauGetFontInfo Structure

Field Name	Datatype	Description
hWndOwner	Integer	Handle of the window that is to act as the parent of the dialog. You can use a null value (0&) if you don't want an owner, but this won't normally be the case. Retrieve either the Access handle (if you want the dialog to be modal) or the handle of a form (if you don't)
hdc	Integer	Device context or information context for the device that will use the fonts. Windows uses this only if you've set the CF_PRINTERFONTS flag. Otherwise, don't set its value
szFontName	String * 255	Chosen font name when the dialog first appears, if the CF_INITTOLOGFONT-STRUCT flag is set. On return from the dialog box, it contains the chosen font name
nSize	Integer	Chosen font size when the dialog first appears, if the CF_INITTOLOGFONT-STRUCT flag is set. On return from the dialog box, it contains the chosen font size (measured in tenths of a point)
nWeight	Integer	Chosen font weight when the dialog first appears, if the CF_INITTOLOGFONT-STRUCT flag is set. On return from the dialog box, it contains the chosen font weight (0–900, in increments of 100)

TABLE 21.6: Fields in the glr_msauGetFontInfo Structure (continued)

Field Name	Datatype	Description
fItalic	Integer	Chosen font italic state when the dialog first appears, if the CF_INITTOLOGFONT-STRUCT flag is set. On return from the dialog box, it contains the chosen font italic state
fUnderline	Integer	Chosen font underline state when the dialog first appears, if the CF_INITTOLOGFONT-STRUCT flag is set. On return from the dialog box, it contains the chosen font underline state
fStrikeout	Integer	Chosen font strikeout state when the dialog first appears, if the CF_INITTOLOGFONT-STRUCT flag is set. On return from the dialog box, it contains the chosen font strikeout state
Flags	Long	Combination of 0 or more flags from Table 21.7 that control the operation of the dialog box. Combine them using the Or operator
rgbColors	Long	Chosen font color when the dialog first appears, if the CF_INITTOLOGFONT-STRUCT flag is set. On return from the dialog box, it contains the chosen font color
szStyle	String * 255	Contains the font style, stored as a string. If you use the CF_USESTYLE flag, you can use this buffer to initialize the font style
nFontType	Integer	Stores the type of font the user selected. Its value will be a combination of values from Table 21.8
nSizeMin	Integer	If you set the CF_LIMITSIZE flag, this integer specifies the lower bound on font sizes
nSizeMax	Integer	If you set the CF_LIMITSIZE flag, this integer specifies the upper bound on font sizes

TABLE 21.7: Possible Values for the Flags Field in the glr_msauGetFontInfo Structure

Constant Name	Value	Description
glrCF_SCREENFONTS	&H1	Displays only screen fonts
glrCF_PRINTERFONTS	&H2	Displays only printer fonts
glrCF_BOTH	&H3	Displays both screen and printer fonts
glrCF_SHOWHELP	&H4	Shows a Help button (not useful from Access)
glrCF_INITTOLOGFONTSTRUCT	&H40	Uses the data passed in to initialize the dialog (font name, size, weight, and so on)
glrCF_USESTYLE	&H80	Initializes the font dialog with data from the szStyle member
glrCF_EFFECTS	&H100	Displays strikeout, underline, and color options
glrCF_APPLY	&H200	Displays an Apply button
glrCF_ANSIONLY	&H400	Limits fonts to ANSI characters (no Symbol fonts)
glrCF_NOVECTORFONTS	&H800	Displays no vector fonts (same as CF_NOOEMFONTS)
glrCF_NOOEMFONTS	&H800	Displays no vector fonts
glrCF_NOSIMULATIONS	&H1000	Displays no GDI simulated fonts
glrCF_LIMITSIZE	&H2000	Limits the range of sizes to values in nSizeMin and nSizeMax members
glrCF_FIXEDPITCHONLY	&H4000	Displays only fixed-pitch fonts
glrCF_WYSIWYG	&H8000	Displays only fonts that are available on the screen and printer
glrCF_FORCEFONTEXIST	&H10000	Displays only fonts explicitly supported by the font data
glrCF_SCALABLEONLY	&H20000	Displays only scalable fonts
glrCF_TTONLY	&H40000	Displays only TrueType fonts
glrCF_NOFACESEL	&H80000	Prohibits selection of a typeface
glrCF_NOSTYLESEL	&H100000	Prohibits selection of a style
glrCF_NOSIZESEL	&H200000	Prohibits selection of a font size

TABLE 21.8: Possible Values for the nFontType Field in the glr_msauGetFontInfo Data Structure

Constant	Value
glrBOLD_FONTTYPE	&H100
glrITALIC_FONTTYPE	&H200
glrREGULAR_FONTTYPE	&H400
glrSCREEN_FONTTYPE	&H2000
glrPRINTER_FONTTYPE	&H4000
glrSIMULATED_FONTTYPE	&H8000

NOTE
We were unable to make most of the options for the font dialog work correctly using MSAU200.DLL. Since this DLL is undocumented and Microsoft is unable to support it, we have to take our findings as "the way it is." We were able to choose a font and retrieve its name and size, but that's about it. Perhaps future versions of MSAU200.DLL will work better in this regard. All the information presented here shows how the dialog box *ought* to work. At this point, as in any other undocumented feature, you're somewhat on your own. We're including this information here only for completeness' sake. If you need to get font information from your users, you'll be far better off using the functions available in MSAU200.DLL that we discuss later in this chapter.

As a simple example, the function in Listing 21.4 pops up the font-choosing dialog box and retrieves a font from the user.

Listing 21.4

```
Function TestGetFont()
    Dim gfi As glr_msauGetFontInfo
    Dim varRetval As Variant
```

```
        gfi.hWndOwner = glr_apiGetActiveWindow()
        gfi.Flags = glrCF_SCREENFONTS Or glrCF_EFFECTS
        gfi.nfontType = glrSCREEN_FONTTYPE

        varRetval = glrGetFont(gfi)
        Debug.Print Trim(gfi.szFontName)
End Function
```

Resetting Help Topics

Although not directly related to MSAU200.DLL, an interesting side-note here is that the example functions in the Wizards that call the Window Common dialogs include an undocumented call to the Access SysCmd() function. The SysCmd() function has ten documented entry points, but the Wizard code uses this call:

```
unused = SysCmd(SYSCMD_CLEARHELPTOPIC)
```

The constant SYSCMD_CLEARHELPTOPIC is defined in the UTILITY.MDA that ships with Access, even though its value (11) is not documented in the Help file. This function call serves a simple purpose: it resets the help engine so that you'll see the main Access help topic if you press the F1 key while the common dialog is currently displayed. We can't think of any other use for this particular entry point to SysCmd(), but you will find it in the functions we use to call into MSAU200.DLL that, in turn, load common dialogs.

Font-Handling Functions

Since MSAU200.DLL's support for the common font dialog is not completely functional, it's convenient that it supplies a great deal of stand-alone functionality in that area. The DLL provides functions to retrieve the count of installed fonts; a list of those fonts; and for each raster (bitmapped) font, a count of the available sizes and a list of those sizes. The next few sections cover the use of these functions. In addition, we've provided a sample form (frmListFonts in CH21.MDB) that ties together all these ideas. Since all these topics will be much clearer with a real example to discuss, you might want to take a moment and exercise frmListFonts before digging into this material. Figure 21.4 shows the form in use.

frmListFonts allows you to view any font in any available point size.

Retrieving a List of Fonts

MSAU200.DLL provides two functions you need in order to fill an array with a list of all the available fonts. The function glr_msauGetFontCount() returns the number of fonts, and glr_msauGetFontList() fills in a passed array with strings representing all those fonts. The code attached to frmListFonts' Open event calls both of these functions directly in order to fill the combo box on the form with a list of fonts. Listing 21.5 shows the portion of the code that handles this.

Listing 21.5

```
Dim hDC As Integer
hDC = glr_apiCreateIC("DISPLAY", "", "", O&)
If hDC <> O Then
    intFonts = glr_msauGetFontCount(hDC)
    If intFonts > O Then
        ReDim afiFonts(O To intFonts - 1) As glrFontInfo
        intFonts = glr_msauGetFontList(hDC, afiFonts(O))
        ' Get rid of the trailing null and spaces NOW.
        For intI = O To intFonts - 1
            afiFonts(intI).strName =
            ➥ glrTruncateString((afiFonts(intI).strName))
        Next intI
    End If
End If
```

```
'
' More code in here...
'
hDC = glr_apiDeleteDC(hDC)
hDC = 0
```

As a first step when you work with fonts, you must retrieve information about the current display device. To do so you call the Windows API function CreateIC() (create information context) or CreateDC() (create device context). Either will do in this case since you're only retrieving information about the display device. Were you interested in modifying any of the device settings, you'd be forced to use CreateDC(), which requires a bit more overhead than CreateIC(). To get the handle you need, you call CreateIC() (aliased as glr_apiCreateIC() in the example), sending to it the name of the device driver ("DISPLAY" in this case), with all the other parameters set to empty strings or 0. This will retrieve for you a device handle referring to the current display device, as shown in the following code fragment:

```
Dim hDC As Integer

hDC = glr_apiCreateIC("DISPLAY", "", "", O&)
```

Once you have a device context, you can request the number of installed fonts from MSAU200.DLL. To call msau_GetFontCount(), just send it the device context as a parameter, and it will return the number of fonts installed for that device:

```
If hDC <> 0 Then
    intFonts = glr_msauGetFontCount(hDC)
```

Once you have the number of installed fonts, you can create an array to hold the list. That array will need to be made up of elements of the type glrFontInfo, as shown here:

```
Type glrFontInfo
    fRasterFont As Integer
    strName As String * 32
End Type
```

where each element stores a True or False value, indicating whether or not the font is a raster font, as well as the name of the font. The code to create the array looks like this:

```
ReDim afiFonts(0 To intFonts - 1) As glrFontInfo
```

To fill in the list of font information, call glr_msauGetFontList(), passing to it the device context and the first element of the array. Since Access creates all its arrays so they are contiguous in memory, passing the first element to the DLL call allows the DLL to fill in all the elements. The function returns the actual number of fonts it filled in and actually fills in the entire array:

```
intFonts = glr_msauGetFontList(hDC, afiFonts(0))
```

As the final step in this process, you need to deal with the extra characters left in the array by the DLL call. Since the DLL treats the strings as though they were null terminated and Access doesn't deal well with null-terminated strings, the function here includes a pass through all the elements of the array, truncating them at the first null character each contains:

```
' Get rid of the trailing null and spaces NOW.
For intI = 0 To intFonts - 1
    afiFonts(intI).strName =
    ➡ glrTruncateString((afiFonts(intI).strName))
Next intI
```

You'll find the code for glrTruncateString() in basMSAU200, so you need to include that module in your application if you also want to use frmListFonts.

Last but not least, you must always release the device (or information) context handle when you're done with it. Windows maintains only a fixed number of these handles, so you must always conclude with code like this:

```
hDC = glr_apiDeleteDC(hDC)
hDC = 0
```

This code both releases the handle and resets its value back to 0 so subsequent code that checks the value of hDC knows that it doesn't represent a device context anymore.

Retrieving a List of Sizes

For TrueType fonts, Windows generally presents you with a list of font sizes that's standardized:

```
8,9,10,11,12,14,16,18,20,22,24,26,28,36,48,72
```

The code attached to frmListFonts maintains an array, aintAllSizes(), that contains those standard sizes. For raster fonts, however, the available sizes are determined by the font itself. Therefore, for raster fonts, the code needs to retrieve the list of specific sizes for the font. The procedure in Listing 21.6, FillFontSizes, fills the global array aintSizes() with the available font sizes for the specified font.

Listing 21.6

```
Sub FillFontSizes(hDC As Integer, ByVal varFaceName As Variant)
    Dim strName As String

    If IsNull(varFaceName) Then
        ReDim aintSizes(0)
        Exit Sub
    End If
    strName = CStr(varFaceName)
    intSizes = glr_msauGetSizeCount(hDC, strName)
    If intSizes > 0 Then
        ReDim aintSizes(intSizes - 1) As Integer
        intSizes = glr_msauGetSizeList(hDC, strName, aintSizes(0))
    End If
End Sub
```

To call FillFontSizes, you pass to it the device context you previously created and the name of the specific font. If the face name is null, of course, the procedure can't do its work and will need to empty out the array and just exit.

```
If IsNull(varFaceName) Then
    ReDim aintSizes(0)
    Exit Sub
End If
```

Next, the procedure needs to determine how many sizes are available for the given font. To do this, it can call the glr_msauGetSizeCount() function provided by MSAU200.DLL. This function takes the device context and a font name and returns the number of available font sizes:

```
strName = CStr(varFaceName)
intSizes = glr_msauGetSizeCount(hDC, strName)
```

Once you have the number of fonts, all you need to do is redimension the global array to be large enough to contain the list of font sizes and then retrieve them. To fill the array with the list of available font sizes, you can call the glr_msauGetSize-List() function in MSAU200.DLL:

```
If intSizes > 0 Then
    ReDim aintSizes(intSizes - 1) As Integer
    intSizes = glr_msauGetSizeList(hDC, strName, aintSizes(0))
End If
```

Just as with the glr_msauGetFontList() function, you pass just the first element of the array to be filled to the glr_msauGetSizeList() function. From that, it can fill in all the other elements.

That's basically all there is to frmListFonts. When the user chooses a font from the list, the AfterUpdate event code requeries the list containing the available sizes for that font. In addition, it sets the properties of the text box that displays the same text to match the chosen values.

To use these functions in your own applications, import the module basMSAU200 from CH21.MDB.

Retrieving National Language Info

Most Windows executables and DLLs contain information about the language and character set for which they were created, among other version-specific information. Table 21.9 lists all the defined language code numbers that Microsoft has documented. Table 21.10 lists all the character sets that Windows currently supports. The combination of these two numbers makes up the language identifier for a version of a product.

Although it's tricky to retrieve this information using API calls directly from Access, it is possible. To simplify the process, MSAU200.DLL provides a single function call, glr_msauGetLanguage(), which tells you both values for any specified file or running module. To use glr_msauGetLanguage(), you must first declare it:

```
Declare Function glr_msauGetLanguage Lib "MSAU200.DLL" Alias
➡ "#14"(ByVal strFileOrMod As String, ByVal fFileName As
➡ Integer, intLang As Integer, intCodePage As Integer) As
➡ Integer
```

TABLE 2 1.9: Windows Language Codes

ID	Language
1052	Albanian
1025	Arabic
1057	Bahasa
2067	Belgian Dutch
2060	Belgian French
1046	Brazilian Portuguese
1026	Bulgarian
3084	Canadian French
1034	Castilian Spanish
1027	Catalan
1050	Croato-Serbian (Latin)
1029	Czech
1030	Danish
1043	Dutch
1035	Finnish
1036	French
1031	German
1032	Greek
1037	Hebrew
1038	Hungarian
1039	Icelandic
1040	Italian
1041	Japanese
1042	Korean
2058	Mexican Spanish
1044	Norwegian—Bokmål
2068	Norwegian—Nynorsk
1045	Polish
2070	Portuguese

TABLE 21.9: Windows Language Codes (continued)

ID	Language
1047	Rhaeto-Romanic
1048	Romanian
1049	Russian
2074	Serbo-Croatian (Cyrillic)
2052	Simplified Chinese
1051	Slovak
1053	Swedish
4108	Swiss French
2055	Swiss German
2064	Swiss Italian
1054	Thai
1028	Traditional Chinese
1055	Turkish
2057	U.K. English
1033	U.S. English
1056	Urdu

TABLE 21.10: Windows' Supported Character Sets

Character Set	Description
0	7-bit ASCII
932	Windows, Japan (Shift—JIS X-0208)
949	Windows, Korea (Shift—KSC 5601)
950	Windows, Taiwan (GB5)
1200	Unicode
1250	Windows, Latin-2 (Eastern European)
1251	Windows, Cyrillic

TABLE 21.10: Windows' Supported Character Sets (continued)

Character Set	Description
1252	Windows, Multilingual
1253	Windows, Greek
1254	Windows, Turkish
1255	Windows, Hebrew
1256	Windows, Arabic

The function takes four parameters, as described in Table 21.11. It returns one of four possible values, depending on the outcome of its efforts. Table 21.12 lists those values.

TABLE 21.11: Parameters for glr_msauGetLanguage()

Parameter	Datatype	On Input	On Output
strFileOrMod	String	Name of a running module or disk file name	Not Used
fFileName	Integer	Flag indicating whether strFileOrMod is a disk file or a running module (True for disk file, False for running module)	Not Used
intLang	Integer	Not Used	Language Code
intCodePage	Integer	Not Used	Character Set

TABLE 21.12: Possible Return Values for glr_msauGetLanguage()

Return Value	Description
0	No Error
−1	The requested module isn't loaded
−2	Out of memory
−3	Unable to retrieve the requested information (Most likely, the file can't be found.)

For example, to find the language version of the currently running copy of Microsoft Access, you could use code like the following:

```
Dim intRetval As Integer
Dim intLang As Integer
Dim intCharSet As Integer

intRetval = glr_msauGetLanguage("MSAIN200", False, intLang,
➡ intCharSet)
If intRetval = 0 Then
    MsgBox "Language: " & intLang & ", Char Set: " &  intCharSet
End If
```

Figure 21.5 shows the resulting message box for the US English version of Access.

FIGURE 21.5:

Message box showing the current language and character set

Retrieving Toolbar Bitmaps

As you've noticed if you've modified the button face of a toolbar button, Access provides a limited set of bitmaps from which to choose. Figure 21.6 shows the 84 that are available when you attempt to modify a toolbar's picture. There are more bitmaps available for you to use on buttons, through the Button Wizard.

Access stores this collection of bitmaps (to which you can't add your own pictures, unfortunately—your toolbars are limited in Access 2.0 to using the bitmaps that Microsoft provided) as a single "clump" in MSAIN200.DLL. Figure 21.7 shows the bitmap as it's stored in the DLL. Storing the bitmaps this way saves on graphics resources, which are in short enough supply with major Windows applications running!

In order to do its work, the Button Builder required some method of retrieving a single bitmap from the "clump," and MSAU200.DLL provides the code necessary

FIGURE 21.6:

Palette of bitmaps available for toolbar buttons

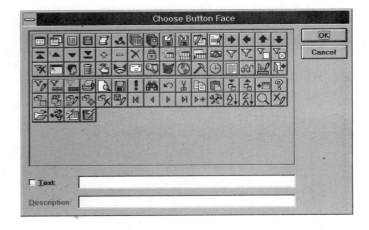

FIGURE 21.7:

The toolbar and button builder bitmaps are stored in a "clump" in MSAIN200.DLL.

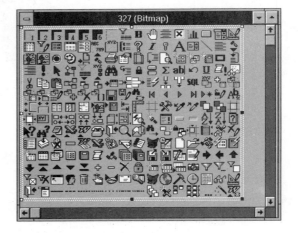

to retrieve that bitmap. To make it possible to use the same bitmaps on all screen resolutions, the function returns a device-independent bitmap. To use the function, you need the following declaration:

```
Declare Function glr_msauGetTBDib Lib "MSAU200.DLL" Alias
➡ "#8"(ByVal lngBmp As Long, ByVal fLarge As Integer,
➡ ByVal strBuf As String) As Integer
```

The function returns 0 if it fails for any reason and a non-zero value if it succeeds.

In addition, you can't use this function without a table that lists all the pictures and their ID values (which indicate to the DLL where to start pulling data from, inside the bitmap). In CH21.MDB you'll find tblTBPictures, which includes all the data you'll need. You must include this table in any application for which you'd like to supply this functionality.

WARNING Since you're including this table in your application, you must be extremely careful to keep the table updated to match the current version of Access. The table we've supplied matches Access 2.0. Anytime the version of Access changes, you'll need to import bw_TblPictures from WZBLDR.MDA, the Button Builder Wizard that ships with Microsoft Access. Since Microsoft maintains complete control over both the table and the bitmap "clump," you have to make sure you have them synchronized. You could, of course, just attach the table bw_TblPictures from WZBLDR.MDA, rename it to tblTBPictures, and use it externally. The problem in this solution is that you can't ship WZBLDR.MDA with applications you distribute using your run-time applications. If you import the table, you aren't fighting that restriction. We decided to import the table and not worry about the distribution problems.

Table 21.13 describes the the three parameters for glr_msauGetTBDib().

TABLE 21.13: Parameters for glr_msauGetTBDib()

Parameter	Datatype	Description
lngBMP	Long Integer	Value from the TBBitmapID column in tblTBPictures, indicating which bitmap to retrieve
fLarge	Integer	Flag: True to use large bitmaps, False to use small bitmaps
strBuf	String	Buffer to hold the bitmap information

It's up to you to make sure that strBuf is large enough to hold all the bitmap information before you call glr_msauGetTBDib(). We recommend that you use the String() or Space() function to ensure that it's initialized to the correct size. For large bitmaps you'll need 488 characters. For small bitmaps you'll need 296 characters. You might use code like the following to set this up:

```
Const LARGEBITMAPSIZE = 488
Const SMALLBITMAPSIZE = 296

' Arbitrarily use large pictures, this time.
fUseSmallPictures = False

strPictureData = String(IIf(fUseSmallPictures, SMALLBITMAPSIZE,
➡ LARGEBITMAPSIZE), " ")
```

To retrieve a specific bitmap from the array of bitmaps in MSAIN200.DLL, you need to find the correct row in tblTBPictures, retrieve the TBBitmapID value from that row, and then call glr_msauGetTBDib(). Listing 21.7 shows code you could use to retrieve a bitmap and use it to replace the picture on a specific button.

Listing 21.7

```
Sub RetrieveDIB(ctl As Control, intPictureID As Integer)
    Dim fUseSmallPictures As Integer
    Dim strPictureData As String
    Dim varRetval As Variant
    Dim db As Database
    Dim rst As Recordset

Const LARGEBITMAPSIZE = 488
Const SMALLBITMAPSIZE = 296

    ' Arbitrarily use large pictures.
    fUseSmallPictures = False

    Set db = DBEngine.WorkSpaces(0).Databases(0)
    Set rst = db.OpenRecordset("Select PictureData,
➡ TBBitmapID from tblTBPictures where PictureID = " &
➡ (intPictureID) & ";", DB_OPEN_SNAPSHOT)

    If rst.RecordCount Then
        If Not IsNull(rst!TBBitmapID) Then
            strPictureData = String(IIf(fUseSmallPictures,
➡ SMALLBITMAPSIZE, LARGEBITMAPSIZE), " ")
```

```
        varRetval = glr_msauGetTBDib((rst!TBBitmapID),
        ➡ Not fUseSmallPictures, strPictureData)
        ctl.PictureData = strPictureData
    Else
        ctl.PictureData = rst!PictureData
    End If
    rst.Close
End If
End Sub
```

In the example code, you first need to find a particular row in tblTBPictures, given the primary key value for a row. The following code does that for you:

```
Set db = DBEngine.WorkSpaces(0).Databases(0)
Set rst = db.OpenRecordset("Select PictureData,
➡ TBBitmapID from tblTBPictures where PictureID = " &
➡ (intPictureID) & ";", DB_OPEN_SNAPSHOT)
```

If you've found the row, you need to check the TBBitmapID column since some of the rows don't pertain to data in the bitmap array but actually store their bitmap information in the PictureData column. For those rows you just copy the data directly out of the table instead of retrieving it from MSAIN200.DLL:

```
If rst.RecordCount Then
    If Not IsNull(rst!TBBitmapID) Then
        strPictureData = String(IIf(fUseSmallPictures,
        ➡ SMALLBITMAPSIZE, LARGEBITMAPSIZE), " ")
        varRetval = glr_msauGetTBDib((rst!TBBitmapID), Not
        ➡ fUseSmallPictures, strPictureData)
        ctl.PictureData = strPictureData
    Else
        ctl.PictureData = rst!PictureData
    End If
    rst.Close
End If
```

In either case, once the procedure has retrieved the data, it places it on the button's face by assigning it to the button's PictureData property. This property is currently undocumented, but you can set or retrieve a button's picture through this property.

Using glr_msauGetTBDib()

If you've used the Command Button Wizard, you know that it supplies you with a list box full of pictures you can place on a button. Its main problem is that you can work with only a single button and its properties at a time. If you need to change the pictures for buttons you've already created, Access does provide a button picture builder, but going through the steps of using the builder for each button can be tedious. Figure 21.8 shows the Command Button Wizard in action.

FIGURE 21.8:
The Command Button Wizard supplies you with a choice of bitmaps for your buttons.

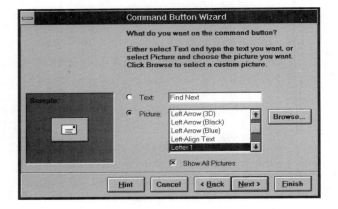

We've created a small tool, frmButtonPix in CH21.MDB, that can take care of this task for you. Using the code shown in Listing 21.7, it can place any picture from tblTBPictures onto any button on any form you have loaded. This can be a very useful design-time tool, and it works fine at run time, too. Figure 21.9 shows frmButtonPix running.

FIGURE 21.9:
frmButtonPix can change the picture on any button on any form.

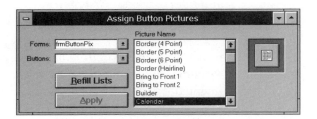

If you want to use frmButtonPix to change the picture on a button permanently, you need to open the form containing that button in design mode, use frmButtonPix to change the button face, and then save the changed form. Changes made to forms at run time are not saved with the form.

On frmButtonPix, most of the code deals with filling the lists containing all the forms and, on each form, all the buttons. Listing 21.8 shows the callback function used to fill the list box with a list of open forms.

Listing 21.8

```
Function ListForms(ctl As Control, lngID As Long, intRow As
➡ Integer, intCol As Integer, intCode As Integer)

    Dim varRetval As Variant

    Select Case intCode
        Case LB_INITIALIZE
            varRetval = True

        Case LB_OPEN
            varRetval = Timer

        Case LB_GETCOLUMNCOUNT
            varRetval = 1

        Case LB_GETROWCOUNT
            varRetval = Forms.Count

        Case LB_GETVALUE
            varRetval = Forms(intRow).Name

    End Select

    ListForms = varRetval
End Function
```

Once you've selected a form from the list, you can select a specific button from that form. Listing 21.9 shows the callback function that fills the list of button names. The only complication here arises from the fact that you don't want to display the names of transparent buttons, but only command buttons can be transparent. Therefore, the LB_INITIALIZE case includes code that checks the type of each control, looping through all the controls on the chosen form, and skips any that aren't command or toggle buttons. Then, if the control is a command button, the function adds the button to the list only if it's not transparent. After the following code, the procedure adds the button name to the list of names if the fAddOne flag has been set to True.

Listing 21.9

```
Function ListButtons(ctl As Control, lngID As Long, intRow
➡ As Integer, intCol As Integer, intCode As Integer)

    Dim varRetval As Variant
    Static intCount As Integer
    Static astrButtons() As String
    Dim intI As Integer
    Dim frm As Form
    Dim fAddOne As Integer
    Dim ctl1 As Control

    Select Case intCode
        Case LB_INITIALIZE
            Erase astrButtons
            intCount = 0
            Set frm = Forms(Me!lstForms)
            For intI = 0 To frm.Count - 1
                fAddOne = False
                Set ctl1 = frm(intI)
                If TypeOf ctl1 Is CommandButton Then
                    fAddOne = Not ctl1.Transparent
                ElseIf TypeOf ctl1 Is ToggleButton Then
                    fAddOne = True
                End If
                If fAddOne Then
                    intCount = intCount + 1
                    ReDim Preserve astrButtons(intCount - 1)
                    astrButtons(intCount - 1) = ctl1.Name
                End If
            Next intI
            varRetval = True
```

```
        Case LB_OPEN
            varRetval = Timer

        Case LB_GETCOLUMNCOUNT
            varRetval = 1

        Case LB_GETROWCOUNT
            varRetval = intCount

        Case LB_GETVALUE
            varRetval = astrButtons(intRow)

    End Select

    ListButtons = varRetval
End Function
```

Since there's no simple way for frmButtonPix to know that you've loaded or closed forms around it, we've also supplied the Refill Lists button on the form. This button allows you to change which forms are currently loaded and then tell frmButtonPix about it.

Finally, once you've selected a form and a button on that form, you can click the Apply button (or double-click on the picture image on the form), and the code will apply the chosen image to the chosen button:

```
Sub cmdApply_Click()
    On Error Resume Next
    Forms(Me!lstForms)(Me!lstButtons).PictureData =
    ➥ Me!cmdSample.PictureData
End Sub
```

To use frmButtonPix in your own applications, import both the form and the table (tblTBPictures). You won't need any other modules since frmButtonPix contains all the code and declarations it needs.

Is That Procedure There?

Digging through the Wizards revealed one more undocumented gem: Access provides a method of determining whether or not a specific procedure exists within a form or report's module. (This tip really has nothing to do with MSAU200.DLL, but since it's one more undocumented trick, this chapter seemed the likely place to put it.) Although this is not functionality that many Access developers will need, and it's *clearly* undocumented and could change in future versions, the Wizards do use it, and chances are that if you're writing development tools yourself, this functionality might be useful.

The Access developers implemented this functionality in a method unlike any other in Access. To ask a form whether or not it contains a procedure, you use the Windows SendMessage() function. Just like any other window, each form maintains its own message-handling queue, which it checks periodically to see if anyone has sent it any messages. This is specifically how each form redraws itself when you resize it: Windows sends it a message that tells it that it needs to redraw. Since you're allowed to create your own messages when writing Windows applications, the Access developers did just that. If you send a form this particular message (by number), along with the name of the procedure you're checking on, it will return either a True (non-zero) or a False (0) value, indicating whether or not the procedure already exists within that form's module.

The code you need, to include this functionality in your own applications, is simple. You first need to include a declaration for the SendMessage() function:

```
Declare Function glr_apiSendMessage Lib "User" Alias
➡ "SendMessage" (ByVal hwnd As Integer, ByVal intMsgId As
➡ Integer, ByVal intParam As Integer, param As Any) As Long
```

To actually do the work, you can use the glrCBFProcExists() function, which takes care of all the details for you. You pass it a form reference and the name of the procedure to check, and it does do the rest:

```
Function glrCBFProcExists(frm As Form, strProcName As String)
➡ As Integer

Const WM_PROCEXISTS = 1434

  glrCBFProcExists = glr_apiSendMessage((frm.hWnd),
  ➡ WM_PROCEXISTS, 0, ByVal strProcName) <> 0

End Function
```

For example, to check whether the module attached to frmListFonts contains a procedure called "FillFontSizes", you could use the expression

```
fProcExists = glrCBFProcExists(Forms!frmListFonts,
➡ "FillFontSizes")
```

After this call, fProcExists will be either True or False, depending on the existence of the requested procedure.

Call WinWord Help

The final function in MSAU200.DLL, glr_msauHelpFileCmd(), will be of little use to most Access developers, and we're mentioning it here just for the sake of completeness. This function allows you to pop up the Word for Windows Help file at a specified page. The Wizards include this functionality so they can open the Word Help file to finish up a mail merge from within Access, started from the Mail Merge Report Wizard.

Unfortunately, the function is hard coded to use only items available from Word-Help.DLL, and you must know the specific page IDs in the Word Help files for this function to be of any use. In case you care to dig in, you must declare the function like this:

```
Declare Function glr_msauHelpfileCmd Lib "MSAU200.DLL" Alias
➡ "#13"(ByVal hwndApp As Integer, ByVal strHelpFile As
➡ String, ByVal intCommand As Integer, ByVal lngData As
➡ Long) As Integer
```

To call the function, you can use code like this:

```
Function TestHelp()
    Dim hWnd As Integer
    Dim fTmp As Integer

' Word mail merge help context id
Const msgMailMerge = 4263
```

```
      hWnd = glr_apiGetActiveWindow()
      fTmp = glr_msauHelpfileCmd(hWnd, "winword.hlp", 1,
      ➥ mscMailMerge)
End Function
```

Since it seems unlikely that you'll ever use this particular function, we'll leave it at that.

Summary

This chapter has introduced the undocumented library MSAU200.DLL and demonstrated how to use each of its entry points. As with any other undocumented feature, the functions in MSAU200.DLL and their use could change with any future release. Everything in this chapter was current as of the writing of this book, and since all the features described here are used by the Access Wizards, chances are they won't change much.

Specifically, the sections in this chapter demonstrated how to

- Check for the existence of a file
- Split a full path reference into component pieces
- Retrieve the full path name for a file
- Create a copy of a file
- Use the File Open/File Save dialogs
- Use the Color Chooser dialog
- Use the Font Chooser dialog
- Retrieve the count of available fonts
- Retrieve the list of available fonts
- Retrieve the count of available font sizes for a font
- Retrieve the list of available font sizes for a font
- Retrieve information about a DLL or executable's national language

- Open the Word Help file to a specific topic
- Retrieve a bitmap from the common button bitmaps
- Reset the selected Help topic
- Check for the existence of a particular procedure in CBF

In addition, we've provided two sample forms, frmListFonts and frmButtonPix, that demonstrate a number of these techniques. You can easily import these forms directly from CH21.MDB into your own applications.

CHAPTER

TWENTY-TWO

Making Sense of Security

- Making your databases secure

- Programmatically manipulating security

- Listing all users with blank passwords

- Encrypting your databases

- Solving common security problems

Access uses a sophisticated workgroup-based security model that you can use to secure data, code, and design objects. Thanks to changes that Microsoft made for version 2.0, you now have a more secure model, finer control over permissions, and the ability to programmatically manipulate account and permission information. If you found Access 1.x's security system confusing, however, you won't find any solace in version 2.0 since it's essentially the same model. But if you take some time to understand the security model and don't expect it to work like simpler database-based models, you'll find that it starts to make a lot of sense and is well suited for securing your databases.

In this chapter we cover Access' security model in detail, outlining how and why it works the way it does and how to avoid common "gotchas." We also show you how to manipulate security programmatically using Access' security objects. In addition, we introduce several generic security functions that serve both as good programming examples and as a ready-to-use package of security management functions.

> **NOTE** Security in Access is a function of the database engine, Jet, not the Access User Interface (UI). (The Jet engine is discussed in Chapters 1 and 16.) While the Access UI provides one means of managing security, Jet maintains security no matter what the client application—Access, Visual Basic, or other programs gaining access through the Access ODBC driver. Thus, in this chapter we use the term *Jet security* rather than *Access security*.

Security Basics

Jet uses a *workgroup-based* security model rather than the more common database-based model that most other desktop database management systems use. Under the simpler file-oriented model, security revolves around a database and is self contained within the confines of that database. Each database has its own security system that is independent of others. In contrast, Jet security is workgroup based, which means that every database used by members of a workgroup shares the same security system.

Security Based on Users, Not Passwords

In addition to being workgroup based, Jet security is based on *users and their permissions*, not passwords. Most desktop databases employ password-based security, if they implement any security features at all. In these systems users enter a password that identifies them to the system as valid users. Every user who shares a given security level shares that same password, so the system is incapable of identifying individual users. Jet's security model, however, requires each user to have both a user name and a password. The password merely verifies that users are who they claim to be. Once verified, the password leaves the picture. With Jet, users manage their own individual passwords, which they can change at will without affecting other users. Passwords can be more secure since they're not shared by gaggles of users.

In a password-based system, each object has passwords associated with it that define its security. For example, the Orders table in Paradox might have a read-only password and a read/write password, so a user named Doug who knew the password to both would have read/write access to the table. With Jet, however, an object doesn't have any associated passwords or permissions. Instead, a user (or a group of users) has an associated set of permissions on a per-object basis. Thus, in Access (Jet), the user Doug or the PowerUsers group of which he is a member might have ReadData and UpdateData permissions for the Orders table.

Two Parts to Security

Jet Security is made up of two parts:

- *User and group accounts and their passwords for a particular workgroup* are stored in the SystemDB file. This file, usually kept centrally on a file server in a multiuser environment, is, by default, called SYSTEM.MDA.

- *Object permissions* are stored in each database.

For example, the security system for a consulting company called Access Only Consulting (AOC), with three employees and four Access databases, might look like that shown in Figure 22.1. The workgroup for this company is defined by their SystemDB file, SYSTEM.MDA. In this file are stored the three user accounts—Joe, Mary, and Sally—and two groups—Managers and Programmers. AOC's SystemDB file would store the user accounts and their passwords, as well as the information that Sally and Joe were members of the Managers group and that Joe and Mary were members of the Programmers group. In Jet, users can be members of multiple groups.

Each of the AOC databases, PROJECTS.MDB, ACCNTNG.MDB, WIZBANG.MDB, and GOVPROJ.MDB, would be tied to the AOC SystemDB file. In each of these databases, Jet stores the access rights to each of the database objects. Thus, for example, the Managers group might have Administer rights on the table tblCustomers in ACCNTNG.MDB, while the Programmers group might have only ReadData and UpdateData rights for this table. The rights for this table and for all the other objects in ACCNTNG.MDB would be stored in the database.

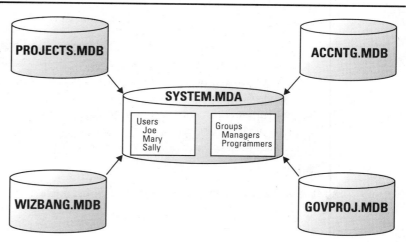

FIGURE 22.1:

Security system for the Access Only Consulting company. SYSTEM.MDA stores three user and two group accounts. Object permissions are stored in each of the four databases.

How to Turn It On

Security in Jet is always on; it can't be turned off. The security system, however, remains invisible until you're ready to use it. This is possible because of the presence of several default user and group accounts.

Overriding Jet's Default Logon Attempt

Sometimes when you are developing an application, it would be nice if you could log on as a user, even when the Admin password is blank. You might want to do this, for example, to test out a user logging system. You can override Jet's attempt to log you on as Admin by using a startup option. For example, you can start Access as user Charles with the password Barkley using the following:

```
MSACCESS.EXE /User Charles /Pwd Barkley
```

Note, however, that this is useful only during testing. Your database will be anything but secure under this scenario.

Every SystemDB file starts out with three predefined group accounts (Admins, Users, and Guests) and two predefined user accounts (Admin and Guest). None of these built-in accounts can be deleted using the Access UI. Jet is able to keep security invisible until needed by using these special accounts. (If you don't take the time to fully understand the special nature of these accounts, you may be leaving yourself open to security breaches. This issue is discussed in detail in the sections "Special Status: Built-In Accounts" and "Common Security Problems and Their Solutions" later in this chapter.)

When a user starts an Access session (or tries to connect to Jet using VB), Jet always attempts to log on the user as the user Admin with a blank password. If this logon attempt fails, only then does Jet prompt the user for a user name and password using the Logon dialog. Thus, as long as you keep the Admin password blank (a zero-length string), security remains invisible. Well, almost. You can still create new users and groups and assign permissions to objects.

Managing Security

You have two ways to manage security with Jet: the Access security menus and data access objects (DAO). They are described in the following sections.

Security Menus

The Access menus provide a simple interface for managing security. They're outlined in the following table:

Menu Command	Use
Permissions	Sets the permissions on new and existing database container objects for user and group accounts
Users	Creates or deletes user accounts, clears account passwords, and adds and removes users from groups
Groups	Creates or deletes group accounts
Change Password	Changes the password of the currently logged-on user (If you're a member of the Admins group, you can use the Users dialog to clear the password of another user.)
Change Owner	Views and changes the owner of each database object. If you have the necessary permissions, you can assign ownership to another user or group. You can also use this command to view, but not change, the owner of the database itself
Print Security	Prints the names of users, groups, or both. Permissions are not included in the reports

You can use the Change Owner command to transfer ownership of an object from one user to another. You can also use this command, which is new to version 2.0, to transfer ownership to a *group* account. The Print Security command is also new but rather disappointing in that it prints only the users and groups in the workgroup, not any permissions for database objects.

Data Access Objects

Prior to version 2.0, Jet security was strictly a user interface affair. Fortunately, with the introduction of version 2.0, Microsoft added the ability to programmatically manipulate security. Using DAO, you can even do things that aren't possible using the Access menus. The DAO security model is discussed in detail in the section "Security DAO in Action" later in this chapter.

Workgroups

Security in Jet revolves around *workgroups*. At the interface level, a workgroup is defined as a group of users who work together. At the Jet level, a workgroup is defined as all users sharing the same SystemDB file.

The SystemDB file is a database library, by default called SYSTEM.MDA (see Chapter 20 for more details on libraries), that Access and Jet use to store a number of pieces of information having to do with users, including

- User account names, their personal identifiers (PIDs), and passwords
- Group account names and their PIDs
- Information regarding which users belong to which groups
- Various user preference settings, including custom toolbar settings
- The list of the last four opened databases (for each user)

In a multiuser environment you can choose to place the SystemDB file either on the file server or on each workstation. Usually, you'll want to place it on the file server, which makes the maintenance of user and group accounts much easier. On the other hand, since the SystemDB file is accessed repeatedly during the execution of an application, you could reduce network traffic by placing a copy of the SystemDB file on each workstation.

> **TIP**
>
> We recommend placing the SystemDB file on the network file server unless performance or network traffic becomes a major concern. If these concerns do arise, you can always change to local SystemDB files. Note, however, that the change may have little noticeable effect on performance and that this effect may be greatly overshadowed by the increased maintenance burden.

Creating a New Workgroup

Microsoft includes a utility program called the Workgroup Administrator (WRKGADM.EXE) that you can use to create a new workgroup (SystemDB file) or to change to another workgroup. If you choose to create a new workgroup, you are met by the Workgroup Owner Information dialog, as shown in Figure 22.2.

Jet is able to uniquely identify your workgroup by running each entry through an encryption algorithm to produce a unique workgroup Security ID (SID). When generating the workgroup SID, the Workgroup program ignores the case of the Name and Organization fields but takes case into account for the Workgroup ID field.

> **TIP**
>
> Since the SystemDB file is such a vital part of security, we recommend regularly backing up this file and storing a copy of it safely off site.
> You should also consider storing a copy of your Workgroup ID in hardcopy form in a secure off-site location.

By default, Jet takes your user and organization name from the Access installation parameters, which you can view using the Help ➤ About Microsoft Access command. This is the default information it displays when you create a new workgroup using the Workgroup Administrator program. But you can change this information to anything you like at this time (but not at any other time). If you do this, no one

FIGURE 22.2:

The information entered into the Workgroup Owner Information dialog is used to uniquely identify a workgroup.

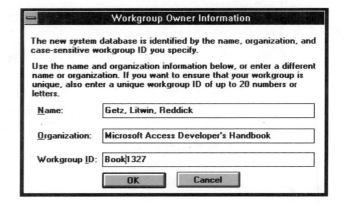

will ever be able to determine what you entered for these two fields. This can be an advantage in that it makes it more difficult for others to re-create a duplicate SystemDB even if they discover your Workgroup ID, but it's also a disadvantage if you fail to keep a record of the entries and need to regenerate the file at a later time.

NOTE The workgroup ID is the 0–20-character string *you* enter. The workgroup SID, however, is a binary ID# that *Jet generates* by combining your Workgroup ID with your user and organization names using an elaborate encryption algorithm.

The third field in the Workgroup Owner Information dialog, Workgroup ID, is the most critical one. You can enter from 0 to 20 numbers or *case-sensitive* letters into this field. Take extra care to keep this entry secret but backed up somewhere off site. If you leave this field blank, you'll be warned, but you won't be prevented from proceeding.

Once you commit your entries to these fields, you will never be able to view or change them again.

WARNING Access creates a default SystemDB named SYSTEM.MDA when you install Access. To create this workgroup, it uses the name and company installation parameters and a *blank* workgroup ID. *This makes the default SystemDB file unsecured!* When you need to secure a database, the first thing you should do is create a brand-new secured SystemDB file.

Jet uses the workgroup SID to uniquely identify the Admins group account—*not* the Admin user account—in the workgroup. The significance of this built-in account is discussed in the section "Special Status: Built-In Accounts" later in this chapter.

Changing Workgroups

You can also use the Workgroup Administrator program to change workgroups. This is really just a convenience issue, however, since the program is merely changing the name of the SystemDB file referenced in the SystemDB topic of the Options section of MSACC20.INI. If you prefer, you can manually change this entry using Notepad or another text editor.

User and Group Accounts

Jet uses user and group accounts to dole out security permissions. Only users and groups can have permissions. Both types of accounts share the same name space, so you need to ensure that all names are unique for a workgroup.

> **TIP**
>
> Microsoft uses the convention whereby user names are singular and group names are plural (for example, the Admin user and the Admins group). We've adopted (and recommend that you adopt) this same account-naming scheme.

In Access, you use the Security ➤ Users command to create and manage user accounts (see Figure 22.3). You use the Security ➤ Groups command to create and delete group accounts.

Only members of the Admins account can add, delete, and change the membership for user and group accounts.

PIDs, SIDs, and Passwords

When you create a new user or group account in Jet, you must enter a non-blank, 4–20 character, case-sensitive *personal identifier* (*PID*). Jet combines the name of the account with the PID to create a *security identifier* (*SID*) for each user or group account. Once you've entered a PID, you can *never* view or change it.

FIGURE 22.3:

The user Joe is a member of the Users, Programmers, and Managers groups.

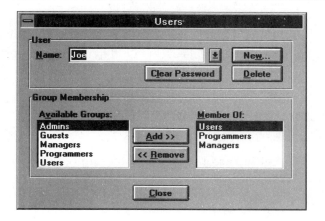

We recommend that only a single database administrator create accounts and PIDs and that this individual keep a written off-site record. This will be useful if someone deletes an account that you need to re-create at a later date. This same person should keep a written off-site record of the user and organization names and the workgroup ID entered into the Workgroup Owner Information dialog, as well as a recent backup of the SystemDB file.

When you create a new user account (not a group account), you must also enter a 0–14-character, case-sensitive password. Unlike PIDs, passwords can be blank. Jet uses passwords only at logon time to verify the identity of a user. Passwords are not part of Jet security except to verify the identity of users.

Only users can change their own passwords, but members of the Admins group can clear another user's password. (This is a restriction of the Access UI—using DAO, an Admins member can change another user's password without knowing the old password.) You *can't* view a password, once it's been entered, using either the UI or DAO.

Both passwords and PIDs are stored in the SystemDB file in an encrypted format.

Jet uses the internally generated account SIDs to uniquely identify user and group accounts across workgroups. Except for some of the special built-in accounts that are discussed in the section "Special Status: Built-In Accounts" a little later in this chapter, Jet treats users in different workgroups with the same name but different PIDs (and thus different SIDs) as distinct users.

Groups Are More than Collections of Users

A group account is more than simply a collection of users. In many situations you can use a group account in place of a user account. The following table contrasts the two types of accounts:

Attribute	User Accounts	Group Accounts
Has associated permissions for objects	Yes	Yes
Has a personal ID (PID)	Yes	Yes
May own objects	Yes	Yes
May log on/has password	Yes	No
May own a database	Yes	No

Although you cannot log on as a group, you can do almost anything else with a group account, including, with the introduction of version 2.0, own objects. (Previously, only users could own objects.) Since group accounts can't be used to log on, however, the only way for a group to gain ownership of an object is to use the Security ➤ Change Owner command. A group account may not own a database.

Special Status: Built-In Accounts

As mentioned earlier in this chapter, the Jet security system includes several built-in accounts that make it possible for security to remain invisible until it's needed. These built-in accounts include the Admin and Guest *users* and the Admins, Users and Guests *groups*. It's important that you understand how these "special status" accounts work; otherwise your database won't be secure.

The two special user accounts and their associated groups are summarized in the following table:

User Account	Member of Groups	Can User Be Deleted?	Same SID for All Workgroups?
Admin	Admins, Users	No	Yes
Guest	Guests	No	Yes

Neither of the special user accounts can ever be deleted from a workgroup.

The three special group accounts and their members are summarized in the following table:

Group Account	Default Members	Can Default User Be Removed?	Same SID for All Workgroups?
Admins	Admin	Yes, but only if another Admin user exists	No
Users	Admin	No	Yes
Guests	Guest	No	Yes

None of the special group accounts can ever be deleted from a workgroup. Each of these accounts is described in more detail in the next few sections.

Admin User

All new workgroups initially contain the Admin user account with a blank password. As mentioned previously, unless a startup option is used to override this behavior, Jet always attempts to log on as the Admin user with a blank password. Only if this logon attempt fails does Jet prompt the user for a user name and password. Since this is the default user account until you change its password, the Admin user will often own the database and all its objects. (Ownership is discussed later in this chapter in the section "Ownership.")

Beginning with Access version 2.0, the Admin user cannot be deleted. (Prior to 2.0 you could delete this user account.) You can, however, remove Admin from the

Admins group as long as Admins has at least one other member. This is one of the steps for making a database secure that are discussed in the section "Common Security Problems and Their Solutions " later in this chapter. *The Admin user will always have the same SID for all workgroups.*

The Admin user is somewhat misnamed; even though it initially owns all objects and is a member of the Admins group, it has no special administrative powers of its own. It might have been more accurate for Microsoft to have named the Admin user account User or DefaultUser.

As long as the Admin user is not the current user when creating objects, it will not have any permissions on newly created objects.

Admins Group

The Admins group is uniquely identified across workgroups. (This differs from all other built-in accounts, which are not unique from one workgroup to another.) In fact, the Admins group draws its SID from the workgroup SID created by the Workgroup Administrator program. Jet requires that there always be at least one member of the Admins group. This requirement makes it impossible to have a workgroup with no administrator.

Members of the Admins group have special, irrevocable administrative rights. (Their membership in Admins, however, *is* revocable by another Admins member.) As long as they are members of Admins, they can grant themselves permissions to all database objects in the databases in their workgroup. (Access, but not the Jet engine, enforces this. It is possible, using DAO, to revoke Administer permission from the Admins group for an object. The object's owner will retain Administer permissions for the object.) In addition, members of Admins always have the ability to manage user and group accounts in their workgroup.

Because of the special, irrevocable nature of the Admins group and the fact that its SID is tied to the workgroup's SID, it is important that you *not* rely on the Access installation program to create your secure SystemDB file. Instead, you must use the Workgroup Administrator program to create a new secure workgroup SID with a non-blank Workgroup ID entry (see the section "Creating a New Workgroup" earlier in this chapter).

By default, when you create a new object, the Admins group gets full permissions to the new object. (You can change this default assignment of permissions by using the Security ➤ Permissions command or DAO.)

Users Group

The Users group is the default group for all Access users. All built-in user accounts, as well as new user accounts created using the Access UI, will be members of the Users group. Access won't allow you to remove any user from the Users group, with the exception of the built-in Guest user. (This is an Access limitation, however, not one that Jet enforces. Using DAO, you can remove user accounts from the Users group. Note, however, that if you do this, these users will no longer be able to log on to Access.)

Along with the Admin user account, it is the presence of the Users group account that allows Jet to keep security invisible until needed. This is possible because the Users group account has the same SID across all workgroups. Thus, if you wish to secure a workgroup, you must remove all object permissions from the Users group and refrain from using it to assign permissions. On the other hand, the easiest way to make a secure database unsecured is to assign full object permissions for each of its objects to the Users group.

By default, the Users group gets full permissions on newly created objects. (You can change this default assignment of permissions.)

Guest User

The built-in Guest account is the sole (default) member of the Guests group. Since its SID is the same across all workgroups, we do not recommend assigning any permissions to this user account. If you do want to create some set of minimum permissions for visiting users, you'd be better off using the Guests *group* to assign these permissions. By default, the Guest account gets no permissions on newly created objects.

Guests Group

The Guests group is a built-in group account you can use as a default no-permissions account. You might use the Guests account, whose SID is the same across all workgroups, to dispense certain minimum rights to *all* users. Use of this account along with Users allows you to maintain two levels of minimum-security permissions. For example, you might assign ReadData permission for all objects (or some subset of objects) to the Guests account and assign UpdateData permission for all objects (or some subset of objects) to the Users account. By default, the Guests group includes one member: Guest.

Also by default, beginning with Access 2.0, the Guests group gets no permissions on newly created objects. (This is a change from version 1.x, where the Guests group received, by default, ReadData permissions on all newly created objects.)

Assigning Permissions

Using the Access UI you assign permissions to database objects with the Security ➤ Permissions command (see Figure 22.4). Although you can change only one type of object at a time, you can select multiple objects (in contiguous or discontiguous groups) in the Permissions dialog. Jet stores the permissions for database objects and their corresponding SIDs in the database itself.

FIGURE 22.4:

The Programmers group account has ReadDesign and ModifyDesign permissions for the basDAOExamples module.

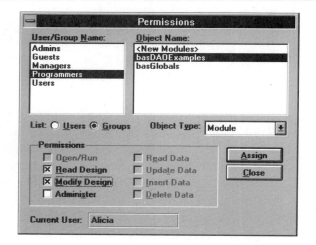

Which Objects Have Which Permissions?

Each database container object in Jet has a set of associated permissions you can set. Each type of object has a different set of settable permissions. For example, tables and queries don't have an Open/Run permission. Instead, they have several permissions that control how data may be read or updated. On the other hand, forms, reports, and macros have no data permissions but do have an Open/Run permission. Table 22.1 lists each object and its permission set.

Permissions exist only for the database itself and database container objects. Similarly, in DAO, only containers and documents have permissions. Controls, columns, parameters, toolbars, and other Jet and Access objects do not have permissions—which means they are not individually securable.

TABLE 22.1: Permission Sets for Each Type of Object

Object	Open/ Run	Read- Design	Modify- Design	Admin- ister	Read- Data	Update- Data	Insert- Data	Delete- Data	OpenEx- clusive
Table		✓	✓	✓	✓	✓	✓	✓	
Query		✓	✓	✓	✓	✓	✓	✓	
Form	✓	✓	✓	✓					
Report	✓	✓	✓	✓					
Macro	✓	✓	✓	✓					
Module		✓	✓	✓					
Database	✓								✓

Version 2.0 has made several changes to permissions:

- The 1.x Execute permission has been renamed to Open/Run.

- The 1.x ModifyData permission has been replaced with three new permissions offering finer update granularity: UpdateData, InsertData, and DeleteData.

- 2.0 introduces an Administer permission. This permission was available previously only to members of the Admins group.

- 2.0 supports two permissions for the database itself: Open/Run and OpenExclusive.

This last change is a significant one. Now you can prevent users from being able to open a database by setting the Open/Run permission for the database to False. In addition, you can use the OpenExclusive permission to block a user from opening a database exclusively.

Permissions are not completely independent of each other; some permissions imply other permissions. For example, you can't have UpdateData permissions if you don't also have ReadDesign and ReadData permissions. Thus, UpdateData permission also implies these other permissions. Table 22.2 shows the interdependencies of permissions for table and query objects. If you have the permission in the first column, you also have the checked permissions to the right.

TABLE 22.2: Relationship between Permissions for Table and Query Objects

Permission	Read-Design	Modify-Design	Administer	Read-Data	Update-Data	Insert-Data	Delete-Data
ReadDesign	N/A						
ModifyDesign	✓	N/A		✓	✓		✓
Administer	✓	✓	N/A	✓	✓	✓	✓
ReadData	✓			N/A			
UpdateData	✓			✓	N/A		
InsertData	✓			✓		N/A	
DeleteData	✓			✓			N/A

Permissions for New Objects

In addition to existing objects, you can set permissions on new objects. You do this by choosing <New *objectname*> in the Access Permissions dialog (see Figure 22.4). Although you can remove all permissions for new objects, this will *not* prevent users from creating new objects. And since they will become the owner of any objects they create, they can always grant themselves Administer rights to any new objects.

Using DAO, however, you *can* prevent users from creating new objects. This is discussed in the section "Security DAO in Action" later in this chapter.

Explicit versus Implicit Permissions

Users in the Jet security model have both implicit and explicit permissions. *Explicit permissions* are those permissions explicitly given to users and associated directly with a user account. *Implicit permissions* are those permissions users inherit because of their membership in a group.

A user's set of permissions for an object will be based on the intersection of that user's explicit permissions and implicit permissions. A user's security level is always the *least restrictive* of that user's explicit permissions and the permissions of any and all groups to which the user belongs.

For example, say that user Joe has no permissions for the table tblCustomer. Joe also belongs to two groups: Managers and Programmers. The Managers group has Administer permissions (which implies all the other permissions for an object) for tblCustomer, and the Programmers group has only ReadDesign permissions for tblCustomer. Joe will have Administer permissions for tblCustomer because this is the least restrictive (or highest) permission for tblCustomer.

If you're a member of the Admins group, you can directly view and set the explicit permissions of users using the Access UI or DAO, but you can't do the same with implicit permissions. Instead, you view implicit permissions by noting the group membership of a user and then looking at the permissions for each of these groups. In order to change implied permissions, you must either modify the permissions for each of the groups to which a user belongs or add or remove the user from groups.

A common mistake made by the naive administrator is to revoke the explicit permissions of a user for an object without paying attention to the user's implied permissions. That administrator is then horrified to find that the user still has access to that object because of the user's implicit permissions.

Who Can Change Permissions?

The following users can change object permissions:

- Members of the Admins account (for the workgroup in which the database was created) can always change permissions on any users. These rights can never be taken away using the Access UI (but they can be taken away using DAO).

- An object's owner—either the user who created the object or the user or group to which ownership of the object was transferred—can always modify the permissions for the object. This includes the ability of owners to give themselves Administer permissions for the object, even if someone else previously revoked these privileges. These rights can never be taken away.

- Any user with explicit or implicit Administer permissions to the object can change the object's permissions. Another user with Administer rights may take away these rights.

- The database owner—the user who created the database—can always open a database and create new objects in it, even if the owner's rights to all the database's objects have been revoked. (The Access UI will allow members of the Admins group to *think* they have revoked the Open/Run permission from the database owner, but the owner will still be able to open the database.) The only way to remove these rights is to import all of a database's objects and delete the original database.

What Happens to Permissions for Deleted Accounts?

When you delete a user or group account from a workgroup for an account that still has associated permissions, those permissions remain in the database. This can be a security concern; if someone can re-create the account and its PID, that person has a *backdoor pass* into your secured database. Thus, it's important that you remove all permissions (and transfer any objects the to-be-deleted account owns to a new owner) before deleting an account.

If someone re-creates an account with the same name but a *different* PID, Jet treats that account as a completely different account. It will not inherit any of the old account's permissions, because its SID is different from the SID of the old account.

TIP

The CurrentUser( ) function returns only the name of a user and therefore cannot be counted on to distinguish between users with the same name but different SIDs (either in the same workgroup at different points in time or across workgroups). This might be an issue when you are using the value of CurrentUser( ) to branch in your code or log activity to a file.

When you use the Security ➤ Change Owners command to list the owner of an object whose account has been deleted, Access lists the owner as "<Unknown>".

Ownership

In addition to the permissions that are granted to accounts, you need to be aware of ownership because database owners and object owners have special privileges.

Who Owns a Database?

The user who creates a database is the database's owner. This user maintains special irrevocable rights to the database. As mentioned previously, this user will always be able to open the database. Only user accounts, not group accounts, can own databases.

Database ownership cannot be changed, but you can always create a new database using a different user account and import all the database's objects into another database. (This is how the Microsoft Security Wizard works; see the section "The Security Wizards" later in this chapter.) If you then delete the original database and rename the new database to the name of the original, you have effectively transferred its ownership. The account used to transfer ownership must have Read-Design and ReadData (where applicable) permissions to each of the database's objects.

You can use the Access Security ➤ Change Owners command to view, but not change, the database owner.

Who Owns a Database's Objects?

In addition to each database having an owner, each database container object has an owner. Initially, this is the user who created the object and may or may not be the same user account as the database owner.

A new feature in version 2.0 is that you can now view and change the ownership of database objects to another account, including a group account. You do this using the Access Security ➤ Change Owner command (see Figure 22.5).

FIGURE 22.5:

Using the Change Owner dialog, Alicia is about to change the ownership for three tables from Paul to the Managers group.

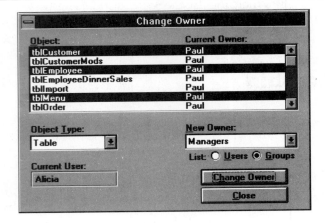

The new owner for an object may be a *group account*. This is especially useful when you are managing OwnerAccess queries, which are discussed in the next section.

OwnerAccess Queries

Queries created in Access QBE have a property, RunPermissions, that governs whether Jet uses the query user's permissions or the owner's permissions when checking the security permissions for each of the source tables in a query. In Access SQL, this property translates to the "WITH OWNERACCESS OPTION" clause.

This property allows you to present data to users who lack access rights to the underlying tables. Using this feature, you can effectively apply column-level and row-level security to a table.

For example, using an Owner Access query, you could let members of the Programmers group view and update all the columns in the tblEmployee table except for the Salary field. To do this, you would perform the following steps:

1. Remove all permissions to tblEmployee for the Programmers group.

2. Using an account that has ReadData and Update Data permissions to tblEmployee, create a query, qryEmployee, that includes all the columns from tblEmployee except Salary.

3. Set the RunPermissions of qryEmployee to "Owner's" (or include the "WITH OWNERACCESS OPTION" clause in the SQL statement for the query).

One problem with OwnerAccess queries is that Jet allows only the query's owner to save changes to the query. Even users with Administer rights to the query are prevented from saving changes to the query. This can present a problem if you are sharing the management of these queries among multiple users. In this case you may wish to transfer ownership of the query to a group account. You will, however, have to be the object's owner to change ownership.

TIP

If you're not the owner of an OwnerAccess query, you won't be able to save changes to the design or change the ownership of the query, even if you have Administer rights to the query. This can be problematic, especially if you are at an off-site location and need to modify the design of an OwnerAccess query. One way around this problem is to open the query in SQL view, copy its SQL statement to the clipboard, close the query, delete it, create a new query with the same name, paste the SQL statement into the new query, and save it using the old name. You will now be the owner of the new query, which will be identical to the old. (In order to use this work-around, you must have at least ModifyDesign permissions to the query and ReadData permissions to each of its source tables.)

Encryption

Although Microsoft did a lot with the introduction of version 2.0 of Access to shore up some of the 1.x security holes—the main hole was plugged by making the database system tables read-only—it is *not* impenetrable. A very knowledgeable hacker equipped with a low-level disk editor could go in and cut and paste SIDs to assume ownership of a database and its objects. The only way to guard against such a hacker is to encrypt the database. (Hacking your way into a database is far from a trivial task, but there are those who love such a challenge.)

Encrypting a database does not secure it. It is only one of a series of steps to properly secure a database. (These steps are discussed in more detail in the section "Securing a Database—Plugging Up the Holes" later in this chapter.)

Only the database owner or members of the Admins group can encrypt or decrypt a database. Jet uses an RSA- (Rivest, Shamir, and Adleman—the names of the inventors of the algorithm) based encryption algorithm with a key based on your workgroup ID to encrypt the database. Using Access, you can encrypt or decrypt a database using the File ➤ Encrypt/Decrypt Database command. The Access Security Wizard encrypts databases as its final step in securing a database.

It's important that you delete or safely archive all unencrypted versions of the encrypted databases to prevent security intrusions.

Encryption has two negative side effects. First, it reduces database performance (according to Microsoft estimates) by approximately 10 to 15 percent. Second, it makes the database uncompressible by programs such as PKZip, LHA, Stacker, and DoubleSpace. (You won't be prevented from compressing the database, but the compression step won't significantly reduce the size.)

The Security Wizards

Microsoft has created two Wizards for version 2.0 of Access: the Access 2.0 Security Wizard (SECURE20.MDA) and the Access 2.0 Security Conversion Wizard (SECCON20.MDA). Both Wizards are library add-ins. (You can download both Wizards from Microsoft's MSACCESS forum on CompuServe. SECURE20.MDA—but not SECCON20.MDA—is also included on the companion disk.)

WARNING The 2.0 Security Wizard *doesn't* check to see whether you are using the default Access installation SystemDB file, which may contain a blank (unsecured) Workgroup ID. Before running the Wizard, run the Workgroup Administrator application and create a new workgroup (SystemDB file) with User and Organization names that differ from the Access installation names. Choose a reasonably long workgroup ID that is not easily guessed. Remove all unsecured SystemDB files and store them away safely.

The *2.0 Security Wizard* is an update of the 1.1 Security Wizard, which has been completely rewritten using DAO. This Wizard takes a completely unsecured database and creates a new secured database. You must be a member of the Admins group to run the Wizard. The Security Wizard works by performing a number of steps, including the following:

1. It creates a new copy of the database that is owned by the user running the Wizard (who must be a member of the Admins group and cannot be the Admin or Guest user).

2. It transfers ownership of all the database objects to the new owner.

3. It rebuilds attached tables and relationships in the new database.

4. It removes all permissions on objects in the new database for the Users and Guests groups and the Admin and Guest users.

5. It encrypts the database.

The new *Security Conversion Wizard* converts your 1.x SystemDB and 1.x databases to take advantage of the new enhanced security model. It performs a number of steps, some of which require you to exit Access and restart the Wizard. These steps include the following:

1. It copies your user and group accounts from your 1.x-created SystemDB to a 2.0 SystemDB.

2. It requires you to enter new PIDs and passwords for the newly created user and group accounts.

3. It takes one or more databases and re-creates them using the new 2.0 SystemDB.

Databases converted using the Security Conversion Wizard will *not* be encrypted.

Programming Security Using Data Access Objects

So far in this chapter we have focused on defining the Jet security model and showing you how to manipulate it using the Access User Interface. You can also use Jet data access objects (DAO) to manipulate security. In fact, DAO lets you manipulate Jet security in ways that the Access UI does not support.

Programming security with DAO revolves around two object hierarchies that correspond to the division in Jet security discussed in the section "Two Parts to Security" earlier in this chapter.

The User and Groups Hierarchy

You manipulate user and group accounts—the elements of security that are stored in the SystemDB file—using the object hierarchy shown in Figure 22.6.

User and group objects are direct descendants of a workspace object; they are independent of any database objects. This is consistent with the physical location of the user and group account information—in the SystemDB file.

The user and group object hierarchies overlap. Each user object contains a *Groups* collection that contains the names of all the groups to which a user belongs. Similarly, each group object contains a *Users* collection that contains the name of each user belonging to that group.

For example, you might enumerate the members of the Managers group to the Debug window using the function shown in Listing 22.1.

FIGURE 22.6:

Data access objects hierarchy for user and groups

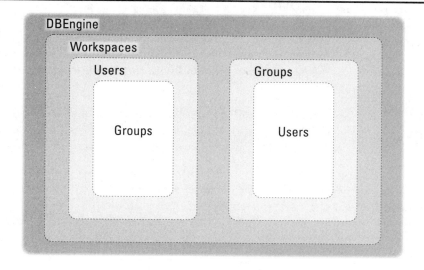

Listing 22.1

```
Function ListManagers()

    Dim wrk As WorkSpace
    Dim gruManagers As Group
    Dim intI As Integer

    Set wrk = DBEngine.Workspaces(0)
    Set gruManagers = wrk.Groups!Managers

    For intI = 0 To gruManagers.Users.Count - 1
        Debug.Print gruManagers.Users(intI).Name
    Next intI

End Function
```

The Collections and Documents Hierarchy

You manipulate object permissions—the elements of security that are stored in databases and move around with the database—using the object hierarchy shown in Figure 22.7.

Unlike user and group objects, permissions are manipulated using container and document objects that *are* descendants of the database object. Again, this is consistent with the physical location of these security elements.

FIGURE 22.7:

Data access objects hierarchy for containers and documents. You use these object collections to manage security permissions.

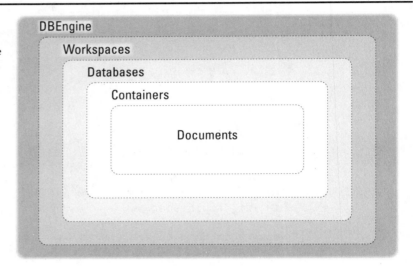

Managing Accounts

Using DAO, you can create, delete, and list user and group accounts. In addition, you can list the groups a user belongs to and the users who are members of a group. You must be a member of the Admins group to perform these activities.

Users Collections and User Objects

There are two types of collections of users: collections of a workspace and collections of a group account. The Users collection for a workspace contains all the user accounts for that workspace. The Users collection for a group account contains all the members of the group.

The Users collection has a single *property*, Count, and three *methods*, described in the following table:

Method	Purpose/Comments
Append	Adds a new user to a collection
Delete	Removes a user from a collection
Refresh	Refreshes the collection. Especially useful in a multiuser setting

You could use the following code to enumerate the names of all the users in the Users collection of the default workspace:

```
Dim wrk As WorkSpace
Dim intI As Integer

Set wrk = DBEngine.Workspaces(0)

Debug.Print "The Users collection has the following ";
➡ wrk.Users.Count; " members:"
For intI = 0 To wrk.Users.Count - 1
   Debug.Print "(" & intI & ") " & wrk.Users(intI).Name
Next intI
```

The Users collection contains User objects. User objects have three *properties*:

Property	Purpose/Comment
Name	Name of the user. Read/write for new users not yet appended to the Users collection. Read-only otherwise
Password	Case-sensitive password for the user account. Write-only for new users not yet appended to the Users collection. Not available otherwise

Property	Purpose/Comment
PID	Case-sensitive personal identifier for the user account. Write-only for new users not yet appended to the Users collection. Not available otherwise

User objects also have two *methods:*

Method	Purpose/Comment
CreateGroup	Creates a new group object. When appended to the user object's Groups collection, this method adds the user to that group
NewPassword	Replaces a password with a new one

To create a new user account, you use the CreateUser method of a workspace object.

Groups Collections and Group Objects

There are two types of collections of groups: collections of a workspace and collections of a user account. The Groups collection for a workspace contains all the group accounts for that workspace. The Groups collection for a user account contains all the groups to which that user belongs.

The Groups collection has a single *property*, Count, and three *methods*, described in the following table:

Method	Purpose/Comments
Append	Adds a new group to a collection
Delete	Removes a group from a collection
Refresh	Refreshes the collection. Especially useful in a multiuser setting

You could use the following code to enumerate the names of all the groups in the Groups collection of the default workspace:

```
Dim wrk As WorkSpace
Dim intI As Integer
```

```
Set wrk = DBEngine.Workspaces(0)

Debug.Print "The Groups collection has the following ";
➥ wrk.Groups.Count; " members:"
For intI = 0 To wrk.Groups.Count - 1
    Debug.Print "(" & intI & ") " & wrk.Groups(intI).Name
Next intI
```

The Groups collection contains Group objects. Group objects have two *properties:*

Property	Purpose/Comment
Name	Name of the group. Read/write for new groups not yet appended to the Groups collection. Read-only otherwise
PID	Case-sensitive personal identifier for the group account. Write-only for new groups not yet appended to the Groups collection. Not available otherwise

Groups don't have passwords; you can't log on as a member of a group. Group objects have a single *method:*

Method	Purpose/Comment
CreateUser	Creates a new user object. When appended to the group object's Users collection, this method adds the user to the group

To create a new group account, you use the CreateGroup method of a workspace object.

Programming Permissions

Permissions are properties of *documents* and their *containers.* Like other DAO collections, the Containers collection and Documents collection have a single property, Count, that indicates the number of objects in the collection. These two collections also have a single method, Refresh, that you can use to make sure the collections are current in a multiuser environment.

Documents and Containers

Container and document objects (discussed in Chapter 6) have several properties. They are listed in Table 22.3.

TABLE 22.3: Properties of Containers and Their Documents

Object	Property	Description
Container	Inherit	A property that determines whether any changes are inherited by new objects. If you set permissions on a container and set Inherit to True, Jet uses these permissions when creating new documents for the container
	Name	Read-only. The name of the container. For example, the Tables container contains a database's tables and queries
	Owner	Read/write. The user or group account that owns the object. By default, all object containers are owned by the engine user (This can be changed, however, using DAO.)
	Permissions	Read/write. A long integer that stores permission information for the container. When you use this property with the Inherit property, you can set permissions for new documents of a container
	UserName	Read/write. When you read or write permissions for a container, the permissions are account specific. By default, this property contains the current user name. You use UserName to view or set permissions for different user and group accounts
Document	Container	Read only. The container to which the document belongs
	DateCreated	Read-only. The date the document was created
	LastUpdated	Read only. The date the document was last changed. For table objects, this is the date the schema was last changed, *not* the date the data was last changed
	Name	Read-only. The name of the document. For example, a form might be named "frmNewOrders"
	Owner	Read/write. The user or group account that owns the object. By default, the owner is the document's creator

TABLE 22.3: Properties of Containers and Their Documents (continued)

Object	Property	Description
	Permissions	Read/write. A long integer that stores permission information for the document
	UserName	Read/write. When you read or write permissions for a document, the permissions are account specific. By default, this property equals the current user. You can use UserName to view or set permissions for different user and group accounts

Permission Constants

Microsoft predefines several database security constants in the Declarations sections of the modules AbcConstants and DataConstants in UTILITY.MDA. Since this library is always loaded, you can use these constants to view and set permissions. They are outlined in Table 22.4.

TABLE 22.4: Security Constants and Their Relationship to Object Permissions

Constant	Value	Object It Applies to	Permission
DB_SEC_NOACCESS	&H0&	All container objects and their containers	No rights
DB_SEC_FULLACCESS	&HFFFFF	All container objects and their containers	Full rights, including Administer
DB_SEC_DELETE	&H10000	All container objects and their containers	Part of the Administer right that allows you to delete an object
DB_SEC_READSEC	&H20000	All container objects and their containers	Part of the Administer right that allows you to read the security of an object
DB_SEC_WRITESEC	&H40000	All container objects and their containers	Part of the Administer right that allows you to write the security of an object
DB_SEC_WRITEOWNER	&H80000	All container objects and their containers	Part of the Administer right that allows you to transfer ownership of an object
DB_SEC_READDEF	&H4&	Table/Query	ReadDesign

TABLE 22.4: Security Constants and Their relationships to Object Permissions (continued)

Constant	Value	Object It Applies to	Permission
DB_SEC_ WRITEDEF	&H8& + DB_SEC_READDEF + DB_SEC_DELETE	Table/Query	WriteDesign
DB_SEC_ RETRIEVEDATA	&H10& + DB_SEC_READDEF	Table/Query	ReadData
DB_SEC_ INSERTDATA	&H20&	Table/Query	InsertData
DB_SEC_ REPLACEDATA	&H40&	Table/Query	UpdateData
DB_SEC_ DELETEDATA	&H80&	Table/Query	DeleteData
DB_SEC_FRMRPT_ READDEF	&H4&	Form/Report	ReadDesign
DB_SEC_FRMRPT_ WRITEDEF	&H8& + DB_SEC_FRMRPT_READ DEF + DB_SEC_DELETE	Form/Report	WriteDesign
DB_SEC_FRMRPT_ EXECUTE	&H100&	Form/Report	Open/Run
DB_SEC_MAC_ READDEF	&HA&	Macro	ReadDesign
DB_SEC_MAC_ WRITEDEF	&H6& + DB_SEC_DELETE	Macro	WriteDesign
DB_SEC_MAC_ EXECUTE	&H8&	Macro	Open/Run
DB_SEC_MOD_ READDEF	&H2&	Module	ReadDesign
DB_SEC_MOD_ WRITEDEF	&H4& + DB_SEC_MOD_READDEF + DB_SEC_DELETE	Module	WriteDesign
DB_SEC_CREATE	&H1&	Container	Right to create new objects
DB_SEC_ DBOPEN	&H2&	Database	Open/Run
DB_SEC_ DBEXCLUSIVE	&H4&	Database	Open Exclusive
DB_SEC_ DBCREATE	&H1&	System Database	Right to create new databases

Note that some of the values are defined as the sum of other permissions. This is how they have been defined in the declarations in SYSTEM.MDA, and it means that the one permission implies (or includes) the other. For example, since DB_SEC_MAC_WRITEDEF equals &H6& + DB_SEC_DELETE, this means that if you have this permission (WriteDesign for a macro), you also have permission to delete the macro.

The use of these constants is discussed in the next few sections.

Reading Permissions

You can read the permissions of an object simply by checking the value of the Permissions property of the object. This returns the long integer corresponding to the user's permissions for the object. For example, you could query the permission of the tblOrder table and store the value in the variable lngPermission with the following assignment statement. (This assumes that you have previously set the db object variable to point to a database.)

```
lngPermission =
    db.Containers!Tables.Documents!tblOrder.Permissions
```

Often, you'll want to check whether a user has some minimum permissions to an object. You can do this using bitwise arithmetic (also referred to by programmers as *bit twiddling*). For example, you could use the function shown in Listing 22.2 to determine whether the user Sally has read permission for tblCustomer.

Listing 22.2

```
Function SallyCanRead()

    Dim db As Database
    Dim doc As Document

    Set db = DBEngine.Workspaces(0).Databases(0)
    Set doc = db.Containers!Tables.Documents!tblCustomer

    doc.UserName = "Sally"
    SallyCanRead = (doc.Permissions And DB_SEC_RETRIEVEDATA)< > 0

End Function
```

If Sally has ReadData permission to tblCustomer, SallyCanRead() returns True; otherwise it returns False. The trick in this example is to use the bitwise And operator to mask off the complete permissions with only the permission you are interested in—in this case, DB_SEC_RETRIEVEDATA (ReadData permission).

> **NOTE**
>
> This function queries permissions for the user Sally—her explicit permissions—only. It doesn't take into account whether she has permission by virtue of her membership in any groups—her implicit permissions. With a little extra code, however, it could. The glrCheckPermission() function introduced in the section "Checking for a Specific Permission" later in the chapter does just this.

Writing Permissions

Writing permissions is similar to reading them. You have two choices when writing the permissions of an object:

- You can replace the existing permissions with a brand-new set of permissions.

- You can add or subtract a permission on top of the existing permissions.

To *replace* a set of permissions, you simply set the permissions to the new value. For example, you could change the permission for tblOrder to give the user Modify-Design permission using the following code:

```
Set doc = db.Containers!Tables.Documents!tblOrder
doc.Permissions = DB_SEC_WRITEDEF
```

You *add* a permission on top of the existing permissions using the bitwise Or operator. For example, you could use the following code to add ModifyDesign permission to the existing set of permissions:

```
Set doc = db.Containers!Tables.Documents!tblOrder
doc.Permissions = doc.Permissions Or DB_SEC_WRITEDEF
```

Using this method of assigning permissions is often preferable because it guards against inadvertently removing other permissions the user may have. For example, if the user also had ReadData permission to tblOrder, that permission would be preserved using this technique. This would not be true in the previous example.

You can *subtract* a permission from a user, while preserving all other permissions, by applying a bitwise And Not to the permission. For example, to take away the same permission from a user, replace the second line in the preceding example with the following:

```
doc.Permissions = doc.Permissions And Not DB_SEC_WRITEDEF
```

Security DAO in Action

The best way to learn DAO is to study the examples of others. To facilitate your learning, we have created a number of generic security utility functions to illustrate some of the possibilities. These functions are all contained in the basSecurityUtilities module of the CH22.MDB database. The next several sections describe these functions in detail.

> **NOTE**
> The functions presented here often work on a single object and a single user, which are passed to the function as parameters. This helps to make these functions generic. Unfortunately, it also makes them inefficient to use if you need to work on many objects or many users. In these cases you'd be better off using less-generic functions that perform bulk security operations.

Creating a New User Account

The function glrNewUser() adds a new user to the workgroup. It takes as its parameters the name of the new user, the new user's PID, and the new user's password. It returns True (–1) if it is successful. This function requires the user running it to be a member of the Admins group. The function can be found in Listing 22.3.

Listing 22.3

```
Function glrNewUser (ByVal pstrName As String, ByVal pstrPID As
➡ String, ByVal pstrPW As String) As Integer

    On Error GoTo glrNewUserErr

    Dim wrk As WorkSpace
    Dim usrNew As User
    Dim strMsg As String
    Dim strProcName As String

    strProcName = "glrNewUser"

    ' Initialize return value
    glrNewUser = False

    Set wrk = DBEngine.Workspaces(0)

    ' Create new user account and append to the Users collection
    Set usrNew = wrk.CreateUser(pstrName, pstrPID, pstrPW)
    wrk.Users.Append usrNew

    ' To be consistent with Access UI, append the account
    ' to the built-in Users group
    usrNew.Groups.Append wrk.CreateGroup("Users")

    ' Success
    glrNewUser = True

glrNewUserDone:
    On Error GoTo 0
    Exit Function

glrNewUserErr:
    Select Case Err
    Case ERR_ACCNT_ALREADY_EXISTS
        strMsg = "An account with the name '" & pstrName &
        ➡ "' already exists."
    Case ERR_BAD_PID
        strMsg = "You must enter a PID of between 4 and 20
        ➡ characters."
    Case ERR_NO_PERMISSION
        strMsg = "You don't have permission to perform this
        ➡ operation."
```

```
Case Else
    strMsg = "Error#" & Err & "--" & Error$
End Select
    MsgBox strMsg, MB_ICONSTOP + MB_OK,
    ➡ "Procedure " & strProcName
Resume glrNewUserDone

End Function
```

Creating a new user is much like creating any new object using DAO. glrNewUser() works by creating a new user object using the CreateUser method of the default workspace. The new user is created when the user's object is appended to the workspace's Users collection. To be consistent with the Access UI—and to make it so the new account will be able to open databases in the workgroup—glrNewUser() finishes by appending the new account to the built-in Users group.

Creating a New Group Account

The function glrNewGroup() is analogous to glrNewUser(). It takes as its parameters the name of the new group and the new group's PID. It returns True if it is successful. This function requires the user running it to be a member of the Admins group. The function can be found in Listing 22.4.

Listing 22.4

```
Function glrNewGroup(ByVal pstrName As String, ByVal pstrPID
➡ As String) As Integer

    On Error GoTo glrNewGroupErr

    Dim wrk As WorkSpace
    Dim strMsg As String
    Dim strProcName As String

    strProcName = "glrNewGroup"

    ' Initialize return value
    glrNewGroup = False

    Set wrk = DBEngine.Workspaces(0)

    ' Create new group account and append to Groups collection
    wrk.Groups.Append wrk.CreateGroup(pstrName, pstrPID)
```

```
    ' Success
    glrNewGroup = True

glrNewGroupDone:
    On Error GoTo 0
    Exit Function

glrNewGroupErr:
    Select Case Err
    Case ERR_ACCNT_ALREADY_EXISTS
        strMsg = "An account with the name '" & pstrName &
        ➡ "' already exists."
    Case ERR_BAD_PID
        strMsg = "You must enter a PID of between 4 and 20
        ➡ characters."
    Case ERR_NO_PERMISSION
        strMsg = "You don't have permission to perform this
        ➡ operation."
    Case Else
        strMsg = "Error#" & Err & "--" & Error$
    End Select
        MsgBox strMsg, MB_ICONSTOP + MB_OK,
        ➡ "Procedure " & strProcName
    Resume glrNewGroupDone

End Function
```

This function is even simpler than glrNewUser() since it doesn't have to deal with a password—there are none for group accounts—and groups can't be members of other groups.

Checking for the Existence and Type of an Account

We originally created two functions to check for account existence, one for groups and one for users, but then decided a more general function that returned the type of account was better. Hence, we created glrGetAccount(), to which you pass the account name. It returns one of the following global constants:

Global Const ACCNT_USER = 1

Global Const ACCNT_GROUP = 2

Global Const ACCNT_NONE = 0

glrGetAccount() can be found in Listing 22.5.

Listing 22.5

```
Function glrGetAccount(ByVal pstrName As String) As Integer

    On Error GoTo glrGetAccountErr

    Dim wrk As WorkSpace
    Dim varAccount As Variant
    Dim intAccount As Integer
    Dim strMsg As String
    Dim strProcName As String

    strProcName = "glrGetAccount"

    ' Initialize return value
    intAccount = ACCNT_NONE

    Set wrk = DBEngine.Workspaces(0)

    ' Turn off event handler and check line by line
    ' to determine the account membership
    On Error Resume Next

    varAccount = wrk.Users(pstrName).Name
    If Err = ERR_NAME_NOT_IN_COLLCTN Then
        intAccount = ACCNT_NONE
    Else
        intAccount = ACCNT_USER
        GoTo glrGetAccountDone
    End If

    ' Reset error variable
    On Error Resume Next

    varAccount = wrk.Groups(pstrName).Name
    If Err = ERR_NAME_NOT_IN_COLLCTN Then
        intAccount = ACCNT_NONE
    Else
        intAccount = ACCNT_GROUP
        GoTo glrGetAccountDone
    End If

glrGetAccountDone:
```

```
        glrGetAccount = intAccount

        On Error GoTo 0
        Exit Function

glrGetAccountErr:
    Select Case Err
    Case ERR_NO_PERMISSION
        strMsg = "You don't have permission to perform this
        ➥ operation."
    Case Else
        strMsg = "Error#" & Err & "--" & Error$
    End Select
        MsgBox strMsg, MB_ICONSTOP + MB_OK,
        ➥ "Procedure " & strProcName
    Resume glrGetAccountDone

End Function
```

glrGetAccount() works by attempting to grab the name of a user account with the passed name. If the error 3265 (ERR_NAME_NOT_IN_COLLCTN) occurs because the user account doesn't exist, glrGetAccount() resumes and attempts to grab the name of a group account with the same name. If both attempts fail, the function returns 0. Like the two previous functions, this function requires the user running it to be a member of the Admins group.

Deleting an Account

The function glrDeleteAccount() deletes an account. You pass it the account name, and it returns True if it succeeds. This function requires the user running it to be a member of the Admins group. glrDeleteAccount can be found in Listing 22.6.

Listing 22.6

```
Function glrDeleteAccount(ByVal pstrName As String) As Integer

    On Error GoTo glrDeleteAccountErr

    Dim wrk As WorkSpace
    Dim usr As User
    Dim intAccount As Integer
    Dim strMsg As String
```

```
    Dim strProcName As String

    strProcName = "glrDeleteAccount"

    ' Initialize return value
    glrDeleteAccount = False

    Set wrk = DBEngine.Workspaces(0)

    ' Call glrGetAccount() to determine account type
    intAccount = glrGetAccount(pstrName)

    Select Case intAccount
    Case ACCNT_USER
        wrk.Users.Delete pstrName
    Case ACCNT_GROUP
        wrk.Groups.Delete pstrName
    Case Else
        GoTo glrDeleteAccountDone
    End Select

    ' Success
    glrDeleteAccount = True

glrDeleteAccountDone:
    On Error GoTo 0
    Exit Function

glrDeleteAccountErr:
    Select Case Err
    Case ERR_NAME_NOT_IN_COLLCTN
        strMsg = "The account '" & pstrName &
        ➡ "' doesn't exist."
    Case ERR_NO_PERMISSION
        strMsg = "You don't have permission to perform this
        ➡ operation."
    Case Else
        strMsg = "Error#" & Err & "--" & Error$
    End Select
        MsgBox strMsg, MB_ICONSTOP + MB_OK,
        ➡ "Procedure " & strProcName
    Resume glrDeleteAccountDone

End Function
```

glrDeleteAccount() begins by calling glrGetAccount() to check whether the account exists and determine its type. If it doesn't exist, the function exits with the return value False. Otherwise it uses the Delete method for the appropriate object. If you don't have permission to delete the account, glrDeleteAccount() displays a dialog and exits.

Adding a User to a Group

Members of the Admins group can use glrAddGroupMember() to add a user to a group. This function takes as its input the name of the user to be added and the name of the group. It returns True if it succeeds. glrAddGroupMember() can be found in Listing 22.7.

Listing 22.7

```
Function glrAddGroupMember(ByVal pstrUser As String, ByVal
➡ pstrGroup As String) As Integer

    On Error GoTo glrAddGroupMemberErr

    Dim wrk As WorkSpace
    Dim usr As User
    Dim gru As Group
    Dim strMsg As String
    Dim intErrHndlrFlag As Integer
    Dim strProcName As String

    Const FLAG_SET_USER = 1
    Const FLAG_SET_GROUP = 2
    Const FLAG_ELSE = 0

    strProcName = "glrAddGroupMember"

    ' Initialize return value
    glrAddGroupMember = False

    ' Initialize flag for determining
    ' context for error handler
    intErrHndlrFlag = FLAG_ELSE

    Set wrk = DBEngine.Workspaces(0)
```

```
' Refresh users and groups collections
wrk.Users.Refresh
wrk.Groups.Refresh

' Check for existence of user
intErrHndlrFlag = FLAG_SET_USER
Set usr = wrk.Users(pstrUser)

' Check for existence of group
intErrHndlrFlag = FLAG_SET_GROUP
Set gru = wrk.Groups(pstrGroup)

intErrHndlrFlag = FLAG_ELSE

' Report error if user already a member of this group
If glrIsMember(pstrUser, pstrGroup) Then
    strMsg = "The user account '" & pstrUser &
    ➥ "' is already a member of the group " & pstrGroup
    ➥ & "."
    MsgBox strMsg, MB_ICONSTOP + MB_OK,
    ➥ "Procedure " & strProcName
    GoTo glrAddGroupMemberDone
End If

' Append user to group
gru.Users.Append gru.CreateUser(pstrUser)

' Success
glrAddGroupMember = True

glrAddGroupMemberDone:
    On Error GoTo 0
    Exit Function

glrAddGroupMemberErr:
    Select Case Err
    Case ERR_NAME_NOT_IN_COLLCTN
        Select Case intErrHndlrFlag
        Case FLAG_SET_USER
            strMsg = "The user account '" & pstrUser &
            ➥ "' doesn't exist."
        Case FLAG_SET_GROUP
            strMsg = "The group account '" & pstrGroup &
            ➥ "' doesn't exist."
        Case Else
```

```
            strMsg = "Error#" & Err & "--" & Error$(Err)
        End Select
    Case ERR_CANT_PERFORM_OPP
        strMsg = "The user account '" & pstrUser &
        ➡ "' is already a member of the group " &
        ➡ pstrGroup & "."
    Case ERR_NO_PERMISSION
        strMsg = "You don't have permission to perform this
        ➡ operation."
    Case Else
        strMsg = "Error#" & Err & "--" & Error$
    End Select
        MsgBox strMsg, MB_ICONSTOP + MB_OK,
        ➡ "Procedure " & strProcName
    Resume glrAddGroupMemberDone

End Function
```

This function, as well as several others in the basSecurityUtilities module, uses a flag, intErrHndlrFlag, to declare the state of the function before executing a statement that may cause an error. The functions use this flag to give better feedback to the user when an error occurs. In glrAddGroupMember(), for example, the flag informs the user whether the nonexistent account is a user or group account.

glrAddGroupMember() refreshes the workspace's collections before checking for membership in case anyone has altered the group membership recently. It then checks for the existence of the user and group accounts and whether the user is already a member of the group. If any of these checks turns up an error, glrAddGroupMember() displays a dialog and exits. Otherwise the CreateUser method is used to append the user to the group.

Checking whether a User Is a Member of a Group

You can check whether a user is a member of a group using glrIsMember(). This function, which works only for members of Admins, takes as its input the name of the user and the group and returns True if the user is a member. The function can be found in Listing 22.8.

Listing 22.8

```
Function glrIsMember(ByVal pstrUser As String, ByVal pstrGroup
➡ As String) As Integer

    On Error GoTo glrIsMemberErr

    Dim wrk As WorkSpace
    Dim usr As User
    Dim gru As Group
    Dim strMsg As String
    Dim intErrHndlrFlag As Integer
    Dim varGroupName As Variant
    Dim strProcName As String

    Const FLAG_SET_USER = 1
    Const FLAG_SET_GROUP = 2
    Const FLAG_CHK_MEMBER = 4
    Const FLAG_ELSE = 0

    strProcName = "glrIsMember"

    ' Initialize return value
    glrIsMember = False

    ' Initialize flag for determining
    ' context for error handler
    intErrHndlrFlag = FLAG_ELSE

    Set wrk = DBEngine.Workspaces(0)

    ' Refresh users and groups collections
    wrk.Users.Refresh
    wrk.Groups.Refresh

    intErrHndlrFlag = FLAG_SET_USER
    Set usr = wrk.Users(pstrUser)

    intErrHndlrFlag = FLAG_SET_GROUP
    Set gru = wrk.Groups(pstrGroup)

    intErrHndlrFlag = FLAG_CHK_MEMBER
    varGroupName = usr.Groups(pstrGroup).Name

    intErrHndlrFlag = FLAG_ELSE
```

```
    If Not IsEmpty(varGroupName) Then
        glrIsMember = True
    End If

glrIsMemberDone:
    On Error GoTo 0
    Exit Function

glrIsMemberErr:
    Select Case Err
    Case ERR_NAME_NOT_IN_COLLCTN
        Select Case intErrHndlrFlag
        Case FLAG_SET_USER
            strMsg = "The user account '" & pstrUser &
            ➥ "' doesn't exist."
        Case FLAG_SET_GROUP
            strMsg = "The group account '" & pstrGroup &
            ➥ "' doesn't exist."
        Case FLAG_CHK_MEMBER
            Resume Next
        Case Else
            strMsg = "Error#" & Err & "--" & Error$
        End Select
    Case ERR_NO_PERMISSION
        strMsg = "You don't have permission to perform this
        ➥ operation."
    Case Else
        strMsg = "Error#" & Err & "--" & Error$
    End Select
        MsgBox strMsg, MB_ICONSTOP + MB_OK,
        ➥ "Procedure " & strProcName
    Resume glrIsMemberDone

End Function
```

This function is similar to glrAddGroupMember(), but instead of adding the user to the group using the CreateUser method, it checks for membership using the following statement:

```
varGroupName = usr.Groups(pstrGroup).Name
```

This statement is attempting to set a variable to the Name property of the group object in the Groups collection of the user object. There's nothing special here about the Name property—any readable property of the group object would suffice.

(With that said, however, you'll find that Name *is* the only readable property of a group or user object.) Because of the symmetry of the Users and Groups collections, glrIsMember() could have also checked for the name of the user object in the Users collection of the group object. The following alternate statement would yield the same result:

```
varUserName = gru.Users(pstrUser).Name
```

Removing a User from a Group

You can use the function glrRemoveGroupMember() to remove a user from a group. Like glrIsMember(), you pass it the user and group account names, and it returns True if it succeeds. You must be a member of the Admins group to use this function. glrRemoveGroupMember() can be found in Listing 22.9.

Listing 22.9

```
Function glrRemoveGroupMember(ByVal pstrUser As String, ByVal
➡ pstrGroup As String) As Integer

    On Error GoTo glrRemoveGroupMemberErr

    Dim wrk As WorkSpace
    Dim usr As User
    Dim gru As Group
    Dim strMsg As String
    Dim intErrHndlrFlag As Integer
    Dim strProcName As String

    Const FLAG_SET_USER = 1
    Const FLAG_SET_GROUP = 2
    Const FLAG_CHK_MEMBER = 4
    Const FLAG_ELSE = 0

    strProcName = "glrRemoveGroupMember"

    ' Initialize return value
    glrRemoveGroupMember = False

    ' Initialize flag for determining
    ' context for error handler
    intErrHndlrFlag = FLAG_ELSE
```

```
        Set wrk = DBEngine.Workspaces(0)

        intErrHndlrFlag = FLAG_SET_USER
        Set usr = wrk.Users(pstrUser)

        ' This next step is not necessary to delete the user, but it
        ' makes for better diagnostic error messages
        intErrHndlrFlag = FLAG_SET_GROUP
        Set gru = wrk.Groups(pstrGroup)

        intErrHndlrFlag = FLAG_CHK_MEMBER
        usr.Groups.Delete pstrGroup

        intErrHndlrFlag = FLAG_ELSE

        ' Success
        glrRemoveGroupMember = True

glrRemoveGroupMemberDone:
    On Error GoTo 0
    Exit Function

glrRemoveGroupMemberErr:
    Select Case Err
        Select Case intErrHndlrFlag
        Case FLAG_SET_USER
            strMsg = "The user account '" & pstrUser &
            ➡ "' doesn't exist."
        Case FLAG_SET_GROUP
            strMsg = "The group account '" & pstrGroup &
            ➡ "' doesn't exist."
        Case FLAG_CHK_MEMBER
            strMsg = "The user account '" & pstrUser &
            ➡ "' isn't a member of the group " & pstrGroup
            ➡ & "."
        Case Else
            strMsg = "Error#" & Err & "--" & Error$
        End Select
    Case ERR_NO_PERMISSION
        strMsg = "You don't have permission to perform this
        ➡ operation."
    Case Else
        strMsg = "Error#" & Err & "--" & Error$
    End Select
    MsgBox strMsg, MB_ICONSTOP + MB_OK,
```

```
        ➡ "Procedure " & strProcName
    Resume glrRemoveGroupMemberDone

End Function
```

glrRemoveGroupMember() works similarly to both glrAddGroupMember() and glrIsMember(). Once the group and user objects have been set and membership has been verified, glrRemoveGroupMember() uses the Delete method to remove the group from the Groups collection of the user object.

Changing Passwords

You can use glrChangePW() to change the password for either the current logged-in user or for another user's account. If you choose the latter, you must be a member of the Admins group. You pass glrChangePW() the name of the account, the old password, and the new password. This function can be found in Listing 22.10.

Listing 22.10

```
Function glrChangePW(ByVal pstrUser As String, ByVal
➡ pstrOldPW As String, ByVal pstrNewPW As String) As Integer

    On Error GoTo glrChangePWErr

    Dim wrk As WorkSpace
    Dim usr As User
    Dim strMsg As String
    Dim strProcName As String

    strProcName = "glrChangePW"

    ' Initialize return value
    glrChangePW = False

    Set wrk = DBEngine.Workspaces(0)

    ' Point to user object
    Set usr = wrk.Users(pstrUser)

    ' Change password. If no permission or
    ' bad PW, the error handler will kick in.
    usr.NewPassword pstrOldPW, pstrNewPW
```

```
        ' Success
        glrChangePW = True

glrChangePWDone:
    On Error GoTo 0
    Exit Function

glrChangePWErr:
    Select Case Err
    Case ERR_NAME_NOT_IN_COLLCTN
        strMsg = "The user account '" & pstrUser &
        ➡ "' doesn't exist."
    Case ERR_NO_PERMISSION
        strMsg = "You don't have permission to perform this
        ➡ operation or you have entered the wrong old
        ➡ password."
    Case Else
        strMsg = "Error#" & Err & "--" & Error$
    End Select
        MsgBox strMsg, MB_ICONSTOP + MB_OK,
        ➡ "Procedure " & strProcName
    Resume glrChangePWDone

End Function
```

glrChangePW() uses the NewPassword method of the user object. When you use this method, you are required to enter the correct old password if the account is the same as the value of CurrentUser(); otherwise you don't have to enter the old password—the string is ignored. This behavior is consistent with the Access UI, where you can clear someone else's password. The difference is that, with DAO, you can both clear the password and set it to a new non-blank value in one step.

Listing All Users with Blank Passwords

A user account with blank passwords is the Achilles heel of a supposedly secure workgroup. Using the Access UI, there's no way for a database administrator to quickly determine which users have left their passwords blank. Using DAO, however, you can accomplish this easily. We have written such a function, glrUsersWith-BlankPW(), which can be found in Listing 22.11.

Listing 22.11

```
Function glrUsersWithBlankPW() As Integer

    On Error GoTo glrUsersWithBlankPWErr

    Dim wrkDefault As WorkSpace
    Dim wrkNew As WorkSpace
    Dim strUser As String
    Dim fNonBlankPW As Integer
    Dim fAnyBlankPWs As Integer
    Dim intI As Integer
    Dim strAccessDir As String
    Dim strMsg As String
    Dim strCR As String
    Dim strProcName As String

    Const FILE_BLANK_PW = "blankpw.txt"
    strCR = Chr$(13) & Chr$(10)

    strProcName = "glrUsersWithBlankPW"

    strAccessDir = SysCmd(SYSCMD_ACCESSDIR) + FILE_BLANK_PW

    ' Initialize flag to track if any blank PWs occur
    fAnyBlankPWs = False

    ' Open output file and create header
    Open strAccessDir For Append As #1
    Print #1, String$(70, "=")
    Print #1, "Users with Blank Passwords      Produced: " & _
    ➡ Format(Now, "mm/dd/yy hh:nn") & "  By: " & CurrentUser()
    Print #1, String$(70, "=")

    Set wrkDefault = DBEngine.Workspaces(0)

    ' Iterate through all users in workgroup
    For intI = 0 To wrkDefault.Users.Count - 1
        strUser = wrkDefault.Users(intI).Name

        ' Skip if special engine-level users
        If strUser <> "Creator" And strUser <> "Engine" Then

            ' Initialize flag that tracks blank PW
            fNonBlankPW = False
```

```
                    ' Create a new workspace and attempt to log on as
                    ' user with blank PW
                    Set wrkNew = DBEngine.CreateWorkspace
                  ➡ ("NewWorkspace", strUser, "")

                    ' If an error occurred on last statement, then
                    ' error handler will set flag to True. Otherwise,
                    ' we were able to log on, so PW must've been blank.
                    If Not fNonBlankPW Then
                        Print #1, strUser
                        fAnyBlankPWs = True
                    End If

                End If

            Next intI

            ' Return True if any passwords are blank

            If fAnyBlankPWs Then
                strMsg = "Accounts with blank passwords were found!" &
              ➡ strCR & strCR
                strMsg = strMsg & "The names have been logged to " &
              ➡ strAccessDir
            Else
                strMsg = "No accounts with blank passwords were found."
              ➡ & strCR & strCR
                strMsg = strMsg & "This fact has been logged to " &
              ➡ strAccessDir
                Print #1, "<NONE>"
            End If
            MsgBox strMsg, MB_ICONINFORMATION + MB_OK, "Procedure " &
          ➡ strProcName

            glrUsersWithBlankPW = fAnyBlankPWs


    glrUsersWithBlankPWDone:
        If Not wrkNew Is Nothing Then wrkNew.Close
        Print #1, String$(70, "=")
        Print #1, ""
        Print #1, ""
        Close #1
```

```
        On Error GoTo 0
        Exit Function

glrUsersWithBlankPWErr:
    Select Case Err
    Case ERR_BAD_ACCNT_OR_PW
        ' Could not log on user account with blank PW
        fNonBlankPW = True
        Resume Next
    Case Else
        strMsg = "Error#" & Err & "--" & Error$
    End Select
        MsgBox strMsg, MB_ICONSTOP + MB_OK, "Procedure " &
        ➡ strProcName
    Resume glrUsersWithBlankPWDone

End Function
```

glrUsersWithBlankPW() works by iterating through the Users collection in the default workspace and then attempting to log on to each account using a blank password. If it is able to log on to an account, it prints the user name to a file.

The function uses SysCmd() with the predefined constant SYSCMD_ACCESSDIR to determine the Access directory path. It then writes to a text file named BLANKPW.TXT in this directory. glrUsersWithBlankPW() prints a header with the name of the current user and the current date and time before printing the offending user account names. If no blank passwords are found, glrUsersWithBlankPW() prints "<NONE>" to the text file.

Jet defines two built-in, but normally hidden, users—Creator and Engine—which have, or more likely just appear to have, blank passwords. For those of you who are immediately thinking "security hole," hold your horses. Even though these Jet-defined users appear in the Users collection, you cannot use them to log on to Access, and they appear to have neither group membership nor any predefined object permissions. In any case, glrUsersWithBlankPW() skips over them.

Reading Permissions

You can read the value of an account's Permissions property using the function glrGetPermission(). This function takes as its input an integer constant denoting the type of object (for example, Table, Query, and so on), the name of the object, and the account name. The object types are defined as the following global constants in the Declarations section of the module:

Global Const OBJ_DATABASE = 0

Global Const OBJ_FORM = 1

Global Const OBJ_MODULE = 2

Global Const OBJ_REPORT = 3

Global Const OBJ_SCRIPT = 5

Global Const OBJ_TABLE = 7

The function returns a long integer corresponding to the object's Permissions property. If you don't have the necessary permissions to view the permissions of the object, glrGetPermission() displays a dialog with the message, "You don't have permission to perform this operation" and returns 0. glrGetPermission() can be found in Listing 22.12.

Listing 22.12

```
Function glrGetPermission(ByVal pintObjType As Integer, ByVal
➡ pstrObjName As String, ByVal pstrAccount As String)As Long

    On Error GoTo glrGetPermissionErr

    Dim wrk As WorkSpace
    Dim db As Database
    Dim con As Container
    Dim doc As Document
    Dim strCurrentUser As String
    Dim strMsg As String
    Dim intErrHndlrFlag As Integer
    Dim strProcName As String

    Const FLAG_SET_ACCNT = 4
    Const FLAG_SET_CON = 5
    Const FLAG_SET_DOC = 6
    Const FLAG_ELSE = 0

    strProcName = "glrGetPermission"
```

```
' Initialize flag for determining
' context for error handler
intErrHndlrFlag = FLAG_ELSE

Set wrk = DBEngine.Workspaces(0)
Set db = wrk.Databases(0)

' If setting permissions for database, you
' actually need to use the MSysDB document
If pintObjType = OBJ_DATABASE Then
    pstrObjName = "MSysDB"
End If

' Point to the right container
intErrHndlrFlag = FLAG_SET_CON
Set con = db.Containers(pintObjType)
intErrHndlrFlag = FLAG_ELSE

' Refresh the container's docs
con.Documents.Refresh

' If user parameter is blank, use current user
If Len(pstrAccount) = 0 Then
    pstrAccount = CurrentUser()
End If

intErrHndlrFlag = FLAG_SET_ACCNT
con.UserName = pstrAccount
intErrHndlrFlag = FLAG_ELSE

' Only point to a document if the name is non-blank
If Len(pstrObjName) > 0 Then
    intErrHndlrFlag = FLAG_SET_DOC
    Set doc = con.Documents(pstrObjName)
    intErrHndlrFlag = FLAG_ELSE
    doc.UserName = pstrAccount
End If

' Get permissions for appropriate type of object
If Len(pstrObjName) = 0 Then
    glrGetPermission = con.Permissions
Else
    glrGetPermission = doc.Permissions
End If
```

```
glrGetPermissionDone:
    On Error GoTo 0
    Exit Function

glrGetPermissionErr:
    Select Case Err
    Case ERR_NO_PERMISSION
        strMsg = "You don't have permission to perform this
        ➡ operation."
    Case ERR_NAME_NOT_IN_COLLCTN
        Select Case intErrHndlrFlag
        Case FLAG_SET_ACCNT
            strMsg = "The account '" & pstrAccount &
            ➡ "' doesn't exist."
        Case FLAG_SET_CON
            strMsg = "Invalid object type constant."
        Case FLAG_SET_DOC
            strMsg = "The object '" & pstrObjName &
            ➡ "' is not in the '" & pintObjType &
            ➡ "' collection."
        Case Else
            strMsg = "Error#" & Err & "--" & Error$
        End Select
    Case ERR_BAD_ACCNT_NAME
        strMsg = "The account '" & pstrAccount &
        ➡ "' doesn't exist."
    Case Else
        strMsg = "Error#" & Err & "--" & Error$
    End Select
        MsgBox strMsg, MB_ICONSTOP + MB_OK, "Procedure " &
        ➡ strProcName
    Resume glrGetPermissionDone

End Function
```

glrGetPermission(), along with the other functions that set and retrieve the values of the Permissions and Owner properties, is flexible in that it allows you to query the permissions on a document object (for example, qryItems), a container (for example, Modules), or the database itself.

If you pass glrGetPermission() a non-blank string for pstrObjName, it determines the permissions for that object.

If instead you pass the function a blank pstrObjName parameter and one of the object constants for the parameter pintObjType, it determines the permissions for the container itself. This is equivalent to determining the permissions for any newly created objects.

If you pass the function a blank pstrObjName parameter and the OBJ_DATABASE constant for the parameter pintObjType, glrGetPermission() determines the permissions for the database itself. glrGetPermission() accomplishes this by using the intrinsic database document name MSysDB. (Although you may be tempted to check the permissions for the Databases container instead, and you can, this is not the same thing. Most important, if you set *these* permissions, they won't stick.)

Once the correct container has been determined, glrGetPermission() sets the container object, con, to point to the appropriate container. This is accomplished with the following statement:

```
Set con = db.Containers(pintObjType)
```

glrGetPermission() then sets the UserName property for the container object. If the pstrAccount parameter was blank, the function uses the name of the current user. Otherwise, it uses the name of the passed user or group account.

If glrGetPermission() will be getting the permissions for a document, it sets the document object, doc, to point to the name of that object and also sets the User-Name property for the document.

Finally, the function returns the value of the Permissions property using the following If...Then...Else statement:

```
If Len(pstrObjName) = O Then
    glrGetPermission = con.Permissions
Else
    glrGetPermission = doc.Permissions
End If
```

Checking for a Specific Permission

While you can use glrGetPermission() to get the *value* of the Permissions property, you may be at a loss as to what to do next. To ascertain the individual permissions, you have to perform bitwise arithmetic on the returned value using one of the built-in DB_SEC constants. Since it's likely that you'd want to check the value against an individual permission, we have also created glrCheckPermission() to make this task easier.

You pass glrCheckPermission() the type of object (for example, Table, Query, and so on), the name of the object, the user name, the permission constant you want to check against, and whether you wish to check explicit *and* implicit permissions (False) or explicit permissions only (True). The function returns True if the user has the permission to the object.

The differences between glrCheckPermission() and glrGetPermission() are worth noting here. First, since glrCheckPermission() looks for both explicit permissions (that is, those for the user account) *and* (optionally) implicit permissions (that is, those for any groups to which the user is a member), it works only with user accounts. Second, you must supply a permissions value to check against. You can use one of the predefined constants from Table 22.4, but because of the nuances of bit-wise arithmetic, you should only use the simple constants that set a single bit, not the constants that are made up of sums of other constants. glrCheckPermission() can be found in Listing 22.13.

Listing 22.13

```
Function glrCheckPermission(ByVal pintObjType As Integer,
➡ ByVal pstrObjName As String, ByVal pstrUser As String,
➡ ByVal plngPermission As Long, ByVal pfExplicitOnly As
➡ Integer) As Integer

    On Error GoTo glrCheckPermissionErr

    Dim wrk As WorkSpace
    Dim db As Database
    Dim con As Container
    Dim doc As Document
    Dim strCurrentUser As String
    Dim usr As User
    Dim strGroupName As String
    Dim strMsg As String
    Dim fPermission As Integer
    Dim intI As Integer
    Dim intErrHndlrFlag As Integer
    Dim strProcName As String

    Const FLAG_SET_USER = 1
    Const FLAG_SET_CON = 5
    Const FLAG_SET_DOC = 6
    Const FLAG_ELSE = 0

    strProcName = "glrCheckPermission"
```

```
' Initialize return value
glrCheckPermission = False

' Initialize flag for determining
' context for error handler
intErrHndlrFlag = FLAG_ELSE

If Len(pintObjType) = 0 Then
    strMsg = "One or more required parameters was blank."
    MsgBox strMsg, MB_ICONSTOP + MB_OK, "Procedure " &
    ➥ strProcName
    GoTo glrCheckPermissionDone
End If

Set wrk = DBEngine.Workspaces(0)
Set db = wrk.Databases(0)

' If setting permissions for database, you
' actually need to use the MSysDB document
If pintObjType = OBJ_DATABASE Then
    pstrObjName = "MSysDB"
End If

' Point to the right container
intErrHndlrFlag = FLAG_SET_CON
Set con = db.Containers(pintObjType)
intErrHndlrFlag = FLAG_ELSE

' Refresh the container's docs
con.Documents.Refresh

' If user parameter is blank, use current user
If Len(pstrUser) = 0 Then
    pstrUser = CurrentUser()
End If

intErrHndlrFlag = FLAG_SET_USER
Set usr = wrk.Users(pstrUser)
intErrHndlrFlag = FLAG_ELSE

con.UserName = pstrUser

' Only point to a document if the name is non-blank
If Len(pstrObjName) > 0 Then
```

```
            intErrHndlrFlag = FLAG_SET_DOC
            Set doc = con.Documents(pstrObjName)
            intErrHndlrFlag = FLAG_ELSE
            doc.UserName = pstrUser
        End If

        ' Initialize permission flag
        fPermission = False

        If plngPermission >= DB_SEC_NOACCESS Then

            ' This will check explicit permissions of either
            ' the document or the container
            If Len(pstrObjName) = 0 Then
                fPermission = ((con.Permissions And plngPermission)
                ➥ <> 0)
            Else
                fPermission = ((doc.Permissions And plngPermission)
                ➥ <> 0)
            End If

            ' If explicit permission not OK, and this is NOT an
            ' explicit-only check, then need to check for implicit
            ' permissions
            If Not fPermission And Not pfExplicitOnly Then
                For intI = False To usr.Groups.Count - 1
                    strGroupName = usr.Groups(intI).Name
                    If Len(pstrObjName) = 0 Then
                        con.UserName = strGroupName
                        fPermission = ((con.Permissions And
                        ➥ plngPermission) <> 0)
                    Else
                        doc.UserName = strGroupName
                        fPermission = ((doc.Permissions And
                        ➥ plngPermission) <> 0)
                    End If
                    If fPermission Then
                        Exit For
                    End If
                Next intI
            End If
        Else
            strMsg = "The permission parameter must be a positive
            ➥ non-zero long number."
            MsgBox strMsg, MB_ICONSTOP + MB_OK, "Procedure " &
```

```
        ➥ strProcName
        GoTo glrCheckPermissionDone
    End If

    glrCheckPermission = fPermission

glrCheckPermissionDone:
    On Error GoTo 0
    Exit Function

glrCheckPermissionErr:
    Select Case Err
    Case ERR_NO_PERMISSION
        strMsg = "You don't have permission to perform this
        ➥ operation."
    Case ERR_NAME_NOT_IN_COLLCTN
        Select Case intErrHndlrFlag
        Case FLAG_SET_USER
            strMsg = "The user account '" & pstrUser &
            ➥ "' doesn't exist."
        Case FLAG_SET_CON
            strMsg = "Invalid object type constant."
        Case FLAG_SET_DOC
            strMsg = "The object '" & pstrObjName &
            ➥ "' is not in the '" & pintObjType &
            ➥ "' collection."
        Case Else
            strMsg = "Error#" & Err & "--" & Error$
        End Select
    Case Else
        strMsg = "Error#" & Err & "--" & Error$
    End Select
        MsgBox strMsg, MB_ICONSTOP + MB_OK, "Procedure " &
        ➥ strProcName
    Resume glrCheckPermissionDone

End Function
```

Most of glrCheckPermission() works similarly to glrGetPermission(). Instead of grabbing the Permissions property value, however, glrCheckPermission() uses the bitwise And operator to mask off the complete permissions with the value of the plngPermission parameter (the permission you wish to check). This is accomplished using the following code:

```
fPermission = ((con.Permissions And plngPermission) <> 0)
```

If the explicit permission check fails (fPermission = False) and the value of the fExplicitOnly flag is False, glrCheckPermission() iterates through the user's Groups collection and sets the UserName property of the document (or container) object for each group to which the user belongs. If one of the implicit permission checks succeeds, the For...Next loop is exited and True is returned. Otherwise, if both the explicit and implicit checks fail, glrCheckPermission() returns False.

Adding or Subtracting Permissions

You can add permissions to or subtract permissions from an object for a user or group account using glrChangePermission(). This function takes as its input the type of object, the name of the object, the account name, the permission value (as in glrCheckPermission(), this value must only have one bit set), and a flag that is set to True to indicate that the passed permission should be added or False to indicate that it should be subtracted. glrChangePermission() returns True if it succeeds. It's shown in Listing 22.14.

Listing 22.14

```
Function glrChangePermission(ByVal pintObjType As Integer,
➡ ByVal pstrObjName As String, ByVal pstrAccount As String,
➡ ByVal plngPermission As Long, ByVal pfState As Integer) As
➡ Integer

    On Error GoTo glrChangePermissionErr

    Dim wrk As WorkSpace
    Dim db As Database
    Dim con As Container
    Dim doc As Document
    Dim strCurrentUser As String
    Dim strMsg As String
    Dim intErrHndlrFlag As Integer
    Dim strProcName As String

    Const FLAG_SET_CON = 5
    Const FLAG_SET_DOC = 6
    Const FLAG_ELSE = 0

    strProcName = "glrChangePermission"

    ' Initialize return value
```

```
glrChangePermission = False

' Initialize flag for determining
' context for error handler
intErrHndlrFlag = FLAG_ELSE

If pfState <> 0 And pfState <> -1 Then
    strMsg = "The pfState parameter must be either True
    ➥ or False."
    MsgBox strMsg, MB_ICONSTOP + MB_OK, "Procedure " &
    ➥ strProcName
    GoTo glrChangePermissionDone
End If

Set wrk = DBEngine.Workspaces(0)
Set db = wrk.Databases(0)

' If setting permissions for database, you
' actually need to use the MSysDB document
If pintObjType = OBJ_DATABASE Then
    pstrObjName = "MSysDB"
End If

' Point to the right container
intErrHndlrFlag = FLAG_SET_CON
Set con = db.Containers(pintObjType)
intErrHndlrFlag = FLAG_ELSE

' Refresh the container's docs
con.Documents.Refresh
' Set the container's inherit property so that
' any changes to it are inherited by new docs
con.Inherit = True

' If user parameter is blank, use current user
If Len(pstrAccount) = 0 Then
    pstrAccount = CurrentUser()
End If

con.UserName = pstrAccount

' Only point to a document if the name is non-blank
If Len(pstrObjName) > 0 Then
    intErrHndlrFlag = FLAG_SET_DOC
    Set doc = con.Documents(pintObjType)
```

```
            intErrHndlrFlag = FLAG_ELSE
            doc.UserName = pstrAccount
        End If

        ' Modify permissions of either the document or the container
        If plngPermission >= DB_SEC_NOACCESS Then

            ' Overlay the new permissions on top of the existing
            ' ones. Use Or to add a permission and And Not to
            ' subtract a permission.
            If Len(pstrObjName) = 0 Then
                If pfState Then
                    con.Permissions = con.Permissions Or
                    ➡ plngPermission
                Else
                    con.Permissions = con.Permissions And Not
                    ➡ plngPermission
                End If
            Else
                If pfState Then
                    doc.Permissions = doc.Permissions Or
                    ➡ plngPermission
                Else
                    doc.Permissions = doc.Permissions And Not
                    ➡ plngPermission
                End If
            End If

        Else
            strMsg = "The permission parameter must be a positive
            ➡ non-zero long number."
            MsgBox strMsg, MB_ICONSTOP + MB_OK, "Procedure " &
            ➡ strProcName
            GoTo glrChangePermissionDone
        End If

        ' Ensure that the UI and other code will see the changes
        con.Documents.Refresh

        ' Success
        glrChangePermission = True

glrChangePermissionDone:
        On Error GoTo 0
        Exit Function
```

```
glrChangePermissionErr:
    Select Case Err
    Case ERR_NO_PERMISSION
        glrChangePermission = False
        Resume glrChangePermissionDone
    Case ERR_NAME_NOT_IN_COLLCTN
        Select Case intErrHndlrFlag
        Case FLAG_SET_CON
            strMsg = "Invalid object type constant."
        Case FLAG_SET_DOC
            strMsg = "The object '" & pstrObjName &
            ➡ "' is not in the '" & pintObjType &
            ➡ "' collection."
        Case Else
            strMsg = "Error#" & Err & "--" & Error$
        End Select
    Case ERR_BAD_ACCNT_NAME
        strMsg = "The account '" & pstrAccount &
        ➡ "' doesn't exist."
    Case Else
        strMsg = "Error#" & Err & "--" & Error$
    End Select
        MsgBox strMsg, MB_ICONSTOP + MB_OK, "Procedure " &
        ➡ strProcName
    Resume glrChangePermissionDone
```

```
End Function
```

glrChangePermission() works similarly to glrGetPermission(). The major difference is that instead of getting the existing permission value, it adds the new permission to or subtracts (based on the value of pfState) it from the existing permission set using the following code:

```
If pfState Then
    doc.Permissions = doc.Permissions Or plngPermission
Else
    doc.Permissions = doc.Permissions And Not plngPermission
End If
```

Setting Permissions

Although glrChangePermission() comes in handy for adding or subtracting permissions to an object for an account, there are times when you'd rather replace the existing set of permissions with a completely new set. In these cases you can use glrSetPermission() instead. It takes as its input the type of object, the name of the object, the account name, and the new permission value. glrSetPermission() returns True if it succeeds. It's shown in Listing 22.15.

Listing 22.15

```
Function glrSetPermission(ByVal pintObjType As Integer, ByVal
➡ pstrObjName As String, ByVal pstrAccount As String, ByVal
➡ plngPermission As Long) As Integer

    On Error GoTo glrSetPermissionErr

    Dim wrk As WorkSpace
    Dim db As Database
    Dim con As Container
    Dim doc As Document
    Dim strCurrentUser As String
    Dim strMsg As String
    Dim intErrHndlrFlag As Integer
    Dim strProcName As String

    Const FLAG_SET_CON = 5
    Const FLAG_SET_DOC = 6
    Const FLAG_ELSE = 0

    strProcName = "glrSetPermission"

    ' Initialize return value
    glrSetPermission = False

    ' Initialize flag for determining
    ' context for error handler
    intErrHndlrFlag = FLAG_ELSE

    Set wrk = DBEngine.Workspaces(0)
    Set db = wrk.Databases(0)

    ' If setting permissions for database, you
    ' actually need to use the MSysDB document
    If pintObjType = OBJ_DATABASE Then
        pstrObjName = "MSysDB"
    End If
```

```
' Point to the right container
intErrHndlrFlag = FLAG_SET_CON
Set con = db.Containers(pintObjType)
intErrHndlrFlag = FLAG_ELSE

' Refresh the container's docs
con.Documents.Refresh

' Set the container's inherit property so that
' any changes to it are inherited by new docs
con.Inherit = True

' If user parameter is blank, use current user
If Len(pstrAccount) = O Then
    pstrAccount = CurrentUser()
End If

con.UserName = pstrAccount

' Only point to a document if the name is non-blank
If Len(pstrObjName) > O Then
    intErrHndlrFlag = FLAG_SET_DOC
    Set doc = con.Documents(pintObjType)
    intErrHndlrFlag = FLAG_ELSE
    doc.UserName = pstrAccount
End If

' Modify permissions of either the document or the container
If plngPermission >= DB_SEC_NOACCESS Then

    ' Replace the existing permissions with the new ones
    If Len(pstrObjName) = O Then
        con.Permissions = plngPermission
    Else
        doc.Permissions = plngPermission
    End If

Else
    strMsg = "The permission parameter must be a positive
    ➥ non-zero long number."
    MsgBox strMsg, MB_ICONSTOP + MB_OK, "Procedure " &
    ➥ strProcName
    GoTo glrSetPermissionDone
End If
```

```
        ' Ensure that the UI and other code will see the changes
        con.Documents.Refresh

        ' Success
        glrSetPermission = True

glrSetPermissionDone:
    On Error GoTo 0
    Exit Function

glrSetPermissionErr:
    Select Case Err
    Case ERR_NO_PERMISSION
        glrSetPermission = False
        Resume glrSetPermissionDone
    Case ERR_NAME_NOT_IN_COLLCTN
        Select Case intErrHndlrFlag
        Case FLAG_SET_CON
            strMsg = "Invalid object type constant."
        Case FLAG_SET_DOC
            strMsg = "The object '" & pstrObjName &
            ➡ "' is not in the '" & pintObjType &
            ➡ "' collection."
        Case Else
            strMsg = "Error#" & Err & "--" & Error$
        End Select
    Case ERR_BAD_ACCNT_NAME
        strMsg = "The account '" & pstrAccount &
        ➡ "' doesn't exist."
    Case Else
        strMsg = "Error#" & Err & "--" & Error$
    End Select
        MsgBox strMsg, MB_ICONSTOP + MB_OK, "Procedure " &
        ➡ strProcName
    Resume glrSetPermissionDone

End Function
```

The main difference between glrChangePermission() and glrSetPermission() is that glrSetPermission() replaces the existing permission set with the passed-in permission. This is accomplished with the following code:

```
con.Permissions = plngPermission
```

You can use glrSetPermission() to set multiple permissions by adding them together and passing the sum of the permissions to the function. For example, you could assign ReadData, InsertData, UpdateData, and DeleteData permissions to the tblPart table for the current user using the following function call:

```
lngWriteData = DB_SEC_RETRIEVEDATA + DB_SEC_INSERTDATA +
➡ DB_SEC_REPLACEDATA + DB_SEC_DELETEDATA
varReturn = glrSetPermission("table", "tblPart", "",
➡ lngWriteData)
```

You could also use this technique when calling glrChangePermission().

Disabling the Creation of New Databases

Jet includes a permission, DB_SEC_DBCREATE, that is not exposed by the Access UI. However, you can set this permission of the Databases container of the SystemDB file (typically, SYSTEM.MDA) using DAO. The function glrSetDbCreate() does just this. You pass it the name of the user or group account—unlike some of the other functions previously described, this one requires you to explicitly name the user to lessen the chances of your shooting yourself in the foot—and a flag that you set to True to set this permission on and to False to set it off. Passing a False parameter will prevent the user or group account from being able to create new databases. (If you use this function for a user account, you'll want to make sure the user doesn't have implicit DB_SEC_DBCREATE permissions.) glrSetDbCreate() can be found in Listing 22.16.

Listing 22.16

```
Function glrSetDbCreate(ByVal pstrAccount As String, ByVal
➡ pfState As Integer) As Integer

    On Error GoTo glrSetDbCreateErr

    Dim wrk As WorkSpace
    Dim strSystemDB As String
    Dim dbSys As Database
    Dim con As Container
    Dim strIniFile As String
    Dim strMsg As String
    Dim strProcName As String
```

```
Dim strBuffer As String
Dim intChars As Integer

strProcName = "glrSetDbCreate"

' Initialize return value
glrSetDbCreate = False

If Len(pstrAccount) = 0 Then
    strMsg = "One or more required parameters was blank."
    MsgBox strMsg, MB_ICONSTOP + MB_OK, "Procedure " &
    ➡ strProcName
    GoTo glrSetDbCreateDone
End If

If pfState <> 0 And pfState <> -1 Then
    strMsg = "The pfState parameter must be either True
    ➡ or False."
    MsgBox strMsg, MB_ICONSTOP + MB_OK, "Procedure " &
    ➡ strProcName
    GoTo glrSetDbCreateDone
End If

strIniFile = SysCmd(SYSCMD_INIFILE)

' Get the path and name of the SystemDB library from
' Access Ini File.
strBuffer = Space(MAX_SIZE)
intChars = glr_apiSecGetPrivateProfileString("Options",
➡ "SystemDB", "", strBuffer, MAX_SIZE, strIniFile)
strBuffer = Left(strBuffer, intChars)

If Len(strBuffer) = 0 Then
    strMsg = "No [Options] topic or SystemDB option in " &
    ➡ strIniFile & "."
    MsgBox strMsg, MB_ICONSTOP + MB_OK, "Procedure " &
    ➡ strProcName
    GoTo glrSetDbCreateDone
End If

strSystemDB = strBuffer

Set wrk = DBEngine.Workspaces(0)
Set dbSys = wrk.OpenDatabase(strSystemDB)
```

```
        Set con = dbSys.Containers!Databases

        con.UserName = pstrAccount

        ' Turn on or off the permission to create new databases
        If pfState Then
            con.Permissions = con.Permissions Or DB_SEC_DBCREATE
        Else
            con.Permissions = con.Permissions And Not
        ➥ DB_SEC_DBCREATE
        End If

        ' Ensure that the UI and other code will see the changes
        con.Documents.Refresh

        ' Success
        glrSetDbCreate = True

glrSetDbCreateDone:
        If Not dbSys Is Nothing Then dbSys.Close
        On Error GoTo 0
        Exit Function

glrSetDbCreateErr:
        Select Case Err
        Case ERR_NO_PERMISSION
            glrSetDbCreate = False
            Resume glrSetDbCreateDone
        Case ERR_NAME_NOT_IN_COLLCTN
            strMsg = "The account '" & pstrAccount &
        ➥ "' doesn't exist."
        Case Else
            strMsg = "Error#" & Err & "--" & Error$
        End Select
            MsgBox strMsg, MB_ICONSTOP + MB_OK, "Procedure " &
        ➥ strProcName
        Resume glrSetDbCreateDone

End Function
```

This function is analogous to glrChangePermission(), except that it works on the Databases container of the SystemDB file. In order to determine the name of the SystemDB file, glrSetDbCreate() uses the Windows API GetPrivateProfileString() function to read in the value from the Access .INI file. Since the name and location of this file vary by Access installation, glrSetDbCreate() uses the SysCmd() function with the predefined SYSCMD_INIFILE constant to get the location of the .INI file first. With the location of the .INI file in hand, the function calls the aliased API function to get the complete path to the SystemDB file.

Once the location of SystemDB has been determined, glrSetDbCreate() creates a database object that points to it with the following Set statement:

```
Set dbSys = wrk.OpenDatabase(strSystemDB)
```

The permission is then set using the following If...Then...Else statement:

```
If pfState Then
    con.Permissions = con.Permissions Or DB_SEC_DBCREATE
Else
    con.Permissions = con.Permissions And Not DB_SEC_DBCREATE
End If
```

Determining Ownership

You can use the function glrObjectOwner() to determine the owner of a document or container object or the database itself. You must be either the object's owner or a member of the Admins group. The function takes as its parameters the object type and the object name. It returns the name of the object's owner. It is shown in Listing 22.17.

Listing 22.17

```
Function glrObjectOwner(ByVal pintObjType As Integer, ByVal
➡ pstrObjName As String) As String

    On Error GoTo glrObjectOwnerErr

    Dim wrk As WorkSpace
    Dim db As Database
    Dim con As Container
    Dim doc As Document
    Dim strMsg As String
    Dim intErrHndlrFlag As Integer
    Dim strProcName As String

    Const FLAG_SET_CON = 5
    Const FLAG_SET_DOC = 6
```

```
        Const FLAG_ELSE = 0

        strProcName = "glrObjectOwner"

        ' Initialize flag for determining
        ' context for error handler
        intErrHndlrFlag = FLAG_ELSE

        Set wrk = DBEngine.Workspaces(0)
        Set db = wrk.Databases(0)

        ' If setting permissions for database, you
        ' actually need to use the MSysDB document
        If pintObjType = OBJ_DATABASE Then
            pstrObjName = "MSysDB"
        End If

        ' Point to the right container
        intErrHndlrFlag = FLAG_SET_CON
        Set con = db.Containers(pintObjType)
        intErrHndlrFlag = FLAG_ELSE

        ' Refresh the container's docs
        con.Documents.Refresh

        ' Check ownership on the document or the container
        If Len(pstrObjName) = 0 Then
            glrObjectOwner = con.Owner
        Else
            intErrHndlrFlag = FLAG_SET_DOC
            Set doc = con.Documents(pstrObjName)
            intErrHndlrFlag = FLAG_ELSE
            glrObjectOwner = doc.Owner
        End If

glrObjectOwnerDone:
    On Error GoTo 0
    Exit Function

glrObjectOwnerErr:
    Select Case Err
    Case ERR_NO_PERMISSION
        strMsg = "You don't have permission to perform this
        ➥ operation."
    Case ERR_NAME_NOT_IN_COLLCTN
```

```
        Select Case intErrHndlrFlag
        Case FLAG_SET_CON
            strMsg = "Invalid object type constant."
        Case FLAG_SET_DOC
            strMsg = "The object '" & pstrObjName &
            ➡ "' is not in the '" & pintObjType &
            ➡ "' collection."
        Case Else
            strMsg = "Error#" & Err & "--" & Error$
        End Select
    Case Else
        strMsg = "Error#" & Err & "--" & Error$
    End Select
        MsgBox strMsg, MB_ICONSTOP + MB_OK, "Procedure " &
        ➡ strProcName
    Resume glrObjectOwnerDone

End Function
```

This function is similar to glrGetPermission(), discussed earlier in this chapter. The main difference is that it returns the name of the owner using the Owner property. You accomplish this (for a document object) using the following assignment statement:

```
glrObjectOwner = doc.Owner
```

Changing Ownership

You can use the glrChangeOwner() function to change the name of the owner account for a single object or for all the objects in the database. It takes as its parameters the object type, the name of the object, and the name of the new owner. It returns True if it succeeds.

If you've passed glrChangeOwner() the constant OBJ_DATABASE, it cycles through all the objects and containers in the database and attempts to change ownership of them all. (Note, however, that this function will *not* change the ownership of the database itself—you can accomplish this only by importing all of the database's objects into a new database.) When you've passed the function the OBJ_DATA-BASE constant, it attempts to change the owner of as many objects as it can—even if some attempts fail. False will be returned even if ownership on some objects *could* be changed. In this case you will have to check the ownership of individual objects to determine which ones failed.

glrChangeOwner() requires the currently logged-on user to be either the owner of all the objects to be changed or a member of the Admins group.

For OwnerAccess queries (see the section "OwnerAccess Queries" earlier in this chapter), glrChangeOwner() won't be able to change the owner unless the currently logged-on user is the owner of the query. The function is shown in Listing 22.18.

Listing 22.18

```
Function glrChangeOwner(ByVal pintObjType As Integer, ByVal
➡ pstrObjName As String, ByVal pstrNewOwner As String) As
➡ Integer

    On Error GoTo glrChangeOwnerErr

    Dim wrk As WorkSpace
    Dim db As Database
    Dim con As Container
    Dim doc As Document
    Dim strMsg As String
    Dim intErrHndlrFlag As Integer
    Dim strProcName As String

    Const FLAG_SET_CON = 5
    Const FLAG_SET_DOC = 6
    Const FLAG_ELSE = 0

    strProcName = "glrChangeOwner"

    ' Initialize return value
    glrChangeOwner = False

    If Len(pstrNewOwner) = 0 Then
        strMsg = "One or more required parameters was blank."
        MsgBox strMsg, MB_ICONSTOP + MB_OK, "Procedure " &
        ➡ strProcName
        GoTo glrChangeOwnerDone
    End If

    ' Initialize flag for determining
    ' context for error handler
    intErrHndlrFlag = FLAG_ELSE
```

```
      Set wrk = DBEngine.Workspaces(0)
      Set db = wrk.Databases(0)

      ' Either change all objects in database or an
      ' individual object.
      ' Changing all objects is handled by ChangeOwnerAll()
      If pintObjType = OBJ_DATABASE Then
          glrChangeOwner = ChangeOwnerAll(pstrNewOwner)
      Else
          ' Point to the right container
          intErrHndlrFlag = FLAG_SET_CON
          Set con = db.Containers(pintObjType)
          intErrHndlrFlag = FLAG_ELSE

          ' Refresh the container's docs
          con.Documents.Refresh

          ' Set ownership on a document or a container
          If Len(pstrObjName) = 0 Then
              con.Owner = pstrNewOwner
          Else
              intErrHndlrFlag = FLAG_SET_DOC
              Set doc = con.Documents(pstrObjName)
              intErrHndlrFlag = FLAG_ELSE
              doc.Owner = pstrNewOwner
          End If

          ' Success
          glrChangeOwner = True

      End If


glrChangeOwnerDone:
      On Error GoTo 0
      Exit Function

glrChangeOwnerErr:
      Select Case Err
      Case ERR_NO_PERMISSION
          strMsg = "You don't have permission to perform this
          ➥ operation."
      Case ERR_NAME_NOT_IN_COLLCTN
          Select Case intErrHndlrFlag
          Case FLAG_SET_CON
```

```
              strMsg = "Invalid object type constant."
        Case FLAG_SET_DOC
              strMsg = "The object '" & pstrObjName &
              ➥ "' is not in the '" & pintObjType &
              ➥ "' collection."
        Case Else
              strMsg = "Error#" & Err & "--" & Error$
        End Select
    Case ERR_BAD_ACCNT_NAME
          strMsg = "The account '" & pstrNewOwner &
          ➥ "' doesn't exist."
    Case Else
          strMsg = "Error#" & Err & "--" & Error$
    End Select
          MsgBox strMsg, MB_ICONSTOP + MB_OK, "Procedure " &
          ➥ strProcName
    Resume glrChangeOwnerDone

End Function
```

When working in single-object mode, glrChangeOwner() works similarly to glrObjectOwner() except that instead of grabbing the name of the owner, it sets the owner name of the object to a new value using the following code:

```
doc.owner = pstrNewOwner
```

When you've passed it the OBJ_DATABASE constant, glrChangeOwner calls the private function ChangeOwnerAll() to iterate through each of the objects in the database using the following nested For...Next loops:

```
For intI = 0 To db.Containers.Count - 1
    Set con = db.Containers(intI)

    For intJ = 0 To con.Documents.Count - 1
        Set doc = con.Documents(intJ)
        doc.Owner = pstrNewOwner
    Next intJ

Next intI
```

Common Security Problems and Their Solutions

The following sections outline several common security problems and how you might go about solving them. Probably the most commonly encountered security issue—and the first one presented here—is how to properly secure a database and each of its objects. We also discuss various strategies for securing only a part of a database (code, data, or schema) and for unsecuring a database.

Securing a Database—Plugging Up the Holes

The best way to take an unsecured database and secure it is to run the Security Wizard. A copy of the Wizard is included on the companion disk of this book.

If you would prefer to do it manually, you must carry out the following steps:

1. Run the Workgroup Administrator application and create a new workgroup (SystemDB file) with User and Organization names that differ from the Access installation names. Choose a reasonably long workgroup ID that is not easily guessed. Remove all unsecured SystemDB files and store them away safely.

2. Log on to Access with a secure user account—not the Admin user—that is a member of the Admins group.

3. Remove the built-in user Admin from the Admins group.

4. Remove all permissions to all objects (including new objects) for the built-in Users group (and the accounts Guests, Admin, and Guest if any permissions have been assigned to them).

5. Close the unsecured database.

6. Create a new blank database and import all of the unsecured database's objects using the Import Database add-in.

7. Rebuild any relationships. (They won't be imported.)

8. Encrypt the database.

NOTE   We strongly recommend using the Security Wizard, which makes it much harder to mess up. Even if you use the Wizard, however, make sure you still follow step 1 (the Wizard won't do this step for you) and create a new secure SystemDB file first.

Unsecuring a Database–Opening the Flood Gates

You can reverse the process of securing a database by following these steps:

1. Log on as a member of the Admins group.
2. Grant full permissions, including Administer permission, to the group Users for all objects in the database.
3. Clear the password for the Admin user.
4. Exit Access.
5. Log on as Admin.
6. Create a new blank database and import all of the secured database's objects using the Import Database add-in.
7. Rebuild any relationships. (They won't be imported.)

The trick to unsecuring a database is to give an unsecured group—Users —full permissions on all the objects and to then transfer ownership of the database and all its objects to an unsecured user—Admin.

Securing Code

To secure Access Basic modules or forms or reports containing Code-Behind-Forms, you first need to follow the steps for securing your database.

You secure module-based code so that users can't see it by removing all permissions to it. Using DAO, you would set the permissions of the modules to DB_SEC_NOACCESS. Users can always run your functions, but you will have to provide objects the user *can* read that hook into the secured functions.

You secure forms and reports with Code-Behind-Forms by removing all permissions but the Open/Run permission. Using DAO, you would set the permissions to DB_SEC_FRMRPT_EXECUTE. This also prevents users from modifying the form or report definitions.

If you will be installing your application at another site, make sure the owner of the objects you wish to secure and the owner of the database are secured users (not Admin or members of the Users or Guests groups).

Grant permissions to the Users group for any objects to which you want users to have access.

Ship the application without the SystemDB with which you created it.

Securing Data

It's likely you'll want to grant database users at least ReadData security on some tables or queries; there's not much sense in your users using a database without access to any of its data. Thus, you need to selectively grant permissions to users.

Follow the steps for securing any database. Set necessary permissions on tables. Then set the necessary permissions on queries and use OwnerAccess queries where needed for column-level or row-level security.

Securing the Database Structure

In some situations you may want to protect your database schema from prying eyes. For example, you might be in a service industry that provides valuable data with a proprietary database structure. In this case the database schema is at least as valuable as the data you provide.

In this scenario users will be able to see the names of the secured tables but will be unable to see the relationships between the tables or the columns in the tables. This works best if the unsecured users will need to have only read-only access to the tables.

You can secure your database schema following these steps:

1. Create a secure SystemDB file.

2. If you are concerned about users being able to see the names of your tables, rename them to nonsense names that have no connection to their content.

3. Split the database into a pair of "data" and "application" databases. (See Chapter 11 for more details.)

4. Remove all relationships in the "data" database if you don't want users to be able to see relationships.

5. Secure both databases using the Security Wizard.

6. Log on as a secure user and open the "data" database. (*Don't* remove Open/Run access to this database for unsecured users. If you do, unsecured users won't be able to read the data from attached tables.)

7. Grant yourself ReadData access for all tables in the "data" database. Make sure no unsecured user or group accounts have any access to these tables.

8. Using the same secure user account, open the "application" database and create OwnerAccess queries that use attached tables pointing to the "data" database.

9. Grant ReadData access to the Users group for the OwnerAccess queries.

10. Set the record source for all other objects in the database to the secured OwnerAccess queries, not the underlying tables.

If you follow these steps, unsecured users will be unable to view either the contents of any of your tables or the OwnerAccess queries. They will, however, still be able to see the names of the tables and open the "data" database.

Summary

In this chapter we have covered security in detail. You should now have a good understanding of the Access/Jet security model and how best to take advantage of it.

You have learned

- The basic structure of the Jet security model
- That security in Access is made up of two components: user and group accounts stored in the SystemDB file and object permissions stored in each database
- How to turn on security
- How to use the Access security menus to manage security
- How to create a secure SystemDB (workgroup) file
- How to manage user and group accounts
- How the special built-in user and group accounts work
- How to manage object permissions for users
- The difference between explicit and implicit permissions
- How object and database ownership works
- What OwnerAccess queries are and how to use them to get column-level and row-level security
- How encryption works and what it has to do with security
- When to use the Security Wizards
- The security object hierarchies
- How the security data access objects work
- What the permission constants are and how to use them to programmatically set permissions
- How to use DAO to create useful functions for manipulating security
- How to solve common security problems

CHAPTER

TWENTY-THREE

Giving Users the Help They Need

- Creating a Help file

- Creating and manipulating .RTF and .HPJ files

- Using Help Author

- Creating context-sensitive help in forms and reports

- Calling help from Access Basic

Creating Help files is a task many developers avoid. This isn't surprising since, in essence, creating a Help file involves learning a new language and yet another set of tools. This means, of course, that you face yet another learning curve. This chapter helps smooth that curve.

Windows Help files run on top of the Windows help engine, WinHelp (WIN-HELP.EXE). You create the Help files, which consist of a series of help topics, and link these topics using hyptertext links.

Users can navigate around a typical Windows Help file using any of the following methods:

- The contents topic
- Context-sensitive help in an application
- Jumps
- Popup windows
- The Search dialog
- The history list
- The Back button
- Browse buttons
- Macros
- Jumps from other Help files
- Calls from the WinHelp() Windows function from Access Basic

An example of a Help file, the main window of the Access Help file, is displayed in in Figure 23.1.

In this chapter we discuss the various steps for preparing professional-quality Help files that give your Access applications that extra edge your users will appreciate.

FIGURE 23.1:
WinHelp main window

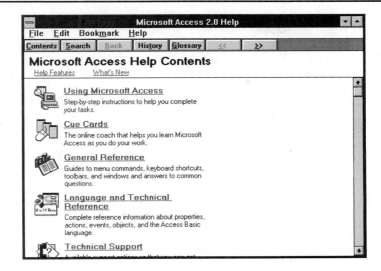

Tools of the Trade

To create a Help file, you need the following tools:

- Rich text editor (for example, Microsoft Word for Windows)
- Help compiler (HC.EXE, HC31.EXE, or HCP.EXE)

In addition, you may need to use some of the following optional tools:

- Hotspot editor (SHED.EXE)
- Multi-resolution bitmap compiler (MRBC.EXE)
- Graphics programs to create and manipulate bitmaps or metafiles
- *Microsoft Help Compiler Guide*
- A third-party help authoring tool

Whether you need all of these tools depends on how complex you want to make your Help file. The help compiler, hotspot editor, multi-resolution bitmap compiler, and *Help Compiler Guide* are all available in the Access Development Toolkit, as well as in several other Microsoft development products. You can also find them on the Microsoft Developer Network CD-ROM.

You can use any word processor that can save a file in rich text format as the editor. Rich text files usually have the extension .RTF. In the section "Using the Windows Help Authoring Tool (WHAT)" later in this chapter we discuss a special tool that simplifies the creation of Help files when using Word for Windows; it makes constructing the .RTF files and .HPJ file much easier.

You may want to include graphics in your Help file. These can be as simple as 4-pixel-wide bullets or as complex as screen shots of your application. For simple bitmaps the Paintbrush program that comes with Windows may be adequate for your needs. For more complex graphics you may need imaging and full-featured drawing programs, such as CorelDraw or Photoshop. You may also need a screen-capture program, such as Collage or Hijaak, if you plan to include screen shots.

The *Help Compiler Guide* is a 171-page book included in the Access Developer's Toolkit and other Microsoft products that include the help compiler.

Parts of a Help File

The process of creating a Help file is sumarized in Figure 23.2. The ultimate result is an .HLP file. To get there you need to start with a number of other files, which are outlined here and described in detail later in the chapter.

The .HPJ File

Each Help file has a project file with the extension .HPJ. This is a text file that describes the components and options that make up the Help file. You run the help compiler against this file to create the .HLP file. The most important part of this file specifies which .RTF files are to be included in the Help file.

.RTF Files

The .RTF files are the meat of the Help file. These files contain the topics that appear in the Help file, and you create them with the rich text editor. The locations of the

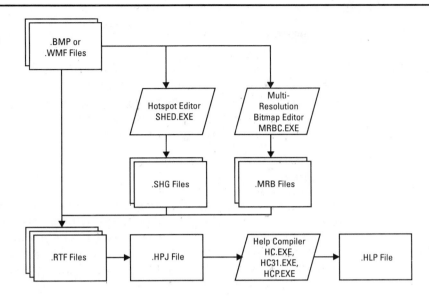

FIGURE 23.2:
Process of building a Help file

files are specified in the .HPJ file. For a small Help file you probably need only one .RTF file. For a larger Help file you may want several. If you have a group of people working on a project, it may make sense for each person to have his or her own .RTF file in which to insert topics.

.BMP Files

Files with the extension .BMP specify device-independent bitmap graphics. You can include these directly in your .RTF files or you can turn them into .MRB or .SHG files.

.WMF Files

Files with the extension .WMF specify Windows metafiles. You can use these files interchangeably with .BMP files. In some cases they may be smaller than .BMP files, but you will need to experiment to be sure.

.SHG Files

Files with the extension .SHG are hypergraphic bitmaps created by the SHED.EXE program from bitmaps or metafiles. These bitmaps can have hotspots embedded in them. For example, if you create a screen shot of your application as a bitmap, you can use SHED to make an .SHG file. Within SHED, you define regions of the bitmap as hotspots. For example, when the user clicks the title bar in the bitmap, the Help system jumps to the title bar help topic. When the user clicks the status bar in the bitmap, the Help system jumps to the status bar help topic, and so forth.

.MRB Files

Files with the extension .MRB contain several bitmaps, each mapped to a different screen resolution. When WinHelp displays a topic that contains an .MRB graphic, it picks the bitmap that corresponds to the screen resolution currently being used. For example, if you include bitmaps for monochrome, EGA, and VGA screens, Win-Help displays the monochrome bitmap on a monochrome screen, the EGA bitmap on an EGA screen, and the VGA bitmap on a VGA screen.

You create these files with the multi-resolution bitmap compiler, MRBC.EXE. See the *Microsoft Help Compiler Guide* for more information on creating these files.

Creating the .RTF Files

Creating the .RTF files is the main task in constructing a Help file. You create an .RTF file by opening a new .RTF file using your word processor. The .RTF file defines the contents of the topics in the Help file, as well as other information related to those topics.

Creating Topics

A Help file is broken into topics. Each topic is one "page" of information. Topics contain the text of the Help file and the jumps between topics, as well as the following properties:

- Title
- ContextString

- Keywords
- BrowseSequence
- BuildTags
- Macros
- Comments

You enter each property by creating a footnote in the .RTF file and using a specific character as the footnote reference mark. For example, to create a context string, you create a pound sign (#) footnote reference mark character in the main text at the point the Help file is to jump to when that context string is referenced.

Each topic in an .RTF file is delimited with a hard page break. In Word for Windows, you create hard page breaks by pressing Ctrl+Enter on the keyboard. The screen in Figure 23.3 shows a typical help topic.

FIGURE 23.3:

Typical help topic created using Word for Windows

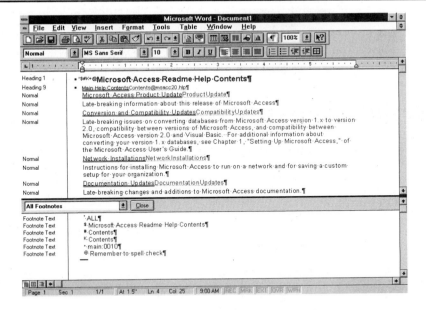

Fonts

You can display help topics in any font available on the system on which the Help file is installed. However, in most cases you cannot count on the user's having a particular font installed unless you ship it with your application or it comes with Windows. Windows 3.1 comes with the following fonts:

- Arial (TrueType)
- Courier New (TrueType)
- Courier in 10, 12, and 15 points (bitmap)
- Modern (vector)
- MS Sans Serif in 8, 10, 12, 14, 18, and 24 points (bitmap)
- MS Serif in 8, 10, 12, 14, 18, and 24 points (bitmap)
- Plotter (vector)
- Roman (vector)
- Script (vector)
- Symbol (TrueType)
- Symbol in 8, 10, 12, 14, 18, and 24 points (bitmap)
- Times New Roman (TrueType)
- WingDings (TrueType)

We recommend that you display your main text in MS Sans Serif 10-point text since this is the most universally available and readable font. You should display topic titles in MS Sans Serif 12-point bold. You can display special effects, like code samples, in the other fonts. If your program must run on systems that have Windows 3.0 installed, you should further restrict yourself to just the bitmap and vector fonts since Windows 3.0 doesn't support TrueType.

Title

Although a title for each topic is not strictly required, we strongly recommend them. If a topic doesn't have a title, it appears in the search list and bookmarks with the text >>Untitled Topic <<, which doesn't look very professional. You can get away with not having titles on topics that are used only as popup windows, but we do not recommend this either because the title also provides information about the topic.

You insert a title by creating a footnote with a dollar sign ($) character as the footnote reference mark immediately after the hard page break. You enter the title string in the footnote text. The footnote text can be 128 characters long, but you should try to keep the title under 40 characters since that is about how many will fit in the Bookmark dialog.

Context Strings

Context strings identify topics in a Help system. Each topic must be unique across all .RTF files in an .HLP file. Although a topic doesn't necessarily require a context string since you can get to topics through a browse sequence or the Search dialog, having one allows hotspots to jump to the topic. (Each hotspot in a Help system uses a context string to tell it what to display when that hotspot is selected.) In general, every topic should have a context string.

Although a topic usually has just one context string identifying it, sometimes it is helpful to have several at different points within the topic. For example, in the Access 2.0 Help file, there is a long list of programming topics. At the top of the list are buttons A–Z and * (see Figure 23.4). When you click one of these buttons, the Help file jumps within the topic to the programming features that start with the letter on the button. This occurs because there are 26 additional context strings within the topic, one for each letter. The * button jumps back to the context string at the start of the topic.

You insert context strings the same way as title strings, except that the footnote reference mark is a pound sign (#). The footnote text can be 255 characters long, but you should keep it under 40 characters or so. Context strings can contain the characters A–Z, 0–9, periods (.), and underlines (_). Spaces are not permitted.

Keywords

Keywords are the entries that appear in the upper part of the Search dialog in the Help file, as shown in Figure 23.5. (Keywords are actually misnamed; they should really be *key phrases* since they can contain multiple words.) After you click the Show Topics button on a keyword (key phrase), the bottom portion of the Search dialog displays all the topic names that have a particular keyword phrase specified.

FIGURE 23.4:

Help topic with multiple context strings

FIGURE 23.5:

Search dialog box

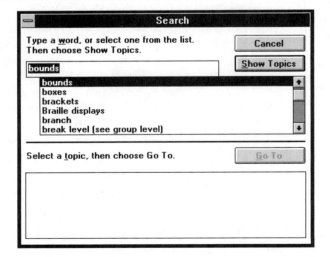

In Figure 23.6 the topics with the titles LBound Function, Option Base Statement, and UBound Function all have the keyword *bound*. Depending on your Help file, the topic title may be repeated in your keywords section.

Topic titles for the bound keyword

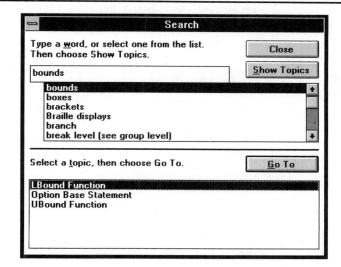

The footnote reference mark for keywords is an uppercase *K*. All ANSI characters except semicolons are permitted in keywords, including accented characters. You can have multiple keywords for each topic by separating them with semicolons. The Search dialog does a case-insensitive search, although the keywords appear in the search list exactly as they appear in the footnote.

Browse Sequence

Most Help systems show buttons on the toolbar for Browse Forward (>>) and Browse Back (<<). If you incorporate these buttons (which we recommend), your users can browse through your topics in a specified order. You set the order with the browse sequence. To get the browse buttons to appear on the toolbar, you must use the BrowseButtons macro in the CONFIG section of the .HPJ file, which is described in the section "The CONFIG Section" later in this chapter.

The footnote reference mark for a browse sequence is the plus (+) sign. You break the text for the browse sequence into two parts, separated by a colon. The first part is the group; the second part is the order. A *group* is a related set of topics that you can traverse by using the browse buttons. When a topic is displayed, the browse buttons traverse topics within the same group, but they never reach a topic that is part of a different group. The *order* is the sequence to be followed within the group. For example:

⁺ `user_interface:0050`.

The order is a string, but it is usually recorded as a number. Because the string will sort in ANSI sequence, not numeric sequence, you must record numbers with leading zeros. You may want to use numbers in increments of five or ten so you can insert another topic later without having to renumber the sequence. For example, if you have three topics in the user_interface sequence, you would set the browse sequence as follows:

Topic	Browse Sequence
Menu	user_interface:0010
Main Window	user_interface:0020
Status Bar	user_interface:0030

Later, if you want to insert a topic called Toolbar between the Menu and Main Window topics, you set the browse sequence for the new topic to user_interface:0015. This saves you from having to renumber the other topics.

Build Tags

Suppose you had three different versions of a program: a retail version, a shareware version, and a registered shareware version. The Help file for all three might be the same except for the license agreements. Keeping three different help projects in sync when changes are required to the Help files can become a nightmare. It makes more sense to keep only one help project and then instruct the Help file compiler to include the appropriate license agreement topic for the build you want to do. You invoke this inclusion and exclusion mechanism with *build tags*.

The footnote reference mark for build tags is the asterisk (*). This reference mark must be the first thing in a topic, immediately after the hard page break and before any other footnote reference marks. This tells the compiler whether it needs to process this particular topic or whether it can skip to the next topic. You enter the build tags into the footnote text. Build tags are case insensitive and can contain alphanumeric characters and the underline character. You can assign multiple tags, separated by semicolons, to a particular topic. For example, if you wanted to include a topic in the shareware and registered shareware versions of a Help file, the footnote might look like this:

```
* SHAREWARE; REGISTERED
```

The help compiler includes any topic that does not contain build tags in all builds of the Help file. You must define all build tags allowed in the Help file in the BUILD-TAGS section of the .HPJ file. The .HPJ file also tells the compiler which set of build tags to include and exclude in the Help file. You do this in the BUILD item in the OPTIONS section of the .HPJ file. The format of the .HPJ file is described in the section "Creating the .HPJ File" later in this chapter. The help compiler has a limit of 30 build tags per Help file.

Macros

The Help system defines a set of functions, called *macros*, to accomplish specific tasks. These macros are described in more detail in the section "Creating Hotspot Macros" later in this chapter. The macro footnote specifies the macros you want executed anytime the topic appears in the help screen. For example, you might want to add the browse buttons when viewing topics that are part of a browse sequence but remove the buttons when viewing topics that aren't. Unfortunately, you can't run a macro when you *leave* a topic, so the only way to remove a button you add in one topic is to put a macro to remove it in every other topic.

The footnote reference mark for macros is the exclamation point (!). For example:

```
! IfThen(Not(IsMark("upbutton")), "CreateButton('up', '&Up',
➡ 'JumpId('helpfile.hlp', 'parenttopic')'); SaveMark('upbutton')")
```

You can specify multiple macros by separating them with a semicolon. Macros can also call other macros, as shown in the preceding example—the IfThen macro calls the Not, CreateButton, and JumpID macros; the Not macro, in turn, calls the IsMark macro. The macros available are shown in Table 23.1. You can find complete documentation on these macros in the *Microsoft Help Compiler Guide*.

TABLE 23.1: Macros Available in Help

Macro Name	Function
About	Displays the About dialog box
AddAccelerator	Assigns a shortcut key to a macro
Annotate	Displays the Annotate dialog box
AppendItem	Appends an item to the end of a menu
Back	Equivalent to clicking the Back button on the toolbar
BookmarkDefine	Displays the Define dialog box
BookmarkMore	Displays the bookmark dialog that appears if the user has more than nine bookmarks
BrowseButtons	Adds the browse buttons to the toolbar
ChangeButtonBinding	Assigns a macro to a button on the toolbar
ChangeItemBinding	Assigns a macro to a menu item
CloseWindow	Closes a main or secondary window
Contents	Displays the contents topic in the current Help file
CopyDialog	Displays the Copy dialog box
CopyTopic	Copies the current topic to the Windows clipboard
CreateButton	Creates a button on the toolbar
DeleteItem	Removes a menu item from a menu
DeleteMark	Deletes a text marker created with SaveMark
DestroyButton	Removes a button from the toolbar
DisableButton	Disables and dims a toolbar button
DisableItem	Disables and dims an item on a menu
EnableButton	Enables a toolbar button disabled with DisableButton
EnableItem	Enables a menu item disabled with DisableItem
ExecProgram	Runs a Windows-based program
Exit	Exits WinHelp
FileOpen	Displays the Open dialog box
FocusWindow	Changes the focus to a main or secondary window
GotoMark	Jumps to a text marker defined by SaveMark

TABLE 23.1: Macros Available in Help (continued)

Macro Name	Function
HelpOn	Displays the Using Help Help file
History	Displays the History dialog box
IfThen	Allows conditional execution of a macro
IfThenElse	Allows conditional execution of two macros
InsertItem	Adds an item to a menu
InsertMenu	Adds a menu to the menu bar
IsMark	Determines whether a text marker has been created with SaveMark
JumpContents	Jumps to the contents topic of another Help file
JumpContext	Jumps to a topic defined by a context identifier
JumpHelpOn	Jumps to the Using Help Help file
JumpId	Jumps to a context string in a Help file
JumpKeyword	Jumps to the first topic that has the specified keyword
Next	Displays the next topic in the browse sequence
Not	Reverses the truth value of the IsMark macro
PopupContext	Displays a popup window showing a topic with a given context identifier
PopupId	Displays a popup window showing a topic with a given context string
PositionWindow	Sets the size and position of a main or secondary window
Prev	Displays the previous topic in a browse sequence
Print	Prints the current topic to the printer
PrinterSetup	Displays the Print Setup dialog box
RegisterRoutine	Registers a function in a DLL with the Help system
SaveMark	Saves a text marker
Search	Displays the Search dialog box
SetContents	Redefines the contents topic to a topic with a given context identifier
SetHelpOnFile	Redefines the Help file displayed when Help On Help is selected

Comments

You can insert comments about a topic for later reference by including text in a foot-note. The footnote reference mark for comments is the "at" (@) symbol.

Creating Non-Scrolling Regions

If you have long topics, you might have text that you always want displayed while the user scrolls through the topic with the scroll bars. You would commonly use this mechanism for the topic title and possibly for a *See Also* hotspot. You specify the text you want included in this non-scrolling region by setting the Keep With Next prop-erty for the paragraphs at the beginning of the topic. The help compiler uses this property as a signal that you want the topic included in the non-scrolling region.

By default, the background color of the non-scrolling region is white. You can set the background color to another color (typically gray) in the WINDOWS section of the .HPJ file, described in the section "Creating the .HPJ File" later in this chapter.

Creating Hotspots

Within a topic, you can create *hotspots* that perform specific actions. These hotspots can

- Jump to another topic in the Help file
- Jump to a topic in another Help file
- Display a popup window with more information about the hotspot
- Perform an action defined by a macro

The hotspot is usually displayed as green text and is underlined with either a dashed or solid underline. A hotspot can also appear in a graphic. For example, if a picture of a dialog is displayed, the user can click on the various parts of the dialog to learn about their functions.

The following sections describe how to create each type of hotspot.

Creating Jumps

To create a jump to another topic in the Help file, you mark the text with a double underline. (You can also use strike-through, but it is harder to read.) Immediately after the underlined text, you give the context string of the location to jump to. You must mark the context string with the *hidden text* font attribute. Word for Windows displays hidden text with a dotted underline. For example:

> When·you·click· <u>Jump</u>JumpTopic , ·the·text·jumps·to·the·context·string· JumpTopic .¶

In this example, the word *Jump* is the text of a hotspot. When you click Jump, the topic with the context string JumpTopic is displayed.

Creating Jumps to Another Help File

You can also jump to a topic in another Help file. The syntax is similar, except that the context string is followed by an @ symbol and the file name of the help topic. For example:

> When·you·press· <u>Jump</u>JumpTopic@file.hlp , ·the·text·jumps·to·the·context·string·
>
> JumpTopic·in·the·specified·Help·file.¶

You may also include a path on the Help file, but we do not recommend this since it forces the file structure to be fixed.

Creating Popup Windows

Sometimes you don't want to jump to another topic. Instead you want to create a small window in place that displays more information on the text (or graphic) that was clicked with the mouse. This is called a *popup window*. You typically use popup windows for definitions of terms. Creating the hotspot for a popup window is similar to a jump, except that the text is only single underlined. For example:

> When·you·click· <u>Popup</u>PopupTopic ·with·the·mouse, ·the·text·displays·the·topic·
>
> with·the·context·string· PopupTopic .¶

The text that is displayed is just like any other topic. You need to keep the text in a popup window relatively short since it cannot be scrolled or moved. Popup windows can contain hotspots that let you jump to other topics or even display another popup window.

The popup topic should not have a non-scrolling region since the help compiler does not allow them in popup topics and changes the topic without producing a warning. It doesn't make sense to include a popup window in a browse sequence or have keywords (using the *K* footnote mark) since you never want to jump to it.

Creating Macro Hotspots

Sometimes you want to execute a macro when you click a hotspot. For example, let's say that for the shareware version of an application, you have a program to print a registration order form. In the Help file you might want to include a hotspot that runs the Registration program. To do so, you double-underline the text and follow it with an exclamation point and the macro. The exclamation point and macro are formatted as hidden text. For example:

```
Register Program!ExecProgram("register.exe",7)¶
```

Inserting Graphics

Sometimes you'll want to insert graphics into your Help files. You can do this with normal graphics or with multi-resolution graphics produced by the multi-resolution bitmap compiler (MRBC.EXE). You can also use hypergraphic bitmaps, where the user can click on part of the bitmap to jump to a topic. You create these bitmaps with the hotspot editor (SHED.EXE). The following sections describe these methods.

Inserting Normal Graphics

You might want to include a graphic in a Help file. For example, you might want to put your corporate logo on the Contents screen. You can insert graphics directly or by reference.

The simplest way to include graphics is directly. You do this by importing the graphics into your topics where you wish them to appear. This has the advantage of letting you see them in context. For most graphics, though, you will want to include them by reference, for ease of maintenance. This method also reduces the size of the Help file since the help compiler includes each graphic in the Help file only once, with all references pointing to the same graphic. To include graphics by reference, you use one of three macros:

- bmc (bitmap character)
- bml (bitmap left)
- bmr (bitmap right)

You enclose the macros in curly braces and follow them with the file name of the bitmap. The bmc bitmap treats the bitmap as one character in the resulting Help file. The baseline of the bitmap aligns with the baseline of the surrounding text.

The bml and bmr macros cause the text to wrap around the graphic, either on the left or on the right. The text is aligned with the upper edge of the graphic and wraps around it. In both cases, the macro should be the first item in the paragraph. Do not put any spaces before the text that uses these macros.

You should be aware that the help compiler strips all bullets, em dashes (—), and superscripts from your .RTF file. It does this without producing a warning message. To create these in your Help file, you must create bitmaps for them and include them with the bmc macro. The Windows Help Authoring Tool, described in the section "Using the Windows Help Authoring Tool (WHAT)" later in this chapter, comes with a number of standard bitmaps.

Here are some examples:

```
{bmc bullet.bmp} The first thing
{bml logo.bmp}Acme Products
{bmr example.bmp}The example on the right shows the problem.
```

You can turn a bitmap into a hotspot the same way you create a text hotspot, except that you single- or double-underline the macro. For example:

```
{bmc okbutton.bmp}OkButtonContext¶
```

Inserting Multi-Resolution Graphics

Multi-resolution graphics are treated the same as normal graphics in every way inside an .RTF file. You create these graphics with the multi-resolution bitmap compiler (MRBC.EXE). The *Help Compiler Guide* includes full documentation on using the MRBC.EXE.

Inserting Hypergraphics

You create *hypergraphics* with the hotspot editor (SHED.EXE). In SHED, you can select regions of a graphic and bind them to jumps, popup windows, or macros. You include a hypergraphic in the Help file with the bmc, bml, and bmr macros, just as you would a normal graphic. When the hypergraphic is displayed, the user can click on a hotspot region and execute the jump, popup window, or macro that is bound to it.

Creating Secondary Windows

A *secondary window* contains information that is supplemental to the main help window. In the Access Help file, a secondary window is used for examples. For example, when viewing the Avg function, clicking the Example hotspot opens a secondary window showing examples for the Avg function. A secondary window does not have a menu. Secondary windows remain open until the user closes them, even if the main help window is closed.

Since secondary windows create another window users have to manage, this can confuse them, especially if they are new to Windows. Be careful that these windows fit cleanly into your overall help scheme.

You specify the look of a secondary window in the .HPJ file. Jumps to a secondary window use a slightly different syntax than the normal jumps. To jump to a topic and have it appear in a secondary window, you must follow the context string with a greater-than (>) sign and the window name of the secondary window, as specified in the WINDOWS section of the .HPJ file. For example:

```
Jump Textcontextstring>secwind¶
```

To jump to a secondary window in another Help file, place the file name first, followed by the window name. For example:

```
Jump·Textcontextstring@file.hlp>windowname¶
```

Creating the .HPJ File

The .HPJ file tells the help compiler how to build the Help file. It specifies the following:

- Which options to use
- Which .RTF files are to be included
- Which build tags are allowed in the .RTF files
- DLL function prototypes
- Which macros are to be run when the Help file opens
- Location of bitmaps
- Numbers to be associated with context strings for context-sensitive help
- Aliases for context strings
- Characteristics of the main and secondary windows

The .HPJ file is a text file you can create with any text editor. You can use Notepad or your word processor. If you use your word processor, you must save the file in MS-DOS text (ASCII text) format. The .HPJ file is laid out like an .INI file, having sections in brackets. Within each section are settings pertaining to the section name. Comments start with a semicolon and continue to the end of the line. Figure 23.7 shows a typical .HPJ file.

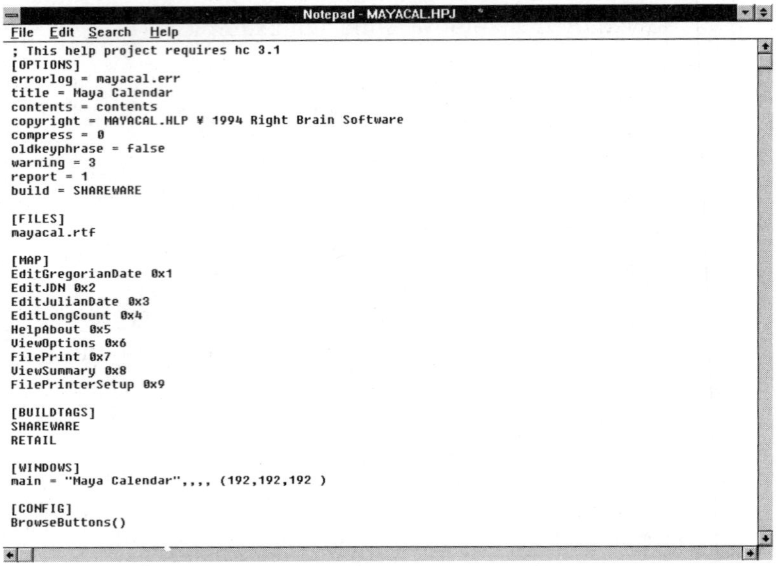

FIGURE 23.7:

Typical .HPJ file

```
                                    Notepad - MAYACAL.HPJ
File   Edit   Search   Help
; This help project requires hc 3.1
[OPTIONS]
errorlog = mayacal.err
title = Maya Calendar
contents = contents
copyright = MAYACAL.HLP ¥ 1994 Right Brain Software
compress = 0
oldkeyphrase = false
warning = 3
report = 1
build = SHAREWARE

[FILES]
mayacal.rtf

[MAP]
EditGregorianDate 0x1
EditJDN 0x2
EditJulianDate 0x3
EditLongCount 0x4
HelpAbout 0x5
ViewOptions 0x6
FilePrint 0x7
ViewSummary 0x8
FilePrinterSetup 0x9

[BUILDTAGS]
SHAREWARE
RETAIL

[WINDOWS]
main = "Maya Calendar",,,, (192,192,192 )

[CONFIG]
BrowseButtons()
```

The OPTIONS Section

The OPTIONS section of the .HPJ file contains options that modify the whole Help file. You separate the option name from its setting with an equal (=) sign. The following sections describe the options within the OPTIONS section.

The BMROOT Option

The BMROOT option designates paths where the help compiler can find bitmaps specified by the bmc, bml, and bmr macros. The format is

BMROOT = *path*[, *path*]

Each path name can specify a drive and path. If the .HPJ file doesn't have a BMROOT option, the help compiler looks for graphics specified by the ROOT option. If you don't use the BMROOT or ROOT option, you must specify each graphic in the BITMAPS section of the .HPJ file.

The BUILD Option

The BUILD option tells the help compiler which topics you want included in the Help file. You need to include this option only if the .RTF files contain build tags. The format is

BUILD=*expression*

The *expression* is the statement that tells the help compiler which build tags to include in the help compiler. The expression can contain the following:

( )	Parentheses
&	Logical And
|	Logical Or
~	Logical Not
tag	Build tag

For example, if you have three build tags, RETAIL, SHAREWARE, and REGISTERED, here are some combinations you might use:

BUILD=RETAIL	Include all topics without tags, plus any with the RETAIL tag
BUILD=SHAREWARE | REGISTERED	Include all topics without tags, plus any that include the SHAREWARE tag or the REGISTERED tag
BUILD=~RETAIL	Equivalent to SHAREWARE | REGISTERED

TIP

Unfortunately, if you use non-scrolling regions and build tags in the same .RTF file, the current version of the help compiler (version 3.10.505) has a bug that produces an error (4813), "Non-scrolling region crosses page boundary." For a work-around that doesn't use build tags, create separate .RTF files that contain the set of topics specific to specific builds. Then create a separate .HPJ file for each build type that references the common and build-specific .RTF files.

The COMPRESS Option

The help compiler is capable of compressing the Help file using file-compression techniques. There are three levels of compression: none, medium, and high. Compressing the Help file reduces its size but increases the amount of time it takes to build the Help file and access the topics. You should turn off compression while working on the Help file and then turn it on before delivering the Help file to the client. Medium compression reduces the size of the Help file by approximately 40 percent, while high compression reduces it by about 50 percent.

The format is

COMPRESS=*setting*

The *setting* can be one of the following:

0, NO, or FALSE	No compression
MEDIUM	Medium compression
1, YES, TRUE, or HIGH	High compression

When using high compression, the help compiler creates a file with a .PH extension. This contains information that speeds up the compression operation the next time you compile the Help file. However, to get maximum compression you need to create a new .PH file when you compile. The OLDKEYPHRASE option, described shortly, determines whether the old .PH file is used or a new one is created.

If your Help file is going to be compressed using another product, such as PKZip or the setup toolkit, you can get a smaller compressed image if the help compiler does not compress the file. However, this takes more room on your user's machine in exchange for the smaller compressed image. You would use this technique if a small distribution size is important.

The CONTENTS Option

In every Help file, one topic is identified as the contents topic. This is the topic you reach when you select Contents from the Help file in an application. You specify this topic with the CONTENTS option. If the CONTENTS option is not present, the compiler makes the first topic it encounters the contents topic. The format is

CONTENTS=*contentstopicstring*

For example:

```
CONTENTS=contents_page
```

The COPYRIGHT Option

You can add a line of text to the About Help dialog box that appears on the Help menu when running help. This line typically contains a copyright notice, but you are free to specify what goes here. You might also show version information or credits. You are limited to one line of text, so you must be concise. The format is

COPYRIGHT=*notice*

For example:

```
COPYRIGHT=APPLICATION © 1996 Right Brain Software
```

The ERRORLOG Option

The ERRORLOG option lets you specify a file where help compiler warnings and errors are to be written. Error messages are also written to the screen. Usually, you name the log file the same as the .HPJ, but with the extension .ERR. For example, if the project file is named APP.HPJ, the option appears as

```
ERRORLOG=app.err
```

The FORCEFONT Option

The FORCEFONT option overrides the font name selections throughout the .HPJ files and substitutes the font specified. The format is

FORCEFONT=*fontname*

The ICON Option

The ICON option specifies an icon that is displayed when the user minimizes the Help file. If this option is not specified, a question mark icon is used. The format is

ICON=*iconfile*

The *iconfile* must be in the Windows standard icon format.

The LANGUAGE Option

The LANGUAGE option changes the sort order in the search keyword lists to something other than the English alphabetic sorting. The only other language currently supported using the normal help compiler is Scandinavian. Microsoft has available different versions of the help compiler for Eastern European and Asian languages. The format is

LANGUAGE=scandinavian

The MAPFONTSIZE Option

The MAPFONTSIZE option allows you to change the size of the fonts specified in the .RTF files to another size. You can specify up to five MAPFONTSIZE option lines in the .HPJ file to specify different mappings. The format is

MAPFONTSIZE=$m[-n]:p$

The *m* argument specifies the font size in the Help file. You can use the format *m–n* to specify a range of font sizes. The *p* argument specifies the font size to which the original is to be mapped. For example:

```
MAPFONTSIZE=8-10:12
```

This line tells the help compiler to change all characters in font sizes 8 through 10 points to 12 points in the compiled Help file. You can use the multiple MAPFONT-SIZE options to specify different ranges, as long as the ranges don't overlap.

The MULTIKEY Option

You can specify several keyword tables in a Help file, but only the normal (K) keywords appear in the search dialog. You can search the other keyword tables by using the Win-Help API, described in the section "Getting to Help from Access Basic" later in this chapter. Refer to the *Help Compiler Guide* for more information on the MULTIKEY option.

The OLDKEYPHRASE Option

The OLDKEYPHRASE option works in conjunction with the COMPRESS option. If the OLDKEYPHRASE option is set to True, the current .PH file is used. If it is set to False, a new .PH file is created. For example:

```
OLDKEYPHRASE=TRUE
```

The OPTCDROM Option

The OPTCDROM option optimizes a Help file for use on a CD-ROM. It speeds access to the topics but slightly increases the size of the Help file. The format is

```
OPTCDROM=1
```

You can also use YES, TRUE, or ON instead of 1.

The REPORT Option

If the REPORT option is turned on, messages are displayed on the screen while the compiler is working to tell you about its progress. The format is

```
REPORT=1
```

You can also use YES, TRUE, or ON instead of 1.

The ROOT Option

The ROOT option specifies the root directory of the help project. If this option is omitted, the help compiler looks for files relative to the .HPJ file. The format is

ROOT=*path*[, *path*]

The TITLE Option

The TITLE option specifies the text that appears on the title bar when help is running. If this option is not specified, the words *Microsoft Help* are displayed. The format is

TITLE=*titletext*

The WARNING Option

The WARNING option specifies the level of errors and warnings the help compiler reports. The format is

WARNING=*warninglevel*

The *warninglevel* setting can be an integer from 1 to 3, where 1 specifies the least number of warnings and 3 the most. For example:

WARNING=3

You should use warning level 3 in most cases so that you can find and fix any problems with your Help file.

The ALIAS Section

The ALIAS section provides a way of remapping context IDs in an Access database to another help topic without changing the database. It works with the MAP section. For example, suppose you have 14 different forms in four databases that have context-sensitive help that refers to the context string invoice_description in the MAP section. If you later took the invoice_description topic and combined it with the statement_description topic, you could avoid changing every form to refer to the statement_description topic. Instead you could put one line in the ALIAS section and recompile the Help file.

The format for items in the ALIAS section is

aliascontextstring = *contextstring*

The *contextstring* must appear in one of the .RTF files. You can have multiple *alias-contextstrings* that refer to the same *contextstring*.

If the ALIAS section appears in the .HPJ file, it must occur before the MAP section.

The BITMAPS Section

If you refer to bitmaps in directories other than those specified by the ROOT or BMROOT options, you must list their file names in the BITMAPS section. For example:

```
[BITMAPS]
BULLET.BMP
SCRNSHOT.BMP
C:\HLP\PROJECT\EXAMPLE.BMP
```

You usually place bitmap files in directories specified by the ROOT or BMROOT option, so you would seldom use the BITMAPS option. You might use it if you had another tool produce a list of files that you would include here.

The BUILDTAGS Section

You must list every build tag in your .RTF files in the BUILDTAGS section. For example:

```
[BUILDTAGS]
RETAIL
SHAREWARE
REGISTERED
```

You can have up to 30 build tags for each help project.

The CONFIG Section

The CONFIG section of the .HPJ file specifies macros that are to be run when the Help file starts. You specify the macros listed in this section in the order in which they are run. For example:

```
[CONFIG]
RegisterRoutine("DISPLAY.DLL", "CopyrightNoticeFunction", "S=U")
```

```
CreateButton("btn_register", "&Register",
➡ "ExecProgram('register.exe', 7)")
BrowseButtons()
```

The RegisterRoutine() macro registers a DLL function, the CreateButton() macro creates a button on the toolbar called Register (with the *R* underlined) that runs the REGISTER.EXE program, and the BrowseButtons() macro puts the << and >> buttons on the toolbar. You should define the BrowseButtons() macro in the CONFIG section of the .HPJ file for most Help files.

The FILES Section

The FILES section of the .HPJ file specifies the .RTF files that are to be compiled. You simply list the files that are to be included in the Help file, or you can include a list of files stored in another file using #*include*:

> #include <*filename*>

If you use the #include option, the contents of *filename* are included in place. The angle brackets are required. An example of a FILES section is shown here:

```
[FILES]
#include <filelist.txt>
MIKE.RTF
BILL.RTF
```

The MAP Section

You use the MAP section of the .HPJ file for context-sensitive help. If you use context-sensitive help in your Help file, you *must* have a MAP section. You use the MAP section to assign numbers to the context strings in the .RTF files. These numbers are used in the HelpContextId property of objects on forms. There are two ways to specify the items in the MAP section:

> *contextstring contextid*

or

> #define *contextstring contextid*

You specify the *contextstring* exactly the way it appears in the context string footnote in the .RTF file. The *contextid* is an unsigned long integer, and you can write it in either decimal or hexadecimal. It must be greater than 0 since Access treats the number 0 as meaning that no context has been declared. You can also use the #include syntax to include a C header file with #define statements. Here is an example MAP section showing the different possible formats:

```
[MAP]
Contents 0x0001
HowToUseTheProgram 2
#define SharewareInformation 0x0003
#include <morectxs.h>
```

The *contextstring* can also specify an alias assigned in the ALIAS section of the .HPJ file.

The WINDOWS Section

The WINDOWS section of the .HPJ file specifies the size, location, and colors of the main and secondary windows. The format is

typename="*caption*",(*left, top, width, height*), *maximized*, (*red, green, blue*),

➡ (*nsred, nsgreen, nsblue*), *topmost*

The following table describes the parameters:

Parameter	Description
typename	Either the word *main*, for the main help window, or a word other than *main*, up to eight characters for a secondary window
caption	For secondary windows, this specifies the text that appears on the title bar for the window. For the main window, it is ignored
left, top, width, and *height*	Position and size of the window. The units are based on the screen's being 1024 units square. Thus, the coordinates (512, 512) are the middle of the screen
maximized	Set to 1 if the Help window is to appear maximized when opened, 0 if not

Parameter	Description
red, *green*, and *blue*	The color of the background of the Help window, in values from 0 to 255
nsred, *nsgreen*, and *nsblue*	The color of the non-scrolling region of the Help window, in values from 0 to 255
topmost	For secondary windows, set to 1 if the window is to remain in front of all other windows; set to 0 if it can move behind other windows

Here is an example of a WINDOWS section:

```
main = "RBS Inventory",(512, 0, 511, 1023),0,, (192, 192, 192), 0
```

This example creates a main window. The caption is set to "RBS Inventory", but since this is a main window, it is ignored. (The Title option is used instead.) The window starts up taking up the right half of the screen. The window is not maximized. It uses the default background color for the main window, and the non-scrolling region appears gray. It is not a top-most window.

Compiling the Help Project

The help compiler is a DOS program. Because of the way it manages memory, you must run it in a DOS window from Windows. The compiler has had different names at different times. The latest version is called HCP.EXE, but older versions are called HC31.EXE or HC.EXE. To compile a project, you simply list the .HPJ file name on the help compiler's command line. For example:

```
HCP PROJECT.HPJ
```

Using the Windows Help Authoring Tool (WHAT)

Now that you've learned how to construct the .RTF files and the .HPJ file, we'll let you in on a little secret: almost nobody actually creates Help files this way! Instead, developers use help authoring tools that simplify the process. Microsoft distributes a free tool called the Windows Help Authoring Tool (WHAT). It's included on the Microsoft Developer Network CD-ROM and is also available for download on CompuServe. This tool is unsupported by Microsoft, meaning that they let you have it for free, but if it doesn't work or you have any problems, they won't help you in any official way.

WHAT consists of two parts:

- A Visual Basic program that maintains the .HPJ file. It also runs Word for Windows and the help compiler by selecting options from the menus.

- A template with Word for Windows macros that facilitates creating .RTF files.

Microsoft HULK

As this book goes to press, the latest edition of the Microsoft Developer Network CD-ROM includes another help authoring tool called HULK (Help Universal Kit). HULK has a slightly different emphasis than WHAT. Besides managing the help project itself, it has tools that help manage and maintain large help projects, such as letting you look for inconsistencies in your topic titles, checking for a variety of errors not reported by the help compiler, and producing reports showing the topics in your Help file. HULK is also unsupported by Microsoft.

Using the Windows Help Project Editor

The Visual Basic program is called WHPE.EXE (Window Help Project Editor, pronounced "whoopee"!). It presents a straightforward interface for manipulating the .HPJ file. Figure 23.8 shows the WHPE window. The menus are summarized in Table 23.2.

FIGURE 23.8:

Windows Help Project Editor window

TABLE 23.2: Menu Items in WHPE

Menu	Option	Description
File	New Project	Creates a new project file
	Open Help Project	Opens an existing .HPJ file
	Save Project	Saves the current .HPJ file
	Save Project As	Saves the current project to a new name
	Run Help on *project name*	Runs WinHelp on the current project. You must compile the project before this is available
	Exit	Closes WHPE.EXE
Edit	Add New or Existing File	Adds an .RTF file to the .HPJ file
	Remove File	Removes an .RTF file from the .HPJ file
	Edit File	Invokes Word for Windows on the file selected in the WHPE main window
	Project	Specifies the TITLE option and CONTENTS option in the .HPJ file. Also lets you select the version of the help compiler to use

TABLE 23.2: Menu Items in WHPE (continued)

Menu	Option	Description
	Comments	Allows you to add comments to the .HPJ file. You can use these as reminders
	Compression	Controls the COMPRESS and OLDKEYPHRASE options of the .HPJ file
	Application Contexts	Provides a user interface for maintaining the MAP section of the .HPJ file, allowing you to define new or modify existing context identifiers
	Graphics	Allows you to maintain the BITMAPS section of the .HPJ file
	Window Definitions	Provides an interface for maintaining the WINDOWS section of the .HPJ file, allowing you to get visual feedback on the size and colors of your windows
Compile	Start	Invokes the help compiler on the project
	View Errors	Displays the errors generated by the help compiler
Help	Contents	Views the WHPE help file
	Search for Help on	Searches the WHPE help file
	How to Use Help	Displays the standard how-to-use-help information
	About Help Project Editor	Displays an about box

WHPE does not provide a user interface for changing some entries in the .HPJ file. However, you can use a text editor to add entries that it does not handle. WHPE does not disturb any entries that it does not manipulate. For example, if you want to add a copyright message, you can use Notepad to edit the .HPJ file and add a COPYRIGHT item in the OPTIONS section.

Using WHAT6.DOT

WHAT includes a template called WHAT6.DOT that contains macros and styles you can use to manipulate the .RTF file. When you open an .RTF file in Word for Windows based on this template, you are presented with the Windows Help Authoring toolbar. (You may have to select View ➤ Toolbars and turn on this toolbar the first time you edit the document.) This toolbar is shown in Figure 23.9. Table 23.3 describes the buttons.

Modifying WHPE.EXE to Work with Word for Windows 6.0

As this book goes to press, the current version of WHPE.EXE on the Microsoft Developer's Network CD-ROM is incompatible with Word for Windows version 6.0. This is the price of an unsupported tool. If you have problems making WHPE work with Word for Windows 6.0, you can patch the executable to make it compatible. To do so: (1) Install Help Author using the setup program in \SMPLS\UNTOOLS\HELPAU on the MSDN CD-ROM. (2) Run Windows Write. (3) Open WHPE.EXE. (4) When Write asks you whether you want to convert the file to a Write document, click the No Conversion button. (5) Select Find ➤ Find. (6) Enter the following text in the Find dialog: ToolsOptionsGeneral.ConfirmConversions = 0. (7) Click OK. (8) Press ←. (9) Very carefully change the entire text that you searched for in step 6 to spaces, using the Del key followed by the spacebar repeatedly. You must not increase or decrease the size of the file by even one character. (10) Save the file.

FIGURE 23.9:

WHAT toolbar

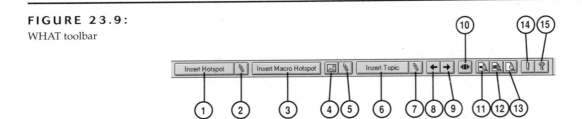

The macros in WHAT6.DOT simplify the process of manipulating the .RTF file since they use dialogs to maintain the footnotes. It is far easier to use the dialogs than to maintain the footnotes by hand since they provide context for each footnote entry. The template also contains some useful styles, which are described in the Help file.

TABLE 23.3: Buttons on the WHAT6.DOT Toolbar

Number	Button	Description
1	Insert Hotspot	Opens a dialog that lets you specify a new jump or popup
2	Edit Hotspot	Opens a dialog that lets you modify an existing jump or popup
3	Insert Macro Hotspot	Inserts text connected to a macro
4	Insert Graphic	Inserts a graphic
5	Edit Graphic	Edits information about a graphic
6	Insert Topic	Inserts a new topic into the .RTF file
7	Edit Topic	Edits an existing topic
8	Start of Topic	Moves to the start of the current topic
9	End of Topic	Moves to the end of the current topic
10	Select Topic	Selects the current topic
11	View Selection	Compiles the selected text and views it in WinHelp
12	View Topic	Compiles the current topic and views it in WinHelp
13	View File	Compiles the entire .RTF file and views it in WinHelp
14	About WHAT	Displays an About dialog
15	On WHAT	Displays a Help file describing the WHAT features

Other Authoring Tools

If having an unsupported tool bothers you, you can use one of the commercial tools sold by third parties that are supported by their respective companies. These come in two categories: macros for major word processors (usually Word for Windows) and stand-alone applications. Some of the better known tools are listed here:

Tool	Description	Company
Doc-To-Help	A set of Word for Windows macros	WexTech Systems, (212) 949-9595

Tool	Description	Company
Help Breeze	A set of Word for Windows macros and Wizards. A slideshow demo is available on CompuServe. Go IBMFF and look for a file named HLPBRZ.ZIP	Solutionsoft, (408) 736-1431
RoboHelp	A set of Word for Windows macros	Blue Sky Software, (800) 677-4946 or (619) 459-6365
Visual Help	A stand-alone tool. You can try a limited version, restricted to three topics, that is otherwise fully functional. It is available on CompuServe. Go IBMFF and look for a file named VH.ZIP	WinWare, (800) 242-4775 or (713) 524-6394
Windows Help Magician	A stand-alone tool. You can try a restricted version, limited to seven topics, that is otherwise fully functional. It is available on CompuServe. Go IBMFF and look for a file named HLPMAG.ZIP	Software Interphase, (401) 397-2340

Creating Context-Sensitive Help for Access Forms and Reports

Once a Help file has been created, getting to it is very easy from Access. For each topic you want to reach from Access, you must create an entry in the MAP section of the .HPJ file. These entries assign numbers called *context identifiers* to the context strings, which identify topics. After the Help file has been compiled, you need to add a few properties to your forms and reports.

Each form or report in Access has a property called HelpFile that specifies the associated Help file. You simply specify the name of the Help file here. Then, in the HelpContextId property, you enter the context identifier you want to reach when the user presses the F1 key.

In addition, you can specify context identifiers for each control on the form. If the context identifier for a control is non-zero, Access uses the topic for that specific control; otherwise it uses the help topic for the form.

Getting to Help from Access Basic

There will be times when you want to get to help from Access Basic. For example, if you create a menu bar that has a Help menu on it, you will want Contents and Search for Help menu items to open the contents page or display the Search dialog for your Help file. To get to help from Access Basic, you need to use the Windows API.

The following code snippet shows the prototypes and all the constants used by the WinHelp Windows API. It also defines the structure if you use the multiple keyword tables. After including these declarations in a module, you can call the WinHelp() function.

```
Declare Function WinHelp Lib "User" (ByVal hWnd As Integer,
➡ ByVal strHelpFile As String, ByVal intCommand As
➡ Integer, anyData As Any) As Integer
```

```
' Commands to pass WinHelp()
Global Const HELP_CONTEXT = &H1 '  Display topic in anyData
Global Const HELP_QUIT = &H2      '  Terminate help
Global Const HELP_CONTENTS = &H3       ' Display Help for a
                                       ' particular topic
Global Const HELP_HELPONHELP = &H4       ' Display help on
                                         ' using help
Global Const HELP_SETCONTENTS = &H5  ' Display Help contents
                                     ' topic
Global Const HELP_CONTEXTPOPUP = &H8 ' Display Help topic in
                                     ' popup window
Global Const HELP_FORCEFILE = &H9    ' Ensure correct Help
                                     ' file is displayed
Global Const HELP_KEY = &H101            ' Display topic for
                                         ' keyword in anyData
Global Const HELP_COMMAND = &H102    ' Execute Help macro
Global Const HELP_PARTIALKEY = &H105 ' Display topic found
                                     ' in keyword list
Global Const HELP_MULTIKEY = &H201
Global Const HELP_SETWINPOS = &H203  ' Display and position
                                     ' Help window

Type MULTIKEYHELP
    intSize As Integer
    strKeylist As String * 1
    strKeyphrase As String * 253 ' Array length is arbitrary;
    ➡ may be changed
End Type
```

After inserting these declarations, you can use the WinHelp() function.

Opening the Help File to the Contents Topic

To open the Help file and display the contents document, use the following syntax:

intRet = WinHelp(Me.hWnd, Me.helpfile, HELP_CONTENTS, ByVal 0&)

The first argument to the WinHelp() function is the handle to the Form window. The second is the name of the Help file where you retrieve the HelpFile property from the form. The third argument is the HELP_CONTENTS constant defined above. The fourth argument is ignored in this context.

Opening the Help File to Any Other Topic

To open the Help file to any topic besides the contents topic, you need to know the context identifier defined in the MAP section of the .HPJ file. You then use the following syntax:

intRet = WinHelp(Me.hWnd, Me.helpfile, HELP_CONTEXT,
➥ ByVal *lngContextId*)

lngContextId contains the context identifier you want.

Opening the Search Dialog

To open the Search dialog for the Help file, you use the following syntax:

intRet = WinHelp(Me.hWnd, Me.helpfile, HELP_PARTIALKEY, ByVal 0&)

Getting Help on Help

Windows provides a standard Help file telling users how the Help system works. You can open this Help file by using the following syntax:

intRet = WinHelp(Me.hWnd, Me.helpfile, HELP_HELPONHELP, ByVal 0&)

Closing Help

In Windows, if a program opens the Help file, it's supposed to close it if the application is closed. So if you call the WinHelp() function, you should set a flag that you opened the Help file. Then, before the window with the hWnd that opened the form is closed, you need to use the following syntax:

If *fWinHelpOpened* Then
    intRet = WinHelp(Me.hWnd, Me.helpfile, HELP_QUIT, ByVal 0&)
End If

If the user has already closed the Help file, this code is ignored.

Tips on Creating Help Files

The following sections give you some guidelines and tips for creating Help files. They offer some things to think about as you plan for and create Help files.

Allocate Time to Create the Help File

Help files are often the last thing you produce, with little time allocated for their production. Creating a good Help file is a time-consuming process—it takes at least as much time as writing a paper document of the same length. You need to build production time into your schedule and/or budget for its creation.

Define Your Audience

An important part of writing any Help file is defining the audience. Are you writing for beginner, intermediate, or advanced users? Do the users have a background in the field, or do you have to explain financial terms if your program does accounting?

Design the Help File Concurrently with the Programming

It helps to design the Help file at the same time you are programming. Sometimes the way you document a program affects its design.

Use Hypermedia, but Don't Overuse It

Use a jump or a popup window only the first time a term appears in a topic. It is not necessary to use these items more often, and it can be confusing. If the term *Accrual* appears six times in a topic, only the first mention should have a popup window defining the concept.

Keep Topics and Paragraphs Short

Information in a Help file can overload a user. You should try to keep topics short enough to fit on one screen. You can use jumps to break a topic into multiple parts. Keep paragraphs in Help files shorter than in printed media.

Enhance a Help File with Subtle Use of Color

You can use the color features of your RTF editor to add color to the text in your Help file. This can enhance the impact of the file. Be careful, though, because too much color will overload the user. Also, do not make the user's distinction of color critical. Remember that approximately 10 percent of the male population is color-blind to some degree.

A Debugging Tip

You may find that adding the SeqTopicKeys item to the Windows Help section of the WIN.INI file helps you debug Help files. For example:

```
[Windows Help]
SeqTopicKeys=1
```

With this item defined when you are viewing a Help file, pressing Ctrl+Shift+→ moves you to the next topic, as defined by the order in which the topics were encountered by the help compiler. You can use this keystroke repeatedly.

Summary

A Help file is the mark of a complete and polished application. This chapter has described the process and tools necessary to complete one, including the following:

- Parts of a Help File
- Creating topics in the .RTF editor
- Creating the .HPJ file

- Compiling the Help file
- Using Help Author
- Creating context-sensitive help in forms and reports
- Calling help from Access Basic
- Tips for creating Help files

APPENDICES

APPENDIX

A

The Leszynski/Reddick Naming Conventions for Microsoft Access

This appendix, written by Stan Leszynski and Greg Reddick (rev. May 25, 1994), is a slightly revised version of guidelines published in the August 1993 issue of *Smart Access,* published by Pinnacle Publishing Inc. (Kent, WA). An update for Access version 2.0 was published in the May 1994 issue of *Smart Access,* and the revisions have been incorporated into this appendix.

If you've ever inherited a project from other developers, you know how frustrating it is to try to dissect their style and maintain their code. When developers code with a common style, however, you can minimize these frustrations. To best share ideas and knowledge, the Access development community will benefit greatly if it adopts a common programming style so that we can benefit from each other's expertise with a minimum of translation overhead. Although Microsoft uses certain naming conventions in the Access documentation, to date they haven't published an official or comprehensive standard. Thus, we've formulated a set of naming conventions to better serve Access users and developers.

These conventions were originally published in the Charter Issue of *Smart Access* in February of 1993. Since then, we've logged thousands of hours of development time and scores of comments from *Smart Access* readers and other users of the conventions, and we continue to improve the style and make it more useful.

Our naming style ties Access conventions closely to Visual Basic conventions because we recognize that many Access developers also use or plan to use Visual Basic for some data access applications. Access and Visual Basic are becoming more similar with each released version. We've written these naming conventions so you can also use them with Visual Basic database applications.

There are two levels to the naming style. Level 1 is comprehensive, but it doesn't clarify objects as explicitly as Level 2. Level 1 is suitable for beginning developers, while Level 2 is intended for more experienced developers and developers involved in complex development projects and multiple-developer environments. You should experiment and choose the level that works best for you.

NOTE Not all parts of the standard have two levels.

If you're already using any previous version of our conventions, you may need to make a few changes to accommodate the enhancements in this revision. Since

Access provides little help in renaming objects, you may wish to leave existing applications as is and apply the revised conventions to new projects, going back to existing applications as time permits.

Naming Conventions: An Overview

Our naming style is based on a method of naming called *Hungarian*, referring to the nationality of its creator, Charles Simonyi (who, incidentally, worked on the first version of Access). Hungarian was first proposed in his doctoral thesis.

Some elements of Hungarian style are used in Microsoft's Visual Basic manuals and Development Kit documentation, among others. Microsoft uses Hungarian internally, and many programmers around the world use it as well. We've adapted the Hungarian style for the Access environment.

In our Access naming style, object names are made up of four parts: prefixes, tag, base name, and qualifier. The four parts are assembled as follows:

[prefixes]tag[Basename][Qualifier]

 **NOTE** The brackets denote that these components are optional; they aren't part of the name.

The tag is the only required component, but in almost all cases the name will also have the base name component since you need to be able to distinguish between two objects of the same type.[1] Here are a few examples:

Name	Prefix	Tag	Base	Qualifier
tblCustomer		tbl	Customer	
aintPartNum	a	int	PartNum	
strCustNamePrev		str	CustName	Prev

Prefixes and tags are always lowercase so your eye goes past them to the first uppercase letter, where the base name begins. This makes the names more readable. The base and qualifier components begin with an uppercase letter.

The *base name* succinctly describes the object, not its class. This is the name you'd likely give the object if you weren't using any particular naming style. For example, in the query name qryPartNum, "PartNum" is the base name; it's an abbreviation for Part Number. *Object tags* are short and mnemonic. *Object prefixes* precede some object names and tags and provide further information. For example, if an integer variable intPartNum is an array of part numbers, the prefix *a* for *array* is added to the front, as in aintPartNum(). Further, a variable that provides an index into the array would use the name of the array prefixed with the index prefix *i*—for example, iaintPartNum.

Applying a naming style like this requires more effort up front, but try to imagine which of these two code samples makes more sense to you a year from now when you want to modify or try to reuse your code:

```
Z = Y(X)
```

or

```
intPart = aintPartNum(iaintPartNum)
```

Object qualifiers may follow a name and further clarify names that are similar. Continuing with our parts index example, if you kept two indexes to the array, one for the first item and one for the last, the variable iaintPartNum above would become two qualified variables -- iaintPartNumFirst and iaintPartNumLast.

Naming Database Objects

Database objects (tables, queries, forms, reports, macros, and modules) are the most frequently referenced items in an Access application. They appear in your macro code, in your Access Basic routines, and in properties. Thus, it's important that you standardize how you name them.

Microsoft's examples in the Northwind Database and Access manuals allow for spaces in object names, but we don't use them in our style. In most database engines and programming languages, including Access Basic, a space is a delimiter character *between* items; it isn't a logical part of an item's name. Also, spaces in field names don't work in most other database platforms or Windows applications, such as SQL Server and Word for Windows. Instead, use upper- and lowercase designations in names, such as tblAccountsPayable. If spacing is still necessary, use the underscore (_) character instead of a space to be consistent with traditionally accepted SQL syntax and with Access 2.x function-naming conventions.

Tags for Database Container Objects

All database container object names in our style have tags. Adding tags to these objects may make them less readable to nondevelopers, but new users will understand their value when they're trying to discern a table from a query in the list box for a New Report Wizard or a form's ControlSource property. This is because Access merges table and query names into one long list. Here are the Level 1 database container object name tags:

Object	Tag	Example
Table	tbl	tblCustomer
Query	qry	qryOverAchiever
Form	frm	frmCustomer
Report	rpt	rptInsuranceValue
Macro	mcr	mcrUpdateInventory
Module[2]	bas	basBilling

At Level 1, the only name qualifier (appended to the name) that we use for database container objects is Sub, which we place at the end of a form or report name for a subform or subreport. The form frmProductSupplier would have the related subform frmProductSupplierSub. This allows objects and their subform or subreport to sort next to each other in the database container.

Level 2 tags, shown here, provide more descriptive information:

Object	Tag	Example
Table	tbl	tblCustomer
Table (lookup)[3]	tlkp	tlkpShipper
Query (select)	qry (or qsel)	qryOverAchiever
Query (append)	qapp	qappNewProduct
Query (crosstab)	qxtb	qxtbRegionSales
Query (DDL)	qddl	qddlInit
Query (delete)	qdel	qdelOldAccount
Query (form filter)	qflt	qfltSalesToday
Query (lookup)[3]	qlkp	qlkpStatus
Query (make table)	qmak	qmakShipTo
Query (SQL pass-through)	qsql	qsqlGetData
Query (totals)	qtot	qtotResult
Query (union)	quni	quniMerged
Query (update)	qupd	qupdDiscount
Form	frm	frmCustomer
Form (dialog)	fdlg	fdlgLogin
Form (menu)	fmnu	fmnuUtility
Form (message)	fmsg	fmsgWait
Form (subform)[4]	fsub	fsubOrder
Report	rpt	rptInsuranceValue
Report (subreport)[4]	rsub	rsubOrder
Macro	mcr	mcrUpdateInventory
Macro (for form)[5]	m[formname]	mfrmCustomer

Object	Tag	Example
Macro (menu)[6]	mmnu	mmnuEntryFormFile
Macro (for report)[5]	m[rptname]	mrptInsuranceValue
Module[2]	bas	basBilling

Using our Level 2 style causes objects with similar functions to sort together in the database container in large applications. Imagine that you have a database container with 100 forms in it (we do!), 30 of which are messages that display during the application. Your users now want all message forms to have red text instead of black, so you must change each of the 30 forms. Having the message forms sort together in the database container (because they've all got the same tag) saves you significant effort trying to discern which forms you need to change.

Choose your table names carefully. Since changes to the names of Access objects do not propagate through the database, it is important to name things correctly when the object is created. For example, changing the name of a table late in the development cycle requires changing all the queries, forms, reports, macros, and modules that refer to that table.

You may want to name each database object that refers to a table with the same base name as the table, using the appropriate tag to differentiate them. For example, if your table is tblCustomer, its primary form would be frmCustomer, its primary report would be rptCustomer, and the macros that drive all of the events would be mfrmCustomer and mrptCustomer. We also suggest that you don't make table names plural (for example, use tblCustomer, not tblCustomers) because a table usually holds more than one record, so it's plural by implication.

Database Object Prefixes

We use four database object prefixes:

- "zz" denotes objects you've deserted but may want to keep in the database for a while for future reference or to reuse later (for example, zzfrmPhoneList). "zz" causes the object name to sort to the bottom of the database container, where it's available but out of the way.

- "zt" denotes temporary objects (for example, ztqryTest).

- "zs" denotes system objects[7] (for example, zstblObjects).
- "_" denotes objects under development (for example, _mcrNewEmployee). An underscore before an object name sorts to the top of the database container to visually remind you that it needs attention. Remove the underscore when the object is ready to use, and it sorts normally.

Tags for Fields

Using tags in field names is a hotly debated issue, even between the authors of this appendix. Greg maintains that tags in field names uniformly apply the naming style across all database elements and further document your work in Access Basic routines and form or report properties. Stan prefers that the database schema remain pure (platform and datatype independent) for migration and connectivity to other products or platforms. He prefers that a field name remain independent of its datatype.

Consider both positions, along with your unique needs, when you choose whether to apply the field name tags shown here:

Field Type	Tag	Example
Binary[8]	bin	binInternal
Byte	byt	bytFloorNum
Counter[9]	lng	lngPKCnt
Currency	cur	curSalary
Date/time	dtm	dtmHireDate
Double	dbl	dblMass
Integer[10]	int	intUnit
Long[11]	lng	lngPopulation
Memo	mem	memComments
Ole	ole	oleEmpPhoto
Single[12]	sng	sngScore

Field Type	Tag	Example
Text[13]	str	strFirstName
Yes/No[14]	ysn	ysnDiscounted

Tags for Control Objects

Access forms and reports automatically assign the field name to the ControlName property when you create a new bound control. Having the control name and field name the same creates some ambiguity in the database schema and in some cases may cause errors in Access Basic code referencing both a control and a field with the same name. To resolve this situation, apply the naming style to form and report controls by inserting the appropriate tag, from the following list, in front of the control name suggested by Access. For example, the control name for a field whose ControlSource is LastName would be txtLastName.

At Level 1, we recognize that users need to know the difference between an active control and a label but may not be concerned with the type of the control. Thus, the control tags are as follows:

Object	Tag	Example
Label	lbl	lblLastName
Other types	ctl	ctlLastName

Level 1 tags provide the minimum differentiation necessary to still prove useful in functions, macros, and program documentation. For example, the preceding control tags allow you to differentiate between labels, which aren't modifiable at run time, and other controls, which accept values from code and users.

Level 2 control tags denote the specific type of the control on the form or report. This makes Access Basic code and macros more explicit with respect to the properties and events of the individual control.

Object	Tag	Example
Chart (graph)	cht	chtSales
Check box	chk	chkReadOnly

Object	Tag	Example
Combo box	cbo	cboIndustry
Command button	cmd	cmdCancel
Frame (object)	fra	fraPhoto
Label	lbl	lblHelpMessage
Line	lin	linVertical
List box	lst	lstPolicyCode
Option button	opt	optFrench
Option group	grp	grpLanguage
Page break	brk	brkPage1
Rectangle (shape)[15]	shp	shpNamePanel
Subform/report	sub	subContact
Text box	txt	txtLoginName
Toggle button	tgl	tglForm

The only prefix for controls, "zs", appears at Level 2. It denotes system-level controls used by the form or code but not displayed to the user. Such controls usually aren't visible at run time, but they may store temporary values or parameters passed to the form.

Naming Access Basic and Macro Objects

Using standardized and descriptive variable, constant, and function names greatly enhances the ability of developers to share, maintain, and jointly develop code.

Procedures and Macros

Access Basic requires that each nonprivate procedure name in a database be unique. For a function called from a property on a form in Access 1.x, construct the function name as follows:

formname_controlname_propertyname[16]

For example:

```
frmEmployee_cmdAdd_Push
```

This tells you that this function is called from the OnPush property of the control cmdAdd on the form frmEmployee. (The "On" prefix is dropped for all On events.) For a property that affects the entire form, just use *formname_propertyname*, as in frmEmployee_Open. If two or more controls on one form execute the same code, create unique functions for each using the naming style in this section; then have each of these functions call the same private function that contains the common code.

In Access 2.x, the event procedure code for controls on a form is stored with the form, so the form name is implied in the function and does not need to be in the function name. Thus, the preceding example becomes

```
cmdAdd_Click
```
[17]

Macro names inside a macro group also use this format. In the macro group mfrmEmployee, the macro txtName_BeforeUpdate contains the actions for the txtName control's BeforeUpdate event. For example, the txtName control on your frmEmployee form would have one of these properties, depending on whether you use global modules (Access 1.x), event procedures (Access 2.x), or macros to implement the task:

1.x code	BeforeUpdate	=frmEmployee_txtName_BeforeUpdate()
2.x code	BeforeUpdate	=txtName_BeforeUpdate()
Macros	BeforeUpdate	mfrmEmployee.txtName_BeforeUpdate

Prefix procedure names in library databases with a unique set of characters to prevent their names from conflicting with any other names from attached libraries.

The prefix should be in uppercase letters, followed by an underscore, and be no more than four letters. For example, we prefix all the library function names for our mail merge utility, Access To Word, with "ATW_". Global constants and variables in a library should use the same prefix since they must also be unique across the entire database name space. Similarly, it is important to use these prefixes in Declare statements to alias all external DLL function and procedure calls.

Tags for Access Basic Variables

Every Access Basic variable should have a type tag from the following list:

Variable Type	Tag	Example
Container	con	Dim conTables As Container
Control	ctl	Dim ctlVapor As Control
Currency	cur	Dim curSalary As Currency
Database	db	Dim dbCurrent As Database
Document	doc	Dim docRelationships As Document
Double	dbl	Dim dblPi As Double
Dynaset	dyn	Dim dynTransact As Dynaset
Flag (Y/N, T/F)[18]	f	Dim fAbort As Integer
Field	fld	Dim fldLastName as Field
Form	frm	Dim frmGetUser As Form
Group	gru	Dim gruManagers as Group
Index	idx	Dim idxOrderId as Index
Integer	int	Dim intRetValue As Integer

Variable Type	Tag	Example
Long	lng	Dim lngParam As Long
Object	obj	Dim objGraph As Object
Parameter	prm	Dim prmBeginDate As Parameter
Property	prp	Dim prpUserDefined As Property
QueryDef	qdf (or qrd)	Dim qdfPrice As QueryDef
Recordset	rec (or rst)	Dim recPeople as Recordset
Relation	rel	Dim relOrderItems as Relation
Report	rpt	Dim rptYTDSales As Report
Single	sng	Dim sngLoadFactor As Single
Snapshot	snp	Dim snpParts As Snapshot
String	str	Dim strUserName As String
Table	tbl	Dim tblVendor As Table
TableDef	tdf (or tbd)	Dim tdfBooking as TableDef
Type (user-defined)	typ	Dim typPartRecord As mtPART_RECORD
User	usr	Dim usrJoe as User
Variant	var	Dim varInput As Variant
Workspace	wrk (or wsp)	Dim wrkPrimary as Workspace
Yes/No[18]	ysn	Dim ysnPaid As Integer

Our style doesn't use datatype suffixes, such as $ and %, on variable names because the Access and Visual Basic documentation recommends against using these suffixes.

Tags for database object variables, such as the Form and Report types, are the same as those used for the objects. This helps when coding because the variable you assign an object to (for example, frmVendor) usually has the same name as the object it references (frmVendor), providing you with consistent object names when coding.

Constants and User-Defined Types

It is common practice in Windows programming to use uppercase names for constants, but the authors differ on how to treat constants. Stan prefers using the uppercase notation and adding a scope prefix (see the next section), so a global constant for a specific error might be gNO_TABLE_ERROR. Greg prefers to treat constants as typed variables without scope—for example, strNoTableError.

In the preceding table we added a variable type tag of "typ" for user-defined types and suggest a convention that matches that of constants because you can think of both user-defined types and user-defined constants as persistent, user-created objects. The recommendations for a user-defined datatype syntax include the following:

- Use uppercase letters (or upper/lower syntax if you use that optional convention for globals).
- Use a tag of "t" in front of the type name to denote that it's a type structure.
- Use "g" and "m" prefixes to denote the scope of the type (see the next section).

Prefixes for Scope

Level 2 of the naming convention introduces scope prefixes for variables and constants. The scope prefix comes before any other prefixes. The rules for prefixes for scope are as follows:

- Variables declared locally with a Dim statement have no prefix.
- Variables declared locally with a Static statement are prefixed with "s", as in sintAccumulate.
- Variables that are declared in the Declarations section of a module using a Dim statement are prefixed with "m", as in mcurRunningSum.
- Variables declared with global scope using a Global statement in the Declarations section have the prefix "g", as in glngGrandTotal.

- Variables that denote parameters passed in to a function (in the parentheses after the function name) have a prefix of "p", as in pstrLastName. Alternately, we sometimes use "r" instead of "p" for values passed to a function by reference and "v" for values passed ByVal, when both types of parameters are used in a single function declaration.

Object qualifiers follow the variable name and further differentiate it from similar names. You'll probably devise a list of qualifiers relevant to the types of applications you develop, but here are some of our common ones:

Variable Property	Qualifier	Example
Current element of set	Cur	iaintCur
First element of set	First	iaintStockFirst
Last element of set	Last	iaintStockLast
Next element of set	Next	strCustomerNext
Previous element of set	Prev	strCustomerPrev
Lower limit of range	Min	iastrNameMin
Upper limit of range	Max	iastrNameMax
Source	Src	lngBufferSrc
Destination	Dest	lngBufferDest

Access Basic Labels

For Access Basic labels, we use a qualifier on the function name to create several standard labels. For On Error GoTo statements, we use the name of the function with the qualifier _Err appended. For example:

```
cmdAdd_Click_Err:
```

Some functions also have a label for jumping to the end of the function because it's more appropriate to leave a function in only one place than to scatter Exit Function statements throughout a routine. We use the Done qualifier, as in

```
cmdAdd_Click_Done:
```

Access Basic Example

Following is an example of an Access Basic routine using the naming conventions. Note these items:

- We put a header in every function that describes, at a minimum, purpose, comments, author's name/date, last revision date and notes, and parameters passed in and/or returned.

- We return to the Done routine from the Error routine to ensure that open objects are closed properly before exiting the function. Simply using Exit Function from an error handler may leave files open and locked.

- The example was originally written for Access 1.x and uses syntax that has been modified in 2.x. (For example, CreateDynaset is now OpenRecordset.)

```
Function EliminateNulls (ByVal vstrFieldName As String,
➡ ByVal vstrTableName As String) As Integer
' What:     Replaces Null values with unique ascending integers
'           A standardized version of a routine from NWIND
' and Chapter 8
' Author: Microsoft   Created: 11/92  Last Revision: 5/25/94
' By: grr/swl
' Passed in:    field name and table name
' Returns:          0/-1

    On Error GoTo EliminateNulls_Err
    Dim db As Database
    Dim dynTableSrc As Dynaset
    Dim varCounter As Variant
    Dim varCriteria As Variant

    EliminateNulls = 0
    Set db = CurrentDB()
    Set dynTableSrc = db.CreateDynaset(vstrTableName)
    varCounter = DMax(vstrFieldName, vstrTableName)
    If IsNull(varCounter) Or IsEmpty(varCounter) Then
        varCounter = 1
    Else
        varCounter = Val(varCounter) + 1
    End If
    varCriteria = vstrFieldName & " = Null"
```

```
' Iterate over all records in the table, throw out records
' with Nulls
dynTableSrc.FindFirst varCriteria
Do Until dynTableSrc.NoMatch
    dynTableSrc.Edit
    dynTableSrc(vstrFieldName) = varCounter
    dynTableSrc.Update
    varCounter = varCounter + 1
    dynTableSrc.FindNext varCriteria
Loop
EliminateNulls = -1

EliminateNulls_Done:                    ' Jump here to clean up and exit
    dynTableSrc.Close
    On Error GoTo 0
Exit Function

EliminateNulls_Err:
    Select Case Err
        ' Handle specific errors here
    Case Else
        ' Generic error handler here
        Resume EliminateNulls_Done
    End Select
End Function
```

Putting Standards into Practice

Naming conventions never replace the judicious use of comments in your table definitions, macro code, or Access Basic routines. Naming conventions are an extension of, not a replacement for, good program-commenting techniques.

Formulating, learning, and applying a consistent naming style require a significant initial investment of time and energy. However, you'll be amply rewarded when you return to your application a year later to do maintenance or when you share your code with others. Once the code is implemented, you'll quickly grow to appreciate the effort you made to standardize the naming of items.

If the entire Access community, including Microsoft, coded to one common naming style, we'd all find it easier to share information about Access. With this in mind, we submit these revised guidelines to the Access community.

> **NOTE**
> Stan Leszynski is president of Kwery Corp., which produces several Access add-on products, including Access To Word and Kwery Control Paks. Stan also manages Leszynski Company, Inc., a consulting group active in database development, which he founded in 1982. He writes and speaks on Access regularly. Stan can be reached at (206) 644-7826 or on CompuServe at 71151,1114. Greg Reddick is a co-author of this book. (See his biography on the back cover of this book.) The authors of this naming convention thank the individuals who submitted comments on and participated in review of the standard presented here.

Notes

[1] Having the tag as the only required part may seem counterintuitive, but in Access Basic you can have code that deals with a generic form passed in as a parameter. In this case you'd use "frm" as the parameter name; the base name isn't required except to distinguish it from a different form object variable in the code.

[2] The module tag "bas" is used to maintain consistency with the file name extension used by Visual Basic modules.

[3] A lookup table or query has information used only to populate combo and list boxes on forms, validate certain fields in another table, or join with short codes or keys to pull descriptive text into reports.

[4] Level 2 recognizes that an advanced user may place a single subform/subreport in several different objects; thus the Level 1 technique of naming the sub-object with the same base name doesn't work.

[5] We prefer to create one macro group for each form and report in the system, so the naming convention adds an "m" to the front of the form or report name to create a hybrid macro name tag.

[6] We suggest you use the menu bar name (File, Edit, Help, and the like) as a qualifier at the end of menu macro names.

[7]System objects are items that are part of the development and maintenance of an application not used by end users, such as error logs, development notes, documentation routines, relationship information, and so on. Note that "zs" is a prefix. It causes the system objects to sort toward the bottom of the database container.

[8]The Access engine supports a datatype called binary, but the Access user interface doesn't expose it to the user. It's still possible to get a field with the binary datatype by importing or attaching certain external tables. Also, some of the system table fields use this datatype.

[9]Internally, Access treats a counter datatype as a long integer with a special property called auto-increment. Since counter fields are often referenced by foreign keys and the datatype in the other table is a long, Greg uses the same tag as a long. Optionally, if you want to distinguish a counter from a long, use the qualifier Cnt at the end of the name.

[10]C programmers may prefer "w".

[11]C programmers may prefer "dw".

[12]Some users find "sgl" more mnemonic.

[13]The tag "str" is used as opposed to "txt" because a text box control uses "txt". C programmers may prefer "sz".

[14]C programmers may prefer "f".

[15]Our style recognizes that Visual Basic uses the term "shape".

[16]Access has a 40-character length limit for function and label names. When using this style, we suggest you use short form and control names (less than 20 characters) to avoid exceeding the limitation.

[17]Access 2.x renamed the *Push* event to *Click*.

[18]Use "ysn" for a variable that stores the value of a field of datatype Yes/No; use "f" to denote a flag variable used to control program flow. "f" is widely used by C and BASIC programmers for true/false variables.

APPENDIX

B

Code Base Reference

Table B.1 in this appendix contains all the generic procedures from the various chapters that will be useful to you in your applications. The matching Help file, GLRCODE.HLP, contains more information on each, including descriptions of the parameters and return values, as well as comments and warnings.

TABLE B.1: Overview of Public Procedures in Sample Databases

Chapter	Declaration	Module	Purpose
3	Function glrSoundex(ByVal pvarSurName As Variant) As Variant	basSoundex	Takes a surname (last name) string and returns a string representing the Russell Soundex code
4	Function glrGetColumnHeadings(ByVal pvarSQL As Variant, pvarErrReturned As Variant) As Variant	basColHead	Takes a SQL statement for a crosstab query and returns the ColumnHeadings property
4	Function glrSetColumnHeadings(pvarSQL As Variant, pvarNewColHead, pvarErrReturned As Variant) As Variant	basColHead	Creates or modifies column headings for a crosstab query
7	Function cmdAddAll_Click(frm As Form)	basMultiPik	In multi-pick list box, code attached to Click event of Add All button on form
7	Function cmdAddOne_Click(frm As Form)	basMultiPik	In multi-pick list box, code attached to Click event of Add One button on form
7	Function cmdDeleteAll_Click(frm As Form)	basMultiPik	In multi-pick list box, code attached to Click event of Delete All button on form
7	Function cmdDeleteOne_Click()	basMultiPik	In multi-pick list box, code attached to Click event of Delete One button on form
7	Function glrAtNew(frm As Form) As Integer	basCarry	Detects whether the current row on the passed-in form is the "new" row

TABLE B.1: Overview of Public Procedures in Sample Databases (continued)

Chapter	Declaration	Module	Purpose
7	Function glrFillAvailable(ctlField As Control, varID As Variant, varRow As Variant, varCol As Variant, varCode As Variant)	basMultiPik	In multi-pick list box, list-filling callback function Access calls to fill the Available list
7	Function glrFillSelected(ctlField As Control, varID As Variant, varRow As Variant, varCol As Variant, varCode As Variant)	basMultiPik	In multi-pick list box, list-filling callback function Access calls to fill the Selected list
7	Sub glrGetSelectedItems(frm As Form, aArray() As Variant)	basMultiPik	In multi-pick list box, retrieves the list of selected items
7	Function glrGetTag(ctl As Control, strTagName As String)	basTags	Retrieves a value from a control's Tag property
7	Sub glrHandlePlusMinusKeys(ctl As Control, intKey As Integer)	basSpin	Increments or decrements numeric or date values in a text box when the gray +/− keys are pressed
7	Function glrIncSearch(ctlTextBox As Control, ctlListBox As Control, strField As String)	basIncSrch	Performs an incremental search in a list box, given the text that's been typed so far in an attached text box
7	Sub glrIncSrchEnd()	basIncSrch	Cleans up after an incremental search, closing the global recordset variable
7	Function glrlstAvailable_DblClick(frm As Form)	basMultiPik	In a multi-pick list box, code attached to the DblClick event of the Available list box
7	Function glrlstSelected_DblClick(frm As Form)	basMultiPik	In a multi-pick list box, code attached to the DblClick event of the Selected list box

TABLE B.1: Overview of Public Procedures in Sample Databases (continued)

Chapter	Declaration	Module	Purpose
7	Function glrMultiPick_OnOpen(frm As Form)	basMultiPik	Code attached to the Open event of the multi-pick form
7	Function glrPutTag(ctl As Control, strTagName As String, varTagValue As Variant)	basTags	Sets a value in a control's Tag property
7	Function glrRestoreValues(strForm As String, strControl As String)	basCarry	Copies a value into a new row that had been saved previously from the previous row. Used in conjunction with glrStoreValues()
7	Function glrSimpleSpin(ctl As Control, intInterval As Integer)	basSpin	Creates spin button controls that allow mouse-driven incrementing and decrementing of numeric or date values
7	Function glrSpin(ctl As Control, intInterval As Integer, varMin As Variant, varMax As Variant, fAllowWrap As Integer)	basSpin	Creates spin button controls that allow mouse-driven incrementing and decrementing of numeric or date values
7	Function glrStoreValues(strForm As String, strControl As String)	basCarry	Stores a value so that it can be restored in the next new row. Used in conjunction with glrRestoreValues
7	Function glrUpdateSearch(ctlTextBox As Control, ctlListBox As Control)	basIncSrch	Sets the value of the text box to match that of the list box in an incremental search. If your user makes a choice directly from the list box, you'll want to update the text box at that point
7	Private Sub SetupArrays()	basMultiPik	In a multi-pick list box, fills the array of available items

TABLE B.1: Overview of Public Procedures in Sample Databases (continued)

Chapter	Declaration	Module	Purpose
8	Function glrDoCalc()	basCalc	Loads frmCalc in dialog mode and returns the calculated value once frmCalc's closed by the user
8	Function glrDoCalendar(varPassedDate As Variant) As Variant	basCalendar	Loads frmCalendar in dialog mode and returns the chosen date once frmCalendar is closed by the user
8	Function glrDoQBF(strFormName As String, fCloseIt As Integer)	basBuildSQL	Loads the specified form as a QBF form
8	Function glrEnableButtons(frm As Form)	basNavigate	Enables and disables buttons as necessary, depending on which is the current record on the form
8	Function glrEnableControlMenuItem(frm As Form, intItem As Integer, fEnable As Integer)	basControlMenu	Enables or disables items on the control menu for a form, depending on the fEnable parameter passed in
8	Function glrFindAccessHWnd()	basWindowRelationships	Finds Access' main windows' hWnd
8	Function glrGetAccessChild(strClass As String) As Integer	basWindowRelationships	Finds the first child of the Access window with the appropriate class name
8	Function glrGetFormInfo(frm As Form)	basSaveSize	Recalls saved form size/position. Call this from the form's Open event

TABLE B.1: Overview of Public Procedures in Sample Databases (continued)

Chapter	Declaration	Module	Purpose
8	Sub glrGetSize(frm As Form, intWidth As Integer, intHeight As Integer)	basFormSize	Gets the size of the inside area of the current form. On the first pass, gets necessary info from Windows about the screen resolution. Otherwise, just calls the Windows API to get the current form size
8	Function glrGetTag(ctl As Control, strTagName As String)	basTags	Retrieves a specific tag name from the requested control's Tag property
8	Function glrNavPrev(frm As Form); Function glrNavFirst(frm As Form); Function glrNavLast(frm As Form); Function glrNavNew(frm As Form); Function glrNavNext(frm As Form)	basNavigate	Moves to the previous, first, last, new, or next row on a form
8	Function glrPutTag(ctl As Control, strTagName As String, varTagValue As Variant)	basTags	Appends the value |strTagName|=|varTagValue| onto the Tag property for the requested control. If the tagName already exists, it is deleted first and then the new value is appended to the end
8	Function glrRemoveCaptionBar(frm As Form)	basCaption	Calls glrRemoveWindowCaptionBar to remove a form's caption bar
8	Sub glrRemoveWindowCaptionBar(ByVal hWnd As Integer)	basCaption	You can use this code, modified from the MS Access Knowledge Base, to remove the caption bar from your forms

TABLE B.1: Overview of Public Procedures in Sample Databases (continued)

Chapter	Declaration	Module	Purpose
8	Function glrResizeForm(frm As Form, fDoResize As Variant)	basFormScale	Called from the Resize event of forms. Attempts to resize the form and all its controls. Doesn't do anything if the current height of the form is 0
8	Function glrSaveFormInfo(frm As Form)	basSaveSize	Saves form position/size. Call this from the form's Close event
8	Function glrScaleForm(frm As Form, intX As Integer, intY As Integer)	basFormScale	Called from the Open event of forms. Attempts to scale the form appropriately for the given screen size, as compared to the size of the screen on which it was designed
8	Function glrSetSystemModal()	basSysModal	Makes the Access window the system modal window, returning the handle of the previous system modal window, if any
9	Function glrBuildDevNames(dr As glr_tagDeviceRec)	basDevNames	Given the printer's device name, driver name, and port, creates an appropriate prtDevNames structure
9	Sub glrCopyDMValues(strOldDM As String, strNewDM As String)	basDevMode	Given an old and a new DevMode structure, copies the nonessential values from the old one to the new one

TABLE B.1: Overview of Public Procedures in Sample Databases (continued)

Chapter	Declaration	Module	Purpose
9	Function glrCrackFields(varValue As Variant, aintFields() As Integer)	basPrintCap	Given the word containing the bit fields for the initialized elements in the driver's DEVMODE structure, fills an array with the values that make up that bit field
9	Function glrGetBinNames(dr As glr_tagDeviceRec, astrBinNames() As String)	basPrintCap	Retrieves the list of bin names, filling in the array astrBinNames()
9	Function glrGetBins(dr As glr_tagDeviceRec, aintList() As Integer)	basPrintCap	Retrieves the list of bin values, filling in the array aintList()
9	Function glrGetCopies(dr As glr_tagDeviceRec)	basPrintCap	Returns the maximum number of copies this printer can support
9	Function glrGetDefaultDM(dr As glr_tagDeviceRec)	basDevMode	For the specified device, gets the default DevMode structure so it can be used with the form whose DevNames property you want to change
9	Function glrGetDevNames(strName As String, intType As Integer, dr As glr_tagDeviceRec)	basDevNames	Retrieves a glr_tagDeviceRec structure neatly filled in with the prtDevNames value from the specified form or report
9	Function glrGetDMSize(dr As glr_tagDeviceRec)	basPrintCap	Gets the size of the DEVMODE structure for this driver
9	Function glrGetDriverVersion(dr As glr_tagDeviceRec)	basPrintCap	Gets the current driver version number
9	Function glrGetDuplex(dr As glr_tagDeviceRec)	basPrintCap	Returns 0 or 1, telling whether or not this printer supports duplex printing

TABLE B.1: Overview of Public Procedures in Sample Databases (continued)

Chapter	Declaration	Module	Purpose
9	Function glrGetEnumResolutions(dr As glr_tagDeviceRec, aptlngList() As typePOINT_LONG)	basPrintCap	Fills the array of pairs of longs (aptlngList()) with the possible printing resolutions for this printer
9	Function glrGetExtraSize(dr As glr_tagDeviceRec)	basPrintCap	Gets the size of the extra portion of the DEVMODE structure for this driver
9	Function glrGetFields(dr As glr_tagDeviceRec)	basPrintCap	Retrieves the bitmap field containing information on which fields in the DEVMODE structure are supported/initialized
9	Function glrGetFileDependencies(dr As glr_tagDeviceRec, astrList() As String)	basPrintCap	Retrieves a list of file dependencies for this printer driver
9	Function glrGetMaxExtent(dr As glr_tagDeviceRec, ptValue As typePOINT_INT)	basPrintCap	Retrieves the max extent for this driver
9	Function glrGetMinExtent(dr As glr_tagDeviceRec, ptValue As typePOINT_INT)	basPrintCap	Retrieves the min extent for this driver
9	Function glrGetOrientation(dr As glr_tagDeviceRec)	basPrintCap	Retrieves the method by which this printer supports landscape printing, if at all
9	Function glrGetPaperNames(dr As glr_tagDeviceRec, astrNames() As String)	basPrintCap	Retrieves an array of strings representing the supported nonstandard paper sizes
9	Function glrGetPapers(dr As glr_tagDeviceRec, aintList() As Integer)	basPrintCap	Retrieves an array of integers representing the standard paper sizes this printer supports

TABLE B.1: Overview of Public Procedures in Sample Databases (continued)

Chapter	Declaration	Module	Purpose
9	Function glrGetPaperSize(dr As glr_tagDeviceRec, aptList() As typePOINT_INT)	basPrintCap	Retrieves an array of point structures, each representing the width and height of a specific paper size this printer supports
9	Function glrGetSpecVersion(dr As glr_tagDeviceRec)	basPrintCap	Gets the spec version to which this driver adheres
9	Function glrGetTrueType(dr As glr_tagDeviceRec)	basPrintCap	Gets information on how this driver supports TrueType fonts
9	Sub glrLoadDriver(strDriver As String)	basPrintCap	After unloading any library this program already has loaded, loads the newly requested driver
9	Function glrParseDevNames(strPrtDevNames As String, dr As glr_tagDeviceRec)	basDevNames	Given the strPrtDevNames string, fills in the appropriate fields in dr
9	Function glrRetrieveDevMode(strName As String, intType As Integer, DM As glr_tagDevMode)	basDevMode	Retrieves a glr_tagDevMode structure neatly filled in with the value from the specified form or report
9	Function glrSetDevMode(strName As String, intType As Integer, DM As glr_tagDevMode)	basDevMode	Sets the prtDevMode property, given a glr_tagDevMode structure neatly filled in with the values for the specified form or report
9	Function glrTrimNull(strString As String) As String	basDevNames	Truncates strings at the first null character the Windows API might happen to have embedded

TABLE B.1: Overview of Public Procedures in Sample Databases (continued)

Chapter	Declaration	Module	Purpose
10	Function glrCheckMenuItem(intSubMenu As Integer, intItem As Integer, fCheckIt As Integer)	basMenuHandling	Checks/unchecks a user-defined menu item (This won't work with Access-controlled menu items!)
10	Function glrCheckSubMenuItem(hMenu As Integer, intItem As Integer, fCheckIt As Integer)	basMenuHandling	Checks/unchecks a user-defined menu item (This won't work with Access-controlled menu items!)
10	Function glrCopyToolbars(strOutput As String)	basCopyToolbars	Copies the user-defined toolbars to a foreign database
10	Function glrEnableMenuBarItem(intItem As Integer, fEnable As Integer)	basMenuHandling	Disables a top-level menu item. Disabling does not change the appearance; it just makes the menu item unavailable
10	Function glrFindAccesshWnd()	basMenuHandling	Retrieves Access' window handle (hWnd)
10	Function glrGetMenuBar()	basMenuHandling	Retrieves the handle for the top-level menu. Since this menu is always attached to Access, not one of its child windows, this seems like a good time to also retrieve Access' window handle and store it in the module variable hWndAccess, which other routines also use
10	Function glrGetMenuBarText(intItem As Integer)	basMenuHandling	Retrieves text from a specific top-level menu
10	Function glrGetMenuBarTitles(astrMenuTitles() As String) As Integer	basMenuHandling	Fills an array with a list of the top-level menu titles

TABLE B.1: Overview of Public Procedures in Sample Databases (continued)

Chapter	Declaration	Module	Purpose
10	Sub glrGetMenuHandles(intSubMenu As Integer, hTopMenu As Integer, hSubMenu As Integer)	basMenuHandling	Gathers the menu handles for the main menu bar and the requested submenu
10	Function glrGetMenuText(hMenu As Integer, intItem As Integer)	basMenuHandling	Retrieves text from a specific menu item
10	Function glrGetMenuTitles(hMenu As Integer, astrMenuTitles() As String)	basMenuHandling	Fills any array with a list of the text in the requested menu
10	Function glrGetSystemMenu(ByVal hWnd As Integer)	basMenuHandling	Gets the handle to the form's system menu
10	Function glrGrayMenuItem(intSubMenu As Integer, intItem As Integer, fEnableIt As Integer) As Integer	basMenuHandling	Enables/disables a user-defined menu item (this won't work with Access-controlled menu items!) by setting it to be "grayed"
10	Function glrGraySubMenuItem(hMenu As Integer, intItem As Integer, fEnableIt As Integer)	basMenuHandling	Grays/ungrays a user-defined menu item (This won't work with Access-controlled menu items!)
10	Sub glrHandlePopup(frm As Form, ByVal intMenu As Integer, ByVal X As Single, ByVal Y As Single)	basMenuHandling	Uses the right mouse button to pop up a user-defined menu. The menu to pop up must be attached to the main menu bar
10	Function glrHiliteMenuBarItem(intItem As Integer, fHilite As Integer)	basMenuHandling	Highlights/unhighlights a top-level menu item
10	Function glrInsertMenuItem(hMenu As Integer, intItem As Integer, intId As Integer, intSubItem As Integer, strText As String)	basMenuHandling	Inserts a new menu item, given all the necessary information
10	Function glrIsItemChecked(intSubMenu As Integer, intSubItem As Integer)	basMenuHandling	Inquires whether a specific item on a top-level submenu is currently checked

TABLE B.1: Overview of Public Procedures in Sample Databases (continued)

Chapter	Declaration	Module	Purpose
10	Function glrIsItemDisabled(intSubMenu As Integer, intItem As Integer)	basMenuHandling	Inquires whether a specific item on the menu bar is currently disabled
10	Function glrIsItemGrayed(intSubMenu As Integer, intItem As Integer)	basMenuHandling	Inquires whether a specific item on a top-level submenu is currently grayed
10	Function glrIsMenuBarItemDisabled(intItem As Integer)	basMenuHandling	Inquires whether a specific item on the menu bar is currently disabled
10	Function glrIsSubItemChecked(hMenu As Integer, intItem As Integer)	basMenuHandling	Inquires whether a specific item on a specific menu is currently checked
10	Function glrIsSubItemDisabled(hMenu As Integer, intItem As Integer)	basMenuHandling	Inquires whether a specific item on a specific menu is currently disabled
10	Function glrIsSubItemGrayed(hMenu As Integer, intItem As Integer)	basMenuHandling	Inquires whether a specific item on a specific menu is currently grayed
10	Function glrRemoveMenubarItem(intItem As Integer, intSubItem As Integer, strText As String)	basMenuHandling	Removes a top-level menu item, returning its action ID or SubMenu handle
10	Function glrRemoveMenuItem(hMenu As Integer, intItem As Integer, intId As Integer, intSubItem As Integer, strText As String)	basMenuHandling	Removes a menu item, returning its action ID or SubMenu handle
10	Function glrRemoveStr(strFindIn As String, strFind As String)	basMenuHandling	Removes all occurrences of a specific string from within another

TABLE B.1: Overview of Public Procedures in Sample Databases (continued)

Chapter	Declaration	Module	Purpose
10	Sub glrResetSystemMenu(ByVal hWnd As Integer)	basMenuHandling	Resets the system menu for a specified window
10	Function glrSetMenuBarText(intItem As Integer, strText As String)	basMenuHandling	Modifies the text for a specific top-level menu item
10	Function glrSetMenuText(hMenu As Integer, intItem As Integer, strText As String)	basMenuHandling	Modifies the text for a specific menu item
10	Sub glrTrackPopup(frm As Form, hSubMenu As Integer, ByVal X As Single, ByVal y As Single)	basMenuHandling	Uses the right mouse button to pop up a user-defined menu, given the menu handle of the menu to pop up (called by glrHandlePopup)
11	Function glrAssignID(frm As Form, ByVal strTableName As String, ByVal strCounterField As String) As Variant	basCounter	Called from the BeforeInsert event of a form to assign a new custom counter value for a field. Removes any record that cannot be saved
11	Function glrGetNextCounter(ByVal strTableName As String) As Long	basCounter	Returns the next custom counter value for a particular table. Counters are stored in the database COUNTER_DB in tables with _ID appended to the name of the table for which they supply counters. Returns −1 if a valid counter value cannot be retrieved because of locking problems
13	Function glrPickNewColor(lngCurrentColor As Long) As Long	basUtilities	Invokes the Windows common dialog to select a color
14	Sub glrAssert(ByVal f As Long)	basError	Asserts that a condition is true

TABLE B.1: Overview of Public Procedures in Sample Databases (continued)

Chapter	Declaration	Module	Purpose
14	Sub glrEnterProcedure(ByVal strProcName As String)	bas Error	Pushes the name of the current procedure onto the call tree stack
14	Sub glrErrorOutput(ByVal intErr As Integer, ByVal varError As Variant)	basError	Reports an error to the screen, via a message box, to the Immediate window and to the file specified by the GLRSTRERRORFILE constant
14	Sub glrExitProcedure(ByVal strProcName As String)	basError	Pops the name of the current procedure from the call tree stack
16	Function glrEndTimer()	basTest	Ends timing and returns the difference between the current time and lngStartTime
16	Function glrRunTests(strFunc1 As String, strFunc2 As String, varReptFunc As Variant, varReptOp As Variant)	basTest	Runs two test cases, comparing their relative timings, and returns a string showing the results of those timings
16	Sub glrStartTimer()	basTest	Starts the timer, storing the value in the module global, lngStartTime
18	Function glrCloseApp(ByVal intApp As Integer) As Integer	basCloseApp	Closes an application started with the Shell() function
18	Function glrUIntFromInt(ByVal intSigned As Integer) As Long	basDDE	Returns a long that contains the unsigned value of an integer
21	Function glrCBFProcExists(frm As Form, strProcName As String) As Integer	basMSAU200	Determines whether a specific procedure already exists in a form's module

TABLE B.1: Overview of Public Procedures in Sample Databases (continued)

Chapter	Declaration	Module	Purpose
21	Function glrFullPath(strFileName As String) As String	basMSAU200	Retrieves the full path for a file, depending on the current directory. A wrapper function for the glr_msauFullPath() function in MSAU200.DLL
21	Function glrGetFileName(gfni As glr_msauGetFileNameInfo, ByVal fOpen As Integer) As Long	basMSAU200	Uses the Windows Common File Open dialog. A wrapper function for glr_msauGetFileName() in MSAU200.DLL
21	Function glrGetFont(gfi As glr_msauGetFontInfo)	basMSAU200	Retrieves font information. A wrapper function for glr_msauGetFont() in MSAU200.DLL
21	Function glrPickNewColor(lngCurrentColor As Long) As Long	basMSAU200	Invokes the Windows common dialog to select a color
21	Sub glrSplitPath(strPath As String, strDrive As String, strDir As String, strFName As String, strExt As String)	basMSAU200	Splits a full path into its component pieces. A wrapper function for the glr_msauSplitPath() function in MSAU200.DLL
21	Function glrTruncateString(strTemp As String)	basMSAU200	Truncates the passed-in string at the first null character (CHR$(0))
22	Function glrAddGroupMember(ByVal pstrUser As String, ByVal pstrGroup As String) As Integer	basSecurityUtilities	Adds a user account to a group
22	Function glrChangeOwner(ByVal pintObjType As Integer, ByVal pstrObjName As String, ByVal pstrNewOwner As String) As Integer	basSecurityUtilities	Changes the owner of an object or all objects in a database

TABLE B.1: Overview of Public Procedures in Sample Databases (continued)

Chapter	Declaration	Module	Purpose
22	Function glrChangePermission(ByVal pintObjType As Integer, ByVal pstrObjName As String, ByVal pstrAccount As String, ByVal plngPermission As Long, ByVal pfState As Integer) As Integer	basSecurityUtilities	Adds or subtracts a user or group account's permission to an object
22	Function glrChangePW(ByVal pstrUser As String, ByVal pstrOldPW As String, ByVal pstrNewPW As String) As Integer	basSecurityUtilities	Changes the password for a user account
22	Function glrCheckPermission(ByVal pintObjType As Integer, ByVal pstrObjName As String, ByVal pstrUser As String, ByVal plngPermission As Long, ByVal pfExplicitOnly As Integer) As Integer	basSecurityUtilities	Determines whether a user has a certain level of permissions for an object. By default, checks both explicit and implicit permissions
22	Function glrDeleteAccount(ByVal pstrName As String) As Integer	basSecurityUtilities	Removes a user or group account
22	Function glrGetAccount(ByVal pstrName As String) As Integer	basSecurityUtilities	Checks for the existence of an account and determines the account type (user or group)
22	Function glrGetPermission(ByVal pintObjType As Integer, ByVal pstrObjName As String, ByVal pstrAccount As String) As Long	basSecurityUtilities	Determines the permissions an account has for an object, a container, or a database. Checks only explicit permissions
22	Function glrIsMember(ByVal pstrUser As String, ByVal pstrGroup As String) As Integer	basSecurityUtilities	Checks whether a user account is a member of a group account
22	Function glrNewGroup(ByVal pstrName As String, ByVal pstrPID As String) As Integer	basSecurityUtilities	Creates a new group account
22	Function glrNewUser(ByVal pstrName As String, ByVal pstrPID As String, ByVal pstrPW As String) As Integer	basSecurityUtilities	Creates a new user account

TABLE B.1: Overview of Public Procedures in Sample Databases (continued)

Chapter	Declaration	Module	Purpose
22	Function glrObjectOwner(ByVal pintObjType As Integer, ByVal pstrObjName As String) As String	basSecurityUtilities	Determines the name of the owner of an object
22	Function glrRemoveGroupMember(ByVal pstrUser As String, ByVal pstrGroup As String) As Integer	basSecurityUtilities	Removes a user account from membership in a group
22	Function glrSetDbCreate(ByVal pstrAccount As String, ByVal pfState As Integer) As Integer	basSecurityUtilities	Enables or disables the permission to create new databases
22	Function glrSetPermission(ByVal pintObjType As Integer, ByVal pstrObjName As String, ByVal pstrAccount As String, ByVal plngPermission As Long) As Integer	basSecurityUtilities	Assigns a permission set for a user or group account for an object
22	Function glrUsersWithBlankPW() As Integer	basSecurityUtilities	Creates a list of all users in the current workgroup with blank (null) passwords

INDEX

Note to the Reader: Throughout this index **boldfaced** page numbers indicate primary discussions of a topic. *Italicized* page numbers indicate illustrations

A

B

C

F

G

H

I

J

K

L

O

P

Q

R

S

T

u

V

W

X

Y

Z

Everything you need to start using the Internet today!

Windows, a modem and this comprehensive book/software package. That's everything you need to start using the Internet now. Includes economical, full-featured, direct Internet connection. Point and click interface. Gopher, World Wide Web, E-mail, Usenet Newsgroups, FTP, Telnet and much more.

Now available wherever computer books are sold.

250 pages.
ISBN 1529-2

Shortcuts to Understanding.

SYBEX, Inc.
2021 Challenger Drive
Alameda, CA 94501
1-800-227-2346
1-510-523-8233

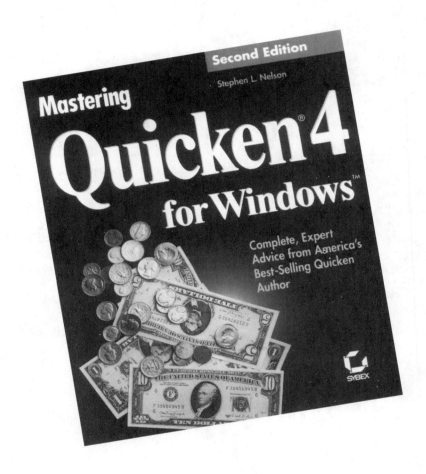

POCKET-SIZED PC EXPERTISE.

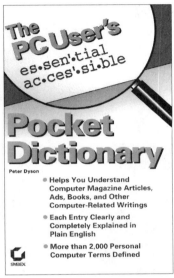

Finding the shortest routes.

Getting to know your way around Access means having the right map—and here it is!
Fundmentals, zoom boxes, customizable button bars, new Wizards, self joins...you'll
find the route to everything you need in this well-written guide.

Now available
wherever computer
books are sold.

335 pages.
ISBN 1548-9

SYBEX

Shortcuts to Understanding.

SYBEX, Inc.
2021 Challenger Drive
Alameda, CA 94501
1-800-227-2346
1-510-523-8233

GET A FREE CATALOG JUST FOR EXPRESSING YOUR OPINION.

Help us improve our books and get a *FREE* full-color catalog in the bargain. Please complete this form, pull out this page and send it in today. The address is on the reverse side.

Name _____ Company _____

Address _____ City _____ State ____ Zip _____

Phone ( )_____

1. How would you rate the overall quality of this book?

- ❑ Excellent
- ❑ Very Good
- ❑ Good
- ❑ Fair
- ❑ Below Average
- ❑ Poor

2. What were the things you liked most about the book? (Check all that apply)

- ❑ Pace
- ❑ Format
- ❑ Writing Style
- ❑ Examples
- ❑ Table of Contents
- ❑ Index
- ❑ Price
- ❑ Illustrations
- ❑ Type Style
- ❑ Cover
- ❑ Depth of Coverage
- ❑ Fast Track Notes

3. What were the things you liked *least* about the book? (Check all that apply)

- ❑ Pace
- ❑ Format
- ❑ Writing Style
- ❑ Examples
- ❑ Table of Contents
- ❑ Index
- ❑ Price
- ❑ Illustrations
- ❑ Type Style
- ❑ Cover
- ❑ Depth of Coverage
- ❑ Fast Track Notes

4. Where did you buy this book?

- ❑ Bookstore chain
- ❑ Small independent bookstore
- ❑ Computer store
- ❑ Wholesale club
- ❑ College bookstore
- ❑ Technical bookstore
- ❑ Other _____

5. How did you decide to buy this particular book?

- ❑ Recommended by friend
- ❑ Recommended by store personnel
- ❑ Author's reputation
- ❑ Sybex's reputation
- ❑ Read book review in _____
- ❑ Other _____

6. How did you pay for this book?

- ❑ Used own funds
- ❑ Reimbursed by company
- ❑ Received book as a gift

7. What is your level of experience with the subject covered in this book?

- ❑ Beginner
- ❑ Intermediate
- ❑ Advanced

8. How long have you been using a computer?

years _____
months _____

9. Where do you most often use your computer?

- ❑ Home
- ❑ Work

- ❑ Both
- ❑ Other _____

10. What kind of computer equipment do you have? (Check all that apply)

- ❑ PC Compatible Desktop Computer
- ❑ PC Compatible Laptop Computer
- ❑ Apple/Mac Computer
- ❑ Apple/Mac Laptop Computer
- ❑ CD ROM
- ❑ Fax Modem
- ❑ Data Modem
- ❑ Scanner
- ❑ Sound Card
- ❑ Other _____

11. What other kinds of software packages do you ordinarily use?

- ❑ Accounting
- ❑ Databases
- ❑ Networks
- ❑ Apple/Mac
- ❑ Desktop Publishing
- ❑ Spreadsheets
- ❑ CAD
- ❑ Games
- ❑ Word Processing
- ❑ Communications
- ❑ Money Management
- ❑ Other _____

12. What operating systems do you ordinarily use?

- ❑ DOS
- ❑ OS/2
- ❑ Windows
- ❑ Apple/Mac
- ❑ Windows NT
- ❑ Other _____

13. On what computer-related subject(s) would you like to see more books?

_____

_____

_____

_____

14. Do you have any other comments about this book? (Please feel free to use a separate piece of paper if you need more room)

_____

_____

_____

_____

PLEASE FOLD, SEAL, AND MAIL TO SYBEX

SYBEX INC.
Department M
2021 Challenger Drive
Alameda, CA
94501

Warranty

Disclaimer

Copy Protection

What's on the Disk?

This disk is a valuable companion to the book. It provides a wealth of information in a readily usable format to aid in your Access development efforts. We've included every significant example presented in the text, and not just the Access Basic code. We've also included all the tables, forms, queries, reports—*everything* to get you up and running instantly. The disk also contains a Windows Help file that, along with Appendix B, details every generic utility function discussed in the book, so you can start calling these functions from your applications with a minimum of effort. In addition to all that, we've included several free utility programs and Access add-ins to make application development even easier.

Just a sampling of what you'll find on the disk:

- A generic query-by-form creator, which works with *any* data input form
- A set of routines for creating screen-resolution-n-independent forms.
- Ready-to-use pop-up calendar and calculator forms you can call from your code
- A set of routines for creating custom right-click menus for your forms
- A set of functions for retrieving and setting printer capabilities
- A wizard that automatically creates tabbed dialog box forms to your specifications
- A routine that prints all user accounts with blank passwords
- SuperSpy freeware program from SoftBlox for spying window classes
- Microsoft's Access 2.0 Security Wizard for making databases absolutely secure

And lots more. For more information about the disk, including installation instructions, see the section "About the Disk" in the Introduction to this book, Appendix B, and the README.TXT file found on the disk.